PERSONAL INJURY AND CLINICAL NEGLIGENCE LITIGATION

PERSONAL INJURY AND CLINICAL NEGLIGENCE LITIGATION

Julie Mardell and Kate Serfozo

Published by

College of Law Publishing,
Braboeuf Manor, Portsmouth Road, St Catherines, Guildford GU3 1HA

© The University of Law 2016

British Library Cataloguing-in-Publication Data
A catalogue record for this book is available from the British Library.

ISBN 978 1 910661 65 9

Typeset by Style Photosetting Ltd, Mayfield, East Sussex
Printed in Great Britain by Polestar Wheatons, Exeter

Preface

The purpose of this book is to provide an introduction to the large and complex area of personal injury and clinical negligence litigation. It does not set out to cover the subject fully, neither does it purport to include all recent developments in this area of law.

Although we hope that this text will be of interest to practitioners, primarily it has been written as an integrated element of the Legal Practice Course elective 'Personal Injury and Clinical Negligence Litigation', and its aim is to provide a framework upon which the course is built. Students are expected to carry out their own research into some aspects of the course and will receive further tuition in others.

The Civil Procedure Rules are amended from time to time and it is important that readers make reference to the most up-to-date provisions which can be found on the Ministry of Justice website. This is a fast-changing area of law, and practitioners must update themselves continually.

In the interests of brevity, we have used the masculine pronoun throughout to include the feminine.

The law is generally stated as at 1 September 2015.

JULIE MARDELL and KATE SERFOZO

Contents

Table of Cases

K

L

M

N

O

P

Y

Table of Statutes

Table of Secondary Legislation

List of Abbreviations

See Chapter 2 for commonly used medical abbreviations.

ACOPs	Approved Codes of Practice
ADR	alternative dispute resolution
AEI	after the event insurance
APIL	Association of Personal Injury Lawyers
AvMA	Action against Medical Accidents
BEI	before the event insurance
CCG	clinical commissioning group
CFA	conditional fee agreement
CICA	Criminal Injuries Compensation Authority
CJA 2009	Coroners and Justice Act 2009
CJCA 2015	Criminal Justice and Courts Act 2015
CMCHA 2007	Corporate Manslaughter and Corporate Homicide Act 2007
CNF	Claim Notification Form
CNST	Clinical Negligence Scheme for Trusts
CPP	court proceedings pack
CPR 1998	Civil Procedure Rules 1998
CPS	Crown Prosecution Service
CRU	Compensation Recovery Unit
CTG	cardiotachograph
DBA	damages-based agreement
DCNF	Defendant Only Claim Notification Form
DPA 1998	Data Protection Act 1998
DWP	Department for Work and Pensions
DSE	display screen equipment
ECG	electrocardiogram
ECHR	European Convention on Human Rights
EL	employers' liability
E&RRA 2013	Enterprise and Regulatory Reform Act 2013
FAA 1976	Fatal Accidents Act 1976
GLO	group litigation order
GMC	General Medical Council
HSE	Health and Safety Executive
HSOA 2008	Health and Safety Offences Act 2008
HSWA 1974	Health and Safety at Work etc Act 1974
LA 1980	Limitation Act 1980
LASPO 2012	Legal Aid, Sentencing and Punishment of Offenders Act 2012
LEI	legal expenses insurance
MIB	Motor Insurers' Bureau
MID	Motor Insurance Database
NHS	National Health Service
NHSLA	NHS Litigation Authority
NMC	Nursing and Midwifery Council
OLA 1957	Occupiers' Liability Act 1957
PALS	Patient Advice and Liaison Service
PAP	pre-action protocol

PAR	police accident report
PD	Practice Direction
PHA 1997	Protection from Harassment Act 1997
PL	public liability
PPE	personal protective equipment
PTSD	post-traumatic stress disorder
QOCS	qualified one way costs shifting
RIDDOR 1995	Reporting of Injuries, Diseases and Dangerous Occurrences Regulations 1995
RTA	road traffic accident
RTA 1988	Road Traffic Act 1988
SSP	statutory sick pay
VWF	vibration white finger
WRA 2012	Welfare Reform Act 2012
WRULD	work-related upper limb disorder

CHAPTER 1

INTRODUCTION TO THE WORK OF A PERSONAL INJURY AND CLINICAL NEGLIGENCE SOLICITOR

LEARNING OUTCOMES

After reading this chapter you will be able to:

- understand the scope and limitations of this book
- explain the similarities and differences between personal injury claims and clinical negligence claims
- set out an outline of the main steps in each type of claim
- explain how these claims are viewed from the perspectives of the claimant, the defendant and their solicitors
- appreciate that solicitors acting for claimants and defendants need to be vigilant in order to spot fraudulent claims, and understand how the courts might deal with dishonest litigants.

1.1 INTRODUCTION

The aim of this text is to provide an introduction to personal injury and clinical negligence litigation. It is assumed, however, that the basic civil litigation procedure has been studied before. Reference to the Legal Practice Guide, *Civil Litigation* and the Civil Procedure Rules 1998 (CPR 1998) may be necessary for those unfamiliar with the essential elements of High Court and county court procedure.

The terms 'personal injury litigation' and 'clinical negligence litigation' are widely used to describe claims for compensation for injuries which a client has suffered. This text will not deal with every type of claim that is encountered in practice, but it should serve as a basic introduction to a fascinating and rapidly developing area of law.

In practice, many personal injury claims will be based on either public liability, where the injury is sustained on property which is accessed by the public, or product liability, where the injury is caused by products made available to the public. However, in this text, the focus will be on the following:

(a) Road traffic accident (RTA) and other highway claims. These are usually the most straightforward type of personal injury claim. See **Chapter 3**.

(b)   Employers' liability claims. This term is used for personal injury claims where the claimant was injured in the course of his employment and his employer is the defendant. Common examples of this type of personal injury claim arise where workers slip on the factory floor, fall from ladders or are caught in moving machinery. More complex cases arise where workers suffer a disease or injury which manifests itself many years after their exposure to dust, fibres, gases, fumes or noxious substances within the workplace. See **Chapter 4**.

(c)   Clinical negligence claims, which arise as a result of the negligence of doctors or other medical professionals, such as nurses, physiotherapists and dentists, or of institutional health providers, such as NHS Trusts or private hospitals. See **Chapter 5**.

(d)   Claims for psychiatric injury. These may arise in the context of any of the above types of claim but the law in relation to claims for nervous shock and occupational stress is complex enough to warrant separate treatment in this text. See **Chapter 6**.

While the basic litigation procedures for personal injury and clinical negligence claims and the skills required of the solicitor are similar, there are differences, some of which are significant. Where the procedure for a clinical negligence claim differs notably from that of a personal injury claim, specific reference is made in the text.

Where a fatality arises from an accident in one of the above areas, special considerations arise. These are discussed in **Chapters 17** and **18**.

1.1.1   Causes of action

In most personal injury and clinical negligence cases, the claim is based on negligence. However, in relation to claims against highway authorities, and in relation to employers' liability claims resulting from incidents occurring prior to 1 October 2013, there may also be a claim arising from breaches of statutory duties. Some of the relevant statutory duties are explored in the text.

In clinical negligence claims against private hospitals and healthcare professionals who have provided advice and treatment on a private basis, there may be a claim in breach of contract. These claims lie beyond the scope of this book.

1.1.2   The CPR and the pre-action protocols

In accordance with the overriding objective set out in r 1 of the CPR 1998, personal injury and clinical negligence solicitors and their clients are required to have regard to the costs involved in pursuing the case, and to deal with the matter expeditiously and proportionately. This philosophy is to be adopted from the early days of the dispute, and reference needs to be made to the relevant pre-action protocol (PAP), which sets out the steps to be taken by the parties prior to the issue of proceedings. The full text of the PAP for Personal Injury Claims and the PAP for the Resolution of Clinical Disputes, both of which were substantially rewritten in April 2015, is set out in **Appendices 2** and **3**.

In April 2010, the Government introduced a new claims process for low value road traffic accident personal injury claims valued between £1,000 and £10,000. In July 2013, the upper financial limit was raised to £25,000 and, in addition, a similar protocol was introduced for low value employers' liability and public liability claims. The aim of these new protocols is to ensure that the process, which includes fixed time periods and fixed recoverable costs, delivers fair compensation to the claimant as soon as possible whilst keeping costs reasonable and proportionate. The Protocols, which apply only when certain criteria are fulfilled, are more prescriptive than other pre-action protocols. Consequently, this process is dealt with in some detail in **Chapter 21**, but is mentioned sparingly in the rest of the book. The full text of the Pre-action Protocol for Low Value Personal Injury (Employers' Liability and Public Liability) Claims is set out at **Appendix 4**.

1.2 PERSONAL INJURY CLAIMS

1.2.1 The claimant's perspective

The aim of the claimant's personal injury solicitor is to prove that the defendant was responsible for the client's injuries and to obtain the appropriate amount of compensation. Therefore, there are two essential elements to a personal injury claim: liability and quantum. This may sound obvious, but it is important that these two elements are paramount in the solicitor's mind throughout the case.

Personal injury claims can take time to progress. At the initial interview, it should be explained to the client how it is anticipated the case will proceed and a realistic timescale should be given (although this can be difficult) as to when the matter might be settled or reach trial. The client should be informed of the basic requirements of the relevant pre-action protocol and the time limits imposed on each side. It is important that the client is kept informed as the matter proceeds. Regular letters should be sent, updating the client on the current position. If a proactive approach is taken, this will avoid difficulties in the future.

1.2.1.1 Liability

It is for the claimant to prove his case; the onus will therefore be on the client to persuade the court that the defendant was in breach of a statutory or common law duty owed to the client. The claimant has to prove, on a balance of probabilities, that:

(a) the defendant owed him a duty of care and/or there was a relevant statutory duty;
(b) the defendant was in breach of that duty;
(c) the breach caused injury and consequential losses which were reasonably foreseeable.

This is further explored in the context of the various types of personal injury claim dealt with in this book in **Chapters 3, 4 and 6**.

1.2.1.2 Quantum

The claimant's solicitor should have as his aim the maximisation of damages for his client, and he must take all legitimate steps to achieve that aim. The assessment of damages is dealt with in **Chapter 15** and, where there has been a fatality, in **Chapter 18**. Most solicitors working in this area acknowledge that a weariness on the part of the victim himself can set in if months pass and the claimant perceives that little has been done, or due to anxiety at having to attend trial. This can result in the client accepting inappropriately low offers rather than instructing the solicitor to progress the matter to trial. This should be acknowledged as a factor to be dealt with by the solicitor, and the client's concerns should be anticipated.

Medical evidence is required by the court to prove the injuries suffered by the client. Instructing a doctor may appear to be a simple task, but the choice of the appropriate doctor is significant as the value of the client's injuries will be based on the medical evidence, including the reports of the medical experts. The instruction of experts is dealt with in **Chapter 11** and a list of important medical specialities is contained in **Chapter 2**.

1.2.2 The defendant's perspective

In many cases the defendant's personal injury solicitor will be instructed only when proceedings have been issued against the defendant. At all times prior to this, where the defendant is insured, the claimant's solicitor will correspond with the defendant's insurance company. Where the insurance company believes that liability will be established, and in some low value cases where it is not economically viable to defend the claim, it will attempt to reach a settlement. The vast majority of claims are settled before trial and a substantial number of these are settled before proceedings are issued.

Many insurance companies require the insured to sign a letter of authority allowing them to act on the insured's behalf and to dispose of the case in any way that the defendant's solicitor sees fit. This is often a formality, as the terms of the insurance policy will allow the insurance company and its solicitor to have control of the case. The role of insurers is explored further at **3.3**.

Increasingly, claims are being defended on the basis that they are entirely fraudulent or that injuries and consequential loss have been fraudulently exaggerated. This is explored further at **1.4** below.

1.3 CLINICAL NEGLIGENCE CLAIMS

1.3.1 The claimant's perspective

The essential aims in a clinical negligence claim are the same as in a personal injury claim, namely, to establish liability and maximise damages. However, these are frequently not the only aims and considerations. The client's trust in a respected profession has been lost, and the client will often lack knowledge and understanding as to what has happened to him. It must be explained to the client that he has to prove his claim, if he is to establish liability. One of the first distinctions which has to be made between personal injury and clinical negligence cases is that the issue of liability is normally far more complicated in the latter, and there is a greater chance that the claimant's claim will fail at trial (see **Chapter 5**). However, the law relating to the quantum of damages is the same in both personal injury and clinical negligence cases.

The costs involved in a clinical negligence case are usually higher than those incurred in a personal injury case. The clinical negligence pre-action protocol will have to be complied with, and the initial investigations prior to commencing the claim will involve the solicitor taking instructions, obtaining the client's medical notes, and then instructing an expert to assess the notes and evidence available. However, it is only then that any preliminary view on liability can be obtained. Unlike a personal injury case, the victim's clinical negligence solicitor will never be able to give a view on liability at the first interview. It will only be when the notes and an expert's view are obtained that any advice on liability can be given to the client.

A common concern expressed by clients is how they will continue to be treated by the doctor/ healthcare professional if there is an ongoing 'doctor/patient' relationship, and advice and support in relation to this may be required. In addition, the solicitor will need to establish whether the client's sole concern is to pursue a damages claim or if he has other objectives, for example to complain to the relevant NHS Trust, to report the alleged misconduct of a healthcare professional to the appropriate regulatory body and to prevent a similar event occurring in the future. In some cases, for example the death of a child, the client may not wish to pursue a claim at all but the other options may be hugely important to him. The options available to the client in such circumstances are set out in **Chapter 5**.

1.3.2 The defendant's perspective

The defendant's clinical negligence solicitor will usually be from a firm instructed by the defendant's indemnity insurers. In the case of most NHS bodies, the NHS Litigation Authority (NHSLA) will choose a solicitor from its panel. The defendant's solicitor will have the same basic aims as those of the defendant's personal injury solicitor. If liability can be refuted then the case will be vigorously defended; if liability is established, the case will be settled. However, there are also special factors that the defendant's clinical negligence solicitor must consider. One important factor is that the defendant is a professional person and, while damages will not be paid by him personally, his reputation, and possibly that of his employer in the case of the NHS, will be brought into question by any admission or finding of negligence on his part. This is one of the reasons why more clinical negligence claims than personal injury claims proceed to trial. Establishing liability in a clinical negligence case is not easy. While the patient may complain that the treatment was unsuccessful, it does not follow that the doctor was negligent, and the arguments available to the defendant's solicitor to refute negligence are wider and more complicated than in a personal injury case.

1.4 FRAUDULENT AND EXAGGERATED CLAIMS

Only the most naive of those acting on behalf of claimants would believe everything every client tells them to be the truth, the whole truth and nothing but the truth. The accounts of even the most honest of people may be tainted by one or more of the following: anger, grief, confusion, a misunderstanding, a sense of indignation, a distorted perspective, an unconscious tendency to exaggerate and, of course, memory loss. Solicitors should always test the evidence of their clients and witnesses, not least of all because a story which does not stack up in the opinion of the solicitor, is likely to be found wanting should the matter be tried in court.

Solicitors acting for claimants may also encounter individuals whose aim it is to make an entirely fraudulent claim, or whose conscious exaggeration of their injuries is such as to amount to fraud. Although, as a matter of professional conduct, it is irrelevant whether a solicitor believes his client's version of events to be true or not, where a solicitor *knows* his client is lying, he should take care not to deceive or mislead the court, or to be complicit in another person's deceiving or misleading the court (SRA Code of Conduct 2011, Outcomes 5.1 and 5.2). Moreover, in circumstances where a reasonably competent lawyer would have realised that the claim was fraudulent and had no reasonable prospect of success, a wasted costs order may be made against the firm (see *Rasoul v (1) Linkevicius (2) Groupama Insurance Company Limited* [2012] Lawtel Document AC0135642).

Defendants, and particularly their insurers, are becoming increasingly wise to such matters, and they are showing a greater inclination to investigate potentially fraudulent claims thoroughly, including using covert surveillance, and to challenge them in court. (Note that fraud should be pleaded in the defence – see **12.8.1.**)

For a fascinating insight into the magnitude of the problem of fraud in relation to RTAs, we recommend the full judgment in the case of *Locke v (1) Stuart (2) Axa Corporate Solutions Services Ltd* [2011] EWHC 399 (QB). This is particularly interesting because the defendant's insurers were able to use Facebook to demonstrate a connection between the claimant in this matter and claimants and defendants in a number of other claims.

Claimants should be aware of the following potential outcomes of dishonesty.

1.4.1 Striking out claim/reduction of damages

Clearly, courts will not award damages in relation to a claim which is entirely fraudulent. However, they have, at times, been reluctant to deprive a claimant of damages to which he is entitled either where he fraudulently attempted to obtain more than his entitlement, or where he lied to support the claim of another claimant. In *Shah v Ul-Haq and Others* [2009] EWCA Civ 542, the Court of Appeal held that there was no rule of law which entitled it to do so.

In *Fairclough Homes Ltd v Summers* [2012] UKSC 26, the Supreme Court disagreed, stating that the court does indeed have jurisdiction to strike out a claim in such circumstances, under CPR, r 3.4(2) for abuse of process, or under its inherent jurisdiction. However, it declined to make such an order, adding that the sanction was so extreme, it could barely envisage when it would be appropriate to do use it.

After *Fairclough*, a number of decisions reflected a more robust approach and a greater willingness to deprive dishonest claimants of damages to which they would have been entitled if the claim had not been fraudulently exaggerated. For example, in *Fari v Homes for Haringey* [2012] Lawtel Document AC0135666, Central London CC, the court struck out the claim of a woman who had grossly exaggerated the nature and extent of her injuries. She was subsequently jailed for contempt.

To bring further clarity to the position, s 57 of the Criminal Justice and Courts Act 2015 (CJCA 2015), enacted in April 2015, states:

(1) This section applies where, in proceedings on a claim for damages in respect of personal injury ('the primary claim')—

    (a) the court finds that the claimant is entitled to damages in respect of the claim, but

    (b) on an application by the defendant for the dismissal of the claim under this section, the court is satisfied on the balance of probabilities that the claimant has been fundamentally dishonest in relation to the primary claim or a related claim.

(2) The court must dismiss the primary claim, unless it is satisfied that the claimant would suffer substantial injustice if the claim were dismissed.

(3) The duty under subsection (2) includes the dismissal of any element of the primary claim in respect of which the claimant has not been dishonest.

1.4.2 Costs sanctions

As a result of qualified one way costs shifting (QOCS – see **9.3**), which was introduced in April 2013, the general rule in personal injury and clinical negligence claims is that a defendant will not be able to recover his own costs if he successfully defends the claim. However, where a claim is found to be *fundamentally dishonest*, or where it is struck out, QOCS will not apply. In *Gosling v Screwfix and another* (Cambridge County Court, 29 March 2014), Mr Gosling was found to be fundamentally dishonest in exaggerating his injuries following an accident at work, thus losing the protection of QOCS and being ordered to pay costs to the defendant on an indemnity basis.

Where a claimant has a genuine claim but the court dismisses it in its entirely due to fundamental dishonesty, s 57(4) of the CJCA 2015 requires the court to record the amount of damages it would have awarded to the claimant for injuries genuinely suffered, but for the dismissal of the claim. When assessing costs in such proceedings, the court must deduct this amount from the amount it would otherwise have ordered the claimant to pay in respect of the costs incurred by the defendant (s 57(5)).

In certain circumstances, courts may be prepared to make an additional order for costs of a punitive nature in order to act as a deterrent (see *Tasneem & Ors v Morley* (CC (Central London), 30 September 2013), when exemplary damages were awarded in recognition of the investigation costs incurred by the defendants' insurer, and *Hassan v (1) Cooper (2) Accident Claims Consultants Ltd* [2015] EWHC 540 (QB), where exemplary damages were calculated by reference to the amount the original claimant had sought to obtain by fraud, including costs).

1.4.3 Contempt proceedings and criminal charges for fraud

Increasingly, defendants are applying for permission to pursue contempt proceedings against claimants who have manufactured or exaggerated claims, and there has been an upturn in the number of individuals being imprisoned for contempt for this type of behaviour. The rules governing contempt are found in CPR 81 and PD 81, and guidance as to its application may be found in *Royal & Sun Alliance Insurance Plc v Kosky* [2013] EWHC 835 (QB).

In *Walton v Kirk* [2009] EWHC 703 (QB), Ms Kirk had claimed damages in excess of £750,000 following a road traffic accident. Liability was admitted by the defendant's insurers, but video surveillance showed that Ms Kirk had grossly exaggerated her injuries. In the ensuing contempt proceedings, it was held that exaggeration of a claim is not automatic proof of contempt. What may matter is the degree of exaggeration and/or the circumstances in which any exaggeration is made. Ms Kirk was found guilty in relation to just one statement, for which she was fined £2,500.

However, in *Motor Insurers' Bureau v Shikell & Others* [2011] EWHC 527 (QB), James Shikell claimed in excess of £1.2 million in respect of a head injury suffered in an RTA. The defendant was granted permission to bring contempt proceedings against Mr Shikell, his father, and a third man, who had signed a witness statement in support of the claim without reading it, for contempt, after surveillance revealed that he was an active, sporty man, with no significant disability. The Shikells were each sentenced to 12 months' imprisonment, and the third man was fined £750.

It should be noted that criminal charges may be brought against anyone who dishonestly makes false representations contrary to s 2 of the Fraud Act 2013. Such charges may arise when the accident was genuine but the claim has been fraudulently exaggerated (see R v W [2013] EWCA Crim 820).

Under s 57(7) of the CJCA 2015, when sentencing a claimant for contempt for fundamental dishonesty in a personal injury claim or in relation to any criminal proceedings resulting from such a claim, or otherwise disposing of such proceedings, the court must have regard to the dismissal of the primary claim. In other words, the claimant has already been punished by the denial of damages to which he would have been entitled had he not been dishonest, and the court is required to take note of this when determining the appropriate sentence.

1.4.4 Other initiatives for combating fraudulent claims

Due to increasing concerns regarding the perceived growth in fraudulent personal injury claims, the Government has introduced a number of other measures in an attempt to tackle the problem:

(a) *Referral fees.* Sections 56–60 of the Legal Aid, Punishment and Sentencing of Offenders Act 2012 (LASPO 2012) create a regulatory offence (but not a criminal offence) for regulated persons, including solicitors, barristers, legal executives, claims management companies and insurers, to pay or receive referral fees in personal injury and fatal accident cases (see SRA Code of Conduct 2011, Outcomes 6.4 and 9.8).

(b) *Inducements to claimants.* Sections 58–61 of the CJCA 2015 prohibit providers of legal services from offering inducements, such as cash, shopping vouchers and iPads, in order to persuade others to make a personal injury claim. Again, this provision does not create a criminal offence, but relevant regulators are required to ensure that appropriate arrangements for monitoring and enforcing the restriction are in place. The SRA has not introduced a specific rule in the SRA Code of Conduct 2011 to deal with inducements but, in an ethics guidance note 'Criminal Justice and Courts Act 2015 (CJCA) – ban on inducements in respect of personal injury claims', it states that firms found to be acting in breach of the ban would be in breach of the SRA Principles 2011, specifically Principles 1, 2, 4, 6 and 7.

(c) *Cold calling and nuisance texts.* Those which relate to the making of personal injury claims are strictly prohibited. Nevertheless, the majority of live calls and spam texts reported to the Information Commissioner's Office (ICO) relate to accident claims. Recent amendments made by s 139 of the Financial Services (Banking Reform) Act 2013 to the Schedule to the Compensation Act 2006 enable regulators to punish rogue claims management companies that use information based on such methods with a fine of up to 20% of their annual turnover, as well as suspending or removing their trading licence. In addition, the requirement for the ICO to show that the call has caused 'substantial damage or substantial distress' has been removed, making it easier for successful action to be taken. Outcome 8.3 of the SRA Code of Conduct 2011 prohibits unsolicited approaches, in person or by telephone, to members of the public.

(d) *askCUE PI.* In view of the fact that most fraudulent claims are low-value RTA claims, as from 1 June 2015, claimants' solicitors are required to check their clients' records held on the askCUE PI database to identify any previous incidents reported to insurers before using the Portal. See para 6.3A of the Pre-Action Protocol for Low Value Personal Injury Claims in Road Traffic Accidents and **Chapter 21** for further information.

(e) *Fixed cost medical reports.* In order to combat fraudulent claims for soft tissue injuries (often referred to as whiplash) following a road traffic accident, where the Claim

Notification Form (CNF) is submitted through the Portal, para 7.8A of the above-mentioned PAP requires the first report from a medical expert to be a fixed cost medical report. Provisions for accredited medical experts and the MedCo Portal (www.medco.org.uk) apply where the CNF is submitted on or after 6 April 2015 (see **Chapter 11**).

1.5 CONCLUSION

Personal injury and clinical negligence litigation is a diverse and expanding area. At its least complex, it may involve a claim for compensation for minor injuries suffered as a result of a road traffic accident, or, at the other extreme, it may involve representing a child who is severely disabled, allegedly as a result of being starved of oxygen at birth.

Overviews of the main steps in a typical personal injury claim and a typical clinical negligence claim are set out in **1.6** below.

This text aims to provide an introduction to personal injury and clinical negligence litigation, but reference should also be made to practitioners' works and original sources. Where appropriate, reference must be made to the CPR 1998 and pre-action protocols.

1.6 OVERVIEWS OF PERSONAL INJURY AND CLINICAL NEGLIGENCE (

1.6.1 Main steps in a typical personal injury claim

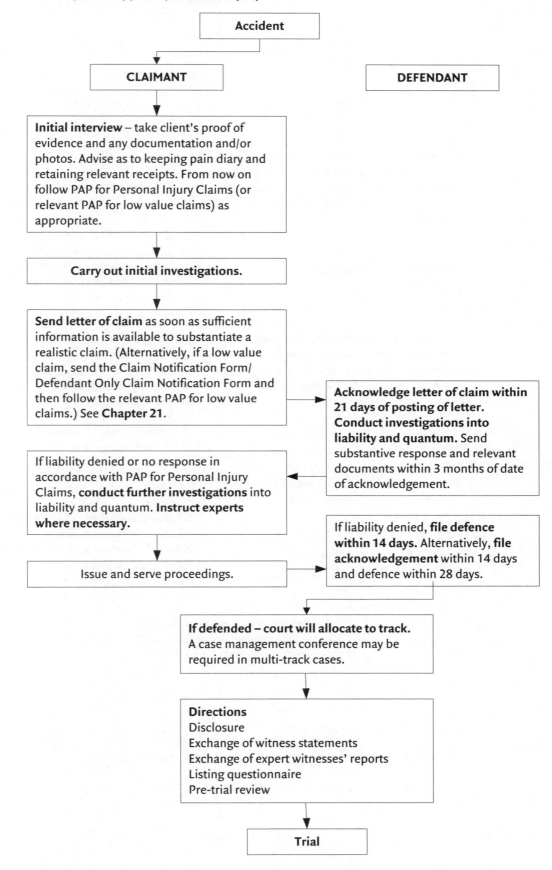

1.6.2   Main steps in a typical clinical negligence claim against an NHS Trust

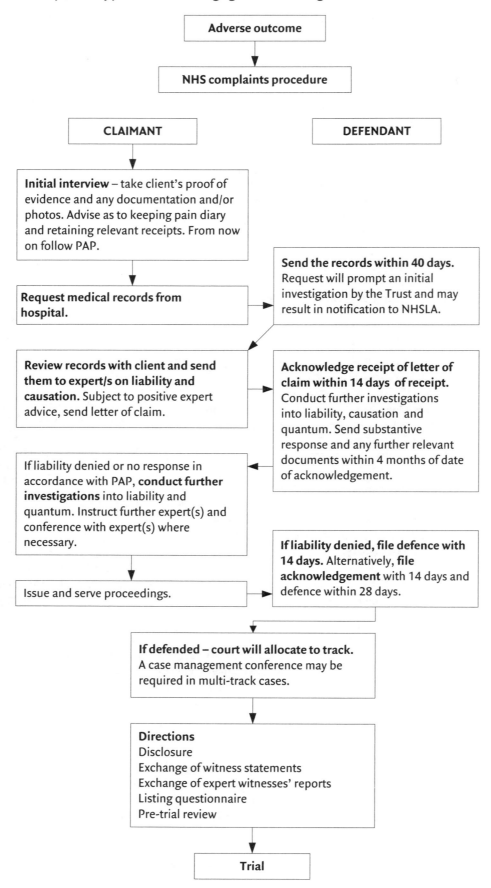

Adverse outcome

NHS complaints procedure

CLAIMANT   **DEFENDANT**

Initial interview – take client's proof of evidence and any documentation and/or photos. Advise as to keeping pain diary and retaining relevant receipts. From now on follow PAP.

Request medical records from hospital.

Send the records within 40 days. Request will prompt an initial investigation by the Trust and may result in notification to NHSLA.

Review records with client and send them to expert/s on liability and causation. Subject to positive expert advice, send letter of claim.

Acknowledge receipt of letter of claim within 14 days of receipt. Conduct further investigations into liability, causation and quantum. Send substantive response and any further relevant documents within 4 months of date of acknowledgement.

If liability denied or no response in accordance with PAP, **conduct further investigations** into liability and quantum. Instruct further expert(s) and conference with expert(s) where necessary.

Issue and serve proceedings.

If liability denied, file defence with 14 days. Alternatively, **file acknowledgement** with 14 days and defence within 28 days.

If defended – court will allocate to track. A case management conference may be required in multi-track cases.

Directions
Disclosure
Exchange of witness statements
Exchange of expert witnesses' reports
Listing questionnaire
Pre-trial review

Trial

CHAPTER 2

PERSONAL INJURY AND CLINICAL NEGLIGENCE TERMINOLOGY

LEARNING OUTCOMES

After reading this chapter you will be able to:

- appreciate the importance to the personal injury/clinical negligence solicitor of acquiring a working knowledge of medical terms and abbreviations, and of understanding the nature of the most common injuries that arise and the scope of different types of medical expertise
- know where to find assistance to acquire such information and knowledge.

2.1 INTRODUCTION

A trainee solicitor who enters the personal injury/clinical negligence department of a legal firm has to cope not only with the pressures of being able to understand fully and advise accurately on the law, but also with a barrage of unfamiliar medical terms. If a trainee is faced on his first day with his colleagues referring to claims dealing with work-related upper limb disorders (WRULD), vibration white finger (VWF), post-traumatic stress disorder (PTSD), etc, and he is unfamiliar with the terminology, he will obviously be at a disadvantage.

There can be no doubt that proficient solicitors who practise in this area have extensive medical knowledge and a detailed understanding of the terms used. This knowledge enables them to comprehend fully clients' complaints, experts' reports and medical notes, and also enables them to explain matters thoroughly to clients. For example, upon receipt of a medical report obtained following a simple road traffic accident, the solicitor must read the report carefully and then send it to the client. If the client subsequently contacts his solicitor stating that he does not understand the terms used in the medical report, it is not acceptable for the solicitor to say, 'Neither do I'!

In addition, it is important for the trainee solicitor to have some knowledge of the areas of medical specialisation, so that appropriate experts can be instructed.

The purpose of this chapter is to assist in the understanding of the terms and abbreviations commonly found in personal injury/clinical negligence work, and of the main areas of specialisation. It should be noted, however, that a medical dictionary is an essential requirement for the personal injury solicitor, and more detailed medical texts may also be of use.

2.2 COMMON INJURIES, CONDITIONS AND MEDICAL TERMS

2.2.1 Orthopaedic injuries

Orthopaedic (bone) injuries are the most common injuries encountered in a personal injury claim. They are normally incurred as a result of falling, or from being involved in a road traffic accident.

The most common terms found in orthopaedic medical reports are as follows:

(a) *Arthrodesis* – means a joint that has been fused, either because of pre-existing joint disease or because of injury as a result of trauma to the joint.

(b) *Arthroplasty* – means that the joint has been reconstructed, often by the use of a joint implant to replace one or more parts of the components of a joint.

(c) *Contusion* – means an injury to the skin and the deeper tissues in the surrounding area which is accompanied by bleeding from damaged blood vessels. The skin, however, is not broken. The simplest form of contusion is a bruise, developing through to a contusion accompanied by a large haematoma, which is a collection of blood under the surface of the skin.

(d) *Dislocation* – means an injury which results in the bones of a joint being out of alignment or connection with one another. There is usually associated ligament and soft tissue damage.

(e) *Fracture* – means a break in the continuity of a bone.

(f) *Sprain* – means an injury in the region of a joint with associated ligament and soft tissue damage.

(g) *Subluxation* – a joint which has subluxed has undergone a partial dislocation, and subluxation is a term which is sometimes used to describe a sprain.

A client who has an orthopaedic injury may also undergo *traction*, ie a system of weights and pulleys is used to pull muscle groups, so as to reduce/immobilise fractures and put the bones back into alignment.

In general, the most common fractures occur to:

(a) *The clavicle (collar bone)* – these fractures are especially common in children and young adults, and are almost always due to falls or direct trauma to the point of the shoulder. Treatment involves wearing a sling until the pain has subsided. Surgical intervention is very rarely required and is usually indicated only if there is a risk to nearby nerves or blood vessels.

(b) *The surgical neck of the humerus (the long bone stretching from the shoulder to the elbow)* – these fractures are usually treated with a sling; but if badly displaced, are surgically treated and fixed with metal pins.

(c) *The shaft of the humerus* – these fractures can occur at any point along the humerus and are usually treated by immobilising the fracture in a plaster of Paris cast for six to eight weeks.

(d) *The radius (the bone running from the elbow to the base of the thumb)* – there are many different types of radial fracture but the most common is the Colles fracture.

(e) *The femur (the thigh bone)* – these fractures can occur at any point along the length of the femur. The most common sites are the neck or the shaft of the femur. Treatment tends to be surgical. Clients with fractures of the shaft of the femur will be placed in a Thomas splint, which immobilises the fracture.

(f) *The tibia and fibula* – these two bones make up the part of the leg from beneath the knee to the ankle. Fracture of these two bones can result from direct or indirect trauma.

(g) *The pelvis* – a number of bones which together form a ring-like structure at the base of the spine. The pelvis contains the vertebrae of the sacral spine and the hip joints, and fractures can occur at any point. Fractures to the pelvis are of two main types: first, isolated fractures of one of the bones which make up the pelvis; and, secondly, double fractures of the bones which make up the pelvic rim.

2.2.2 Hand injuries

In interpreting medical reports regarding hand injuries, a basic understanding of the anatomical position of the hand is required.

The functional parts of the hand are the wrist and the fingers. If the wrist is flexed, the hand is brought forward; if the hand is positioned as if to push someone away, it is said to be extended. The wrist is described as being 'pronated' if the palm of the hand is pointing towards the floor, and is described as being 'supinated' if the hand is positioned to receive something.

If the hand is made into a fist, the fingers are described as flexed; if the hand is opened out as if to receive something, the fingers are described as extended.

The fingers are described as the distal half of the hand, and are made up of three joints. Working from the palm of the hand out towards the end of the fingers, the three joints are the metacarpo-phalangeal joint (the knuckles), the proximal interphalangeal joint, and the distal interphalangeal joint, which is the joint nearest to the finger nails. The thumb has the same number of joints, but appears shorter because it attaches to the hand lower down; 70% of the function of the hand is provided by the thumb.

2.2.3 Head injuries

The following terms are used in relation to head injuries:

(a)   *aphasia* – the loss of power of speech;

(b)   *anosmia* – the loss of the sense of smell;

(c)   *cerebral oedema* – a swelling of the brain;

(d)   *closed head injury* – a head injury in which there is no open skull fracture;

(e)   *concussion* – instantaneous loss of consciousness due to a blow on the head;

(f)   *diffuse axonal injury* – a brain injury which involves shearing of the brain tissue itself;

(g)   *dysphasia* – a difficulty in understanding language and in self-expression;

(h)   *extradural haematoma* – a blood clot which lies immediately above the brain and its protective membranes and below the surface of the skull;

(i)   *Glasgow Coma Scale* – a system of assessing neurological function;

(j)   *hydrocephalus* – a condition which arises due to an increase in the amount of cerebro-spinal fluid within the cranial cavity;

(k)   *hemiplegia* – paralysis of one side of the body;

(l)   *intracerebral* – within the substance of the brain itself;

(m)   *monoplegia* – a paralysis of one limb;

(n)   *open head injury* – a head injury with an associated depressed skull fracture;

(o)   *subdural haematoma* – a blood clot lying in-between the brain and its protective membranes.

2.2.4 Injuries to the skin

The following terms are used to describe injuries to the skin:

(a)   *abrasion* – occurs when the surface of the skin is rubbed off due to a mechanical injury;

(b)   *hypertrophy* – the overgranulation of scar tissue which can lead to disfigurement;

(c)   *laceration* – a wound to the skin which has jagged, irregular edges.

2.2.5 Whiplash/soft tissue injuries

The term 'whiplash injury' is not a medical term at all, but is one which is used by lawyers and the general public to describe a whole range of symptoms suffered, in the main, by someone whose head is thrown forward in a sudden forceful jerk – literally whipped forward – and back. Medical practitioners may prefer to use the terms 'cervical sprain' or 'hyperextension injuries of the neck', and recent legislation uses the term 'soft tissue injury'. This type of injury is commonly associated with road traffic accidents, but it can also result from other accidents (such as tripping and slipping), sporting activities (such as biking and diving) and assaults.

The cause of the injuries associated with whiplash is the stretching and straining of the soft tissues – the tendons, ligaments and muscles – supporting the cervical spine (ie in the neck region). Symptoms can be of widely varying severity, and may include pain and stiffness in the neck, backache, tingling and numbness in the arms and possibly in the hands, headaches, dizziness, ringing in the ears, tiredness, inability to concentrate, memory loss, blurred vision, nausea and reduced libido. Typically, symptoms will not be present immediately after the accident but will develop over one or two days, and may gradually get worse before they start to improve. Most people make a full recovery within days or weeks, but where symptoms are severe, it may take months or even years for them to subside.

As these injuries are to the soft tissues, they cannot be detected by means of an MRI scan, CT scan or an x-ray, and they are otherwise difficult to diagnose accurately. This means that it is sometimes difficult to assess whether a claim is spurious or not.

2.2.6 Work-related upper limb disorders

The term 'repetitive strain injury' is commonly used by the general public to describe musculoskeletal problems of the arm and hand associated with repetitive activity, such as typing or assembly work. However, this term does not accurately reflect the fact that the condition may not be due to repetitive work and may not be the result of a strain. Consequently, the term 'work-related upper limb disorder' (WRULD) is to be preferred.

WRULDs, which are common across a wide range of occupations, may be caused by repetitive or forceful activities, including lifting or carrying heavy objects, poor posture and/or carrying out activities for long periods without adequate breaks. In some cases, a WRULD may be caused by a single strain or trauma resulting, for example, from carrying a heavy load. In other cases, problems are caused by vibration, due to the use of tools such as chainsaws, grinders or drills.

Symptoms include aches, pain, weakness, numbness, tingling, stiffness, swelling and cramp in the arm and hand, including the fingers, wrist, forearm, elbow, shoulder and neck. In many instances, rest or adjustments to the working environment (the desk layout or assembly line) or the way that work is managed will alleviate the symptoms, but in some cases the condition is permanent.

It may be possible for a precise medical diagnosis to be made, for example, carpal tunnel syndrome, tenosynovitis or vibration white finger.

Controversy surrounds claims for WRULDs due to the fact that some specific conditions, such as carpal tunnel syndrome, may be caused by factors not related to the workplace and because some WRULDs are non-specific (ie, a medical diagnosis is not possible).

2.2.7 Industrial deafness

Industrial deafness claims are brought by those who have suffered hearing loss due to exposure at work to a high level of noise for a long period of time. For example, employees working in the steel industry, shipbuilding or other manufacturing industry may suffer from industrial deafness. Expert medical evidence is required to prove the loss of hearing, and evidence relating to the employees' working conditions is also required. Employers should, for example, have a system of assessing the risk from noise, provide ear protectors and have clearly marked zones where ear protection must be worn.

2.2.8 Asbestos related conditions

Where people are exposed to asbestos, dust or fibres may be inhaled which can move to the lungs or to the pleura, which is the membrane surrounding the lungs. Where this occurs, a number of conditions of varying severity may arise.

Asbestosis is a form of *pneumoconiosis*, which is a general term applied to any chronic form of inflammation of the lungs affecting people who are liable to inhale irritating substances or particles at work. Asbestosis occurs due to the inhalation of mainly blue or brown asbestos dust, which leads to the development of widespread scarring of the lung tissue and causes severe breathing difficulties. The main hazard, however, is the potential for the development of a type of cancer called mesothelioma, which affects the lungs, the pleura or, more rarely, the ovaries.

Pleural plaques are areas of fibrosis, sometimes partly calcified, on the pleura. Typically, there are no symptoms, but there is evidence to conclude that individuals who have pleural plaques have an increased risk of developing mesothelioma.

Where these areas of fibrosis are more widespread, they can prevent the lungs from working properly and thereby cause difficulties with breathing. This is known as pleural thickening

2.2.9 Occupational asthma

Occupational asthma may develop following exposure to a precipitating factor in the workplace, for example flour.

Asthma is a breathing disorder characterised by a narrowing of the airways within the lungs. The main symptom is breathlessness and an associated cough. It is an extremely distressing condition and, if left untreated, can be fatal.

2.2.10 Occupational dermatitis

Dermatitis is an inflammation of the skin, which is usually caused by direct contact with some irritating substance.

Occupational dermatitis is the most common of all the occupational diseases.

2.2.11 Occupational stress

Following the case of *Walker v Northumberland County Council* [1995] 1 All ER 737, in which a social services officer received compensation for stress induced by his employment (he suffered a nervous breakdown), a number of occupational stress claims have been brought before the courts. Careful consideration needs to be given as to whether the particular client will satisfy the necessary criteria to persuade the court to award damages in these circumstances. Occupational stress is considered in more detail in **Chapter 6**.

2.2.12 Post-traumatic stress disorder

Post-traumatic stress disorder (PTSD) has become more prominent in recent years. This expression refers to a psychological illness in which the claimant suffers from a variety of symptoms, which may include flashbacks, panic attacks, palpitations, chest pain, nausea, constipation, diarrhoea, insomnia, eating disorders, extreme fatigue and loss of libido.

It is important that medical evidence is obtained to support the injury, so that the defendants cannot make the allegation that the claimant has simply been 'shaken up'. This type of injury must be considered by the claimant's solicitor, even if the client concentrates only on his physical injuries when he is asked at the first interview what injuries he has suffered as a result of the accident. Post-traumatic stress is considered in more detail in **Chapter 6**.

2.2.13   Obstetrics

A normal labour and delivery take place in three stages. The first stage refers to the period of time it takes the cervix to dilate fully to 10 cms, and this is the longest stage of labour. The full dilation of the cervix is also associated with the rupture of the amnion, which is the tough fibrous membrane lining the cavity of the womb during pregnancy, containing amniotic fluid which supports the foetus. The rupture of the amnion is often referred to as 'the breaking of the waters'. The second stage of labour is the actual birth of the baby. The third stage is the delivery of the placenta.

If a baby is deprived of oxygen, it is said to have become 'hypoxic'. Hypoxia refers to a state where there is an inadequate supply of oxygen to maintain normal tissue function. If a baby is deemed to be in danger, it will be intubated and ventilated. This involves the insertion of an endotracheal tube into the baby's trachea to facilitate the maintenance of the baby's airway.

Once a baby is born, it is assessed using the Apgar score. This is a method of assessing a baby's condition by giving a score of 0, 1 or 2 to each of five signs: colour, heart rate, muscle tone, respiratory effort, and response to stimulation. A total score of 10 is the best Apgar score. If a baby is described as 'apnoeic', it means that it is not breathing; 'bradycardia' refers to the fact that the baby's heart is beating too slowly.

Perinatal mortality refers to the death of a foetus after the 28th week of pregnancy and to the death of the newborn child during the first week of life.

2.2.14   Cerebral palsy

Cerebral palsy is a general term used by medical practitioners to refer to a set of neurological conditions occurring in infancy or early childhood which affect movement and coordination. There are several different types of varying severity, the main ones being:

(a)   *Spastic cerebral palsy* – some of the muscles in the body are tight, stiff and weak, making control of movement of the affected arm or leg difficult. The degree of spasticity can vary significantly from case to case, but in the most severe cases the muscles in the affected limb may become permanently contracted.

(b)   *Athetoid (dyskinetic) cerebral palsy* – characterised by involuntary slow, writhing movements of the limbs and sometimes sudden muscle spasms. Sufferers have difficulty holding items or staying in one position.

(c)   *Ataxic cerebral palsy* – problems include difficulty with balance, causing unsteadinesss when walking, shaky movements of the hands, making writing difficult, and speech difficulties.

(d)   *Mixed cerebral palsy* – a combination of two or more of the above.

In addition to the above symptoms, there may a lack of coordination of the muscles of the mouth, causing speech and feeding problems, visual and hearing problems, and epilepsy. The symptoms often lead others to conclude that the sufferer has learning difficulties, but the condition does not, of itself, affect intelligence.

In a minority of cases (thought to be about 1:10) cerebral palsy is caused by problems during labour and birth, such as lack of oxygen or trauma. In the majority of the remaining cases, the damage arises while the baby is developing in the womb, as a result of genetic problems, malformations of the brain or maternal infection, such as rubella or toxoplasmosis. Infantile infections (especially encephalitis or meningitis) can also be causative.

Cerebral palsy is not a progressive condition, but the strains it places upon the body can lead to further problems in later life. There is no cure, but sufferers can benefit greatly from physiotherapy, occupational therapy, speech therapy and conductive education.

2.3 AREAS OF MEDICAL SPECIALITY

In dealing with his caseload, the personal injury and clinical negligence lawyer may require expert evidence to be given by a wide range of medical specialists. The following are amongst the most common areas of expertise. In order to avoid offending medical experts, it is useful to remember that consultant surgeons are known as 'Mr' 'Mrs' or 'Ms', rather than 'Dr'.

(a) *Anaesthesia* – either renders the patient unconscious (general anaesthesia) or removes sensation in a specific area (local anaesthesia), thereby enabling surgery or other procedures to be performed without the patient incurring pain and distress. An anaesthetist assesses the patient's fitness to undergo anaesthesia, chooses and administers the appropriate drugs, monitors the patient during the operation or procedure, and supervises the recovery period. He also plays a major role in pain management. A consultant anaesthetist will usually have 'FRCA' (Fellow of the Royal College of Anaesthetists) after his name.

(b) *Cardiology* – the study of the diseases of the heart. A cardiologist is a physician who specialises in this branch of medicine. A cardiac surgeon carries out surgical procedures in relation to the heart. If a cardiac surgeon has also been trained in the field of vascular surgery (relating to diseases affecting the arteries and veins) and/or thoracic surgery (relating to diseases inside the thorax – the chest – including the oesophagus and the diaphragm), he will be a cardiovascular, cardiothoracic or cardiovascular thoracic surgeon. A consultant cardiologist will usually have 'MRCP' or 'FRCP' (Membership or Fellowship of one of the Royal Colleges of Physicians) after his name. A cardiac surgeon will have 'FRCS' (Fellow of the Royal College of Surgeons) after his name.

(c) *Dermatology* – deals with the diagnosis and treatment of disorders of the skin, such as eczema, psoriasis, dermatitis and skin infections, and those affecting the hair and nails. A consultant dermatologist will usually have 'MRCP' or 'FRCP' after his name.

(d) *Geriatric medicine* – relates to disorders and diseases associated with old age (usually over 65) and their social consequences. A consultant geriatrician will usually have 'MRCP' or 'FRCP' after his name.

(e) *Gynaecology* – deals with the female pelvic and urogenital organs in both the normal and diseased state. It encompasses aspects of contraception, abortion and in vitro fertilisation (IVF). Practitioners may also specialise in obstetrics (see below). A consultant gynaecologist will have 'MRCOG' or 'FRCOG' (Membership or Fellowship of the Royal College of Obstetricians and Gynaecologists) after his name.

(f) *Haematology* – the study and treatment of blood and blood disorders, such as blood clotting deficiencies, leukaemia, myeloma, lymphoma, and Hodgkin's Disease. A haematologist also deals with blood transfusions and treatments involving warfarin and heparin. A consultant haematologist will have FRCPath' (Fellowship of one of the Royal Colleges of Pathologists) after his name.

(g) *Medical oncology* – the treatment of cancer. Clinical oncologists are largely concerned with radiotherapy, whilst medical oncologists deal with the medical management of those suffering from the disease. They liaise with primary care providers, clinical oncologists and other health professionals, and providers of palliative care. The consultant oncologist may have 'MRCP' or 'FRCP', or 'FRCR' (Fellow of the Royal College of Radiologists) or 'FRCS' after his name.

(h) *Neurology* – the study of the nervous system and its disorders, ie the patient's nerves, sensory and motor functions and reflexes, and will cover injuries to the brain, neck and back, neurodegenerative disorders, epilepsy and multiple sclerosis. A consultant neurologist will have 'MRCP' or 'FRCP' after his name. A neurosurgeon operates on the brain and spine, and deals with trauma and injuries to both, with brain tumours and haemorrhages, and with spinal nerve problems. A consultant neurosurgeon will have 'FRCS' after his name.

(i)   *Obstetrics* – covers pregnancy and birth, and is concerned with the health of the mother and of the foetus from conception to delivery. The obstetrician will also deal with sterilisations and infertility, cervical cancer, tumours of the ovaries and endometriosis. Both doctors and nurses can specialise in obstetrics. A consultant obstetrician will have 'MRCOG' or 'FRCOG' after his name.

(j)   *Occupational health* – this deals with the effect of work on the individual's health, both mental and physical, and the effect of ill-health on the individual's work. Specialists identify and treat specific occupational illnesses and diseases, and deal with the prevention of ill-health caused by chemical, biological, physical and psychological factors arising in the workplace. The term 'occupational health' covers a number of areas, and therefore there are various specialists, including occupational physicians, occupational psychologists, occupational health nurses, occupational hygienists, disability managers, workplace counsellors, health and safety practitioners, and workplace physiotherapists. The consultant occupational physician will usually have 'FFOM' (Fellow of the Faculty of Occupational Medicine) after his name. Others specialising in this area may have a Diploma in Occupational Medicine (DOccMED).

(k)   *Ophthalmology* – the diagnosis and treatment of disorders of the eye. The consultant ophthalmologist will usually have 'FRCOphth' (Fellow of the Royal College of Ophthalmologists) after his name.

(l)   *Orthopaedics* – this is concerned with injuries to and disorders of the bones and muscles. Surgeons who work in this area may specialise in certain parts of the body – the knee, the hip, the spine etc. The orthopaedic surgeon will have FRCS after his name, possibly followed by (Orth) and/or (Tr & Orth) signifying his specialism in orthopaedics and trauma.

(m)   *Paediatrics* – diseases and illness affecting children. A paediatrician may have a sub-speciality, eg a paediatric neurologist, a paediatric surgeon, etc. The consultant paediatrician will normally have 'MRCP' or 'FRCP' after his name, and may have 'FRCPCH' (Fellow of the Royal College of Paediatrics and Child Health).

(n)   *Palliative care* – the care of patients suffering from a terminal illness, including pain control and psychological and spiritual care, and the provision of services either at home or in a hospital, hospice or day centre. It also encompasses support for the family of the patient, which continues into the bereavement period.

(o)   *Pathology* – the science of the changes which the body goes through as a result of disease. A pathologist examines body samples in order to diagnose disease and undertakes post-mortem examinations in order to determine the cause of death. The consultant pathologist will have 'FRCPath' after his name.

(p)   *Physiotherapy* – the use of exercise, manipulation, and heat in the treatment of disease or injury, which is often essential in the rehabilitation process. All physiotherapists will have either 'MCSP' (Member of the Chartered Society of Physiotherapy) or 'FCSP' (Fellow of the Chartered Society of Physiotherapy) after their names, and must be registered with the Health Professions Council, the regulatory body for physiotherapists.

(q)   *Psychiatry* – the branch of medical science which treats mental disorder and disease, and which helps with the management of individuals with learning disabilities. A psychiatrist deals with depression, PTSD, drug and substance abuse, schizophrenia, etc. A consultant psychiatrist will have 'MRCPsych' or 'FRCPsych' (Member or Fellow of the Royal Colleges of Psychiatrists) after his name.

(r)   *Psychology* – the scientific study of how people think, how and why they act, react and interact as they do. It covers memory, rational/irrational thought, intelligence, learning, personality, perception and emotions. Psychology is used in promoting rehabilitation and assessing rehabilitation needs following an accident. There are a number of different branches, including educational psychology (concerned with children's learning and development), clinical psychology (concerned with reducing psychological stress in those suffering from depression, mental illness, brain injuries and the after effects of trauma), health psychology (concerned with behaviour relating to health, illness and care) and occupational psychology (relating to how people perform at work). Psychologists are not medically qualified but rather have a graduate degree in psychology plus an accredited postgraduate qualification leading to chartered status.

(s)   *Rheumatology* – medical speciality concerned with the study and management of diseases of the joints and connective tissue, including rheumatoid arthritis, osteoarthritis, osteoporosis, whiplash and repetitive strain injury. A consultant rheumatologist will have 'MRCP' or 'FRCP' after his name.

2.4   COMMON ABBREVIATIONS USED IN MEDICAL RECORDS

AAL	Anterior axillary line
ACTH	Adrenocorticotrophic hormone
ADH	Antidiuretic hormone
AE	Air entry
AF	Atrial fibrillation
AFB	Acid fast bacillus (TB)
AFP	Alpha-fetoprotein
AJ	Ankle jerk (reflex)
Alk	Alkaline (phos = phosphatase)
An	Anaemia
ANF	Antinuclear factor
Anti-D	This gamma globulin must be given by injection to Rhesus negative mother who delivers/ aborts Rhesus positive child/foetus to prevent mother developing antibodies which could damage a subsequent Rhesus positive baby
Apgar	Apgar score: means of recording baby's condition at and shortly after birth by observing and 'scoring' (0, 1 or 2) 5 parameters
AP	Anteroposterior
APH	Antepartum haemorrhage
ARM	Artificial rupture of membranes (labour)
ASO	Antistreptolysin O
ATN	Acute tubular necrosis
A/V	(a) Anteverted
	(b) Arterio venous
AXR	Abdominal x-ray (plain)
Ba	Barium
BD	To be given/taken twice a day
BJ	Biceps jerk (reflex, see AJ)
BMJ	British Medical Journal
BMR	Basal metabolic rate
BO	Bowels open
BP	British Pharmacopoeia
BP	Blood pressure
BS	(a) Breath sounds
	(b) Bowel sounds
	(c) Blood sugar
C_2H_5OH	Alcohol
ca	Carcinoma/cancer
Ca	Calcium
Caps	Capsules
CAT scan	Computed axial tomograph scan
CBD	Common bile duct
cc	(a) Carcinoma (cancer)
	(b) Cubic centimetre

CCF	Congestive cardiac failure
Ch VS	Chorionic villus sampling
CI	Contraindications
Cl	Clubbing (of finger or toe nails)
CLL	Chronic lymphocytic leukaemia
CML	Chronic myeloid leukaemia
CMV	Cytomegalovirus
CN I-XII	Cranial nerves 1 – 12
CNS	Central nervous system
C/O	Complaining of
CO_2	Carbon dioxide
COETT	Cuffed oral endotracheal tube
COT	Cuffed oral tube (an endotracheal tube used for ventilating a patient who cannot breathe unaided)
CPD	Cephalo-pelvic disproportion (baby too large to fit through pelvis)
CSF	Cerebro-spinal fluid
CT	Computerised tomography
CTG	Cardiotocograph (trace during labour of baby's heart and mother's contractions)
CVA	Cardiovascular accident (stroke)
CVP	Central venous pressure
CVS	Cardiovascular system
Cx	Cervix
CXR	Chest x-ray
Cy	Cyanosis
DB	Decibel
D&C	Dilation (cervical) and curettage
DM	Diabetes mellitus
DNA	Deoxyribonucleic acid (also 'did not attend')
DOA	Dead on arrival
D&V	Diarrhoea and vomiting
DVT	Deep venous thrombosis
D/W	Discussed with
Dx	Diagnosis
ECG	Electrocardiography
ECT	Electroconvulsive therapy
EDC	Expected date of confinement
EDD	Expected date of delivery
EEG	Electroencephalogram/graph (brain scan)
ENT	Ear, nose and throat
ERCP	Endoscopic retrograde choledochopancreatico/graphy/scope
ERPC	Evacuation of retained products of conception
ESR	Erythrocyte sedimentation rate (blood)
ETR	Examined through clothes
EtoH	Alcohol
ET(T)	Endotracheal (tube)
EUA	Examined under anaesthesia
FB	(a) Finger's breadth
	(b) Foreign body
FBC	Full blood count
FBS	Foetal blood sampling (a procedure which is carried out during labour to check on the baby's condition)
FH	Family history
FHH	Foetal heart heard
FHHR	Foetal heart heard regular
FHR	Foetal heart rate
FMF	Foetal movements felt

FSE	Foetal scalp electrode
FSH	Follicle-stimulating hormone
G	gram
GA	General anaesthesia
GB	Gall bladder
GFR	Glomerular filtration rate
GI	Gastro-intestinal
GIT	Gastro-intestinal tract
G6PD	Glucose 6 phosphate dehydrogenase
GP	General practitioner
GTT	Glucose tolerance test (for diabetes)
GU	Genito-urinary
GUT	Genito-urinary tract
h	Hour
Hb	Haemoglobin
Hct	Haemocrit
HOCM	Hypertrophic obstructive cardiomyopathy
HPC	History of presenting complaint
HRT	Hormone replacement therapy
HS	Heart sounds
HVS	High vaginal swab
Hx	History
ICP	Intracranial pressure
ICS	Intercostal space
IDA	Iron deficiency anaemia
IDDM	Insulin dependent diabetes mellitus
Ig	Immunoglobulin
IJ	Internal jugular vein
IM	Intramuscular
ISQ	In status quo
IT	Intrathecal
ITP	Idiopathic thrombocytopenic purpura
ITU	Intensive therapy unit
iu	International unit
IUCD	Intrauterine contraceptive device
IV	Intravenous
IVC	Inferior vena cava
IVI	Intravenous infusion (drip)
IVU	Intravenous urography
Ix	Investigations
J	Jaundice
°JACCO	No jaundice, anaemia, cyanosis, clubbing or oedema
JVP	Jugular venous pressure
K^+	Potassium
kg	Kilogram
KJ	Knee jerk (reflex, see AJ)
kPa	Kilopascal, approximately 7.5 mmHg
L	(a) Litre
	(b) Left
LA	Local anaesthesia
LBBB	Left bundle branch block
LFTs	Liver function tests
LH	Luteinising hormone
LIF	Left iliac fossa
LIH	Left inguinal hernia

LMN	Lower motor neurone
LMP	First day of the last menstrual period
LN	Lymph node
LOA	Left occiput anterior (position of baby's head at delivery, see also LOP, ROA, ROP, LOL, ROL, OA, OP)
LOC	Loss of consciousness
LOL	Left occipitolateral (see LOA)
LOP	Left occiput posterior (see LOA above)
LP	Lumbar puncture
LS	Letter sent
LSCS	Lower segment caesarean section (the 'normal' type of caesarean section)
LSKK	Liver, spleen and kidneys
LUQ	Left upper quadrant
LVF	Left ventricular failure
LVH	Left ventricular hypertrophy
mane	In the morning
mcg	Microgram
MCL	Mid clavicular line
MCV	Mean cell volume
μg	Microgram
mg	Milligram
mist	mixture
mitte 1/12	Supply/give/send/provide
ml	Millilitres
mmHg	Millimetres of mercury (pressure)
mMol	Millimol
MRI	Magnetic resonance imaging (=NMRI)
MS	Multiple sclerosis
MSU	Mid stream urine
N&V	Nausea and vomiting
Na	Sodium
$NaHCO_3$	Sodium bicarbonate
NAD	Nothing abnormal diagnosed/detected
NBM	Nil by mouth
ND	Notifiable disease
ng	Nanogram
NG	(a) Naso-gastric
	(b) Carcinoma/cancer (neoplastic growth)
NMCS	No malignant cells seen
NMR	Nuclear magnetic resonance (scan)
noct/nocte	At night
NOF	Neck of femur
N/S	Normal size
NSAID	Non-steroidal anti-inflammatory drugs
O_2	Oxygen
OA	(a) Occipito-anterior (see LOA)
	(b) Osteoarthritis
OCP	Oral contraceptive pill
OE	On examination
OP	Occipito-posterior (see LOA)
Orthop.	Orthopnoea (breathlessness on lying flat)
P	Pulse
P or π	Period
PA	Posteroanterior
PAN	Polyarteritis nodosa

PC	Post cibum (after food)
pCO_2	Partial pressure of carbon dioxide (normally in blood)
PCV	Packed cell volume
PERLA	Pupils are equal and react to light and accommodation
PE	(a) Pulmonary embolism
	(b) Pre eclampsia
PEFR	Peak expiratory flow rate
PET	Pre-eclamptic toxaemia
pg	Picogram
pH	Acidity and alkalinity scale. Low is acidic. High is alkaline. pH7 is about neutral
PH	Past/previous history
PID	(a) Pelvic inflammatory disease
	(b) Prolapsed intervertebral disc
PIP	Proximal interphalangeal
PL	Prolactin
PMH	Past/previous medical history
PND	Paroxysmal nocturnal dyspnoea
PN (R)	Percussion note (resonant)
po	Per os (by mouth)
pO_2	Partial pressure of oxygen (normally in blood)
POH	Past/previous obstetric history
POP	Plaster of Paris
PoP	Progesterone only pill
PPH	Post-partum haemorrhage
pr	Per rectum (by the rectum)
prn	As required – of eg, pain killers
PRV	Polycythaemia rubra vera
PTH	Parathyroid hormone
PTT	Prothrombin time
PU	Peptic ulcer
PV	Per vaginam (by the vagina)
QDS	To be given/taken 4 times a day
R	Right *or* respiration
RA	Rheumatoid arthritis
RBBB	Right bundle branch block
RBC	Red blood cell (erythrocyte)
RE	Rectal examination
Rh	Rhesus factor
RIC	Raised intracranial pressure
RIF	Right iliac fossa
RIH	Right inguinal hernia
ROA	Right occiput anterior (see LOA)
ROL	Right occipito-lateral (see LOA)
ROM	Range of movement
ROP	Right occiput posterior (see LOA)
RS	Respiratory system
RT	Radiotherapy
RTA	Road traffic accident
RTI	Respiratory tract infection
RUQ	Right upper quadrant
SB	Serum bilirubin
S/B	Seen by
SBE	Subacute bacterial endocarditis
SC	Subcutaneous
S/D	Systolic/diastolic (heart and circulation)

SE	Side effects
SH	Social history
SJ	Supinator jerk (reflex: see AJ)
SL	Sub linguinal (under the tongue)
SLE	Systemic lupus erythematosus
SOA	Swelling of ankles
SOB (OE)	Shortness of breath
SOS	(a) if necessary
	(b) see other sheet
SROM	Spontaneous rupture of membranes
stat	Immediately
Supp	Suppositories
SVC	Superior vena cava
SVD	Spontaneous vaginal delivery
SVT	Supraventricular tachycardia
SXR	Skull x-ray
Ts and As	Tonsils and Adenoids
TCI 2/52	To come in (to be admitted to hospital), in 2 weeks' time
tds	To be given/taken 3 times a day
TGH	To go home
THR	Total hip replacement
TIA	Transient ischaemic attack
TJ	Triceps jerk (reflex: see AJ)
TPR	Temperature, pulse and respiration
TSH	Thyroid stimulating hormone
TTA	To take away
TVF	Tactile vocal fremitus
TX	Transfusion
UC	Ulcerative colitis
U&E	Urea and electrolytes (biochemical tests)
UG	Urogenital
UMN	Upper motor neurone
URTI	Upper respiratory tract infection
USS	Ultra sound scan
UTI	Urinary tract infection
VA	Visual acuity
VE	Vaginal examination
VF	Ventricular fibrillation
VT	Ventricular tachycardia
V/V	Vulva and vagina
VVs	Varicose veins
WBC	White blood corpuscle/white blood cell count
WCC	White blood cell count
WR	Wasserman reaction
wt	Weight
XR	X-ray

2.5   DIAGRAMMATIC REPRESENTATION OF THE HUMAN SKELETON

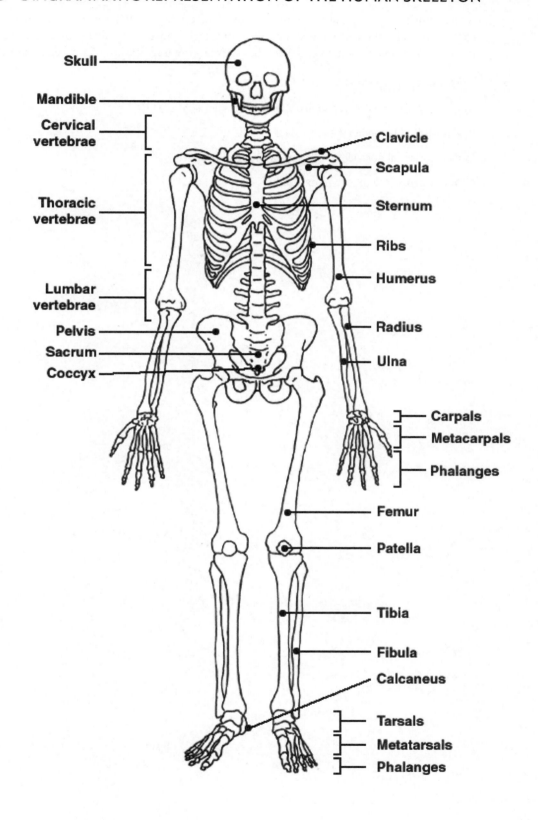

2.6 CONCLUSION

A basic understanding of the medical terms involved in personal injury and clinical negligence cases can assist the trainee when reading medical reports, and also provides an insight into the client's problems which can often be useful in the negotiation of any settlement.

2.7 FURTHER READING

Kemp and Kemp, *The Quantum of Damages* (Sweet & Maxwell)

Black's Medical Dictionary (A & C Black Publishers Ltd)

Dorland's Medical Abbreviations (W B Saunders Company)

Other appropriate medical textbooks

ROAD TRAFFIC AND OTHER HIGHWAY CLAIMS: THE LAW

LEARNING OUTCOMES

After reading this chapter you will be able to:

- describe how liability for road traffic accidents may be established
- set out the circumstances in which a claimant might be held to be contributorily negligent and how damages might be reduced in such circumstances
- explain the role of insurance and insurers in this type of claim
- explain the role of the Motor Insurers Bureau, and the impact of the Uninsured Drivers Agreement 1999 and the Untraced Drivers Agreement 2003
- set out the statutory duties of highway authorities and the defence under s 58 of the Highways Act 1980.

3.1 INTRODUCTION

According to the Department of Transport's statistics bulletin, *Reported Road Casualties in Great Britain: Main Results 2014*, which is based on accidents reported the police in 2014, 1,774 people were killed in road traffic accidents. The number of people seriously injured was 22,807 and the overall number of casualties of all severities was 194,477. Not surprisingly therefore, road traffic accidents form a large part of the personal injury lawyer's casework.

A road user may be liable to an injured person, or to the estate or dependants of a deceased person, on the basis of common law negligence. A highways authority may be liable to such people on the basis of negligence and/or breach of statutory duty.

3.2 ESTABLISHING LIABILITY FOR ROAD TRAFFIC ACCIDENTS

3.2.1 The duty of one road user to another

All road users have a duty of care to avoid causing injury to others who it may reasonably be anticipated may be injured by their actions or failure to act. The term 'road user' includes not only those driving motor vehicles or riding motorbikes or bicycles, but also their passengers, pedestrians and owners of roadside property, such as signs and bollards, and the highway itself, which in most cases will be the local highway authority.

Clearly, a driver has a duty to drive carefully so as not to cause injury to his passengers or other road users, but other examples include the duty of a driver not to park his vehicle where it might constitute a danger, the duty of a pedestrian not to step into the path of a vehicle, and the duty of the highway authority to keep the highway in good repair.

This duty of care is well established and, in the majority of cases, will not be in dispute between the parties.

3.2.2   The standard of care

The standard of care is that of the ordinary skilful driver, and it is not lowered to take account of the fact that the driver is a learner driver (see *Nettleship v Weston* [1971] 2 QB 691).

A driver is not entitled to assume that other road users will always exercise reasonable care and skill, but he is not 'bound to anticipate folly in all its forms' (*London Passenger Transport Board v Upson* [1949] AC 1555). Neither is the duty so high that it equates to a guarantee of the claimant's safety. In *Ahanonu v South East Kent Bus Company Limited* [2008] EWCA Civ 274, where the claimant had been trapped between the defendant's double-decker bus and a metal bollard, the Court of Appeal reversed the finding that a driver of the bus had been negligent. Lord Justice Laws said that the judge had imposed a counsel of perfection on the bus driver, thereby distorting the nature of the driver's duty, which was no more or less than a duty to take care.

This view was reiterated in *Stewart v Glaze* [2009] EWHC 704 (QB), where a driver was found not liable for injuries incurred by the claimant, who had stepped into the path of his car without warning. The judge commented that it was important to ensure the court was not guided by '20:20 hindsight'. In *Smith v Co-operative Group Ltd & Another* [2010] EWCA Civ 725, the Court of Appeal considered the case of a 13-year-old newspaper boy, who had, without looking, cycled out of a driveway across a pavement and into the path of a lorry. The defendant lorry driver had braked and swerved but could not avoid hitting the claimant. The defendant admitted that he had not sounded his horn, but relied on expert evidence that this would not have prevented the accident from occurring. The judge found against the defendant (although the claimant was held to be 60% contributory negligent), ignoring the expert evidence, and instead relying on his own opinion that, if the defendant had sounded his horn when the claimant was halfway across the pavement, the claimant would have reacted by stopping or cycling out of the way. In allowing the appeal, the Court of Appeal demonstrated its unwillingness to impose a standard of driving on motorists which amounts to a counsel of perfection. It held that the defendant had not been negligent in failing to sound his horn at the same time as being involved in emergency braking and swerving to avoid a collision.

3.2.3   Breach of duty

Each case must turn on its own facts. It is for the court to decide whether there has been any breach of the duty to take reasonable care in relation to other road users. When trying to answer this vital question, personal injury lawyers should consider legislation designed to regulate the conduct of road users and the Highway Code.

3.2.3.1   Are there any relevant criminal convictions?

Evidence of the defendant being convicted of a relevant criminal offence is of particular importance to the claimant's solicitor in order to establish breach of duty. Likewise, a relevant conviction of the claimant may assist the defendant's solicitor in negating liability or establishing contributory negligence. A conviction will be relevant where it relates to how the accident was caused or to the quantification of damages. So, for example, a defendant who was driving without insurance at the time of the accident may have been in breach of the criminal law, but a conviction for this offence will not be relevant for the purposes of civil proceedings. Convictions arising from the accident should be set out in the police accident report (see **10.10.3.1**). The following issues are some, but by no means all, of the matters for which you should look out:

(a) *Vehicle maintenance*:

  (i) Under s 40 of the Road Traffic Act 1988 (RTA 1988), it is an offence to use, cause or permit another to use a motor vehicle on a road when its condition is such that its use involves a danger of injury to any person.

  (ii) Under s 41A of the RTA 1988, a person who uses a motor vehicle, or causes or permits such a vehicle to be used on a road when the vehicle does not comply with regulations governing the construction and use of brakes, steering-gear or tyres, is guilty of an offence. Current regulations relating to tyres specify a minimum tread depth, prohibit the mix of radial and cross-ply tyres, and require tyres to be inflated to the correct pressure for the vehicle.

(b) *Poor driving.* The most important issues of relevance are as follows:

  (i) Speeding. Driving at a speed in excess of the limit is not necessarily in itself sufficient evidence of negligence (*Quinn v Scott* [1965] 2 All ER 588). Neither will driving below the speed limit automatically negate liability (*Richardson v Butcher* [2010] EWHC 214 (QB)). Under the Highway Code, drivers should adjust their driving to the prevailing conditions and circumstances. So they must take account of the weather, available light, road layout, weight of traffic, parked vehicles or other obstructions, the presence of cyclists and motorcyclists, and the likelihood of pedestrians, particularly children, crossing the road. A driver who fails to adjust his speed in appropriate circumstances risks prosecution for dangerous or careless driving.

  (ii) Dangerous driving. Under s 2 of the RTA 1988, it is an offence to drive dangerously on a road or other public place. For the purposes of this section, a person drives dangerously if the way he drives falls far below what would be expected of a competent and careful driver, and it would be obvious to a competent and careful driver that driving in that way, or driving the vehicle in its current state, would be dangerous. (For causing death by dangerous driving, careless driving or whilst under the influence of alcohol, see **17.3.1.**)

  (iii) Careless driving. Under s 3 of the RTA 1988, it is an offence to drive without due care and attention. A person will drive in this way if the way he drives falls below what would be expected of a competent and careful driver.

(c) *The influence of alcohol or drugs.* Under the RTA 1988, a person commits an offence if he:

  (i) drives, attempts to drive, or is in charge of a motor vehicle on a road or other public place, when he is unfit to do so through drink or drugs (s 4);

  (ii) drives or is in charge of a vehicle after consuming so much alcohol that the proportion of it in his breath, blood or urine exceeds the prescribed limit (s 5). The current prescribed limits for alcohol are 35 microgrammes of alcohol in 100 millilitres of breath; 80 milligrammes of alcohol in 100 millilitres of blood; and 107 milligrammes of alcohol in 100 millilitres of urine; or

  (iii) drives or is in charge of a vehicle whilst there is a concentration of specified controlled drugs in excess of specified limits (s 5A). The relevant drugs and associated limits are set out in the Drug Driving (Specified Limits) (England and Wales) Regulations 2014 (SI 2014/2868).

(d) *The use of mobile phones.* Under s 41D of the RTA 1988, it is an offence to drive or supervise the driving of a motor vehicle whilst holding a hand-held mobile telephone or other interactive communication device contrary to the relevant regulations. Although it is currently not an offence to use a hands-free telephone, should an accident occur whilst the driver is using such equipment, a prosecution for careless or dangerous driving might arise.

(e) *The wearing of seat belts and child restraints.* Under s 14 of the RTA 1988, it is an offence to drive or ride in a motor vehicle on a road without wearing a seat belt as prescribed by regulations made by the Secretary of State. In accordance with the Motor Vehicles (Wearing of Seat Belts) Regulations 1993 (SI 1993/176) (as amended), the driver must ensure that seat belts are worn, where they are available, by all passengers under the age of 14. Under s 15 of the RTA 1988, the driver must ensure that children are strapped into an appropriate child restraint. The current regulations apply only to children who are both under 1.35 metres in height and under 12 years old.

(f)   *The wearing of safety helmets.* Under s 16 of the RTA 1988, it is an offence to ride on a motor cycle without a safety helmet in accordance with the relevant regulations. Followers of the Sikh religion who are wearing a turban are exempt from this requirement.

3.2.3.2   Are there any breaches of the Highway Code?

A failure on the part of any road user to observe a provision of the Highway Code does not of itself render that person liable to criminal proceedings. Some of the rules set out in the Code, identified by the use of the words 'must' or 'must not', reflect statutory requirements, the breach of which amounts to a criminal offence, whilst others, which are in the nature of guidance, do not. In accordance with s 38(7) of the RTA 1988, all breaches of the Code may be relied upon in the civil courts to establish breach of duty. However, a breach of the Highway Code does not create a presumption of negligence but is merely one of the circumstances which the court will consider when establishing whether a breach of duty has occurred (*Powell v Phillips* [1972] 3 All ER 864, CA; *Goad v Butcher & Another* [2011] EWCA Civ 158).

The personal injury solicitor requires a good knowledge of the Code. Although the printed version must be used for all legal proceedings, you can access an adapted on-line version at www.gov.uk/highway-code.

3.2.3.3   *Res ipsa loquitur*

The maxim *res ipsa loquitur* is sometimes thought of as a rule of law whereby the burden of proof shifts from the claimant to the defendant. This is a misunderstanding: it is, in fact, a rule of evidence, and the burden of proof remains on the claimant throughout. Roughly translated as 'the thing speaks for itself', the maxim means that the facts of the case are sufficient proof in themselves. It may be applied in circumstances where the claimant is unable to adduce any evidence as to how or why the accident happened, but is able to show that:

(a)   the accident is such that, in the ordinary course of events, it would not have occurred without negligence; and

(b)   whatever inflicted or caused the damage was under the sole management and control of the defendant.

In such circumstances, where it appears to be more likely than not that the defendant's breach of duty led to the accident, the maxim enables the court to conclude that the claimant has established a prima facie case against the defendant. It is therefore sometimes said that the evidential burden shifts to the defendant. In order to avoid liability, the defendant must either give an explanation of what happened which is inconsistent with negligence or, where he is unable to give such an explanation, demonstrate that he exercised all reasonable care.

In *Ng Chun Pui & Others v Le Chuen Tat & Another* [1988] RTR 298, a coach driven by the first defendant and owned by the second defendant left the carriageway, crossed a grass verge and collided with a public bus travelling in the opposite direction. One passenger in the bus was killed and its driver and other passengers were injured. In the absence of any evidence of any mechanical defect within the defendant's coach, the claimants did not offer any evidence as to how the accident arose but relied on the maxim *res ipsa loquitur*. However, the court accepted evidence put on behalf of the defendants that the driver had been obliged to react to another, untraced vehicle, which had cut in front of him, causing him to brake and swerve, and that this reaction did not constitute a breach of duty. (Reading the full text of the judgment in this case may prove useful for furthering comprehension of *res ipsa loquitur*.)

It is not common for liability in road traffic accidents to be established on the basis of the maxim *res ipsa loquitur*, as there will usually be evidence from the claimant, in the form of eye-witness testimony and/or expert opinion, as to how and why the accident occurred. One case in which it was successfully used is *Widdowson v Newgate Meat Corporation & Others* (1997) *The Times*, 4 December. The claimant, who was suffering from mental disorder, had been walking at the side of a dual carriageway just before midnight, when he was hit by a van driven by an employee of the respondent company. Neither the claimant, who could not be considered a reliable witness, nor the driver of the van gave evidence. Having heard evidence from a psychiatrist on behalf of the claimant, the Court of Appeal held that despite the claimant's mental illness, he was aware of road safety issues, was not a risk-taker and did not have any suicidal tendencies. Moreover, it was 'pure surmise' that he fell into the van's path as a result of losing his balance. Consequently, the defendants had failed to put forward a plausible explanation.

3.2.4 Vicarious liability

Under the doctrine of vicarious liability, an employer is liable for damage caused by the negligence of an employee whilst acting in the course of his employment. So, if an employee is driving whilst carrying out work for his employer and causes a road traffic accident due to his negligence, the employer will be liable for any resulting personal injury or damage to property.

You will find a more detailed analysis of vicarious liability at **4.4**.

3.2.5 Causation

The claimant will have to prove that the breach of duty caused the loss and damage complained of. He will have to show that 'but for' the defendant's breach, the injuries would not have arisen. Causation will be disputed where the defendant argues:

(a) that the cause of the injury was not the defendant's breach of duty but the claimant's own negligence. In *Whittle v Bennett* [2006] EWCA Civ 1538, a car driven by the defendant in excess of the speed limit and too close to the car in front, was involved in a collision with the claimant's car. Although the defendant's actions were negligent, the court held that the accident was caused by the gross negligence of the claimant, who had been attempting a U-turn manoeuvre on a busy single-carriage 'A' road. Courts frequently find that the negligence of the defendant and the claimant have played a part in causation, and apportion damages accordingly (see **3.2.6**).

(b) that the accident could not have caused the injuries complained of. In recent years, it has become increasingly common for insurers to defend on this basis in low-velocity impact claims. This type of accident, where damage to the vehicles may be no more than a scratch, typically results in whiplash, where there are no visible signs of injury. In some instances, defendants are going further than disputing the severity of the injuries; they are making positive allegations that the claimant has fabricated the claim. The Court of Appeal considered these types of cases in *Kearsley v Klarfeld* [2005] EWCA Civ 1510 and *Casey v Cartwright* [2006] EWCA Civ 1280, and gave guidelines as to how they should be dealt with. These guidelines are beyond the scope of this book.

3.2.6 Contributory negligence

The claimant has a duty to take care of his own safety and to take reasonable precautions against risks of injury of which he was aware or ought to have been aware. His actions or failure to act might amount to a breach of this duty, and the court may conclude that the claimant was fully or partly responsible for the injury suffered. Section 1(1) of the Law Reform (Contributory Negligence) Act 1945 states:

> Where any person who suffers damage as a result partly of his own fault and partly of the fault of any other person or persons, ... the damages recoverable in respect thereof shall be reduced to such an extent as the court thinks just and equitable having regard to the claimant's share in the responsibility for the damage.

Therefore, the court will reduce the amount of damages payable by the defendant to the claimant only where the defendant is able to prove, on the balance of probabilities:

(a)   that the claimant was at fault;

(b)   that the fault was causative of the injury suffered; and

(c)   that it would be just and equitable for the claimant's damages to be reduced.

When determining the extent to which damages will be reduced, the court will apportion responsibility between the parties by looking at the relative causative potency of what each of the parties has done and their respective blameworthiness. (You may find it useful to read the full judgment in *Eagle v Chambers* [2003] EWCA Civ 1107.)

It would be rare for a court to find a pedestrian more responsible than a driver of a vehicle (and therefore reduce damages by more than 50%), unless the pedestrian suddenly moved into the path of the vehicle in circumstances where the driver could not have anticipated such a thing to happen. The court will consider all the relevant circumstances, including whether the driver was driving in a manner appropriate for the prevailing conditions, whether he was aware that pedestrians were about and might step into the road, and the age of the pedestrian. Children are not expected to exercise the degree of care reasonably expected of an adult. Very young children will never be held to have been negligent, and those under the age of 12 are seldom held to be so. However, in the case of *Ehrari v Curry & Another* [2006] EWCA Civ 120, the claimant, who was 13 years old at the time of the accident, was held to be 70% to blame for the accident which had left her brain-damaged. The defendant driver had been travelling at no more than 20 miles per hour when the claimant stepped into the road without looking.

In the following types of cases, the courts will follow the precedents set in the cases cited:

(a)   Where a driver or passenger fails to wear a seat belt, damages will be reduced by 25% in cases where the injury would not have happened at all, or by 15% where the injuries would have been less severe (*Froom v Butcher* [1976] QB 286). From time to time, defendants attempt to argue that the court should depart from these guidelines, but the case of *Stanton v Collinson* [2010] EWCA Civ 81 highlights the court's reluctance to do so. In this case, the teenage claimant was a front seat passenger in a car driven by his friend. Neither the claimant nor the girl sitting on his lap wore a seatbelt, and when the driver lost control and crashed into an oncoming car the claimant sustained serious brain damage. In spite of the claimant's reckless behaviour, the Court of Appeal held that there was no contributory negligence as the defendant had failed to supply medical evidence proving the causal link between the claimant's failure to wear a safety belt and his injuries.

(b)   Where a motor cyclist fails to wear a crash helmet, damages will be reduced by 15% (*O'Connell v Jackson* [1972] 1 QB 270) or, where the helmet's chin strap is not fastened, by 10% (*Capps v Miller* [1989] 1 WLR 839).

(c)   Where a passenger allows himself to be carried in a vehicle when he knows the driver is drunk and should not be driving, damages will be reduced by 20% (*Owens v Brimmel* [1977] QB 859).

(d)   Although there is no legal compulsion for a cyclist to wear a helmet, and there has not been a case where damages have been reduced as a result of a cyclist's failure to wear a helmet, in *Smith v Finch* [2009] EWHC 53 (QB) the judge appeared to suggest that such a failure would amount to contributory negligence. On the facts of this case, however, the wearing of a helmet would have made no difference to the injuries sustained by the claimant.

If the claimant has contributed to his own injuries in more than one way, the court will not necessarily calculate the overall reduction simply by adding the normal percentage reductions together. So, in *Gleeson v Court* [2007] EWHC 2397 (QB), where the claimant had allowed herself to be driven in a car when she was aware that the driver was drunk (20% reduction) and had sat in the boot of the hatchback car (25% reduction), the overall reduction was 30%.

The reduction of damages as a result of contributory negligence will be a theoretical, rather than an actual, disadvantage to the motorist who has the benefit of fully comprehensive insurance which includes personal injury cover, as his own insurer, being bound to indemnify him for his own injuries irrespective of blame, will cover any shortfall in damages recovered from the defendant. However, few pedestrians, particularly children, will have relevant insurance cover, and therefore they will suffer a loss in real terms from any finding of contributory negligence.

3.3   INSURANCE

3.3.1   Statutory provisions and types of policy

Under s 143(1) of the RTA 1988, any person who drives, or causes or permits another person to drive a motor vehicle on a road or other public place, must have a policy of insurance which, at the very least, covers third party risks. The minimum protection afforded by what is commonly known as a Road Traffic Act policy or third party insurance covers:

(a)   the death or bodily injury of a third party;

(b)   damage to property belonging to a third party up to £1,000,000; and

(c)   any emergency treatment, ie medical or surgical examination or treatment which is required by those suffering an injury (including a fatal injury) immediately following the accident.

A common type of policy, known as Third Party Fire & Theft, provides this minimum cover, plus cover for the policyholder's own vehicle should it be damaged or destroyed by fire or stolen. Neither of these types of policies indemnifies the policyholder where his own vehicle is damaged due to his own negligence, or where nobody was at fault. More importantly, neither do they cover the policyholder for injuries that he might himself suffer in such circumstances. It is perhaps little understood by the public at large how common road traffic accidents are, how devastating the resulting injuries can be, and just how important adequate financial compensation is for someone suffering long-term disability.

Policies which are commonly known as 'fully comprehensive' cover the minimum risks and damage to the policyholder's property. They might also cover the injury or death of the policyholder and legal expenses arising from taking or defending proceedings following an accident, but terms do vary and should be checked carefully.

3.3.2   Road Traffic Act 1988, ss 151–152

Sometimes, a situation will arise where the defendant was driving a vehicle which was covered by a policy of insurance at the time of the accident, but the insurer may have grounds to avoid paying damages to the claimant. This may arise where:

(a)   the driver of the vehicle who was responsible for the accident was insured to drive that vehicle under the terms of the policy, but the insurance company was entitled to cancel the policy due to a breach of its terms, eg driving whilst under the influence of alcohol, a failure to disclose a material fact, eg the existence of previous driving convictions or a medical condition, such as diabetes or epilepsy, or a failure to report the accident; or

(b)   the driver of the vehicle was not insured to drive the vehicle, eg where a family member or friend of the policyholder drove the vehicle, with or without the policyholder's permission, or a thief drove the vehicle.

In any of the above situations, the claimant should not be dissuaded from issuing a claim against the driver on the grounds that damages will not be recovered even if judgment is obtained. Under s 151 of the RTA 1988, the insurance company will be obliged to pay out on the judgment to the claimant, provided notice of the proceedings is given to the insurer, under s 152 of the Act, before or within seven days of commencement of the proceedings. Because it is not always clear at the start of proceedings whether or not any of the above situations applies, those acting for claimants in road traffic accident cases should always send out the required notice to the insurer of the vehicle (see **12.3.2**).

Under s 151(4), there is an exception in relation to third parties who were willing passengers in a vehicle they knew or had reason to believe had been stolen.

3.3.3 The insurer's role in civil proceedings

Although a claimant is able to issue proceedings directly against the negligent driver's insurers instead of or in addition to the driver (see **10.3.1.2**), many solicitors acting for claimants will proceed only against the driver. If the claimant succeeds in obtaining judgment against the defendant driver, the insurer is obliged to pay out. Consequently, in order to protect their own position, insurers insert a clause into their policies which enables them to initiate or defend proceedings in the name of the insured. This means that the insurer will choose which firm of solicitors to use and will give instructions as to how the matter should be dealt with, including the making and accepting of any offers to settle.

3.3.4 Obtaining insurance details

Where an accident has resulted in personal injury, under s 154 of the RTA 1988, all drivers involved must supply details of their insurance to others involved in the accident. It is a criminal offence either to refuse to supply this information, or to supply false information.

In addition, the Motor Insurers' Bureau (see **3.4**) maintains the Motor Insurance Database (MID), a centralised database of motor insurance policy information of all insured UK vehicles. Insurers who underwrite motor insurance for vehicles on UK roads are obliged to be members of the MIB and to submit the policy details of all vehicles to the MID. For a small fee, those who have suffered injury and/or loss due to a motor accident, or their representatives, may make an on-line enquiry to obtain information regarding the insurance details of other vehicles involved (www.askmid.com).

Since November 2014, those involved in RTAs are able to use a smart mobile phone or device to check the insurance details of the other driver at the roadside. The 'askMID Roadside' service is free and can be accessed through the website mentioned above.

3.4 THE MOTOR INSURERS' BUREAU

It is not uncommon for individuals to suffer personal injury as the result of the negligence of an uninsured driver or a driver who cannot be traced. The Motor Insurers' Bureau (MIB) was founded in 1946 with the specific purpose of entering into agreements with the Government to compensate victims of negligent and uninsured drivers. All motor insurers are obliged under the RTA 1988 to be a member of the MIB and to contribute to the fund from which compensation is paid. These contributions are funded by the premiums paid by their policyholders.

The relevant agreements, explanatory notes and application forms may be found on the MIB's website at www.mib.org.uk.

3.4.1 The Uninsured Drivers Agreement 2015

The Uninsured Drivers Agreement 2015 ('the 2015 Agreement') relates to claims arising from the negligence or intentional assaults of uninsured drivers who can be identified, where the incident occurred on or after 1 August 2015. Accidents occurring prior to this date are governed by older Agreements, the details of which can be found on the MIB's website.

Under the 2015 Agreement, the MIB is obliged to satisfy any judgment obtained against the defendant driver which remains unsatisfied for more than seven days, subject to the exceptions, limitations and preconditions set out in the Agreement. However, where it deems appropriate, the MIB will settle the claim prior to proceedings being commenced.

The form of the application to the MIB will depend upon the value of the claim. Where this is no more than £25,000 and is within the scope of the Pre-Action Protocol for Low Value Personal Injury Claims in Road Traffic Accidents, the claimant should complete and send the Claim Notification Form (RTA1) through the Portal, as set out in **Chapter 21**. Section H of RTA1 should be completed when there is an uninsured driver and the MIB is to be involved. Otherwise, the application should be made by completing and returning the MIB's standard form, either online or by post and, in either case, supplying any documents in support.

Where the MIB declines to settle the matter and proceedings are necessary, the claimant's solicitors must name the MIB as second defendant (see clause 13(1) of the 2015 Agreement). If this is not done, the MIB will not usually incur a liability to the claimant. However, a claimant may not name the MIB as a party to the proceedings if he initially and reasonably believes liability to be covered by an identifiable insurer. In such a case, if he gives notice of the commencement of the proceedings to the MIB, notifies them promptly as soon as he realises that the insurer has no responsibility, consents to the MIB being joined to the proceedings and promptly supplies relevant documentation to the MIB, the MIB cannot avoid liability on the basis of clause 13(1) (see clause 13(2)).

The onerous reporting requirements which are found in previous MIB Agreements have been omitted from the 2015 Agreement.

3.4.1.1 Exclusions from the 2015 Agreement

The MIB is not obliged to satisfy compensation claims where (inter alia):

(a) the claimant has received, or is entitled to receive or demand, payment or indemnity in respect of his losses from any other person, including an insurer, with the exception of the Criminal Injuries Compensation Authority; or

(b) the claim relates to damage to a motor vehicle and, at the time of the damage, the vehicle was not insured and the claimant knew or ought to have known that that was the case; or

(c) the person suffering death, injury or loss was voluntarily allowing himself to be carried in the vehicle and, before the start of his journey in the vehicle (or after such start if he could reasonably be expected to have alighted from the vehicle), he knew or had reason to believe that the vehicle:

  (i) had been stolen or unlawfully taken, or

  (ii) was being used without insurance (for more details, see clause 8); or

(d) death, injury or damage to property was caused by an act of terrorism (clause 9).

In March 2015, the Court of Appeal held in *Delaney v Secretary of State for Transport* [2015] EWCA Civ 172 that the exclusion of compensation (found in previous MIB Agreements), where a passenger knew or ought to have known that the vehicle was being used in the course or furtherance of a crime, was contrary to European law. Consequently, this provision and the provision which excluded claims where the passenger knew or ought to have known that the vehicle was being used as a means of escape from or avoidance of lawful apprehension are omitted from the 2015 Agreement.

3.4.1.2   Assignment of judgment and undertakings

In accordance with clause 15 of the 2015 Agreement, the MIB is not obliged to settle the judgment unless the claimant:

(a)   assigns the unsatisfied judgment and any order for costs made against the uninsured driver to the MIB. This enables the MIB to pursue him for the amount paid to the claimant;

(b)   undertakes to repay to the MIB any part of the judgment which is set aside, or any compensation received by the claimant from other sources (except the Criminal Injuries Compensation Authority) in respect of the same incident.

3.4.2   The Untraced Drivers Agreement 2003

The Untraced Drivers Agreement 2003 ('the 2003 Agreement') relates to accidents occurring on or after 14 February 2003 and requires the MIB to consider applications for compensation for victims of 'hit and run' cases where the owner or driver cannot be traced. The 2003 Agreement has been amended by five supplementary agreements, the most recent dated 3 July 2015 and affecting claims relating to accidents occurring on or after 1 August 2015. Unfortunately, there is no consolidated text, which makes life difficult for the unwary. The Department of Transport and the MIB are currently in discussion about a new Untraced Drivers Agreement.

The 2003 Agreement applies where:

(a)   the death of, or bodily injury to, a person or damage to property of a person has been caused by, or arisen out of, the use of a motor vehicle on a road or other public place in Great Britain; and

(b)   the event giving rise to the death, bodily injury or damage to property occurred on or after 14 February 2003; and

(c)   the death, bodily injury or damage to property occurred in circumstances giving rise to liability of a kind which is required to be covered by a policy of insurance.

Clearly, in this type of incident, where the identity of the person responsible for the accident is not known, it is not possible to commence civil proceedings. Where a person who has suffered injury and loss wishes to claim under the 2003 Agreement, he must make an application to the MIB either online, or by post using the relevant form which can be downloaded from the MIB's website.

3.4.2.1   Exclusions from the Agreement

The 2003 Agreement does not apply (inter alia) where:

(a)   the person suffering death, injury or damage was voluntarily allowing himself to be carried in the vehicle and before the commencement of his journey in the vehicle (or after such commencement if he could reasonably be expected to have alighted from the vehicle) he knew or ought to have known that the vehicle:

(i)   had been stolen or unlawfully taken, or

(ii)   was being used without insurance;

(b)   the claimant has received, or is entitled to receive or demand, payment or indemnity in respect of his losses from any other person, including an insurer, with the exception of the Criminal Injuries Compensation Authority;

(c)   the claim is for damages to a vehicle and, at the time of the incident, that vehicle was uninsured, and the person suffering the damage either knew or ought to have known that that was the case. This prevents an applicant benefiting from the 2003 Agreement when his own vehicle was being driven unlawfully.

As with the Uninsured Drivers Agreement 2015, appropriate amendments were made in relation to exclusions following the *Delaney* case (see **3.4.1.1**).

3.4.2.2 Time limit for making an application

The periods of limitation set out in the Limitation Act 1980 apply (see **Chapter 7**).

3.4.2.3 Requirements

The applicant, or person acting on behalf of the applicant, must have reported the event to the police (clause 4(3)(c)):

(a) in the case of claims for death or bodily injury alone, not later than 14 days after the event occurred; and

(b) in the case of claims for property damage, not later than five days after the event occurred.

Evidence of the report must be supplied in the form of the crime or incident number, and the applicant must have co-operated with the police in any investigation they conducted.

3.4.2.4 Investigation of claims

The MIB is under an obligation to make an award only if it is satisfied, on the balance of probabilities, that the death, bodily injury or damage was caused in such circumstances that the unidentified person would (had he been identified) have been held liable to pay damages to the applicant in respect of it.

The MIB shall investigate the claim and reach a decision as to whether it must make an award to the applicant, and where it decides to make an award, it will determine the amount. Where the MIB gives notice to the applicant that it has decided to make him an award, it shall pay the award within 14 days of a written confirmation from the applicant that he accepts the award.

3.4.2.5 Compensation

The MIB shall award a sum equivalent to the amount which it would have awarded to the applicant for general and special damages if the applicant had brought successful proceedings to enforce a claim for damages against the unidentified person. In calculating the sum payable, the MIB shall adopt the same method of calculation as the court would adopt in calculating damages (clause 8).

It will include in the award a sum representing interest on the compensation payable at a rate equal to that which a court would award a successful litigant (clause 9).

3.4.2.6 Contribution towards legal costs

In accordance with clause 10 and the Schedule, the MIB will make a contribution to the claimant's costs. Where the award of damages does not exceed £150,000, the contribution towards the cost of legal advice will be 15% of the amount of the award, subject to a minimum of £500 and a maximum of £3,000 (plus VAT and reasonable disbursements). If the damages exceed £15,000, the contribution will be 2% of the award.

3.5 DUTIES OF THE HIGHWAY AUTHORITY

Claims against highway authorities include those made by pedestrians who have tripped or slipped on pavements or pathways, and those made by motorists who have been injured in accidents caused by the poor state of roads. Solicitors acting for claimants injured in road traffic accidents should always consider the possibility that a highways authority may be liable to their client in addition to or instead of another road user.

3.5.1 Who is the relevant highway authority?

The local highway authority will be the local county council, metropolitan district council, unitary authority or, in London, either Transport for London or the relevant London borough council. The Secretary of State for Transport or, for roads in Wales, the Secretary of State for Wales, is the highway authority for most motorways and trunk roads.

Section 36(6) of the Highways Act 1980 (HA 1980) requires every council to keep an up-to-date list of all roads and traffic routes within its area for which it is responsible. Section 36(7) states that any person may consult the list at the council offices free of charge. Consequently, if there is any doubt as to whether it is the council who has responsibility or whether the road is in private ownership and privately maintainable, recourse can be made to the records.

It is common for neighbouring councils to enter into agency agreements, whereby one council undertakes maintenance of certain highways on behalf of the other. Ultimate responsibility remains with the statutory highway authority, and legal proceedings should be issued accordingly.

3.5.2 Duty to maintain the highway

3.5.2.1 Duty under statute and common law

Under s 41(1) of the HA 1980, a highway authority has a duty to maintain (which includes a duty to repair) any highway which is maintainable at the public expense. Section 36(2) defines a highway 'maintainable at public expense' as:

(a)   a highway constructed by a highway authority;

(b)   a highway constructed by a council within its own area, or a highway constructed outside of its area for which it has agreed to be responsible;

(c)   a trunk road;

(d)   a footpath or bridleway created or diverted by the local authority.

Highway authorities have a similar duty to maintain highways under common law (see *Dabinett v Somerset County Council* [2006] LTL 20/4/2007), and breaches of both statutory and common law duties are commonly pleaded in particulars of claim. Highway authorities also have duties in common law nuisance and under s 150(1) of the HA 1980 to remove obstructions from the highway, but these are outside the ambit of this text.

3.5.2.2 Flooding and snow and ice

Is the duty to maintain the highway limited to the surface of the road itself? In *Department of Transport, Environment and the Regions v Mott Macdonald Ltd & Others* [2006] EWCA Civ 1089, the Court of Appeal considered whether the highway authority was liable to the claimants, who had all been injured in road accidents caused by a dangerous accumulation of water on the surface of the highway, due to the longstanding blockage of the drains serving the road. In overturning the judge's decision, the Court concluded that the duties of a highway authority are not confined to the repair and the keeping in repair of the surface of the highway, and that it is obliged to maintain the drains in good repair. This duty is not limited to the repair of physical damage to the drains, but extends to the clearance of blockages. However, you should note that where a statutory authority, such as Thames Water or Severn Trent, has adopted responsibility for the drains in accordance with an agreement under the Water Industry Act 1991, it will be that authority, rather than the highway authority, which will be responsible for any accident resulting from a failure to maintain the drains.

Does the highway authority have a duty to prevent or remove the accumulation of snow or ice on the highway? It appears that there is no such duty under common law (*Sandhar v The Department of Transport, Environment and the Regions* [2004] EWHC 28 (QB)). However, s 150 of the HA 1980 requires authorities to remove any obstruction of the highway resulting from 'accumulation of snow or from the falling down of banks on the side of the highway, or from any other cause'. In addition, s 41(1A) requires highway authorities to ensure 'so far as is reasonably practicable, that safe passage along a highway is not endangered by snow and ice', and this would appear to include the need to undertake preventative gritting as well as clearing away accumulations of snow and ice. What is reasonably practicable is ultimately a matter for the courts, but one would expect highway authorities to be able to demonstrate that they have, at the very least, planned and implemented a winter maintenance plan in accordance with *Well-maintained Highways – Code of Practice for Highway Maintenance Management* (see **3.5.3**).

3.5.2.3   The role of contractors

Although the general rule is that employers are not liable for the torts of their independent contractors, statutory duties are non-delegable. Consequently, a highway authority which delegates responsibility for the repair and maintenance of a highway, does not escape liability to a claimant who is injured due to the negligent failure of the contractor to discharge its responsibilities.

3.5.2.4   The role of statutory undertakers

There are organisations, such as those dealing with gas, electricity, water, cable TV and telephones, which have apparatus on or under the highway. Such statutory undertakers are entitled to break up the highway under licences granted by the highway authority. They are, of course, required to take measures to ensure the highway is safe whilst the works are being carried out and to make good the highway following the completion of the works. Nevertheless, the responsibility to ensure that the highway does not pose a danger to road users remains with the highway authority and, subject to a successful defence under s 58 of the HA 1980, a claim against it for injuries caused by the dangerous condition of the highway will be successful. Where there is a possibility that a s 58 defence may be successful, claimants should commence proceedings against both the highway authority and the statutory undertaker. Where proceedings are commenced against the highway authority only, those acting for the authority should consider whether it is appropriate to issue an additional claim under CPR, Part 20, in order to pass all or part of the blame to the statutory undertaker (see **12.12**).

3.5.3   Breach of duty

In order to succeed in a claim against the highways authority, a claimant will have to prove:

(a)   that the condition of the highway made it a foreseeable danger to road users; and

(b)   the condition of the highway was due to the failure of the highways authority to maintain it; and

(c)   that the damage was caused by the dangerous condition of the highway.

In applying the forseeability test, the danger must be foreseeable to a road user having reasonable care for his own safety. In *Rider v Rider* [1973] 1 All ER 294, Sachs LJ concluded that:

> The highway authority must provide not merely for model drivers, but for the normal run of drivers to be found on their highways, and that includes those who make the mistakes which experience and common sense teach us are likely to occur.

When considering whether the highway authority has failed to maintain the highway, reference should be made to *Well-maintained Highways – Code of Practice for Highway Maintenance Management* produced by the UK Roads Liaison Group (which is currently being revised). Although the recommendations set out in the Code are not mandatory, courts are likely to treat them as relevant considerations when determining whether a breach has occurred.

Highway authorities are required to carry out safety inspections in order to identify all defects which are likely to create a danger to road users. Section 9.4 of the Code deals with the safety inspection regime, the frequency of which is largely determined by the category of the road, footway or cycle path within the highway network hierarchy. For example, as a starting point, strategic routes should be inspected once every month, whereas local access roads may be inspected just once a year. Other factors, such as the volume of traffic use and the number of accidents, are then taken into account, which may either increase or decrease the frequency of inspections.

During inspections, all observed defects posing a risk to road users must be recorded and the appropriate level of risk determined. Category 1 defects represent an immediate hazard or a risk of short-term structural deterioration, and should be dealt with at the time of inspection, if reasonably practicable, or, if not, within a maximum of 24 hours. A temporary resolution, such as warning notices or cordoning off the hazard, may be used, but a permanent repair should be carried out within 28 days.

3.5.3.1   The statutory defence

Under s 58 of the HA 1980, a highway authority may, in its defence, prove that it had taken such care as in all the circumstances was reasonably required to ensure that the highway was not dangerous for traffic. For the purposes of such a defence, the court will attempt to balance the public and private interests, and will have regard to the following matters:

(a)   the character of the highway, and the traffic which was reasonably to be expected to use it;

(b)   the standard of maintenance appropriate for a highway of that character and used by such traffic;

(c)   the state of repair in which a reasonable person would have expected to find the highway;

(d)   whether the highway authority knew, or could reasonably have been expected to know, that the condition of the part of the highway to which the action relates was likely to cause danger to users of the highway;

(e)   where the highway authority could not reasonably have been expected to repair that part of the highway before the cause of action arose, what warning notices of its condition had been displayed.

A highway authority will not necessarily be liable for injuries resulting from an accident which occurred shortly after a defect in the highway arose, but it will need to provide evidence that systems of regular inspection and maintenance were in place in order to detect each defect and repair it within a reasonable time. Where the highways authority had departed from the frequency of inspections set out in the Code of Practice for that type of highway, it would need to satisfy the court that the departure was based on proper evidence-based considerations (see *AC (1) DC (2) TR (3) v Devon County Council* [2012] EWHC 796 (QB)). If it is able to show that the frequency of inspections was appropriate for the nature and character of that particular highway and that, at the time of the last inspection before the accident, the defect was not present or not considered to be dangerous, it is likely to be successful in its defence. If, however, it had been aware of the defect but had taken an unreasonable time to effect the necessary repairs, the defence will not succeed. What is a 'reasonable time' will depend on the nature of the defect and the potential consequences to road users of failing to repair it.

3.5.4   Tripping and slipping cases

Tripping and slipping claims against highway authorities under s 41 of the HA 1980 (and other land owners) are very common, and they have increased in recent years. They may arise, for example, as a result of uneven or unstable paving stones, broken or missing kerbstones, potholes, protruding tree roots, missing manhole covers and highway surfaces which have become slippery, such as where there is an abundance of moss or wet leaves, or an accumulation of snow or ice.

As with other claims regarding the highway, the courts have been at pains to point out that each case should turn on its own facts and that the trial judge should determine whether the highway is in a dangerous condition. The court in *Littler v Liverpool Corporation* [1968] 2 All ER 343 gave the following guidance:

> The test ... is reasonable foreseeability of danger. A length of pavement is only dangerous if, in the ordinary course of human affairs, danger may reasonably be anticipated from its continued use by the public who usually pass over it. It is a mistake to isolate and emphasise a particular difference in levels between flagstones unless that difference is such that a reasonable person who noticed and considered it would regard it as presenting a real source of danger. Uneven surfaces and differences in level between flagstones of about an inch may cause a pedestrian ... to trip and stumble, but such characteristics have to be accepted.

When considering the point at which differing levels in a highway become dangerous to pedestrians, practitioners sometimes do refer to one inch as being the appropriate measurement. However, claimants have been successful where the difference has been as little as one-eighth of an inch (*Pitman v Southern Electricity Board* [1978] 3 All ER 901).

3.6 CONCLUSION

Road traffic accident claims are the most common type of personal injury claims, and they are, in the main, fairly straightforward. This means that the trainee solicitor or junior solicitor is likely to be dealing with this type of case when he is first introduced to personal injury work. It is useful to be aware that many low value claims will be handled, on behalf of claimants and defendants, by individuals who have no legal qualifications, sometimes with minimal training and supervision. If the solicitor has a thorough understanding of the legal principles which govern RTA claims, he will bring clarity to the procedure and will be better able to bring about the optimum conclusion for his client.

3.7 FURTHER READING AND RELEVANT WEBSITES

Uninsured Drivers Agreement 2015

Untraced Drivers Agreement 2003

<www.mib.org.uk>

<www.askmid.com>

<www.ukroadsliaisongroup.org>

EMPLOYERS' LIABILITY CLAIMS: THE LAW

LEARNING OUTCOMES

After reading this chapter you will be able to:

- explain the duty of care owed by an employer to an employee at common law
- explain how an employer may be liable to an employee for breach of statutory duty
- identify breaches of key health and safety regulations
- explain how an employer may be vicariously liable for the negligence of an employee
- understand the defences that are likely to be relied upon in a workplace claim
- explain the role of the Health and Safety Executive in enforcing health and safety in the workplace.

4.1 INTRODUCTION

For accidents which occurred before 1 October 2013, an employer may be personally liable to an injured employee on the basis of:

(a) common law negligence; and/or

(b) breach of statutory duty, for example under the Health and Safety at Work, etc Act 1974 (HSWA 1974), the Occupiers' Liability Act 1957 (OLA 1957) or European Directives covering safety by way of regulations under the HSWA 1974.

The heads of liability are not mutually exclusive. For example, in certain circumstances the employer may be liable to the injured employee under both heads, while in other circumstances the employer may be liable only in common law negligence but not otherwise. The employer may also be vicariously liable to the injured employee where the injury was caused by a tort (eg, negligence) of another employee who was acting in the course of his employment. We consider these heads of liability below, together with the defences which are most likely to be relied upon.

For accidents which occur on or after 1 October 2013, the Enterprise and Regulatory Reform Act (E&RRA) 2013 removes the right to bring a civil claim for breach of nearly all health and safety regulations, and so for such claims employers will only be personally liable on the basis of common law negligence. We discuss the likely impact of this major change in the law below (see **4.3.3**).

In addition to civil liability, an employer who breaches health and safety regulations may face a criminal prosecution. This is also considered below, together with the role of the Health and Safety Executive (HSE) in investigating accidents.

4.2 THE EMPLOYER'S COMMON LAW DUTY OF CARE

An employer is under a duty to take reasonable care of his employees' health and safety in the course of their employment. This includes providing health checks (especially if employees are engaged in hazardous work), equipment to protect employees from injury, and medical equipment in order to mitigate the effects of any injury.

This duty to take 'reasonable care' was explained by Lord Wright in *Wilsons & Clyde Coal Co v English* [1938] AC 57 as requiring an employer to exercise due care and skill in four particular areas, ie to provide:

(a)   competent staff;
(b)   adequate plant and equipment;
(c)   a safe system of work; and
(d)   safe premises.

Many of the common law duties are confirmed or strengthened by statute and regulations, but common law rules are an important indication of how courts are likely to interpret new regulations. Each of the four areas identified by Lord Wright is discussed in further detail below.

4.2.1 Competent staff

In many cases the employer will be vicariously liable for the negligence of an employee which results in injury to a fellow worker. An employer may also be personally liable under its common law duty. The duty is on the employer to take reasonable care to provide competent fellow workers. Whether the employer has failed to take reasonable care may depend upon the knowledge that he has (or ought to have) of the workmate's incompetence or inexperience, etc. In *Hudson v Ridge Manufacturing Co* [1957] 2 QB 348, the employers were held liable for continuing to employ a man who over a space of four years had habitually engaged in horseplay such as tripping people up. On the day in question he tripped the claimant, as a result of which the claimant injured his wrist. The court held that as this potentially dangerous misbehaviour had been known to the employers for a long time, and as they had failed to prevent it or remove the source of it, they were liable to the claimant for failing to take proper care of his safety.

However, in other cases involving practical jokes by fellow workers the employers have been held not liable on the basis that they could not reasonably have foreseen the behaviour that caused the injury (*Smith v Crossley Bros* (1951) 95 Sol Jo 655; *Coddington v International Harvester Co of Great Britain* (1969) 113 SJ 265).

4.2.2 Adequate plant and equipment

Accidents may also occur either because no plant or equipment is provided, or because inadequate equipment is provided. For example, if an employee suffers injuries falling from a makeshift means of gaining access to high shelves, the employer will be liable if no ladder has been provided for this purpose.

'Plant' simply means anything used in the course of work. It will include everything from large and complicated machinery (eg, a paper mill) to the most basic equipment (eg, an office chair). The duty rests on the employer to take reasonable steps to provide adequate equipment and materials to do the job, and then to maintain that equipment. For example, if an office swivel chair gives way under an employee, the employer may be liable for failing to maintain the chair, or for having inadequate provision for maintenance or renewal. The employer will also be vicariously liable if employees fail to maintain or repair such plant or equipment.

The duty to maintain plant and equipment in good order is now supplemented by the Provision and Use of Work Equipment Regulations 1998 (SI 1998/2306) (see **4.3.2.3**). When considering whether plant has been adequately maintained, the court will look to current practice, which will be different according to the type of equipment involved. Depending on the type of equipment, all or any of the following matters may be relevant, and evidence should be looked for, both when using the PAP and at the disclosure stage of litigation:

(a)   inspection and servicing records;

(b)   reports of defects, breakdown or poor running;

(c)   replacing worn-out parts or equipment;

(d)   steps taken to repair or replace equipment shown to be defective.

The frequency and method of inspection or testing that employers should adopt will depend on the nature of the equipment in question. Items which are subject to stress, such as ropes, should be inspected and, if necessary, replaced more regularly than items which are subject simply to ordinary wear and tear, such as floor coverings.

The requirement to provide adequate plant also extends to a duty to make reasonable provision of safety and protective equipment, eg goggles, safety gloves and shoes. This duty at common law is now supplemented by the Personal Protective Equipment at Work Regulations 1992 (SI 1992/2966) (see **4.3.2.4**).

If an employee is injured as a result of a latent defect in the equipment he is using, he may also be able to rely on the Employer's Liability (Defective Equipment) Act 1969, which imposes a form of strict liability on the employer. Section 1(1) provides:

> Where ... an employee suffers personal injury in the course of his employment in consequence of a defect in equipment provided by his employer for the purposes of the employer's business and the defect is attributable wholly or partly to the fault of a third party (whether identified or not) the injury shall be deemed to be also attributable to negligence on the part of the employer.

4.2.3   Safe system of work

The duty to provide a safe system of work is very wide and will be a question of fact to be considered in each case. It covers such things as:

(a)   the physical layout of the plant;

(b)   the method by which work is carried out;

(c)   the sequence in which work is to be carried out;

(d)   the provision of instructions;

(e)   the taking of any safety precautions;

(f)   the provision of proper warnings and notices (*Speed v Thomas Swift & Co* [1943] KB 557).

The employer must take care to see that the system is complied with, bearing in mind the fact that an employee may become careless after a time, especially if the work is of a repetitive nature (*General Cleaning Contractors Ltd v Christmas* [1953] AC 180).

EXAMPLES

In *General Cleaning Contractors Ltd v Christmas* [1953] AC 180, the claimant window cleaner was instructed by his employers in the sill method of cleaning windows. He was to hold on to the window sash whilst cleaning. A window closed on his fingers and he fell to the ground. It was held that the employers were in breach of their duty to provide a safe system of work, as they should have told the claimant to test the sashes to see if they were loose, and should have provided him with wedges.

In *Morgan v Lucas Aerospace Ltd* [1997] JPIL 4/97, 280–1, the claimant was employed in the defendants' factory to clean waste swarf (oil contaminated with metal waste) from trays underneath machinery. He had been given no formal training. Swarf caught in the machine cut through his heavy-duty glove, causing a gash to the claimant's hand. The claimant alleged this injury was caused by the defendants' failure to provide and maintain a safe system of work. In the first instance, it was held that the defendants were not absolved from the duty to provide a safe glove merely because it was difficult or expensive to obtain. If no better glove could be obtained at a reasonable price, the whole system was unsafe. The defendants appealed. On appeal, it was held that it was not necessary for the claimant to prove what alternative system of work could be adopted and which would have been safer. The claimant proved that the defendants allowed an unsafe practice to be adopted which they ought to have known to be unsafe and which they could have altered. If the gloves provided were the best available, the obligation of the defendants was to devise a system which would remove or reduce the risk of injury.

In *Johnson v Warburtons Ltd* [2014] EWCA Civ 258. The claimant was injured when his foot slipped on steps as he was exiting a side door of his lorry. There were two steps, which were steep, vertically uneven but horizontally deep. In order to use the steps a hinged flap had to be lifted vertically and secured with a catch. This was not a purpose built 'grab-point' but could be used as a handhold. There was no handrail. As he exited the lorry the claimant came down the stairs facing forwards. He was not holding onto the flap, his foot slipped off the bottom step and he fell into a gully breaking his ankle.

The steps themselves had been introduced to avoid the need for drivers to jump on and off partially deployed tail lifts, and had been specifically approved by the HSE prior to the accident. The defendant's newer fleet of lorries had been modified so that access was via three rather than two steps, however the evidence was that this was because three steps would be more comfortable to use and not due to any safety considerations. There was no specific risk assessment regarding use of the steps. Subsequent to the accident a guide was produced which suggested that the flap could be used as a handhold and that, if it was, it should be secured in an upright position.

The Claimant put his case two ways: (i) that the steps were unsuitable and posed an inherent risk of injury – they were not a safe system of work; or (ii) if that was wrong, the steps were so unsafe that drivers should have been trained in their use and advised to use the flap as a handhold.

The Court of Appeal upheld the decision of the judge at first instance who found that no training was needed and no risk assessment necessary because the need to take care was obvious.

4.2.4 Safe premises

It is accepted that the duty of care extends to the provision of safe premises. The duty applies not only to premises occupied by the employer, but also to premises occupied by a third party where the employee is working temporarily (*General Cleaning Contractors Ltd v Christmas* [1953] AC 180; *Wilson v Tyneside Window Cleaning Co* [1958] 2 QB 110). The duty is supplemented by the Workplace (Health, Safety and Welfare) Regulations 1992 (SI 1992/3004) (see **4.3.2.6**).

Slipping and tripping cases are frequent causes of negligence claims at work, as is shown by the amount of advice and preventative information available to employers from the HSE. The employer must act reasonably to ensure that floors and means of access are reasonably safe.

4.2.5 The requirement of 'reasonableness'

It should be remembered that the duty on the employer is not absolute but merely a duty to take reasonable care. Generally a high standard will be required, but it will vary according to the circumstances.

The standard of care demanded of an employer was summarised by Swanwick J in *Stokes v Guest Keen and Nettlefold Bolts & Nuts Ltd* [1968] 1 WLR 1776:

> The overall test is still the conduct of the reasonable and prudent employer, taking positive thought for the safety of his workers in the light of what he knows or ought to know; where there is a recognised and general practice which has been followed for a substantial period in similar circumstances without mishap, he is entitled to follow it, unless in the light of common sense or newer knowledge it is clearly bad; but where there is developing knowledge, he must keep abreast of it and not be too slow to apply it ...

Section 16 of the HSWA 1974 authorises Approved Codes of Practice (ACOPs), which set out guidance as to what is good practice in a particular trade and, as such, are a reflection of current informed thinking in the health and safety industry. Similarly, Guidance Notes issued by the HSE, although not binding, will be indicative of whether good working practices were being followed. It will be difficult for an employer to argue that a risk could not be foreseen where information was available in documents published by the HSE.

In *Stokes*, Swanwick J went on to say that an employer

> must weigh up the risk in terms of the likelihood of injury occurring and the potential consequences if it does; and he must balance against this the probable effectiveness of the precautions that can be taken to meet it and the expense and inconvenience they involve.

The employer must take into account the likelihood and potential gravity of an injury. It must then consider the measures necessary, and the cost involved in taking those measures, to avert the risk of injury. In *Latimer v AEC Ltd* [1953] AC 643, the claimant was one of 4,000 employees at the defendant's factory. During a night shift, the claimant slipped on the factory floor, the surface of which had become oily following recent flooding after a thunderstorm. The House of Lords held that it was reasonable for the defendant to put on the night shift rather than close the factory until the oily surface had been rendered safe.

The duty of care is owed to each employee individually, and so all the circumstances relevant to each employee must be taken into account. A good illustration of this is the case of *Paris v Stepney Borough Council* [1951] AC 367, in which the employers were held to be negligent for failing to supply goggles to a one-eyed workman, even though it was not necessary to provide goggles to fully-sighted workers.

4.2.6 Personal nature of duty

The employer will escape liability only if he shows that both he and the person to whom he delegated the duty exercised reasonable care in the discharge of that duty (*Davie v New Merton Board Mills Ltd* [1959] AC 604). Therefore, the duty is not discharged, for example, merely by delegating it to an apparently competent manager, if that manager in fact fails to act competently (*Sumner v William Henderson & Sons Ltd* [1964] 1 QB 450; *McDermid v Nash Dredging & Reclamation Co Ltd* [1987] 2 All ER 878).

An employer can remain liable for the safety of an employee, even while the employee is under the control of someone else. For example, where a worker on a building site is injured whilst working on a different building site under the control and instruction of different contractors, because he had been sent to work for the contractors by his own employer, his employer can be found liable for failing to ensure that he was properly trained and for failing to maintain a safe system of work, even though the employer had no control over management of that site (*Morris v Breaveglen* [1993] ICR 766, CA).

In certain circumstances both an independent contractor and an occupier of a building may also owe a duty of care to the employee of one of its subcontractors. See *EH Humphries (Norton) Ltd, Thistle Hotels v Fire Alarm Fabrication Services Ltd* [2006] EWCA Civ 1496. The judge was entitled to find in the circumstances that the defendant's right to supervise the work so as to ensure that it was carried out safely, imposed on it a duty of care which extended to the employees of the subcontractor who actually carried out the work. The defendant had been negligent in failing to obtain from the subcontractor a proper method statement of the work to be carried out, or a proper risk assessment.

4.3   BREACH OF STATUTORY DUTY

The relationship between an employer and employee is usually closely regulated by statute. The basic principles are set out below.

Legislation generally falls into one of the following categories:

(a)   The HSWA 1974, ss 2 and 3 impose obligations on employers and the self-employed to ensure, so far as reasonably practicable, the health and safety of their employees and members of the public who might be affected by their activities. A breach of s 2 or s 3 will usually give rise to criminal liability (see **4.9.3**).

(b)   Regulations (made under the HSWA 1974, s 15, to comply with EU Directives). A failure to comply with regulations may lead to a criminal prosecution by the HSE; and for accidents occurring before 1 October 2013, a breach of such regulations could also give rise to a civil claim for breach of statutory duty. However, for accidents which occur after that date, s 69 of the E&RRA 2013 has removed the right to bring a civil claim for a breach of nearly all such regulations, although a breach may be relied on as evidence of negligence (see **4.3.3**).

In addition, s 16 of the HSWA 1974 authorises Approved Codes of Practice (ACOPs), which set out what is good practice in a particular trade. Unlike a breach of the 1974 Act or regulations, a failure to observe an ACOP will not give rise to criminal liability, but it will be admissible in evidence in criminal proceedings. These Codes will also be admissible in civil proceedings as evidence of good practice in the trade and, as such, are a reflection of current informed thinking in the health and safety industry. Similarly, Guidance Notes issued by the HSE, although not binding, will be indicative of whether good working practices were being followed.

4.3.1   Civil liability for breach of statutory duty

To be successful in a civil claim based on a breach of statutory duty, the injured employee must show that:

(a)   the breach is actionable in a civil court;
(b)   the duty is owed to the claimant by the defendant;
(c)   the claimant's loss is within the mischief of the Act;
(d)   the defendant is in breach of the duty;
(e)   the breach caused the loss.

4.3.1.1   Is the breach of duty actionable in a civil court?

Although a breach of statutory duty is primarily a crime, under s 47(2) of the HSWA 1974 it may also give rise to civil liability, except where the statute expressly provides otherwise. However, for accidents which occur on or after 1 October 2013, s 69 of the E&RRA 2013 amends s 47(2) to provide that there is no right of action for breach of statutory duty in relation to a health and safety regulation, except to the extent that regulations made under s 47 make provision for this (see further **4.3.3** below). To date the only exceptions that have been provided are for pregnant workers and new mothers under the Health and Safety at Work etc Act 1974 (Civil Liability) (Exceptions) Regulations 2013 (SI 2013/1867).

4.3.1.2 Has the defendant breached his statutory duty?

The standard required of the employer to fulfil his statutory duty is a question of construction of the statute. The common words used are as follows:

(a) *'Shall'* or *'shall not'*: these words impose an absolute duty (or 'strict') obligation to do (or not to do) the act or thing in question. It is not permissible to argue that it is impracticable, difficult or even impossible to do it (or not to do it).

(b) *'So far as reasonably practicable'*: when judging whether there has been a breach, the court will balance the risk against any sacrifice (eg, in terms of time, trouble or money) required to avoid the risk. In *Davies v Health & Safety Executive* [2002] EWCA Crim 2949, [2003] IRLR 170, the court considered s 40 of the HSWA 1974, which deals with the interpretation of 'reasonably practicable'. Section 40 imposes on the defendant the burden of proving to the court that it was not reasonably practicable to do more than was in fact done to satisfy the duty (the reverse burden of proof). This was attacked by the defendant as being incompatible with the presumption of innocence in Article 6(2) of the European Convention for the Protection of Human Rights and Fundamental Freedoms (ECHR) 1950. On appeal, the Court found that Article 6(2) was not breached, and confirmed that a defendant who wishes to raise a defence of reasonable practicability does have the legal burden of calling positive evidence to prove that it was not possible to have done more to prevent the death or injury. The Court justified this stance by observing that the defence should not be difficult for a defendant to prove, as he will have this information to hand, whereas it would be unreasonable to place this burden on the prosecution.

(c) *'As far as practicable'*: this duty is stricter than 'reasonably practicable' but not an absolute duty. Lord Goddard, in *Lee v Nursery Furnishings Ltd* [1945] 1 All ER 387, described it as something that is 'capable of being carried out in action' or 'feasible'. Once something is found to be practicable then it must be done, no matter how inconvenient or expensive it may be to do it.

4.3.2 Health and safety legislation

It is not possible to set out here all the legislation currently in force; what follows is a summary of some of the regulations that are most frequently relied on in claims for personal injury.

4.3.2.1 Management of Health and Safety at Work Regulations 1999

The revised Management of Health and Safety at Work Regulations 1999 (SI 1999/3242) came into force on 29 December 1999 and replaced the Management of Health and Safety at Work Regulations 1992. These Regulations implement European Health and Safety Directives relating to the employer's obligations in respect of health and safety for workers, and in relation to minimum health and safety requirements for the workplace as to fire safety.

The main provisions regarding employer's duties are as follows:

Risk assessment (reg 3)

All employers are required to make a suitable and sufficient assessment of the risks to health and safety of their employees, and of persons who are not in their employment but who are affected by the conduct of their undertaking. Having made an assessment of the health and safety risks, it is incumbent upon the employer to try to diminish the risks that have been identified. If the employer has five or more employees, there is a duty to record the risk assessment (reg 3(6)), and to note any significant findings of the assessment and whether any group of employees is identified as being especially at risk. The assessment should be made by asking employees how they carry out their functions, together with taking advice from a relevant health and safety expert and ergonomists. The assessment should be updated and reviewed regularly.

The duty on employers to carry out a risk assessment is likely to be one of the areas highlighted by personal injury lawyers to substantiate whether or not the employer has acted reasonably to provide a safe system of work and to establish the question of foreseeability of harm in negligence claims. In *Allison v London Underground Ltd* [2008] EWCA Civ 71, the Court of Appeal held that the employers were held liable when the claimant, a tube train driver, suffered an injury as a result of prolonged use of a traction brake controller. In his judgment Smith LJ asked:

> How is the court to approach the question of what the employer ought to have known about the risks inherent in his own operations? In my view, what he ought to have known is (or should be) closely linked with the risk assessment which he is obliged to carry out under regulation 3 of the 1999 Regulations. That requires the employer to carry out a suitable and sufficient risk assessment for the purposes of identifying the measures he needs to take ... [W]hat the employer *ought* to have known will be what he *would* have known if he had carried out a suitable and sufficient risk assessment.

Smith LJ went on to say:

> Plainly, a suitable and sufficient risk assessment will identify those risks in respect of which the employee needs training. Such a risk assessment will provide the basis not only for the training which the employer must give but also for other aspects of his duty, such as, for example, whether the place of work is safe or whether work equipment is safe.

The question of whether an employer has carried out a suitable and sufficient risk assessment will be a central issue in establishing liability in many cases. However, in the recent case of *West Sussex County Council v Fuller* [2015] EWCA Civ 189, the Court of Appeal held that, despite a failure by the appellant local authority to carry out a risk assessment before asking the claimant to deliver post around the office, the claimant's case failed because there was no causal connection between the task concerned and the injuries she sustained when she tripped on a stair whilst delivering the post.

Principles of prevention (reg 4)

According to reg 4, the principles of prevention of risk to be applied are to:

(a)   avoid risks;

(b)   evaluate the risks which cannot be avoided;

(c)   combat the risks at source;

(d)   adapt the work to the individual, especially as regards the design of workplaces, choice of work equipment, and choice of working and production methods, with a view to alleviating monotonous work and work at a pre-determined rate to reduce their effects on health;

(e)   adapt to technical progress;

(f)   replace the dangerous by the non-dangerous or less dangerous;

(g)   develop a coherent overall prevention policy which covers technology, organisation of work, working conditions, social relationships and the influence of factors relating to the working environment;

(h)   give collective protective measures priority over individual protective measures; and

(i)   give appropriate instruction to employees.

Review of health and safety arrangements (reg 5)

Employers must make appropriate arrangements for the planning, organisation, control, monitoring and review of preventative and protective measures.

Health surveillance (reg 6)

Employers are required to have an appropriate policy on risk surveillance, having regard to the findings of risks identified by the risk assessment. For example, if the risk assessment of employees showed that there were risks to health from airborne dust, that identified risk should be kept under review by regular health checks for rises in respiratory problems in employees.

Health and safety assistance (reg 7)

Employers must appoint competent persons to assist the employer in carrying out compliance with statutory safety provisions. The Regulations require a safety audit to be carried out by accredited auditors who are suitably qualified. The audit will identify potential hazards in the workplace.

Information for employees (reg 10)

Employers must give information which is comprehensible to employees on health and safety risks and protective measures that should be adopted.

Employers' duties to 'outside workers' (reg 12)

Employers must provide information to 'outside workers' relating to hazards and the protective and preventative measures being taken.

Employee capabilities and health and safety training (reg 13)

Employers must provide adequate health and safety training to employees when first recruited and subsequently on being exposed to new risks. Such training should be repeated periodically.

Risk assessment for new or expectant mothers (reg 16)

For the purpose of reg 16, 'new or expectant mother' means an employee who is pregnant, who has given birth within the previous six months or who is breastfeeding. Where the workforce includes women of child-bearing age and the work is of a kind which could involve risk to the health and safety of a new or an expectant mother, or of the baby, the risk assessment required by reg 3 must include an assessment of that risk. If at all possible, the employee's working conditions or hours of work should be altered so as to avoid the risk. If it is not reasonable or possible to avoid the risk by these means, the employer may suspend the employee from work for so long as is necessary to avoid the risk.

Where a new or an expectant mother works at night and obtains a certificate from a registered medical practitioner or registered midwife showing it is necessary for her health and safety that she should not work for any period identified in the certificate, the employer shall suspend her from work for so long as is necessary for her health and safety.

Protection of young employees (reg 19)

A 'young person' means any person who has not attained the age of 18. In relation to young persons, reg 19 states that employers are under a duty to ensure that young persons are protected from risks which arise as a consequence of the young persons' lack of experience, or absence of awareness of existing or potential risks, or the fact that young persons have not yet fully matured. Subject to this, employers are not allowed to employ young persons for work which is beyond their physical or psychological capacity, or involves harmful exposure to agents which are toxic, carcinogenic, cause heritable genetic damage or harm to an unborn child, or which in any other way may chronically affect human health. Employers must not allow young persons to work where they may be involved in harmful exposure to radiation; nor must employers expose young employees to the risk of accidents which it may reasonably be assumed cannot be recognised or avoided by young persons owing to their insufficient attention to safety, or lack of experience or training.

Duties of employees (reg 14)

Although the main thrust of the Regulations is to confirm the obligations on employers in relation to health and safety, there are also obligations on employees, who have a duty to:

(a) use machinery, equipment, dangerous substances or other equipment in accordance with the training and instructions which have been given to them by their employer; and

(b) inform the employer of anything which the employee considers to represent a danger to health and safety, or any shortcomings in the employer's arrangements for health and safety.

4.3.2.2 Health and Safety (Display Screen Equipment) Regulations 1992 (as amended)

The Health and Safety (Display Screen Equipment) Regulations 1992 (SI 1992/2792) are applicable to new display screen equipment (DSE) as from 1 January 1993, and to existing DSE from 1 January 1996. However, the requirement of ongoing risk assessment applies to both old and new DSE as from 1 January 1993.

The main provisions are as follows:

(a) Employers must make a risk assessment of workstations used by display screen workers and reduce risks identified (reg 2).

(b) Employers must ensure that display screen workers take adequate breaks, and must ensure that an appropriate eyesight test is carried out by a competent person (reg 5).

(c) Employers must provide users with adequate health and safety training in the use of any workstation upon which they may be required to work (reg 6).

(d) Employers must also provide adequate health and safety information to DSE operators, which should cover such things as information and reminders of how to reduce risks, such as early reporting of problems and provision of adjustable furniture (reg 7).

The main health problems associated with DSE operation are:

(a) general fatigue caused by poor workstation design;

(b) upper limb disorders, such as peritendonitis or carpal tunnel syndrome. Repetitive strain injury (RSI) is the most common problem experienced by keyboard users;

(c) eyesight problems, such as temporary fatigue, sore eyes and headaches.

Employers should have, and be able to show that they have, an adequate policy designed to reduce risks associated with DSE work. The policy should identify hazards, such as visual fatigue, and action to be taken to reduce risk, such as provision of eyesight tests, screen filters and training in workstation adjustment.

4.3.2.3 Provision and Use of Work Equipment Regulations 1998 (as amended)

The Provision and Use of Work Equipment Regulations 1998 (SI 1998/2306) replace the Provision of Work Equipment Regulations 1992. The Regulations apply to any machine, appliance, apparatus, tool or installation for use at work (reg 2) in all types of workplaces. The Regulations are intended to ensure the provision of safe work equipment and its safe use. The main provisions are as follows:

(a) The employer shall ensure the suitability of work equipment for the purpose for which it is provided. The equipment must be suitable, by design and construction, for the place in which it will be used and for the intended purpose (reg 4).

(b) The employer must ensure that the equipment is maintained in an efficient state (reg 5(1)) and, if machinery has a maintenance log, that the log is kept up to date (reg 5(2)).

The wording of reg 5(1) was considered by the Court of Appeal in *Stark v Post Office* [2000] ICR 1013. The claim concerned an accident at work, where a postman was thrown from a bicycle provided by his employer when part of the front brake snapped in two. It was accepted that the defect to the bicycle would not have been detected by a rigorous inspection. Nevertheless, the Court found that the form of words used in the regulation gave rise to a finding of strict liability in relation to the provision of work equipment.

In *Ball v Street* [2005] EWCA Civ 76, the Court of Appeal reinforced the view that reg 5(1) gives rise to liability where injury is caused by machinery that is not in an efficient state of repair. The claimant was a farmer who was injured when part of a hay bailing machine fractured and ricocheted into his left eye. The Court found that notwithstanding that this was a 'freak accident', it was only necessary for the claimant to prove that the equipment failed to work efficiently and that that failure caused the accident. The Court found that the machine was no longer in good repair, neither was it in an efficient state, and such failure caused the accident. The imposition of an absolute duty by the Regulations was designed to render the task of an injured workman easier by simply requiring him to prove that the mechanism of the machine, that is the significant part of the machine, failed to work efficiently or was not in good repair and that such failure caused the accident. In this context 'efficient' refers to its state of repair from a health and safety standpoint and not from that of productivity.

Despite this apparent strict line taken by the courts, there have been examples where defendants have escaped liability. In *Smith v Northamptonshire County Council* [2008] EWCA Civ 181, the appellant local authority appealed against a decision that it was strictly liable under the Provision and Use of Work Equipment Regulations 1998, reg 5(1), for failure to maintain an access ramp used by the respondent employee (S) at a person's home. S was employed by the local authority as a carer/driver. As part of her duties she was required to collect a person (C) from her home and take her by minibus to a day centre. As S was pushing C in a wheelchair down a ramp which led out from C's house, S stepped on the edge of the ramp which gave way, causing her to stumble and injure herself. The ramp had been installed by the NHS some years previously. The Court of Appeal allowed the appeal on the basis that the duty to maintain could not normally apply to something which was part of someone else's property. It could furthermore not normally apply to something in relation to which access was limited, and in relation to which, if some maintenance was necessary, consent to carry out the work was required. S's appeal to the House of Lords was dismissed. Their Lordships confirmed that control over the use of equipment is not enough. Control over the equipment must be demonstrated. This could not be achieved simply from the fact that an employer has assessed and inspected the piece of equipment in question.

(c) If the work equipment must be assembled and installed correctly in order for it to be safe to use, the employer must ensure that:

    (i)   it is inspected after installation and prior to being put into service; or

    (ii)   it is inspected after assembly at its new location (reg 6(1)).

(d) The employer must ensure that employees have adequate health and safety information, and, if appropriate, written instruction in the use of equipment (reg 8).

(e) The employer must ensure that anyone using the equipment has had adequate training, including as to any risks which use may entail and precautions to be adopted (reg 9). In particular, the ACOP attached to these Regulations states that induction training is particularly important when young people first enter the workplace.

(f) Employers must ensure the protection of persons from dangerous parts of machinery in the following order of precedence (reg 11):

    (i)   by fixed guards if practicable; but if not

    (ii)   by other guards or other protection devices if practicable; but if not

    (iii)   by use of jigs, holders, push-sticks or similar protective devices where practicable; but if not

(iv)   by providing information, instruction, training and supervision as is necessary.

(g)   Employers must ensure that where equipment or the substances produced are at a very high or low temperature, there must be protection to prevent injury to any person (reg 13).

(h)   Employers must ensure that, where appropriate, equipment is provided with one or more easily accessible stop controls, and, where appropriate, emergency stop controls, and that they are clearly visible and identifiable (regs 15, 16 and 17 respectively).

(i)   Employers must ensure that, where appropriate, the equipment is provided with suitable means to isolate it from all sources of energy. This must be clearly identifiable and readily accessible. Appropriate measures must be taken to ensure that reconnection of the energy source to the equipment does not expose any person using the equipment to any risk (reg 19).

(j)   The equipment must be suitably stabilised and suitably lit (regs 20 and 21 respectively).

(k)   When maintenance is being carried out, equipment must be shut down if reasonably practicable (reg 22).

(l)   The equipment must be suitably marked with appropriate health and safety information and warning devices as appropriate (regs 23 and 24).

(m)   Due to the rising number of accidents arising out of the use and misuse of forklift trucks, there are comprehensive regulations relating to the use of mobile work equipment. The Regulations require employers to ensure that employees are not carried on mobile equipment unless it is both suitable and incorporates reasonably practicable safety features (reg 25). They also seek to reduce the risk of equipment rolling over or overturning by placing on the employer an obligation to increase the stability of the equipment by making structural alterations if necessary (regs 26–28).

4.3.2.4   Personal Protective Equipment at Work Regulations 1992 (as amended)

The Personal Protective Equipment at Work Regulations 1992 (SI 1992/2966) make provision for the supply of protective and safety equipment, eg: eye-protectors, respirators, gloves, clothing for adverse weather conditions, safety footwear, safety hats, high-visibility jackets, etc.

The main provisions are as follows:

(a)   Employers must ensure that suitable personal protective equipment (PPE) is provided to employees at risk to their health and safety while at work. Such PPE is not suitable unless (reg 4(4)):

(i)   it is appropriate to the risk involved, the conditions at the place where the exposure to the risk may occur, and the period for which it is worn;

(ii)   it takes account of ergonomic requirements and the health of persons who may wear it, and of the characteristics of the workstation of each such person.

(b)   Before choosing PPE the employer should make an assessment to ensure that it is suitable and compatible with other work equipment used at the same time (reg 6).

(c)   Employers must ensure that PPE is maintained in efficient working order and good repair (reg 7). The obligation to supply protective equipment relates to identified risks. The Regulations will not be concerned with risks other than those necessitating protective equipment, and no absolute duty was intended to be imposed by reg 7(1) in relation to other risks (see *Fytche v Wincanton Logistics* [2003] EWCA Civ 874). In *Fytche*, the claimant suffered frostbite in the little toe of his right foot because there was a small hole in his boot where the steel cap met the sole. The steel-capped boots were PPE within the 1992 Regulations. The Court found that the boots were provided for the purpose of protecting the employee's foot from falling objects, and therefore his claim must fail.

(d)   Employers must ensure that where PPE is provided, employees obtain such information, instruction and training as is adequate to ensure that they know what risks the PPE will avoid or limit, the purpose of the PPE, and any action they must take to ensure efficient working of the PPE, and must ensure that this information is available to employees (reg 9).

4.3.2.5 Manual Handling Operations Regulations 1992 (as amended)

The Manual Handling Operations Regulations 1992 (SI 1992/2793), reg 2(1), provides a definition of 'manual handling operations' as any transporting of a load (including the lifting, carrying and moving thereof) by hand or bodily force. Over one-quarter of accidents reported to the HSE involve manual handling. Despite moves toward mechanisation in industry, there are still many jobs, such as packaging and warehouse work, requiring the day-to-day lifting of heavy objects. Many claims are brought by health service staff, who may have to lift and carry heavy patients as part of their everyday duties.

The Regulations make provision as follows:

(a) So far as reasonably practicable, employers must avoid the need for employees to undertake any manual handling involving risk of injury (reg 4(1)(a)).

(b) If avoidance is not reasonably practicable, employers must make an assessment of manual handling risks, and try to reduce risk of injury. The assessment should address the task, the load, the working environment and the individual's capability (reg 4(1)(b)).

In *Brazier v Dolphin Fairway Ltd* [2005] EWCA Civ 84, at the time of the alleged injury the claimant was trying to lift down a wooden 6-feet by 6-feet pallet from a stack of pallets which was about 6-feet high. That was the system of work at C's place of employment and was known to his employers. There was a witness statement on behalf of the employers so indicating, and also using words to the effect that the pallets were 'fairly lightweight'.

The judge dismissed the claim on the basis that there was no evidence as to the weight of the pallet that was being lifted down. He said: 'I have no means of knowing how heavy it was or whether it was heavy enough to give rise to a foreseeable risk of injury.' He then went on to say that there was evidence that the pallet was roughly 6-feet by 6-feet, '... but I am completely at sea as to the forces and the strains which the claimant had to undergo. I have no expert engineering evidence which tells me anything about the forces of the strains.' The judge took the view that there was no evidence that the system of work that was being employed was unsafe.

On appeal (granting leave to appeal) the Court of Appeal found that it was arguable that the judge made an error of principle. Smith LJ put it like this:

> There comes a point when one does not need detailed evidence or expert evidence. The judge had evidence of a man being required to lift down a 6-feet by 6-feet wooden pallet; a pallet which when in use had to be strong enough to take considerable weight and be used with a fork lift truck. It seems to me to be arguable that no further evidence was needed to decide that a system which required someone to bring down such an object from a height of 6-feet would place that person at risk of injury.

(c) If it is not reasonably practicable to avoid manual handling operations which involve risk of injury, employers must take steps to reduce manual handling to the lowest level reasonably practicable (reg 4(1)(b)(ii)). In the context of assessing manual handling risks for the purpose of complying with reg 4, the correct approach is for the employer to consider the particular task in the context of the particular place of work and the particular employee who has to perform that task: see *O'Neill v DSG Retail Ltd* [2002] EWCA Civ 1139. In this case the employer conceded that it had failed to give adequate training once it had recognised it was necessary to increase awareness of the risks in manual handling, and therefore it had failed to reduce the risk of injury 'to the lowest level reasonably practicable' (as required by reg 4(1)(b)(ii)).

(d) Employees must be provided with information on the weight of each load, and the heaviest side of any load (reg 4(1)(b)(iii)).

Regulation 4 was amended by the Health and Safety (Miscellaneous Amendments) Regulations 2002 (SI 2002/2174) by the addition of the following paragraph:

> (3)   In determining for the purposes of this regulation whether manual handling operations at work involve a risk of injury and in determining the appropriate steps to reduce that risk regard shall be had in particular to—
>
> (a)   the physical suitability of the employee to carry out the operations;
>
> (b)   the clothing, footwear or other personal effects he is wearing;
>
> (c)   his knowledge and training;
>
> (d)   the results of any risk assessment carried out pursuant to regulation 3 of the Management of Health and Safety at Work Regulations 1999;
>
> (e)   whether the employee is within a group of employees identified by that assessment as being especially at risk; and
>
> (f)   the results of any health surveillance provided pursuant to regulation 6 of the Management of Health and Safety at Work Regulations 1999.

Employees have a duty to make full use of any system of work provided by the employer to reduce manual handling risks (reg 5). As to the meaning of 'so far as reasonably practicable' in reg 4(1), see *Hawkes v Southwark LBC* [1998] EWCA Civ 310. In this case, it was found that the defendant had not carried out any risk assessment as required under the Regulations. The judge made it clear that the burden of proving what was 'reasonably practicable' lay on the defendant and that failure to carry out an assessment did not by itself prove liability, rather it was the failure to take appropriate steps to reduce risk of injury to the lowest level reasonably practicable that was at issue. See also the Lifting Operations and Lifting Equipment Regulations 1998 (SI 1998/2307), which deal with health and safety requirements with respect to lifting equipment.

4.3.2.6   Workplace (Health, Safety and Welfare) Regulations 1992

The Workplace (Health, Safety and Welfare) Regulations 1992 (SI 1992/3004) apply to all workplaces except ships, aircraft and trains, construction sites and mining operations (reg 3). The Regulations are concerned with the way in which the building and the facilities within it may affect employees.

The main provisions are as follows:

(a)   Workplace equipment, devices and systems must be maintained in efficient working order and good repair (reg 5).

(b)   There must be adequate ventilation (reg 6).

(c)   The indoor temperature during working hours must be reasonable, and thermometers must be provided to enable employees to determine the temperature (reg 7).

(d)   Workplaces must have suitable lighting, which, if reasonably practicable, should be natural light (reg 8).

(e)   Workplaces, including furniture, fittings, floors, walls and ceilings, must be kept sufficiently clean. So far as is reasonably practicable, waste materials must not be allowed to accumulate (reg 9).

(f)   Every workstation must be arranged so that it is suitable for any person likely to work there (reg 11).

(g)   Every floor or traffic route surface must be suitable for the purpose for which it is used. In particular, it must have no hole or slope, or be uneven or slippery so as to expose any person to a risk to his health or safety. So far as reasonably practicable, every floor or traffic route must be kept free of obstructions or articles which may cause a person to slip, trip or fall (reg 12). The claim in *Coates v Jaguar Cars Ltd* [2004] EWCA Civ 337 concerned an accident that occurred as the claimant was going up a number of steps at the defendant's factory. The claimant tripped on the third stair, causing him to fall and break his arm. The claimant contended that this amounted to a breach of reg 12 as, if there had been a handrail, he would not have fallen. The Court of Appeal held that there had been no reason to find that the steps posed any real risk provided that those who had used them used a sufficient degree of care, as had been the case for any other steps of this nature. The judge at first instance was correct to have dismissed the claim.

(h) Suitable and sufficient sanitary conveniences must be provided at readily accessible places. They must be adequately lit and ventilated, and kept in a clean and tidy condition (reg 20).

(i) Suitable and sufficient washing facilities must be provided, including showers if required by the nature of the work for health reasons (reg 21).

(j) An adequate supply of wholesome drinking water must be provided at the workplace, which should be readily accessible and conspicuously marked where necessary.

4.3.2.7　Work at Height Regulations 2005

The Work at Height Regulations 2005 (SI 2005/735) impose health and safety requirements with respect to work at height where there is a risk of a fall liable to cause personal injury. They contain minimum safety and health requirements for the workplace, including minimum health and safety requirements at temporary or mobile construction sites.

Meaning of work at height

Working at height is defined in reg 2(1) as:

(a) work in any place, including a place at or below ground level;

(b) obtaining access to or egress from such place while at work, except by a staircase in a permanent workplace,

where, if measures required by these Regulations were not taken, a person could fall a distance liable to cause personal injury.

To whom do the Regulations apply?

The Regulations apply to employers, to the self-employed and to any person under an employer's control. This means that the Regulations apply not only to employees working under their employer's control, but also to contractors to the extent that they are under the control of building owners.

Duties relating to the organising and planning of work at height

Every employer is under a duty to ensure that work at height is properly planned, supervised and carried out in a safe manner, subject to its being reasonably practicable to do so. This duty includes the selection of work equipment in accordance with reg 7 (reg 4).

Persons undertaking work at height must be competent, or, if being trained, supervised by a competent person (reg 5).

Requirement for Management Regulations risk assessment

There are prescribed steps to be taken to avoid risk from work at height, including provision of a risk assessment under reg 3 of the Management Regulations (see **4.3.2.1**), which should:

(a) identify whether it is reasonably practicable to carry out the work safely otherwise than at height; and if not

(b) provide sufficient work equipment for preventing, so far as is reasonably practicable, a fall occurring and to minimise the distance or consequences should a fall occur (reg 6 and Sch 1).

Duties relating to the selection of work equipment

When selecting work equipment for use in work at height, the person concerned must give collective protection measures priority over personal protection measures; and must also take account of:

(a)   the working conditions and the risks to the safety of persons at the place where the work equipment is to be used;

(b)   in the case of work equipment for access and egress, the distance to be negotiated;

(c)   the distance and consequences of a potential fall;

(d)   the duration and frequency of use;

(e)   the need for easy and timely evacuation and rescue in an emergency;

(f)   any additional risk posed by the use, installation or removal of that work equipment, or by evacuation and rescue from it (reg 7).

The Regulations also impose duties for the avoidance of risks from fragile surfaces, falling objects and danger areas, requiring that such areas are clearly indicated (regs 9–11); and require the inspection of certain work equipment and of places of work at height (regs 12 and 13 and Sch 7).

4.3.2.8   Control of Substances Hazardous to Health Regulations 2002

The Control of Substances Hazardous to Health Regulations 2002 (SI 2002/2677) came into force on 21 November 2002, and revoke and replace the 1994 Regulations. They provide a comprehensive and systematic approach to the control of hazardous substances at work, which include chemicals, airborne dusts, micro-organisms, biological agents and respiratory sensitisers.

The main duties on employers are as follows:

Duty to carry out a formal risk assessment

Regulation 6 provides that

an employer shall not carry on any work which is liable to expose any employees to any substance hazardous to health unless he has made a suitable and sufficient assessment of the risks created by that work to the health of those employees and of the steps that need to be taken to meet the requirements of these Regulations.

The assessment should be reviewed if circumstances change. In *Naylor v Volex Group Plc* [2003] EWCA Civ 222, the claimant was exposed to a hazardous substance during her employment with the defendant, and as a result suffered from industrial asthma. The defendant had carried out a risk assessment based on standards provided by the HSE which were subsequently withdrawn. The Court of Appeal held that in those circumstances a new risk assessment should have been carried out, and that the defendant was therefore in breach of reg 6.

Duty to prevent or control exposure to risks

Regulation 7 provides that the employer must ensure that the exposure of employees to hazardous substances is either prevented or, where this is not reasonably practicable, adequately controlled.

In *Dugmore v Swansea NHS Trust* [2003] 1 All ER 333, the claimant developed a severe allergy to latex as a result of wearing surgical gloves. The Court of Appeal held that the defendant should have provided vinyl gloves and was in breach of its duty to control the claimant's exposure to latex under reg 7.

The prevention or adequate control of the exposure to hazardous substances must be secured by measures other than the provision of personal protective equipment so far as is reasonably practicable. This means that the employer's first act should be to control the process or substance hazardous to health by, for example, closing off the process or machine, or by providing suitable exhaust ventilation.

Duty to ensure proper use of and to maintain personal protective equipment

Regulation 8 provides that employers must take reasonable steps to ensure that any control measure or personal protective equipment is used or applied properly.

There is also a duty on every employee to make full and proper use of such equipment, and to report any defect in it to his employer.

Regulation 9 provides that employers must ensure that any control measure is maintained in an efficient state, in efficient working order and in good repair. For example, where respiratory equipment is provided, the employer must ensure that thorough examinations and tests of that equipment are carried out at suitable intervals.

Duty to monitor exposure of employees

Regulation 10 requires monitoring to ensure the maintenance of adequate control to substances hazardous to health, or to protect the health of employees. Certain substances and processes require monitoring at specified intervals, and the results of all monitoring must be recorded and kept for at least five years. Where the monitoring relates to the personal exposure of individual employees, the records must be kept for at least 40 years.

Duty to provide health surveillance of employees where necessary

Regulation 11 requires suitable health surveillance where it is appropriate (ie, where a particular task is known to make employees susceptible to a particular injury or disease). Medical surveillance is required for certain substances or processes, and a health record must be kept in respect of each employee under surveillance for at least 40 years.

Duty to provide information and training to employees regarding hazardous substances

Regulation 12 requires an employer to provide its employee with such information, instruction and training as is suitable and sufficient for the employee to know the risks to health created by such exposure, and the precautions which should be taken.

4.3.3 The impact of the Enterprise and Regulatory Reform Act 2013

The E&RRA 2013 is part of the Government's response to concerns that the UK had in recent years acquired a so-called 'compensation culture', and that health and safety legislation needed reform.

Section 69 of the E&RRA 2013 amends s 47(2) of the HSWA 1974 to remove civil liability for all breaches of statutory duty which occur on or after 1 October 2013. Evidence of a breach of statutory duty might still be relied on to support a claim in negligence, but it will not constitute a cause of action in its own right. This means that an employee injured during the course of his employment will only be able to pursue a claim in common law negligence (see **4.2** above). For new accidents occurring after 1 October 2013, we should still expect reference to the health and safety regulations within letters of claim, claim notification forms and particulars of claim, but with the argument that those breaches of the regulations should be seen as evidence of a breach of the common law duty to take reasonable care.

The concept of 'strict liability' will therefore disappear from employers' liability claims, and claimants such as Mr Stark, the postman in *Stark v Post Office* (see **4.3.2.3** above), will no longer be successful. Furthermore, as the claim can only be brought in negligence, the burden of proof will remain with the claimant employee throughout, rather than, as sometimes occurs under the regulations, part of that burden being on the defendant employer to show that it took all reasonably practicable steps to comply with a regulation (see **4.3.1.2**).

Where the accident occurred before 1 October 2013, a claimant employee may still make a claim both in common law negligence and for breach of statutory duty. It is usually difficult, but not impossible, to show that if the employer has complied with regulations, he has nevertheless been negligent. In *Bux v Slough Metals Ltd* [1974] 1 All ER 262, the employer was found to have complied with regulations that required the provision of goggles to its employees, and so had complied with its statutory duty, but it had failed to instruct the employee to wear the goggles and so was in breach of its common law duty. (See also *Franklin v Gramophone Co Ltd* [1948] 1 KB 542; *Close v Steel Co of Wales* [1962] AC 367.)

Equally, the employer may be liable for breach of statutory duty even though he has not been negligent. In *Hide v The Steeplechase Company (Cheltenham) Limited & Ors* [2013] EWCA Civ 545, the claimant jockey brought a claim in common law negligence and under reg 4 of the Provision and Use of Work Equipment Regulations 1998 (see **4.3.2.3**) for damages for injuries sustained following a fall during a race. The claim under reg 4 was based on the allegation that the guard rail with which the claimant collided was not suitable for the purpose for which it was provided. The claim failed at first instance, as the judge held that the common law concept of 'reasonable forseeability' was imported into reg 4. He decided that the way in which Mr Hide fell was unusual, and that the defendant had complied with the requirements laid down by the British Horseracing Authority. Therefore the rail was suitable under reg 4. The claimant appealed and was successful. The Court of Appeal held that the words 'reasonably forseeability' had to be construed in a way which was consistent with the limited concept of forseeability envisaged by the EU Directives. It should not construed in the same way as the classic concept of 'reasonably foreseeable' in common law negligence. The Court of Appeal held that the burden was on the defendant to show that the incident was not 'reasonably foreseeable', ie that it was due to unforeseeable circumstances beyond its control, or to exceptional events the consequences of which could not be avoided. The defendant could not do this, and so the Court of Appeal held that although there was no negligence, there was a breach of reg 4.

It will be a while before the impact the E&RRA 2013 has made on employers' liability claims can be assessed, as it may take several years for the accidents to which it applies to make their way through the claims system. It is likely that fewer defendants (such as those in *Hide v The Steeplechase Company (Cheltenham) Ltd*) will be held liable where they have done all that is reasonable to make the workplace safe. However, there may well be additional costs incurred in a range of EL claims because of the need to investigate whether or not the employer has done all that is reasonable to provide a safe workplace. For example, in a claim involving machinery, it is likely that claimants' lawyers will want disclosure of records relating to the maintenance and operation of the machine, and will also wish to involve expert engineers to investigate the machinery and work systems in place in order to establish whether the employer took reasonable care.

4.4 VICARIOUS LIABILITY

4.4.1 Definition

An employer will be vicariously liable for his employee's torts if committed in the course of his employment. Therefore, it falls to be established:

(a)   whether the tort was committed by an employee; and

(b)   whether that employee was acting in the course of (ie, within the scope of) his employment.

4.4.2 'Course of employment'

The employee must have committed the tort 'in the course of his employment', which is less clear than might at first appear. There are many cases on the point, but the nearest to a formulation of a rule is that the employer will be liable for acts of employees if they perform an authorised act in an unauthorised way, but will not be liable for acts not sufficiently connected with authorised acts. This is examined in further detail at **4.4.3** below.

4.4.3   Disobedience of orders by employees

Having established that an employer will be liable for acts of his employees if they are acting within the course of their employment, it is necessary to examine the situation where the employee disobeys the orders of his employer in relation to the way he carries out his work. In *Rose v Plenty* [1976] 1 All ER 97, a milkman had been told by his employers not to allow children to help him on his rounds. Subsequently he allowed a child to assist him, and the child was injured while riding on the milk float due to the milkman's negligent driving. On appeal to the Court of Appeal, the employer was found to be vicariously liable. The Court held that the employee was doing his job but was using a method that his employers had prohibited. Nonetheless, he was still found to be working within the scope of his employment as it was performed for the benefit of the defendant's business.

Contrast the above with *Lister and Others v Hesley Hall Ltd* [2001] 2 All ER 769. The facts of the case were that the warden of the school abused boys while they were resident at the school. The House of Lords held the defendant vicariously liable for the acts of its employee. The Lords said that the court should not concentrate on the nature of the actual act complained of (abuse) but on the closeness of the connection between the nature of the employment and the tort complained of. They found that the defendant employed the warden to care for the claimants. The abuse took place while he was carrying out the duties required by his employment. On that basis, the proximity between the employment and the tort complained of was very close, and therefore the defendant ought to be liable.

The Court of Appeal applied the reasoning in *Lister and Others v Hesley Hall Ltd* in the subsequent case of *Mattis v Pollock* [2003] EWCA Civ 887. There, the claimant was stabbed by a doorman of a nightclub who was employed by the defendant nightclub owner. The Court found that the defendant expected the doorman to carry out his duties in an aggressive manner; and where an employee was expected to use violence while carrying out his duties, the likelihood of establishing that an act of violence fell within the scope of his employment was greater.

In the recent case of *Mohamud v WM Morrison Supermarkets Plc* [2014] EWCA Civ 116, the claimant was kicked and punched by the defendant's employee (Mr Khan) at a petrol station, in what the judge described as a 'brutal and unprovoked' attack. The claimant brought a claim against the defendant for damages for the injuries he had sustained, on the basis that it was vicariously liable for the actions of its employee who worked at the petrol station.

The trial judge held that Morrison Supermarkets were not vicariously liable, and the Court of Appeal agreed. The Court held that the application of the test for vicarious liability in *Lister* was fact sensitive, and that, in seeking to determine whether the test was satisfied, a court had to focus closely on the facts of the case and pay careful attention to the closeness of the connection between the employee's wrongdoing and the duties he was employed to do.

The required connection was not present on the facts of this case. The assault had taken place at a time when Mr Khan's supervisor had told him not to follow the claimant out of the petrol station. Mr Khan had made a positive decision to leave the petrol station and follow the claimant, and he had for 'no good or apparent reason' carried out the attack 'purely for reasons of his own'.

Further, the duties imposed on Mr Khan in terms of his interaction with customers were relatively limited, and involved no element of authority over them or responsibility for keeping order. The case could be distinguished from cases involving vicarious liability where the employee was given duties involving the clear possibility of confrontation and the use of force, or was placed in the situation where an outbreak of violence was likely, such as a night club doorman. Mr Khan's duties included no element of keeping order over customers.

More recently, in *Graham v Commercial Bodyworks Ltd* [2015] EWCA Civ 47, the claimant's case failed as the act of negligence by the co-worker was found not to have occurred in the 'course of employment'. The facts of the case were that the co-worker sprayed a highly flammable agent onto the claimant's overalls and then lit a cigarette, causing the claimant's overalls to set alight.

4.5 OCCUPIERS' LIABILITY

4.5.1 Occupiers' liability to lawful visitors

The OLA 1957 replaces common law rules concerning the duty owed by an occupier to a lawful visitor.

Under s 1(1), 'occupier' is given the same meaning as at common law (s 1(2)), the test for which was said by Lord Denning, in *Wheat v E Lacon & Co Ltd* [1966] AC 522, to be 'who is in sufficient control?'.

A 'visitor' is a person who would be treated as an invitee or a licensee at common law (s 1(2)), and who therefore is a lawful visitor (as opposed to a trespasser). The duty of care extends not only to the visitor's person, but also to his property (s 1(3)).

4.5.2 The nature of the duty of care

The common duty of care is a duty to take such care as in all the circumstances of the case is reasonable to see that the visitor will be reasonably safe in using the premises for the purposes for which he is invited or permitted by the occupier to be there (s 2(2)).

The common duty of care does not impose on an occupier any obligation to a visitor in respect of risks willingly accepted as his by the visitor (s 2(5)).

4.5.3 Discharging the duty of care

The duty is to take 'such care as ... in all the circumstances ... is reasonable', taking into account the degree of care, and of want of care, which would ordinarily be looked for in such a visitor (s 2(3)). So, for example, an occupier must expect children to be less careful than adults. A warning may discharge the duty of care if it is enough to enable the visitor to be reasonably safe (s 2(4)).

In *Tomlinson v Congleton Borough Council and Another* [2002] EWCA Civ 309, [2003] 2 WLR 1120, the claimant was injured when diving into a lake despite signs prohibiting swimming and warning that to do so was dangerous. The defendants argued that the risk of danger was an obvious one which the claimant had willingly accepted; that they owed the claimant no duty of care; or if they did, that it had been discharged by the display of warning notices.

The Court of Appeal agreed with the court of first instance and found in favour of the claimant. The House of Lords overturned the Court of Appeal decision on the basis that it would be unreasonable to impose a duty to protect people from self-inflicted injuries that they sustained when voluntarily taking risks in the face of obvious warnings. Even if the local authority had owed the claimant a duty of care, that duty would not extend to preventing the claimant from diving or warning him against dangers that were obvious. Their Lordships took the view that it was not appropriate to find in favour of the claimant and thereby impose a duty on local authorities to protect those foolish enough to ignore clear warnings. This would be at the expense of the vast majority of people, who might find that they were barred from all manner of recreational activities on public land for fear that they might injure themselves and decide to sue the local authority.

4.5.4 Employing an independent contractor

Where injury is caused to a visitor by a danger due to the faulty execution of any work of construction, maintenance or repair by an independent contractor employed by the occupier, the occupier will not be treated by this reason alone as answerable for the danger if in all the circumstances (s 2(4)(b)):

(a)   he had acted reasonably in entrusting the work to an independent contractor; and

(b)   he had taken such steps (if any) as he reasonably ought in order to satisfy himself that:

    (i)   the contractor was competent, and

    (ii)   that the work had been properly done.

The duty of care under the Act is therefore delegable to an independent contractor. This should be contrasted with the personal nature of the common duty of care owed to an employee, which is non-delegable (see *Wilsons & Clyde Coal Co v English* [1938] AC 57; and **4.2.6** above).

4.5.5   Exclusion or modification of duty of care

By s 2(1) of the OLA 1957, an occupier may extend, restrict, modify or exclude his duty to any visitor. However, this must be read subject to s 2 of the Unfair Contract Terms Act 1977, under which, in the case of business liability:

(a)   a person cannot by reference to any contract term, or to a notice given to persons generally or to particular persons, exclude or restrict his liability for death or personal injury resulting from negligence;

(b)   in the case of other loss or damage, a person cannot so exclude or restrict his liability for negligence except in so far as the term or notice satisfies the requirement of reasonableness.

4.6   REMOTENESS OF DAMAGE

The defendant will be liable to the claimant only if it can be proved that it was foreseeable that the claimant would suffer damage of the kind that the claimant did in fact suffer. The claimant will generally recover for:

(a)   damage which was reasonably foreseeable; or

(b)   damage which can be shown to flow as a direct consequence of the breach.

Once damage is established as foreseeable (no matter how small), the claimant can recover for the full extent of the injury even if this was unforeseeable (*Smith v Leech Brain & Co Ltd* [1962] 2 QB 405).

4.7   CAUSATION

Whether the claimant can establish causation is a question of fact to be decided by the judge in each case. The basic test both for common law negligence and breach of statutory duty is the 'but for' test. In *Clough v First Choice Holidays and Flights Ltd* [2006] EWCA Civ 15 at [44], Sir Igor Judge said that the term 'but for'

> encapsulates a principle understood by lawyers, but applied literally, or as if the two words embody the entire principle, the words can mislead. ... The claimant is required to establish a causal link between the negligence of the defendant and his injuries, or, in short, that his injuries were indeed consequent on the negligence.

The claimant is not required to show that the breach is the sole cause of the loss; it is sufficient if the breach materially contributed to the loss (*Bonnington Castings Ltd v Wardlaw* [1956] AC 613). To determine who caused the accident, the courts apply common sense to the facts of the case. If a number of people can be shown to have been at fault, that does not necessarily mean that they all caused the accident; it is a question of looking at the facts and deciding which factors are too remote and which are not (*Stapley v Gypsum Mines Ltd* [1953] AC 663).

In most straightforward personal injury claims the issue of causation will be clear. However, this may not be so in occupational disease cases, where two or more defendants have negligently exposed an employee to work practices that may prove injurious to health. This was the situation in the House of Lords' ruling in *Fairchild v Glenhaven Funeral Services Ltd and Others; Fox v Spousal (Midlands) Ltd; Matthews v Associated Portland Cement Manufacturers (1978) Ltd and Others* [2002] UKHL 22, [2002] 3 All ER 305. Here, during the course of his career with more than one employer, the claimant had been exposed to asbestos dust which in later years manifested itself as mesothelioma, for which there is no cure. The House of Lords found that where there had been employment with more than one employer and:

(a)   both employers had a duty to take reasonable care to prevent the claimant from inhaling asbestos dust; and

(b)   both were in breach of that duty; and

(c)   the claimant did subsequently suffer from mesothelioma,

then the claimant could recover damages from both former employers. In these circumstances it was not necessary to satisfy the 'but for' causation test. It was enough that the claimant was able to prove that a defendant had materially increased his risk of injury. In his speech to the House, Lord Bingham of Cornhill said that 'such injustice as may be involved in imposing liability on a duty breaking employer is heavily outweighed by the injustice of denying redress to a victim'.

The case of *Barker v Corus (UK) plc & Others* [2006] UKHL 20 was another House of Lords decision following hot on the heels of *Fairchild v Glenhaven Funeral Services*. In *Barker v Corus*, the House of Lords concluded that where it was established that a number of employers were liable, on the basis that they had negligently exposed an employee to asbestos and thereby created a risk of mesothelioma which did in fact occur, those employers should be liable to the claimant only to the extent of the share of the risk created by their breach of duty. To understand this case it is necessary to take a step back to the previous state of the law. Prior to this judgment, if there were a number of employers all of whom were negligent to some degree, the claimant would simply sue all of them and claim joint and several liability (ie sue all potential defendants for 100% of the loss and let them apportion the blame between them). This allowed the claimant to gain damages in full from one defendant in circumstances where the others might be insolvent or uninsured. Not surprisingly, defendants and their insurers were keen to resist this.

The facts of the case are as follows. The employer (Corus) appealed against a decision of the Court of Appeal in respect of its liability for damages for negligently exposing Mr Barker to asbestos dust, from which he ultimately died, having contracted mesothelioma. During his career he had worked at three stages where he was exposed to asbestos dust. The first two episodes were due to breaches of duty by his then employers. However, the third instance occurred when he was self-employed, and arose from his failure to take reasonable care for his own safety.

The Court of Appeal held that the defendant was jointly and severally liable with the first employer, but subject to a 20% reduction for B's contributory negligence while he was self-employed.

The defendant submitted that it should not be liable at all as a matter of causation, since there had been a period when B, and no one else, had been responsible for his exposure to asbestos dust; and submitted, amongst other things, that it should be severally liable only according to the share of the risk created by its breach of duty.

By a majority decision the House of Lords held that a defendant who is found liable under the *Fairchild* exception to the usual rule of causation, will be liable only to the extent that it contributed to the risk.

The Supreme Court has since disapproved the decision in *Barker* in *Durham v BAI (Run Off) Ltd (in scheme of arrangement)* [2012] 2 All ER (Comm) 1187, in which Lord Mance summarised the correct interpretation of *Fairchild* as follows:

[T]he rule can now be stated as being that when a victim contracts mesothelioma each person who has, in breach of duty, been responsible for exposing the victim to a significant quantity of asbestos dust and thus creating a 'material increase in risk of the victim contracting the disease will be held to be jointly and severally liable in respect of the disease.

Fairchild constitutes an exception to the normal principles of causation. In the House of Lords judgment it was accepted that there might well be instances when the same principle should be applied to other circumstances. However, those circumstances are likely to be strictly controlled by the courts.

In *Sanderson v Hull* [2008] All ER (D) 39 (Nov), the claimant alleged that she had been infected by the campylobacter bacterium as a result of her employer's breach of duty during the course of her employment as a turkey plucker. At first instance the judge held that her case fell within the *Fairchild* exception. However, the Court of Appeal disagreed. The Court did not accept that this was a case where it was impossible for the claimant to show that 'but for' negligence on the part of her employer there would have been no injury. The appeal judges stated that the conditions set out in *Fairchild* in respect of mesothelioma cases, which might justify a relaxation of the test, were not intended to exclude the application of the exception to other diseases, but an essential element is the impossibility of the claimant satisfying the 'but for' test: mere difficulty of proof is not enough. More recently, in *Heneghan v Manchester Dry Docks Limited* [2014] EWHC 4190 (QB), the *Fairchild* exception was held to apply where the claimant developed lung cancer from exposure to asbestos.

4.7.1 The Compensation Act 2006

Because of the implications of the House of Lords' ruling in *Barker v Corus*, Parliament acted quickly to negate its effect in the form of s 3 of the Compensation Act 2006, which came into force on 26 July 2006. The effect of s 3 is that where mesothelioma is contracted as a result of negligent exposure to asbestos in the course of employment with more than one employer, the employers will be jointly and severally liable for the damage caused. This means that the employee can claim compensation in full from any one of the negligent employers, who may in turn claim against the remaining employers for a contribution according to their share of the blame. The effect of s 3 has of course now been confirmed in case law by *Durham v BAI* (see above **4.7**).

4.8 THE MESOTHELIOMA ACT 2014 AND THE DIFFUSE MESOTHELIOMA PAYMENT SCHEMES

Mesothelioma is a cancer of the lining of internal organs, such as the lungs, and almost always arises from exposure to asbestos. Life expectancy from diagnosis is between eight and nine months, on average. The long time that mesothelioma takes to develop – sometimes 40 to 50 years after exposure before symptoms appear – means that some workers were negligently exposed to asbestos at work but their employers are no longer in existence to make a claim against. Insurance records from the time are also often incomplete. The Diffuse Mesothelioma Payment Schemes (DMPS) have been introduced in response to the difficulties faced by sufferers in obtaining compensation through a civil claim for damages and the fact that death usually occurs within months of diagnosis. There are two such schemes in operation at present, both of which are administered by the DWP.

The Mesothelioma Act 2014 established the latest DMPS, which provides for lump sum payments to be made to sufferers who were exposed to asbestos either negligently or in breach of statutory duty by their employer(s) and who are unable to bring a claim for damages because they cannot trace the employer or that employer's EL insurer. It is funded by a levy on insurance companies and applies where mesothelioma was diagnosed after 25 July 2012.

The DMPS 2008, which is a 'no fault' scheme, continues to operate where the diagnosis is before 25 July 2012. It applies where the mesothelioma is unrelated to the employment of the sufferer (for instance, where the claimant was self-employed), or to a family member who was exposed via the worker's overalls.

The details of these schemes are beyond the scope of this textbook but can be found by consulting the schemes themselves on the gov.uk website.

4.9 DEFENCES

4.9.1 *Volenti non fit injuria*

Where the defence of *volenti non fit injuria* applies, if a person engages in an event, being aware of and accepting the risks inherent in that event, he cannot later complain of, or seek compensation for, an injury suffered during the event. In order to establish the defence, the claimant must be shown not only to have perceived the existence of danger, but also to have appreciated it fully and voluntarily accepted the risk.

In *ICI v Shatwell* [1965] AC 656, two brothers, both experienced shotfirers, agreed to test detonators without obeying safety regulations imposed by their employers. Both were injured when one of the detonators exploded. One of the brothers sued his employer on the basis that ICI were vicariously liable for injuries caused to him by the negligence of his fellow worker. The Court held that ICI were not liable. Shatwell had voluntarily consented to a risk of which he was well aware. The Court went on to say that the defence of *volenti non fit injuria* should be available where the employer is not himself in breach of statutory duty and is not vicariously in breach of any statutory duty through neglect of some person of superior rank to the claimant and whose commands the claimant is bound to obey, or who has some special and different duty of care.

It is important to note that in *ICI v Shatwell* there was no breach of statutory duty by the employers. The defence is not available to an employer on whom a statutory obligation is imposed as against liability for his own breach of that obligation.

While *volenti non fit injuria* may be a defence in theory, in practice it is rarely successful; an employee will not often consent freely to run the risk of injury with full knowledge of that risk. The only real defence to a work-based claim will therefore be contributory negligence.

4.9.2 Claimant's contributory negligence

The contributory negligence of the claimant may sometimes reduce the damages to be awarded against the defendant. It is for the judge to decide the proportion of responsibility of the claimant and to reduce the amount of damages accordingly.

The Law Reform (Contributory Negligence) Act 1945, s 1 provides:

> [If] any person suffers damage as a result partly of his own fault and partly of the fault of any other person ... damages recoverable in respect thereof shall be reduced by such extent as the court thinks just and equitable having regard to the claimant's share in responsibility for the damage.

'Fault' is defined by s 4 as 'negligence, breach of statutory duty, or other act or omission which gives rise to a liability in tort or, apart from this Act, gives rise to the defence of contributory negligence'.

The question for the court, when considering contributory negligence, is whether the claimant acted reasonably in taking the risk (*AC Billings & Son Ltd v Riden* [1968] AC 240). Whether the claim is in negligence or for breach of statutory duty, there cannot be a finding of 100% contributory negligence (see *Anderson v Newham College of Further Education* [2002] EWCA Civ 505).

In assessing the claimant's conduct, allowance will be made for his working conditions. Mere inadvertence by the employee will generally not be sufficient for contributory negligence, for example where the employee is engrossed in his work or is in a hurry to get on with his job.

The relative age and experience of the claimant will also be a relevant consideration for the court when deciding questions of contributory negligence. Disobedience or reckless disregard for the employer's orders are far more likely to give rise to a finding of contributory negligence.

In *Eyres v Atkinsons Kitchens & Bathrooms* [2007] EWCA Civ 365, the defendant was the claimant's employer. The claimant asserted that the defendant was liable in negligence and/or for breach of statutory duty because it caused or permitted him to drive when he was too tired after having worked excessively long hours without a proper break.

At the time of the accident, the claimant was a 20-year-old kitchen fitter employed by the defendant. Long hours, resulting in good money, were accepted by all the defendant's employees to be normal. If the work took them far from their factory base, the fitters, including the claimant, tended to prefer a long drive back to Bradford and getting home late rather than staying away overnight. The claimant was held to be 25% to blame for his injuries because he had not been wearing a seat belt. The Court was asked to consider the degree of culpability of the claimant, as he had, whilst driving, become tired and liable to fall asleep.

The Court concluded that the claimant had to bear some further responsibility for the accident, but went on to say that the claimant was in that predicament because his employer had put him there. His employer was next to him, fast asleep. His employer was doing nothing to guard against the very risk of injury from which he ought to have been saving his employee. Bearing in mind the relative blameworthiness of the parties' respective faults and their degrees of responsibility, the judge assessed the claimant's overall contributory negligence at 33%.

In *Sherlock v Chester City Council* [2004] EWCA Civ 201, the claimant was a joiner who lost his thumb and index finger in an accident when using a circular saw provided by his employer. He claimed that his employer was both negligent, for failing to carry out an appropriate risk assessment, and in breach of statutory duty in relation to breaches of reg 3 of the Management of Health and Safety at Work Regulations 1999, reg 20 of the Provision and Use of Work Equipment Regulations 1998, and reg 4 of the Manual Handling Operations Regulations 1992. On appeal to the Court of Appeal, Arden LJ considered whether it was appropriate for there to be findings of contributory negligence in a breach of statutory duty case:

> There may be some justification for the view [that the findings of contributory negligence are not appropriate] in cases of momentary inattention by an employee. But where a risk has been consciously accepted by an employee, it seems to me that different considerations may arise. That is particularly so where the employee is skilled and the precaution in question is neither esoteric nor one which he could not take himself ... In those circumstances it seems to me that the appellant can properly be required to bear the greater responsibility. I would assess his responsibility for the accident at 60 per cent.

When considering contributory negligence, it should be remembered that many statutory duties apply to employees and not employers. For example, the Management of Health and Safety at Work Regulations 1999, reg 14 places a duty on employees to use equipment in accordance with training and instructions.

4.10 ENFORCEMENT OF HEALTH AND SAFETY AT WORK

The function of enforcement is carried out by:

(a)   the HSE, which deals broadly with industrial working environments;

(b)   various specialist agencies appointed on behalf of the HSE (eg, the Hazardous Installations Directorate);

(c)   local authorities, which deal broadly with non-industrial working environments such as the retail, office, leisure and catering sectors.

4.10.1   Health and safety inspectors

Health and safety inspectors have wide powers to enter premises and carry out investigations. As a result of an investigation revealing a contravention, an inspector may:

(a)   issue an improvement notice requiring any contravention to be remedied;

(b)   serve a prohibition notice requiring the contravention to be remedied and fixing a time after which the activity is prohibited unless remedied;

(c)   commence a criminal prosecution (which may give rise to a relevant conviction that can be used against the employer by the employee in subsequent civil proceedings).

4.10.2   The employer's duty to report, maintain and implement safety provisions

The following are the principal requirements imposed on an employer:

(a)   An employer who employs five or more persons must have written details of his policy in regard to the organisation, control, monitoring and review of health and safety measures.

(b)   An employer is under a duty to report certain accidents, diseases and dangerous occurrences to the HSE via its website at <www.riddor.gov.uk>. This enables the HSE to consider an investigation of the incident. Only accidents resulting in death or injury which leads to a worker being unable to work for seven days or more need to be reported to the HSE. All occurrences which result in a worker being unable to work for three days or more must be recorded, and details of the injuries must be kept in an accident book. The records must be kept for at least three years.

(c)   The employer may (and in certain circumstances must) have a safety representative to represent the health and safety interests of the employees. Such a representative has wide powers to investigate potential hazards and dangerous occurrences, and to follow up complaints made by employees.

(d)   In addition to the safety representative, the employer may (and in certain circumstances must) have a safety committee, the function of which includes:

(i)   the studying of accidents and notifiable diseases in order to recommend corrective measures to management;

(ii)   making recommendations on safety training;

(iii)   examining reports of the HSE and safety representatives;

(iv)   making recommendations on developing/changing safety rules.

(e)   Where an employee is injured at work and claims benefit, in certain circumstances the employer is obliged to complete Form B176 to be sent to the Department of Work and Pensions.

(f)   Subject to certain exceptions, an employer is required by the Employers' Liability (Compulsory Insurance) Act 1969 to take out insurance against liability to his own employees.

4.10.3   Employers' liability – enforcement through criminal proceedings

Criminal prosecutions may be brought against both the company and individual directors for breaches of the HSWA 1974.

Section 2(1) is the key provision of the HSWA 1974. It states that '[i]t shall be the duty of every employer to ensure, so far as is reasonably practicable, the health, safety and welfare at work of all his employees'.

The Court of Appeal established in R *v Gateway Foodmarkets Ltd* [1997] 3 All ER 78 that the HSWA 1974, s 2(1) imposed a duty of strict liability. This is qualified only by the defence that the employer has done everything reasonably practicable to ensure that no person's health and safety are put at risk. The defendants appealed against their conviction for failing to do everything reasonable to ensure the safety of their employees. The facts of the case were that a supermarket manager died after falling down an open lift shaft which he had been trying to repair. He had entered the room to free the lift, which had become jammed, by hand – a regular though unauthorised practice of which head office was unaware – but failed to notice that the trap door had been left open by contractors. The Court dismissed the company's appeal and held that s 2(1) of the Act was to be interpreted so as to impose liability in the event of a failure to ensure safety unless all reasonable precautions had been taken not only by the company itself, but also by its servants and agents on its behalf.

In R v HTM Ltd [2006] EWCA Crim 1156, the Court reaffirmed that a defendant to a charge under the ss 2, 3 or 4 of the HSWA 1974, could adduce evidence in support of its case that it had taken all reasonable steps to eliminate the likelihood of the relevant risk occurring. In a preparatory hearing, the judge ruled that evidence of foreseeability was admissible as it was relevant to the case alleged against the defendant, particularly with regard to the reasonable practicability of its ensuring the health, safety and welfare of its employees, and that the Management of Health and Safety at Work Regulations 1999, reg 21 did not preclude the defendant from relying upon any act or default of its employees in its defence. The defendant was entitled to put before the jury evidence to show that what had happened was purely the fault of one or both of its employees. If the jury were persuaded that everything had been done by or on behalf of the defendant to prevent the accident from happening, the defendant would be entitled to be acquitted: R v Gateway Foodmarkets Ltd applied.

In the case of R v Tangerine Confectionery and Veolia [2011] EWCA Crim 2015, the Court of Appeal gave further guidance on the relevance of foreseeability in such cases. The appeals involved two companies which had been convicted of offences under the HSWA 1974. Tangerine Confectionary had been prosecuted after an employee was killed attempting to unblock a sweet-making machine. It was convicted of a breach of s 2 of the HSWA 1974 and fined £300,000. However, it appealed on the basis that the risk of the employee's making an inexplicable decision not to isolate the machine before entering it was not foreseeable, and therefore the employer could not have been expected to guard against it. Veolia, a waste company, was convicted of breaches of ss 2 and 3 of the HSWA 1974 and fined £225,000, following an accident in which a worker collecting litter from the roadside was killed when hit by a car driven by a member of the public. Veolia appealed on the basis that the risk arose from the negligent driving of a member of the public and was not something over which the employer had any control. Both appeals were rejected by the Court of Appeal, which held that foreseeability of risk is relevant but it is only the risk that needs to be foreseeable (such as an employee's being crushed by the arms of a sweet-making machine) and not the mechanics of the actual events which occurred.

Following concern at the low level of fines being imposed for offences under the HSWA 1974, the Court of Appeal has given guidance on the factors to be taken into account by courts when considering the appropriate penalty for this type of offence. In R v Howe & Son (Engineers) Ltd [1999] 2 All ER 249, the Court stated that the aim of the Act was to ensure safety for employees and the public, and therefore fines needed to be large enough to convey that message. In general, they should not be so large as to put the employer out of business. In determining seriousness, the court should consider:

(a)   how far short of the appropriate standard the defendant had been;
(b)   that the standard of care was the same for small organisations as for large;
(c)   the degree of risk and extent of danger involved; and
(d)   the defendant's resources and the effect of a fine on its business.

Aggravating factors could include:

(a)   failure to heed warnings;
(b)   deliberate breach of regulations in pursuit of profit or saving money; and
(c)   loss of life.

Mitigating factors could include:

(a)   early admission of responsibility;

(b)   a plea of guilty;

(c)   taking action to remedy any breach brought to the company's notice; and

(d)   a good safety record.

The Court further held that it was incumbent upon a defendant seeking to make representations about its financial position to provide copies of accounts to the court and the prosecution in good time.

The above guidelines were considered by the Court of Appeal in R v Rollco Screw & Rivet Co Ltd [1999] 2 Cr App R (S) 436. The defendant company and two of its directors protested that the length of time given for payment of fines was inappropriate, and that no distinction should be made between personal and corporate defendants (as there was a risk of double penalty if directors and shareholders were the same people). On appeal, the Court agreed that a personal defendant's period of punishment had to remain within acceptable boundaries; this was not true of a corporate defendant, as the same sense of anxiety was unlikely and a fine could be ordered to be payable over a longer period. The level of fines must make it clear that directors had a personal responsibility; there was a risk of double penalty in smaller companies where directors were also shareholders and would be the principal losers.

The Health and Safety Offences Act 2008 (HSOA 2008), which came into force on 16 January 2009, was introduced as a result of concern that sentences under the HSWA 1974 were too lenient. The HSOA 2008 does not create any new offences, but it raises the maximum penalties available to the courts in respect of many health and safety offences. Previously such offences were punishable only by fines (maximum £5,000 in the magistrates' court). Under the HSOA 2008, most offences under the HSWA 1974 (and regulations made under it) will also carry a sentence of imprisonment for 12 months following prosecution in the magistrates' court, and for two years following prosecution in the Crown Court. The maximum fine that may be imposed in the magistrates' court increases to £20,000; fines imposed by the Crown Court are unlimited.

Where an accident results in death and the evidence indicates that a serious criminal offence other than a health and safety offence may have been committed, the HSE is required to liaise with the Crown Prosecution Service in deciding whether to prosecute. This is dealt with in more detail in **Chapter 17**.

4.11 CONCLUSION

Although the E&RRA 2013 will undoubtedly have an impact on this area of personal injury litigation, it may be several years before claims for accidents that occurred after 1 October 2013 actually come before the courts, and so for the time being both negligence and breach of statutory duty will continue to be relied on for those accidents that pre-date the E&RRA 2013. Even for accidents that occur after 1 October 2013, breaches of statutory duty will continue to be an important part of a claimant's case in establishing negligence against an employer, and so it remains important for claimants' solicitors to consider possible breaches of regulations in order to maximise the clients' chances of success.

Defendants' solicitors need to be alert to possible arguments of contributory negligence on the part of the claimant, although there is generally less scope for substantial reductions for contributory negligence in work-based claims than in RTA claims. It is important that the solicitors for both sides regularly review the evidence available, including all relevant health and safety documentation which can often hold the key to establishing liability and which it is essential to obtain at an early stage.

An example of an EL case may be found in **Appendix 1**.

4.12 FURTHER READING AND RELEVANT WEBSITES

The above is merely an overview of the law as it relates to liability in EL claims. For a more detailed consideration of the subject, reference should be made to the following sources of information:

Redgrave, Hendy and Ford, *Redgrave's Health and Safety* (Butterworths)

Munkman, *Employer's Liability* (Butterworths)

Tolley's Health and Safety at Work Handbook (Tolley)

<www.hse.gov.uk>

<www.riddor.gov.uk>

<www.gov.uk>

CHAPTER 5

CLINICAL NEGLIGENCE: THE LAW

LEARNING OUTCOMES

After reading this chapter you will be able to:

- set out the nature and scope of the duty of care owed by institutional health providers and individual medical practitioners

- explain how the *Bolam* test is used to determine whether there has been a breach of duty

- appreciate that causation is a more complicated issue in clinical negligence cases than in personal injury cases

- set out the role of the NHS Litigation Authority, the structure of the NHS and the operation of the NHS complaints procedure.

5.1 INTRODUCTION

Clinical negligence claims arise when a medical practitioner, such as a doctor, nurse, midwife or dentist, or an institutional health provider, such as an NHS or Foundation Trust or a private hospital, breaches his or its duty of care to the claimant, who is injured as a result of the breach. The claimant may seek legal advice following an adverse outcome from medical treatment, for example an unexpected injury or condition, a worsening of the original condition, an increased length of stay in hospital, a subsequent unplanned re-admission, a transfer to the intensive care unit, or perhaps even the death of the patient. However, whereas in the case of an accident on the highway or in the workplace it is generally a straightforward matter to establish breach and causation, this is not so in clinical negligence claims. The fact that the claimant has had an unexpected or disappointing outcome from the medical treatment he received does not necessarily mean that the healthcare provider failed to act with reasonable care and skill. Even where a breach can be established, it may not be possible to show that the breach caused the injury, as the underlying medical condition may have led to the same outcome for the patient in any event.

From the outset, the claimant's solicitor will need to manage his client's expectations with sympathetic tact and diplomacy. His client may struggle to understand why the case is not as clear-cut as he had imagined and, in the absence of a very careful explanation, may feel that the solicitor is simply incompetent. The client may have objectives other than compensation, such as an explanation as to what went wrong, an apology, the punishment of those responsible and the assurance that similar mistakes will not happen in the future. These options should be explored with him and the shortcomings of each option highlighted. For instance, the NHS complaints procedure will not lead to the payment of compensation. The NHS complaints procedure and the disciplinary procedures followed by the General Medical Council and the Nursing and Midwifery Council are dealt with in **5.9** and **5.11** below.

Clinical negligence claims are, in the main, more complex than personal injury claims, and should therefore be handled only by those solicitors who have the required specialist skills. For a number of reasons, including the implicit allegations of professional incompetence, the high levels of compensation awards and the need for NHS bodies in particular to maintain the confidence and support of the public, claims are frequently defended.

Where a patient has been treated privately and a certain outcome had been anticipated, such as in the case of cosmetic surgery or dentistry, a claim may be brought for breach of contract. However, most claims against NHS bodies and private doctors and hospitals are brought under the tort of negligence. If the claim is to be successful, the claimant must show, on a balance of probabilities, that the essential elements are proved, ie:

(a)　that the medical practitioner or institutional health provider owed him a duty of care;

(b)　that the medical practitioner or institutional health provider breached that duty;

(c)　that he suffered injury and losses as a result of that breach of duty, which were reasonably foreseeable.

Each of these three elements is examined in detail below.

5.2　THE DUTY OF CARE

5.2.1　The medical practitioner

It is clear that a doctor, nurse, midwife or other medical practitioner owes a duty of care to his patients. This is unlikely to be a matter in dispute between the parties. The duty of care owed by a doctor is wide-ranging but would encompass, for example:

(a)　properly assessing the patient's condition by taking account of the symptoms, the patient's views and an examination, where necessary;

(b)　working within the limits of personal competence;

(c)　keeping professional knowledge and skills up to date;

(d)　prescribing drugs or administering treatment only where in possession of adequate knowledge of the patient's health and where satisfied that the drugs or treatment are appropriate for the patient's needs;

(e)　keeping clear, accurate and legible records;

(f)　being readily accessible when on duty;

(g)　consulting and taking advice from colleagues, where necessary; and

(h)　referring a patient to another practitioner, where this in the patient's best interests.

5.2.2　The institutional health provider

Where a medical practitioner is an employee of an NHS or Foundation Trust, the institutional health provider will be vicariously liable for its employees' breaches of duty. However, the NHS or Foundation Trust itself owes a duty of care to the patient, and can be sued for negligence without the claimant having to prove negligence on the part of an individual medical practitioner. The leading case in this area is *Wilsher v Essex Area Health Authority [1988]*

AC 1074, in which it was held that an institutional health provider has a duty to provide services of doctors of sufficient skill and that there was no reason why a health authority could not be liable for a failure to provide such services.

The duty of care owed by an institutional health provider encompasses, for example:

(a)   the provision of staff with the appropriate levels of knowledge, experience and ability;

(b)   the provision of adequate instruction, training and supervision of staff;

(c)   the provision of equipment which is reasonably suitable for the patient's needs and is maintained in good working order;

(d)   ensuring that the working conditions within the hospital are not such that they lead to levels of fatigue or stress which pose a risk to the patient; and

(e)   ensuring that appropriate systems are in place for the storage and retrieval of patients' records.

In respect of private treatment, the doctors and some other healthcare providers will usually be independent contractors. Where it is their breach of duty which has led to the claim, vicarious liability is not applicable. A private hospital is vicariously liable for the breaches of duty of its own employees, such as nurses, and it will also owe a duty to provide appropriate services and equipment.

5.3   BREACH OF THE DUTY OF CARE

5.3.1   The *Bolam* test

Some errors made by doctors are clearly in breach of their duty of care, for example where a swab is left in the patient during an operation, where the wrong limb is amputated or where an incorrect drug is administered. Such errors are known as 'never events' in the NHS and, when they arise, liability is unlikely to be disputed. However, difficulty arises in cases where a medical practitioner exercises his professional judgement and decides to take one course of action rather than another, or perhaps decides not to act at all. In the realms of diagnosis and treatment, there is scope for genuine differences of opinion, and a doctor will not necessarily be negligent because the decisions he took did not result in the outcome the patient was hoping for.

Consequently, in clinical negligence claims, the normal 'reasonable man' test is modified. In order to show a breach of duty, the claimant must show that the doctor has followed a course of action which is not supported by any reasonable body of medical opinion. This has become known as the *Bolam* test after the case of *Bolam v Friern Hospital Management Committee* [1957] 1 WLR 582, in which it was held that:

> The test as to whether there has been negligence or not is not the test of the man on top of the Clapham omnibus because he has a special skill. The test is the standard of the ordinary skilled man exercising and professing to have that special skill. A man need not possess the highest expert skill; it is well established law that it is sufficient if he exercises the ordinary skill of an ordinary competent man exercising that particular art ... A doctor is not guilty of negligence if he has acted in accordance with a practice accepted as proper by a reasonable body of medical men skilled in that particular art ... a doctor is not negligent, if he is acting in accordance with such a practice, merely because there is a body of opinion which takes the contrary view.

Thus, if the defendant NHS body can show that the doctor it employed acted in accordance with a reasonable body of opinion, it will have a defence to the claim. The word 'reasonable' is important, because it is possible that a sizeable group of doctors might hold firm and honest beliefs which are rejected by their peers, for example because they are outdated or have been disproved.

This point was addressed when the House of Lords considered the *Bolam* test in *Bolitho v City and Hackney Health Authority* [1997] 3 WLR 1151 (see **5.5.4** for the facts of this case). It held:

> The court is not bound to hold that a defendant doctor escapes liability for negligent treatment or diagnosis just because he leads evidence from a number of medical experts who are genuinely of the opinion that the defendant's treatment or diagnosis accorded with sound medical practice. ... The court has to be satisfied that the exponents of the body of opinion relied upon can demonstrate that such opinion has a logical basis.

Practitioners sometimes refer to the *Bolam* test as the 10% rule. It is said that if 10% of the doctors in the country would have taken the same course of action, and that action has a logical basis, then it will not be a negligent act.

The following further clarifications should be noted:

(a)   A medical practitioner will be judged in accordance with the reasonable body of opinion which existed at the time of the alleged negligent act. It would be inequitable to consider medical practice which exists at the time of trial, as advances in knowledge and practice are almost inevitable.

(b)   A medical practitioner will normally be judged in accordance with the opinion of practitioners of the same rank and experience. So the standard of an obstetric senior registrar is assessed by reference to the opinion of other obstetric senior registrars rather than that of a consultant obstetrician. However, a medical practitioner has a responsibility to ensure that he practises within the confines of his own knowledge and experience, and he should seek the advice of more knowledgeable and experienced clinicians where appropriate. Where he fills a more demanding role, a higher standard of care may be applied (see *Wilsher v Essex Area Health Authority* [1988] AC 1074). Moreover, an NHS body will be in breach of duty if it fails to provide medical practitioners of the required level of skill and experience for the task in hand.

5.4   RES IPSA LOQUITUR

The maxim *res ipsa loquitur* may be applied in clinical negligence cases in circumstances where the claimant is unable to adduce any evidence as to how or why the injury has occurred but asserts that it would not have occurred in the absence of the defendant's negligence (see **3.2.3.3**).

In *Cassidy v Ministry of Health* [1951] 2 KB 343, the claimant attended a hospital due to a problem affecting two fingers on one hand, but following an operation and post-operative treatment, the whole hand was affected. The court held that he was entitled to rely on the maxim *res ipsa loquitur* and that the defendant had failed to explain how the injury could have occurred without negligence.

The approach to *res ipsa loquitur* in clinical negligence litigation was reviewed by the Court of Appeal in *Ratcliffe v Plymouth and Torbay Health Authority* [1998] PIQR P170. Dismissing the claimant's appeal, the Court expressed surprise at the suggestion that courts were having difficulty in assessing the applicability of the doctrine to cases involving allegations of clinical negligence, and reviewed the relevant principles in detail.

Lord Justice Brooke made the following points:

(a)   The maxim applies where the claimant relies on the happening of the thing itself to raise the inference of negligence, which is supported by ordinary human experience, and with no need for expert evidence.

(b)   The maxim can be applied in that form to simple situations in the clinical negligence field (a surgeon cutting off a right foot instead of the left; a swab left in the operation site; a patient who wakes up in the course of a surgical operation despite a general anaesthetic).

(c)   In practice, in contested clinical negligence cases the evidence of a claimant which establishes the *res* is likely to be buttressed by expert evidence to the effect that the matter complained of does not ordinarily occur in the absence of negligence.

(d) The position may then be reached at the close of the claimant's case that the judge would be entitled to infer negligence on the defendant's part unless the defendant can then adduce some evidence which discharges the inference.

(e) This evidence may be to the effect that there is a plausible explanation of what may have happened which does not rely on negligence on the defendant's part.

(f) Alternatively, the defendant's evidence may satisfy the judge on the balance of probabilities that he did exercise proper care. If the untoward outcome is extremely rare, or is impossible to explain in the light of the current state of medical knowledge, the judge will be bound to exercise great care in evaluating the evidence before making such a finding.

The judgment goes some way in explaining why *res ipsa loquitur* is not commonly pleaded in such cases. Whilst it is commonplace for a claimant not to have full knowledge of what had occurred, particularly if the procedure was an operation carried out under anaesthetic, in practical terms, few cases are brought to trial without full disclosure of relevant information being supplied by the defendant, and both sides will rely on expert evidence. Consequently, by the time the matter comes to trial, most claimants will be able to particularise allegations of negligence and the trial opens 'not in the vacuum of available evidence and explanation' as sometimes occurs in road traffic accident cases. The court will be able to decide the case on the evidence which is presented.

5.5 CAUSATION

In a clinical negligence claim, the claimant will argue that, as a result of the negligent treatment by the doctor or hospital, he suffered an unexpected injury or condition, his pre-existing injury or condition became worse, he failed to recover from that condition, or the chances of him recovering diminished. Where a patient has died, his estate or dependants may argue that the death was caused by negligent treatment.

However, the issue of causation which is likely to be admitted (subject to liability) in personal injury cases, is likely to be hotly disputed by the defendant in clinical negligence cases. In personal injury cases, the claimant is normally fit and well prior to the accident, and it is clearly the accident which caused the injury. In contrast, in clinical negligence cases, the adverse outcome complained of can arise as a result of many different variables, and it may be difficult to show that 'but for' the breach, this outcome would not have arisen.

Also in contrast with personal injury cases, in clinical negligence cases, the term 'liability' is usually confined to matters relating to breach of duty. 'Causation' is dealt with separately and the evidence of a further medical expert may be required. Consequently, where the defendant admits liability prior to trial, the claimant's solicitor should seek confirmation that the defendant also admits causation.

5.5.1 The 'but for' test

The claimant has to satisfy the court, on a balance of probabilities, that, but for the defendant's breach of duty, he would not have suffered the injury complained of. If, for example, a failure to treat a patient has made no difference because he would have died in any event, his death will not have been caused by negligence.

In *Barnett v Chelsea and Kensington Hospital Management Committee* [1969] 1 QB 428, three night-watchmen attended a casualty department complaining of vomiting after drinking tea three hours previously. The men were sent home with instructions to go to bed, and if necessary to call their own doctors. They went away but one of them died later that night, and the cause of death was subsequently found to be arsenic poisoning. In an action brought by the widow, the defendant was found to be in breach of duty. However, the court found that the deceased would have died of the poisoning even if he had been treated with all the necessary care.

Therefore, the claimant had failed to establish on the balance of probabilities that the defendant's negligence caused the deceased's death.

The claimant does not have to prove that the defendant's breach of duty was the sole cause of the injury. It is enough for him to show that the breach made a material (ie something more than minimal) contribution towards the injury. In *Bailey v Ministry of Defence* [2008] EWCA Civ 883, the claimant, who underwent a medical procedure at the defendant's hospital, was not properly resuscitated and, due to the subsequent deterioration in her condition, had to undergo three further procedures shortly after. It was argued on her behalf that she would have needed only one additional procedure had she been properly resuscitated after the first operation. As a result of weakness due to the procedures, and the development of pancreatitis, which was a natural complication not attributable to negligence, the claimant inhaled vomit, went into cardiac arrest and suffered brain damage. The Court of Appeal upheld the trial judge's finding that it was not possible to say whether the weakness had been caused mainly by the negligence or by the pancreatitis, that each had contributed materially to the overall weakness, and it was that overall weakness that caused her inability to respond to the vomit and her subsequent injuries. Consequently, the finding against the defendant was upheld.

It is possible for the court to hold more than one type of healthcare professional jointly responsible for personal injuries that result from negligence. This is well illustrated in the case of *Prendergast v Sam and Dee Ltd* (1989) *The Times*, 14 March, in which a pharmacist misread a prescription and gave the claimant a drug which resulted in irreversible brain damage. The pharmacist was held to be 75% responsible, and the doctor who wrote the prescription was held to be 25% at fault because his handwriting was illegible.

5.5.2 Causation and loss of a chance

As the claimant must prove causation on a balance of probabilities, the courts have held that a claimant cannot claim for the loss of a prospect of recovery where the chance of recovery is less than probable. In *Hotson v East Berkshire Health Authority* [1987] AC 750, a 13-year-old boy, was climbing a tree to which a rope was attached when he lost his grip and fell 12 feet to the ground. He was subsequently taken to hospital, where the staff failed to diagnose a fracture and sent him home to rest. When he returned to the hospital, the correct diagnosis was made. As a result of the initial failure to give a correct diagnosis, he was left with a disability of the hip and a risk of future osteoarthritis. At first instance, the trial judge found that if the health authority had correctly diagnosed and treated the claimant when he first attended hospital, there was a high probability (which he assessed at a 75% risk) that his injury would have followed the same course it had followed. In other words, the doctor's delay in making the correct diagnosis had denied the claimant a 25% chance that, if given immediate treatment, he would have made a complete recovery. Accordingly, the claimant was awarded 25% of the appropriate damages. The defendant's appeal to the Court of Appeal was dismissed, but the House of Lords overturned the decision. The claimant had failed to prove causation as the lost chances of recovery, being less than 50%, were less than probable.

This approach was confirmed in the case of *Gregg v Scott* [2005] UKHL 2. The claimant, Mr Gregg, visited his GP, Dr Scott, because he had discovered a lump under his left arm. Dr Scott negligently misdiagnosed the lump as a lipoma or benign fatty tumour and therefore as non-cancerous. Nine months later, the claimant went to a new GP who was more cautious and referred him on to a specialist. It was then that he discovered that he had cancer of a lymph gland. By that time the tumour had spread and he had to undergo painful chemotherapy. The claimant sued Dr Scott, alleging that he should have referred the claimant to hospital and that, if he had done so, the condition would have been diagnosed earlier and there would have been a significant likelihood of a cure. Although the claimant could claim for the extra pain and suffering caused by the defendant, the claimant tried to sue on the basis that he had suffered a loss due to diminished chances of surviving the cancer. On appeal to the House of Lords, their Lordships found in favour of the defendant on the basis that the claimant was unable to prove that his negligence had caused or materially contributed to the injury. It had not been shown that, on the balance of probabilities, the delay in commencing the claimant's treatment had affected the course of his illness or his prospects of survival, which had never been as good as even. Further, liability for the loss of a chance of a more favourable outcome should not be introduced into personal injury claims.

5.5.3 Causation and failure to attend

In *Bolitho v City and Hackney Health Authority* [1997] 3 WLR 1151, the House of Lords considered causation in the context of a doctor's breach of duty in failing to attend a child. The child claimant (aged 2 years) who had been treated for croup at St Bartholomew's Hospital, was discharged but then readmitted. He suffered episodes of extreme breathing difficulties and, during one such episode, the nurse called for a doctor to attend. The senior registrar was dealing with a clinic and was unable to attend, and the senior house officer did not attend either because the batteries of her pager were flat. The child subsequently suffered cardiac arrest which led to brain damage. The defendant accepted that the failure to attend the child was in breach of duty, but it disputed that the failure was causative of any damage. It was agreed that if the child had been intubated (to create an airway), the child would not have suffered the cardiac arrest and consequently would not have incurred brain damage. The senior registrar gave evidence to the effect that she would not have intubated had she attended. There was a dispute between experts called by the parties as to whether intubation would have been the appropriate course of action to take in those circumstances, bearing in mind the risks associated with that procedure. The House of Lords dealt with the case by taking a two-stage approach:

(a) The court first considered what the doctor would have done if she had attended the child. This was a fact-finding exercise and the *Bolam* test was not relevant at this stage. From the senior registrar's evidence, it was accepted by the court that she would not have intubated the child and that the senior house officer would not have done so without her permission.

(b) The court went on to consider whether the failure to intubate would have been negligent. At this point the *Bolam* test was relevant, and the court found that a reasonable body of medical opinion would support the registrar's decision not to intubate.

Consequently, their Lordships found in favour of the defendant.

5.6 CONSENT

The patient's consent is required by the medical practitioner before any sort of operation is performed or treatment (such as an injection of drugs or manipulation of a limb) administered. The consent must be freely given and informed. It need not be in writing, although, in relation to surgical procedures, it invariably will be, and the patient will be asked to sign a consent form. However, it should be noted that a signed consent form is evidence that consent was given but not necessarily that consent was valid, ie freely given by someone with capacity, following full disclosure of all the relevant facts.

The standard NHS consent forms are drafted widely so as to allow a surgeon to deal with any procedure that he deems to be necessary, in the patient's best interests, during the course of the operation. However, the surgeon would be justified in carrying out such additional measures only where they were closely related to the initial procedure, or where they became necessary due to an emergency.

In *Williamson v East London and City Health Authority* [1998] Lloyd's Rep Med 6, the claimant agreed to an operation to replace a leaking silicone breast implant. Immediately prior to the operation, the surgeon noted that the situation was worse than had originally been thought, but did not tell the claimant that she intended to carry out a more extensive procedure than she had initially planned, and no further consent form was signed. A mastectomy was performed without the patient's consent and the patient sued the health authority. The court found that the clinician did not properly or sufficiently inform the claimant of her intention to increase the scope of the operation, the claimant had not consented to the operation, and accordingly damages were awarded in respect of the claimant's pain and suffering.

Where treatment is less risky, oral consent is common. It may also be implied by the very fact that the patient has consulted the doctor.

If the medical practitioner acts without consent, this may lead to a criminal prosecution for battery and to civil proceedings under the tort of trespass to the person (or battery in particular). The basis of these actions is that the interference with the physical integrity of the patient was intentional. (A consideration of the tort of battery lies beyond the scope of this book.)

However, where the medical practitioner seeks the consent of the patient and advises him, in broad terms, of the nature of the operation or treatment, but fails to advise him of all the associated risks, the consent may not be fully 'informed' but it will not be invalidated (see *Chatterton v Gerson* [1981] QB 432). This failure to advise fully may lead to civil proceedings in negligence (see **5.6.4**).

Where the patient suffers from a mental incapacity and thereby falls under Pt IV of the Mental Health Act 1983, his consent is not required for any medical treatment necessary for the management of his mental disorder. (A consideration of the treatment of those who are mentally incapacitated also falls outside the scope of this book.)

5.6.1 Emergency treatment

In some instances, for example in emergencies, consent may not be possible. Where treatment is necessary to save the life or preserve the health of the patient in such circumstances, a failure to obtain consent will not render the doctor liable in civil or criminal proceedings (see *Connolly v Croydon Health Services NHS Trust* [2015] EWHC 1339 (QB)).

5.6.2 Consent by children

Section 8(1) of the Family Law Reform Act 1969 provides a presumption that a child may give valid consent for medical treatment at the age of 16. This area of the law was examined closely in *Gillick v West Norfolk and Wisbech Area Health Authority and Department of Health and Social Security* [1986] AC 112, in which it was held that the important point is the degree of understanding by the child of what is going to happen.

5.6.3 Refusal of consent

The basic proposition is that an adult of sound mind has the right to autonomy and self-determination, and therefore can refuse to consent to medical treatment, even where this may lead to his death. Many of the reported cases deal with women who are in the later stages of pregnancy, and where the medical practitioners, concerned to protect the foetus as well as the mother, apply for a declaration from the court that it would be lawful to carry out the required medical procedure without the mother's consent. These cases show that the court is not able to take the interests of a foetus into account. In *St George's Hospital NHS Trust v S; R v Collins and others, ex p S* [1998] 3 All ER 673, the Court of Appeal said:

> In our judgment while pregnancy increases the personal responsibilities of a woman it does not diminish her entitlement to decide whether or not to undergo medical treatment. Although human, and protected by the law in a number of different ways ... an unborn child is not a separate person from its mother. Its need for medical assistance does not prevail over her rights. She is entitled not to be forced to submit to an invasion of her body against her will, whether her own life or that of her unborn child depends on it. Her right is not reduced or diminished merely because her decision to exercise it may appear morally repugnant. The declaration in this case involved the removal of the baby from

within the body of her mother under physical compulsion. Unless lawfully justified, this constituted an infringement of the mother's autonomy. Of themselves, the perceived needs of the foetus did not provide the necessary justification.

In the case of *Re MB (An Adult: Medical Treatment)* (1997) 38 BMLR 175, a woman who was 40 weeks pregnant and in labour refused to consent to a caesarean section because she had a phobia about needles and therefore could not consent to anaesthesia. Her life and that of her unborn child were therefore at risk. The Court of Appeal held that a competent woman could choose to reject medical intervention, even on irrational grounds, ie where the decision was so outrageous in its defiance of logic or of morally accepted standards that no sensible person could have arrived at it. However, in this case, the appellant's fear of needles had made her incapable of making a decision in relation to anaesthesia and had therefore rendered her temporarily incompetent.

5.6.4 Failure to advise of risk

5.6.4.1 Breach of duty

In order that consent to the proposed treatment may be fully informed, the medical practitioner must, so far as is possible, advise the patient of the risks involved in treatment and the likelihood and nature of any side-effects. Where a patient asks a question, the medical practitioner must answer the question honestly. Clearly, a failure to advise a patient about a substantial risk of grave adverse consequences will be negligent, whether or not the patient asks a specific question; but what about where the risks are very small and there is no specific question?

Until fairly recently, the decision in the case of *Sidaway v Board of Governors of the Bethlem Royal Hospital and Maudsley Hospital* [1985] AC 871 governed the nature of the obligation placed upon the doctor to tell the patient about the risks of proposed treatments and procedures. In that case, it was held by the majority that the *Bolam* test should be applied. In other words, if a reasonable body of clinicians would not have advised the patient of the risk in those circumstances, there was no breach of duty. The decision sat uneasily with the general recognition that the relationship between doctor and patient was, in practice, becoming less paternalistic and more co-operative.

In *Montgomery v Lanarkshire Health Board* [2015] UKSC 11, the Supreme Court held that the analysis of the law by the majority in *Sidaway* was unsatisfactory. Following *Montgomery*, the situation is as follows:

(a) An adult of sound mind is entitled to determine which, if any, of the available forms of treatment to undergo, and consent to such treatment must be obtained before treatment interfering with her bodily integrity is undertaken.

(b) Medical practitioners are under a duty to take reasonable care to ensure that patients are aware of any material risks involved in any recommended treatment, and of any reasonable alternative or variant treatments. There are exceptions: for example, where an unconscious patient requires urgent treatment, where a patient makes it clear he does not wish to be informed of the risks, and where a doctor reasonably believes that disclosure would be seriously detrimental to the patient's health.

(c) The test of materiality is whether, in the circumstances, a reasonable person in the patient's position would be likely to attach significance to the risk, or the doctor was (or should reasonably be) aware that the particular patient would be likely to attach significance to it. The *Bolam* test is not relevant.

5.6.4.2 Causation

In a case where informed consent has not been obtained, the claimant must demonstrate, using the 'but for' test, that the breach of duty has caused the injury (see **5.5.1**). In many instances, it will be a straightforward matter for the court to determine whether or not the patient would have consented to the operation anyway. If a patient, made fully aware of the risks involved in the recommended procedure or treatment, would have consented, causation is not established; if the patient would not have so consented, causation is established.

However, sometimes the matter is not so straightforward. In *Chester v Afshar* [2004] UKHL 41, the House of Lords modified conventional causation principles on policy grounds. The claimant, who consulted the defendant consultant neurosurgeon for back pain, was not warned of a small (1–2%) risk that the proposed operation, no matter how expertly performed, could result in a serious complication, causing partial paralysis. The operation was not performed negligently but, unfortunately, the risk materialised. The difficulty in this case was that the claimant was unable to say that she would never have had the operation had she known of the risk; merely that she would not have had it as soon as she did, as she would have explored other options first. Moreover, the failure to warn had not increased the risk, which was inherent in the operation and liable to occur randomly, irrespective of the degree of care and skill of the surgeon. Consequently, the 'but for' test strictly applied could not be satisfied. The House of Lords found in the claimant's favour and, in so doing, veered away from conventional causation principles. Their Lordships justified their ruling on policy grounds, on the basis that the loss arose from the violation of the patient's right to make an informed choice due to the failure to warn.

5.7   THE ROLE OF THE NHS LITIGATION AUTHORITY

The NHS Litigation Authority (NHSLA) handles clinical negligence claims against NHS bodies and administers a risk-pooling scheme, the Clinical Negligence Scheme for Trusts (CNST), which provides unlimited cover for members of the scheme and their employees against such claims. (Health professionals who provide advice and treatment on a private basis and self-employed health professionals, such as GPs, are not covered by the scheme and must carry their own indemnity insurance.) Membership of the CNST is voluntary, but all NHS and Foundation Trusts are currently members of the scheme. Independent sector providers of NHS care can also join. Members contribute to the scheme in accordance with the level of risk they pose. For example, hospitals that perform high-risk procedures, such as obstetrics, have higher levels of contributions than those which do not.

The NHSLA relies on a panel of solicitors' firms which are specialised in clinical negligence litigation to handle defence work on their behalf. Fewer than 2% of cases referred to the NHSLA are concluded at trial.

The *NHSLA Reporting Guidelines* set out a framework within which claims managers working for Trusts report cases of alleged clinical negligence to the NHSLA. Various situations – such as the discovery of an incident which might lead to a large value claim (at least £5,000), a disclosure request suggesting the possibility of a claim of whatever value, or the receipt of a letter of claim – require notification to be given within specified time limits. The purpose of timely notification is to enable to NHSLA to carry out appropriate investigations and to consider whether any pro-active steps, such as an early admission, offer or apology, could be taken to avoid proceedings being issued.

As of July 2014, the NHSLA offers a mediation service in all suitable cases involving a fatality or the care of the elderly. This voluntary and confidential service is provided by independent and accredited mediators, the purpose being to find a solution without the need for litigation.

5.8   THE STRUCTURE OF THE NHS

Solicitors acting for clients who have suffered as a result of poor NHS treatment must acquire an understanding of the structure of the NHS, and the responsibilities of each body within that structure, to enable them to determine where complaints should be addressed and the identity of the appropriate defendant, should proceedings be necessary.

On 1 April 2013, as a result of the implementation of the provisions of the Health and Social Care Act 2012, fundamental changes were made, the full extent of which is beyond the scope of this book. However, a basic diagrammatical structure showing the bodies relevant to the personal injury solicitor is provided at **5.15,** and an outline of the responsibilities of those bodies is as follows:

(a) The Department of Health, under the leadership of the Secretary of State for Health, is responsible for standards of health and social care and is accountable to Parliament. It provides strategic leadership to the health and care system, the basis of which is set out in the NHS Mandate published by the Secretary of State in November 2012.

(b) NHS England (formerly the NHS Commissioning Board) is an independent body which has a statutory obligation to pursue the objectives found in the NHS Mandate. It is responsible for improving health outcomes for people in England by driving up the quality of care, by commissioning specialist services and primary care (GP services, dental services, pharmacy, and certain aspects of optical services), through the local area teams, and by allocating resources to, and overseeing the work of, the clinical commissioning groups (see below).

(c) Clinical commissioning groups (CCGs) are responsible for a substantial part of the NHS commissioning budget, namely that relating to the provision of secondary care. This includes planned hospital care, rehabilitative care, urgent and emergency care, most community health services and mental health and learning disability services. Services may be commissioned from any provider that meets NHS standards and costs, including charities and private sector providers.

There are 211 CCGs, overseen by 27 NHS England local area teams (including 10 specialised commissioning hubs responsible for those who have very rare conditions), which are themselves overseen by four regional offices. All GP practices must belong to a CCG, and each CCG board must include at least one hospital doctor, a nurse and a member of the public.

(d) Providers of primary and secondary care. These will be the defendants in civil proceedings, and complaints about the services provided will usually be made directly to them, at least in the first instance.

(i) Primary care. This is the first point of contact for most people experiencing health problems and is delivered by a wide range of independent contractors, such as GPs, dentists, opticians and pharmacists. It also includes NHS walk-in centres, NHS 111 and the NHS Direct telephone service.

Those who are not primary care providers (see (ii)–(iv) below) are sometimes referred to as secondary care providers.

(ii) Hospital care. Hospitals in England are managed by acute trusts, many of which are NHS Hospital Trusts. However, Foundation Trusts were introduced in 2004 with the aim of decentralising health services and tailoring them to meet the needs of the local population. They have more financial and operational freedom than NHS Hospital Trusts, and the aim is that all NHS Trusts, including those providing community care or mental health services (see below), will have become Foundation Trusts by 2016.

(iii) Community care services. Care trusts manage integrated services between health and social care which arise from joint working agreements between the NHS and local authorities. Services include those provided by district nurses and health visitors.

(iv) Mental health services. Mental health trusts (the majority of which have foundation status) oversee the specialist care required by those with mental health problems, such as severe anxiety or psychotic illness. Services include counselling, psychological therapies, community and family support and more specialist care. Services may be provided in partnership with other primary and secondary care providers and local authorities.

The Care Quality Commission is the independent regulator of all health and social care services in England. It makes sure that the care provided by hospitals, dentists, ambulances, care homes and services in people's own homes and elsewhere meets national standards of quality and safety by regulating, monitoring and inspecting those services and sharing its findings with the public.

In March 2013, the Department of Health published the NHS Constitution (the 'Constitution'), which establishes the principles and values of the NHS in England. It sets out the rights and responsibilities of patients, public and staff, and the pledges which the NHS is committed to achieve. Further information is set out in the NHS Constitution Handbook (the 'Handbook'). The Secretary of State for Health, NHS bodies, private and voluntary sector providers of NHS services, and local authorities exercising their public health functions are statutorily obliged to take account of the Constitution. NHS England and clinical commissioning groups are obliged to promote the Constitution.

5.9 THE NHS COMPLAINTS PROCEDURE

In April 2009, the Government introduced a simplified two-stage process for handling complaints about NHS services in accordance with the Local Authority Social Services and National Health Service Complaints (England) Regulations 2009 (SI 2009/309) ('the Regulations'). The procedure, which is set out at **5.9.1** applies to complaints concerning all NHS staff, whether they are GPs, hospital doctors, nursing staff, ambulance crew, administrators or cleaners. The procedure is not relevant where treatment has not been funded by the NHS, even where that treatment was provided in an NHS hospital. A complaint by a patient may encompass any expression of dissatisfaction, from a complaint about the food or politeness of staff, to one about diagnosis or treatment (ie a clinical complaint), and may be made orally, in writing or electronically.

The purpose of the complaints procedure is to enable complaints to be dealt with simply and swiftly, at a local level if at all possible. The Government recognises that speedy resolution of the complaint to the complainant's satisfaction may avoid the instigation of civil proceedings, especially where the adverse outcome has not resulted in particularly serious consequences for a patient.

When advising a client about the right to complain in relation to NHS care, and how to go about it, there are a number of matters for the solicitor to explain:

(a)   The complaints procedure does not provide for the payment of compensation to the complainant, although some NHS Trusts operate a policy of offering limited compensation, and the proposed NHS Redress Scheme would, in the unlikely event it were to become operational, provide a formal basis for such payments (see **5.10**). Therefore, particularly in relation to those who have suffered severe injury and consequential financial loss, the complaints procedure is unlikely to provide a complete solution in itself.

(b)   In spite of (a) above, generally it is advisable to exhaust the complaints procedure before commencing proceedings. In addition to ensuring that the complainant's voice does not go unheard, the complaints procedure will ensure that the matter is investigated quickly by the relevant NHS body, while events are still fresh in the minds of those involved. This may provide the claimant's solicitor with valuable information for civil proceedings, should they be necessary. In the past, it was common for the complaints procedure to be suspended as soon as legal proceedings were commenced, or where there was a stated intention to commence proceedings. This should no longer happen.

(c) In accordance with the guidance *Openness and honesty when things go wrong: the professional duty of candour*, issued by the General Medical Council and the Nursing and Midwifery Council in June 2015, healthcare professionals must tell the patient (or their advocate, carer or family) when things go wrong. They should also apologise, offer an appropriate remedy or support to put matters right, and give a full explanation of the short- and long-term effects of what has happened. It should be noted that an apology, an offer of treatment or other redress does not, of itself, amount to an admission of negligence (Compensation Act 2006, s 2).

(d) The purpose of the procedure is to satisfy complaints, rather than apportion blame amongst staff, and it is separate from disciplinary procedures. A complaint may bring the shortcomings of individual members of staff to the notice of the management of an NHS body, which may then consider taking action in accordance with its internal disciplinary procedures. Negligence amounting to gross misconduct may lead to dismissal and/or a referral of the matter by the NHS body to an individual's professional body. However, a complainant should not assume that this will happen, and he may wish to seize the initiative and bring the matter to the attention of the appropriate professional body himself (see **5.11**).

(e) There are various sources of information and bodies that will provide assistance regarding the complaints procedure:

  (i)   Basic information as to how to complain and how the complaint will be dealt with may be found on the NHS website (www.nhs.uk).

  (ii) Each NHS Trust has its own complaints policy, and this is normally found on the Trust's own website. For example, the Surrey and Sussex Healthcare NHS Trust's 'Patient Complaints Management Policy and Procedure' may be found at www.surreyandsussex.nhs.uk/wp-content/uploads/2013/02/0384complaints.pdf.

  (iii) There is a Patient Advice and Liaison Service (PALS) within each Trust, which is staffed by NHS employees and volunteers. Its role is to provide confidential advice and assistance to patients, their relatives, visitors to the hospital and staff members, with the aim of resolving problems and concerns quickly, wherever possible. It does not investigate formal complaints but it can provide advice as to the complaints procedure, and it will refer complainants on to the Independent Complaints Advocacy Service. The website of the National Network of NHS Patient Advice and Liaison Services may be found at www.pals.nhs.uk, although some individual PALS have their own websites.

  (iv) The Independent Complaints Advocacy Service (ICAS) is an organisation which is independent of the NHS. Its staff, known as advocates, can assist with all stages of the complaints procedure, for example writing letters of complaint, contacting third parties on the complainant's behalf and attending meetings with him. Its website may be found at www.seap.org.uk/icas.

  (v)   The Citizens Advice Bureau and NHS Direct can also provide help and assistance.

The complaints procedure involves two stages, local resolution and, if the complainant remains dissatisfied, referral to the Health Service Commissioner. However, complaints may be made to the Care Quality Commission or to the local Clinical Commissioning Group where appropriate.

5.9.1 Local resolution

Local resolution is seen by the Government and the NHS Executive as the main thrust of the complaints procedure. Complaints are most likely to be voiced to staff on the spot, and it is these front-line staff or their departmental managers who are the people best placed to make the initial response. The aim is to resolve problems and answer concerns of patients and their families immediately and informally if possible, thereby reducing the need for legal proceedings and the associated cost to the public purse.

Regulation 3 requires each NHS body to make arrangements for the handling and consideration of complaints. These arrangements must be such as to ensure that

(a)   complaints are dealt with efficiently;

(b)   complaints are properly investigated;

(c)   complainants are treated with respect and courtesy;

(d)   complainants receive, so far as is reasonably practicable—

    (i)   assistance to enable them to understand the procedure in relation to complaints; or

    (ii)   advice on where they may obtain such assistance;

(e)   complainants receive a timely and appropriate response;

(f)   complainants are told the outcome of the investigation of their complaint; and

(g)   action is taken if necessary in the light of the outcome of a complaint.

Each NHS body must designate a person, known as a 'responsible person' to be responsible for ensuring compliance with the arrangements and, in particular, ensuring that action is taken if necessary in the light of the outcome of the complaint. This will be the Chief Executive Officer, although he may authorise others to act on his behalf. Each NHS body must also designate a person as a 'complaints manager', to be responsible for managing the procedures for handling and considering complaints. The responsible person and the complaints manager may be the same person.

A complaint should be made within 12 months of the date the matter complained of occurred or, if later, the date when it came to the notice of the complainant. However, the time limit shall not apply where the NHS body is satisfied that the complainant had good reasons for not making the complaint within the time limit and, notwithstanding the delay, it is still possible to investigate the complaint effectively and fairly.

Unless a complaint is made orally and is resolved to the complainant's satisfaction not later than the next working day after the day on which the complaint was made, a complaint must be dealt with in accordance with the procedures set out in the Regulations. This means that the NHS body should:

(a)   acknowledge the complaint not later than three working days after the day on which it receives the complaint;

(b)   investigate the complaint in a manner appropriate to resolve it speedily and efficiently, and, during the investigation, keep the complainant informed, as far as reasonably practicable, as to the progress of the investigation;

(c)   as soon as reasonably practicable after completing the investigation, send a response to the complainant setting out how the complaint has been considered, its conclusions, a confirmation that it is satisfied that any necessary action has been taken or is proposed to be taken, and details of the complainant's right to take his complaint to the Health Service Commissioner;

(d)   provide the response within six months commencing on the day on which the complaint was received, or such longer period as may be agreed by the NHS body and the complainant, or set out in writing to the complainant the reasons why this has not been possible and provide a response as soon as possible thereafter.

Each NHS body must maintain systems for monitoring complaints, and must prepare an annual report which is made available to any person on request.

5.9.2   The Parliamentary and Health Service Ombudsman and the Public Service Ombudsman for Wales

The Parliamentary and Health Service Ombudsman ('the Ombudsman') deals with complaints arising in England about the NHS and other government departments and public organisations (www.ombudsman.org); the Public Service Ombudsman for Wales (www.ombudsman-wales.org.uk) deals with complaints about public services in Wales. There are separate ombudsmen for Scotland and Northern Ireland.

The Ombudsman, who is independent of the NHS and the Government, will investigate complaints where the NHS body has refused to investigate a complaint on the basis that it is outside the time limit, or where a complaint has been dealt with by NHS complaints procedure and the complainant is still dissatisfied. Complaints which have not been through the local resolution process are unlikely to be considered by the Ombudsman. The complaint should generally be made within one year of the event complained of, although there is discretion to extend this limit in cases where there is good reason for the delay.

Where the Ombudsman finds in favour of the complainant, in accordance with the Principles of Remedy, she will recommend that the health authority offers a remedy which will return the complainant to the position he would have been in had the service provided to him been of the proper standard, or compensate him appropriately where this is not possible.

The remedies which may be recommended by the Ombudsman include:

(a)   an apology, an explanation, and acknowledgment of responsibility;

(b)   remedial action, such as reviewing or changing a decision on the service given to the complainant, revising published material, revising procedures to prevent recurrence of that particular problem, training or supervising staff, or any combination of these;

(c)   financial compensation.

Although the Ombudsman has no power to enforce her recommendations, they are generally followed.

The Ombudsman publishes annual reports regarding her investigations, which are available on the website.

5.10   PLANS FOR REFORM

In June 2003, the Chief Medical Officer (CMO) published his recommendations for reform of the system for handling and responding to clinical negligence claims in a Consultation Paper entitled *Making Amends*. The aim of the NHS Redress Act 2006 was to give effect to the recommendations for an NHS Redress Scheme, which would provide those who had allegedly suffered harm as a result of the negligence of the NHS with an alternative to legal proceedings. Although no firm proposals were ever made, it was widely thought that the Scheme initially would be targeted at straightforward lower value claims, probably up to a value of £20,000. In the event, although the Scheme was introduced in Wales, it was not introduced in England. It is now thought that the Scheme will not be implemented in England; instead, the Government will adopt an approach similar to that for low value RTA, employers' liability and public liability claims (see **Chapter 21**) for low value clinical negligence claims.

5.11   DISCIPLINARY PROCEEDINGS

Those who have been injured or who have lost a loved one as a result of a clinical error may be keen to see those responsible punished, and the solicitor will need to give advice regarding the appropriate disciplinary procedures. A detailed consideration of the conduct of the proceedings lies beyond the scope of this book.

5.11.1   Disciplinary proceedings against doctors

Doctors must be registered with the General Medical Council (GMC) in order to practise medicine in the UK. The GMC has responsibility for investigating complaints about doctors, and it can take action if the doctor's fitness to practise is impaired due to any of the following grounds:

(a)   misconduct;

(b)   poor performance;

(c)   receipt of a criminal conviction or caution;

(d)   physical or mental ill-health;

(e)   determination by a regulatory body either in the British Isles or overseas.

The GMC's procedures are divided into two separate stages: 'investigation' and 'adjudication'. At the investigation stage, cases are investigated to assess whether the matter is sufficiently serious to warrant referral for adjudication. The adjudication stage consists of a hearing of those cases which have been referred to a Fitness to Practise Panel.

A Fitness to Practise Panel may come to any of the following conclusions:

(a)   the doctor's fitness to practise is not impaired and no further action should be taken;

(b)   the doctor's fitness to practise is not impaired but he is required to give an undertaking, eg to have further training or to work only under supervision;

(b)   the doctor's fitness to practise is not impaired but a warning should be issued;

(c)   the doctor's fitness to practise is impaired and –

    (i)   conditions should be placed on the doctor's registration (for example, restricting the doctor to certain areas of practise or stating that he must be supervised), or

    (ii)   the doctor's name should be suspended from the medical register, or

    (iii)   the doctor's name should be erased from the medical register.

An appeal may be made by either side within 28 days.

5.11.2 Disciplinary proceedings against nurses and midwives

The Nursing and Midwifery Council (NMC) is the regulatory body for nurses and midwives. The NMC has a duty to investigate once an allegation has been made against a member to the effect that his fitness to practise is impaired due to:

(a)   misconduct;

(b)   lack of competence;

(c)   a conviction or caution;

(d)   physical or mental ill-health; or

(e)   where a different healthcare profession has already determined that he is unfit to practise.

The sanctions which may be imposed at the end of the procedure are as follows:

(a)   the issue of a caution;

(b)   the removal of the practitioner from the register for a specified period, after which he may apply for his name to be restored; or

(c)   the removal of the practitioner from the register indefinitely.

5.12 CRIMINAL PROCEEDINGS

The CPS may bring a prosecution for manslaughter against a medical practitioner following an incidence of gross clinical negligence which results in the death of a patient (see **17.3.3**).

5.13 CONCLUSION

Clinical negligence claims are, in the main, more complex than personal injury claims and should be handled only by those practitioners who have the required specialist skills. The claimant's chances of success are less than in personal injury claims, largely due to the increased difficulties in establishing breach of duty (see the *Bolam* test) and causation.

The claimant's solicitor's job may be made more difficult by his client's ambivalent attitude towards taking action against medical practitioners, particularly where a relationship with those practitioners is on-going. A sound knowledge of the NHS complaints procedure and the procedures of the relevant disciplinary bodies is required.

5.14 FURTHER READING AND RELEVANT WEBSITES

The General Medical Council's website: <www.gmc-uk.org>

The Care Quality Commission's website: <www.cqc.org.uk>

The NHS Mandate: <https://www.gov.uk/government/uploads/system/uploads/attachment_data/file/127193/mandate.pdf.pdf>

The NHS Constitution: <http://www.nhs.uk/choiceintheNHS/Rightsandpledges/NHSConstitution/Documents/2013/the-nhs-constitution-for-england-2013.pdf>

The Handbook to The NHS Constitution: <https://www.gov.uk/government/uploads/system/uploads/attachment_data/file/152200/dh_132959.pdf.pdf>

5.15 DIAGRAM – STRUCTURE OF THE NHS

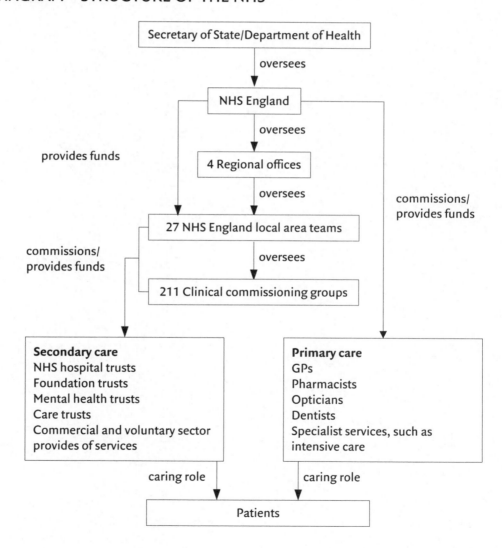

CLAIMS FOR PSYCHIATRIC INJURY

LEARNING OUTCOMES

After reading this chapter you will be able to:

- explain what is meant by the term 'nervous shock'
- identify whether a person is a primary or a secondary victim
- understand the control mechanisms that apply to claims brought by secondary victims
- explain what must be established in order to make a claim for occupational stress.

6.1 INTRODUCTION

Not all accidents result in physical injury. Claims for psychiatric injury or illness have risen markedly in recent years, and are usually awarded in a claim arising from an accident (so-called 'nervous shock 'claims) or as a consequence of occupational stress. The purpose of this chapter is to examine some particular issues that arise when dealing with these types of claim.

6.2 CLAIMS FOR NERVOUS SHOCK

There have been a number of high-profile nervous shock cases arising out of disasters such as Hillsborough, which involved a crush at the Sheffield Wednesday FC stadium in 1989. In the Hillsborough case, a number of claims were brought against the police by spectators and relatives of the victims who were present at the stadium or who had seen the disaster unfolding on the television (*Alcock v Chief Constable of South Yorkshire Police* [1992] 1 AC 310). Other claims were brought by police officers who had been on duty in the stadium and who were traumatised by what they saw (*White v Chief Constable of South Yorkshire* [1999] 2 AC 455). These cases establish certain 'control mechanisms' that limit liability for psychiatric injury.

6.2.1 What is nervous shock?

In order to claim for psychiatric injury there must be expert medical evidence that the claimant has suffered a recognised psychiatric illness which is more than temporary grief, fright or emotional distress. In recent years the courts have recognised a wide range of psychiatric injuries, including chronic fatigue syndrome (*Page v Smith* [1996] AC 155), pathological grief disorder (*Vernon v Bosley* [1997] 1 All ER 577) and post-traumatic stress disorder (PTSD) (*Alcock v Chief Constable of South Yorkshire* Police [1992] 1 AC 310). In establishing whether a claimant has suffered a recognisable psychiatric illness, a medical expert is likely to refer to two main systems of classification of psychiatric illnesses currently used in the UK:

(a)   the *Diagnostic and Statistical Manual of Mental Disorders of the American Psychiatric Association*, 4th edn (DSM IV); and

(b)   *The World Health Organisation International Classification of Mental and Behavioural Disorders*, 10th edn (ICD-10).

The most common psychiatric illness that arises is PTSD following a life-threatening experience or exposure to the sudden death of a close relative, the symptoms of which are listed at **2.2.12**.

6.2.2   Primary and secondary victims

In order to bring a claim for negligently inflicted psychiatric illness, a person must fall into one of two categories established by the House of Lords in *Alcock v Chief Constable of South Yorkshire Police* [1992] 1 AC 310. Primary victims will normally be involved in the events as participants, but it will be relatively rare for a primary victim directly involved in the events not to suffer any physical injury as well. Secondary victims are normally witnesses of injury caused to primary victims, and have not suffered physical injury themselves but have suffered psychologically from what they saw or heard. The key importance of this classification between primary and secondary victims is that if the claimant can show that he is a primary victim then he is likely to be treated more favourably by the courts.

6.2.2.1   Primary victims

A primary victim must show that some personal injury (ie, physical injury or psychiatric injury) was reasonably foreseeable as a result of the defendant's negligence so as to bring him within the scope of the defendant's duty of care. No distinction should be made between a physical or a psychiatric injury.

The case of *Page v Smith* [1996] AC 155 was the first time that the House of Lords had considered a claim brought by a primary victim. The claimant's car was involved in a collision with a car driven by the defendant. The collision was not severe and the claimant suffered no physical injuries, but he claimed damages on the basis that shortly after the accident he suffered a recurrence of chronic fatigue syndrome from which he had suffered 20 years before. The House of Lords held that as a participant in the accident he was a primary victim, and therefore it was not necessary for him to show that the psychiatric harm he suffered was foreseeable in a person of normal fortitude. It made no difference that the claimant was predisposed to psychiatric illness – the normal 'egg-shell skull' rule applied so that the defendant had to take his victim as he found him.

In *Corr v IBC Vehicles* [2006] EWCA Civ 331, the claimant brought proceedings under the Fatal Accidents Act following the suicide of her husband, who had been badly injured in a factory accident whilst employed by the defendant. He suffered PTSD which resulted in deep depression, and some six years after the accident he committed suicide by jumping off the roof of a multi-storey car park. The Court of Appeal held that the claimant did not need to establish that at the time of the accident the deceased's suicide had been reasonably foreseeable, as the suicide flowed from the psychiatric illness for which the defendant was admittedly responsible.

In *Johnstone v NEI International Combustion Limited* [2007] UKHL 39, the House of Lords rejected claims by workers who had been negligently exposed to asbestos by the defendants and who had developed clinical depression as a consequence of being told that they had pleural plaques which indicated a risk of future illness. It was argued on behalf of the claimants that they should be regarded as primary victims and should therefore be entitled to recover damages regardless of whether or not psychiatric injury was a foreseeable consequence of the defendants' negligence. The House of Lords rejected this argument on the basis that the illness had been caused by the fear of the possibility of an unfavourable event which had not actually happened and was therefore not actionable.

6.2.2.2 Secondary victims

A secondary victim must show that it was reasonably foreseeable that a person of reasonable fortitude would have suffered some psychiatric injury. Foreseeability of psychiatric injury is of critical importance to secondary victims, as they will normally be outside the scope of persons who might suffer foreseeable physical injury.

In addition to the test of reasonable fortitude, *Alcock v Chief Constable of South Yorkshire Police* [1992] 1 AC 310 established that a secondary victim must satisfy three further control mechanisms if he is to succeed in a claim for damages for psychiatric injury:

(a)   *A close tie of love and affection to the immediate victim.* In *Alcock*, the claimants were various relations of the immediate victims, some of whom had been present at the Hillsborough football stadium and some of whom had watched the disaster unfold on television. The House of Lords held that there is a rebuttable presumption of sufficiently close ties between spouses, parents and children, but that in all other cases the closeness of the tie had to be proved. One claimant had been present at the ground and witnessed the incident in which his two brothers were killed, but his claim failed because he did not produce evidence of a close tie of love and affection to his brothers. However, in a subsequent case, damages were awarded to the half-brother of one of the Hillsborough victims because the judge found evidence that he was particularly close to his half brother.

(b)   *Closeness in time and space to the incident or its aftermath.* In *Alcock*, several claimants were not present at the ground but went there subsequently to identify the bodies of their relatives. The earliest had arrived between eight and nine hours after the accident, which was held by the House of Lords not to be part of the immediate aftermath.

Subsequent decisions have seen a relaxation in the courts' approach to what constitutes the immediate aftermath. In *Walters v North Glamorgan NHS Trust* [2002] EWHC 321 (QB), [2002] All ER (D) 65, the mother of a baby claimed psychiatric injury as a result of witnessing her child's decline and death due to misdiagnosis at the treating hospital. The period from first onset of injury to death was 36 hours. The claimant issued proceedings against the hospital for damages. The court found that although clearly not a primary victim, she could succeed as a secondary victim if her psychiatric injury was induced by shock as a result of the sudden appreciation by sight or sound of a horrifying event or its immediate aftermath. The court found that the whole period of 36 hours could be seen in law as a horrifying event, and the claimant was therefore entitled to recover damages. In *Galli-Atkinson v Seghal* [2003] EWCA Civ 697, the claimant appealed to the Court of Appeal following a decision dismissing her claim for nervous shock. The facts of the case were such that the claimant was present at the immediate aftermath of a road traffic accident at which her daughter had died. At that time she was told of the death of her daughter, but did not see the body until some hours later in the mortuary. It was only when she viewed the body that the claimant broke down and suffered the psychiatric condition that formed the basis of her claim. On appeal, the Court found that, provided events retained sufficient proximity, the subsequent viewing of the body could be seen as part of the aftermath of the incident, and on that basis the claim could succeed. In *Taylor v Novo Ltd* [2013] EWCA Civ 194, the claimant's mother suffered a head injury at work which the claimant did not witness. Some three weeks later, the claimant witnessed her mother die as a result of a pulmonary embolism which was caused by the original injury. The claimant brought a claim for damages for psychiatric injury which succeeded at first instance. However, the Court of Appeal reversed the decision, holding that the lack of physical and temporal connection between the sudden and unexpected death and the original accident meant that the claim had to fail. In *Wild & Another v Southend University Hospitals NHS Foundation Trust* [2104] EWHC 4053 (QB), a father's claim following the discovery that his unborn son had died in the womb failed. Negligence was admitted by the defendant, on the basis of a failure to note foetal growth rate at antenatal appointments, and it was accepted that, but for the negligence of the hospital staff, labour would have been induced earlier and the baby would have survived. The mother's claim for psychiatric injuries as a primary victim was settled, but the father's claim as a secondary victim failed. The judge concluded that the father's experience was analogous to those who witnessed the Hillsborough disaster unfolding on television in *Alcock* and experienced distress and anxiety about their loved ones, but held that being present when the baby's death was confirmed did not qualify as 'witnessing horrific events leading to death or serious injury'.

(c)   *The claimant must suffer 'nervous shock' through witnessing a sudden shocking event with his own unaided senses.* In *Alcock*, the House of Lords confirmed that the secondary victim must establish that his illness was induced by a shock or, in the words of Lord Ackner, 'the sudden appreciation by sight or sound of a horrifying event, which violently agitates the mind'. Some of the claimants in *Alcock* had watched the events at Hillsborough unfold via live television broadcasts. This was held to be insufficient to satisfy the test of proximity, because watching the events on television was not felt to be equivalent to witnessing the events at first hand. More recently, in *Ronayne v Liverpool Women's NHS Foundation Trust* [2015] EWCA Civ 588, the claimant brought a claim for damages, alleging that he was a secondary victim and had sustained PTSD caused by the shock of seeing his wife's deterioration in hospital due to injuries caused by the Trust's negligence. The claimant's wife had recently undergone a hysterectomy but, due to a negligently misplaced suture, developed septicaemia and peritonitis and was admitted to the A&E department for emergency surgery. During the next 36 hours, the claimant witnessed her deterioration, which resulted in her being connected to a ventilator, drips and monitors and becoming swollen, with her 'arms, legs and face blown up because of the amount of fluid'. He subsequently described his wife's appearance as resembling 'the Michelin man''. The claimant succeeded at first instance but the defendant appealed, arguing that there was no qualifying 'event', in the sense that it was neither sudden nor sufficiently shocking. The Court of Appeal overturned the trial judge's decision, holding that the judge was wrong to regard the events of the 36 hours as one event and distinguished this case from that of *Walters* (above), which Tomlinson LJ described as 'a seamless tale with an obvious beginning and an equally obvious end'. In contrast, Mr Ronayne had suffered a 'series of events over a period of time' which did not have the necessary element of suddenness. The Court of Appeal also found that the appearance of the claimant's wife in hospital was as would ordinarily be expected of a person in hospital in the same circumstances and that, by objective standards, it was not horrifying.

6.2.2.3   Employee victims

In *White v Chief Constable of South Yorkshire* [1999] 2 AC 455, the claimants were police officers who were severely traumatised by their duties at the aftermath of the Hillsborough Stadium disaster. They claimed compensation for their psychiatric injury against the police service. It was conceded that none of the claimants had been exposed to any personal physical danger, but their case was that the Chief Constable was vicariously liable for the negligence of the police officer who caused the catastrophe by admitting the crowd in to the pens. The claimants argued that by the negligent creation of the horrific situation, the Chief Constable was in breach of his duty not to expose the claimants to unnecessary risk of injury and was consequently liable for their injuries. The House of Lords rejected their claims and confirmed that unless employees can show a risk of physical injury (and therefore fall into the category of primary victims), they will be treated as secondary victims and subject to the control tests established in *Alcock* (see **6.2.2.2**). Part of the reason for this was undoubtedly public policy – since all the claims for compensation by relatives of the victims had already been rejected, it could – and did – cause a public furore if police officers were compensated in less deserving cases. The effect of this decision is that the *Alcock* test applies to all psychiatric injury claims where personal injury is not reasonably foreseeable; employees do not get special consideration.

In *Young v Charles Church (Southern) Ltd* (1997) 39 BMLR 146, it was established that an employee who suffered psychiatric illness after seeing a workmate electrocuted close to him could recover damages against his employer as a primary victim because of the risk to himself of physical injury. The court decided that the ambit of the regulations was not limited to physical electrocution. The statute gave protection to employees from kinds of injury which could be foreseen as likely to occur when the electrical cable or equipment was allowed to become a source of danger to them. This included mental illness caused to the claimant by the shock of seeing his workmate electrocuted in circumstances where he was fortunate to escape electrocution himself.

Contrast the above case with *Hunter v British Coal* [1999] QB 89, CA. The claimant was a driver in a coalmine. His vehicle struck a hydrant, causing it to leak. With the help of a workmate, he tried to stop the flow but failed. He left the scene in search of help. When the claimant was 30 metres away, the hydrant burst, and he was told that someone was injured. On his way back to the scene, he was told that the workmate who had been helping him had died. The claimant thought he was responsible and suffered nervous shock and depression. He brought proceedings for damages against his employers. It was held that a claimant who believes he has been the cause of another's death in an accident caused by the defendant's negligence could recover damages as a primary victim if he was directly involved as a participant in the incident. However, a claimant who was not at the scene could not recover damages as a primary victim merely because he felt responsible for the incident. In this case, the claimant was not involved in the incident in which the workmate died as he was 30 metres away and suffered psychiatric injury only on being told of the death some 15 minutes later. Therefore, there was not sufficient proximity in time and space with the incident. Also, the illness triggered by the death was not a foreseeable consequence of the defendant's breach of duty of care, as it was an abnormal reaction to being told of the workmate's death, triggered by an irrational feeling that the claimant was responsible.

6.2.2.4   Professional rescuers

Before *White v Chief Constable of South Yorkshire and Others* [1999] 2 AC 455 it had been thought that rescuers were automatically to be treated as primary victims. However, in *White* the House of Lords rejected the police officers' claims for psychiatric injury, stating that there was no authority for placing rescuers in a special position. The decision was based on two factors:

(a)   the problem of applying a definition to delineate the class of rescuers that could claim; and

(b)   the fact that, if the law did allow the claims to succeed, the result would be unacceptable to the ordinary person, who would think it wrong that police officers should have the right to compensation for psychiatric injury out of public funds when bereaved relatives did not. Fairness demanded that the appeal be allowed, and the claims were therefore dismissed.

A rescuer who is not exposed to danger of physical injury, or who does not believe himself to have been so exposed, is therefore classified as a secondary victim who must satisfy the control mechanisms set out in *Alcock* before he can recover damages for pure psychiatric injury.

In *Stephen John Monk v (1) PC Harrington Ltd (2) HTC Plant Ltd (3) Multiplex Constructions Ltd* [2008] EWHC 1879 (QB), the claimant had been working as a self-employed foreman on site during the construction of Wembley Stadium. While he was working, a temporary platform fell 60 feet onto two fellow workers. One of the men died from his injuries shortly after the accident, the other suffered a broken leg. Having arrived at the scene of the accident, the claimant tried to help both men and, specifically, to comfort the man with the broken leg. Thereafter, as a result of the accident, he began to suffer from symptoms of PTSD, which ultimately caused him to stop work. The defendant admitted liability for the accident, and the claimant claimed damages for psychiatric injury on the grounds that his involvement in the accident was such that he fulfilled the necessary conditions to recover compensation as a rescuer; and even if he was unable to bring himself within the rescuer category of primary victim, he could nevertheless establish the necessary proximity to the accident, which he believed he had caused, in order that he could be regarded as an unwilling participant.

While it was accepted by the court that the claimant had provided significant help and comfort to the injured men, and that this assistance entitled him to be regarded as a rescuer, the claimant could not show on the evidence that he had reasonably believed that he was putting his own safety at risk. He could not therefore establish himself as a primary victim on the basis of his acts as a rescuer. As for the second ground advanced by the claimant – that he was a primary victim as an unwilling participant – it was held that he had to show that his injuries were induced by a genuine belief that he had caused another person's injury or death, and there was no reasonable basis for such a belief in this case. Therefore, it was not reasonably foreseeable that someone in his position would suffer psychiatric injury as a result of such a belief.

6.2.2.5   Bystanders as victims

A 'mere bystander' will be unable to claim damages for pure psychiatric injury as he will be unable to satisfy control mechanisms for a secondary victim outlined at **6.2.2.2** above. This is well illustrated by the case of *McFarlane v EE Caledonia Ltd* [1994] 2 All ER 1, which arose out of the Piper Alpha oil rig disaster. The claimant had been off duty on a support vessel some 550 metres away when he witnessed the explosions and consequent destruction of the oil rig, which resulted in the death of 164 men. His claim failed as he was not himself in any danger, and it had not been shown that it was reasonably foreseeable that a man of ordinary fortitude would have suffered a psychiatric injury as a result of what he saw.

6.3   OCCUPATIONAL STRESS

6.3.1   The meaning of occupational stress

Stress is a feature of nearly every workplace, and indeed is often seen as desirable to motivate and encourage people. However, too much pressure can lead to psychological problems and physical ill-health.

In trying to come to some workable definition of 'occupational stress', Hale LJ, in *Hatton v Sutherland; Barber v Somerset County Council; Jones v Sandwell Metropolitan Borough Council; Bishop v Baker Refractories Ltd* [2002] EWCA Civ 76, [2002] 2 All ER 1, referred to three documents which she said the Court had found particularly helpful:

(a)   *Stress in the Public Sector – Nurses, Police, Social Workers and Teachers* (1988) defines stress as 'an excess of demands upon an individual in excess of their ability to cope'.

(b)   *Managing Occupational Stress: a Guide for Managers and Teachers in the School Sector* (Education Service Advisory Committee of the Health and Safety Commission, 1990) defines stress as 'a process that can occur when there is an unresolved mismatch between the perceived pressures of the work situation and an individual's ability to "cope"'.

(c)   The HSE booklet *Stress at Work* (1995) defines stress as follows:

> The reaction people have to excessive pressures or other types of demand placed upon them. It arises when they worry that they can't cope …

> Stress is not the same as ill health. But in some cases, particularly where pressures are intense and continue for some time, the effect of stress can be more sustained and far more damaging, leading to longer term psychological problems and physical ill health.

In *Hatton v Sutherland*, the judge concluded that harmful levels of stress are more likely to occur in situations where people feel powerless or trapped, and are therefore much more likely to affect people at junior levels; and, secondly, stress is a psychological phenomenon which can lead to either physical or mental ill-health, or both.

6.3.2   Duty of care

In *Petch v Commissioners of Customs and Excise* [1993] ICR 789, it was accepted that the ordinary principles of employers' liability applied to claims for psychiatric illness arising from employment. Although the claim in *Petch* failed, Colman J, in *Walker v Northumberland County Council* [1995] 1 All ER 737, applied the same principles in upholding the claim. In this case, Mr Walker was a conscientious but overworked manager of a social work area office, with a heavy and emotionally demanding work-load of child abuse cases. Although he complained and asked for help and for extra leave, the judge held that his first mental breakdown was not foreseeable. There was liability, however, when he returned to work with a promise of extra help, which did not materialise, and he experienced a second breakdown only a few months later.

Petch and *Walker* have both been cited with approval by the Court of Appeal in *Garrett v Camden LBC* [2001] EWCA Civ 395.

6.3.3   Reasonable foreseeability, breach of duty and causation – the *Hatton* guidelines

In *Hatton v Sutherland* [2002] EWCA Civ 76, the Court of Appeal set out guidance for courts to follow in occupational stress cases which was approved by the House of Lords in *Barber v Somerset* [2004] UKHL 13. Hale LJ set out the guidance as follows:

(1) There are no special control mechanisms applying to claims for psychiatric (or physical) illness or injury arising from the stress of doing the work the employee is required to do. The ordinary principles of employer's liability apply.

(2) The threshold question is whether this kind of harm to this particular employee was reasonably foreseeable: this has two components (a) an injury to health (as distinct from occupational stress) which (b) is attributable to stress at work (as distinct from other factors).

(3) Foreseeability depends upon what the employer knows (or ought reasonably to know) about the individual employee. Because of the nature of mental disorder, it is harder to foresee than physical injury, but may be easier to foresee in a known individual than in the population at large. An employer is usually entitled to assume that the employee can withstand the normal pressures of the job unless he knows of some particular problem or vulnerability.

(4) The test is the same whatever the employment: there are no occupations which should be regarded as intrinsically dangerous to mental health.

(5) Factors likely to be relevant in answering the threshold question include:

   (a) The nature and extent of the work done by the employee. Is the workload much more than is normal for the particular job? Is the work particularly intellectually or emotionally demanding for this employee? Are demands being made of this employee unreasonable when compared with the demands made of others in the same or comparable jobs? Or are there signs that others doing this job are suffering harmful levels of stress? Is there an abnormal level of sickness or absenteeism in the same job or the same department?

   (b) Signs from the employee of impending harm to health. Has he a particular problem or vulnerability? Has he already suffered from illness attributable to stress at work? Have there recently been frequent or prolonged absences which are uncharacteristic of him? Is there reason to think that these are attributable to stress at work, for example because of complaints or warnings from him or others?

(6) The employer is generally entitled to take what he is told by his employee at face value, unless he has good reason to think to the contrary. He does not generally have to make searching enquiries of the employee or seek permission to make further enquiries of his medical advisers.

(7) To trigger a duty to take steps, the indications of impending harm to health arising from stress at work must be plain enough for any reasonable employer to realise that he should do something about it.

(8) The employer is only in breach of duty if he has failed to take the steps which are reasonable in the circumstances, bearing in mind the magnitude of the risk of harm occurring, the gravity of the harm which may occur, the costs and practicability of preventing it, and the justifications for running the risk.

(9)   The size and scope of the employer's operation, its resources and the demands it faces are relevant in deciding what is reasonable; these include the interests of other employees and the need to treat them fairly, for example, in any redistribution of duties.

(10)   An employer can only reasonably be expected to take steps which are likely to do some good: the court is likely to need expert evidence on this.

(11)   An employer who offers a confidential advice service, with referral to appropriate counselling or treatment services, is unlikely to be found in breach of duty.

(12)   If the only reasonable and effective step would have been to dismiss or demote the employee, the employer will not be in breach of duty in allowing a willing employee to continue in the job.

(13)   In all cases, therefore, it is necessary to identify the steps which the employer both could and should have taken before finding him in breach of his duty of care.

(14)   The claimant must show that that breach of duty has caused or materially contributed to the harm suffered. It is not enough to show that occupational stress has caused the harm.

(15)   Where the harm suffered has more than one cause, the employer should only pay for that proportion of the harm suffered which is attributable to his wrongdoing, unless the harm is truly indivisible. It is for the defendant to raise the question of apportionment.

(16)   The assessment of damages will take account of any pre-existing disorder or vulnerability and of the chance that the claimant would have succumbed to a stress related disorder in any event.

Young v Post Office [2002] EWCA Civ 661 was decided after *Hatton v Sutherland* and considered whether it is the responsibility of the claimant to inform the employer if he is unable to cope, and whether the claimant will be contributorily negligent if he fails to do so. The claimant had worked for the Post Office for a number of years and had been promoted to workshop manager. He had no direct line manager, and when a new computer system was introduced he was expected to familiarise himself with it without formal training. The claimant began to show signs of stress and eventually suffered a nervous breakdown, and subsequently took four months off work to recover. Arrangements were made to allow the claimant to return to work gradually and on a flexible basis. When the claimant returned to work he quickly shouldered the burden of the management position that had led to his breakdown. Seven weeks later the claimant was again unable to continue due to stress and left. The defendants contended that they had done all that they could in offering a less stressful work pattern for the claimant. On appeal, the Court found for the claimant, as it was plainly foreseeable that there might be a recurrence if appropriate steps were not taken when the claimant returned to work, and the employer owed a duty to take such steps. Although the employer had told the claimant that he could adopt a flexible approach to his work, the reality was that he was a hardworking and conscientious employee, and it was foreseeable that he would quickly revert to overworking, and the employer had a duty to ensure that help was on hand. Regarding the allegation of contributory negligence, the Court found that this was not relevant in this case and would be unusual but was 'theoretically possible'.

The High Court decision in *Barlow v Broxbourne Borough Council* [2003] EWHC 50 (QB), [2003] All ER (D) 208 (Jan), provides an example of the application of the principles set out by the Court of Appeal in *Hatton v Sutherland*. B had initially been employed as a gardener and had obtained several promotions to become senior operations manager in 1993. B's claim was based on two broad grounds: systematic victimisation and 'general' bullying. He alleged that from approximately 1997 he had been deliberately victimised and bullied by senior members of the council's staff, which had caused him to suffer emotional distress and psychological injury. The alleged 'victimisation' and 'bullying' had included receipt of lengthy letters detailing B's non-performance, threats of disciplinary action and, at times, abusive language. Medical experts for each party were agreed that B had suffered a moderately severe depressive episode. Consequently, B had been unable to continue working for the council. B argued that he had been exposed to such stress at work that he had developed a stress-related illness which had prevented him from remaining in the council's employ. However, B's claim failed on the following grounds:

(a)   The actions of the council and its employees did not give rise to a foreseeable risk of injury. Hale LJ's guidelines in *Hatton v Sutherland* applied. In the circumstances, it was not necessary for the court to consider causation issues.

(b)   The council could not have reasonably known or foreseen that the conduct complained of by B would have caused him harm.

(c)   Nothing in B's behaviour, at the time, had given any cause for concern about the risk of psychiatric illness.

This judgment assists the defendant by confirming that the alleged incidents of bullying and/ or harassment must be considered in context. In the context of the claimant's working environment, the use of bad language (which was not disputed at trial) and the actions of his line managers in highlighting areas of non-performance, did not amount to victimisation or bullying.

In *Intel Corporation (UK) Limited v Daw* [2007] EWCA Civ 70, Pill LJ approved of the guidance in *Hatton* but warned courts against following it too slavishly:

> A very considerable amount of helpful guidance is given in *Hatton*. That does not preclude or excuse the trial judge either from conducting a vigorous fact-finding exercise, as the trial judge in this case did, or deciding which parts of the guidance are relevant to the particular circumstances. The reference to counselling services in *Hatton* does not make such services a panacea by which employers can discharge their duty of care in all cases. The respondent, a loyal and capable employee, pointed out the serious management failings which were causing her stress and the failure to take action was that of management. The consequences of that failure are not avoided by the provision of counsellors who might have brought home to management that action was required. On the judge's findings, the managers knew it was required.

This approach was endorsed by the Court of Appeal in *Dickins v O2 plc* [2008] EWCA Civ 1144, when the Court upheld the trial judge's decision to award the claimant damages for injury caused by occupational stress.

Ms Dickins' job involved the preparation of management and regulatory accounts. She found one particular audit in February 2002 'extremely stressful'. She had a short holiday but returned to work exhausted, and on 11 March 2002 she asked her line manager for a different and less stressful job. As there were no vacancies available at the time, Ms Dickins was told that the matter would be reviewed in three months. On 23 April 2002 she requested a six-month sabbatical. She said she was stressed out, was having a real struggle to get out of bed in the mornings and to get to work on time because she felt so drained of physical and mental energy, and she did not know how long she could carry on before being off sick. She was advised to access O2's confidential counselling helpline, and was told that her request for a sabbatical would be considered. On 30 May 2002 Ms Dickins repeated her concerns during her appraisal and was referred to occupational health, albeit with some delay. Before any appointment was fixed she suffered a breakdown and never returned to work.

The Court of Appeal upheld the judge's finding that psychiatric injury was reasonably foreseeable from 23 April 2002 onwards. There was sufficient indication of impending harm to health, given the claimant's description of the seriousness of her symptoms and the important background context that these problems had not come 'out of the blue'. The fact that the claimant had been mentioning difficulties over a period of time was significant, given that she was usually a conscientious employee.

The Court of Appeal also agreed with the trial judge that the defendant employer was in breach of duty in not sending her home and in not making an immediate referral to occupational health.

In *Connor v Surrey County Council* [2010] EWCA Civ 286, the claimant, a head teacher in a primary school, was awarded damages against the defendant local education authority for its failure to have regard to the effect of its conduct on her health or to give her the support she needed, which resulted in her suffering severe depression. The defendant raised in its defence the issue of foreseeability of injury, and argued that there were no signs of impending harm to the claimant's health, particularly as she had not been absent from work prior to her breakdown. However, the judge held that the fact that the claimant had not been absent from work was irrelevant; the risk was apparent from comments made by the claimant and others, and action should have been taken to respond to it. The decision at first instance was upheld by the Court of Appeal.

It seems clear from these decisions that, in an appropriate case, it may not be necessary to show that the claimant has previously suffered a breakdown if his words and actions in the recent past would alert a reasonable employer to the risk of illness. Furthermore, whereas *Hatton* had indicated that an employer who offered a confidential counselling service was unlikely to be found in breach of duty, the recent cases cast doubt over whether the provision of such a service will exonerate an employer. More recently, in *Yapp v Foreign and Commonwealth Office* [2014] EWCA Civ 1512, the Court of Appeal held that the claimant's claim for psychiatric injuries should fail. In a judgment that provides an extremely useful summary of the authorities on this subject, Underhill LJ stated that it would 'be exceptional that an apparently robust employee, with no history of any psychiatric ill-health, will develop a depressive illness as a result even of a very serious setback at work', but that 'each case depends on its own facts, and in principle the employer's conduct in a particular case might be so devastating that it was foreseeable that even a person of ordinary robustness might develop a depressive illness as a result'.

6.3.4 Causation

Having established a breach of duty, it is still necessary to prove that the particular breach of duty caused the harm. Where there are several different possible causes (as will often be the case with stress-related illness), the claimant may have difficulty proving that the employer's breach of duty was one of them. This will be a particular problem if, as in *Garrett v Camden LBC* [2001] EWCA Civ 395, the main cause was a vulnerable personality which the employer knew nothing about. However, the employee does not have to prove that the breach of duty was the sole cause of his ill-health: it is enough to show that it made a material contribution (see *Bonnington Castings Ltd v Wardlaw* [1956] AC 613). Expert medical evidence will be crucial in determining causation.

6.3.5 Damages

The *Hatton* guidelines (see **6.3.3**) suggested that an employer found liable for psychiatric injury caused by occupational stress should pay only for that proportion of the injury caused by his wrongdoing and not for any part of the injury caused by other factors. However, in *Dickins v O2*, the Court of Appeal was critical of the trial judge's decision to reduce the total damages by 50% for the other non-tortious factors which had contributed to the claimant's illness. In the Court's view, albeit *obiter*, the injury was indivisible, and so an employer should be liable for the whole injury if it is proved that the tort has made more than a minimal contribution to the injury.

Although further guidance by the Court of Appeal on the whole issue of apportionment can be expected, for the time being it seems that no reduction should be made for the other stresses which contributed to a claimant's illness. A more appropriate route may be for defendants to argue that particular heads of damage (eg loss of future earnings) should be discounted to reflect the fact that a claimant might in any event have suffered a breakdown at some time in the future.

6.4 CLAIMS UNDER THE PROTECTION FROM HARASSMENT ACT 1997

The Protection from Harassment Act 1997 (PHA 1997) provides an alternative course of action for employees who experience harassment in the workplace caused by a colleague.

Section 1 of the PHA 1997 provides that 'a person must not pursue a course of conduct: (a) which amounts to harassment of another, and (b) which he knows or ought to know amounts to harassment of another'.

Although there is not a specific definition of harassment, the PHA 1997 does stipulate that references to harassing a person include alarming or causing the person distress; a course of conduct must involve at least two occasions; and that conduct includes speech (s 7).

In contrast to a claim in common law, under the PHA 1997 a claimant needs only to prove that he has experienced 'anxiety' as a result of the harassment. This is a significantly lower hurdle than establishing 'a recognisable psychiatric condition' required for a successful non-physical injury claim under established common law principles. In addition, a claimant has six years to bring a claim, rather than three years (s 6).

In *Majrowski v Guy's and St Thomas's NHS Trust* [2006] UKHL 34 the House of Lords held that to succeed under the PHA 1997, a claimant must show that the conduct complained of is 'oppressive and unacceptable' as opposed to merely unattractive, unreasonable or regrettable. The primary focus is on whether the conduct is oppressive and unacceptable, albeit the court must keep in mind that it must be of an order which 'would sustain criminal liability'.

In *Veakins v Kier Islington Ltd* [2009] EWCA Civ 1288 the Court of Appeal allowed the claimant's appeal in a harassment at work claim as the trial judge had applied the wrong legal test.

The claimant was an electrician employed by the defendant for two years before she went on long-term sick leave with depression after which she never returned to work. She alleged that she was victimised by her supervisor for some two to three months during which her supervisor had made it clear that she did not like her, had singled her out from other employees for no reason and had 'made her life hell'.

The trial judge decided that the claimant's allegations, even though unchallenged by the defendant, did not amount to harassment under the PHA 1997. Relying on the Court of Appeal decision in *Conn v Council and City of Sunderland* [2007] EWCA Civ 1492 the trial judge held that this conduct would not justify any criminal prosecution and dismissed the claim.

The claimant's appeal to the Court of Appeal was allowed. The Court of Appeal agreed that the conduct must be grave to constitute harassment under the PHA 1997 but the judge had failed to apply the primary legal test set out by the in House of Lords in *Majrowski*. Under that primary test the judge was required to consider whether the conduct had crossed the boundary from the 'unattractive and unreasonable' to conduct which is 'oppressive and unacceptable'.

On the undisputed evidence of the claimant, the Court of Appeal held that this was such a case where the conduct was extraordinary and that boundary had been crossed. The trial judge had undervalued the evidence. The claimant's account was of victimisation, demoralisation and reduction of a substantially reasonable and usually robust woman to a state of clinical depression. This was, the Court of Appeal felt, to have self-evidently crossed the line into conduct which is 'oppressive and unreasonable'.

6.5 CONCLUSION

The main points to bear in mind when bringing a claim for psychiatric injury are as follows:

* To claim damages for nervous shock there must be evidence of a recognised psychiatric illness.
* It is necessary to identify whether the client is a primary victim (directly involved in the accident) or a secondary victim (a witness/bystander).
* If the client is a secondary victim, he must satisfy the control mechanisms laid down in *Alcock* to establish closeness to the victim and the incident itself.

- There are no special control mechanisms in claims for occupational stress – the ordinary principles of employers' liability apply.
- The injury to the individual employee must have been reasonably foreseeable.
- In order to establish a breach of duty, it will be necessary to identify the steps the employer could and should have taken to prevent harm.
- The provision of a counselling service will not automatically exonerate an employer.

6.6　FURTHER READING AND RELEVANT WEBSITES

Butterworths Personal Injury Litigation Service

Marshall, *Compensation for Stress at Work* (Jordans)

Law Commission Consultation Paper, *Liability for Psychiatric Illness* 1995 (Law Com No 137)

<www.hse.gov.uk/stress>

LIMITATION OF ACTIONS

LEARNING OUTCOMES

After reading this chapter you will be able to:

- set out the law as it relates to limitation in cases involving a claim for personal injuries and a claim following a fatal accident
- appreciate that the court may use its discretion to disapply the limitation period, and set out the factors which it takes into consideration
- apply the law to real-life situations.

7.1 INTRODUCTION

The law relating to limitation is fairly complex and can cause difficulties for the unwary. Each year, there is a steady flow of case law relevant to this area, partly because clients seek legal advice far too late, but also because solicitors sometimes breach the duty of care owed to their clients by failing to ensure that proceedings are issued within the limitation period. Consequently, one of the first priorities for the claimant's solicitor will be to identify when the limitation period ends and, having established this, to mark the file with that date and enter it into the diary system.

The principal statute dealing with limitation issues is the Limitation Act 1980 (LA 1980).

For the purpose of limitation in a personal injury claim, 'personal injury' includes any disease and any impairment of a person's physical or mental condition (s 38).

7.2 THE LIMITATION PERIOD

Under ss 11 and 12 of the LA 1980, where a claimant claims damages for negligence, nuisance or breach of duty, and that claim consists of or includes a claim for personal injuries, the claimant must normally commence his claim (ie the claim form must be issued, or received by the court in order to be issued) within three years from:

(a)   the date on which the cause of action accrued; or

(b)   the date of knowledge (if later) of the person injured (s 11(4); see **7.3** below).

When calculating the three-year period (generally referred to as the 'primary' limitation period), the day on which the cause of action accrued is excluded (s 2). Therefore, in a simple road traffic accident case, generally the claimant has three years from the incident (excluding the date of the incident) in which to commence the claim. If the last date of this period is a Saturday, Sunday or Bank Holiday, the time is extended until the next day when the courts are open and the claim can be issued.

Where the three-year period has expired, the claimant is not prohibited from commencing proceedings, although if he does so, the defendant may seek to have the claim struck out on the grounds that it is statute barred. However, the claimant may apply to the court for the limitation to be disapplied under s 33 of the LA 1980 (see **7.8**).

7.3   DATE OF KNOWLEDGE

A claimant may work in an environment which exposes him to injurious dust particles such as asbestos dust or coal dust. It may be many years before an illness or disease manifests itself, and it may be some time later before the claimant realises what the cause of his illness is. Similarly, in a clinical negligence context, a patient may be fully aware of his pain and suffering but assumes that it is entirely due to an underlying illness, rather than due to negligent advice from or treatment by a doctor. In such circumstances, it is not unusual for a claimant to issue proceedings many years after the expiry of the three-year limitation period and to seek to rely on a later date of knowledge under s 14 of the LA 1980. Where he seeks to do so, the burden of proof rests with the claimant.

7.3.1   Section 14 of the Limitation Act 1980

Section 14 of the LA 1980 defines 'date of knowledge' for the purpose of ss 11 and 12 as follows:

(1)   In sections 11 and 12 of this Act references to a person's date of knowledge are references to the date on which he first had knowledge of the following facts—

   (a)   that the injury in question was significant; and

   (b)   that the injury was attributable in whole or in part to the act or omission which is alleged to constitute negligence, nuisance or breach of duty; and

   (c)   the identity of the defendant; and

   (d)   if it is alleged that the act or omission was that of a person other than the defendant, the identity of that person and the additional facts supporting the bringing of an action against the defendant;

   and knowledge that any acts or omissions did or did not, as a matter of law, involve negligence, nuisance or breach of duty is irrelevant.

(2)   For the purposes of this section an injury is significant if the person whose date of knowledge is in question would reasonably have considered it sufficiently serious to justify his instituting proceedings for damages against a defendant who did not dispute liability and was able to satisfy a judgment.

(3)   For the purposes of this section a person's knowledge includes knowledge which he might reasonably have been expected to acquire—

   (a)   from facts observable or ascertainable by him; or

   (b)   from facts ascertainable by him with the help of medical or other appropriate expert advice which it is reasonable for him to seek;

   but a person shall not be fixed under this subsection with knowledge of a fact ascertainable only with the help of expert advice so long as he has taken all reasonable steps to obtain (and, where appropriate, to act on) that advice.

7.3.2   The meaning of knowledge and the starting of the clock

In *Halford v Brookes* [1991] 3 All ER 559, it was stated that knowledge does not mean 'know for certain and beyond the possibility of contradiction', but rather 'know with sufficient confidence to justify embarking on the preliminaries to issue of proceedings, such as submitting a claim to the proposed defendant, taking legal advice and other advice and collecting evidence'.

Consequently, the date of a claimant's knowledge is the date on which the claimant first knew enough of the various matters set out in s 14(1) to begin to investigate whether he has a claim against the defendant. For example, where a specialist told the claimant that he had an inhaled disease or industrial injury and the only source for this could be his work for the defendants (*Corbin v Penfold Metalizing* [2000] Lloyd's Rep Med 247), or where the claimant was told by a community worker that his deafness could have been caused by his work in a mill (*Ali v Courtaulds Textiles Limited* [1999] Lloyd's Rep Med 301).

It should be noted that knowledge will be present even though the claimant's psychological condition leads to a state of denial. In *TCD v (1) Harrow Council (2) Worcester County Council (3) Birmingham City Council* [2008] EWHC 3048 (QB), the clamant sought damages in relation to child abuse suffered from 1975 and 1981. The fact that her psychological or mental state 'may have meant that she was in denial and/or could not face reliving her abuse for the purposes of the claim', was not relevant for the purposes of determining her knowledge (although it was relevant in relation to the exercise of discretion under s 33 – see **7.8**).

Although it may be possible to identify a specific date when it is clear that the claimant had the requisite knowledge, the court may determine that the claimant should have acquired this knowledge at an earlier date.

7.3.3   Actual and constructive knowledge

Where a claimant wishes to rely on a later date of knowledge, he will seek to fix that date as being the date when he actually acquired the requisite knowledge. This is known as 'actual knowledge'. The defendant, though, may argue that the claimant had actual knowledge of these matters at an earlier date and/or *should* have obtained knowledge at an earlier date, and that the claimant is thereby fixed with 'constructive knowledge'.

7.3.3.1   Actual knowledge

When considering the question of actual knowledge, claimants will often seek to rely on a date when they were told that their injury or illness was caused by the defendant's actions, usually by a doctor or a solicitor. However, the court may determine that a claimant had actual knowledge at an earlier date.

In *Spargo v North Essex District Health Authority* [1997] 8 Med LR 125, the court held that a subjective test was to be applied, namely 'What did the claimant know?' and not 'What would a reasonable layman realise?' The facts of the case were that the claimant had been diagnosed as suffering from selective brain damage and was compulsorily detained in hospital from 1975 until 1981. The proceedings were not issued until 1993, although the claimant had first consulted solicitors in 1986. At this time she did not know whether she had a case but felt clear in her own mind that her suffering was attributable to a mistaken diagnosis. It was held on appeal that because the claimant was clear in her own mind that a connection existed between her suffering and the misdiagnosis when she first sought legal advice in 1986, it was not necessary for the court to enquire further whether a rational lay person would have been willing to say that he knew of a connection between the suffering and the misdiagnosis without first obtaining a medical confirmation.

In *Ministry of Defence v AB and others* [2012] UKSC 9, the Supreme Court looked at limitation as a preliminary issue in the context of nine conjoined cases. The claimants, all veteran servicemen, claimed that they had suffered numerous illnesses as a result of exposure to ionising radiation during nuclear tests carried out by the British Government in the 1950s. At first instance, it was held that actual and constructive knowledge arose only when each veteran had been made aware of the Rowland Study in 2007, which was the first credible scientific evidence that the exposure could cause the illnesses complained of. Although, applying that test, none of the cases was statute barred, five of the veterans had already formed a strong belief that exposure to radiation had caused their illnesses, and this was sufficient to amount to actual knowledge. These cases would have been statute barred had the court not exercised its discretion under s 33 to disapply the limitation period (see **7.8** below).

The Court of Appeal and the Supreme Court determined that the wrong approach had been taken in relation to the date of knowledge, and that the discretion to disapply the limitation period should not be exercised. The claimants had argued that they had not *known* that their illnesses were attributable to the acts or omissions of the defendant more than three years prior to issue of proceedings; they might have believed this to be the case, but the Act required knowledge. However, the Court of Appeal unanimously and the Supreme Court by a majority held that a reasonable belief (ie more than a fanciful suggestion) that the defendant was responsible amounted to knowledge. All that was required was sufficient knowledge to justify further investigation and commencement of the preliminaries to making a claim.

For the purposes of establishing knowledge, it was irrelevant that the claimants were still not in a position, after many years of investigation and campaigning, to establish causation. However this, and the lapse of time, led to the Court determining that time should not be extended under s 33.

It is possible that a claimant may be fixed with actual knowledge of certain facts even if a medical expert has advised him that this was not the case. In *Sniezek v Bundy (Letchworth) Ltd* (2000) LTL, 7 July, the Court of Appeal ruled that the claimant had the knowledge from the date when he went to complain to his doctor of severe symptoms but was assured that there was no link between the illness and his work. The Court decided that the claimant knew that his severe throat symptoms, which had persisted for five years, were a significant injury, and that he had always attributed them to his work. The fact that a doctor subsequently advised him that this was not the case, did not change the fact that he had actual knowledge.

7.3.3.2 Constructive knowledge

Where a claimant is not fixed with actual knowledge, he may be fixed with constructive knowledge in accordance with s 14(3) of the LA 1980.

In accordance with s 14(3) (see **7.3.1**), a claimant cannot argue that he did not have the requisite knowledge due to his ignorance of the law, or because he failed to make further enquiries or seek appropriate advice. The test is an objective one: knowledge which would have been obtained by a reasonable man in the same circumstances as the claimant will be imputed to the claimant. So, there is an assumption that a reasonable man who had suffered a significant injury would be sufficiently curious about the cause of the injury that he would seek expert advice (see *Adams v Bracknell Forest BC* [2004] UKHL 29), unless there were reasons why a reasonable man in his position would not have done so (see *Johnson v Ministry of Defence* [2012] EWCA Civ 1505).

In *Collins v Secretary of State for Business, Innovation and Skills and Stenna Line Irish Sea Ferries Ltd* [2014] EWCA Civ 717, the claimant, who had been exposed to asbestos when he worked as a docker between 1947 and 1967, and who had developed lung cancer in 2002 (although he had made a full recovery), commenced proceedings in 2012. At first instance, the court determined that actual knowledge took place in 2009, when the claimant saw an advertisement by personal injury solicitors, but that constructive knowledge had occurred in 2003, after he had been diagnosed with cancer and allowing time for him recover from the shock of diagnosis. This was on the basis that a reasonable man would have asked his doctor about the possible causes of the cancer, and that it was inevitable that the doctor would have mentioned the claimant's exposure to asbestos. The Court of Appeal upheld this decision. This case is also important in relation to the exercise of the court's discretion to disapply the limitation period under s 33 of the LA 1980 (see **7.8**).

The objective nature of the test was confirmed by the House of Lords in *A v Hoare* [2008] UKHL 6, when it was said that the correct approach was to ask what the claimant knew about his injury, add any 'objective' knowledge which might be imputed to him under s 14(3) and then ask whether a reasonable person with that knowledge would have considered the injury sufficiently serious to justify his instituting proceedings. Once the court has determined what the claimant knew and what he should be treated as having known, the actual claimant drops out of the picture, and judges should not consider the claimant's intelligence. Consequently, the effect of any psychological injuries resulting from the breach of duty upon what the claimant could reasonably have been expected to do is irrelevant when considering constructive knowledge. (However, this will be considered by the court when deciding whether to exercise its discretion under s 33 to disapply the limitation period – see **7.8**.)

In *Forbes v Wandsworth Health Authority* [1997] QB 402, the claimant, who suffered from poor circulation, underwent surgery for a by-pass operation. This was not a success and a further by-pass was performed the next day. Unfortunately, the second operation was too late to be successful and the claimant was told that it was necessary to amputate his leg to prevent gangrene, to which he agreed. The sole allegation was that the authority had been negligent not to perform the second operation sooner. The claimant did not seek advice until seven years after the limitation period had expired. The Court of Appeal held by a majority that the claimant was deemed to have constructive knowledge as soon as he had time to overcome the shock of the injury, take stock of his disability and seek advice.

In *Kew v Bettamix Ltd (formerly Tarmac Roadstone Southern Ltd) & Others* [2006] EWCA Civ 1535, the claimant issued proceedings in respect of injuries suffered from his exposure to vibrating equipment during his employment with the defendants. As early as 1991 the claimant had experienced numbness in his fingers, but had thought this was due to his age. On 29 March 2000, following a routine occupational health care assessment, he was informed by means of a letter from an occupational physician that his symptoms might be attributable to his exposure to vibration at work. The Court held that it was necessary for the claimant to have sufficient knowledge to make it reasonable for him to seek to acquire further knowledge of the link between his injury and his prior working conditions. He did not have such knowledge until 29 March 2000, when he received the physician's letter. Although he was not told about the causative link at that time, he knew that there was a real possibility that his working conditions had caused his symptoms, and a reasonable man would have investigated further. He was therefore fixed with constructive knowledge at that date.

In *Pearce v Doncaster MBC* [2008] EWCA Civ 1416, the Court of Appeal considered the knowledge of a man who claimed damages from the local authority for its failure to take him into care when he was a child. The claimant's actual knowledge arose when he saw his care records, shortly before issuing proceedings. However, constructive knowledge took place several years earlier, when he had requested his files but had failed to take up the appointment to view them, even though the authority had offered to pay his train fare.

In *Whiston v London Strategic Health Authority* [2010] EWCA Civ 195, the claimant suffered from cerebral palsy caused at the time of his birth, but he was highly intelligent and lived a full life. The claimant's mother had told him that he had been delivered by forceps and that he had been starved of oxygen at birth, but she did not tell him that she thought the junior doctor attending her may have been at fault until 2005, when she was prompted to do so by a deterioration in the claimant's condition. Proceedings were commenced in 2006, when the claimant was 32 years old, more than 11 years after the expiry of the limitation period. Although the Court of Appeal accepted that a person who suffers from a disability at birth is more likely to be accepting of his disability, and therefore less likely to ask questions, than a person who suffers an injury during adult life, it held that a reasonable man in his position would have wanted to know more about the circumstances of his birth and would have asked his mother, particularly as she was a nurse and a trained midwife. Consequently, it concluded that the claimant had constructive knowledge of the facts which he discovered from his mother in 2005 no later than when he was in his early 20s, in about 1998.

It is not necessary for the court to specify an exact date when constructive knowledge took place. In *White v EON and Others* [2008] EWCA Civ 1436, the claimant claimed damages for vibration white finger (VWF) caused whilst working for the defendant between 1962 and 1996. He argued that he first had the requisite knowledge in the summer of 2003, when he saw an advert from a claims company describing the symptoms of VWF. At first instance, the judge dismissed his claim on the basis that he knew he had a significant injury and it was reasonable for him to have obtained medical advice which would have led to his linking that injury to his employment. Consequently, he had constructive knowledge at the end of 1996. On appeal, the claimant's argument that it was illogical for the judge to have plucked the end of 1996 as the date of constructive knowledge, because nothing significant happened at that point to have led to that knowledge, was dismissed by the Court of Appeal. The Court held that the end of 1996 was the *latest time* at which the claimant could be fixed with constructive knowledge, as the claimant's symptoms had reached a plateau by that time.

The issue of constructive knowledge of the identity of the defendant was considered in *Henderson v Temple Pier Co Ltd* [1998] 1 WLR 1540. In this case, it was held that, where a claimant instructed solicitors to bring a claim for damages, on the proper construction of s 14(3) of the LA 1980 the claimant was fixed with constructive knowledge of facts which the solicitor ought to have acquired.

7.3.4   The injury was 'significant'

In order to determine whether the claimant was aware that the injury was significant, further guidance is provided in s 14(2). This states that an injury is significant if the claimant would reasonably have considered it sufficiently serious to justify instituting proceedings against a defendant who did not dispute liability and was able to satisfy a judgment.

In *McCoubrey v Ministry of Defence* [2007] EWCA Civ 17, the Court of Appeal considered the case of a soldier who, during a training exercise in 1993, had been deafened by a thunderflash which had been thrown negligently into his trench. The claimant had known almost immediately that he had suffered the injury, and this had been confirmed by medical examinations. However, he had continued working in the army without complaint until 2003, when he was told that he could not accompany his unit to Iraq because of his disability. At that stage, he became aware of the consequences of the injury, consulted solicitors and issued proceedings. It was held that time had started to run in 1993, as soon as the claimant had become aware of his deafness. When determining whether an injury is 'significant', the court should consider the gravity of the injury and not its effect, or perceived effect, on the personal life or career of the claimant.

If an injury is significant, the fact that the symptoms attributable to it subsequently became worse is irrelevant for purpose of determining when knowledge took place (see *Brooks v J & P Coates (UK) Ltd* [1984] 1 All ER 702). The date of knowledge is not affected by the fact that the consequences turned out to be more serious than was initially thought.

Moreover, in cases of multiple illnesses arising from the same course of events, time starts to run as soon as the claimant has knowledge of the first injury that could be said to be significant, irrespective of whether he might learn of other injuries much later.

7.3.5   Attributable to the act or omission

'Attributable' means 'capable of being attributable to' and not necessarily 'caused by'. The knowledge of the 'act or omission' does not necessarily include knowledge that the act or omission is actionable in law. For example, if the claimant has asthma but does not know that this is due to his working conditions, time does not start to run. However, if he is aware that his asthma is capable of being attributed to those working conditions, time starts to run even though he may not know that his employer may have been to blame.

In *Dobbie v Medway Health Authority* [1994] 1 WLR 1234, CA, Mrs Dobbie had surgery to remove a lump in her breast. It was only during the operation that the surgeon took the decision to perform a mastectomy (removal of the breast), as he believed the lump was cancerous. In fact, the lump was not cancerous and the mastectomy had been unnecessary. Mrs Dobbie accepted at the time that the surgeon had acted reasonably and it was her good fortune that the lump was not cancerous. It was only several years later, when she heard about a similar case, that Mrs Dobbie took legal advice and commenced proceedings. The Court of Appeal held that she knew of the removal of her breast and the psychological and physical harm which followed within months of the operation, and she knew it to be significant. She also knew that her injury was the result of an act or omission of the health authority and, therefore, time began to run even though she did not appreciate until later that this act or omission may have been negligent.

7.3.6 The identity of the defendant

In most cases the claimant will know who is responsible for his injuries, but s 14(1)(c) will assist a claimant where there is a delay in identifying the defendant, eg in the case of a hit and run motor accident (assuming an application is not made to the Motor Insurers' Bureau – see **3.4**).

The identity of the defendant may prove problematic in cases involving corporate groups. In *Simpson v Norwest Holst Southern Ltd* [1980] 2 All ER 471, the claimant worked on a building site, and his contract of employment stated that he was employed by Norwest Holst Group. However, this did not identify his employer because at least four companies made up Norwest Holst Group, including Norwest Holst Ltd and Norwest Construction Co Ltd, and the claimant's payslips stated simply that his employer was 'Norwest Holst'. In the circumstances, the Court of Appeal found for the claimant, on the basis that neither the contract nor the payslips identified the employer, and it was not reasonable to expect the claimant to request further particulars of the identity of his employer prior to the expiry of his primary limitation period. For a case on similar facts, see *Rush v JNR (SMD) Ltd* (CA, 11 October 1999), where it was held that knowledge of a number of potential defendants was not sufficient knowledge for the purpose of s 14.

7.4 PERSONS UNDER A DISABILITY

Under s 38(2) of the LA 1980, a person is under a disability while he is an infant (a person who has not attained the age of 18) or lacks capacity (within the meaning of the Mental Capacity Act 2005) to conduct legal proceedings.

Under s 28(6), while a person is under a disability, he may bring a claim at any time up to three years from the date when he ceased to be under a disability. Consequently, where a child is injured, limitation does not start to run until he reaches his 18th birthday and it expires on his 21st birthday.

Where a person is disabled within the meaning of the Mental Capacity Act 2005, the start of the limitation period is delayed only if he was so disabled when the cause of action first accrued. If the disability comes into existence after that date, time continues to run. However, under s 33(3) of the LA 1980 (see **7.8**) the court will have regard to any period or periods of disability when it considers its discretion to disapply the limitation period.

7.5 LIMITATION IN ASSAULT CASES

Until January 2008, the limitation period in relation to acts of deliberate assault, including indecent assault, followed the House of Lords' decision in the case of *Stubbings v Webb* [1993] AC 498, which involved child abuse at a children's home. The House of Lords held that deliberate assault did not fall under s 11(1) actions for 'negligence, nuisance or breach of duty' but under s 2, and therefore the correct limitation period was six years from the date of the cause of action (or the age of 18 in the case of a child) rather than three years. However, there was no discretion to disapply the period under s 33, which led to unfairness in cases where the victim had been a child or otherwise vulnerable at the time of the assault and, as a result, lacked the psychological capacity to bring a claim.

The House of Lords departed from this approach in R v Hoare [2008] UKHL 6, the facts of which were as follows. In 1988, the claimant had been subjected to a serious sexual assault by Hoare, who was subsequently convicted of attempted rape and sentenced to life imprisonment. The claimant had not brought civil proceedings against him within the six-year limitation period as Hoare did not have the financial means to pay any damages that the court might award. However, in 2004, whilst on day release from prison, Hoare purchased a lottery ticket and won over £7 million. When the claimant heard of the defendant's windfall, she commenced proceedings against him, seeking to rely on the court's discretion to disapply the limitation period under s 33. The House of Lords heard the claimant's appeal against the decision that her claim was statute barred, together with four other cases, all relating to the abuse of children in children's homes.

Their Lordships held that *Stubbings* had been wrongly decided, and they extended the meaning of claims under 'negligence, nuisance or breach of duty' to include deliberate assault. Consequently, the limitation period in assault cases was three years. They remitted the matter to the judge, for him to reconsider whether the court was able to exercise its discretion under s 33 to disapply this limitation period (see **7.8**).

7.6   CLAIMS FOLLOWING FATAL ACCIDENTS

Claims on behalf of the deceased's estate and on behalf of his dependants are generally brought together. Nevertheless, there are slight differences in how limitation is dealt with.

7.6.1   Claims under the Law Reform (Miscellaneous Provisions) Act 1934

Where a claim is brought on behalf of the deceased's estate, s 11(5) of the LA 1980 provides that if the injured person died before expiration of the limitation period of three years as set out in s 11(4), the limitation period is three years from:

(a)   the date of death; or

(b)   the date of the personal representative's knowledge,

whichever is the later. If there is more than one personal representative and they have differing dates of knowledge, time runs from the earliest date of knowledge (s 11(7)).

If the injured person died after the expiry of the primary limitation period under s 11(4) without commencing proceedings for the personal injuries he had suffered, or if he died before the expiration of the primary limitation period and his personal representatives failed to commence proceedings within three years of death or date of later knowledge, the claim is statute-barred. However, in both instances, the court does have a general discretion to override the above provisions and disapply the limitation period under s 33 of the LA 1980 (see **7.8**).

7.6.2   Claims under the Fatal Accidents Act 1976

In relation to claims brought by the dependants of the deceased, s 12(2) of the LA 1980 provides that if the injured person died before the expiration of the limitation period of three years as set out in s 11(4), the limitation period is three years from:

(a)   the date of death; or

(b)   the date of knowledge of the person for whose benefit the claim is brought,

whichever is the later.

Where there is more than one dependant, the limitation period is applied separately to each one, taking into account the date of knowledge of each dependant. Moreover, if any dependant is a child, time does not start to run for that dependant until he reaches 18, and the claim will not become time-barred until he is 21.

If the dependants fail to commence their claim within the three-year limitation period, an application can be made under s 33 to disapply the limitation period.

Where the injured person failed to commence a personal injury claim within three years of the cause of action and subsequently died as a result of his injuries, a claim under the FAA 1976 cannot be brought by the dependants. This is because s 12(1) of the LA 1980 provides that a claim under the FAA 1976 cannot be brought if death occurred when the person injured could no longer maintain a claim and recover damages in respect of the injury, whether because of a limitation problem or for any other reason. In other words, the dependants of the deceased are not in a better position than the deceased would have been. When considering whether a claim brought by the deceased person would have been time-barred, no account may be made of the possibility that the court would have exercised its discretion under s 33 to disapply the limitation period. However, the court may exercise its discretion to disapply the primary limitation period in respect of the dependants' action. See s 12(1) of the LA 1980.

7.7 OTHER PERIODS OF LIMITATION

Although in the vast majority of personal injury cases the three-year rule will apply, it is possible that a special rule applies, for example in regard to claims relating to aircraft under the Carriage by Air Act 1961 or the Warsaw Convention, or relating to vessels used for navigation under the Maritime Conventions Act 1911 or the Merchant Shipping Act 1995. In these cases, the limitation period is generally two years.

The most common form of special rule is in respect of contributions between tortfeasors under the Civil Liability (Contribution) Act 1978, where no claim to recover a contribution may be brought after the expiration of two years from the date on which the right accrued. This is generally the date on which judgment was given against the person who is seeking the contribution, or the date when he pays or agrees to pay compensation.

7.8 THE COURT'S DISCRETION TO OVERRIDE THE LIMITATION PERIOD

Section 33 of the LA 1980 gives the court a wide and unfettered discretion to disapply the three-year limitation period. Section 33(1) provides that:

> If it appears to the court that it would be equitable to allow an action to proceed having regard to the degree to which—
>
> (a)   the provisions of section 11 or 11A or 12 of this Act prejudice the plaintiff or any person whom he represents; and
>
> (b)   any decision of the court under this subsection would prejudice the defendant or any person whom he represents;
>
> the court may direct that those provisions shall not apply to the action, or shall not apply to any specified cause of action to which the action relates.

The onus rests upon the claimant to show why the limitation period should be disapplied (*Halford v Brookes* [1991] 3 All ER 559).

Under s 33(3), the court is required to have regard to all the circumstances of the case, and it will attempt to balance the needs of the parties by seeking to avoid prejudice caused to the claimant by depriving him of the right to continue with the claim, or prejudice caused to the defendant by allowing the matter to continue when he has been deprived of the ability to defend himself.

The court is specifically directed to six factors, which are outlined below:

(a)   the length and reasons for the delay on the part of the claimant;

(b)   the effect of any delay on the cogency of the evidence;

(c)   the conduct of the defendant following the date of the cause of action;

(d)   the duration of any disability (within the meaning of the Mental Capacity Act 2005) suffered by the claimant after the cause of action arose;

(e)   the conduct of the claimant after he became aware that he might have a claim against the defendant;

(f)   the steps taken by the claimant to obtain medical, legal or other expert advice, and the nature of any advice received.

'Delay' in s 33(3)(a) and (b) is the delay since the expiry of the limitation period. However, the court may consider the overall delay when having regard to all the circumstances of the case. See *McDonnell & Another v Walker* [2009] EWCA Civ 1257 and *Cairn-Jones v Tyler* [2010] EWCA Civ 1642.

Guidance in relation to s 33(3)(a) was provided by the Court of Appeal in *Coad v Cornwall and Isles of Scilly Health Authority* [1997] 1 WLR 189, CA. The Court held that it must apply a subjective test when determining why the claimant had delayed, the length of the delay and whether the reason was good or bad. There was no requirement for the claimant to provide a 'reasonable' explanation.

In *Collins v Secretary of State for Business, etc* (see **7.3.3.2**), in a decision which is thought to have serious implications for long-tail disease claims, the Court of Appeal confirmed that the period of time between the defendant's breach of duty and the commencement of the limitation period (ie a later date of knowledge) must be part of 'the circumstances of the case' within the meaning of s 33(3), although the weight attached to pre-knowledge delay will be less than that attached to post-knowledge delay. There had been a period of some 50 years between the alleged breaches of duty and the date of constructive knowledge, and this lengthy delay had a detrimental effect on the cogency of the evidence. Taking this and other issues into account, the judge at first instance had been correct to refuse to exercise his discretion.

When considering s 33(3)(b), the extent to which evidence is less cogent, the Court of Appeal highlighted the importance of written evidence when memories of witnesses are unreliable due to the lapse of time (see *Farthing v North East Essex Health Authority* [1998] Lloyd's Rep Med 37, CA). In 1981, the claimant had had a hysterectomy which was negligently performed, but proceedings were not issued until 1995. When considering her application under s 33, the court found that due to the lapse of time a number of the witnesses had died, or had moved abroad and could recall little of the events in question. However, the Court of Appeal further found that because there was considerable evidence available in the form of the medical records and a letter from the surgeon to the claimant's GP written shortly after the operation, there would be little need for reliance on memory alone and consequently the appeal should be allowed.

In *McArdle v Marmion* [2013] NIQB 123, the court exercised its discretion where there had been an inexcusable and unjustifiable delay of 17 years, because the large amount of evidence collected at the time of the accident meant the ability to conduct a defence had not been diminished.

In *TCD v Harrow Council and Others* (see **7.3.2**), it was argued on behalf of the claimant that she had been unable to confront some aspects of the abuse to the extent that would be necessary for the purposes of litigation, and that she had delayed proceedings until her children were older. Nevertheless, the judge repeated what was said in *Hoare* (see **7.5**), that not everyone who brings a late claim for damages for sexual abuse, however genuine his or her complaint, can expect the court to exercise the s 33 discretion favourably. He refused to exercise his discretion in relation to the claims against two of the authorities on the grounds that the long delay meant that evidence was not forthcoming and the defendants were therefore severely prejudiced. (Discretion was not exercised in relation to the third claim due to the weakness of the claim.)

In relation to s 33(3)(c), where the court is satisfied that the defendants have brought upon themselves the prejudice that they claim to suffer, that should be taken into account and the prejudice should be significantly discounted. In the case of *Hammond v West Lancashire Health Authority* [1998] Lloyd's Rep Med 146, CA, the defendants claimed prejudice to their case as they had destroyed the deceased's x-rays after three years had elapsed. The Court held that the destruction of the x-rays was a policy implemented by the defendants, and which had no regard for the time limits of the LA 1980. Consequently, although the prejudice caused to their case should still be taken into account, it would be significantly discounted.

These factors are guidelines only, and the court is entitled to take into account any other matter which it considers to be relevant. For example, the time of notification of the claim to the defendant is of extreme importance in ascertaining prejudice, although there is no specific reference to this in s 33. In addition, the court is entitled to consider the ultimate prospects of the claim being successful. In *TCD v Harrow Council and Others* (see above), the judge refused to grant discretion in relation to the case against Worcester County Council on the grounds that the claim had no realistic prospects of success. (Also see *Forbes v Wandsworth Health Authority* at **7.3.3.2**).

In the case of *Hoare* (see **7.5**), the House of Lords remitted the matter to the judge to reconsider the application of s 33 in accordance with the opinions of their Lordships. In *A v Hoare* [2008] EWHC 1573 (QB), the parties agreed that the main reason why the claimant had not commenced proceedings within the limitation period was because the defendant had been impecunious and, because he had been serving a life sentence, this was unlikely to change. She had commenced proceedings in 2004, almost 14 years after expiry of the three-year limitation period, principally because she had learned that the defendant had won £7 million on the lottery. It was also agreed that there was no reported authority on the court being asked to exercise its discretion under s 33 on the grounds that the defendant was impecunious. However, the judge determined that this was a relevant factor when considering the exercise of the discretion to disapply the limitation period. In doing so, he took into account the fact that the defendant's own actions were the cause of his impecuniosity. The judge found in favour of the claimant and exercised his discretion under s 33. (The full judgment in this case may aid understanding of the application of s 33.)

Where the proceedings are brought against the defendant outside the limitation period as a result of the negligence of the claimant's solicitor, and the claim is not allowed to proceed, the claimant may have a claim against his own solicitor. It has been argued by defendants that the fact that the claimant has a cast-iron claim against his own solicitor provides an overwhelming reason why the limitation period should not be disapplied; the claimant will not be prejudiced because he can pursue an alternative claim against his solicitor (rather than the defendant). However, although the ability to claim against the solicitor is a factor for the court to bear in mind, it is not an absolute bar against disapplying the limitation period.

The court considered this issue in *Steeds v Peverel Management Services Ltd* [2001] EWCA Civ 419. In this case, solicitors issued proceedings 49 days outside of the limitation period. On appeal, the court found that the district judge at first instance was wrong to treat the claimant's good claim against his own solicitors as justification for refusing to exercise a discretion under s 33. The better view was that the existence of a claim against his own solicitors was a relevant factor in weighing the degree of prejudice suffered by the defendant in not being able to rely on the limitation period as a defence. To that end, it would always be relevant to consider when the defendant first had notification of the claim. On the facts of the case, the judgment was set aside and the court exercised its discretion under s 33, as it was unlikely that the defendants were caused any appreciable prejudice and it was equitable to allow the claim to continue allowing for all of the circumstances of the case.

However in *McDonnell v Walker* (see above), the Court of Appeal refused to disapply the limitation period as the defendant had been forensically disadvantaged by a substantial period of inexcusable delay.

It has also been argued by defendants that the loss of the limitation defence itself, and the subsequent requirement to pay damages, is a prejudice which must be taken into account by the court when considering the exercise of the s 33 discretion. In *Cain v Francis; McKay v Hamlani* [2008] EWCA Civ 1451, both road traffic accident claims, the Court of Appeal considered the so-called 'windfall defence', which arises where the defendant has no defence other than one based on limitation due to the claimant's solicitors failing to issue proceedings on time. In each case, the defendant had admitted liability but, in the course of negotiating damages, the claimant's solicitors had missed the limitation deadline. In *Cain*, where there was a delay of just one day, the judge refused to exercise his discretion; in *McKay*, the delay was one year, but the judge exercised his discretion and allowed the case to proceed. In order to establish a consistency of approach, as opposed to a 'lottery for litigants', the Court of Appeal dealt with both cases together.

The Court of Appeal held that the defendant had a right to a fair opportunity to defend himself and had a complete procedural defence under s 11, which would remove the obligation for him to pay damages. However, fairness and justice meant that the obligation to pay damages should be removed only if the passage of time had significantly damaged the defendant's opportunity to defend himself. Parliament could not have intended the financial consequences for the defendant to be a consideration relevant to the exercise of discretion under s 33. The important factor is whether the defendant is able to defend himself, and therefore it would always be important to consider when the defendant was notified of the claim against him, and whether it was still possible for him to investigate the claim and gather evidence. This judgment has brought clarity to this area, and is likely to result in the court exercising its discretion under s 33 in more claims which were issued late but where the defendant's ability to defend himself is not prejudiced.

7.9   DEALING WITH LIMITATION ISSUES IN PRACTICE

Failure to issue proceedings within the limitation period is a major source of negligence claims against solicitors. Although this chapter includes the law and procedure relevant to an application under s 33 to override the limitation period (see **7.8** above), prevention is better than cure. It is therefore essential that the claimant's solicitor establishes a routine of checking and rechecking the limitation period on the files for which he is responsible. There may also be many other files for which he is not responsible, but which may pass through his hands on a regular basis. Such files are often the source of limitation problems, as one solicitor may assume (wrongly) that the responsibility for checking limitation resides with someone else, and the date of limitation may go unnoticed. To avoid this, the solicitor should adopt a routine of checking for limitation on every file in which he is involved.

Needless to say, as the expiry of the limitation period provides the defendant with a significant, although not always watertight defence, those acting for defendants should always keep a watchful eye open for limitation issues.

7.9.1   Initial instructions

At the first interview, the claimant's solicitor should note the date of the cause of action and calculate the limitation period from this date. This can be verified by checking, for example, the relevant hospital A&E notes, the employer's accident report book, or police reports. If he is satisfied that there is sufficient time for him to investigate the matter and commence proceedings within the limitation period, he should mark the file with the expiry date and enter the date into the file management system, to ensure that limitation does not become a problem at a later stage.

If the limitation period has already expired, the solicitor will need to take account of this fact when carrying out the risk assessment. Where there appear to be no grounds for relying on a later date of knowledge or persuading the court to exercise its discretion under s 33, the client should be advised accordingly. *Carlton v Fulchers (a Firm)* [1997] PNLR 337, CA, provides a valuable illustration as to how a solicitor can be found to be negligent due to a failure to be aware of limitation problems. In this case, even though the claimant did not consult the solicitor until after the three-year limitation period had expired, the solicitor was held liable due to his failure to advise of the possibility of an application under s 33.

Where the primary limitation period has expired and there are good arguments relating to later knowledge and/or s 33, the claimant's solicitor should issue proceedings without further delay. He may delay the service of the claim form and follow the procedure as set out in **7.9.2**.

In clinical negligence cases, where there is a possibility of public funding, further delays resulting from applying for such funding must be avoided, and therefore the solicitor should apply for emergency assistance from the Community Legal Service.

7.9.2 Protective proceedings and standstill agreements

The court does not have the power to extend the limitation period before it has expired, so in circumstances where the claimant's solicitor has insufficient time to investigate the matter and carry out the steps set out in the relevant pre-action protocol before time runs out, the options available to him to secure his client's position are:

(a)   obtain the defendant's agreement not to plead a limitation defence;

(b)   enter a standstill agreement with the defendant; or

(c)   commence protective proceedings.

Obtaining the defendant's agreement not to plead a limitation defence effectively places the parties in the position they would be in if proceedings were commenced within the limitation period. However, as many defendants would not be prepared to enter into such an agreement, the remaining options are more likely.

Where the parties enter a standstill agreement, the defendant agrees not to rely on a limitation defence from a specified date, usually the date of the agreement, until he serves notice on the claimant that he wishes to restart the clock. This has the effect of freezing time at the specified date. Generally, agreements specify that a month's notice must be given by the defendant. The case of *Gold Shipping Navigation Co SA v Lulu Maritime Ltd* [2009] EWHC 1365 (Admlty), regarding a shipping dispute, demonstrates how important it is to take care when drawing up such an agreement. In that case, clumsy drafting almost prevented one party from pursuing its claim.

The claimant's solicitor may initiate protective proceedings in order to safeguard his client's position. The steps which should be taken are as follows:

(a)   The claim form should be issued, which will stop the clock for limitation purposes, but should not be served upon the defendant. Under CPR, r 7.5(2), where it is to be served within the jurisdiction, it must be served within four months of being issued. This provides the claimant's solicitor with some time to investigate the matter and comply with the protocol. The particulars of claim must be served upon the defendant within 14 days after service of the claim form (CPR, r 7.4(1)(b)), but it too must be served within four months of the claim form being issued (CPR, r 7.4(2)).

(b)   The claimant's solicitor should contact the defendant and notify him of the situation without delay. The date when the defendant first became aware of the claim or potential claim will be a relevant factor if the court is asked to consider whether the time limit should be disapplied under s 33.

(c)   Both parties should then follow the relevant protocol. However, there may not be time to follow the protocol to the letter, eg there may not be time to allow the defendant three months to investigate the matter.

(d)   Where time allowed for service of the claim form is about to expire, the claimant's solicitor should make an interim application to the court for an extension of the time limit relating to service (CPR, r 7.6). The application must be made in accordance with Part 23 and supported by evidence. It is vital that this application is made within the four months allowed for service of the claim form, as the powers of the court to grant an extension where the application is made after the expiry of this period are limited to when the court has been unable to serve the claim form, the claimant has taken all reasonable steps to serve it but has been unable to do so and, in either case, the application for the extension has been made promptly (CPR, r 7.6(3)).

(e)   Where an application is made within the four-month time period, it is likely that the court will grant an extension of time for the service of the claim form. If so, it will also make directions in order to manage the case properly.

7.9.3   Commencing proceedings

Rule 16.4(a) of the CPR states that the particulars of claim should include a concise statement of the facts on which the claimant relies. It therefore follows that where a claim is issued outside the primary limitation period, the particulars of claim should, where relevant, include a statement that the claimant relies on a later date of knowledge, and the date should be specified.

It will be for the claimant to prove the later date of knowledge, and therefore this issue should be addressed in the witness statements of the claimant and any other witness who can give evidence on this point.

In practice, where there is a limitation problem and the parties have discussed this prior to commencement, the claimant's solicitor will deal with the limitation issue in the particulars of claim. However, if the matter has not been discussed before issue, some solicitors acting for claimants will not pre-empt a defence by raising the limitation problem in the particulars of claim, on the basis that it is not in their client's interests to do so. If the defendant is not aware of the existence of the rules relating to limitation, or does not notice that the limitation period has expired, he may admit the claim.

7.9.4   The defence

The defendant's solicitor should carefully check each particulars of claim for limitation problems. Where the claim form was issued outside the primary limitation period, he will need to address the issue in the defence. Where the claimant has relied on a later date of knowledge and the defendant seeks to rely on an earlier date of knowledge, whether actual or constructive, he should give details.

The defendant will have to prove any earlier date of knowledge he seeks to rely on. It is unlikely that he will be able to call witnesses of his own in this regard; rather, he will be obliged to extract the necessary information from the claimant and any other witness during cross-examination.

7.9.5   Dealing with limitation as a preliminary issue

In most cases, the limitation problem will be dealt with as a preliminary issue. The defendant should consider bringing the issue to a head either by applying for the claim to be stayed under CPR, r 3.1(f) or, in a clear case, by applying for summary judgment under CPR, r 24.2(a)(i). The claimant should respond by giving notice of his intention to ask the court to exercise its discretion to disapply the limitation period under s 33. Both parties should address the matter fully in the supporting witness statements. This will enable the court to consider the matter before trial.

If the defendant does not bring the matter to the court's attention by making an application, the claimant's solicitor should consider doing so by making an application under s 33.

Whilst the courts will normally seek to deal with limitation as a preliminary issue wherever feasible, there will be circumstances where it is not appropriate to do so. In the case of *J, K & P v Archbishop of Birmingham & Trustees of the Birmingham Archdiocese of the Roman Catholic Church* [2008] LTL, 21 August, which involved the alleged victims of child sexual abuse, the court held that it was not appropriate due to the large overlap of evidence and the additional stress on the victims having to give their evidence twice.

7.10 CONCLUSION

Practitioners must be alert to limitation issues and maintain a good working knowledge of the key sections of the LA 1980. The courts' interpretation of the statutory provisions, particularly in relation to actual and constructive knowledge and the discretion to disapply the limitation period, is something of a moveable feast, and therefore practitioners must keep an eye out for relevant case law.

Sound case management processes and an exemplary diary system are essential for claimants' solicitors. There is claimant's limitation checklist at **7.11** below.

7.11 CLAIMANT'S LIMITATION CHECKLIST

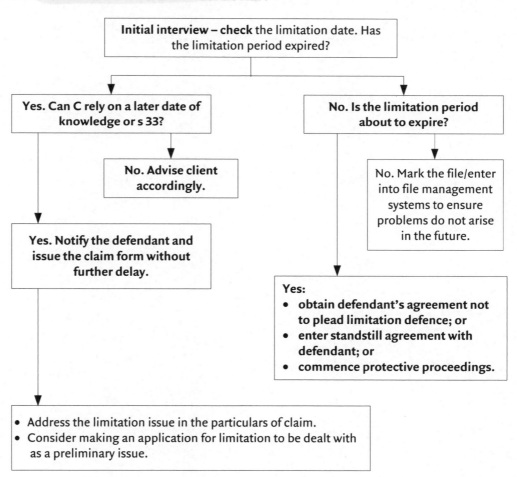

The First Interview

LEARNING OUTCOMES

After reading this chapter you will be able to:

- identify the important matters that must be dealt with during the first interview
- identify any urgent action that needs to be taken
- take a proof of evidence.

8.1 INTRODUCTION

The first interview is the cornerstone of the solicitor/client relationship, and it is therefore worthwhile making the effort to get it right. The Law Society's Practice Note on initial interviews, dated 6 October 2011, contains useful guidance on this topic and may be obtained from The Law Society website. Reference should also be made to *Skills for Lawyers*, which deals with how to conduct an interview. The interview will normally last at least an hour. The client should tell his own story, and the solicitor will often complete a long and detailed accident questionnaire, prior to drafting a proof of evidence. Detailed preparation at this stage will save a great deal of time later. The matters that should be considered in preparation for this first interview are examined below.

You should note that conduct requirements, such as checking for conflicts of interest and obtaining evidence of identity, are not dealt with in this book, but should be strictly followed.

8.2 FUNDING

Many people are wary of solicitors' charges, and are reluctant even to approach a solicitor in order to enquire about making a personal injury or clinical negligence claim. Consequently, some firms offer a free, fixed fee or reduced cost initial interview, in which they can give preliminary advice about the viability of the claim and provide information about costs and funding options.

Should the solicitor be instructed in relation to the matter, in accordance with Outcome 1.13 of the SRA Code of Conduct 2011, he must ensure the client receives, at the time of engagement, the best information possible about the likely overall cost of the matter. This includes information about funding options, disbursements which may arise and potential liability for inter parties costs. Funding is discussed in more detail in **Chapter 9**.

8.3 URGENT MATTERS

If an urgent matter comes to light during the first interview, the solicitor should bear in mind the question of funding prior to making lengthy or expensive investigations on the client's behalf, and should consider making an application for emergency public funding if appropriate.

8.3.1 Limitation

Limitation is discussed in detail in **Chapter 7**. At the first interview in a personal injury or clinical negligence claim, it may become apparent that:

(a)   the three-year primary limitation period is about to expire (see **7.2**). If so, the solicitor should consider entering into a standstill agreement with the defendant or issuing protective proceedings immediately (see **7.9.2**);

(b)   the three-year primary limitation period has recently expired. If so, consideration should be given to issuing proceedings as soon as possible, including in the claim form or particulars of claim, a request for a direction that the limitation period should be disapplied (see **7.8**). Thereafter, the solicitor should inform the defendant without delay that proceedings have been issued, to minimise any claim by the defendant of prejudice due to the passage of time;

(c)   there is a question as to the client's 'date of knowledge' of the injury complained of. The client should be questioned closely regarding the earliest date on which he realised he might have a cause of action, and how he came to that conclusion. The client's medical records should be obtained without delay in order to confirm the precise date of knowledge. Proceedings can then be issued as in point (b) above, and thereafter it can be argued that the limitation period has not yet expired because the client's date of knowledge of the injury is within the last three years. If this is not successful, an application should be made for the court to exercise its discretion and disapply the limitation period (see **7.8**).

Having established when the primary limitation period is due to expire, it is important that the time limit is recorded separately from the file in a diary system. The file itself may be similarly marked with the date on which limitation expires. This double recording of the primary limitation period is good practice, as failure to issue the claim within the limitation period is a common pitfall, and one which may lead to a negligence claim by the claimant against his solicitor.

8.3.2 Photographs

In most personal injury cases, persons seeking advice following an accident will do so relatively soon after the accident occurs. If this is the case, a task, which is often overlooked, will be to secure photographic evidence.

8.3.2.1 The client

The client may attend the interview with an array of bruises and abrasions (soft tissue injuries). These will heal or fade relatively quickly, and an important piece of the claimant's evidence will be lost. The claimant's solicitor should therefore ensure that good colour photographs are taken of the client's injuries for subsequent disclosure. Such photographs will form very tangible evidence of the severity of the injuries sustained, when the case comes to be considered some months or years in the future. In cases where the client may suffer embarrassment at being photographed, or indeed in any case where a degree of sensitivity is needed, specialist medical photographers are available, for example at larger teaching hospitals.

8.3.2.2   The location of the accident

In road traffic cases, it is usually necessary to visit and take photographs of the location of the accident as soon as possible after the accident, because the layout of the road may change as time passes and/or the road may appear different depending on whether it is photographed in summer or in winter, especially if there are lots of trees or vegetation which could obscure a driver's view (see **10.10.5**).

Where accidents at work are concerned, it is good practice to obtain photographs of any machinery or equipment involved. Any delay may mean that the equipment involved is replaced and/or disposed of. Similarly, if the accident involves allegations of a defect in a floor surface, it would be helpful to obtain photographic evidence of that floor surface before it is corrected.

8.4   ADVISING THE CLIENT

It is important for the solicitor not to lose sight of the fact that the client has come into his office seeking some meaningful advice, which he hopes will lead him to a decision as to whether he has an actionable case against some other party. The client therefore needs to have the best information available, in a form that he can understand, so that he can make an informed decision as to what to do next. It is best to set out the strengths and weaknesses of the case, based on what has been said by the client. The importance of the limitation period should be explained to the client if this is likely to be an issue. The solicitor should also explain to the client that it is for him to prove his case by evidence and that anything short of this is not enough. He should be informed of the basis of his case, and the level of proof needed by the court to prove it. The client should be left in no doubt that it is his case, to be proved by his evidence, and that he bears the risk that his case may fail. As such, he should think seriously prior to instructing his solicitor to issue proceedings. The solicitor should give an indication as to whether he believes that the case is likely to succeed, but he should make it clear that the assessment is based on the limited information available at this early stage. In any event, if the solicitor is considering taking the client's case but will be paid under a CFA or a DBA, it will be necessary for the solicitor to conduct an assessment of risk at an early stage in order to decide whether or not to accept the client's instructions on that basis.

It may be that the solicitor advising the client will be required to produce to his superiors a report, from which his superiors will make a risk assessment in relation to whether or not the client should be accepted on a CFA or DBA basis. The risk assessment report may also consider such things as whether it is proposed that the client covers his own disbursements, or whether the firm is prepared to fund them on the client's behalf. The client is likely to press for an indication of the likely level of damages that may be recovered. Giving a firm indication based on inadequate information should be resisted. Instead, the solicitor should explain to the client why an assessment would be premature at this stage. The solicitor will not be in a position to assess the value of the claim until medical evidence dealing with diagnosis and prognosis has been obtained.

One reason for not giving a provisional indication of the likely level of damages is that the client may be found to have been contributorily negligent. This principle should be explained to the client, first to try to elicit whether the client has any reason to believe that it will be relevant to his claim and, secondly, to act as a warning to the client that it is likely that the opposition will try to allege that he was contributorily negligent.

The client should also be advised that he must prove every head (or type) of loss against his opponent. Although it is the case that the client is able to claim all he has lost as a direct result of the accident, he must also be in a position to prove every head of that loss to the court if he wishes to recover damages in respect of it. It should therefore be explained to the client that damages are made up of general damages (for pain, suffering and loss of amenity) and special damages (everything the client has had physically to pay for and other quantifiable losses as a direct result of the accident). For a detailed analysis of the subject of damages, see **Chapter 15**.

It will assist greatly, when it comes to proving his losses, if the client has kept a detailed record or account of his out-of-pocket expenses. To this end, the client should be advised at the first interview to keep all receipts for expenses incurred as a direct result of the accident, and that it is his responsibility to do so. Common examples are prescriptions, the cost of items lost or damaged beyond repair in the accident, and taxi fares to the out-patient or physiotherapy departments. Similarly, with respect to general damages for pain and suffering, although the client's distress may be keen at the first interview, by the time of trial his recollection may have dimmed, to the extent that he has forgotten many of the minor losses of function he suffered in the early stages of recovery from his injuries. The client should therefore be advised to keep a diary if he does not already do so, to record, for example, the fact that he is unable to sleep due to pain, or is unable to dress himself unaided or to do housework, and to record how long these disabilities last. Any number of tasks, either recreational or work-related, should be recorded so that they are not forgotten later when it comes to preparing the client's witness statement.

It is particularly important in clinical negligence cases that the client is made aware of the difficulties in pursuing the claim, and especially that he must establish not only a breach of duty, but also that the breach was causative of the damage that resulted (rather than the underlying illness or injury being the root cause of the loss). If the client is paying for the litigation privately, the high costs involved must be explained to him clearly. The solicitor should also explain the difficulty in giving a preliminary view on liability without first obtaining all the client's medical notes and at least one expert's views.

8.5   THE CLIENT'S PROOF OF EVIDENCE

Client questionnaires are used frequently in personal injury work. The questionnaires are designed to elicit certain basic information about the client and the accident. Increasingly, law firms 'capture' these basic data about the client by keying the details into a case management system. This has the advantage that once 'captured', the data are available for use subsequently throughout the life of the claim.

The client's proof of evidence should not be confused with the client's witness statement. Although they are both statements taken from the client, they serve different functions. The proof is the 'rough copy', which may include irrelevant material and suspicions or 'versions' rather than facts provable by the client in court. The witness statement contains only those matters which the witness can prove, and is disclosed to the opposition at the relevant stage in the proceedings.

The function of the proof is to obtain the fullest possible detail from the client, and only later to sift out what is strictly admissible as evidence. The proof can be taken at the end of the first interview when the client is still present, or from notes made at the time in conjunction with the questionnaire.

8.5.1   Contents of the proof

The proof should commence with the client's full name, address, date of birth and National Insurance number. It should state his occupation and whether he is married. If he was admitted to hospital, it should state his hospital number. The proof is intended for use by the client's solicitor and barrister, and, subsequently, in the preparation of the client's witness statement; as such, it should be the fullest possible statement from the client relating to the incident, the events immediately following the incident and its long-term effects. The client should begin his narrative at the earliest point in time that he feels to be relevant.

Following the client's personal details, the proof should next detail the date, time and location of the incident. It should then follow through chronologically and meticulously:

(a)   the events leading up to the incident;

(b)   the circumstances of the accident, including a clear explanation of the mechanics of the accident itself;

(c)   what happened immediately after the incident;

(d)   why the client feels that the incident was caused by the negligence of some other person;

(e)   what medical treatment was given and injuries incurred; and

(f)   how the client feels that the incident has affected his day-to-day life.

The solicitor should bear in mind that the proof will form the basis of the witness statement, and that, usually, the witness statement will be ordered to stand as the witness's evidence-in-chief at the trial. It is important, therefore, that the proof is detailed in its description of how the incident actually happened, and the effect the incident has had on the client's day-to-day life. All aspects of the client's life should therefore be considered in the proof. The following areas should always be covered, including an estimate in weeks or months of how long the incapacity affected the client's life, or confirmation that the incapacity is still continuing:

(a)   Everyday tasks which he is unable to do for himself, eg dressing, bathing, housework, shopping, driving. This will be important if a claim is made for loss incurred in employing someone else to carry out these tasks.

(b)   Recreational activities such as sports, hobbies, gardening, DIY in maintaining the home and the family car. The client's inability to participate in sports will have an effect on his loss of amenity claim for general damages. The client should also be asked whether he is a member of any sports team or club, and about any prizes or trophies he has won as further evidence of his level of commitment. The inability to carry out jobs of maintenance around the home will similarly affect his claim for loss of amenity. If the client gives evidence that DIY is a hobby, details should be obtained of any projects he has undertaken. This will also affect his special damages claim for the labour element of the cost of having to employ someone else to fulfil those tasks in the future.

(c)   Whether and to what extent the injury has affected his sex life. This area of loss of amenity should always be broached with the client, as the stress of an accident can often bring about a degree of sexual dysfunction, even if the injury itself would not immediately suggest that such was the case.

(d)   Specifically, whether the incident will affect the client's ability to continue with his employment, and the extent to which he is affected. It may be obvious that the client will never work again, or will be unable to work in his pre-incident position but will have to retrain, or that he intends to return to his pre-incident employment but is unsure whether he will cope. Details should also be obtained as to the client's position if he were to be made redundant, and the degree of difficulty he would have in obtaining similar employment elsewhere because of his injuries.

It is important that all of the above issues are considered and, if relevant, that they are covered in the proof in some detail, as there is little point in the client and/or his solicitor knowing the extent to which the incident has ruined the client's life, if this is not articulated sufficiently to the court. If a matter is not covered in the client's witness statement, the chances are the court will never hear of it; and if the court is not made aware of all relevant matters, the claimant's solicitor has not achieved one of his main aims, that of maximising the client's damages.

Before finishing the proof in personal injury cases, the client should always be asked whether he has had any pre-existing incident injury which may affect the current case.

The proof should always end with the client's signature and the date on which it was prepared so that, if the client dies prior to the conclusion of the case, the proof will still be of use evidentially.

8.5.2 Proofs in relation to different types of incident

The following types of incident will require the proof to cover certain areas in particular detail.

8.5.2.1 Road traffic incidents

When taking the proof in the case of a road incident, it is important first to have in mind the stretch of road in question. A large-scale map of the area in question is invaluable at this stage, as it will cut short any unproductive argument as to how or where, for example, the road bends. If the client has difficulty explaining how the incident happened, it can be useful to get him to draw a sketch of the relative position of the vehicles involved, or to use toy cars to illustrate what happened. Care should be taken to ensure that the client is entirely clear about the following matters:

(a)   the direction in which he was travelling; ·

(b)   the time of day;

(c)   whether there was anyone else in the car with him;

(d)   the weather conditions;

(e)   the speed of travel;

(f)   familiarity with the car;

(g)   familiarity with the road;

(h)   whether there were any witnesses;

(i)   the make and registration numbers of all vehicles involved;

(j)   who he believes to be responsible for the incident and why;

(k)   what happened immediately after the incident;

(l)   exactly what he said to anyone after the incident;

(m)   exactly what anyone said to him, and whether anyone else heard what was said;

(n)   whether the police were called and, if not, why not;

(o)   if the police were called, which police force and the name of the officer attending;

(p)   whether the client is aware of any pending prosecutions (eg, whether he was warned that he might be prosecuted, or that he might be needed as a witness in the prosecution of the other driver);

(q)   whether he is comprehensively insured and the amount of excess he has to pay on his own insurance policy (his uninsured loss);

(r)   whether he is the owner of the vehicle, and details of the owner if he is not.

If the client wrote anything down at the time of the incident, such as the name and address of the other driver(s), this should be retained. If he explains what happened, for example by referring to the offside and nearside of his vehicle, the solicitor should check that he understands what is meant by those terms. Clients may believe that they have to speak to their solicitor using words which they would not normally use in everyday speech, and consequently they may use words that they do not fully understand. For the avoidance of doubt, the solicitor should check with the client that when referring to a vehicle's 'offside' the client means the driver's side, and that 'nearside' refers to the side of the vehicle nearest the gutter.

In road traffic cases, it is vitally important to trace and interview witnesses as soon as possible. It is unlikely that the witnesses will be known to the client and they may prove difficult to trace if not contacted immediately, and in any event their memory of the events will fade quickly and will therefore be of less use evidentially. The question of whether there are any independent third party witnesses is of central importance, because the case will be much easier to prove if an independent witness can be found who is prepared to give evidence to a court that he saw the incident and believes that the cause of the incident was the fault of the other driver. If the client does not have any details of witnesses, the police accident report may have statements from witnesses whom the solicitor can contact. The police should be notified of all incidents involving personal injury, and will prepare a report on the incident including witness statements (see **10.10.3.1**).

8.5.2.2 Tripping/slipping incidents on public roads and pavements

Tripping and slipping incidents occurring on public roads and pavements are governed by s 41 of the Highways Act 1980, under which the highway authority (usually the local district council responsible for the area in which the fall or trip took place) has a duty to maintain the highway, which includes the pavements used by the public (see **3.5**). It is for the claimant to show that the highway was not reasonably safe. Uneven paving stones or the sites of road improvements with poor temporary surfaces usually claim the most victims. Local authorities sometimes contract out such road works to independent contractors, in which case it may be advisable to sue both the contractor responsible for the safety of the site and the local authority which delegated the improvement work to them. If the client can show that the highway was not reasonably safe, the authority must show that it has taken such care as in all the circumstances was reasonably required to ensure that the highway was not dangerous.

Applying the above rule to the client's proof, it will be necessary to ask the client:

(a)   the time of day;

(b)   the weather conditions;

(c)   whether he was in a hurry or was running at the time of the incident;

(d)   whether he was carrying anything which obscured his view;

(e)   whether there was a warning sign to take care and, if so, what the sign said;

(f)   whether there were any witnesses;

(g)   what sort of shoes the client was wearing; and

(h)   the exact location of the incident.

It will then be necessary to procure photographs of the location without delay, as the local authority may act quickly to repair the relevant area as soon as it becomes aware of a possible claim, in order to show that it has taken such care as in all the circumstances was reasonably required.

8.5.2.3 Incidents at work

The nature of the work process that gave rise to the incident must be thoroughly understood from the outset if the case is to be dealt with properly. The client should be asked to explain:

(a)   his job title;

(b)   what that involves in the work process;

(c)   the level of training or instruction received;

(d)   the level of seniority he held;

(e)   the level of supervision over him;

(f)   whether he can recall any written or oral confirmation of his work duties;

(g)   a description of his usual duties;

(h)   what he was doing on the day in question that gave rise to the incident;

(i)   whether anything out of the ordinary occurred that day;

(j)   details of other similar incidents known to the claimant;

(k)   any representations made by a trade union about the machine or system of work;

(l)   any comments made at health and safety meetings;

(m)   any witnesses to the incident or the unsafe practice.

Trips and slips make up a large proportion of incidents in the workplace and therefore, in addition to the above questions, the client should be asked such questions as are relevant from **8.5.2.2** above.

> **EXAMPLE**
>
> John is an instrument artificer employed to work at a chemical plant. Part of his duties is to check the temperature of certain chemicals stored in large tanks above ground on the site. On the day of the accident, John climbed to the top of a storage tank and removed the outer cover. Without warning, John was blown backwards by excess pressure in the tank, causing him to fall from the tank approximately 4 metres to the ground. Because the chemical was corrosive on contact with the skin, John suffered burns to his face and hands, as well as a damaged spine and broken left leg. John tells you that he has done the same task many times before without incident, but he believes that whoever last checked that particular tank failed adequately to secure the inner seal, so that when he next opened the outer seal the sudden change in pressure was like releasing a cork from a bottle. John tells you that he is usually accompanied by a fellow employee when doing these checks, as the company's safety policy requires this. On the day of the incident, his colleague had telephoned in sick, but the duty manager had not called in anyone else to take his place. John also tells you that the company used to have a nurse on site to deal with minor injuries, but when the last nurse ceased to be employed she was not replaced. John believes that this was because of the expense involved. John also believes that his burns would not be so severe if he had received first aid more quickly.

In the above example, if, when describing any part of his duties, John becomes unclear, he should be asked to explain it again, perhaps drawing a sketch to assist his narrative. It is important that there is no misunderstanding at this stage, as the solicitor will probably use this information as the basis for his statement of case. In addition, if the solicitor is unsure from the client's explanation precisely how the incident happened, it is also likely that a judge will be similarly confused. It is therefore vitally important that any ambiguity is resolved at this point. If ambiguity remains, facilities should be sought for a site inspection. Where the place of work is privately-owned property, and may be a dangerous environment for the visitor, the solicitor must always seek permission from the employer for a site inspection. The inspection can be carried out with the claimant's expert engineer if the accident involves a piece of machinery.

In the above example, it is necessary to include in the proof John's suspicions as to:

(a)   the cause of the incident;

(b)   disregard of safety policy; and

(c)   his belief that the burns were worsened by delay in treatment.

All these matters will have to be checked, however, as the chemical engineer who inspects the plant may conclude that the incident had a completely different cause, possibly involving contributory negligence by John himself. It may be apparent to the engineer that the tank is fitted with a large pressure gauge that John should have checked prior to opening the tank. Similarly, the company safety policy may specify that rubber gloves and a full face mask must be worn when working with corrosive chemicals, and that the burn time for that particular chemical is less than 30 seconds, in which case having medical personnel on site would have made no difference to John's injuries.

8.5.2.4   Clinical negligence claims

In a clinical negligence claim, the client is likely to be in a more confused or uncertain position than in a personal injury matter. While a client is normally able to explain, for example, what occurred during a road traffic incident, he may not understand the treatment and care he received from a medical practitioner. The terminology will be unfamiliar and, in the case of alleged negligence during hospital treatment, the client may not be able to recall or identify the doctors or nurses who treated him.

When obtaining a proof in a clinical negligence case, it is important that every detail is obtained, such as what exactly was said when the claimant attended at the hospital or when the client was asked to sign the consent form.

Unless the alleged negligent act arises out of an illness not previously suffered by the client, full details of any previous medical problems should be obtained. Other matters contained in the proof could be as follows:

(a)   the symptoms which led the client to seek medical advice;

(b)   the information given by the client to the doctor;

(c)   any questions asked by the doctor (eg, where the client went to his GP complaining of headaches, whether the doctor asked the client if he had hit his head or whether the client had been sick – questions which would lead a competent GP to suspect a severe head injury);

(d)   whether the client was given details of a diagnosis at that time;

(e)   what form of treatment was prescribed;

(f)   whether the treatment was explained to the client, and whether he was warned of any potential risks and the likely consequences of not receiving treatment;

(g)   the name of the doctor who treated the client and his status;

(h)   whether the client was receiving treatment from different doctors;

(i)   whether the client asked for a second opinion;

(j)   whether any witnesses were present at the consultation;

(k)   any previous medical problems which could have affected the client;

(l)   whether the client has complained to the hospital/doctor;

(m)   whether the client has received any reply or relevant correspondence;

(n)   whether an apology has been received.

This should be followed by details of the injury in the normal fashion.

In certain cases, it can be useful to ask what prompted the client to contact a solicitor. In some cases, the client is advised by other medical professionals to seek legal advice as they believe that a mistake may have been made.

> **EXAMPLE**
>
> A client injures his leg playing football and attends at the local A&E department. The department is busy and, although the client is sent for an x-ray, the house officer fails to spot the fracture and discharges the client immediately. The client is in considerable pain for a number of weeks and eventually visits his GP, who refers him back to the hospital for another x-ray. In such circumstances, the client may be told that in fact the leg is fractured and that it was missed when the client first attended. Such information is clearly of assistance in assessing liability.

8.6   WELFARE BENEFITS

It will be necessary to advise the client of the welfare benefits he may be entitled to receive because of the incident. It may be months or years before the claim is settled, and if the client is unfit for work, he may experience financial difficulties and feel pressured into accepting the first offer of compensation from the defendant. The solicitor should give the client general advice on the types of benefits that may be available to him in view of his inability or decreased capacity to work, and to assist with the costs of mobility issues, household tasks and child care requirements.

The law relating to state welfare benefits is complex and subject to frequent amendment. In particular, the Welfare Reform Act 2012 (WRA 2012) is bringing in sweeping reforms over the next few years. Details of the benefits which may be available are beyond the scope of this book. If the solicitor is not fully familiar with the current situation regarding available benefits, and the firm does not have a welfare rights adviser, he should give only general advice and tell the client to contact Jobcentre Plus (an agency of the Department for Work and Pensions (DWP)) for further information. The client must act quickly when seeking benefits, as it is not always possible to back-date them.

The client should be advised that where he does qualify for benefits, if his claim is successful there may be some recoupment under the Social Security (Recovery of Benefits) Act 1997. This area is considered in detail in **Chapter 16.**

Lastly, when considering eligibility for benefits, it is necessary to have regard to whether the receipt of compensation will take the claimant out of financial eligibility for means-tested benefits. In *Beattie v Secretary of State for Social Security* [2001] 1 WLR 1404, Charles Beattie was injured in a road traffic accident and rendered quadriplegic. He sued by his litigation friend and Court of Protection receiver, Stephen Beattie. The claimant appealed a decision of the Social Security Commissioner that he was not entitled to income support because payments 'falling to be treated as income' under a structured settlement took him beyond the limit on income for the purpose of claiming income support. This issue was appealed because guidance from the Public Trust Office suggested that, as long as the compensation was held on trust and payments were made on a discretionary basis and were not used to fund items that would normally be paid for using benefits, then those payments would not affect benefit entitlement. In *Beattie* the court ruled that the agreement, as part of the structured settlement, to make regular payments for a fixed number of years was in fact an annuity and was therefore 'capital treated as income' under reg 41(2) of the Income Support (General) Regulations 1987 (SI 1987/1967). The essential difference in this case is that the compensation was paid to the Court of Protection, which would hold the money for the benefit of the patient, rather than simply held on discretionary trust.

8.7 REHABILITATION, EARLY INTERVENTION AND MEDICAL TREATMENT

Where the client has not fully recovered from his injuries at the time of the first interview, the solicitor should explore the possibility of rehabilitation with him. It has long been recognised that a claimant's long-term prognosis can be dramatically improved by the intervention of rehabilitative treatment at the earliest possible opportunity. Examples of such early treatment include surgery, physiotherapy, counselling, occupational therapy, speech therapy and also adaptations to the claimant's home to make his life easier.

The problem in the past was that many claimants were not able to find the funds to pay for the necessary treatment until after their claims for damages for personal injuries were settled. However, over time, insurance companies began to see the clear benefits of early intervention for themselves, even if liability had not yet been determined. Extra sessions of physiotherapy, for example, might speed up the claimant's recovery rate to enable him to return to work earlier than otherwise expected, if he was expected to return to work at all, and this might result in a smaller claim for damages.

The Rehabilitation Code (the 'Code'), which was drafted as a collaborative effort between insurers and personal injury lawyers, was first introduced in 1999 and updated in 2007. A revised Rehabilitation Code is due to become operational from 1 December 2015 (see **Appendix 5**). Its aim, as set out in the introduction to the Code, is to promote the use of rehabilitation and early intervention in the claims process so that the injured person makes the best and quickest possible medical, social and psychological recovery. The Code is designed to apply whatever the severity of the injury suffered by the client.

The Code provides a framework within which all those involved in the claim can work together to ensure that the claimant's needs are assessed at an early stage and appropriate treatment provided as a matter of priority. Both claimants' solicitors and insurers are required to consider whether rehabilitation is appropriate and, if so, to raise the matter with the other party. It should be noted that the provisions of the Code are not mandatory and that the aims of the Code might be achieved by means of an alternative framework agreed between the parties.

For the details of the provisions of the Code, you are referred to the Code itself. Further assistance can be found in APIL's Best practice guide to rehabilitation, 2nd edn (2008).

8.8 CONCLUSION

If the first interview is handled correctly, it should save the solicitor a great deal of time in the future. As personal injury litigation is 'front loaded', much of the essential work is covered during or shortly after the first interview. If essential matters have been missed, old ground will need to be covered again, which will lead to delay and upset for the client, and may allow the opposition to gain the advantage. An overview of matters to be considered is set out below at **8.10**.

8.9 FURTHER READING

The Law Society Initial Interviews Practice Note, 6 October 2011

APIL Best practice guide to rehabilitation, 2nd edn (2008)

8.10 OVERVIEW OF MATTERS TO BE CONSIDERED AT THE FIRST INTERVIEW

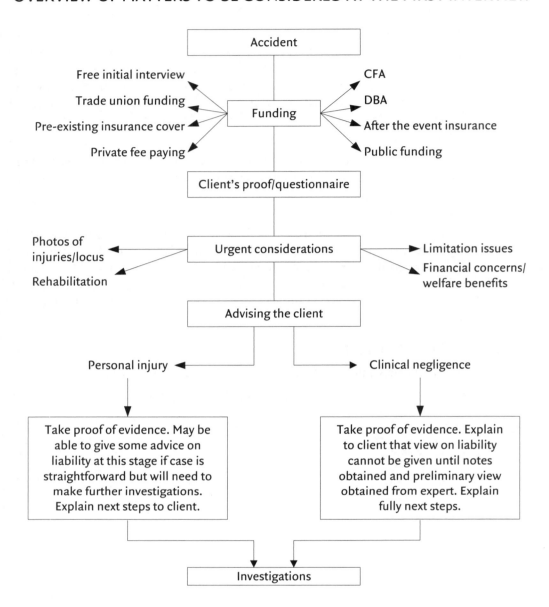

CHAPTER 9

METHODS OF FUNDING AND QUALIFIED ONE WAY COSTS SHIFTING

LEARNING OUTCOMES

After reading this chapter you will be able to:

- describe the methods of funding available to a client
- explain how a conditional fee agreement operates
- explain how a damages-based agreement operates
- understand how qualified one way costs shifting works.

9.1 INTRODUCTION

The ways in which personal injury and clinical negligence claims may be funded and costs recovered by both sides have undergone many changes following the Legal Aid, Sentencing and Punishment of Offenders Act 2012 (LASPO 2012), which came into operation on 1 April 2013. The so-called 'big bang' introduced a new method of funding in the form of damages-based agreements (DBAs) and placed restrictions on the recovery of costs by prohibiting in all but a few cases the recovery of success fees and insurance premiums, applying a new system of qualified one way costs shifting (QOCS). This chapter aims to summarise the methods of funding that are now available and to describe how the new regime of QOCS will be applied.

9.2 METHODS OF FUNDING

9.2.1 Advising the client – the Code of Conduct

The SRA Code of Conduct 2011 (the 'Code') sets out several 'Outcomes', which relate to how a solicitor should advise a client about costs and funding his claim. In particular, Outcome 1.6 requires that you only enter into fee agreements with your client that are legal, and which you consider are suitable for the client's needs and take account of the client's best interests. Outcome 1.13 provides that a solicitor must ensure that a client receives the best possible information about the likely overall cost of his matter, both at the outset and as the matter progresses. The Code also sets out a number of 'Indicative Behaviours' (IBs) which, if followed, indicate that a solicitor has complied with the Code. These IBs include:

(a) warning about any other payments for which the client may be responsible (IB 1.15);

(b) discussing how the client will pay, including whether public funding may be available, whether the client has insurance that might cover the fees, and whether the fees may be paid by someone else such as a trade union (IB 1.16);

(c) where acting for a client under a fee arrangement governed by statute, such as a conditional fee or a damages-based agreement, giving the client all relevant information relating to that arrangement (IB 1.17).

Solicitors should therefore bear in mind these Outcomes and IBs when advising on the funding options outlined below.

9.2.2 Public funding

9.2.2.1 Is legal aid still available?

The majority of personal injury and clinical negligence cases are now outside the scope of public funding, with the exception of:

(a) claims involving neurological injury to a child resulting in severe disability, which arises during pregnancy, childbirth, or in the eight week postnatal period; and

(b) cases which the Director of Legal Aid Casework determines to be 'exceptional' on the basis that to deny legal aid would be a breach of the individual's human rights.

The detail of how to apply for legal aid in such cases is beyond the scope of this book and so what follows is a brief summary.

9.2.2.2 Funding in clinical negligence cases

The LASPO 2012 removed all claims for damages for clinical negligence from the scope of civil legal aid, with one exception: clinical negligence during pregnancy, child birth or the postnatal period (eight weeks), which causes a child to suffer severe disability due to a neurological injury.

The conditions which must be met are set out in LASPO 2012, Sch 1, Pt 1, para 23. They are that:

(a) clinical negligence caused a neurological injury to the individual (V) and, as a result of the neurological injury, V is severely disabled; and

(b) the clinical negligence occurred:
   (i) while V was in his or her mother's womb; or
   (ii) during or after V's birth but before the end of the following period:
     • if V was born before the beginning of the 37th week of pregnancy, the period of eight weeks beginning with the first day of what would have been that week; or
     • if V was born during or after the 37th week of pregnancy, the period of eight weeks beginning with the day of V's birth.

Paragraph 23(5) provides that 'disabled' means 'physical or mentally disabled' and defines 'birth' as 'the moment when an individual first has a life separate from his or her mother'.

The most common scenario is likely to be obstetric negligence where mismanagement of a mother's labour leads to deprivation of oxygen to the baby resulting in brain injury. Alternatively it could be that a serious illness (eg meningitis) is not diagnosed in the early weeks of a baby's life either by a GP or hospital staff.

In addition to falling within the scope of claims described above, it will be necessary for the client to satisfy both financial criteria (under the Civil Legal Aid (Financial Resources and Payment for Services) Regulations 2013 (SI 2013/480)) and merits criteria which are contained in the Civil Legal Aid (Merits Criteria) Regulations 2013 (SI 2013/104). There are essentially two levels of funding which may be granted – Investigative Help and Full Representation.

Investigative Help

Investigative Help will be granted only where the prospects of success on a claim are not clear and substantial work needs to be undertaken before the prospects of success can be determined accurately. Certificates limited to Investigative Help will be subject to a limitation that the certificate covers only the obtaining of medical notes and records, obtaining one medical report per specialism, complying with all steps under the clinical disputes pre-action protocol, considering relevant evidence with counsel or an external solicitor with higher court advocacy rights and experts if necessary, and thereafter obtaining counsel's opinion, up to and including settling proceedings if counsel so advises.

Investigative Help may be refused if it is more appropriate for the client to pursue the NHS complaints procedure than litigation.

Criteria for granting of Full Representation

To qualify for full representation, both the 'cost–benefit' criteria and the 'merits' criteria must be met. In terms of merits, the prospects of success must not be 'poor' or 'borderline' but must be at least 'moderate' (50–60%). The cost–benefit criteria which relate to likely costs versus likely damages are as follows:

(a)   1:1 – for cases with 80% or more prospects of success, the likely damages must at least break even with and should exceed the likely cost in cases with very good prospects of success.

(b)   1:2 – for 60–80% prospects of success, ie the prospects of success are good, likely damages must be at least twice the likely cost.

(c)   1:4 – for cases with 50–60% prospects of success, ie the prospects of success are moderate, likely damages must be at least four times the likely cost.

If the prospect of success and the cost–benefit criteria set out above are satisfied, the solicitor should make an application for Full Representation after the investigative stage. The certificate will then be issued, and will normally be limited to all steps up to and including exchange of statements and reports and CPR Part 35 questioning of experts, and thereafter obtaining counsel's opinion or the opinion of an external solicitor with higher court advocacy rights.

In the event that the claimant wishes to proceed to full trial, the cost–benefit criteria above are reapplied to the case; if the criteria are satisfied then application can be made once again to amend the scope of the Full Representation certificate to cover the cost of trial.

9.2.2.3 'Exceptional funding'

If a case falls outside the scope of legal aid, funding may still be provided if the case is deemed 'exceptional'.

Section 10(3) of LASPO 2012 sets out the test for determination of exceptional funding as follows:

> (3)   For the purposes of subsection (2), an exceptional case determination is a determination—
>
> > (a)   that it is necessary to make the services available to the individual under this Part because failure to do so would be a breach of—
> >
> > > (i)   the individual's Convention rights (within the meaning of the Human Rights Act 1998), or
> > >
> > > (ii)   any rights of the individual to the provision of legal services that are enforceable EU rights, or
> >
> > (b)   that it is appropriate to do so, in the particular circumstances of the case, having regard to any risk that failure to do so would be such a breach

The Lord Chancellor has issued guidance for both inquest and non-inquest cases which would otherwise not qualify for legal aid. Inquest cases are discussed further in **Chapter 17**. As for non-inquest cases, the guidance makes it clear that the overarching question is 'whether the withholding of legal aid would make the assertion of the claim practically impossible or lead to an obvious unfairness in proceedings'. This threshold is very high.

The same means criteria apply to legal aid under the exceptional funding scheme as to general cases, and it will only be available to those claimants of qualifying means who do not have any form of alternative funding, such as before the event (BTE) insurance, and are unable to secure a conditional fee agreement (CFA) or a DBA. The type of claim that is most likely to succeed in an application for exceptional funding is a clinical negligence claim of moderate to high value where the claimant has failed to find a solicitor to accept it as a CFA or a DBA because its merits appear to be moderate rather than good. All clinical negligence claims require medical expert evidence on breach of duty, causation and quantum and involve complex issues of law. It may therefore be possible to assert that the claimant could not represent himself and should therefore qualify for exceptional funding.

9.2.3   Conditional fee agreements

The decline in legal aid has led to a huge increase in CFAs. Under s 58 of the Courts and Legal Services Act 1990 (CLSA 1990), a solicitor and client can agree that the client will have to pay his own solicitor's costs only in certain agreed circumstances or conditions, the condition usually being that the client wins his case (hence 'conditional fee agreement').

Conditional fee agreements have undergone important changes following LASPO 2012, and so what follows is a summary of the position that is in force since those changes came into operation on 1 April 2013. The Law Society has issued a new model CFA, together with a guidance note that should be followed when drafting a CFA.

9.2.3.1   Formal requirements

A CFA is enforceable only if it meets the requirements of ss 58 and 58A of the CLSA 1990, which provide that a CFA:

(a)   must be in writing;

(b)   must state the percentage success fee to be applied (up to a maximum of 100%); and

(c)   may not be used in family and criminal proceedings.

The CFA must be signed by the client and by the legal representative.

There are no statutory requirements regarding information to be given to the client over and above the requirements of the SRA Code of Conduct 2011 (see **9.2** above). Any breaches of the Code will be a professional conduct issue and therefore a matter for the SRA to deal with, but it will not render the CFA unlawful/unenforceable. However, a breach of the CLSA 1990 will render a CFA unenforceable and will prevent the solicitor from recovering any costs.

9.2.3.2   The success fee

If the claim is successful, the solicitor will normally expect to receive an enhanced fee to reflect his 'success'. The enhancement on the fee is a percentage increase on the solicitor's normal fee and not a percentage of damages. The percentage increase on the solicitor's fee is agreed in writing between the client and the solicitor prior to the litigation, and will take into account a number of factors discussed below (see **9.2.5**), including the likelihood of winning the case.

The success fee can be up to 100% of the basic fee. However, for CFAs entered into from 1 April 2013, art 5 of the Conditional Fee Agreements Order 2013 (SI 2013/689) imposes a cap on the recoverable success fee in personal injury and clinical negligence claims of 25% of general damages and past losses less any benefits recoupable by the Compensation Recovery Unit (see **Chapter 16**). This means that the success fee cannot be taken from damages for future losses, such as future care costs.

9.2.3.3   Recovery of the success fee

Prior to 1 April 2013, if the client won his case and the opponent was ordered to pay his costs, these would include the success fee to the extent that it was 'reasonable'. However, for CFAs entered into from that date, s 44 of LASPO 2012 provides that the success fee may no longer be claimed from the other side and so will now be paid by the client out of his damages. As success fees are no longer recoverable as part of costs, the requirement to notify your opponent that you have entered into a CFA (or taken out after the event insurance (AEI)) has gone.

9.2.3.4 Conditional fees and counsel

Where there is a CFA between client and solicitor, counsel's fees are usually dealt with in one of two ways:

(a)   The solicitor enters into a separate CFA with the barrister, in which case:

   (i)   if the client wins the case, the barrister's basic fee will be recovered as a disbursement from the opponent. The solicitor will pay the barrister's 'uplift' agreed in the barrister's CFA, but will have regard to this expense when agreeing his own fee 'uplift' with the client;

   (ii)   if the client loses the case, he will owe the barrister nothing.

(b)   There is no CFA between the barrister and the solicitor, in which case:

   (i)   if the client wins the case and has been paying the barrister's fees on account (ie, up front), there will be no extra success fee to pay, and the barrister's fees can be recovered from the opponent as before;

   (ii)   if the client wins the case and has not been paying the barrister's fees on account, the solicitor will recover that disbursement from the opponent. Because of this greater outlay by the solicitor (and greater financial loss to the firm in the event that the client loses), the solicitor will charge an extra success fee in the event that the client wins;

   (iii)   if the client loses the case and has not been paying the barrister's fees on account, the solicitor is liable to pay them, and will not be able to pass this loss on to the client.

9.2.4   Damages-based agreements

Damages-based agreements were introduced as a method of funding for civil litigation by s 45 of LASPO 2012. Under a DBA, solicitors are not paid if they lose a case, but they may take a percentage of the damages recovered for their client as their fee if the case is successful. Damages-based agreements differ from CFAs because, under a DBA, the payment received by the lawyer is calculated as a percentage of the damages awarded to the client, rather than as an uplift on the lawyer's base costs.

In order to be enforceable, the DBA must comply with s 58AA of the CLSA 1990 and the Damages-Based Agreements Regulations 2013 (SI 2013/609) (DBA Regulations 2013). In summary, to be enforceable the DBA must:

(a)   be in writing;

(b)   specify:

   (i)   the claim or proceedings or parts of them to which the agreement relates;

   (ii)   the circumstances in which the representative's payment, expenses and costs, or part of them, are payable; and

   (iii)   the reason for setting the amount of the payment at the level agreed; and

(c)   not provide for a payment above an amount which, including VAT, is equal to 25% of the combined sums awarded for general damages for pain, suffering and loss of amenity (PSLA) and past pecuniary losses.

9.2.4.1   How do DBAs work?

Costs are recoverable on what is known as the 'Ontario model', since the regime is based on the system that operates in Ontario, Canada. Regulation 4 of the DBA Regulations 2013 states:

(1)   ... a damages-based agreement must not require an amount to be paid by the client other than—

    (a)   the payment, net of—

        (i)   any costs (including fixed costs under Part 45 of the Civil Procedure Rules 1998); and

        (ii)   where relevant, any sum in respect of disbursements incurred by the representative in respect of counsel's fees that have been paid or are payable by another party to the proceedings by agreement or order; and

    (b)   any expenses incurred by the representative, net of any amount which has been paid or is payable by another party to the proceedings by agreement or order.

In other words, the claimant's recoverable costs will be assessed in the conventional way, ie how many hours were reasonably spent on the case, what is a reasonable rate for those hours, etc. If the fee agreed with the lawyer is higher than the figure arrived at through that exercise, the claimant will have to pay the shortfall out of the damages.

EXAMPLE 1

The claimant (C) has entered into a DBA with his solicitor which provides for a contingency fee of 25% and is awarded damages of £100,000. C owes the solicitor £25,000.

If the costs recoverable from the defendant are assessed at £15,000, then C has to pay his solicitor the excess £10,000 out of his damages – ie, C receives £90,000 of the damages.

Accordingly, the existence of a DBA will not increase the amount of the defendant's costs liability. It may, however, decrease the defendant's costs liability. The indemnity principle applies to DBAs, so that the claimant cannot recover more in costs than he is liable to pay his own lawyer. Therefore, if the agreed contingency fee is lower than the figure arrived at through a traditional costs assessment, the defendant will only have to pay the lower amount.

EXAMPLE 2

Continuing the scenario in Example 1 above, if the assessed costs are £30,000 then the defendant only has to pay the lower contingency fee figure of £25,000 due to the indemnity principle, and there is nothing further for C to pay his lawyer.

9.2.4.2 The 25% cap

Regulation 4(2) of the DBA Regulations 2013 provides that:

(2)   In a claim for personal injuries—

    (a)   the only sums recovered by the client from which the payment shall be met are—

        (i)   general damages for pain, suffering and loss of amenity; and

        (ii)   damages for pecuniary loss other than future pecuniary loss, net of any sums recoverable by the Compensation Recovery Unit of the Department for Work and Pensions; and

    (b)   ... a damages-based agreement must not provide for a payment above an amount which, including VAT, is equal to 25% of the combined sums in paragraph (2)(a)(i) and (ii) which are ultimately recovered by the client.

EXAMPLE 3

Mr Brown enters into a DBA with his solicitor which provides for a contingency fee of 25%. Mr Brown is awarded £70,000 damages for PSLA, £30,000 for past loss of earnings and £400,000 for future loss of earnings. The contingency fee will be £25,000 (25% of the combined sums for PSLA and past loss of earnings). The £400,000 awarded to Mr Brown for future losses cannot be touched.

The 25% cap will apply only to claims or proceedings at first instance, not to appeals.

9.2.5   Risk assessment for CFAs and DBAs

In order to decide:

(a)   whether to take a potential claim on *at all* on a CFA or DBA basis; and

(b)   once the decision has been made to accept the client's case on that basis, what is the appropriate level of fee to apply to the agreement,

it will be necessary for the claimant's solicitor to undertake assessment of the risk of the potential claim in every case.

The method of risk assessment adopted will differ from one firm to another, with some adopting paper-based systems and others utilising computer software to capture basic information and assist in speeding up the risk assessment process. Whichever method is used, the underlying principles are the same.

Principles of risk assessment

The *Oxford English Dictionary* defines 'risk' as 'the chance or possibility of loss or bad consequence'. If a solicitors' firm accepts a case on a 'no win, no fee' basis, it exposes itself to the risk of loss in not getting paid for the work it has done on behalf of the client. However, this is only half of the equation. There is equally the chance of a successful outcome. So risk assessment can be seen as the process of balancing the risk of losing against the chance of winning. That is easy enough to say, but rather more difficult to quantify objectively in a way that gives predictable and workable results. Nevertheless, this is exactly what a personal injury practitioner has to do when deciding whether or not to take a case on a CFA or DBA basis.

Practice of risk assessment

In practice, the skill of the personal injury practitioner will be in his ability to spot the factors relevant to risk and then go on to assess the severity of that risk. The majority of firms make use of a checklist for this purpose, which may be paper- or electronically based.

The factors relevant to risk (or hazards) will include anything that could harm the claim. The risk will be the percentage chance that the factor will actually occur.

Common risk factors will include:

(a)   *The facts*: is the client a credible witness and are there any other witnesses who will confirm his version?

(b)   *Liability*: will the client be able to show that there was a relevant duty of care and that this duty has been breached?

(c)   *Causation*: will the client be able to show that the injuries sustained are causally linked to the accident?

(d)   *Limitation*: are there any issues due to limitation of claims or delay (ie 'stale' evidence)?

(e)   *The potential defendant*: is the opponent a 'viable' source of damages – does he carry insurance or have funds to meet a damages claim, and have insurance details been confirmed?

(f)   *Loss and damage*: can the losses sustained be proved by way of medical and other forms of evidence?

The second stage in the risk assessment is to assess the chance of each of the above risk factors actually occurring and harming the viability of the case. To do this, each factor needs to be categorised or 'scored' in some way. This can be done by giving each factor a percentage, or a score between 1 and 10 or, more simply still, by assessing it as a high, medium or low risk.

Based on the result (or score) from the above assessment, a risk assessment co-ordinator (usually a partner in the firm) will judge whether to accept the case on a conditional fee basis and, if so, on what level of success fee. In the event that he is unable to do so, because of insufficient information being available, he will pass the file back to the case worker for further investigation, for example obtaining witness statements or contacting the police for clarification of key issues.

In the event that the claim is accepted on a CFA or DBA basis, it is essential to record the reasoning behind the decision and the reason for the success fee claimed, as this will be needed in the event that the claim is successful and either the client (or the opponent in the case of a CFA entered into prior to 1 April 2013) wishes to challenge the level of the success fee.

9.2.6 After the event insurance

The client's potential liability to pay the other side's costs and disbursements and his own disbursements can be insured against by what is often referred to as 'after the event' insurance (AEI). The risk of having to pay the other side's costs has greatly diminished following the introduction of qualified one way costs shifting (see **9.3** below) but nevertheless there may still be potential costs that an unsuccessful client may be liable to pay.

As the name suggests, AEI is taken out only once the need for the legal action has become apparent but before the proceedings have commenced. Here, the insurance is not against the risk of litigation but merely against the risk of having to pay the other side's costs and disbursements should the litigation fail, and it can cover the cost of the party's own disbursements as well. This type of insurance can be obtained alongside a CFA, a DBA or on its own. If necessary, many AEI insurers will arrange a loan to the client to fund both the disbursements and the cost of the AEI premium. If he wins, the interest on the loan is not recoverable from his opponent but is usually deducted from the damages recovered.

9.2.6.1 Can the premium be recovered?

As with success fees, for AEI policies entered into before 1 April 2013 the AEI premium for insuring against liability to pay the other side's costs and disbursements is recoverable from the loser provided it is reasonable. However, for policies entered into after 1 April 2013, the premium will not be recoverable from the other side.

Clinical negligence proceedings are treated as a special category. Regulation 3 of the Recovery of Costs Insurance Premiums in Clinical Negligence Proceedings (No 2) Regulations 2013 (SI 2013/739) states:

> (1) A costs order made in favour of a party to clinical negligence proceedings who has taken out a costs insurance policy may include provision requiring the payment of an amount in respect of all or part of the premium of that policy if—
>
> > (a) the financial value of the claim for damages in respect of clinical negligence is more than £1,000; and
> >
> > (b) the costs insurance policy insures against the risk of incurring a liability to pay for an expert report or reports relating to liability or causation in respect of clinical negligence (or against that risk and other risks).
>
> (2) The amount of the premium that may be required to be paid under the costs order shall not exceed that part of the premium which relates to the risk of incurring liability to pay for an expert report or reports relating to liability or causation in respect of clinical negligence in connection with the proceedings.

Therefore, in clinical negligence cases, a party may recover the cost of an AEI premium taken out to cover the risk of having to pay for his own or the other side's costs in relation to obtaining expert evidence on liability and causation (but not quantum). The reasoning behind this exception to the normal rules is that clinical negligence claimants should not be deterred from pursuing their case by the unusually heavy burden of expert evidence required in such cases.

9.2.6.2 Staged AEI premiums

There are many different types of AEI policy, and it is important to shop around to find one that is appropriate for a client's particular case. One popular form of AEI is where the premiums are 'staged'.

The way this works is as follows: with traditional AEI insurance, the underwriter considers the level of risk of the claimant losing and sets a premium accordingly. In so doing, he bears in mind that the majority of claims are settled either pre- or post-issue, but long before trial. Another big tranche of claims will fight on at least until directions are complied with (so that each side has had the benefit of full disclosure from the opposition) and will then settle before being set down for trial. Only a small number of claims will go on to trial. By staging premiums at these trigger points (pre-issue, on setting down for trial, commencement of trial), the insurer can set a lower premium earlier on (accurately reflecting the risk) and an appropriately larger premium only for those cases that do not settle at an early stage. Clearly, a claim which does not settle until trial has a much greater prospect of going to trial, and is therefore much more likely actually to fail on liability and land the insurer with a big bill for the other side's costs. Hence the nearer the claim is to trial, the higher the AEI premium should be.

9.2.7 Legal expenses insurance

The client may have legal expenses insurance (known as 'before the event' or 'BTE' insurance) as a part of either his home or motor insurance policy, or as an extra service from his credit card provider, or as an extra for which he has paid an additional premium. This is something that the client may either be unaware of or have forgotten, and it is therefore important that this is considered at the first interview.

Where the client has the benefit of a BTE insurance policy, the presumption is that he will use it rather than take out additional insurance in the form of an AEI policy. There is no need to enter into a CFA or DBA because BTE insurance generally covers both sides' costs. However, the level and type of cover available under the BTE policy should be checked to make sure it is suitable. Many BTE policies have a limit of indemnity of £25,000, which may not be sufficient to cover the larger multi-track cases. If the cover is insufficient then it may well be reasonable to enter into a CFA or DBA and to take out AEI instead.

In *Sarwar v Alam* [2001] EWCA Civ 1401, the claimant had taken out an AEI policy when there was the opportunity to benefit from an existing legal expenses insurance policy or BTE insurance. In the costs-only proceedings, the issue was whether the AEI premium was recoverable. The Court of Appeal gave guidance that although a solicitor is not obliged to embark on a 'treasure hunt' in relation to pre-existing insurance, a solicitor should develop a practice of sending a standard letter requesting sight of:

(a) any relevant motor insurance policy;

(b) any household insurance policy;

(c) any stand-alone BTE insurance policy belonging to the client and/or any spouse or partner living in the same household, and, if possible, their driver (if they are an injured passenger), in advance of the first interview.

A decision then needs to be made about whether any legal expenses insurance policy is satisfactory. The Court emphasised that the decision related to small road traffic accident claims with a quantum of £5,000 or less and that enquiries should be proportionate. (See also *Kilby v Gawith* [2008] WLR (D) 163.)

As with union-funded work (see **9.2.8** below), the insurer may have nominated firms of solicitors who must be instructed to undertake the insured's claim. If the insured is free to instruct the solicitor of his choice, it is usual for the insurer to require the solicitor to report to it regularly on the progress of the case. In terms of confidentiality, it is essential for the solicitor to explain to the client at the outset that a term of the insurance is that the insurer has the right to receive reports on the viability of the case and whether or not it is worthwhile to continue with it. The progress of the case can be slowed down considerably by the obligation on the solicitor to report back to the insurer to seek approval (and therefore funding) to continue with the claim to the next stage.

9.2.7.1 Choice of solicitor under legal expenses insurance policies

The Insurance Companies (Legal Expenses Insurance) Regulations 1990 (SI 1990/1159) give effect to Directive 87/344/EEC. The Regulations cover, amongst other things, BTE insurance cover in respect of road traffic accidents. Regulation 6 of the 1990 Regulations specifies:

> 6. Freedom to choose a lawyer
>
> (1) Where under a legal expenses insurance contract recourse is had to a lawyer ... to defend, represent or serve the interests of the insured in any *enquiry or proceedings*, the insured shall be free to choose that lawyer (or other person). (emphasis added)

The interpretation given to the term 'enquiry or proceedings' will determine whether or not the insured person does have freedom to choose his lawyer. Some insurance companies providing legal expenses insurance (LEI) cover put a narrow interpretation on it, saying that only when there are actual court proceedings is there any freedom for the policy holder to choose. The insurer will often prefer to refer the insured's claim to its panel of solicitors only, effectively concentrating the bulk of claims to so-called 'panel firms'. Not all LEI providers operate panels of preferred solicitors but many do, citing quality assurance and consistency of claims handling as the rationale for insisting on operating panels to which to channel claims. Non-panel firms see this as damaging to their position, as they may be forced to advise clients that they should avail themselves of pre-existing LEI cover rather than take up the non-panel solicitors' offer to work on the basis of a CFA or DBA. The non-panel solicitors will often take the view that the wording of reg 6(1) of the 1990 Regulations should be given a wide interpretation, and 'enquiry or proceedings' will encompass the work undertaken at pre-issue stage under the pre-action protocol. Their justification for this is due to the 'front loading' of litigation, where much of the work and advice is, of necessity, conducted before the issue of proceedings.

A case which illustrates many of the points outlined above is *Chappell v De Bora's of Exeter* (SCCO, 2004). This is a Supreme Court Costs Office case in which the costs claim of a non-panel local firm of solicitors was allowed despite the existence of pre-existing LEI. The facts briefly are as follows. The claimant's claim was in respect of the personal injuries she suffered when she fell down some steps at the defendant's shop in Exeter. The claimant, who lived near Exeter, instructed solicitors in Exeter. They entered into a CFA with a success fee of 71%. They also arranged a policy of AEI and corresponded with DAS, the legal expenses insurers with whom the claimant had an existing BTE insurance policy. DAS said that, under the terms of her policy with them, the claimant was obliged to instruct solicitors who were on their panel for any work which had to be done before the issue of proceedings, although she was entitled to instruct the solicitors of her choice for the purpose of the proceedings themselves should proceedings be necessary. The claimant's solicitors (who were not on the DAS panel) undertook the usual pre-proceedings work, including sending the letter of claim, taking witness evidence and obtaining two medical reports. The defendant's solicitors eventually offered to settle the matter for £31,156 plus costs. This offer was accepted, but the issue of costs could not be agreed and, following detailed assessment, the defendant was given permission to appeal on the issue of whether it was reasonable for the claimant to enter into a CFA with a success fee and AEI with the solicitors of her choice, when BTE insurance was available but the claimant's chosen solicitors were not on the BTE insurers' panel.

The defendant's counsel submitted that the onus was on the claimant to show why it was reasonable, on the standard basis, that the more expensive route of proceedings under a CFA with AEI should have been adopted. He submitted that solicitors on the DAS panel up and down the country conducted very many cases no less serious and complex than the present case on a regular basis. He accepted what the Master of the Rolls had said in *Sarwar v Alam* (see **9.2.7** above).

> In this case we are concerned only with a relatively small personal injury claim in a road traffic accident. We are not concerned with claims which look as if they will exceed about £5,000, and we are not concerned with any other type of BTE claim. We have no doubt that, if a claimant possesses pre-existing BTE cover which appears to be satisfactory for a claim of that size, then in the ordinary course of things that claimant should be referred to the relevant BTE insurers.

The claimant's counsel submitted that this was not a straightforward case and that the amount of the damages, in excess of £31,000, reflected those complexities. It had been reasonable for the claimant to go to solicitors in Exeter to handle her case rather than to solicitors in Bristol or Salisbury. He submitted that the costs which the district judge had allowed were proportionate in relation to a multi-track case of this nature. The judge concluded that it was reasonable in a case of this kind for the claimant to instruct the solicitors of her choice in Exeter rather than DAS panel solicitors, the nearest of whom would have been many miles away from where she lived. Accordingly, he dismissed the appeal in so far as it related to the claimant's choice of solicitor.

9.2.8 Trade unions

If the client has had an accident at work and belongs to a trade union, he may be entitled to receive free access to legal advice as part of his membership. This is something of which the client may not be aware initially, and the solicitor should therefore cover this point at the first interview.

If the client is entitled to advice through his union, the union may have its own legal department or nominated solicitors whom it always uses. If this is the case, the solicitor first consulted by the client is unlikely to be instructed, but should nevertheless advise the client to seek advice from his union on this point. The advantage to the client, if he is able to procure the support of union funding, is that, provided he has paid his membership fees to the union, he will have the full financial support of the union behind him. His solicitor will still have to convince the union as to the merits of the case, and will also be obliged to report on the case prior to proceeding with it. However, the claimant will not have to worry that part of his damages may be taken away to pay his legal expenses, as would be the case if he were funded either through public funding or via a CFA or DBA.

9.2.9 Private fee-paying clients

Some clients will have no alternative but to fund their cases privately, or may choose to do so in any event. In such circumstances the solicitor is required under the Code of Conduct to explain to the client fully his liability for costs and disbursements. The solicitor should give the best information on costs that he can, including likely disbursements and the hourly rate that the solicitor proposes to charge (as to which see **9.2.1** above and **Legal Foundations**, Professional Conduct).

9.3 QUALIFIED ONE WAY COSTS SHIFTING

On 1 April 2013, 'qualified one way costs shifting' (QOCS) was introduced for personal injury and clinical negligence claims. This means that although a defendant will still generally be ordered to pay the costs of a successful claimant, subject to certain exceptions, a defendant will not recover his own costs if he successfully defends the claim. The new rules are contained in CPR, rr 44.13–44.17 and PD 44 General Rules About Costs, paras 12.1–12.7.

9.3.1 When will QOCS apply?

Rule 44.13(1) provides that QOCS applies to proceedings which include a claim for damages:

(a)   for personal injuries;

(b)   under the Fatal Accidents Act 1976; or

(c)   which arises out of death or personal injury and survives for the benefit of an estate by virtue of s 1(1) of the Law Reform (Miscellaneous Provisions) Act 1934.

It also applies where a person brings a counterclaim or an additional claim for such damages.

9.3.2   How does it work?

Rule 44.14 sets out the basic rule that:

(1)   ... orders for costs made against a claimant may be enforced without the permission of the court but only to the extent that the aggregate amount in money terms of such orders does not exceed the aggregate amount in money terms of any orders for damages and interest made in favour of the claimant.

(2)   Orders for costs made against a claimant may only be enforced after the proceedings have been concluded and the costs have been assessed or agreed.

Rule 44.14 does permit costs orders to be made and enforced against claimants, but only to the extent that those costs do not exceed the total damages the claimant recovers. Therefore the effect is that a claimant who loses (and so has no damages against which an order for costs can be enforced) will not have to pay the defendant's costs. However, it does not preclude a successful claimant being deprived of all or part of his costs, or ordered to pay the defendant's costs, in other circumstances. Enforcement of any such costs order cannot take place until after the conclusion of the proceedings. The intention is to enable costs orders to be made in the usual way against a claimant who fails to beat a Part 36 offer, loses an application or fails to comply with court orders and directions.

9.3.3   Exceptions when QOCS will not apply

Rules 44.15 and 44.16 set out the exceptions:

(a)   *The claim is found on the balance of probabilities to be 'fundamentally dishonest'.* Practice Direction Costs, para 12.4 provides that the court will normally direct that allegations of fundamental dishonesty will be determined at trial. The intention is that sham accidents and other totally dishonest claims will lose the protection of QOCS. In *Gosling v Screwfix and another* (Cambridge County Court, 29 March 2014), it was held that the claim was fundamentally dishonest for the purposes of QOCS and, as a result, the claimant was ordered to pay the defendant's costs on the indemnity basis. The judge found that the claimant had suffered an injury and had not been dishonest about the accident circumstances. However, the claimant had significantly exaggerated the extent of his ongoing symptoms, and the effect of the discovery of this deceit reduced the value of his claim by half.

The term 'fundamental dishonesty' has now been incorporated into s 57 of the Criminal Justice and Courts Act 2015 (see **1.4**) which will apply to all proceedings issued on or after 13 April 2015. If a claim is struck out under this section, the court must record the amount that the claimant would have received for any genuine element of the claim if it had not been dismissed. The claimant will be ordered to pay the defendant's costs, but the amount recorded for the genuine element will be deducted from the amount that the claimant will have to pay.

(b)   *The claim is struck out as disclosing no reasonable grounds for bringing the proceedings, or as an abuse of process, or for conduct likely to obstruct the just disposal of the proceedings.*

(c)   *The proceedings include a claim which is made for the financial benefit of a person other than the claimant.* Practice Direction Costs gives examples of such claims as subrogated claims for damages for the repair of a motor vehicle in an RTA or for credit hire of a replacement vehicle where the beneficiary of the claim is the claimant's insurer. The intention here is to prevent insurers persuading a lay claimant to make a claim for a minor personal injury and to include the claim for repairs or car hire, thereby enabling the insurer to obtain the benefit of QOCS. In such a case, the rules expressly give the court the power to make a costs order against a person other than the claimant, ie generally the injured claimant will retain the QOCS protection for the injury element of the claim.

It is expected that there will be some satellite litigation with regard to the interpretation of these new rules.

9.4 CONCLUSION

Personal injury lawyers are facing challenging times following the implementation of these new rules on costs and funding, and it will take time before we can assess their true impact.

The introduction of QOCS was aimed at counter-balancing the impact on personal injury claimants of the decision to abolish recoverability of CFA success fees and, in particular, ATE insurance premiums. The intention behind QOCS is to make ATE insurance unnecessary for personal injury actions, since the claimant will not be liable for the defendant's costs if the claim fails. It is not clear how effective this will be in practice, however, for the following reasons:

(a) The fact that the claimant can lose the QOCS protection where the defendant has made a Part 36 offer means that the claimant will potentially be back on risk for costs whenever a Part 36 offer is made, though only up to the amount of the claimant's damages. If ATE cover is available in respect of this risk, and is taken out, the premium will not be recoverable.

(b) After the event insurance is also taken out, normally, to cover own disbursements as well as adverse costs. The Government has carved out from the reforms the cost of ATE premiums to cover expert reports on liability and causation in clinical negligence cases, but the cost of ATE cover in respect of other disbursements will not be recoverable.

Not surprisingly, there was a significant increase in the number of CFAs and AEI policies entered into immediately before 1 April 2013. So far the profession has not shown any enthusiasm for DBAs.

CHAPTER 10

INVESTIGATING THE CLAIM AND PRELIMINARY STEPS

LEARNING OUTCOMES

After reading this chapter you will be able to:

- set out the main requirements of the pre-action protocols for personal injury claims, disease and illness claims, and clinical disputes, and the Practice Direction on pre-action conduct
- identify the appropriate defendant in personal injury and clinical negligence cases
- set out the preliminary steps in such cases
- draft an appropriate letter of claim on behalf of the claimant
- respond appropriately on behalf of the defendant
- appreciate the different types of evidence which may be available and understand how to go about collecting such evidence.

10.1 INTRODUCTION

During the first interview, the claimant's solicitor will have taken a proof of evidence from his client, who may have been able to supply additional evidence, such as documents or photographs. However, in all but the most straightforward low value personal injury cases, further information will be required before the claimant's solicitor is able to send either the Claim Notification Form (CNF) in a case falling within the scope of one of the low value pre-action protocols, or a letter of claim in all other cases. In all cases where settlement is not reached prior to commencement, full investigations must be made before proceedings are issued.

The defendant may contact his solicitor immediately after the incident which has given rise to the potential claim, but in many cases the defendant's solicitor or the defendant's insurer's solicitor will become involved only after the letter of claim or the CNF has been received. In any event, the defendant's solicitor must also make full investigations and, where a claim is to be defended, gather evidence in support of his client's case.

Solicitors acting for both parties should be keen to gather evidence quickly, while events are fresh in the minds of clients and witnesses, and before real and documentary evidence is repaired, misplaced or destroyed. In this chapter, the investigations that should be made will be outlined. This chapter will also deal with the procedural steps that must be taken before proceedings are issued. In this regard, the parties and their solicitors are guided by the relevant pre-action protocols (PAPs).

10.2 PRE-ACTION PROTOCOLS

Solicitors dealing with personal injury and clinical negligence claims must be familiar with the PAPs relating to these claims and the associated Practice Direction. There are a number of protocols, and it is important to ensure that the correct one is consulted for each individual claim. Sanctions may be imposed by the court for non-compliance with the requirements of the PAPs, although it is unlikely to be concerned with minor or technical shortcomings.

The protocols considered in this book are as follows:

(a) PAP for Personal Injury Claims (revised April 2015). This is primarily designed for PI claims which are likely to be allocated to the fast track, and to the entirety of such claims (for example, to any property damage resulting from the incident causing the injury). It does not apply to cases which would properly fall under any of the other PAPs listed below; but, if a case commenced under either of the Low Value PAPs ((d) and (e) below) exits the Portal for any reason, it would then fall under this PAP. This PAP is equally appropriate to higher value claims, and the spirit (if not the letter) of the PAP should be followed for claims which could potentially be allocated to the multi-track. This PAP is set out in full in **Appendix 2**.

(b) PAP for Disease and Illness Claims. This is the correct protocol to use for all personal injury claims where the injury takes the form of an illness or disease, eg mesothelioma, asthma or dermatitis, which arises through working in or occupying premises or using products (and which do not fall under the PAP for Low Value Personal Injury (Employers' Liability and Public Liability) Claims). These claims are likely to be complex and therefore unsuitable for fast track procedures, even where the value is less than £25,000. This PAP is not reproduced in this book, but may be found on the Ministry of Justice website. (CPR, PD 3D, which gives further assistance in relation to mesothelioma claims, is beyond the scope of this book.)

(c) PAP for the Resolution of Clinical Disputes (revised April 2015). This is the correct protocol to use for claims against hospitals, GPs, dentists and other healthcare providers (both NHS and private) which involve an injury that is alleged to be the result of clinical negligence. The PAP recognises that it is in the interests of everyone involved – patients, healthcare professionals and providers – that patients' concerns, complaints and claims are dealt with quickly, efficiently and professionally, and that the patient/clinician relationship is preserved if at all possible, not least because the patient may need further treatment. This PAP is set out in full in **Appendix 3**.

(d) PAP for Low Value Personal Injury Claims in Road Traffic Accidents. This is the correct protocol to use where a claim for general and special damages for personal injury resulting from an RTA (excluding damage to the vehicle and hire costs) is valued at no more than £25,000, the value for pain, suffering and loss of amenity exceeds £1,000, and the CNF was sent on or after 31 July 2013. (The previous version of this PAP, dealing with claims of up to £10,000, shall continue to have effect in respect of any claim where the CNF was sent before 31 July 2013.) There are exclusions, set out in para 4.5 of the PAP, such as where the claimant or defendant is either a personal representative of a deceased person or is a protected party (for protected party, see **Chapter 20**).

Claims commenced under this PAP may cease to be governed by it in a number of circumstances, such as where the defendant defends the claim or admits negligence but alleges contributory negligence (other than simple failure to wear a safety belt). The PAP is not reproduced in this book, but the main elements of the PAP and the associated practice direction are set out in **Chapter 21**.

(e)   PAP for Low Value Personal Injury (Employers' Liability and Public Liability) Claims. This is the correct protocol to use where damages for personal injury in an employers' liability or public liability claim are valued at no more than £25,000 and the accident occurred on or after 31 July 2013 or, in a disease claim, no letter of claim was sent before 31 July 2013 (although there are exclusions – see para 4.3 of the PAP). As in (d) above, there are circumstances where claims commenced under this PAP may cease to be governed by it. This PAP is set out in full in **Appendix 4** and is covered in more depth in **Chapter 21**.

In addition to these protocols, there is a Practice Direction on pre-action conduct ('PD Pre-action Conduct') which describes the conduct the court will normally expect of the prospective parties prior to the start of the proceedings.

The PAPs deal with such matters as the letter of claim and the defendant's response, but before the claimant's solicitor can think about writing the letter of claim, he will need to investigate the matter further and ensure that he has identified the correct defendant.

10.3   IDENTIFYING THE DEFENDANT

One of the first issues for the claimant's solicitor to deal with is the identification of the defendant and, in many cases, this will be straightforward. However, this question should always be addressed carefully by the claimant's solicitor, as sometimes the issue may not be as simple as it appears, and it is crucial to issue proceedings within the primary limitation period against the correct defendant.

Generally, there is little point in pursuing a claim against a defendant unless he is insured, or has the means with which to pay the judgment sum. It is important to note that, for the purposes of the two PAPs for low value claims, the CNF will be sent to the insurer and it will be necessary, therefore, to make a reasonable attempt to identify the insurer. The means of doing so are set out at **10.3.1** and **10.3.2** below.

10.3.1   Road traffic incidents and other highway claims

In a road traffic accident claim, it is necessary to establish not only the name of the driver of the vehicle and his insurance position, but also the name of the owner of the vehicle and of his insurer. Under the Fourth EU Motor Insurance Directive, it is a requirement that the insurer of a vehicle must be readily identifiable from the vehicle registration number. Therefore, when trying to trace the owner and insurer of a vehicle involved in a road traffic accident, if the claimant has taken down the registration of the other driver's vehicle, the solicitor should be able to trace the insurance details. The UK insurance industry has met this requirement by introducing the Motor Insurance Database (MID), which provides details of all vehicles and their associated insurance policies. Individual firms of solicitors can apply for a licence to operate the MID system, allowing them almost instant access to insurance details of third parties, accessed by means of the vehicle registration mark. A savvy client may have used the 'askMID Roadside' service to obtain these details at the time of the accident (see **3.3.4**).

10.3.1.1   Driving in the course of employment

Frequently, the driver may be using a vehicle owned and insured by his employer. In such cases, the claim would normally be issued against the employer (or vehicle operator in the case of commercial vehicles). If it is unclear whether or not the driver was acting within the course of employment, it is usual to sue both the driver and the employer. Similarly, if protective proceedings are necessary to avoid the claim being statute-barred under the LA 1980 (see **7.9.2**), and there is insufficient time to investigate the issue of vicarious liability properly, the claim should be issued against both driver and employer.

10.3.1.2 Insured drivers – naming the insurer as defendant

Under reg 3 of the European Communities (Rights against Insurers) Regulations 2002 (SI 2002/3061), where a claimant has a claim in tort against an insured person arising out of an accident, he has a direct right of action in the courts against the driver's insurer. This means that he can issue proceedings against the insurer alone, or in addition to the driver. How this is dealt with in practice varies. Some solicitors acting for claimants always issue proceedings directly against insurers where they are able to do so; some never do so. On a practical level, it is unlikely to make any measurable difference to how the proceedings are conducted or to the final outcome. Where a driver is insured, it will be the insurance company and its solicitors who will determine how the proceedings are conducted, and it will be the insurance company who will pay up, should liability be established, whether or not it is named as a defendant. Under the terms of the policy, the driver will be obliged to cooperate with the insurer in defending the matter, including giving evidence at trial if necessary, whether or not he is named as a defendant.

10.3.1.3 Invalid insurance – Road Traffic Act 1988, ss 151 and 152

Sometimes, a situation will arise where a vehicle was covered by a policy of insurance at the time of the accident, but the policy did not cover the driver or the insurer has grounds to void the policy. The claimant should not be dissuaded from commencing proceeding against the driver on the grounds that he may be impecunious, as the insurance company will be obliged to pay out on the judgment to the claimant, provided the correct notice is given (see **3.3** and **12.3.2**).

10.3.1.4 Uninsured drivers

Where an accident occurring on or after 1 August 2015 is caused by an uninsured driver, an application should be made to the Motor Insurers' Bureau (MIB) under the Uninsured Drivers' Agreement 2015, and under previous versions of the Agreement for accidents occurring before that date (see **3.4.1**). If the MIB declines liability, proceedings should be commenced against the driver, as first defendant, and the MIB, as second defendant. If the driver is found to be liable, the MIB must satisfy the judgment, provided the claimant has followed the steps set out in the Agreement.

10.3.1.5 Untraced drivers

Where the accident is caused by a 'hit and run' driver who cannot be traced, it will not be possible to commence court proceedings. Instead, an application should be made to the MIB on behalf of the injured party under the Untraced Drivers Agreement 2003. This scheme is considered in **3.4.2**.

10.3.1.6 Highway authorities, statutory undertakers and other owners of the highway

Where there are indications that the actions or omissions of a highway authority, statutory undertaker or some other owner of the highway have caused or contributed to the claimant's accident, enquiries may be made of the local council in order to identify who that body is. Every council is obliged to keep and allow access to records detailing the ownership of highway land within its area (see **3.5.1**); and it will also have information about any activities of statutory undertakers on highway land, as the council operates a licensing system (see **3.5.2.4**). Whilst highway authorities and statutory undertakers will always have public liability insurance, other owners of the highway may not.

10.3.2 Employers' liability claims

If an incident occurs at work, notwithstanding that the incident was caused by another employee or someone acting as agent for the employer, provided that person was acting in the course of employment, it is usual to sue the employer only (see **4.4**). (Although the defendant will generally be the employer, a claim may also be made against the occupier of the premises, or against the person with control of the premises if different from the employer. This lies beyond the scope of this book.) All employers should have appropriate insurance, although a minority of rogue employers may not, and the claimant's solicitor should carry out a database search through the Employers' Liability Tracing Office in order to establish the identity of the insurer.

10.3.3 Cases involving negligence of doctors and medical staff

10.3.3.1 Claims arising out of NHS hospital treatment

If the claim arises out of treatment in a hospital by an employee of the NHS, the relevant NHS Trust or Foundation Trust is named as the defendant. It is not appropriate to sue individual doctors or nurses in the direct employment of the Trust.

In order to identify the name and address of the relevant Trust, a search can be made on the NHS website at <www.nhs.uk> by typing in the name of the hospital.

The National Health Service Litigation Authority (NHSLA) is responsible for handling all clinical negligence claims against NHS bodies and their employees, who are indemnified under the Clinical Negligence Scheme for Trusts. The NHSLA has a panel of firms of solicitors to deal with such claims on its behalf (see **5.7**).

10.3.3.2 General practitioners

General practitioners (GPs) are almost always self-employed, and they contract their services to the NHS. A GP is liable for his own acts and for the acts of his employees. General practitioners often operate in partnerships, and in such cases, the claim may be issued against the individual GP concerned or against the partnership. General practitioners will carry indemnity insurance from an organisation such as the Medical Defence Union or the Medical Protection Society.

10.3.3.3 Private hospitals and clinics

If the claim arises out of treatment in a private hospital or clinic, the decision as to who should be named as the defendant will depend upon the basis of the claim. The doctors and some other healthcare providers will usually be independent contractors. Where it is their breach of duty which has led to the claim, the claim should be issued against them as individuals, as vicarious liability is not applicable. They will be indemnified by their own medical defence organisations.

The hospital or clinic will provide premises and equipment for the use of independent contractors and will employ the staff who run and administer the hospital or clinic, and this will usually include nursing staff. If the claim arises as a result of defective or inadequate premises or equipment or the actions of employees, the hospital or clinic should be named as defendant. It will carry its own insurance. The hospital or clinic will advise the claimant's solicitor as to the position of individuals who are employed or who otherwise use their premises.

10.3.3.4 Private treatment from dentists

A dentist treating private patients is not under any statutory or professional requirement to have insurance cover in respect of professional negligence – although the majority are insured.

10.4 CLINICAL NEGLIGENCE CLAIMS – PRELIMINARY STEPS

The PAP for the Resolution of Clinical Disputes assumes that the patient's medical records will be provided to him by the health care provider *before* the letter of claim is sent. It may also be necessary for the claimant's solicitor to instruct an expert to look at the records and advise as to liability and/or causation prior to the letter of claim.

10.4.1   Obtaining medical records

The claimant's solicitor should obtain a copy of his client's records from his GP and from the hospital where he was treated, in order to build up a full picture of his client's health prior to the incident and of the treatment he received. The GP's records should contain notes of symptoms, medication and treatment, referrals to hospital, reports back from hospital doctors and referrals to other professionals such as occupational therapists, physiotherapists or community nurses. The hospital records will contain details of the client's admission, his consents to treatment, x-rays, photographs, print-outs from monitoring equipment, nursing records and comments made by the doctors who were treating him.

The claimant's solicitor should ensure that he obtains all the notes, not just those which are supplied and marked relevant to the matter in hand, as background history may be highly relevant. In *Wickham v Dwyer* (1995) *Current Law Weekly*, 1 January, the court held that it was for the expert to determine whether or not there was any information of any irrelevance contained within the notes, and therefore it was fair to allow the solicitors and experts access to the full notes.

Until all records have been traced and disclosed, the solicitor will not be in a position to instruct an expert to review the evidence and form a view on liability and/or causation. Early and full disclosure is the key to successful clinical negligence litigation as, without this, it may be impossible for the claimant and his solicitor to know exactly what happened.

10.4.1.1   Right of access to medical records

Records of living individuals

The Data Protection Act 1998 (DPA 1998) gives the right to living individuals to access their personal health records. For the purposes of the Act, 'records' may be handwritten or in a computerised form, and will include imaging records, such as x-rays, photographs and print-outs from monitoring equipment.

Records of deceased individuals

The Access to Health Records Act 1990 governs access to the health records of individuals who have died. Access may be requested only by a personal representative or a person who may have a claim arising out of the death.

10.4.1.2   Procedure for obtaining access to medical records

Paragraph 3.2 of the PAP for the Resolution of Clinical Disputes states that a request for records by the claimant should:

(a)   provide sufficient information to alert the defendant where an adverse outcome has been serious or has had serious consequences or may constitute a notifiable safety incident;

(b)   be as specific as possible about the records which are required for an initial investigation of the claim (including, for example, a continuous copy of the CTG trace in birth injury cases); and

(c)   include a request for any relevant guidelines, analyses, protocols or policies and any documents created in relation to an adverse incident, notifiable safety incident or complaint.

Paragraph 3.3 states that the requests should be made using the Law Society and Department of Health approved standard form, which can be found at Annex A of the PAP, adapted as necessary. The form requires the solicitor to obtain his client's signature to indicate the client's informed consent to the release of the records.

Paragraph 3.4 states that the copy records should be provided within 40 days of the request and for a cost not exceeding the charges permissible under the Access to Health Records Act 1990 and/or the Data Protection Act 1998. Payment may be required in advance by the healthcare provider. If the defendant is unable to comply with this time limit, the problem should be explained quickly and details given of what is being done to resolve it (para 3.6). Ultimately, an application can be made to the court under r 31.16 of the CPR for an order for pre-action disclosure. The court has the power to impose costs sanctions for unreasonable delay in providing records (para 3.7).

Under para 3.8, if either party requires additional health records from a third party healthcare provider, co-operation from that third party is expected. Rule 31.17 of the CPR sets out the procedure for applying to the court for pre-action disclosure by third parties (see **10.10.3**).

10.4.1.3   The content of medical records

Medical records may be in paper or electronic form and will, of course, vary from case to case. The following is a sample of the records that a solicitor may expect to receive from a hospital:

(a)   *Admission details/record sheet.* These should give the date and the time of admission, the record number, the name of the ward and the name of the consultant in charge of the case.

(b)   *In-patient notes.* These include casualty notes (where appropriate), personal details of the patient, a detailed history of the patient and of the initial examination, daily progress and record notes, discharge notes, a copy of the letter to the GP giving details of the patient's treatment and a general report to the GP.

(c)   *Nursing records.* Nursing records are detailed notes made by nursing staff including temperature charts, vital signs, test results, results of all investigations carried out, and details of drugs prescribed and taken.

(d)   *Letters of referral.* These include referrals from GPs, responses to GPs following consultation or complaint of a missed appointment, and comments on the patient's demeanour and attitude.

(e)   *Records of x-rays.* These include other films taken. Copies of the x-rays and films themselves are not supplied automatically (only the record of the fact that the x-ray was carried out) and copies of the films will have to be obtained separately.

(f)   *Anaesthetic details.* These are details of the examination of the patient prior to an operation, a record of the drugs administered during pre-medication and during the operation itself.

(g)   *Patient consent forms.* These forms show what treatments the patient consented to have performed on him.

(h)   *Internal enquiry reports.* Where an internal enquiry has been held and the dominant purpose of that enquiry was not in contemplation of litigation, the enquiry notes will be discoverable.

(i)   *Obstetric cases.* The following documents should also be supplied:

(i)   progress of labour cards;

(ii)   cardiotachograph (CTG) traces showing foetal contractions;

(iii)   partogram (showing labour in chart form);

(iv)   ante-natal records;

(v)   neo-natal records;

(vi)   paediatric notes.

Information that a solicitor may expect to receive from a GP will include the doctor's own notes, reports of any investigations requested by him, letters of referral to hospitals or consultants and any responses, letters from hospital regarding out-patient clinic attendances and treatment, and in-patient discharge summaries.

10.4.1.4   Examining the records

The solicitor should ensure (as far as possible) that the notes or records supplied to him are complete and are in chronological order, which will show the pattern of the disease or problem and its treatment, and may also highlight missing documents or records. Where the claimant's solicitor suspects that a document or documents may be missing, or where documents have been badly copied or are otherwise illegible, he should raise the issue with the records holder, since an incomplete set of records may distort the overall picture and thus give a false impression of the claim. It may be necessary to make an appointment with the GP or hospital to inspect the original documents. It is also helpful for the solicitor to go through the records with the client to ensure that the treatment shown on the records accords with the client's recollection of what actually occurred. The records should be supplied to the solicitor and not direct to the expert, so that the solicitor has an opportunity to check them through before instructing the expert to prepare his report.

10.4.2   Instructing an expert on liability and/or causation

In clinical negligence cases, it will be necessary to instruct one or more medical experts to consider the claimant's medical records and provide an opinion on matters relating to breach of duty and causation. Frequently, it will be appropriate to do this before the letter of claim is sent. In due course, other medical experts will deal with issues relating to quantum. Expert evidence is dealt with in **Chapter 11**.

10.5   EMPLOYERS' LIABILITY CLAIMS FOR DISEASE AND ILLNESS – PRELIMINARY STEPS

Disease and illness claims are very difficult to establish, particularly the so-called 'long-tail' claims, where the illness or disease manifests itself many years after exposure to the causative substance or working conditions (see **4.7**). It will not be possible for the claimant's solicitor to assess whether there is a claim with a reasonable chance of success until he has seen all relevant medical records and has obtained his occupational records from the potential defendant, who will be either the claimant's current employer or a former employer. These notes will enable the claimant's solicitor to draw up a chronology of events and map the progress of the disease. He may need a medical expert to advise as to causation before the letter of claim is sent.

Medical records should be obtained as outlined in **10.4**.

10.5.1   Obtaining occupational records

In accordance with para 4 of the PAP for Disease and Illness Claims, the claimant's solicitor should write to the potential defendant, the client's employer or former employer, requesting his occupational records, including health and personnel records, before the letter of claim is sent. The DPA 1998 applies. Sufficient information should be given in the letter of request to alert the potential defendant or his insurer to the fact that a potential disease claim is being investigated. A specimen letter and request form to be used for this purpose is set out at Annexes A and A1 of the Protocol.

Records should be provided within a maximum of 40 days of the request, free of charge. The Protocol suggests that as a matter of good practice, the potential defendant should also disclose any product data documents which the claimant has requested which may resolve a causation issue. Where documents are not provided within 40 days and no information is forthcoming from the defendant to explain the reasons for the delay, the claimant should apply to the court for an order for pre-action disclosure (see **10.10.2**).

The claimant's solicitor should also seek to obtain relevant occupational records held by other bodies or individuals who have employed the claimant in the past.

10.6   LETTER OF NOTIFICATION

In many instances, the potential defendant will be aware of the possibility of a claim before the letter of claim is sent. Where this is not the case, the claimant's solicitor may wish to give the potential defendant early notification before he is in possession of sufficient information to enable him to send the letter of claim, as follows:

(a)   Personal injury claims: In accordance with para 3.3 of the PAP for Personal Injury Claims, this will not start the clock ticking for the purposes of the time limit set for the defendant's response. However, the Letter of Notification should be acknowledged by the proposed defendant within 14 days of receipt.

(b)   Clinical negligence cases: A template for the recommended contents is set out in Annex C1 to the PAP for the Resolution of Clinical Disputes. On receipt, the defendant should acknowledge receipt within 14 days, identify who will be dealing with the matter, and consider what investigations/preliminary steps need to be taken and what information could be passed to the claimant in order to narrow the issues or facilitate early resolution. In addition, a copy of the letter should be sent to the NHSLA or any relevant medical defence organisation or indemnity provider.

10.7   LETTER OF CLAIM

10.7.1   Purpose

The purpose of the letter of claim is:

(a)   to notify the likely defendant of the proposed claim and to set out sufficient information to enable him to assess liability and the likely size and heads of claim without necessarily addressing quantum in detail;

(b)   to obtain details of the defendant's insurers (where not already known). In personal injury claims, the claimant must send two copies of the letter to the defendant with a request that one copy is forwarded to the defendant's insurers, which ensures that the insurers are involved at the earliest possible date. In clinical negligence cases against an NHS Trust, a copy of the letter of claim should be sent by the claimant to the NHS Litigation Authority; and

(c)   to request access to relevant documents which the defendant might hold and which the claimant has not yet seen.

10.7.2   Contents

The precise wording contained in the three PAPs differs, and therefore reference to the relevant protocol should be made in order to determine precisely what the letter of claim should contain in each type of case. Each PAP has a specimen letter of claim set out in the Appendices, which should be followed, although the required detail will depend on the facts of each case. However, as a general approach, the letter should contain the following:

(a)   a clear summary of the facts on which the claim is based;

(b)   the main allegations of negligence/breach of statutory duty (and an outline of the causal link where this is likely to be in dispute);

(c)   an indication of the nature of all of the injuries that have been sustained, including current condition and prognosis where relevant;

(d)   an indication of other financial losses; and

(e)   a request for early disclosure of relevant documentation held by the defendant. It is best practice for the claimant's solicitor to assist the defendant by identifying those documents which he believes are material (see **10.10.1**).

In the majority of cases, witness statements and the reports of experts would not be enclosed with the letter of claim. However, where the claimant's solicitor feels that such evidence demonstrates a very strong case on liability, he may decide that disclosure at this stage may lead to an admission of liability by the defendant.

The claimant's solicitor may make an offer to settle in the letter of claim, by setting out what his client would be willing to accept in full and final settlement of the matter. However, in many cases, a detailed investigation into quantum will not have been undertaken by the claimant's solicitor, and therefore an offer should not be made.

The letter of claim does not have the same status as a statement of case, and so the claimant will not be held to the content of the letter. Nevertheless, the claimant's solicitor should be as accurate as possible, in order to avoid credibility issues if the matter goes to trial.

10.8   CLAIMS NOTIFICATION FORM – LOW VALUE CLAIMS

Where a claim falls under one of the low value claims PAPs (see **10.2** above and **Chapter 21**), the claimant's solicitor commences the process by completing and sending the Claim Notification Form (CNF) to the defendant's insurer electronically through the Portal at www.claimsportal.org.uk and, in the case of EL or public liability (PL) claims, sending the Defendant Only CNF (DCNF) to the defendant electronically through the Portal. In EL or PL cases where it is not possible to serve the defendant electronically, and in RTA cases, the DCNF should be sent to the defendant by first class post at the same time as sending the CNF to the insurer, or as soon as practicable thereafter.

All boxes in the CNF and DCNF which are marked as mandatory must be completed, and a reasonable attempt made to complete those boxes which are not marked as mandatory. The statement of truth in the CNF must be signed by the claimant or the claimant's legal representative where the client has authorised him to do so and the representative can provide written evidence of that authorisation. Where the claimant is a child, the statement of truth may be signed by the parent or guardian. On the electronically completed CNF, the person may enter his name in the signature box to satisfy this requirement.

See Document 2 in **Appendix 1** for a completed CNF.

10.9   RESPONSE TO THE LETTER OF CLAIM OR CNF

10.9.1   Personal injury claims

In personal injury claims where the claim does not fall under one of the new low value protocols, the defendant has 21 calendar days of the date of the posting of the letter of claim to send a preliminary response to the claimant. In this letter, the defendant should identify his insurer, if any, and highlight any significant omissions from the letter of claim. If there is no reply from the defendant or his insurer within that period, the claimant is entitled to issue proceedings.

The defendant has three months from the date of acknowledging the claim to investigate the matter and provide a substantive response. Where the claim is denied, reasons for the denial and any alternative versions of events should be set out. Any documents material to the issues (which are not privileged) should be enclosed. The individual PAPs give further information as to what information should be included.

See Document 4 of the Case Study in **Appendix 1** for an example of a defendant's letter denying liability.

10.9.2 Clinical negligence claims

In clinical negligence claims, the defendant has less time to respond. The letter of claim must be acknowledged within 14 days of receipt and the person dealing with the matter should be identified. Where the claim is denied, full reasons for the denial should be provided within four months of the letter of claim. A template for the letter of response is at Annex C3 of the PAP for the resolution of clinical disputes (see **Appendix 4**).

10.9.3 Low value claims

Where one of the low value PAPs applies, the insurer must send to the claimant's solicitor an electronic acknowledgement of the CNF the day after its receipt. It must then complete the 'Insurer Response' section of the CNF and send it to the claimant within 15 business days of the acknowledgment in the case of RTAs and 30 days in the case of EL and PL cases. Where the defendant denies liability, he must give brief reasons.

If the insurer fails to respond within this time limit, denies liability, alleges contributory negligence (other than failure to wear a seatbelt in a RTA) or states that the information in the CNF is inadequate, the claim exits the low value PAP and continues in accordance with the relevant non-low value PAP. In accordance with para 2.10A of the PAP for Personal Injury Claims, where this happens, the CNF can be used as a letter of claim, unless the defendant notifies the claimant that there is inadequate information on the CNF. The insurer/defendant then has 30 days from the date of acknowledgment of the claim to investigate the matter and serve a full response on the claimant.

10.10 ACQUIRING EVIDENCE IN RESPECT OF LIABILITY

Although the claimant's solicitor will have obtained sufficient evidence to justify the dispatch of the CNF or letter of claim, where the defendant denies liability, he will need to obtain further evidence in order to ensure that liability can be proved at trial, if need be.

10.10.1 Documents held by the defendant

The claimant's solicitor will have no difficulties in obtaining documents which are in the possession of his client, or documents to which the public have access. However, many of the documents which will give real insight into the causes of the accident will be in the possession of the proposed defendant.

The PAPs are designed to encourage parties to have an open-handed approach to litigation, and this requires each party to allow the other to see relevant documents at an early stage. In clinical negligence claims and in occupational disease and illness claims, the relevant PAPs envisage that the claimant will obtain medical records or occupational health records prior to the sending of the letter of claim (see **10.4** and **10.5**). In all other cases, where the defendant denies liability, he should enclose with his letter of reply copies of all documents in his possession which are material to the issues between the parties and which would be likely to be ordered to be disclosed by the court, either on an application for pre-action disclosure or on disclosure during proceedings. In clinical negligence and occupational disease and illness claims, the defendant should disclose any relevant documents he has not yet disclosed.

10.10.1.1 Documents relevant to personal injury claims

Annex C to the PAP for personal injury claims contains lists of documents which are likely to be in the defendant's possession in various types of claim, and in the letter of claim the claimant's solicitor should set out which documents he requires, should liability not be admitted. However, Annex C does not provide an exhaustive list of what the defendant may have and there might be other relevant documents, including, for example, minutes of meetings, memorandums between in-house departments or individuals, and reports. With experience, the personal injury solicitor will obtain an understanding of the types of documents which might be available in certain circumstances, but the claimant's solicitor should always listen carefully to what his client and other witnesses have to say, as they may know of the existence of documentation without understanding its relevance.

It is important to remember that, for the purpose of disclosure, the term 'document' is not restricted to written documents but includes anything in which information of any description is recorded. It therefore includes audiotapes, videotapes, photographs and electronic documents such as e-mails. Footage from CCTV cameras is becoming increasingly available, and in workplace claims, it is possible that the employer had installed a CCTV camera in, for example, a factory, warehouse or supermarket, which has captured images of the accident.

10.10.1.2   Documents relevant to employer liability claims

A list of documents which the defendant employer may be expected to have following an accident at work are set out in Annex C to the PAP for personal injury claims. However, the following documents may require an explanation:

(a)   *The Accident Book.* Under the Reporting of Injuries, Diseases and Dangerous Occurrences Regulations 1995 (RIDDOR 1995) (SI 1995/3163), employers are required to keep an accident book of an approved type where details of all accidents that occur on the premises must be recorded. The claimant's solicitor should not only ask the employer for a copy of the relevant page from the accident book, but should also consider whether the book itself should be inspected for evidence of similar incidents in the past.

   See Document 5 of the Case Study in **Appendix 1** for an example of a report from an employer's accident book.

(b)   *RIDDOR report to the HSE.* Employers are required to report certain classes of injury or disease sustained by people at work and specified dangerous occurrences. The RIDDOR 1995 require the responsible person (ie the safety officer/manager) to inform the HSE electronically, and to follow it up with written confirmation within 10 days. The defendant should retain a copy of the report in its files.

   The reportable occurrences include:

   (i)   the death of any person;

   (ii)   any person suffering a specified major injury;

   (iii) any person suffering an injury which is not major but which results in him being away from work or unable to do the full range of his normal duties for more than seven days;

   (iv)   any person suffering from a work related disease;

   (v)   where there has been a dangerous occurrence. Dangerous occurrences are listed in Sch 2 to RIDDOR 1995 and include such things as dangerous occurrences involving overhead electric lines, biological agents and radiation generators, as well as occurrences in mines, at quarries, on the railways and at off-shore installations.

   See Document 6 of the Case Study in **Appendix 1** for an example of a report to the HSE – RIDDOR.

10.10.2   Application for pre-action disclosure and inspection

Where the claimant's solicitor believes the proposed defendant has relevant documentation which he has not disclosed in compliance with the protocol, and he has failed to respond to written requests to do so, an application for disclosure prior to the start of proceedings should be made under s 33 of the Senior Courts Act 1981 or s 52 of the County Courts Act 1984. The application must be supported by appropriate evidence, and the procedure is the same in both the High Court and county court. Under r 31.16, the court may make an order for disclosure only where:

(a)   the respondent is likely to be a party to subsequent proceedings;

(b)   the applicant is also likely to be a party to the proceedings;

(c)   if proceedings had started, the respondent's duty by way of standard disclosure, set out in rule 31.16, would extend to the documents or classes of documents of which the applicant seeks disclosure; and

(d)   disclosure before proceedings have started is desirable in order to—

  (i)   dispose fairly of the anticipated proceedings; or

  (ii)   assist the dispute to be resolved without proceedings; or

  (iii)   save costs.

An order under r 31.16 will specify the documents or class of documents which the respondent must disclose and require him, when making such disclosure, to specify any of those documents which he no longer has, or which he claims the right or duty to withhold from inspection. The order may also specify the time and place for disclosure and inspection to take place.

10.10.3   Documents held by third parties

Relevant documents may also be held by third parties. In some instances, for example where documents are held by the police or the HSE, the claimant's solicitor will generally be able to obtain copies, although he may be frustrated by the delay. Where documents contain the claimant's personal data, for example occupational records held by someone other than the proposed defendant, he is entitled to see them under the DPA 1998.

In other cases, where a third party holds documents and it is under no statutory obligation to disclose them, the claimant's solicitor should make a polite request, offering to pay all the reasonable costs associated with providing access to or copies of the documents. If the third party refuses to cooperate, generally the claimant's solicitor cannot apply to the court for an order of disclosure and inspection until proceedings have commenced (see CPR, r 31.17). The court does have an equitable power to make a pre-action order for disclosure against third parties, but this will be exercised only in rare circumstances, a consideration of which lies beyond the scope of this book.

10.10.3.1   Documents relevant to RTAs – the police accident report

In the case of a road traffic incident, it may be useful to obtain a copy of the police accident report (PAR), if one exists. Some police forces use different terminology, eg 'collision report'. The following should be borne in mind:

(a)   The PAR will contain statements from the parties and a sketch plan, as well as the police officer's comments on the condition of the vehicles, the road surface, the weather conditions and details of any criminal proceedings that have been commenced as a result of the accident. It may also include photographs and witness statements. Some PARs contain more useful information than others and, bearing in mind that a fee will be payable, it may be advisable to ask what the PAR does contain before seeking to obtain a copy.

(b)   In order to obtain a copy of the PAR, the solicitor should contact the accident records department at the police force headquarters for the area in which the accident occurred (not the police officer assigned to the case). The letter should include details of the date, time and place of the accident, the registration numbers of the vehicles and the full names of those involved.

(c)   The PAR will not be released until the conclusion of any criminal investigation and proceedings. If the defendant is convicted of an offence which is relevant to the issue of negligence, it is likely that he (or more likely his insurers) will want to settle the proceedings, and therefore it will not be necessary to obtain a copy of the PAR.

(d)   A fee is payable for the PAR. The amount of the fee varies, depending upon the relevant police force, the length and nature of the report and the type of accident.

(e)   On payment of a further fee, the police officer who prepared the PAR may be interviewed, in the presence of a senior officer. (If the matter goes to trial, police officers will give evidence in civil proceedings, but they must be witness summonsed and a further fee will be payable.)

(f)   If there is no PAR, it is still possible to obtain copies of police notebooks and witness statements on payment of a fee. Because reports may be destroyed (in some cases after as little as one year), a request for a report should be made promptly, notwithstanding that the report will not actually be released until the conclusion of criminal investigations.

10.10.3.2   Documents relevant to work-based claims – HSE reports

Health and Safety Executive reports are the equivalent of police reports in the field of industrial incidents. Generally, the same rules apply as with police reports, although, due to lack of resources, a report may only be available in the case of very serious injury or death.

The HSE officer responsible for the factory or workplace concerned should be approached with a request for a copy of his report. As with the PAR, the HSE report will not be available until after any criminal prosecution has been dealt with. If the HSE is unwilling to provide a copy of its report voluntarily, it may be necessary to wait until after proceedings have been commenced and then make an application for non-party disclosure.

The HSE will also have other relevant documentation, such as the RIDDOR and correspondence with the defendant regarding the incident. However, the defendant should have a copy of these documents in its own files and may possibly have a copy of the HSE report. All these documents should be disclosed to the claimant with other relevant documents it holds.

10.10.4   Real evidence

Real evidence is a material object, such as a piece of machinery, an article of personal protective clothing, etc, which is relevant to the issues of the case. Where it is practicable for the item to be produced at court, the claimant's solicitor should take appropriate steps to obtain the item, instruct an expert to examine it where necessary, and then put it into safe-keeping until it is required. If it is impracticable for an item (eg a large piece of machinery) to be produced at court, photographs should be taken.

10.10.5   Photographs and sketch plans of the location of the accident

In road traffic cases, it is usually necessary to produce photographs and sketch plans of the location of the accident for two reasons. First, the layout of the road may change between the date of accident and the date of trial, and/or the road may appear different depending on whether it is photographed in summer or in winter, especially if there are lots of trees or vegetation which could obscure a driver's view. Secondly, it may be necessary to try to show the location from the perspective of the car drivers at the time. An aerial view or plan of a road junction will do nothing, for example, to prove to a court how badly the approach of a vehicle was obscured by trees and bushes or roadside property. The solicitor should not lose sight of the fact that he must be able to prove to the court what could or could not be seen from a particular vantage point. It is open to the court to visit the site of the accident, but this may not be practicable, and in any event, it would take an inordinate amount of time. The solicitor should always visit the site if possible, in order to get a feel for the case.

Police accident reports (see **10.10.3.1**) often contain good quality photographs which can be purchased on payment of an extra fee per print, and which may prove helpful in showing not only the severity and location of the damage to each vehicle, but also the final position on the road in which the vehicles were immediately following the accident. This evidence may assume significance at a later date, or may contradict the oral evidence of the witnesses. It is, however, important to read the PAR closely, as it will confirm whether or not the vehicles were moved from their original resting position prior to the taking of the photographs.

In road traffic cases, the photographer should mark on a plan the precise location from which each photograph was taken and the direction in which the camera was pointing.

Site visits in non-road traffic cases are no less important. For example, in a case where the client has tripped on a broken pavement, it is not uncommon for the local authority, upon receiving intimation of a possible claim, to send a team of operatives to mend the offending paving stone. It is therefore vitally important to secure good quality photographs of the pavement, etc as soon as possible, usually on the same day that the client is interviewed. Photographs must contain some indication of scale, and it is therefore necessary to place an item, such as a ruler, within the photograph.

In modern times, the availability of mobile telephones with inbuilt cameras means that claimants or their friends or family members may have taken relevant photographs of the site at or about the time of the accident. Whilst such photographs may have some use, particularly in low-value cases, it is not good practice to entrust the taking of photographs to the client, who may underestimate the importance of the task and forget about it until it is too late. Photographs taken by the client may be out of focus, underexposed or otherwise taken in a manner which will not help the client's case. A good example of this can be found in *Flynn v Leeds City Council*, 10 September 2004, where the claimant was injured when she tripped on the edge of an uneven paving stone. She claimed that the discrepancy between the heights of the paving stones was over an inch and that the pavement was therefore dangerous to pedestrians. Photographs of the paving stones, with the alleged discrepancy highlighted by the presence of a 50 pence piece and a ruler, had been taken by the claimant's partner, who happened to be a litigation solicitor. The defendant claimed that these photographs appeared to have been 'massaged slightly'. The judge did not feel that anything sinister was being suggested, but he accepted that the 50 pence piece appeared to be leaning at an angle and that there may have been some slight excavation of material between the paving stones. The claimant failed to prove that the discrepancy between the paving stones was a dangerous one and the judge found in favour of the defendant.

10.10.6 Evidence of criminal convictions

If the proposed defendant is charged with a criminal offence in relation to the incident which caused the injury to the claimant, ideally the claimant's solicitor should attend the proceedings to note the evidence. The date of the proceedings may be obtained from the police or the HSE, as appropriate.

Any resulting conviction of the defendant which is relevant to the issues in civil proceedings (ie relevant when seeking to prove or disprove negligence or breach of statutory duty) may be referred to in the civil proceedings (Civil Evidence Act 1968, s 11). In an RTA claim, for example, a conviction for speeding or dangerous driving arising out of the incident itself is a relevant conviction. However, a conviction for driving without insurance at the time of the accident, or a previous conviction for driving with excess alcohol in the blood, is not a relevant conviction, as it does not prove that the defendant was negligent at the time of the accident.

For the purposes of the civil proceedings, the defendant will be taken to have committed the offence 'unless the contrary is proved'. The defendant may seek to argue that he should not have been convicted, but if he does so, the burden of proving this on the balance of probabilities will pass to him. In most cases where there is a relevant conviction, the defendant will seek to settle the matter.

Where a claimant is convicted for failing to wear a safety belt or a safety helmet, the conviction is relevant to the issue of damages as it indicates contributory negligence.

Should the matter go to trial, the party seeking to rely on the conviction will need to produce a certificate from the convicting court in order to prove the conviction.

10.10.7　Evidence of lay witnesses

Witnesses should be contacted and interviewed by the claimant's solicitor as soon as possible. The defendant's solicitor, in the normal course of events, will be instructed at a later date than the claimant's solicitor, but he too should contact and interview witnesses without delay. Where a witness is not interviewed at an early stage, his memory of the events may fade or he may become untraceable. If the claimant was injured at work and the witness is a fellow employee of the claimant, he may be concerned about his employer's reaction and become increasingly reluctant to speak to the claimant's solicitor. Witnesses to road incidents are often initially enthusiastic, but later decide that they have little to gain and would rather not get involved. For this reason, the solicitor should not delay in contacting the witness and obtaining a proof of evidence, or at the very least a letter confirming what he saw and/or heard and that he is prepared to make a statement to that effect.

In a straightforward case, it may not be necessary to interview the witness. If his letter of response is sufficiently clear, a proof can be prepared from it and from any questionnaire he may also have been sent. A copy of the proof should be forwarded for approval and signature by the witness. This should be accompanied by a stamped addressed envelope and covering letter, requesting the witness to read the proof carefully and make any amendments or additions that he feels to be necessary before signing and dating the document for return in the envelope provided. The witness is a volunteer to the client's cause and should be thanked accordingly for the time and trouble he has taken on the client's behalf.

The proof of evidence, once converted into a formal witness statement and exchanged with the other side, will form the basis of the witness's evidence to be relied on at trial and will stand as his evidence-in-chief. Furthermore, the statement may have to be used at the trial under the Civil Evidence Act 1995 if the witness subsequently becomes unavailable. Consequently, it should contain all the relevant evidence the witness can give and, needless to say, it should be the truth. In accordance with r 22.1 of the CPR, the witness statement must conclude with a statement of truth, and this must be signed by the witness himself.

In an EL case, it may be advisable for the claimant's solicitor to obtain statements from individuals, such as shop stewards or co-workers, who, although they may not have seen the accident, may know of other similar accidents in the past, or be able to give background information on policy changes that may have taken place within the organisation. In road incident or tripping cases, people living or working adjacent to the location of the incident may be able to give useful information relating to similar incidents that have happened in the past, and even as to the identities of past claimants in similar incidents, or information on how long the defect has been in existence.

10.10.8　Expert evidence

Almost all cases will involve some expert evidence. There may be a requirement for non-medical experts, such as engineers or RTA reconstruction experts, but most experts will be from the medical field. In clinical injury cases, experts will be required in respect of liability, causation and quantum. In most personal injury cases, the evidence of a medical expert will relate to quantum rather than liability, although there will be some cases where a medical opinion in relation to causation will be required, for example where the claimant has suffered a disease or illness. Consequently, the claimant's solicitor will not normally seek to obtain a report from a medical expert until he is satisfied that the claimant has a strong case on liability, or liability has been admitted by the defendant. See **Chapter 11** for a detailed consideration of the role of experts.

10.11 ACQUIRING EVIDENCE IN RESPECT OF QUANTUM

10.11.1 Evidence of lost earnings

The client's loss of earnings is likely to form a significant part of his claim for special damages. See **Chapter 15** for a detailed consideration of this point.

10.11.1.1 Obtaining details from employers

In an EL claim against the claimant's current employer, a request for details of the claimant's earnings should be set out in the letter of claim. In other cases, the claimant's solicitor should write to the client's employer to ask for details of earnings for 13 weeks prior to the incident and for a copy of the client's contract of employment. The loss of earnings details should be set out to show weekly earnings (both gross and net) so as to reveal a pattern over 13 weeks.

10.11.1.2 Self-employed clients

Documentary evidence in the form of the client's previous year's trading accounts (or longer if appropriate) should be obtained if possible, together with other evidence of contracts or offers of work that had to be turned down as a result of the incident. The client's accountant, business associates and colleagues in the same area of work should be approached to assist in this.

10.11.1.3 Unemployed clients

Even if the client is unemployed, evidence should be obtained of his last employer and of the likelihood of his obtaining suitable work which he could have undertaken but for the accident, as evidence of earning capacity. Colleagues in the same area of business and employment agencies should be approached for evidence of availability of work within the client's specialism and the level of possible earnings.

10.11.2 Evidence of other special damages

During the first interview with his client, the claimant's solicitor should ask him to keep details of any articles damaged in the accident, repair costs, private medical treatment, journeys to hospital, parking tickets, etc which have resulted from the accident, and to retain any relevant quotes, invoices, receipts or tickets. Where the defendant admits liability, or where the court finds in favour of the claimant, many of these items will be admitted by the defendant, provided evidence is produced.

10.11.3 Evidence of pain, suffering and loss of amenity

10.11.3.1 Medical records

It may be necessary to obtain copies of the claimant's medical records from his GP and/or from a hospital where he was treated (see **10.4.1**) in order to prove the extent of the claimant's suffering and, if necessary, disprove that any pre-existing condition contributed to the injuries suffered by the claimant.

10.11.3.2 Medical experts

Medical experts provide crucial evidence for the assessment of general damages for pain, suffering and loss of amenity. In a fairly straightforward case, one medical expert of an appropriate specialisation will be able to deal with all aspects of liability and quantum in his report. In more complex cases, such as where the claimant has suffered major brain trauma, several experts might be required, including, for example, a neurologist, a neuropsychologist, an occupational therapist, and an expert on the need for care and general support.

10.11.3.3 Lay witnesses

The claimant's own testimony is important. During the first interview, the claimant's solicitor should ask his client to keep a pain diary. The claimant should set out the extent of his suffering and its effect on his life in his witness statement.

The evidence of members of the claimant's family, friends and work colleagues may also provide a valuable insight into the impact of the accident.

10.11.3.4 Photographs

Photographs of the injuries immediately after the accident, during the various stages of recovery and as at the date of trial, where they are continuing, are also very useful.

10.12 CONCLUSION

The claimant's solicitor is obliged, under the overriding objective found in r 1 of the CPR and under the PAPs, to be fully prepared before proceedings are commenced. Once proceedings have been issued, the court will actively manage the case and will require the parties to deal with each step of the proceedings in accordance with the timetable it lays down in the order for directions. Where a solicitor fails to prepare adequately prior to issue and consequently is unable to comply with the directions within the specified time limits, the court may impose cost penalties.

The essential element when gathering evidence at the preliminary stage is to act quickly. A failure to act on the client's instructions as soon as they are received can have disastrous consequences for the subsequent conduct of the litigation. In extreme cases, this may seriously prejudice the client's chances of success and can amount to negligence on the part of the solicitor.

INSTRUCTING EXPERTS

LEARNING OUTCOMES

After reading this chapter you will be able to:

- understand the role of experts in personal injury and clinical negligence cases

- appreciate the different types of expert who might be instructed

- explain the expert's overriding duty to the court and the court's case management powers in relation to experts

- write a letter of instruction to an expert.

11.1 INTRODUCTION

In almost every personal injury or clinical negligence case, the claimant's solicitor will instruct at least one medical expert. Commonly, an expert will prepare a report on the claimant's injuries for quantum purposes, which is often referred to as a report on condition and prognosis. In clinical negligence and disease and illness claims, medical evidence will not only be required in order to assist the court in assessing damages, but will also be necessary in order to prove liability and/or causation. Indeed, the claimant's solicitor may be unable to understand precisely what happened to the claimant, and therefore advise him in relation to the claim, until such evidence has been obtained. In some personal injury cases, other types of experts, such as accident reconstruction experts or engineers, may be required for liability purposes.

The purpose of this chapter is to examine the role of experts and the matters that must be considered when instructing an expert in a personal injury or clinical negligence case.

With regard to the procedural law, the practitioner must have a sound grasp of CPR Part 35 and the accompanying Practice Direction, which govern the use of experts in civil trials. In addition, the Guidance for the Instruction of Experts in Civil Claims 2014 (the 'Guidance') provides guidance on the interpretation of and compliance with Part 35 and PD 35 in the interests of good practice.

11.1.1   Who is an expert?

An expert is an individual with a high level of skill, knowledge and experience in a particular area which is outside the knowledge of the court. The expert will be permitted to give his opinion when the court would otherwise be unable properly to understand the factual evidence which has been placed before it and requires the expert's assistance in order to determine a matter of dispute between the parties. This evidence should be presented in a clear and concise way so that the court can use the information to reach its own conclusions.

The court is not obliged to accept the evidence of an expert. In *Armstrong and Another v First York Ltd* [2005] EWCA Civ 277, the Court of Appeal held that the trial judge had been entitled to reject the evidence of a forensic motor vehicle engineer who had been jointly instructed by the parties. The two claimants had allegedly sustained neck and spinal injuries when their car had been hit by a bus owned by the defendant. The expert's evidence was that there had been insufficient force generated by the impact to cause the injuries claimed. Although the trial judge found that the expert's evidence had been flawless, this could not be reconciled with his belief that the claimants were credible and honest witnesses. Consequently, he was entitled to find that there must have been a flaw in the expert's evidence, even though he had not been able to identify that flaw. In the Court of Appeal case of *Huntley v Simmons* [2010] EWCA Civ 54, Waller LJ stated that:

> the evidence of experts is important evidence but it is nevertheless only evidence which the judge must assess with all other evidence. Ultimately issues of fact and assessment are for the judge. Of course if there is no evidence to contradict the evidence of experts it will need very good reason for the judge not to accept it and he must not take on the role of expert so as to, in effect, give evidence himself. So far as Joint Statements are concerned parties can agree the evidence but (as happened in this case) it can be agreed that the joint statements can be put in evidence without the need to call the two experts simply because they do not disagree; but either party is entitled to make clear that the opinion expressed in the joint statement is simply evidence that must be assessed as part of all the evidence.

In *Stewart v Glaze* [2009] EWHC 704 (QB), the judge said that although the expert could be of considerable assistance, it was the primary factual evidence which was of the greatest importance, and that expert evidence should not be elevated into a fixed framework or formula against which the defendant's actions were to be judged rigidly with mathematical precision.

11.1.2   The expert's overriding duty to the court

Rule 35.3 of the CPR states that it is the duty of experts to help the court on matters within their expertise, and that this duty overrides any obligation to the person from whom experts have received instructions or by whom they are paid.

Paragraph 2 of PD 35 gives the following guidance as to the nature of that duty:

2.1   Expert evidence should be the independent product of the expert uninfluenced by the pressures of litigation.

2.2   Experts should assist the court by providing objective, unbiased opinion on matters within their expertise, and should not assume the role of an advocate.

2.3   Experts should consider all material facts, including those which might detract from their opinions.

2.4   Experts should make it clear:

(a)   when a question or issue falls outside their expertise; and

(b)   when they are not able to reach a definite opinion, for example because they have insufficient information.

2.5   If, after producing a report, an expert changes his view on any material matter, such change of view should be communicated to all the parties without delay, and when appropriate to the court.

Paragraphs 9 to 15 of the Guidance set out further guidance on the duties and obligations of experts. In particular, para 10 provides that experts are under an obligation to assist the court in dealing with cases in accordance with the overriding objective set out in r 1 of the CPR.

Paragraph 11 of the Guidance offers a test for independence as being, 'Would the expert express the same opinion if given the same instructions by an opposing party?', and goes on to say that experts should not take it upon themselves to promote the point of view of the party instructing them or engage in the role of advocates or mediators.

In accordance with para 3.1 of PD 35, the expert's report should be addressed to the court and not to the party from whom the expert has received instructions.

11.2 CASE MANAGEMENT AND THE USE OF EXPERTS

11.2.1 General principles

Rule 35.1 states that expert evidence should be 'restricted to that which is reasonably required to resolve the proceedings', and solicitors should be mindful that the court's permission is required before a party may call an expert or put in evidence an expert's report (CPR, r 35.4(1)). In determining whether a party should be entitled to use an expert, the court will be governed by the overriding objective found in r 1 of the CPR, in particular ensuring that the parties are on an equal footing, saving expense and dealing with the case in ways which are proportionate.

Specific new rules apply to whiplash claims under the RTA Low Value Protocol and are set out in **Chapter 21**. For all other types of claim, the following should be noted:

(a) Generally, permission will be sought in the directions questionnaire. When permission is sought, parties must provide an estimate of the costs of the proposed expert evidence and identify the field in which expert evidence is required, the issues the expert will address and, where practicable, the name of the proposed expert (CPR, r 35.4(2)). Where permission is granted, it shall be in relation only to the expert named or the field identified, and the issues which may be addressed may also be specified. Where a claim has been allocated to the small claims track or the fast track, permission will normally be given for evidence from only one expert on a particular issue (CPR, r 35.4(3A)). If necessary, further directions relating to the use of experts may be given on listing or upon the application of a party.

(b) Usually, the claimant's solicitor will be obliged to instruct an expert before permission is given by the court for the use of that expert. In clinical negligence and disease and illness claims, it will be necessary for the claimant's solicitor to instruct an expert in order to advise in relation to liability and/or causation before the letter of claim is sent and, in almost all cases, a medical report will be attached to the particulars of claim. This is well understood by the court, and there is unlikely to be a problem in obtaining permission for the use of such an expert. Solicitors instructed by both claimants and defendants should give careful consideration as to whether it is necessary to instruct any other expert prior to permission being given. The court may decide that expert evidence is not required at all, or may determine that a single joint expert should be used. The client should be informed of the risks of instructing an expert before permission has been given, ie that he may not be permitted to use the expert's evidence and costs relating to that expert will not be recoverable even where the client is successful in the claim.

(c) The PAP for Personal Injury Claims encourages the joint selection of experts, mostly medical experts for quantum purposes but also experts dealing with liability, where appropriate (PAP, para 7.2). In accordance with para 7.3, before a party instructs an expert, he must provide his opponent with a list of one or more experts whom he considers to be suitable for the case. In many cases, the claimant's solicitor will do this in the letter of claim and three names are usually supplied. The defendant then has 14 days within which to communicate any objections he has to any expert appearing on the list, and the claimant's solicitor is thereby able to select a mutually acceptable expert. The expert is instructed only by the claimant's solicitor (and in this respect, joint selection differs from joint instruction as envisaged by CPR, r 35.7 – see (d) below), but there is a presumption in fast track cases that the defendant will not be permitted to instruct his own expert in relation to that issue. Where the defendant objects to all the experts suggested by the claimant, he may instruct his own expert. However, if the matter proceeds, the court will consider whether the defendant acted reasonably in this regard.

In *Edwards-Tubb v JD Wetherspoon Plc* [2011] EWCA Civ 136, the claimant, Mr Edwards-Tubb, brought a claim arising out of a fall at work in October 2005. His employer, JD Wetherspoon, accepted liability. The issue related to damages and causation.

The claimant in the pre-action letter of claim gave notice to the defendant of three medical experts he wished to instruct. The defendant raised no objection and the claimant obtained a report from one of those experts, Mr Jackson. It was accepted that this was not a joint instruction and the report would remain privileged unless and until disclosed.

Proceedings were issued close to limitation. Shortly before service, the claimant disclosed a medical report from a Mr Khan, who was not originally nominated. The defendant sought an order that disclosure of the original report by Mr Jackson should be made a condition of the permission which the claimant needed to rely on Mr Khan.

The main issue before the Court of Appeal was whether the Court's power to impose a condition on the permission granted to rely on a particular expert could be utilised to require the disclosure of another expert report. The Court concluded that, before the claimant could rely on the second expert report, he should disclose the findings of the first expert report.

The Court was mindful of the duty under CPR, r 35.4 to discourage 'expert shopping'. In the circumstances of the case, expert A had been instructed for the purposes of the litigation. A factor which held significant weight for the Court of Appeal was that the parties had embarked upon the pre-action protocol procedure of co-operation in the selection of experts. This is not something which is generally undertaken under the pre-action protocol for the resolution of clinical disputes, and it remains to be seen whether the Court would impose such a condition upon a request for leave to rely upon a particular expert where there has been no pre-action discussion in relation to the instruction of experts.

(d) Where the parties wish to submit expert evidence on a particular issue, the court has the power, under CPR, r 35.7, to direct that a single joint expert be used. See **11.2.2** below.

(e) A party will be entitled to use the report or call the expert at trial only if the report has been disclosed to the other parties to the action in accordance with CPR, r 35.13.

(f) At trial, expert evidence is to be given by means of a written report unless the court gives permission for the expert to give oral evidence. In small claims and fast track cases, permission will be given for an expert to attend a hearing only if it is necessary in the interests of justice (CPR, r 35.5).

(g) In accordance with para 11.1 of PD 35, at any stage in the proceedings the court may direct that some or all of the experts from like disciplines shall give their evidence concurrently. This is known as hot-tubbing and may include, for example, the judge inviting the experts, in turn, to give their views, or the judge questioning one witness and then asking the other witness to comment on the answers given.

11.2.2 The single joint expert

A 'single joint expert' is defined in CPR, r 35.2(2) as an expert instructed to prepare a report for the court on behalf of two or more parties (including the claimant) to the proceedings. Under CPR, r 35.7, where two or more parties wish to submit expert evidence on a particular issue, the court may direct that the evidence on that issue be given by a single joint expert. In fast track cases, the court is likely to direct that a single joint expert be used unless there is good reason not to do so (PD 28, para 3.9(4)). Similar wording is used in PD 29, para 4.10(4) in relation to multi-track cases, but the insertion of the words 'on any appropriate issue' reflects the reality that there will be more issues in a multi-track case which will not be suitable for a single joint expert to determine. Paragraph 34 of the Guidance provides that, in the early stages of a dispute, when investigations, tests, site inspections, photographs, plans or other preliminary expert tasks are necessary, consideration should be given to the instruction of a single joint expert, especially where such matters are not expected to be contentious. Generally, single joint experts are more likely to be used to determine issues in relation to quantum than issues relating to liability or causation. In clinical negligence and illness and disease cases, it is recognised that single joint experts are less likely to be acceptable to the parties, and the pre-action protocols state that the courts are less prescriptive as to the use of experts in these types of claim.

Where the parties are unable to agree who the single joint expert should be, the court may select an expert from a list provided by the parties, or direct how the expert should be selected (CPR, 35.7(2)). Paragraph 37 of the Guidance requires parties to try to agree instructions to single joint experts, but allows for each party to give instructions in default of such an agreement. Where each party gives instructions to the expert, he should supply a copy of those instructions to the other side (CPR, r 35.8). Unless the court otherwise directs, the instructing parties are jointly and severally liable for the expert's fees and expenses.

11.2.3   Directions relating to the use of experts

In fast track cases, standard directions given on allocation in relation to expert evidence will order the use of the written report of a single joint expert or, where permission is given for the parties to use their own experts, order the disclosure of experts' reports by way of simultaneous exchange (usually within 14 weeks of allocation). Where the reports are not agreed, a discussion between the experts in accordance with CPR, r 35.12(1) and the preparation of a report under r 35.12(3) (PD 28, para 3.9) are required. In addition, the court may direct that a party put written questions to an expert instructed by another party or to a single joint expert about his report (CPR, r 35.6). Bearing in mind the tight timetable between allocation and trial (30 weeks), little time will be available for these steps.

Directions in multi-track cases are tailored to the requirements of each individual case and are likely to be more complex. Where the parties are permitted to use their own experts on any issue, typical directions will include:

(a)   exchange of reports, either simultaneously or sequentially;

(b)   the service of written questions to the experts and the service of answers;

(c)   the agreement of expert reports where possible;

(d)   where agreement is not possible, a without prejudice meetings between the experts in order to try to resolve the matters upon which they are unable to agree, and the subsequent filing of a report setting out the points upon which they agree and disagree;

(e)   permission for the experts to give oral evidence at trial or that the reports shall stand as evidence.

The time allowed for each step outlined above will be dependent upon the complexities of the individual case and, in some cases, the availability of the experts themselves.

11.3   AREAS OF EXPERTISE

The number and variety of experts available to prepare reports are often surprising to those unfamiliar with this area. The following are examples of experts who provide reports.

11.3.1 Medical experts

Medical experts are usually required in order to assist the court in relation to the assessment of damages. In other words, they will report on the condition and prognosis of the claimant and the cost of living with the particular injury suffered by the claimant. In a simple, low-value case, a report from a general practitioner may be sufficient, but in a complex, high-value case, experts in several areas of medical expertise may be required. The types of medical experts who may assist in this regard are numerous, but may include doctors of various specialities, occupational therapists, behavioural therapists, speech therapists and physiotherapists.

In clinical negligence cases, it will be necessary to instruct an expert to advise in relation to liability and possibly causation. A consultant should be instructed with expertise in the same speciality as the doctor who is alleged to have been negligent.

A list of the most common areas of medical expertise can be found at **2.3**.

11.3.2 Other experts

In road traffic accidents, the following types of experts may be helpful in order to establish liability:

(a)   accident investigators to reconstruct the events leading up to the road traffic accident;

(b)   mechanical engineers to examine the vehicles involved in the accident, to identify damage or to investigate if any mechanical defects were present in the vehicle.

In employers' liability cases, the following types of experts may be helpful to establish liability:

(a)   general consulting engineers to provide reports on machinery, systems of work, slipping accidents;

(b)   mining engineers;

(c)   ergonomics experts;

(d)   bio-engineers;

(e)   pharmacologists.

When dealing with quantum, in addition to doctors of the appropriate speciality, the following experts may be useful in relation to condition and prognosis and the costs of living with a particular injury:

(a)   occupational therapists;

(b)   behavioural therapists;

(c)   speech therapists;

(d)   physiotherapists;

(e)   employment consultants.

When dealing with quantum, the following experts may be useful in relation to financial loss and the investment of damages:

(a)   employment consultants;

(b)   accountants;

(c)   actuaries.

11.3.3 Specific experts

The following types of experts warrant further attention.

11.3.3.1 Accident reconstruction experts

In more serious RTA claims, an accident reconstruction expert may be required. If the claimant's solicitor is instructed immediately following the accident, the accident reconstruction expert should be contacted without delay and requested to attend the scene of the accident in order to examine any skid marks, etc. It may also be appropriate for the expert to examine the vehicles involved in the accident, and the claimant's solicitor should take appropriate steps to ensure that the vehicles are not disposed of or repaired prior to the expert carrying out his examination. The evidence of tachographs will be particularly useful. The reconstruction expert will want to see the PAR and any associated reports prepared by the police, such as a police reconstruction report, and proofs of evidence from anyone involved in the accident or anyone who witnessed the accident. He will then be in a position to provide an opinion as to the cause of the accident.

11.3.3.2 Consulting engineers

Many personal injury claims involve machinery or systems of work (especially EL claims), and in such cases it may be thought appropriate for a consulting engineer to be instructed to prepare a report on the machinery involved or the system of work undertaken.

> **EXAMPLE**
>
> A client is injured while driving a fork-lift truck and alleges that the steering wheel failed to respond while he was driving it. It is part of the client's case that the employer failed adequately to maintain the fork-lift truck. If the truck has not been modified prior to the solicitor being instructed, a consulting engineer may be instructed to examine the vehicle and its maintenance records. The solicitor will therefore obtain an expert's view as to whether the appropriate system of maintenance was adopted and attempt to identify the cause of the accident.

The expert will need to inspect the machinery, and the permission of the proposed defendants (who are normally the claimant's employers in such cases) is required. If this is not granted then it will be necessary to apply to court for an order for preservation and inspection.

Where both parties are given permission to instruct their own experts, it is common for them to attend the scene of the accident at the same time in order to conduct a joint inspection. This has the advantage of saving costs and time, as the engineers can agree on measurements and technical details.

11.3.3.3 Clinical case managers

In certain high-value/severe injury cases, a clinical case manager may be appointed to consider the claimant's appropriate care regime. In *Wright (by her litigation friend Karen Fay) v Kevin Sullivan* [2005] EWCA Civ 656, it was held that the clinical case manager would owe a duty to the claimant to work in his best interests and should not be jointly appointed. The evidence given by such a witness is evidence of fact and not expert opinion.

11.4 HOW TO FIND AN EXPERT

New rules relating to whiplash claims under the Low Value RTA Protocol provide that an accredited medical expert must be selected via the MedCo Portal (see **Chapter 21**). In all other cases, there is no such restriction on who may be instructed, and it is vital that the solicitor responsible instructs the correct person to provide expert evidence in the case. Many firms will have their own in-house directory of experts, which should be referred to in the first instance. Frequently, other fee-earners will have inserted comments about the expert alongside the entry in the directory. Information such as how well the expert gave evidence in court, can be extremely useful. If an in-house directory of experts is not available or is inappropriate then other sources can be used.

The following sources may also be of use:

(a)   The Association of Personal Injury Lawyers. This organisation provides information to members on appropriate experts.

(b)   Action against Medical Accidents (AvMA).

(c)   The Academy of Expert Witnesses.

(d)   The Society of Expert Witnesses.

(e)   Expert Witness Institute.

(f)   The *New Law Journal* and *Solicitor's Journal* regularly issue expert witness supplements which carry advertisements from experts who are prepared to provide reports for the purposes of litigation.

(g)   Many professional institutes also prepare a directory of expert witnesses.

(h)   The Medico-Legal Society publishes reports which may reveal the name of a suitable expert.

11.4.1   The use of medical agencies

Increasingly, solicitors rely on medical agencies to source suitable experts to write reports. The rise in popularity of medical agencies has come about due to the growth of large personal injury practices which accept claims from clients anywhere in England and Wales. It is necessary to find a medical expert (or better still a choice of experts in the same specialism) who is sufficiently local to the home of the client. Without the assistance of a national agency to co-ordinate this search, this would represent something of a headache for the claimant's solicitor.

Medical agencies are able to provide a choice of experts local to the client, and they will send copies of the CVs of those experts direct to the solicitor, together with an indication of the waiting time for preparation of the report. Subject to the arrangement they have with the instructing solicitor, they may also attempt to agree the choice of expert with the defendant insurer direct, obtain the client's medical records, arrange the medical appointment for the client and forward the subsequent report direct to the solicitor. The agency will charge a fee for this service which, if reasonable, will be allowed as part of the disbursements incurred on the claim at assessment of costs stage.

In the case of *Woollard v Fowler* [2006] EWHC 90051 (Costs), 12 April 2006, the court held that it was entirely proper that a payment made by a solicitor to such an agency should be treated as a disbursement under the fixed costs regime in section II of Part 45 of the CPR 1998, and therefore as recoverable in full from the losing party.

The PAP for personal injury claims states that where a claimant wishes to use a medical agency, the defendant's prior consent should be sought and, if the defendant so requests, the medical agency should provide in advance the names of the doctors whom they are considering instructing (para 7.4).

11.5   KEY QUALITIES TO LOOK FOR IN AN EXPERT

A number of key qualities must be looked for when selecting an expert:

(a)   Is the individual appropriately qualified to deal with the matter and does he have the relevant practical experience in the area? If not, the court is unlikely to consider him to be an expert.

(b)   Can the expert be regarded as impartial? In *Liverpool Roman Catholic Archdiocesan Trust v Goldberg* [2001] Lloyd's Rep PN 518, the evidence of an expert was disregarded due to his close relationship with the defendant.

(c)   Is the expert usually instructed on behalf of defendants when you are instructed by a claimant, or vice versa? Although all experts have an overriding duty to the court and should give the same evidence in a particular case no matter who is instructing them, it is unwise to instruct an expert who has an impressive record of appearing against the type of client you are representing.

(d) Does the expert have sufficient time to deal with the case properly? A good expert will refuse instructions when he has insufficient time, but this will not always happen. Whether the case is a personal injury or clinical negligence claim, the expert will have to spend considerable time on the matter, either examining the papers or the claimant, or inspecting a vehicle, a piece of machinery or the scene of the accident.

(e) Can the expert provide a clear and comprehensive report?

(f) Does the expert have experience in litigation of this type? Does he prepare reports and attend at trial regularly to give evidence? Only a small percentage of cases proceed to trial, and thus an expert may claim to have been involved in, say, 200 cases but may have given evidence in only a few of them (especially as, in the fast track, expert evidence is normally given in written form). It cannot be assumed that the case will settle and, however good the written report might be, convincing oral testimony (where allowed by the court) and the ability to withstand tough cross-examination are essential. The expert's general reputation should be checked with his colleagues who practise in the same area.

11.6 PRELIMINARY ENQUIRIES OF THE EXPERT

Once a party has decided to instruct an expert in relation to any issue in a case and an appropriate expert has been identified, the solicitor should approach the expert with a number of preliminary enquiries, in order to establish whether he is willing and able to act in relation to the matter. Some health practitioners may be reluctant to provide reports for claimants in clinical negligence cases, and their views on this must be obtained. Even if the expert has been used by the solicitor before, it is good practice to send a preliminary letter to establish whether the proposed expert has any personal or professional connection with others who may be involved in the case, such as one of the parties, a health professional who is alleged to have been negligent or experts instructed by another party. Even though experts have an overriding duty to the court, it is preferable to avoid any possibility of bias or allegations of bias.

The preliminary letter to the expert might usefully cover the following matters:

(a) request confirmation that the expert deals with the appropriate speciality, has the necessary qualifications and experience, and is familiar with the general duties of an expert;

(b) request confirmation that he is willing to accept instructions to provide a report and, where time is an important consideration, details of when the report will be available;

(c) request confirmation that the expert is prepared to carry out any necessary post-initial report work, such as attending conference with counsel and attending experts' meetings;

(d) request confirmation that he would be willing to provide oral evidence to support his written report, if required;

(e) inform the expert of the identity of the potential defendant and, in a clinical negligence claim, the name of any health professional who is alleged to have been negligent;

(f) obtain details of the expert's charging rate and/or to explain that the client has the benefit of public funding; and

(g) confirm on whose behalf the solicitor is acting (but without giving any view on liability).

(h) where the expert is a medical expert and relevant medical records have been obtained, confirm that this is the case (however, they must not be forwarded to the expert at this stage);

If the expert is prepared to act in response to an initial letter of enquiry then a full letter of instruction should be sent.

11.7   LETTER OF INSTRUCTION

The nature of the letter of instruction to a medical expert will, of course, be determined by what it is the expert is required to do.

11.7.1   Instructing medical experts in relation to quantum

Generally, in an RTA claim or an EL claim not involving illness or disease, the only medical expert instructed will be required to examine the claimant in order to provide a condition and prognosis report for quantum purposes. Medical experts will also be required for quantum purposes in clinical negligence and disease and illness claims. The specimen letter of instruction to a medical expert which is set out at Annex D to the PAP for personal injury claims (see **Appendix 2**) is suitable for this purpose.

It may be necessary to provide the expert with copies of the claimant's medical records where they relate to the injuries sustained and/or the treatment received by the claimant as a result of the defendant's negligence, or where there is a pre-existing condition which may have an impact on the assessment of damages.

The heading of the letter should contain: the client's full name, address, date of birth, date of the accident, his telephone number and, if considered appropriate, details of the hospital where the client was treated. It is important that the letter of instruction makes it clear on whose behalf the solicitor is acting and whether the notice of appointment should be sent directly to the claimant or via his solicitor.

Where a defendant is given permission to instruct an expert to examine the claimant and provide a report on condition and prognosis, specific questions included in the letter of instruction may require the expert to comment, for example, on the reasonableness of the special damages claim, ie did the client reasonably need assistance with gardening and, if so, for how long?

11.7.2   Instructing medical experts in relation to liability and causation

In clinical negligence and disease and illness claims, it will be necessary to instruct a medical expert of an appropriate speciality to advise in relation to liability and/or causation. These experts may not need to examine the claimant and their expert opinion will be primarily based on the claimant's medical records, copies of which should be enclosed. The letter of instruction may include the following matters:

(a)   a chronology of the events/factual resumé to which the expert can refer. A concise overview of the events should be available for the expert to consider;

(b)   a brief explanation of the relevant standard of care, with reference to the *Bolam* test as modified by *Bolitho* (see **5.3**). In the case of *Sharpe v Southend Health Authority* [1997] 8 Med LR 299, the Court of Appeal stated that an expert in a clinical negligence case should make it clear in his report whether the approach adopted by the defendant was in accordance with a responsible body of medical practitioners, even if he himself would have adopted a different approach. If it is not known that the expert is aware of this point, then this must also be mentioned in the letter of instruction;

(c)   a reminder that it will be necessary to establish a causational link between the identified negligence and injury;

(d)   an offer for the expert to meet the claimant if he so wishes. This may not be necessary but the facility should be made available;

(e)   the date by which the report is needed;

(f)   who is responsible for the fee;

(g)   a request that the expert consider whether all relevant notes have been disclosed and, if not, what further notes should be obtained;

(h)   a request that the expert advise as to whether any other type of expert evidence is required in addition to his own;

(i)   a request that the expert make reference to medical publications to support his case. The expert should be asked to refer to texts and authoritative works that were available at the time of the incident (see *Breeze v Ahmed* [2005] EWCA Civ 223);

(j)   specific questions that the expert is required to answer;

(k)   a reminder that the expert may be required to attend a conference with counsel at the appropriate time;

(l)   a reminder as to how the doctor should structure the report.

The medical notes must not be sent to the expert without first being checked by the solicitor to ensure that they are complete and in order. Identical ring binders should be prepared, with copies of paginated medical notes included, in date order, indexed and divided into relevant sections. A ring binder of notes should be prepared for each expert, counsel and the solicitor.

11.8 THE EXPERT'S REPORT

Practice Direction 35, para 3.2 states that an expert's report must:

(1)   give details of the expert's qualifications;

(2)   give details of any literature or other material which the expert has relied on in making the report;

(3)   contain a statement setting out the substance of all facts and instructions given to the expert which are material to the opinions expressed in the report or upon which those opinions are based;

(4)   make clear which of the facts stated in the report are within the expert's own knowledge;

(5)   say who carried out any examination, measurement, test or experiment which the expert has used for the report, give the qualifications of that person, and say whether or not the test or experiment has been carried out under the expert's supervision;

(6)   where there is a range of opinion on the matters dealt with in the report –

    (a)   summarise the range of opinion, and

    (b)   give reasons for his own opinion;

(7)   contain a summary of the conclusions reached;

(8)   if the expert is not able to give his opinion without qualification, state the qualification; and

(9)   contain a statement that the expert –

    (a)   understands his duty to the court, and has complied with that duty; and

    (b)   is aware of the requirements of Part 35, this practice direction and the Guidance for the Instruction of Experts in Civil Claims 2014.

In relation to the requirement for a statement of the substance of the instructions given to the expert, it should be noted that r 35.10(4) specifically states that the instructions are not privileged. However, the court will not normally allow cross-examination of the expert on the instructions, unless it believes the statement is inaccurate (see also *Lucas v Barking, Havering and Redbridge Hospitals NHS Trust* [2003] EWCA Civ 1102, [2003] All ER (D) 379 (Jul)).

Once an expert's report has been received, it should be read (and understood) by the solicitor and sent to the client for his approval. It should then be disclosed to the other party in accordance with the order for directions.

A specimen medical report may be found in **Appendix 1** at Document 8.

11.9   CONFERENCE WITH EXPERT AND COUNSEL WHERE EXPERT INSTRUCTED BY ONE PARTY

11.9.1   The initial conference prior to proceedings being issued

11.9.1.1   Personal injury

An initial conference prior to proceedings being issued is not normally necessary in personal injury cases, but consideration should be given to this approach if the claimant is resistant to the solicitor's advice that the claim is likely to fail, or if the matter is unusually complicated.

11.9.1.2   Clinical negligence and illness and disease claims

In clinical negligence and illness and disease cases, because the issues involved are likely to be complex, it may be appropriate to arrange a conference with the expert, counsel and the client after the initial medical report on liability and/or causation has been provided. This will provide an opportunity to examine all the issues in full, to test the expert's evidence and ensure that he is the appropriate person to be instructed, and to determine whether proceedings should be issued. An initial conference at this stage is also appropriate when the medical report is unfavourable and it appears that the claim should not proceed.

The conference also provides a valuable opportunity to satisfy the client that every possibility has been investigated, that he is not being sidelined by the legal process and that there is no medical conspiracy against him.

Consideration should be given to instructing counsel to produce a written advice following the conference, to ensure that all matters have been dealt with. During the conference, a detailed note should be taken of matters covered. This note should be sent to all the experts who attended the conference to confirm that it accurately records the views they expressed.

If the case is going to proceed, the next stage is the drafting of the letter of claim which is to be sent to the potential defendant.

11.9.2   Conference with counsel after proceedings issued

11.9.2.1   Personal injury

In the vast majority of personal injury cases, proceedings will be issued without the need for a conference with counsel, and many low-value cases proceed to trial without such a conference. In more complex personal injury cases, the solicitor and counsel will want to be sure that the expert has studied all the papers sent to him, has understood the facts of the case, and that he has excellent communication skills. These and other matters can be assessed at a conference.

11.9.2.2   Clinical negligence

In addition to the conference prior to the issue of proceedings in a clinical negligence case, it is common to have a further conference after the exchange of lay witness statements to check whether all the experts can still support the case. A further conference is normally arranged prior to the trial to review matters.

11.10   CONCLUSION

The role that the expert has in a personal injury or clinical negligence case is a significant one. The importance of the selection of the correct individual cannot be overestimated. The key points are summarised below at **11.12**.

11.11   FURTHER READING

Pre-action Protocol for Personal Injury Claims

Pre-action Protocol for the Resolution of Clinical Disputes

Guidance for the Instruction of Experts in Civil Claims 2014

11.12   KEY POINTS

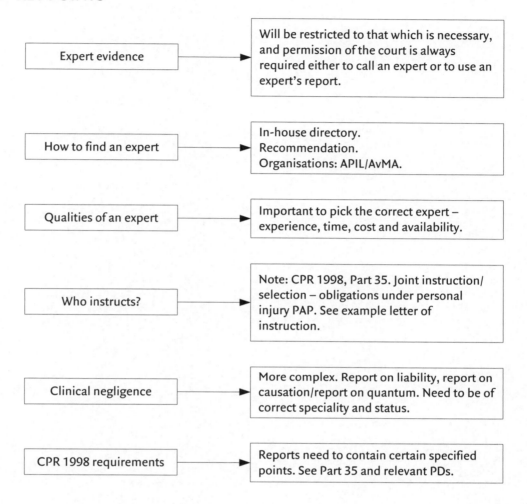

COMMENCEMENT OF PROCEEDINGS

LEARNING OUTCOMES

After reading this chapter you will be able to:

- set out the main matters to be considered before and upon the issue of proceedings
- explain where and how proceedings are issued
- draft appropriate Particulars of Claim and Defence
- explain what additional claims are and how such claims are made.

12.1 INTRODUCTION

Where the defendant has denied liability, or where he has failed to respond within the time limits set out in the relevant PAP (see **10.2**), the claimant is entitled to commence proceedings by issuing and serving the claim form.

It is usually to the claimant's advantage to begin proceedings early for the following reasons:

(a) To avoid problems with the limitation period. In personal injury litigation, proceedings must normally be commenced within three years of the accident occurring (see **Chapter 7**). Ongoing negotiations with the proposed defendant/defendant's insurers do not have the automatic effect of extending the limitation period, and in any event, negotiations may continue after proceedings have been commenced.

(b) To avoid further delay in so-called 'long-tail' occupational disease and illness claims, and in some clinical negligence claims where claimants will be relying on a later date of knowledge in order to overcome limitation problems. Claimants may have suffered from poor health for many years, and it is important that their claims are progressed with expedition.

(c)   To exert pressure on the defendant/defendant's insurers to act in relation to the claim. In personal injury cases, it will often precipitate the defendant's file moving from the insurance company claims department to the insurer's nominated solicitors, who may be more willing to negotiate.

(d)   In practice, judgment usually carries entitlement to interest and costs. A settlement achieved prior to the commencement of proceedings does not carry such an entitlement (although the claimant's solicitor will always include in any such settlement an element in respect of interest and costs). After proceedings have been issued, if there is any argument by the defendant as to how much of the claimant's costs he should pay on settlement, the claimant's solicitor can have his costs assessed by the court.

(e)   Commencing proceedings enables the claimant to apply to the court for an interim payment in the event that a voluntary payment cannot be negotiated.

12.2 PRE-ISSUE CHECKLIST

Unless the limitation period is about to expire (in which case see **7.9.2**), proceedings should not be commenced until the claimant's solicitor is satisfied that:

(a)   the period allowed by the relevant PAP for the defendant to respond to the letter of claim (or the CNF/DCNF in a case falling under one of the low value protocols) has expired and either the defendant has not responded or the defendant has denied liability;

(b)   a full investigation of the matter has been conducted and the claimant's solicitor is in possession of all relevant evidence in relation to liability and quantum;

(c)   a re-evaluation of the risk assessment has been carried out which takes into account the defendant's response to the letter of claim, the documents supplied by him and other evidence obtained following the dispatch of the letter of claim. Where the risk assessment indicates that the claim is unlikely to succeed, the claimant's solicitor should not issue proceedings but should try to settle the matter, if at all possible;

(d)   the requirements of the relevant PAP have been complied with. In particular, an approach has been made to the proposed defendant with the aim of settling the matter without the need for litigation;

(e)   the claimant's solicitor is ready to process the claim once proceedings have started, in accordance with the directions and the associated timetable which will be set out by the court on allocation. The court will actively manage the claim and, in fast track cases in particular, there will be limited time to prepare for each stage of the proceedings. The court will not be best pleased if the claimant's solicitor is unable to keep to the timetable due to inadequate preparation prior to issue;

(f)   where the client has before the event insurance (BEI) or after the event insurance (AEI), the insurer has given permission for proceedings to be commenced;

(g)   the claimant understands the situation and has given his instructions for the matter to proceed.

12.3 MATTERS TO CONSIDER UPON ISSUE

Additional steps must be taken in certain circumstances before, at the time of, or shortly following the issue of proceedings. The claimant's solicitor needs to be suitably organised before proceedings are issued, as the consequences of failing to carry out the required steps may be severe.

12.3.1 Medical report and schedule of past and future loss and expense

A medical report and a schedule setting out past and future loss and expense should be served with the particulars of claim. Medical experts can be extremely busy and there may be a lengthy delay in obtaining an appointment for the claimant. Schedules in relation to substantial claims may be complex and cannot be put together overnight. Bearing in mind the fact that the particulars of claim must be served within 14 days of service of the claim form, the claimant's solicitor should be wary of issuing proceedings until these documents are available.

12.3.2 Notice in road traffic cases: Road Traffic Act 1988, ss 151 and 152

In RTA claims, where the claimant is entitled to require an insurance company to settle the judgment under s 151 of the Road Traffic Act 1988 (see **3.3.2** and **10.3.1.3**), the claimant must give the insurer notification of the claim under s 152, either before or within seven days of the commencement of the claim. It makes sense to give this notification as soon as possible, although some solicitors may choose to wait until commencement and then serve the notice on the insurers with a copy of the claim form and particulars of claim. There is no prescribed form for the notice.

12.4 ISSUING PROCEEDINGS

12.4.1 Where to issue

All tort proceedings may be issued in the county court. Proceedings which include a claim for damages for personal injury may be commenced in the High Court only where the total claim is worth at least £50,000 unless an enactment requires it to be commenced in the High Court (CPR, PD 7A, paras 2.2 and 2.3).

When calculating the value of the claim for commencement purposes, the claimant must disregard interest and costs, any possible counterclaim or finding of contributory negligence which may be made against him, and any recoupment of benefits by the Compensation Recovery Unit (CPR, r 16.3(6)).

The procedure for issuing proceedings is dealt with in *Civil Litigation*, but it is worth saying here that all designated money claims which are to be commenced in the county court must be issued in the County Court Money Claims Centre.

12.4.2 Claim form – statements of value

In accordance with CPR, r 16.2(c), where the claimant is making a claim for money, the claim form must contain a statement of value in accordance with CPR, r 16.3. This will be used to determine the amount of the court fee to be paid by the claimant upon issue of proceedings, and will assist the court to allocate the matter to the appropriate track.

As it will not be possible to state a precise amount, but it should be possible to give an approximation of how much is likely to be received, the statement would be that the claimant expects to recover:

(a) not more than £10,000;

(b) more than £10,000 but not more than £25,000; or

(c) more than £25,000.

See Document 10 of the Case Study in **Appendix 1** for an example of a claim form.

If a claim is to be issued in the High Court, it must state that the claimant reasonably expects to recover £50,000 or more; or must state that some other enactment provides that the claim may be commenced in the High Court and specify that enactment (CPR, r 16.3(5)(c)).

In a claim for personal injuries, the claimant must state on the claim form whether the amount which he reasonably expects to recover in general damages for pain, suffering and loss of amenity is either not more than £1,000 or more than £1,000 (CPR, r 16.3(3)). This is to enable the court to allocate the claim to the correct track should a defence be filed (see **13.3**).

12.5 PARTICULARS OF CLAIM

The particulars of claim must be contained in or served with the claim form, or be served on the defendant by the claimant within 14 days after service of the claim form. In any event, particulars of claim must be served on the defendant no later than the latest time for serving a claim form (ie, within four months after date of issue of the claim form).

It is vital that the particulars of claim are drafted carefully. They should set out the basis of the claim clearly, accurately and comprehensively. If they do not do this, the worst case scenario is that the claim will be struck out for failing to disclose reasonable grounds for bringing the claim (CPR, r 3.4(2)(a)) or summary judgment will be given against the claimant (CPR, r 24.2). At the very least, the claimant's solicitor will give an impression of sloppiness or incompetence.

12.5.1 Structure and content of the particulars of claim

The formalities set out in PD 5, para 2.2 and the main principles of drafting are discussed in **Civil Litigation**. A suggested structure for particulars of claim in a personal injury case can be found at **12.15** below, and an example is included in the Case Study at **Appendix 1(11)**. Particulars of claim in clinical negligence cases and in more complex personal injury cases are generally drafted by counsel.

Rule 16.4 of the CPR and PD 16 deal with the contents of the particulars of claim. The particulars must include, *inter alia*:

(a)   a concise statement of the facts on which the claimant relies. When drafting, it is useful to remember that the claimant will need to prove that the defendant owed him a duty of care and/or there was a statutory duty, that this duty was breached by the defendant, and that this caused injury and loss which was reasonably foreseeable. As far as is reasonably possible, the particulars should deal with these elements in separate, consecutively numbered paragraphs, with one allegation in each paragraph and in a chronological order.

Although the CPR allow references to evidence and statutory provisions, the particulars should deal with the 'bare bones' of the claim, and it is therefore preferable not to include these details unless the information is specifically required. Four examples of where evidence or statutory provisions should be set out are as follows:

(i)   Where the claimant wishes to rely on the evidence of a medical expert, a medical report should be attached to the particulars (see (e) below).

(ii)   Where the claimant alleges breach of statutory duty, such as in an employer's liability case, the relevant statutory provisions should be set out.

(iii)   Where the claimant relies on a criminal conviction of the defendant (see (b) below).

(iv)   Where the claimant is seeking an order for provisional damages (see (g) below);

(b)   where the claimant is relying on a relevant conviction of the defendant, the nature of the conviction, the date of conviction, the name of the convicting court and the issue in the claim to which it relates;

(c)   where the claimant is relying on a later date of knowledge for the purposes of limitation (see **Chapter 7**), details of the date of knowledge (PD 16, para 8.2);

(d)   for the purposes of assessing damages, the claimant's date of birth and brief details of his injuries. The main points of the medical report can be summarised for this purpose but, especially in a high-value claim, it is important to ensure that all the relevant information is included, ie the immediate impact of the accident, the duration of any stay in hospital, the number and nature of any operations or other treatments, continuing pain and disability, the practical effects on the claimant's life, disability in the labour market, loss of congenial employment, etc;

(e) if the claimant wishes to rely on the evidence of a medical expert, a report detailing the injuries, which must be served with or attached to the particulars of claim. In a soft tissue injury claim, the medical report must be a fixed cost medical report (PD 16, para 4.3A);

(f) details of past and future expenses and losses, which should be provided in a schedule attached to the particulars;

(g) if the claimant is seeking provisional damages, a statement to that effect and his grounds for claiming them. Further guidance as to what must be set out is found in PD 16, para. 4.4, namely:

    (i) that the claimant is seeking the award under either s 32A of the Senior Courts Act 1981, or s 51 of the County Courts Act 1984,

    (ii) that there is a chance that at some future time he will develop some serious disease or suffer some serious deterioration in his physical or mental condition, and

    (iii) the disease or type of deterioration in respect of which an application may be made at a future date;

(h) where the claim relates to a fatal accident, a statement by the claimant covering:

    (i) the fact that it is brought under the FAA 1976,

    (ii) the dependants on whose behalf the claim is made,

    (iii) the date of birth of each dependant, and

    (iv) details of the nature of the dependency claim;

(i) where the claimant seeks interest, this must be pleaded by reference to the Senior Courts Act 1981 or the County Courts Act 1984, depending on whether the claim is to be issued in the High Court or the county court. The amount of interest which may be claimed, and the period for which it may be claimed, differs in relation to special damages and damages for pain, suffering and loss of amenity (see **15.6**). Consequently, where the amount sought is considerable or the calculation of damages complex, the plea for interest may be set out in detail. However, it is common practice, particularly in low value claims, to claim interest at such rates and for such periods as the court thinks fit.

The particulars of claim and the schedule of special damages must also contain a statement of truth, ie that the claimant (and if the claimant is acting as a litigation friend, the litigation friend) believes that the facts stated in the document are true. This may be signed by the claimant (or litigation friend), or by the solicitor on his behalf (CPR, r 22).

See Document 11 of the Case Study in **Appendix 1** for an example of Particulars of Claim, Document 8 for an example of a medical report and Document 12 for a Schedule of Past and Future Expenses and Losses.

12.6　SERVICE OF PROCEEDINGS

After the claim form has been issued, it must be served within four months after the date of issue. This may be extended, however, with leave of the court. If the claim form is to be served out of the jurisdiction, the period is six months.

See *Civil Litigation* for the rules governing the service of court documents.

12.7　ACKNOWLEDGEMENT OF SERVICE

The defendant may respond to the claim by:

(a) defending the claim; or

(b) admitting the claim; or

(c) acknowledging service of the claim form.

If the defendant makes no response to the claim, the claimant may enter default judgment.

Where the defendant is unable to file a defence in time, he may gain extra time by acknowledging service. The time for acknowledgement of service is 14 days from the service of the claim form, unless the claim form indicates that the particulars of claim are to follow separately, in which case the defendant does not have to acknowledge service until 14 days after service of those particulars of claim. The acknowledgement of service form must be signed by the defendant or his legal representative, and must include an address for service for the defendant which must be within the jurisdiction.

On receipt of such an acknowledgement of service, the court must notify the claimant in writing of this.

12.8   THE DEFENCE

The defendant must file a defence within 14 days of service of the particulars of claim, or, if the defendant has filed an acknowledgement of service, within 28 days after service of the particulars of claim.

The parties may agree an extension of time for filing of the defence of up to 28 days. The defendant must give the court written notice of any such agreement.

12.8.1   Contents of the defence

The defence must deal with every allegation set out in the particulars of claim by admitting, denying or not admitting (neither admitting nor denying) each allegation. This will be an easier task if the particulars have dealt with one allegation per paragraph.

The following should also be noted.

(a)   Where allegations are denied, the defendant must give reasons for that denial and, where relevant, give his own version of the facts. If the defendant disputes the claimant's statement of value, he must give reasons for doing so and, if possible, give his own estimate of value.

(b)   Where the defendant wishes to make an allegation of fraud, and there is reasonable evidence to establish a prima facie case of fraud, this must be specifically pleaded in the defence.

(c)   Where the defendant wishes to rely on the fact that he took all reasonable care or on a statutory defence, such as s 58 of the Highways Act 1980, he should say so.

(d)   Where the defendant claims that the claimant was himself negligent, and therefore contributed to the accident or increased the severity of his injuries, the particulars of the claimant's negligence should be set out in the defence.

(e)   The defendant should give details of the expiry period of any limitation period on which he wishes to rely (PD 16, para 14.1).

(f)   If the claimant has attached a medical report to his particulars of claim, the defendant should state whether he admits, denies or does not admit the matters contained in it, and give reasons for any matters he denies. For example, the defendant may claim that the claimant has failed to mitigate loss, that the injuries were not caused by the alleged negligence but rather by some pre-existing condition, or that the claimant has fraudulently made or exaggerated the claim. If the defendant has obtained his own medical report on the claimant, he should attach it to the defence.

(g)   If the claimant has attached a schedule of past and future expenses and losses to his particulars of claim, the defendant must include with his defence a counter-schedule stating which items he agrees, disputes, or neither agrees nor disputes but has no knowledge of. If items are disputed, an alternative figure must be supplied.

(h) The defence must contain a statement that the defendant, or, if the defendant is conducting proceedings with a litigation friend, the litigation friend, believes the facts stated in it are true. The statement of truth may be signed either by the defendant (or litigation friend), or by his legal adviser.

(i) Unless the defendant has already acknowledged service, the defendant must give an address for service which is within the jurisdiction.

12.9 THE COUNTERCLAIM

If a defendant wishes to make a counterclaim against a claimant, he should file his counterclaim with his defence (CPR, r 20.4). Provided the counterclaim is filed at the same time as the defence, the defendant will not need permission of the court to make the counterclaim. Generally, the counterclaim will form part of the same document as the defence and will follow on from the defence.

12.10 THE REPLY TO DEFENCE AND DEFENCE TO COUNTERCLAIM

The claimant may file a reply to the defence, but if he does not do so, he will not be deemed to admit the matters raised in the defence. The reply must respond to any matters in the defence which have not been dealt with in the particulars of the claim, and must contain a statement of truth.

The claimant may file a reply and a certificate of reply when he files his directions questionnaire (see **13.2**). If he does serve a reply, he must also serve it on all other parties.

Where there is a counterclaim and the claimant disputes the counterclaim, he must file a defence to it within the usual 14-day period. This will be way of a reply to the defence and a defence to the counterclaim. If the claimant does not file a defence to the counterclaim, the defendant will be entitled to enter judgment in respect of the counterclaim.

The particulars of claim, defence and reply are said to be the statements of case. No subsequent statements of case may be filed without the court's leave.

12.11 AMENDMENT TO STATEMENTS OF CASE

Sometimes, the claimant's solicitor may need to amend the particulars of claim. Where this arises before the particulars have been served on the defendant, the amendments may be made without the court's permission. On occasion, the defence may highlight a need for an amendment, for example the need to add a further defendant, or even to pursue a different defendant. Amendments may be made at any time after service, provided the defendant gives his written consent. Where consent is not forthcoming, the permission of the court must be sought (see CPR, rr 17 and 23).

In *Goode v Martin* [2001] EWCA Civ 1899, [2002] 1 WLR 1828, the claimant sought permission to amend her statement of claim after the expiry of the limitation period. The amendment consisted of a response to the defendant's version of events and no new facts were being introduced. The claimant also argued that if the amendment could not be allowed under a conventional approach to r 17.4, a less conventional approach should be adopted to comply with Article 6 of the European Convention on Human Rights.

The court found that because the claimant's new cause of action arose out of the same facts that were in issue in the original claim, she should be allowed to add to her claim the alternative plea proposed. The Court of Appeal agreed with the claimant that to prevent the claimant from putting her alternative case before the court would impose an impediment on her access to the court that would have to be justified. It was possible to interpret r 17.4 in such a way as to allow the claimant's amendment, and that should be done to comply with Article 6 of the Convention.

12.12 ADDITIONAL CLAIMS (CPR, PART 20)

Part 20 of the CPR and PD 20 deal with counterclaims by the defendant against the claimant (see **12.9**) and other additional claims, namely counterclaims against the claimant and some other person, and claims by the defendant against any person (whether or not already a party) for contribution or indemnity or some other remedy (CPR, r 20.2(1)). Where an additional claim involves an individual or a body who was not already a party to the proceedings, the claim is commonly known as 'third party proceedings'.

In accordance with s 1(1) of the Civil Liability (Contribution) Act 1978, 'any person liable in respect of any damage suffered by another person may recover contribution from any other person liable in respect of the same damage (whether jointly with him or otherwise)'.

The 'contribution' which a defendant may seek from a third party may be either:

(a)   *an indemnity* – this arises though a contractual relationship between the defendant and the third party (such as where a product supplied by the defendant to the claimant causes injury to the claimant, but was manufactured and supplied to the defendant by the third party), or a statutory obligation placed on the third party (such as where a gas company fails to reinstate a road properly and the claimant, who was injured in a road traffic accident caused by defects in the road surface, brings proceedings against the local highway authority). The claimant has a cause of action against the defendant, but the court may order the third party to recompense the defendant in respect of the full amount of the damages he is ordered to pay the claimant. The important point to note is that an indemnity does not exonerate the defendant; the defendant remains liable to the claimant. Consequently, if the third party were to become insolvent, the claimant would be able to recover the judgment sum from the defendant; or

(b)   *a contribution* – this arises where either or both of two parties, the defendant and the third party, have been negligent or in breach of contract or of statutory duty (such as in a road traffic accident where the claimant, who was a passenger in Car A, issues proceeding against the defendant, the driver of Car B, but the defendant alleges that the driver of Car A, the third party, was fully or partially responsible for the accident). In such a case, the defendant seeks a contribution which may be equal to or less than the claimant's loss.

It is common for defendants to claim both an indemnity and a contribution in the alternative.

12.12.1 Making an 'additional claim'

Where a defendant wishes to make a counterclaim against someone other than the claimant, or where he wishes to claim an indemnity or a contribution from someone else in respect of the damages which he may be ordered to pay to the claimant, his solicitor should take the appropriate steps set out in CPR, Part 20 and PD 20 to ensure that the court is able to apportion blame and liability to pay compensation. The appropriate steps for each type of claim are as follows:

(a)   a defendant who wishes to seek damages (ie counterclaim) against someone who is not already a party to the proceedings. He must apply to the court for an order that that person be added as an additional party. The application may be made without notice unless the court orders otherwise (CPR, r 20.5);

(b)   a defendant who wishes to seek a contribution or an indemnity from a co-defendant. Once he has filed his acknowledgement of service or defence, the defendant may proceed with his additional claim against the co-defendant by filing a notice stating the nature and grounds of his claim and serving it upon the co-defendant. Provided he serves the notice with his defence, he will not require the court's permission. Otherwise, he must seek leave (CPR, r 20.6);

(c)   a defendant who wishes to seek a contribution or an indemnity in respect of the claimant's losses from someone who is not already a party to the proceedings (commonly known as 'third party proceedings'). The defendant must issue an additional claim and serve it on the third party, together with particulars of claim, the forms for defending and admitting the claim and acknowledging service, a copy of the statements of case which have been served in the main claim, and any other document the court directs. Provided the claim is issued before or at the same time as the defence is filed, the court's permission is not required. Otherwise, leave will be necessary (CPR, r 20.7);

(d)   where an additional claim has been made against a third party, when that third party wishes to seek a contribution or an indemnity from someone else, whether or not already a party. Where a new party is introduced, the procedure is the same as in (b) above.

12.12.2   Obtaining permission to issue an additional claim

Where permission is required for an additional claim, an application notice must be filed and served, together with a copy of the proposed additional claim and a witness statement setting out the matters contained in PD 20, paras 2.1 to 2.3, namely:

(a)   the stage the proceedings have reached;

(b)   the nature of the additional claim to be made, or details of the question or issue which needs to be decided;

(c)   a summary of the facts on which the additional claim in based;

(d)   the name and address of the proposed additional party;

(e)   where there has been a delay, an explanation for the delay. The court will be concerned to ensure that the late introduction of an additional party will not cause prejudice to any existing party; and

(f)   a timetable of the proceedings to date.

12.12.3   Case management in relation to an additional claim

The court will be keen to ensure that counterclaims and other additional claims are managed in the most convenient and effective manner. Where the defendant to an additional claim files a defence, a case management hearing will take place to enable the court to consider the future conduct of the proceedings. In accordance with PD 20, para 5.3, the court may treat the hearing as a summary judgment hearing, order that the Part 20 proceedings be dismissed and/or make appropriate directions.

12.12.4   Example of an additional claim

Carol was injured in a road traffic accident when her car was hit by a vehicle driven by Darren. Darren had failed to stop at a junction. Carol (the claimant) issued proceedings in negligence against Darren (the defendant). The day before the accident, Darren had taken his car to be serviced by Tyrone, who had fitted new brake pads. Darren alleges that when he tried to apply his brakes they failed to work, and this was the cause of the accident. Darren makes an additional claim against Tyrone (the third party). Tyrone alleges that the brakes failed because the brake pads he fitted to Darren's car, which were purchased from Fab-Brakes Limited, were defective. Tyrone makes an additional claim against Fab-Brakes Limited (the fourth party).

12.13   GROUP LITIGATION

Engaging in group litigation is time-consuming, difficult and (therefore) costly. Group litigation results when there are a number of prospective claimants who have a common interest or common defendant arising out of a common incident. An example of group litigation is that brought by a number of families following the drowning of 51 passengers of the pleasure boat *Marchioness*, which sank after being hit by the dredger *Bowbelle* on the Thames in 1989.

The relevant rule of the CPR 1998 governing group litigation can be found at Part 19, with its accompanying PD 19B. Part 19 provides for the making of a group litigation order (GLO) at the request of the parties where there are, or are likely to be, a number of similar claims. The aim of the GLO is to 'steer' the group litigation by ensuring that the case is managed to suit the needs of multi-party litigation.

The GLO seeks to ensure that all cases that are eligible to join the group do so and are then all treated in like manner to ensure consistency of result. The GLO must include specific directions for the maintenance of a group register, specify the GLO issues, and appoint a particular court and particular judge to oversee the case management process. By giving one court/judge 'ownership' of the management process, the case can be more effectively managed than if all potential claimants were allowed to issue and deal with their case at any court of their choosing. The managing judge appointed to the group litigation will quickly amass specialist knowledge in relation to that particular group litigation, and will therefore be able to deal with matters as they arise more quickly and effectively.

The details of group litigation are beyond the scope of this book but recourse should be had, as a starting point, to PD 19B and to The Law Society's Multi-party Action Information Service.

12.14 CONCLUSION

Generally, it is in the claimant's interests for proceedings to be commenced as early as possible. Nevertheless, the claimant's solicitor should ensure that the matter has been investigated as thoroughly as possible, and that all preliminary steps to protect the client's position and to comply with the overriding objective set out in r 1 and the relevant pre-action protocol are complied with prior to issue of proceedings.

Practitioners require a good working knowledge of the rules which govern whether the proceedings should be commenced in the county court or High Court, and where and how they should be issued. A sound understanding of what should be contained in the Particulars of Claim and the Defence, and competent drafting skills are essential.

12.15 SUGGESTED STRUCTURE OF PARTICULARS OF CLAIM IN PERSONAL INJURY CASE

Court inserts case number

IN THE HIGH COURT OF JUSTICE ETC

Parties

PARTICULARS OF CLAIM

- Describe parties to establish duty of care if necessary

- Succinctly describe what happened

- Allege breach of statutory duty/duty of care

PARTICULARS OF BREACH OF STATUTORY DUTY

Where relevant, set out the breaches with specific reference to the relevant statutory provisions. Be as comprehensive as possible.

PARTICULARS OF NEGLIGENCE

Set out what the defendant did or did not do which constitutes negligence. Be as specific as possible. Where you have set out breaches of statutory duty, state here 'The Claimant repeats the allegations of breach of statutory duty as allegations of negligence', then particularise negligence.

- Criminal conviction (if relevant) – nature of conviction, date of conviction, name of convicting court and the issue in the claim to which it relates

- Allege injury and loss caused

PARTICULARS OF INJURY

- Date of birth
- Summary of injuries, treatment and continuing effect on claimant
- Weakening in labour market (*Smith v Manchester*)
- Refer to attached medical report(s)

PARTICULARS OF LOSS

- Refer to attached schedule

- Claim for interest

- Remedies sought (the prayer)
  AND THE CLAIMANT CLAIMS

- Statement of truth

- Ending

Note: in EL cases where the accident occurred on or after 1 October 2013, save in limited circumstances, breach of statutory duty does not give rise to civil liability. Consequently, there will not be Particulars of Breach of Statutory Duty. However, such breaches may be cited to support allegations of negligence.

CASE MANAGEMENT AND INTERIM APPLICATIONS

LEARNING OUTCOMES

After reading this chapter you will be able to:

- explain why and how and upon what criteria claims are allocated to the appropriate track, and the court's role in managing cases

- set out the standard directions together with the timeframe for fast track cases, and explain how directions are dealt with in multi-track cases

- explain what an interim payment is, the grounds and procedure for obtaining an interim payment, and how the amount of an interim payment is determined.

13.1 INTRODUCTION

Case management is one of the key elements of the CPR 1998. The overriding objective of the Rules, as set out in CPR, r 1.1, is to enable the court to deal with cases justly and at proportionate cost. In accordance with CPR, r 1.4, the court must further the overriding objective by actively managing cases, and r 1.3 requires solicitors and their clients to assist the court in furthering the overriding objective. Dealing with cases justly and at proportionate cost includes allotting to each case an appropriate share of the court's resources (r 1.1(2)(e)), which, in the first instance, requires the court to ensure that cases are dealt with in the appropriate court and are allocated to the appropriate track. It also means that the court will enforce compliance with rules, practice directions and orders (r 1.1(2)(f)), and it has various sanctions at its disposal in order to enable it to do so.

The bulk of the activities which require active management by the court arise in the period between the filing of the defence and trial, or earlier settlement. During this period, the case is allocated to the appropriate track and the parties receive from the court a set of directions, setting out a number of steps which must be taken within specified time limits. The aim of these directions is to encourage settlement and, where this is not possible, ensure the matter is properly prepared for trial.

This chapter contains a brief account of some of the main issues relating to case management and interim applications which are relevant to personal injury and clinical negligence cases. See *Civil Litigation* for a more in-depth consideration of this area.

13.2 DIRECTIONS QUESTIONNAIRE

Where a claim is defended, upon receipt of the defence, the court will make a provisional decision regarding the appropriate track for the case and will serve on the parties a notice of the proposed allocation (CPR, r 26.3). The factors relevant to allocation are set out at **13.3** below.

The notice of the proposed allocation requires each party to complete the relevant directions questionnaire (N180 for small track cases; N181 for fast track and multi-track cases), return it to the court office stated in the notice and serve copies on all other parties by the date specified on the notice. Parties are advised as to where the directions questionnaire may be obtained, unless a party is not legally represented, in which case a copy of the questionnaire will be enclosed with the notice.

Where a case is suitable for allocation to the fast track or multi-track, parties are also required to file proposed or agreed directions (see **13.5** and **13.6** below).

See Document 16 of the Case Study at **Appendix 1** for an example of a directions questionnaire.

13.2.1 Stay to allow settlement of case

A party returning his directions questionnaire may request a stay of up to one month while the parties try to settle the case. Where all parties request a stay, or where the court, of its own initiative, considers such a stay would be appropriate, the court will direct a stay for one month. The court may also extend the period of the stay until such a date or such a period as it considers appropriate. If proceedings are settled during the stay, the claimant must inform the court.

13.2.2 Transfer of proceedings between courts

The court has the power to transfer cases between the High Court and the county courts and within district registries of the High Court (CPR, r 30.1). It may do so of its own volition, or upon application by a party to the proceedings. Where the matter has been commenced in the county court and a party believes that it is suitable for trial in the High Court or vice versa, it should set out its reasons in the directions questionnaire.

The court may transfer designated money claims issued in the County Court Money Claims Centre (see **12.4.1**) to the claimant's preferred court or the defendant's home court as appropriate (CPR, r 26.2(A)). Parties should set out in the directions questionnaire the court in which they would like the matter to be dealt with, and should reach an agreement on this point, if possible.

13.3 ALLOCATION TO TRACK

In accordance with CPR, r 26.6, personal injury and clinical negligence claims are allocated to the appropriate track within a three-tier system largely in accordance with the value of the claim as a whole and the value of the claim for damages for 'personal injuries' suffered, ie that part of the damages which relates to pain, suffering and loss of amenity.

The *small claims track* is the normal track where:

(a)   the value of the claim as a whole is not more than £10,000; and

(b)   the value of any claim for damages for personal injuries is not more than £1,000.

The *fast track* is the normal track for any claim for which the small claims track is not the normal track and which has a value of not more than £25,000. However, such a case will be allocated to the fast track only if the court considers that:

(a)   the trial is likely to last for no longer than one day; and

(b)   oral expert evidence at trial will be limited to one expert per party in relation to a maximum of two expert fields.

The *multi-track* is the normal track for any claim for which the small claims track or the fast track is not the normal track.

Once the court has allocated a claim to a track, it will notify all parties, and it will also serve them with copies of the allocation questionnaire provided by all other parties and a copy of any further information provided by a party about his case.

Factors taken into account

When allocating a case, the court may take into account the following factors (CPR, r 26.8(1)):

(a)   the financial value of the claim (or amount in dispute if different);

(b)   the nature of remedy sought;

(c)   the likely complexity of the facts, law or evidence;

(d)   the number of parties or likely parties;

(e)   the value of any counterclaim or other claim and the complexity of any matters relating to it;

(f)   the amount of oral evidence that may be required;

(g)   the importance of the claim to persons who are not parties to the proceedings;

(h)   the views expressed by the parties;

(i)   the circumstances of the parties.

When assessing the value of the claim for the purposes of track allocation, the court will disregard any amounts not in dispute, interest, costs and any possible finding of contributory negligence which may be made against the claimant (CPR, r 26.8(2)).

If the statements of case are later amended and it becomes clear that the case has been allocated to an inappropriate track, the court may subsequently re-allocate a claim to a different track (CPR, r 26.10).

13.4   THE SMALL CLAIMS TRACK

The small claims track has been specifically designed to enable individuals to pursue or defend a claim without the need to instruct solicitors. A consideration of the procedure for these claims is beyond the scope of this book.

13.5   THE FAST TRACK

Case management of cases allocated to the fast track (see CPR Part 28) will generally be by directions given at allocation and, later, on the filing of the pre-trial checklists (listing questionnaires). The court will seek to give directions without the need for a hearing wherever possible, and sanctions will be imposed upon parties or their legal representatives whose default makes a hearing necessary.

Generally, the court will give standard directions for the management of the case, based on what is set out below, which will not be more than 30 weeks from allocation to trial. Although the parties may seek to agree directions, they are unlikely to be approved if they are not based on the following:

Disclosure	4 weeks
Exchange of witness statements	10 weeks
Exchange of experts' reports	14 weeks
Pre-trial checklists, listing questionnaires sent out by court	20 weeks
Pre-trial checklists, listing questionnaires filed by parties	22 weeks
Trial	30 weeks

When giving directions relating to the trial, the court may fix a trial date but would more usually set a 'trial period', a three-week period within which the trial will take place.

13.6   THE MULTI-TRACK

Where the value of the claim is more than £25,000, or where other factors make it unsuitable for the fast track, the claim will be allocated to the multi-track (see CPR Part 29). Claims will range from those which are just above the financial limit and which are fairly straightforward, to those of high value where the issues, evidence and law are extremely complex, and the court will adopt a flexible approach in order to manage the claim in accordance with its needs. When allocating a case to the multi-track, the court will either:

(a)   use the information contained in the directions questionnaires and any draft directions submitted by the parties in order to give directions for case management and set a timetable; or

(b)   fix a case management conference or a pre-trial review, or both, when it will hear from the parties and then give such directions relating to management of the case as it thinks fit.

In accordance with CPR, r 29.1(2), when drafting case management directions, both the parties and the court should take as their starting point any relevant model directions and standard directions, which can be found online at www.justice.gov.uk/courts/procedure-rules/civil, and adapt them as appropriate to the circumstances of the particular case.

13.7   THE CASE MANAGEMENT CONFERENCE AND PRE-TRIAL REVIEW

Where the court decides that directions cannot be given without hearing directly from the parties, it may, at any time after the filing of the defence, fix a date for a case management conference and/or, after the return of the directions questionnaires, set a date for a pre-trial review. Where a party is legally represented, any case management conference or pre-trial review called by the court must be attended by a legal representative who is familiar with the case and has the authority to take decisions regarding the management of the case. It is therefore important that the solicitors have obtained their client's instructions regarding all matters which are likely to be dealt with at the hearing. The court will expect the parties to be in a position to deal with all outstanding matters regarding the conduct of the case, and to reach an agreement regarding these matters wherever possible. It is increasingly common for case management conferences to be conducted over the telephone.

13.7.1   Case management in relation to an additional claim

Where the defendant to an additional claim (see **12.12**) files a defence, a case management hearing will take place to enable the court to consider the future conduct of the proceedings and give appropriate directions. It is obliged to ensure, in so far as it is practicable, that the original claim and all additional claims are managed together (CPR, r 20.13). In accordance with PD 20, para 5.3, at the hearing the court may:

(a)   treat the hearing as a summary judgment hearing;

(b)   order that the additional claim be dismissed;

(c)   give directions about the way any claim, question or issue set out in or arising from the additional claim should be dealt with;

(d)   give directions as to the part, if any, the additional defendant will take at the trial of the claim;

(e)   give directions about the extent to which the additional defendant is to be bound by any judgment or decision to be made in the claim.

Paragraph 7 of PD 20 sets out how parties should be described in the proceedings when there are additional claims. In summary, the claimant and defendants in the original claim should be referred to as such, and additional parties should be referred to as 'Third Party' or 'Fourth Party', depending on the order in which they were joined to the proceedings.

13.8   DISCLOSURE AND INSPECTION OF DOCUMENTS

Recent changes to the rules relating to disclosure and inspection of documents in multi-track cases require parties to file and serve a disclosure report, which includes an estimate of the costs associated with the disclosure process. However, it should be noted that where a multi-track claim includes a claim for personal injuries, it is exempt from this requirement. Consequently, parties are not required to give more than standard disclosure in fast track and multi-track cases unless the court directs otherwise (see CPR, r 31.5).

Standard disclosure means that a party is required to disclose only:

(a)   the documents on which he relies;

(b)   the documents which could adversely affect his own case, adversely affect another's case or support another party's case; and

(c)   all documents which he is required to disclose by any Practice Direction.

The court may dispense with or limit standard disclosure, and the parties can agree in writing to dispense with or limit any part of standard disclosure. The duty of standard disclosure continues throughout the proceedings, and if a document comes to a party's notice at any time, that party must immediately notify every other party. Privileged documents, however, should not be disclosed.

13.8.1   Procedure

Each party must make and serve a list of documents, which must identify the documents 'in a convenient order and manner as concisely as possible'. The list must indicate documents which are no longer in the parties' control and state what has happened to those documents.

The list must include a disclosure statement by the party:

(a)   setting out the extent of the search made to locate the documents;

(b)   certifying that he understands the duty of disclosure and that, to the best of his knowledge, he has carried out that duty.

13.8.2   Specific disclosure

Where a party believes that the other party has failed to carry out his duty of disclosure and inspection under CPR Part 31, he may apply for an order for specific disclosure under CPR, r 31.12. An order for specific disclosure can require a party to disclose specified documents or classes of documents, or carry out a search for specified documents and disclose any documents located as a result of that search.

An application for specific disclosure must be supported by evidence. The court will order specific disclosure only if necessary to dispose fairly of the claim or save costs.

For applications for an order for pre-action disclosure, see **10.10.2**.

13.9   THE EVIDENCE OF LAY WITNESSES

As part of its management powers, the court will decide the issues on which it requires evidence, the nature of that evidence and the way in which the evidence should be placed before the court (see CPR Part 32).

Facts should normally be proved at the trial by oral evidence of witnesses, and at any other hearing by the written evidence of witnesses. The court may allow a witness to give evidence by any means, which includes by means of a video link.

13.9.1   Procedure

According to CPR, r 32.4(1): 'A witness statement is a written statement signed by a person which contains the evidence which that person would be allowed to give orally.' A witness statement must comply with the requirements set out in PD 32 (CPR, r 32.8).

The court will normally give directions that each party serve the witness statements of the oral evidence on which he intends to rely at the trial. The directions usually envisage that simultaneous exchange will take place, but that court may give directions as to the order in which such witness statements are to be served and whether or not the statements are to be filed.

If a witness statement has been served and a party wishes to rely on that evidence at trial, the party must call the witness to give oral evidence unless the court otherwise orders.

13.9.2   Statements to stand as evidence-in-chief

Where a witness is called to give oral evidence, his statement shall stand as evidence-in-chief, unless the court orders otherwise (CPR, r 32.5(2)).

The witness giving the oral evidence may amplify the witness statement, and give evidence in relation to new matters that have arisen since the statement was served. However, he may do this only if the court considers there is a good reason not to confine his evidence to the contents of the statement that has been served.

Evidence in proceedings other than at the trial should be by witness statement, unless the court or a particular Practice Direction otherwise directs.

13.9.3   Witness summary

Where a party is required to serve a witness statement and he is unable to obtain such a statement, for example because the witness refuses to communicate with the party's solicitor, he may apply to the court for permission to serve only a witness summary instead (CPR, r 32.9). This application should be made without notice. The witness summary is a summary of the evidence which would otherwise go into a witness statement, or, if the evidence is not known, matters about which the party serving the witness summary will question the witness.

Where a witness statement or a witness summary is not served, the party will not be able to call that witness to give oral evidence unless the court allows it.

13.10   EXPERT EVIDENCE

The duties of experts in relation to court proceedings and the directions which the courts are likely to make are dealt with in Part 35 of the CPR (see **Chapter 11** generally and **11.2** for case management and the use of experts).

13.11 USE OF PLANS, PHOTOGRAPHS AND MODELS AT TRIAL

Where a party wishes to use evidence such as plans, photographs or models, or other evidence:

(a)   which is not contained in a witness statement, affidavit or expert's report;

(b)   which is not given orally at trial;

(c)   which has already been disclosed in relation to hearsay evidence;

the party wishing to use the evidence must disclose his intention to do so not later than the latest date for serving witness statements (CPR, r 33.6).

If the evidence forms part of expert evidence, it must be disclosed when the expert's report is itself served on the other party. Having disclosed such evidence, the party must give every other party an opportunity to inspect it and agree its admission without further proof.

13.12 PRE-TRIAL CHECKLIST (LISTING QUESTIONNAIRE)

In accordance with the order for directions, the court will send each party a listing questionnaire to complete and return to the court by the date specified in the notice of allocation (CPR, r 28.5 (fast track); CPR, r 29.6 (multi-track)). The date specified for filing a listing questionnaire is not more than eight weeks before the trial date.

If a party fails to file a completed listing questionnaire within the time limit, or fails to give all of the information, or the court thinks it is necessary, the court may fix a listing hearing or give such other directions as it thinks appropriate.

On receipt of the parties' listing questionnaires, the court may decide to hold a pre-trial review, or cancel a pre-trial review if it has already decided to hold one, having regard to the circumstances of the case.

Using the information given in the listing questionnaires or at the pre-trial review or listing hearing, the court will set a timetable for the trial, including confirming or fixing the trial date and setting out any further steps that need to be taken by the parties prior to the trial.

The court will give each party at least three weeks' notice of the trial date. Only in exceptional circumstances will the notice period be shorter than this.

13.13 VARIATION OF CASE MANAGEMENT TIMETABLE

The parties may agree in writing to extend the dates for the carrying out of any steps set out in the directions subject to CPR, r 29.5. This states that if a party wishes to vary any of the dates which the court has fixed for:

(a)   the case management conference;

(b)   the pre-trial review;

(c)   the return of listing questionnaires;

(d)   the trial;

he may do so only with leave of the court. The parties should not agree to make any other variations to the timetable which would make it impossible for them to comply with the time limits set for the above steps.

13.14 INTERIM APPLICATIONS

Interim applications are applications which are made by either party between the issue of proceedings and trial. The general rules governing such applications are set out in CPR Part 23, but practitioners should be aware that some types of application are governed by specific rules. For a detailed consideration of interim applications, see **Civil Litigation**. This text will deal with the following types of application:

(a)   interim payments;

(b)   specific disclosure – see **13.8.2** above; and

(c)   specific disclosure against a non-party.

13.15   INTERIM PAYMENTS

An interim payment is a payment made to the claimant, prior to the conclusion of the matter, in partial settlement of the claim. It is defined as 'a payment on account of any damages, debt or other sum (excluding costs) which that party may be held liable to pay to or for the benefit of another party to the proceedings if a final judgment or order of the court in the proceedings is given or made in favour of that other party' (Senior Courts Act 1981, s 32(5) and County Courts Act 1984, s 50(5)).

In a multi-track case where liability has been admitted or proven, or where the claimant can demonstrate a strong case on liability, an interim payment will assist in mitigating the effects of financial hardship caused by the often lengthy period between the accident and the determination of the claim. Interim payments are particularly important where the claimant has suffered catastrophic injuries or disablement and requires access to a substantial sum of money in order to pay for accommodation and/or a care regime.

An interim payment cannot be made in a small claims track case and, whilst not forbidden in a fast track case, will be rarely made due both to the value of the claim and to the relatively short period of time from issue of proceedings to trial. For interim payments in cases falling under one of the low value pre-action protocols, see **21.4**.

Where the grounds for making an order are satisfied, the court has a discretionary power to order that the defendant make an interim payment under r 25.6 of the CPR. The order may specify that such payment be made by instalments, and more than one order may be made during the lifetime of a claim. Where the claimant is a child or a protected party (see **Chapter 20**), the payment will usually be made to the Court of Protection.

In accordance with CPR, r 25.9, where an interim payment has been made either voluntarily or pursuant to a court order, unless the defendant agrees, this shall not be disclosed to the trial judge until all questions of liability and quantum have been decided.

13.15.1   Grounds for making the order

In accordance with CPR, r 25.7(1), the court may order an interim payment only if:

(a)   the defendant admits liability; or

(b)   the claimant has a judgment for damages to be assessed; or

(c)   if the matter were to proceed to trial, the claimant would obtain judgment for a substantial amount of money.

The court will take into account the defendant's ability to pay the interim payment before making an order.

In a claim where there are two or more defendants, the court may make an order for interim payment against any of them if it is satisfied that, if the claim went to trial, the claimant would obtain judgment for substantial damages against at least one of the defendants although it cannot determine which. It will do so only where all the defendants are either insured or they are a public body, or liability will be met by the MIB.

Although a claimant will normally set out in his application why the interim payment is required, he is not obliged to show that there is a *need* for the payment. In *Stringman v McCardle* [1994] 1 WLR 1653, Stuart-Smith LJ said: 'It should be noted that the plaintiff does not have to demonstrate any particular need over and above the general need that a plaintiff has to be paid his or her damages as soon as reasonably may be done.'

13.15.2   Procedure

Before making an application to the court for an interim payment, the claimant's solicitor should contact the defendant's solicitor and request that the defendant make a voluntary interim payment. The defendant may be amenable to such a request; if the payment is to fund treatment or rehabilitation costs, this may reduce the final award of damages and interest payments will be reduced. However, where the claimant is a child or protected party, the permission of the court is required before an interim payment is made (PD 25B, para 1.2).

A claimant may not seek an interim payment until after the time for acknowledging service has expired.

The application should be made using Form N244 and must be supported by evidence. Although the evidence may be set out on the application form itself, generally it will be set out in a witness statement. Paragraph 2.1 of PD25B states that the evidence must deal with the following:

(1)   the sum of money sought by way of an interim payment,

(2)   the items or matters in respect of which the interim payment is sought,

(3)   the sum of money for which final judgment is likely to be given,

(4)   the reasons for believing that the conditions set out in rule 25.7 are satisfied,

(5)   any other relevant matters,

(6)   in claims for personal injuries, details of special damages and past and future loss, and

(7)   in a claim under the Fatal Accidents Act 1976, details of the person(s) on whose behalf the claim is made and the nature of the claim.

Paragraph 2.2 of PD 25B states that any documents in support of the application should be exhibited, including, in personal injuries claims, the medical report(s).

The application notice and witness statement in support must be served on the defendant (the respondent) at least 14 days before the return date for the application. If the defendant wishes to rely on a witness statement in response to the application, he must file and serve a copy of that witness statement at least seven days before the hearing; and if the claimant (the applicant) wishes to file a further witness statement in reply, he must do so at least three days before the hearing.

Where the claimant has been in receipt of recoverable benefits which will fall to be repaid by the defendant to the Compensation Recovery Unit (CRU) (see **Chapter 16**), the defendant should obtain a certificate of recoverable benefits and file this with the court.

13.15.3   The amount of the interim payment

When dealing with an application for an interim payment, the court will seek to avoid making an overpayment which may lead to the claimant having to repay money to the defendant (see **13.15.4**). In accordance with CPR, r 25.7(4) and (5), the amount of the interim payment must not exceed a reasonable proportion of the likely amount of the final judgment, taking into account contributory negligence and any relevant set-off or counterclaim.

Where there is a large discrepancy between what the claimant and the defendant believe will be ultimately awarded, the court will first look at the amount of special damages which have already accrued and the amount of special damages which will arise prior to the date of trial. There can be a large degree of certainty as to the likely amount of damages to be awarded in this respect. The court will then attempt to determine what the court is likely to award in respect of pain, suffering and loss of amenity, etc, and future loss of earnings and costs of care, which is much more speculative.

Defendants have sought to limit the size of interim payments by arguing:

(a)   that allowing substantial interim payments to cover the cost of purchasing new accommodation and/or an expensive care regime, in circumstances where the defendant argues that the accommodation or care regime is excessive for the claimant's needs, distorts the 'level playing field' against defendants. When quantum is ultimately considered by the court, it is considerably harder for the defendants to argue this point when the accommodation has already been purchased and the care regime is up and running, and where expert witnesses are able to give evidence as to how the claimant's needs are being met. In *Spillman v Bradfield Riding Centre* [2007] EWHC 89, the claimant, a minor, suffered serious head injuries when she was kicked by a horse at the defendant's riding school. The application for an interim payment to fund special care and to enable her parents to purchase a larger house, which they argued was necessary for her benefit, was rejected at first instance. At appeal, the defendant unsuccessfully argued that if the interim payment was ordered in the amount sought by the claimant, the head of damage would become self-fulfilling as, at the date of trial, the claimant would have benefitted from the accommodation and care to which the defendants argued she was not entitled;

(b)   that allowing a substantial interim payment may prevent the court at trial from awarding periodical payments (see **15.5**) because there will be insufficient damages left to be paid. This argument is particularly relevant to cases where the claimant's life expectancy has been reduced significantly. Where it is likely that the final judgment would involve an order for periodical payments to be made, the court has to consider what is the 'likely amount' for the purposes of CPR, r 25.7(4). In *Braithwaite v Homerton University Hospitals Foundation Trust* [2008] EWHC 353 (QB), the court held that the amount of the final judgment was the capital sum plus a periodical sum payable during the life of the claimant. Consequently, the court must be confident that the amount of the proposed interim payment is not in excess of the capital sum ultimately awarded at trial.

There is no rule as to what constitutes a 'reasonable proportion', but decided cases appear to suggest that the courts will order a maximum of 75% of the likely final award of damages.

For guidance in cases where an interim payment is sought and where the final judgment is likely to include a periodical payment order, see the Court of Appeal's judgment in *Cobham Hire Services Ltd v Eeles* [2009] EWCA Civ 204.

It should be noted that where recoverable benefits have been received by the claimant, he will receive the interim payment net of the amount of the benefits. The defendant will pay an amount equal to the recoverable benefits to the CRU.

13.15.4   Repayment and variation

In accordance with r 25.8 of the CPR, where a defendant has made an interim payment either voluntarily or pursuant to an order, the court may order that all or part of that sum be repaid by the claimant, or that the defendant be reimbursed by another defendant.

In addition, where a defendant makes an interim payment which it transpires exceeds his liability under the final judgment, the court may award interest on the overpaid amount from the date the interim payment was made.

13.16   SPECIFIC DISCLOSURE OF DOCUMENTS HELD BY A THIRD PARTY

Once proceedings have been commenced, the court may make an order for specific disclosure of documents against a non-party under CPR, r 31.17(3), only where:

(a)   the documents of which disclosure is sought are likely to support the case of the applicant or adversely affect the case of one or other of the parties to the proceedings; and

(b)   disclosure is necessary to dispose fairly of the claim or save costs.

The application must be supported by appropriate evidence. An order under r 31.17 will specify the documents or class of documents which must be disclosed, and require the respondent to make disclosure or specify any of those documents which are no longer in his possession or for which he claims the right or duty to withhold from inspection. The order may specify a time and place for such disclosure and inspection.

13.17   CONCLUSION

When proceedings are defended, upon completion of the directions questionnaires, the case will be allocated to the appropriate track, and may be transferred from the court of issue to another court where appropriate. The court will then actively manage the matter in accordance with the overriding objective set out in CPR, r 1, and will require the parties and their solicitors to co-operate fully in achieving that objective. The parties will be expected to do their best to settle the matter as soon as possible and without the need for a court hearing.

Directions will be issued as are appropriate for the track to which the case has been allocated, and practitioners must do all they can to ensure that steps are taken within the specified time limits.

Solicitors acting for claimants and defendants may make interim applications to the court in relation to diverse issues such as time extensions, specific disclosure and interim payments, either where agreement cannot be reached between the parties or where the CPR require the court's involvement. Where possible, such applications should be made at the time of case management conferences, pre-trial reviews or at the same time as other applications, in order to save court time and costs.

Sound case management systems and procedures are essential, as judges are increasingly intolerant of avoidable delays and mistakes which lead to unnecessary applications.

CHAPTER 14

NEGOTIATIONS, ALTERNATIVE DISPUTE RESOLUTION AND TRIAL

LEARNING OUTCOMES

After reading this chapter you will be able to:

- understand how to prepare for and conduct a negotiation on behalf of the client
- draw up an appropriate consent order
- draft a Part 36 offer including provisional damages or periodical payments
- identify steps necessary to prepare a case for trial.

14.1 INTRODUCTION

Over 90% of personal injury claims and many clinical negligence claims settle without trial. It is usually the case that the solicitor's skill in arguing his client's claim with the other side's representative, rather than his ability to argue the case at trial, will determine the level of damages. For this reason, the personal injury solicitor is more likely to become a skilled negotiator than a trial advocate.

In order to avoid a potential negligence claim, it is imperative that the claimant solicitor is absolutely sure that the client's medical prognosis is clear prior to proceeding to settle the claim, or to advising the client that it is appropriate to settle the claim. In this regard the solicitor will rely heavily on the medical report and the prognosis for recovery contained within it. It should be stressed to the client that the prognosis is only an estimate, and if the client does not feel that he has recovered then the solicitor cannot advise the client to settle his claim prematurely. It should be pointed out to the client that the compensation offered by the defendant is a 'once and for all payment', and he therefore cannot (normally) return at a future date to obtain further compensation if the prognosis for recovery should prove to be incorrect.

This chapter aims to summarise the main factors to take into account when negotiating, and considers other methods of alternative dispute resolution (ADR) which may be used in personal injury and clinical negligence cases (including cases within the low value protocols). Inevitably there will be cases which are not capable of settlement and which must proceed to trial, in which case it is vital to prepare properly as a poorly presented case will not impress a judge. The steps that should be taken to prepare the case for trial are also explained below. (but note that, for cases which are proceeding within the low value protocols, different procedures apply and reference should instead be made to **Chapter 21**)

14.2 PROFESSIONAL CONDUCT

As a matter of conduct, a solicitor does not have ostensible authority to settle a client's claim until after proceedings have been issued. It is imperative for the solicitor to seek the client's specific instructions prior to settling a claim. For example, even if the client instructs his solicitor that he can settle his claim as long as the client receives at least £1,000, the solicitor should, when negotiating with the defence, stipulate that any agreement is 'subject to his client's instructions'. In this way, if the client should change his mind (which he may do at any time), the solicitor will not have committed the client to the settlement irrevocably. A solicitor acting for the defendant must be careful not to exceed any authority he has been given to settle by his insurance client.

Negotiations should always be entered into on an expressly 'without prejudice' basis. When talking to an insurer in person or on the telephone, it is advisable for the solicitor to preface anything he says by stating expressly at the outset that the entire conversation is without prejudice to his client's claim.

14.3 NEGOTIATING WITH INSURANCE COMPANIES AND DEFENCE SOLICITORS

Claims can be settled by agreement being reached between the parties at any stage. The pre-action protocols encourage early disclosure of information to facilitate this. Claimant solicitors have in the past considered that defendant insurers will not make reasonable offers for settlement prior to issue of proceedings. For this reason, many claimant solicitors have tended to issue proceedings first and negotiate second. This strategy is not encouraged by the CPR 1998. The pre-action protocols require that attempts be made to settle disputes. For a detailed consideration of the protocols, see **Chapter 10**.

When negotiating with the defendant's insurer or its solicitor, a firm approach should be taken by the claimant's solicitor. He must be alert to the fact that the insurer is in business to make money for its shareholders, and its employees are employed to ensure that as little money as possible is paid out in damages. Therefore, the claimant's solicitor should not delay in issuing proceedings, after the pre-action protocol has been complied with if the defendant has failed or refused to make an acceptable response. Failure to do so is likely to be a failure to act in the best interests of the client.

14.4 PREPARING FOR THE NEGOTIATION

Prior to any negotiation, the solicitor should first familiarise himself with the file, noting specifically any matters likely to increase the level of damages, such as the risk of osteoarthritis or permanent scarring. There is a risk that the solicitor will fail to remember the file adequately because he may be running many very similar claims at any one time. When reviewing the file it is good practice to build up a profile of the severity of the injuries by reading the medical reports and client's statement. Matters relevant to each head of loss should be noted, so that the solicitor has a list of areas of loss without having to make reference to the specifics of the claim itself.

> **EXAMPLE**
>
> Client A is aged 56. She suffered injuries to her left shoulder and abrasions to both arms and legs when she tripped over a loose paving stone in her local high street. She is a keen gardener and likes to attend aerobics once a week, and enjoys walking her dog in the countryside near her home. Her husband took early retirement due to ill-health and is not able to assist her much, but he has been driving her to the doctor and to physiotherapy, and has been helping her bathe and dress herself. Day-to-day cleaning of the house and gardening has been undertaken by friends and relations.
>
> The profile in such a case would be:
>
> *General damages claim:*
>
> (a) female aged 56, therefore likely to take some time for injuries to mend, danger of osteoarthritis revealed in medical report;
>
> (b) report revealed split fracture to the clavicle (collar bone) together with a tear to the *latissimus dorsi* (muscle beneath the shoulder) and associated soft tissue damage;
>
> (c) medical intervention involved substantial and uncomfortable strapping to render the injury immobile followed by light physiotherapy. Physiotherapy continued for 20 weeks;
>
> (d) reasonably fit, unable to undertake pastimes such as aerobics and walking in countryside for X weeks.
>
> *Special damages:*
>
> (a) clothes and personal items lost or damaged in the accident;
>
> (b) mileage claim for travel to and from hospital/physiotherapy;
>
> (c) prescription charges;
>
> (d) daily care necessary;
>
> (e) husband unable to care on his own due to his own ill-health;
>
> (f) cleaning of house and garden maintenance undertaken by others.

Having built up such a profile, the next stage is for the solicitor to become familiar with the likely level of damages to be awarded in such a claim. Such familiarity comes with experience. The method of approach to calculation of damages is considered in detail in **Chapter 15**.

In addition to reviewing quantum, the solicitor must ensure he has a good grasp of the facts of the accident and the evidence supporting the case on liability. The solicitor must undertake a thorough review of all pleadings, witness statements and other documents disclosed, and consideration should be given to possible arguments of contributory negligence.

The client should be aware that any form of litigation carries with it a certain amount of risk that the claim will fail because the evidence may not come up to proof at trial. Because of this 'litigation risk', it is likely that the defence solicitor will seek some reduction in damages because the claimant is being spared the upset and risk of failure at trial.

If acting for the defendant, the solicitor must obtain a certificate of recoverable benefit from the DWP before making any offer in settlement so that any relevant benefits can be taken into account.

14.5 CONDUCTING THE NEGOTIATION

The technique of negotiation is contained in *Skills for Lawyers*. When conducting negotiations, it is worth bearing in mind the following:

(a) Settlement should not be entered into prematurely. If proceedings are never issued and the defendant's insurers make clear that they do not contest the case, argument will centre on quantum, and it will be fairly safe to negotiate. If, however, the matter is contested, it is unwise to negotiate prior to disclosure of each side's evidence. For this reason, many solicitors believe that settlement should not be contemplated prior to the exchange of witness evidence. Once the solicitor has considered the evidence, he can then assist the client to make an informed decision as to whether he should accept a settlement.

(b)   The solicitor must never negotiate when unprepared. The file must be considered thoroughly prior to proceeding with negotiations. If the solicitor receives a surprise telephone call from a defendant insurer seeking a settlement, it is better for the solicitor to call back later, after having considered the case afresh.

(c)   The defence should be invited to put forward its settlement figure with supporting argument as to why that figure is correct. Comments should be kept to a minimum and further negotiations postponed while the offer is considered. This is easiest to do if negotiating over the telephone, as negotiation can be cut short and re-established later with minimum difficulty. The telephone has the added advantage that the person making an offer cannot see the reaction of the recipient of the call, and will be unable to gauge how well or how badly the offer is received. The claimant's solicitor should never disclose his valuation of the claim first in negotiations, and should not reveal any figures until he believes the defendant is putting forward a realistic amount.

(d)   The defence opening offer is unlikely to be the best it is prepared to come up with. All offers must, however, be put to the client. A solicitor has a duty to act in the best interests of his client, and this includes obtaining the best possible settlement figure.

(e)   An offer by the defence to pay the claimant's costs to date should not sway the solicitor into advising his client to accept an offer. If the defence is offering to settle, it is effectively admitting (albeit without prejudice) that there is merit in the claim, and it would normally be obliged to pay the claimant's reasonable costs if the case went to trial.

(f)   Often the solicitor has specific instructions to try to settle the case on the client's behalf. In such circumstances, he may seek confirmation that a settlement will be agreed as long as the client will receive at least £x. If this is the case, the solicitor must be careful not to jump at the first offer simply because it will secure for the client the minimum that he requires and will usually also secure payment of the solicitor's costs.

(g)   Consideration of the defendant's offer should not be rushed. Any attempt to force an agreement quickly should be regarded as spurious. The defence would not have made an offer if it was happy to take the case to trial. Therefore, regardless of whether a time limit is placed on the offer, it is likely that unless fresh evidence comes to light strengthening the defence case, an offer once made will remain open. By making an offer at all the defence is saying that it would far rather pay than fight.

(h)   When negotiating, defendant insurers will often offer to 'split the difference' if agreement cannot be reached on a particular head of loss. This is a favourite tactic that the claimant solicitor should consider carefully before accepting. On the face of it, it may appear to be a generous offer, bringing negotiations to a speedy conclusion. On closer scrutiny, it may be a ploy which results in the loss of a substantial portion of the client's legitimate expectation in a particular head of damages.

14.6   NEGOTIATING IN CLINICAL NEGLIGENCE CLAIMS

When considering negotiation in the context of clinical negligence claims, the following additional points should be borne in mind.

(a)   In many cases, the NHS complaints procedure will already have been put to use, and there may therefore be greater clarity as regards the issues of the claim.

(b) It is unlikely that any negotiations with a view to settlement will be made prior to full recourse to the clinical disputes PAP. Only after both sides have had access to full disclosure and expert opinion will it be possible for any meaningful negotiation to take place.

(c) In straightforward claims of low value, negotiating tactics as outlined above may be appropriate. In relation to more complex claims, it is more likely that there would be a meeting of the parties' solicitors, with or without experts, to try to narrow as many issues as possible. In appropriate cases, counsel for both sides may be asked to discuss the case informally to try to narrow areas in dispute.

14.7 ALTERNATIVE DISPUTE RESOLUTION

The use of ADR is likely to become more important in the resolution of disputes, as the overriding objective (stated in Part 1 of the CPR 1998) encourages its prompt use as a way of furthering the overriding objective and to aid prompt settlement. Most disputes are capable of resolution either by discussion and negotiation, or by trial on the issues. The rules encourage the use of alternatives to litigation as a first resort and of litigation as a last resort. **Civil Litigation** explains ADR in detail.

14.7.1 Different types of ADR

All of the methods of ADR are mechanisms which aim to bring the parties together to obtain a consensual agreement rather than a ruling which is forced upon them. The main types of ADR available today are as follows.

14.7.1.1 Mediation

In mediation, a neutral third party is chosen by the parties as their intermediary (mediator). The mediator is likely to meet the opposing parties separately to try to establish some common ground before finally bringing the parties together to try to reach an agreement.

14.7.1.2 Conciliation

Conciliation is a similar process to mediation. However, the conciliator is likely to take a more interventionist approach by taking a more central role. He will often consider the case as put forward by both sides, and then suggest terms of settlement which he feels to be most appropriate.

14.7.1.3 The mini-trial

The format and content of a mini-trial is much more like a trial. It will be chaired by a neutral mediator who will sit with a representative from each party.

14.7.2 Case management conference

At the case management conference/pre-trial review, the parties will be told to confirm whether the question of ADR has been considered and also to confirm, if it has not, why this is the case.

When considering the conduct of the parties, the judge is entitled to consider the parties' unreasonable refusal to use ADR, as this is central to the ethos of how to deal with disputes in accordance with Part 1 of the CPR 1998. Where ADR has been refused, or where a party has later failed to co-operate with ADR, the court is entitled to take that into account when considering what costs order to make, or whether to make any costs order at all.

14.7.3 ADR and personal injury claims

Use of the pre-action protocol will ensure that the parties are better able to obtain a greater depth of knowledge about the case against them than in the past. Full use of pre-action disclosure, and preliminary disclosure of key documents, will enable each side to obtain a far better view of the issues of the case in relation to liability, and will therefore allow them to make a far better and earlier assessment of their client's case.

At the stage where the parties complete their directions questionnaire, they will be asked whether they would like their proceedings to be stayed while they try to settle the case by way of ADR.

Because the court is very likely to ask whether the parties are interested in attempting ADR, and whether the possibility of ADR has been discussed with the client prior to any case management conference, it follows that the solicitor will need to ask his client at an early stage whether he would be interested in pursuing the matter by way of ADR, and must explain to the client what this will entail.

In *Halsey v Milton Keynes General NHS Trust* [2004] EWCA Civ 576, the Trust refused to refer the matter to mediation as it was of the steadfast view that there had been no negligence and therefore referral to ADR would increase costs and delay. The claim was dismissed by the court. When the court came to consider the question of costs, it stated that when deciding whether a successful party had acted unreasonably in refusing to agree to ADR, the court should bear in mind the advantages of ADR over the court process and have regard to all of the circumstances of the particular case. The following factors were found to be of relevance:

(a)   the nature of the dispute;

(b)   the merits of the case;

(c)   the extent to which other settlement methods had been attempted;

(d)   whether the costs of ADR would be disproportionately high;

(e)   whether any delay in setting up and attending the ADR would have been prejudicial;

(f)   whether the ADR had a reasonable prospect of success.

14.7.4 The timing of ADR

It is likely that in complicated cases ADR will not be appropriate until such time as statements of case and disclosure of documents by both sides have been dealt with. Only then will ADR be a practical alternative to a trial. It is therefore likely that parties in cases which were initially felt to be unsuitable for ADR may find that ADR is a possibility once the case is at the case management conference stage.

14.7.5 Procedure following failed ADR

Where the parties have attempted ADR and this has failed to produce a settlement, the parties are likely to wish to fall back on their original court proceedings or intended court proceedings.

At this stage, if proceedings have already been issued, the solicitor for the claimant will need to apply promptly for further directions in the case so that the matter may proceed swiftly to trial.

However, although ADR may fail to produce a settlement, it may produce a degree of information about the other side's case which prior to ADR had not been clear. If this is so, it may be that an offer to settle or payment should be considered by either party or both parties.

14.7.6 ADR in clinical negligence cases

Although the majority of clinical negligence claims do settle, due to their relative complexity they often do so at a very late stage. The NHSLA, which handles large clinical negligence claims, encourages the use of ADR, and the Clinical Disputes Forum has also produced a guide on the use of mediation in clinical negligence disputes.

The guidance aims to:

(a)   ensure that the use of ADR is considered by clients and solicitors at key points in clinical negligence claims;

(b)   require solicitors to report to their regional office at various stages in the litigation, explaining why ADR has not been pursued if appropriate;

(c)   explain the approach regional offices should take in deciding whether to limit a certificate to work necessary to progress ADR;

(d)   help the parties set up mediation.

14.7.6.1   When should ADR be considered in clinical negligence claims?

The parties should keep the possibilities of ADR in mind at all times. However, at the outset of litigation ADR is not likely to be appropriate until the PAP for use in clinical negligence claims has been complied with, because the client and his solicitor are unlikely to have information available to enter into a fair settlement of the claim.

Once the clinical negligence PAP has been complied with, solicitors should consider with their clients the use of ADR at the following stages:

(a)   prior to issue of proceedings;

(b)   before and immediately after a case management conference;

(c)   before and immediately after pre-trial review;

(d)   whenever the other side offers ADR;

(e)   whenever the new parties are specifically asked to consider ADR by the court.

If at any of the above points it is decided by the client or solicitor not to pursue ADR, the reason for that decision should be recorded on the solicitor's file.

14.7.6.2   Cases where ADR may not be appropriate

The following types of claims may not be suitable for ADR:

(a)   where essential basic information (such as relevant medical records, key expert evidence on liability and causation) is not available;

(b)   where there is no clear prognosis for the condition of the client and time is needed to see how the client progresses before settlement can be considered;

(c)   ADR is unnecessary as all parties are already negotiating effectively;

(d)   proceedings need to be issued urgently in order for the claim to be within the relevant limitation period;

(e)   the claim includes a future cost of care claim and information is needed as to quantum before any settlement can be discussed;

(f)   the case is a 'test case' and requires a ruling from a court in order to lay down a precedent for future claims;

(g)   ADR would not be a cost-effective way of dealing with the claim because there is no reason to believe that the claim will be resolved more quickly or cheaply by using it.

14.7.7   NHS complaints procedure

The complaints procedure (which is dealt with in detail in **Chapter 5**) is designed specifically to provide an explanation to patients in cases where they have felt sufficiently concerned about the healthcare received to make a complaint. The procedure is not designed or able to give compensation to patients. It is useful if the only or main issue at stake is for an explanation or an apology to be obtained, or simply to find more information to help the patient to come to terms with an event, or to help him decide whether he should take further action and, if so, what form this should take.

14.7.8 Mediation

Mediation may be appropriate in some cases where the parties agree. This may be seen as particularly useful when there are allegations of clinical negligence, as ADR will be conducted in private, and this is something which is likely to appeal to medical practitioners who may not wish the allegations to be made public and reportable, as would be the case if the matter were to proceed in open court to a trial.

14.8 FUNDING ANY SETTLEMENT

In nearly all personal injury cases, there will not be a problem with the financing of any settlement, as the defendant will have been required to be insured in respect of the potential liability and a commercial insurer will normally meet any settlement.

In clinical negligence cases too, the defendant will normally not have a problem with the financing of any settlement but the administration of the settlement can be rather more complicated in certain cases. The NHSLA administers the Scheme and Clinical Negligence Scheme for Trusts (CNST). The CNST came into being as a result of concern over the financing of damages claims, and the object of the scheme is to protect NHS Trusts and improve the quality of risk management. The CNST is not an insurance scheme but a mutual fund (see **5.7** above).

The administration of any settlement is normally of little concern to claimant solicitors, but many practitioners become frustrated by the delays which can arise with insurance companies in personal injury cases and also the NHSLA, as they operate a system whereby certain levels of claims have to be given specific approval.

14.9 COURT ORDERS

It is good practice to obtain a court order formally stating the terms of the settlement. A settlement on behalf of a minor should always be contained in a court order (see **Chapter 20**). The court will charge a fee for sealing the consent order.

14.9.1 Advantages of obtaining a court order

The advantages of obtaining an order are:

(a)   payment of interest and costs can be dealt with specifically;

(b)   if the amount stated in the order is not paid, the order can be enforced in the same way as any other judgment;

(c)   if costs cannot be agreed, they can be assessed by the court if there is provision in the order;

(d)   if the client has legal aid funding, he will need an order for legal aid assessment.

The order should contain a provision that the claim be stayed rather than dismissed, and the stay should contain provision for a return to court in the event that the terms of the stay are not complied with.

14.9.2 Drawing up the consent order

The procedure for drawing up a consent order is:

(a)   it must be drawn up in the agreed terms;

(b)   it must be expressed as being 'by consent';

(c)   it must be signed by solicitors or counsel for the parties;

(d)   it must be presented to the court for entry and sealing.

An order takes effect from the date given, unless the court orders otherwise. An order for payment of money (including costs) must be complied with within 14 days, unless the order or any rule of the CPR specifies otherwise. When drafting a consent order, the guiding principle is that the order shows where the money is to come from to satisfy the order and where that money will go.

> **EXAMPLE**
>
> In a case where a settlement is achieved by which the defendant agrees to pay £3,000 plus costs to be assessed if not agreed, the order should state:
>
> (a) that the claim is stayed on payment of £3,000;
>
> (b) that the £3,000 is to be paid by the defendant within a given timescale (usually 14 days);
>
> (c) where the money is to go (in this case to the claimant). In a case involving a minor the money will usually be ordered to be invested by the court;
>
> (d) who is to bear the costs. If this has been agreed, the figures should be stated with a time limit for payment. Usually, the provision will be for costs to be assessed if not agreed;
>
> (e) whether legal aid assessment is needed; and
>
> (f) liberty to apply – which simply allows the parties to return to the court if there is subsequently a disagreement as to what the terms of the order mean or because the terms have not been complied with.

If there had been an interim payment in the above example, this should also be reflected in the terms of the order. The order should state that the amount agreed in full and final settlement takes into account the interim payment, specifying the amount and the date it was given, or the date of the court order so ordering it to be paid. An example of a consent order may be found in **Appendix 1** at Document 22.

14.10 PART 36 OFFERS

If negotiations do not result in a settlement, consideration should be given to making a Part 36 offer in order to place the opponent under some pressure as to costs. For a detailed discussion of the form, content and costs consequences of Part 36 offers, you should refer to *Civil Litigation*.

In personal injury cases, in addition to the above basic requirements as to content, further information must be set out in the offer if the claim involves future pecuniary loss, provisional damages or the deduction of State benefits. That information is summarised below.

14.10.1 Special provisions applicable to Part 36 offers and personal injury claims for future pecuniary loss

It is possible to make an offer to settle a claim involving future pecuniary loss either by way of a lump sum, or by way of periodical payments or a combination of both (see **Chapter 15**). To be treated as a Part 36 offer with all the costs consequences that follow, the offer must explicitly set out the amounts which relate to the lump sum and periodical payments, and the duration of the periodical payments. If the offer is accepted, in addition to serving a notice of acceptance, the claimant must apply to the court for an order for an award of damages in the form of periodical payments. This must be done within seven days of the date of acceptance.

Rule 36.18 provides as follows:

(3) A Part 36 offer to which this rule applies may contain an offer to pay, or an offer to accept—

    (a) the whole or part of the damages for future pecuniary loss in the form of—

        (i) a lump sum; or

        (ii) periodical payments; or

        (iii) both a lump sum and periodical payments;

    (b) the whole or part of any other damages in the form of a lump sum.

(4)   A Part 36 offer to which this rule applies—

(a)   must state the amount of any offer to pay the whole or part of any damages in the form of a lump sum;

(b)   may state—

(i)   what part of the lump sum, if any, relates to damages for future pecuniary loss; and

(ii)   what part relates to other damages to be accepted in the form of a lump sum;

(c)   must state what part of the offer relates to damages for future pecuniary loss to be paid or accepted in the form of periodical payments and must specify—

(i)   the amount and duration of the periodical payments;

(ii)   the amount of any payments for substantial capital purchases and when they are to be made; and

(iii)   that each amount is to vary by reference to the retail prices index (or to some other named index, or that it is not to vary by reference to any index); and

(d)   must state either that any damages which take the form of periodical payments will be funded in a way which ensures that the continuity of payment is reasonably secure in accordance with section 2(4) of the Damages Act 1996 or how such damages are to be paid and how the continuity of their payment is to be secured.

(5)   Rule 36.6 applies to the extent that a Part 36 offer by a defendant under this rule includes an offer to pay all or part of any damages in the form of a lump sum.

(6)   Where the offeror makes a Part 36 offer to which this rule applies and which offers to pay or to accept damages in the form of both a lump sum and periodical payments, the offeree may only give notice of acceptance of the offer as a whole.

(7)   If the offeree accepts a Part 36 offer which includes payment of any part of the damages in the form of periodical payments, the claimant must, within 7 days of the date of acceptance, apply to the court for an order for an award of damages in the form of periodical payments under rule 41.8.

14.10.2   Special provisions applicable to Part 36 offers and provisional damages

If the claim is for provisional damages (see **15.4**), an offer to settle must specify whether or not the offeror is offering to agree to the making of an award for provisional damages. If he is, the offer must state

(a)   the damages offered;

(b)   the conditions to trigger a further claim;

(c)   the period within which such further claim may be made.

Once the offer is accepted, the claimant must, within seven days, apply to the court for an order.

Rule 36.19 provides:

(1)   An offeror may make a Part 36 offer in respect of a claim which includes a claim for provisional damages.

(2)   Where he does so, the Part 36 offer must specify whether or not the offeror is proposing that the settlement shall include an award of provisional damages.

(3)   Where the offeror is offering to agree to the making of an award of provisional damages the Part 36 offer must also state—

(a)   that the sum offered is in satisfaction of the claim for damages on the assumption that the injured person will not develop the disease or suffer the type of deterioration specified in the offer;

(b)   that the offer is subject to the condition that the claimant must make any claim for further damages within a limited period; and

(c)   what that period is.

(4)   Rule 36.6 applies to the extent that a Part 36 offer by a defendant includes an offer to agree to the making of an award of provisional damages.

(5)   If the offeree accepts the Part 36 offer, the claimant must, within 7 days of the date of acceptance, apply to the court for an order for an award of provisional damages under rule 41.2.

14.10.3 Compensation recovery and Part 36 offers – deduction of benefits

A Part 36 offer in a personal injury claim may state that the offer is made without regard to any liability for recoverable benefits, ie it is a net offer and the compensator will pay benefits in addition.

Alternatively, the offer should state that it is intended to include any deductible CRU benefits.

According to r 36.22, the offer must state:

(a)   the amount of gross compensation before CRU benefits are offset;

(b)   the name of any deductible benefit;

(c)   the amount of any deductible benefit by which the gross amount is reduced; and

(d)   the net amount of compensation after deduction.

Remember, when calculating what benefits can be offset, that specific benefits can be offset only against certain heads of claim and must not exceed the amount claimed under that head. Where it is agreed or alleged that the claimant was contributorily negligent, the damages from which benefits can be offset must be net of the deduction for contributory negligence.

For the purpose of establishing whether the claimant has failed to beat a Part 36 offer, the sums to be considered are those after deduction of the deductible benefits. In other words, the court will look at what sum the claimant was offered net of benefits and what sum he recovered net of benefits.

Where the claimant accepts a Part 36 offer out of time and the CRU repayment has increased, the court may direct that the additional benefits should be deducted from the net offer.

14.10.4 QOCS and Part 36

Rule 44.14 of the CPR allows a costs order to be made against a claimant who fails to beat a defendant's offer to settle. The usual order will require the claimant to pay the defendant's costs from the end of the relevant offer period. However, the claimant's liability for the defendant's costs in these circumstances will be capped at the level of damages and interest recovered by the claimant (see **9.3.2**). After the event insurance may be available to cover this risk but any insurance premium will not be recoverable.

14.11 PREPARATION FOR TRIAL

14.11.1 Outstanding orders

Once it becomes apparent that the case will proceed to trial as no satisfactory Part 36 offer has been received, the claimant's solicitor should undertake a thorough stocktaking of the file to ensure that all directions or other orders of the court have been complied with. Any outstanding matters in the claimant's own file should be attended to without further delay, and any outstanding matters for the defendant to attend to should be chased by issuing an interim application for judgment in default of compliance with the direction/other order if necessary.

14.11.2 Experts

Experts' reports will usually have been exchanged in accordance with directions. Provision of joint experts and agreed expert evidence is dealt with in **Chapter 11**.

14.11.3 Use of counsel

The solicitor may not have instructed counsel before this stage if the claim has been straightforward. If the case has been complex, as is likely in a clinical negligence case, counsel will probably have been involved at an early stage, from drafting documents to advising on evidence. It is usual for the barrister who drafted the statements of case also to be briefed for the trial. As counsel will be handling the witnesses at trial, it may be thought to be appropriate to send the witness statements to counsel for approval before exchange to ensure that an important area concerning the conduct of the case at trial is not overlooked. It may be more cost-efficient to brief counsel for the trial than for the solicitor himself to attend. However, with trial on the fast track limited to one day, and with fixed costs of trial, it may be that many more solicitor-advocates will undertake the advocacy of this type of claim.

If the case involves complex elements, such as clinical negligence, catastrophic injuries, or difficult questions of fact or law, consideration should be given to whether it would be appropriate to instruct leading counsel; junior counsel will usually advise the solicitor if he thinks that this would be appropriate. The solicitor should advise the client accordingly of the extra cost involved and, if the client is funded by legal aid, seek authority to instruct leading counsel. The client should also be advised that if leading counsel is instructed, and this is disallowed on assessment, the cost will ultimately be borne by the client in the form of the statutory charge on the client's damages.

14.11.4 Narrowing the issues

When preparing for trial the solicitor should ask himself, 'What do I have to prove?' A review should be made of the case file to ascertain areas of agreement which are no longer in issue. One useful device may be a list comprising two columns: the left-hand column listing the facts which have to be proved (eg, that the claimant was driving the car; that an accident occurred; the date of the accident; the place of the accident; an itemised list of the losses, etc); and the right-hand column indicating whether the fact is admitted by the opponent.

Admissions will normally be found in the statements of case or in open correspondence.

14.11.5 Schedule of special damages

Note that CPR, PD 22, para 1.4(3) requires that a statement of truth is included in a schedule or counter-schedule of expenses and losses, and in any amendments to such a schedule or counter-schedule, whether or not the schedule is contained in a statement of case.

The claimant's solicitor must check that the schedule of special damages is up to date, and if necessary, serve an updated schedule of special damages. Ideally, this should be the final schedule (although it may have to be revised again if there is a significant delay before the trial), the purpose of which is to identify the areas of agreement and disagreement between the parties. With this in mind, the following format could be usefully employed (the figures are merely for illustration):

Item of claim	Claimant's figure	Defendant's figure	Discrepancy
Purchase of wheelchair	£350	£350	Nil
Loss of future earnings	£50,000 (multiplicand = £5,000, multiplier = 10)	£32,000 (multiplicand = £4,000, multiplier = 8)	£18,000

The defendant's solicitor should be sent the updated schedule of special damages, with a covering letter requesting that he agrees it or specifies the items he is not prepared to agree, and giving a time limit for the reply. It should be pointed out that if he fails to reply, the claimant's solicitors will have to issue a witness summons for any persons necessary to prove the amounts claimed, and the claimant will ask for the costs of this exercise be paid by the defendant in any event.

In clinical negligence claims, where special damages claims are likely to involve substantial amounts of money, it is more likely that the defence will seek to query items claimed as special damages. For this reason the directions will normally require that the defendant also provide a counter-schedule of special damages itemising the areas of disagreement.

14.11.6   Trial bundles

In both the High Court and the county court, bundles of documents upon which the parties intend to rely must be lodged within the appropriate time, for use by the trial judge.

The bundle must be paginated and indexed. The medical records must be complete and in good order to enable medical experts to study them easily. X-rays or scans included in the bundle should be clearly identified. Scans may be several feet long and should be professionally copied if possible. The index to the trial bundle is normally agreed with the defendant.

The quality of preparation of bundles varies enormously, and this can have serious implications for the client's case if preparation is not undertaken properly. Although there are rules governing the content of the bundles, there is very little guidance on how the documents should be presented. When preparing the bundle the aim should be to enable whoever is conducting the trial to turn to any document at any time with the minimum of fuss or delay, and that all others concerned with the case can do likewise. The more documents there are in the bundle, the more difficult this task becomes. In a straightforward road traffic claim, there will be few documents and, as such, the bundle should be relatively easy to prepare. In serious cases involving multiple injuries or in clinical negligence cases, however, the documents are likely to extend to many hundreds of pages. In such cases, it is even more important that the court is not hindered by trying to find documents that should be readily to hand. Poor preparation of the case will not impress the judge, neither will it go unnoticed. Documents will need to be split into a number of smaller bundles which are easier to handle. Using colour-coded lever arch files is often a good method, with a separate file for each class of document. As a matter of courtesy, if counsel has been instructed, the solicitor may wish to send the proposed index to the core bundle of documents to counsel in advance of the trial, so that counsel has the opportunity to ask for further items to be included if necessary.

14.11.7   Use of visual aids

Plans, photographs and models can be of enormous value at the trial as an aid to clarity, thereby shortening the length of the trial (avoiding long testimony of a witness) and saving costs. A judge may more readily understand the testimony of a witness if that witness is allowed to refer to a plan or photograph. Medical experts can often supply good quality colour diagrams, anatomical illustrations or models to make their testimony more comprehensible. In clinical negligence cases, it is worth the extra time and effort to find good visual aids. A judge is unlikely to have in-depth medical knowledge, and attempts to help the judge fully comprehend the circumstances giving rise to the alleged negligence are likely to be gratefully received.

Visual aids must be disclosed to the opponent in advance. No plan, photograph or model will be receivable in evidence at trial unless the party wishing to use the evidence discloses it no later than the latest date for serving witness statements.

A video-recording is more useful than photographs in the case of 'movement'. Two common examples are:

(a)   a video-recording of an industrial process;

(b)   a video-recording showing the difficulties of the claimant in coping with his injuries (a 'day in the life'). Although the claimant should call, in addition to his own evidence, members of his family or friends to give evidence as to how he manages with his injuries (evidence of his bodily and mental condition before and after the accident), a video film (eg, showing the medical assistance required, such as physiotherapy or even surgery) may illustrate the situation more graphically.

If the photographs or other visual aids are agreed, they are admissible in the absence of the maker. If the aids are not agreed, the maker must be called to prove their authenticity.

The solicitor should ensure at the trial that there are enough copies of photographs for the use of the judge, advocates and witnesses.

14.12 THE TRIAL

14.12.1 The morning of the trial

The solicitor should arrive early to ensure that he has time:

(a)   to check with the clerk to the court that the court has the trial bundles, and place a bundle in the witness-box;

(b)   to ensure that counsel has arrived and consider any last-minute questions he may have;

(c)   to meet the client on his arrival and attempt to put him at his ease;

(d)   to introduce counsel to the client (if they have not already met in conference);

(e)   to ensure that an interview room is reserved for the pre-trial conference with counsel.

14.12.2 Advice to clients and witnesses

The case will often turn on how well or how badly the witnesses give their evidence, and how they are perceived by the judge. The client and other witnesses should be reminded that they will not be able to take their statements into the witness-box. The solicitor should run through the procedure to be adopted when giving oral evidence with the witnesses, as follows:

(a)   explain the procedure on taking the oath, and whether the client wishes to affirm;

(b)   remind the witness that all responses should be addressed to the judge regardless of who asked the question; and

(c)   that the judge must be addressed in the appropriate manner; and

(d)   go through the order in which the witnesses will be examined.

Each witness's statement will normally stand as evidence-in-chief, in which case the witness's evidence will move to being cross-examined almost immediately.

It is important to allay the client's fears about giving oral evidence. The solicitor should advise the client to speak slowly and directly to the judge, just as if there was no one else in the room. The judge will be writing notes, and therefore the witness should watch the judge's pen and resume speaking only when the judge has finished writing.

It is unlikely that the client and lay witnesses will have given evidence before. They should be advised that if they do not understand the question they should say so, and to take their evidence slowly, answer only the question put to them and not to engage in questioning opposing counsel or offer unsolicited opinions of their own. It is up to the solicitor to keep his witnesses in check and ensure that they do not embarrass the client or harm his case.

14.12.3 Conduct of the trial

Counsel (if instructed) will have the conduct of the trial, and the solicitor's function will be to sit behind counsel and take full notes of evidence. For the purpose of costing, a note should be made of the start time, any adjournments and the time the trial finishes. The questions asked by counsel should be noted, as well as the responses given, as counsel will not be able to make any notes himself while on his feet.

14.12.4   Order of evidence

Although evidence is usually given by the claimant first, followed by the defence, in clinical negligence cases all witnesses of fact may be called first, followed by witnesses giving evidence of opinion. This is because the facts themselves are often complex and it assists the judge greatly if the facts are laid out clearly by hearing evidence from the witnesses of fact for the claimant, followed directly by those of the defence. The object is to clarify the areas of disagreement so that experts can concentrate their efforts there, and shorten the length of trial. However, the parties must apply to the trial judge on the first day of the trial to use this procedure, as the order of evidence in the judge's court will be decided by the individual judge as a matter of discretion.

14.12.5   Judgment

The solicitor should take a careful note of the judgment delivered by the judge at the end of the case, as it may be crucial if the client decides to appeal.

Counsel must be made aware of any specific orders which may be necessary. In addition, counsel must be informed about any Part 36 offers which may have a bearing on costs.

The solicitor should also check the pre-trial orders to see if costs were reserved in any interim proceedings, and if so, that this is brought to the attention of the judge so that a costs order can be made in relation to that application.

The judgment should be fully explained to the client, which can be undertaken by counsel.

14.12.6   The order

Following trial in the county court, the court will draw up the order, which should be checked carefully to ensure that it reflects the judge's decision, as mistakes are sometimes made by the court staff.

14.13   CONCLUSION

Most cases settle, and taking a case to trial will be the exception rather than the rule in personal injury litigation. The court, as we have seen, actively encourages parties to negotiate and attempt to settle at every opportunity. Nevertheless, every case must be approached from the standpoint that it will go to trial, and must be prepared accordingly. It is important to keep a case under review as the case progresses. In particular, any Part 36 offers should be kept under review and, if necessary, withdrawn if further evidence comes to light which alters your views of quantum and /or liability.

14.14   FURTHER READING

Civil Court Practice (the Green Book) (Butterworths)

Civil Procedure (the White Book) (Sweet & Maxwell)

Skills for Lawyers (CLP)

CHAPTER 15

THE QUANTIFICATION OF DAMAGES

LEARNING OUTCOMES

After reading this chapter you will be able to:

- explain what special damages are and how the main items of loss are calculated
- explain what general damages for pain, suffering and loss of amenity are, and how such damages are quantified
- explain what general damages for future financial loss are and how they are calculated
- draft a schedule of past and future expenses and losses
- set out and apply the law in relation to provisional damages
- explain the court's power to make an order for periodical payments and set out the procedure for obtaining such an order
- set out how interest is calculated in personal injury and clinical negligence claims.

15.1 INTRODUCTION

In November 2012, a teenage girl left paralysed following a road traffic accident was awarded a lump sum plus annual payments thought to total over £23 million over her lifetime, in what is believed to be the highest personal injury award in England and Wales. Of course, the vast majority of claims are settled or determined for considerably smaller amounts, most within the fast track limit of £25,000.

The aim of the claimant's solicitor is to establish liability against the defendant and to achieve the highest possible level of damages for his client (without falsifying or exaggerating the claim). The primary aim of the defendant's solicitor is to defeat the claimant's claim. However, if he cannot prevent his client being found liable for the claimant's injuries and loss, his fallback position is to minimise the level of damages his client is obliged to pay. It therefore follows that the task of valuing the claimant's losses is just as important to those representing defendants as it is to those representing claimants. Although the claimant and defendant will usually only be interested in the final amount of the award, the personal injury solicitor must fully understand the various heads of damages which the court can order, to ensure that he can achieve the best possible result for his client. However, even the most experienced personal injury lawyer will be able to quantify the damages only approximately, and therefore solicitors should take care to manage their client's expectations. It is a wise claimant's solicitor who gives his client a slightly lower assessment of the likely damages, and a wise defendant's solicitor who gives his client a slightly higher assessment.

In negligence, the aim of the award of damages is to restore the claimant to the position that he was in prior to the accident. Of course, it is impossible to take away the pain and suffering associated with a personal injury, particularly as, in many cases, there will be lasting physical and/or psychological disability. The award of monetary compensation is the only remedy available to the court and, particularly in cases of catastrophic injury, claimants and their families will cope better with the physical, mental, social and financial consequences of the injuries where appropriate monetary compensation is received.

In most cases, the claimant will receive a lump sum award in full and final settlement of his claim, which means he will not be able to return to court at a later date to seek additional compensation (see provisional damages and periodical payments at **15.4** and **15.5** below for exceptions to this rule). It is therefore important that the claimant's solicitor is thorough in his investigations to identify all losses. Where the case is determined at trial, damages are assessed as at the date of the trial (or, in 'split trials', at a later hearing), and therefore detailed and up-to-date evidence, such as an updated loss of earnings calculation and medical report, should be provided to the court. Most claims are settled through negotiation, but it is equally important for the claimant's solicitor to have detailed and up-to-date evidence available whenever quantum is discussed with the defendant's solicitor.

15.1.1 Heads of damage

The following heads of damage can be claimed in personal injury and clinical negligence cases:

(a) Special damages (also known as past pecuniary loss). These are the financial losses which the claimant has incurred prior to trial, and they are capable of fairly precise calculation.

(b) General damages. These are damages that cannot be calculated precisely and therefore require the application of certain formulaic approaches plus a little educated guesswork. They can be split into two categories:

   (i) Non-pecuniary loss. This is the element of the compensation award that does not reflect financial losses at all but rather reflects the claimant's pain, suffering and loss of amenity.

   (ii) Future pecuniary loss. Although this element of the compensation reflects financial losses, such as future loss of earnings or the cost of the care which the claimant will require, it cannot be calculated precisely as it is impossible to say with precision, for example, how long the claimant will live, what he would have earned had he not been injured or how much his care requirements will cost in future years.

Terminology may create problems for the unwary, as some practitioners use the term 'special damages' when referring to all items of pecuniary loss, both past and future, and the term 'general damages' is used routinely in case reporting to mean pain, suffering and loss of amenity only. It goes without saying that, when negotiating a settlement, solicitors must be precise about the nature of the damages to which they are referring. In this text, we shall give the terminology its traditional meaning as set out in (a) and (b) above.

The distinction between special damages and the two heads of general damages is significant not only in the method of calculation, but also with regard to the level of interest awarded by the court (see **15.6**).

15.2 SPECIAL DAMAGES – 'PAST PECUNIARY LOSS'

Special damages are the items of financial loss incurred by the claimant between the date of the accident and the date of trial which can be specifically calculated.

The main heads of special damages are:

(a)   loss of earnings;

(b)   clothing and personal effects;

(c)   cost of medical care and expenses;

(d)   cost of care and quasi-nursing services;

(e)   cost of DIY, gardening and housework services;

(f)   cost of aids and appliances;

(g)   cost of alternative and/or adapted accommodation;

(h)   transport costs.

In RTA cases, there may also be:

(i)   cost of repairs to or replacement of the claimant's vehicle;

(j)   vehicle recovery and storage charges;

(k)   loss of use of a motor vehicle or hire of a substitute vehicle;

(l)   loss of a no claims bonus and wasted road fund licence.

You should note that some of the above heads will also be relevant to any general damages claim for future pecuniary loss.

15.2.1   Loss of earnings up to the date of the trial

In most cases, there will be a claim for loss of earnings up to the date of trial. The claimant is entitled to recover his net loss of earnings, ie what he would have earned after tax, National Insurance and contractual pension payments.

In many cases, where the claimant was in regular employment, it will be reasonably straightforward to determine precisely how much the claimant has lost. In other cases, the calculation will not be so precise. For example, where the claimant's pre-accident wages varied markedly from week to week, or where there has been a fairly lengthy period of time between the accident and trial and the claimant argues that he would have been promoted to a more lucrative position had he still been working.

15.2.1.1   Calculating loss of earnings

The starting point in the calculation is to determine the claimant's average net wage for the period immediately prior to the accident. The common approach is to obtain, from the claimant's wage slips or bank statements or from his employer, details of his earnings for the 13-week period prior to the accident. Where that 13-week period is not representative of the claimant's average pre-accident wage, a longer period, for example six months, should be considered. Whatever period is looked at, appropriate adjustments should be made to take account of any overtime, bonus payments, benefits such as company cars or commission that the claimant would have earned had he been at work. Further adjustments should be made to take account of any pay increase, promotion, or further benefits which the claimant would have obtained during the period from the date of the action to trial.

In some cases, such as where the claimant had obtained a job immediately prior to the accident and a clear pattern of pre-accident wages cannot be provided, or where there has been a lengthy period between the date of the accident and the assessment of damages, it may be useful to obtain details of a comparative earner. This involves identifying someone who was in a similar post and earning a similar salary to the claimant immediately prior to the accident, and determining what his earnings pattern had been and, where appropriate, tracking his career progression and salary increases during the period up to trial. Clearly, it would be most useful if the comparative earner is employed by the claimant's employer, but where this is not possible, a comparative earner from a similar business or organisation can be used.

Some claimants have more complex employment histories, such as where they worked on short-term contracts or were self-employed. In such circumstances, more detailed enquiries must be made in order to provide evidence of income lost before the trial. Self-employed claimants should be asked to supply copies of their accounts and/or tax returns for the year prior to the accident, or a longer period if one year's figures are not representative. This information may be difficult to obtain, leaving scope for those representing defendants to argue that losses have been exaggerated. It may be necessary to obtain a report from an accountant (the term 'forensic accountant' is often used for those who specialise in this area).

In an attempt to establish details of how much the claimant would have earned between the accident and trial in cases where an erratic employment history is presented, reference can be made to the Annual Survey of Hours and Earnings produced by the Office for National Statistics, which is a statistical analysis of earnings throughout the country. The Survey can provide details of average earnings for particular industries or occupations on a national or regional basis, and can be useful in attempting to persuade the defendant to accept that the claimant would have received a particular wage.

Very few employees receive no income whatsoever while absent from work, and so the calculation of the claimant's lost earnings is not simply a case of multiplying the net weekly loss by the number of weeks' absence. Such an approach would place the claimant in a better financial position than he would have been in had the accident not occurred. A detailed examination of what income the claimant received while absent from work is required, as certain types of income have to be credited in calculating the net loss figure.

15.2.1.2 Items which must be accounted for in the calculation

The following are the most common items which must be accounted for in the net loss of earnings figure (for both past and future loss of earnings calculations), ie these amounts must be deducted from the net salary in order to calculate the total loss of earnings:

(a) *Tax refunds received due to absence from work as a result of the accident.* A claimant who is an employee will generally pay income tax on the Pay As You Earn (PAYE) system. To a certain extent this system is a payment of tax in advance, as it assumes that the claimant's earnings will continue throughout the whole of the forthcoming year. In the event of the claimant's absence from work, he may then have paid too much tax. In this case, the claimant may receive a tax rebate via his employer. An amount equivalent to the whole of the rebate has to be given credit for in the calculation of wage loss (*Hartley v Sandholme Iron Co Ltd* [1975] QB 600). Occasionally, instead of a 'cash-in-hand' tax rebate, the claimant may receive a tax credit against future tax liability, so that on his return to work he pays no tax for a period (a 'tax holiday'). A sum equivalent to this tax credit also has to be given credit for in the calculation of the wage loss (*Brayson v Wilmot-Breedon* [1976] CLY 682).

(b) *Sums paid to the claimant by his employer.* Whether sums equivalent to such payments fall to be deducted from the damages depends on the basis of the payment and the identity of the tortfeasor.

The following are the most common situations:

(i)   The sum is paid under a legal obligation (eg, under the claimant's contract of employment) and is not refundable by the claimant to his employer. An amount equivalent to the whole of the payment should be deducted from the damages.

(ii) The sum is paid under a legal obligation (eg, under the contract of employment) and must be repaid by the claimant to his employer out of any damages the claimant receives from the defendant. Such a payment is effectively a loan and, as such, is not deducted when assessing the damages.

    (iii)   The sum is paid *ex gratia* by the employer who is not the tortfeasor. Such a payment is effectively a 'charitable' payment and is not to be deducted when assessing the damages (*Cunningham v Harrison* [1973] 3 All ER 463).

    (iv)   The sum is paid *ex gratia* by the employer who is the tortfeasor. An amount equivalent to the whole of the payment may (in certain circumstances) be deducted from the damages (*Hussain v New Taplow Paper Mills Ltd* [1988] AC 514).

    (v)   The claimant receives statutory sick pay (SSP) from his employer. This is not a recoverable benefit to the DWP (see **Chapter 16**), and therefore an amount equivalent to the whole payment should be deducted (the contract of employment may need to be examined in case the employer is entitled to claw back the SSP in some way). See also *Palfrey v Greater London Council* [1985] ICR 437.

(c)   *Any saving to an injured person attributable to his maintenance wholly or partly at public expense.* This would apply where the claimant was, for example, admitted into an NHS hospital, a nursing home or other institution. The savings must be calculated and set off against any claim for income lost as a result of the injuries (Administration of Justice Act 1982, s 5). In practice, this deduction is overlooked because in most cases the sums saved are *de minimis*. (While in hospital the claimant will generally have to meet the same household expenses such as rent, mortgage and council tax; any saving will usually be only in regard to the cost of food. This saving is then so small as to be ignored.)

(d)   *Redundancy payments.* An equivalent amount is to be deducted in full from the damages calculation when redundancy occurs as a result of the injury caused by the accident (*Colledge v Bass Mitchells & Butlers* [1988] 1 All ER 536).

(e)   *Benefits outside the ambit of the Social Security (Recovery of Benefits) Act 1997.* A sum equivalent to certain benefits received by the claimant as a result of the accident will be deducted from the judgment sum or negotiated settlement by the defendant and paid directly to the Compensation Recovery Unit (see **Chapter 16**). However, when calculating the award, benefits which are not subject to offsetting are potentially deductible. In *Clenshaw v Tanner* [2002] EWCA Civ 1848, the Court of Appeal held that as the claimant was not required to reimburse the local authority for receipt of housing benefit, if he was allowed to recover for loss of earnings in full, he would be overcompensated to the extent of the housing benefit. Consequently, the housing benefit payments were deducted from the loss of earnings award. It therefore follows that, potentially, other benefits, such as council tax benefit, child tax credit, working tax credit, motability payments, etc are deductible.

15.2.1.3   Items which are not accounted for

The following items are the most common payments to be left out of account in assessing an award for loss of past (and future) earnings:

(a)   *State retirement pension.* The State retirement pension is ignored in assessing an award for loss of past and future earnings (*Hewson v Downs* [1970] 1 QB 73).

(b)   *Pensions received.* The general rule is that if the claimant receives a pension, this cannot be set against the claim for loss of earnings. However, if there is a separate claim for loss of pension rights, for example since the claimant is unable to work he will receive less pension in the future, any pension he does receive may be offset against the claim for loss of pension rights (*Parry v Cleaver* [1970] AC 1; *Smoker v London Fire and Civil Defence Authority* [1991] 2 All ER 449; *Longden v British Coal Corporation* [1997] 3 WLR 1336.

(c)   *Insurance moneys.* Where a claimant has taken out an insurance policy specifically to cover him against the risk of sustaining personal injuries, or where such cover is an incidental' benefit to other types of insurance, such as motor insurance, he may receive a payment as a result of injuries caused by the defendant's negligence. In such cases, the payment is usually a fixed sum according to the type of injury; for example, in the event of a loss of a specified limb, the insurance company will pay the insured the sum of £5,000.

The claimant need not give credit for moneys received under such a policy against the damages payable by the defendant, provided he paid for or contributed to the policy premiums. The justification is that the defendant should not benefit from the fact that the claimant had the foresight to take out the cover and pay the premium (*Bradburn v Great Western Railway Co* (1874) LR 10 Exch 1; *McCamley v Cammell Laird Shipbuilders Ltd* [1990] 1 All ER 854). Where the claimant does not pay for or contribute to the policy, as where the employer sets up a non-contributory group personal accident insurance policy, credit must be given (see *Pirelli v Gaca* [2004] EWCA Civ 373).

In cases where credit does not have to be given to the defendant, the terms of the insurance policy should be checked carefully. There will often be a provision (particularly in motor insurance) which obliges a policyholder to reimburse the insurance company for any sum it paid to him under the policy in respect of a loss for which he receives compensation from a third party. In such a case, the claimant will not receive any financial benefit from commencing proceedings, but the insurance company may insist on commencing and conducting proceedings in his name.

(d) *Charitable payments.* If money is received by the claimant as a charitable payment (even if it is on an informal basis such as the proceeds of a collection taken among his friends) then the claimant is not required to give credit for such payment against the damages received. The justification is that as a matter of policy, people should not be discouraged from making such payments to the victims of accidents. However, the exact circumstances and sources of the *ex gratia* payment must be considered. In *Williams v BOC Gases Ltd* [2000] PIQR Q253, the Court of Appeal held that where an employer (who was the tortfeasor) made an *ex gratia* payment on termination of the claimant's employment on the basis that it was to be treated as an advance against any damages that might be awarded in respect of any claim the claimant had against the employer, credit had to be given for that amount in a subsequent personal injury claim.

15.2.2 Clothing and personal effects

Where the claimant has been injured as a result of an accident, there may be damage to items of clothing and other personal effects, such as mobile telephones, laptop computers, watches, etc. Where such items are damaged beyond repair, the claimant is entitled to claim their pre-accident value, and appropriate documentary evidence (such as receipts or valuations) should be provided. Solicitors acting for defendants will be keen to ensure that items have not been overvalued by the claimant and that discounts are given in respect of items which were not brand-new at the time of the accident. This type of loss does not arise in clinical negligence cases.

15.2.3 Cost of medical care and expenses

The claimant is entitled to recover all medical expenses reasonably incurred as a result of the defendant's breach of duty, for example prescriptions, over-the-counter drugs, and private medical care and treatment. However, where the claimant has been treated as an in-patient, only the cost of the medical care may be claimed; he cannot claim for the 'hotel' element included in the cost of staying in hospital, for example the proportion of the fees that relate to the provision of meals, heating and lighting (*Lim Poh Choo v Camden and Islington Area Health Authority* [1979] 2 All ER 910).

Treatment may be in relation to essential matters (such as a colostomy), non-emergency, non-life threatening matters (such as dealing with bed sores), or incidental treatments (such as IVF, required, for example, where a claimant is unable to father a child naturally due to a spinal cord injury). The courts will allow the costs of numerous types of therapeutic care, such as psychiatric assistance, physiotherapy and occupational therapy, and may allow the cost of alternative medical treatments, such as acupuncture. The availability of free NHS treatment is ignored (Law Reform (Personal Injuries) Act 1948, s 2(4); see also *Eagle v Chambers* [2004]

EWCA Civ 1033), although a claimant cannot be treated free under the NHS and then claim for private treatment.

In cases where there are long waiting lists under the NHS, if the claimant does not himself raise the matter, the claimant's solicitor should suggest that the client undergo private medical treatment in an attempt to speed the recovery period. Indeed, where the claimant has a strong case on liability, the defendant's solicitors may well suggest this, as prompt treatment may reduce the level of damages ultimately payable by the defendant. Reference should be made to the Rehabilitation Code (Annex D to the PAP for Personal Injury Claims; see **Appendix 2**), which requires the parties to co-operate in order to assess and provide for the claimant's rehabilitation needs.

> **EXAMPLE**
>
> A 10-year-old girl is injured and has to undergo major abdominal surgery at the local hospital, which leaves her with a large surgical incision. As part of her general damages award she will claim for pain and suffering relating to the scarring. It is also likely that she will claim that she will suffer psychological problems in relation to the embarrassment of wearing swimming costumes throughout her teenage years and perhaps in later life. In such a case, the claimant should undergo specialist plastic surgery in an attempt to reduce the significance of the scarring and the potential psychological problems, which, in turn, will reduce the level of damages that the defendant will pay.

Future private medical care may also be claimed as part of the future pecuniary loss head of general damages (see **15.3.5**), provided it is reasonably likely to be incurred.

15.2.4   Cost of care and quasi-nursing services

In cases where the claimant is seriously injured, the cost of providing care and quasi-nursing services may form a substantial part of both the special damages claim for past pecuniary losses and the general damages claim for future pecuniary losses (see **15.3.5**). The cost of such services may also form part of the special damages claim where injuries have been less severe. In most cases, at least some of the care will have been provided gratuitously, by a member of the claimant's family or a close friend. As with medical care and expenses, the claimant is under no obligation to use care services provided by the NHS.

15.2.4.1   Professional care

Where care services are provided on a commercial basis, they can be recovered from the defendant provided they are reasonable in amount and are reasonably incurred as a result of the injuries. The claimant will bear the burden of proving that he needed or will need the level of care provided.

15.2.4.2   Gratuitous care

In relation to gratuitous care, the carer is unable to make a claim against the defendant due to the general principle that a third party cannot claim in respect of losses he has incurred as a result of the claimant's injuries. However, the claimant may recover the value of care services provided to him on a gratuitous basis, so long as such services were rendered necessary by the negligence of the defendant. In other words, the care provided must be over and above that which the claimant would have normally received from the carer. So, for example, where a mother is severely injured and her child slightly injured in a road traffic accident as a result of the defendant's negligence, it is not possible for the child to claim damages for the care element from the defendant, as the mother would normally provide such care. The appropriate course is for the mother to include, as part of her damages claim, the costs of the care of the child which she can no longer provide herself (see *Buckley v Farrow and Buckley* [1997] PIQR Q78).

The value of gratuitous services may be claimed by the claimant irrespective of whether the third party has been put to actual expense in providing those services, for example by incurring loss of earnings, and it is unnecessary for there to be any agreement between the claimant and the third party as to reimbursement for the services.

Initially, courts were reluctant to award damages for the cost of gratuitous care except in the most serious cases. However, in *Giambrone & Others v JMC Holidays Ltd (formerly t/a Sunworld Holidays Ltd)* [2004] EWCA Civ 158, holiday makers who had developed gastro-enteritis at the defendant's hotel, which persisted for more than 14 days, were able to recover for gratuitous care provided by family members once they had returned home. The Court of Appeal rejected the defendant's argument that an award for the value of such services should be made only in serious cases or where the claimant could point to a demonstrable financial expense in providing the necessary care. Consequently, claimants' solicitors should always include a claim for gratuitous care when it has been provided.

As has already been said, the claim for the value of the services is made by the claimant, not by the third party, as it is the claimant's loss (his need for the services) which is being compensated. However, although it is the claimant who obtains the award for the value of the services, the damages are held by him in trust for the carer. Therefore, where the carer is also the defendant (eg, where a wife is injured as a result of her husband's negligent driving and the husband provides quasi-nursing services to her), the claimant cannot recover the value of those services from the defendant/carer, as the claimant would have to repay the damages to the defendant/carer (*Hunt v Severs* [1994] 2 All ER 385, HL).

15.2.4.3   The valuation of gratuitous care

In the case of professional services, the claimant is entitled to the reasonable fee payable for those services; but in the case of gratuitous care where no fee is incurred, the valuation may be more problematical. Each case will be assessed on its own facts.

Where the relative or spouse has given up work in order to look after the claimant, and has thereby incurred loss of earnings, the lost earnings will be recoverable, provided they were reasonably incurred.

Where there is no loss of income by the third party, the court will normally take account of what it would cost to employ professional help. In this regard, there has been a recent tendency to favour the standard hourly rate paid at spinal point 8 of the National Joint Council for Local Government Services table. This rate, currently £7.19 per hour, which represents the earnings of home care workers, may be weighted to take account of location and also whether care is provided during the night or in extremely difficult circumstances. (See *Massey v Tameside & Glossop Acute Services NHS Trust* [2007] EWHC 317 (QB), where the court found that the flat rate at spinal point 8 did not adequately recompense a mother who provided particularly demanding services during the night and at weekends to her claimant son.) In addition, the court will normally apply a discount of somewhere between 20 and 30%, to reflect the absence of tax and National Insurance deductions, travelling costs to and from work, the profit element associated with commercial care services and the fact that professional carers might be more efficient.

If the claimant seeks a rate in excess of the commercial rate, he has the onus of proving the higher value (*Rialas v Mitchell* (1984) *The Times*, 17 July, where the claimant justified care at home which was approximately twice the cost of care in an institution) (see also *Fitzgerald v Ford* [1996] PIQR Q72).

15.2.5   Cost of DIY, gardening and housework services

The claimant is entitled to recover from the defendant the reasonable costs of obtaining DIY, gardening and housework services which he used to provide for himself but has been unable to do as a result of the accident. The services may be provided commercially or gratuitously, and there may be a claim for past loss under special damages and/or a general damages claim for future loss.

15.2.6 Costs of aids and appliances

The claimant may require specific aids or equipment to enable him to cope better with his disabilities. Such items will result in one-off payments, and where this expense has been incurred before the trial, it will form part of the claim for special damages. However, such items may be required at regular intervals after trial and throughout the claimant's life, and therefore the replacement cost must be included within any future loss calculation.

The types of aids and appliances which a claimant may require are too numerous to list here, but the following are a few examples:

(a) adaptations to the family car to allow the claimant to drive;

(b) wheelchairs (defendants may argue that these can be provided free by the State, in which case claimant's solicitors should argue that these would not be suitable);

(c) special beds;

(d) incontinence pads;

(e) odour control in the house due to incontinence;

(f) hoists, to assist in moving the claimant in and out of bed;

(g) tilting chairs;

(h) exercise equipment, such as stationary cycles;

(i) therapy balls, to help with mobility.

15.2.7 Cost of alternative accommodation and/or adaptations

Where a disabled claimant is living at home, it is possible that the accommodation he had prior to the accident is no longer suitable. It may require alterations and adaptations, such as the installation of ramps for a wheelchair or a hoist for access to the bath, alterations to the internal layout of the premises to facilitate access to bedrooms and bathrooms, or the creation of extra storage space to accommodate wheelchairs and other aids or appliances. It may be necessary to create accommodation for a resident nurse or carer. Where such alterations and adaptations do not add value to the accommodation, the cost may be recovered in full from the defendant. If the expense has been incurred prior to trial, it will form part of the special damages calculation. If not, it will form part of the future loss calculation.

Some alterations, such as an extension, may be expensive, but they will add value to the accommodation and, in such cases, the added value must be accounted for in the claim for damages.

In some circumstances, the claimant's existing home may be incapable of adaptation and it is not unreasonable for him to move to more suitable accommodation. Provided that accommodation is reasonable for his needs, he will be entitled to purchase a home which is more expensive than his previous one. Clearly, the claimant will incur expenses in the move which are recoverable from the defendant. However, if he were entitled to recover from the defendant the purchase price of the more expensive new property less the proceeds from the sale of his previous home, he would be overcompensated. He would benefit from a more expensive house than perhaps he would otherwise have been able to buy, and the capital value of the property would remain intact on his death and represent a windfall to his estate.

In such circumstances, the solution developed by the courts is to say that the loss is not a straightforward capital loss, ie the cost of buying a larger house less the proceeds from the sale of the previous house, but rather the loss of the net income which that capital sum would have earned had it been invested. This lost income is not calculated by reference to a normal commercial rate of interest but in accordance with the rate set by the Court of Appeal in *Roberts v Johnstone* [1988] 3 WLR 1247. The rate of 2.5% per annum represents the real rate of return on a risk-free investment.

The loss to the claimant is calculated as follows:

- Past loss: extra capital outlay x 2.5% (rate of return) x number of years of loss
- Future loss: extra capital outlay x 2.5% x whole life multiplier (obtained from the Ogden tables) – see **15.3.4.2**
- In either case, add any cost of conversion less any enhancement value

---

EXAMPLE

The claimant, Abdul, was 39 at the time of the trial and has, as a result of catastrophic injuries, been confined to a wheelchair. Prior to the accident, he had lived in a third-floor flat, which was wholly unsuitable for his needs following the accident. Consequently, a year before the trial, he sold his former flat for £200,000 and moved to a bungalow, which he purchased for £300,000. The bungalow was more or less suitable for his needs, but a number of adaptations were required, including alterations to the bathroom and the installation of a ramp to the front door, which cost a further £15,000. In addition, an extension was built, costing £55,000, in order to accommodate a full-time carer. The extension has added £60,000 to the value of the bungalow. The other adaptations have not altered the valuation in any way.

Cost of replacement accommodation:	£300,000	
LESS: value of current house:	£200,000	
Capital difference	£100,000	
@2.5% of £100,000	£2,500	
Past loss - £2,500 x 1		**£2,500**
Future loss - Multiplier (Table 1, Pecuniary loss for life, male; aged 39 at trial) = 26.86		
£2,500 x 26.86		**£67,150**
ADD conversion costs		**£70,000**
		£137,150
LESS increase in value		**£60,000**
Future loss		£77,150
Total loss claimable:		**£79,650**

15.2.8 Travelling costs

The claimant is entitled to claim reasonable travelling costs, whether by private car or other transport, such as buses, trains and taxis, which have arisen as a result of the accident. The costs of travelling to hospitals, doctors, physiotherapists, etc are all claimable. Although the cost of travelling to a medical expert for the purposes of the litigation is more properly claimed as legal costs rather than as damages, it is common to see them in the claim for special damages.

Where the claimant uses his own vehicle, there is usually a dispute between the parties regarding the reasonable amount payable for mileage. Claimants may seek to rely on the amount HM Revenue and Customs allows employees to claim for business mileage before tax is charged – currently 45p per mile for up to 10,000 miles per year and 25p per mile for any additional miles. The defendant may seek to rely on figures based on running costs, such as those provided by the AA and the RAC, which tend to be lower.

In many cases, family members and friends will incur additional travelling expenses, for example by visiting the claimant whilst he is in hospital. The claimant is able to claim such expenses as part of his loss (because he has a need for the visit), but it will be necessary to prove that they were reasonably incurred as a result of his injuries. Consequently, only those expenses which exceed what the family member or friend would have ordinarily spent on visiting the claimant can be recovered.

EXAMPLE

The claimant, Peter, lived with his girlfriend, Sally, prior to the accident. Ordinarily, Sally would not have incurred any expense in seeing him, so all travelling expenses associated with visiting him in hospital can be claimed. On the other hand, if she had lived several miles away from Peter, a claim could be made only in respect of the costs which were over and above the normal travelling costs. If the hospital is further away than Peter's house, or she visits him more frequently than she would have otherwise done, a claim should be made for the additional expense.

Where there is a claim for future travelling costs, these can be calculated by means of a multiplicand and multiplier (see **15.3.4**). A claim for parking charges should also be made where appropriate.

15.2.9 Repairs to or replacement of the claimant's vehicle; recovery and storage costs

Where the claimant's vehicle is damaged beyond repair, he is entitled to claim its pre-accident value, less any salvage price obtained. Where the vehicle has been repaired, he is entitled to the reasonable costs of the repairs. The claimant will also be able to claim any reasonable costs incurred in recovering the vehicle from the accident site and storage costs prior to repair or disposal. As the claimant is under an obligation to mitigate his losses, he should not allow his vehicle to languish in storage facilities for too long or he may find he is unable to recover all of the associated charges.

15.2.10 Loss of use of a motor vehicle or hire of substitute vehicle

Where the claimant's vehicle is damaged and is off the road for a number of weeks while being repaired, the claimant may claim damages for the 'loss of use' of his vehicle. A weekly amount should be claimed, and this will reflect the level of inconvenience and hardship incurred by the claimant's having to rely on other means of transport. Special damages claims for loss of use of a motor vehicle have decreased in recent years, as the claimant is more likely to hire a substitute vehicle and claim the associated costs. However, such claims are still relevant where the claimant is no longer able to drive, and in such cases there might also be a general damages claim for the future loss of use of a motor vehicle.

Although it is clear that car hire charges incurred while the claimant's vehicle is being repaired can be claimed, the claimant must show that he has acted reasonably. The defendant should challenge the claim where the claimant has hired a more expensive type of vehicle than that involved in the accident, or has continued to hire a vehicle after his own vehicle has been repaired. Also, if the hire car is hired at the more expensive daily rate rather than at the cheaper weekly rate, then the defendant should argue that only the weekly rate should be recovered, although the claimant may be able to show a good reason for using the daily rate (see *Usher v Crowder* [1994] CLY 1494). In relation to the reasonableness of the basic daily hire rate, see *Stevens v Equity Syndicate Management Ltd* [2015] EWCA Civ 93.

In certain circumstances, the claimant may use a vehicle supplied by a 'credit hire' company, but for any such agreement to be enforceable, it must comply with the Consumer Credit Act 1974 (or be exempt), the hire charges should be at the 'market rate' (*Dimond v Lovell* [2000] 2 WLR 1121) and the period of hire should be reasonable (*Opoku v Tintas* [2013] All ER (D) 81 (Jul)).

Where a claim for hire charges is made, generally, a claim for loss of use will not be made as the claimant has not been without a vehicle.

15.2.11   No-claims bonus

Under the terms of an insurance policy, a no-claims bonus (NCB) will entitle the policyholder to a discount on his annual premiums where he has not made any claims under the policy for a specified period. Where there is a NCB of five years or more, the policyholder may be entitled to a discount of as much as 60% to 75% and, as premiums are becoming increasingly expensive, the loss of the NCB may represent a significant monetary loss to the claimant. The claimant will lose the NCB where, as a result of his being involved in an accident, the insurance company has to make payments to either the claimant or a third party under the terms of the policy, and is unable to recoup such losses from anyone else. As it is a NCB and not a no-fault bonus, it is immaterial whether the claimant was at fault or not. Where the claimant has lost his NCB, or is at risk of doing so, the loss should be included in the claim for damages. If, ultimately, the claimant's insurer is able to recover all its losses from the defendant (or more usually the defendant's insurer), the NCB will not be lost and the defendant's solicitor should ensure that the claim for the NCB is withdrawn.

15.2.12   Evidence of items of special damages

It is for the claimant to prove all items of special damages, and details should be set out in the appropriate witness statement(s). Where damaged items are capable of repair or services are required, the claimant should obtain two or three estimates in order to demonstrate that the costs incurred are reasonable. A decision to use a more expensive service provider should be explained in full. The claimant should be reminded at the outset of the case that he should retain documentary evidence (such as receipts, estimates and valuations) wherever possible. Defendants' solicitors should challenge items that cannot be supported by appropriate evidence. Where there is no documentary evidence, it is open to the claimant to attempt to prove the loss by his own oral testimony at trial, but see *Hughes v Addis* [2000] LTL, 23 March, where the Court of Appeal upheld the judge's decision not to allow petrol costs where no receipts were supplied.

15.3   GENERAL DAMAGES

General damages are those which are not capable of precise mathematical calculation. They may be divided into:

(a)   pain, suffering and loss of amenity (sometimes known as non-pecuniary loss); and

(b)   financial losses incurred from the date of trial (or date of assessment of damages) for as long as court deems the losses will continue into the future (sometimes known as future pecuniary loss).

The main heads of general damages are:

(a)   pain, suffering and loss of amenity;

(b)   handicap in the labour market;

(c)   loss of congenial employment;

(d)   future loss of earnings;

(e)   future cost of medical expenses and care/non-medical care and aids and appliances;

(f)   lost pension.

15.3.1   Pain, suffering and loss of amenity

15.3.1.1   Damages for pain and suffering

Awards of damages under this head are designed to compensate the claimant for the pain and suffering attributable to any physical injury and psychological illness caused by the defendant's actions, from the moment of the accident to the date of trial, when damages are assessed, and, where appropriate, future pain and suffering.

The award is made on the basis of a subjective test, ie a consideration of the pain and suffering of this particular claimant.

15.3.1.2 Damages for loss of amenity

Strictly speaking, there is a separate head of damages known as 'loss of amenity', but compensation for this loss is usually included with compensation for pain and suffering. This element is designed to compensate the claimant for the loss of enjoyment of life which has resulted from the accident. Examples under this head include interference with the claimant's sex life, or the loss or impairment of his enjoyment of holidays, sports, hobbies and other pursuits.

The award for loss of amenity is based on an objective test (in contrast to pain and suffering), and thus may be awarded irrespective of whether the claimant is personally aware of his loss, for example if he is unconscious (*West v Shephard* [1964] AC 326).

Although the test is primarily objective, it does have subjective overtones in so far as the court will have regard to the claimant's former lifestyle. This may be particularly pertinent where the claimant was formerly a very active person (eg a keen sportsman) and can no longer pursue his sport. Although his pain and suffering may be the same as that of another person with a similar disability, his loss of amenity may be greater and, as such, the total award for pain and suffering and loss of amenity may be greater.

Damages for loss of congenial employment (see **15.3.3**) may also be argued under this head, but increasingly, the courts are making separate reference to these types of damages.

15.3.1.3 Quantification of damages for pain, suffering and loss of amenity

There is no minimum award which must be made for pain, suffering and loss of amenity (however, only exceptionally would an injury not be worth, for example, £500 or £750); neither is there any maximum.

The award is incapable of precise mathematical calculation. The solicitor's first step is to examine the claimant's witness statement and the medical report in order to identify details of the following:

(a) The claimant's life prior to the accident. This will be relevant to the loss of amenity claim.

(b) The pain and suffering associated with the accident itself and the immediate aftermath. What were the injuries? How did the claimant react? Was he taken to hospital by ambulance?

(c) Any periods of time the claimant was in hospital, and the number and nature of any operations or other medical procedures he had to undergo.

(d) The short-term/long-term prognosis. Will the claimant recover in full? If not, what will his continuing pain/disabilities be, and how long will they continue?

(e) Is there a risk of any future degeneration (eg, osteoporosis)?

(f) What has been/will be the effect of the injuries on the claimant's lifestyle?

In attempting to value the claim, courts will refer to the awards made in comparable cases, so the solicitor's next step is to carry out the relevant research. As no two cases are exactly alike (for example, there may be differences in relation to the sex and age of the claimant, the injuries suffered and the effect on the claimant's life), this is not as straightforward as it might appear.

A useful starting point is the Judicial College's *Guidelines for the Assessment of General Damages in Personal Injury Cases*, currently in their 12th edition, published in October 2013. The *Guidelines* are commonly used by personal injury lawyers and judges to obtain a ball-park figure for the claimant's injuries. (An on-line version of the *Guidelines* may be found on Lawtel Personal Injury.) The *Guidelines* are based on an analysis of previous judgments and provide an easy reference to broad categories of injuries, such as head injuries, psychiatric damages, injuries affecting the senses, injuries to internal organs, etc. These categories are further divided, so, for example, the section on orthopaedic injuries is divided into neck injuries, back injuries, shoulder injuries, etc. Lastly, each of these sub-categories is divided into severe, serious, moderate and minor classifications, with an indication of what each of these types of injuries are worth.

You should note that the 12th edition was published early in order to take account of the 10% uplift in general damages resulting from the revised decision of the Court of Appeal in *Simmons v Castle* [2012] EWCA Civ 1039 (see further below).

You should not base your assessment of the claimant's losses solely on the *Guidelines* but rather should make reference to specific comparable cases. The importance of comparable cases was stressed by the Court of Appeal in *Dureau v Evans* [1996] PIQR Q18, when it commented on the limited assistance provided by the *Guidelines* in relation to claimants who have suffered multiple injuries. Similarly, in *Reed v Sunderland Health Authority* (1998) *The Times*, 16 October, it was held that while the *Guidelines* were an important source of information, they did not have the force of law, and the Court of Appeal is unlikely to overturn a decision if the *Guidelines* are not followed precisely (see *Davis v Inman* [1999] PIQR Q26).

Traditionally, solicitors looking for comparable cases would use specialist sources, such as:

(a)　Kemp and Kemp, *The Quantum of Damages* (Sweet & Maxwell);

(b)　*Butterworths Personal Injury Service*;

(c)　*Personal Injuries and Quantum Reports* (Sweet & Maxwell);

(d)　*Current Law* (Sweet & Maxwell);

(e)　*Personal and Medical Injuries Law Letter* (IBC).

However, increasingly, solicitors are using on-line services, such as Butterworth's PI or Lawtel (which includes access to Kemp and Kemp), to identify comparable cases.

Once a comparable case has been found, the relevant figure is that relating to pain, suffering and loss of amenity. Remember the difficulties associated with terminology. Frequently, the case reports will helpfully set out a figure for pain, suffering and loss of amenity, but sometimes they will refer to 'general damages'. If it is clear from the facts of the case that there are no future losses, or alternatively a figure for future losses appears, it is safe to assume that the term 'general damages' is the award for pain, suffering and loss of amenity. If it is unsafe to make such an assumption, further investigations will need to be made.

There will be differences between the claimant's situation and the circumstances of the claimants in the comparable case so, once the relevant figure in the comparable case has been identified, adjustments will need to be made in order to take account of the following matters:

(a)　*Sex* – for example, traditionally, female claimants have received more for facial scarring than male claimants. This seems to be based on the assumption that a woman's appearance is of greater importance than that of a man and that women suffer more as a result of disfigurement. Although the Judicial College has maintained the gender differences in the 12th edition, it acknowledges that it is doubtful whether gender itself can be a proper or lawful factor to take into account. In her Foreword to the *Guidelines*, The Rt Hon Dame Janet Smith DBE suggests that judges should put the matter of gender out of their minds when assessing damages, and should state that they have done so when giving judgment.

(b)　*Age of the victim* – in cases of permanent disability, younger victims tend to get more compensation than older victims as the young will suffer longer. On the other hand, some injuries will have a more severe impact on an older claimant than on a younger one.

(c) *Loss of amenity* – this is heavily influenced by whether the victim had a previously active lifestyle.

(d) *Limb injuries* – injuries to dominant limbs attract higher awards than injuries to non-dominant limbs.

(e) *Inflation* – previous awards must be inflated to present-day values. The inflation table in Kemp and Kemp, *The Quantum of Damages*, can be used for that purpose although on-line sources, such as the one on Lawtel PI, provide both original and inflated figures in their quantum reports. Lawtel also has an on-line calculator which is very easy to use.

(f) *2000 uplift* – in the case of *Heil v Rankin and Another* [2000] 2 WLR 1173, the Court of Appeal considered the level of damages for pain and suffering, concluded that they were too low, and stated that there should be staged increases for all future cases where the value of awards for pain and suffering was in excess of £10,000. Consequently, when seeking to rely on a pre-March 2000 case in excess of £10,000, a conversion table (such as that found in *Quantum* 2/2000, 18 April 2000 (Sweet & Maxwell)), must be used to update the award, which will then need to be inflated to present-day values. The inflated figures provided in Lawtel's quantum reports take account of *Heil v Rankin*, and their on-line calculator will do this automatically, where relevant. The latest edition of the *JC's Guidelines* also takes the increases into account.

(g) *2013 uplift* – following the Court of Appeal's revised decision in *Simmons v Castle* [2012] EWCA Civ 1039, in order to mitigate the effects of the reforms to the civil litigation costs regime, a 10% uplift is to be applied for damages for pain, suffering and loss of amenity in all cases where judgment is given after 1 April 2013, except where the claimant has entered into a CFA before that date (LASPO 2012, s 44(6)). The idea is that this increase will be used by the claimant to pay for any success fee owed to his solicitor, as this will no longer be recoverable from a losing defendant. The 12th edition of the *Guidelines* has two columns, one providing figures for general damages with the uplift, and one without. The column with the uplift relates to those transitional cases funded by a CFA entered into before 1 April 2013 with a recoverable success fee. It is important that you use the correct column for each case.

When carrying out the research relating to a client who has sustained multiple injuries, it is extremely unlikely that a comparable case will be found. The accepted approach is to identify the most serious injury, find a comparable award for that injury and then take account of awards made for the other injuries. It will not normally be appropriate simply to bolt the separate awards together, as the court will seek to compensate the claimant for the totality of his pain and suffering, and some discount will be required in recognition of this.

15.3.1.4   Damages where there are pre-existing injuries or conditions

One of the arguments that the defendant may use to bar or limit recovery of loss for pain and suffering is that the whole or part of the claimant's injuries or disabilities is due to a pre-existing condition.

The egg-shell skull rule, which states that the defendant 'must take the victim as he finds him', means that a defendant will not escape liability in situations where the claimant had pre-existing injuries which made him more vulnerable to further injury. However, it does not mean that the defendant will be liable for the full extent of any injuries or disabilities suffered by the claimant. Rather, the defendant will be liable for the full extent of the *aggravation or exacerbation* of the claimant's pre-existing conditions. Where the defendant is able to show that the claimant would eventually have suffered similar symptoms in any event, damages will be restricted to those arising during the acceleration period, ie the period of time by which the symptoms have been brought forward by reason of the defendant's negligence.

> **EXAMPLE**
>
> Samantha suffered from a degenerative condition of the spine prior to her involvement in a RTA caused by the defendant's negligence. The defendant argues that this condition would eventually have generated the symptoms of which Samantha is now complaining, and that his actions have merely accelerated her disabilities. The defendant is able to prove that, but for his actions, her symptoms would have developed in five years' time in any event. The court will apply the 'acceleration period' approach and the defendant will be liable only for a five-year period for injury, loss and damage.

15.3.1.5 Evidence

Although the medical evidence will be the primary matter to which the court will have regard in determining the award for pain, suffering and loss of amenity, the claimant will also give evidence of his injuries at trial. It is important that details are contained within the client's witness statement. It is surprising how many clients forget the exact details of the difficulties they had immediately post-accident or post-operation, and it is good practice for the claimant's solicitor to suggest that a diary is kept by the client, detailing the pain and practical difficulties that were suffered. It may also be helpful to obtain evidence from others, such as the claimant's spouse and family members, or his employer, as to the effect of the injuries on the claimant.

15.3.2 Handicap in the labour market

The purpose of this award is to compensate the claimant for the potential difficulties he may face in obtaining another job, should he lose his current job, as a result of his injuries. For the court to award such damages, the claimant should have suffered a 'weakening' of his competitive position in the open labour market. In practice, this is referred to as a *Smith v Manchester* claim (see *Smith v Manchester Corporation* (1974) 17 KIR 1).

In deciding whether this type of award is appropriate, the court will:

(a)   consider whether there is a 'substantial' or 'real' risk that the claimant will lose his present job at some time before the estimated end of his working life; and if there is

(b)   assess and quantify the present value of the loss which the claimant will suffer if that risk materialises. In doing so, the court will have regard to the degree of risk, the time when it is likely to materialise and the factors, both favourable and unfavourable, which may affect the claimant's chance of getting another job at all or an equally well-paid job.

When seeking to establish whether there is a risk that the claimant will lose his job, the courts have given the words 'substantial' or 'real' a liberal interpretation, so that what is required to be shown is that the risk is 'real' rather than 'speculative'. The risk might lie in the nature of the injuries themselves, which might make it impossible for the claimant to continue in that line of work. If this is the case, the matter should be addressed in the medical report, and the claimant may also give evidence in his witness statement. Alternatively, the risk might lie in matters that have nothing to do with the injuries, such as business restructuring. The client's trade union will have details of any redundancies that have been made by the employer in recent years, and it may also be able to provide information about the employer's future plans, of which the client may not have been aware. If the client does not belong to a trade union, evidence should be obtained from the client's workmates or managers. (If the defendant is the claimant's employer, such information should be obtained from the defendant's insurers or solicitor.) The solicitor representing the defendant must obtain clear evidence concerning the claimant's job security in an attempt to refute the *Smith v Manchester* claim.

Once the first test has been satisfied, the court will attempt to quantify the risk and calculate the appropriate damages. The court has to anticipate what would be the claimant's chances of getting an equally well-paid job if he was forced onto the labour market. This head of damages is notoriously hard to quantify as the court will consider each individual case on its own facts, but a common approach is to award between zero to two years' net loss of earnings as at the date of trial. However, the Court of Appeal in *Foster v Tyne and Wear County Council* [1986] 1 All ER 567 stated that there was no 'conventional' figure for damages under this head, and awarded a sum equivalent to four years' net salary.

Examples of cases where a *Smith v Manchester* award may be considered appropriate include the following:

(a)   The claimant has returned to work after the accident and thus he has no continuing loss of earnings claim. However, there is a risk that he will lose his job in the future and will have difficulty in obtaining a job as well paid due to his injuries. A *Smith v Manchester* award will be claimed.

(b)   The claimant has returned to work and is earning, say, 20% less than he did prior to the accident. As a result, he will have a continuing partial loss of earnings claim that could be calculated by using the multiplier/multiplicand approach (see **15.3.4**). In addition, the court is satisfied that he will lose his job and will have difficulty in obtaining another equally well-paid job due to his injuries. A *Smith v Manchester* award will be claimed.

(c)   The claimant is still absent from work at the time of the trial as a result of the injuries suffered in the accident, but he expects to return to his job in a few years when he has recovered further. The medical evidence suggests that, should he lose his job, he may still have problems in obtaining equally well-paid work due to his injuries. In these circumstances, a *Smith v Manchester* award will be claimed.

This type of award is not normally appropriate where the claimant will never be able to return to work, as he will be compensated by his claim for future lost earnings. However, the number of cases where the claimant is unable to work at all in the future will be small.

A *Smith v Manchester* award should normally be claimed in the particulars of claim (*Chan Wai Tong v Li Ping Sum* [1985] AC 446). However, the Court of Appeal, in *Thorn v Powergen* [1997] PIQR Q71, upheld a decision allowing a *Smith v Manchester* award in a case where it had not been claimed specifically but was found by the trial judge to be implied due to the nature of the injuries revealed by the medical evidence.

Evidence must be obtained concerning the claimant's future job prospects, including any skills he possesses (eg, a labourer of 50 years of age with no qualifications will find it difficult to retrain if he loses his job), the prospects of the industry in which the claimant works and any unusual local problems that may be relevant to the claimant. It may be necessary to instruct an employment consultant to provide information about these matters, or to obtain relevant information from other sources, for example the Annual Survey of Hours and Earnings. The expert would consider the client's injuries and personal qualifications, and analyse employment statistics and local press advertisements in order to report on the severity of the handicap on the labour market. In other cases, the trial judge will be aware of the employment situation in his area and be able to formulate the appropriate award.

Any evidence relating to handicap on the labour market claim must be included within the medical report and the witness statements for exchange.

15.3.3   Loss of congenial employment

The concept of compensating the claimant for a loss of job satisfaction has been accepted by the courts for some time. In *Morris v Johnson Matthey & Co Ltd* (1967) 112 SJ 32, a precious metal worker, aged 52, sustained a serious injury to his left hand, which left him incapable of continuing his craft. His employers found him alternative employment as a storeman, which he described as 'at times rather boring'. Edmund-Davies LJ stated:

> [T]he joy of the craftsman in his craft is beyond price. But the court has to give some monetary value to the loss of craft. The court should give consideration to the fact that a craftsman had to replace his craft with humdrum work.

Traditionally, the award was incorporated within the award for pain, suffering and loss of amenity, but it is now well established that the court will normally make a separate award under this heading. Generally, those who received such awards were deprived of jobs which have a vocational element or where a period of training is required, such as firemen, nurses, members of the armed forces, dancers, actors, and craftsmen such as carpenters. Those employed in repetitive manual work, such as factory workers, are unlikely to be able to convince a court that they found their job rewarding. However, claimants' solicitors should listen carefully to what their clients have to say on this point, as courts will judge each case on its facts. In *McCrae v (1) Chase International Express Ltd (2) Justin Smith* [2003] LTL, 14 March, the Court of Appeal overturned an award made to a motor-cycle courier on the basis that it was not satisfied with the evidence in support of the claim, but said that that an award might otherwise have been appropriate. In *Lane v The Personal Representatives of Deborah Lake (Deceased)* [2007] All ER (D) 258, the defendant tried to argue that this award should be reserved for policemen, firemen, etc, but this was rejected by the judge on the basis that such an award 'should be confined to those who truly have suffered a loss under this head and not be awarded merely by reference to the type of employment nor automatically as an extra'.

Awards tend to be in the range of £5,000 to £10,000. In *Willbye (by her mother and next friend) v Gibbons* [2003] EWCA Civ 372, the Court of Appeal reduced an award of £15,000 which had been made to a girl who had been 12 years old at the time of the accident and who had wanted to become a nursery nurse. It said that it was important to keep this head of damages in proportion and reduced the award to £5,000. Nevertheless, higher awards will be made in appropriate circumstances. The highest award so far was made in *Appleton v Medhat Mohammed El Safty* [2007] EWHC 631 (QB), to a footballer who had been playing for West Bromwich Albion before clinical negligence cut short his career. The Court of Appeal found the facts of this case to be exceptional and awarded £25,000.

Any evidence relating to a loss of congenial employment claim must be included within the witness statements for exchange. In particular, the claimant must give full details of the nature of his previous employment, any training or qualifications required, his career progression, etc, so that the loss of job satisfaction can be proved.

15.3.4 Future loss of earnings

Damages for loss of earnings after the date of trial will be assessed as general damages. The court will need to determine what the claimant would have earned, had he not been injured, up to the time he would have ordinarily retired or for a specified period, if he is expected to recover sufficiently to be able to work in the future. Even the most straightforward case will require the court to tackle uncertainty, and the more complex the case, the more 'crystal ball gazing' will be required.

Under the conventional method of calculating future loss of earnings, a lump sum award will be calculated using a multiplier and a multiplicand. The object is to assess the amount of money which can be invested today which will represent a fund which should last for precisely the period of the lost earnings. In other words, the capital sum is invested, the claimant periodically draws out from the fund what he would have earned throughout the period of loss, and the fund gradually decreases until it is exhausted at the very end of the period of loss. That is, at least, the theory.

15.3.4.1 The multiplicand

The multiplicand is the figure which represents the claimant's annual loss, so where a claimant is not able to work at all, it will be the net annual earnings that he would have received had he not been injured. Where the claimant is able to work but will earn less than his pre-accident salary, the multiplicand is the difference between the two net annual earnings. The items to be included or ignored in the calculation of the multiplicand are the same as for pre-trial earnings, as identified at **15.2.1**.

15.3.4.2   The multiplier

The multiplier is based on the period of likely future loss. This will depend on the facts of the case. For example, in the case of a male claimant who will never work again, the period of loss will normally extend until his likely retirement age (normally 60 or 65). The period of loss is taken from the date of trial, as pre-trial losses will be claimed as special damages.

The period of loss is then converted into a multiplier. Following the House of Lords' decision in the joint appeals of *Page v Sheerness Steel Co Ltd; Wells v Wells; Thomas v Brighton Health Authority* [1998] 3 WLR 329, it can now be assumed that the starting point when attempting to identify the multiplier is to use the Government's actuarial tables (the Ogden Tables; see **Appendix 5**). The current version of the Ogden Tables, the 7th edition, was published in August 2011.

The multipliers in Tables 1 to 26 are based on mortality rates for the United Kingdom, with different tables for males and females, and a discount to take account of accelerated receipt (ie the claimant will receive a lump sum which he can invest).

In order to find the appropriate multiplier, the solicitor will;

(a)   identify the correct table from Tables 3 to 14 by using the claimant's sex and anticipated retirement age had it not been for the accident;

(b)   find the claimant's age at the date of trial along the left-hand vertical column;

(c)   find the correct discount rate along the top horizontal line. In 2001, the Lord Chancellor set the 'discount rate' that should be referred to when using the Ogden Tables at 2.5%, which is said to represent the real rate of return (ie, after tax and making allowance for inflation) calculated over the appropriate period of time. The Ministry of Justice is currently considering whether the rate should be changed. It is open to the courts under s 1(2) of the Damages Act 1996 to adopt a different rate if there are exceptional circumstances;

(d)   identify the appropriate multiplier, which can be found where the relevant vertical and horizontal columns meet;

(e)   consider whether further discounts are appropriate to take account of other 'risks and vicissitudes of life', such as the possibility that there would be periods when the claimant would not have been earning due to ill-health or loss of employment. The factors which are to be taken into account are as follows:

     (i)   whether the claimant was employed or not at the time of the accident. Employed includes being self-employed or being on a government training scheme;

     (ii)   whether the claimant was disabled or not at the time of the accident. A claimant is disabled if he has an illness or a disability which has or is expected to last for over a year or is a progressive illness, satisfies the Equality Act 2010 definition that the impact of the disability substantially limits his ability to carry out normal day-to-day activities, *and* his condition affects either the kind or the amount of paid work he can do;

     (iii)   the claimant's level of educational attainment at the time of the accident. There are three levels: degree or equivalent and higher, GCSE grades A to C up to A levels and equivalent, and below GCSE grade C or CSE grade 1 or no qualifications.

Section B of the Ogden Tables gives further information regarding these discounts and how they should be applied (see **Appendix 5**).

15.3.4.3   The calculation

In order to determine the amount for future loss of earnings, the multiplicand is multiplied by the amended multiplier.

> **EXAMPLE**
>
> Simon was 43 when the accident occurred and 45 at trial. He was employed as a labourer prior to the accident, earning £20,000 per annum. He was not disabled, had no qualifications and was due to retire 65.
>
> (a)   As he is male and his retirement age is 65, the correct table is Table 9;
>
> (b)   Using his age at trial, 45, and the 2.5% rate of return, a multiplier of 15.27 is identified.
>
> (c)   Account for risks other than mortality, ie for Simon being employed, not disabled and having no qualifications. Table A is the correct table as Simon is male, would have retired at 65, and was not disabled. Identify the correct age bracket on the left hand side (45–49) and, across the top, identify the correct column. This is the third column (headed O), as he was employed but without qualifications. The correct discount figure is 0.86.
>
> (d)   The amended multiplier is 15.27 x 0.86 = 13.13
>
> (e)   The future loss of earnings 13.13 x £20,000 = £262,600

15.3.4.4   Career progression and loss of earnings

In cases where the period of loss will continue for many years into the future, it is particularly important to ensure that account is taken of likely periodic changes to the claimant's income. The claimant will want to point to anticipated career progressions where, for example, he was a junior doctor, a trainee solicitor or a junior officer in the armed forces. In such cases, the court will either:

(a)   determine an average multiplicand, based upon the likely earnings throughout the period of loss, which will then be applied to the full period of the loss; or

(b)   use stepped multiplicands for each stage of the claimant's career. Generally, this will result in a lower multiplicand at the beginning and possibly at the very end of the period of loss, with one or more higher multiplicands to represent the likely career progression that would have been followed.

In *Collett v Smith and Middlesborough Football & Athletics Company (1986) Ltd* [2008] EWHC 1962 (QB), the court was required to assess damages in relation to a young man whose promising football career had been cut short, at the age of 18, as a result of a negligent tackle. In assessing damages for future loss of earnings at £3,854,328, the court was obliged to make decisions on such issues as the level at which he would have played football and at what remuneration, how long he would have played for, whether his career would have otherwise have been cut short by injury and whether he would have gone on to work as a coach or manager.

The amount of 'crystal ball gazing' which the court will of necessity have to undertake in this exercise is increased in cases where the claimant was a child at the time of the accident. If the child is old enough to have attended school, taken a few exams and shown some interest in one career or another, it might be possible to anticipate a likely career progression. With a younger child, this will be much more difficult. The court will take into account the following evidence, where available:

(a)   the nature of the employment of the claimant's parents and siblings;

(b)   any qualifications obtained so far;

(c) evidence from the claimant's former teachers, club leaders, sports trainers, etc regarding the claimant's abilities and personality;

(d) neuropsychological evidence of the claimant's pre-accident IQ;

(e) the claimant's own evidence and personality, as demonstrated in the witness-box.

15.3.4.5 Evidence

The importance of expert evidence in such a case is vital. Medical evidence can provide an indication as to what work the claimant will be capable of undertaking, both at present and in the future. This, together with evidence of the claimant's employment prospects, will assist the court in determining what will happen to the claimant in the future, which, while often appearing unsatisfactory to many clients, is usually the approach that the court will take.

15.3.5 Future cost of medical expenses, care and quasi-nursing services, and aids and appliances

In cases of catastrophic injury, it is possible that the claim for the cost of future care and quasi-nursing services will exceed the claim for future loss of earnings. This is because the need for care will often continue beyond the claimant's normal retirement age, plus the fact that specialist care is extremely expensive. It must be remembered that the cost and type of care may change in the future. For example, a severely injured child's costs of care will increase as he becomes older because it is unlikely that his parents will be able to look after him when they are elderly and, as such, increased professional help will be required.

The calculation for the future cost of care is carried out in the same way as set out in **15.3.4**. However, when identifying the multiplier, the correct table will be either Table 1 or Table 2, depending upon whether the claimant is male or female. In addition, following the House of Lords' decision in *Page v Sheerness Steel Co Ltd; Wells v Wells; Thomas v Brighton Health Authority* (see **15.3.4.2**), it is not appropriate to discount whole life multipliers.

The cost of medical expenses and aids and appliances may also be dealt with using a multiplier from Tables 1 or 2 and a multiplicand where a continuing need can be demonstrated. For example, the claimant may include the cost of a wheelchair as part of his special damages claim. That wheelchair will not last the claimant for the rest of his life, and therefore the replacement cost will need to be annualised. So, where the cost of a wheelchair is £1,000 and it would have a life span of five years, the multiplicand would be £200. Generally, the annual cost of items relevant to the same period of loss are added together to produce one multiplicand.

Alternatively, the claimant may require an operation which will not need to be repeated, or an appliance which will not need to be replaced. In such cases, a one-off payment should be included in the claim.

15.3.6 Loss of pension

In more serious cases, where the claimant does not return to work or returns on a lower wage, consideration must be given to a claim for lost pension. The claimant's pension is normally based upon his period of service with the company and the salary that he would have earned at retirement age. Reference should be made to specialist texts on this subject.

15.4 PROVISIONAL DAMAGES

15.4.1 The problem which provisional damages are intended to solve

When the court awards damages or the parties agree a settlement, it will be on the basis of a full and final settlement of the claim. Consequently, the normal rule is that the claimant is unable to return to court to ask for a further award to be made, even where his condition has seriously deteriorated.

This being the case, the claimant's solicitor should ensure that the claimant is properly compensated, by ensuring that expert medical evidence deals with any deterioration that is likely to arise in the future. Where the court is satisfied that the claimant is more than 50% likely to suffer a specified deterioration in his condition, the court will award damages on the basis that the deterioration will occur and a provisional damages order is not appropriate. The problem lies in cases where the deterioration, although possible, is less than probable.

> **EXAMPLE**
>
> Fred is injured. At the time of the trial he has no loss of sight, but there is a 10% possibility that in the future he will lose the sight in one eye. Bearing in mind that quantum for pain and suffering and loss of amenity for the total loss of sight in one eye is approximately £30,000, how does the judge award damages to Fred?
>
> If the judge awards £3,000 (10% of £30,000) and Fred does lose the sight in his eye in the future, Fred will be under-compensated by £27,000 but cannot return to court for more damages. If Fred does not lose the sight in his eye in the future, Fred is unjustly enriched by £3,000 and the defendant cannot recover the excess damages.

Provisional damages are aimed at solving the above problem by providing an exception to the basic rule. In certain limited circumstances the claimant can be compensated for his injuries with the proviso that if a specific condition occurs in the future, he will be allowed to return to court so that further damages may be awarded.

15.4.2   The statutory provisions

Rule 41.2 of the CPR states that the court may make an order for provisional damages, provided the claim is included in the particulars of claim and the court is satisfied that s 32A of the Senior Courts Act 1981 or s 51 of the County Courts Act 1984 applies.

In accordance with s 32A of the Senior Courts Act 1981, an order for provisional damages may be made where there is:

> a chance that at some definite or indefinite time in the future the injured person will, as a result of the act or omission which gave rise to the cause of action, develop some serious disease or suffer some serious deterioration in his physical or mental condition.

A similar provision is found in s 51 of the County Courts Act 1984.

If the court considers that there is a suitable case for provisional damages (see CPR, Part 41 and PD 41), it will:

(a)   assess damages on the assumption that the injured person will not develop the disease or suffer the deterioration in his condition;

(b)   identify the disease or deterioration that has been disregarded;

(c)   stipulate a period (which may be indefinite) during which the claimant may return to court for further damages if he develops the disease or suffers the deterioration;

(d)   make an order that relevant documents are to be kept by the court.

If the claimant subsequently suffers the specified disease or deterioration within the specified time frame, he may apply to the court for further damages. The order will set out with precision the circumstances which must arise before the claimant is allowed to return to court, as it will wish to avoid a situation where there is a subsequent dispute as to whether the proper circumstances had arisen.

15.4.2.1   'Chance'

The expression 'chance' is not defined in the legislation. It clearly indicates something less than a probability, ie less than 50% likelihood, and in *Curi v Colina* [1998] EWCA Civ 1326, the Court of Appeal said there had to be a 'possibility but no more than a possibility'. However, it must be measurable rather than merely fanciful (*Willson v Ministry of Defence* [1991] 1 All ER 638, where it was held that the possibility that the claimant would incur further injury from a fall as a result of an ankle injury was not evidence of 'serious deterioration' as it might not ever happen).

In order to be measurable, the chance should be expressed in terms of a percentage figure. The courts have been prepared to make an order for provisional damages where the likelihood of deterioration has been expressed in terms of single figure percentages, but an award should not be made where the risk is *de minimis*. In *Chewings v (1) Williams & (2) Abertawe Bro Morgannwg University NHS Trust* [2009] EWHC 2490 (QB), the claimant sought provisional damages, reserving the right to claim further damages should he suffer a below the knee amputation of his right leg. One of the issues for the court to determine was whether the risk of amputation was more than fanciful. In allowing the award, the court held that the chance of amputation was more than fanciful and, although it was difficult to ascribe a precise percentage to it, if it were necessary to do so, it would be about 2%.

If there is doubt as to whether the case is appropriate for a provisional damages claim then advice from a solicitor or barrister with expertise in this area should be sought.

15.4.2.2 'Serious deterioration'

'Serious deterioration' is not defined in the legislation. In *Willson*, it was held that 'serious deterioration' meant:

(a)   a clear and severable risk of deterioration (not merely the natural progression of the injury); and

(b)   something beyond ordinary deterioration.

On the facts of *Willson*, the court held that the chance of arthritis was merely a natural progression of the injury and was not a suitable case for provisional damages. The most common examples of conditions in which provisional damages have been awarded in practice are where there is the chance of the claimant suffering from epilepsy, or from a disease such as cancer or asbestosis as a result of exposure to a dangerous substance.

15.4.3 Procedural approach

The claim for provisional damages must be included in the particulars of claim, and if the possibility of provisional damages emerges after these documents have been served, the documents must be amended. Part 16 of the CPR 1998 and the accompanying Practice Direction set out the necessary information which must be included. Where a case settles before proceedings are issued and the parties agree that an order for provisional damages should be made, the matter should be brought before the court using Part 8 proceedings.

The court will be slow to make an order for provisional damages, on the basis that finality is better for all parties. Evidence is therefore very important, and the medical report should address the issues with precision. In particular, it should set out the nature of the deterioration, the chance of deterioration by means of a percentage figure and an anticipated time frame.

The only basis for an award of provisional damages is a court order. Any application by consent for an award of provisional damages should follow the procedure set out in Part 23 of the CPR 1998.

If the specified disease or deterioration occurs within the specified period, the claimant must give at least 28 days' written notice to the defendant of his intention to apply for further damages.

Ideally, such an application should be made within the time limit set out in the original order. However, although the CPR do not expressly authorise an extension where an application is made after the expiry of the time limit, they do not exclude it. In *Blythe v Ministry of Defence* [2013] All ER (D) 326 (Nov), CA, the Court of Appeal held that the facts of a case might justify an extension in such circumstances in furtherance of the overriding objective.

15.4.4   The claimant's and defendant's perspectives

Even where the claimant's claim falls within the realm of provisional damages, the claimant may not want to pursue this option, preferring instead that the claim is satisfied once and for all by the award of a lump sum. The defendant will also usually prefer the matter to be dealt with by one lump sum award, and will therefore be prepared to negotiate an additional amount to take account of the risk of deterioration in an attempt to persuade the claimant to abandon his claim for provisional damages.

The claimant's solicitor must advise his client of the implications of each option, preferably in writing, and obtain his instructions, again preferably in writing. The claimant must appreciate that if he chooses to accept a lump sum in full and final settlement, he will not be able to return to court to ask for additional compensation should his condition deteriorate, no matter how serious the deterioration is. Alternatively, if the court makes an order for provisional damages, he will be able to return to court only if the specified deterioration occurs within the specified time limit.

Solicitors must ensure that they preserve their own files for the appropriate length of time.

15.4.5   Provisional damages and the Fatal Accidents Act 1976

Section 3 of the Damages Act 1996 allows an application to the court under the FAA 1976 where a person is awarded provisional damages and subsequently dies.

15.4.6   Provisional damages and Part 36 of the CPR

Where there is a claim for provisional damages and the defendant makes a Part 36 offer, the offer notice must specify whether or not the settlement includes the making of a provisional damages award (see **14.10.2**).

15.5   PERIODICAL PAYMENTS

15.5.1   The problems which periodical payments are intended to solve

The assessment of damages, particularly in relation to future pecuniary loss, depends upon matters which are uncertain and unpredictable. Consequently, a lump sum payment may result in the following:

(a)   over-compensation, leading to unfairness to the defendant. A claimant may die early and his beneficiaries be unjustly enriched;

(b)   under-compensation, leading to a lack of financial security for the claimant. Where a claimant will be dependent on care for many years, the money may run out;

(c)   a lack of prudence on the part of the claimant or his family. Few have experience of managing large sums of money, and inappropriate spending or unwise investment may dissipate the fund;

(d)   a lack of flexibility. The general rule is that the claimant cannot return to court if his condition deteriorates (unless there is an order for provisional damages, see **15.4** above).

These problems will be less severe where the court orders periodical payments to be made. Here, the court will assess the annual needs of the claimant in order to calculate the amount of the periodic payments; the payments rise in accordance with inflation and are paid, free of tax, to the end of claimant's life. In addition, the management and administration involved in the investment of damages is transferred from the claimant to the defendant, but as the payments must be secure, the continuity of the payments is guaranteed.

15.5.2   The statutory provisions

15.5.2.1   The court's power to make an order for periodical payments

Under s 2 of the Damages Act 1996 (as amended by s 100 of the Courts Act 2003), where an order for damages includes an amount for future pecuniary loss in respect of personal injury, the court must consider whether an order for periodical payments is appropriate. Where there is a claim for damages in respect of future pecuniary loss, such as the future loss of earnings or the future costs of care, the court can order that the damages wholly or partly take the form of periodical payments, and it can do so without obtaining the consent of the parties.

The court can make an order for periodic payments in respect of other damages, such as past pecuniary loss and pain, suffering and loss of amenity, only where both parties consent (s 2(2)).

Under s 2(3), the court can make such an order only where it is satisfied that the continuity of payment is reasonably secure. Section 2(4) states that a payment is 'reasonably secure' where:

(a) it is protected by a guarantee given under s 6 of or the Schedule to the Act;

(b) it is protected by a scheme under s 213 of the Financial Services and Markets Act 2000; or

(c) the source of payment is a government or health service body.

Where none of the above applies, a defendant may be able to prove that payment is reasonably secure by purchasing a life annuity for the claimant's benefit, which would be protected by the Financial Services Compensation Scheme or by some other means.

15.5.2.2 The order

Under CPR, r 41.8(1), where the court awards damages in the form of periodical payments, it must specify:

(a) the annual amount awarded, how each payment is to be made during the year and at what intervals;

(b) the amount awarded for future—

    (i) loss of earnings and other income; and

    (ii) care and medical costs and other recurring or capital costs;

(c) that the claimant's annual future pecuniary losses, as assessed by the court, are to be paid for the duration of the claimant's life, or such other period as the court orders; and

(d) that the amount of the payments shall vary annually by reference to the retail prices index, unless the court orders otherwise under section 2(9) of the 1996 Act.

15.5.2.3 Indexation

Under s 2(8) of the Damages Act 1996, the payments will rise by reference to the Retail Price Index (RPI), although s 2(9) allows for s 2(8) to be disapplied. There has been much controversy as to whether the RPI is the appropriate index as it is based on prices, which historically have not risen as sharply as wages. In the provision of care services, it has been wages that have been driving the cost up, and it is therefore argued that the Aggregate Annual Survey of Hours and Earnings (ASHE 6115) is the appropriate index to use. In *Tameside and Glossop Acute Services NHS Trust v Thompstone* [2008] EWCA Civ 5, the Court of Appeal settled this debate by endorsing the use of ASHE 6115.

15.5.2.4 Variation

In accordance with the Damages (Variation of Periodical Payments) Order 2005 (SI 2005/841), where the court is satisfied that, at some time in the future, the claimant will:

(a) as a result of the act or omission which gave rise to the cause of action, develop some serious disease or suffer some serious deterioration; or

(b) enjoy some significant improvement in his physical or mental condition, where that condition had been adversely affected as a result of that act or omission;

the court can include in an order for periodical payments an order that they may be varied. The consent of the parties is not required. The wording is similar to that used for provisional damages (see **15.4**), and it is thought that the courts will apply the same strict criteria before including a provision for variation in a periodical payments order.

15.5.3 Procedural approach

In accordance with CPR, r 41.5, the party should address whether or not it considers periodical payments to be appropriate in its statement of case and set out the particulars of the circumstances it relies on. If a statement of case does not address the matter at all, or does not set out sufficient particulars, the court may order the party to rectify the situation.

The power to make an order for periodical payments must be exercised in accordance with CPR, r 41.7, which states that when considering whether to make such an order, the court must have regard to 'all the circumstances of the case and in particular the form of award which best meets the claimant's needs, having regard to the factors set out in the practice direction'. The relevant Practice Direction, PD 41B, para 1, states that these factors include:

(1)   the scale of the annual payments taking into account any deductions for contributory negligence;

(2)   the form of the award preferred by the claimant including

(a)   the reasons for the claimant's preference; and

(b)   the nature of any financial advice received by the claimant when considering the form of the award; and

(3)   the form of the award preferred by the defendant including the reasons for the defendant's preference.

Although the court must have regard to the wishes of the parties, ultimately it must decide what order best meets the claimant's needs, and this may not necessarily coincide with what the claimant prefers. The claimant's solicitor must instruct an independent financial adviser to report on the form of order which he considers is in the best interests of the claimant. However, in the *Tameside* case (see **15.5.2.3**), the Court of Appeal stated that it was able to have regard to the defendant's preferences without the need for the defendant to call evidence on this point. It went on to say that only in rare cases would it be appropriate for the defendant to call expert evidence in order to seek to demonstrate that the form of order preferred by the claimant would not best meet his needs.

15.5.4 The claimant's and defendant's perspectives

Generally speaking, claimants are not keen on the idea of periodical payments, preferring all damages to be paid as a lump sum. This gives them more control over their finances, and may be particularly important to the claimant who is keen to provide for his family in the event of his death. Defendants differ in their approach, and some may be deterred by the need to manage the fund on behalf of the claimant. However, where cases involve large claims for the cost of future care, defendants will usually prefer periodical payments, because they will assist with cash-flow and will prevent large over-payments where the claimant dies early.

15.6 INTEREST

A claim for interest should be included in the court proceedings. In the majority of personal injury cases, the court will award interest (simple, not compound) in addition to the basic damages. The purpose of an interest award is to compensate the claimant for having to wait to receive his compensation. Interest in a personal injury claim is generally awarded in accordance with the following guidelines:

(a)   Special damages carry interest at half the short-term investment/special account rate from the date of the accident to the date of trial. For the seven years prior to February 2009, the special account rate remained at 6%. It has since been reduced three times to its current rate of 0.5%. In *Roberts v Johnstone* [1989] QB 878, it was held that damages for unpaid past services of care and attendance should be awarded in a similar manner to any other items of special damages.

It should also be noted that following the case of *Wadley v Surrey County Council* (2000) *The Times*, 7 April, the House of Lords confirmed that when calculating interest on special damages, the court should disregard deductible State benefits; interest is claimed on the gross amount.

(b) Damages for pain and suffering and loss of amenity carry interest from date of service of proceedings to the date of trial at 2% per annum, following the case of *Felmai Lawrence v Chief Constable of Staffordshire* (2000) *The Times*, 25 July.

(c) Damages for future losses carry no interest (as, by definition, the losses have not yet been incurred).

(d) General damages for a handicap on the labour market carry no interest.

It should be noted that these are general guidelines, but the court does have a discretion to depart from them in exceptional cases. In Kemp and Kemp, *The Quantum of Damages*, it is argued that while the general approach for special damages stated above is appropriate for regular losses between the accident and trial (eg, weekly wage loss), it is not satisfactory where the claimant had incurred a large, one-off item of expenditure shortly after the accident. In such circumstances, he would be under-compensated by the application of the normal interest rule, and therefore, it is argued, interest should be awarded at the full rate on such items.

Interest is awarded to mitigate the effects of delay. However, if the delay is the fault of the claimant, this may be a 'special reason' not to award full interest (*Birkett v Hayes* [1982] 2 All ER 70). This point was raised in the case of *Beahan v Stoneham* [2001] LTL, 16 May, where an appeal from an assessment of damages in a claim for personal injuries was allowed in part where the trial judge failed to reduce interest on damages. The matter concerned a case where there was a significant delay in proceeding with the claim (see also *Spittle v Bunney* [1988] 1 WLR 847). The court held that the judiciary should be more ready to mark their disapproval of delay in this matter.

15.6.1 Calculation of interest

The calculation of interest on general damages should not present any problem. However, the calculation of interest on special damages can be more difficult. Traditionally, solicitors used the Nelson–Jones table, which is printed annually in the *Law Society's Gazette*. However, on-line calculators are quicker and easier to use.

The inclusion of interest on the settlement of a case must not be forgotten by the claimant's solicitor.

15.7 THE SCHEDULE OF PAST AND FUTURE LOSS AND EXPENSE

In accordance with PD 16, para 4.2, the claimant must attach to his particulars of claim a schedule setting out details of any past and future expenses and losses (see **12.5.1** and **Appendix 1(12)**). Where the defendant disputes the information contained in the schedule, he should serve a counter-schedule. Both the schedule and the counter-schedule should be revised for the trial.

15.8 CONCLUSION

Subject to liability being established, the aim of the claimant's solicitor is to recover the highest possible award of damages on behalf of his client (without falsifying or exaggerating the claim), and the aim of the defendant's solicitor is to minimise the award. Both require an in-depth understanding of the rules which govern what may be recovered under the heads of special damages for pecuniary losses incurred up to the date of the trial or earlier settlement, and general damages for non-pecuniary loss and future pecuniary loss.

The claimant's solicitor should make thorough enquiries of his client to ensure that all pecuniary losses and expenses are included in the schedule of loss, as the client may not appreciate the true cost of his losses and expenditure thus far or the possible financial implications stretching out into the future. The schedule should be updated as required as the matter progresses. The defendant's solicitor should not be afraid to challenge the inclusion of items of loss or the amounts claimed where it is appropriate to do so.

General damages for pain, suffering and loss of amenity, and for handicap in the labour market and loss of congenial employment, are not capable of precise mathematical calculation. Nevertheless, the courts have adopted an approach to quantifying these heads of damage which aims to ensure, in so far as possible, that comparable cases receive comparable amounts in damages. The starting point for practitioners when calculating an appropriate award for pain, suffering and loss of amenity is the *Guidelines for the Assessment of General Damages in Personal Injury Cases*, but research of reported cases involving similar injuries will also be necessary.

Future pecuniary losses, such as the loss of earnings or the cost of care, are calculated by means of a multiplicand, a figure representing the claimant's annual loss, and a multiplier, a figure which is based on a best guess of how long the incapacity will continue into the future and is found by reference to the Ogden Tables.

In the vast majority of cases, lump sum damages are awarded in full and final settlement of the claim, which means that the award cannot be changed in the event that the claimant makes a substantial recovery or suffers an unexpected deterioration. However, an exception to this rule exists where the court makes an order for provisional damages, enabling the claimant to return to court to seek a further award of damages in the event that a specified condition or deterioration occurs within a specified time period. A further exception arises where the court makes an order for periodical payments, where an annual sum is paid to the claimant in accordance with his needs, usually in addition to lump sum damages. Such payments may be increased, decreased or stopped on the application of either party, where the claimant's needs have changed.

Proceedings should always include a claim for interest, as this may be a considerable amount, but practitioners should be aware that different rules apply to different heads of damage and that there is no interest on future losses.

15.9 FURTHER READING

Kemp and Kemp, *The Quantum of Damages* (Sweet & Maxwell)

Ogden Tables (7th edn)

Judicial College, *Guidelines for the Assessment of General Damages in Personal Injury Cases* (OUP)

RECOVERY OF BENEFITS AND NHS CHARGES

LEARNING OUTCOMES

After reading this chapter you will be able to:

- explain how the Compensation Recovery Unit (CRU) recovers benefits paid to a claimant as a result of an accident or disease
- explain how the cost of NHS treatment provided to a claimant as a result of an accident or disease is recovered from a defendant who is found liable
- identify which benefits may be set off against each head of damage by way of 'like for like' offsetting
- describe the steps that each party must take in order to comply with the CRU system.

16.1 INTRODUCTION

Where a claimant has received State benefits as a result of an accident or disease and is subsequently awarded compensation, the Department for Work and Pensions (DWP) will seek to recover those benefits from the defendant (or his insurer) via a system operated by the Compensation Recovery Unit (CRU). The CRU is also responsible for collecting from a defendant the cost of any NHS treatment that a claimant has received following an accident. The purpose of this chapter is to explain how these systems of recovery operate and how they may affect a compensation payment.

16.2 RECOVERY OF BENEFITS – KEY FEATURES OF THE SYSTEM

The legislation on the recovery scheme is predominantly contained in the Social Security (Recovery of Benefits) Act 1997 ('the 1997 Act'). The key features of the scheme are as follows:

(a)   No person should be compensated twice in respect of the same accident or disease.

(b)   A defendant cannot make a compensation payment (other than an exempt payment) without first applying to the CRU for a Certificate. The defendant (or 'compensator') must pay to the DWP an amount equal to the total amount of the recoverable benefits on the Certificate when he pays compensation to the claimant.

(c)   In some circumstances it may be possible for the compensator to deduct some or all of the amount he has had to repay to the DWP from the compensation award (a practice known as 'offsetting'; see **16.4**).

(d)   The compensator is responsible for repayment of *all* relevant benefits paid to the injured person, regardless of whether he is able to offset the full amount out of that person's damages. However, recovery of a lump sum paid cannot exceed the amount of compensation paid.

The main regulations relevant to the scheme are found in the Social Security (Recovery of Benefits) Regulations 1997 (SI 1997/2205), as amended by paras 148–152 of Sch 7 to the Social Security Act 1998.

16.3 KEY DEFINITIONS

There are several key definitions in the 1997 Act:

16.3.1 The meaning of 'compensation payment'

A compensation payment is a payment made by a person (whether on his own behalf or not) to or in respect of any other person in consequence of any accident, injury or disease suffered by the other (s 1 of the 1997 Act). This is a very wide definition and is designed to cover payments made by the defendant or his insurer.

16.3.2 The meaning of 'compensator'

The compensator means the person, company or agent who is paying the compensation, usually an insurance company, on behalf of the insured.

16.3.3 The meaning of 'recoverable benefit'

A recoverable benefit is any listed benefit which has been or is likely to be paid in respect of an accident, injury or disease (s 1 of the 1997 Act).

'Recoverable benefits' are listed in Sch 2 to the 1997 Act and are reproduced at **16.4.2**.

16.3.4 The meaning of 'relevant period'

Recovery of benefits can occur only in respect of losses during what the 1997 Act terms 'the relevant period'.

The relevant period begins on:

(a)   the day following an accident or injury; or

(b)   in the case of a disease, the date on which a listed benefit was first claimed in consequence of the disease.

The relevant period ends on:

(a)   the day a compensation payment is made in final discharge of a claim; or

(b)   the date five years after the relevant period begins, whichever comes first.

16.4 COMPENSATION SUBJECT TO OFFSETTING

16.4.1 Heads of damage subject to offsetting

Offsetting of recoverable benefits is allowed only against specified areas of loss. The three specified areas subject to offsetting are:

(a) compensation for loss of earnings;

(b) compensation for cost of care; and

(c) compensation for loss of mobility.

Scope for offsetting is further limited by the fact that it is only allowed on a 'like-for-like' basis (see below at **16.4.2**).

Therefore, the overall effect of the legislation is that, in relation to benefits:

(a) it allows offsetting only against certain items of special damage; and

(b) it ensures that general damages for pain suffering and loss of amenity, loss of congenial employment, handicap on the labour market and all future losses are protected from offsetting.

The position in relation to lump sums, however, is different (see below at **16.4.3**).

16.4.2 'Like-for-like' offsetting

Having established that only special damages can be the subject of offsetting, Sch 2 to the 1997 Act further safeguards special damages as it allows only 'like-for-like' offsetting. This means that only benefits which closely correspond to the relevant head of loss can be set against damages awarded in respect of that head of loss, as set out in the table below. For example, you will see that attendance allowance can be recouped only from compensation for cost of care, and not from compensation for loss of earnings.

EXAMPLE

A claimant agrees to accept compensation totalling £100,000 which is broken down as follows: £40,000 for pain, suffering and loss of amenity (PSLA), £30,000 for loss of earnings, and £30,000 for the cost of care.

The Certificate shows that the claimant has received incapacity benefit totalling £5,000, income support totalling £10,000 and attendance allowance amounting to £10,000.

The compensator (the defendant's insurer) may not offset any of the benefits against the PSLA element of the award, but may offset the incapacity benefit and income support against the loss of earnings award. He therefore deducts a total of £15,000 from the loss of earnings sum, leaving £15,000 to be paid to the claimant.

Similarly the compensator may offset the £10,000 attendance allowance against the damages for cost of care, leaving £20,000 to be paid to the claimant.

The claimant has settled his claim for £100,000 but following offsetting he receives £75,000 (he has already received the remaining £25,000 in benefits so double compensation is avoided).

In addition to paying the claimant £75,000, the compensator must now pay £25,000 to the DWP, representing the amount of recoverable benefits.

If compensation for cost of care is less than the amount actually paid out in listed benefits during the relevant period, the claimant will receive nothing in respect of that head of loss; *however*, any excess in benefits for cost of care which has not so far been offset, cannot be offset against any other head of compensation. In this instance, the burden of paying off the excess falls on the compensator (usually the insurance company) and will be refunded to the DWP, so that the State will always achieve 100% recovery, the only question being how much will be out of compensation, and how much will be paid by the compensator.

Table to illustrate like-for-like offsetting

Head of compensation	Benefit
1. Compensation for earnings lost during relevant period	Disablement Pension Employment and Support Allowance Incapacity Benefit Income Support Industrial Injuries Disablement Benefit Invalidity Pension and Allowance Jobseeker's Allowance Reduced Earnings Allowance Severe Disablement Allowance Sickness Benefit Unemployability Supplement Unemployment Benefit Universal Credit
2. Compensation for cost of care incurred during the relevant period	Attendance Allowance Care Component of Disability Living Allowance Disablement Pension increase for Constant Attendance Allowance Exceptionally Severe Disablement Allowance Living Component of Personal Independence Payment
3. Compensation for loss of mobility during the relevant period	Mobility Allowance Mobility Component of Disability Living Allowance Mobility Component of Personal Independence Component

The DWP Guidance Note Z1 provides further details of damages that do and do not fall within Sch 2.

In *Griffiths and Others v British Coal Corporation and the Department of Trade and Industry* [2001] 1 WLR 1493, it was held that an award of interest on damages for past loss of earnings fell within the expression 'compensation for earnings lost' in Sch 2 to the 1997 Act and was therefore subject to reduction on account of payments by the defendant to the DWP. In the same case, it was also held that any compensation for services in the nature of care, gratuitously rendered, fell within the term 'compensation for cost of care incurred during the relevant period', and allowed the defendant to set off the benefits paid against the damages.

16.4.3   Lump sum payments

The Child Maintenance and Other Payments Act 2008 introduced changes to the Social Security (Recovery of Benefits) Act 1997, which provides for the recovery of lump sum payments. The lump sum payments covered by the scheme include:

(a)   lump sum payments made under the Pneumoconiosis etc (Worker's Compensation) Act 1979; and

(b)   payments under the 2008 Diffuse Mesothelioma Scheme and the Diffuse Mesothelioma Payment Scheme 2014 to people who have contracted diffuse mesothelioma as a result of asbestos exposure in the UK.

In contrast to the system applied to benefits (see **16.4.2** above), under the provisions of the Social Security (Recovery of Benefits) (Lump Sum Payments) Regulations 2008 the compensator can deduct any amount in respect of a lump sum from any part of the compensation award. However, lump sum payments must be offset against damages for pain and suffering first. Furthermore, if the amount of compensation is less than the lump sum payment, the CRU can only recover an amount up to the equivalent of the gross compensation award. The compensator is liable to repay lump sum payments before repaying recoverable benefits.

EXAMPLE

An award of compensation totalling £60,000 is agreed and broken down as follows: £15,000 for pain, suffering and loss of amenity (PSLA), £25,000 in respect of loss of earnings and £20,000 in respect of loss of mobility.

The CRU certificate lists lump sums totalling £20,000, Income Support totalling £15,000, and Disability Living Allowance (Mobility Component) totalling £10,000.

The compensator must offset the £20,000 lump sum payment from the PSLA first, which would leave an outstanding balance of £5,000. He may then offset from any of the remaining heads of damage, ie the compensator may offset the outstanding balance of £5,000 plus the £15,000 Income Support from the loss of earnings head of damage and the £10,000 DLA (Mobility) from the loss of mobility head of damage.

The claimant has settled his claim for a total of £60,000. Following offsetting, he receives £15,000 from the compensator in addition to the £45,000 he has already received from the state benefits system. Double compensation is thereby avoided.

The compensator pays £15,000 to the claimant and £45,000 to the CRU representing the amount of recoverable benefits and lump sums.

16.5 CONTRIBUTORY NEGLIGENCE

Since 'compensation payment' is defined as the sum falling to be paid to the claimant, it follows that the relevant sum from which benefits can be deducted is that which is paid to the claimant after any deduction for the claimant's contributory negligence. However, the compensator remains liable to pay the full amount of any benefits listed on the certificate regardless of contributory negligence (*Williams v Devon County Council* [2003] EWCA Civ 365). This may have the result after trial that the compensator has to pay a total sum in excess of that which the court has awarded by way of damages.

EXAMPLE

Assume that on a full liability basis the claimant's damages are valued at £10,000 for pain, suffering and loss of amenity (PSLA) and £10,000 for loss of earnings (LE), and that the certificate of recoverable benefit shows that he has received £7,500 in incapacity benefit.

If the claimant is 25% contributorily negligent, the calculation is as follows:

Total damages awarded £15,000 (£7,500 PSLA plus £7,500 LE)

Benefits deducted £7,500 (from LE award)

Defendant pays claimant £7,500

Defendant repays benefits to CRU £7,500

If the Claimant is 50% contributorily negligent, the calculation is as follows:

Total damages awarded £10,000 (£5,000 PSLA plus £5,000 LE)

Benefits deducted £5,000 (from LE award)

> Defendant pays claimant £5,000
>
> Defendant repays benefits to CRU £7,500
>
> In this second calculation, as a result of the finding of 50% contributory negligence, the amount of recoverable benefits now exceeds the sum awarded for the relevant head of damage (LE) against which they can be deducted. However, the defendant must still repay the full amount of benefits to the CRU.

16.6 PROCEDURE

16.6.1 Notifying the CRU

(a)   Section 4 of the 1997 Act requires the compensator to inform the CRU not later than 14 days after receiving the claim.

The notification is made on Form CRU 1 which is sent to the CRU. The information required by the compensator to complete Form CRU 1 includes:

(i)   the full name and address of the claimant;

(ii)   (if known) the date of birth and National Insurance number of that person;

(iii) the date of the accident or injury (or in the case of disease, the date of diagnosis);

(iv)   the nature of the accident, injury or disease (as alleged by the claimant);

(v)   (if known) the name and address of the claimant's employer and his payroll number at the relevant time;

(vi)   the name and address of any NHS hospital the claimant has attended as a result of the accident.

(b)   On receipt of Form CRU 1, the CRU will send Form CRU 4 to the defendant. This has a two-fold function:

(i)   it acknowledges receipt of the notification of claim; and

(ii)   the compensator should retain it safely on the file as it will be needed later to obtain the Certificate (ie, the details of the benefit paid or to be paid to the claimant).

(c)   The claim then progresses to the settlement stage.

(d)   When ready to make an offer of compensation, the compensator submits Form CRU 4 to obtain a Certificate.

(e)   The CRU acknowledges receipt of Form CRU 4 (within 14 days).

(f)   The CRU sends the Certificate to the compensator. A copy will also be sent to the claimant's solicitor. The compensator will then settle the compensation claim and pay the relevant amount to the CRU within 14 days of the settlement. The compensator will also complete and send to the CRU Form CRU 102 detailing the outcome of the claim.

Despite the requirement that the CRU be informed of the claim within 14 days of notification of the claim, this is sometimes overlooked by insurance companies. If proceedings are issued and the insurer instructs solicitors, Form CRU 1 should be completed immediately, if this has not already been done. In such circumstances, it may be appropriate for the address of the compensator given on Form CRU 1 to be care of the solicitors, to ensure that the Certificate is forwarded to the solicitors, who are likely to make the compensation payment to the claimant.

When the matter is lodged with the CRU, the claimant's solicitor will be notified and a Form CRU 4R will also be sent to the claimant's representative, which can be used to obtain benefit information (the claimant's solicitor can also obtain benefit details by writing to the DWP). It is important that, prior to negotiating any settlement or accepting any payment into court, the claimant himself examines the benefit details to ensure that they are correct. It is therefore essential to send a copy of the CRU certificate to the client.

16.6.2 The Certificate

The provision central to the whole system is that no compensation is to be paid until the defendant has obtained a Certificate setting out the recoverable benefits and lump sums. If compensation is paid without obtaining a Certificate, the CRU can still take steps against the defendant to recover the benefits.

The defendant obtains the Certificate by completing and returning Form CRU 4 to the CRU. The defendant must ensure that all the information required by Forms CRU 1 and CRU 4 is given, after which the CRU will acknowledge the form in writing and send the Certificate to the defendant and a copy to the claimant.

The Certificate details:

(a)   the amount of relevant benefits paid or likely to be paid by a specified date;

(b)   the details of any continuing benefit;

(c)   the amount of each recoverable lump sum;

(d)   the amount to be repaid in the event of a compensation payment being made;

(e)   the date the certificate ceases to be valid.

An example of a Certificate may be found at **Appendix 1(14)**.

16.7 EXEMPT PAYMENTS

Schedule 1, Pt 1 to the 1997 Act and reg 2 of the Social Security (Recovery of Benefits) Regulations 1997, list the payments which are exempt from offsetting under the Act. These include payments by or under the following:

(a)   the FAA 1976;

(b)   Criminal Injuries Compensation Authority payments;

(c)   vaccine damage payments;

(d)   the Macfarlane Trust (established partly under funds from the Secretary of State to the Haemophilia Society) the Eileen Trust and the trust established for persons suffering from variant Creutzfeld-Jakob disease;

(e)   British Coal, in accordance with the NCB Pneumoconiosis Compensation Scheme;

(f)   cases of hearing loss, where the loss is less than 50db in one or both ears;

(g)   the National Health Service (Injury Benefits) Regulations 1974 (SI 1974/1547) and subsequent amendments;

(h)   criminal court compensation orders, s 35 of the Powers of Criminal Courts Act 1973;

(i)   certain trust funds (in particular 'disaster funds', where more than half of the fund is raised by public subscription);

(j)   certain private insurance contracts between the victim and his insurer entered into before the contract;

(k)   any redundancy payment already accounted for in the assessment of damages;

(l)   any amount which is referable to costs;

(m)   any contractual amount paid to an employee by an employer in respect of incapacity for work (eg, occupational sick pay);

(n)   any small payment, as defined in Pt II of Sch 1 to the Social Security (Recovery of Benefits) Act 1997. There are currently no small payment exceptions;

(o)   payment made from the Skipton Fund for the benefit of certain persons suffering from hepatitis C;

(p)   payments made from the London Bombings Relief Charitable Fund established for the benefit of victims, families or dependants of victims of the terrorist attacks carried out in London on 7 July 2005.

16.8 MULTIPLE DEFENDANTS ('COMPENSATORS')

In certain cases, the claimant will sue two or more defendants, and as such, all defendants are jointly and severally liable to reimburse the CRU. However, in practice, it is usual for a sharing agreement to be made as between defendants, whereby the defendants reach an agreement as to how they are to pay the claimant and the CRU.

16.9 CLINICAL NEGLIGENCE

The rules relating to the recovery of benefit apply to clinical negligence claims. Due to their complexity, especially with regard to causation, the CRU has set up a specialist group to deal with the claims, and makes a special request that compensators inform the CRU about clinical negligence claims as soon as the pre-action correspondence is received.

16.10 PART 36 OFFERS

A party who wishes to make a Part 36 offer must first apply for a Certificate of Recoverable Benefit (see **16.6.2**) from the CRU.

Rule 36.22(3) of the CPR 1998 requires a defendant who makes an offer to state whether or not the offer is intended to include any deductible benefits.

Rule 36.22(6) requires the offer to state:

(a)   the amount of the gross compensation;

(b)   the name and amount of any deductible benefit by which that gross amount is reduced; and

(c)   the net amount of compensation after the reduction.

Although Part 36 does not spell it out, guidance from case law suggests that the offer should therefore particularise the various heads of damage and indicate the amount of benefits to be deducted against each head (*Williams v Devon County Council* [2003] EWCA Civ 365).

16.11 INTERIM PAYMENTS

It should be noted that if an interim payment is made, the compensator is liable to repay any relevant recoverable benefits at that stage. Therefore a Certificate of Recoverable Benefit (see **16.6.2**) should be obtained before any voluntary payment or hearing of an application for an interim payment takes place.

16.12 APPEALS SYSTEM

An appeal may be made on the grounds that:

(a)   any amount, rate or period in the Certificate is incorrect;

(b)   the Certificate shows benefits or lump sums not paid in consequence of the accident, injury or disease;

(c)   benefits and or lump sums listed have not been paid to the injured person;

(d)   the compensation payment made was not as a consequence of the accident, injury or disease.

An appeal can be made only after final settlement of the compensation claim and payment of the recoverable benefits has been made. The basic time limit for the appeal is one month from the date on which the compensator makes the full payment of recoverable benefits; it is dealt with by an independent tribunal administered by the Appeals Service.

An appeal can be made by:

(a)   the person who applied for the certificate, ie, the compensator; or

(b)   the injured person whose compensation payment has been reduced.

There is a less formal procedure that can be adopted, known as a 'review'. This can be requested at any time, and as a result the CRU will look at the matter again and clear the benefits that are listed as recoverable.

16.13 RECOVERY OF NHS CHARGES

The CRU operates a similar recovery scheme on behalf of the Government in respect of the cost of NHS treatment given as a result of an accident. Initially the scheme applied only to road traffic accidents, but this was expanded to include all types of accident as from 29 January 2007. The main details of the scheme are as follows.

16.13.1 Key features of the scheme

The legislation is contained primarily in the Road Traffic (NHS Charges) Act 1999 ('the 1999 Act') and the Health and Social Care (Community Health and Standards) Act 2003 ('the 2003 Act'). The purpose of this legislation is to provide a national administration system, the aim of which is to ensure that costs of treatment are, in fact, recovered in as many cases as is possible.

The 1999 Act allows for recovery of NHS treatment charges as a result of a road traffic accident which occurs on or after 5 April 1999. This includes MIB cases. It allows for NHS charges to be calculated according to a tariff. The tariff allows for:

(a)   a set fee for patients treated in A&E departments or out-patient clinics (the fee will be the same regardless of the number of out-patient appointments);

(b)   a daily rate for patients admitted to hospital.

Part 3 of the 2003 Act makes provision for an expanded scheme to recover the costs of providing treatment to an injured person where that person has made a successful personal injury compensation claim against a third party. This allows recovery of NHS hospital costs in all cases where personal injury compensation is paid, not just following road traffic accidents, but also, for example, following accidents at work. It applies to all accidents which occur on or after 29 January 2007.

The expanded scheme builds on the existing scheme introduced by the 1999 Act. In addition, the 2003 Act allows the recovery of NHS ambulance service costs for the first time. The scheme applies to injuries only; diseases are excluded from the scheme, unless the disease in question has been contracted as a direct result of an injury that falls within the scope of the scheme. Costs of treatment given by general practitioners in the primary care setting are also not included in the scheme.

16.13.2 Procedure

In many ways, the NHS costs recovery scheme mirrors the benefit recovery scheme considered above. However, unlike the benefit recovery scheme, the NHS costs recovery scheme will not affect the amount of damages recovered by the claimant, and if the injury occurs on or after 29 January 2007, the 2003 Act makes provision to take into account contributory negligence, eg a finding of 25% contributory negligence will reduce the NHS charges by 25%.

The procedure to follow is as follows:

(a)   The compensator will apply to the CRU in the usual way by completing Form CRU 1, and must ensure that the form contains the name and address of the hospital where treatment was provided.

(b)   The CRU will send Form CRU 4 to the compensator to acknowledge receipt of Form CRU 1.

(c)   The case progresses to the settlement stage.

(d)   When ready to make an offer to the claimant, the compensator submits Form CRU 4.

(e)   The CRU will provide a Certificate of NHS Charges at the same time as the Certificate of Recoverable Benefit. The Certificate of NHS Charges will specify the name of the NHS Trust or Health Board where the treatment took place, the number of days' admission, the appropriate NHS treatment and ambulance charges.

(f)   The compensator must pay to the CRU the amount shown on the Certificate of NHS Charges within 14 days of making the compensation payment.

The appeal and review procedures for NHS costs recovery are designed to mirror the appeal and review provisions governing benefit recovery under the Social Security (Recovery of Benefits) Act 1997, as to which, see **16.12** above.

16.14   CONCLUSION

Solicitors should exercise care when dealing with this area, to ensure that it is clear whether any offer put forward is net or gross of benefits, and that the benefit figures are correct. In *Hilton International v Martin-Smith* [2001] LTL, 12 February, it was held that where a party made an error of judgement (in this case, in relation to the amount stated on the Certificate), it did not follow that the court would permit that party to escape its consequences. Similarly, solicitors acting for defendants also need to ensure that benefits listed as recoverable benefits are as a consequence of the accident (see *Eagle Star Insurance v Department of Social Development (Northern Ireland)* (only persuasive) (2001) NICE, 12 February). See also *Williams v Devon County Council* [2003] EWCA Civ 365, [2003] All ER (D) 255 (Mar), concerning details to be included on a Part 36 notice; and *Bruce v Genesis Fast Food Ltd* [2003] EWHC 788 (QB), concerning whether defendants are entitled to take the benefit of any reduction in recoverable benefits when an appeal takes place.

An overview of the recovery of benefits system is set out at **16.16** below.

16.15   FURTHER READING

DWP Guidance Note Z1, *Recovery of benefits and or lump sums and NHS charges*

Kemp and Kemp, *The Quantum of Damages* (Sweet & Maxwell)

16.16   OVERVIEW OF RECOVERY OF BENEFITS

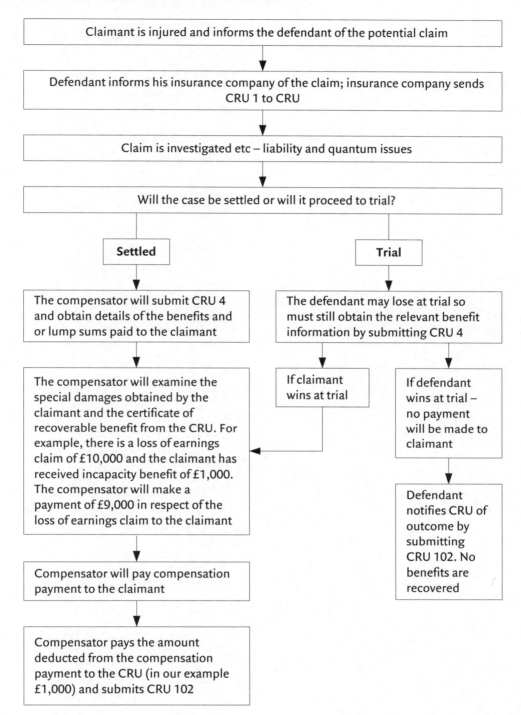

Claimant is injured and informs the defendant of the potential claim

Defendant informs his insurance company of the claim; insurance company sends CRU 1 to CRU

Claim is investigated etc – liability and quantum issues

Will the case be settled or will it proceed to trial?

Settled

Trial

The compensator will submit CRU 4 and obtain details of the benefits and or lump sums paid to the claimant

The defendant may lose at trial so must still obtain the relevant benefit information by submitting CRU 4

If claimant wins at trial

If defendant wins at trial – no payment will be made to claimant

The compensator will examine the special damages obtained by the claimant and the certificate of recoverable benefit from the CRU. For example, there is a loss of earnings claim of £10,000 and the claimant has received incapacity benefit of £1,000. The compensator will make a payment of £9,000 in respect of the loss of earnings claim to the claimant

Defendant notifies CRU of outcome by submitting CRU 102. No benefits are recovered

Compensator will pay compensation payment to the claimant

Compensator pays the amount deducted from the compensation payment to the CRU (in our example £1,000) and submits CRU 102

POST-DEATH INVESTIGATIONS

LEARNING OUTCOMES

After reading this chapter you will be able to:

- explain the purpose of an inquest
- take appropriate steps to prepare to represent a client at an inquest
- understand the procedure involved and verdicts that may be given at an inquest
- advise on the possible criminal prosecutions that might follow a fatal accident.

17.1 INTRODUCTION

The personal injury/clinical negligence solicitor must, on occasion, advise either the family of an accident victim who has died, or the person who it is claimed is responsible for the death. There are two main processes in which the solicitor may become involved:

(a) the coroner's inquest; and

(b) a criminal prosecution for:

    (i) manslaughter (corporate or individual);

    (ii) death by dangerous or careless driving; or

    (iii) offences under the HSWA 1974.

Although each process has its own purpose, post-death investigations offer an important opportunity to gain evidence on liability for the civil claim, and we consider both processes below.

17.2 INQUESTS

17.2.1 The Coroners and Justice Act 2009

There has been pressure for many years for reform of the coroner system. This has largely been due to a series of high-profile disasters, such as Hillsborough in 1989, where the coroner's verdict at the inquest into the deaths of the 96 victims was simply 'accidental death', which meant that no one has ever properly been held to account. After years of campaigning by the Hillsborough families, those verdicts were eventually quashed by the High Court in December 2012 and new inquests into the Hillsborough deaths are now taking place.

In the 1990s, coroners came under further, intense public scrutiny for their actions. For example, there were many concerns raised over the coroner in the *Marchioness* disaster, who ordered the hands of the victims to be cut off for identification purposes. Then there was the

Shipman case, where the faking of patients' death certificates brought home the shortcomings of the death certification process.

The Shipman Inquiry (2003) and the Fundamental Review of Death Certification and Investigation (2003) found the level of service provided to bereaved people was inconsistent; family and friends were not always involved in coroners' investigations; there was a lack of leadership and training for coroners; and there was insufficient medical knowledge in the system as a whole.

After years of consultation, the Coroners and Justice Act 2009 (CJA 2009) finally came into force on 25 July 2013, together with three new sets of rules which regulate the day-to-day conduct of inquests:

- Coroners (Inquests) Rules 2013 (SI 2013/1616) (the 'Inquests Rules');
- Coroners (Investigations) Regulations 2013 (SI 2013/1629) (the 'Investigations Regulations'); and
- Coroners Allowances, Fees and Expenses Regulations 2013 (SI 2013/1615) (the 'Expenses Regulations').

The CJA 2009 introduces a national coroner service for England and Wales, headed by a new Chief Coroner, HHJ Peter Thornton QC. The intention behind the CJA 2009 is to improve the experience of bereaved people coming into contact with the coroner system, giving them rights of appeal against coroners' decisions and setting out the general standards of service they can expect to receive. It is hoped that the new system will be simpler and quicker and will result in a coroner service that meets both the interests of bereaved families and the wider public interest in terms of the quality and effectiveness of investigations. The system also aims to ensure that the knowledge gained from death investigation is applied for the prevention of avoidable death and injury in the future.

17.2.2   What is an inquest?

An inquest is a fact-finding inquiry to establish:

- who has died; and
- how, when and where the death occurred.

It is important to understand that the purpose of an inquest is not to establish any matter of liability or blame. Although it receives evidence from witnesses, an inquest does not have prosecution and defence teams, like a criminal trial; the coroner and all those with 'proper interests' simply seek the answers to the above questions.

An inquest is usually opened soon after a death to record that a death has occurred, to identify the deceased, and to enable the coroner to issue the authority for the burial or cremation to take place without any unnecessary delay. It will then be adjourned until any other investigations and any inquiries instigated by the coroner have been completed. It will usually take an average of 27 weeks to conclude this work, but some cases can take longer than this if the inquiries prove to be complicated. The inquest will then be resumed and concluded. Under the old system, it could sometimes take years before an inquest was held, but r 8 of the Inquests Rules now states that a coroner must complete an inquest within six months of the date on which the coroner is made aware of the death, or as soon as is reasonably practicable after that date.

Sometimes, the coroner may hold one or more hearings before the inquest itself, known as pre-inquest hearings (or pre-inquest reviews), where the scope of the inquest and any matters of concern, including about the arrangements for the hearing, can be considered. The coroner usually invites the properly interested persons and/or their legal representatives to the pre-inquest hearing, where they have the opportunity to make representations to the coroner.

17.2.3 Personnel involved at an inquest

17.2.3.1 The coroner

The coroner is responsible for the inquest procedure, and although appointed by the local government body responsible for the area where the coroner sits (subject to the consent of the Chief Coroner and the Lord Chancellor), he is an independent judicial officer. To be eligible for appointment as a coroner, a person must now have possessed a relevant legal qualification (barrister/solicitor) for a period of five years. A number of coroners are qualified both as doctors and solicitors/barristers, although this is not a strict requirement of obtaining the post. Those who are legally qualified only normally have significant knowledge of medical matters.

In certain cases, the coroner may sit with an 'assessor', who is a person with specialist knowledge of the matters being considered, for example a consultant anaesthetist in a case where a patient died due to an airway not being maintained. However, the assessor must remain under the control of the coroner and cannot give expert evidence (see R v Surrey Coroner, ex p Wright [1997] 2 WLR 16).

17.2.3.2 The coroner's officer

The coroner is assisted by the coroner's officer, who is usually a serving or ex-police officer and is often the first person with whom the personal injury solicitor will communicate about the case. The coroner's officer will obtain evidence relating to the accident, or liaise with the police if they are carrying out investigations. His role is important to the solicitor, as he can provide information regarding the investigations which are being carried out and details of the incident, and may provide details of any witnesses the coroner intends to call.

The coroner's officer will notify the relevant parties and/or their solicitors of the inquest date.

17.2.3.3 The assistant coroner

There is one senior coroner for each coroner area, assisted by one or more assistant coroners, who normally stand in when the senior coroner is absent. An assistant coroner will have the same qualifications as a senior coroner but will usually be part time and paid a fee for sitting rather than a salary.

17.2.4 Circumstances which lead to an inquest

The circumstances in which a coroner will become involved in a death are set down in s 1 of the CJA 2009.

If the senior coroner is informed that a dead body is within his jurisdiction (it is the fact that there is a body in his jurisdiction and not where the death occurred that is important), the coroner must as soon as practicable conduct an investigation into the person's death, if the coroner has reason to suspect that a person has died:

(a)   a violent or unnatural death; or
(b)   where the cause of death is unknown; or
(c)   while in custody or otherwise in state detention.

A violent death is normally regarded as one where an injury has occurred, and will normally be apparent, for example when a factory operative falls into machinery and dies.

An unnatural death is not legally defined and it will be a question for the coroner to decide. Certain coroners believe that the phrase should be given its 'ordinary meaning'.

The coroner decides whether the death is natural or unnatural at his discretion, and this decision may need to be challenged. For example, in R v Poplar Coroner, ex p Thomas [1993] 2 WLR 547, a woman died following an asthma attack after there had been a considerable delay in an ambulance reaching her. There was evidence that if she had reached hospital earlier, she might have survived. Was this an unnatural death? The Court of Appeal overturned the decision of the Divisional Court that it was an unnatural death and stated that 'unnatural' was an ordinary word, the meaning of which should be left to the coroner (unless his decision was unreasonable). If a solicitor believes that the death was unnatural, the coroner's officer must be contacted immediately and informed of the solicitor's interest.

Normally, the police, the GP or the hospital will contact the coroner's officer and inform the coroner of the death. However, on occasion, the relatives of the deceased will contact the coroner's officer, for instance if they believe that there has been an act of clinical negligence. Once the coroner has been informed of the death, the coroner's officer will make preliminary enquiries, and the coroner may then require a post-mortem examination to be made.

Section 6 of the CJA 2009 provides that a senior coroner who conducts an investigation into a person's death must (as part of the investigation) hold an inquest into the death. However, s 4 of the CJA 2009 provides an exception to this rule where a post-mortem examination reveals the cause of death before the inquest begins and the coroner thinks that it is not necessary to continue the investigation. This power to discontinue cannot be used where the deceased died a violent or unnatural death or died in custody. A senior coroner who discontinues an investigation into a death under s 4 must, if requested to do so in writing by an interested person, give to that person as soon as practicable a written explanation as to why the investigation was discontinued.

17.2.5   Post-mortem examinations

Although no absolute obligation is placed upon the coroner, usually he will request that a post-mortem takes place.

Section 14 of the CJA 2009 states that where it is alleged that the death was caused wholly or partly by clinical negligence of a medical practitioner, that practitioner:

(a)   must not make, or assist at, an examination under this section of the body; but

(b)   is entitled to be represented at such an examination.

The coroner must inform the relatives of the deceased, the GP and the hospital (if the deceased died in hospital) of the arrangements for the post-mortem. These are normally referred to as the 'interested parties' and they may be represented at the post-mortem by a doctor.

The post-mortem report is vital evidence, and an immediate request should be made to the coroner for a copy. The report may contain evidence which will assist in establishing civil liability. For example, if the death resulted from a road traffic accident, the pathologist will give a detailed description of the injuries, and photographs will be taken of the body. The pathologist's investigations in respect of this may be vital in indicating the events which occurred prior to the accident, for example whether the deceased was wearing a seat belt. In fatal accident at work cases, the pathologist's report may also be of use in identifying whether the cause of the death resulted from exposure to dangerous materials at work, such as coal dust or asbestos.

If acting for the defendant, the post-mortem may reveal whether there are any intervening illnesses from which the deceased may have died. This may then be used in negotiations, in an attempt to reduce the multiplier in the dependency calculation (see **Chapter 18**). In addition, in a road traffic case, it is important to check the blood alcohol levels to see if the deceased had been drinking at the time of the accident. Such evidence may provide important arguments regarding liability and quantum.

17.2.6   Funding representation at the inquest

The Lord Chancellor has issued guidance on Exceptional Funding for Inquests under s 10 of LASPO 2012. This provides that it may still be possible for a solicitor (with an appropriate contract) to provide assistance to a member of the deceased family under the Legal Help scheme for the initial preparations for an inquest. Legal Help can cover all of the preparatory work associated with the inquest, which may include preparing written submissions to the coroner. Legal Help can also fund someone to attend the inquest as a 'Mackenzie Friend', to offer informal advice in court, provided that the coroner gives permission.

Funding for representation at an inquest is not generally available because an inquest is a relatively informal inquisitorial process, rather than an adversarial one. There are two grounds for granting legal aid exceptionally for representation at an inquest:

(a)   it is required by Article 2 of the ECHR; or

(b)   where the Director makes a 'wider public interest determination' in relation to the individual and the inquest.

Article 2 inquests are dealt with below at **17.2.17**. A 'wider public interest determination' is a determination that, in the particular circumstances of the case, the provision of advocacy for the individual for the purposes of the inquest is likely to produce significant benefits for a class of person, other than the applicant and members of the applicant's family. In the context of an inquest, the most likely wider public benefits are the identification of dangerous practices, systematic failings or other findings that identify significant risks to the life, health or safety of other persons.

In general, applicants for legal aid must satisfy the eligibility limits as set out in regulations. However, there is a discretion to waive the financial eligibility limits relating to inquests if, in all the circumstances, it would not be reasonable to expect the family to bear the full costs of legal assistance at the inquest. Whether this is reasonable will depend in particular on the history of the case and the nature of the allegations to be raised against agents of the state, the applicant's assessed disposable income and capital, other financial resources of the family, and the estimated costs of providing representation.

As legal aid is only available in exceptional cases, all possible alternative sources of finance should be considered (eg, in a fatal road traffic accident, the deceased's legal expenses insurance may cover the cost of representation for the estate). Immediate enquiries must be made in respect of any claim on any insurance policy and, if appropriate, prior authorisation should be obtained from the insurer. Enquiries should also be made as to whether a trade union will fund representation at the inquest, or whether any *pro bono* service may be able to provide assistance.

Interestingly, in the case of *King (Administratrix of the Estate of Robert Gadd deceased) v Milton Keynes General NHS Trust* [2004] LTL, 4 June, it was held that when assessing the costs of civil proceedings, the court did have jurisdiction to award the costs of attending at an inquest if the material purpose was to obtain information or evidence for use in civil proceedings. Similarly, in *Stewart and Hubbard v Medway NHS Trust* [2004] LTL, 20 September, the cost of counsel attending an inquest in a clinical negligence case was held to be recoverable. More recently, in *Roach v Home Office* [2009] EWHC 312 (QB), it was held that the costs of attendance at an inquest by both solicitor and counsel were recoverable as costs incidental to subsequent civil proceedings.

If there is a possibility of a clinical negligence claim being brought, any doctor who is required to give evidence will be represented by the NHSLA solicitors or his defence union. Similarly, in a personal injury case, if a civil claim is likely to follow as a result of the death, the employer (eg, in a factory accident) or the driver of the other vehicle (in a road traffic accident) will be represented by solicitors instructed by their respective insurers.

17.2.7   Preparation for the hearing

Rule 13 of the Inquests Rules provides that, where an interested person asks for disclosure of a document, the coroner must provide that document as soon as is reasonably practicable. This includes post-mortem examination reports, any other report provided to the coroner during the course of the investigation and any other document the coroner considers relevant to the investigation.

In some cases, the coroner may hold a 'pre-inquest review' to allow the parties and the coroner to consider matters prior to the actual inquest. The coroner may summarise the evidence that he proposes to call and give the parties the opportunity to suggest any other witnesses that they may wish to call.

Normally, statements will be taken from the proposed witnesses by the coroner's officer or police, and it can be of considerable advantage if these can be obtained beforehand.

It is also important to make enquiries of such bodies as the police, trade union or HSE, which may be able to provide general background information. The more information that is obtained prior to the hearing the better.

When the pathologist gives evidence, he will undoubtedly use medical language, and it is important that the solicitor is able to understand the evidence which is given. Thus, research should be carried out prior to the inquest, so as to become familiar with the potential medical terms that may be used. Consideration should also be given to making a request that blood and tissue samples taken at the post-mortem are preserved, as they may provide important information

In a clinical negligence case, the deceased's medical records should be obtained (see *Stobart v Nottingham Health Authority* [1992] 3 Med LR 284). Once received, they should be placed in an ordered, paginated file, and legible copies made. If the solicitor is instructed by an insurance company on behalf of the deceased's estate, in-depth research should be carried out into the nature of the illness, the usual treatment which is prescribed for the illness, and the usual consequences of and recovery time for the illness. This research will include relevant medical literature, and copies should be taken of any appropriate material. Medical school libraries are generally very helpful with this form of research, and can provide assistance and copying facilities. Research may reveal whether the treatment fell below the level which can be expected and required of the medical staff.

In addition, a solicitor may seek assistance from an expert who can advise him on how to examine any medical experts giving evidence on behalf of the doctor. Informed examination will test a witness's evidence, and may be useful if civil proceedings are later issued. It is important for the claimant's solicitor to make such detailed preparation, because solicitors acting for a doctor will be experienced in this field and have access to a wide range of sources, including many experts.

17.2.8   Procedure at the inquest

The inquest is formally opened without any significant evidence being given, and the formalities are carried out by the coroner sitting alone (who, for example, will take initial evidence, evidence of identification of the body, issue an order for disposal of the body and adjourn until a more suitable time). Evidence will be called concerning the death at the resumed full hearing, with legal representatives for both sides attending. If appropriate, a jury (see **17.2.9**) will also be in attendance at that time.

Schedule 1 to the CJA 2009 sets out several situations in which a coroner may suspend an investigation and inquest into a death. These relate to when it is likely that certain criminal proceedings will be brought (eg, murder, manslaughter or death by careless or dangerous driving). Rule 25(4) of the Inquests Rules states that a coroner must adjourn an inquest and notify the Director of Public Prosecutions if, during the course of an inquest, it appears to the coroner that the death of the deceased is likely to have been due to a homicide offence and that a person may be charged in relation to that offence.

In such a case, the claimant's solicitor should attend the criminal proceedings and take notes of the trial (see below), as useful evidence may be obtained which can assist in identifying any civil liability for the death.

The majority of evidence at the resumed inquest will usually be given orally by witnesses on oath, but the coroner has power to admit documentary evidence if he believes that the evidence is unlikely to be disputed. However, it is possible to object to such a decision, and a solicitor should do this where he believes that a witness should be called to answer questions (see also R (Bentley) v HM Coroner for Avon [2001] EWHC 170 (Admin), [2001] LTL, 23 March). Rules 17 and 18 of the Inquests Rules provide that a coroner may direct that evidence is to be given by video link or from behind a screen when it is in the interests of justice or national security to do so.

The actual order of calling the witnesses lies entirely within the discretion of the coroner. However, it is often the pathologist who is the first substantive witness to give evidence. The coroner will normally then examine each witness so that the evidence is heard in the same order as the events leading to the death occurred. The solicitor should make careful notes, as these witnesses may need to be contacted in relation to a potential civil claim. If the witness does not give evidence in accordance with his previous written statement to the coroner, and the interested party is not aware of this, then the coroner must deal with this point (see R v HM Coroner for Inner London North District, ex p Cohen (1994) 158 JP 644, DC). Once the coroner has dealt with the witness, each interested party (or his legal representatives) will be allowed to question him. A witness is examined by his own representative last (Inquests Rules, r 21).

An 'interested person' entitled to examine witnesses at an inquest includes:

(a)   a spouse, civil partner, partner, parent, child, brother, sister, grandparent, grandchild, child of a brother or sister, stepfather, stepmother, half-brother or half-sister;

(b)   a personal representative;

(c)   a medical examiner exercising functions in relation to the death of the deceased;

(d)   any beneficiary under a policy of insurance issued on the life of the deceased;

(e)   the insurer who issued such a policy of insurance;

(f)   any person whose act or omission, or that of his agent or servant, may, in the opinion of the coroner, have caused, or contributed to, the death of the deceased, or whose employee or agent may have done so;

(g)   any person appointed by a trade union to which the deceased belonged at the time of his death, if the death of the deceased may have been caused by an injury received in the course of his employment or by an industrial disease;

(h)   a person appointed by, or a representative of, an enforcing authority, or any person appointed by a government department to attend the inquest;

(i)   the chief officer of police;

(j)   any other person that the senior coroner thinks has a sufficient interest.

The questioning of witnesses at the inquest can be a difficult matter as the strict purpose of the inquest is limited to finding:

(a)   who the deceased was;

(b)   how, when and where the deceased came by his death;

(c)   the particulars required by the Registration Acts to be registered concerning the death.

The Divisional Court has repeatedly reaffirmed that these are the only matters with which the coroner's court is concerned, and the coroner will wish to concentrate on these fundamental points. However, there can be no doubt that many solicitors attend the inquest with a slightly wider agenda, that of trying to identify who was liable for the death and to examine the evidence surrounding the case. Much will depend upon the individual coroner as to the types of questions which are allowed, but the coroner will always limit questions concerned with civil liability.

To prevent the inquest apportioning blame, r 22 of the Inquests Rules specifically provides that a witness is not obliged to answer any questions tending to incriminate himself. The witness may be called to the witness box and asked merely to give his name and address. On occasion, no further questions will be put to him. However, practice varies widely on this point, and in R v Lincolnshire Coroner, ex p Hay (1999) 163 JP 666, it was held that the privilege against self-incrimination did not give the witness complete immunity against further questioning. The privilege against self-incrimination is against criminal proceedings (and not civil proceedings), and this should be borne in mind when the coroner is deciding if the witness is entitled to claim self-incrimination. The solicitor may have to remind the coroner about this point. If the coroner allows the witness to be questioned, it is for the witness's representative to make the objection if a question is put which might lead to self-incrimination. If the witness answers the question, he will waive the privilege.

17.2.9 Juries

The general rule is that an inquest must be held without a jury, but s 7(2) and (3) of the CJA 2009 sets out the exceptions to this rule.

A jury must be summoned where:

(a) the deceased died while in custody or otherwise in state detention, and the death was violent or unnatural, or of unknown cause;

(b) where the death was as a result of an act or omission of a police officer or member of a service police force (defined in s 48) in the purported execution of his duties; or

(c) where the death was caused by an accident, poisoning or disease which must be reported to a government department or inspector. This includes, for example, certain deaths at work.

Although a jury is not required in any other case, the coroner will be able to summon one in any case where he believes there is sufficient reason for doing so.

Section 8 of the CJA 2009 provides that the jury must consist of between seven and 11 people. The senior coroner calls people to attend for jury service by issuing a summons stating the time that they are needed and the place that they must attend. At the outset, the coroner will require jury members to swear they will make a true determination according to the evidence.

A jury will initially be directed by the senior coroner to reach a unanimous determination or finding. If the coroner thinks that the jury have deliberated for a reasonable time without reaching a unanimous verdict, under s 9(2) of the CJA 2009, he may accept a determination or finding on which the minority consists of no more than two persons. The jury spokesperson should announce publicly how many agreed. If there is no agreement by the required number of jurors, the coroner may discharge the jury and summon a completely new jury and the case will be heard again.

17.2.10 Summing up and directions to the jury

If a jury are present, the coroner will sum up the evidence to the jury after the witnesses have given evidence and will direct the jury on points of law. In R v HM Coroner for Inner London South District, ex p Douglas-Williams (1998) 162 JP 751, it was held that, in complex cases, it would be good practice for the coroner to prepare a written statement of matters which the law requires in relation to possible verdicts. If such a policy is followed, a solicitor should ask to inspect the statement prior to summing up. If no jury are present, the coroner normally sums up by means of a revision of the evidence and states his conclusions.

17.2.11 Reports to prevent future deaths

Sometimes an inquest will show that something could be done to prevent other deaths. If so, at the end of the inquest, the coroner is now under a duty to draw this to the attention of any person or organisation that may have the power to take action under para 7(1) of Sch 5 to the CJA 2009 and r 28 of the Investigations Regulations, which states that any report must be sent to the Chief Coroner and every interested person who the coroner believes should receive it. Anyone who receives such a report must send the coroner a written response. These reports (which were previously referred to as rule 43 reports), and the responses to them, are copied to all interested persons and to the Lord Chancellor. A summary of the reports is published twice a year by the Ministry of Justice.

17.2.12 Determinations and findings

Under the CJA 2009, the old terminology of 'inquisition' and 'verdict' has gone. Section 10 of the CJA 2009 requires the coroner – or the jury, where there is one – to make a 'determination' at the end of the inquest as to who the deceased was, and how, when and where the deceased came by his death. This is broadly equivalent to the requirements under the old rules. In an investigation where Article 2 of the ECHR is engaged, the coroner must also include a determination, or direct a jury to include a determination, as to the circumstances of the death.

Section 10(1)(b) also requires the coroner or jury to make a 'finding' at the end of the inquest about the details required for registration of the death. This will normally be, for example, a short finding, such as accident or misadventure, suicide, industrial disease, natural causes, drug related. Where no clear cause of death has been established, the finding will be known as 'open'. Increasingly, coroners make use of 'narrative' findings in which they sum up (usually in a few sentences) how the person came to die.

Section 10(2) makes clear that a determination may not be worded in such a way as to appear to determine any question of criminal liability of any named person or to determine any question of civil liability.

A Record of an Inquest (the 'Record') is completed by the coroner at the end of the inquest, which is signed by the coroner and jury members who concur with it. The form requires five matters to be dealt with:

(a)   the name of the deceased;

(b)   the medical cause of death;

(c)   how, when and where (and where Article 2 applies, in what circumstances the deceased came by his death);

(d)   the conclusion of the jury/coroner as to the death; and

(e)   the particulars required by the Births and Deaths Registration Act 1953.

The standard Record form gives a list of suggested conclusions, of which the most significant in personal injury/clinical negligence cases are:

(a)   accident or misadventure (the courts have taken the view that any distinction between the two words is undesirable);

(b)   alcohol/drug related;

(c)   industrial disease;

(d)   lawful/unlawful killing;

(e)   natural causes;

(f)   open;

(g)   road traffic collision;

(h)   stillbirth;

(i)   suicide.

The following points should be noted in relation to possible conclusions:

(a) Accident/accidental death. Even if such a verdict is given, it does not mean that a civil case cannot be brought.

(b) An open conclusion means simply that there is insufficient evidence to reach a conclusion.

(c) Suicide or unlawful killing. The standard of proof required for a suicide or unlawful killing conclusion to be returned is that of 'beyond reasonable doubt'. See R (*on the application of Neil Sharman*) *v HM Coroner for Inner London* [2005] EWHC 857 (Admin), concerning the returning of a verdict of unlawful killing; and R (*on the application of Anderson and Others*) *v HM Coroner for Inner North Greater London* [2004] EWHC 2729 (Admin).

All other conclusions require a burden of proof based on the balance of probabilities.

In *R (O'Connor) v HM Coroner for the District of Avon* [2009] EWHC 854 (Admin), it was held that a coroner's verdict of unlawful killing predicated a finding equivalent to that required for a conviction of at least manslaughter in a criminal trial, and that insanity, if properly raised in the evidence, had to be disproved to the criminal standard to sustain a verdict of unlawful killing.

The Divisional Court has made it clear that the coroner's court does not decide the responsibility for the death. Therefore, conclusions in the coroner's court are framed so as not to identify any individual as being responsible (see also *R v HM Coroner for Derby and South Derbyshire, ex p John Henry Hart Jnr* (2000) 164 JP 429 and *R v Director of Public Prosecutions, ex p Manning and Another* [2000] 3 WLR 463).

17.2.13 Transcripts

At the conclusion of the inquest, the coroner's officer will collect any documents or copy statements which were used during the hearing. A copy of the transcript of the case may be obtained on payment of a fee. (See also R (*on the application of the Ministry of Defence*) *v Wiltshire and Swindon Coroner* [2005] EWHC 889 (Admin).)

17.2.14 Representing the family

The inquest can be difficult for lay persons to understand. Lay persons will be unfamiliar with the role of the coroner and may expect that the purpose of the inquest is not to establish how the deceased died but to establish fault.

The procedure that the coroner will follow during the inquest must be explained to the family of the deceased. It will be necessary to discuss the evidence with them and, in particular, to discuss the conclusion. The 'finding' should be explained thoroughly, and the deceased's family should be reminded that the purpose of the inquest and the conclusion is not to apportion blame but to establish by what means the deceased came by his death.

17.2.15 Representing the potential defendant

17.2.15.1 Clinical negligence cases

Requesting records and taking statements

The solicitor for the health authority or NHS Trust should obtain all relevant records, and obtain statements from any medical and nursing staff who have been called by the coroner to give evidence at the inquest.

The solicitor should help the staff by reviewing their statements prior to submission to the coroner. He should ensure that the statements contain only relevant facts and do not offer any opinion which the witness is not competent to give. For example, a house officer should not give an opinion on whether specific parts of the treatment contributed to the death but should restrict his statement to the facts alone.

If it appears from the statements that disciplinary action might be taken against a member of the medical staff (eg, because a mistake in treatment has been made), that person should be advised to seek his own representation from his defence organisation as his interests will conflict with those of the hospital.

The solicitor should advise the medical and nursing staff that the original records will be available at the inquest, and that they are permitted to refer to these.

Purpose, form and limits of inquest

The solicitor should advise the medical and nursing staff about the purpose and form of an inquest, and encourage an attitude of openness and co-operation at the inquest.

Expert evidence

The solicitor may consider obtaining a specialist opinion on the issues arising at the inquest from a hospital consultant (but not from a consultant who is directly involved in the case).

17.2.15.2 Personal injury cases

In a personal injury case, as soon as the solicitor is instructed, he will make contact with the insured and attempt to investigate the matter further. This will normally involve attending at the insured's premises, if the accident was work-based, or at the scene of the accident with the insured, in the case of a road traffic accident. The defendant's solicitor will be under strict instructions from the insurer to formulate a view on liability and attempt to find out as much as possible about the deceased, so that some idea can be obtained about quantum. In a road traffic accident, the inquest will provide early access to the police investigation report (which may have involved a partial reconstruction), and useful information, such as whether a seat belt was worn, may become apparent. In the case of an industrial accident, the solicitor investigating the case will normally be concerned with the system of work used or the employment history of the deceased. This may be particularly useful in asbestosis claims, where it may become apparent that the deceased's main exposure to asbestos was during his employment with another employer.

17.2.16 Publicity at the inquest

There is often publicity attached to inquests. Reporters may request an interview with the key witnesses and, in particular, the family. The appropriate advice to witnesses is at the discretion of the solicitors acting for the parties. Usually, the solicitor representing the hospital or doctors will decline to say anything to the press, to avoid saying anything amounting to an admission in subsequent proceedings, or which may be upsetting to the family. The solicitor should also advise the doctors and nursing staff not to make any comments to the media. In some cases, it may be appropriate, from a public relations point of view, for the hospital to issue a brief statement offering sympathy to the family following the death of the deceased.

If the family wishes to express its anger in a more public forum, the press is usually happy to provide this opportunity. If there are any concerns to which the inquest gave rise, these could be expressed to the press. It is important, however, that the family's solicitor does not get carried away on the tide of emotion and risk slandering any of the individuals concerned.

17.2.17 'Article 2' inquests

Where employees of the state potentially bear responsibility for loss of life (whether by their actions or omissions), the right to life in Article 2 of the ECHR may be engaged. For Article 2 to be engaged, there must be reasonable grounds for thinking that the death may have resulted from a wrongful act on behalf of the state. An example might be a death in custody, either in prison or under police detention, or a death which occurs in an NHS hospital.

In such a case, the state is under an obligation to initiate an effective public investigation by an independent body. The House of Lords (now Supreme Court) ruled that, while a criminal investigation and prosecution may not discharge this obligation, an inquest is likely to do so. The inquest must, however, determine not only the identity of the deceased and when, where and how the death occurred, but also in what circumstances (see R *v HM Coroner for the Western District of Somerset & Another, ex parte Middleton* [2004] UKHL 10). The limited ambit of a 'standard' inquest will not satisfy the obligation on the state.

Whether this more detailed form of inquest will be required will depend on the precise circumstances of the particular case. Only those inquests that are concerned with a possible breach of Article 2 by an agent of the state have this wider scope; other types of inquest may be more limited.

17.3   CRIMINAL PROSECUTIONS

Where an accident results in a fatality, a criminal prosecution of those thought to be responsible will often follow. The procedure adopted in the magistrates' courts and Crown Court for such a prosecution is dealt with in **Criminal Litigation**.

If such a prosecution occurs, the claimant's solicitor should attend at court to obtain details of the circumstances of the accident and take notes of the evidence. If a conviction is obtained, this will be very useful for the civil proceedings, and in these circumstances the relevant insurance company will often settle any claim.

Many insurance policies provide for the cost of defending such criminal charges, and the insurance company will nominate solicitors to act on the insured's behalf. The defendant's insurers will use the proceedings to establish a view on civil, as well as criminal liability

17.3.1   Criminal prosecution following a fatal road traffic accident

The four offences which may be prosecuted now following a fatal road traffic accident are as follows:

(a)   *Causing death by dangerous driving* (RTA 1988, s 1). Under s 2 of the RTA 1988, a person is to be regarded as driving dangerously if the standard of driving falls 'far below what would be expected of a competent and careful driver and it would be obvious to a competent and careful driver that driving in that way would be dangerous'. The Sentencing Guidelines Council has issued a definitive guideline on sentencing (the 'Guideline') which gives examples of driving behaviour likely to result in this charge. They include aggressive driving, racing or competitive driving, speeding, and using a hand-held mobile phone when the driver was avoidably and dangerously distracted by that use.

The maximum penalty in the Crown Court is 14 years' imprisonment with a minimum disqualification of two years.

(b)   *Causing death by careless driving when under the influence of drink or drugs,* or having failed without reasonable excuse either to provide a specimen for analysis or to permit the analysis of a blood sample (RTA 1988, s 3A).

According to s 3ZA of the RTA 1988, careless driving is driving that 'falls below what would be expected of a competent and careful driver'. In comparison with dangerous driving, the level of culpability in the actual manner of driving is lower, but that culpability is increased by the fact that the driver has driven after consuming drugs or alcohol.

The maximum penalty in the Crown Court is 14 years' imprisonment with a minimum disqualification of two years.

(c)   *Causing death by careless or inconsiderate driving* (RTA 1988, s 2B). Careless driving is described in (b) above. Under s 3ZA of the RTA 1988, a person is to be regarded as driving without reasonable consideration for other persons, 'only if those persons are inconvenienced by his driving'. Examples of careless driving given in the Guideline include overtaking on the inside, emerging from a side road into the path of another vehicle, and tuning a car radio. Examples of inconsiderate driving include flashing of lights to force drivers in front to give way and driving with undipped headlights.

The maximum penalty for this offence is five years' imprisonment with a minimum of 12 months' disqualification.

(d)   *Causing death by driving: unlicensed, disqualified or uninsured drivers* (RTA 1988, s 3ZB). This charge is likely to be prosecuted alongside one of the more serious offences outlined in (a) to (c) above, and is self-explanatory. It carries a maximum penalty of two years' imprisonment with a minimum disqualification of 12 months.

17.3.2   Criminal prosecution following an accident at work

Following a fatal accident at work, the HSE may bring a prosecution under the HSWA 1974 (see **4.9**). It is also possible for an individual (such as a director of a company) to be prosecuted for gross negligence manslaughter.

Where the evidence indicates that a serious criminal offence other than a health and safety offence may have been committed, the HSE is required to liaise with the CPS in deciding whether to prosecute. Health and safety offences are usually prosecuted by the HSE, or by the local authority responsible for enforcement. The CPS may also prosecute health and safety offences, but usually does so only when prosecuting other serious criminal offences, such as manslaughter, arising out of the same circumstances.

There is also the possibility that the CPS could bring a prosecution against an employer for corporate manslaughter under the Corporate Manslaughter and Corporate Homicide Act 2007, which is discussed in more detail below (see **17.3.4**).

17.3.3   Criminal prosecution following clinical negligence

The CPS may bring a prosecution for manslaughter against an individual (such as a doctor or nurse) following a clinical negligence incident which results in the death of a patient. Such a charge will be on the basis that the breach of duty committed was so great as to constitute gross negligence and therefore merits criminal sanctions rather than just a duty to compensate the victim (see R v Adomako [1995] 1 AC 171).

Over the years, a number of doctors have been convicted of manslaughter by gross negligence. In 2003, two senior house officers were so convicted following the death of a man who had been placed in their post-operative care. Following a routine knee operation at Southampton University Hospital, the patient contracted an infection and subsequently died of toxic shock syndrome. The doctors had failed to deal with the clear signs of serious illness, take appropriate blood samples, administer antibiotics or consult senior colleagues. Their appeal against a suspended sentence of 18 months each was dismissed by the Court of Appeal (R v Misra; R v Srivastava [2004] EWCA Crim 2375).

Following their conviction, the CPS also instigated criminal proceedings against the NHS Trust (R v Southampton University Hospitals NHS Trust [2006] EWCA Crim 2971) for its failure to discharge its duty under s 3 of the HSWA 1974. This section requires an employer to conduct his undertakings in such a way as to ensure, so far is reasonably practical, that persons not in his employment and who may be affected (in this instance a patient) are not exposed to risks to their health and safety. The Trust had failed to provide enough junior doctors in the Trauma and Orthopaedic Department, and had failed to implement systems for the adequate supervision of staff by consultants. The Trust pleaded guilty, and the initial fine of £100,000 was reduced on appeal to £40,000 on the grounds that the judge had not taken account of the early guilty plea and that the public would suffer as a result of a large fine.

It is also now possible that an NHS Trust, Foundation Trust or health authority could be prosecuted for corporate manslaughter (see **17.3.4** below).

17.3.4   Corporate Manslaughter and Corporate Homicide Act 2007

17.3.4.1   The background

The Corporate Manslaughter and Corporate Homicide Act 2007 (CMCHA 2007) came into force on 6 August 2008 in response to problems applying the existing offence of manslaughter by gross negligence to organisations rather than to individuals. The main problem under existing criminal law was that, in order for a company or other organisation to be guilty of gross negligence manslaughter, it was necessary for a senior individual (the 'controlling mind'), who might be said to embody the company, to be guilty of the offence. This is sometimes referred to as the 'identification doctrine'.

The matter was examined in *Attorney-General's Reference (No 2 of 1999)* [2000] 2 Cr App R 207, which concerned a train collision at Southall in 1997 in which seven passengers died and 151 were injured. Great Western Trains was prosecuted for manslaughter on the basis that it had allowed the train to be operated with two important safety devices switched off, as a result of which the driver of the train had failed to notice a warning signal. The company was acquitted as there was no human being with whom the company could be identified. On a reference by the Attorney-General, the Court of Appeal stated that the identification doctrine remained the only basis in common law for corporate liability in gross negligence manslaughter.

As a result of the identification doctrine there were very few successful prosecutions for corporate manslaughter. The only successful prosecutions were of small, owner-managed companies, where it was not difficult to pinpoint a senior individual who effectively ran the company, such as in *Kite and Others* (1994) *Independent*, 9 December, where four teenagers drowned while canoeing during an adventure holiday.

The failures of the law led to a sustained campaign for reform, which finally resulted in the offence of corporate manslaughter being introduced by the CMCHA 2007. The offence is intended to work in conjunction with other forms of accountability, such as gross negligence manslaughter for individuals and other health and safety legislation.

17.3.4.2   The offence

Section 1 of the CMCHA 2007 states:

(1)   An organisation to which this section applies is guilty of an offence if the way in which its activities are managed or organised—

    (a)   causes a person's death; and

    (b)   amounts to a gross breach of a relevant duty of care owed by the organisation to the deceased.

(2)   An organisation is guilty of an offence ... only if the way in which its activities are managed or organised by its senior management is a substantial element in the breach referred to in subsection (1).

To prove the offence, therefore, the CPS must prove:

(a)   the defendant is a qualifying *organisation*;

(b)   the organisation *causes* a person's death;

(c)   there was a *relevant duty of care* owed by the organisation to the deceased;

(d)   there was a *gross breach* of that duty; and

(e)   a substantial element of that breach was in the way those activities were managed or organised *by senior management*; and

(f)   that the defendant does not fall within one of the *exemptions* for prosecution under the Act.

Therefore the court will have to consider how the fatal activity was managed, or organised, throughout the organisation, including any systems and processes for managing safety and how these were operated in practice. A substantial part of the failure within the organisation must have been at a senior level.

Meaning of 'organisation'

Section 1(2) states the offence applies to the following bodies:

(a)   a corporation;

(b)   a department or other body listed in Sch 1;

(c)   a police force; and

(d)   a partnership, or trade union or employer's association that is an employer.

Crown immunity has been a long-established legal doctrine that means that Crown bodies (such as government departments) cannot be prosecuted. Section 11(1) now allows prosecutions under the Act to apply to such bodies. Schedule 1 sets out a list of government departments to which the offence applies.

The Act also applies to a wide range of statutory public bodies which are not part of the Crown, including local authorities and NHS bodies.

Causation

It is not necessary for the management failure to have been the sole cause of death. The prosecution will need to show that 'but for' the management failure (including the substantial element attributable to senior management), the death would not have occurred. The law does not, however, recognise very remote causes, and in some circumstances the existence of an intervening event may mean that the management failure is not considered to have caused the death.

Relevant duty of care

Section 2(1) requires that the relevant duty of care is to be one that is owed under the law of negligence. The Act does not create new duties in addition to those already owed in the civil law of negligence.

The duty must be a relevant one for the offence. Relevant duties are set out in s 2(1) of the Act and include:

(a)   employer and occupier duties;

(b)   duties owed in connection with:

    (i)   supplying goods and services (whether or not for consideration),

    (ii)   construction and maintenance work (note that simply because there is a statutory duty to perform an act, this does not create a relevant duty of care; thus although a highways authority has a duty to maintain and repair roads (HA 1980, s 41), the failure to do so does not give rise to a duty of care to a motorist in negligence. However a negligent repair would do so),

    (iii)   other activities on a commercial basis, and

    (iv)   using or keeping plant, vehicles or other things.

Gross breach

Once a relevant duty of care has been established, any breach must fall far below what could reasonably be expected of the organisation in the circumstances (s 1(4)(b)).

This is a matter for the jury to decide, and s 8 sets out factors for the jury to consider. Section 8(2) states that the jury must consider whether health and safety legislation was breached and, if so:

(a)   how serious the breach was (s 8(2)(a)); and

(b)   how much of a risk of death it posed (s 8(2)(b)).

Meaning of 'senior management'

The term 'senior management' is defined in s 1(4) to mean those persons who play a *significant* role in the management of the whole of, or a *substantial* part of, the organisation's activities.

This covers both those in the direct chain of management and those in, for example, strategic or regulatory compliance roles.

Neither 'significant' nor 'substantial' is defined, but the former is likely to be limited to those whose involvement is influential, and will not include those who simply carry out the activity.

Whether the activity in question is itself a 'substantial' part of the company's activities will be of great importance in determining if the offence applies, especially where a company has multiple businesses or is a national organisation with regional managers. The test of senior management is wider than the former 'controlling mind', which effectively restricted the offence to actions of directors. A regional manager would probably count, but this may itself depend on the number of regions, the number of higher tiers of management, the diversity of the organisation's activities and his own job description.

Exemptions

Corporate manslaughter does not apply to certain public and government functions where there exist wider questions of public policy. So, for example, the Act exempts the military, the police and the emergency services when conducting certain activities, including dealing with emergencies, terrorism and violent disorder.

17.3.4.3 Punishment for corporate manslaughter and health and safety offences causing death

The Sentencing Council issued the Definitive Guideline on Corporate Manslaughter and Health and Safety Offences which cause death (the 'Guideline') in February 2010. It sets out the key principles relevant to assessing the seriousness of such offences and the factors that should be taken into account in deciding on an appropriate sentence. The Guideline applies only to organisations which commit serious health and safety offences. It does not apply to individuals.

The possible sentencing options for such offences are:

(a) *Unlimited fine*. The Guideline states that fines must be punitive and sufficient to have an impact on the defendant and that the appropriate fine for the offence of corporate manslaughter will seldom be less than £500,000. For health and safety offences causing death, the appropriate fine will usually be at least £100,000.

(b) *Publicity order*. This is available only for offences of corporate manslaughter. A publicity order may require publication of:

(i) the fact of the conviction;

(ii) specified particulars of the offence;

(iii) the amount of any fine; and

(iv) the terms of any remedial order (see (c) below).

The Guideline states that a publicity order should ordinarily be imposed in a case of corporate manslaughter. The order should specify the place where the public announcement is to be made (for example, a newspaper or a website) and consideration should also be given to the size of any notice or advertisement required.

(c) *Remedial order*. A remedial order can be made for both corporate manslaughter and health and safety offences. The guideline points out that a defendant ought, by the time of the sentencing, to have remedied any dangerous practices, and if it has not will be deprived of significant mitigation. Nevertheless, if it still appears to be necessary, a judge may make a remedial order requiring a defendant to address the cause of the accident. The order should be sufficiently specific to make it enforceable.

17.3.4.4 Corporate manslaughter convictions

To date, there have been fewer than 15 successful prosecutions for corporate manslaughter, but over half of those have been in the last year, which suggests that there is now much greater confidence in the CPS to bring such prosecutions. The first company to be convicted under the CMCHA 2007 was Cotswold Geotechnical Holdings Ltd, which was fined £385,000 in February 2011 following the death of an employee who was crushed to death when the sides of an excavated pit collapsed as he was collecting samples. Although the fine was less than the suggested starting-point fine of £500,000 (see **17.3.4.3**), the court took account of the fact that the company was in financial difficulties, and the fine was in fact 116% of the company's turnover.

The second conviction was in May 2012 against JMW Farms, based in Northern Ireland. This was the first corporate manslaughter conviction in Northern Ireland. The company was convicted under the CMCHA 2007 following the death of its employee, Robert Wilson, on 15 November 2010. Mr Wilson, who was 45 years old, was working at a farm, when he was crushed by a large metal bin, which had fallen from the raised forks of a forklift. The vehicle was being driven by one of the company's directors, Mark Wright. The bin had not been properly attached to the forklift. JMW Farms was fined £187,500 plus £13,000 costs.

In July 2012, Lion Steel Equipment Ltd became the third company in the UK to be convicted of corporate manslaughter, and was fined £480,000 and ordered to pay prosecution costs of £84,000. The case followed the death of an employee who suffered fatal injuries when he fell through a fragile roof at its site in Hyde, Cheshire in May 2008. The company admitted the offence, part way through the trial, on the basis that all charges against its directors would be dropped (three men had been charged with gross negligence manslaughter and health and safety charges).

Until recently, the fines imposed have all been below the £500,000 lower threshold suggested by the Sentencing Guidelines Council, due to the size of the companies involved. The first company to receive a fine in excess of this threshold was CAV Aerospace Ltd, which was found guilty of corporate manslaughter on 31 July 2015 following the death of employee Paul Bowers. Mr Bowers died after a stack of metal sheets collapsed on top of him in a warehouse. The metal sheets, which had been delivered to the warehouse at the company's request, collapsed as a result of the dangerously high levels of stock in the warehouse. The senior management of CAV Aerospace Ltd had received repeated warnings over a number of years and had been warned, ahead of the fatal accident, that there were potentially disastrous consequences if nothing was done about it. The company was fined £600,000.

Most of the convictions so far have followed guilty pleas by the company, usually in exchange for the dropping of charges against individual directors and, in several of the more recent convictions, publicity orders were made which required the publication of details of the convictions in trade magazines and local newspapers.

After a slow start, the number of prosecutions for corporate manslaughter appears to be on the increase, with approximately 50 cases currently under consideration by the CPS or waiting to come to trial. These include the case of Maidstone NHS Trust, which will be the first hospital to be charged with corporate manslaughter. The charge follows the death of Frances Cappuccini, who died in 2012 after giving birth by emergency Caesarean section at Pembury Hospital in Tunbridge Wells. Two individual doctors who treated Mrs Cappuccini have also been charged with gross negligence manslaughter. The trial is due to take place in January 2016.

17.4 CONCLUSION

Inquests and criminal prosecutions are important processes which may be used to gather evidence at an early stage, and the outcome of a criminal prosecution may be extremely influential in establishing liability in a civil claim for compensation. From a personal injury solicitor's point of view, this can be very demanding work, as the client is likely to make considerable demands of the solicitor, both professionally and emotionally. A summary of the main points is set out below at **17.6**.

17.5 FURTHER READING

Matthews, *Jervis on Coroners* (Sweet & Maxwell) and the cumulative supplement

Cooper, *Inquests* (Hart Publishing)

Forlin & Smail (eds), *Corporate Liability: Work Related Deaths and Prosecutions* (Bloomsbury Professional)

17.6 INVESTIGATING FATAL ACCIDENTS

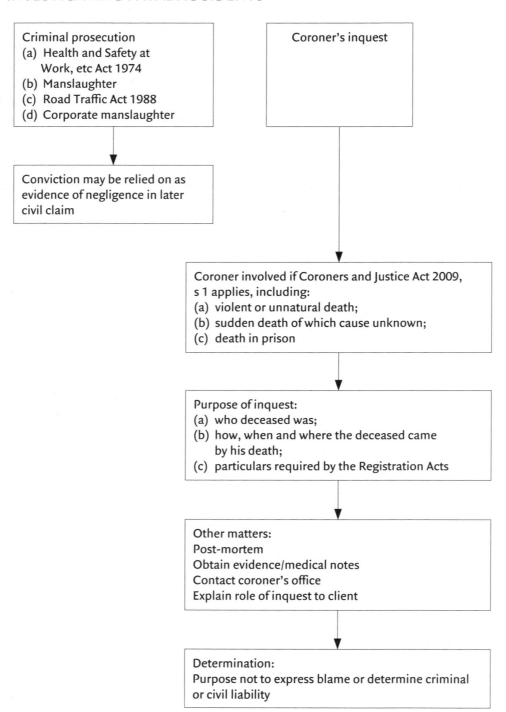

CHAPTER 18

INTRODUCTION TO FATAL ACCIDENT CLAIMS — PROCEDURE AND QUANTIFICATION

> **LEARNING OUTCOMES**
>
> After reading this chapter you will be able to:
>
> - understand the causes of action available to the estate and dependants of the deceased after a fatal accident
> - identify who may claim as a dependant of the deceased
> - advise on the heads of damage which may be claimed by the estate of the deceased
> - calculate the amount of a dependency claim
> - identify who may claim bereavement damages and the amount of those damages.

18.1 INTRODUCTION

This chapter sets out the basic principles involved in assessing damages in personal injury and clinical negligence cases where the victim has died before trial.

There are two elements to a claim in such circumstances:

(a) the Law Reform (Miscellaneous Provisions) Act 1934 (LR(MP)A 1934), which allows a claim for the benefit of the deceased's estate; and

(b) the Fatal Accidents Act 1976 (FAA 1976), which allows a claim for the benefit of the dependants and those entitled to an award of bereavement damages.

While the Acts provide two separate causes of action, they are commonly brought together and, to some extent, may overlap. The methods of valuing damages which may be claimed under each Act are considered below.

In certain cases, specific statutes provide for recompense for the deceased's family, such as the Carriage by Air Act 1961 in cases of death arising out of civil aviation accidents. These are not dealt with in this text.

18.2 CAUSE OF ACTION

The LR(MP)A 1934 provides (for the benefit of the deceased's estate) for the continuation of the cause of action to which the deceased was entitled the instant before he died (LR(MP)A 1934, s 1(2)). It does not create a separate cause of action.

The FAA 1976 does create a separate cause of action for the dependants (and those entitled to the award of bereavement damages), but it is based on the pre-condition that the deceased, had he lived, would have been able to sue successfully (FAA 1976, s 1).

Three things follow from this, namely:

(a)   if the deceased had no cause of action then the estate and the dependants have no cause of action;

(b)   any defence that could have been used against the deceased can be used against the estate and the dependants;

(c)   if the deceased was contributorily negligent then the damages of the estate and the dependants are reduced accordingly.

EXAMPLE 1

Tom is driving his car when it collides with a car driven by Sharon. Tom dies as a result of his injuries. He is survived by his widow, Elaine, and his son, Christopher. The accident is entirely the fault of Tom. As a result, neither Tom's estate, nor Elaine or Christopher has any right of action against Sharon.

EXAMPLE 2

Lucy is killed in an accident at work. She is survived by her husband, Michael, and daughter, Patricia. Lucy and her employers are equally to blame for the accident. Although Lucy's estate, Michael and Patricia may claim against the employers, the damages awarded to each will be reduced by 50%.

In the case of *Jameson and Another v Central Electricity Generating Board and Another* [2000] AC 455, the House of Lords held that in a case where the second co-defendant had paid a compensation payment to the injured person when he was still alive (on a less than full liability basis), this did prevent the dependants bringing a claim under FAA 1976 against the first co-defendant (who was a concurrent tortfeasor) and did amount to a settlement of claim.

Pleadings may be amended to plead a fatal accident claim if the deceased dies during the course of proceedings which were commenced in his name when he was alive. However, once judgment is given or a claim is settled by a living claimant, there can be no subsequent claim by dependants. This is well illustrated by the case of *Thompson v Arnold* [2007] EWHC 1875 (QB). Mrs Thompson commenced proceedings against her GP, Dr Arnold, who had incorrectly diagnosed a lump in her breast as benign. The case was settled for £120,000, in full and final settlement, in January 2000. Mrs Thompson died in April 2002 and, in April 2005, her husband and two daughters as her dependants sought to bring a claim against the defendant under the FAA 1976. Their claim was dismissed on the basis of the previous settlement made by Mrs Thompson during her lifetime. If there is a possibility that a claimant might die of their injuries during the course of proceedings, the best approach (as suggested by Langstaff J in *Thompson v Arnold*) may be to seek an interim payment of equal value to a lifetime award, together with an adjournment of the case. This will preserve the dependant's right to claim under the FAA 1976 in the event of death. Alternatively, a claim for provisional damages could be made (see **15.4**). Section 3 of the Damages Act 1996 makes it clear that a provisional damages award does not bar a claim under the FAA 1976, although the award will be taken into account in assessing damages payable to the dependants under the 1976 Act.

18.3 THE APPOINTMENT OF PERSONAL REPRESENTATIVES

Fatal accident claims are normally representative actions. This means that the personal representative normally brings a claim simultaneously on behalf of the estate under the LR(MP)A 1934 and on behalf of the dependants under the FAA 1976. The grant of probate or letters of administration should therefore be obtained before the claim is commenced.

18.4 DAMAGES UNDER THE LAW REFORM (MISCELLANEOUS PROVISIONS) ACT 1934

Generally, the damages awarded to the estate under the LR(MP)A 1934 are based on the losses for which the deceased could have claimed at the instant before he died. In essence, the estate inherits the deceased's right to sue in respect of the death. Any head of damages that is duplicated between the LR(MP)A 1934 and the FAA 1976 is recoverable only once.

The following heads of damages may be appropriate.

18.4.1 Pain, suffering and loss of amenity (PSLA)

Chapter 1 of the 12th edition of the *Guidelines for the Assessment of General Damages* in *Personal Injury Cases* allows for an element of PSLA for the period between injury and death. There are four brackets:

(A) **Full Awareness – £16,940 to £19,250**

Severe burns and lung damage coupled with full awareness initially then fluctuating consciousness for 4 to 5 weeks and intrusive treatment.

(B) **Followed by Unconsciousness – £8,470 to £11,330**

Severe burns and lung damage causing excruciating pain but followed by unconsciousness after 3 hours and death two weeks later; or very severe chest and extensive orthopaedic injuries from which recovery was being made, but complications supervened.

(C) **Immediate Unconsciousness/Death after Six Weeks – £6,820**

Immediate unconsciousness after injury, and death occurring after six weeks.

(D) **Immediate Unconsciousness/Death within One Week – £1,100 to £2,255**

Immediate unconsciousness, or unconsciousness following very shortly after injury, and death occurring within a week.

Previously, there was no guidance in this area, with parties having to search for authorities in each case, and defendants often argued that there could really be no pain with immediate unconsciousness, so reaching a conclusion that no PSLA award should be made. For example, in *Hicks v Wright* [1992] 2 All ER 65, no damages under this head were awarded to victims of the Hillsborough disaster for the short period of terror and pain they experienced before death. It would seem likely that if those cases were being valued today they would be awarded something for PSLA.

Chapter 1 does not apply, for example, to cases relating to asbestos exposure or other cancer claims where reference will continue to be made to the awards for those underlying conditions.

Although the above brackets are a useful starting point, every case will be unique and so the amount of the award for pain, suffering and loss of amenity will depend upon the actual level of pain and the length of time over which the pain was experienced. Reference should therefore still be made to case law in order to obtain a more accurate valuation. For example, in *Fallon v Beaumont*, 16 December 1993, CC (Leeds), a 22-year-old man was involved in a high-speed road accident, during which the car in which he was a passenger exploded and burst into flames. He was trapped in the burning car until the emergency services arrived, and was conscious throughout. He died 30 days later. He would have had significant insight into the gravity of his situation and an award of £10,000 (the equivalent of about £16,500 at today's values) was made for pain and suffering.

The Court of Appeal case of *Kadir v Mistry* [2014] All ER (D) 247 concerned a claim for damages for the distress caused by the knowledge of the deceased that she was going to die as a result of the delay by her GP to diagnose that she was suffering from cancer. Section 1(1) of the Administration of Justice Act 1982 provides:

> In an action under the law of England and Wales or the law of Northern Ireland for damages for personal injuries—
>
> (a)   no damages shall be recoverable in respect of any loss of expectation of life caused to the injured person by the injuries; but
>
> (b)   if the injured person's expectation of life has been reduced by the injuries, the court, in assessing damages in respect of pain and suffering caused by the injuries, shall take account of any suffering caused or likely to be caused to him by awareness that his expectation of life has been so reduced.

The appellant/claimant, as personal representative of the deceased's estate, appealed against a decision awarding no damages for pain, suffering and loss of amenity, or for mental anguish, arising from the admitted negligent failure of the respondent/defendant general practitioners to diagnose his late wife with stomach cancer as early as they should have done.

For several months the deceased had been visiting the defendants complaining of various stomach-related symptoms until, in March 2008, she was diagnosed with stomach cancer. She was advised that the cancer was too advanced to treat, and thereafter she received only palliative care until she died in August 2008. She was 32 years old and had four small children. The claimant claimed against the defendant on behalf of himself and the children under the FAA 1976, and on behalf of the deceased's estate under the LR(MP)A 1934.

The defendants admitted liability for the delay in the diagnosis and the consequent delay in treatment.

The claimant gave evidence that in March 2008 the family was told by doctors that the deceased might have survived if she had been diagnosed sooner, and that during a home visit in May 2008 she asked her GP why she was not diagnosed earlier and whether she would have survived if she had been. The trial judge found that if the defendants had not been negligent the deceased would have been diagnosed in June or July 2007, and would probably have lived until July or August 2010. He found that if the deceased had been diagnosed earlier she would have suffered the same symptoms as she did, albeit later, and would have had to endure intensive and gruelling treatments, so he awarded no damages for pain, suffering and loss of amenity. He also rejected the claim under s 1(1)(b) of the Administration of Justice Act 1982 for damages in respect of mental anguish caused or likely to be caused by the deceased's awareness that her life expectation had been reduced.

Allowing the claimant's appeal, the Court of Appeal held that it was important to bear in mind that there were no special rules for the assessment of damages in cases under the 1934 Act: the court was required to undertake the conventional exercise, namely, decide what pain was occasioned by the negligence. If the court was looking at a living claimant facing an early death, like the deceased, the court inevitably had to compare the facts as they occurred with the likely facts if there had been no negligence. On that basis, the fact that the deceased would have had the same symptoms two years later was relevant, as was the pain of treatment. The judge had been correct on the evidence to refuse the claim for pain, suffering and loss of amenity.

The word 'awareness' in s 1(1)(b) of the 1982 Act did not mean strictly certain knowledge. As a matter of ordinary humanity, if there was good reason for the anguish, it could be inferred that the sufferer would have suffered some. The claimant had given evidence that the deceased had believed that the delay had caused the cancer to spread. The issue of why she was not diagnosed earlier was a live question during her last months. There was plainly material that gave rise to the proper inference that she feared on good objective grounds that her life expectancy had been reduced by the delayed diagnosis. It was necessary to prove that she knew that it was reduced.

No cases had been found that were relevant to the assessment of damages under s 1(1)(b) of the 1982 Act for the deceased's suffering occasioned by her awareness of her reduced life expectancy. On the evidence, her mental anguish was proved for the three-month period from May 2008 until her death. It was important to recognise that there was no psychiatric injury, but there were other important elements: in particular, she was a young woman with four small children; her anguish must have been exacerbated by her knowledge that they would be left without her and that she would not see them grow up. It was proper to take those factors into account. Adopting a broad-brush approach, £3,500 would do justice.

18.4.2 Loss of income

The estate is entitled to claim the lost net earnings of the deceased from the time of the accident until death, calculated in the same way as for a living claimant (see **15.2.1**). No claim can be made for loss of income in respect of any period after that person's death (LR(MP)A 1934, s 1(2)(a)(ii), as amended by the Administration of Justice Act 1982).

18.4.3 Funeral expenses

Funeral expenses are specifically provided for in s 1(2)(c) of the LR(MP)A 1934. The expenses may be claimed provided they are:

(a)   reasonable; and

(b)   incurred by the estate.

What is 'reasonable' will depend on the individual circumstances of the case, including the social standing and racial origin of the deceased. In *Gammell v Wilson* [1982] AC 27, the court drew a distinction between the cost of the funeral service and a headstone (which was allowed), and the cost of a wake and a memorial to the deceased (which was not allowed).

In *Brown v Hamid* [2013] EWHC 4067 (QB), no award was allowed for funeral expenses on the basis that they would have been incurred shortly in any event. The court found that, even if the defendant had not been negligent, the deceased would have survived for only another 12 months.

If the expenses are incurred by a dependant of the deceased rather than by the deceased's estate, the dependant may claim the expenses as part of the fatal accidents claim.

On a practical note, it is important to obtain receipts in order to prove all the expenses incurred. Many insurers are amenable to making an immediate interim payment in relation to the funeral expenses, in order to relieve the dependants of some of the immediate expenses and to prevent interest accruing on those expenses.

18.4.4 Value of services rendered by third parties

Services rendered by third parties may include, for example: nursing services rendered by a relative to the deceased up to the time of death; expenses incurred by a third party in assisting in bringing the deceased's body home from abroad; or the costs incurred by relatives in visiting the hospital. The quantum is the proper and reasonable cost of supplying the need. (For the general principles involved, see **Chapter 15**.)

18.4.5   Other losses

Other losses may include, for example, damage to chattels, such as the car the deceased was driving at the time of the incident, or the clothing which he was wearing.

18.4.6   Distribution of damages

Damages under the LR(MP)A 1934 pass to the deceased's estate, and from there to the deceased's beneficiaries according to the deceased's will or the rules of intestacy.

Damages under the LR(MP)A 1934 are, in appropriate cases (eg, where there was a long interval between the accident and the death, and the deceased had been in receipt of recoverable benefits), subject to the Social Security (Recovery of Benefits) Act 1997 (see **Chapter 16**), but are not subject to any other losses or gains to the estate, such as the receipt of insurance money (LR(MP)A 1934, s 1(2)).

18.4.7   Conclusion

In the case of instantaneous death, damages under the LR(MP)A 1934 will normally be limited to damages for funeral expenses and damage to chattels. Where there is a period of survival, the damages may be more extensive but will normally still be severely curtailed by the inability of the estate to claim the lost future income of the deceased.

18.5   DAMAGES UNDER THE FATAL ACCIDENTS ACT 1976

In general terms, there are three possible heads of damages, namely:

(a)   a dependency claim for the financial losses suffered by the dependants of the deceased;

(b)   an award of bereavement damages; and

(c)   a claim for the funeral expenses, if paid by the dependants.

18.5.1   Loss of dependency

To succeed in a dependency claim, the claimant

(a)   must be a dependant as defined by the FAA 1976; and

(b)   must have had a reasonable expectation of financial benefit from the deceased.

18.5.1.1   The statutory meaning of 'dependant'

'Dependant' is defined in s 1(3) of the FAA 1976 as follows:

(a)   the wife or husband or former wife or husband of the deceased;

(aa)   the civil partner or former civil partner of the deceased;

(b)   any person who:

(i)   was living with the deceased in the same household immediately before the date of the death; and

(ii)   had been living with the deceased in the same household for at least two years before that date; and

(iii)   was living during the whole of that period as the husband or wife or civil partner of the deceased;

(c)   any parent or other ascendant of the deceased;

(d)   any person who was treated by the deceased as his parent;

(e)   any child or other descendant of the deceased;

(f)   any person (not being a child of the deceased) who, in the case of any marriage to which the deceased was at any time a party, was treated by the deceased as a child of the family in relation to that marriage;

(fa)   any person (not being a child of the deceased) who, in the case of any civil partnership in which the deceased was at any time a civil partner, was treated by the deceased as a child of the family in relation to that civil partnership;

(g)   any person who is, or is the issue of, a brother, sister, uncle or aunt of the deceased.

The requirement to come within the statutory definition of 'dependant' has resulted in adverse judicial comment (see *Shepherd v Post Office* (1995) *The Times*, 15 June), and the introduction of the cohabitee as a possible claimant ((b) above) by the Administration of Justice Act 1982 was controversial.

In *Fretwell v Willi Betz*, 8 March 2001, the definition of a 'dependant' was challenged, by virtue of the Human Rights Act 1998. The case was settled without any admission as regards the claimant's status as a 'dependant' (the argument concerned a child of the girlfriend who was living with the deceased prior to the accident), but it does illustrate the possibility of using the Human Rights Act 1998 to challenge the narrow statutory definition of a 'dependant' (see also *Ogur v Turkey* (2001) 31 EHRR 912).

The requirement to have been living together for two years prior to the death should be noted, and evidence should be obtained on this point if it is anticipated that the defendant will challenge this (see *Kotke v Saffarini* [2005] EWCA Civ 221). The FAA 1976 contains a provision that the cohabitee's lack of enforceable right to support is to be taken into account (FAA 1976, s 3(4)). This may mean that a cohabitee will receive less compensation than a lawful spouse, as the court may use a lower multiplier in determining the dependency claim. For example, a multiplier of 13 was used for a cohabiting couple, instead of 15 which would have been used if they were married.

18.5.1.2   Further provisions with regard to the meaning of 'dependant'

Section 1(4) of the FAA 1976 (as amended by the Administration of Justice Act 1982) provides:

> ... former wife or husband ... includes a reference to a person whose marriage to the deceased has been annulled or declared void as well as a person whose marriage to the deceased has been dissolved.

Section 1(5) of the FAA 1976 (as amended by the Administration of Justice Act 1982) provides:

(a)   any relationship by affinity shall be treated as a relationship by consanguinity, any relationship of the half blood as a relationship of the whole blood, and the stepchild of any person as his child;

(b)   an illegitimate person shall be treated as the legitimate child of his mother and reputed father.

Thus, for example, the stepbrother of the deceased is treated as his true brother; the uncle of a wife is treated as the husband's uncle.

The Adoption Act 1976 provides that, generally, an adopted child is treated as the natural child of the adopters.

18.5.1.3   Identifying the dependants

It is important to identify all prospective dependants, as s 2(3) of the FAA 1976 provides that 'not more than one action shall lie' and, as a result, only one claim will be brought. A defendant is entitled to full particulars of all those on whose behalf the claim is being brought. In practice, the particulars of the dependants are set out in the court documentation and generally include details of:

(a)   the age of the dependants;

(b)   their relationship with the deceased;

(c)   the nature of the dependency (eg, the dependant was a minor son wholly supported by the deceased father who was the family breadwinner and who had good promotion prospects).

On occasions, the defendants will argue that a claimant is not a true 'dependant' under the FAA 1976, and this is often resolved by the court ordering a trial of the point as a preliminary issue.

18.5.1.4   The requirement of 'financial loss'

It is not sufficient that the claimant merely satisfies the statutory meaning of 'dependant'. It must be shown in addition that there is a reasonable likelihood that the claimant has or will suffer financial loss as a result of the death of the deceased. In the case of *Thomas v Kwik Save Stores Ltd* (2000) *The Times*, 27 June, the Court of Appeal reaffirmed the principle that, when awarding damages under the FAA 1976, the court was concerned with the financial loss and not the emotional dependency of the claimant on the deceased.

In many cases, the dependants will have a clear and immediate financial loss. For example, where a husband was maintaining his wife and children before his death, the fact that they will suffer financial loss as a result of the husband's death is obvious. In addition to the loss of the deceased's earnings, consideration should be given to whether the dependents have lost any fringe benefits to which he was entitled, such as a company car.

The loss may still be regarded as 'financial' even if there was no expenditure by the deceased, provided the support can be quantified in monetary terms (eg, where the deceased's elderly mother was allowed to live rent-free in the deceased's house before his death, the mother would be able to claim a quantifiable financial loss). If the deceased regularly did DIY, gardening or other jobs around the house, the dependants can claim for the loss of those gratuitous services. In *Crabtree v Wilson* [1993] PIQR Q24 the court valued the deceased's work around the home at £1,500 per annum.

In the case of *Cox v Hockenhull* [1999] 3 All ER 577, the Court of Appeal held that the important point in assessing the dependency was to identify the loss the claimant has suffered as a result of a death. In that case, the deceased's income had been certain State benefits which she and her husband had relied upon. The Court allowed the husband's claim for dependency on the basis that he was dependent on certain benefits that had been received prior to the death and which he no longer obtained after his wife was killed in a road traffic accident.

18.5.1.5   The loss must be as a result of a personal family relationship with the deceased

If the loss to the dependant is, in reality, a loss attributable to a business relationship with the deceased, the claim for loss of dependency will fail (*Burgess v Florence Nightingale Hospital for Gentlewomen* [1955] 1 QB 349).

EXAMPLE

Tom is killed in a car accident as a result of the negligent driving of Keith. Tom is survived by his widow, Sally, and his 6-month-old son, Brian. Tom was the sole financial support of Sally and Brian. Tom worked in business with his brother, Joe. As a result of Tom's death, the business fails and Joe suffers heavy financial losses. Tom's married sister, Edwina, is very upset at the news of her brother's death.

Sally and Brian may claim as defined dependants who suffer financial losses as a result of a family relationship with Tom.

Joe cannot claim because, although he is a defined dependant, his financial losses are as a result of a business relationship with Tom.

Edwina cannot claim because, although she is a defined dependant, she has suffered no financial losses (merely grief and sorrow).

18.5.2   Assessing loss of dependency – the traditional method

The award for loss of dependency is ascertained by a multiplicand and multiplier system. The multiplicand is the net annual loss of the dependants; the multiplier is based on the number of years' loss of dependency (ie, the length of time that the claimant would have been dependent on the deceased).

18.5.2.1   The multiplicand – the net annual loss to the dependants

The deceased wage earner

The starting point is to calculate the amount of the deceased's earnings and deduct the estimated amount representing the sum that would have been spent by the deceased on his own personal and living expenses. The remaining balance will be the dependency multiplicand.

The deceased's net annual earnings must be calculated as at the date of the trial (*Cookson v Knowles* [1979] AC 556). No allowance is made for inflation (*Auty v National Coal Board* [1985] 1 All ER 930), but the deceased's future earning capacity (eg, as result of promotion) must be taken into account. For example, a trainee doctor may have been earning a relatively modest income at the date of death, but his earnings would clearly have increased substantially on qualifying and again on becoming a consultant. Evidence will be needed in support of this, and the best evidence may be from a comparative employee or employees who have gone, or who are going through, the same career structure as the deceased would have done. This evidence could be obtained, for example, from the deceased's trade union or employer.

Conversely, there may be evidence of likely loss of earning capacity, for example because of redundancy.

Calculating the dependency figure

There are two approaches that the courts have considered:

(a)   The 'old' system for calculating the dependency figure is to add up all the financial benefits received by the dependants from the deceased. It is necessary to produce a list of the items which contributed to the annual value of dependency and for the claimant to provide documentary evidence, bills, etc for the year prior to the death. A proportion is then deducted for the deceased's own expenses. For example, the following items have been considered: How much housekeeping money was paid to the wife? How much was spent on the deceased's food? How much was spent on the food for the rest of the family? Who paid how much for the children's shoes, etc? This type of calculation is very difficult and in practice is rarely attempted.

(b)   The customary modern practice, which was established in the case of *Harris v Empress Motors* [1983] 3 All ER 561, is to deduct a percentage from the net income figure to represent what the deceased would have spent exclusively on himself. Conventional percentages are adopted. Where the family unit was husband and wife, the usual figure is one-third. Where the family unit was husband, wife and children, the usual figure is one-quarter. However, it is important to note that each case must be judged on its own facts. The court is willing to depart from the conventional figures where there is evidence that they are inappropriate (*Owen v Martin* [1992] PIQR Q151), for example where the deceased was particularly frugal or a spendthrift. In such circumstances, less or more than the conventional figure should be deducted (see also *Coward v Comex Houlder Diving Ltd*, 18 July 1988, CA and *Dhaliwal v Personal Representatives of Hunt (Deceased)* [1995] PIQR Q56, CA).

Furthermore, it is quite possible that different multiplicands may have to be selected according to different times in the period of dependency. Had he lived, the deceased's financial affairs would not have remained constant throughout his life. Similarly, therefore, the multiplicand will not remain constant either. For example, in the case of a husband with wife and children, 75% of the husband's earnings may be the appropriate initial multiplicand while his children are likely to be dependent. However, from the point where the children can be expected to become independent the multiplicand may be merely two-thirds of the husband's earnings (see also *Coward v Comex Houlder Diving Ltd*, above).

Frequently, both husband and wife would have been earning at the time of death, and in such circumstances the approach adopted is to calculate the dependency as two-thirds or three-quarters (as the case may be) of the total joint net income, less the continuing earnings of the surviving spouse.

> **EXAMPLE**
>
> Mike and Susan both earn £50,000 pa net. They have no children. Mike dies in an accident at work. Two-thirds of their joint income is approximately £66,600 (£100,000 x 66%), but Susan's earnings of £50,000 must be deducted to calculate her dependency claim. Susan's annual loss of dependency is therefore £16,000.

Services rendered by the deceased

The deceased may have been contributing to the support of the family not only in terms of a percentage of his earnings, but also by rendering services to the family free of charge. Examples of such services include:

(a)   DIY jobs (eg, painting the house annually);

(b)   vegetable gardening (therefore saving on grocery bills);

(c)   nursing services to a sick member of the family;

(d)   contributions to childcare.

On the deceased's death, such free services will be lost. The family will have to pay for the services (eg, by employing a decorator) and thus incur a loss. The value of these services can add considerably to the multiplicand. Evidence must be obtained, for example by quotations from the appropriate source.

In *Beesley v New Century Group Ltd* [2008] EWHC 3033 (QB), the claimant's husband had died from malignant mesothelioma as a result of his employment with the defendant company. The court made an award of damages for loss of 'intangible benefits' in respect of the extra value to be attached to help such as domestic services provided by a husband. The court held that there were considerable advantages in having jobs around the house and garden done by a husband in his own time and at his own convenience, rather than having to employ a professional. Accordingly, it awarded the claimant £2,000. See also *Manning v King's College Hospital NHS Trust* [2008] EWHC 3008 (QB), in which similar sums were awarded to the husband and children of the deceased for the loss of personal attention of a wife and mother, 'in recognition that what is lost goes beyond the material'.

The deceased non-wage earner

Where the deceased was a wage earner, the valuation of the multiplicand in the dependency claim is predominantly based on a proportion of the deceased's earnings (see above). This is so whether the deceased was male or female (eg, whether husband, father, wife or mother). It is not uncommon, however, that the deceased was not in paid employment. In this case, the value of the services rendered to the family becomes the vital issue. For example, if the deceased was the wife and mother of the family, and was not a wage earner at the date of her death, the services rendered by her to the family might be quantified in the terms of employing a housekeeper to provide the same services. In *Regan v Williamson* [1976] 1 WLR 305, Watkins J said that in this context 'the word "services" [has] been too narrowly construed. It should at least include an acknowledgement that a wife and mother does not work to set hours, and, still less, to rule'. Accordingly, a value in excess of a housekeeper was awarded in that case. In *Mehmet v Perry* [1977] 2 All ER 529, the claimant widower, on the death of his wife, reasonably gave up his job in order to look after his young children. The starting point for the value of the services of the deceased wife was taken as the husband's loss of earnings.

Claims by parents, if children unmarried

A claim can be made by a parent (who is often unemployed or ill) who was dependent on the support from his unmarried child. When the court considers this type of case, it will have regard to the fact that the child may have married and the financial assistance provided by the child may have ceased.

18.5.2.2   The multiplier – the period of loss

Having calculated the multiplicand, the other side of the equation is to calculate the number of years' loss of dependency.

Commencement of period of loss

The starting point for the number of years' loss is the date of death (not the date of trial: *Graham v Dodds* [1983] 2 All ER 953; *White v ESAB Group (UK) Ltd* [2002] All ER (D) 02 (Jan) and *ATM v MS* (2002) *The Times*, 3 July). However, see the 7th edition of the Ogden Tables for further commentary on this point.

End of the period of loss

In the case of a deceased wage earner, prima facie the number of years' loss will extend to the end of the deceased's working life (ie, usually up to what would have been the deceased's retiring age). Direct evidence should be called on this point. It must be remembered that certain items of loss, such as the claim for the cost of DIY, may extend beyond retirement age, as the deceased would not necessarily have stopped doing DIY when he retired from work.

However, each case will turn upon its own facts, and the period of dependency may end before or after what would have been the normal date of the deceased's retirement. For example, where the deceased was a professional person, he might have been expected to work and support his dependants beyond normal retirement age. Equally, if the deceased would have enjoyed a pension, it may be argued that he would have continued to provide for his dependants beyond normal retirement age (although evidence would be needed to substantiate this: *Auty v National Coal Board* [1985] 1 All ER 930; see **Chapter 15**).

Conversely, the period of dependency may stop before what would have been the normally expected retirement age of the deceased. For example, if the deceased was already in a poor state of health, he may not have been expected to work until normal retirement age, and the financial support for the dependants would therefore have ended earlier. Similarly, if the dependant himself is in a poor state of health and has a short life-expectancy, the period of dependency will be shorter.

What if the dependant's shorter life expectancy has been caused by the negligence of the defendant? This was the case in *Haxton v Philips Electronics UK Ltd* [2014] All ER (D) 138 (Jan). The claimant had developed mesothelioma as a result of handling her husband's work clothes, which had become impregnated with asbestos fibres during his employment with the defendant. After her husband's death from mesothelioma, the claimant issued proceedings against the defendant seeking damages (i) as a dependant, and (ii) in her own right. The defendant admitted liability and damages were agreed, except in respect of her personal claim where she sought a sum to compensate her for the fact that her reduced life expectancy had resulted in a lower dependency claim. Although the claim failed at first instance, the Court of Appeal allowed the claimant's appeal and awarded her an additional £200,000.

Effect of likely divorce or remarriage

Where there is a claim by a widow as dependant, the likelihood that the marriage would have ended in divorce may be taken into account in assessing the period of dependency. In *Owen v Martin* [1992] PIQR Q151, the judge adopted a multiplier of 15, but the Court of Appeal reduced this to 11 on the basis that the widow's attitude towards her marriage vows, as shown by her personal history, led the court to believe that the marriage might not have lasted the whole of the natural life of the deceased. The court should take this approach only provided there is some evidence of likelihood of divorce (*Wheatley v Cunningham* [1992] PIQR Q100). See also *D and D v Donald* [2001] PIQR Q44, concerning an extra-marital affair. In *O'Loughlin v Cape Distribution Ltd* [2001] EWCA Civ 178, [2001] JPIL 191, the court confirmed that there was no prescribed method by which damages for loss of dependency had to be identified. The key factor was showing economic loss. However, the widow's prospects of remarriage or actual remarriage are to be ignored (FAA 1976, s 3(3)). Therefore, the period of the widow's dependency on her deceased husband is calculated without regard to the fact that she is or may be financially supported by a new husband.

Conversion of the period of loss to a multiplier

Once the number of years' loss of dependency has been ascertained, this is then converted to a multiplier using the Ogden Tables (see **Chapter 15**) .

18.5.2.3   The multiplication

Having established the appropriate multiplicand and the overall multiplier, one method of calculating the award for loss of dependency is as follows:

(a)   Pre-trial losses – calculate the actual number of years' loss from the date of death until the trial and apply to the multiplicand (or multiplicands).The resulting amount(s) will be treated as special damages and will attract interest.

(b)   Future losses – deduct the number of pre-trial years from the overall multiplier and apply the balance of the multiplier to the multiplicand (or multiplicands).

EXAMPLE

Tom Brown is killed in a road traffic accident. At the time of his death, Tom was 30 years old. Tom has left a widow, Lucy, aged 29, and twin boys, Mark and James, aged 9. Tom was a DIY enthusiast, and performed many decorating and maintenance tasks in the family home. The value of the services to the family was £750 per year. Prior to the accident, Tom was in good health and was expected to work until he was 65. His net annual earnings at trial have been calculated as £10,000. The case comes to trial three years after the accident.

A simplified schedule of loss for the above example is set out below:

Tom Brown's date of birth	January 1983
Date of accident/death	January 2013
Date of schedule/trial	January 2016

1. BEREAVEMENT DAMAGES   £12,980

2. FUNERAL EXPENSES   £1,390

3. PAST LOSSES FROM DATE OF DEATH TO DATE OF SCHEDULE/TRIAL

A. Past loss of earnings

Net pre-accident wage £10,000 pa

Reduction for deceased's own needs: 25% so multiplicand = £7,500

1 January 2013 to 1 January 2016 (3 years)   3 x £7,500 = £ 22,500

B. Other services to family (eg, gardening, housework, DIY)

3 × £750 = £2,250

TOTAL PAST LOSS OF DEPENDENCY   £24,750

4. FUTURE LOSSES

A. Future loss of dependency – earnings

Multiplicand = £7,500

Multiplier based on Tom Brown retiring at 65 = 19.84 (22.84 – 3 years elapsed since death)

£7,500 x 19.84 = **£148,800**

B. Future non-financial dependency – gardening, DIY etc

Multiplicand = £750

Multiplier of 26.60 (29.60 – 3 years elapsed since death)

£750 x 26.60 = **£19,950**

TOTAL FUTURE LOSS OF DEPENDENCY   £168,750

SUMMARY

Past (ie pre-trial) losses	£24,750
Future losses	£168,750
Bereavement damages	£12,980
Funeral expenses	£1,390
TOTAL	**£207,870**

In addition, interest is claimed on the pre-trial loss to the date of trial at half the short-term rate, and on bereavement damages and funeral expenses at the full short-term investment account rate.

The significant factors in the calculation are as follows:

(a)   The length of loss of earnings dependency is likely to be based on Tom's age of 30 and his retirement age of 65, that is a period of 35 years. This is likely to produce an overall multiplier of 22.84 using table 9 of the Ogden Tables (see **Appendix 5**).

(b)   There is a separate multiplicand based on the value of the services. The length of this dependency would be longer than the earnings dependency, on the assumption that Tom would have continued to provide these services throughout his lifetime Using table 1 of the Ogden Tables this produces a multiplier of 29.60.

(c)   In practice, the multipliers are likely to be further reduced to take account of contingencies other than mortality (see **Chapter 15** and **Appendix 5**).

(d)   Three years have elapsed from the date of death to the date of this schedule. These three years must be deducted from the overall multipliers which are calculated from the date of death (not the date of trial as in straightforward personal injury cases). Losses in this period are treated as special damages and will attract interest.

(e)   The calculation may be split into various sub-calculations to reflect, for example, that for the first nine years after the accident (but for his death) Tom would have been supporting a wife and children (therefore he might have been expected to spend one-quarter of his net earnings on his own maintenance), but for the remaining 26 years of his working life (after the children became independent) he would have been supporting only a wife (and therefore he might be expected to spend one-third of his net earnings on his own maintenance). Another reason for splitting the calculation may be to reflect any increased earnings because of promotion.

The above example is given merely to illustrate the general principles of quantifying a claim. It will be appreciated that, in practice, it will be rare that a person's working and family life can be predicted with such certainty, and other methods of calculating the loss of dependency (eg, nil discount tables issued by the Government's Actuary's Department) have been advocated.

It should also be remembered that different multipliers must be applied to items that would not have ceased at the age of 65. Detailed instructions need to be obtained from the client on this point. In practice, therefore, the facts of a particular case are usually such as to defy precise mathematical calculation. The assessment of dependency damages is a difficult matter, and the court has to anticipate what would have occurred in the future. To assist the court, as much evidence as possible should be obtained.

18.5.3 Apportionment of the dependency

Whenever there is more than one dependant under the FAA 1976, the court must apportion the damages between them. Where a claim is made by a surviving spouse and child, the court's approach is often to assess the claim for dependency of the widow alone, and then to apportion a small amount ('pocket money') to the child. This approach may be justified on the basis that:

(a)   the surviving spouse will be expected to provide for the child out of her damages;

(b)   compared to the surviving spouse, the period of dependency of the child will often be short (ending probably between the ages of 16 to 21 depending on whether the child is expected to go on to higher education); and

(c)   it avoids repeated applications to the court for the release of invested funds for the benefit of the child.

However, the court is keen to protect the child's interest, and this approach may not be followed in every case. For example, if the surviving spouse is a known spendthrift and cannot be trusted to provide for the child, the court may assess the claims of the surviving spouse and child separately (see *H and Another v S* [2002] EWCA Civ 792, [2003] QB 965, concerning the protection of any damages for child dependants).

Where the claim involves a minor dependant (or any other protected party), the court's approval of any settlement should be sought, as it will be necessary to satisfy the court that the child's interests are protected.

18.5.4 Bereavement

18.5.4.1 The claimants

The claim for bereavement is open only to a limited class (not just 'dependants' generally: see **18.5.1.1**). The possible claimants are:

(a)   the spouse or civil partner of the deceased; or

(b)   the parents of a legitimate unmarried deceased minor;

(c)   the mother of an illegitimate unmarried deceased minor.

It should be noted that a cohabitee is excluded from the definition, despite the fact that a cohabitee can pursue a dependency claim, as noted above. Furthermore, a child is not entitled to the award of bereavement on the death of his parent; and in a case where both parents can claim, the damages are divided equally between them (FAA 1976, s 1A(4)). However, in *Navaei v Navaei*, 6 January 1995, the mother was negligent, and this resulted in the death of her daughter. The father claimed all of the bereavement damages and stated that they should not be shared with the mother. He argued that if he were to be paid only half of the damages, the mother/tortfeasor would be benefiting contrary to public policy. The court held that in bringing a claim under the FAA 1976, a claimant is under a duty to act on behalf of all dependants and the father was allowed only half the damages.

In the case of *Griffiths and Others v British Coal Corporation* (QBD, 23 February 1998), it was held that the FAA 1976 did not require an apportionment of damages for bereavement where there were two causes of death (in this case, smoking and exposure to mine dust), and therefore the claimant recovered the full statutory sum.

The claim for the bereavement award by parents depends on the deceased being a minor at the date of death, not at the date of the accident (*Doleman v Deakin* (1990) *The Times*, 30 January).

18.5.4.2 The amount of the bereavement award

The award is a fixed amount of £12,980. Many people have criticised the level of award. In certain cases, especially those with a media interest, defendants have offered a figure higher than the statutory minimum, so as to avoid allegations by the press that they have undervalued a life. Once entitlement is established, defendants are often amenable to paying this part of the claim early by way of an interim payment.

18.5.5 Funeral expenses

Funeral expenses may be claimed if reasonable and paid by a dependant (FAA 1976, s 3(5)). The question of reasonableness will be a decision on the facts of each case. Reference should be made to previous case law in circumstances where the client puts forward an unusual claim, so as to determine whether the court will regard the claim as reasonable or otherwise.

If the funeral expenses are paid by the estate then they are claimed as part of a LR(MP)A 1934 claim (see **18.4.3**). Clearly, funeral expenses cannot be claimed under both the LR(MP)A 1934 and the FAA 1976.

18.5.6 Disregarding benefits

Section 4 of the FAA 1976 provides:

> In assessing damages in respect of a person's death in an action under this Act, benefits which have accrued or will or may accrue to any person from his estate or otherwise as a result of his death shall be disregarded.

For example, if a dependant receives insurance money as a result of the deceased's death, the dependant does not have to give credit for that money against the FAA 1976 damages. Similarly, if damages awarded to the estate under a LR(MP)A 1934 claim end up in the hands of a dependant by reason of the deceased's will or rules of intestacy, those damages do not necessarily reduce any FAA 1976 damages which may be awarded to that dependant.

See also *H and Another v S* [2002] EWCA Civ 792, [2003] QB 965, concerning support now being given by a surviving parent who was unlikely to have supported the children if the death had not occurred.

18.5.7 Recoupment and offsetting of benefits

Any payment made in consequence of a claim under the FAA 1976 is not subject to recoupment under the Social Security (Recovery of Benefits) Act 1997 (see **Chapter 16**).

18.6 INTEREST

Interest on the bereavement damages may be awarded at the full short-term investment rate (*Sharman v Sheppard* [1989] CLY 1190) from the date of death. Interest on funeral expenses is usually awarded at the full rate from the date that they were paid.

The remaining pecuniary losses to the date of the trial are treated as special damages in a fatal injury claim, and therefore are often awarded interest at half the short-term investment rate, although it is arguable that interest can be awarded at the full rate in certain circumstances (see **15.6**). Future pecuniary loss attracts no interest.

18.7 PENSION LOSS

Investigations should be made as to whether there will be a reduced pension fund available to the deceased's dependants due to the early death, and this should be included within the claim if appropriate (see also **15.3.6**). It is likely that an expert accountant will need to be instructed to assist in the calculation of such losses.

18.8 LOSS OF CONSORTIUM

In recent years, there has been a growing trend for separate awards under this head of damages, which is also sometimes referred to as 'loss of intangible benefits'.

It originated in a parent and child context in *Regan v Williamson* [1976] 1 WLR 305, where the sum awarded to the children for loss of services of a mother was increased to reflect the loss of the personal attention and affection which the mother provided and which could not be replaced by a housekeeper or nanny. In *Mehmet v Perry* [1977] 2 All ER 529, separate awards under this head were made to the children and also to the husband.

In *Beesley v New Century Group Ltd* [2008] EWHC 3033 (QB), the principle was extended to loss of a husband, on the basis that Mrs Beesley had lost not only the domestic services that her husband had provided but also the extra value that was derived from having such help provided by a husband and friend rather than an outside contractor.

The sums awarded tend to be fairly modest (between £2,000 and £4,000, depending on the circumstances), on the basis that there is some overlap between this head and bereavement damages (see **18.5.4**) and, in the more recent case of *Brown v Hamid* [2013] EWHC 4067 (QB), the judge declined to make a separate award for loss of consortium where the deceased had a limited life expectancy. Nevertheless, the principle of making awards for loss of intangible benefits is now well established, and consideration should always be given to including such a claim in a fatal case.

18.9 CONDUCT

To avoid conflicts of interest arising, it is good practice to ensure that none of the dependants who could be to blame in whole or part for the accident that resulted in the death are appointed as personal representatives.

The conduct of a fatal accident claim clearly requires sympathy and diplomacy on the part of the solicitor. There are frequently conflicts of personality between the dependants and personal representatives, and this is compounded by the fact that only one claim can be brought in respect of the fatal accident. If, after the fatal accident, it comes to light that the deceased had more than one dependent family, it can be anticipated that any interviews with the deceased's wife may be difficult!

18.10 CONCLUSION

Acting on behalf of the relatives in a fatal accident claim requires the personal injury/clinical negligence solicitor to have tact, sympathy and a detailed understanding of the law involved. It should be appreciated that each case will be dealt with on its own facts, and only broad principles have been established by the case law in this area. In fatal accident cases the court is required to anticipate what would have occurred in the future, which will be different in every case. An overview of damages which may be claimed in fatal cases is set out at **18.12** below.

18.11 FURTHER READING

Kemp and Kemp, *The Quantum of Damages* (Sweet & Maxwell)

18.12   OVERVIEW OF DAMAGES IN FATAL CLAIMS

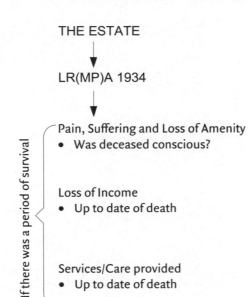

THE ESTATE

↓

LR(MP)A 1934

↓

If there was a period of survival

Pain, Suffering and Loss of Amenity
- Was deceased conscious?

Loss of Income
- Up to date of death

Services/Care provided
- Up to date of death

Damages to personal items
- Eg car, clothing, jewellery

Funeral expenses
- If not claimed under FAA

THE DEPENDANTS

↓

FAA 1976

↓

Bereavement
- £12,980
- Spouse/parent?

Dependency
- Who are the dependants?
- Nature of dependency, eg wages/diy/childcare?

Multiplicand
- Husband and wife ⅔
- Husband, wife and children ¾

Multiplier
- Assess at date of death
- Split between pre- and post-trial

Funeral expenses
- If not claimed under LR(MP)A

Loss of consortium/intangible benefits
- Loss of wife/mother/husband/father
- No set figure (£2,000 – £4,000 approx)

CRIMINAL INJURIES COMPENSATION AUTHORITY

LEARNING OUTCOMES

After reading this chapter you will be able to:

- set out the criteria for eligibility to make a claim under the Criminal Injuries Compensation Scheme 2013, and the relevant procedure
- explain how compensation is calculated
- explain when compensation may be withheld or reduced.

19.1 INTRODUCTION

Those who have suffered injury as a result of acts of violence may be unable to take civil proceedings to recover damages, because those responsible are either unknown or have insufficient means to pay compensation. However, blameless victims of crimes of violence in Great Britain who have suffered injuries and associated loss can apply for compensation from a government-funded scheme known as the Criminal injuries Compensation Scheme 2012 (the 'Scheme'), which is administered by the Criminal Injuries Compensation Authority (CICA). The Scheme is relevant for applications received on or after 27 November 2012.

The types of payment which may be available under the Scheme are:

(a) injury payments, which are calculated by reference to a tariff (see **19.4.1**);

(b) loss of earnings payments (see **19.4.2**);

(c) special expenses payments in respect of injury-related requirements which are not available free of charge from any other source (see **19.4.3**); and

(d) various payments relating to fatal injuries, which are beyond the scope of this book.

The maximum award payable in relation to one incident, before any reduction (see **19.5**), is £500,000, which may fall short of the actual losses suffered by the applicant. However, the Scheme is not designed to provide full financial recompense, but rather to provide some compensation, where there would not otherwise be any, out of the public purse and in recognition of public sympathy for the victim. It is for this reason that the victim must be 'blameless' (see **19.5** below).

The Scheme is both comprehensive and complex and consequently only the basics are dealt with here. For more information, you can find the Scheme, the 2008 Scheme (relevant for applications received prior to 27 November 2012), the application forms and the Guide to the 2012 Compensation Scheme (the 'Guide') on the CICA website at <www.cica.gov.uk>.

It should be noted that CICA will not cover the costs of making an application under the Scheme and therefore the client will need to fund the matter himself should he want a solicitor to deal with the application on his behalf. The client should be advised that free independent advice and help to make the application may be available from Victim Support, Citizens Advice, law centres or welfare rights organisations.

19.2   ELIGIBILITY

In order to be eligible for compensation under the Scheme, an applicant must show that he has sustained a criminal injury which is directly attributable to his being a direct victim of a crime of violence committed in a 'relevant place' (para 4). In the vast majority of cases, and for the purposes of this book, 'relevant place' means Great Britain (para 8), but it also covers, for example, British-controlled aircraft and Her Majesty's ships (see Annex C of the Schedule).

Compensation may also be paid to those who have sustained an injury while taking an exceptional and justified risk in order to remedy or prevent a crime (para 5), to those who have sustained a mental injury as a result of witnessing or being involved in the immediate aftermath of an incident in which a loved one is injured (para 6), or to a qualifying relative of a victim who died as a result of a crime of violence (para 7), but these matters are beyond the scope of this book.

19.2.1   What is a crime of violence?

There is no legal definition of what amounts to a 'crime of violence', but types of crimes of violence which may lead to a payment are set out in Annex B of the Scheme. The following are included, provided the perpetrator acts intentionally or recklessly:

(a)   a physical attack;

(b)   any other act or omission of a violent nature which causes physical injury to a person, eg withholding something that another person needs to stay alive;

(c)   a threat against a person, causing fear of immediate violence in circumstances which would cause a person of reasonable firmness to be put in such fear;

(d)   a sexual assault to which a person did not in fact consent; or

(e)   arson or fire-raising.

However, a crime of violence will not be considered to have been committed for the purposes of the Scheme if an injury:

(a)   resulted from suicide or attempted suicide, unless the suicidal person acted with intent to cause injury to another person;

(b)   resulted from the use of a vehicle, unless the vehicle was used with intent to cause injury to a person (see *Alexander Smith v Criminal Injuries Compensation Authority* (2015), where a man struck by a cyclist on a zebra crossing succeeded in his claim, as the cyclist had ridden his bicycle at him with the intent to injure him);

(c)   resulted from an animal attack, unless the animal was used with intent to cause injury to a person;

(d)   was sustained in the usual course of sporting or other activity to which a person consented by taking part in the activity; or

(e)   was sustained in *utero* as a result of harmful substances willingly ingested by the mother during pregnancy, with intent to cause, or being reckless as to, injury to the foetus.

19.2.2 Residency and nationality

The applicant must meet one of the following residency requirements (paras 10–13):

(a) ordinarily resident in the UK on the date of the incident;

(b) a British citizen;

(c) a close relative of a British citizen;

(d) a national of a Member State of the European Union (EU) or the European Economic Area (EEA);

(e) a family member of an EU/EEA national who has the right to be in the UK;

(f) a national of a State party to the Council of Europe Convention on the Compensation of Victims of Violent Crimes (CETS No 116, 1983);

(g) a member of Her Majesty's armed forces, or an accompanying close relative of an armed forces member;

(h) someone identified as a potential victim of human trafficking on or before the date of the application; or

(i) someone who made an application for asylum to remain in the UK on or before the date of the application for an award.

19.2.3 Matters which may prevent eligibility

It is not necessary for the assailant to have been convicted of an offence in connection with the injury (para 9), and in some cases, the applicant will not know the identity of the offender. However, the following matters will prevent eligibility being established (in relation to accidents happening after 1 October 1979 only):

(a) the applicant has already applied for compensation for the same criminal injury under this or any other Criminal Injuries Compensation Scheme (para 18);

(b) the applicant and the person who caused the injury were adults living together as members of the same family at the time and will continue to do so (para 20); or

(c) the person who injured the applicant could benefit from the award as a result of a continuing link between that person and the applicant (para 21).

19.2.4 Time limit

Applications should be made as soon as reasonably practicable and, where the applicant was 18 or over at the date of the incident causing the injury, it must be made within two years of the date of the incident (para 87).

Where the applicant was under 18 at the time of the incident, it is advisable that an application is made on his behalf as soon as possible, as it may be more difficult to provide the relevant evidence at a later stage. However, the following time limits apply:

(a) If the incident was reported to the police before the applicant turned 18, but no application was made on his behalf, the claim must be made before the applicant reaches 20.

(b) If the incident took place before the applicant reached 18 but was not reported at the time, an application may be made up to two years of the date when the incident was first reported to the police.

In both of the above instances, an application will not be accepted unless the claims officer is satisfied that the evidence presented in support of the application means that it can be determined without further extensive enquiries (para 88).

In relation to applicants of any age, in exceptional circumstances, ie where the circumstances of the injury meant that the application could not reasonably have been made within the time limit, CICA may extend the time limit provided it can make a decision without further extensive enquiries (para 89). It does not normally consider the applicant's lack of knowledge of the Scheme to be an 'exceptional reason'.

19.3   PROCEDURE

Applications must be made by filling in CICA's application form and submitting it online or by supplying the relevant details over the telephone. Initially, a regional casework team will handle the application but, once CICA has all the relevant evidence, a claims officer will be assigned to the claim and he will determine the matter on the balance of probabilities.

At all times, the applicant must comply with his obligations as set out in paras 91 and 92 of the Scheme. In other words, he must comply with any direction or condition imposed by the claims officer, assist the claims officer as far as reasonably practicable, and provide all information and evidence relevant to the application.

The onus is on the applicant to prove that he is eligible for a payment, and therefore evidence that the applicant meets the residency requirements and basic medical evidence of the injury suffered must be provided. The applicant must also provide signed consent for the release of all records relevant to the application to CICA. These might include:

(a)   evidence the applicant gave to the police about the incident. The applicant must supply the unique police reference number in the application form. CICA will obtain confirmation from the police that the incident was reported to them and that the applicant's behaviour was not a contributory factor;

(b)   criminal records;

(c)   medical records; and

(d)   where loss of earnings and/or special expenses payments are being claimed, information from the Department for Work and Pensions and/or HM Revenue and Customs.

CICA may require further medical evidence, in which case the applicant will be required to meet the costs of providing initial medical evidence up to maximum of £50. If further medical evidence is required, such as where injuries are complex, the application involves a claim for mental illness, or where there may be pre-existing conditions, the applicant will be required to see his existing doctor or an expert arranged by CICA, and the costs of will be met by CICA. If the applicant wishes to provide his own medical evidence, CICA will cover the cost only if it relies on the evidence to determine the claim.

19.4   COMPENSATION CALCULATION

Compensation is based on a tariff award for the injuries suffered and, where relevant, compensation for lost earnings and/or special expenses. The minimum award that may be made is £1,000 and the maximum award that may be made in respect of one application is £500,000, before any deductions (para 31).

Where injuries are not sufficiently serious to fall under the Scheme, the Hardship Fund introduced by the Government may provide some temporary assistance to very low-paid workers suffering financial hardship as a result of being unable to work due to being a victim of violent crime.

19.4.1   The injury payment (paras 32–41)

In order to determine whether compensation is payable for a certain injury and to calculate the amount due, the claims officer will consult the Tariff of Injuries set out in Annex E of the Scheme. This list sets out descriptions of approximately 400 different types of injuries and, in relation to each one, specifies both the level of seriousness – by means of a figure from 1 (being the least serious) to 20 – and the associated fixed amount of compensation. A Level 1 injury is valued at £1,000 and a Level 20 injury is valued at £250,000. Part A of the tariff shows the amount payable in respect of physical and mental injuries. (Part B, which shows the amount payable in respect of fatal injuries, and injuries resulting from sexual and physical abuse, is beyond the scope of this book.)

The following should be noted:

(a)   Compensation is not payable under the Scheme unless the injury appears in Appendix 3, although where an injury does not appear in the list, but is of an equivalent seriousness to an injury which does appear, CICA may refer the matter to the Secretary of State for consideration for inclusion.

(b)   Where an applicant is eligible for an injury payment in respect of an injury requiring an operation, no separate payment will be made in respect of scarring arising from that operation (para 35).

(c)   Where an applicant's injury includes the acceleration or exacerbation of an existing condition, the payment will only compensate for the degree of acceleration or exacerbation, will be calculated by reference to such tariff injuries as the claims officer considers appropriate, and will not be paid at all unless the relevant payment is £1,000 or more (para 36).

In order to calculate the total tariff award where there are two or more injuries, the three most serious injuries must be identified and the associated tariffs added together as follows:

(a)   100% of the tariff for the highest rated injury; plus

(b)   30% of the tariff for the second highest injury; plus, where relevant

(c)   15% of the tariff for the third highest injury.

No compensation is payable in respect of any additional injuries (para 37).

19.4.2   Compensation for lost earnings (paras 42–49)

Where an applicant is entitled to a tariff payment and has been unable to work or may be prevented from working in the future as a direct result of the injury, he may also be entitled to be compensated for lost earnings provided he satisfies the following conditions (para 43):

(a)   He must be unable to do any paid work or have a very limited capacity to do such work, ie he can work only a few hours of paid work per week. Where the applicant has capacity to do paid work, but the type of work he is able to do is limited as a result of his injuries, a loss of earnings payment will not be made.

(b)   He must be able to demonstrate that he was in work at the time of the accident, or show that he had either an established work history, or a good reason for not having such a work history, for the three years immediately prior to the accident. A good reason may be that he was in full time education, or that he was unable to work due to his age or caring responsibilities.

Payments for loss of earnings are made at a fixed weekly rate, which is the rate of Statutory Sick Pay (SSP) in force at the date when a decision is made regarding the application (currently £88.45). No such compensation is payable for the first 28 weeks following the date of the accident, and therefore the period to which a loss of earnings payment will relate begins on the first day of the 29th week (para 44).

A loss of earnings payment may relate to earnings lost before an application is determined (past loss of earnings) and any losses which may continue after the determination (future loss of earnings).

A loss of earnings payment in respect of past loss of earnings will be calculated by multiplying the weekly rate of SSP at the date of determination by the number of weeks from the beginning of week 29, treating part weeks as full weeks, and ending on the day the application is determined (para 47).

Payment for future loss of earnings will be calculated by:

(a)   multiplying the weekly rate of SSP at the date of determination by the number of weeks of the period of entitlement. That period begins on the day after the date on which the application is determined and ends when the applicant is no longer incapable of working, or he reaches retirement age or, where the criminal injury has resulted in a life expectancy below the state pension age, the expected end of the applicant's life (para 48);

(b)   discounting the payment so calculated in accordance with the Tables in Annex F, which set out:

(i)   multipliers to be applied to account for the accelerated receipt of payments, which are found by reference to the number of years of future loss (Table A);

(ii)   discount factors to be applied to a lump sum in respect of loss which starts at a future date, which are also found by reference to the number of years of future loss (Table B); and

(iii)   assumptions in relation to life expectancy, which are calculated by reference to the applicant's age at the date of determination (or death in the case of fatality) (Table C).

19.4.3   Compensation for special expenses (paras 50–56)

Compensation may be paid for special expenses incurred as a result of the injury from the date of the injury, but only where the applicant is eligible for an injury payment and has lost earnings or earnings capacity for longer than 28 weeks.

A special expenses payment will only be made in relation to expenses of the types listed in para 52, such as the applicant's own property or equipment used as a physical aid which was damaged in the incident, NHS prescriptions and dentists or optician's charges, special equipment such as wheelchairs or specially-adapted vehicles, the costs of adaptations to the applicant's home, and costs arising from the administration of the applicant's affairs due to his lack of mental capacity, provided the following conditions apply (para 51):

(a)   they were/will be necessarily incurred by the applicant on or after the date of the injury as a direct result of the criminal injury giving rise to the injury payment;

(b)   provision, or similar provision, is not available free of charge from another source; and

(c)   the cost is reasonable.

Where the need for special equipment is likely to continue, a claims officer will:

(a)   assess the cost of replacement, taking into account the number of likely replacements;

(b)   deduct the amount for which the applicant's existing equipment could be sold on each occasion; and

(c)   apply an appropriate discount factor in accordance with Table B of Annex F to take account of the fact that a lump sum will be paid in respect of loss which will arise in the future.

Where the need for any other special expenses of a type specified in para 52 is likely to continue, a claims officer will assess the annual cost of the expense and apply the relevant Tables in Annex F (para 53).

A special expenses payment may be withheld or reduced to take account of the receipt of, or entitlement to, social security benefits or insurance payments (paras 54–56), the details of which are beyond the scope of this book.

19.5   WITHHOLDING OR REDUCTION OF AWARD

The Scheme is funded by the Government on the basis that the public are sympathetic to innocent victims of crime and wish to see them supported. Consequently, compensation may be refused or discounted in respect of applications by those who may be seen as morally undeserving of support. In addition, the Scheme must be protected from fraudulent claims and applicants should not be permitted to be over-compensated.

Compensation may be withheld or reduced in the following circumstances:

(a)   where the applicant has failed to report the incident to the police, or has thereafter failed to co-operate with the police or with the CICA (paras 22–24). Generally, the applicant must make a formal report to the police immediately following the incident, and this must be done by the applicant in person, unless his injuries prevent him from doing so. Co-operation with the police includes making a statement, attending identity procedures and giving evidence in court, if required. Co-operation with the CICA includes supplying complete and truthful information, and attending independent medical examinations, if required;

(b)   where the applicant behaved inappropriately either before, or during or after the incident (para 25). This will include where the applicant's consumption of alcohol or illegal drugs caused him to act aggressively or to provoke the attack, where he voluntarily took part in a fight, where he threw the first punch, or where his use of abusive language or gestures led to the incident. However, this does not include where intoxication through alcohol or drugs made the applicant more vulnerable to becoming a victim of a crime of violence. So an applicant who was sexually assaulted whilst intoxicated may still be eligible to receive a full award;

(c)   where the applicant has unspent criminal convictions (para 26). Annex D sets out how CICA will determine what effect an unspent criminal conviction will have in respect of the withdrawal or reduction of an award. However, in general terms, an unspent conviction which attracted a custodial or community sentence will result in the withdrawal of the award, whilst a lesser sentence (other than endorsements, penalty points or fines resulting from motoring offences) will result in a reduction in the amount of the award;

(d)   where the applicant's character, other than in relation to an unspent conviction, makes it appropriate (para 27). CICA will consider evidence relating to involvement with illegal drugs or other crimes, tax evasion or benefit fraud, anti-social behaviour orders and cautions or reprimands;

(e)   where the applicant receives or is awarded criminal injuries compensation or a similar payment, receives an order for damages from a civil court, agrees the settlement of a damages claim, or receives a compensation order or offer made during criminal proceedings (para 85); or

(f)   in relation to payments for special expenses only, where the applicant has received State benefits or insurance payments in respect of the injury (paras 54–56 – see **19.4.3**).

19.6   EXAMPLE

Last year, Jacob was attacked in Birmingham city centre as he made his way home from work. He was punched to the ground and kicked repeatedly by assailants who have not been identified. He suffered a depressed fracture of the skull, for which he required surgery, his jaw was dislocated and a front tooth was knocked out. The tooth has been replaced, but his other injuries are continuing to cause him significant difficulties. In addition, he has completely lost his sense of smell. Jacob was unable to work for 40 weeks, but he has now returned to his previous job as a shop assistant. His salary throughout the period when he was unable to work would have been £250 per week, but Jacob received only statutory sick pay of £88.45 per week during this period.

Tariff for injuries: depressed fracture of skull requiring operation = £4,600 (Level A6); dislocated jaw causing continuing significant disability = £3,500 (Level A5); loss of one front tooth = £1,500 (Level A2); total loss of smell = £11,000 (Level A8). Only the three most serious injuries may be considered.

Calculation: 100% of £11,000 (loss of smell) = £11,000; 30% of £4,600 (fractured skull) = £1,380; 15% of £3,500 (dislocated jaw) = £525.

Total for injury = £12,905.

Lost salary: Nothing for first 28 weeks. Thereafter, 12 weeks at the SSP rate of £86.70 per week = £1,040.40. The SSP he has already received is not deductible.

Total payment: £12,905 + £1,040.40 = £13,945.40.

19.7 CONCLUSION

Generally, those who have suffered injury as a result of an act of violence are unable to take civil proceedings against the perpetrator as their attacker is unlikely to have the financial means to pay damages. Where such a situation exists, and it is not possible to hold another individual or body, such as an employer, responsible for the perpetrator's actions, the Criminal Injuries Compensation Scheme may provide compensation to the victim.

As the costs associated with making an application are not recoverable by the applicant, the solicitor should advise him that free assistance may be available elsewhere. However, if the client instructs the solicitor to make the application on his behalf, the solicitor should ensure that he falls within the criteria set out in the Scheme rules and that the procedure for making a claim is followed correctly.

Compensation for injuries suffered is based on a tariff which sets out a comprehensive list of injuries of varying seriousness. Where such an award is made and the victim is unable to work for more than 28 weeks, past and future loss of earnings from the 29th week may also be awarded, as may items of special expense. The total claim cannot exceed £500,000.

Awards may be withheld or reduced as a result of the applicant's conduct before, during or after the incident.

19.8 FURTHER READING AND RELEVANT WEBSITES

Criminal Injuries Compensation Scheme 2012 and A Guide to the Criminal Injuries Compensation Scheme 2012 (Criminal Injuries Compensation Authority)

<www.justice.gov.uk/guidance/compensation-schemes/cica/index.htm>

CHAPTER 20

CLAIMS ON BEHALF OF CHILDREN AND PROTECTED PARTIES

LEARNING OUTCOMES

After reading this chapter you will be able to:

- identify a child and a protected party

- understand who might act as a litigation friend, what their duties are, how they are appointed and when their appointment ceases

- appreciate the court's role in sanctioning settlements involving children and protected parties

- set out how the money recovered on behalf of a child or protected party will be dealt with.

20.1 INTRODUCTION

The Civil Procedure Rules (CPR), Part 21 and PD 21 set out special provisions relating to proceedings brought or defended by children and protected parties, ie those who lack the mental capacity to conduct proceedings on their own behalf. Many of these provisions apply equally to children and protected parties, for example:

(a) proceedings will usually be conducted on behalf of the child or protected party by a litigation friend (see **20.3**);

(b) the court must approve any settlement of a claim made on behalf of a child or protected party (see **20.4**); and

(c) the court will direct how damages recovered on behalf of a child or protected party will be dealt with (see **20.5**).

20.1.1 Who is a child/protected party?

A child is a person who is not yet 18 years old.

A protected party is a person who lacks capacity, within the meaning of the Mental Capacity Act 2005, to conduct proceedings. In accordance with s 2 of the 2005 Act, a person lacks capacity in relation to a matter if at the material time he is unable to make a decision for himself in relation to the matter because of an impairment of, or a disturbance in the functioning of, the mind or brain. It is irrelevant whether the impairment or disturbance is permanent or temporary and a person's age or appearance, or his condition or an aspect of his behaviour, which might lead others to make unjustified assumptions about his capacity, are not of themselves sufficient to establish incapacity.

The principles to be applied when dealing with questions of capacity are set out in s 1 of the 2005 Act as follows:

> (2)   A person must be assumed to have capacity unless it is established that he lacks capacity.
>
> (3)   A person is not to be treated as unable to make a decision unless all practicable steps to help him to do so have been taken without success.
>
> (4)   A person is not to be treated as unable to make a decision merely because he makes an unwise decision.
>
> (5)   An act done, or decision made, under this Act for or on behalf of a person who lacks capacity must be done, or made, in his best interests.
>
> (6)   Before the act is done, or the decision is made, regard must be had to whether the purpose for which it is needed can be as effectively achieved in a way that is less restrictive of the person's rights and freedom of action.

The case of *Dunhill (a protected party by her litigation friend Paul Tasker) v Burgin* [2014] UKSC 18 illustrates how important it is for practitioners to consider whether a party to the proceedings might lack capacity to deal with them. The claimant was an adult woman who had been injured as a result of a road traffic accident, and the modest claim bought on her behalf was settled in the sum of £12,500. Although it was known that she had suffered brain damage, it appears that none of the legal advisers gave any thought as to whether or not she had the capacity to deal with the litigation. Consequently, a litigation friend was not appointed and the court was not asked to approve the settlement. Several years later (when it was realised that a more realistic valuation of the claim might exceed £2,000,000), the Court of Appeal determined that an application made on the claimant's behalf to set aside the settlement, on the grounds of her lack of capacity to manage her affairs at that time and the absence of court approval, should succeed. This decision was subsequently upheld by the Supreme Court.

20.2 LIMITATION

Under s 28(6) of the Limitation Act 1980, where a person under a disability (ie a child or an individual lacking mental capacity) has a cause of action, the three-year limitation period does not start to run until he ceases to be under a disability.

For a child who is not also a protected party, this is when he reaches his 18th birthday, which means that he has until his 21st birthday to commence proceedings.

For a protected party, provided he was incapacitated at the time when the cause of action accrued, disability ceases if and when he regains mental capacity. Where mental incapacity arises after the limitation period has commenced, it will not prevent time from continuing to run. However, an application may be made under s 33 of the LA 1980 to disapply the limitation period (see **7.8**).

20.3 THE LITIGATION FRIEND

A protected party may not conduct proceedings without a litigation friend, and a child must have a litigation friend unless the court orders otherwise (CPR, r 21.2). The court will make an order permitting a child to conduct litigation without a litigation friend only where it is satisfied that the child has sufficient maturity and understanding to deal with the proceedings (*Gillick v West Norfolk & Wisbech Area Health Authority* [1985] UKHL 7).

20.3.1 Who may be the litigation friend?

In accordance with CPR, r 21.4, the following individuals may be a litigation friend:

(a)   in the case of a protected party, a deputy appointed by the Court of Protection under the Mental Capacity Act 2005 with power to conduct proceedings on the protected party's behalf;

(b)   in all other cases, someone who:

    (i)   can fairly and competently conduct proceedings on behalf of the child or protected party,

    (ii)   has no interests adverse to that of the child or protected party (eg, if a child is injured in a road traffic accident while a passenger in a car being driven by his father, the mother should act as litigation friend as the father may become a defendant in the proceedings), and

    (iii)   where the child or protected party is a claimant, undertakes to pay any costs which the child or protected party may be ordered to pay in relation to the proceedings, subject to any right he may have to be repaid from the assets of the child or protected party.

This is the case whether the litigation friend is appointed without a court order or with a court order (see CPR, r 21.6(5)).

In circumstances where there is no one suitable and willing to act as the litigation friend, the Official Solicitor will so act subject to his costs being covered.

20.3.2   How is a litigation friend appointed?

A court order will be required where a party to the proceedings other than the child or protected party applies for a litigation friend to be appointed, or where a new litigation friend is to be substituted for an existing one.

In other cases, a person who wishes to be appointed must follow the procedure set out in CPR, r 21.5:

(a)   A deputy appointed by the Court of Protection with power to conduct proceedings on a protected party's behalf must file an official copy of the order of the Court of Protection which confers his power to act.

(b)   Any other person must file a certificate of suitability stating he satisfies the conditions specified in r 21.4(3).

This must be done at the time the claim is made if he acts for a claimant, and at the time he first takes a step in the proceedings if he acts for a defendant.

Practice Direction 21, para 2.2 requires the certificate of suitability to be set out in Form N235. The person seeking appointment must state:

(a)   that he consents to act;

(b)   that he knows or believes that the claimant/defendant is a child/lacks capacity to conduct the proceedings;

(c)   in the case of a protected party, the grounds of his belief and, if his belief is based upon medical opinion or the opinion of another suitably qualified expert, attach any relevant document to the certificate;

(d)   that he can fairly and competently conduct proceedings on behalf of the child or protected party and has no interest adverse to that of the child or protected party; and

(e)   where the child or protected party is a claimant, that he undertakes to pay any costs which the child or protected party may be ordered to pay in relation to the proceedings, subject to any right he may have to be repaid from the assets of the child or protected party.

The certificate of suitability must be verified by a statement of truth.

20.3.3 When does the litigation friend's appointment cease

In accordance with CPR, r 21.9, when a child who is not a protected party reaches the age of 18, the litigation friend's appointment ceases. Where a protected party regains capacity to deal with the proceedings himself, the litigation friend's appointment continues until it is ended by court order.

Within 28 days after the cessation of the appointment, the child or protected party must serve on other parties and file at court a notice stating that the appointment of his litigation friend has ceased, giving his address for service, and stating whether or not he intends to carry on the proceedings. If he fails to do so, on application, the court may strike out his claim or defence.

Where litigation is continuing, the title of the proceedings should be amended in order to reflect the change in the claimant's circumstances, eg 'A B (formerly a child but now of full age)'.

20.4 COURT'S APPROVAL OF SETTLEMENTS

Where a claim involves a child or a protected party, under CPR, r 21.10 no settlement, compromise or payment (including any voluntary interim payment) and no acceptance of money paid into court shall be valid without the court's approval. This approval is necessary to ensure that the claim is not settled for less than it is worth and that the award is invested appropriately or, where there are future pecuniary losses, periodical payments are considered. Moreover, if such approval to a settlement is not obtained, a child claimant upon reaching 18, or a protected party upon regaining capacity, may issue proceedings against the defendant or, alternatively, issue proceedings against the litigation friend for negligently dealing with his claim.

If an agreement is made between the parties prior to proceedings being issued and the sole purpose of issuing proceedings is to obtain the court's approval, the solicitor must follow the procedure set out in Part 8 of the CPR, and a specific request must be included with the claim form for approval of the settlement. In addition, a draft consent order must be provided to the court using Practice Form N292.

20.4.1 The approval hearing

The aim of the hearing is to ensure that the settlement agreed is a reasonable one and is in the best interests of the child or protected party. The documents which the court will expect to be provided at the hearing will vary, depending on whether the application is made pre- or post-issue, and on the individual facts of the case, but will include some or all of the following:

(a)   the birth certificate of the child or protected party;

(b)   where proceedings have been commenced, the statements of case and other documents already on the court file;

(c)   evidence on liability (information as to whether liability is in dispute or the extent to which the defendant admits liability) and documents such as the PAR, inquest report and details of any prosecutions brought;

(d)   an up-to-date calculation of past and future losses (with supporting documentation);

(e)   up-to-date medical and quantum reports;

(f)   the litigation friend's certificate of suitability;

(g)   the litigation friend's approval of the settlement;

(h)   an interest calculation to date;

(i)   Court Funds Office Form 320 (request for investment);

(j)   a copy of an opinion on the merits of the agreed settlement given by counsel or a solicitor acting for the child or protected party;

(k)   a draft consent order.

20.5 CONTROL OF MONEY RECOVERED BY OR ON BEHALF OF A CHILD OR PROTECTED PARTY

The court will make directions as to how money recovered by or on behalf of a child or protected party should be dealt with, which may include (PD 21, para 8.1) that:

(a)   the money be paid into court for investment;

(b)   certain sums be paid direct to the child or protected beneficiary, his litigation friend or his legal representative for the immediate benefit of the child or protected beneficiary or for expenses incurred on his behalf; and

(c)   the application in respect of the investment of the money be transferred to a local district registry.

20.5.1 Children

Where the case has been concluded by settlement, the court will forward to the Court Funds Office a request for investment decision and the Public Trustee's investment managers will make the appropriate investment.

Where the matter has been concluded at trial, unless the amount is small (in which case it will be paid to the litigation friend to be placed in a building society account or similar for the benefit of the child), the court will direct that the money be paid into court and placed into the special investment account until further investment directions can be given by the court.

The court may appoint the Official Solicitor to be a guardian of the child's estate. Those with parental responsibility must agree, unless the court decides that their agreement can be dispensed with.

When the child reaches 18, any money invested in court must be paid out to him.

20.5.2 Protected parties

Before directions are made in a case involving a protected party, the court must determine whether the protected party is a protected beneficiary, ie he lacks the capacity to manage and control the money he has received. Where he is judged to be a protected beneficiary, the Court of Protection has jurisdiction to make decisions about how to deal with money recovered in his best interests. The Court of Protection is entitled to make charges for the administration of funds, and provision must be made for such charges in any settlement reached (PD 21, para 10.1).

Where the sum to be administered on behalf of the protected beneficiary is less than £30,000, it may be retained in court and invested on his behalf. If it is £30,000 or more, unless the person with authority as an attorney under a registered enduring power of attorney, the donee of a lasting power of attorney, or the deputy appointed by the Court of Protection has been appointed to administer or manage the protected beneficiary's financial affairs, the court will direct the litigation friend to apply to the Court of Protection for the appointment of a deputy, after which the fund will be dealt with as directed by the Court of Protection (PD 21, para 10.2).

20.6 CONCLUSION

This chapter merely outlines the most important issues which need to be considered when dealing with a claim involving a child or a protected party. It does not include everything that must be considered, for example the issue of the costs which may be recovered by the claimant's solicitor in these matters. The court always requires solicitors to deal with personal injury and clinical negligence claims competently and professionally, but it will be less tolerant of inadequacies in the services provided when dealing with claims involving children and protected parties. It is therefore incumbent on solicitors to ensure that they are familiar with the relevant issues and the court rules which govern them.

CHAPTER 21

THE PRE-ACTION PROTOCOLS FOR LOW VALUE RTA, EL AND PL CLAIMS

LEARNING OUTCOMES

After reading this chapter you will be able to:

- appreciate when the RTA or EL/PL Protocol for low value claims applies
- understand how to commence a claim through the Claims Portal
- describe the further stages that a claim may go through once commenced
- identify the fixed costs that may be claimed at the end of each stage
- understand how to make an offer to settle under the RTA or EL/PL Protocols
- understand what happens to a case which exits the Portal.

21.1 INTRODUCTION

On 31 July 2013, two new Pre-Action Protocols for Low Value Personal Injury Claims in Road Traffic Accidents (the 'RTA Protocol') and Employers' Liability and Public Liability Claims (the 'EL/PL Protocol') came into force, extending the previous Protocol which had been in force for RTAs from £10,000 to £25,000 and introducing a new procedure for EL or PL claims valued at up to £25,000. Further changes to the RTA Protocol came into force on 6 April 2015, implementing the Government's reform of low value whiplash claims. Solicitors who are instructed to act in RTA, EL or PL cases need to understand how to run these so called 'Portal' claims and so must be familiar with the Protocols, Practice Direction 8B, and the accompanying regime of fixed costs which are outlined in this chapter.

21.2 APPLICATION OF THE PROTOCOLS

21.2.1 When will the RTA Protocol apply?

Paragraph 4.1 of the RTA Protocol states that it will apply where:

(a)   a claim for damages arises from a road traffic accident where the Claim Notification Form (CNF) is submitted on or after 31 July 2013;

(b)   the claim includes damages in respect of personal injury;

(c)   the claimant values the claim at no more than the 'Protocol Upper Limit' (see below); and

(d)   if proceedings were started, the small claims track would not be the normal track for that claim.

The 'Protocol Upper Limit' is defined in para 1.2 as:

(a)   £25,000 where the accident occurred on or after 31 July 2013; or

(b)   £10,000 where the accident occurred on or after 30 April 2010 and before 31 July 2013.

The value is on a full liability basis including pecuniary losses but excluding interest. Paragraph 4.3 states that a claim may include vehicle related damages, but these are excluded for the purposes of valuing the claim.

'Vehicle related damages' are defined as damages for the pre-accident value of the car, vehicle repair, insurance excess and vehicle hire (para 1.1(18)). 'Pecuniary losses' are defined as past and future expenses and losses (para 1.1(14)).

Paragraph 4.5 sets out a number of claims to which the RTA Protocol will not apply, including:

(a)   claims made to the MIB under the Untraced Drivers Agreement 2003; and

(b)   where the claimant or defendant acts as the personal representative of a deceased person or is a protected party.

21.2.2   When will the EL/PL Protocol apply?

Paragraph 4.1 of the EL/PL Protocol states that it applies where:

(a)   either:

   (i)   the claim arises from an accident occurring on or after 31 July 2013; or

   (ii)   in a disease claim, no letter of claim has been sent to the defendant before 31 July 2013;

(b)   the claim includes damages in respect of personal injury;

(c)   the claimant values the claim at not more than £25,000 on a full liability basis including pecuniary losses but excluding interest ('the upper limit'); and

(d)   if proceedings were started, the small claims track would not be the normal track for that claim.

Paragraph 4.3 sets out claims to which the EL/PL Protocol will not apply, most notably:

(a)   claims where the claimant or defendant is the personal representative of a deceased person or a protected party;

(b)   claims arising out of the harm, abuse or neglect of a child/protected party;

(c)   mesothelioma claims; and

(d)   disease claims where there is more than one employer defendant.

21.3   THE THREE STAGES

Both the RTA and the EL/PL Protocols set out a three-stage process. Stages 1 and 2 are pre-litigation. The court becomes involved only at Stage 3. A summary of each stage is set out below. From 6 April 2015, where a claim is brought under the RTA Protocol for a soft tissue injury, there are additional requirements to follow, primarily in relation to obtaining medical evidence (see **21.4**).

21.3.1   Stage 1

(a)   To begin the process, the claimant must complete and send the Claim Notification Form (CNF) to the defendant's insurer. It must be sent electronically via www.claimsportal.org.uk. From 1 June 2015, para 6.3A of the RTA Protocol requires a claimant's legal representative to undertake a search of askCUE PI and to enter the unique reference number generated by that search in the 'additional information' box in the CNF (see **1.4**).

(b) At the same time, the Defendant Only CNF must be sent to the defendant by first class post. This is the only exception to para 5.1 of both Protocols, which provides that all information required by the Protocols must be sent electronically.

There are further detailed provisions to follow in para 6.1 of the EL/PL Protocol where the identity of the insurer is not known or there is no insurance. It is sometimes difficult to establish the identity of insurers in EL/PL claims (due to the passage of time that sometimes elapses before claims are brought), but para 6.1(3) states that the claimant must make a reasonable attempt to identify the insurer and, in an EL claim, must carry out a database search through the Employers' Liability Tracing Office.

(c) The insurer must send to the claimant an electronic acknowledgement the day after receipt of the CNF.

(d) The insurer must complete the 'Insurer Response' section of the CNF and send it to the claimant within:

    (i)   15 days for an RTA claim;

    (ii)   30 days for an EL claim;

    (iii)   40 days for a PL claim.

(e) If the insurer admits liability, the insurer must pay the Stage 1 fixed costs (see below) within 10 days of receiving the Stage 2 settlement pack (see Stage 2 below).

(f) If the insurer does not respond, denies liability, alleges contributory negligence (other than failure to wear a seatbelt in an RTA case) or asserts that the information in the CNF is inadequate, then the claim exits the Protocol and the claimant may continue the claim under the existing procedure.

(g) Both Protocols provide that, before the end of Stage 1, the insurer must apply to the CRU for a certificate of recoverable benefits.

21.3.2 Stage 2

Liability having been admitted, the process now turns to valuation of the claim and settlement.

(a) In an EL claim, the defendant must within 20 days of the admission of liability provide earnings details to verify the claimant's loss of earnings. Under both Protocols, the claimant now obtains a medical report. There is no time limit for doing this.

(b) When ready to value the claim, the claimant sends the Stage 2 settlement pack to the insurer. This includes:

    (i)   the medical report(s);

    (ii)   any medical records or photographs served with medical reports;

    (iii)   evidence of all special damages claimed;

    (iv)   receipts for disbursements (eg the cost of the medical report);

    (v)   any witness statements; and

    (vi)   an offer of settlement.

Non-medical reports are not expected to be required as part of the Stage 2 pack, but may be obtained where reasonably required to value the claim. In most cases, witness statements, whether from the claimant or otherwise, will not be required as part of the Stage 2 pack, but they may be provided where reasonably required to value the claim.

(c) The insurer must respond within 15 days by accepting the offer or making a counter-offer (the 'initial consideration period').

(d) If the claim is not settled, there follows a 20-day negotiation period (the 'negotiation period').

(e)   Both the initial period and the negotiation period may be extended by agreement.

(f)   An offer to settle by either party will automatically include an agreement to pay Stage 2 fixed costs and disbursements. In some cases, additional advice may be obtained from counsel or a specialist lawyer to assist in valuing any claim over £10,000, recoverable as a disbursement, but this should not be the norm.

(g)   If the insurer does not respond to the Stage 2 settlement pack, the claim exits the RTA or the EL/PL Protocol.

(h)   If the insurer responds but the claim is not settled, the claimant's solicitor prepares a court proceedings pack (CPP) and sends it to the insurer or its nominated solicitor to check for accuracy. The pack includes both parties' comments on disputed heads of damage and both parties' final offers. The insurer has five days to check the pack.

(i)   In addition, except where the claimant is a child, the insurer must pay to the claimant its final offer of damages (net of any CRU benefits and interim payments already made) plus Stage 1 and 2 fixed costs and disbursements within 15 days of receiving the CPP.

21.3.3   Stage 3

(a)   The claimant issues proceedings under CPR, Part 8 in accordance with Practice Direction 8B.

(b)   The defendant must acknowledge service within 14 days.

(c)   It is assumed that the final assessment of damages will be a paper exercise which neither party will attend. However, either party may request an oral hearing.

(d)   The court will notify both parties of the date when a district judge will assess damages.

21.4   SOFT TISSUE INJURY CLAIMS UNDER THE RTA PROTOCOL

21.4.1   Definition of 'soft tissue injury claim'

Paragraph 16A of the RTA Protocol defines a soft tissue injury as:

> a claim brought by an occupant of a motor vehicle where the significant physical injury caused is a soft tissue injury and includes claims where there is a minor psychological injury secondary in significance to the physical injury.

Where such a claim is brought, the RTA Protocol sets out additional requirements, the aim of which (according to para 3.2) is to ensure that:

(a)   the use and cost of medical reports is controlled;

(b)   in most cases only one medical report is obtained;

(c)   the medical expert is normally independent of any medical treatment; and

(d)   offers are made only after a fixed cost medical report has been obtained and disclosed.

21.4.2   Defendant's account of the accident

Although, in most cases where liability is admitted, the defendant's account of an accident will not be relevant, para 6.19A of the RTA Protocol provides that '... in limited cases where it is considered appropriate, the defendant may send their account to the claimant electronically at the same time as the CNF response'.

This will no doubt be of most relevance in so-called 'low velocity' crashes, where the severity of the injuries suffered by the claimant is disputed, and will be used to ask the medical expert to comment on the diagnosis and prognosis based on the defendant's alternative version of events.

21.4.3   Medical reports in soft tissue injury claims

The Protocol provides for fixed cost medical reports, which are defined at para 1.1(10A) as:

> ... a report in a soft tissue injury claim which is from a medical expert who, save in exceptional circumstances –

(a)   has not provided treatment to the claimant;

(b)   is not associated with any person who has provided treatment; and

(c)   does not propose or recommend treatment that they or an associate then provide.

It sets out details of a new system for obtaining such reports through an IT Hub known as 'MedCo', which will allocate an independent accredited expert. The relevant provisions in the Protocol are:

7.8A   In addition to paragraphs 7.1 to 7.7, and subject to paragraph 7.8B, in a soft tissue injury claim –

(1)   the first report must be a fixed cost medical report from an accredited medical expert selected for the claim via the MedCo Portal (website at: www.medco.org.uk); and

(2)   where the defendant provides a different account under paragraph 6.19A, the claimant must provide this as part of the instructions to the medical expert for the sole purpose of asking the expert to comment on the impact, if any, on diagnosis and prognosis if –

(a)   the claimant's account is found to be true; or

(b)   the defendant's account is found to be true.

7.8B   In a soft tissue injury claim –

(1)   it is expected that only one medical report will be required;

(2)   a further medical report, whether from the first expert instructed or from an expert in another discipline, will only be justified where –

(a)   it is recommended in the first expert's report; and

(b)   that report has first been disclosed to the defendant; and

(3)   where the claimant obtains more than one medical report, the first report must be a fixed cost medical report from an accredited medical expert selected via the MedCo Portal and any further report from an expert in any of the following disciplines must also be a fixed cost medical report –

(a)   Consultant Orthopaedic Surgeon;

(b)   Consultant in Accident and Emergency Medicine;

(c)   General Practitioner registered with the General Medical Council;

(d)   Physiotherapist registered with the Health and Care Professions Council.

21.4.4   Stage 2 settlement pack

In addition to the documents set out at **21.3.2(b)** above, the settlement pack in a soft tissue injury claim must contain the invoice for obtaining the fixed cost medical report and any invoice for the cost of obtaining medical records. Furthermore, para 7.32A provides that:

> ... In a soft tissue injury claim, the Stage 2 Settlement Pack is of no effect unless the medical report is a fixed cost medical report. Where the claimant includes more than one medical report, the first report obtained must be a fixed cost medical report from an accredited medical expert selected via the MedCo Portal and any further report from an expert in any of the disciplines listed in paragraph 7.8B(3)(a) to (d) must also be a fixed cost medical report.

21.5   INTERIM PAYMENTS

Paragraph 7 of both the RTA Protocol and the EL/PL Protocol set out identical procedures for obtaining an interim payment at Stage 2. The claimant must send to the defendant an interim settlement pack (ISP), medical reports and evidence of pecuniary losses and disbursements.

Where the claimant seeks an interim payment of £1,000, the defendant must pay £1,000 within 10 days of receiving the ISP. If the interim payment sought is greater than £1,000, the defendant may offer less than is requested but must pay at least £1,000 to the claimant within 15 days of receiving the ISP.

21.6 FIXED COSTS

The fixed costs regime in the amended CPR, Part 45 provides for fixed costs to be paid at the end of each stage of the RTA and EL/PL Protocols. The costs are set out in Tables 6 and 6A as follows:

TABLE 6

Fixed costs in relation to the RTA Protocol

Where the value of the claim for damages is not more than £10,000		Where the value of the claim for damages is more than £10,000, but not more than £25,000	
Stage 1 fixed costs	£200	Stage 1 fixed costs	£200
Stage 2 fixed costs	£300	Stage 2 fixed costs	£600
Stage 3 Type A fixed costs	£250	Stage 3 Type A fixed costs	£250
Stage 3 Type B fixed costs	£250	Stage 3 Type B fixed costs	£250
Stage 3 Type C fixed costs	£150	Stage 3 Type C fixed costs	£150

TABLE 6A

Fixed costs in relation to the EL/PL Protocol

Where the value of the claim for damages is not more than £10,000		Where the value of the claim for damages is more than £10,000, but not more than £25,000	
Stage 1 fixed costs	£300	Stage 1 fixed costs	£300
Stage 2 fixed costs	£600	Stage 2 fixed costs	£1300
Stage 3 Type A fixed costs	£250	Stage 3 Type A fixed costs	£250
Stage 3 Type B fixed costs	£250	Stage 3 Type B fixed costs	£250
Stage 3 Type C fixed costs	£150	Stage 3 Type C fixed costs	£150

Type A, B and C fixed costs?

Type A fixed costs are the legal representative's Stage 3 costs for a paper hearing and under both Protocols are £250.00.

Type B

Type B costs are additional advocate's costs for conducting an oral Stage 3 hearing and are also £250 for RTA cases and the same for EL/PL Protocol cases, giving a total fee of £500 for an oral Stage 3 hearing in all portals.

Type C

Type C fixed costs are the costs for the advice on the amount of damages where the claimant is a child and are £150 in both Protocols.

All fixed costs at all stages are exclusive of VAT, and a further allowance may be made for disbursements such as medical reports and court fees under CPR, r 45.19. Where the claim is a soft tissue injury claim, limits are placed on the amount that can be claimed for a medical report as follows:

(2A) In a soft tissue injury claim to which the RTA Protocol applies, the only sums (exclusive of VAT) that are recoverable in respect of the cost of obtaining a fixed cost medical report or medical records are as follows –

(a) obtaining the first report from an accredited medical expert selected via the MedCo Portal: £180;

(b)   obtaining a further report where justified from an expert from one of the following disciplines –

(i)   Consultant Orthopaedic Surgeon (inclusive of a review of medical records where applicable): £420;

(ii)   Consultant in Accident and Emergency Medicine: £360;

(iii)   General Practitioner registered with the General Medical Council: £180; or

(iv)   Physiotherapist registered with the Health and Care Professions Council: £180;

(c)   obtaining medical records: no more than £30 plus the direct cost from the holder of the records, and limited to £80 in total for each set of records required. Where relevant records are required from more than one holder of records, the fixed fee applies to each set of records required;

(d)   addendum report on medical records (except by Consultant Orthopaedic Surgeon): £50; and

(e)   answer to questions under Part 35: £80.

(2B)   Save in exceptional circumstances, no fee may be allowed for the cost of obtaining a report to which paragraph (2A) applies where the medical expert –

(a)   has provided treatment to the claimant;

(b)   is associated with any person who has provided treatment; or

(c)   proposes or recommends treatment that they or an associate then provide.

(2C)   The cost of obtaining a further report from an expert not listed in paragraph (2A)(b) is not fixed, but the use of that expert and the cost must be justified.

(2D)   Where appropriate, VAT may be recovered in addition to the cost of obtaining a fixed cost medical report or medical records.

21.7   OFFERS TO SETTLE

If settlement is not reached in a Portal claim, both parties must state their final offer in the CPP prior to the claim being issued. Section II of CPR, Part 36 is a new section regulating such offers to settle where the parties have followed the RTA or EL/PL Protocols and the claim has proceeded to a hearing at Stage 3.

21.7.1   Form and content of offer

Under CPR, r 36.25(1), an offer to settle under these provisions is called a 'Protocol offer'. Rule 36.25(2) provides that, to be valid, a Protocol offer must:

(a)   be set out in the CPP; and

(b)   contain the final total amount of the offer from both parties.

Rule 36.26 provides that the offer is deemed to be made on the first business day after the CPP is sent to the defendant. Under CPR, r 36.27, the offer is treated as being exclusive of all interest.

21.7.2   Costs consequences following judgment

As usual, the court will not know the amount of any Protocol offer until the claim has been decided. Rule 36.29 sets out three possible outcomes of the Stage 3 hearing, together with the costs consequences of each outcome:

(a)   *Claimant is awarded damages less than or equal to the defendants offer.* The court will order the claimant to pay the defendant's Stage 3 fixed costs and interest on those costs.

(b)   *Claimant is awarded more than the defendant's offer but less than the claimant's offer.* The court will order the defendant to pay the claimant's fixed costs .

(c)   *Claimant is awarded equal to or more than the claimant's own offer.* The court will order the defendant to pay interest on the whole of the damages at a rate not exceeding 10% above base rate for some or all of the period starting with the date on which the offer was made. In addition, the defendant will be ordered to pay the claimant's fixed costs, interest on those costs at a rate not exceeding 10% above base rate and an additional 10% of the amount awarded (pursuant to CPR, r 36.17(4)(d)).

21.8 WHAT IF A CLAIM EXITS THE PORTAL?

Claims which are started in the Portal may exit the process, for instance because an allegation of contributory negligence is made, or one party fails to follow the relevant Protocol. Claims which no longer continue under the Protocols cannot subsequently re-enter the process. Where this happens, the Protocols provide that the claims will proceed under the relevant PAP. Both the Personal Injury PAP and the Disease and Illness Claims PAP provide that in such a case the CNF will serve as the letter of claim.

21.8.1 Fixed costs apply to claims which exit the Portal

Section IIIA of CPR, Part 45 now contains a new, secondary fixed costs scheme which applies to all claims which exit the RTA or the EL/PL Protocol except for disease claims, the costs of which will be payable on the usual standard basis after they exit the Portal. The detail of these fixed costs is not set out here but may be found in CPR, Part 45. They increase depending on the stage the claim reaches before settlement and are slightly more generous than the fixed costs which apply to claims which stay in the Portal.

21.8.2 Costs consequences of Part 36 offers after a claim exits the Portal

Two new provisions have been added to CPR, Part 36 to cover the costs consequences of acceptance of a Part 36 offer or a protocol offer after a claim has left the Portal (CPR, r 36.20), and the costs consequences for a claimant who obtains a judgment less advantageous than an offer made by the defendant after exiting the portal (CPR, r 36.21). The rules are complex but in summary they provide as follows:

CPR, r 36.20 – costs consequences of acceptance

(a) Where a Part 36 offer is accepted within the relevant period, the claimant (C) is entitled to fixed costs as set out in Section IIIA of CPR, Part 45. The level of those costs will depend upon the stage the case has reached at the date on which the notice of acceptance is served (CPR, r 36.20(2)).

(b) Where C accepts a Part 36 offer after the relevant period, C will be entitled to the fixed costs applicable at the date on which the relevant period expired, but C will be liable for the defendant's (D's) costs from the date of expiry of the relevant period to the date of acceptance (CPR, r 36.20(4)).

(c) Where a protocol offer is made and is subsequently accepted after a claim exits the portal:

    (i) C is entitled to Stage 1 and 2 fixed costs; and

    (ii) C is liable for D's costs from the date on which the protocol offer is deemed to be made until the date of acceptance (CPR, r 36.20(5)).

CPR, r 36.21 – costs consequences following judgment

(a) Where C fails to obtain a judgment more advantageous than D's Part 36 offer and a split order for costs is made pursuant to CPR, r 36.21 (2) after a claim has exited the Portal:

    (i) C will be entitled to fixed costs for the stage applicable at the date on which the relevant period expired; and

    (ii) C will be liable for D's costs from the date on which the relevant period expired to the date of judgment (CPR, r 36.21(2)).

(b) Where C fails to obtain a judgment more advantageous than D's protocol offer:

    (i) C is entitled to Stage 1 and 2 fixed costs; and

    (ii) C is liable to pay D's costs from the date on which the protocol offer is deemed to be made until the date of judgment (CPR, r 36.21(3)).

In all cases, where an order for costs is made in favour of a defendant under either CPR, r 36.20 or CPR, r 36.21, the amount of those costs will not exceed the fixed costs set out in the tables in Section III of CPR, Part 45.

21.8.3 Claimants who unreasonably fail to follow the Protocols

In order to prevent a claimant from trying to circumvent the rules and deliberately exiting the Portal in order to secure higher costs, CPR, r 45.24 provides as follows:

(1)   This rule applies where the claimant –

    (a)   does not comply with the process set out in the relevant Protocol; or

    (b)   elects not to continue with that process,

and starts proceedings under Part 7.

(2)   Subject to paragraph (2A), where a judgment is given in favour of the claimant but –

    (a)   the court determines that the defendant did not proceed with the process set out in the relevant Protocol because the claimant provided insufficient information on the Claim Notification Form;

    (b)   the court considers that the claimant acted unreasonably –

        (i)   by discontinuing the process set out in the relevant Protocol and starting proceedings under Part 7;

        (ii)   by valuing the claim at more than £25,000, so that the claimant did not need to comply with the relevant Protocol; or

        (iii)   except for paragraph (2)(a), in any other way that caused the process in the relevant Protocol to be discontinued; or

    (c)   the claimant did not comply with the relevant Protocol at all despite the claim falling within the scope of the relevant Protocol,

the court may order the defendant to pay no more than the fixed costs in rule 45.18 together with the disbursements allowed in accordance with rule 45.19.

The new para (2A) provides that, where a judgment is given in favour of the claimant but the claimant did not undertake a search of askCUE PI in accordance with para 6.3A(2) of the RTA Protocol, the court may not order the defendant to pay the claimant's costs and disbursements, save in exceptional circumstances.

21.8.4 'Escaping' fixed costs

CPR, r 45.29J provides that 'if it considers that there are exceptional circumstances making it appropriate to do so the court will consider a claim for an amount of costs (excluding disbursements) which is greater than the fixed recoverable costs'. There is no definition of what will be deemed 'exceptional', but the sorts of cases which will qualify are likely to be rare.

If the court is persuaded that exceptional circumstances exist, it will assess the costs. However, the applicant should beware: if the assessed costs are less than 20% greater than the fixed costs, then the court will only allow the lower of assessed costs and fixed recoverable costs and may order that the applicant pay the costs of the assessment (CPR, rr 45.29K and 45.29L).

21.9 LIMITATION AND PORTAL CLAIMS

Where the limitation period is about to expire and therefore there is insufficient time to comply with the Portal procedure, a Part 8 claim form should be issued using the Stage 3 procedure (see **21.3.3** above) in order to protect the client's position. It will then be necessary to apply to the court for a stay of proceedings to enable the parties to comply with the Portal procedure. If the claim is not subsequently settled and exits the Portal, an application may then be made to lift the stay and to request directions for trial.

21.10 CONCLUSION

The extension of Portal claims to all RTA, EL and PL claims up to £25,000, and the reduction in costs that can now be claimed, has been controversial. Many have suggested that whilst the Portal might work for RTAs, which are on the whole relatively straightforward, the complexity in the law relating to EL and PL claims make them unsuitable for such a process. The figures suggest that approximately one-third of RTA claims exit the Portal as a result of allegations of contributory negligence. Although only time will tell, many practitioners believe that the figure for claims exiting the EL/PL Portal is likely to be much higher; and although it is still early days, the most recent statistics suggest that the drop out rate is closer to 50% for EL, PL and EL disease claims.

The amendments to the CPR and Protocols to implement the whiplash reforms are also in their infancy, and it remains to be seen whether they will have the desired effect of decreasing costs and discouraging bogus or exaggerated claims.

APPENDICES

APPENDIX 1

Employers' Liability Case Study

INTRODUCTION

The following case study is illustrative of the low-value personal injury cases which form the bulk of the personal injury lawyer's caseload. The documentation charts the basic procedural steps, from instruction, through commencement of proceedings, to settlement. It does not cover all eventualities and not all documents which would be relevant to the case have been provided. As the accident occurred after 30 July 2013, the Pre-action Protocol for Low Value Personal Injury (Employers' Liability and Public Liability) Claims applies.

The claim proceeds as follows:

1. The claimant, Neil Worthing, instructs a firm of solicitors, Goodlaw, in relation to an injury he has suffered whilst in the employment of Guildshire Engineering Limited. A proof of evidence is taken (**Document 1**). The matter is funded by means of a CFA backed up by an AEI policy.

2. Using the Portal, the claimant's solicitors send the Claims Notification Form (CNF) electronically to the Defendant's insurer, Bright Insurance Co Ltd (**Document 2**). At the same time, the Defendant Only Claim Form is sent to the Defendant by first class post.

3. Bright Insurance Co Ltd sends an electronic acknowledgement and instructs Winter Wood & Co, to act on its behalf. A response is sent electronically via the Portal, denying the claim (**Document 3**). The matter therefore exits the Portal and, henceforward, the Pre-action Protocol for Personal Injury Claims applies. The CNF stands as the Letter of Claim.

4. The defendant's solicitors write to the claimant's solicitors setting out their reasons for denying the claim (**Document 4**) and enclosing relevant documents, including the accident report (**Document 5**) and the RIDDOR report (**Document 6**).

5. The claimant's solicitors write to the defendant's solicitors with the aim of appointing a jointly selected medical expert (**Document 7**). They provide three names.

6. The defendant does not raise any objection to those named, one is instructed and a medical report is obtained (**Document 8**).

7. Following receipt of the medical report, the assistant solicitor acting for the claimant conducts research into what the claimant would be entitled to in respect of general damages for pain, suffering and loss of amenity, and he sends a memo to his supervising solicitor setting out his findings (**Document 9**).

8. A claim form is issued (**Document 10**) (through the County Court Money Claims Centre), and served with the particulars of claim (**Document 11**), the Schedule of Past and Future Expenses and Losses (**Document 12**) and the medical report.

9. The defendant's solicitors notify the Compensation Recovery Unit (CRU) of the claim by means of Form CRU 1 (**Document 13**). They receive a CRU certificate of repayable benefits (CRU 100) (**Document 14**) which shows that there are no recoverable benefits. A copy is forwarded to the claimant's solicitors.

10. The defence is filed (**Document 15**). The case is provisionally allocated to the fast track and is transferred to the County Court at Christlethorpe.

11. Directions questionnaires are completed by both sides (**Document 16**).

12. Directions are given (**Document 17**).

13. Following disclosure of witness statements, solicitors for the parties discuss a possible settlement, and the claimant subsequently indicates to his solicitors that he wants to

settle. The assistant solicitor acting for the claimant sends a memo to his supervising solicitor (**Document 18**).

14   The defendant's solicitors send a Part 36 offer letter to the claimant's solicitors (**Document 19**). The assistant solicitor acting for the claimant consults his client and contacts the defendant's solicitors, asking them for an improved offer. He notes this in a memo to his supervising solicitor (**Document 20**).

15   The claimant's solicitors write to the defendant's solicitors accepting the updated offer (**Document 21**) and enclosing a draft consent order (**Document 22**).

DOCUMENT 1 – PROOF OF EVIDENCE

I, Neil Matthew Worthing, of 22 Elstead House, Griffin Road, Christlethorpe, Guildshire GU48 1XX will say:

1. My date of birth is 14 December 1992 and I am 21 years old. My National Insurance number is WK987999X. I am single and I have lived in rented accommodation at the above address since 11 June 2013.

2. I am currently a full-time student at Queen Margaret's College, Guildshire, where I am studying law. This is the final year of my degree course. Throughout my years of study, I have taken temporary jobs during the summer breaks in order to help fund my studies.

3. In June 2014, after the end of term, I was able to get a temporary contract with Guildshire Engineering Limited (GEL) at their factory at 77 Blizzard Lane, Christlethorpe, Guildshire, GU59 2YZ. They manufacture metal tools for industrial use. I was to work on their production line as a process engineer. The contract was to run for 10 weeks from Monday 9 June to Friday 15 August and my take home pay was £296 per week.

4. When I arrived at the factory on 9 June, I was shown where I was to work by the foreman, Tony Benson. He gave me a short demonstration on how to use the machinery, gave me some written health and safety information, and told me that the Health and Safety Representative would talk to me when he came back from holiday the following Monday. Everything went very well the first week until the last day.

5. On Friday 13 June 2014, at about 2.30pm, Tony asked me to help Jerry Packman, another process engineer, to move several boxes of widgets from one part of the factory to another. We were to use two metal trolleys, which had handles on each end, to transport the boxes. He told us the boxes were heavy, so we were to move each box between us and keep our backs straight when we were doing it. He said we were to put only four boxes on each trolley. Jerry was mucking about when Tony was talking to us, and Tony told him to listen and behave himself. Jerry is great fun and a bit of a practical joker, but he seems to be in trouble quite a lot.

6. We stacked the first trolley with four boxes and then I pushed it about three feet further forward. The boxes were heavy so it took considerable effort on my part to move the trolley. Jerry then moved the second trolley to about a foot behind the first one, and we stacked that with four boxes. There was only one box left, so we decided to put this box on the second trolley. Once the fifth box was loaded, Jerry tried to move the trolley, but it wouldn't budge at all. It looked quite funny as Jerry is quite small and skinny. I was standing to the side of the first trolley with my left hand on the handle. I told Jerry to stop being such a weed and to push harder. Suddenly, the trolley he was pushing shot forward and the thumb of my left hand was caught between the handles of the two trolleys. It was excruciatingly painful. The accident happened at around 2.45 pm.

7. I immediately went to see the first aider, Alison Jacobs, who examined my thumb and said she thought it might be broken. My hand was already swelling up, and I was in great pain and very distressed. As I am left handed, I was worried about being able to write. Also I was concerned about my ability to play the piano, which is my great passion. I perform as a pianist in the restaurant at the Swan Lake Hotel on Tuesday, Thursday, and Friday evenings from 7pm to 11pm, for which I am paid £80 each Tuesday and Thursday evening and £100 each Friday evening.

8. As I was unable to drive, Alison Jacobs drove me to the A&E department at Guildshire Hospital. By the time we arrived, the pain and swelling in my thumb had increased. My left thumb was x-rayed, which confirmed that it had been fractured. A plaster cast was applied to my thumb up to my elbow and I was given a sling. I wore this plaster for two weeks and then a splint for a further two weeks.

9.   Obviously I could not go to work. On Wednesday 18 June, I received a call from Tony Benson. He sounded quite cross. He said that the accident had been due to me mucking about with Jerry and that I hadn't carried out his instructions. He said that he would send me two weeks' wages, which was more than generous and that my services were no longer needed.

10.   A few days later, I received a cheque from GEL in the sum of £592.00 for two weeks' wages – for the week I had worked and for one other week. Because of the injury, I was incapable of working for about four weeks, but when I had recovered enough to work, I was unable to find another job for what remained of the summer break. In addition, I lost money due to being unable to play the piano at the Swan Lake Hotel for a period of 12 weeks. Luckily, they took me back once I was able to play again. I did not claim benefits as I did not think I would be entitled to any.

11.   I was unable to cook or clean, or do anything much after the accident. Consequently, my mother came and stayed with me for two weeks to look after me. She doesn't work, so she didn't lose any money, but it was very inconvenient for her and quite embarrassing for me.

12.   I had a course of five physiotherapy treatments at Guildshire Hospital. I incurred travelling expenses attending these physiotherapy treatments. I travelled in my own car to the hospital, which is a round trip of 10 miles from my flat.

13.   I was then advised to continue with a course of exercises at home. I still do these exercises on a daily basis as I still have restricted movement in my thumb. It continues to give me pain, especially in cold weather, or if I knock or catch it accidentally. Sometimes, it locks when I am trying to grip with my left hand. I can play the piano, but it does hurt towards the end of the four-hour period when I am playing at the hotel. It also hurts when I have been writing for a while, which obviously I have to do at college.

14.   Jerry rang me a few weeks after the accident to apologise and to ask how I was. He told me that he had never received any information or training regarding stacking boxes or moving trolleys, and that GEL had recently had foam placed over the metal handles of all the trolleys in the factory. I asked him if he would give evidence on my behalf, if I took it to court, and he said that was unlikely as he thought he would have to give evidence on behalf of his employer.

Signed *Neil Worthing*   15 September 2014

DOCUMENT 2 – CLAIM NOTIFICATION FORM (EL1)

This is a formal claim against you, which must be acknowledged by email immediately and passed to your insurer.

Claim notification form (EL1)
Low value personal injury claims in
employers' liability - accident only (£1,000 - £25,000)

Before filling in this form you are encouraged to seek independent legal advice.

Date sent | 1 | 8 | / | 0 | 9 | / | 2 | 0 | 1 | 4 |

Items marked with (✱) are optional and the claimant must make a reasonable attempt to complete those boxes. All other boxes on the form are mandatory and must be completed before being sent.

What is the value of your claim? ☐ up to £10,000   ☑ up to £25,000

Please tick here if you are not legally represented? ☐   *If you are not legally represented please put your details in the claimant's representative section.*

Claimant's representative - contact details	Defendant's details
Name	**Defendant's name**
Goodlaw Solicitors	Guildshire Engineering Limited
Address	**Defendant's address***
4 College Road Christlethorpe Guildshire	77 Blizzard Lane Christlethorpe Guildshire
Postcode G U 1 4 D Z	Postcode G U 5 9 2 Y Z
Contact name	**Policy number reference (If not known insert not known)**
Mrs Belinda Braithwaite	Not known
Telephone number	**Insurer/Compensator name (if known)**
01483 606099	Bright Insurance Co. Ltd.
E-mail address	
bbraithwaite@goodlaw.co.uk	
Reference number	
BB/WORTH/14/426	

EL1 Claim notification form (04.13)

Section A — Claimant's details

☑ Mr.   ☐ Mrs.   ☐ Ms.

☐ Miss   ☐ Other

Claimant's name

Neil Matthew Worthing

Address

22 Elstead House
Griffin Road,
Christlethorpe,
Guildshire

Postcode G U 4 8 | 1 X X

Date of birth

1 4 / 1 2 / 1 9 9 2

Is this a child claim? ☐ Yes ☑ No

National Insurance number

W K 9 8 7 9 9 9 X

If the claimant does not have a National Insurance number, please explain why

Occupation

Student

Date of accident

1 3 / 0 6 / 2 0 1 4

If exact accident date is not known please select the most appropriate date and provide further details in Section B 1.1

Section B — Injury and medical details

1.1 Please provide a brief description of the injury sustained as a result of the accident

The Claimant's thumb on his left hand was fractured when it was crushed between the metal handles of two industrial trolleys. A plaster cast was applied from the thumb up to the elbow, which remained in place for two weeks. For a further two weeks, a splint was in place.

There is some remaining stiffness of the thumb joint, tenderness, and occasional locking of the joint.

this section continues over the page ⇨

1.2 Has the claimant had to take any time off work as a result of the accident? ☑ Yes ☐ No

1.3 Is the claimant still off work? ☐ Yes ☑ No

If No, how many days in total was the claimant off work? `45`

1.4 Has the claimant sought any medical attention? ☑ Yes ☐ No

If Yes, on what date did they first do so? `1 3 / 0 6 / 2 0 1 4`

1.5 Did the claimant attend hospital as a result of the accident? ☑ Yes ☐ No

If Yes, please provide details of the hospital(s) attended

> Guildshire Hospital, Grove Road, Guildshire, Christlethorpe, GU34 1HH

1.6 If hospital was attended, was the claimant detained overnight? ☐ Yes ☑ No

If Yes, how many days were they detained?

Section C — Rehabilitation

2.1 Has a medical professional recommended the claimant should undertake any rehabilitation such as physiotherapy? ☑ Yes ☐ No ☐ Medical professional not seen

If Yes, please provide brief details of the rehabilitation treatment recommended and any treatment provided including name of provider

> As recommended by the consultant at Guildshire Hospital, the claimant underwent a course of 5 physiotherapy treatments at Guildshire Hospital. He continues to do a number of exercises at home, as recommended by the physiotherapist.

2.2 Are you aware of any rehabilitation needs that the claimant has arising out of the accident? ☑ Yes ☐ No

If Yes, please provide full details

> The claimant needs to continue to carry out the exercises as mentioned above for the foreseeable future.

Section D — Accident time, location and description

3.1 Estimated time of accident (24 hour clock)

> 2.45

3.2 Where did the accident happen?

> The factory floor at the defendant's factory at Blizzard Lane, Christlethorpe, Guildshire.

3.3 At the time of the accident the claimant was

☑ working at the claimant's own place of work

☐ working in the workplace of another employer

☐ Other (please specify)

>

3.4 Please explain how the accident happened

> The claimant, who is a student, was working at the defendant's factory on a 10 week temporary contract.
>
> At the time of the accident, he and another process engineer, Jerry Packman, were moving boxes of widgets from one part of the factory to another, using two metal trolleys. Once stacked with boxes of widgets, the trolleys were very heavy and difficult to move.
>
> Mr Packman pushed one of the trolleys with some force, causing it to suddenly shoot forward. The claimant had been resting his hand on the handle of the other trolley, and his left thumb was caught in the impact between the handles of the two trolleys.

3.5 Was the accident reported?   ☑ Yes   ☐ No   ☐ Not known

If Yes, please confirm the date the accident was
reported and to whom it was reported (if known)

> 16/06/2014 - RIDDOR submitted to Health & Safety Executive

4

Section E — Liability

4.1 Why does the claimant believe that the defendant was to blame for the accident?

> The accident was caused by the negligence of the defendant, its servants or agents because it:-
>
> 1. failed to provide competent fellow workers. Mr Packman was known to the Defendant to be a practical joker. He behaved in a reckless manner in pushing the trolley with force without ascertaining that it was safe to do so. The defendant is vicariously liable for Mr Packman's actions.
>
> 2. failed to provide adequate equipment. In view of the likelihood of hands becoming trapped between the handles of trolleys, the handles should have been covered in foam or another suitable material in order to minimise injury. It is understoof that the handles were so covered by the defendant following this accident.
>
> 3. failed to provide a safe system of work in that insufficient thought had been given to the method by which boxes of widgets should be moved. There were insufficient instructions, safety precautions, warnings and supervision.
>
> In support of the above breaches of duty, the claimant relies on the following breaches of statutory duty.
>
> The Defendant failed:-
>
> (a) to make a proper risk assessment regarding the moving of trolleys contrary to reg 3(1) of the Management of Health and Safety at Work Regulations 1999 (the "Management Regulations") and reg 4(1) (b)(i) of the Manual Handling Operations Regulations 1992 (the "Manual Handling Regulations");
>
> (b) to provide information to its employees on health and safety risks and protective measures contrary to reg 10 of the Management Regs and reg 8 of the Provision and Use of Work Equipment Regulations 1998 (the Work Equipment Regulations");
>
> (c) to provide adequate health and safety training to its employees contrary to reg 13 of the Management Regulations and reg 9 of the Work Equipment Regulations;
>
> (d) to ensure the suitability of the trolleys for the purpose for which they were provided contrary to reg 4 of the Work Equipment Regulations .
>
> (e) to ensure that its employees received proper information and training on how to handle loads correctly in the process of moving loaded trolleys contrary to reg 4(1)(b)(ii) of the Manual Handling Regulations;
>
> (f) to take appropriate steps to reduce the risk of injury to employees arising out of the activity mentioned in (e) above to the lowest practicable level contrary to reg 4(1)(b)(ii) of the Manual Handling Regulations.

5

Section F — Funding

5.1 Has the claimant undertaken a funding arrangement within the meaning of CPR rule 43.2(1)(k) of which they are required to give notice to the defendant?

☐ Yes   ☑ No

If Yes, please tick the following boxes that apply:

☐ The claimant has entered into a conditional fee agreement in relation to this claim, which provides for a success fee within the meaning of section 58(2) of the Courts and Legal Services Act 1990

Date conditional fee arrangement was entered into   ☐☐ / ☐☐ / ☐☐☐☐

☐ The claimant has taken out an insurance policy to which section 29 of the Access to Justice Act 1999 applies.

Name of insurance company

Address of insurance company

Policy number

Policy date   ☐☐ / ☐☐ / ☐☐☐☐

Level of cover

Are the insurance premiums staged?   ☐ Yes   ☐ No

If Yes, at which point is an increased premium payable?

☐ The claimant has an agreement with a membership organisation to meet their legal costs.

Name of organisation

Date of agreement   ☐☐ / ☐☐ / ☐☐☐☐

☐ Other, please give details

Section G — Other relevant information

7

Section H — Statement of truth

Your personal information will only be disclosed to third parties, where we are obliged or permitted by law to do so. This includes use for the purpose of claims administration as well as disclosure to third-party managed databases used to help prevent fraud, and to regulatory bodies for the purposes of monitoring and/or enforcing our compliance with any regulatory rules/codes.

Where the claimant is a child the signature below will be by the child's parent or guardian or by the legal representative authorised by them.

☑ I am the claimant's legal representative. The claimant believes that the facts stated in this claim form are true. I am duly authorised by the claimant to sign this statement.

☐ I am the claimant. I believe that the facts stated in this claim form are true.

Signed

Belinda Braithwaite

Date

| 1 | 8 | / | 0 | 9 | / | 2 | 0 | 1 | 4 |

Position or office held
(if signed on behalf of firm or company)

Associate Solicitor

☑ I have retained a signed copy of this form including the statement of truth.

DOCUMENT 3 – RESPONSE TO CNF

Claim notification form (EL1)
Low value personal injury claims in
employers' liability - accident only (£1,000 - £25,000)

Compensator response

Section A — Liability

Please select the relevant statement

Defendant admits: Accident occured

Caused by the defendant's breach of duty

Caused some loss to the claimant, the nature and extent of which is not admitted

The defendant has no accrued defence to the claim under the Limitation Act 1980

☐ The above are admitted

☐ The defendant makes the above admission but the claim will
exit the process due to contributory negligence

If the defendant does not admit liability please provide reasons below

At all material times, the defendant complied with its common law duties to the claimant. It provided competent fellow workers who were adequately trained, instructed and supervised. The trolleys were suitable and safe when used appropriately. Safe systems of work were in place. All statutory obligations were followed.

The accident was caused by the claimant's own actions in suggesting that one of the trolleys be overloaded with boxes of widgets, in direct contravention of instructions given to him, and in not behaving in a mature and sensible manner.

Section B — Services provided by the compensator - Rehabilitation

Is the compensator prepared to provide
rehabilitation?   ☐ Yes   ☐ No

Has the compensator provided rehabilitation?   ☐ Yes   ✔ No

If Yes, please provide full details below

Section C — Response information

Date of notification	1 8 / 0 9 / 2 0 1 4
Date of response to notification	1 5 / 1 0 / 2 0 1 4

Defendant's compensator details

Address

Bright Insurance Co. Ltd.
Peacock House
Regents Lane
London WC2 SW4

Contact name

Ralph East

Telephone number

01966 485485

E-mail address

ralpheast@brightinsurance.co.uk

Reference number

GuildshireEL/RE/4321/14

DOCUMENT 4 – LETTER OF DENIAL

Winter Wood & Co Solicitors

Rembrandt House,
Lee Lane, Brampton
Guildshire, GU7 8TU
DX 26438 GUILDSHIRE
Tel: 01483 432143
Fax: 01483 432156

Goodlaw Solicitors
DX 3214 GUILDSHIRE

Our ref: NG/GELTD/14/A48
Your ref: BB/WORTH/14/426
Date: 7/11/2014

Dear Sirs

YOUR CLIENT: Mr Neil Worthing
OUR CLIENT: Guildshire Engineering Limited
ACCIDENT DATE: 13 June 2014

We act for Guildshire Engineering Limited in relation to the above mentioned matter, which has now exited the Portal. As you are aware, our client disputes liability in this matter. Consequently, in furtherance of the Pre-action Protocol for Personal Injury Claims, we write to set out a detailed response to the matters raised in the CNF.

Although it is accepted that Mr Worthing did suffer an injury on 13 June at our client's premises, the causes of the accident are disputed.

- Our client strongly disputes the allegations that it failed to provide competent fellow workers. Our client provides training to each individual employee in accordance with its legal obligations and insists on the highest levels of behaviour and discipline from its staff. It is our understanding that it was at Mr Worthing's suggestion that an extra box of widgets was placed on one of the trolleys, in direct contravention of the instructions given to him. This made the trolley difficult to manoeuvre, which led directly to the accident. It was your client's inappropriate behaviour which caused his injury.

- The trolleys were, at the time of the alleged accident, suitable in every respect for their intended purpose. Whilst it is true that our client has since placed foam on the handles of the trolleys, this is in no way an acceptance that they were previously unsuitable. These adaptations had been discussed prior to the alleged accident not due to safety issues but because the handles are thin and uncomfortable to push. It is unreasonable to suggest that all hard surfaces in a factory should be covered in foam.

- It is disputed that our client failed to provide a safe system of work. Our client carried out risk assessments as required by Regulation 3 of the Management of Health and Safety at Work Regulations in relation to all activities conducted in their premises. A copy of the pre and post-accident risk assessments are attached. You will note that trolleys are dealt with in paragraph 14.10 of both documents and that no specific risks are identified. There are no risks associated with pushing a trolley provided the person doing the pushing behaves sensibly. It is our client's contention that Mr Worthing was not behaving sensibly at the time of the accident.

- Mr Worthing was provided with appropriate health and safety information and training, both generally and in relation to manual handling. The foreman, Mr Benson, gave him written information on all relevant matters on the first day of Mr Worthing's employment with our client and he also gave specific instructions as to how the boxes of widgets should be moved. In particular he told Mr Worthing that no more than four boxes should be placed on a trolley at one time, which your client chose to ignore. Mr Benson did not give instructions or training on how to push the trolley as this is a matter of common sense.

In addition to the risk assessment mentioned above, we enclose the following documents:

- Copy of your client's contract of employment. Please note the requirement for employees to read the health and safety information and the standards of behaviour required by all employees at all times.
- Copies of all health and safety documents supplied to your client
- Accident book entry
- First aider report
- RIDDOR report to the HSE
- Earnings information

There are no further relevant documents to disclose.

Mr Worthing was dismissed by our client due to his unreasonable behaviour.

This was an unfortunate accident for which we have every sympathy with your client. Nevertheless, we have no offers to make to settle this matter as we do not consider that our client was negligent.

Please note that, should you wish to continue with this matter, we are instructed to accept service of proceedings on our client's behalf.

Yours faithfully,

Winter Wood & Co

DOCUMENT 5 – ACCIDENT REPORT

EMPLOYEE ACCIDENT REPORT

Report number (consecutive)	
1. About the person who had the accident	
Name	NEIL MATTHEW WORTHING
Address	22 ELSTEAD HOUSE, GRIFFIN ROAD, CHRISTLETHORPE, GUILDSHIRE GU48 1XX
Position	PROCESS ENGINEER

2. About you, the individual filling in this record

If you did not have the accident, write your name and position

Name ALISON JACOBS   Position SECRETARY AND FIRST AIDER

3. Details of the accident

When it happened.   Date 13/06/14   Time 2.45pm (approx)

Where it happened. State location Factory floor

How did the accident happen? Give the cause if possible.   Mr Worthing and another process engineer were using two trolleys to transport components from one part of the factory to another when the thumb of Mr Worthing's left hand became trapped between the handles of the two trolleys.

If the person who had the accident suffered an injury, give details Crushed left thumb - fractured

Signed by Alison Jacobs   Dated 13/06/14

4. For the employer only

Complete this box if the accident is reportable under the Reporting of Injuries, Diseases and Dangerous Occurrences Regulations 1995 (RIDDOR).

How was it reported? On-line, electronically

Signed by Alison Jacobs   Dated 16/06/14

DOCUMENT 6 – RIDDOR

 HSE

Health and Safety
Executive

Report of an injury

Note: this is a preview of your form and does NOT represent the submitted details of your notification, which will include the Notification number for reference

About you and your organisation

Notifier name	Mr Adam Kilbride		
Job title	Works Manager		
Organisation name	Guildshire Engineering Limited		
Address	77 Blizzard Lane Christlethorpe GUILDSHIRE GU59 2YZ		
Phone no	01483 454545	Fax Number	01483 454546
Email Address	akilbride@GEL.co.uk		

Where did the incident happen

The incident happened at the above address

About the incident

Incident Date	13/06/2014	Incident Time	14:45
In which local authority did the incident occur (Country, Geographical Area and Local Authority)?			
England, Guildshire, Christlethorpe			
In which department or where on the premises did the incident happen?			
Factory Floor			
What type of work was being carried out (generally the main business activity of the site)?			
All other Manufacturing - Casting of metals - Light metals			

The enforcing authority for the address where the incident happened is HSE

About the kind of accident

Kind of accident	Lifting and handling injuries
Work process involved	Production, manufacturing or processing
Main factor involved	Loss of control of machinery, transport or equipment
What happened	Mr Worthing and a co-worker, Mr Jerry Packman, were transporting boxes of metal parts across the factory floor using two trolleys when his left thumb was caught between the metal handles of the two trolleys.

	It is believed that some horseplay was involved. Mr Packman has been given a written warning regarding his behaviour and Mr Worthing is no longer employed by this company.

About the injured person

Injured persons name	Mr Neil Matthew Worthing		
Injured persons address	22 Elstead House Griffin Road CHRISTLETHORPE Guildshire GU48 1XX		
Phone no	07777 888444	What was their occupation or job title?	Process engineer (temporary contract)
Gender	Male	Age	21
Work Status	The injured person was one of my employees.		

About the injured person's injuries

Severity of the injury	Injury preventing the injured person from working for more than 7 days		
Injuries	Fracture	Part of the body affected	Finger or fingers

DOCUMENT 7 – LETTER PROPOSING MEDICAL EXPERT

Goodlaw Solicitors

4 College Road, Christlethorpe, Guildshire, GU1 4DZ
DX 3214 GUILDSHIRE; Tel: 01483 606060; Fax: 01483 606099

Winter Wood & Co Solicitors
DX 26438 GUILDSHIRE

Our ref: BB/WORTH/14/426
bbraithwaite@goodlaw.co.uk
Your ref: NG/GELTD/14/A48
Date: 18 November 2014

Dear Sirs,

OUR CLIENT: Mr Neil Worthing
YOUR CLIENT: Guildshire Engineering Limited
ACCIDENT DATE: 13 June 2014

Further to the above matter and in accordance with the pre-action protocol, we write to inform you of our intention to instruct one of the following consultant orthopaedic surgeons to examine our client and prepare a report for these proceedings:

1.   Mr G D Cookson, MB ChB, FRCS (Tr & Orth), Crown House, Victoria Drive, Sandford, Storeshire, SS56 6YP.

2.   Mr R B Alimi, MB ChB, FRCS (Orth), BSc (Hons), Hampton Hospital, Hampton, Hillshire HS1 89P.

3.   Mrs F Field, MB ChB, FRCS (Orth) FRCS (Ed), The Shambles, Greenway, Heston, Scarshire SS35 1QW.

If you have any objections to any of the above, please let us know before 6 December.

Yours faithfully,

Goodlaw Solicitors

DOCUMENT 8 – MEDICAL REPORT

Mr G D Cookson MB ChB, FRCS (Tr & Orth),

Consultant Orthopaedic Surgeon
Crown House, Victoria Drive, Sandford, Storeshire, SS56 6YP
Tel: 01354 787878; Fax: 01358 675675

Our ref: GDC/14/23/WORTHING
Your ref: BB/WORTH/14/426
9 January 2015

This Medical Report is addressed to the Court

1. **Qualifications**

1.1 I am a consultant Orthopaedic and Trauma Surgeon with over 35 years' experience in this field. I became a consultant in 1986. My full CV is attached to this report.

2. **Instructions**

2.1 This medical report was produced on the instructions of Goodlaw Solicitors set out in their letter dated 8 December 2014. I was requested to examine their client, Mr Neil Worthing, who had been injured in an accident at work. The injury was said to be a fracture of the left thumb.

2.2 I interviewed and examined Mr Worthing at Crown House on 7 January 2015. I was also provided with photocopies of his medical records from his GP and from the A&E Department at Guildshire Hospital.

3. **History**

3.1 Mr Worthing is a 22-year-old law student. He is single and lives in rented accommodation with other students. He is left handed.

3.2 Last summer, he was working at a factory owned by Guildshire Engineering Limited on a temporary basis. On 13 June 2014, he was moving boxes of metal components, when his thumb was trapped between the metal handles of two trolleys. He said that the trolleys had been pushed together with some force.

3.3 Immediately after the accident, he was seen by the First Aider at the workplace, who examined his hand and took him to the A&E department at Guildshire Hospital. An examination and x-ray revealed a fracture of the left thumb and, on the advice of the on-call orthopaedic registrar, a POP was applied to the thumb up to the elbow. He was advised to take painkillers and was discharged with a sling. He had difficulty sleeping for the first week and took Nurofen tablets regularly for the first two weeks. He returned to the Fracture Clinic at Guildshire Hospital two weeks after the accident when the plaster was changed to a thumb spika. He was then bandaged for a further two weeks. Mr Worthing subsequently underwent a course of 5 physiotherapy treatments at the hospital.

3.4 Mr Worthing tells me he was unable to work for one month, by which time he had lost his temporary position at the factory. He was unable to find alternative employment for the remainder of the summer vacation. He was unable to play the piano to the standard required by the hotel for a period of 12 weeks.

4. **Previous medical history**

Mr Worthing is a fit and healthy young man. There is nothing in his medical records which could have any bearing at all on the current injury.

5. **Present condition**

Mr Worthing told me that he is still experiencing pain across the back of the metacarpo-phalangeal joint of his left thumb and that the joint often felt stiff. He said that it would sometimes lock, especially if he was holding objects tightly, and on occasions he would drop them. Writing or playing the piano for long periods of time would cause pain and discomfort. Mr Worthing has to do both of these activities on a regular basis as he is a student and plays the piano at a hotel several evenings a week on a commercial basis. He can drive without difficulty. His sleep is not disturbed unless he has been playing the piano at the hotel. On those occasions, he sometimes has to take pain killers in order to get a good night's sleep.

6. **On examination**

The left thumb was not swollen, bruised or discoloured. However, there was light tenderness over the dorsal aspect of the MCP joint. Ligaments and tendons to the thumb appeared to be intact. Resisted movements of the MCP and IP joints of the thumb were possible without pain. He felt, however, that he could not bend the left thumb as well as the right thumb. The grip and pinch grip of the left hand appeared to be normal.

7. **Diagnosis and opinion**

7.1 Undisplaced avulsion fracture base of proximal phalanx radial side left thumb with bruising to IP joint.

7.2 In my opinion, an injury of this nature would have prevented Mr Worthing from working for one month following the accident and from playing the piano competently for a period of three months following the accident.

7.3 Mr Worthing appears to have made a good but not complete recovery from the injury. There appears to be some slight stiffness of the MCP joint of the left thumb with tenderness over the dorsal aspect but resisted movements are pain free. Gripping appears to cause some pain and discomfort, the thumb occasionally 'locks' and he sometimes drops objects.

7.4 On a balance of probabilities, I believe that his symptoms will gradually settle over a period of 18 months from the accident. He will not develop osteoarthritic changes in his left thumb, IP or MCP joints as a result of the injury sustained on 13 June 2014 and his ability to work and pursue leisure activities will not be disadvantaged as a result of these injuries 18 months post-accident.

8. **Declaration**

8.1 I understand that my overriding duty is to the court, both in preparing reports and in giving oral evidence.

8.2 I have set out in my report what I understand from those instructing me to be the questions in respect of which my opinion as an expert is required.

8.3 I have done my best, in preparing this report, to be accurate and complete. I have mentioned all matters which I regard as relevant to the opinions I have expressed. All of the matters on which I have expressed an opinion lie within my field of expertise.

8.4 I have drawn to the attention of the court all matters, of which I am aware, which might adversely affect my opinion.

8.5 Wherever I have no personal knowledge, I have indicated the source of factual information.

8.6 I have not included anything in this report which has been suggested to me by anyone, including the lawyers instructing me, without forming my own independent view of the matter.

8.7 Where, in my view, there is a range of reasonable opinion, I have indicated the extent of that range in the report.

8.8 At the time of signing the report I consider it to be complete and accurate. I will notify those instructing me if, for any reason, I subsequently consider that the report requires any correction or qualification.

8.9 I understand that this report will be the evidence that I will give under oath, subject to any correction or qualification I may make before swearing to its veracity.

8.10 I have attached to this report a summary of my instructions. [not reproduced]

I believe that the facts I have stated in the report are true and that the opinions I have expressed are correct.

Signed *G D Cookson*   Dated 09/01/15

DOCUMENT 9 – MEMORANDUM RE DAMAGES

From:	Ravinder Omar, Assistant Solicitor, Goodlaw
Sent:	23/01/15
To:	Belinda Braithwaite, Associate Solicitor, Goodlaw
Subject:	Neil Worthing case – general damages

Hi Belinda,

I have now had the chance to read through the medical report provided by Mr Cookson and, as you have requested, I have researched the general damages position.

With regard to the Guidelines, although we are dealing with a fracture of the thumb on the dominant hand here, I do not believe the injury is serious enough to fall under (x) moderate injury to the thumb, which suggests an award of up to £10,175. Instead, I suggest the injury falls within heading (y) Severe Dislocation of the Thumb, indicating an award of between £3,190 to £5,500. However, the Defendant may argue it falls within heading (z) Minor Injuries to the Thumb – a fracture which has recovered in six months except for residual stiffness and some discomfort – indicating an award in the region of up to £3,190. Suggest we argue client's injury is more serious than this – continuing pain from writing/playing the piano and still dropping things.

I looked up similar injuries in Kemp and on Lawtel PI but there isn't really anything that is completely on a par with the client's injuries:

- Pearson v Snax 24 Ltd [2006] – older lady dislocated middle joint of right thumb, also a laceration. Looks as if right hand is dominant hand (though it doesn't say!). This seems to be a more serious injury as she was left with constant stiffness, a loss of grip and 50% flexion of the interphalangeal joint – injury permanent and she had also suffered from minor arthritis. PSLA £4,500 (£5,905 RPI).

- Jones v Manchester City Council [2004] – lady – soft tissue strain to dominant right thumb. Satisfactory recovery after 18 months but permanent minor loss of function with intermittent swelling and aching, slight loss of grip strength. Injury less serious than Mr W's but some permanent loss of function. PSLA £3,500 (£4,805 RPI).

- Lawrence v Scott Ltd [1998] – older male – crush injury to dominant thumb, fracture of terminal phalanx of thumb – similar sort of injury. No significant pain after 6 months, permanent slight deformity, minor scarring, continuing cold intolerance. Couldn't do DIY for 10 weeks or swimming for 6 mths. PSLA £2,500 (£4,011 RPI).

- Moore v Johnstone [1987] – older male fractured interphalangeal joint of non-dominant thumb. Left with slight loss of grip in left hand. Small amount of discomfort experienced when practising hobby or archery. Difficulty in picking up small components and operating certain types of lathes. Similar type of injury, but to non-dominant thumb. However, damages also cover concussion to head. PSLA £2,300 (£5,960 RPI).

Suggest we aim for top end of heading (y) – £5,500. Do you agree?

Ravi

DOCUMENT 10 – CLAIM FORM

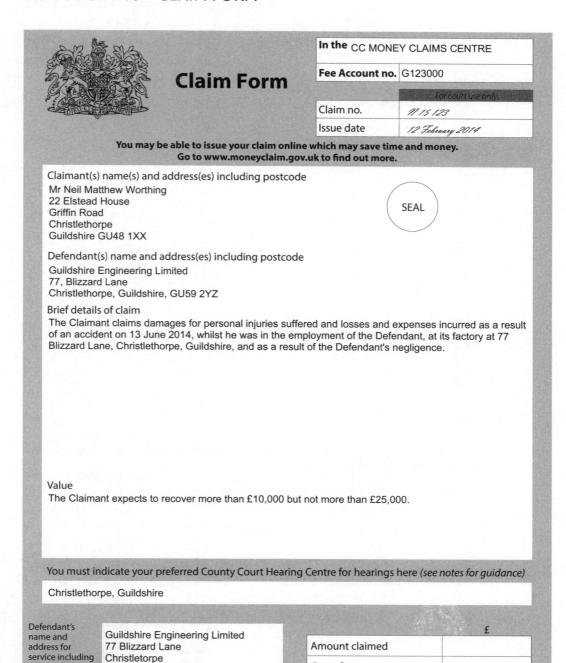

Claim Form

In the CC MONEY CLAIMS CENTRE	
Fee Account no.	G123000

	For court use only
Claim no.	*N 15 123*
Issue date	*12 February 2014*

You may be able to issue your claim online which may save time and money.
Go to www.moneyclaim.gov.uk to find out more.

Claimant(s) name(s) and address(es) including postcode
Mr Neil Matthew Worthing
22 Elstead House
Griffin Road
Christlethorpe
Guildshire GU48 1XX

SEAL

Defendant(s) name and address(es) including postcode
Guildshire Engineering Limited
77, Blizzard Lane
Christlethorpe, Guildshire, GU59 2YZ

Brief details of claim
The Claimant claims damages for personal injuries suffered and losses and expenses incurred as a result of an accident on 13 June 2014, whilst he was in the employment of the Defendant, at its factory at 77 Blizzard Lane, Christlethorpe, Guildshire, and as a result of the Defendant's negligence.

Value
The Claimant expects to recover more than £10,000 but not more than £25,000.

You must indicate your preferred County Court Hearing Centre for hearings here *(see notes for guidance)*

Christlethorpe, Guildshire

Defendant's name and address for service including postcode	Guildshire Engineering Limited 77 Blizzard Lane Christletorpe Guildshire GU59 2YZ		£
		Amount claimed	
		Court fee	455.00
		Legal representative's costs	
		Total amount	**£455.00**

For further details of the courts www.gov.uk/find-court-tribunal.
When corresponding with the Court, please address forms or letters to the Manager and always quote the claim number.

N1 Claim form (CPR Part 7) (05.14)   © Crown Copyright 2014

	Claim No.	*11 15 123*

Does, or will, your claim include any issues under the Human Rights Act 1998?   ☐ Yes   ☑ No

Particulars of Claim (attached)~~(to follow)~~
The Claimant confirms that he has complied with the Pre-action Protocol for Personal Injury Claims and Section IV of the Practice Direction on Pre-action Conduct insofar as it applies.

Statement of Truth
*(I believe)(The Claimant believes) that the facts stated in these particulars of claim are true.
* I am duly authorised by the claimant to sign this statement

Full name Ravinder Omar

Name of claimant's legal representative's firm Goodlaw Solicitors

signed *R Omar*   position or office held Solicitor
~~*(Claimant)(Litigation friend)~~   (if signing on behalf of firm or company)
(Claimant's legal representative)
                              delete as appropriate

Goodlaw Solicitors
4 College Road
Christlethorpe
Guildshire GU1 4DZ
romar@goodlaw.co.uk
DX 3214 GUILDSHIRE
Tel 01483 606060/Fax 01483 606099

Claimant's or claimant's legal representative's address to which documents or payments should be sent if different from overleaf including (if appropriate) details of DX, fax or e-mail.

DOCUMENT 11 – PARTICULARS OF CLAIM

Claim No: N 15 123

IN THE COUNTY COURT AT CHRISTLETHORPE

BETWEEN

MR NEIL MATTHEW WORTHING   Claimant

and

GUILDSHIRE ENGINEERING LIMITED   Defendant

PARTICULARS OF CLAIM

1.   The Defendant is a manufacturer of industrial tools. At all material times, the Claimant was employed by the Defendant as a process engineer at their factory at 77, Blizzard Lane, Christlethorpe, Guildshire, GU59 2YZ.

2.   At all times, the provisions of the Management of Health and Safety at Work Regulations 1999 ("the Management Regulations"), the Manual Handling Operations Regulations 1992 (the 'Manual Handling Regulations') and the Provision and Use of Work Equipment Regulations 1998 ("the Work Equipment Regulations") applied.

3.   On 13 June 2014, at approximately 2.45pm, whilst acting in the course of his employment, the Claimant and a co-worker Mr Jeremy Packman, were in the process of moving boxes of widgets from one part of the factory to another. They were transporting the boxes on two trolleys both of which had metal handles on each side. The Claimant was standing at the side of the first trolley, with his left hand on the handle, when the second trolley was pushed forward by Mr Packman with force, causing it to slam into the first trolley. The Claimant's left thumb was trapped between the handles of the two trolleys.

4.   The accident was caused or contributed to by the negligence of the Defendant, its servants or agents acting in the course of their employment.

PARTICULARS OF NEGLIGENCE

The Defendant was negligent in that it:

(a)   failed to provide a safe system of work in that the Claimant was not given adequate information, instruction and training in relation to manual handling and health and safety matters;

(b)   failed to provide safe or adequate plant in that the trolleys were not reasonably safe. The handles of the trolleys should have been covered with foam or an alternative appropriate material in order to minimise the risk of injury to employees;

(c)   failed to provide the Claimant with competent fellow workers. The Defendant was aware that Mr Packman was prone to practical jokes and horseplay within the workplace;

(d)   exposed the Claimant to a foreseeable risk of injury;

(e)   breached the following statutory obligations in that the Defendant, its servants or agents:

(i)   failed to make a suitable and sufficient assessment of the risks to health and safety of their employees in relation to the moving of the trolleys contrary to reg 3(1) of the Management Regulations and reg 4(1)(b)(i) of the Manual Handling Regulations;

(ii)   failed to provide information to the Claimant and/or Mr Packman on health and safety risks and protective measures that should be adopted, contrary to reg 10 of the Management Regulations and, specifically, failed to provide information and instruction in the use of equipment, namely the trolleys, contrary to reg 8 of the Work Equipment Regulations;

(iii) failed to provide adequate health and safety training to the Claimant and/or Mr Packman contrary to reg 13 of the Management Regulations and, specifically, failed to provide adequate training in the use of equipment contrary to reg 9 of the Work Equipment Regulations;

(iv)   failed to ensure the suitability of work equipment, namely trolleys, for the purpose for which they were provided contrary to reg 4 of the Work Equipment Regulations. 4(b) above is repeated;

(v)   failed to ensure that the Claimant and/or Mr Packman received proper information and training on how to handle loads correctly in the process of moving loaded trolleys contrary to reg 4(1)(b)(ii) of the Manual Handling Regulations;

(vi)   failed to take appropriate steps to reduce the risk of injury to the Claimant arising out of undertaking the operation set out above to the lowest practicable level contrary to reg 4(1)(b)(ii) of the Manual Handling Regulations.

5.   By reason of the matters aforesaid the Claimant has suffered pain and injury and sustained loss and damage.

PARTICULARS OF INJURY

The Claimant, who was born on 14 December 1992, suffered a fracture to his left thumb. He has made a good but not complete recovery and continues to suffer from some joint stiffness and tenderness. It is anticipated that he will make a full recovery within 18 months of the accident. Further details of the Claimant's injuries and prognosis are provided in the attached medical report of Mr GD Cookson, Consultant Orthopaedic Surgeon, dated 9 January 2015.

PARTICULARS OF PAST AND FUTURE EXPENSES AND LOSSES
See Schedule attached.

6.   The Claimant claims interest on damages pursuant to Section 69 of the County Courts Act 1984 at such rates and for such periods as the Court shall think fit.

AND the Claimant seeks:

(a)   Damages; and

(b)   Interest pursuant to paragraph 6.

DATED this 9th day of February 2015   SIGNED *Goodlaw Solicitors*

STATEMENT OF TRUTH

I believe that the facts stated in these Particulars of Claim are true.

Signed: *Neil Worthing*

Full name: Neil Matthew Worthing, Claimant

Dated: 9th February 2015

The Claimant's solicitors are Goodlaw Solicitors of 4 College Road, Christlethorpe, Guildshire, GU1 4DZ, where they will accept service of proceedings on behalf of the Claimant.

To: the Defendant
To: the Court Manager

DOCUMENT 12 – SCHEDULE OF PAST AND FUTURE EXPENSES AND LOSSES

Claim No: N 15 123

IN THE COUNTY COURT AT CHRISTLETHORPE

BETWEEN

MR NEIL MATTHEW WORTHING	Claimant
and	
GUILDSHIRE ENGINEERING LIMITED	Defendant

SCHEDULE OF PAST AND FUTURE EXPENSES AND LOSSES

The Claimant (d.o.b 14 December 1992) was employed by the Defendant and injured at the Defendant's premises on 13 June 2014, when his left thumb was trapped between the metal handles of two trolleys. He suffered a fracture of the left thumb. His hand and arm were placed in a plaster of paris casing for two weeks and his thumb was bandaged for two weeks thereafter. He underwent five physiotherapy treatments, was unable to work for the remaining nine weeks of his contract with the Defendant, or play the piano at the Swan Lake Hotel for twelve weeks.

Loss of earnings

Guildshire Engineering Ltd

Pre-accident weekly net wage = £296

9 weeks @ £296		£2,664	
Less received from employers	£296		
Net loss of earnings		£2,368	

Swan Lake Hotel

Pre-accident weekly net wage = £260

12 weeks @ £260		£3,120	
Total net loss of earnings			£5,488

Travelling expenses

Journeys to and from hospital/outpatients

2 x trips to have PoP/bandages removed			
5 x trips for physiotherapy			
Total 7 x trips			
(10 miles @ 45p per mile £4.50 per trip)	£31.50		
Car parking 7 x £2	£14		
Total			£45.50

Cost of care

4 hours per day for 14 days @ £7 per hour	£392
TOTAL	£5,925.50

STATEMENT OF TRUTH

I believe the facts stated in this schedule are true

Signed: *Neil Worthing*

Dated this 9th day of February 2015

DOCUMENT 13 – FORM CRU 1

Department for Work & Pensions

Notification of a claim for compensation
Please use block capitals when completing this form

Injured person's details

All parts marked with an asterisk are mandatory requirements as set out in regulations 3,6 & 7 of the Social Security (Recovery of Benefits) Regulations 1997

National Insurance (NI) number
WK987999X

* Date of birth
14/12/1992

Office use   V   NV

* Surname
WORTHING

Date of death (if applicable)

Office use   V   NV

* First forename
NEIL

* Address
22 ELSTEAD HOUSE, GRIFFIN ROAD, CHRISTLETHORPE, GUILDSHIRE

Other forename(s)
MATTHEW

* Postcode GU48 1XX

Any other known surname(s) for example maiden name

Title
MR

Sex (F for female, M for male)
M

Reason for claim as alleged by the injured person

If accident or alleged clinical negligence:

* Date of accident/incident 13/06/2014

*Accident/incident – details of injury sustained resulting from the accident and condition/reason for which compensation is claimed (include specific part injured, left or right where appropriate)

FRACTURED LEFT THUMB ARISING FROM AN ACCIDENT AT WORK WHEN THUMB WAS TRAPPED BETWEEN THE HANDLES OF 2 METAL TROLLEYS

If disease:

* Name of disease – if compensation is also being claimed for condition(s) prior to disease being diagnosed, give those details as well

Office use:
Disease code

Type of liability

Tick appropriate box
Employer - ☑   Clinical negligence - ☐   Public - ☐   Motor - ☐   Other - ☐

Compensator details

Name of compensator or compensator's representative
WINTER WOOD & CO. SOLICITORS

On behalf of: (enter name of compensator if representative's details given opposite)
BRIGHT INSURANCE CO. LTD.

Full postal address
REMBRANT HOUSE
LEE LANE
BRAMPTON, GUILDSHIRE
DX 26438 GUILDSHIRE

Postcode GU7 8TU

Your reference (maximum of 24 characters)
NG/GELTD/14/A48

Name of insured / policy holder or car registration
GUILDSHIRE ENGINEERING LIMITED

Telephone
01483 432143

Fax
01483 432156

CRU1
04-2015

Injured person's representative details

Name of representative

GOODLAW SOLICITORS

Reference (maximum of 24 characters)

BB/WORTH/14/426

Full postal address

4 COLLEGE ROAD
CHRISTLETHORPE
GUILDSHIRE
DX 3214 GUILDSHIRE

Postcode GU1 4DZ

Telephone

01483 606060

Fax

01483 960609

Hospital details
All incidents on or after 29.01.07
Road Traffic Accidents only before 29.01.07

All parts marked with an asterisk are mandatory requirements as set out in Regulation 7 of the Road Traffic (NHS Charges) Regulations 1999 and Regulation 5 of the Personal Injuries (NHS Charges) (General) and Road Traffic (NHS Charges) (Amendment) Regulations 2006

Did the injured person receive NHS treatment because of the incident?

*Yes ☑ No ☐ Not Yet Known ■

Is the compensator the same as the Trust?

*Yes ☐ No ☑
(If yes do not complete hospital details)

Details of the hospital(s) the injured person attended or admitted to in order of attendance.

* Name of hospital (1) (if applicable)

GUILDSHIRE HOSPITAL

Name of hospital (2) (if applicable)

* Address (if applicable)

GROVE ROAD,
CHRISTLETHORPE,
GUILDSHIRE

Postcode GU34 1HH

Address

Postcode

For Road Traffic accidents before 29.01.07:If you are claiming exemption from recovery of NHS charges on the grounds of nil requirement to carry compulsory insurance, (section 144, Road Traffic Act 1988) state category of exemption here: ☐

Employment details
Only complete in disease cases or if date of accident is before 06.04.1994

Was the injured person absent from work prior to 06.04.1994 as a result of the disease/condition(s) for which compensation has been claimed?   Yes ☐ No ☐
If yes, please give name and address of employer(s) and employee payroll number here:

What to do now

Send this form to: Compensation Recovery Unit
Durham House
Washington
Tyne & Wear
NE38 7SF
email: cru1@dwp.gsi.gov.uk

Fax: 0191 2252324

Date:

CRU USE	STB	IS	DLA	PIP	Scrutinised by
BPO	ESA	JSA	AA	UC	
	DISB			DWA	....

CRU1
04-2015

DOCUMENT 14 – CRU CERTIFICATE

DWP Department for Work and Pensions

CRU
DX68560
Washington 4

Compensation Recovery Unit
Durham House
Washington
Tyne & Wear
NE38 7SF

Tel.: 0191-2252377
Fax.: 0191-2252366
Typetalk:-1800101912252377

Our Ref: NLB – 416

Your Ref: BB/WORTH/14/426

Date : 23/02/2015

Below is a copy of the Certificate of Recoverable Benefits sent to Winter Wood & Co.

Please note: This is for information only – no payment is required from you

CRU101

Certificate of Recoverable Benefits

Date of issue: 23/02/2015

Your ref: NG/GELTD/14/A48

Our ref: NBL – 416

Injured person: NEIL M WORTHING

This certificate shows the amount due to the Department for Work and Pensions (DWP), as a result of an accident or injury which occurred on 13/06/2014 to the person named above and is issued in response to your request for a Certificate of Recoverable Benefits which was received on 20/02/2015.

The amount due is NIL. No recoverable benefits have been paid.

This Certificate is valid until 20/08/2016.

Authorized by   S Peters Compensation Recovery Unit
On behalf of the Secretary of State

Issue No. 19988776

CRU100

DOCUMENT 15 – DEFENCE

Claim No: N 15 123

IN THE COUNTY COURT AT CHRISTLETHORPE

BETWEEN

MR NEIL MATTHEW WORTHING　　　　　Claimant

and

GUILDSHIRE ENGINEERING LIMITED　　　　　Defendant

DEFENCE

---

1. Paragraphs 1 and 2 of the Particulars of Claim are admitted.

2. As to Paragraph 3, save that it is admitted that the Claimant suffered some accidental injury on 13 June 2014 at the Defendant's premises, the Defendant is unable to admit or deny the remaining allegations and requires the Claimant to prove them.

3. It is denied that the Defendant, its servant or agent, was negligent as alleged in paragraph 4 or at all.

4   As to the Particulars of Negligence in Paragraph 4:

    (i)   4(a) and 4(e)(i)(ii)(iii)(v) and (vi) are denied. In order to ensure a safe system of work was in operation at all times, the Defendant carried out a suitable and sufficient risk assessment on 27 April 2013, a copy of which is attached to this Defence. The Claimant and Mr Packman were provided with appropriate health and safety information and training both generally and in relation to manual handling, orally and in writing. A copy of the written information relevant to this matter is attached to this Defence. The Claimant and Mr Packman received specific instructions not to place more than 4 boxes of widgets on each trolley. In the circumstances, it was not reasonable for the Defendant to provide instructions on how to push a trolley, that being a matter of common sense;

    (ii)   4(b) and 4(e)(iv) are denied. The trolleys were suitable for the purpose for which they were provided;

    (iii) 4(c) is denied. It is admitted that the Defendant was aware of Mr Packman's nature as stated in 4(c), but it is denied that the Defendant failed to provide the Claimant with competent fellow workers. The health and safety information and training mentioned in 4(i) above is provided to all employees, and was provided to Mr Packman. This included clear instructions that practical jokes and horseplay on the Defendant's premises would not be tolerated, and that any such incidents that did arise would lead to investigation and disciplinary action where appropriate. To the Defendant's knowledge, no incidents of horseplay had taken place on the Defendant's premises for at least two years prior to this incident.

    (iv)   4(d) is denied. 4(i) to (iii) are repeated.

5. Further or in the alternative, if, which is not admitted, the Claimant's thumb became trapped between the handles of the trolleys as alleged and this was caused wholly or partly by any inappropriate behaviour on the part of Mr Packman, which is denied, Mr Packman was acting contrary to instructions given to him by the Defendant and was therefore not acting in the course of his employment.

6. Further or in the alternative, if, which is not admitted, the Claimant's thumb became trapped between the handles of the trolleys as alleged, the accident was wholly caused or alternatively materially contributed to by his own negligence.

PARTICULARS OF NEGLIGENCE

The Claimant:

(a)   stacked the second trolley with five boxes instead of four as instructed;

(b)   engaged in horseplay with Mr Packman and encouraged him to behave irresponsibly;

(c)   failed to exercise reasonable care for his own safety.

7.   The Defendant denies that any pain, injury, loss or damage alleged in Paragraph 5 was caused by any negligence by the Defendant as alleged or at all. The Defendant is not in a position to agree or dispute the contents of the attached medical report of Mr Cookson or the alleged losses and expenses set out in the attached Schedule. Consequently, the Defendant puts the Claimant to strict proof in relation to all damages claimed.

DATED this 18th day of February 2015   SIGNED *Winter Wood & Co*

STATEMENT OF TRUTH

The Defendant believes that the facts stated in this Defence are true.

I am duly authorised by the Defendant to sign this statement.

Full name: Jacob Hudson

Signed: *J Hudson*   Position held: Managing Director
18th February 2015

The Defendant's solicitors are Winter Wood & Co, Rembrandt House, Lee Lane, Brampton, Guildshire, GU7 8TU where they will accept service of proceedings on behalf of the Defendant.

To: The Claimant
To: The Court Manager

(Note to readers – the attachments referred to in this Defence are not reproduced)

DOCUMENT 16 – DIRECTIONS QUESTIONNAIRE

Directions questionnaire (Fast track and Multi-track)

▶ Print form   ▶ Reset form

In the	Claim No.
CHRISTLETHORPE C.C.	N 15 123

To be completed by, or on behalf of,

Mr Neil Matthew Worthing

who is [1ˢᵗ][2ⁿᵈ][3ʳᵈ][   ][Claimant][Defendant][Part 20 claimant] in this claim

---

You should note the date by which this questionnaire must be returned and the name of the court it should be returned to since this may be different from the court where the proceedings were issued.

If you have settled this claim (or if you settle it on a future date) and do not need to have it heard or tried, you must let the court know immediately.

If the claim is not settled, a judge will allocate it to an appropriate case management track. To help the judge choose the most just and cost-effective track, you must now complete the directions questionnaire.

You should write the claim number on any other documents you send with your directions questionnaire. Please ensure they are firmly attached to it.

A Settlement

Notes

Under the Civil Procedure Rules parties should make every effort to settle their case before the hearing. This could be by discussion or negotiation (such as a roundtable meeting or settlement conference) or by a more formal process such as mediation. The court will want to know what steps have been taken. Settling the case early can save costs, including court hearing fees.

For legal representatives only

I confirm that I have explained to my client the need to try to settle; the options available; and the possibility of costs sanctions if they refuse to try to settle.

☑ I confirm

For all

Your answers to these questions may be considered by the court when it deals with the questions of costs: see Civil Procedure Rules Part 44.

1. Given that the rules require you to try to settle the claim before the hearing, do you want to attempt to settle at this stage?   ☐ Yes ☑ No

2. If Yes, do you want a one month stay?   ☐ Yes ☑ No

3. If you answered 'No' to question 1, please state below the reasons why you consider it inappropriate to try to settle the claim at this stage.

Reasons:

Attempts to settle were made pre-issue but were unsuccessful. There is no possibility of settlement at this stage, but both parties will reconsider the matter following exchange of documents/witness statements.

The court may order a stay, whether or not all the other parties to the claim agree. Even if you are requesting a stay, you must still complete the rest of the questionnaire.

More information about mediation, the fees charged and a directory of mediation providers is available online from www.civilmediation.justice.gov.uk This service provides members of the public and businesses with contact details for national civil and commercial mediation providers, all of whom are accredited by the Civil Mediation Council.

B Court

B1. (High Court only)

The claim has been issued in the High Court. Do you consider it should remain there?   ☐ Yes   ☐ No

If Yes, in which Division/List?

```

```

If No, in which County Court hearing centre would you prefer the case to be heard?

```

```

B2. Trial (all cases)

Is there any reason why your claim needs to be heard at a court or hearing centre?   ☑ Yes   ☐ No

If Yes, say which court and why?

```
Christlethorpe County Court, as this is local to both parties and their
legal representatives.
```

High Court cases are usually heard at the Royal Courts of Justice or certain Civil Trial Centres. Fast or multi-track trials may be dealt with at a Civil Trial Centre or at the court where the claim is proceeding.

C Pre-action protocols

You are expected to comply fully with the relevant pre-action protocol.

Have you done so?   ☑ Yes   ☐ No

If you have not complied, or have only partially complied, please explain why.

```

```

Before any claim is started, the court expects you to have complied with the relevant pre-action protocol, and to have exchanged information and documents relevant to the claim to assist in settling it. To find out which protocol is relevant to your claim see: www.justice.gov.uk/guidance/courts-and-tribunals/courts/procedure-rules/civil/menus/protocol.htm

D Case management information

D1. Applications

Have you made any application(s) in this claim?   ☐ Yes   ☑ No

If Yes, what for? (e.g. summary judgment, add another party).

```

```

For hearing on ☐☐ / ☐☐ / ☐☐☐☐

D2. Track

If you have indicated in the proposed directions a track attached which would not be the normal track for the claim, please give brief reasons below for your choice.

```

```

D1. Applications

It is important for the court to know if you have already made any applications in the claim (or are about to issue one), what they are for and when they will be heard. The outcome of the applications may affect the case management directions the court gives.

D2. Track

The basic guide by which claims are normally allocated to a track is the amount in dispute, although other factors such as the complexity of the case will also be considered. Leaflet *EX305 – The Fast Track and the Multi-track*, explains this in greater detail.

2

D | Case management information (continued)   Notes

D3. Disclosure of electronic documents (multi-track cases only)

If you are proposing that the claim be allocated to the multi-track:

1. Have you reached agreement, either using the Electronic Documents   ☐ Yes   ☐ No
    Questionnaire in Practice Direction 31B or otherwise, about the scope
    and extent of disclosure of electronic documents on each side?

2. If No, is such agreement likely?   ☐ Yes   ☐ No

3. If there is no agreement and no agreement is likely, what are
    the issues about disclosure of electronic documents which the
    court needs to address, and should they be dealt with at the Case
    Management Conference or at a separate hearing?

    ┌───┐
    │   │
    │   │
    │   │
    │   │
    └───┘

D4. Disclosure of non-electronic documents (all cases)

What directions are proposed for disclosure?

┌───┐
│   │
│   │
│   │
│   │
│   │
└───┘

For all multi-track cases, except personal injury.

Have you filed and served a disclosure report (Form N263)   ☐ Yes   ☐ No
(see Civil Procedure Rules Part 31).

Have you agreed a proposal in relation to disclosure that meets the   ☐ Yes   ☐ No
overriding objective?

If Yes, please ensure this is contained within the proposed directions
attached and specify the draft order number.

┌───┐
│   │
└───┘

E | Experts

Do you wish to use expert evidence at the trial or final hearing?   ☑ Yes   ☐ No   There is no presumption that expert evidence is necessary,
                                                                                                 or that each party will be entitled to their own expert(s).
Have you already copied any experts' report(s) to the other party(ies)? ☐ None yet obtained   Therefore, the court requires a short explanation of your
                                                                          ☑ Yes   ☐ No   proposals with regard to expert evidence.

Do you consider the case suitable for a single joint expert in any field? ☑ Yes   ☐ No

E Experts (continued)

Please list any single joint experts you propose to use and any other experts you wish to rely on.
Identify single joint experts with the initials 'SJ' after their name(s). Please provide justification of
your proposal and an estimate of costs.

Expert's name	Field of expertise (e.g. orthopaedic surgeon, surveyor, engineer)	Justification for expert and estimate of costs
Mr. G D Cookson (SJ)	Consultant orthopaedic surgeon	Evidence as to diagnosis of injury and likely duration of pain / disability. £780.00 including VAT

F Witnesses

Which witnesses of fact do you intend to call at the trial or final hearing including, if appropriate, yourself?

Witness name	Witness to which facts
Mr Neil Worthing - Claimant	The lack of information / training he received from the Defendant; the accident; the injury and associated losses and expenses.

G Trial or Final Hearing

How long do you estimate the trial or final hearing will take?

[✔] less than one day   [ ] one day   [ ] more than one day

    3   Hrs   [ ] State number of days

Give the best estimate you can of the time that the court will need to decide this case. If, later you have any reason to shorten or lengthen this estimate you should let the court know immediately.

Are there any days within the next 12 months when you, an expert or an essential witness will not be able to attend court for trial or final hearing?

You should only enter those dates when you, your expert(s) or essential witnesses will not be available to attend court because of holiday or other commitments.

If Yes, please give details

Name	Dates not available
Mr Worthing Mr Cookson	1-12 June 2015 - exams 10-21 August 2015 - holiday

You should notify the court immediately if any of these dates change.

H Costs

Do not complete this section if:

1) you do not have a legal representative acting for you

2) the case is subject to fixed costs

If your claim is likely to be allocated to the Multi-Track form Precedent H must be filed at in accordance with CPR 3.13.

I confirm Precedent H is attached. ☐

I Other information

Do you intend to make any applications in the future?   ☐ Yes   ☑ No

If Yes, what for?

In the space below, set out any other information you consider will help the judge to manage the claim.

J Directions

You must attempt to agree proposed directions with all other parties. **Whether agreed or not a draft of the order for directions which you seek must accompany this form.**

All proposed directions for multi-track cases must be based on the directions at www.justice.gov.uk/courts/procedure-rules/civil

All proposed directions for fast track cases must be based on CPR Part 28.

Signature

Goodlaw, Solicitors

[Legal Representative for the][1st][2nd][3rd][   ]
[Claimant][Defendant][Part 20 claimant]

Date
0 4 / 0 3 / 2 0 1 5

Please enter your name, reference number and full postal address including details of telephone, DX, fax or e-mail

Goodlaw Solicitors 4 College Road Christlethorpe Guildshire		If applicable
	Telephone no.	01483 606060
	Fax no.	01483 606099
	DX no.	DX3214 GUILD.
Postcode G U 1 4 D Z	Your ref.	BB/WORTH14/426

E-mail	bbraithwaite@goodlaw.co.uk

▶ Print form   ▶ Reset form

DOCUMENT 17 – NOTICE OF ALLOCATION TO FAST TRACK AND DIRECTIONS

To: the Claimant's
Solictor

Goodlaw Solicitors
4 College Road
Christlethorpe
Guildshire
GU1 4DZ

In the	COUNTY COURT AT CHRISTLETHORPE
Claim Number	N 15 123
Claimant (including ref)	Mr Neil Matthew Worthing
Defendant (including ref)	Guildshire Engineering Limited
Date	21/04/15

Warning: you must comply with the terms imposed upon you by this order otherwise your case is liable to be struck out or some other sanction imposed. If you cannot comply you are expected to make formal application to the court before any deadline imposed upon you expires.

On 21 April 2015, DISTRICT JUDGE BILLINGHURST, sitting in the County Court at Christlethorpe, considered the papers in the case and **ordered** that:

1. This case is allocated to the fast track

2. (a) Standard disclosure by lists between the parties by 4:00pm on 26 May 2015 and CPR 31.21 shall apply in the event of default.

    (b) Inspection of documents by 4:00pm on 9 June 2015

3. (a) Statements of witnesses as to fact to be exchanged by 4:00pm on 7 July 2015

    (b) Witness statements shall stand as evidence in chief.

    (c) Evidence shall not be permitted at trial from a witness whose evidence has not been served in accordance with this order.

4. (a) The Claimant is permitted to rely on the written report of Mr G D Cookson.

    (b) The Defendant shall raise any questions of the said expert in writing by 4:00pm on 21 July 2015 which shall be responded to by 4:00pm on 17 August 2015.

5. (a) The Claimant shall serve an updated schedule of damages by 4:00pm on 25 August 2015 and the Defendant shall serve any counter schedule by 4:00pm on 1 September 2015 both incorporating an estimate of the general range of damages.

    (b) Within 7 days of the exchange of schedules the parties shall communicate and shall agree subject to liability the range of general damages and the extent to which the general damages are agreed and shall agree a case summary setting out the extent of agreement and of disagreement giving reasons for the disagreement.

6. The parties shall file a Listing Questionnaire by 4:00pm on 29 September 2015 together with the case summary directed at 5(b) above.

7. (a) The matter be listed for trial before a District Judge in a 3 week trial window commencing 2 November 2015 with an estimated length of hearing of 3 hours.

    (b) The Claimant shall lodge the trial bundle by no later than 5 days prior to the date of trial.

Dated 21 April 2015

The court office at the County Court at CHRISTLETHORPE is open between 10am and 4pm Monday to Friday. When corresponding with the court, please address forms or letters to the Court Manager and quote the claim number. Tel: 01483 123123 Fax: 01483 123345.

DOCUMENT 18 – MEMORANDUM RE OFFER

From: Ravinder Omar, Assistant Solicitor, Goodlaw

Sent: 11/07/15

To: Belinda Braithwaite, Principal Solicitor, Goodlaw

Subject: Neil Worthing case – settlement

Hi Belinda

Just to let you know that we exchanged witness statements with the defendant last week. In his statement Jerry Packman, the guy who was loading the trolleys with Mr W, confirms that it was Mr W who suggested putting the extra box onto the second trolley. He also says that it was Mr W who started messing about with the trolleys, that Mr W pushed his trolley at Mr P's trolley first and then stood about laughing as Mr P tried to push his trolley. That's when the accident happened. In addition, contrary to what he told our client, he is now saying that he did have H&S/manual handling training.

I discussed this with Rosie Smith at Winter Wood on Friday. I said that they couldn't avoid liability. Just handing over H&S info to Mr W isn't sufficient instruction and training, particularly as he has never worked in a factory before. They haven't got any evidence to back up their statement that the foam on the handles was sorted out before the accident and Mr Packman was messing about too. She more or less said she agreed and that she would be talking to her client about making a Part 36 offer on a 25% contrib. basis. The certificate obtained from the CRU shows that there are no repayable benefits. (There are NHS charges which relate to the treatment our client received at hospital, but the defendant has to pay that.)

She was unhappy about our claim for gratuitous care, saying that the number of hours claimed and the amount per hour are unreasonable. She didn't like our mileage rates either but I don't think they'll quibble over a few pounds.

I couldn't get hold of Mr W until this morning. He admitted that Mr P's account was accurate. He is keen to settle and understands that the defendant will want to knock a bit off for contributory negligence. I told him we would wait and see what they offered and then we would talk again.

What do you think?

Ravi

DOCUMENT 19 – PART 36 OFFER LETTER

Winter Wood & Co Solicitors

Rembrandt House,
Lee Lane, Brampton
Guildshire, GU7 8TU
DX 26438 GUILDSHIRE
Tel: 01483 432143
Fax: 01483 432156

Goodlaw Solicitors
DX 3214 GUILDSHIRE

Our ref: NG/GELTD/14/A48
Your ref: BB/WORTH/14/426

Date: 14 July 2015

Dear Sirs

YOUR CLIENT: Mr Neil Worthing
OUR CLIENT: Guildshire Engineering Limited
ACCIDENT DATE: 13 June 2014
PART 36 OFFER – without prejudice save as to costs

We are instructed by our client to put forward the following offer which is made without prejudice save as to costs pursuant to Part 36 of the Civil Procedure Rules 1998:

1.   Our client agrees to pay your client the sum of £6,600 inclusive of interest in full and final settlement of all claims your client has or may have against our client in this matter.

2.   Our client agrees in addition to pay your client's reasonable costs, including costs that have been incurred up to 21 days after the date you receive this letter, as agreed or, if not agreed within 14 days, to be assessed by detailed assessment.

3.   This offer is open for acceptance for 21 days from the date you receive this letter.

We await hearing from you.

Yours faithfully,

Winter Wood & Co

DOCUMENT 20 – MEMORANDUM RE PART 36 OFFER

From: Ravinder Omar, Assistant Solicitor Goodlaw

Sent: 17/07/2015

To: Belinda Braithwaite, Principal Solicitor, Goodlaw

Subject: Neil Worthing

Hi Belinda

I telephoned Mr W to inform him of the offer. I talked him through the options and advised him that I thought it was reasonable but perhaps a little on the low side. We agreed that I would speak to the defendant's solicitors to see if I can get them to improve their offer but if not, he wanted to accept their offer.

I then spoke to Rosie Smith at Winter Wood & Co. Their offer is based on generals of £4,000, 25% contributory negligence and some reduction in the claim for gratuitous care. After some negotiation she agreed to increase the offer to £7,000 which I accepted on Mr W's behalf. I will send a consent order to finalise the matter.

I rang Mr W to tell him the good news – he is delighted!

Ravi

DOCUMENT 21 – ACCEPTANCE LETTER

Goodlaw Solicitors

4 College Road, Christlethorpe, Guildshire, GU1 4DZ
DX 3214 GUILDSHIRE; Tel: 01483 606060; Fax: 01483 606099

Winter Wood & Co Solicitors
DX 26438 GUILDSHIRE

Your ref: NG/GELTD/14/A48
bbraithwaite@goodlaw.co.uk
Our ref : BB/WORTH/14/426
Date: 20 July 2015

Dear Sirs,

OUR CLIENT: Mr Neil Worthing
ADDRESS: 22 Elstead House, Griffin Road, Guildshire, GU48 1XX
ACCIDENT DATE: 13 June 2014

Further to our telephone conversation with Rosie Smith we confirm that our client is prepared to accept your offer of £7,000 in full and final settlement of his claim plus our costs to be assessed if not agreed. Please sign and return the enclosed consent order which we will then file at court.

Yours faithfully

Goodlaw Solicitors

DOCUMENT 22 – DRAFT CONSENT ORDER

Claim No: N 15 123

IN THE COUNTY COURT AT CHRISTLETHORPE

BETWEEN

MR NEIL MATTHEW WORTHING   Claimant

and

GUILDSHIRE ENGINEERING LIMITED   Defendant

CONSENT ORDER

Upon the parties agreeing to settle this matter

AND BY CONSENT

IT IS ORDERED THAT

1. The Defendant pay the Claimant the sum of £7,000 by 4pm on Monday 17 August 2015;
2. Upon payment, claim N 15 123 be stayed;
3. The Defendant pay the Claimant's costs of this matter to be assessed on the standard basis if not agreed.
4. Liberty to apply.

We consent to the terms of this order.

We consent to the terms of this order.

Goodlaw Solicitors

Winter Wood & Co Solicitors

Dated 31 July 2015

Dated 30 July 2015

Pre-action Protocol for Personal Injury Claims

1. Introduction

1.1

1.1.1 This Protocol is primarily designed for personal injury claims which are likely to be allocated to the fast track and to the entirety of those claims: not only to the personal injury element of a claim which also includes, for instance, property damage. It is not intended to apply to claims which proceed under—

    (a)   the Pre-Action Protocol for Low Value Personal Injury Claims in Road Traffic Accidents from 31 July 2013;

    (b)   the Pre-Action Protocol for Low Value Personal Injury (Employers' Liability and Public Liability) Claims;

    (c)   the Pre-Action Protocol for the Resolution of Clinical Disputes; and

    (d)   the Pre-Action Protocol for Disease and Illness Claims.

1.1.2 If at any stage the claimant values the claim at more than the upper limit of the fast track, the claimant should notify the defendant as soon as possible. However, the "cards on the table" approach advocated by this Protocol is equally appropriate to higher value claims. The spirit, if not the letter of the Protocol, should still be followed for claims which could potentially be allocated multi-track.

1.2   Claims which exit either of the low value pre-action protocols listed at paragraph 1.1.1(a) and (b) ("the low value protocols") prior to Stage 2 will proceed under this Protocol from the point specified in those protocols, and as set out in paragraph 1.3.

1.3

1.3.1 Where a claim exits a low value protocol because the defendant considers that there is inadequate mandatory information in the Claim Notification Form ("CNF"), the claim will proceed under this Protocol from paragraph 5.1.

1.3.2 Where a defendant—

    (a)   alleges contributory negligence;

    (b)   does not complete and send the CNF Response; or

    (c)   does not admit liability,

    the claim will proceed under this Protocol from paragraph 5.5.

1.4

1.4.1 This Protocol sets out conduct that the court would normally expect prospective parties to follow prior to the commencement of proceedings. It establishes a reasonable process and timetable for the exchange of information relevant to a dispute, sets standards for the content and quality of letters of claim, and in particular, the conduct of pre-action negotiations. In particular, the parts of this Protocol that are concerned with rehabilitation are likely to be of application in all claims.

1.4.2 The timetable and the arrangements for disclosing documents and obtaining expert evidence may need to be varied to suit the circumstances of the case. Where one or both parties consider the detail of the Protocol is not appropriate to the case, and proceedings are subsequently issued, the court will expect an explanation as to why the Protocol has not been followed, or has been varied.

1.5   Where either party fails to comply with this Protocol, the court may impose sanctions. When deciding whether to do so, the court will look at whether the parties have complied in substance with the relevant principles and requirements. It will also consider the effect any non-compliance has had on another party. It is not likely to be concerned with minor or technical shortcomings (see paragraphs 13 to 15 of the Practice Direction on Pre-Action Conduct and Protocols).

Early Issue

1.6 The Protocol recommends that a defendant be given three months to investigate and respond to a claim before proceedings are issued. This may not always be possible, particularly where a claimant only consults a legal representative close to the end of any relevant limitation period. In these circumstances, the claimant's solicitor should give as much notice of the intention to issue proceedings as is practicable and the parties should consider whether the court might be invited to extend time for service of the claimant's supporting documents and for service of any defence, or alternatively, to stay the proceedings while the recommended steps in the Protocol are followed.

Litigants in Person

1.7 If a party to the claim does not have a legal representative they should still, in so far as reasonably possible, fully comply with this Protocol. Any reference to a claimant in this Protocol will also mean the claimant's legal representative.

2. Overview of Protocol – General Aim

2.1 The Protocol's objectives are to—

(a)   encourage the exchange of early and full information about the dispute;

(b)   encourage better and earlier pre-action investigation by all parties;

(c)   enable the parties to avoid litigation by agreeing a settlement of the dispute before proceedings are commenced;

(d)   support the just, proportionate and efficient management of proceedings where litigation cannot be avoided; and

(e)   promote the provision of medical or rehabilitation treatment (not just in high value cases) to address the needs of the Claimant at the earliest possible opportunity.

3. The Protocol

An illustrative flow chart is attached at Annexe A which shows each of the steps that the parties are expected to take before the commencement of proceedings.

Letter of Notification

3.1 The claimant or his legal representative may wish to notify a defendant and/or the insurer as soon as they know a claim is likely to be made, but before they are able to send a detailed Letter of Claim, particularly, for instance, when the defendant has no or limited knowledge of the incident giving rise to the claim, or where the claimant is incurring significant expenditure as a result of the accident which he hopes the defendant might pay for, in whole or in part.

3.2 The Letter of Notification should advise the defendant and/or the insurer of any relevant information that is available to assist with determining issues of liability/suitability of the claim for an interim payment and/or early rehabilitation.

3.3 If the claimant or his legal representative gives notification before sending a Letter of Claim, it will not start the timetable for the Letter of Response. However the Letter of Notification should be acknowledged within 14 days of receipt.

4. Rehabilitation

4.1 The parties should consider as early as possible whether the claimant has reasonable needs that could be met by medical treatment or other rehabilitative measures. They should discuss how these needs might be addressed.

4.2 The Rehabilitation Code (which can be found at: http://www.iua.co.uk/IUA_Member/ Publications) is likely to be helpful in considering how to identify the claimant's needs and how to address the cost of providing for those needs.

4.3 The time limit set out in paragraph 6.3 of this Protocol shall not be shortened, except by consent to allow these issues to be addressed.

4.4 Any immediate needs assessment report or documents associated with it that are obtained for the purposes of rehabilitation shall not be used in the litigation except by consent and shall in any event be exempt from the provisions of paragraphs 7.2 to 7.11 of this Protocol. Similarly, persons conducting the immediate needs assessment shall not be a compellable witness at court.

4.5 Consideration of rehabilitation options, by all parties, should be an on going process throughout the entire Protocol period.

5. Letter of Claim

5.1 Subject to paragraph 5.3 the claimant should send to the proposed defendant two copies of the Letter of Claim. One copy of the letter is for the defendant, the second for passing on to the insurers, as soon as possible, and, in any event, within 7 days of the day upon which the defendant received it.

5.2 The Letter of Claim should include the information described on the template at Annexe B1. The level of detail will need to be varied to suit the particular circumstances. In all cases there should be sufficient information for the defendant to assess liability and to enable the defendant to estimate the likely size and heads of the claim without necessarily addressing quantum in detail.

5.3 The letter should contain a clear summary of the facts on which the claim is based together with an indication of the nature of any injuries suffered, and the way in which these impact on the claimant's day to day functioning and prognosis. Any financial loss incurred by the claimant should be outlined with an indication of the heads of damage to be claimed and the amount of that loss, unless this is impracticable.

5.4 Details of the claimant's National Insurance number and date of birth should be supplied to the defendant's insurer once the defendant has responded to the Letter of Claim and confirmed the identity of the insurer. This information should not be supplied in the Letter of Claim.

5.5 Where a claim no longer continues under either low value protocol, the CNF completed by the claimant under those protocols can be used as the Letter of Claim under this Protocol unless the defendant has notified the claimant that there is inadequate information in the CNF.

5.6 Once the claimant has sent the Letter of Claim no further investigation on liability should normally be carried out within the Protocol period until a response is received from the defendant indicating whether liability is disputed.

Status of Letters of Claim and Response

5.7 Letters of Claim and Response are not intended to have the same formal status as a statement of case in proceedings. It would not be consistent with the spirit of the Protocol for a party to 'take a point' on this in the proceedings, provided that there was no obvious intention by the party who changed their position to mislead the other party.

6. The Response

6.1 Attached at Annexe B2 is a template for the suggested contents of the Letter of Response: the level of detail will need to be varied to suit the particular circumstances.

6.2 The defendant must reply within 21 calendar days of the date of posting of the letter identifying the insurer (if any). If the insurer is aware of any significant omissions from the letter of claim they should identify them specifically. Similarly, if they are aware that another defendant has also been identified whom they believe would not be a correct defendant in any proceedings, they should notify the claimant without delay, with reasons, and in any event by the end of the Response period. Where there has been no reply by the defendant or insurer within 21 days, the claimant will be entitled to issue proceedings. Compliance with this paragraph will be taken into account on the question of any assessment of the defendant's costs.

6.3 The defendant (insurer) will have a maximum of three months from the date of acknowledgment of the Letter of Claim (or of the CNF where the claim commenced in a portal) to investigate. No later than the end of that period, The defendant (insurer) should reply by no later than the end of that period, stating if liability is admitted by admitting that the accident occurred, that the accident was caused by the defendant's breach of duty, and the claimant suffered loss and there is no defence under the Limitation Act 1980.

6.4 Where the accident occurred outside England and Wales and/or where the defendant is outside the jurisdiction, the time periods of 21 days and three months should normally be extended up to 42 days and six months.

6.5 If a defendant denies liability and/or causation, their version of events should be supplied. The defendant should also enclose with the response, documents in their possession which are material to the issues between the parties, and which would be likely to be ordered to be disclosed by the court, either on an application for pre-action disclosure, or on disclosure during proceedings. No charge will be made for providing copy documents under the Protocol.

6.6 An admission made by any party under this Protocol may well be binding on that party in the litigation. Further information about admissions made under this Protocol is to be found in Civil Procedure Rules ("CPR") rule 14.1A.

6.7 Following receipt of the Letter of Response, if the claimant is aware that there may be a delay of six months or more before the claimant decides if, when and how to proceed, the claimant should keep the defendant generally informed.

7. Disclosure

7.1 Documents

7.1.1 The aim of early disclosure of documents by the defendant is not to encourage 'fishing expeditions' by the claimant, but to promote an early exchange of relevant information to help in clarifying or resolving issues in dispute. The claimant's solicitor can assist by identifying in the Letter of Claim or in a subsequent letter the particular categories of documents which they consider are relevant and why, with a brief explanation of their purported relevance if necessary.

7.1.2 Attached at Annexe C are specimen, but non-exhaustive, lists of documents likely to be material in different types of claim.

7.1.3 Pre-action disclosure will generally be limited to the documents required to be enclosed with the Letter of Claim and the Response. In cases where liability is admitted in full, disclosure will be limited to the documents relevant to quantum, the parties can agree that further disclosure may be given. If either or both of the parties consider that further disclosure should be given but there is disagreement about some aspect of that process, they may be able to make an application to the court for pre-action disclosure under Part 31 of the CPR. Parties should assist each other and avoid the necessity for such an application.

7.1.4 The protocol should also contain a requirement that the defendant is under a duty to preserve the disclosure documents and other evidence (CCTV for example). If the documents are destroyed, this could be an abuse of the court process.

Experts

7.2 Save for cases likely to be allocated to the multi-track, the Protocol encourages joint selection of, and access to, quantum experts, and, on occasion liability experts e.g. engineers. The expert report produced is not a joint report for the purposes of CPR Part 35. The Protocol promotes the practice of the claimant obtaining a medical report, disclosing it to the defendant who then asks questions and/or agrees it and does not obtain their own report. The Protocol provides for nomination of the expert by the claimant in personal injury claims.

7.3 Before any party instructs an expert, they should give the other party a list of the name(s) of one or more experts in the relevant speciality whom they consider are suitable to instruct.

7.4 Some solicitors choose to obtain medical reports through medical agencies, rather than directly from a specific doctor or hospital. The defendant's prior consent to this should be sought and, if the defendant so requests, the agency should be asked to provide in advance the names of the doctor(s) whom they are considering instructing.

7.5 Where a medical expert is to be instructed, the claimant's solicitor will organise access to relevant medical records – see specimen letter of instruction at Annexe D.

7.6 Within 14 days of providing a list of experts the other party may indicate an objection to one or more of the named experts. The first party should then instruct a mutually acceptable expert assuming there is one (this is not the same as a joint expert). It must be emphasised that when the claimant nominates an expert in the original Letter of Claim, the defendant has a further 14 days to object to one or more of the named experts after expiration of the 21 day period within which they have to reply to the Letter of Claim, as set out in paragraph 6.2.

7.7 If the defendant objects to all the listed experts, the parties may then instruct experts of their own choice. It will be for the court to decide, subsequently and if proceedings are issued, whether either party had acted unreasonably.

7.8 If the defendant does not object to an expert nominated by the claimant, they shall not be entitled to rely on their own expert evidence within that expert's area of expertise unless—

(a)   the claimant agrees;

(b)   the court so directs; or

(c)   the claimant's expert report has been amended and the claimant is not prepared to disclose the original report.

7.9 Any party may send to an agreed expert written questions on the report, via the first party's solicitors. Such questions must be put within 28 days of service of the expert's report and must only be for the purpose of clarification of the report. The expert should send answers to the questions simultaneously to each party.

7.10 The cost of a report from an agreed expert will usually be paid by the instructing first party: the costs of the expert replying to questions will usually be borne by the party which asks the questions.

7.11 If necessary, after proceedings have commenced and with the permission of the court, the parties may obtain further expert reports. It would be for the court to decide whether the costs of more than one expert's report should be recoverable.

8. Negotiations following an admission

8.1

8.1.1 Where a defendant admits liability which has caused some damage, before proceedings are issued, the claimant should send to that defendant—

(a)   any medical reports obtained under this Protocol on which the claimant relies; and

(b)   a schedule of any past and future expenses and losses which are claimed, even if the schedule is necessarily provisional. The schedule should contain as much detail as reasonably practicable and should identify those losses that are ongoing. If the schedule is likely to be updated before the case is concluded, it should say so.

8.1.2 The claimant should delay issuing proceedings for 21 days from disclosure of (a) and (b) above (unless such delay would cause his claim to become time-barred), to enable the parties to consider whether the claim is capable of settlement.

8.2   CPR Part 36 permits claimants and defendants to make offers to settle pre-proceedings. Parties should always consider if it is appropriate to make a Part 36 Offer before issuing. If such an offer is made, the party making the offer must always try to supply sufficient evidence and/or information to enable the offer to be properly considered.

The level of detail will depend on the value of the claim. Medical reports may not be necessary where there is no significant continuing injury and a detailed schedule may not be necessary in a low value case.

9. Alternative Dispute Resolution

9.1

9.1.1 Litigation should be a last resort. As part of this Protocol, the parties should consider whether negotiation or some other form of Alternative Dispute Resolution ("ADR") might enable them to resolve their dispute without commencing proceedings.

9.1.2 Some of the options for resolving disputes without commencing proceedings are—

- (a)   discussions and negotiation (which may or may not include making Part 36 Offers or providing an explanation and/or apology);
- (b)   mediation, a third party facilitating a resolution;
- (c)   arbitration, a third party deciding the dispute; and
- (d)   early neutral evaluation, a third party giving an informed opinion on the dispute.

9.1.3 If proceedings are issued, the parties may be required by the court to provide evidence that ADR has been considered. It is expressly recognised that no party can or should be forced to mediate or enter into any form of ADR but unreasonable refusal to consider ADR will be taken into account by the court when deciding who bears the costs of the proceedings.

9.2   Information on mediation and other forms of ADR is available in the Jackson ADR Handbook (available from Oxford University Press) or at—

http://www.civilmediation.justice.gov.uk/

http://www.adviceguide.org.uk/england/law_e/law_legal_system_e/law_taking_legal_action_e/alternatives_to_court.htm

10. Quantification of Loss - Special damages

10.1   In all cases, if the defendant admits liability, the claimant will send to the defendant as soon as reasonably practicable a schedule of any past and future expenses and losses which he claims, even if the schedule is necessarily provisional. The schedule should contain as much detail as reasonably practicable and should identify those losses that are ongoing. If the schedule is likely to be updated before the case is concluded, it should say so. The claimant should keep the defendant informed as to the rate at which his financial loss is progressing throughout the entire Protocol period.

11. Stocktake

11.1   Where the procedure set out in this Protocol has not resolved the dispute between the parties, each party should undertake a review of its own positions and the strengths and weaknesses of its case. The parties should then together consider the evidence and the arguments in order to see whether litigation can be avoided or, if that is not possible, for the issues between the parties to be narrowed before proceedings are issued. Where the defendant is insured and the pre-action steps have been taken by the insurer, the insurer would normally be expected to nominate solicitors to act in the proceedings and to accept service of the claim form and other documents on behalf of the defendant. The claimant or their solicitor is recommended to invite the insurer to nominate the insurer to nominate solicitors to act in the proceedings and do so 7 to 14 days before the intended issue date.

Annex A: Illustrative flow chart

ANNEXE A - ILLUSTRATIVE FLOWCHART OF LIKELY PROGRESSION OF THE CLAIM UNDER THIS PROTOCOL

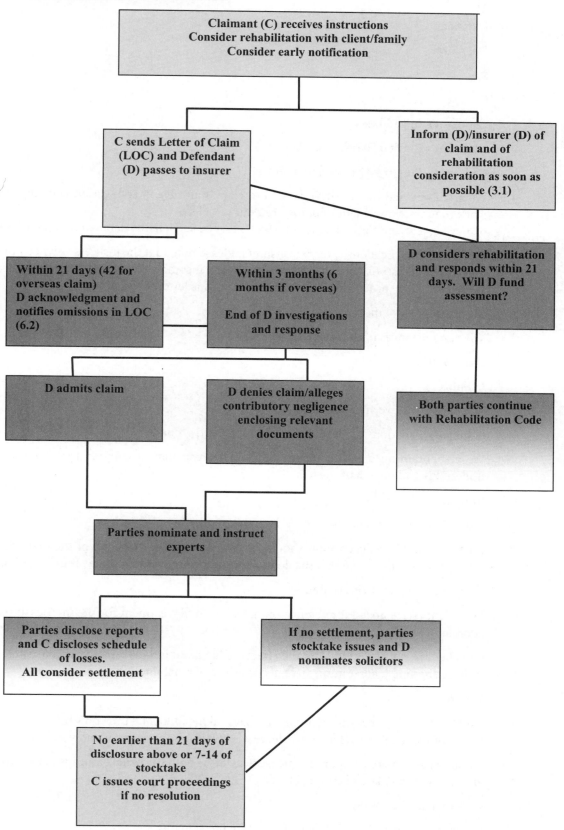

Annex B: Templates for letters of claim and response

B1 Letter of Claim

To

Defendant

Dear Sirs

Re:

Claimant's full name

Claimant's full address

Claimant's Clock or Works Number

Claimant's Employer (name and address)

We are instructed by the above named to claim damages in connection with an **accident at work/road traffic accident/tripping accident**
on day of **(year)** at **(place of accident which must be sufficiently detailed to establish location)**

Please confirm the identity of your insurers. Please note that the insurers will need to see this letter as soon as possible and it may affect your insurance cover and/or the conduct of any subsequent legal proceedings if you do not send this letter to them.

Clear summary of the facts

The circumstances of the accident are:

(brief outline)

Liability

The reason why we are alleging fault is:

(simple explanation e.g. defective machine, broken ground)

We are obtaining a police report and will let you have a copy of the same upon your undertaking to meet half the fee.

Injuries

A description of our clients' injuries is as follows:

(brief outline) The description should include a non-exhaustive list of the main functional effects on daily living, so that the defendant can begin to assess value / rehabilitation needs.

(In cases of road traffic accidents)

Our client (state hospital reference number) received treatment for the injuries at name and address of hospital).

Our client is still suffering from the effects of his/her injury. We invite you to participate with us in addressing his/her immediate needs by use of rehabilitation.

Loss of Earnings

He/She is employed as (occupation) and has had the following time off work
(dates of absence). His/Her approximate weekly income is (insert if known).

If you are our client's employers, please provide us with the usual earnings details which will enable us to calculate his financial loss.

Other Financial Losses

We are also aware of the following (likely) financial losses:

Details of the insurer

We have also sent a letter of claim to **(name and address)** and a copy of that letter is attached. We understand their insurers are **(name, address and claims number if known)**.

At this stage of our enquiries we would expect the documents contained in parts **(insert appropriate parts of standard disclosure list)** to be relevant to this action.

A copy of this letter is attached for you to send to your insurers. Finally we expect an acknowledgment of this letter within 21 days by yourselves or your insurers.

Yours faithfully

B2 Letter of response

To Claimant's legal representative

Dear Sirs

Letter of Response

[Claimant's name] v [Defendant's name]

Parties

We have been instructed to act on behalf of [defendant] in relation to your client's accident on [   ]. We note that you have also written to [defendant] in connection with this claim. We [do/do not] believe they are a relevant party because [   ]. [In addition we believe your claim should be directed against [defendant] for the following reasons:

Liability

In respect of our client's liability for this accident we admit the accident occurred and that our client is liable for loss and damage to the claimant the extent of which will require quantification.

Or

admit the accident occurred but deny that our client is responsible for any loss or damage alleged to have been caused for the following reasons:–

Or

do not admit the accident occurred either in the manner described in your letter of claim [or at all] because:

Limitation

[We do not intend to raise any limitation defence]

Documents

We attach copies of the following documents in support of our client's position:

You have requested copies of the following documents which we are not enclosing as we do not believe they are relevant for the following reasons:

[It would assist our investigations if you could supply us with copies of the following documents]

Next Steps

In admitted cases

Please advise us which medical experts you are proposing to instruct.

Please also supply us with your client's schedule of past and future expenses [if any] which are claimed, even if this can only be supplied on a provisional basis at present to assist us with making an appropriate reserve.

If you have identified that the claimant has any immediate need for additional medical treatment or other early rehabilitation intervention so that we can take instructions pursuant to the Rehabilitation Code.

In non-admitted cases

Please confirm we may now close our file. Alternatively, if you intend to proceed please advise which experts you are proposing to instruct.

Alternative Dispute Resolution

Include details of any options that may be considered whether on a without prejudice basis or otherwise.

Yours faithfully

Annex C: Pre-Action Personal Injury Protocol Standard Disclosure Lists

RTA CASES

SECTION A

In all cases where liability is at issue–

(i)   documents identifying nature, extent and location of damage to defendant's vehicle where there is any dispute about point of impact;

(ii)   MOT certificate where relevant;

(iii)   maintenance records where vehicle defect is alleged or it is alleged by defendant that there was an unforeseen defect which caused or contributed to the accident.

SECTION B

Accident involving commercial vehicle as defendant–

(i)   tachograph charts or entry from individual control book;

(ii)   maintenance and repair records required for operators' licence where vehicle defect is alleged or it is alleged by defendant that there was an unforeseen defect which caused or contributed to the accident.

SECTION C

Cases against local authorities where highway design defect is alleged—

(i)   documents produced to comply with Section 39 of the Road Traffic Act 1988 in respect of the duty designed to promote road safety to include studies into road accidents in the relevant area and documents relating to measures recommended to prevent accidents in the relevant area;

(ii)   any Rule 43 reports produced at the request of a coroner pursuant to Schedule 5 of the Coroners & Justice Act 2009, for accidents occurring in the same locus as one covered by an earlier report.

HIGHWAY TRIPPING CLAIMS

Documents from Highway Authority for a period of 12 months prior to the accident–

(i)   records of inspection for the relevant stretch of highway;

(ii)   maintenance records including records of independent contractors working in relevant area;

(iii)   records of the minutes of Highway Authority meetings where maintenance or repair policy has been discussed or decided;

(iv)   records of complaints about the state of highways;

(v)   records of other accidents which have occurred on the relevant stretch of highway.

WORKPLACE CLAIMS

GENERAL DOCUMENTS

(i)   accident book entry;

(ii)   other entries in the book or other accident books, relating to accidents or injuries similar to those suffered by our client (and if it is contended there are no such entries please confirm we may have facilities to inspect all accident books);

(iii)   first aider report;

(iv)   surgery record;

(v)   foreman/supervisor accident report;

(vi)   safety representative's accident report;

(vii)   RIDDOR (Reporting of Injuries, Diseases and Dangerous Occurrences Regulations) reported to HSE or relevant investigatory agency;

(viii)   back to work interview notes and report;

(ix)   all personnel/occupational health records relating to our client;

(x)   other communications between defendants and HSE or other relevant investigatory agency;

(xi)   minutes of Health and Safety Committee meeting(s) where accident/matter considered;

(xii)   copies of all relevant CCTV footage and any other relevant photographs, videos and/or DVDs;

(xiii)   copies of all electronic communications/documentation relating to the accident;

(xiv)   earnings information where defendant is employer;

(xv)   reports to DWP;

(xvi)   manufacturer's or dealers instructions or recommendations concerning use of the work equipment;

(xvii)   service or maintenance records of the work equipment;

(xviii)   all documents recording arrangements for detecting, removing or cleaning up any articles or substances on the floor of the premises likely to cause a trip or slip;

(xix)   work sheets and all other documents completed by or on behalf of those responsible for implementing the cleaning policy and recording work done;

(xx)   all invoices, receipts and other documents relating to the purchase of relevant safety equipment to prevent a repetition of the accident;

(xxi)   all correspondence, memoranda or other documentation received or brought into being concerning the condition or repair of the work equipment/the premises;

(xxii)   all correspondence, instructions, estimates, invoices and other documentation submitted or received concerning repairs, remedial works or other works to the work equipment/the premises since the date of that accident;

(xxiii)   work sheets and all other documents recording work done completed by those responsible for maintaining the work equipment/premises;

(xxiv)   all relevant risk assessments;

(xxv)   all reports, conclusions or recommendations following any enquiry or investigation into the accident;

(xxvi)   the record kept of complaints made by employees together with all other documents recording in any way such complaints or actions taken thereon;

(xxvii)   all other correspondence sent, or received, relating to our client's injury prior to receipt of this letter of claim;

(xxviii)   documents listed above relating to any previous/similar accident/matter identified by the claimant and relied upon as proof of negligence including accident book entries;

WORKPLACE CLAIMS – DISCLOSURE WHERE SPECIFIC REGULATIONS APPLY

SECTION A - Management of Health and Safety at Work Regulations 1999

Documents including—

(i)   Pre-accident Risk Assessment required by Regulation 3(1);

(ii)   Post-accident Re-Assessment required by Regulation 3(2);

(iii)   Accident Investigation Report prepared in implementing the requirements of Regulations 4, and 5;

(iv)   Health Surveillance Records in appropriate cases required by Regulation 6;

(v)   documents relating to the appointment of competent persons to assist required by Regulation 7;

(vi)   documents relating to the employees health and safety training required by Regulation 8;

(vii)   documents relating to necessary contacts with external services required by Regulation 9;

(viii) information provided to employees under Regulation 10.

SECTION B– Workplace (Health Safety and Welfare) Regulations 1992

Documents including—

(i)   repair and maintenance records required by Regulation 5;

(ii)   housekeeping records to comply with the requirements of Regulation 9;

(iii)   hazard warning signs or notices to comply with Regulation 17 (Traffic Routes).

SECTION C – Provision and Use of Work Equipment Regulations 1998

Documents including—

(i)   manufacturers' specifications and instructions in respect of relevant work equipment establishing its suitability to comply with Regulation 4;

(ii)   maintenance log/maintenance records required to comply with Regulation 5;

(iii)   documents providing information and instructions to employees to comply with Regulation 8;

(iv)   documents provided to the employee in respect of training for use to comply with Regulation 9;

(v)   risk assessments/documents required to comply with Regulation 12;

(vi)   any notice, sign or document relied upon as a defence to alleged breaches of Regulations 14 to 18 dealing with controls and control systems;

(vii)   instruction/training documents issued to comply with the requirements of Regulation 22 insofar as it deals with maintenance operations where the machinery is not shut down;

(viii) copies of markings required to comply with Regulation 23;

(ix)   copies of warnings required to comply with Regulation 24.

SECTION D – Personal Protective Equipment at Work Regulations 1992

Documents including—

(i)   documents relating to the assessment of the Personal Protective Equipment to comply with Regulation 6;

(ii)   documents relating to the maintenance and replacement of Personal Protective Equipment to comply with Regulation 7;

(iii)   record of maintenance procedures for Personal Protective Equipment to comply with Regulation 7;

(iv)   records of tests and examinations of Personal Protective Equipment to comply with Regulation 7;

(v)   documents providing information, instruction and training in relation to the Personal Protective Equipment to comply with Regulation 9;

(vi) instructions for use of Personal Protective Equipment to include the manufacturers' instructions to comply with Regulation 10.

SECTION E – Manual Handling Operations Regulations 1992

Documents including—

(i) Manual Handling Risk Assessment carried out to comply with the requirements of Regulation 4(1)(b)(i);

(ii) re-assessment carried out post-accident to comply with requirements of Regulation 4(1)(b)(i);

(iii) documents showing the information provided to the employee to give general indications related to the load and precise indications on the weight of the load and the heaviest side of the load if the centre of gravity was not positioned centrally to comply with Regulation 4(1)(b)(iii);

(iv) documents relating to training in respect of manual handling operations and training records.

SECTION F – Health and Safety (Display Screen Equipment) Regulations 1992

Documents including—

(i) analysis of work stations to assess and reduce risks carried out to comply with the requirements of Regulation 2;

(ii) re-assessment of analysis of work stations to assess and reduce risks following development of symptoms by the claimant;

(iii) documents detailing the provision of training including training records to comply with the requirements of Regulation 6;

(iv) documents providing information to employees to comply with the requirements of Regulation 7.

SECTION G – Control of Substances Hazardous to Health Regulations 2002

Documents including—

(i) risk assessment carried out to comply with the requirements of Regulation 6;

(ii) reviewed risk assessment carried out to comply with the requirements of Regulation 6;

(iii) documents recording any changes to the risk assessment required to comply with Regulation 6 and steps taken to meet the requirements of Regulation 7;

(iv) copy labels from containers used for storage handling and disposal of carcinogenics to comply with the requirements of Regulation 7(2A)(h);

(v) warning signs identifying designation of areas and installations which may be contaminated by carcinogenics to comply with the requirements of Regulation 7(2A)(h);

(vi) documents relating to the assessment of the Personal Protective Equipment to comply with Regulation 7(3A);

(vii) documents relating to the maintenance and replacement of Personal Protective Equipment to comply with Regulation 7(3A);

(viii) record of maintenance procedures for Personal Protective Equipment to comply with Regulation 7(3A);

(ix) records of tests and examinations of Personal Protective Equipment to comply with Regulation 7(3A);

(x) documents providing information, instruction and training in relation to the Personal Protective Equipment to comply with Regulation 7(3A);

(xi) instructions for use of Personal Protective Equipment to include the manufacturers' instructions to comply with Regulation 7(3A);

(xii) air monitoring records for substances assigned a maximum exposure limit or occupational exposure standard to comply with the requirements of Regulation 7;

(xiii) maintenance examination and test of control measures records to comply with Regulation 9;

(xiv)   monitoring records to comply with the requirements of Regulation 10;

(xv)   health surveillance records to comply with the requirements of Regulation 11;

(xvi)   documents detailing information, instruction and training including training records for employees to comply with the requirements of Regulation 12;

(xvii) all documents relating to arrangements and procedures to deal with accidents, incidents and emergencies required to comply with Regulation 13;

(xvii) labels and Health and Safety data sheets supplied to the employers to comply with the CHIP Regulations.

SECTION H – Construction (Design and Management) Regulations 2007

Documents including—

(i)   notification of a project form (HSE F10) to comply with the requirements of Regulation 7;

(ii)   Health and Safety Plan to comply with requirements of Regulation 15;

(iii)   Health and Safety file to comply with the requirements of Regulations 12 and 14;

(iv)   information and training records provided to comply with the requirements of Regulation 17;

(v)   records of advice from and views of persons at work to comply with the requirements of Regulation 18;

(vi)   reports of inspections made in accordance with Regulation 33;

(vii)   records of checks for the purposes of Regulation 34;

(viii) emergency procedures for the purposes of Regulation 39.

SECTION I – Construction (Health, Safety & Welfare) Regulations 1996

Documents including—

(i)   documents produced to comply with requirements of the Regulations.

SECTION J – Work at Height Regulations 2005

Documents including—

(i)   documents relating to planning, supervision and safety carried out for Regulation 4;

(ii)   documents relating to training for the purposes of Regulation 5;

(iii)   documents relating to the risk assessment carried out for Regulation 6;

(iv)   documents relating to the selection of work equipment for the purposes of Regulation 7;

(v)   notices or other means in writing warning of fragile surfaces for the purposes of Regulation 9;

(vi)   documents relating to any inspection carried out for Regulation 12;

(vii)   documents relating to any inspection carried out for Regulation 13;

(viii) reports made for the purposes of Regulation 14;

(ix)   any certificate issued for the purposes of Regulation 15.

SECTION K – Pressure Systems and Transportable Gas Containers Regulations 1989

(i)   information and specimen markings provided to comply with the requirements of Regulation 5;

(ii)   written statements specifying the safe operating limits of a system to comply with the requirements of Regulation 7;

(iii)   copy of the written scheme of examination required to comply with the requirements of Regulation 8;

(iv)   examination records required to comply with the requirements of Regulation 9;

(v)   instructions provided for the use of operator to comply with Regulation 11;

(vi)   records kept to comply with the requirements of Regulation 13;

(vii)   records kept to comply with the requirements of Regulation 22.

SECTION L – Lifting Operations and Lifting Equipment Regulations 1998

Documents including—

(i) records kept to comply with the requirements of the Regulations including the records kept to comply with Regulation 6.

SECTION M – The Noise at Work Regulations 1989

Documents including—

(i) any risk assessment records required to comply with the requirements of Regulations 4 and 5;

(ii) manufacturers' literature in respect of all ear protection made available to claimant to comply with the requirements of Regulation 8;

(iii) all documents provided to the employee for the provision of information to comply with Regulation 11.

SECTION N – Control of Noise at Work Regulations 1989

Documents including—

(i) documents relating to the assessment of the level of noise to which employees are exposed to comply with Regulation 5;

(ii) documents relating to health surveillance of employees to comply with Regulation 9;

(ii) instruction and training records provided to employees to comply with Regulation 10.

SECTION O – Construction (Head Protection) Regulations 1989

Documents including—

(i) pre-accident assessment of head protection required to comply with Regulation 3(4);

(ii) post-accident re-assessment required to comply with Regulation 3(5).

SECTION P – The Construction (General Provisions) Regulations 1961

Documents including—

(i) report prepared following inspections and examinations of excavations etc. to comply with the requirements of Regulation 9.

SECTION Q – Gas Containers Regulations 1989

Documents including—

(i) information and specimen markings provided to comply with the requirements of Regulation 5;

(ii) written statements specifying the safe operating limits of a system to comply with the requirements of Regulation 7;

(iii) copy of the written scheme of examination required to comply with the requirements of Regulation 8;

(iv) examination records required to comply with the requirements of Regulation 9;

(v) instructions provided for the use of operator to comply with Regulation 11.

SECTION R – Control of Noise at Work Regulations 2005

Documents including—

(i) risk assessment records required to comply with the requirements of Regulations 4 and 5;

(ii) all documents relating to steps taken to comply with regulation 6;

(iii) all documents relating to and/or arising out of actions taken to comply including providing consideration of alternative work that the claimant could have engaged to comply with Regulation 7.

SECTION S – Mine and Quarries Act 1954

Documents including—

(i) documents produced to comply with requirements of the Act.

SECTION T – Control of Vibrations at Work Regulations 2005

Documents including—

(i)   risk assessments and documents produced to comply with requirements of Regulations 6 and 8;

(ii)   occupational health surveillance records produced to comply with Regulation 7.

ANNEX D: Letter of instruction to medical expert

Dear Sir,

Re: **(Name and Address)**

D.O.B.–

Telephone No.–

Date of Accident –

We are acting for the above named in connection with injuries received in an accident which occurred on the above date. A summary of the main facts of the accident circumstances is provided below. The main injuries appear to have been **(describe main injuries and functional impact on day to day living as in Letter of Claim).**

In order to assist with the preparation of your report we have enclosed the following documents:

Enclosures

1. Hospital Records
2. GP records
3. Statement of Events

We have not obtained [ ] records yet but will use our best endeavours to obtain these without delay if you request them.

We should be obliged if you would examine our Client and let us have a full and detailed report dealing with any relevant pre-accident medical history, the injuries sustained, treatment received and present condition, dealing in particular with the capacity for work and giving a prognosis.

It is central to our assessment of the extent of our Client's injuries to establish the extent and duration of any continuing disability. Accordingly, in the prognosis section we would ask you to specifically comment on any areas of continuing complaint or disability or impact on daily living. If there is such continuing disability you should comment upon the level of suffering or inconvenience caused and, if you are able, give your view as to when or if the complaint or disability is likely to resolve.

If our client requires further treatment, please can you advise of the cost on a private patient basis.

Please send our Client an appointment direct for this purpose. Should you be able to offer a cancellation appointment please contact our Client direct. We confirm we will be responsible for your reasonable fees.

We are obtaining the notes and records from our Client's GP and Hospitals attended and will forward them to you when they are to hand/or please request the GP and Hospital records direct and advise that any invoice for the provision of these records should be forwarded to us.

In order to comply with Court Rules we would be grateful if you would insert above your signature, the following statement: "I confirm that I have made clear which facts and matters referred to in this report are within my own knowledge and which are not. Those that are within my own knowledge I confirm to be true. The opinions I have expressed represent my true and complete professional opinions on the matters to which they refer".

In order to avoid further correspondence we can confirm that on the evidence we have there is no reason to suspect we may be pursuing a claim against the hospital or its staff.

We look forward to receiving your report within _____ weeks. If you will not be able to prepare your report within this period please telephone us upon receipt of these instructions.

When acknowledging these instructions it would assist if you could give an estimate as to the likely time scale for the provision of your report and also an indication as to your fee.

Yours faithfully,

Pre-action Protocol for the Resolution of Clinical Disputes

1 INTRODUCTION

1.1 This Protocol is intended to apply to all claims against hospitals, GPs, dentists and other healthcare providers (both NHS and private) which involve an injury that is alleged to be the result of clinical negligence. It is not intended to apply to claims covered by—

(a) the Pre-Action Protocol for Disease and Illness Claims;

(b) the Pre-Action Protocol for Personal Injury Claims;

(c) the Pre-Action Protocol for Low Value Personal Injury Claims in Road Traffic Accidents;

(d) the Pre-Action Protocol for Low Value Personal Injury (Employers' Liability and Public Liability) Claims; or

(e) Practice Direction 3D – Mesothelioma Claims

1.2 This Protocol is intended to be sufficiently broad-based and flexible to apply to all sectors of healthcare, both public and private. It also recognises that a claimant and a defendant, as patient and healthcare provider, may have an ongoing relationship.

1.3 It is important that each party to a clinical dispute has sufficient information and understanding of the other's perspective and case to be able to investigate a claim efficiently and, where appropriate, to resolve it. This Protocol encourages a cards-on-the-table approach when something has gone wrong with a claimant's treatment or the claimant is dissatisfied with that treatment and/or the outcome.

1.4 This Protocol is now regarded by the courts as setting the standard of normal reasonable pre-action conduct for the resolution of clinical disputes.

1.5

1.5.1 This Protocol sets out the conduct that prospective parties would normally be expected to follow prior to the commencement of any proceedings. It establishes a reasonable process and timetable for the exchange of information relevant to a dispute, sets out the standards for the content and quality of letters of claim and sets standards for the conduct of pre-action negotiations.

1.5.2 The timetable and the arrangements for disclosing documents and obtaining expert evidence may need to be varied to suit the circumstances of the case. Where one or more parties consider the detail of the Protocol is not appropriate to the case, and proceedings are subsequently issued, the court will expect an explanation as to why the Protocol has not been followed, or has been varied.

Early Issue

1.6

1.6.1 The Protocol provides for a defendant to be given four months to investigate and respond to a Letter of Claim before proceedings are served. If this is not possible, the claimant's solicitor should give as much notice of the intention to issue proceedings as is practicable. This Protocol does not alter the statutory time limits for starting court proceedings. If a claim is issued after the relevant statutory limitation period has expired, the defendant will be entitled to use that as a defence to the claim. If proceedings are started to comply with the statutory time limit before the parties have followed the procedures in this Protocol, the parties should apply to the court for a stay of the proceedings while they so comply.

1.6.2 The parties should also consider whether there is likely to be a dispute as to limitation should a claim be pursued.

Enforcement of the Protocol and sanctions

1.7   Where either party fails to comply with this Protocol, the court may impose sanctions. When deciding whether to do so, the court will look at whether the parties have complied in substance with the Protocol's relevant principles and requirements. It will also consider the effect any non-compliance has had on any other party. It is not likely to be concerned with minor or technical shortcomings (see paragraph 4.3 to 4.5 of the Practice Direction on Pre-Action Conduct and Protocols).

Litigants in Person

1.8   If a party to a claim does not seek professional advice from a solicitor they should still, in so far as is reasonably possible, comply with the terms of this Protocol. In this Protocol "solicitor" is intended to encompass reference to any suitably legally qualified person.

In so far a party to a claim becomes aware that another party is a litigant in person, they should send a copy of this Protocol to the litigant in person at the earliest opportunity.

2 THE AIMS OF THE PROTOCOL

2.1   The general aims of the Protocol are –

(a)   to maintain and/or restore the patient/healthcare provider relationship in an open and transparent way;

(b)   to reduce delay and ensure that costs are proportionate; and

(c)   to resolve as many disputes as possible without litigation.

2.2   The specific objectives are–

(a)   to encourage openness, transparency and early communication of the perceived problem between patients and healthcare providers;

(b)   to provide an opportunity for healthcare providers to identify whether notification of a notifiable safety incident has been, or should be, sent to the claimant in accordance with the duty of candour imposed by section 20 of the Health and Social Care Act 2008 (Regulated Activities) Regulations 2014;

(c)   to ensure that sufficient medical and other information is disclosed promptly by both parties to enable each to understand the other's perspective and case, and to encourage early resolution or a narrowing of the issues in dispute;

(d)   to provide an early opportunity for healthcare providers to identify cases where an investigation is required and to carry out that investigation promptly;

(e)   to encourage healthcare providers to involve the National Health Service Litigation Authority (NHSLA) or their defence organisations or insurers at an early stage;

(f)   to enable the parties to avoid litigation by agreeing a resolution of the dispute;

(g)   to enable the parties to explore the use of mediation or to narrow the issues in dispute before proceedings are commenced;

(h)   to enable parties to identify any issues that may require a separate or preliminary hearing, such as a dispute as to limitation;

(i)   to support the efficient management of proceedings where litigation cannot be avoided;

(j)   to discourage the prolonged pursuit of unmeritorious claims and the prolonged defence of meritorious claims;

(k)   to promote the provision of medical or rehabilitation treatment to address the needs of the claimant at the earliest opportunity; and

(l)   to encourage the defendant to make an early apology to the claimant if appropriate.

2.3 This Protocol does not—

(a) provide any detailed guidance to healthcare providers on clinical risk management or the adoption of risk management systems and procedures;

(b) provide any detailed guidance on which adverse outcomes should trigger an investigation; or

(c) recommend changes to the codes of conduct of professionals in healthcare.

3 THE PROTOCOL

3.1 An illustrative flowchart is attached at Annex A which shows each of the stages that the parties are expected to take before the commencement of proceedings.

Obtaining health records

3.2 Any request for records by the claimant should–

(a) provide sufficient information to alert the defendant where an adverse outcome has been serious or has had serious consequences or may constitute a notifiable safety incident;

(b) be as specific as possible about the records which are required for an initial investigation of the claim (including, for example, a continuous copy of the CTG trace in birth injury cases); and

(c) include a request for any relevant guidelines, analyses, protocols or policies and any documents created in relation to an adverse incident, notifiable safety incident or complaint.

3.3 Requests for copies of the claimant's clinical records should be made using the Law Society and Department of Health approved standard forms (enclosed at Annex B), adapted as necessary.

3.4

3.4.1 The copy records should be provided within 40 days of the request and for a cost not exceeding the charges permissible under the Access to Health Records Act 1990 and/or the Data Protection Act 1998. Payment may be required in advance by the healthcare provider.

3.4.2 The claimant may also make a request under the Freedom of Information Act 2000.

3.5 At the earliest opportunity, legible copies of the claimant's medical and other records should be placed in an indexed and paginated bundle by the claimant. This bundle should be kept up to date.

3.6 In the rare circumstances that the defendant is in difficulty in complying with the request within 40 days, the problem should be explained quickly and details given of what is being done to resolve it.

3.7 If the defendant fails to provide the health records or an explanation for any delay within 40 days, the claimant or their adviser can then apply to the court under rule 31.16 of the Civil Procedure Rules 1998 ('CPR') for an order for pre-action disclosure. The court has the power to impose costs sanctions for unreasonable delay in providing records.

3.8 If either the claimant or the defendant considers additional health records are required from a third party, in the first instance these should be requested by or through the claimant. Third party healthcare providers are expected to co-operate. Rule 31.17 of the CPR sets out the procedure for applying to the court for pre-action disclosure by third parties.

Rehabilitation

3.9 The claimant and the defendant shall both consider as early as possible whether the claimant has reasonable needs that could be met by rehabilitation treatment or other measures. They should also discuss how these needs might be addressed. An immediate needs assessment report prepared for the purposes of rehabilitation should not be used in the litigation except by consent.

(A copy of the Rehabilitation Code can be found at: http://www.iua.co.uk/IUA_Member/ Publications)

Letter of Notification

3.10 Annex C1 to this Protocol provides a template for the recommended contents of a Letter of Notification; the level of detail will need to be varied to suit the particular circumstances.

3.11

3.11.1 Following receipt and analysis of the records and, if appropriate, receipt of an initial supportive expert opinion, the claimant may wish to send a Letter of Notification to the defendant as soon as practicable.

3.11.2 The Letter of Notification should advise the defendant that this is a claim where a Letter of Claim is likely to be sent because a case as to breach of duty and/or causation has been identified. A copy of the Letter of Notification should also be sent to the NHSLA or, where known, other relevant medical defence organisation or indemnity provider.

3.12

3.12.1 On receipt of a Letter of Notification a defendant should—

    (a) acknowledge the letter within 14 days of receipt;

    (b) identify who will be dealing with the matter and to whom any Letter of Claim should be sent;#

    (c) consider whether to commence investigations and/or to obtain factual and expert evidence;

    (d) consider whether any information could be passed to the claimant which might narrow the issues in dispute or lead to an early resolution of the claim; and

    (e) forward a copy of the Letter of Notification to the NHSLA or other relevant medical defence organisation/indemnity provider.

3.12.2 The court may question any requests by the defendant for extension of time limits if a Letter of Notification was sent but did not prompt an initial investigation.

Letter of Claim

3.13 Annex C2 to this Protocol provides a template for the recommended contents of a Letter of Claim: the level of detail will need to be varied to suit the particular circumstances.

3.14 If, following the receipt and analysis of the records, and the receipt of any further advice (including from experts if necessary – see Section 4), the claimant decides that there are grounds for a claim, a letter of claim should be sent to the defendant as soon as practicable. Any letter of claim sent to an NHS Trust should be copied to the National Health Service Litigation Authority.

3.16 This letter should contain—

    (a) a clear summary of the facts on which the claim is based, including the alleged adverse outcome, and the main allegations of negligence;

    (b) a description of the claimant's injuries, and present condition and prognosis;

    (c) an outline of the financial loss incurred by the claimant, with an indication of the heads of damage to be claimed and the scale of the loss, unless this is impracticable;

    (d) confirmation of the method of funding and whether any funding arrangement was entered into before or after April 2013; and

    (e) the discipline of any expert from whom evidence has already been obtained.

3.17 The Letter of Claim should refer to any relevant documents, including health records, and if possible enclose copies of any of those which will not already be in the potential defendant's possession, e.g. any relevant general practitioner records if the claimant's claim is against a hospital.

3.18 Sufficient information must be given to enable the defendant to focus investigations and to put an initial valuation on the claim.

3.19 Letters of Claim are not intended to have the same formal status as Particulars of Claim, nor should any sanctions necessarily apply if the Letter of Claim and any subsequent Particulars of Claim in the proceedings differ.

3.20 Proceedings should not be issued until after four months from the letter of claim. In certain instances it may not be possible for the claimant to serve a Letter of Claim more than four months before the expiry of the limitation period. If, for any reason, proceedings are started before the parties have complied, they should seek to agree to apply to the court for an order to stay the proceedings whilst the parties take steps to comply.

3.21 The claimant may want to make an offer to settle the claim at this early stage by putting forward an offer in respect of liability and/or an amount of compensation in accordance with the legal and procedural requirements of CPR Part 36 (possibly including any costs incurred to date). If an offer to settle is made, generally this should be supported by a medical report which deals with the injuries, condition and prognosis, and by a schedule of loss and supporting documentation. The level of detail necessary will depend on the value of the claim. Medical reports may not be necessary where there is no significant continuing injury and a detailed schedule may not be necessary in a low value case.

Letter of Response

3.22 Attached at Annex C3 is a template for the suggested contents of the Letter of Response: the level of detail will need to be varied to suit the particular circumstances.

3.23 The defendant should acknowledge the Letter of Claim within 14 days of receipt and should identify who will be dealing with the matter.

3.24 The defendant should, within four months of the Letter of Claim, provide a reasoned answer in the form of a Letter of Response in which the defendant should—

    (a)   if the claim is admitted, say so in clear terms;

    (b)   if only part of the claim is admitted, make clear which issues of breach of duty and/or causation are admitted and which are denied and why;

    (c)   state whether it is intended that any admissions will be binding;

    (d)   if the claim is denied, include specific comments on the allegations of negligence and, if a synopsis or chronology of relevant events has been provided and is disputed, the defendant's version of those events;

    (e)   if supportive expert evidence has been obtained, identify which disciplines of expert evidence have been relied upon and whether they relate to breach of duty and/or causation;

    (f)   if known, state whether the defendant requires copies of any relevant medical records obtained by the claimant (to be supplied for a reasonable copying charge);

    (g)   provide copies of any additional documents relied upon, e.g. an internal protocol;

    (h)   if not indemnified by the NHS, supply details of the relevant indemnity insurer; and

    (i)   inform the claimant of any other potential defendants to the claim.

3.25

3.25.1 If the defendant requires an extension of time for service of the Letter of Response, a request should be made as soon as the defendant becomes aware that it will be required and, in any event, within four months of the letter of claim.

3.25.2 The defendant should explain why any extension of time is necessary.

3.25.3 The claimant should adopt a reasonable approach to any request for an extension of time for provision of the reasoned answer.

3.26 If the claimant has made an offer to settle, the defendant should respond to that offer in the Letter of Response, preferably with reasons. The defendant may also make an offer to settle at this stage. Any offer made by the defendant should be made in accordance with the legal and procedural requirements of CPR Part 36 (possibly including any costs incurred to date). If an offer to settle is made, the defendant should provide sufficient medical or other evidence to allow the claimant to properly consider the offer. The level of detail necessary will depend on the value of the claim.

3.27 If the parties reach agreement on liability, or wish to explore the possibility of resolution with no admissions as to liability, but time is needed to resolve the value of the claim, they should aim to agree a reasonable period.

3.28 If the parties do not reach agreement on liability, they should discuss whether the claimant should start proceedings and whether the court might be invited to direct an early trial of a preliminary issue or of breach of duty and/or causation.

3.29 Following receipt of the Letter of Response, if the claimant is aware that there may be a delay of six months or more before the claimant decides if, when and how to proceed, the claimant should keep the defendant generally informed.

4 EXPERTS

4.1 In clinical negligence disputes separate expert opinions may be needed—
- on breach of duty;
- on causation;
- on the patient's condition and prognosis;
- to assist in valuing aspects of the claim.

4.2 It is recognised that in clinical negligence disputes, the parties and their advisers will require flexibility in their approach to expert evidence. The parties should co-operate when making decisions on appropriate medical specialisms, whether experts might be instructed jointly and whether any reports obtained pre-action might be shared.

4.3 Obtaining expert evidence will often be an expensive step and may take time, especially in specialised areas of medicine where there are limited numbers of suitable experts.

4.4 When considering what expert evidence may be required during the Protocol period, parties should be aware that the use of any expert reports obtained pre-action will only be permitted in proceedings with the express permission of the court.

5 ALTERNATIVE DISPUTE RESOLUTION

5.1 Litigation should be a last resort. As part of this Protocol, the parties should consider whether negotiation or some other form of alternative dispute resolution ('ADR') might enable them to resolve their dispute without commencing proceedings.

5.2 Some of the options for resolving disputes without commencing proceedings are—
- (a) discussion and negotiation (which may or may not include making Part 36 Offers or providing an explanation and/or apology)
- (b) mediation, a third party facilitating a resolution ;
- (c) arbitration, a third party deciding the dispute;
- (d) early neutral evaluation, a third party giving an informed opinion on the dispute; and
- (e) Ombudsmen schemes.

5.3 Information on mediation and other forms of ADR is available in the Jackson ADR Handbook (available from Oxford University Press) or at—

http://www.civilmediation.justice.gov.uk/

http://www.adviceguide.org.uk/england/law_e/law_legal_system_e/law_taking_legal_action_e/alternatives_to_court.htm

5.4   If proceedings are issued, the parties may be required by the court to provide evidence that ADR has been considered. It is expressly recognised that no party can or should be forced to mediate or enter into any form of ADR, but a party's silence in response to an invitation to participate in ADR might be considered unreasonable by the court and could lead to the court ordering that party to pay additional court costs.

6 STOCKTAKE

6.1

6.1.1 Where a dispute has not been resolved after the parties have followed the procedure set out in this Protocol, the parties should review their positions before the claimant issues court proceedings.

6.1.2 If proceedings cannot be avoided, the parties should continue to co-operate and should seek to prepare a chronology of events which identifies the facts or issues that are agreed and those that remain in dispute. The parties should also seek to agree the necessary procedural directions for efficient case management during the proceedings.

Annex A   ILLUSTRATIVE FLOWCHART

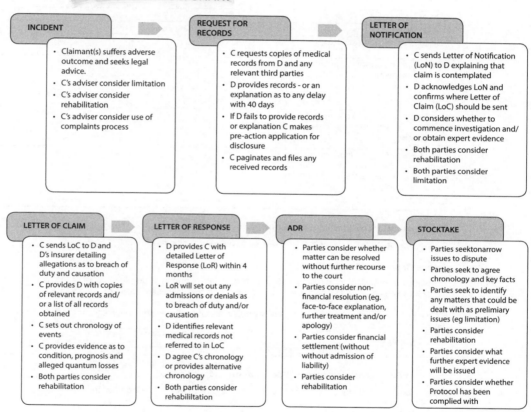

Annex B   FORM FOR REQUESTING MEDICAL RECORDS

Consent form
(Releasing health records under the Data Protection Act 1998)

About this form

In order to proceed with your claim, your solicitor may need to see your health records. Solicitors usually need to see all your records as they need to assess which parts are relevant to your case. (Past medical history is often relevant to a claim for compensation.) Also, if your claim goes ahead, the person you are making the claim against will ask for copies of important documents. Under court rules, they may see all your health records. So your solicitor needs to be familiar with all your records.

Part a – your, the health professionals' and your solicitor's or agent's details

Your full name:	
Your address:	
Date of birth:	
Date of incident:	
Solicitor's or agent's name and address:	
GP's name and address (and phone number if known):	
Name (and address if known) of the hospitals you went to in relation to this incident :	
If you have seen any other person or organisation about your injuries (for example, a physiotherapist) or have had any investigations (for example, x-rays) please provide details.	

Part b – your declaration and signature

Please see the 'Notes for the client' over the page before you sign this form.

To health professionals

I understand that filling in and signing this form gives you permission to give copies of all my GP records, and any hospital records relating to this incident, to my solicitor or agent whose details are given above.

Please give my solicitor or agent copies of my health records, in line with the Data Protection Act 1998, within 40 days.

Your signature: [   ]   Date: [/   /   ]

Part c – your solicitor's or agent's declaration and signature

Please see the 'Notes for the solicitor or agent' over the page before you sign this form.

To health professionals

I have told my client the implications of giving me access to his or her health records. I confirm that I need the full records in this case.   I enclose the authorised fee for getting access to records.

Solicitor's or agent's signature: [   ]   Date: [/   /   ]

Notes for the client

Your health records contain information from almost all consultations you have had with health professionals. The information they contain usually includes:

- why you saw a health professional;
- details of clinical findings and diagnoses;
- any options for care and treatment the health professional discussed with you;
- the decisions made about your care and treatment, including evidence that you agreed; and
- details of action health professionals have taken and the outcomes.

By signing this form, you are agreeing to the health professional or hospital named on this form releasing copies of your health records to your solicitor or agent. During the process your records may be seen by people who are not health professionals, but they will keep the information confidential.

If you are making, or considering making, a legal claim against someone, your solicitor will need to see copies of all your GP records, and any hospital records made in connection with this incident, so he or she can see if there is anything in your records that may affect your claim. Once you start your claim, the court can order you to give copies of your health records to the solicitor of the person you are making a claim against so he or she can see if any of the information in your records can be used to defend his or her client.

If you decide to go ahead with your claim, your records may be passed to a number of people including:

- the expert who your solicitor or agent instructs to produce a medical report as evidence for the case;
- the person you are making a claim against and their solicitors;
- the insurance company for the person you are making a claim against;
- any insurance company or other organisation paying your legal costs; and
- any other person or company officially involved with the claim.

You do not have to give permission for your health records to be released but if you don't, the court may not let you go ahead with your claim and, in some circumstances, your solicitor may refuse to represent you.

If there is very sensitive information in the records, that is not connected to the claim, you should tell your solicitor. They will then consider whether this information needs to be revealed.

Notes for the solicitor or agent

Before you ask your client to fill in and sign this form you should explain that this will involve his or her full health records being released and how the information in them may be used. You should also tell your client to read the notes above.

If your client is not capable of giving his or her permission in this form, this form should be signed by:

- your client's litigation friend;
- someone who has enduring power of attorney to act for your client; or
- your client's receiver appointed by the Court of Protection.

When you send this form to the appropriate records controller please also enclose the authorised fees for getting access to records.

If you find out at any stage that the medical records contain information that the client does not know about (for example, being diagnosed with a serious illness), you should discuss this with the health professional who provided the records.

Unless your client agrees otherwise, you must use his or her health records only for the purpose for which the client signed this form (that is, making his or her claim). Under the Data Protection Act you have responsibilities relating to sensitive information. The entire health record should not be automatically revealed without the client's permission and you should not keep health records for any longer than you need them. You should return them to the client at the end of the claim if they want them. Otherwise, you are responsible for destroying them.

Notes for the medical records controller

This form shows your patient's permission for you to give copies of his or her full GP record, and any hospital records relating to this incident, to his or her solicitor or agent. You must give the solicitor or agent copies of these health records unless any of the exemptions set out in The Data Protection (Subject Access Modification) (Health) Order 2000 apply. The main exemptions are that you must not release information that:

- is likely to cause serious physical or mental harm to the patient or another person; or
- relates to someone who would normally need to give their permission (where that person is not a health professional who has cared for the patient).

Your patient's permission for you to release information is valid only if that patient understands the consequences of his or her records being released, and how the information will be used. The solicitor or agent named on this form must explain these issues to the patient. If you have any doubt about whether this has happened, contact the solicitor or agent, or your patient.

If your patient is not capable of giving his or her permission, this form should be signed by:

- a 'litigation friend' acting for your patient;
- someone with 'enduring power of attorney' to act for your patient; or
- a receiver appointed by the Court of Protection.

You may charge the usual fees authorised under the Data Protection Act for providing the records.

The BMA publishes detailed advice for doctors on giving access to health records, including the fees that you may charge. You can view that advice by visiting www.bma.org.uk/ap.nsf/Content/accesshealthrecords.

This form is published by the Law Society and British Medical Association. (2nd edition, October 2004)

Annex C   TEMPLATES FOR LETTERS OF NOTIFICATION, CLAIM AND RESPONSE

C1 Letter of Notification

To

Defendant

Dear Sirs

Letter of Notification

Re: [Claimant's Name, Address, DoB and NHS Number]

We have been instructed to act on behalf of [Claimant's name] in relation to treatment carried out/care provided at [name of hospital or treatment centre] by [name of clinician(s) if known] on [insert date(s)].

The purpose of this letter is to notify you that, although we are not yet in a position to serve a formal Letter of Claim, our initial investigations indicate that a case as to breach of duty and/or causation has been identified. We therefore invite you to commence your own investigation and draw your attention to the fact that failure to do may be taken into account when considering the reasonableness of any subsequent application for an extension of time for the Letter of Response.

Defendant

We understand that you are the correct defendant in respect of treatment provided by [name of clinician] at [hospital/surgery/treatment centre] on [date(s)]. If you do not agree, please provide us with any information you have that may assist us to identify the correct defendant. Failure to do so may result in costs sanctions should proceedings be issued.

Summary of Facts and Alleged Adverse Outcome

[Outline what is alleged to have happened and provide a chronology of events with details of relevant known treatment/care.]

Medical Records 58

[Provide index of records obtained and request for further records/information if required.]

Allegations of Negligence

[Brief outline of any alleged breach of duty and causal link with any damage suffered.]

Expert Evidence

[State whether expert evidence has been obtained or is awaited and, if so, the relevant discipline.]

Damage

[Brief outline of any injuries attributed to the alleged negligence and their functional impact.]

Funding

[If known, state method of funding and whether arrangement was entered into before or after April 2013.]

Rehabilitation

As a result of the allegedly negligent treatment, our client has injuries/needs that could be met by rehabilitation. We invite you to consider how this could be achieved.

Limitation

For the purposes of limitation, we calculate that any proceedings will need to be issued on or before [date].

Please acknowledge this letter by [insert date 14 days after deemed receipt] and confirm to whom any Letter of Claim should be sent. We enclose a duplicate of the letter for your insurer.

Recoverable Benefits

The claimant's National Insurance Number will be sent to you in a separate envelope.

We look forward to hearing from you.

Yours faithfully,

C2 Letter of Claim

To

Defendant

Dear Sirs

Letter of Claim

[Claimant's name] –v- [Defendant's Name]

We have been instructed to act on behalf of [Claimant's name] in relation to treatment carried out/care provided at [name of hospital or treatment centre] by [name of clinician(s) if known] on [insert date(s)]. Please let us know if you do not believe that you are the appropriate defendant or if you are aware of any other potential defendants.

Claimant's details

Full name, DoB, address, NHS Number.

Dates of allegedly negligent treatment

- include chronology based on medical records.

Events giving rise to the claim:

- an outline of what happened, including details of other relevant treatments to the client by other healthcare providers.

Allegation of negligence and causal link with injuries:

- an outline of the allegations or a more detailed list in a complex case;
- an outline of the causal link between allegations and the injuries complained of;
- A copy of any supportive expert evidence (optional).

The Client's injuries, condition and future prognosis

- A copy of any supportive expert report (optional);
- Suggestions for rehabilitation;
- The discipline of any expert evidence obtained or proposed.

Clinical records (if not previously provided)

We enclose an index of all the relevant records that we hold. We shall be happy to provide copies of these on payment of our photocopying charges.

We enclose a request for copies of the following records which we believe that you hold. We confirm that we shall be responsible for your reasonable copying charges. Failure to provide these records may result in costs sanctions if proceedings are issued.

The likely value of the claim

- an outline of the main heads of damage, or, in straightforward cases, the details of loss;
- Part 36 settlement offer (optional);
- suggestions for ADR.

Funding

[State method of funding and whether arrangement was entered into before or after April 2013.]

We enclose a further copy of this letter for you to pass to your insurer. We look forward to receiving an acknowledgment of this letter within 14 days and your Letter of Response within 4 months of the date on which this letter was received. We calculate the date for receipt of your Letter of Response to be [date].

Recoverable Benefits

The claimant's National Insurance Number will be sent to you in a separate envelope.

We look forward to hearing from you.

Yours faithfully

C3 Letter of Response

To

Claimant

Dear Sirs

Letter of Response

[Claimant's name] –v- [Defendant's Name]

We have been instructed to act on behalf of [defendant] in relation to treatment carried out/ care provided to [claimant] at [name of hospital or treatment centre] by [name of clinician(s) if known] on [insert date(s)].

The defendant [conveys sympathy for the adverse outcome/would like to offer an apology/ denies that there was an adverse outcome].

Parties

It is accepted that [defendant] had a duty of care towards [claimant] in respect of [details if required] treatment/care provided to [claimant] at [location] on [date(s)].

However, [defendant] is not responsible for [details] care/treatment provided to [claimant] at [location] on [date(s)] by [name of clinician if known].

Records

We hold the following records...

We require copies of the following records...

Failure to provide these records may result in costs sanctions if proceedings are issued.

Comments on events and/or chronology:

We [agree the chronology enclosed with the Letter of Claim] [enclose a revised chronology of events].

We enclose copies of relevant [records/Protocols/internal investigations] in respect of the treatment/care that [claimant] received.

Liability

In respect of the specific allegations raised by the claimant, the defendant [has obtained an expert opinion and] responds as follows:-

[each allegation should be addressed separately. The defendant should explain which (if any) of the allegations of breach of duty and/or causation are admitted and why. The defendant should also make clear which allegations are denied and why].

Next Steps

The defendant suggests...

[e.g. no prospect of success for the claimant, resolution without admissions of liability, ADR, settlement offer, rehabilitation].

Yours faithfully,"

Pre-action Protocol for Low Value Personal Injury (Employers' Liability and Public Liability) Claims

SECTION I - INTRODUCTION

Definitions

1.1 In this Protocol—

(1) 'admission of liability' means the defendant admits that—

    (a) the breach of duty occurred;

    (b) the defendant thereby caused some loss to the claimant, the nature and extent of which is not admitted; and

    (c) the defendant has no accrued defence to the claim under the Limitation Act 1980;

(2) 'bank holiday' means a bank holiday under the Banking and Financial Dealings Act 1971;

(3) 'business day' means any day except Saturday, Sunday, a bank holiday, Good Friday or Christmas Day;

(4) 'certificate of recoverable benefits' has the same meaning as in rule 36.22(1)(e)(i) of the Civil Procedure Rules 1998.

(5) 'child' means a person under 18;

(6) 'claim' means a claim, prior to the start of proceedings, for payment of damages under the process set out in this Protocol;

(7) 'claimant' means a person starting a claim under this Protocol; unless the context indicated that it means the claimant's legal representative;

(8) 'clinical negligence' has the same meaning as in section 58C of the Courts and Legal Services Act 1990;

(9) 'CNF' means a Claim Notification Form;

(10) 'deductible amount' has the same meaning as in rule 36.22(1)(d) of the Civil Procedure Rules 1998;

(11) 'defendant' includes, where the context indicates, the defendant's insurer or legal representative;

(12) 'disease claim' means a claim within sub-paragraph (14)(b);

(13) 'employee' has the meaning given to it by section 2(1) of the Employers' Liability (Compulsory Insurance) Act 1969;

(14) 'employers' liability claim' means a claim by an employee against their employer for damages arising from—

    (a) a bodily injury sustained by the employee in the course of employment; or

    (b) a disease that the claimant is alleged to have contracted as a consequence of the employer's breach of statutory or common law duties of care in the course of the employee's employment, other than a physical or psychological injury caused by an accident or other single event;

(15) 'legal representative' has the same meaning as in rule 2.3(1) of the Civil Procedure Rules 1998;

(16) 'medical expert' means a person who is—

    (a) registered with the General Medical Council;

    (b) registered with the General Dental Council; or

(c)   a Psychologist or Physiotherapist registered with the Health Professions Council;

(17)   'pecuniary losses' means past and future expenses and losses; and

(18)   'public liability claim'—

(a)   means a claim for damages for personal injuries arising out of a breach of a statutory or common law duty of care made against—

(i)   a person other than the claimant's employer; or

(ii)   the claimant's employer in respect of matters arising other than in the course the claimant's employment; but

(b)   does not include a claim for damages arising from a disease that the claimant is alleged to have contracted as a consequence of breach of statutory or common law duties of care, other than a physical or psychological injury caused by an accident or other single event;

(19)   'Type C fixed costs' has the same meaning as in rule 45.18(2) of the Civil Procedure Rules 1998; and

(20)   'vulnerable adult' has the same meaning as in paragraph 3(5) of Schedule 1 to the Legal Aid, Sentencing and Punishment of Offenders Act 2012

1.2   A reference to a rule or practice direction, unless otherwise defined, is a reference to a rule in the Civil Procedure Rules 1998 ('CPR') or a practice direction supplementing them.

1.3   Subject to paragraph 1.4 the standard forms used in the process set out in this Protocol are available from Her Majesty's Courts and Tribunals Service ('HMCTS') website at www.justice.gov.uk/forms/hmcts—

(1)   Claim Notification Form ('Form EL1', 'Form ELD1' and 'Form PL1'– which are referred to in this Protocol as 'the CNF');

(2)   Defendant Only Claim Notification Form ('Form EL2', 'Form ELD2' and 'Form PL2');

(3)   Medical Report Form ('Form EPL3');

(4)   Interim Settlement Pack Form ('Form EPL4');

(5)   Stage 2 Settlement Pack Form ('Form EPL5');

(6)   Court Proceedings Pack (Part A) Form ('Form EPL6'); and

(7)   Court Proceedings Pack (Part B) Form ('Form EPL7').

1.4   The information required in Form EPL3 may be provided in a different format to that set out in that Form.

Preamble

2.1   This Protocol describes the behaviour the court expects of the parties prior to the start of proceedings where a claimant claims damages valued at no more than £25,000 in an employers' liability claim or in a public liability claim. The Civil Procedure Rules 1998 enable the court to impose costs sanctions where this Protocol is not followed.

Aims

3.1   The aim of this Protocol is to ensure that—

(1)   the defendant pays damages and costs using the process set out in the Protocol without the need for the claimant to start proceedings;

(2)   damages are paid within a reasonable time; and

(3)   the claimant's legal representative receives the fixed costs at each appropriate stage.

Scope

4.1   This Protocol applies where—

(1)   either—

(a)   the claim arises from an accident occurring on or after 31 July 2013; or

    (b)   in a disease claim, no letter of claim has been sent to the defendant before 31 July 2013;

  (2)   the claim includes damages in respect of personal injury;

  (3)   the claimant values the claim at not more than £25,000 on a full liability basis including pecuniary losses but excluding interest ('the upper limit'); and

  (4)   if proceedings were started the small claims track would not be the normal track for that claim.

      (Rule 26.6 provides that the small claims track is not the normal track where the value of any claim for damages for personal injuries (defined as compensation for pain, suffering and loss of amenity) is more than £1,000.)

4.2 This Protocol ceases to apply to a claim where, at any stage, the claimant notifies the defendant that the claim has now been revalued at more than the upper limit.

4.3 This Protocol does not apply to a claim—

  (1)   where the claimant or defendant acts as personal representative of a deceased person;

  (2)   where the claimant or defendant is a protected party as defined in rule 21.1(2);

  (3)   in the case of a public liability claim, where the defendant is an individual ('individual' does not include a defendant who is sued in their business capacity or in their capacity as an office holder);

  (4)   where the claimant is bankrupt;

  (5)   where the defendant is insolvent and there is no identifiable insurer;

  (6)   in the case of a disease claim, where there is more than one employer defendant;

  (7)   for personal injury arising from an accident or alleged breach of duty occurring outside England and Wales;

  (8)   for damages in relation to harm, abuse or neglect of or by children or vulnerable adults;

  (9)   which includes a claim for clinical negligence;

  (10) for mesothelioma;

  (11) for damages arising out of a road traffic accident (as defined in paragraph 1.1(16) of the Pre-Action Protocol for Low Value Personal Injury Claims in Road Traffic Accidents).

4.4 The fixed costs in rule 45.18 apply in relation to a claimant only where a claimant has a legal representative.

SECTION II – GENERAL PROVISIONS

Communication between the parties

5.1 Subject to paragraphs 6.1 and 6.2, where the Protocol requires information to be sent to a party it must be sent via www.claimsportal.org.uk (or any other Portal address that may be prescribed from time to time). The claimant will give an e-mail address for contact in the Claim Notification Form ("CNF"). All written communications not required by the Protocol must be sent by e-mail.

5.2 Where the claimant has sent the CNF to the wrong defendant, the claimant may, in this circumstance only, resend the relevant form to the correct defendant. The period in paragraph 6.12 starts from the date that the form was sent to the correct defendant.

Time periods

5.3 A reference to a fixed number of days is a reference to business days as defined in paragraph 1.1(3).

5.4 Where a party should respond within a fixed number of days, the period for response starts the first business day after the information was sent to that party.

5.5 All time periods, except those stated in—

  (1)   paragraph 6.11 (response);

:)   paragraph 7.34 (the further consideration period),

may be varied by agreement between the parties.

.. here this Protocol requires the defendant to pay an amount within a fixed number of days the claimant must receive the cheque or the transfer of the amount from the defendant before the end of the period specified in the relevant provision.

Limitation period

5.7   Where compliance with this Protocol is not possible before the expiry of the limitation period the claimant may start proceedings and apply to the court for an order to stay (i.e. suspend) the proceedings while the parties take steps to follow this Protocol. Where proceedings are started in a case to which this paragraph applies the claimant should use the procedure set out under Part 8 in accordance with Practice Direction 8B ("the Stage 3 Procedure").

5.8   Where the parties are then unable to reach a settlement at the end of Stage 2 of this Protocol the claimant must, in order to proceed to Stage 3, apply to lift the stay and request directions in the existing proceedings.

Claimant's reasonable belief of the value of the claim

5.9   Where the claimant reasonably believes that the claim is valued at between £1,000 and £25,000 but it subsequently becomes apparent that the value of the claim is less than £1,000, the claimant is entitled to the Stage 1 and (where relevant) the Stage 2 fixed costs.

Claimants without a legal representative

5.10   Where the claimant does not have a legal representative, on receipt of the CNF the defendant must explain—

(1)   the period within which a response is required; and

(2)   that the claimant may obtain independent legal advice.

Discontinuing the Protocol process

5.11   Claims which no longer continue under this Protocol cannot subsequently re-enter the process.

SECTION III – THE STAGES OF THE PROCESS

Stage 1   Completion of the Claim Notification Form

6.1   (1)   The claimant must complete and send—

(a)   the CNF to the defendant's insurer, if known; and

(b)   the Defendant Only Claim Notification Form ("Defendant Only CNF") to the defendant,

but the requirement to send the form to the defendant may be ignored in a disease claim where the CNF has been sent to the insurer and the defendant has been dissolved, is insolvent or has ceased to trade.

(2)   If—

(a)   the insurer's identity is not known; or

(b)   the defendant is known not to hold insurance cover,

the CNF must be sent to the defendant's registered office or principal place of business and no Defendant Only CNF is required.

(3)   Where the insurer's identity is not known, the claimant must make a reasonable attempt to identify the insurer and, in an employers' liability claim, the claimant must have carried out a database search through the Employers' Liability Tracing Office.

(4)   In a disease claim, the CNF should be sent to the insurer identified as the insurer last on risk for the employer for the material period of employment.

6.2   If the CNF or Defendant Only CNF cannot be sent to the defendant via the prescribed Portal address, it must be sent via first class post; and this must be done, in a case where the CNF is sent to the insurer, at the same time or as soon as practicable after the CNF is sent.

6.3   All boxes in the CNF that are marked as mandatory must be completed before it is sent. The claimant must make a reasonable attempt to complete those boxes that are not marked as mandatory.

6.4   Where the claimant is a child, this must be noted in the relevant section of the CNF.

6.5   The statement of truth in the CNF must be signed either by the claimant or by the claimant's legal representative where the claimant has authorised the legal representative to do so and the legal representative can produce written evidence of that authorisation. Where the claimant is a child the statement of truth may be signed by the parent or guardian. On the electronically completed CNF the person may enter their name in the signature box to satisfy this requirement.

Rehabilitation

6.6   The claimant must set out details of rehabilitation in the CNF. The parties should at all stages consider the Rehabilitation Code which may be found at: http://www.judiciary.gov.uk/about-the-judiciary/advisory-bodies/cjc/pre-action-protocols

Failure to complete the Claim Notification Form

6.7   Where the defendant considers that inadequate mandatory information has been provided in the CNF that shall be a valid reason for the defendant to decide that the claim should no longer continue under this Protocol.

6.8   Rule 45.24(2) sets out the sanctions available to the court where it considers that the claimant provided inadequate information in the CNF.

Response

6.9   The defendant must send to the claimant an electronic acknowledgment the next day after receipt of the CNF.

6.10   If the claimant has sent the CNF to the defendant in accordance with paragraph 6.1(2)—

(a)   the defendant must send to the claimant an electronic acknowledgment the next day after receipt of the CNF and send the CNF to the insurer at the same time and advise the claimant that they have done so;

(b)   the insurer must send to the claimant an electronic acknowledgment the next day after its receipt by the insurer;
and

(c)   the claimant must then submit the CNF to the insurer via the Portal as soon as possible and, in any event, within 30 days of the day upon which the claimant first sent it to the defendant.

6.11   The defendant must complete the 'Response' section of the CNF ("the CNF response") and send it to the claimant—

(a)   in the case of an employers' liability claim, within 30 days of the step taken pursuant to paragraph 6.1; and

(b)   in the case of a public liability claim, within 40 days of the step taken pursuant to paragraph 6.1.

Application for a certificate of recoverable benefits

6.12 The defendant must, before the end of Stage 1, apply to the Compensation Recovery Unit (CRU) for a certificate of recoverable benefits.

Contributory Negligence, liability not admitted or failure to respond

6.13 The claim will no longer continue under this Protocol where the defendant, within the relevant period in paragraph 6.11 —

(1)   makes an admission of liability but alleges contributory negligence;

(2)   does not complete and send the CNF response;

(3)   does not admit liability; or

(4)   notifies the claimant that the defendant considers that—

(a)   there is inadequate mandatory information in the CNF; or

(b)   if proceedings were issued, the small claims track would be the normal track for that claim.

6.14 Where the defendant does not admit liability the defendant must give brief reasons in the CNF response.

6.15 Where paragraph 6.13 applies the claim will proceed under the relevant Pre-Action Protocol and the CNF will serve as the letter of claim (except where the claim no longer continues under this Protocol because the CNF contained inadequate information). Time will be treated as running under the relevant Pre-Action Protocol from the date the form of acknowledgment is served under paragraph 6.9 or 6.10.

(For admissions made in the course of the process under this Protocol, see rule 14.1B.)

(Paragraph 2.10A of the Pre-Action Protocol on Personal Injury and paragraph 6.10A of the Pre-Action Protocol for Disease and Illness Claims provide that the CNF can be used as the letter of claim except where the claim no longer continues under this Protocol because the CNF contained inadequate information.)

Stage 1 fixed costs

6.16 Except where the claimant is a child, where liability is admitted the defendant must pay the Stage 1 fixed costs in rule 45.18 within 10 days after receiving the Stage 2 Settlement Pack.

6.17 Where the defendant fails to pay the Stage 1 fixed costs within the period specified in paragraph 6.16 the claimant may give written notice that the claim will no longer continue under this Protocol. Unless the claimant's notice is sent to the defendant within 10 days after the expiry of the period in paragraph 6.16 the claim will continue under this Protocol.

Stage 2 Medical reports

7.1 The claimant should obtain a medical report, if one has not already been obtained.

7.2 It is expected that most claimants will obtain a medical report from one expert but additional medical reports may be obtained from other experts where the injuries require reports from more than one medical discipline.

7.3 The claimant must check the factual accuracy of any medical report before it is sent to the defendant. There will be no further opportunity for the claimant to challenge the factual accuracy of a medical report after it has been sent to the defendant.

7.4 (1)   The medical expert should identify within the report—

(a)   the medical records that have been reviewed; and

(b)   the medical records considered relevant to the claim.

(2)   The claimant must disclose with any medical report sent to the defendant any medical records which the expert considers relevant.

7.5   Any relevant photograph(s) of the claimant's injuries upon which the claimant intends to rely should also be disclosed with the medical report.

Subsequent medical reports

7.6   A subsequent medical report from an expert who has already reported must be justified. A report may be justified where—

(1)   the first medical report recommends that further time is required before a prognosis of the claimant's injuries can be determined; or

(2)   the claimant is receiving continuing treatment; or

(3)   the claimant has not recovered as expected in the original prognosis.

Non-medical reports

7.7   (1)   In most cases, a report from a non-medical expert will not be required, but a report may be obtained where it is reasonably required to value the claim.

(2)   Paragraph 7.2 applies to non-medical expert reports as it applies to expert medical reports.

Specialist legal advice

7.8   In most cases under this Protocol, it is expected that the claimant's legal representative will be able to value the claim. In some cases with a value of more than £10,000, an additional advice from a specialist solicitor or from counsel may be justified where it is reasonably required to value the claim.

Details of loss of earnings

7.9   In an employers' liability claim, the defendant must, within 20 days of the date of admission of liability, provide earnings details to verify the claimant's loss of earnings, if any.

Witness Statements

7.10   In most cases, witness statements, whether from the claimant or otherwise, will not be required. One or more statements may, however, be provided where reasonably required to value the claim.

Stay of process

7.11   Where the claimant needs to obtain a subsequent medical report or a report from a non-medical expert the parties should agree to stay the process in this Protocol for a suitable period. The claimant may then request an interim payment in accordance with paragraphs 7.12 to 7.20.

Request for an interim payment

7.12   Where the claimant requests an interim payment of £1,000, the defendant should make an interim payment to the claimant in accordance with paragraph 7.17.

7.13   The claimant must send to the defendant the Interim Settlement Pack and initial medical reports (including any recommendation that a subsequent medical report is justified) in order to request the interim payment.

7.14   The claimant must also send evidence of pecuniary losses and disbursements. This will assist the defendant in considering whether to make an offer to settle the claim.

7.15   Where an interim payment of more than £1,000 is requested the claimant must specify in the Interim Settlement Pack the amount requested, the heads of damage which are the subject of the request and the reasons for the request.

7.16   Unless the parties agree otherwise—

(a)   the interim payment of £1,000 is only in relation to general damages; and

(b)   where more than £1,000 is requested by the claimant, the amount in excess of £1,000 is only in relation to pecuniary losses.

Interim payment of £1,000

7.17   (1)   Where paragraph 7.12 applies the defendant must pay £1,000 within 10 days of receiving the Interim Settlement Pack.

(2)   Sub-paragraph (1) does not apply in a claim in respect of a disease to which the Pneumoconiosis etc. (Workers' Compensation) Act 1979 applies unless there is a valid CRU certificate showing no deduction for recoverable lump sum payments.

Interim payment of more than £1,000

7.18   Subject to paragraphs 7.19 and 7.21, where the claimant has requested an interim payment of more than £1,000 the defendant must pay—

(1)   the full amount requested less any deductible amount which is payable to the CRU;

(2)   the amount of £1,000; or

(3)   some other amount of more than £1,000 but less than the amount requested by the claimant,

within 15 days of receiving the Interim Settlement Pack.

7.19   Where a payment is made under paragraphs 7.18(2) or (3) the defendant must briefly explain in the Interim Settlement Pack why the full amount requested by the claimant is not agreed.

7.20   Where the claim is valued at more than £10,000, the claimant may use the procedure at paragraphs 7.12 to 7.19 to request more than one interim payment.

7.21   Nothing in this Protocol is intended to affect the provisions contained in the Rehabilitation Code.

Application for a certificate of recoverable benefits

7.22   Paragraph 7.23 applies where the defendant agrees to make a payment in accordance with paragraph 7.18(1) or (3) but does not yet have a certificate of recoverable benefits or does not have one that will remain in force for at least 10 days from the date of receiving the Interim Settlement Pack.

7.23   The defendant should apply for a certificate of recoverable benefits as soon as possible, notify the claimant that it has done so and must make the interim payment under paragraph 7.18(1) or (3) no more than 30 days from the date of receiving the Interim Settlement Pack.

Request for an interim payment where the claimant is a child

7.24   The interim payment provisions in this Protocol do not apply where the claimant is a child. Where the claimant is a child and an interim payment is reasonably required proceedings must be started under Part 7 of the CPR and an application for an interim payment can be made within those proceedings.

(Rule 21.10 provides that no payment, which relates to a claim by a child, is valid without the approval of the court.)

7.25   Paragraph 7.24 does not prevent a defendant from making a payment direct to a treatment provider.

Interim payment – supplementary provisions

7.26   Where the defendant does not comply with paragraphs 7.17 or 7.18 the claimant may start proceedings under Part 7 of the CPR and apply to the court for an interim payment in those proceedings.

7.27   Where the defendant does comply with paragraph 7.18(2) or (3) but the claimant is not content with the amount paid, the claimant may still start proceedings. However, the court will order the defendant to pay no more than the Stage 2 fixed costs where the court awards an interim payment of no more than the amount offered by the defendant or the court makes no award.

7.28   Where paragraph 7.26 or 7.27 applies the claimant must give notice to the defendant that the claim will no longer continue under this Protocol. Unless the claimant's notice is sent to the defendant within 10 days after the expiry of the period in paragraphs 7.17, 7.18 or 7.23 as appropriate, the claim will continue under this Protocol.

Costs of expert medical and non-medical reports and specialist legal advice obtained

7.29   (1)   Where the claimant obtains more than one expert report or an advice from a specialist solicitor or counsel—

   (a)   the defendant at the end of Stage 2 may refuse to pay; or

   (b)   the court at Stage 3 may refuse to allow,

the costs of any report or advice not reasonably required.

   (2)   Therefore, where the claimant obtains more than one expert report or obtains an advice from a specialist solicitor or counsel—

   (a)   the claimant should explain in the Stage 2 Settlement Pack why they obtained a further report or such advice; and

   (b)   if relevant, the defendant should in the Stage 2 Settlement Pack identify the report or reports or advice for which they will not pay and explain why they will not pay for that report or reports or advice.

Submitting the Stage 2 Settlement Pack to the defendant

7.30   The Stage 2 Settlement Pack must comprise—

   (1)   the Stage 2 Settlement Pack Form;

   (2)   a medical report or reports;

   (3)   evidence of pecuniary losses;

   (4)   evidence of disbursements (for example the cost of any medical report);

   (5)   any non-medical expert report;

   (6)   any medical records/photographs served with medical reports; and

   (7)   any witness statements.

7.31   The claimant should send the Stage 2 Settlement Pack to the defendant within 15 days of the claimant approving —

   (1)   the final medical report and agreeing to rely on the prognosis in that report; or

   (2)   any non-medical expert report,

whichever is later.

Consideration of claim

7.32   There is a 35 day period for consideration of the Stage 2 Settlement Pack by the defendant ("the total consideration period"). This comprises a period of up to 15 days for the defendant to consider the Stage 2 Settlement Pack ("the initial consideration period") and make an offer. The remainder of the total consideration period ("the negotiation period") is for any further negotiation between the parties.

7.33   The total consideration period can be extended by the parties agreeing to extend either the initial consideration period or the negotiation period or both.

7.34   Where a party makes an offer 5 days or less before the end of the total consideration period (including any extension to this period under paragraph 7.32), there will be a further period of

5 days after the end of the total consideration period for the relevant party to consider that offer. During this period ("the further consideration period") no further offers can be made by either party.

Defendant accepts offer or makes counter-offer

7.35   Within the initial consideration period (or any extension agreed under paragraph 7.33) the defendant must either accept the offer made by the claimant on the Stage 2 Settlement Pack Form or make a counter-offer using that form.

7.36   The claim will no longer continue under this Protocol where the defendant gives notice to the claimant within the initial consideration period (or any extension agreed under paragraph 7.33) that the defendant—

(a)   considers that, if proceedings were started, the small claims track would be the normal track for that claim; or

(b)   withdraws the admission of causation as defined in paragraph 1.1(1)(b).

7.37   Where the defendant does not respond within the initial consideration period (or any extension agreed under paragraph 7.33), the claim will no longer continue under this Protocol and the claimant may start proceedings under Part 7 of the CPR.

7.38   When making a counter-offer the defendant must propose an amount for each head of damage and may, in addition, make an offer that is higher than the total of the amounts proposed for all heads of damage. The defendant must also explain in the counter-offer why a particular head of damage has been reduced. The explanation will assist the claimant when negotiating a settlement and will allow both parties to focus on those areas of the claim that remain in dispute.

7.39   Where the defendant has obtained a certificate of recoverable benefits from the CRU the counter offer must state the name and amount of any deductible amount.

7.40   On receipt of a counter-offer from the defendant the claimant has until the end of the total consideration period or the further consideration period to accept or decline the counter offer.

7.41   Any offer to settle made at any stage by either party will automatically include, and cannot exclude—

(1)   the Stage 1 and Stage 2 fixed costs in rule 45.18;

(2)   an agreement in principle to pay a sum equal to the Type C fixed costs of an additional advice on quantum of damages where such advice is justified under paragraph 7.8;

(3)   an agreement in principle to pay relevant disbursements allowed in accordance with rule 45.19; or

(4)   where applicable, any success fee in accordance with rule 45.31(1) (as it was in force immediately before 1 April 2013).

7.42   Where there is a dispute about whether an additional advice on quantum of damages is justified or about the amount or validity of any disbursement, the parties may use the procedure set out in rule 46.14.

(Rule 46.14 provides that where the parties to a dispute have a written agreement on all issues but have failed to agree the amount of the costs, they may start proceedings under that rule so that the court can determine the amount of those costs.)

Withdrawal of offer after the consideration period

7.43   Where a party withdraws an offer made in the Stage 2 Settlement Pack Form after the total consideration period or further consideration period, the claim will no longer continue under this Protocol and the claimant may start proceedings under Part 7 of the CPR.

Settlement

7.44 Except where the claimant is a child or paragraphs 7.46 and 7.47 apply, the defendant must pay—

(1) the agreed damages less any—

(a) deductible amount which is payable to the CRU; and

(b) previous interim payment;

(2) any unpaid Stage 1 fixed costs in rule 45.18;

(3) the Stage 2 fixed costs in rule 45.18;

(4) where an additional advice on quantum of damages is justified under paragraph 7.8, a sum equal to the Type C fixed costs to cover the cost of that advice;

(5) the relevant disbursements allowed in accordance with rule 45.19; and

(6) where applicable, any success fee in accordance with rule 45.31(1) (as it was in force immediately before 1 April 2013),

within 10 days of the parties agreeing a settlement.

(Rule 21.10 provides that the approval of the court is required where, before proceedings are started, a claim is made by a child and a settlement is reached. The provisions in paragraph 6.1 of Practice Direction 8B set out what must be filed with the court when an application is made to approve a settlement.)

7.45 Where the parties agree a settlement for a greater sum than the defendant had offered during the total consideration period or further consideration period and after the Court Proceedings Pack has been sent to the defendant but before proceedings are issued under Stage 3,

(1) paragraph 7.44 applies; and

(2) the defendant must also pay the fixed late settlement costs in rule 45.23A.

Application for certificate of recoverable benefits

7.46 Paragraph 7.47 applies where, at the date of the acceptance of an offer in the Stage 2 Settlement Pack, the defendant does not have a certificate of recoverable benefits that will remain in force for at least 10 days.

7.47 The defendant should apply for a fresh certificate of recoverable benefits as soon as possible, notify the claimant that it has done so and must pay the amounts set out in paragraph 7.44 within 30 days of the end of the relevant period in paragraphs 7.32 to 7.34.

Failure to reach agreement - general

7.48 Where the parties do not reach an agreement on the damages to be paid within the periods specified in paragraphs 7.32 to 7.34, the claimant must send to the defendant the Court Proceedings Pack (Part A and Part B) Form which must contain—

(a) in Part A, the final schedule of the claimant's losses and the defendant's responses comprising only the figures specified during the periods in paragraphs 7.32 to 7.34, together with supporting comments and evidence from both parties on any disputed heads of damage; and

(b) in Part B, the final offer and counter offer from the Stage 2 Settlement Pack Form.

7.49 Comments in the Court Proceedings Pack (Part A) Form must not raise anything that has not been raised in the Stage 2 Settlement Pack Form.

7.50 The defendant should then check that the Court Proceedings Pack (Part A and Part B) Form complies with paragraphs 7.48 to 7.49. If the defendant considers that the Court Proceedings Pack (Part A and Part B) Form does not comply it must be returned to the claimant within 5 days with an explanation as to why it does not comply.

7.51   Where the defendant intends to nominate a legal representative to accept service the name and address of the legal representative should be provided in the Court Proceedings Pack (Part A) Form.

7.52   Where the defendant fails to return the Court Proceedings Pack (Part A and Part B) Form within the period in paragraph 7.50, the claimant should assume that the defendant has no further comment to make.

Non-settlement payment by the defendant at the end of Stage 2

7.53   Except where the claimant is a child the defendant must pay to the claimant—

(1)   the final offer of damages made by the defendant in the Court Proceedings Pack (Part A and Part B) Form less any—

(a)   deductible amount which is payable to the CRU; and

(b)   previous interim payment(s);

(2)   any unpaid Stage 1 fixed costs in rule 45.18;

(3)   the Stage 2 fixed costs in rule 45.18; and

(4)   the disbursements in rule 45.19(2) that have been agreed.

7.54   Where the amount of a disbursement is not agreed the defendant must pay such amount for the disbursement as the defendant considers reasonable.

7.55   Subject to paragraphs 7.56 and 7.57 the defendant must pay the amounts in paragraph 7.53 and 7.54 within 15 days of receiving the Court Proceedings Pack (Part A and Part B) Form from the claimant.

7.56   Paragraph 7.57 applies where the defendant is required to make the payments in paragraph 7.53 but does not have a certificate of recoverable benefits that remains in force for at least 10 days.

7.57   The defendant should apply for a fresh certificate of recoverable benefits as soon as possible, notify the claimant that it has done so and must pay the amounts set out in paragraph 7.53 within 30 days of receiving the Court Proceedings Pack (Part A and Part B) Form from the claimant.

7.58   Where the defendant does not comply with paragraphs 7.55 or 7.57 the claimant may give written notice that the claim will no longer continue under this Protocol and start proceedings under Part 7 of the CPR.

General provisions

7.59   Where the claimant gives notice to the defendant that the claim is unsuitable for this Protocol (for example, because there are complex issues of fact or law or where claimants contemplate applying for a Group Litigation Order) then the claim will no longer continue under this Protocol. However, where the court considers that the claimant acted unreasonably in giving such notice it will award no more than the fixed costs in rule 45.18.

Stage 3   Stage 3 Procedure

8.1   The Stage 3 Procedure is set out in Practice Direction 8B.

The 2015 Rehabilitation Code

INTRODUCTION

The Code promotes the collaborative use of rehabilitation and early intervention in the compensation process. It is reviewed from time to time in response to feedback from those who use it, taking into account the changing legal and medical landscape.

The Code's purpose is to help the injured claimant make the best and quickest possible medical, social, vocational and psychological recovery. This means ensuring that his or her need for rehabilitation is assessed and addressed as a priority, and that the process is pursued on a collaborative basis. With this in mind, the claimant solicitor should always ensure that the compensator receives the earliest possible notification of the claim and its circumstances whenever rehabilitation may be beneficial.

Although the objectives of the Code apply whatever the clinical and social needs of the claimant, the best way to achieve them will vary depending on the nature of the injury and the claimant's circumstances. The Code recognises that the dynamics of lesser-injury cases are different to those further up the scale. A separate process is set out for claims below £25,000 (in line with the Civil Procedure Rules definition of low value). Separate provision is also made for soft tissue injury cases as defined in paragraph **1.1(16A)** of the Pre-Action Protocol for Low Value Personal Injury Claims in Road Traffic Accidents.

It is important to stress, however, that even low value injuries can be life-changing for some people. The projected monetary value of a claim is only a guide to the rehabilitation needs of the injured person. Each case should be taken on its individual merits, and the guidelines for higher-value injuries will sometimes be more appropriate for those in the lowest category.

Sections 1 to 3 set out the guiding principles and the obligations of the various parties, and apply to all types of injury. After that, the sections diverge significantly depending on the size of claim.

Although the Code deals mainly with the Immediate Needs Assessment, it encourages all parties to adopt the same principles and collaborative approach right up until the case is concluded. In doing so, it does not stipulate a detailed process. Rather, it assumes that the parties will have established the collaborative working relationships that render a prescriptive document unnecessary.

Ten 'markers' that can affect the rehabilitation assessment, and therefore the treatment, are to be found in the Glossary at the end of the Code. They should be considered in all cases.

With the more serious injuries, it is envisaged that Case Managers will have an essential role to play in assessing the claimant's needs and then overseeing treatment. This Code should be read in conjunction with the Guide for Case Managers and those who Commission them, published separately.

1. **Role of the Code**

    1.1 The purpose of the personal injury claims process is to restore the individual as much as possible to the position they were in before the accident. The Code provides a framework for the claimant solicitor and compensator to work together to ensure that the claimant's health, quality of life, independence and ability to work are restored before, or simultaneously with, the process of assessing compensation.

    1.2 Although the Code is recognised by the relevant CPR Pre-Action Protocols, achieving the aims are more important than strict adherence to its terms. Therefore, it is open to the parties to agree an alternative framework to achieve the early rehabilitation of the claimant.

1.3   Where there is no agreement on liability, the parties may still agree to use the Code. The health and economic benefits of proceeding with rehabilitation at an early stage, regardless of agreement on liability, may be especially strong in catastrophic and other severe cases. Compensators should consider from the outset whether there is a possibility or likelihood of at least partial admission later on in the process so as not to compromise the prospects for rehabilitation.

1.4   In this Code, the expression 'the compensator' includes any person acting on behalf of the compensator. 'Claimant solicitor' includes any legal representative acting on behalf of the claimant. 'Case Manager' means a suitably qualified rehabilitation case manager.

2.   The Claimant Solicitor

2.1   The claimant solicitor's obligation to act in the best interests of their client extends beyond securing reasonable financial compensation, vital as that may be. Their duty also includes considering, as soon as practicable, whether additional medical or rehabilitative intervention would improve the claimant's present and/or longer-term physical and mental well-being. In doing so, there should be full consultation with the claimant and/or their family and any treating practitioner where doing so is proportionate and reasonable. This duty continues throughout the life of the case, but is most important in the early stages.

2.2   It is the duty of a claimant solicitor to have an initial discussion with the claimant and/or their family to identify:

(1)   Whether there is an immediate need for aids, adaptations, adjustments to employment to enable the claimant to perform their existing job, obtain a suitable alternative role with the same employer or retrain for new employment. They should, where practical and proportionate, work with the claimant's employers to ensure that the position is kept open for them as long as possible.

(2)   The need to alleviate any problems related to their injuries.

2.3   The claimant solicitor should then communicate these needs to the compensator by telephone or email, together with all other relevant information, as soon as practicable. It is the intention of this Code that both parties will work to address all rehabilitation needs on a collaborative basis.

2.4   The compensator will need to receive from the claimant solicitor sufficient information to make a well-informed decision about the need for rehabilitation assistance, including detailed and adequate information on the functional impact of the claimant's injuries. There is no requirement for an expert report at this early stage. The information should, however, include the nature and extent of any likely continuing disability and any suggestions that may have already been made concerning rehabilitation and/or early intervention. It should be communicated within 21 days of becoming aware of those injuries or needs once the compensator is known.

2.5   Upon receiving a rehabilitation suggestion from the compensator, the claimant solicitor should discuss it with the claimant and/or their family as soon as practical and reply within 21 days.

2.6   Many cases will be considered under this Code before medical evidence has actually been commissioned or obtained. It is important in these situations that rehabilitation steps are not undertaken that might conflict with the recommendations of treating clinical teams. It is equally important that unnecessary delay is avoided in implementing steps that could make a material difference to the injured person or their family. Early engagement with the compensator is crucial to discuss such issues.

2.7   Whilst generally in catastrophic and other particularly severe cases, it is recommended that an appropriately qualified Case Manager should be appointed before any rehabilitation commences, this may not always be possible even though it should be a priority. Methods of selecting Case Managers are described in paragraphs 7.3 and 7.4. The aim when appointing a Case Manager should be to ensure that any proposed rehabilitation plan they recommend is appropriate and that the goals set are specific and attainable. The Case Manager should, before undertaking an Immediate Needs Assessment (INA) as part of the claims process, make every attempt to liaise with NHS clinicians and others involved in the claimant's treatment, and to work collaboratively with them, provided this does not unduly delay the process. If possible, they should obtain the claimant's rehabilitation prescription, discharge summary or similar, including any A&E records and/or treating consultant's report and medical records.

3. The Compensator

3.1 It is the duty of the compensator, from the earliest practicable stage, to consider whether the claimant would benefit from additional medical or rehabilitative treatment. This duty continues throughout the life of the case, but is most important in the early stages.

3.2 If the claimant may have rehabilitation needs, the compensator should contact the claimant solicitor as soon as practicable to seek to work collaboratively on addressing those needs. As set out in paragraph 2.5, the claimant solicitor should respond within 21 days.

3.3 Where a request to consider rehabilitation has been communicated by the claimant solicitor, the compensator should respond within 21 days, or earlier if possible, either confirming their agreement or giving reasons for rejecting the request.

3.4 Nothing in this Code modifies the obligations of the compensator under the Protocols to investigate claims rapidly and, in any event, within the relevant liability response period.

LOWER-VALUE INJURIES

4. The Assessment Process – lower-value injuries

4.1 Different considerations apply for soft-tissue injury cases compared to other lower-value cases of £25,000 or below. In all cases, the claimant's solicitor should consider, with the claimant and/or the claimant's family, whether there is a need for early rehabilitation. The results of that discussion should be recorded in section C of the electronic Claims Notification Form, which will be transmitted through the Ministry of Justice Claims Portal to commence the claim. That form requires details of any professional treatment recommendations, treatment already received (including name of provider) and ongoing rehabilitation needs.

4.2 For lower-value injuries generally, this might involve physiotherapy, diagnostics and consultant follow-up, psychological intervention or other services to alleviate problems caused by the injury. In soft-tissue injury cases, in particular, it is understood that there is not always necessarily a requirement for a rehabilitation intervention. It is considered likely that, where there is an initial intervention, it will focus on treating any physical need, for example through physiotherapy.

In all cases, the claimant solicitor should communicate with the compensator as soon as practical about any rehabilitation needs, preferably by electronic means. The mechanism of completion and transmission of the Claims Notification Form should facilitate this process and should take place before any significant treatment has been commenced, subject always to any overriding medical need for urgent treatment.

4.3 Nothing in this Code alters the legal principles that:

1. Until there has been a liability admission by a compensator (through the Compensator's Response in the Claims Portal), the claimant can have no certainty about the prospect of recovery of any treatment sums incurred.

2. Until the compensator has accepted a treatment regime in which the number and price of sessions have been agreed, the level of recovery of any such sums will always be a matter for negotiation (most likely through exchange of offers in the portal system), unless the subject of a Court order.

3. Where a claimant has decided not to take up a form of treatment that is readily available in favour of a more expensive option, the reasonableness of that decision may be a factor that is taken into account on the assessment of damages.

4.4 Unless there is a medico-legal report containing full recommendations for rehabilitation, which both parties are happy to adopt, an initial Triage Report (TR) should be obtained to establish the type of treatment needed. In most cases, the Triage Report will be the only report required. Where both the claimant's solicitor and the compensator agree that further reports are required, the assessment process is likely to have two further stages:

(i)   A subsequent Assessment Report (AR) provided by the healthcare professional who is actually treating the claimant;

(ii) A Discharge Report (DR) from the treating healthcare professional to summarise the treatment provided.

It is, however, understood within the Code that a treatment discharge summary should routinely be included within the claimant's treatment records.

It is always possible for the Assessment Report (AR) and Discharge Report (DR) to be combined into one document.

4.5 The Triage Report (TR) assessment should be undertaken by an appropriately qualified and experienced person who is subject to appropriate clinical governance structures. Guidance on this may be obtained by reading the British Standards Institute standard PAS 150 or the UKRC Standards. It is permissible under the Code that the assessor providing the Triage Report could also be appointed to implement the recommendations.

4.6 The person or organisation that prepares the Triage and, if appropriate, Assessment and Discharge Reports and/or undertakes treatment should, save in exceptional circumstances, be entirely independent of the person or organisation that provided any medico-legal report to the claimant. In soft-tissue injury cases, the parties are referred to Part 45.29I of the Civil Procedure Rules.

4.7 The Triage and the preparation of any subsequent Assessment and Discharge Report and/or the provision of any treatment may be carried out or provided by a person or organisation having a direct or indirect business connection with the solicitor or compensator only if the other party agrees. The solicitor or compensator will be expected to reveal to the other party the existence and nature of such a business connection before instructing the connected organisation.

4.8 The assessment agency will be asked to carry out the Triage Report in a way that is appropriate to the needs of the case, which will in most cases be a telephone interview within seven days of the referral being received by the agency. It is expected that the TR will be very simple, usually just an email.

4.9 In all cases, the TR should be published simultaneously or made available immediately by the instructing party to the other side. This applies also to treatment reports (AR and DR) where the parties have agreed that they are required. Both parties will have the right to raise questions on the report(s), disclosing such correspondence to the other party.

4.10 It is recognised that, for the Triage Report to be of benefit to the parties, it should be prepared and used wholly outside the litigation process. Neither side can rely on the report in any subsequent litigation unless both parties agree in writing. Likewise, any notes, correspondence or documents created in connection with the triage assessment process will not be disclosed in any litigation. Anyone involved in preparing the Triage Report or in the assessment process shall not be a compellable witness at court. This principle is also set out in the Protocols.

4.11 The compensator will usually only consider rehabilitation that deals with the effects of the injuries that have been caused in the relevant accident. They will not normally fund treatment for other conditions that do not directly relate to the accident unless these conditions have been exacerbated by it or will impede recovery.

5.   The Reports – lower-value injuries

5.1   It is expected under the Code that all treatment reporting described in this section will be concise and proportionate to the severity of the injuries and likely value of the claim.

5.2   The Triage Report should consider, where relevant, the ten 'markers' identified at the end of this Code and will normally cover the following headings:

1.   The injuries sustained by the claimant;
2.   The current impact on their activities of daily living, their domestic circumstances and, where relevant, their employment;
3.   Any other relevant medical conditions not arising from the accident;
4.   The past provision and current availability of treatment to the claimant via the NHS, their employer or health insurance schemes;
5.   The type of intervention or treatment recommended;
6.   The likely cost and duration of treatment;
7.   The expected outcome of such intervention or treatment.

5.3   The Triage Report will not provide a prognosis or a diagnosis.

5.4   The assessment reports (TR, or any AR or DR) should not deal with issues relating to legal liability and should therefore not contain a detailed account of the accident circumstances, though they should enable the parties to understand the mechanism by which the injury occurred.

5.5   Where agreed as needed, any Assessment Report (AR) will normally have the following minimum headings:

1.   Nature, symptoms and severity of injury(ies);
2.   Relevance of any pre-existing conditions or injuries;
3.   Primary rehabilitation goal and anticipated outcome;
4.   Expected duration, number, type and length of treatment sessions;
5.   Impact of injuries upon work and or activities of daily living and barriers to recovery and return to work.

5.6   Where agreed as needed, such as where a treatment discharge summary is considered inadequate, any Discharge Report (DR) will normally have the following minimum headings:

1.   Current nature, symptoms and severity of injury(ies);
2.   Whether the primary rehabilitation goal has been attained;
3.   Number, type and length of treatment sessions/appointments attended or missed/DNAs (Did Not Attend);
4.   Current impact of injuries on work or activities of daily living;
5.   Whether the claimant has achieved, as far as possible, a full functional recovery;
6.   Whether additional treatment is required to address the claimant's symptoms.

In cases where no AR or DR has been agreed, it is expected that the notes and discharge summary of the treatment provider will contain the necessary information.

5.7   The provision as to the report being outside the litigation process is limited to the Triage Report and any notes or correspondence relating to it. Any notes and reports created during the subsequent treatment process will be covered by the usual principle in relation to disclosure of documents and medical records relating to the claimant.

5.8   The compensator will normally pay for the TR within 28 days of receipt. Where the claimant's solicitor and the compensator have agreed that such reports are required, the compensator will also pay for any AR and DR within 28 days of receipt. In either case, the compensator may challenge bills that they believe to be excessive or disproportionate.

5.9   The reporting agency should ensure that all invoices are within reasonable market rates, are clear and provide the following detail:

1.   Type of treatment provided, e.g. telephonic CBT, face-to-face physiotherapy;

2.   Dates of treatments/sessions attended and DNAs of treatment sessions;

3.   Total number of treatments delivered and whether those treatments were provided remotely or in person;

4.   Total cost and whether this is for treatment provided or an estimate of future cost.

5.10   Where any treatment has been organised prior to notification to or approval by the compensator, any invoice submitted to the compensator will also need to be accompanied by a discharge summary recording treatment outcome in addition to the information contained in paragraph 5.9 The need for the discharge summary to be included in the treatment records is covered in paragraph 4.4.

5.11   The parties should continue to work together to ensure that the recommended rehabilitation proceeds smoothly and that any further rehabilitation needs continue to be assessed.

6.   Recommendations – lower-value injuries

6.1   The compensator will be under a duty to consider the recommendations made and the extent to which funds will be made available to implement the recommendations. The claimant will be under no obligation to undergo intervention, medical or investigation treatment. Where intervention treatment has taken place, the compensator will not be required to pay for treatment that is unreasonable in nature, content or cost.

6.2   The compensator should provide a response to the claimant's solicitor within15 business days from the date when the TR is disclosed. If the Insurer's Response Form is transmitted via the portal earlier than 15 business days from receipt of the CNF and the TR, the response should be included in the Response Form. The response should include: (i) the extent to which the recommendations have been accepted and rehabilitation treatment will be funded; (ii) justifications for any refusal to meet the cost of recommended rehabilitation and (if appropriate) alternative recommendations. As stated in paragraph 4.3, the claimant may start treatment without waiting for the compensator's response, but at their own risk as to recovering the cost.

6.3   The compensator agrees that, in any legal proceedings connected with the claim, they will not dispute the reasonableness or costs of the treatment they have funded, provided the claimant has undertaken the treatment and it has been expressly agreed and/or the treatment provider has been jointly instructed. If the claim later fails, is discontinued or contributory negligence is an issue, it is not within the Code to seek to recover such funding from the claimant unless it can be proven that there has been fraud/ fundamental dishonesty.

6.4   Following on from implementation of the assessment process, the parties should consider and agree at the earliest opportunity a process for ensuring that the ongoing rehabilitation needs of the claimant are met in a collaborative manner.

MEDIUM, SEVERE AND CATASTROPHIC INJURIES

7. **The Assessment Process – medium, severe and catastrophic injuries**

   7.1   The need for and type of rehabilitation assistance will be considered by means of an Immediate Needs Assessment (INA) carried out by a Case Manager or appropriate rehabilitation professional, e.g. an NHS Rehabilitation Consultant. (For further information about Case Managers, refer to the Glossary and The Guide for Case Managers and those who Commission them, published separately.)

   7.2   The Case Manager must be professionally and suitably qualified, experienced and skilled to carry out the task, and they must comply with appropriate clinical governance. With the most severe life-changing injuries, a Case Manager should normally be registered with a professional body appropriate to the severity of the claimant's injuries. The individual or organisation should not, save in exceptional circumstances, have provided a medico-legal report to the claimant nor be associated with any person or organisation that has done so.

   7.3   The claimant solicitor and the compensator should have discussions at the outset to agree the person or organisation to conduct the INA, as well as topics to include in the letter of instruction. The INA should go ahead whether or not the claimant is still being treated by NHS physicians, who should nonetheless be consulted about their recommendations for short-term and longer-term rehabilitation. A fundamental part of the Case Manager's role is to make immediate contact with the treating clinical lead to assess whether any proposed rehabilitation plan is appropriate.

   7.4   The parties are encouraged to try to agree the selection of an appropriately qualified independent Case Manager best suited to the claimant's needs to undertake the INA. The parties should then endeavour to agree the method of instruction and how the referral will be made. When considering options with the claimant, a joint referral to the chosen Case Manager may maximise the benefits of collaborative working. Any option chosen by the parties is subject to the claimant's agreement. In all situations, the parties should seek to agree early implementation of reasonable recommendations and secure funding. In circumstances where trust has been built, it is recommended that the parties agree to retain the Case Manager to co-ordinate the implementation of the agreed rehabilitation plan.

   7.5   With catastrophic injuries, it is especially important to achieve good early communication between the parties and an agreement to share information that could aid recovery. This will normally involve telephone or face-to-face meetings to discuss what is already known, and to plan how to gain further information on the claimant's health, vocational and social requirements. The fact that the claimant may be an NHS in-patient should not be a barrier to carrying out an INA.

   7.6   No solicitor or compensator may insist on the INA being carried out by a particular person or organisation if the other party raises a reasonable objection within 21 days of the nomination. Where alternative providers are offered, the claimant and/or their family should be personally informed of the options and the associated benefits and costs of each option.

   7.7   Objections to a particular person or organisation should include possible remedies such as additional information requirements or alternative solutions. If the discussion is not resolved within 21 days, responsibility for commissioning the provider lies ultimately with the claimant as long as they can demonstrate that full and timely co-operation has been provided.

   7.8   A rehabilitation provider's overriding duty is to the claimant. Their relationship with the claimant is therapeutic, and they should act totally independently of the instructing party.

7.9   The assessment may be carried out by a person or organisation having a direct or indirect business connection with the solicitor or compensator only if the other party agrees. The solicitor and compensator must always reveal any business connection at the earliest opportunity.

7.10   The assessment process should provide information and analysis as to the rehabilitation assistance that would maximise recovery and mitigate the loss. Further assessments of rehabilitation needs may be required as the claimant recovers.

7.11   The compensator will usually only consider rehabilitation that deals with the effects of injuries for which they are liable. Treatment for other conditions will not normally be included unless it is agreed that they have been exacerbated by the accident or are impeding the claimant's recovery.

8.   **The Immediate Needs Assessment (INA) Report – medium, severe and catastrophic injuries**

8.1   The Case Manager will be asked to carry out the INA in a way appropriate to the case, taking into account the importance of acting promptly. This may include, by prior appointment, a telephone interview. In more complex and catastrophic cases, a face-to-face discussion with the claimant is likely.

8.2   As well as the ten 'markers' identified in the Glossary at the end of this Code, the INA should consider the following points, provided doing so does not unduly delay the process:

    a.   The physical and psychological injuries sustained by the claimant and the subsequent care received or planned;

    b.   The symptoms, disability/incapacity arising from those injuries. Where relevant to the overall picture of the claimant's rehabilitation needs, any other medical conditions not arising from the accident should also be separately noted;

    c.   The availability or planned delivery of interventions or treatment via the NHS, their employer or health insurance schemes;

    d.   Any impact upon the claimant's domestic and social circumstances, including mobility, accommodation and employment, and whether therapies such as gym training or swimming would be beneficial;

    e.   The injuries/disability for which early intervention or early rehabilitation is suggested;

    f.   The type of clinical intervention or treatment required in both the short and medium term, and its rationale;

    g.   The likely cost and duration of recommended interventions or treatment, their goals and duration, with anticipated outcomes;

    h.   The anticipated clinical and return-to-work outcome of such intervention or treatment.

8.3   The INA report will not provide a medical prognosis or diagnosis, but should include any clinically justifiable recommendations for further medical investigation, compliant with NICE guidelines and, where possible, aligned to the NHS Rehabilitation prescription, discharge report or similar. Where recommendations are in addition to or deviate from the NHS recommendations, these should be explained with appropriate justification provided.

8.4   The INA report should not deal with issues relating to legal liability, such as a detailed account of the accident circumstances, though it should enable the parties to understand the mechanism by which the injury occurred.

8.5   The Case Manager will, on completion of the report, send copies to the claimant solicitor and compensator simultaneously. Both parties will have the right to raise questions on the report, disclosing such correspondence to the other party. It is, however, anticipated that the parties will discuss the recommendations and agree the appropriate action to be taken. Subject to the claimant's consent, their GP and/or treating clinical team will also be informed of the INA and its recommendations once funding to proceed has been obtained. In most cases, the INA will be conducted, and the report provided, within 21 days from the date of the letter of referral to the Case Manager.

8.6 For this assessment report to be of benefit to the parties, it should be prepared and used wholly outside the litigation process, unless both parties agree otherwise in writing.

8.7 The report, any correspondence related to it and any notes created by the assessing agency will be deemed to be covered by legal privilege and not disclosed in any proceedings unless the parties agree. The same applies to notes or documents related to the INA, either during or after the report submission. Anyone involved in preparing the report or in the assessment process will not be a compellable witness at court. (This principle is also set out in the Protocols.)

8.8 Any notes and reports created during the subsequent case management process post-INA will be covered by the usual principle in relation to disclosure of documents and medical records relating to the claimant. However, it is open to the parties to agree to extend the provisions of the Code beyond the INA to subsequent reports.

8.9 The compensator will pay for the INA report within 28 days of receipt.

9. Recommendations – medium, severe and catastrophic injuries

9.1 When the Immediate Needs Assessment (INA) report is received, the compensator has a duty to consider the recommendations and the extent to which funds are made available to implement them. The compensator is not required to pay for treatment that is unreasonable in nature, content or cost. The claimant will be under no obligation to undergo treatment.

9.2 The compensator should respond to the claimant solicitor within 21 days of receiving the INA report. The response should include: (i) the extent to which it accepts the recommendations and is willing to fund treatment; and (ii) justifications for any refusal, with alternative recommendations.

9.3 The compensator will not dispute the reasonableness or costs of the treatment, as long as the claimant has undertaken the treatment and it was expressly agreed in advance (or the treatment provider had been jointly instructed). Where there is disagreement, general interim payments are recommended to provide continuity of services with an understanding that recovery of such sums is not guaranteed and will always be a matter for negotiation or determination by a court. Where a claimant has decided not to take up a form of treatment that is readily available in favour of a more expensive option, the reasonableness of that decision may be a factor that is taken into account on the assessment of damages. If the claim later fails or is discontinued or contributory negligence is an issue, the compensator will not seek to recover any agreed rehabilitation funding it has already provided unless it can be proven that there has been fraud/fundamental dishonesty.

9.4 Following implementation of the INA, the parties should consider and attempt to agree, as soon as possible, a collaborative process for meeting the claimant's ongoing rehabilitation needs.

9.5 The overriding purpose of the INA should be to assess the claimant's medical and social needs with a view to recommending treatment rather than to obtain information to settle the claim.

GLOSSARY – THE TEN 'MARKERS'

The ten 'markers' referred to in this Code that should be taken into account when assessing an injured person's rehabilitation needs are summarised below:

1. Age (particularly children/elderly);
2. Pre-existing physical and psycho-social comorbidities;
3. Return-to-work/education issues;
4. Dependants living at home;
5. Geographic location;
6. Mental capacity;
7. Activities of daily living in the short-term and long-term;
8. Realistic goals, aspirations, attainments;
9. Fatalities/those who witness major incidence of trauma within the same accident;
10. Length of time post-accident.

September 2015

The working parties that drew up the 2015 Rehabilitation Code included representatives of ABI, APIL, CMSUK, FOIL, IUA, MASS and PIBA. Although it is for the parties involved in personal injury claims to decide when and how to use the Code, it is envisaged that it should become operational from December 1, 2015.

APPENDIX 6

Actuarial Tables – Extracts

SECTION B: CONTINGENCIES OTHER THAN MORTALITY

26. As stated in paragraph 19, the tables for loss of earnings (Tables 3 to 14) take no account of risks other than mortality. This section shows how the multipliers in these tables may be reduced to take account of these risks.

27. Tables of factors to be applied to the existing multipliers were first introduced in the Second Edition of the Ogden Tables. These factors were based on work commissioned by the Institute of Actuaries and carried out by Professor S Haberman and Mrs D S F Bloomfield (*Work time lost to sickness, unemployment and stoppages: measurement and application* (1990), Journal of the Institute of Actuaries 117, 533-595). Although there was some debate within the actuarial profession about the details of the work, and in particular about the scope for developing it further, the findings were broadly accepted and were adopted by the Government Actuary and the other actuaries who were members of the Working Party when the Second Edition of the Tables was published and remained unchanged until the 6th edition.

28. Some related work was published in 2002 by Lewis, McNabb and Wass (*Methods of calculating damages for loss of future earnings*, Journal of Personal Injury Law, 2002 Number 2). For the publication of the 6th Edition of the Ogden Tables, the Ogden Working Party was involved in further research into the impact of contingencies other than mortality carried out by Professor Richard Verrall, Professor Steven Haberman and Mr Zoltan Butt of City University, London and, in a separate exercise, by Dr Victoria Wass of Cardiff University. Their findings were combined to produce the tables of factors given in section B of the 6th edition and repeated here.

29. The Haberman and Bloomfield paper relied on data from the Labour Force Surveys for 1973, 1977, 1981 and 1985 and English Life Tables No. 14 (1980-82). The Labour Force Survey (LFS) was originally designed to produce a periodic cross-sectional snapshot of the working age population and collects information on an extensive range of socio-economic and labour force characteristics. Since the winter of 1992/3, the LFS has been carried out on a quarterly basis, with respondents being included in the survey over 5 successive quarters. The research of Professor Verrall *et al* and Dr Wass used data from the Labour Force Surveys conducted from 1998 to 2003 to estimate the probabilities of movement of males and females between different states of economic activity, dependent on age, sex, employment activity and level of disability. These probabilities permit the calculation of the expected periods in employment until retirement age, dependent on the initial starting state of economic activity, disability and educational attainment. These can then be discounted at the same discount rate that is used for obtaining the relevant multiplier from Tables 3 to 14, in order to give a multiplier which takes into account only those periods the claimant would be expected, on average, to be in work. These discounted working life expectancy multipliers can be compared to those obtained assuming the person remained in work throughout, to obtain reduction factors which give the expected proportion of time to retirement age which will be spent in employment.

30. The factors described in subsequent paragraphs are for use in calculating loss of earnings up to retirement age. The research work did not investigate the impact of contingencies other than mortality on the value of future pension rights. Some reduction to the multiplier for loss of pension would often be appropriate when a reduction is being applied for loss of earnings. This may be a smaller reduction than in the case of loss of earnings because the ill-health contingency (as opposed to the unemployment contingency) may give rise to significant ill-health retirement pension rights. A bigger reduction may be necessary in cases where there is significant doubt whether pension rights would have continued to accrue (to the extent not already allowed for in the post-retirement multiplier) or in cases where there may be doubt over the ability of the pension fund to pay promised benefits. In the case of a defined contribution pension scheme, loss of pension rights may be allowed for simply by increasing the future earnings loss (adjusted for contingencies other than mortality) by the percentage of earnings which the employer contributions to the scheme represent.

31. The methodology proposed in paragraphs 33 to 42 describes one method for dealing with contingencies other than mortality. If this methodology is followed, in many cases it will be appropriate to increase or reduce the discount in the tables to take account of the nature of a particular claimant's disabilities. It should be noted that the methodology does not take into account the pre-accident employment history. The methodology also provides for the possibility of valuing more appropriately the possible mitigation of loss of earnings in cases where the claimant is employed after the accident or is considered capable of being employed. This will in many cases enable a more accurate assessment to be made of the mitigation of loss. However, there may be some cases when the *Smith v Manchester Corporation* or *Blamire* approach remains applicable or otherwise where a precise mathematical approach is inapplicable.

32. The suggestions which follow are intended as a 'ready reckoner' which provides an initial adjustment to the multipliers according to the employment status, disability status and educational attainment of the claimant when calculating awards for loss of earnings and for any mitigation of this loss in respect of potential future post-injury earnings. Such a ready reckoner cannot take into account all circumstances and it may be appropriate to argue for higher or lower adjustments in particular cases. In particular, it can be difficult to place a value on the possible mitigating income when considering the potential range of disabilities and their effect on post work capability, even within the interpretation of disability set out in paragraph 35. However, the methodology does offer a framework for consideration of a range of possible figures with the maximum being effectively provided by the post injury multiplier assuming the claimant was not disabled and the minimum being the case where there is no realistic prospect of post injury employment.

The deduction for contingencies other than mortality

33.   Under this method, multipliers for loss of earnings obtained from Tables 3 to 14 are multiplied by factors to allow for the risk of periods of non-employment and absence from the workforce because of sickness.

34.   The research by Professor Verrall *et al* and Dr Wass referred to in paragraphs 28 and 29 demonstrated that the key issues affecting a person's future working life are employment status, disability status and educational attainment.

35.   The definitions of employed/not employed, disabled/not disabled and educational attainment used in this analysis and which should be used for determining which factors to apply to the multipliers to allow for contingencies other than mortality are as follows:

Employed — Those who at the time of the accident are employed, self-employed or on a government training scheme

Not employed — All others (including those temporarily out of work, full-time students and unpaid family workers)

Disabled — A person is classified as being disabled if all three of the following conditions in relation to the ill-health or disability are met:

(i)   has an illness or a disability which has or is expected to last for over a year or is a progressive illness

(ii)   satisfies the Equality Act 2010 definition that the impact of the disability substantially limits the person's ability to carry out normal day-to-day activities

(iii)   their condition affects either the kind or the amount of paid work they can do

Not disabled — All others

Normal day-to-day activities are those which are carried out by most people on a daily basis, and we are interested in disabilities/health problems which have a substantial adverse effect on respondent's ability to carry out these activities.

There are several ways in which a disability or health problem may affect the respondent's day to day activities:

Mobility – for example, unable to travel short journeys as a passenger in a car, unable to walk other than at a slow pace or with jerky movements, difficulty in negotiating stairs, unable to use one or more forms of public transport, unable to go out of doors unaccompanied.

Manual dexterity – for example, loss of functioning in one or both hands, inability to use a knife and fork at the same time, or difficulty in pressing buttons on a keyboard

Physical co-ordination – for example, the inability to feed or dress oneself; or to pour liquid from one vessel to another except with unusual slowness or concentration.

Problems with bowel/bladder control – for example, frequent or regular loss of control of the bladder or bowel. Occasional bedwetting is not considered a disability.

Ability to lift, carry or otherwise move everyday objects (for example, books, kettles, light furniture) – for example, inability to pick up a weight with one hand but not the other, or to carry a tray steadily.

Speech – for example, unable to communicate (clearly) orally with others, taking significantly longer to say things. A minor stutter, difficulty in speaking in front of an audience, or inability to speak a foreign language would not be considered impairments.

Hearing – for example, not being able to hear without the use of a hearing aid, the inability to understand speech under normal conditions or over the telephone.

Eyesight – for example, while wearing spectacles or contact lenses – being unable to pass the standard driving eyesight test, total inability to distinguish colours (excluding ordinary red/green colour blindness), or inability to read newsprint.

Memory or ability to concentrate, learn or understand – for example, intermittent loss of consciousness or confused behaviour, inability to remember names of family or friends, unable to write a cheque without assistance, or an inability to follow a recipe.

Perception of risk of physical danger – for example, reckless behaviour putting oneself or others at risk, mobility to cross the road safely. This excludes (significant) fear of heights or underestimating risk of dangerous hobbies.

Three levels of educational attainment are defined for the purposes of the tables as follows:

D   Degree or equivalent or higher

GE-A   GCSE grades A to C up to A levels or equivalents

O   Below GCSE C or CSE 1 or equivalent or no qualifications

The following table gives a more detailed breakdown of the allocation of various types of educational qualification to each of the three categories above and are based on the allocations used in the research by Professor Verrall *et al* and Dr Wass.

Categories of highest educational attainment

D Degree or equivalent or higher	GE-A GCSE grades A to C up to A levels or equivalent	O Below GCSE C or CSE 1 or equivalent or no qualifications
Any degree (first or higher)	A or AS level or equivalent	CSE below grade 1
Other higher education qualification below degree level	O level, GCSE grade A-C or equivalent	GCSE below grade C
Diploma in higher education		
NVQ level 4 or 5	NVQ level 2 or 3	NVQ level 1 or equivalent
HNC/HND, BTEC higher etc	BTEC/SCOTVEC first or general diploma	BTEC first or general certificate
	OND/ONC, BTEC/SCOTVEC national	SCOTVEC modules or equivalent
RSA higher diploma	RSA diploma, advanced diploma or certificate	RSA other
Teaching, Nursing etc	GNVQ intermediate or advanced	GNVQ/ GVSQ foundation level
	City and Guilds craft or advanced craft	City and Guilds other
	SCE higher or equivalent Trade apprenticeship	YT/ YTP certificate
	Scottish 6th year certificate (CSYS)	Other qualifications
		No qualification
		Don't know

Note: "educational attainment" is used here as a proxy for skill level, so that those in professional occupations such as law, accountancy, nursing etc who do not have a degree ought to be treated as if they do have one.

36.   The research also considered the extent to which a person's future working life expectancy is affected by individual circumstances such as occupation and industrial sector, geographical region and education. The researchers concluded that the most significant consideration was the highest level of education achieved by the claimant and that, if this was allowed for, the effect of the other factors was relatively small. As a result, the Working Party decided to propose adjustment factors which allow for employment status, disability status and educational attainment only. This is a change from earlier editions of the Ogden Tables where adjustments were made for types of occupation and for geographical region.

37.   A separate assessment is made for (a) the value of earnings the claimant would have received if the injury had not been suffered and (b) the value of the claimant's earnings (if any) taking account of the injuries sustained. The risk of non-employment is significantly higher post-injury due to the impairment. The loss is arrived at by deducting (b) from (a).

38. In order to calculate the value of the earnings the claimant would have received, if the injury had not been suffered, the claimant's employment status and the disability status need to be determined as at the date of the accident (or the onset of the medical condition) giving rise to the claim, so that the correct table can be applied. For the calculation of future loss of earnings (based on actual pre-accident earnings and also future employment prospects), Tables A and C should be used for claimants who were not disabled at the time of the accident, and Tables B and D should be used for those with a pre-existing disability. In all of these tables the three left hand columns are for those who were employed at the time of the accident and the three right hand columns are for those who were not.

39. In order to calculate the value of the actual earnings that a claimant is likely to receive in the future (i.e. after settlement or trial), the employment status and the disability status need to be determined as at the date of settlement or trial. For claimants with a work-affecting disability at that point in time, Tables B and D should be used. The three left hand columns will apply in respect of claimants actually in employment at date of settlement or trial and the three right hand columns will apply in respect of those who remain non-employed at that point in time.

40. The factors in Tables A to D allow for the interruption of employment for bringing up children and caring for other dependants.

41. In the case of those who at the date of the accident have not yet reached the age at which it is likely they would have started work, the relevant factor will be chosen based on a number of assessments of the claimant's likely employment had the injury not occurred. The relevant factor from the tables would be chosen on the basis of the level of education the claimant would have been expected to have attained, the age at which it is likely the claimant would have started work, together with an assessment as to whether the claimant would have become employed or not. The work multiplier will also have to be discounted for early receipt using the appropriate factor from Table 27 for the number of years between the claimant's age at the date of trial and the age at which it is likely that he/she would have started work.

42. Tables A to D include factors up to age 54 only. For older ages the reduction factors increase towards 1 at retirement age for those who are employed and fall towards 0 for those who are not employed. However, where the claimant is older than 54, it is anticipated that the likely future course of employment status will be particularly dependent on individual circumstances, so that the use of factors based on averages would not be appropriate. Hence reduction factors are not provided for these older ages.

Table A
Loss of Earnings to pension Age 65 (Males – Not disabled)

Age at date of trial	Employed			Not employed		
	D	GE-A	O	D	GE-A	O
16-19		0.90	0.85		0.85	0.82
20-24	0.92	0.92	0.87	0.89	0.88	0.83
25-29	0.93	0.92	0.89	0.89	0.88	0.82
30-34	0.92	0.91	0.89	0.87	0.86	0.81
35-39	0.90	0.90	0.89	0.85	0.84	0.80
40-44	0.88	0.88	0.88	0.82	0.81	0.78
45-49	0.86	0.86	0.86	0.77	0.77	0.74
50	0.83	0.83	0.83	0.72	0.72	0.70
51	0.82	0.82	0.82	0.70	0.70	0.68
52	0.81	0.81	0.81	0.67	0.67	0.66
53	0.80	0.80	0.80	0.63	0.63	0.63
54	0.79	0.79	0.79	0.59	0.59	0.59

Table B
Loss of Earnings to pension Age 65 (Males – Disabled)

Age at date of trial	D	Employed GE-A	O	D	Not employed GE-A	O
16-19		0.55	0.32		0.49	0.25
20-24	0.61	0.55	0.38	0.53	0.46	0.24
25-29	0.60	0.54	0.42	0.48	0.41	0.24
30-34	0.59	0.52	0.40	0.43	0.34	0.23
35-39	0.58	0.48	0.39	0.38	0.28	0.20
40-44	0.57	0.48	0.39	0.33	0.23	0.15
45-49	0.55	0.48	0.39	0.26	0.20	0.11
50	0.53	0.49	0.40	0.24	0.18	0.10
51	0.53	0.49	0.41	0.23	0.17	0.09
52	0.54	0.49	0.41	0.22	0.16	0.08
53	0.54	0.49	0.42	0.21	0.15	0.07
54	0.54	0.50	0.43	0.20	0.14	0.06

Table C
Loss of Earnings to Pension Age 60 (Females – Not disabled)

Age at date of trial	D	Employed GE-A	O	D	Not employed GE-A	O
16-19		0.81	0.64		0.77	0.59
20-24	0.89	0.82	0.68	0.84	0.76	0.60
25-29	0.89	0.84	0.72	0.83	0.75	0.61
30-34	0.89	0.85	0.75	0.81	0.75	0.63
35-39	0.89	0.86	0.78	0.80	0.74	0.63
40-44	0.89	0.86	0.80	0.78	0.72	0.60
45-49	0.87	0.85	0.81	0.72	0.64	0.52
50	0.86	0.84	0.81	0.64	0.55	0.43
51	0.85	0.84	0.81	0.60	0.51	0.40
52	0.84	0.84	0.81	0.56	0.46	0.36
53	0.83	0.83	0.81	0.50	0.41	0.32
54	0.83	0.83	0.82	0.44	0.35	0.27

Table D
Loss of Earnings to Pension Age 60 (Females – Disabled)

Age at date of trial	Employed			Not employed		
	D	GE-A	O	D	GE-A	O
16-19		0.43	0.25		0.35	0.19
20-24	0.64	0.44	0.25	0.58	0.33	0.17
25-29	0.63	0.45	0.25	0.50	0.32	0.16
30-34	0.62	0.46	0.30	0.44	0.31	0.15
35-39	0.61	0.48	0.34	0.42	0.28	0.14
40-44	0.60	0.51	0.38	0.38	0.23	0.13
45-49	0.60	0.54	0.42	0.28	0.18	0.11
50	0.60	0.56	0.47	0.23	0.15	0.10
51	0.61	0.58	0.49	0.21	0.14	0.09
52	0.61	0.60	0.51	0.20	0.13	0.08
53	0.62	0.62	0.54	0.18	0.11	0.07
54	0.63	0.66	0.57	0.16	0.09	0.06

The factors in Tables A to D will need to be reviewed if the discount rate changes.

Different pension ages

43.   The factors in the preceding tables assume retirement at age 65 for males and age 60 for females. It is not possible to calculate expected working life times assuming alternative retirement ages from the LFS data, since the employment data in the LFS are collected only for the working population, assumed aged between 16 and 64 for males and between 16 and 59 for females. Where the retirement age is different from age 65 for males or age 60 for females, it is suggested that this should be ignored and the reduction factor and the adjustments thereto be taken from the above tables for the age of the claimant as at the date of trial with no adjustment i.e. assume that the retirement age is age 65 for males and age 60 for females. However, if the retirement age is close to the age at the date of trial, then it may be more appropriate to take into account the circumstances of the individual case.

44.   It should be noted that the reduction factors in Tables A, B, C and D are based on data for the period 1998 to 2003. Whilst the reduction factors and adjustments allow for the age-specific probabilities of moving into, or out of, employment over future working life time, based on data for the period 1998-2003, the methodology assumes that these probabilities remain constant over time; there is no allowance for changes in these age-specific probabilities beyond this period. It is also assumed that there will be no change in disability status or educational achievement after the date of the accident. Future changes in the probabilities of moving into, and out of, employment are especially difficult to predict with any certainty. It is the intention that the factors should be reassessed from time to time as new data become available.

Table 1   Multipliers for pecuniary loss for life (males)

Age at date of trial	Multiplier calculated with allowance for projected mortality from the 2008-based population projections and rate of return of											Age at date of trial
	−2.0%	−1.5%	−1.0%	−0.5%	0.0%	0.5%	1.0%	1.5%	2.0%	2.5%	3.0%	
0	264.76	195.32	147.14	113.22	88.96	71.35	58.34	48.60	41.17	35.41	30.89	0
1	259.11	191.95	145.15	112.06	88.31	71.00	58.18	48.54	41.18	35.46	30.96	1
2	252.28	187.68	142.46	110.35	87.22	70.30	57.73	48.24	40.98	35.33	30.87	2
3	245.58	183.46	139.78	108.64	86.12	69.58	57.26	47.94	40.78	35.19	30.78	3
4	239.02	179.29	137.12	106.93	85.01	68.86	56.78	47.62	40.56	35.05	30.68	4
5	232.59	175.19	134.48	105.22	83.89	68.12	56.30	47.29	40.34	34.90	30.58	5
6	226.29	171.15	131.87	103.52	82.78	67.39	55.80	46.96	40.12	34.75	30.47	6
7	220.14	167.18	129.29	101.83	81.66	66.65	55.31	46.63	39.89	34.59	30.36	7
8	214.13	163.28	126.74	100.15	80.55	65.90	54.80	46.28	39.65	34.42	30.24	8
9	208.23	159.43	124.21	98.48	79.43	65.15	54.29	45.93	39.41	34.25	30.13	9
10	202.47	155.64	121.71	96.81	78.31	64.39	53.78	45.58	39.16	34.08	30.00	10
11	196.83	151.92	119.23	95.15	77.19	63.63	53.25	45.22	38.91	33.90	29.87	11
12	191.33	148.26	116.79	93.50	76.07	62.86	52.72	44.85	38.65	33.72	29.74	12
13	185.95	144.67	114.37	91.87	74.96	62.09	52.19	44.47	38.39	33.53	29.61	13
14	180.69	141.14	111.98	90.24	73.84	61.32	51.65	44.10	38.12	33.34	29.47	14
15	175.56	137.67	109.62	88.63	72.73	60.55	51.11	43.71	37.84	33.14	29.32	15
16	170.55	134.27	107.30	87.02	71.61	59.77	50.56	43.32	37.57	32.94	29.17	16
17	165.66	130.93	105.00	85.44	70.51	58.99	50.01	42.93	37.28	32.73	29.02	17
18	160.89	127.66	102.74	83.86	69.41	58.22	49.46	42.53	37.00	32.52	28.87	18
19	156.25	124.45	100.52	82.31	68.31	57.44	48.91	42.14	36.71	32.31	28.71	19
20	151.72	121.31	98.32	80.76	67.22	56.66	48.35	41.73	36.41	32.10	28.55	20
21	147.28	118.22	96.15	79.23	66.13	55.88	47.78	41.32	36.11	31.87	28.39	21
22	142.94	115.17	94.00	77.70	65.04	55.09	47.21	40.90	35.81	31.64	28.22	22
23	138.69	112.17	91.87	76.18	63.94	54.30	46.63	40.48	35.49	31.41	28.04	23
24	134.54	109.22	89.77	74.67	62.85	53.51	46.05	40.05	35.17	31.17	27.86	24
25	130.49	106.33	87.69	73.17	61.76	52.71	45.46	39.61	34.85	30.92	27.67	25
26	126.54	103.50	85.65	71.69	60.68	51.91	44.87	39.17	34.51	30.67	27.48	26
27	122.69	100.72	83.63	70.22	59.59	51.11	44.28	38.73	34.18	30.42	27.28	27
28	118.90	97.98	81.63	68.74	58.51	50.30	43.67	38.27	33.83	30.15	27.08	28
29	115.20	95.28	79.64	67.28	57.42	49.49	43.06	37.81	33.48	29.88	26.87	29
30	111.59	92.63	77.69	65.83	56.34	48.68	42.45	37.34	33.12	29.60	26.65	30
31	108.09	90.04	75.78	64.40	55.27	47.87	41.83	36.87	32.76	29.32	26.44	31
32	104.68	87.52	73.89	62.99	54.20	47.06	41.22	36.40	32.39	29.04	26.21	32
33	101.36	85.04	72.04	61.60	53.15	46.26	40.60	35.92	32.02	28.75	25.99	33
34	98.10	82.61	70.21	60.21	52.09	45.45	39.98	35.44	31.65	28.46	25.75	34
35	94.92	80.21	68.39	58.83	51.03	44.63	39.35	34.95	31.26	28.15	25.51	35
36	91.82	77.86	66.60	57.46	49.98	43.82	38.71	34.45	30.87	27.84	25.27	36
37	88.78	75.55	64.83	56.10	48.93	43.00	38.07	33.95	30.47	27.53	25.01	37
38	85.81	73.27	63.08	54.74	47.87	42.18	37.42	33.44	30.06	27.20	24.75	38
39	82.89	71.03	61.35	53.39	46.82	41.35	36.77	32.91	29.65	26.86	24.48	39
40	80.05	68.83	59.63	52.05	45.76	40.51	36.11	32.39	29.22	26.52	24.20	40
41	77.27	66.67	57.94	50.72	44.71	39.68	35.44	31.85	28.79	26.17	23.91	41
42	74.56	64.55	56.28	49.41	43.67	38.84	34.77	31.31	28.35	25.81	23.62	42
43	71.92	62.47	54.63	48.10	42.62	38.01	34.10	30.76	27.91	25.45	23.32	43
44	69.34	60.43	53.01	46.81	41.59	37.17	33.42	30.21	27.45	25.08	23.01	44
45	66.82	58.43	51.41	45.52	40.55	36.33	32.73	29.65	26.99	24.70	22.69	45
46	64.36	56.46	49.83	44.25	39.52	35.49	32.05	29.08	26.53	24.31	22.37	46
47	61.96	54.53	48.28	42.99	38.49	34.65	31.35	28.51	26.05	23.91	22.04	47
48	59.63	52.64	46.74	41.74	37.47	33.81	30.66	27.94	25.57	23.51	21.70	48
49	57.35	50.79	45.24	40.50	36.45	32.97	29.97	27.36	25.09	23.10	21.36	49
50	55.14	48.99	43.76	39.29	35.45	32.14	29.27	26.78	24.60	22.69	21.01	50
51	52.99	47.23	42.31	38.09	34.45	31.31	28.58	26.19	24.11	22.27	20.65	51
52	50.90	45.51	40.89	36.91	33.47	30.48	27.88	25.61	23.61	21.85	20.29	52
53	48.87	43.83	39.49	35.74	32.49	29.67	27.19	25.02	23.11	21.42	19.92	53
54	46.90	42.19	38.12	34.60	31.53	28.85	26.50	24.43	22.61	20.99	19.55	54
55	44.99	40.60	36.79	33.47	30.58	28.04	25.81	23.85	22.11	20.56	19.18	55
56	43.15	39.04	35.48	32.37	29.64	27.25	25.13	23.26	21.60	20.12	18.80	56
57	41.35	37.53	34.19	31.28	28.71	26.45	24.45	22.67	21.09	19.68	18.42	57
58	39.59	36.04	32.93	30.19	27.78	25.65	23.76	22.08	20.58	19.23	18.02	58
59	37.87	34.57	31.67	29.11	26.85	24.85	23.07	21.47	20.05	18.77	17.62	59
60	36.17	33.12	30.42	28.04	25.92	24.04	22.36	20.86	19.51	18.30	17.20	60
61	34.52	31.69	29.19	26.97	25.00	23.23	21.65	20.24	18.96	17.81	16.77	61
62	32.91	30.30	27.98	25.92	24.08	22.43	20.95	19.62	18.41	17.33	16.34	62
63	31.36	28.95	26.80	24.89	23.17	21.63	20.25	19.00	17.86	16.84	15.90	63
64	29.85	27.63	25.65	23.88	22.28	20.85	19.55	18.38	17.31	16.35	15.47	64
65	28.40	26.37	24.54	22.90	21.42	20.08	18.87	17.77	16.77	15.86	15.03	65
66	27.02	25.14	23.46	21.94	20.57	19.33	18.20	17.17	16.24	15.38	14.60	66
67	25.68	23.96	22.41	21.01	19.74	18.59	17.54	16.58	15.70	14.90	14.16	67
68	24.38	22.81	21.39	20.10	18.93	17.86	16.88	15.99	15.17	14.42	13.73	68
69	23.13	21.69	20.39	19.21	18.12	17.14	16.23	15.40	14.64	13.93	13.29	69

continued

34

Table 1   **Multipliers for pecuniary loss for life (males)** *continued*

Age at date of trial	Multiplier calculated with allowance for projected mortality from the 2008-based population projections and rate of return of											Age at date of trial
	−2.0%	−1.5%	−1.0%	−0.5%	0.0%	0.5%	1.0%	1.5%	2.0%	2.5%	3.0%	
70	21.91	20.60	19.41	18.32	17.32	16.41	15.58	14.81	14.10	13.44	12.84	70
71	20.70	19.52	18.43	17.44	16.53	15.69	14.92	14.21	13.55	12.94	12.38	71
72	19.52	18.44	17.46	16.56	15.72	14.96	14.25	13.60	12.99	12.43	11.91	72
73	18.34	17.38	16.49	15.67	14.92	14.22	13.57	12.97	12.42	11.90	11.42	73
74	17.18	16.32	15.52	14.79	14.10	13.47	12.89	12.34	11.83	11.36	10.92	74
75	16.04	15.27	14.56	13.90	13.29	12.72	12.19	11.70	11.24	10.81	10.40	75
76	14.93	14.25	13.62	13.03	12.48	11.97	11.50	11.05	10.64	10.25	9.88	76
77	13.86	13.26	12.70	12.18	11.70	11.24	10.82	10.42	10.05	9.69	9.36	77
78	12.83	12.31	11.82	11.36	10.93	10.53	10.15	9.79	9.46	9.15	8.85	78
79	11.86	11.40	10.97	10.57	10.19	9.84	9.50	9.19	8.89	8.61	8.34	79
80	10.94	10.55	10.17	9.82	9.49	9.18	8.88	8.60	8.34	8.09	7.85	80
81	10.10	9.75	9.43	9.12	8.83	8.56	8.30	8.05	7.82	7.60	7.38	81
82	9.33	9.03	8.74	8.47	8.22	7.98	7.75	7.53	7.33	7.13	6.94	82
83	8.62	8.36	8.11	7.88	7.65	7.44	7.24	7.05	6.87	6.69	6.53	83
84	7.97	7.74	7.53	7.32	7.13	6.94	6.76	6.59	6.43	6.28	6.13	84
85	7.36	7.16	6.98	6.80	6.63	6.47	6.31	6.16	6.02	5.88	5.75	85
86	6.79	6.62	6.46	6.31	6.16	6.02	5.88	5.75	5.62	5.50	5.39	86
87	6.25	6.11	5.97	5.83	5.71	5.58	5.46	5.35	5.24	5.14	5.04	87
88	5.74	5.62	5.50	5.38	5.27	5.16	5.06	4.96	4.87	4.78	4.69	88
89	5.26	5.15	5.05	4.95	4.86	4.76	4.68	4.59	4.51	4.43	4.35	89
90	4.81	4.72	4.64	4.55	4.47	4.39	4.31	4.24	4.17	4.10	4.03	90
91	4.40	4.32	4.25	4.17	4.10	4.04	3.97	3.91	3.85	3.79	3.73	91
92	4.01	3.94	3.88	3.82	3.76	3.70	3.65	3.59	3.54	3.49	3.44	92
93	3.65	3.59	3.54	3.49	3.44	3.39	3.34	3.30	3.25	3.21	3.17	93
94	3.33	3.29	3.24	3.20	3.16	3.11	3.07	3.03	2.99	2.96	2.92	94
95	3.06	3.02	2.98	2.94	2.91	2.87	2.84	2.80	2.77	2.74	2.71	95
96	2.83	2.79	2.76	2.72	2.69	2.66	2.63	2.60	2.57	2.54	2.52	96
97	2.62	2.59	2.56	2.53	2.50	2.48	2.45	2.42	2.40	2.37	2.35	97
98	2.44	2.41	2.38	2.36	2.34	2.31	2.29	2.27	2.24	2.22	2.20	98
99	2.27	2.25	2.22	2.20	2.18	2.16	2.14	2.12	2.10	2.08	2.06	99
100	2.11	2.09	2.07	2.06	2.04	2.02	2.00	1.98	1.97	1.95	1.93	100

Table 2 **Multipliers for pecuniary loss for life (females)**

Age at date of trial	Multiplier calculated with allowance for projected mortality from the 2008-based population projections and rate of return of											Age at date of trial
	−2.0%	−1.5%	−1.0%	−0.5%	0.0%	0.5%	1.0%	1.5%	2.0%	2.5%	3.0%	
0	285.20	208.39	155.57	118.70	92.57	73.74	59.95	49.69	41.92	35.94	31.26	0
1	279.01	204.72	153.41	117.45	91.86	73.36	59.76	49.62	41.91	35.97	31.32	1
2	271.81	200.28	150.65	115.73	90.77	72.67	59.33	49.34	41.73	35.86	31.24	2
3	264.75	195.89	147.91	114.00	89.68	71.97	58.88	49.05	41.55	35.73	31.16	3
4	257.83	191.56	145.19	112.28	88.58	71.27	58.43	48.75	41.35	35.60	31.08	4
5	251.06	187.30	142.49	110.56	87.49	70.56	57.97	48.45	41.15	35.47	30.99	5
6	244.43	183.11	139.83	108.85	86.38	69.85	57.50	48.14	40.95	35.34	30.89	6
7	237.94	178.98	137.18	107.15	85.28	69.13	57.03	47.83	40.74	35.19	30.80	7
8	231.59	174.92	134.57	105.46	84.18	68.40	56.55	47.51	40.52	35.05	30.70	8
9	225.38	170.93	131.98	103.77	83.07	67.67	56.06	47.18	40.30	34.90	30.60	9
10	219.31	167.00	129.43	102.10	81.97	66.94	55.57	46.85	40.08	34.75	30.49	10
11	213.37	163.14	126.90	100.43	80.86	66.20	55.07	46.52	39.85	34.59	30.38	11
12	207.57	159.34	124.40	98.78	79.76	65.46	54.57	46.18	39.62	34.42	30.27	12
13	201.89	155.60	121.92	97.13	78.65	64.71	54.07	45.83	39.38	34.26	30.15	13
14	196.33	151.93	119.48	95.49	77.55	63.96	53.55	45.47	39.13	34.09	30.03	14
15	190.91	148.32	117.06	93.86	76.44	63.21	53.03	45.12	38.88	33.91	29.90	15
16	185.61	144.77	114.67	92.25	75.34	62.45	52.51	44.75	38.62	33.73	29.77	16
17	180.42	141.28	112.31	90.64	74.24	61.70	51.99	44.38	38.37	33.55	29.64	17
18	175.36	137.86	109.98	89.05	73.14	60.94	51.46	44.01	38.10	33.36	29.51	18
19	170.42	134.50	107.68	87.46	72.05	60.17	50.92	43.63	37.83	33.16	29.37	19
20	165.60	131.20	105.42	85.89	70.96	59.41	50.38	43.25	37.56	32.97	29.22	20
21	160.88	127.95	103.17	84.33	69.86	58.64	49.84	42.86	37.28	32.76	29.08	21
22	156.26	124.76	100.95	82.78	68.77	57.86	49.28	42.47	36.99	32.56	28.92	22
23	151.72	121.60	98.74	81.22	67.67	57.08	48.72	42.06	36.70	32.34	28.76	23
24	147.29	118.50	96.56	79.68	66.57	56.29	48.16	41.65	36.40	32.12	28.60	24
25	142.97	115.46	94.41	78.15	65.48	55.50	47.58	41.23	36.09	31.89	28.43	25
26	138.74	112.47	92.28	76.63	64.38	54.71	47.01	40.81	35.78	31.66	28.26	26
27	134.61	109.53	90.18	75.12	63.29	53.92	46.43	40.38	35.46	31.42	28.08	27
28	130.57	106.65	88.11	73.62	62.20	53.12	45.84	39.95	35.14	31.18	27.90	28
29	126.63	103.81	86.05	72.13	61.11	52.32	45.25	39.51	34.81	30.93	27.71	29
30	122.78	101.02	84.03	70.65	60.02	51.52	44.65	39.06	34.47	30.68	27.51	30
31	119.02	98.29	82.03	69.18	58.94	50.71	44.05	38.61	34.13	30.41	27.31	31
32	115.34	95.60	80.06	67.72	57.86	49.90	43.44	38.15	33.78	30.15	27.11	32
33	111.75	92.97	78.11	66.27	56.77	49.09	42.83	37.68	33.42	29.87	26.89	33
34	108.24	90.37	76.18	64.83	55.69	48.27	42.21	37.21	33.06	29.59	26.67	34
35	104.80	87.81	74.27	63.40	54.61	47.45	41.58	36.73	32.69	29.31	26.45	35
36	101.45	85.31	72.39	61.98	53.53	46.63	40.95	36.24	32.31	29.01	26.22	36
37	98.17	82.84	70.53	60.57	52.46	45.81	40.31	35.75	31.93	28.71	25.98	37
38	94.97	80.42	68.69	59.17	51.38	44.98	39.67	35.25	31.54	28.40	25.74	38
39	91.83	78.04	66.88	57.78	50.31	44.15	39.03	34.74	31.14	28.09	25.48	39
40	88.77	75.71	65.08	56.39	49.24	43.31	38.37	34.23	30.73	27.76	25.23	40
41	85.78	73.41	63.31	55.02	48.17	42.48	37.71	33.71	30.32	27.43	24.96	41
42	82.86	71.16	61.56	53.66	47.10	41.64	37.05	33.18	29.90	27.09	24.69	42
43	80.01	68.94	59.84	52.31	46.04	40.80	36.38	32.65	29.47	26.75	24.41	43
44	77.23	66.77	58.14	50.97	44.98	39.95	35.71	32.11	29.03	26.39	24.12	44
45	74.52	64.65	56.46	49.64	43.93	39.11	35.03	31.56	28.59	26.03	23.82	45
46	71.87	62.56	54.81	48.32	42.87	38.27	34.35	31.01	28.14	25.67	23.52	46
47	69.28	60.51	53.17	47.02	41.83	37.42	33.67	30.45	27.69	25.29	23.21	47
48	66.77	58.50	51.57	45.73	40.79	36.58	32.98	29.89	27.23	24.91	22.90	48
49	64.32	56.54	50.00	44.46	39.76	35.74	32.30	29.33	26.76	24.53	22.58	49
50	61.93	54.62	48.44	43.20	38.73	34.90	31.61	28.76	26.29	24.14	22.25	50
51	59.60	52.73	46.91	41.95	37.71	34.06	30.91	28.19	25.81	23.74	21.92	51
52	57.33	50.88	45.40	40.71	36.69	33.22	30.22	27.61	25.33	23.33	21.57	52
53	55.11	49.07	43.92	39.49	35.68	32.38	29.52	27.02	24.84	22.92	21.22	53
54	52.96	47.30	42.46	38.28	34.68	31.55	28.82	26.44	24.34	22.50	20.87	54
55	50.86	45.57	41.02	37.09	33.68	30.71	28.12	25.84	23.84	22.07	20.51	55
56	48.83	43.88	39.61	35.91	32.69	29.88	27.42	25.25	23.34	21.64	20.14	56
57	46.84	42.22	38.23	34.75	31.71	29.05	26.72	24.65	22.83	21.21	19.76	57
58	44.89	40.60	36.86	33.59	30.74	28.22	26.01	24.05	22.31	20.76	19.37	58
59	42.99	38.99	35.50	32.44	29.76	27.39	25.29	23.43	21.78	20.30	18.98	59
60	41.12	37.41	34.16	31.30	28.78	26.55	24.57	22.81	21.24	19.83	18.57	60
61	39.30	35.86	32.83	30.16	27.80	25.70	23.84	22.18	20.69	19.35	18.15	61
62	37.52	34.33	31.52	29.03	26.83	24.86	23.11	21.54	20.13	18.86	17.72	62
63	35.79	32.84	30.24	27.92	25.86	24.02	22.38	20.90	19.57	18.37	17.28	63
64	34.11	31.39	28.98	26.83	24.91	23.19	21.65	20.26	19.01	17.87	16.84	64
65	32.50	29.99	27.76	25.77	23.98	22.38	20.93	19.63	18.45	17.38	16.40	65
66	30.94	28.64	26.58	24.73	23.07	21.58	20.23	19.00	17.89	16.88	15.96	66
67	29.44	27.32	25.43	23.72	22.18	20.78	19.52	18.38	17.34	16.39	15.52	67
68	27.99	26.05	24.30	22.72	21.29	20.00	18.83	17.76	16.78	15.89	15.07	68
69	26.57	24.80	23.19	21.74	20.42	19.22	18.13	17.13	16.22	15.39	14.62	69

continued

Table 2   Multipliers for pecuniary loss for life (females) *continued*

Age at date of trial	Multiplier calculated with allowance for projected mortality from the 2008-based population projections and rate of return of											Age at date of trial
	−2.0%	−1.5%	−1.0%	−0.5%	0.0%	0.5%	1.0%	1.5%	2.0%	2.5%	3.0%	
70	25.19	23.57	22.10	20.76	19.55	18.44	17.43	16.50	15.65	14.87	14.15	70
71	23.83	22.35	21.01	19.79	18.67	17.65	16.72	15.86	15.07	14.35	13.68	71
72	22.47	21.14	19.92	18.81	17.79	16.85	16.00	15.20	14.48	13.80	13.18	72
73	21.13	19.93	18.83	17.82	16.89	16.04	15.25	14.53	13.86	13.24	12.66	73
74	19.80	18.72	17.73	16.82	15.99	15.21	14.50	13.84	13.23	12.66	12.13	74
75	18.48	17.53	16.64	15.83	15.08	14.38	13.74	13.14	12.58	12.06	11.58	75
76	17.20	16.35	15.57	14.84	14.17	13.55	12.97	12.43	11.92	11.45	11.01	76
77	15.95	15.21	14.51	13.87	13.28	12.72	12.20	11.72	11.27	10.84	10.45	77
78	14.75	14.10	13.50	12.93	12.40	11.91	11.45	11.02	10.62	10.24	9.88	78
79	13.62	13.05	12.52	12.03	11.56	11.13	10.72	10.34	9.98	9.64	9.32	79
80	12.56	12.07	11.61	11.17	10.77	10.38	10.02	9.69	9.37	9.07	8.78	80
81	11.58	11.15	10.75	10.37	10.02	9.68	9.36	9.06	8.78	8.51	8.26	81
82	10.67	10.30	9.95	9.62	9.31	9.02	8.74	8.48	8.23	7.99	7.76	82
83	9.83	9.51	9.21	8.92	8.65	8.39	8.15	7.92	7.70	7.49	7.29	83
84	9.06	8.78	8.52	8.27	8.03	7.81	7.59	7.39	7.19	7.01	6.83	84
85	8.34	8.10	7.87	7.65	7.45	7.25	7.06	6.88	6.71	6.55	6.40	85
86	7.66	7.45	7.25	7.07	6.89	6.72	6.56	6.40	6.25	6.11	5.97	86
87	7.01	6.84	6.67	6.51	6.36	6.21	6.07	5.93	5.80	5.68	5.56	87
88	6.41	6.26	6.11	5.98	5.85	5.72	5.60	5.48	5.37	5.26	5.16	88
89	5.84	5.71	5.59	5.47	5.36	5.25	5.15	5.05	4.95	4.86	4.77	89
90	5.31	5.20	5.10	5.00	4.90	4.81	4.72	4.64	4.55	4.47	4.40	90
91	4.82	4.73	4.64	4.55	4.47	4.40	4.32	4.25	4.18	4.11	4.04	91
92	4.37	4.29	4.22	4.15	4.08	4.01	3.95	3.89	3.83	3.77	3.71	92
93	3.97	3.90	3.84	3.78	3.72	3.67	3.61	3.56	3.51	3.46	3.41	93
94	3.62	3.56	3.51	3.46	3.41	3.36	3.31	3.27	3.22	3.18	3.14	94
95	3.32	3.27	3.23	3.18	3.14	3.10	3.06	3.02	2.98	2.94	2.91	95
96	3.06	3.02	2.98	2.94	2.91	2.87	2.84	2.80	2.77	2.74	2.71	96
97	2.84	2.80	2.77	2.74	2.70	2.67	2.64	2.61	2.58	2.56	2.53	97
98	2.64	2.61	2.58	2.55	2.52	2.49	2.47	2.44	2.42	2.39	2.37	98
99	2.45	2.42	2.40	2.37	2.35	2.32	2.30	2.28	2.26	2.23	2.21	99
100	2.27	2.25	2.22	2.20	2.18	2.16	2.14	2.12	2.10	2.08	2.06	100

Table 7   Multipliers for loss of earnings to pension age 60 (males)

Age at date of trial	Multiplier calculated with allowance for projected mortality from the 2008-based population projections and rate of return of											Age at date of trial
	−2.0%	−1.5%	−1.0%	−0.5%	0.0%	0.5%	1.0%	1.5%	2.0%	2.5%	3.0%	
16	69.28	61.13	54.18	48.26	43.18	38.81	35.03	31.77	28.93	26.46	24.29	16
17	66.90	59.22	52.65	47.02	42.18	38.00	34.38	31.24	28.50	26.11	24.01	17
18	64.58	57.34	51.13	45.79	41.18	37.19	33.73	30.71	28.07	25.75	23.72	18
19	62.30	55.49	49.63	44.57	40.19	36.38	33.06	30.17	27.62	25.39	23.42	19
20	60.08	53.68	48.15	43.36	39.20	35.57	32.40	29.62	27.17	25.02	23.11	20
21	57.90	51.89	46.68	42.15	38.21	34.75	31.72	29.06	26.71	24.64	22.80	21
22	55.76	50.13	45.23	40.95	37.21	33.93	31.04	28.50	26.25	24.25	22.47	22
23	53.66	48.40	43.79	39.76	36.22	33.11	30.36	27.93	25.77	23.85	22.14	23
24	51.61	46.69	42.37	38.57	35.23	32.28	29.66	27.35	25.28	23.44	21.80	24
25	49.60	45.01	40.96	37.40	34.24	31.45	28.97	26.76	24.79	23.02	21.44	25
26	47.64	43.35	39.57	36.22	33.25	30.61	28.26	26.16	24.28	22.59	21.08	26
27	45.71	41.72	38.19	35.06	32.27	29.77	27.55	25.56	23.77	22.16	20.71	27
28	43.82	40.12	36.83	33.90	31.28	28.93	26.83	24.94	23.24	21.71	20.32	28
29	41.97	38.54	35.48	32.74	30.29	28.09	26.10	24.32	22.70	21.25	19.92	29
30	40.15	36.99	34.14	31.59	29.30	27.24	25.37	23.69	22.16	20.78	19.52	30
31	38.38	35.46	32.83	30.46	28.32	26.39	24.64	23.05	21.61	20.29	19.10	31
32	36.65	33.96	31.53	29.33	27.34	25.53	23.89	22.40	21.04	19.80	18.67	32
33	34.96	32.48	30.24	28.21	26.36	24.68	23.15	21.75	20.47	19.30	18.23	33
34	33.30	31.03	28.97	27.09	25.38	23.82	22.39	21.09	19.89	18.79	17.78	34
35	31.67	29.60	27.71	25.98	24.40	22.96	21.63	20.42	19.30	18.27	17.32	35
36	30.07	28.19	26.46	24.88	23.43	22.09	20.87	19.74	18.69	17.73	16.84	36
37	28.51	26.80	25.23	23.78	22.45	21.22	20.09	19.04	18.08	17.18	16.35	37
38	26.98	25.43	24.01	22.69	21.48	20.35	19.31	18.34	17.45	16.61	15.84	38
39	25.48	24.08	22.80	21.60	20.50	19.47	18.52	17.63	16.81	16.04	15.32	39
40	24.00	22.76	21.60	20.52	19.52	18.59	17.72	16.91	16.15	15.44	14.78	40
41	22.56	21.45	20.41	19.45	18.54	17.70	16.91	16.17	15.48	14.84	14.23	41
42	21.15	20.16	19.24	18.38	17.57	16.81	16.10	15.43	14.80	14.21	13.66	42
43	19.76	18.90	18.08	17.31	16.59	15.92	15.28	14.68	14.11	13.58	13.07	43
44	18.41	17.65	16.93	16.26	15.62	15.02	14.45	13.91	13.41	12.93	12.47	44
45	17.08	16.42	15.79	15.20	14.64	14.12	13.61	13.14	12.69	12.26	11.85	45
46	15.78	15.21	14.67	14.16	13.67	13.21	12.77	12.35	11.95	11.58	11.22	46
47	14.50	14.02	13.56	13.12	12.70	12.30	11.92	11.55	11.21	10.88	10.56	47
48	13.26	12.85	12.46	12.08	11.73	11.38	11.06	10.75	10.45	10.16	9.89	48
49	12.03	11.69	11.37	11.05	10.75	10.47	10.19	9.93	9.67	9.43	9.19	49
50	10.83	10.56	10.29	10.03	9.78	9.55	9.32	9.10	8.88	8.68	8.48	50
51	9.66	9.44	9.22	9.01	8.81	8.62	8.43	8.25	8.08	7.91	7.75	51
52	8.51	8.34	8.17	8.00	7.84	7.69	7.54	7.40	7.26	7.12	6.99	52
53	7.38	7.25	7.12	7.00	6.87	6.76	6.64	6.53	6.42	6.32	6.21	53
54	6.27	6.18	6.08	5.99	5.90	5.82	5.73	5.65	5.57	5.49	5.41	54
55	5.18	5.12	5.05	4.99	4.93	4.87	4.81	4.75	4.69	4.64	4.58	55
56	4.12	4.07	4.03	3.99	3.95	3.91	3.87	3.84	3.80	3.76	3.73	56
57	3.06	3.04	3.02	2.99	2.97	2.95	2.93	2.91	2.89	2.86	2.84	57
58	2.03	2.02	2.01	2.00	1.99	1.98	1.97	1.96	1.95	1.94	1.93	58
59	1.01	1.00	1.00	1.00	1.00	0.99	0.99	0.99	0.99	0.98	0.98	59

Table 8   Multipliers for loss of earnings to pension age 60 (females)

Age at date of trial	Multiplier calculated with allowance for projected mortality from the 2008-based population projections and rate of return of											Age at date of trial
	−2.0%	−1.5%	−1.0%	−0.5%	0.0%	0.5%	1.0%	1.5%	2.0%	2.5%	3.0%	
16	70.04	61.77	54.73	48.72	43.57	39.14	35.32	32.02	29.14	26.64	24.45	16
17	67.65	59.85	53.18	47.48	42.57	38.33	34.67	31.49	28.72	26.29	24.17	17
18	65.30	57.96	51.66	46.24	41.57	37.52	34.01	30.96	28.28	25.94	23.88	18
19	63.01	56.10	50.15	45.02	40.57	36.71	33.35	30.41	27.84	25.58	23.59	19
20	60.76	54.27	48.66	43.80	39.57	35.90	32.68	29.87	27.39	25.21	23.28	20
21	58.56	52.46	47.18	42.58	38.58	35.08	32.01	29.31	26.93	24.83	22.97	21
22	56.40	50.69	45.71	41.37	37.58	34.25	31.32	28.74	26.46	24.44	22.64	22
23	54.29	48.94	44.26	40.17	36.58	33.42	30.64	28.17	25.98	24.04	22.31	23
24	52.21	47.21	42.83	38.98	35.58	32.59	29.94	27.59	25.50	23.63	21.97	24
25	50.18	45.51	41.41	37.79	34.59	31.75	29.24	27.00	25.00	23.21	21.61	25
26	48.19	43.84	40.00	36.60	33.59	30.91	28.53	26.40	24.49	22.78	21.25	26
27	46.24	42.20	38.61	35.43	32.59	30.07	27.81	25.79	23.98	22.34	20.87	27
28	44.33	40.58	37.24	34.26	31.60	29.22	27.09	25.17	23.45	21.89	20.49	28
29	42.46	38.98	35.87	33.09	30.60	28.37	26.36	24.55	22.91	21.43	20.09	29
30	40.63	37.41	34.53	31.94	29.61	27.51	25.62	23.91	22.37	20.96	19.69	30
31	38.83	35.86	33.19	30.79	28.62	26.65	24.88	23.27	21.81	20.48	19.27	31
32	37.08	34.34	31.87	29.64	27.62	25.79	24.13	22.62	21.24	19.98	18.83	32
33	35.35	32.84	30.57	28.50	26.63	24.93	23.37	21.96	20.66	19.48	18.39	33
34	33.67	31.37	29.28	27.37	25.64	24.06	22.61	21.29	20.07	18.96	17.93	34
35	32.01	29.91	28.00	26.25	24.65	23.18	21.84	20.60	19.47	18.43	17.46	35
36	30.40	28.48	26.73	25.13	23.66	22.30	21.06	19.91	18.86	17.88	16.98	36
37	28.81	27.08	25.48	24.02	22.67	21.42	20.28	19.21	18.23	17.32	16.48	37
38	27.26	25.69	24.24	22.91	21.68	20.54	19.48	18.50	17.60	16.75	15.97	38
39	25.73	24.32	23.02	21.81	20.69	19.65	18.68	17.78	16.95	16.17	15.44	39
40	24.24	22.98	21.81	20.72	19.70	18.76	17.88	17.05	16.29	15.57	14.90	40
41	22.78	21.66	20.61	19.63	18.71	17.86	17.06	16.31	15.61	14.96	14.34	41
42	21.35	20.35	19.42	18.55	17.73	16.96	16.24	15.56	14.93	14.33	13.77	42
43	19.95	19.07	18.24	17.47	16.74	16.05	15.41	14.80	14.23	13.69	13.18	43
44	18.58	17.81	17.08	16.40	15.75	15.15	14.57	14.03	13.52	13.03	12.57	44
45	17.24	16.57	15.93	15.33	14.77	14.23	13.73	13.25	12.79	12.36	11.95	45
46	15.92	15.34	14.80	14.28	13.79	13.32	12.87	12.45	12.05	11.67	11.30	46
47	14.63	14.14	13.67	13.23	12.80	12.40	12.01	11.65	11.30	10.96	10.64	47
48	13.37	12.95	12.56	12.18	11.82	11.48	11.15	10.83	10.53	10.24	9.96	48
49	12.13	11.79	11.46	11.14	10.84	10.55	10.27	10.00	9.75	9.50	9.26	49
50	10.92	10.64	10.37	10.11	9.86	9.62	9.39	9.17	8.95	8.74	8.54	50
51	9.73	9.51	9.29	9.08	8.88	8.69	8.50	8.31	8.14	7.97	7.80	51
52	8.57	8.39	8.22	8.06	7.90	7.75	7.60	7.45	7.31	7.17	7.04	52
53	7.43	7.30	7.17	7.04	6.92	6.80	6.68	6.57	6.46	6.36	6.25	53
54	6.31	6.21	6.12	6.03	5.94	5.85	5.76	5.68	5.60	5.52	5.44	54
55	5.21	5.14	5.08	5.02	4.95	4.89	4.83	4.77	4.72	4.66	4.61	55
56	4.13	4.09	4.05	4.01	3.97	3.93	3.89	3.85	3.82	3.78	3.74	56
57	3.07	3.05	3.03	3.00	2.98	2.96	2.94	2.92	2.89	2.87	2.85	57
58	2.03	2.02	2.01	2.00	1.99	1.98	1.97	1.96	1.95	1.94	1.93	58
59	1.01	1.01	1.00	1.00	1.00	1.00	0.99	0.99	0.99	0.99	0.98	59

Table 9   **Multipliers for loss of earnings to pension age 65 (males)**

Age at date of trial	Multiplier calculated with allowance for projected mortality from the 2008-based population projections and rate of return of											Age at date of trial
	−2.0%	−1.5%	−1.0%	−0.5%	0.0%	0.5%	1.0%	1.5%	2.0%	2.5%	3.0%	
16	81.11	70.46	61.56	54.09	47.80	42.47	37.95	34.08	30.77	27.92	25.46	16
17	78.49	68.41	59.95	52.82	46.80	41.68	37.32	33.59	30.38	27.61	25.21	17
18	75.93	66.39	58.35	51.56	45.80	40.89	36.69	33.09	29.98	27.29	24.96	18
19	73.42	64.40	56.78	50.31	44.80	40.10	36.06	32.58	29.58	26.97	24.70	19
20	70.97	62.45	55.22	49.07	43.81	39.30	35.42	32.07	29.16	26.64	24.43	20
21	68.57	60.53	53.68	47.83	42.82	38.50	34.78	31.55	28.74	26.30	24.15	21
22	66.21	58.63	52.16	46.60	41.82	37.70	34.13	31.02	28.31	25.95	23.87	22
23	63.90	56.77	50.65	45.38	40.83	36.89	33.47	30.49	27.88	25.59	23.57	23
24	61.64	54.93	49.15	44.16	39.84	36.08	32.81	29.94	27.43	25.22	23.27	24
25	59.43	53.12	47.68	42.95	38.85	35.27	32.14	29.39	26.98	24.85	22.96	25
26	57.26	51.35	46.22	41.75	37.86	34.45	31.46	28.84	26.52	24.47	22.65	26
27	55.14	49.60	44.77	40.56	36.87	33.63	30.78	28.27	26.05	24.07	22.32	27
28	53.06	47.87	43.34	39.37	35.88	32.81	30.10	27.70	25.57	23.67	21.98	28
29	51.02	46.17	41.92	38.18	34.89	31.98	29.40	27.11	25.08	23.26	21.63	29
30	49.03	44.50	40.52	37.01	33.90	31.15	28.70	26.52	24.58	22.84	21.28	30
31	47.08	42.86	39.14	35.84	32.92	30.32	28.00	25.93	24.07	22.41	20.91	31
32	45.17	41.25	37.78	34.69	31.94	29.49	27.29	25.33	23.56	21.97	20.54	32
33	43.31	39.67	36.43	33.54	30.96	28.65	26.58	24.72	23.04	21.53	20.16	33
34	41.48	38.11	35.10	32.40	29.99	27.81	25.86	24.10	22.51	21.07	19.77	34
35	39.69	36.57	33.78	31.27	29.01	26.97	25.14	23.48	21.97	20.60	19.36	35
36	37.94	35.06	32.47	30.14	28.03	26.13	24.41	22.84	21.42	20.13	18.95	36
37	36.22	33.57	31.18	29.02	27.06	25.28	23.67	22.20	20.86	19.64	18.52	37
38	34.54	32.11	29.90	27.90	26.08	24.43	22.92	21.55	20.29	19.13	18.08	38
39	32.89	30.66	28.64	26.79	25.11	23.57	22.17	20.88	19.70	18.62	17.62	39
40	31.27	29.24	27.38	25.69	24.13	22.71	21.41	20.21	19.11	18.09	17.16	40
41	29.69	27.84	26.14	24.59	23.16	21.85	20.64	19.53	18.50	17.55	16.68	41
42	28.14	26.46	24.92	23.50	22.19	20.98	19.87	18.84	17.88	17.00	16.18	42
43	26.62	25.10	23.70	22.41	21.22	20.11	19.09	18.14	17.26	16.44	15.68	43
44	25.13	23.77	22.50	21.33	20.25	19.24	18.30	17.43	16.62	15.86	15.16	44
45	23.68	22.45	21.32	20.26	19.28	18.36	17.51	16.71	15.97	15.27	14.62	45
46	22.25	21.16	20.14	19.19	18.31	17.48	16.71	15.98	15.30	14.67	14.07	46
47	20.86	19.89	18.98	18.14	17.34	16.60	15.90	15.24	14.63	14.05	13.50	47
48	19.49	18.64	17.84	17.08	16.38	15.71	15.09	14.50	13.94	13.42	12.92	48
49	18.15	17.41	16.70	16.04	15.41	14.82	14.27	13.74	13.24	12.77	12.33	49
50	16.85	16.20	15.58	15.00	14.46	13.94	13.44	12.98	12.53	12.11	11.71	50
51	15.57	15.01	14.48	13.98	13.50	13.04	12.61	12.20	11.81	11.44	11.09	51
52	14.32	13.84	13.39	12.95	12.54	12.15	11.77	11.42	11.08	10.75	10.44	52
53	13.09	12.69	12.30	11.94	11.59	11.25	10.93	10.62	10.33	10.05	9.78	53
54	11.89	11.56	11.24	10.93	10.63	10.35	10.08	9.82	9.57	9.33	9.10	54
55	10.71	10.44	10.18	9.92	9.68	9.45	9.22	9.00	8.79	8.59	8.40	55
56	9.56	9.34	9.13	8.93	8.73	8.54	8.35	8.17	8.00	7.84	7.67	56
57	8.43	8.26	8.09	7.93	7.77	7.62	7.47	7.33	7.19	7.06	6.93	57
58	7.32	7.19	7.06	6.94	6.82	6.70	6.59	6.48	6.37	6.26	6.16	58
59	6.22	6.13	6.03	5.94	5.85	5.77	5.68	5.60	5.52	5.45	5.37	59
60	5.14	5.08	5.01	4.95	4.89	4.83	4.77	4.71	4.66	4.60	4.55	60
61	4.09	4.04	4.00	3.96	3.92	3.89	3.85	3.81	3.77	3.74	3.70	61
62	3.04	3.02	3.00	2.98	2.95	2.93	2.91	2.89	2.87	2.85	2.83	62
63	2.02	2.01	2.00	1.99	1.98	1.97	1.96	1.95	1.94	1.93	1.92	63
64	1.00	1.00	1.00	1.00	0.99	0.99	0.99	0.99	0.98	0.98	0.98	64

Table 10   Multipliers for loss of earnings to pension age 65 (females)

Age at date of trial	Multiplier calculated with allowance for projected mortality from the 2008-based population projections and rate of return of											Age at date of trial
	−2.0%	−1.5%	−1.0%	−0.5%	0.0%	0.5%	1.0%	1.5%	2.0%	2.5%	3.0%	
16	82.26	71.41	62.34	54.74	48.34	42.93	38.33	34.41	31.05	28.16	25.66	16
17	79.62	69.34	60.72	53.47	47.34	42.14	37.71	33.91	30.66	27.85	25.41	17
18	77.03	67.31	59.12	52.20	46.34	41.35	37.08	33.42	30.26	27.53	25.16	18
19	74.50	65.30	57.53	50.95	45.34	40.55	36.45	32.91	29.86	27.21	24.91	19
20	72.02	63.33	55.96	49.70	44.34	39.75	35.81	32.40	29.45	26.88	24.64	20
21	69.59	61.39	54.41	48.45	43.34	38.95	35.16	31.88	29.03	26.54	24.37	21
22	67.20	59.48	52.87	47.21	42.34	38.15	34.51	31.35	28.60	26.20	24.08	22
23	64.87	57.59	51.35	45.98	41.35	37.33	33.85	30.82	28.16	25.84	23.79	23
24	62.58	55.73	49.84	44.75	40.35	36.52	33.19	30.27	27.72	25.47	23.49	24
25	60.34	53.91	48.35	43.53	39.35	35.70	32.51	29.72	27.27	25.10	23.19	25
26	58.14	52.11	46.87	42.32	38.35	34.88	31.84	29.16	26.80	24.72	22.87	26
27	55.99	50.33	45.41	41.11	37.35	34.05	31.15	28.60	26.33	24.33	22.54	27
28	53.88	48.59	43.96	39.91	36.36	33.23	30.46	28.02	25.85	23.93	22.21	28
29	51.82	46.87	42.53	38.72	35.36	32.39	29.77	27.44	25.36	23.51	21.86	29
30	49.80	45.18	41.12	37.53	34.36	31.56	29.06	26.84	24.87	23.09	21.51	30
31	47.82	43.52	39.72	36.35	33.37	30.72	28.35	26.25	24.36	22.66	21.14	31
32	45.88	41.88	38.33	35.18	32.38	29.87	27.64	25.64	23.84	22.22	20.77	32
33	43.98	40.27	36.96	34.01	31.38	29.03	26.92	25.02	23.31	21.77	20.38	33
34	42.12	38.68	35.60	32.85	30.39	28.18	26.19	24.39	22.78	21.31	19.98	34
35	40.30	37.11	34.26	31.70	29.40	27.32	25.45	23.76	22.23	20.84	19.57	35
36	38.51	35.58	32.93	30.56	28.41	26.47	24.71	23.12	21.67	20.35	19.15	36
37	36.76	34.06	31.62	29.42	27.42	25.61	23.96	22.47	21.10	19.86	18.72	37
38	35.05	32.57	30.32	28.28	26.43	24.74	23.21	21.81	20.52	19.35	18.28	38
39	33.38	31.10	29.04	27.16	25.44	23.88	22.44	21.14	19.93	18.83	17.82	39
40	31.73	29.66	27.76	26.04	24.45	23.00	21.68	20.46	19.33	18.30	17.35	40
41	30.12	28.24	26.51	24.92	23.47	22.13	20.90	19.77	18.72	17.76	16.86	41
42	28.55	26.84	25.26	23.81	22.48	21.25	20.12	19.07	18.10	17.20	16.37	42
43	27.01	25.46	24.03	22.71	21.50	20.37	19.33	18.36	17.46	16.63	15.85	43
44	25.49	24.10	22.81	21.62	20.51	19.48	18.53	17.64	16.82	16.05	15.33	44
45	24.02	22.77	21.61	20.53	19.53	18.60	17.73	16.92	16.16	15.45	14.79	45
46	22.57	21.46	20.42	19.45	18.55	17.71	16.92	16.18	15.49	14.84	14.23	46
47	21.15	20.17	19.24	18.38	17.57	16.81	16.10	15.43	14.81	14.22	13.66	47
48	19.77	18.90	18.08	17.31	16.59	15.92	15.28	14.68	14.11	13.58	13.08	48
49	18.41	17.65	16.93	16.26	15.62	15.02	14.45	13.91	13.41	12.93	12.47	49
50	17.08	16.42	15.80	15.21	14.65	14.12	13.62	13.14	12.69	12.26	11.85	50
51	15.78	15.21	14.67	14.16	13.67	13.21	12.77	12.35	11.96	11.58	11.22	51
52	14.51	14.02	13.56	13.12	12.70	12.30	11.92	11.56	11.21	10.88	10.56	52
53	13.26	12.85	12.46	12.09	11.73	11.39	11.06	10.75	10.45	10.17	9.89	53
54	12.04	11.70	11.37	11.06	10.76	10.47	10.20	9.93	9.68	9.43	9.20	54
55	10.84	10.56	10.30	10.04	9.79	9.55	9.32	9.10	8.89	8.68	8.49	55
56	9.67	9.44	9.23	9.02	8.82	8.63	8.44	8.26	8.09	7.92	7.75	56
57	8.52	8.34	8.17	8.01	7.85	7.70	7.55	7.40	7.26	7.13	7.00	57
58	7.39	7.25	7.13	7.00	6.88	6.76	6.65	6.53	6.43	6.32	6.22	58
59	6.28	6.18	6.09	5.99	5.91	5.82	5.73	5.65	5.57	5.49	5.41	59
60	5.19	5.12	5.05	4.99	4.93	4.87	4.81	4.75	4.69	4.64	4.58	60
61	4.11	4.07	4.03	3.99	3.95	3.91	3.87	3.84	3.80	3.76	3.73	61
62	3.06	3.04	3.02	2.99	2.97	2.95	2.93	2.91	2.88	2.86	2.84	62
63	2.03	2.02	2.01	2.00	1.99	1.98	1.97	1.96	1.95	1.94	1.93	63
64	1.01	1.00	1.00	1.00	1.00	0.99	0.99	0.99	0.99	0.98	0.98	64

Index

Ecology and Landscape Development:
A History of the Mersey Basin

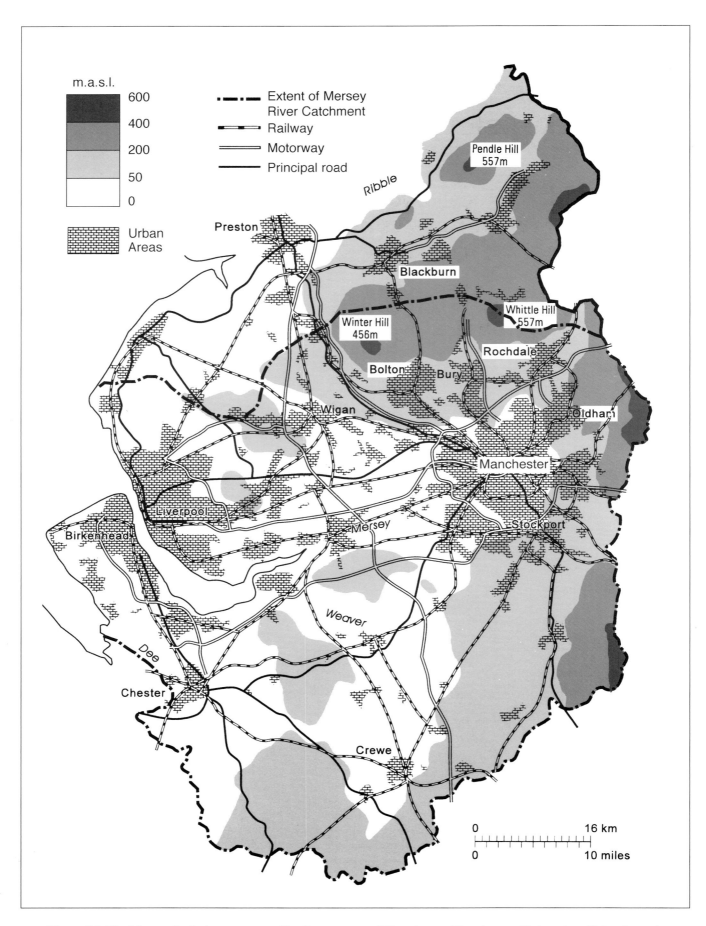

Figure 0.1. The Mersey Basin (map prepared by Department of Planning and Landscape, University of Manchester).

Ecology and Landscape Development:
A History of the Mersey Basin

PROCEEDINGS OF A CONFERENCE
HELD AT MERSEYSIDE MARITIME MUSEUM,
LIVERPOOL, 5–6 JULY 1996

Edited by E.F. Greenwood

LIVERPOOL UNIVERSITY PRESS

NATIONAL MUSEUMS & GALLERIES ON MERSEYSIDE

First published 1999 by Liverpool University Press
copyright © 1999 The Board of Trustees of
the National Museums & Galleries on Merseyside

The right of E.F. Greenwood
to be identified as the editor of this work
has been asserted by him in accordance with
the Copyright, Design and Patents Act, 1988

British Library Cataloguing-in-Publication Data
A British Library CIP record is available

ISBN 0-85323-653-4

Design and production: Janet Allan

Typeset in 10/12pt Palatino by
XL Publishing Services, Lurley, Tiverton
Printed by Redwood Books, Trowbridge

Contents

Forewords

As Chairman of the Mersey Basin Campaign I was honoured to be invited to give the opening address to the conference which gave rise to this publication.

The Mersey Basin Campaign is, like the rest of north-west England, a consequence of the history that the conference traced. We are dealing with the basin's geography, geology and hydrology as well as the effects of its economic past and its hopes for the future. The conference and the papers published here amply illustrate the scale and variety of those topics.

There have been so many influences on the nature and landscape and its flora and fauna. Few of the influences have been planned and, until relatively recently, almost none sought to shape the future environment positively. Those influences, both natural and man-made are explored in great detail through these conference papers. Fascinating as that is in its own right, perhaps the true value of the papers lies in the pointers they can give about how we move on.

Understanding the ingredients that have brought us to where we are today is an essential part of the process of taking us towards tomorrow. That future is in the hands of a wide range of individuals and organisations with many different roles. The biggest question is perhaps, not so much what they will do and what they will decide, but how will they work together? The Mersey Basin Campaign is one organisation which invites partners, whose objectives overlap, to co-operate – I believe that the conference in 1996, and the chapters published here, also encourage that process.

Brian Alexander
Chairman, Mersey Basin Campaign
December 1997

One of the main aims in 1986 of the newly created National Museums & Galleries on Merseyside was the promotion of its scholarly and scientific programmes. The Trustees quickly established a Scholarship Committee under the Chairmanship of Sir David Wilson. It seemed particularly important to the Trustees that they should procure a study of man's impact on the animals, plants and natural features of the Merseyside landscape.

Eric Greenwood, as Liverpool Museum's leading natural historian, was asked to co-ordinate the preparation of this study and to find a way of funding it. A tall order indeed! Nevertheless Eric achieved all this through meticulous preparation of the conference held in July 1996.

On behalf of NMGM's Trustees and staff I would like to acknowledge both the importance and practical value of this benchmark survey. The result is a tribute to Eric Greenwood's determination and tenacity as the organiser and editor of the many distinguished papers presented by the experts who attended and gave papers to this important gathering.

Richard Foster
Director, National Museums & Galleries on Merseyside
October 1998

Sea - Level Tendencies

Thousands of Years B.P.	14	13	12	11	10	9	8	7	6	5	4	3	2	1

Stage

PLEISTOCENE ← | → HOLOCENE

Devensian (Glacial) (115,000 to 10,000 B.P., peak 17,000 B.P.)

Flandrian (Interglacial) — Early | Mid | Late

Chronozone — Godwin Zones / P.A.Z. Pollen Assemblage Zones

Late Devensian 1: L De II, L De I | IV/Fa/a | V/Flb/b | VIa/Flc/c | VIb/Fld/d | VIc/Fld | VIIa/Fll/e | VIIb | VIII

Flandrian III

Loch Lomond Stadial | Preboreal | Boreal | Atlantic | Sub-Boreal | Sub-Atlantic (Brett-Sermander Units)

Major Vegetation

Herbs | Birch, Herbs | Birch Pine Hazel | Hazel Pine | Pine Hazel Elm | Oak Elm Alder | Oak, Alder (heather, grasses and herbs increasing)

Elm Decline 5250 B.P.

Climate (*Sharp Deterioration)

Cold | Warm | Cold | Warm and dry | Warm and wet | Cooler and drier | Warmer and drier | *Cool and wet

Soils

Raw, unstable soil profiles | Stabilised profiles | Unstable profiles | Maturing soil profiles base-rich | Stable, base-rich forest soils | Increasing acidity and podsolisation

Sea-Level Tendencies

Transgressive (+VE): 1 2 3 4 5 6 7 8 9 10 11 12
Regressive (-VE): 1 2 3 4 5 6 7 8 9 10 11 12

Actual Levels:
Sea-Level Very Low | -20m - -15m OD | High Sea-Level? | Period of Rapid Rise | 0 - +2m OD | +2 - +3.5m OD | High levels +3.5 - 5m OD | *Dune Slack Peat

Wetlands

None | Some moss peat deposition | Start of mossland formation in lake basins | Creation of coastal mosses inland raised bog growth | Extension of coastal mosses creation of meres | 'Recurrence surfaces' rapid bog growth | Truncation of bog profiles by erosion

Geology — Dated Events at SEFTON COAST (Minero/biogenic sediment'n.)

End of till deposition | Periglacial sands and gravels | Shirdley Hill Sand deposition | S.H. Sand redistribution and organic inclusions (continues through Flandrian) | DH I, DH II, DH III | Marine alluvium 'Downholland Silt' | Sand dune building | S1 | River valley alluvium | S? | V. | S2 | Sand dune building

Human Influence

Final Paleolithic & Mesolithic | *Poulton-le-Fylde Elk | Neolithic | evidence of settlement (Little Crosby) | Early Bronze | Late Bronze + Iron Age | Rom. Occ. | Medieval

Clearance / Drainage / Plantation (Cl / D / Pl)

Cl | *Cereal Cultivation Locally | Cl | D | Pl

Physical/climate side notes: Ice Cover | Very Cold | None | High Sea-Level? — Cold | Warm | Cold — Raw, unstable soil profiles | Stabilised profiles

Introduction

E.F. GREENWOOD

Shortly after the National Museums & Galleries on Merseyside (NMGM) was formed in April 1986, two of the trustees with special interests in natural science, Professors A.D. Bradshaw and R.J. Berry, asked me (as Keeper of the Liverpool Museum) what particular research topic I would like to see developed.

I explained that the NMGM with its broad subject base was in an excellent position to lead a study of the interactions between humans and other living organisms on Merseyside since the last 'ice age'. The Mersey Basin embraced an area where human intervention had a long history and in the last few hundred years had caused pollution as severe as anywhere in the world. It was a profoundly altered landscape. Yet, the area also contained regions of wildscape, ranging from open moorland on the Pennine hills through woods and moors to the estuaries and Liverpool Bay, and was home to various forms of rare wildlife on at least a European scale that have found a refuge and sanctuary. I believed an integrated study would provide many lessons for the future. Furthermore, I did not believe that such a study of an urban and industrial region had taken place anywhere in the world.

During the following years interest in the wildlife of the urban environment and the ecological processes involved has developed world-wide, particularly in Europe, North America and in the UK. Often the studies reveal a lack of knowledge of what plants and animals occur or of those that do occur, how they have survived human activity or indeed to what extent their existence depends upon humans. Indeed it is possible that more is known of the remote islands of the world than of the most densely populated city regions.

Within the Mersey Basin the ten years between 1986 and 1996 saw a number of studies that made a profound difference in our understanding of the changes that took place in the prehistoric period. However, our understanding of settlement changes that took place from the 'Dark Ages' until written documents became available remains less certain with almost no information about plants and animals. Even during the last 200 years information for all but the better known groups of plants and animals is remarkably thin.

Nevertheless, there have been many recent studies in the region and, whilst it was not possible to fund an integrated research programme, it did prove possible to bring together many of those who have worked in the region during the last few years. Their work was presented at a conference attended by some 170 participants, held at the Merseyside Maritime Museum on 5 and 6 July 1996. The written versions of their papers are published in this volume.

In response to the requests of participants references are included at the end of each chapter. Also, common names are used in preference to Latin ones. Nomenclature follows the following texts: flowering plants and ferns, *New Flora of the British Isles* by C. Stace, Cambridge University Press (1991); birds, *The Birdwatcher's Yearbook and Diary 1994* edited by J.E. Pemberton, Buckingham Press (1993); mammals, *The Handbook of British Mammals*, 3rd edn, edited by G.B. Corbet and S. Harris, Blackwell Scientific Publications for Mammal Society, Oxford (1991); fish, *A list of the Common and Scientific names of fishes of the British Isles*, Academic Press, London (1992); reptiles and amphibians, A *Field Guide to the Reptiles and Amphibians of Britain and Europe* by E.N. Arnold and J.A. Burton, Collins, London (1985).

To help understanding of the major events in the region over the last 15,000 years Figure 1.1 from *The Sand Dunes of the Sefton Coast* edited by D. Atkinson and J. Houston, NMGM, Liverpool (1993) is reproduced here (Figure 0.2). However, authors have used both calibrated radiocarbon dates and calendar years. Standardised dates can be obtained by reference to the papers by M. Stuiver and P.J. Reimer (1993) Extended ^{14}C database and revised CALIB 3.0 ^{14}C age calibration program. *Radiocarbon*, **35**, 215–30. A map of the Mersey Basin is also included (Figure 0.1).

In addition the following abbreviations are used: sp for species (singular), spp. for species (plural), ssp. for sub-species (singular) and sspp. for sub-species (plural).

Figure 0.2. (left) Major events in the sub-region over the last 15,000 years in context (courtesy of J.B.Innes). Dating is in ^{14}C years BP (Years Before Present: present taken conventionally to be AD 1950). The table shows some of the interrelationships between climate, vegetation, sea-level trends and human activity over the Holocene period. Further explanation of the table is given in chapters two, three and four of *The Sand Dunes of the Sefton Coast* (Atkinson & Houston, 1993).

Acknowledgements

Conferences and their proceedings do not just happen and I am particularly grateful to Professors A.D. Bradshaw and R.J. Berry for their help, guidance and continued support. I am also grateful to Julian Taylor, George Barker and David Atkinson who at various times with Professor Bradshaw formed an *ad hoc* steering group to organise the conference. I am also indebted to the British Ecological Society, the Mersey Basin Campaign, the University of Liverpool and NMGM for financial support and to a number of other organisations who provided support in kind. I am also very grateful to the chairs for the various sessions who provided valuable assistance by refereeing the chapters. Special thanks are due to all the contributors who made the conference so successful and who have provided a unique assemblage of information and analysis of one of the most urbanised yet fascinating parts of the world. Finally I am greatly indebted to my secretary, Barbara Rowan, for much typing and incorporating all the alterations to the scripts.

E.F. GREENWOOD

The Background Setting

F. OLDFIELD

Concern about the consequences of future climatic change and their impact on our environment and life support systems is now almost universal. Even if scepticism persists about the reality of 'greenhouse warming', the inevitability of climatic change cannot be denied – climate varies naturally on all timescales and every aspect of the world we see around us changes in response to these variations. Although they are global, the way the variations are expressed and their regional impact are highly differentiated. This makes it of exceptional importance to understand, at a regional level, the way our environment has changed in the past, and to use this knowledge realistically in any consideration of the potential effects of future climatic change. Nowhere is this more important than in a region like the Mersey Basin where the combination of a large population, a highly developed modern infrastructure and a low-lying, naturally dynamic coastal zone makes planning for a future where environmental conditions are likely to change quite dramatically a major and complex responsibility. The past does not provide simple analogues for a future world, but it is the only source of evidence we have for what has actually happened and for what may happen in response to climate changes on the timescales and of the magnitude of those predicted for the next century. We therefore value greatly the contributions to this first session of the conference and the chapters that follow, setting out the nature of past changes in the local environment and the ecological and human responses to these.

CHAPTER ONE

The influence of a changing climate

B. HUNTLEY

Introduction

In examining the ecological and landscape history of any region it is essential to consider the potential influences of climate change. Although ecologists frequently have viewed climate as an unchanging part of the environment to which organisms and ecosystems are adapted, and archaeologists frequently have taken a similarly static view of climate when examining the history of human influences upon landscapes, whenever records of environmental history are examined climate change is seen to be a ubiquitous feature. The minute-to-minute variations of the aerial environment experienced by a leaf simply are the highest frequency component of a spectrum of such changes that extends through the familiar diurnal and annual cycles and onward to much longer timescales. Ultimately, at timescales of 10^7 to 10^8 years we find records of global climate changes that relate to the rearrangement of the continents and to the major orogenic periods of geological history. In the present context, however, where our concern is with environmental history since the last glacial stage that ended about 12,000 years ago, it is those climate changes that have characteristic periodicities of 10^3 to 10^5 years that are most relevant. These are the climate changes that are associated with the alternating glacial and interglacial stages of the most recent Quaternary geological period (the last c.2.4 Ma).

These climate changes have been the subject of a considerable research effort and are now relatively well-documented, at least in the western North Atlantic region, for the last 130,000 years – the period spanning the last interglacial and glacial stages as well as the Holocene or post-glacial period. Not only have Quaternary scientists documented the changes, but they also have developed a number of hypotheses as to their underlying causes and mechanisms. These hypotheses have to some extent been evaluated by collaborative studies using atmospheric general circulation models (AGCMs) to simulate past climates (COHMAP 1988; Kutzbach & Gallimore 1988; Kutzbach & Guetter 1986; Wright et al. 1993). Two key hypotheses will be introduced below as the evolution of palaeoclimate since the last glacial maximum, some 21,000 years ago, is

described. Firstly, the Milankovitch hypothesis relates to the role of changes in the quantity and especially the seasonal distribution of solar radiation reaching the earth (Berger et al. 1984; Hays, Imbrie & Shackleton 1976), and secondly the 'ocean conveyor belt' hypothesis attempts to account for the magnitude of the resulting climate changes through a proposed oceanic circulation feedback mechanism (Broecker & Denton 1989; Imbrie et al. 1993; Imbrie et al. 1992).

In order to appreciate the approach that I have adopted it is important to see the Mersey Basin in its geographical context not only within Great Britain but also much more widely. The map presented in Figure 1.1 attempts to illustrate a number of the key features of this context; these include major features of the present-day circulation both of the North Atlantic ocean and of the atmosphere above it. The location of the Mersey Basin closer to the eastern margin of this map is an appropriate reflection of the latitudinal position in which it lies. The most characteristic feature of the atmospheric circulation in such middle latitudes is the westerly airflow, so that the climate of any location is influenced most strongly by areas to its west. Nonetheless, the map extends also to include Scandinavia because, as we shall see, 'down-stream' features also can exert an influence upon climate. It is impossible to consider the influence of climatic change upon this small region of western England without seeing it in such a context, not least because only in this way can we understand which of these climate changes would be ubiquitous throughout the British Isles or even much of north-western Europe. Indeed it will become apparent that the Mersey Basin is much too small a region to have any climate changes that affect this region alone. Viewed in this context it also immediately becomes apparent that most of the climate changes to which an area such as the Mersey Basin is subjected arise entirely from causes external to the region; indeed I shall argue that some of these changes arise from causes external to Earth itself. It further should become apparent that, arising as they do from external causes, the impact of these climatic changes is inescapable, whether by ecosystems or human communities.

Thus, although this chapter is written in the context of a discussion focused upon the ecology and landscape development of the Mersey Basin, its content in general would be equally applicable to most of Great Britain. Indeed it might be sub-titled '*Climate change in the western North Atlantic Region since the Last Glacial Maximum – a context for considerations of the environmental history of British landscapes*'. The chapter is organised into four principal sections that deal in chronological order with the period since the last glacial maximum; it ends with a short Coda that reiterates and summarises the key points to emerge.

Climate at the last glacial maximum

The last glacial maximum was *c.*21,000 years ago;* however, conditions broadly comparable to those at the time of maximum ice extent prevailed for perhaps 6,000 years or more and the phase of most rapid melting of the major ice sheets did not start until *c.*14,500 BP. Figure 1.2 presents the palaeogeographical context for the Mersey Basin at the time of the last glacial maximum and should be compared with Figure 1.1. The most important factors that impinge directly upon the region under consideration are the local ice sheet developed within the British Isles and the lowering of sea-level that results in the present Mersey Basin becoming, at least during the early stages of deglaciation, the head-waters of a tributary to a fluvial system occupying the northern part of the Irish Sea. However, it is also important to note the changed ocean and atmospheric circulation patterns, the position of the sea-ice margin in the north-eastern North Atlantic and the fact that the British Isles are not islands but the western margin of the European mainland. In addition, we must be aware that the atmospheric concentrations of naturally occurring 'greenhouse gases', CO_2 and CH_4, were markedly lower not only than today but also than pre-industrial concentrations that prevailed during most of the Holocene (Chappellaz *et al.* 1990; Lorius *et al.* 1988). The seasonal insolation values, in contrast, were more or less the same as today (COHMAP 1988).

Although to some extent the climate at this time is rendered irrelevant by the presence of an ice sheet covering the present Mersey Basin (Boulton *et al.* 1977; Devoy 1995), it is worthwhile to note a number of features that account for the climatic conditions leading to the growth of this ice sheet, and changes in which during the subsequent deglaciation will be important causes of the climate prevailing in the area during that period. Foremost amongst these, perhaps, are the two major last glacial ice sheets developed in north-eastern North America (Laurentide ice sheet) and in Fennoscandia. The thickness of these ice sheets (1,000–2,000m) was such that they were able to influence the atmospheric circulation in much the same way as would major mountain ranges. Although more recent

palaeoclimate model results have not simulated the split in the jet stream seen in the COHMAP results (Kutzbach *et al.* 1993), the Laurentide ice sheet nonetheless had a substantial impact upon atmospheric circulation over the North Atlantic and downstream into Europe. The Fennoscandian ice sheet similarly affected the upstream circulation over the western North Atlantic and over the British Isles, as well as having an impact upon atmospheric circulation across Europe as a whole. These changes are represented on the maps (Figures 1.1 and 1.2) by shifts in the path of the winter jet stream; this in turn, however, relates to climate conditions at the surface because the predominant path taken by storm systems ('depressions') as they cross the North Atlantic and enter Europe is determined by the position of this atmospheric feature.

A second key contrast between the two maps (Figures 1.1 and 1.2) relates to the oceanic circulation within the North Atlantic. The two key classes of feature shown on the maps are the, generally more familiar, surface currents and the mid- and deep-water currents. Whereas today the North Atlantic Drift (often inaccurately referred to as the 'Gulf Stream') passes north-eastwards to the west of the British Isles and finally is dissipated in the Norwegian Sea, the equivalent surface current at the last glacial maximum crossed the Atlantic in a more or less easterly direction, reaching Europe in the latitude of southern Iberia. Although some question arises as to the extent to which a component of this warm surface flow

Figure 1.1. (right) The geographical context of the Mersey Basin at the present day
A schematic illustration of major atmospheric and ocean circulation features that affect the environment of the Mersey Basin (indicated by a black dot) today. The mean position of the January storm track is shown, along with the warm (A Gulf Stream; B North Atlantic Drift) and cold (C East Greenland Current; D Labrador Current) surface currents in the North Atlantic and the generalised path of the North Atlantic Deep Water (NADW) flow. The present extents of ice sheets and of permanent sea ice also are shown. (Redrawn and schematised from various sources.)

Figure 1.2. (right) The palaeogeographic context of the Mersey Basin at the last glacial maximum
A schematic illustration of major atmospheric and ocean circulation features that affected the Mersey Basin (indicated by a black dot) at the last glacial maximum. The mean January storm track is shown splitting around the major ice sheets as in the palaeoclimate simulation made by Kutzbach *et al.* (1993). The surface currents are schematised from various sources whilst the generalised path of a deep water flow generated by the 'boreal heat pump' (Imbrie *et al.* 1992) also is indicated. The extents of the last glacial ice sheets and of permanent sea ice are redrawn schematically from a variety of sources. The approximate position of the coastline is shown by the thin black line, the present geographical features being retained in grey for reference.

---

* Throughout this chapter ages are given in calendar years; where the ages of events have been determined by ^{14}C dating the calibration procedure of Stuiver and Reimer (1993) has been used to estimate their calendar age.

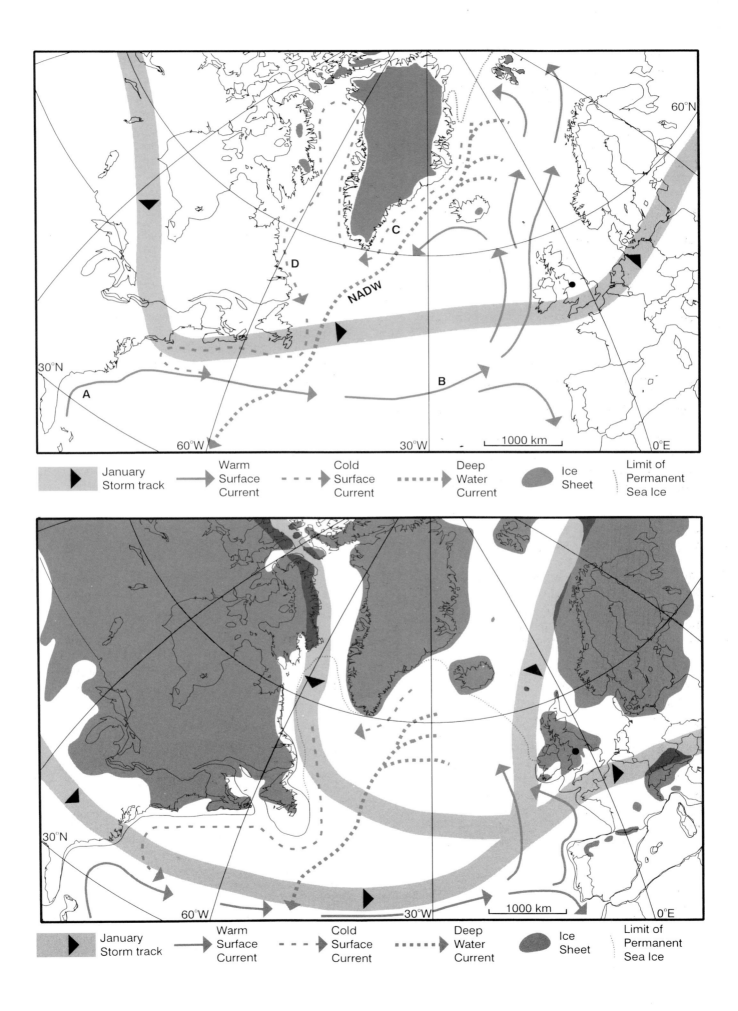

January Storm track   **Warm Surface Current**   **Cold Surface Current**   **Deep Water Current**   **Ice Sheet**   **Limit of Permanent Sea Ice**

may then have travelled northwards up the western seaboard of Europe, there is no doubt as to the principal consequence of this changed surface circulation, namely that the bulk of the North Atlantic surface was much cooler during the last glacial maximum than it is today. As a result, air masses crossing the ocean arrived in Europe cooler and also drier, because less moisture was evaporated from the cooler ocean surface. The extents both of permanent and of seasonal sea ice also were much greater. This was a secondary consequence of the cooler surface, combined with a reduction in the salinity of the surface waters as compared with today, because they had not been concentrated by evaporation to the same extent as are the warmer modern surface waters derived from the tropical Atlantic and Mediterranean. The extensive seasonal formation of sea ice promoted further cooling of conditions over those areas; the winter temperatures in Europe were as a result particularly strongly affected (Atkinson, Briffa & Coope 1987; Guiot et al. 1993a).

In a global context North Atlantic surface temperatures exhibit greater cooling during glacial maximum times than does any other ocean region (CLIMAP Members 1976). Both as a consequence of this cooling, and of the associated reduction in surface salinity, as well as a partial cause of these phenomena, North Atlantic Deep Water (NADW) formation did not occur in the Norwegian Sea during the glacial maximum and the strength of the southward flowing deep water current in the Atlantic was reduced. However, it has been hypothesised by Imbrie et al. (1992) that the sinking motion that occurs in the northern North Atlantic (the 'boreal heat pump') was strengthened during the glacial maximum, leading to the formation both of an intermediate water current that flowed southward to upwell once again in the tropical Atlantic and of a deep water flow southward, albeit at lesser depths than the NADW flow during interglacial times and of much reduced volume compared to that of NADW at the present day.

The markedly lowered CO_2 concentration, c.190ppmv compared to a pre-industrial value of c.280ppmv and a present day value of c.355ppmv, also affected the climate as a consequence of the reduced 'greenhouse effect' and would have had direct ecophysiological effects upon terrestrial vegetation.

Together, these various factors resulted in winter temperatures at least 25°C, and perhaps as much as 35°C, cooler in north-west Europe (Atkinson et al. 1987; Guiot et al. 1993a). Summer temperatures also were markedly reduced, although not by a comparable amount. There also was a reduction in moisture supply that had its greatest impact in southern Europe and in those areas downstream of the British and especially the Fennoscandian ice sheets; orographic precipitation over the ice sheets coupled to the sinking and hence warming of the air on their downstream sides produced very dry conditions in these areas.

Climate during deglaciation and the transition to the Holocene

The onset of rapid melting of the ice sheets about 14,500 years ago heralds a period of c. 5,000 years of complex environmental changes and associated climate fluctuations. Amongst the relatively well-established phenomena occurring during this time we may include the following:

1. summer insolation in the northern hemisphere rose to a maximum of c.8% more than present at c.12,000 years ago, whereas winter insolation fell to a minimum of c.5% less than today at the same time (COHMAP 1988);

2. the principal ice sheets melted rapidly during two periods, c.14,000 to 12,000 years ago and c.11,000 to 10,000 years ago (Fairbanks 1989); between these two periods was an interval when the principal ice sheets were more or less stable (Denton & Hughes 1981). In the British Isles, however, whereas the local ice sheet had melted completely during the first major phase of melting, there was local redevelopment of an ice-cap in the western highlands of Scotland (Sissons 1981) and of corrie glaciers as far south and west as the mountains of Wales and eastern Ireland (Watts 1977). These small areas of ice rapidly melted with the onset of the second phase of melting;

3. sea-level responded to the rapid ice sheet melting, exhibiting two principal periods of particularly rapid rise coinciding with the phases of rapid melting (Fairbanks 1989). In areas of ice sheet accumulation during the glacial the effective sea-level rise was apparently higher because the isostatic rebound of the earth's crust proceeded less rapidly than the eustatic sea-level rise. Thus the maximum incursion of the sea onto areas around the Irish Sea that today are land areas occurred during the late-glacial period, i.e., during the time of deglaciation (Wingfield 1995);

4. atmospheric concentrations of CO_2 rose to their Holocene levels of c.280ppmv; some evidence suggests that this rise was irregular and that levels may have fluctuated quite markedly during this interval (White et al. 1994), perhaps even rising above their Holocene value (Beerling et al. 1993);

5. surface circulation patterns in the North Atlantic exhibited complex changes (Ruddiman & McIntyre 1981). Initially a north-eastward flow of warm surface water became established, although this did not penetrate as far to the north-east as does the present-day North Atlantic Drift. This trend was reversed following the first phase of rapid ice sheet melting so that during the period when ice once again accumulated in the British Isles the surface ocean circulation probably resembled most strongly that at the glacial maximum (Broecker & Denton 1989). Thereafter the surface circulation changed to something closely

resembling that which we see today. This relatively simple pattern corresponds to the simple sequence of zones recognised in many stratigraphic records, i.e. glacial – late-glacial interstadial – late-glacial stadial ('Younger *Dryas*') – post glacial (Holocene). However, many terrestrial records for this interval provide evidence for additional fluctuations within the late-glacial interstadial and/or the early post glacial (Huntley 1994; Watts 1977); the limited temporal resolution of many ocean records may mask additional changes in surface circulation patterns associated with these events.

6. both the extent of sea ice and the deep circulation of the North Atlantic also exhibit complex changes during this period that intimately link to the changes in surface circulation (Broecker & Denton 1989; Imbrie *et al.* 1992);

7. finally, atmospheric circulation and, as a result, the climate of Great Britain were undergoing substantial changes as a result of all of these other phenomena (Kutzbach & Guetter 1986; Kutzbach *et al.* 1993).

Following the retreat of the British ice sheet, the Mersey Basin, in common with much of the remainder of England, initially was occupied by tundra-like vegetation dominated by Arctic–Alpine herbaceous and dwarf-shrub taxa. During the late-glacial interstadial taller woody taxa arrived, first Juniper (*Juniperus*) and later Birch (*Betula*). Subsequently these were displaced during the late-glacial stadial; tundra-like vegetation prevailed once again at that time (Birks 1965). A wider variety of woody taxa rapidly arrived during the early Holocene, Juniper and Birch soon being displaced by more thermally-demanding tree and shrub taxa characteristic of the modern nemoral forest zone of Europe, e.g. Hazel (*Corylus*), Elm (*Ulmus*) and Oak (*Quercus*) (Huntley & Birks 1983).

In contrast to this vegetation development, fossil beetle assemblages changed in composition extremely rapidly following deglaciation; a variety of taxa that today exhibit strongly southern distributions and which in some cases no longer extend as far north as the British Isles, e.g., *Asaphidion cyanicorne* Pand., *Bembidion ibericum* Pioch. (two species found in late-glacial interstadial deposits at Glanllynnau, North Wales, see Coope & Brophy 1972), were present almost immediately. This contrast has often in the past been interpreted as indicating a lag in the response of vegetation to an early and very rapid climatic change. There even have been attempts to explain why this might occur, including the hypothesis that soil development was the limiting factor rather than dispersal and migration (Pennington 1986). Such hypotheses, however, overlook, or were formulated before we had become aware of, some of the environmental changes that characterise this period. In particular, the enhanced seasonal contrast in insolation, peaking 12,000 years ago, would have favoured the development of warm microhabitats which might

have been exploited by warmth-demanding beetles (Andersen 1993); at the same time the effective temperatures experienced by taller woody taxa may have been insufficient to meet their growth requirements, or, more likely, the extreme winter cold to which they were exposed may have prevented their survival (Huntley 1991). The relatively low atmospheric concentration of CO_2 also would have limited tree growth as well as rendering them more susceptible to moisture deficiency; this is unlikely to have had any effect upon beetles.

Thus, as the Mersey Basin became ice free it experienced a climate that was very cold in winter, with much stronger seasonal contrast in temperature and the development of microhabitats that were extremely warm in summer as a result of enhanced insolation. The amount of precipitation probably was less than today, although so too was the overall evaporative demand; nonetheless the climate probably was effectively drier than today. Sub-Arctic trees and shrubs colonised the area during the latter part of the late-glacial interstadial whilst Reindeer (*Rangifer tarandus*), Elk (*Alces alces*), Wild Horse (*Equus ferus*) and even Giant Deer (*Megaceros giganteus*) – now extinct, still roamed the landscape (Stuart 1982). Seasonally frozen ponds became very warm during the short intense summers of the interstadial, enabling them to support relatively warmth-demanding plants and invertebrates, and locally on the landscape warmth-demanding terrestrial invertebrates and even perhaps low-growing herbaceous plants occurred in suitable microhabitats at this time. The return of tundra during the late-glacial stadial, corresponding to the development of corrie glaciers in the mountains of the English Lake District and of North Wales, indicates a return of colder conditions associated with changed circulation of the North Atlantic and of the atmosphere above. This cold phase persisted for at most 1,000 years, probably not much more than 500 years, before the onset of the rapid climate change which coincides with the beginning of the Holocene.

Climate during the Holocene

The beginning of the post-glacial period is marked by one of the most rapid palaeoenvironmental changes seen during the late Quaternary. The magnitude of this event, however, has tended to obscure the fact that the environment has continued to change, albeit exhibiting changes of much smaller magnitude, throughout the Holocene. This ongoing pattern of change is what we should expect, nonetheless, given that the various components of the climate system in particular have not been static during the Holocene.

The changes in some of these components are well documented. Thus, although the seasonal contrast in insolation peaked 12,000 years ago, there was still a substantial divergence from today during the early Holocene and the difference in insolation alone 6,000 years ago remained sufficient to cause substantial differences in climate between then and now (COHMAP 1988;

Kutzbach & Guetter 1986; Kutzbach *et al.* 1993). Only during the second half of the Holocene have insolation values approached relatively closely those of today.

The major northern hemisphere ice sheets had not completely melted at the beginning of the Holocene; remnants of the Fennoscandian ice sheet persisted until less than 9,000 years ago and the Laurentide ice sheet did not completely melt until *c.*7,000 years ago. Although by the early Holocene these ice sheets no longer were thick enough to disturb atmospheric circulation directly, they remained as areas of relatively high albedo and consequently continued to impact indirectly upon atmospheric circulation in the higher northern latitudes.

Just as the ice sheets continued to melt, so the sea level continued to rise, albeit much more slowly than previously. From the view point of the Mersey Basin an important sequence of events was that associated with the evolution of the connections between the Irish Sea and the Atlantic. The connection in the north was established already during the late-glacial period *via* the deepwater channel in the Gulf of Corryvrecken (Wingfield 1995), whilst the early rapid sea-level rise also flooded the southern part of the basin, albeit temporarily. Subsequently, the isostatic rebound of the land overtook sea-level rise such that by 13,000 years ago a land connection apparently was re-established between south-west England and south-east Ireland. This land connection then migrated northward so that *c.*11,000 years ago the area of the Irish Sea into which the Mersey opens shifted from being open to the Atlantic via a relatively narrow northern channel to being open to the Celtic Sea to the south. The remaining land connection was subsequently flooded and both the northern and southern connections were open by *c.*10,500 years ago (Wingfield, 1995); thereafter sea water once again could circulate through the Irish Sea basin and, as today, it is likely that some warmer surface waters from the North Atlantic began to move through this channel. From the more general view point of Great Britain as a whole, the key events were the initial flooding of the southern North Sea *c.*11,000 years ago, apparently via the English Channel, and the subsequent isolation of Great Britain from the European mainland *c.*8,000 years ago as the waters flooding the northern North Sea met those encroaching from the south (Funnel 1995). These events had consequences both for the environment of Britain, as ocean water circulated into and through the North Sea and English Channel, and for the biota because any immigrant taxa subsequently had to cross a sea barrier in order to colonise Britain.

Changes in other components of the climate system either are unknown and/or less firmly established. Thus, for example, the Holocene record of surface conditions and overall circulation in the North Atlantic is insufficiently well resolved to be able to determine whether or not, and to what extent, there may have been a stronger north-eastward circulation during the early Holocene. Simulation experiments using a model which couples a very simple representation of the upper ocean to a rather low resolution AGCM, however, have suggested that the North Atlantic surface may have been warmer than today during the early Holocene as a result of the enhanced summer insolation and that this warming extended to the north-east leading to delayed onset of surface freezing and a reduced duration and extent of sea ice cover (Kutzbach & Gallimore 1988). Similar uncertainty surrounds the atmospheric CO_2 concentration during the Holocene. To date the published records from ice cores lack resolution in this critical interval; either they are relatively short highly-resolved records of the late Holocene or else they are long records extending back to the last interglacial or beyond. Recent work (J. Jouzel, pers. comm.), however, has shown evidence that the early Holocene levels may have been lower than previously thought, perhaps *c.*240ppmv as opposed to the immediate pre-industrial concentration of *c.*280ppmv. Although such a 40ppmv reduction may seem small, it is 45–50% of the overall change in concentration between glacial and pre-industrial times and physiologically is potentially important to many plants.

This array of ongoing changes is reflected in an ongoing pattern of change in the Holocene climate. Thus the climate of Great Britain during the first half of the Holocene was generally more strongly seasonal or 'continental' in character. Initially winter temperatures rose relatively slowly compared to an apparent rapid increase in overall growing season warmth (B. Huntley, unpublished results); this inference from the palaeovegetation record is supported independently by evidence from AGCM simulations as well as by other forms of palaeoenvironmental proxy evidence. It appears that the residual areas of the last glacial ice sheets had a persistent effect and that this reinforced the reduced winter season insolation resulting in the cooler winter conditions. High summer insolation, however, coupled to the now warmer North Atlantic surface, brought persistent warm anticyclonic conditions in summer. The same warm summer conditions also shifted the mean summer storm track northwards so that Great Britain and other areas at similar latitudes in western Europe received less summer precipitation (Guiot, Harrison & Prentice 1993b), and hence less precipitation in total. The reduced total precipitation is reflected in the records of lake levels which were relatively low across this part of Europe during the early millennia of the Holocene; that at least a significant part of the reduction was in summer precipitation is suggested both by the model results and by the evidence of an impact upon vegetation which is sensitive principally to moisture availability during the growing season (B. Huntley, unpublished results).

The subsequent overall trend during the mid- and late Holocene periods has been of reduced seasonal contrast, corresponding to the reduced seasonal insolation contrast, and of increasing moisture levels as the summer storm track has migrated towards its present mean position. Despite this overall pattern, however, we should no longer persist in using the concept of a post-glacial 'climatic optimum'. We should avoid this term for two reasons. The first is an essentially philosophical reason, namely that we cannot consider any conditions to be 'optimal' without identifying from what point of view they are optimal. Early Holocene climate in Britain may have been optimal for the development of diverse nemoral forests over most of England and Wales and even a large part of Scotland; however, they were not optimal for those warmth-demanding beetles which thrived only briefly during the early part of the late-glacial interstadial and they certainly were optimal neither for blanket mire communities in our uplands nor for the Arctic–Alpine component of our flora. More subtly, the conditions also apparently were not optimal for the expansion north-westwards of the range of nemoral trees such as Beech (*Fagus*) or Hornbeam (*Carpinus*), both of which do not appear to have colonised Great Britain until the later Holocene (Huntley & Birks 1983).

The second reason for avoiding the term relates to the observed independence amongst the principal climate variables; the time of warmest winters certainly did not correspond to the time of maximum growing season warmth, nor did the latter correspond to the time of maximum moisture availability. Thus we must define which aspect of climate is 'optimal' before we discuss a 'climatic optimum'. Because such a definition only can be made arbitrarily, it is pointless to do so.

It would be inappropriate to close any discussion of climate change during the Holocene without some consideration of the evidence for variations on centennial to millennial time scales that cannot be accounted for by the overall trends in insolation nor, to date, by any of the other known long-term changes which I have outlined above. The most recent and well-known of these variations is that which we refer to as the 'Little Ice Age' and that reached its maximum expression in the 17th and 18th centuries. This relatively cool interval lasting several centuries is but the most recent of a long series of such events which have occurred throughout the Holocene (Grove 1988). These events alternate with relatively warmer intervals of which the last was the so-called 'Medieval warm period' of the 11th to 14th centuries. Another similar phenomenon frequently discussed at least in the older palaeoecological literature is that of so-called 'recurrence surfaces' seen in peat bogs. These surfaces reflect intervals of relatively dry conditions on the bog surface, with a high degree of humification of the peat, followed apparently rather abruptly by a switch to relatively moist conditions leading to a rapid increase in the rate of accumulation of the peat and a sharp reduction in its degree of humification (Barber *et al.* 1994). Such surfaces also might reflect relatively cool periods, promoting moist conditions on the mire surface and rapid peat accumulation, alternating with relatively warmer and/or drier periods. The short-lived expansion of Scots Pine (*Pinus sylvestris*) onto blanket mire surfaces in the far north of Scotland around 4,500 years ago represents another example of the impact upon vegetation of such climate fluctuations during the Holocene (Gear & Huntley 1991).

The causes of such fluctuations remain controversial; what is clear, however, is that whatever their causes the expression we see in terms of climate variation must have been mediated through the same phenomena of atmospheric and ocean circulation as mediate the larger magnitude and longer-term changes onto which they are superimposed. Thus, whilst the most popular explanation is in terms of variations in solar output related to sunspot number, this would exercise its impact by changing the quantity of energy reaching the atmosphere as well as the land and ocean surfaces, and thus by changing the extent of heating of these different components of the climate system, which in turn would affect the atmospheric and ocean circulation. Alternative explanations that call upon injections of volcanic dust to the atmosphere or changes in the levels of naturally-occurring 'greenhouse gases' similarly rely upon the same underlying mechanisms of changes in the earth's energy balance and hence in atmospheric and ocean circulation.

In the context of the Mersey Basin it is important to remember the overall trends in Holocene climate and that these have been overlain by higher-frequency variations. The wide development of blanket peat across the southern Pennines, in the upper parts of the Mersey catchment, for example, corresponds to the development of a generally more oceanic climate during the later Holocene. In examining any records of increased or decreased human settlement, and especially activities in what today is the agriculturally marginal zone, this overall trend also must be borne in mind; so too, however, must the fluctuations around this trend which are recorded in the peat stratigraphy of western England as well as in historical documents and other such sources (Lamb 1982).

Recent, present and future climate changes

Just as climate change has provided the continuously varying backdrop to the development of the landscape and of human settlement and agricultural activities in Britain, the landscape and human activities are also vulnerable to the recent and ongoing changes in climate. The general warming since the end of the 'Little Ice Age' may well have contributed to the present-day susceptibility of Pennine blanket peat to erosion, for example. Contemporary agriculture continues to be vulnerable to the year-to-year variations in climate, as does the water-supply industry, etc. Coastal communities are affected by storms and by the continuing rise in sea-level; no part of the landscape and no human activity is completely isolated from the impact of variations in climate.

Although such interannual or even centennial climate variations may be dismissed as of limited magnitude and impact, post-industrial revolution and especially 20th-century human society in the developed world has begun to exert a major influence on the global climate (Houghton *et al.* 1996). These changes, plus associated changes in sea-level and the direct impacts of the changes in atmospheric CO_2 concentration which are a principal cause of these climate changes together will exert a profound influence upon the future development of the landscape of the Mersey Basin and upon human activities therein. Thus in the future we may see the cultivation of new crops, the establishment of new species currently with more southern distribution patterns, and the complete loss of blanket peat cover in the Pennine uplands. We also are likely to see coastal erosion and flooding. It is certain that there will be more frequent conflicts between those concerned with the conservation of the landscape and of natural ecosystems and those whose principal interest is in 'development'. Thus in the future the landscape of the Mersey Basin will face increased pressures arising both directly and indirectly from human activities.

Coda

To the extent that this account of the changing climate and its influence upon the Mersey Basin has a conclusion, it is to emphasise the extent to which factors external to the region ultimately determine its environment and thus impact upon its landscape and upon human activities in the region. It readily may be accepted that the history of the vegetation, of the landscape or of human activities in the region over the period since the last glacial maximum cannot be considered without placing them in the context of climate changes. These latter changes, however, were driven by changes in insolation, in atmospheric composition and in the circulation of both the oceans and atmosphere – changes which were external to the region. In the future the same will be true. The climate of the region will continue to change and it is likely that it will change profoundly during the next century – once again, however, the principal causes will lie outside the region itself. The fundamental conclusion is that no region may be considered to be isolated from 'Global Changes' and thus, to the extent that future changes are anthropogenic in origin, no region can afford to ignore its potential role in limiting these changes; nor, in an historical context, can the impact of climate changes be ignored by those whose focus is upon the palaeoecological, archaeological or even historical records.

Acknowledgements

I am grateful to the organisers of this conference for their invitation to present this paper and for their forbearance when the manuscript was delivered later than they had requested. The ideas presented owe much to discussions with many colleagues and students over many years; I am grateful to them all for sharing their views upon issues of global environmental change, past, present and future. A first draft of the manuscript was critically read by Jacqui Huntley.

References

Andersen, J. (1993). Beetle remains as indicators of the climate in the Quaternary. *Journal of Biogeography*, **20**, 557–62.
Atkinson, T.C., Briffa, K.R. & Coope, G.R. (1987). Seasonal temperatures in Britain during the past 22,000 years reconstructed using beetle remains. *Nature*, **325**, 587–93.
Barber, K.E., Chambers, F.M., Maddy, D., Stoneman, R. & Brew, J.S. (1994). A sensitive high-resolution record of late Holocene climatic change from a raised bog in northern England. *The Holocene*, **4**, 198–205.
Beerling, D.J., Chaloner, W.G., Huntley, B., Pearson, J.A. & Tooley, M.J. (1993). Stomatal density responds to the glacial cycle of environmental change. *Proceedings of the Royal Society of London Series B*, **251**, 133–38.
Berger, A., Imbrie, J., Hays, J., Kukla, G. & Saltzman, B. (eds) (1984). *Milankovitch and Climate*. NATO Advanced Studies Institute Series: Vol. 126. D. Reidel Publishing Company, Dordrecht/Boston, Netherlands/USA.
Birks, H.J.B. (1965). Late-Glacial deposits at Bagmere, Cheshire and Chat Moss, Lancashire. *New Phytologist*, **64**, 270–85.
Boulton, G.S., Jones, A.S., Clayton, K.M. & Kenning, M.J. (1977). A British ice-sheet model and patterns of glacial erosion and deposition in Britain. *British Quaternary Studies: Recent Advances* (ed. F.W. Shotton), pp. 231–46. Clarendon Press, Oxford.
Broecker, W.S. & Denton, G.H. (1989). The role of ocean-atmosphere reorganizations in glacial cycles. *Geochimica Cosmochimica Acta*, **53**, 2465–501.
Chappellaz, J., Barnola, J.M., Raynaud, D., Korotkevich, Y.S. & Lorius, C. (1990). Ice-core record of atmospheric methane over the past 160,000 years. *Nature*, **345**, 127–31.
CLIMAP Members (1976). The surface of the ice-age earth. *Science*, **191**, 1131–37.
COHMAP (1988). Climatic changes of the last 18,000 years: Observations and model simulations. *Science*, **241**, 1043–52.
Coope, G.R. & Brophy, J.A. (1972). Late Glacial environmental changes indicated by a coleopteran succession from North Wales. *Boreas*, **1**, 97–142.
Denton, G.H. & Hughes, T.J. (eds) (1981). *The Last Great Ice Sheets*. Wiley, New York, USA.
Devoy, R.J.N. (1995). Deglaciation, Earth crustal behaviour and sea-level changes in the determination of insularity: a perspective from Ireland. *Island Britain: a Quaternary perspective*. Geological Society Special Publication: Vol. 96 (ed. R.C. Preece), pp. 181–208. The Geological Society, London.
Fairbanks, R.G. (1989). A 17,000-year glacio-eustatic sea level record: Influence of glacial melting rates on the Younger Dryas event and deep-ocean circulation. *Nature*, **342**, 637–42.
Funnel, B.M. (1995). Global sea-level and the (pen-)insularity of late Cenozoic Britain. *Island Britain: a Quaternary perspective*. Geological Society Special Publication: Vol. 96 (ed. R.C. Preece), pp. 3–13. The Geological Society, London.
Gear, A.J. & Huntley, B. (1991). Rapid changes in the range limits of Scots Pine 4000 years ago. *Science*, **251**, 544–47.
Grove, J.M. (1988). *The Little Ice Age*. Methuen, London.
Guiot, J., de Beaulieu, J.L., Cheddadi, R., David, F., Ponel, P. & Reille, M. (1993a). The Climate in Western Europe During the Last Glacial Interglacial Cycle Derived from Pollen and Insect Remains. *Palaeogeography Palaeoclimatology Palaeoecology*, **103**, 73–93.
Guiot, J., Harrison, S.P. & Prentice, I.C. (1993b). Reconstruction of Holocene precipitation patterns in Europe using pollen and lake-level data. *Quaternary Research*, **40**, 139–49.
Hays, J.D., Imbrie, J. & Shackleton, N. (1976). Variations in the earth's orbit: pacemaker of the ice age. *Science*, **194**, 1121–32.
Houghton, J.T., Meira Filho, L.G., Callander, B.A., Harris, N., Kattenberg, A. & Maskell, K. (eds) (1996). *Climate Change 1995: The Science of Climate Change*. Cambridge University Press, Cambridge.
Huntley, B. (1991). How plants respond to climate change:

migration rates, individualism and the consequences for plant communities. *Annals of Botany*, **67**, 15–22.

Huntley, B. (1994). Late Devensian and Holocene palaeoecology and palaeoenvironments of the Morrone Birkwoods, Aberdeenshire, Scotland. *Journal of Quaternary Science*, **9**, 311–36.

Huntley, B. & Birks, H.J.B. (1983). *An atlas of past and present pollen maps for Europe: 0–13000 B.P.* Cambridge University Press, Cambridge.

Imbrie, J., Berger, A., Boyle, E.A., Clemens, S.C., Duffy, A., Howard, W.R., Kukla, G., Kutzbach, J., Martinson, D.G., McIntyre, A., Mix, A.C., Molfino, B., Morley, J.J., Peterson, L.C., Pisias, N.G., Prell, W.L., Raymo, M.E., Shackleton, N.J. & Toggweiler, J.R. (1993). On the structure and origin of major glaciation cycles. 2. The 100,000-year cycle. *Paleoceanography*, **8**, 699–735.

Imbrie, J., Boyle, E.A., Clemens, S.C., Duffy, A., Howard, W.R., Kukla, G., Kutzbach, J., Martinson, D.G., McIntyre, A., Mix, A.C., Molfino, B., Morley, J.J., Peterson, L.C., Pisias, N.G., Prell, W.L., Raymo, M.E., Shackleton, N.J. & Toggweiler, J.R. (1992). On the structure and origin of major glaciation cycles. 1. Linear responses to Milankovitch forcing. *Paleoceanography*, **7**, 701–38.

Kutzbach, J.E. & Gallimore, R.G. (1988). Sensitivity of a coupled atmosphere/mixed layer ocean model to changes in orbital forcing at 9000 years B.P. *Journal of Geophysical Research*, **93**, 803–21.

Kutzbach, J.E. & Guetter, P.J. (1986). The influence of changing orbital parameters and surface boundary conditions on climatic simulations for the past 18 000 years. *Journal of the Atmospheric Sciences*, **43**, 1726–59.

Kutzbach, J.E., Guetter, P.J., Behling, P.J. & Selin, R. (1993). Simulated climatic changes: results of the COHMAP climate-model experiments. *Global Climates since the Last Glacial Maximum* (eds H.E. Wright, Jr., J.E. Kutzbach, T. Webb, III, W.F. Ruddiman, F.A. Street-Perrott, & P.J. Bartlein), pp. 24–93. University of Minnesota Press, Minneapolis, USA.

Lamb, H.H. (1982). *Climate, history and the modern world.* Methuen, London.

Lorius, C., Barkov, N.I., Jouzel, J., Korotkevich, Y.S., Kotylyakov, V.M. & Raynaud, D. (1988). Antarctic ice core: CO_2 and climatic change over the last climatic cycle. *Eos*, **69**, 681–84.

Pennington, W. (1986). Lags in adjustment of vegetation to climate caused by the pace of soil development: Evidence from Britain. *Vegetatio*, **67**, 105–18.

Ruddiman, W.F. & McIntyre, A. (1981). The mode and mechanism of the last deglaciation: oceanic evidence. *Quaternary Research*, **16**, 125–34.

Sissons, J.B. (1981). The last Scottish ice sheet: facts and speculative discussion. *Boreas*, **10**, 1–17.

Stuart, A.J. (1982). *Pleistocene Vertebrates in the British Isles.* Longman, London.

Stuiver, M. & Reimer, P.J. (1993). Extended ^{14}C database and revised CALIB radiocarbon calibration program. *Radiocarbon*, **35**, 215–30.

Watts, W.A. (1977). The Late Devensian vegetation of Ireland. *Philosophical Transactions of the Royal Society of London Series B*, **280**, 273–93.

White, J.C.W., Ciais, P., Figge, R.A., Kenny, R. & Markgraf, V. (1994). A high-resolution record of atmospheric CO_2 content from carbon isotopes in peat. *Nature*, **367**, 153–56.

Wingfield, R.T.R. (1995). A model of sea-levels in the Irish and Celtic seas during the end-Pleistocene to Holocene transition. *Island Britain: a Quaternary perspective.* Geological Society Special Publication: Vol. 96 (ed. R.C. Preece), pp. 209–42. The Geological Society, London.

Wright, H.E., Jr., Kutzbach, J.E., Webb, T., III, Ruddiman, W.F., Street-Perrott, F.A. & Bartlein, P.J. (eds) (1993). *Global Climates since the last glacial maximum.* University of Minnesota Press, Minneapolis, USA.

CHAPTER TWO

The land of the Mersey Basin: sea-level changes

A.J. PLATER, A.J. LONG, D. HUDDART, S. GONZALEZ
AND M.J. TOOLEY

The causes of these changes (of sea level) were then alluded to. The abrading influence of the sea, the probabilities of sudden convulsions of nature, the general rise of level of the ocean, were examined and rejected as inadequate to account for the phenomena under examination. The hypothesis which seemed to the writer the only satisfactory one was, that the land along the coast line has been for a long period in course of a gradual and slow depression in its level (Picton 1849).

Introduction

The coast of the Mersey Basin contains a wealth of evidence for past sea-level change and shoreline evolution. This evidence has attracted coastal geomorphologists, archaeologists and palaeobotanists for many years, the results of which have led to the development of a series of methodological and conceptual advances of local, regional and international importance.

In this paper we provide an introduction to the evidence for sea-level change and coastal evolution in the Mersey Basin, and explore three of the important research themes that have developed in the region. The first of these themes is the evidence for the 'Hillhouse Coast'; a shoreline variously thought to be formed during the mid-Holocene or the Late Pleistocene. The second theme considered is the pattern and cause of coastal change in the region. Here we reappraise the research in which the changes in coastal stratigraphy were attributed to oscillations in sea-level, and examine more recent (and earlier) evidence that the build-up and breakdown of coastal barriers may have been more influential in controlling coastal change. The final theme is the degree to which the past record of coastal change can be used as an analogue for the future evolution of the area.

Late-Quaternary sea-level changes

At the maximum of the last major glaciation (the Devensian cold stage) approximately 18,000 BP, global sea-level was approximately 120m lower than today (Fairbanks 1989). Consequently, vast tracts of land which are currently under water would have been sub-aerially exposed. The eastern shelf of the Irish Sea Basin, for example, would have been occupied by ice lobes which deposited glacial sediment as they retreated in response to subsequent climatic warming (Thomas 1985; Bowen et al. 1986). In the simplest model, cooler temperatures resulted in lower sea-level, through the large-scale storage of water in ice sheets and alpine glaciers during cold periods, whilst warming was characterised by sea-level rise (Fairbridge 1961).

However, in addition to the climatically-driven change in sea-level, the earth's crust has also responded to the redistribution of ice and water over its surface via isostatic adjustment. Hence, the loading of the crust by the Irish Sea ice during the Devensian brought about subsidence. This has prompted some workers (Eyles & Eyles 1984: Eyles & McCabe 1989) to suggest that much of the late-Devensian was characterised by glacio-marine deposition as crustal subsidence was of the same order of magnitude as eustatic (global) sea-level change. Although this interpretation is the subject of considerable debate (Thomas 1985; Thomas & Dackombe 1985; Austin & McCarroll 1992; McCarroll & Harris 1992; Huddart & Clark 1993), the interplay of eustatic sea-level change and glacio-isostatic crustal movements has governed sea-level trends in the Mersey Basin during the late-Quaternary (Tooley 1978a, 1982, 1985; Shennan 1989; Lambeck 1991, 1993; Wingfield 1992, 1993, 1995; Devoy 1995; Zong & Tooley 1996).

The sea-bed sediments of the eastern Irish Sea bear witness to the reworking of glacial deposits in the surf zone as sea-level rose rapidly during the early part of the present interglacial (the Holocene or Flandrian). The eastern shelf of the Irish Sea is armoured with a bed of coarse gravels and gravelly sands which remained after the fines had been winnowed out and carried eastward by the advancing surf (Wright et al. 1971). This ample supply of sediment enhanced the potential for coastal barriers to form in the nearshore zone, which, in turn, may have reduced the wave energy in the coastal zone and enabled tidal sedimentation to predominate (e.g., Eicher 1978; Leeder 1982). Consequently, the coastal lowlands of the Mersey Basin, i.e., those of the Sefton coast, northern Wirral and the Mersey Estuary, possess a sedimentary record of significant shoreline changes during the Holocene (Tooley 1978a, 1982; Kenna 1986; Innes *et al*. 1990; Bedlington 1995).

Whilst sea-level was rising as a result of ice melt and thermal expansion of the oceans, the earth's crust will also have undergone uplift as the ice sheet loading was removed. Geodynamic models of the crust, coupled with reconstructions of ice sheet thickness, enable glacio-isostatic uplift to be predicted. Lambeck (1991) suggested that the late-Pleistocene (16,000 to 12,000 BP) was characterised by rapid relative sea-level fall as the crust rose faster than the eustatic sea-level trend (Figure 2.1). This proposition, if correct, is of crucial significance in the evolution of the Mersey Basin coast.

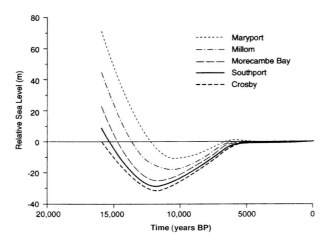

Figure 2.1. Relative sea-level curves for north-west England from geodynamic modelling of the earth's crust and eustatic sea-level trends (Lambeck, 1991).

The Hillhouse Coast

Approaches to sea-level reconstructions make use of a variety of physical evidence. In Britain, extensive use has been made of morphological and stratigraphic evidence; the former predominating (although not exclusively) in the study of Holocene sea-level change in Scotland (e.g., Sissons & Dawson 1981) and the latter in England and Wales (e.g., Tooley 1978a). Indeed, these two approaches are governed to some degree by the nature of late-Quaternary glacio-isostatic crustal movements; uplift in the north raising coastal features above the present level of the sea, and subsidence in the south resulting in the submergence of former coastal environments.

Evidence for high sea-level stands is present in the Isle of Man (Synge 1977; Thomas 1977), but raised morphological features are rare in the Mersey Basin. However, Wright (1914) postulated the presence of a post-glacial shoreline (the 25-foot raised beach) extending from the Lleyn peninsula, across the coast of the Wirral and into south-west Lancashire. Gresswell (1957) documented a morphological feature over much of the Lancashire coast which he identified as an ancient shoreline fronted by relict beach sands (the Shirdley Hill Sand) and tidal silts (the Downholland Silt). It was proposed that this

'Hillhouse Coast' marked the location of the coast during the mid-Holocene (6,000 to 5,000 BP).

Tooley (1978a) tested this hypothesis by collecting new litho-, bio- and chronostratigraphic data from the Lancashire lowlands during the 1970s, and, as a result, called the coastal origin of this morphological feature into question. First, Gresswell (1957) identified the Hillhouse Coast at altitudes above +5m O.D. (above mean sea-level), but Tooley (1976, 1978a) argued that this was too high to be a mid-Holocene shoreline since his sea-level graph for north-west England (Figure 2.2) suggested that the level of mean high water spring tides at 5,000 BP stood at approximately +2m O.D. Secondly, the Shirdley Hill Sand in south-west Lancashire extends *c*.20km inland from the present coast and is recorded at altitudes ranging from -14m to +120m O.D. Thirdly, investigation of the Shirdley Hill Sand suggested it was reworked cover sand rather than beach deposits, and that it was of late-glacial age (Godwin 1959; Tooley & Kear 1977; Wilson, Bateman & Catt 1981; Innes, Tooley & Tomlinson 1989). In contrast, evidence from the Hightown area reveals that deposits initially recorded as Shirdley Hill Sand may be coastal deposits of mid-Holocene age (Huddart 1992; Pye, Stokes & Neal 1995).

If one believes the results of recent geodynamic modelling (Lambeck 1991, 1993; Wingfield 1992, 1995), the Hillhouse Coast could be a Late Pleistocene coastal feature, with relative sea-level being close to +5m O.D. in the region of Crosby and Southport at approximately 16,000 BP (Lambeck, 1991). If this were the case, parts of the Shirdley Hill Sand could be beach sands which were reworked during the cold conditions of the late-glacial (the Younger Dryas or Loch Lomond stadial periods *c*.10,500 BP). A late-glacial coastal origin for some of the sand deposit was postulated by Tooley (1985), whilst Innes (1986) and Innes *et al*. (1989) suggested that this may have been followed by aeolian reworking. Indeed, thermoluminescence dating of Shirdley Hill Sand from Mere Sands Wood, near Rufford, revealed a minimum age for the onset of sand deposition of 11,730 ±1,510 BP, with further periods of deposition and/or reworking between 8,740 ±2,060 and 6,940 ±1,110 BP (Bateman 1995).

The Hillhouse Coast and the Shirdley Hill Sand could once again be the focus of investigation into late-Pleistocene and Holocene sea-level trends. Clearly, the geodynamic models need to be validated with reference to the available morphological and stratigraphic data. Although it might prove difficult to improve on the equivocal evidence from south-west Lancashire, research may extend northward to Cumbria where the modelled post-glacial relative sea-level raises the potential for marine inundation of the coastal lake basins of the Lake District during the late-Devensian.

Holocene coastal change

Irrespective of the status of the Hillhouse Coast, the coastal lowlands of the Mersey Basin possess a rich record of Holocene sea-level change. The buried peats of the Mersey, Wirral and Sefton were investigated more than one hundred years ago in the reconstruction of past environments (de Rance 1869, 1872, 1877; Reade 1871, 1872, 1881, 1908; Morton 1887, 1888, 1891). Attention also focused on the nature and trends of past vegetation (Travis 1908, 1922; Travis 1926, 1929; Erdtman 1928). However, the complex intercalation of biogenic and minerogenic units proved an interesting challenge, and were interpreted in the context of coastal (primarily land level) change by Binney & Talbot (1843), Picton (1849), Reade (1871), Morton (1888) and Blackburn (in Cope, 1939). Subsequently, Tooley (1970, 1974, 1976, 1978a, 1978b, 1982, 1985) undertook detailed stratigraphic and micropalaeontological work which established the West Derby region (Formby, Hightown and Downholland Moss) as one of the classic sites for Holocene sea-level reconstructions in the UK. Upward transitions from brackish-water minerogenic horizons to biogenic sediments deposited in close proximity to the shore were used as indicators of negative sea-level change, whilst the reverse provided evidence of sea-level rise. The sequence of stratigraphic intercalations in the Lancashire mosslands enabled the reconstruction of sea-level trends for north-west England from approximately 8,000 to 4,500 BP (Figure 2.2).

The resulting Holocene sea-level curve for north-west England was established using evidence from the West Derby and the Fylde in Amounderness and Morecambe Bay study areas (Tooley 1978a), and has been correlated with records from other parts of Britain and north-western Europe in the study of eustatic sea-level trends. Fairbridge (1961) had argued that minor oscillations in eustatic sea-level could be linked with fluctuations in climate, whilst Jelgersma (1966) rejected oscillating sea-level trends on the basis of the inadequacy and insufficiency of available data. Tooley (1978a) acknowledged the presence of oscillations in the north-west of England sea-level curve, but he proposed that low amplitude fluc-

tuations reflected local factors, such as sediment compaction, and high amplitude oscillations were primarily eustatic in origin. Indeed, the rapid rise in sea-level preserved in the sediments of Downholland Moss between c.8,000 and c.6,800 BP is present in other examples from north-western Europe, and has also been observed in recent work on the sedimentary record of Morecambe Bay (Zong & Tooley, 1996).

In the context of glacio-isostatic crustal movement, Shennan (1989) has shown from analysis of the sea-level curves from both southern and northern Lancashire that there was a marked decrease in the rate of uplift at c.5,000 BP. Further north, the rate of uplift in Morecambe Bay decreased at c. 6,000 BP but has continued at a low rate of rise to the present day (Shennan 1989; Zong & Tooley, 1996). Thus, it would appear that glacio-isostatic uplift is now complete in the region of the Mersey Basin. However, if uplift was related to the collapse of a glacial forebulge, subsidence may eventually follow. Wingfield (1993) believes that this forebulge-related subsidence may have passed through the region c.8000 BP, but this does not account for the changes observed in the relative sea-level trends during mid-Holocene.

There is also considerable debate concerning the reconstruction of mid- to late-Holocene sea-level trends from the stratigraphic record of the Mersey Basin. During the early-Holocene, the coast was characterised by an extensive intertidal sandflat in the west with mudflats and fringing saltmarsh to the east. There was vertical aggradation of these sedimentary environments under rising sea-level in the early- to mid-Holocene, resulting in alternating phases of marine and terrestrial sedimentation. However, Neal, Huddart & Pye (pers. comm.) suggest that more local factors could also have been important in explaining the alternating stratigraphy. Foraminiferal evidence suggests that the periodic breaching of an offshore barrier (Pye & Neal 1993a) may have provided a local control on coastal sedimentation, and enabled marked changes in the connection with the

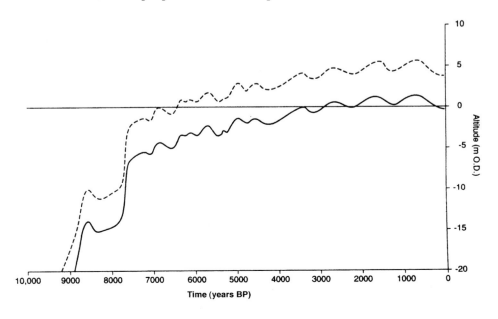

Figure 2.2. Relative sea-level curve for west Lancashire (Tooley, 1978a). The dashed line shows the trend of MHWST and the solid line represents mean sea-level.

open sea to take place. Stratigraphic sequences on the Wirral (Kenna 1986; Innes *et al.* 1990; Bedlington, 1995), have revealed a similar sequence of changes in coastal sedimentation which have been interpreted in the context of Holocene sea-level rise. Although this spatial continuity might support the interpretation of regional-scale changes brought about via sea-level trends, the Wirral and Sefton coasts may have supported similar barriers and back-barrier environments and, therefore, experienced similar periods of inundation resulting from barrier breaching. Indeed, Binney and Talbot (1843) had originally interpreted the Downholland Moss sequence in the context of coastal barrier evolution:

> After a time, a second bank of sand similar to the first one described was thrown up, which stopped the ingress of the sea and the egress of the fresh water, so as to cause a second morass which has produced the upper bed of peat.

Recent research has suggested the persistence of a barrier in the Sefton region for much of the Holocene (Pye & Neal 1993a, 1993b; Huddart 1992; Neal 1993; Neal *et al.* pers. comm.). Although radiocarbon ages from organic deposits which are overlain by dune sand range between 4,545 ±90 (Tooley 1970) and 3,380 ±60 BP (Pye & Neal 1993a), sand barrier formation was underway as early as 5,100 BP (Pye & Neal 1993a). Furthermore, the pattern of drainage channels on Altcar and Downholland Mosses associated with tidal sediments deposited between 6,000 and 5,600 BP, implies a north-south trending barrier in the Formby-Ainsdale region at this time (Huddart 1992). Indeed, Pye & Neal (1993a) propose that the earliest dunes in the region, which formed between 5,800 and 5,700 BP, may have become established on an emergent offshore sand bank which was in existence by 6,800 BP. Consequently, the main body of evidence presented by Tooley (1978a) (with the exception of the earliest period of transgression, DM-I) may have been laid down in this low energy environment which was buffered from high wave energy by the protective barrier complex.

The extent of this back-barrier environment has been the subject of recent investigation. In addition to the above evidence, the clear palaeoenvironmental and archaeological linkages between the stratigraphic records of the Wirral and Sefton coast (Gonzalez, Huddart & Roberts 1996) suggest that the coastal margins of Liverpool Bay may have been occupied by an extensive coastal plain in the lee of a discontinuous nearshore barrier complex during the mid-Holocene. In this context, the preservation of human and animal (Aurochs (*Bos primigenius*), Red Deer (*Cervus elaphus*), Roe Deer (*Capreolus capreolus*), Horse (*Equus caballus*) and crane) footprints in Holocene sediments in the foreshore at Formby Point is of particular importance in relation to the coastal evolution of the Mersey Basin. The footprints are located in the intertidal zone of the beach, with at least two stratigraphic sets of prints in sediments which exhibit a change from a nearshore, intertidal environment (lower footprints) to a terrestrial dune and dune slack (upper footprints). The stratigraphic evidence indicates a Neolithic/Bronze age for the footprints (Roberts, Gonzalez & Huddart 1996) and a ^{14}C date from an associated layer of Alder (*Alnus*) roots gives a *terminus ante quem* of 3,649 ±109 BP. The footprints show remarkable preservation (Figure 2.3), independent of sediment type, which indicates a rapid rate of sedimentation. Hence, this type of evidence is rare; Caldicot Levels in the Severn Estuary being the only other intertidal site in the UK where human and animal footprints have been reported in Holocene sediments (Aldhouse-Green *et al.* 1992).

Figure 2.3. Human footprint and cattle hoofprint from Formby Point foreshore, Blundell Avenue, 17 January 1996 (*Photo: S. Gonzalez*).

The sedimentary environment in which these footprints were made is characteristic of a mesotidal system (Hayes 1979) in which morphology is controlled by a combination of wave energy and tidal processes in the back-barrier. If this proves to be the case, the lowland stratigraphy of the Mersey Basin will also possess a sedimentary record of significant palaeotidal change during the Holocene because the present spring tidal range is approximately 8.4m (Admiralty Tide Tables 1995). The required increase in tidal range (mesotidal regimes are characterised by a spring tidal range of between 2.0 and

4.0m according to Davies 1964) would necessitate a critical review of the evidence for Holocene sea-level change in north-western England. If spring tidal range has increased by up to 4m (or possibly even more) over the last 6,000 years, then eustatic mean sea-level may have been 2m higher than has been assumed for 6,000 BP from the reconstructed curves. Consequently, glacio-isostatic crustal movements could prove to be very different to those determined for the mid- to late-Holocene (Shennan 1989).

The significance of coastal barrier systems in the evolution of the Mersey Basin does not stop with the interpretation of back-barrier stratigraphy. Indeed, the youngest phase of Holocene sea-level change (Transgression V from the West Derby region) proposed by Tooley (1978a) is represented by the occurrence of a fossil dune slack peat, dated to 2,335 ±120 BP, at an altitude of +5.08m O.D. in the dunes of Formby Foreshore. Similar organic deposits have revealed ages of 2,510 ±120 (Pye 1990), 2,260 ±60 (Pye & Neal 1993a), 3,200 ±60 and 2,680 ±50 BP (Innes & Tooley 1993), and the optically-stimulated luminescence dating of podsolized dune sand yielded an age between 3,200 and 2,500 BP (Pye, Stokes & Neal 1995). These data provide evidence of dune stability which, in turn, gives equivocal evidence of sea-level change (Fairbridge 1961; van Straaten 1965; Jelgersma *et al*, 1970; Tooley 1978a, 1990; Innes & Frank 1988), i.e., there is some debate as to whether dunes are stable during periods of static or rising sea-level, and the ages give only the timing of change and not the altitude of sea-level. Further periods of dune stability are recorded in Lancashire between 1,795 ±240 and 1,370 ±85 BP, and at approximately 800 BP (Tooley 1978a, 1990; Innes & Tooley 1993). Indeed, this most recent period is also recorded in the coastal dunes of the Wirral peninsula, where dates from soils and peats overlain by aeolian sand range from 925 ±50 to 540 ±40 BP (Kenna 1986). The fact that these phases of dune stability can be correlated with similar trends found in western Europe suggests some climatic control, although this may be an indirect control via sea-level change (Tooley 1990).

The barrier control on coastal evolution is a common feature of many coasts. Consequently, the interpretation of lowland stratigraphy in the context of sea-level change is fraught with difficulty, especially when the rate of sea-level rise is low (Plater & Shennan 1992). Although the coastal lowland stratigraphy of the Mersey Basin may well be regarded as a classic record of coastal evolution brought about by Holocene sea-level rise, perhaps it should be viewed as a sedimentary record with which to investigate the relative importance of coastal processes and factors which operate over differing timescales and spatial extent.

Reverse uniformitarianism

At the end of the 18th century, James Hutton proposed that the key to interpreting the geological past was through present-day processes operating over much longer timescales than had been considered previously – the concept of uniformitarianism. The reverse of this approach has provided researchers with an essential justification for the study of late-Quaternary sea-level change. The wealth of data on sea-level change in the region of the Mersey Basin, and in particular the detail provided by the coastal dune stratigraphy for the last 3,000 years or so, provides an excellent context for assessing the consequences of present and future sea-level change. Tide gauge data from the region (Woodworth 1992) reveal rates of relative sea-level rise of the order of 2mm yr[-1] for the latter part of the 20th century. These rates of change are likely to increase to approximately 7mm yr[-1] by the end of the next century (Houghton, Jenkins & Ephraums 1990). The Holocene sea-level data illustrate that the predicted changes represent a marked acceleration of the most recent rates of change, but that similar rates of sea-level rise were experienced during the early part of the present interglacial.

The problem with using the early-Holocene as an analogue for what the next century holds for the coastal lowlands of the Mersey Basin is that sediment sources were less restricted at that time, the vegetation cover was very different, and the role of human societies in maintaining the coast was far less significant than today. Although humans may be able to reduce the immediate impacts of sea-level rise through the control of coastal erosion and the construction of flood defences, engineered coastlines may well be more vulnerable than previously assumed. If the response of the present-day coast to extreme events, such as storm surges, can be considered as an indication of vulnerability to sea-level rise, it would appear that the coastal dunes are more robust than anthropogenically-protected lowland environments. Indeed, coastal environments in which the sediments are able to respond to future sea-level rise may fare better than static walls and revetments. This is of some significance where the lowlands of the Mersey Estuary are concerned, and the managed retreat of society from these areas may be the only option towards the end of the next century.

A further consequence of adopting the uniformitarianism approach at the turn of the century was that catastrophic change was given less significance. However, recent research initiatives, such as IGCP 367 (late-Quaternary coastal records of rapid change: application to present and future conditions) have once again highlighted the importance of understanding low-frequency, high-magnitude events such as storm surges and tsunami. Indeed, a report by the Department of the Environment (DoE 1991) illustrated that a 0.2m rise in mean sea-level significantly increases the frequency of extreme water level events for the east and, in particular, south coasts of England. This followed the earlier findings of Rossiter (1962), who demonstrated that a 0.15m rise in mean sea-level would reduce the return interval of extreme water level events on the west coast by a factor of three.

It is unlikely that the temporal and spatial resolution

of Holocene or late-Pleistocene sea-level reconstructions will match the needs of coastal planners and managers in the immediate future. However, if research is to progress in improving the information available for sustained habitation of coastal lowlands, the sediments of the Mersey Basin offer an excellent testing ground for new techniques.

Acknowledgements

The authors should like to acknowledge all those who commented on the text, as well as the various researchers whose work is included in this review. Sandra Mather is thanked for the redrafting of the figures included in the text, Ian Qualtrough for reproducing the photograph, Frank Oldfield for his editorship, and Eric Greenwood for the opportunity to consider the research on the coastal evolution of the Mersey Basin in a broader context.

References

Admiralty Tide Tables (1995). *Volume 1 – European Waters*. The Hydrographer of the Navy.

Aldhouse-Green, S.H.R., Whittle, A.W.R., Allen, J.R.L., Caseldine, A.E., Culver, S.J., Day, M., Lundquist, J. & Upton, D. (1992). Prehistoric human footprints from the Severn Estuary at Uskmouth and Magor Pill, Gwent, Wales. *Archaeologia Cambrensis*, **141**, 14–55.

Austin, W.E.N. & McCarroll, D. (1992). Foraminifera from the Irish Sea glacigenic deposits at Aberdaron, Western Lleyn, North Wales: palaeoenvironmental implications. *Journal of Quaternary Science*, **7**, 311–17.

Bateman, M.D. (1995). Thermoluminescence dating of the British coversand deposits. *Quaternary Science Reviews*, **14**, 791–98.

Bedlington, D. (1995). *Holocene sea-level changes and crustal movements in North Wales and Wirral*. PhD thesis, University of Durham.

Binney, E.W. & Talbot, J.H. (1843). On the petroleum found in the Downholland Moss, near Ormskirk. Paper read at the Fifth Annual General Meeting of the Manchester Geological Society, 6 October 1843. *Transactions of the Manchester Geological Society*, **7**, 41–48.

Bowen, D.Q., Rose, J., McCabe, A.M. & Sutherland, D.G. (1986). Correlation of Quaternary glaciations in England, Ireland, Scotland and Wales. *Quaternary Science Reviews*, **5**, 299–340.

Cope, F.W. (1939). Oil occurrences in south-west Lancashire (with a Biological Report by K.B. Blackburn). *Bulletin of the Geological Survey of Great Britain*, **2**, 18–25.

Davies, J.L. (1964). A morphogenic approach to the World's shorelines. *Zeitschrift für Geomorphologie*, **8**, 127–42.

de Rance, C.E. (1869). *The geology of the country between Liverpool and Southport*. Explanation of Quarter Sheet 90SE of the 1 inch Geological Survey Map of England and Wales. Memoir of the Geological Survey of the United Kingdom, HMSO, London.

de Rance, C.E. (1872). *Geology of the country around Southport, Lytham Southshore*. Explanation of the Quarter Sheet 90NE. Memoir of the Geological Survey of the United Kingdom, HMSO, London.

de Rance, C.E. (1877). *The superficial geology of the country adjoining the coast of south-west Lancashire*. Memoir of the Geological Survey of the United Kingdom, HMSO, London.

Department of the Environment (1991). *The Potential Effects of Climate Change in the United Kingdom*. United Kingdom Climate Change Impacts Review Group, HMSO, London.

Devoy, R.J.N. (1995). Deglaciation, earth crustal behaviour and sea-level changes in the determination of insularity: a perspective from Ireland. *Island Britain: a Quaternary Perspective* (ed. R.C. Preece), pp. 181–208. Geological Society Special Publication No. 96.

Eicher, D.L. (1978). *Geologic Time*. Prentice-Hall, New Jersey, USA.

Erdtman, G. (1928). Studies in the post-arctic history of the forests of North-west Europe. I. Investigations in the British Isles. *Geologiska Föreningens i Stockholm Förhandlingar*, **50(2:373)**, 123–92.

Eyles, C.H. & Eyles, N. (1984). Glaciomarine sediments of the Isle of Man as a key to late Pleistocene stratigraphic investigations in the Irish Sea Basin. *Geology*, **12**, 359–64.

Eyles, N. & McCabe, A.M. (1989). The Late Devensian (<22,000 BP) Irish Sea Basin: the sedimentary record of a collapsed ice sheet margin. *Quaternary Science Reviews*, **8**, 307–51.

Fairbanks, R.G. (1989). A 17000-year glacio-eustatic sea level record. *Nature*, **342**, 637–42.

Fairbridge, R.W. (1961). Eustatic changes in sea-level. *Physics and Chemistry of the Earth*, **4**, 99–185.

Godwin, H. (1959). Studies of the postglacial history of British vegetation. XIV. Late Glacial deposits at Moss Lake, Liverpool. *Philosophical Transactions of the Royal Society of London, Series B*, **242**, 127–49.

Gonzalez, S., Huddart, D. & Roberts, G. (1996). Holocene development of the Sefton Coast: a multidisciplinary approach to understanding the archaeology. *Proceedings of the Archaeological Sciences Conference 1995* (eds. A. Sinclair, E. Slater & J. Gowlett), pp. 289–99. Oxford University Archaeological Monograph Series, Oxbow Books, Oxford.

Gresswell, R.K. (1957). Hillhouse Coastal Deposits in South Lancashire. *Liverpool and Manchester Geological Journal*, **2**, 60–78.

Hayes, M.O. (1979). Barrier island morphology as a function of tidal and wave regime. *Barrier Islands* (ed. S.P. Leatherman), pp. 1–27. Academic Press, London.

Houghton, J.T., Jenkins, G.J. & Ephraums, J.J. (eds) (1990). *Climate Change: The IPCC Scientific Assessment*. Cambridge University Press, Cambridge.

Huddart, D. (1992). Coastal environmental changes and morphostratigraphy in southwest Lancashire, England. *Proceedings of the Geologists' Association*, **103**, 217–36.

Huddart, D. & Clark, R. (1993). Conflicting interpretations from the glacial sediments and landforms in Cumbria. *Proceedings of the Cumberland Geological Society*, **5(4)**, 419–36.

Innes, J.B. (1986). The history of the Shirdley Hill Sand revealed by examination of associated organic deposits. *Proceedings of the North England Soils Discussion Group*, **21**, 31–43.

Innes, J.B. & Frank, R.M. (1988). Palynological evidence for Late Flandrian coastal changes at Druridge Bay, Northumberland. *Scottish Geographical Magazine*, **104(1)**, 14–23.

Innes, J.B. & Tooley, M.J. (1993). The age and vegetational history of the Sefton coast dunes. *The Sand Dunes of the Sefton Coast* (eds. D. Atkinson & J. Houston), pp. 3–20. National Museums & Galleries on Merseyside in association with Sefton Metropolitan Borough Council, Liverpool.

Innes, J.B., Tooley, M.J. & Tomlinson, P.R. (1989). A comparison of the age and palaeoecology of some sub-Shirdley Hill Sand peat deposits from Merseyside and south-west Lancashire. *Naturalist*, **114**, 65–69.

Innes, J.B., Bedlington, D.J., Kenna, R.J.B. & Cowell, R.W. (1990). A preliminary investigation of coastal deposits at Newton Carr, Wirral, Merseyside. *Quaternary Newsletter*, **62**, 5–12.

Jelgersma, S. (1966). Sea-level changes during the last 10,000 years. *World Climate 8000 to 0 B.C.* (ed. J.E. Sawyer), pp. 54–69. Proceedings of the International Symposium, Royal Meteorological Society, London.

Jelgersma, S., de Jong, J., Zagwijn, W.H. & van Regteren Altena, J.F. (1970). The coastal dunes of the western Netherlands; geology, vegetational history and archaeology. *Mededelingen Rijks Geologische Dienst N.S.*, **21**, 93–167.

Kenna, R.J.B. (1986). The Flandrian sequence of north Wirral (N.W. England). *Geological Journal*, **21**, 1–27.

Lambeck, K. (1991). Glacial rebound and sea-level change in the British Isles. *Terra Nova*, **3**, 379–89.

Lambeck, K. (1993). Glacial rebound of the British Isles – II. A high-resolution, high-precision model. *Geophysical Journal International*, **115**, 960–90.

Leeder, M.R. (1982). *Sedimentology: Process and Product*. George Allen and Unwin, London.

McCarroll, D. & Harris, C. (1992). The glacigenic deposits of western Lleyn, North Wales: terrestrial or marine? *Journal of Quaternary Science*, **7**, 19–29.

Morton, G.H. (1887). Stanlow, Ince and Frodsham Marshes. *Proceedings of the Liverpool Geological Society*, **5**, 349–51.

Morton, G.H. (1888). Further notes on the Stanlow, Frodsham and Ince Marshes. *Proceedings of the Liverpool Geological Society*, **6**, 50–55.

Morton, G.H. (1891). *Geology of the Country around Liverpool, including the North of Flintshire*. George Philip and Son, London.

Neal, A. (1993). *Sedimentology and morphodynamics of a Holocene coastal dune barrier complex, north-west England*. Unpublished PhD thesis, University of Reading.

Picton, J.A. (1849). The changes of sea-levels on the west coast of England during the historic period. (Abstract) *Proceedings of the Literary and Philosophical Society of Liverpool*, 36th Session, **5**, 113–15.

Plater, A.J. & Shennan, I. (1992). Evidence of Holocene sea-level change from the Northumberland coast, eastern England. *Proceedings of the Geologists' Association*, **103**, 201–16.

Pye, K. (1990). Physical and human influences on coastal dune development between the Ribble and Mersey estuaries, northwest England. *Coastal Dunes: Form and Process* (eds. K.F. Nordstrom, N.P. Psuty & R.W.G. Carter), pp. 339–59. Wiley, Chichester.

Pye, K. & Neal, A. (1993a). Late Holocene dune formation on the Sefton Coast, northwest England. *The Dynamics and Environmental context of Aeolian Sedimentary Systems* (ed. K. Pye), pp. 201–17. Geological Society Special Publication No. 72, Geological Society Publishing House, Bath.

Pye, K. & Neal, A. (1993b). Stratigraphy and age structure of the Sefton dune complex: preliminary results of field drilling investigations. *The Sand Dunes of the Sefton Coast* (eds D. Atkinson & J. Houston), pp. 41–44. National Museums & Galleries on Merseyside in association with Sefton Metropolitan Borough Council, Liverpool.

Pye, K., Stokes, S. & Neal, A. (1995). Optical dating of aeolian sediments from the Sefton coast, northwest England. *Proceedings of the Geologists' Association*, **106**, 281–92.

Reade, T.M. (1871). The geology and physics of the Post-Glacial Period, as shown in deposits and organic remains in Lancashire and Cheshire. *Proceedings of the Liverpool Geological Society*, **2**, 36–88.

Reade, T.M. (1872). The post-glacial geology and physiography of west Lancashire and the Mersey estuary. *Geological Magazine*, **9(93)**, 111–19.

Reade, T.M. (1881). On a section of the Formby and Leasowe Marine Beds, and Superior Peat Bed, disclosed by cuttings for the outlet sewer at Hightown. *Proceedings of the Liverpool Geological Society*, **4(4)**, 269–77.

Reade, T.M. (1908). Post-Glacial beds at Great Crosby as disclosed by the new outfall sewer. *Proceedings of the Liverpool Geological Society*, **10(4)**, 249–61.

Roberts, G., Gonzalez, S. & Huddart, D. (1996). Intertidal Holocene footprints and their archaeological significance. *Antiquity*, **70(269)**, 647–51.

Rossiter, J.R. (1962). Tides and storm surges. *Proceedings of the Royal Society of London, Series A*, 265, 328–30.

Shennan, I. (1989). Holocene crustal movements and sea-level changes in Great Britain. *Journal of Quaternary Science*, **4**, 77–89.

Sissons, J.B. & Dawson, A.G. (1981). Former sea-levels and ice limits in Wester Ross, northwest Scotland. *Proceedings of the Geologists' Association*, **92**, 115–24.

van Straaten, L.M.J.U. (1965). Coastal barrier deposits in South- and North-Holland, in particular in the areas around Scheveningen and Ijmuiden. *Mededelingen van de Geologische Stichting N.S.*, **17**, 41–76.

Synge, F.M. (1977). Records of sea-levels during the late devensian. *Philosophical Transactions of the Royal Society of London, Series B*, **280**, 211–28.

Thomas, G.S.P. (1977). The Quaternary of the Isle of Man. *The Quaternary History of the Irish Sea* (eds C. Kidson & M.J. Tooley), pp. 155–78. Geological Journal Special Issue No. 7, Seel House Press, Liverpool.

Thomas, G.S.P. (1985). The Quaternary of the northern Irish Sea Basin. *The Geomorphology of North-West England* (ed. R.H. Johnson), pp. 143–58. Manchester University Press, Manchester.

Thomas, G.S.P. & Dackombe, R.V. (1985). Comment on 'Glaciomarine sediments of the Isle of Man as a key to late pleistocene stratigraphic investigations in the Irish Sea Basin'. *Geology*, **13**, 445–47.

Tooley, M.J. (1970). The peat beds of the south-west Lancashire coast. *Nature in Lancashire*, **1**, 19–26.

Tooley, M.J. (1974). Sea-level changes during the last 9000 years in north-west England. *Geographical Journal*, **140**, 18–42.

Tooley, M.J. (1976). Flandrian sea-level changes in west Lancashire and their implications for the 'Hillhouse coast-line'. *Geological Journal*, **11(2)**, 37–52.

Tooley, M.J. (1978a). *Sea-level Changes: north-west England during the Flandrian stage*. Clarendon Press, Oxford.

Tooley (1978b). Interpretation of Holocene sea level changes. *Geologiska Föreningens i Stockholm Förhandlingar*, **100(2)**, 203–12.

Tooley, M.J. (1982). Sea-level changes in northern England. *Proceedings of the Geologists' Association*, **93**, 43–51.

Tooley, M.J. (1985). Sea-level changes and coastal morphology in north-west England. *The Geomorphology of North-West England* (ed. R.H. Johnson), pp. 94–121. Manchester University Press, Manchester.

Tooley, M.J. (1990). The chronology of coastal dune development in the United Kingdom. *Catena Supplement*, **18**, 81–88.

Tooley, M.J. & Kear, B. (1977). Shirdley Hill Sand Formation. *The Isle of Man, Lancashire coast and Lake District* (ed. M.J. Tooley), pp. 9–12. Guidebook for Excursion A4, X INQUA Congress, Geoabstracts, Norwich.

Travis, C.B. (1926). The peat and forest bed of the south-west Lancashire coast. *Proceedings of the Liverpool Geological Society*, **14**, 263–77.

Travis, C.B. (1929). The peat and forest beds of Leasowe, Cheshire. *Proceedings of the Liverpool Geological Society*, **15**, 157–78.

Travis, W.G. (1908). On plant remains in peat in the Shirdley Hill Sand at Aintree, south Lancashire. *Transactions of the Liverpool Botanical Society*, **1**, 47–52.

Travis, W.G. (1922). On peaty beds in the Wallasey Sand-Hills. *Proceedings of the Liverpool Geological Society*, **13(3)**, 207–14.

Wilson, P., Bateman, R.M. & Catt, J.A. (1981). Petrography, origin and environment of deposition of the Shirdley Hill Sand of southwest Lancashire, England. *Proceedings of the Geologists' Association*, **92**, 211–29.

Wingfield, R.T.R. (1992). Quaternary changes of sea level and climate. *The Irish Sea*, pp. 56–66. Irish Sea Forum Seminar Report, Global Warming and Climatic Change, Liverpool University Press, Liverpool.

Wingfield, R.T.R. (1993). Modelling Holocene sea levels in the Irish and Celtic seas. *Proceedings of the international Coastal*

Congress, ICC-Kiel '92 (eds. H. Sterr, J. Hofstede & H.-P. Plag), pp. 760–72. Peter Lang, Frankfurt am Main, Germany.

Wingfield, R.T.R. (1995). A model of sea level in the Irish and Celtic Seas during the end-Pleistocene to Holocene transition. *Island Britain: a Quaternary Perspective* (ed. R.C. Preece), pp. 209–42. Geological Society Special Publication No. 96, Geological Society, London.

Woodworth, P.L. (1992). Sea-level changes. *The Irish Sea*, pp. 21–28. Irish Sea Forum Seminar Report, Global Warming and Climatic Change, Liverpool University Press, Liverpool.

Wright, W.B. (1914). *The Quaternary Ice Age*. Macmillan, London.

Wright, J.E., Hull, J.H., McQuillin, R. & Arnold, S.E. (1971). *Irish Sea investigations 1969–1970*. Institute of Geological Sciences, Report No. 71/19, HMSO, London.

Zong, Y. & Tooley, M.J. (1996). Holocene sea-level changes and crustal movements in Morecambe Bay, northwest England. *Journal of Quaternary Science*, **11(1)**, 43–58.

CHAPTER THREE

Vegetational changes before the Norman Conquest

J.B. INNES, M.J. TOOLEY AND J.G.A. LAGEARD

Introduction

This paper summarises the history of vegetation change in the Mersey Basin from the time of the earliest available evidence until the Norman Conquest, since when humans have dominated the processes which control vegetation distributions. With the limited exception of some wetland communities, vegetation has been so greatly modified or controlled by human agricultural and industrial activities as to be virtually artificial. These recent anthropogenic plant associations will be discussed in other chapters in this volume. The balance between natural and cultural influences on the vegetation has only in the last millennium swung so decisively towards man, and for most of the past vegetation distributions were subject predominantly to external natural environmental forces and to internal processes of community succession, with human impacts localised and limited in effect. With the adoption of increasingly intensive systems of food production in the later Holocene human influence on vegetation patterns grew until the cultural factor assumed dominance over natural factors in determining the vegetation cover, laying the basis for the present artificial situation.

Over 80 pollen diagrams of varying detail are available from organic lake and mire sediments in the study area, and these are listed in Table 3.1 and shown on Figure 3.1. Despite a lack of sites in some urban areas, the distribution of these archives of palaeobotanical diversity (Barber 1993) is representative enough to allow comparative study of regional vegetation history (Behre 1981; Bradshaw 1988). Pollen nomenclature follows Moore *et al.* (1991) adjusted to follow Stace (1991). Radiocarbon dating allows broad age correlation between diagrams, but in its absence similar pollen changes can be compared ecologically, but can not be assumed to be synchronous. All dates quoted in this chapter are in uncalibrated radiocarbon years before present (BP). Vegetation changes provide a sensitive measure of the rate and scale of variation in a range of environmental factors, some like climate operating as gradual processes over longer time periods and others occurring as rapid, even catastrophic, disturbance events.

Three main natural factors in combination have determined the past vegetation in the Mersey Basin: soils, climate and drainage. The highest parts of the Pennine watershed probably escaped ice cover, but the Mersey Basin was almost entirely occupied by either lowland ice sheets or upland glaciers during the maximum Devensian cold period around 18,000 years ago, wiping clean the vegetation record. Glaciation and periglacial processes have created drift and fluvioglacial deposits which include clays, fine and coarse sands and gravels (Johnson 1985). Centres of sand and gravel sediments within the clay drift plain are the Shirdley Hill Sands of south-west Lancashire and Merseyside, gravels in the river valleys of the Irwell and other rivers, and the sands of Delamere Forest and east Cheshire. Upon these diverse parent materials formed soils of differing textures and drainage (Kear 1985) and, spatially highly variable, these form the basis for diversity in natural and cultural vegetation patterns within the region (Innes & Tomlinson 1983, 1991). Impedance of drainage and the deflection of vegetation successions into wetland pathways (Shimwell 1985; Tallis 1991) added a further important element of diversity to the floral history. Altitudinal variation and its effect on soils and climate, and hence vegetation, is another major influence on natural vegetation patterns.

The vegetation history of the Mersey Basin is considered under four major categories: a) pre-Holocene vegetation communities, b) Holocene woodland communities, c) specialised Holocene vegetation communities, and d) woodland disturbance and post-woodland vegetation communities. The first represents the long pre-Holocene period (>c.10,000 BP) with mainly open vegetation under very cold climatic conditions of varying severity. The second examines the establishment of woodland communities during the ameliorating post-glacial climate of the early and mid Holocene (c.10,000 to c.5,000 BP). The third considers natural non-woodland vegetation such as wetland, coastal or moorland and the fourth examines the late-Holocene period (<c.5,000 BP) of woodland disturbance caused by man's increasingly severe impacts compounded by natural environmental degeneration, leading to the spread of various kinds of post-woodland vegetation across almost the entire region.

Pre-Holocene communities

Pre-Late-Devensian vegetation >c.15,000 BP

The temperate Holocene period is untypical of conditions during the great majority of the past several hundred thousand years, with glacial cold phases and cold adapted vegetation lasting much longer than brief temperate interglacials. Floras from interglacials predating the Devensian ice sheet have been reported from Staffordshire on the southern fringe of the region

(Worsley 1985). At Trysull deposits may be Hoxnian (c.240,000 BP), while probable Ipswichian (c.120,000 BP) peat at Four Ashes contained evidence for Oak (Quercus), Alder (Alnus), Hazel (Corylus), Yew (Taxus) and Holly (Ilex). From Oakwood Quarry near Chelford in Cheshire comes a pollen assemblage of terrestrial herbs reflecting a cold-climate, treeless landscape from the earlier stages of the Devensian glacial before the main ice advance. At Farm Wood Quarry, Chelford, organic sediments younger than the Oakwood deposits contained Pine

Mire sites of the Mersey Basin

1	Alt Mouth	Tooley 1978		39	Bagmere	Birks 1965a
2	Downholland Moss	Tooley 1978		40	Lindow Moss	Birks 1965b
3	Ince Blundell	Cowell & Innes 1994		41	Wybunbury Moss	Green & Pearson 1977
4	Sniggery Wood	Cowell & Innes 1994		42	Cranberry Moss	Tallis 1973
5	Flea Moss Wood	Cowell & Innes 1994		43	Peckforton Mere	Twigger 1983
6	Waterloo	Cowell & Innes 1994		44	Danes Moss	Birks 1962 unpub.
7	Rimrose Brook	Innes 1991		45	Congleton Moss	Leah et al. 1997
8	Moss Lake, Liverpool	Godwin 1959		46	Cock's Moss	Leah et al. 1997
9	Bidston Moss	Cowell & Innes 1994		47	Walker's Heath	Leah et al. 1997
10	Park Road, Meols	Cowell & Innes 1994		48	Mere Moss Wood	Leah et al. 1997
11	Newton Carr	Cowell & Innes 1994		49	Abbots Moss	Gray unpub.
12	Bull Lane, Aintree	Innes 1992		50	Whitemore, Bosley	Johnson et al. 1970
13	Simonswood Moss	Cowell & Innes 1994		51	Goyt Moss	Tallis 1964b
14	Knowsley Park	Cowell & Innes 1994		52	Wessenden	Tallis 1964b
15	Holiday Moss	Baxter 1983		53	Deep Clough	Tallis & McGuire 1972
16	Firswood Road	Tooley 1978		54	Snake Pass	Tallis 1964a
17	Bickerstaffe Moss	Kear 1968		55	Didsbury Intake	Tallis & Johnson 1980
18	Rainford Brook	Innes unpub.		56	Laddow Rocks	Tallis & Johnson 1980
19	Prescot	Cowell & Innes 1994		57	Bradwell Sitch	Tallis & Johnson 1980
20	Parr Moss	Cowell & Innes 1994		58	Charlesworth Landslips	Franks & Johnson 1964
21	Holland Moss	Cundill 1981		59	Seal Edge Coombes	Johnson et al. 1990
22	Reeds Moss	Baxter 1983		60	Lady Clough Moor	Tallis 1975
23	Mossborough Moss	Baxter 1983		61	Rishworth Moor	Bartley 1975
24	Skelmersdale	Baxter 1983		62	Tintwistle Knarr	Tallis & Switsur 1990
25	Haskayne	Baxter 1983		63	Robinson's Moss	Tallis & Switsur 1990
26	Bangor's Green	Baxter 1983		64	Alport Moor	Tallis & Switsur 1990
27	Berrington's Lane	Baxter 1983		65	Salvin Ridge	Tallis 1985
28	Red Moss	Hibbert et al. 1971		66	Featherbed Top	Tallis 1985
29	Hale	Baxter 1983		67	Featherbed Moss	Tallis & Switsur 1973
30	Helsby Marsh	Tooley 1978		68	Kinder	Tallis 1964a, 1964b
31	Ditton Brook	Innes unpub.		69	Bleaklow	Conway 1954
32	Risley Moss	Hibbert 1977		70	Soyland Moor	Williams 1985
33	Chat Moss	Birks 1964, 1965a		71	West Moss	Tallis & McGuire 1972
34	Nook Farm	Hall et al. 1995		72	Bar Mere	Schoenwetter 1982
35	Dunham Massey	Baxter 1983		73	Clieves Hills	Tooley 1978
36	Holcroft Moss	Birks 1965b		74	White Moss	Lageard 1992
37	Hatchmere	Birks unpub. 1975		75	Madeley	Yates & Moseley 1958
38	Flaxmere	Tallis 1973		76	Farm Wood, Chelford	Simpson & West 1958
				77	Oakwood Quarry, Chelford	Worsley 1985

Other mire sites mentioned in the text
78 Hoscar Moss (Cundill 1984), 79 Martin Mere (Tooley 1985a), 80 Extwistle Moor (Bartley & Chambers 1992), 81 Lismore Fields (Wiltshire & Edwards 1993)

Table 3.1. Names and major references for pollen analytical sites located on Figure 3.1.

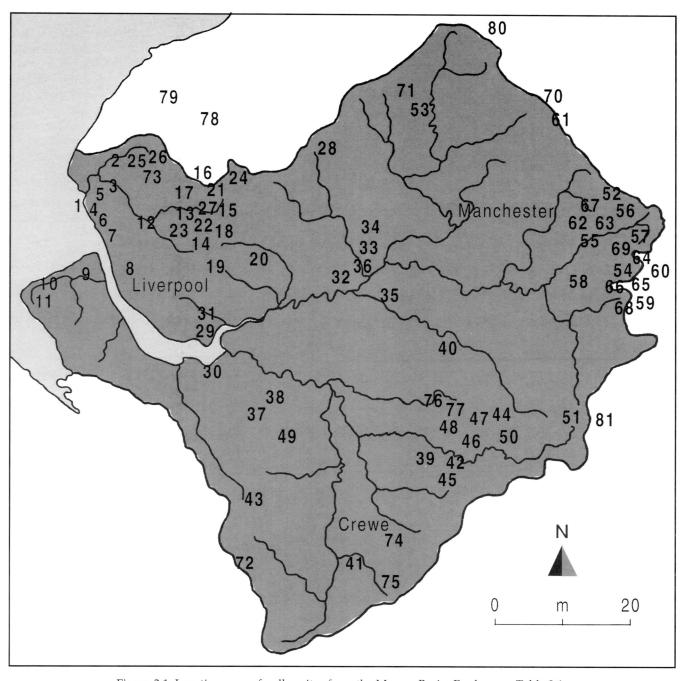

Figure 3.1. Location map of pollen sites from the Mersey Basin. For key see Table 3.1.

(*Pinus*), Spruce (*Picea*) and Birch (*Betula*) pollen and Spruce stumps, suggesting a briefly warmer climate with boreal woodland (Simpson & West 1958), radiocarbon dating suggesting a date older than 60,000 BP (Worsley 1985). Spruce is not native to Britain in the Holocene.

Late-Devensian vegetation *c.*15,000–*c.*10,000 BP

Soon after the retraction of ice cover around 15,000 BP pioneer polar desert vegetation of mosses and lichens and then turf and short herb communities with grasses (Poaceae), sedges (Cyperaceae), Clubmoss (*Lycopodium*), Dock (*Rumex*) and Mugwort (*Artemisia*) colonised the newly exposed ground surfaces (Pennington 1977),

together with a wide range of ruderal and specialised cold tolerant herbs like Rockrose (*Helianthemum*), Thrift (*Armeria*) and Goosefoot family (Chenopodiaceae). There were abundant habitats for aquatic herbs such as Alternate-flowered Water-milfoil (*Myriophyllum alterniflorum*). Rapidly changing successional vegetation characterised this initial period of environmental transition. Heath and dwarf shrub communities of Juniper (*Juniperus*), Crowberry (*Empetrum*), Dwarf Birch (*Betula nana*) and Willow (*Salix*) became established gradually, via tall herb associations, due to climatic amelioration after 13,000 BP (Walker *et al.* 1994), although herbs would still have been common as a more complete and diverse plant cover developed. In sheltered localities stands of tree birch developed and expanded until between 12,000 and 11,000 BP there was open Birch woodland in parts of the lowlands, with a rich tall herb field layer. At lowland sites like Bagmere and Chat Moss (Birks 1965a) and Moss Lake, Liverpool (Godwin 1959), mature Birch woodland did not develop in the Windermere (Allerød) interstadial between 12,000 and 11,000 BP, tree (mainly Birch) pollen reaching 25% of total pollen at most. Interstadial age pollen diagrams from beneath Shirdley Hill Sand east of Liverpool (e.g., Skelmersdale) and in north Cheshire (e.g. Dunham Massey) suggest very open herb and low shrub dominated vegetation and limited Birch woodland (Baxter 1983).

Climatic deterioration began about 12,500 BP, even as shrub and tree cover was spreading, culminating between 11,000 and 10,000 BP in the extremely cold late-glacial (Loch Lomond) stadial with unstable soils, during which tundra-type herb vegetation and Crowberry dwarf heath replaced the Juniper and Birch shrub woodland. Mugwort is characteristic of this zone, with grasses, sedges, Dock, Lesser Clubmoss (*Selaginella*) and many ruderal weed taxa. Peats beneath late-glacial coversand (Shirdley Hill Sand) reactivated at this time (Tooley 1978; Innes 1986), record pollen data of this age, as at Clieves Hills near Ormskirk at 10,455±110 BP. At higher altitude a channel at Whitemoor, Bosley (Johnson *et al.* 1970) is dominated by Dwarf Birch, grasses and sedges, with a rich herb flora including glacial taxa like Iceland-purslane (*Koenigia islandica*).

Holocene woodland communities

The development of early Holocene woodland c.10,000 – c.7,000 BP

Climatic amelioration at the end of the late-glacial swiftly replaced open ground tundra herb flora with a succession of transitional early Holocene communities. The classical pattern followed grass sward through tall herb associations with Dock, Crowberry dominated heath, Juniper shrub to Birch woodland of an increasingly closed nature. Willow and Aspen (*Populus*) were important initially until shaded out by tree Birches. Thermophilous herbs like Meadowsweet (*Filipendula*) were briefly abundant in the few centuries of warm climate before canopy closure. The immigration of forest taxa began with the arrival of Hazel, joining Birch as co-dominant, supplanting it in places, and creating a denser canopy which suppressed Juniper, Willow and the lower elements of the transitional flora. The timing of the great increase of Hazel pollen, which may include pollen of Bog-myrtle (*Myrica*), varies but the Hatchmere date of 9,580±140 BP (Switsur & West 1975) is probably representative for much of the lowlands. At White Moss in south-east Cheshire (Lageard 1992) the Hazel pollen rise occurs rather later, between 9,230±85 BP and 8,625±50 BP, with percentages of more than 25% by the latter date. Thermophilous trees Elm (*Ulmus*) and Oak, migrated into the area after 9,000 BP, out-competing Birch on the better soils, although the timing of their introduction

varies from site to site. The major regional palaeobotanical event of mid-Flandrian I, however, was the spread of Pine, delaying the expansion of the broadleaf forest trees. It is difficult to assess the abundance of Pine before this spread. At White Moss Lageard (1992) showed that although large quantities of sub-fossil Pine wood were discovered during peat extraction, Pine pollen rarely exceeded 20% of the total pollen count. Low Pine pollen counts need not mean the absence of pinewoods, but it seems likely that high Pine counts must mean that the tree was locally common, and on this basis there seems to have been a diachronous spread of Pine in the Mersey Basin. At White Moss on sandy soils, Pine woodland became established at 8,625±50 BP and Pine remained common in the region until about 6,000 BP. On Shirdley Hill Sand at Knowsley Park Moss a similar early date for the Pine pollen rise of 8,880±90 BP occurred (Cowell & Innes 1994). Pine dominance was delayed on heavier clay soils, however, as at Red Moss (Hibbert *et al.* 1971) at 8196±150 BP, but other long pollen records suggest that eventual Pine abundance occurred everywhere in the region (e.g., Wybunbury Moss, Green & Pearson 1977). Pine tolerates a wide range of soil types and was not supplanted by deciduous trees until the rise of Alder and climatic and successional changes at the start of mid-Holocene Flandrian II. Although Pine persisted in some favourable areas these processes culminated with its exclusion from regional forests due to competition from broadleaved trees.

The establishment of mid-Holocene forest c.7,000 – c.5,000 BP

The optimum temperature and rainfall conditions of the mid-Holocene favoured the maximum extension of tree growth in the region. In contrast to the immigration of tree taxa in the earlier Holocene, once established the stable forest ecosystem of Flandrian II offered few opportunities for new tree species and was an almost steady state, highly stable community. It was not unchanging, for even if a long term stable 'climax' situation had been reached there was still change going on within the forest community mosaic, if only very slowly, with senescent individuals being naturally replaced by new plants and successions being set in motion. A mature, long established and undisturbed woodland may seem unchanging, but in reality the spatial distribution of woodland components must change due to individual plant mortality so that while the community structure is maintained, the distribution of different tree species and stands will gradually alter. The thermophilous Lime (*Tilia*) achieved maximum expansion during Flandrian II and was common in lowland areas, even co-dominant with Oak and Elm in places, although in the Mersey Basin it was unlikely to have been the major deciduous tree (Greig 1982). It was certainly more common than the poor representation its low pollen production affords it on pollen diagrams. The deciduous forest extended almost to the highest altitudes (Tallis & Switsur 1983, 1990), with no real altitudinal gradients in taxa abundance. Hazel, likely to be more successful if the forest canopy were more open on higher ground, shows similarly high values on the watershed (Robinson's Moss) and on lowland sandy soils (Wybunbury Moss). On heavier soils (Holcroft Moss and Lindow Moss, Birks 1965b) Hazel values tend to be lower. Site factors seem to have been generally more important than altitude.

The defining feature of Flandrian II is the rise to high pollen frequencies of Alder which occurred about 7,000 BP (7,107±120, Red Moss, Hibbert *et al.* 1971; 7403±114, Hatchmere, Switsur & West 1975), although there was considerable variation between sites (Bennett & Birks 1990), for example at White Moss where the Alder rise was delayed until 5,890±45 BP (Lageard 1992). Even allowing for its high pollen productivity, it must have been a very common tree and was favoured by the humid, oceanic conditions of the climatic optimum, seemingly replacing Pine directly in many cases. Abundant around water bodies such as the channel deposit at Whitemoor, Bosley (Johnson *et al.* 1970), and in river valleys flood plains such as the River Alt at Ince Blundell (Cowell & Innes 1994), it must also have found favourable habitats throughout the damp closed canopy forest. The more representative extra-local and regional pollen rain observed from the centres of some large raised bogs or lakes (Wybunbury Moss, Green & Pearson 1977; Holcroft Moss, Birks 1965b), or from the blanket peats near the Pennine watershed (Alport Moor, Tallis 1991) contains Oak and Alder pollen in similar proportions, as do sites from the sandy coastal plain away from centres of Alder carr growth (Sniggery Wood, Innes & Tooley 1993).

The establishment of Alder and Lime completed the assembly of the natural climax post-glacial mixed Oak forest. Site conditions, mainly edaphic factors, decided the relative importance of the components of this forested ecosystem but in most situations across the study area considerable homogeneity existed, with limited regional variability. At all sites Oak, Alder and Hazel were commonest, and most clearly so at higher altitudes, with Elm a lesser but very important member of the deciduous forest community, rivalling Oak on better soils. Ash (*Fraxinus*) was present from early times but was rare until the more open woods of later Flandrian II, being unable to supplant the other mixed Oak forest trees until the inertia of the primary forest was broken, mainly by disturbance.

In a few favourable areas Pine remained common, as on light sandy soils near the coast, on fluvioglacial outwash or shallow accumulating peats (Lageard 1992) and in some high altitude locations like the Bradwell Sitch landslip site in upper Longdendale (Tallis & Johnson 1980). In some cases Pine's replacement by deciduous trees, often Alder, was merely delayed into the first half of Flandrian II, as at White Moss where the major decline of Pine occurred at 5,890±45 BP. On a few nutrient poor sites, or where fire was a common factor, Pine remained locally important into the later Holocene.

Late-Holocene woodland (<*c.*5,000 BP)

It is difficult to evaluate any natural developments which took place in the late Holocene, Flandrian III, woodlands of the Mersey Basin, as the vegetation history of this more recent period has been so heavily influenced by the activities of man. Natural climatic and edaphic changes did occur, however, which caused woodland composition changes. Major climatic deterioration around 4,000 BP appears to have caused the final displacement of Pine from its last refuges in marginal, low nutrient locations (Bennett 1984; Gear & Huntley 1991). During Flandrian III there are pollen records from several sites (e.g., Red Moss, Hibbert *et al.* 1971), some at quite high altitudes (e.g., Franks & Johnson 1964), for the arrival of Beech (*Fagus*) and Hornbeam (*Carpinus*) in the region in low numbers, these trees being more suited to conditions well to the south. Human disturbance would have assisted their immigration and the spread of other secondary trees like Ash and Birch. At varying times around *c.*3,500 BP, Lime became much less important in the regional woodlands. This will have been due partly to climatic degeneration (Lamb 1981) during the late-Holocene, and partly as the result of human activity (Turner 1962).

Macrofossil evidence of the former forest

Although only preserved in exceptional circumstances of rapid burial by sand, alluvium or peat, sub-fossil tree stumps and trunks can be used as an indication of the former forest's extent or structure and can be used to test the conclusions reached from pollen analysis. Oak and Pine appear to have been the main taxa which colonised marginal environments throughout the region in the mid and late Holocene. Their remains are common in and beneath upland (Tallis & Switsur 1983, 1990), coastal (Kenna 1986; Pye & Neal 1993) and inland mossland (Lageard *et al.* 1995) peats. Three-dimensional recording of Pine stumps at White Moss has shown that the colonisation and demise of trees on peat sites was a protracted and complex process and not a simple single phase event. While not representative of regional dryland forest communities, sub-fossil tree remains may prove to be an important source of data on prehistoric woodland structure and ecology in the Mersey Basin.

Specialised Holocene communities

Wetland vegetation

The closed mid-Holocene forest contained few areas of open vegetation and floral diversity. Exceptions were the coastal intertidal zone, exposed locations above the tree line in the Pennines and areas where fire or other disturbance initiated successional communities. Wetlands also added a major element of long-term diversity to the vegetation mosaic. Although the distribution of surviving wetlands in the Mersey Basin suggests only a localised presence (Shimwell 1985; Howard-Davis *et al.* 1988; Hall *et al.* 1995), before systematic modern drainage wetlands of many kinds would have been widespread, controlled by climate and by local topographical and hydrological factors, each supporting different wetland plant communities (Moore *et al*. 1984). Hydroseral succession through open water aquatic, reedswamp, fen, fen-carr and fenwood vegetation (Walker 1970; Rodwell 1991) would have started at different times and proceeded at different rates in each location, creating a mosaic of wetlands at different stages of succession at any one time.

The final stage in vegetation succession for many basin wetlands would have been to mossland bog due to falling nutrient levels and increasing acidity, although recent surveys of mire stratigraphy (Wells 1992; Wells *et al*. 1993) suggest that ombrotrophic raised bog with an acid tolerant flora dominated by Bogmoss (*Sphagnum*) was not always reached. Many successions remained as intermediate mire systems, often growing together over shallow slopes from several centres, characterised by a less acid Cottongrass (*Eriophorum*) community (Hall & Folland 1970). Valley mires and river flood plain mires which were minerotrophic were maintained as mesotrophic fen and fen-carr systems, often dominated by Alder. The Gowy valley in Cheshire is a good example of long term persistence of fen-reedswamp wetland vegetation (Shimwell 1985) but before human drainage and clearance most of the lower parts of the region's watercourses would have been similar. Superabundance of Alder pollen in diagrams from such sites is common, as in the valley of the Rimrose Brook near Liverpool (Innes 1991) or at Ince Blundell in the Alt valley (Cowell & Innes 1994) where it maintains values of 80% of total pollen for thousands of years. Dense fen woodland was a long term feature of the region's coastal and mere fringe vegetation (Lageard 1992). Human clearance of the riverine Alder fen-carr and fenwood in later prehistoric and early historic times would have led to the establishment of flood plain grassland of a type determined by both hydrology and management, being maintained by grazing and adapted to inundation, both natural and due to run off effects of human activity in the catchment. Systematic drainage in the historic period has greatly impoverished the floral diversity provided by wetland habitats, probably causing the regional extinction of some wetland plants, e.g., Rannoch-rush (*Scheuchzeria palustris*) (Tallis & Birks 1965).

Coastal vegetation

The coastal zone is a transitional area of natural plant diversity, and was much more so in the past than today, when almost all the coastal wetlands have been reclaimed for agriculture and industry. Sea-level rise since deglaciation (Tooley 1978, 1985a, 1985b; Plater *et al*. 1993) established the coast near its present position by the mid-Holocene. Subsequent minor coastal changes have caused some spatial relocation of the associated plant communities.

A suite of wetland environments and vegetation types may be recognised (Tooley 1978) which have a seral relationship based upon salinity tolerance and altitude relative to tide level. Most specialised are intertidal environments in which halophyte plants are characteristic, some open ground herbs like Thrift (*Armeria*), Sea Plantain (*Plantago maritima*) and Chenopodiaceae finding favourable habitats denied to them across the landscape as a whole since the demise of the late-glacial tundra communities. The zonation of low, mid and high saltmarsh communities above the unvegetated sand and mudflat can show a complex spatial arrangement due to local intertidal topography (Shennan 1992). Halophytes of the Chenopodiaceae and Caryophyllaceae families, with Thrift and saltmarsh grasses, dominate the low salt-marsh. In the high saltmarsh less often inundated by the tide near the transition to brackish and freshwater conditions, less halophyte taxa like Lesser Bullrush (*Typha angustifolia*) dominate.

In areas of the coastal lowland above high tide the elevation of groundwater tables caused the formation of a zone of freshwater wetland environments between the higher dryland and the intertidal zone, comprising lagoons, marshes, swamps, fens and meres. This perimarine freshwater zone (Tooley 1978) supported extremely rich and diverse eutrophic successional aquatic, reedswamp, fen and carr communities (Lind 1949; Rodwell 1991), accepting nutrient rich drainage from the hillslopes inland. Many small meres came into existence, some ephemeral as a result of seasonal flooding, and although several such as Martin Mere (Tooley 1978, 1985a) became permanent features in the landscape, all were subject to rapid water level changes which caused fluctuations in their wetland vegetation type. Changes in sea level or breaching of coastal barriers often replaced this freshwater ecosystem with intertidal floras, as at Helsby Marsh and Downholland Moss (Tooley 1978), or at Ince Blundell, Crosby or Park Road, Meols (Cowell & Innes 1994). Coastal wetland vegetation has also been subject to alteration by human activity (Jones 1988; Jones *et al*. 1993) even before the modern severe drainage of most of the perimarine zone and the grazing of saltmarshes. Fire was a factor from early times and charcoal is present in many of the sediments, as at Downholland Moss (Tooley 1978) and Formby Moss (Wells 1992), particularly those of the reedswamp phase.

Blown sand dunes form a third major coastal environment, and support specialised vegetation communities (Carter 1988), originating around Liverpool Bay between 5,000 and 4,000 years ago after the stabilisation and then temporary regression of sea level (Innes & Tooley 1993; Pye & Neal 1993). The dune barriers have undergone periods of relative stability and instability since then, with wetland dune slack vegetation forming during the former and sand overblowing fringing perimarine wetlands during the latter, for example burying the westward edge of Downholland Moss at 4,090±170 BP (Tooley 1978). Distinctive dry and wet dune slack pollen floras have been recorded by O'Garra (1976) analogous to pollen data from fossil slack deposits at Lifeboat Road, Formby (Innes & Tooley 1993) and characterised by taxa like Sea-milkwort (*Glaux maritima*), Sea-buckthorn (*Hippophaë rhamnoides*), Juniper and Willow.

Heather (*Calluna vulgaris*) and Pine were common on the sandy dune fringe soils.

Heath, moorland and grassland vegetation

Heathlands and moorlands form specialised low stature vegetation communities dominated by dwarf shrubs of the heath family (Ericaceae), as well as grasses and sedges. In the Mersey Basin dry heathlands are a lowland feature (Gimingham 1972), with conditions in the cooler, wetter uplands leading to the formation of blanket mire (Chambers 1988; Moore 1988), or wet moorland with Heather and Bracken (*Pteridium aquilinum*). Crowberry heath was the dominant vegetation during colder periods of the late-glacial with less stable soils, particularly during transitional phases between open ground tundra communities and scrub woodland (Walker *et al.* 1994). The Holocene spread of closed forest over almost the entire region severely restricted the habitat of heath and moor vegetation but it is likely that soils formed on sand and gravel in Cheshire (Tallis 1973; Reynolds 1979) and north of the River Mersey (Kear 1985) maintained some heathland during the Holocene. At Knowsley Park (Cowell & Innes 1994) on the Shirdley Hill Sand of Merseyside high Crowberry pollen counts persist until about 8,650 BP, after which a continuous high Heather curve occurs throughout the rest of the Holocene. Although its composition changed, heath vegetation was able to coexist with the Holocene woodland on sandy soils as an understorey but perhaps also as climax vegetation in places. Coastal blown sand also provided refuge habitats for heath associations, as at Sniggery Wood, Sefton (Cowell & Innes 1994), and almost all of the region's lowland bogs were colonised by Heather during their drier phases from at least Flandrian II onwards. Crowberry also colonised dry bog surfaces in the later Holocene (Wybunbury Moss, Green & Pearson 1977). The survival inland of dry heath probably depended on the recurrence of fire (Wells 1992), as well as the promotion of acidification and paludification by human activity (Dimbleby 1962).

The key vegetational feature in the Mersey Basin uplands was the spread of blanket peat and Heather moor, reviewed by Tallis (1991), replacing the previously existing woodland. In places peat moor began to form in the mid-Holocene, perhaps after woodland fire disturbance (Simmons & Innes 1985), but the major expansion of Heather moor took place about 4,000 BP (Rishworth Moor, Bartley 1975; Bradwell Sitch, Tallis & Johnson 1980) probably as a response to climatic and soil deterioration (Birks 1988). Human activity (Bartley & Chambers 1992) would have accelerated the process.

Woodland disturbance and post-woodland communities

Disturbed soils

Soil instability after natural environmental disturbance was important allowing the survival of ruderal weed and early seral dryland communities within the Holocene closed forest. Landslides were an important source of such disturbance in both the late-glacial cold phase (Johnson *et al.* 1990), and throughout the Holocene (Tallis & Johnson 1980). Land subsidence due to underground salt solution (Reynolds 1979), tree windthrow after severe storms or sand dune mobilisation would have led to similar seral vegetation. Sand formations like the Shirdley Hill Sands remained naturally unstable well into the early Holocene after their main deposition in the late-glacial cold phase (Tooley 1978; Innes 1986). Innes *et al.* (1989) have described a peat lens with a tundra weed pollen flora within Shirdley Hill Sand at Holiday Moss, dated to 9,120±60 BP, when on clay soils at nearby Red Moss (Hibbert *et al.* 1971) closed Birch and Pine woodland with some Hazel was well established. In the earlier Holocene, coversands provided reservoirs of floral diversity which contrasted strongly with the forests which colonised the rest of the region. By the mid Holocene the sands supported open woodland and heathland.

Throughout the Mersey Basin in the later Holocene, cultural vegetation disturbance became by far the most common cause of soil instability and erosion and the creation of open ground habitats. Lowland mosses contain inwash stripes of eroded soil which are evidence of catchment devegetation, as at Peckforton Mere and Bar Mere (Twigger 1983) by the mid-Cheshire ridge, where much of the Iron Age and Roman period soil was eroded and redeposited, with major floral changes. Mid-Holocene woodland disturbance caused reworking of Shirdley Hill Sand (Tooley 1978; Innes 1992), promoting a scrub, heath and grassland flora. In the uplands at Deep Clough (Tallis & McGuire 1972) in Bronze Age and later times heavy erosion of catchment soils occurred. The promotion of post disturbance ruderal weed and regeneration associations is a key feature of late Holocene vegetation history.

Fire disturbance

Fire was a potent instrument of ecological change, deflecting vegetation successions, increasing plant diversity and changing vegetation patterns. Whether employed by humans or due to natural events such as lightning strike, fire was a major environmental force throughout the Holocene and was also present in earlier periods. Indeed, fire was an integral part of vegetation evolution over a very long time period and some plant taxa and associations are highly favoured by it, while occasional low intensity burning promotes most plant communities' regeneration and health.

Fire was a consistent factor in the vegetation history of the Mersey Basin, as both macro- and microscopic charcoal are preserved in sediments of all ages from all parts of the region. Abundant conifer charcoal occurred as long ago as 60,000 BP at Chelford, presumably due to natural fire and probably changing Spruce to Pine woodland (Simpson & West 1958). Microscopic charcoal particles occur in peats from the earliest Holocene onwards and often show an increased concentration at horizons where major vegetation changes occur. They may reflect longer distance transport and so measure the regularity of extra-local or regional burning. Macroscopic charcoal layers also occur, presumably due to higher intensity fires or burning very close to the sediment site (Cundill 1981). Fire probably caused major changes, particularly where pollen evidence suggests an abrupt decline of tree taxa, as at many lowland sites like Simonswood Moss (Cowell & Innes 1994) and Walkers Heath (Leah *et al.* 1997), and in the uplands as at Lady Clough Moor (Tallis 1975).

The botanical effects of fire in established woodland are to replace trees with a range of transitional habitats and successional vegetation communities. Newly open ground is rapidly colonised by pioneer weeds and ruderals, some like Cow-wheat (*Melampyrum*) and Bracken strongly responsive to post-fire conditions. Shrubs, particularly Hazel, are greatly favoured because of increased access to sunlight as members of the woodland edge community around the margins of the clearing or as part of the secondary regeneration community on the cleared area itself. Eventual regeneration of tree cover suppresses the heliophyte successional taxa. Long term alteration in woodland structure may occur, with secondary forest trees like Ash and Birch replacing primary deciduous taxa. While the effects of a single fire may appear ephemeral, the cumulative effects of many such events over millennia, as is suggested by the charcoal record from the Mersey Basin, may have been quite profound. Simmons & Innes (1985) discussed the degenerative potential of repetitive disturbance in the spread of bog and moorland, at least at altitude. A more positive consequence during the mid-Holocene may have been the replacement of steady state homogeneous deciduous forest by a mosaic structure with tracts of primary forest, areas of more open secondary woodland and patches of seral communities at various stages of regeneration, creating local centres of diversity and species richness. While individual patches would regenerate, the creation of new open areas would have maintained the mosaic structure and the overall balanced pattern of the forest.

The Elm decline

Despite intensive study the decline in Elm pollen frequencies which occurred *c.*5,000 years BP, although later in the upland (Robinson's Moss 4,875±60, Tallis & Switsur 1990) than the lowland (Knowsley Park Moss 5,290±80, Cowell & Innes 1994), remains an enigmatic feature of the Holocene pollen record. While an earlier or 'primary' Elm Decline was recognised on a few pollen diagrams (Rishworth Moor, 5,490±140, Bartley 1975) in which little but the fall in Elm pollen occurs, most Elm Declines from the Mersey Basin are accompanied by other pollen changes which indicate woodland opening. Other tree taxa also decline and weed and shrub pollen increase. This woodland clearance or 'landnam' phase implicates human activity as a likely cause. In some cases cereal pollen (Cowell & Innes 1994) or charcoal (Cundill 1984) also occur but usually indicators are restricted to

plants of grassy clearings like Poaceae, Ribwort Plantain (*Plantago lanceolata*) and Bracken. Woodland management practices, like stripping and lopping of Elm branches for foddering of stock, could have had the effect of reducing Elm pollen frequencies by reducing flowering, and once opened the woodland could have been kept open as long as beasts were herded there. Perry & Moore (1987) showed that pollen changes very like those of the Elm Decline, including a rise in Ribwort Plantain and other weeds, took place after the modern death and fall of Elms killed by disease. Disease may have caused many of the examples of Elm pollen reduction in the Mersey Basin, in places combined with human activity, and with other factors like climate change and soil deterioration of lesser importance. Whatever its cause the Elm Decline heralded real vegetation changes. The forest seems to have become less dense and secondary trees like Ash, Birch and Hazel more important.

The anthropogenic phase

Although human disturbance of woodland occurred prior to the Elm Decline, it is man's subsequent development of agricultural food production that defines the succeeding anthropogenic phase, during which the environmental results of forest clearance and the maintenance of cultural sub-climax vegetation became the dominant features of vegetation history. The history of human settlement, forest clearance and agriculture will be considered in detail by Cowell (chapter four, this volume) and so this section is restricted to a brief examination of the kind of vegetation change produced by this activity.

Forest clearance and pastoralism

Forest opening occurred in late Flandrian II and the earlier part of Flandrian III, presumably due to the agricultural activity of Neolithic and Bronze Age people. Many episodes of clearance lack cereal pollen and while negative evidence is inconclusive, cereal pollen being poorly transported and of low productivity, much of earlier prehistoric agriculture may have been pastoral, involving exploitation of a managed woodland ecosystem which included pollarding and coppicing of selected trees. The creation of grassy clearings in the woodland produces a classic 'landnam' pollen signature, with a fall in primary tree pollen like Elm and Oak, increased grass pollen and the appearance of Ribwort Plantain, encouraged by grazing and trampling by stock. Regeneration of a more open woodland with Ash, Birch and Hazel follows relaxation of grazing pressure, with Heather or Bracken colonisation in areas of poorer soils. A cycle of limited woodland opening then regeneration without cereal cultivation is familiar from the heavier clay soils of the region, as in the Bronze Age at Parr Moss, St Helens (Cowell & Innes 1994). The impact was greater in the upland, and pollen from Bronze Age soils sealed beneath barrows in the Rossendales (Tallis & McGuire 1972) shows a post clearance vegetation with some heathland on acidifying soils.

Arable cultivation

The vegetational effects of arable cultivation are very significant in that crop cultivation promotes land clearance and the spread of open ground, yet includes a tendency towards reduced vegetation diversity through the selection of a limited number of preferred food plants, so that in its later more intensive forms it aims towards areas of land maintained as almost monocultural climax vegetation. This was unachievable before modern times, and in later prehistoric periods arable land-use led to specialised diverse herbaceous associations of a kind not seen since late-glacial tundra communities. Localised cereal cultivation may have been present in the Mersey Basin since the earliest Neolithic, as cereal type pollen grains have been recorded several centuries before the dates for the Elm Decline. Although wild grasses with pollen of cereal type have been present throughout the Holocene, these early examples cluster around 5,800 BP (Cowell & Innes 1994; Williams 1985; Wiltshire & Edwards 1993) within well-defined forest clearance episodes.

The pollen data suggest that arable cultivation provided habitats for many more weeds of broken ground and ruderal conditions than did pastoralism. Even in the Neolithic, on favourable soils such as the sandstone fringing Prescot Moss about 4,520 BP (Innes & Tomlinson 1995) the weed assemblage moves beyond the Ribwort Plantain dominated grassland group and includes many which later came to be classified as arable indicators, including Dock, Mugwort, Common Knapweed (*Centaurea nigra*), Goosefoot family, Thistle (*Cirsium*), Greater and Hoary Plantains (*Plantago major* and *P. media*), Mayweed (*Matricaria*)-type and Chickweeds (*Stellaria* spp.). This arable community is well illustrated in Cheshire in the Iron Age pollen spectra from Lindow Moss (Oldfield *et al.* 1986; Branch & Scaife 1995), and on the sandstone ridges around Bar Mere and Peckforton Mere (Twigger 1983) where major replacement of oakwoods by cultivation occurred. Later crop plants diversified from Wheat and Barley (*Triticum/ Hordeum*) types into other cereals such as Oat (*Avena*) and Rye (*Secale*), and other crops such as Hemp (*Cannabis sativa*), Flax (*Linum usitatissimum*) and Broad Bean (*Vicia faba*), and crop weeds which had earlier occurred sporadically, such as Cornflower (*Centaurea cyanus*), Corn Spurrey (*Spergula arvensis*), Knotgrass (*Polygonum aviculare*) and spurges (*Euphorbia*), become more common. Arable communities declined between Roman times and the Norman Conquest. One aspect of arable agriculture which promoted vegetation diversity was the creation of fields and their boundaries to keep stock from the valuable crop. Shrubs such as Holly (*Ilex*), Hawthorn (*Crataegus*), Blackthorn (*Prunus*) and others, which could be hedge taxa, often increase during arable pollen phases.

Conclusions

Significant elements of floristic diversity were present in the Mersey Basin before major human disturbance of ecosystems occurred in the later Holocene. Altitude, geology and soil variations encouraged differing patterns of natural vegetation across the region even in pre-Holocene times, and the increasingly severe human effects were superimposed upon a landscape already a complex mosaic of vegetation communities. Some areas like the mere and mire landscape of Cheshire were floristically very rich and are important on a more than regional basis, requiring more detailed research. Concentration is needed in parts of the region which have few pollen records (Figure 3.1), and the systematic work of the North West Wetlands Survey should identify sites of high potential here and elsewhere. The present record relies on a few researchers to whom a great vote of thanks is owed, but who naturally focused upon their own research areas. A more even distribution of data is required from which to plan future work. Where sediment distribution allows, past time periods for which little botanical information exists should receive closer attention in future.

Acknowledgements

We thank Colin Wells and Elizabeth Huckerby (North West Wetlands Survey) for making unpublished data available. JGAL acknowledges the support of a NERC research studentship, grants from Cheshire County Council and the British Ecological Society (Small Ecological Project Grant No. 1145). Vicki Innes produced the manuscript. Figure 3.1 was drawn in the Department of Geography, University of Durham.

Dedication

This paper is dedicated to the memory of Elizabeth Emma Innes.

References

Barber, K.E. (1993). Peatlands as scientific archives of past biodiversity. *Biodiversity and Conservation*, **2**, 474–89.

Bartley, D.D. & Chambers, C. (1992). A pollen diagram, radiocarbon ages and evidence of agriculture on Extwistle Moor, Lancashire. *New Phytologist*, **121**, 311–20.

Bartley, D.D. (1975). Pollen analytical evidence for prehistoric forest clearance in the upland area west of Rishworth, West Yorkshire. *New Phytologist*, **74**, 375–81.

Baxter, J. (1983). *Vegetation History of the Shirdley Hill Sand in Southwest Lancashire*. PhD thesis. U.C.W. Aberystwyth.

Behre, K-E. (1981). The interpretation of anthropogenic indicators in pollen diagrams. *Pollen et Spores*, **23**, 225–45.

Bennett, K.D. & Birks, H.J.B. (1990). Postglacial history of Alder (*Alnus glutinosa* (L.) Gaertn.) in the British Isles. *Journal of Quaternary Science*, **5**, 123–33.

Bennett, K.D. (1984). The Postglacial history of *Pinus sylvestris* in the British Isles. *Quaternary Science Reviews*, **3**, 133–55.

Birks, H.J.B. (1964). Chat Moss, Lancashire. *Memoirs and Proceedings of the Manchester Literary and Philosophical Society*, **106**, 1–24.

Birks, H.J.B. (1965a). Late-Glacial deposits at Bagmere, Cheshire and Chat Moss, Lancashire. *New Phytologist*, **64**, 270–75.

Birks, H.J.B. (1965b). Pollen analytical investigations at Holcroft Moss, Lancashire and Lindow Moss, Cheshire. *Journal of Ecology*, **53**, 299–314.

Birks, H.J.B. (1988). Long term ecological change in the British uplands. *Ecological Change in the Uplands* (eds M.B. Usher & D.B.A. Thompson), pp. 37–56, Blackwell, Oxford.

Bradshaw, R.H.W. (1988). Spatially-precise studies of forest dynamics. *Vegetation History* (eds B. Huntley & T. Webb III), pp. 725–51, Kluwer Academic Publishers, Dordrecht Netherlands.

Branch, N.P. & Scaife, R.G. (1995). The stratigraphy and pollen analysis of peat sequences associated with the Lindow III bog body. *Bog Bodies: New Discoveries and New Perspectives* (eds R.C. Turner & R.G. Scaife), pp. 19–30. British Museum Press, London.

Carter, R.W.G. (1988). *Coastal Environments*. Academic Press, London.

Chambers, F.M. (1988). Archaeology and the flora of the British Isles: the moorland experience. *Archaeology and the Flora of the British Isles* (ed. M. Jones) pp. 107–15, Oxford University Committee for Archaeology Monograph 14, Oxford.

Conway, V.M. (1954). Stratigraphy and pollen analysis of southern Pennine blanket peats. *Journal of Ecology*, **42**, 117–47.

Cowell, R. & Innes, J.B. (1994). *The Wetlands of Merseyside*. North West Wetlands Survey **1**. Lancaster Imprints **2**, Lancaster.

Cundill, P.R. (1981). The history of vegetation and land use of two peat mosses in south-west Lancashire. *The Manchester Geographer*, **2**, 35–44.

Cundill, P.R. (1984). Palaeobotany and archaeology on Merseyside: additional evidence. *Circaea*, **2**, 129–31.

Dimbleby, G.W. (1962). *The Development of British Heathlands and their Soils*. Oxford Forestry Memoirs 23.

Franks, J.W. & Johnson, R.H. (1964). Pollen analytical dating of a Derbyshire landslip: the Cown Edge Landslides, Charlesworth. *New Phytologist*, **63**, 209–16.

Gear, A.J. & Huntley, B. (1991). Rapid changes in the range limits of Scots pine 4000 years ago. *Science*, **251**, 544–47.

Gimingham, C.H. (1972). *Ecology of Heathlands*. Chapman & Hall, London.

Godwin, H. (1959). Studies in the Postglacial history of British vegetation. XIV. Late Glacial deposits at Moss Lake, Liverpool. *Philosophical Transactions of the Royal Society of London B*, **242**, 127–49.

Green, B.H. & Pearson, M.C. (1977). The ecology of Wybunbury Moss, Cheshire II. Post-Glacial history and the formation of the Cheshire mere and mire landscape. *Journal of Ecology*, **65**, 793–814.

Greig, J. (1982). Past and present limewoods of Europe. *Archaeological Aspects of Woodland Ecology* (eds M. Bell & S. Limbrey), pp. 23–55. British Archaeological Reports International Series, 146, Oxford.

Hall, B.R. & Folland, C.J. (1970). *Soils of Lancashire*. Memoirs of the Soil Survey of Great Britain 5, Harpenden.

Hall, D., Wells, C.E. & Huckerby, E. (1995). *The Wetlands of Greater Manchester*. North West Wetlands Survey **2**. Lancaster Imprints **3**, Lancaster.

Hibbert, F.A., Switsur, V.R. & West, R.G. (1971). Radiocarbon dating of Flandrian pollen zones at Red Moss, Lancashire. *Proceedings of the Royal Society of London B*, **177**, 161–76.

Howard-Davis C., Stocks C. & Innes, J.B. (1988). *Peat and the Past. A Survey and Assessment of the Prehistory of the Lowland Wetlands of North-West England*. English Heritage and Lancaster University, Lancaster.

Innes, J.B. (1986). The history of the Shirdley Hill Sand revealed by examination of associated organic deposits. *Proceedings of the North of England Soils Discussion Group*, **21**, 31–43.

Innes, J.B. (1991). A preliminary report on pollen analyses from Rimrose Brook. *An Archaeological Assessment of the Rimrose Valley, Sefton* (eds R.W. Cowell & S.M. Nicholson), pp. 3–4. Liverpool Museum, Liverpool.

Innes, J.B. (1992). Pollen analysis of a radiocarbon dated peat bed within Shirdley Hill sand at Aintree, Merseyside. *The Manchester Geographer*, **11**, 44–51.

Innes, J B. & Tooley, M.J. (1993). The Age and Vegetational History of the Sefton Coast Dunes. *The Sand Dunes of the Sefton Coast* (eds D. Atkinson & J. Houston), pp. 35–40. National Museums & Galleries on Merseyside in association with Sefton Metropolitan Borough Council, Liverpool.

Innes, J.B. & Tomlinson, P.R. (1983). An approach to palaeobotany and survey archaeology in Merseyside. *Circaea*, **1**, 83–93.

Innes, J.B. & Tomlinson, P.R. (1991). Environmental Archaeology in Merseyside. *Journal of the Merseyside Archaeological Society*, **7**, 1–20.

Innes, J.B. & Tomlinson, P.R. (1995). Radiocarbon dates from Warrington Road, Prescot. *Journal of the Merseyside Archaeological Society*, **9**, 61–4.

Innes, J.B., Tooley, M.J. & Tomlinson, P.R. (1989). A comparison of the age and palaeoecology of some sub-Shirdley Hill Sand peat deposits from Merseyside and south-west Lancashire. *Naturalist*, **114**, 65–9.

Johnson, R.H. (1985). The imprint of glaciation on the west Pennine uplands. *The Geomorphology of North-west England* (ed. R.H. Johnson), pp. 237–62. Manchester University Press, Manchester.

Johnson, R.H., Franks, J.W. & Pollard, J.E. (1970). Some Holocene faunal and floral remains in the Whitemoor meltwater channel at Bosley, east Cheshire. *North Staffordshire Journal of Field Studies*, **10**, 65–74.

Johnson, R.H., Tallis, J.H. & Wilson, P. (1990). The Seal Edge Coombes, north Derbyshire – a study of their erosional and depositional history. *Journal of Quaternary Science*, **5**, 83–94.

Jones, C.R., Houston, J.A. & Bateman, D. (1993). A history of human influence on the coastal landscape. *The Sand Dunes of the Sefton Coast* (eds D. Atkinson & J. Houston), pp. 3–20. National Museums & Galleries on Merseyside in association with Sefton Metropolitan Borough Council, Liverpool.

Jones, R.L. (1988). The impact of early man on coastal plant communities in the British Isles. *Archaeology and the Flora of the British Isles* (ed. M. Jones) pp. 96–106. Oxford University Committee for Archaeology Monograph 14, Oxford.

Kear, B.S. (1968). *An investigation into soils developed on the Shirdley Hill Sand in south-west Lancashire*. MSc thesis, University of Manchester.

Kear, B.S. (1985). Soil development and soil patterns in north-west England. *The Geomorphology of North-west England* (ed. R.H. Johnson), pp. 80–93, Manchester University Press, Manchester.

Kenna, R.J.B. (1986). The Flandrian sequence of North Wirral (N.W. England). *Geological Journal*, **21**, 1–27.

Lageard, J.G.A. (1992). *Vegetational history and palaeoforest reconstruction at White Moss, south Cheshire, UK*. PhD Thesis, Keele University.

Lageard, J.G.A., Chambers, F.M. & Thomas P.A. (1995). Recording and reconstruction of wood macrofossils in three-dimensions. *Journal of Archaeological Science*, **22**, 561–67.

Lamb, H.H. (1981). Climate from 1000BC to 1000AD. *The Environment of Man: the Iron Age to the Anglo Saxon Period* (eds M. Jones and G. Dimbleby), pp. 53–65. British Archaeological Reports (British Series), **87**, Oxford.

Leah, M., Wells, C.E., Huckerby, E. & Appleby, C. (1997). *The Wetlands of Cheshire*. North West Wetlands, Survey 4. Lancaster Imprints 5, Lancaster.

Lind, E.M. (1949). The history and vegetation of some Cheshire meres. *Memoirs and Proceedings of the Manchester Literary and Philosophical Society*, **90**, 17–36.

Moore, P.D. (1988). The development of moorlands and upland mires. *Archaeology and the Flora of the British Isles* (ed. M. Jones), pp. 116–22. Oxford University Committee for Archaeology Monograph 14, Oxford.

Moore, P.D., Merryfield, D.L. & Price, M.D.R. (1984). The vegetation and development of British mires. *European Mires* (ed. P.D. Moore) pp. 203–35, Academic Press, London.

Moore, P.D., Webb, J.A. & Collinson, M.E. (1991). *Pollen Analysis*. Blackwell, Oxford.

O'Garra, A. (1976). *Dune slack systems – vegetation and morphological development at Ainsdale*. BSc thesis, Department of Geography, University of Liverpool.

Oldfield, F., Higgit, S.R., Richardson, N. & Yates, G. (1986). Pollen, charcoal, rhizopod and radiometric analysis. *Lindow Man, the Body in the Bog* (eds I.M. Stead, J.B. Bourke and D. Brothwell), pp. 82–5. Guild Publishing, London.

Pennington, W. (1977). The late-glacial flora and vegetation of Britain. *Philosophical Transactions of the Royal Society of London B*, **280**, 247–71.

Perry, I. & Moore, P.D. (1987). Dutch elm disease as an analogue of Neolithic Elm Decline. *Nature*, **326**, 72–73.

Plater, A.J., Huddart, D., Innes, J.B., Pye, K., Smith, A.J. & Tooley, M.J. (1993). Coastal and sea-level changes. *The Sand Dunes of the Sefton Coast* (eds D. Atkinson & J. Houston), pp. 23–34. National Museums & Galleries on Merseyside in association with Sefton Metropolitan Borough Council, Liverpool.

Pye, K. & Neal, A. (1993). Stratigraphy and Age Structure of the Sefton Dune Complex: Preliminary Results of Field Drilling Investigations. *The Sand Dunes of the Sefton Coast* (eds D. Atkinson & J. Houston), pp.41–4. National Museums & Galleries on Merseyside in association with Sefton Metropolitan Borough Council, Liverpool.

Reynolds, C.S. (1979). The limnology of the eutrophic meres of the Shropshire–Cheshire plain. *Field Studies*, **5**, 93–173.

Rodwell, J.S. (ed.) (1991). *British Plant Communities*. Volume 2 *Mires and Heaths*. Cambridge University Press, Cambridge.

Schoenwetter, J. (1982). Environmental archaeology of the Peckforton Hills. *Cheshire Archaeological Bulletin*, **8**, 10–11.

Shennan, I. (1992). Late Quaternary sea-level changes and crustal movements in eastern England and eastern Scotland: an assessment of models of coastal evolution. *Quaternary International*, **15/16**, 161–73.

Shimwell, D.W. (1985). The distribution and origins of the lowland mosslands. *The Geomorphology of North-west England* (ed. R.H. Johnson), pp. 299–312, Manchester University Press, Manchester.

Simmons, I.G. & Innes, J.B. (1985). Late Mesolithic land-use and its environmental impacts in the English uplands. *Biogeographical Monographs*, **2**, 7–17.

Simpson, I.M. & West, R.G. (1958). On the stratigraphy and palaeobotany of a Late-Pleistocene organic deposit at Chelford, Cheshire. *New Phytologist*, **57**, 239–50.

Stace, C. (1991). *New Flora of the British Isles*. Cambridge University Press, Cambridge.

Switsur, V.R. & West, R.G. (1975). University of Cambridge Natural Radiocarbon Measurements XIII. *Radiocarbon*, **17**, 35–51.

Tallis, J.H. (1964a). The pre-peat vegetation of the southern Pennines. *New Phytologist*, **63**, 363–73.

Tallis, J.H. (1964b). Studies on southern Pennine peats. I. The general pollen record. *Journal of Ecology*, **52**, 323–31.

Tallis, J.H. (1973). The terrestrialisation of lake basins in North Cheshire, with special reference to the development of a 'Schwingmoor' structure. *Journal of Ecology*, **61**, 537–67.

Tallis, J.H. (1975). Tree remains in southern Pennine blanket peats. *Nature*, **256**, 482–4.

Tallis, J.H. (1985). Mass movement and erosion of a southern Pennine blanket peat. *Journal of Ecology*, **73**, 282–315.

Tallis, J.H. (1991). Forest and moorland in the south Pennine upland in the mid-Flandrian period. III. The spread of moorland – local, regional and national. *Journal of Ecology*, **79**, 401–15.

Tallis, J.H. & Birks, H.J.B. (1965). The past and present distribution of *Scheuchzeria palustris* (L.) in Europe. *Journal of Ecology*, **53**, 287–98.

Tallis, J.H. & Johnson R.H. (1980). The dating of landslides in Longdendale, north Derbyshire, using pollen-analytical techniques. *Timescales in Geomorphology* (eds R.A. Cullingford, D.A. Davidson & J. Lewin), pp. 189–205, Wiley, Chichester.

Tallis, J.H. & McGuire, J. (1972). Central Rossendale: the evolution of an upland vegetation. I. The clearance of woodland. *Journal of Ecology*, **60**, 721–37.

Tallis, J.H. & Switsur, V.R. (1973). Studies on the southern Pennine peats. VI. A radiocarbon dated pollen diagram from Featherbed Moss, Derbyshire. *Journal of Ecology*, **61**, 743–51.

Tallis, J.H. & Switsur, V.R. (1983). Forest and moorland in the south Pennine uplands in the mid-Flandrian period. I. Macrofossil evidence of the former forest cover. *Journal of Ecology*, **71**, 585–600.

Tallis, J.H. & Switsur, V.R. (1990). Forest and moorland in the south Pennine uplands in the mid-Flandrian period. II. The hillslope forests. *Journal of Ecology*, **78**, 857–83.

Tooley, M.J. (1978). *Sea-Level Changes in North West England During the Flandrian Stage*. Clarendon Press, Oxford.

Tooley, M.J. (1985a). Sea-level changes and coastal morphology in north-west England. *The Geomorphology of North-west England* (ed. R.H. Johnson), pp. 94–121, Manchester University Press, Manchester.

Tooley, M.J. (1985b). Climate, sea level and coastal changes. *The Climatic Scene. Essays in Honour of Gordon Manley* (eds M.J. Tooley & G.M. Sheail), pp. 206–34, George Allen and Unwin, London.

Turner, J. (1962). The *Tilia* decline: an anthropogenic interpretation. *New Phytologist*, **61**, 328–41.

Twigger, S.N. (1983). *Environmental Change in Lowland Cheshire*. Unpublished report. Department of Prehistoric Archaeology, University of Liverpool.

Walker, D. (1970). Direction and rate of some Post-glacial hydroseres. *Studies in the Vegetational History of the British Isles* (eds D.Walker and R.G. West), pp. 117–39. Cambridge University Press, Cambridge.

Walker, M.J.C., Bohncke, S.J.P., Coope, G.R., O'Connell, M., Usinger, H. & Verbruggen, C. (1994). The Devensian/Weichselian Late-glacial in northwest Europe (Ireland, Britain, north Belgium, The Netherlands, north-west Germany). *Journal of Quaternary Science*, **9**, 109–18.

Wells, C.E. (1992). Stratigraphic survey in Merseyside and West Lancashire borderlands. *North West Wetlands Survey Annual Report 1992* (ed. R. Middleton), pp. 43–7. Lancaster University Archaeological Unit, Lancaster.

Wells, C.E., Huckerby, E. & Hall D. (1993). Archaeological and palaeoecological survey in Greater Manchester. *North West Wetland Survey Annual Report 1993* (ed. R. Middleton), pp. 29–35, Lancaster University Archaeological Unit, Lancaster.

Williams, C.T. (1985). *Mesolithic Exploitation Patterns in the Central Pennines. A Palynological Study of Soyland Moor*. British Archaeological Reports (British Series), 139, Oxford.

Wiltshire, P.E.J. & Edwards, K.J. (1993). Mesolithic, early Neolithic, and later prehistoric impacts on vegetation at a riverine site in Derbyshire, England. *Climate Change and Human Impact on the Landscape* (ed. F.M. Chambers), pp. 157–68, Chapman & Hall, London.

Worsley, P. (1985). Pleistocene history of the Cheshire–Shropshire plain. *The Geomorphology of North-west England* (ed. R.H. Johnson), pp. 201–21, Manchester University Press, Manchester.

Yates, E.M. & Moseley, F. (1958). Glacial lakes and spillways in the vicinity of Madeley, North Staffordshire. *Quarterly Journal of the Geological Society of London*, **113**, 409–28.

CHAPTER FOUR

The human influence to the Norman Conquest

R.W. COWELL

Introduction

This paper covers 9,000 years since the last Ice Age and incorporates three distinct phases of human exploitation of the Mersey Basin environment. It is a time, however, which has left little direct impact on today's landscape, other than that seen in the bare peat covered uplands of the Basin (chapter eleven, this volume) and in some shadowy links between the nature of the agricultural lowlands and landscape changes taking place in the final part of the period covered here. The prehistoric and early historic land-use of the area therefore largely provides a contrasting picture to the nature of the landscape in the succeeding period, which was the one in which many features of today's landscape originated (chapter five, this volume).

The earliest forest c.9,500–c.3,200 BP

The occupation of this part of England during the late stages of the last Ice Age has left no trace within the Mersey Basin, although sites of mobile hunter-gatherers of this period are known in the uplands of Derbyshire and North Wales, and parts of northern Lancashire and Cumbria (Jacobi 1980). The earliest evidence for inhabitants in the Mersey region comes from shortly after the final retreat of the ice c.10,000 years ago, with the development of the wooded landscape of the Mesolithic period.

There were probably two main ways in which the mobile hunter-gatherer communities of this period exploited the landscape. One was in residential areas, places where a family, or group of families, might stay for a period of time; the second was in various types of smaller, specialist sites associated with hunting and gathering expeditions away from the residential areas (Smith 1992).

The coastal areas of Sefton and Wirral (Figure 4.1) are the main residential locations in the Basin (Cowell & Innes 1994). Mesolithic settlement of the Basin coincided with loss of land due to rising sea-level, so that by c.6,000 BP the approximate line of the present coast would have been reached for the first time (chapter two, this volume). The coastline provided a rich variety of resources that would have been available almost all year round. Estuarine muds would have been important for wildfowl breeding and nesting, while inshore fishing would have been possible in the estuaries. Backing onto these habitats were freshwater reedswamps and fens where wildfowl, fish, and aquatic animals would have been plentiful.

Apart from rich coastal environments, after c.7,500 BP, the local hunter-gatherers lived in an environment where large areas of swamp and subsequently fen, now covered by peatland, occupied inland hollows and waterlogged gradients across large areas of the lowlands north of the Mersey (Birks 1964, 1965; Cowell & Innes 1994; Hall et al. 1995; Hibbert, Switsur & West 1971; Howard-Davis, Stocks & Innes 1988; chapter three, this volume) and within smaller basins south of the river in Cheshire. By c.7,000 BP, Alder fenwood was common around wetlands, rivers and on the lower slopes of the uplands.

Elsewhere during this period, mixed deciduous woodland had come to dominate the landscape, resulting in a dense forest that must have hindered easy movement within it. Deciduous woodland also clothed the Pennines, in general to altitudes above c.500m, above which Hazel (Corylus) and Birch (Betula) scrub probably predominated, although in some poorly drained areas, particularly at higher altitudes, the increased rainfall of this period also led to the initiation of peat (chapter eleven, this volume).

This expanse of dryland woods, interspersed with carr wetlands and the mixed vegetation along the upper tree limit in the Pennines, would have provided rich habitats with plentiful grazing for Aurochs (Bos primigenius), Wild Boar (Sus scrofa), and Deer as well as edible plants, berries, and nuts for humans. The exploitation of this landscape may have been different in the lowlands and the adjoining uplands from the coasts. In the interior lowlands of the Basin, the nature of Mesolithic activity is generally dispersed and largely concentrated in the main river valleys, such as those of the Rivers Mersey and Weaver and tributaries like the Ditton (Barnes 1982; Cowell 1991, 1992). Most of these sites may represent small camps for specialist task groups.

The Pennines have produced the greatest concentra-

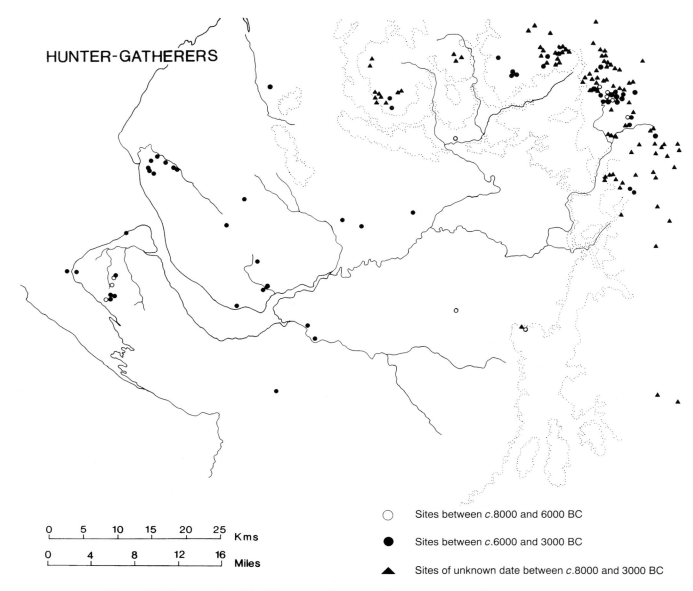

HUNTER-GATHERERS

○	Sites between c.8000 and 6000 BC
●	Sites between c.6000 and 3000 BC
▲	Sites of unknown date between c.8000 and 3000 BC

Figure 4.1. Sites associated with hunter-gatherers in the Mersey Basin, from c.9,500–5,500 BP.

tion of Mesolithic sites in the country. They are found mainly between the 366m and 488m contours (Jacobi, Tallis & Mellars 1976), with the greatest concentration in a fairly restricted area between Saddleworth and Marsden, where the Pennines are at their narrowest (Barnes 1982; Stonehouse 1989, 1994; Wymer & Bonsall 1977). Most of the upland sites are interpreted as summer hunting camps, occupied by a limited number of people (Mellars 1976), although Williams (1985) argues for an intensive form of managed grazing over many centuries in parts of the Pennines.

Pollen diagrams suggest that in the early part of the period the woodland cover was not being altered to any degree (Cowell & Innes 1994; Hibbert et al. 1971; chapter three, this volume). Disturbance to the woodland cover in the lowlands of the Mersey Basin before c.6,000 BP is only found in coastal areas. This suggests that hunter-gatherers were undertaking activities at the natural clearings around the edges of swamps or fens without

affecting the woodland or disturbing the ground to any great degree. It is only during the 6th millennium BP that evidence from pollen diagrams shows broken ground and associated small dips in the woodland cover becoming more common. This occurs both in the coastal and central areas of the Basin.

There is evidence that burning of the woodlands may have been taking place in the uplands (chapter eleven, this volume) as well as in the lowlands of Merseyside (Cowell & Innes 1994) and Greater Manchester (Hall et al. 1995), probably after c.7,000 BP. In the uplands, hunting sites are often associated with an increase of Heather (Calluna) and charcoal flecks in the artefact layers at altitudes which probably mark the upper limits of tree cover. Manipulation of the edges of the forest, where browse is more plentiful, would have been accomplished more easily and there may have been a deliberate policy of woodland management rather than the use of accidental natural events (Mellars 1976).

In the more thinly exploited interior lowlands, if the extensive evidence for burning represents a deliberate policy of firing woodland, then it would have to have been undertaken by small groups of hunters, operating away from the main residential areas, part of whose function might have been to clear scattered areas for future hunting expeditions.

Whether or not the woodland burning during this period was associated with human actions, it appears to have had an effect on the ecological succession of these habitats (chapter eleven, this volume; Hall *et al.* 1995, p. 116). In the uplands, mire development may have resulted naturally at the higher altitudes, but may have been encouraged by human activity at the forest margins where clearance activity was more concentrated, leading to impoverishment of the soil and the onset of peat formation during the deteriorating climate of this period. At lower altitudes and across the lowlands generally woodland regeneration was the norm.

The impact of agriculture: after *c.*5,400 BP

The introduction of agriculture, traditionally associated with the Neolithic period, is a potentially important development in the vegetational history of the Basin. A number of sites, mainly coastal, in north-western England show woodland disturbances accompanied by cereal type pollen at the beginning of the 6th millennium BP. This is interpreted as the adoption of one part of the agricultural process by Mesolithic hunters (Cowell & Innes 1994; Williams 1985), before the adoption nationally of the full Neolithic cultural and economic repertoire many centuries later. Thus, small areas might have been planted as a slightly more predictable adjunct to the normal round of seasonal hunting and gathering.

The adoption of cultivation in the Mersey Basin, however, seems to have had little effect on the vegetation cover of the lowlands, which remained much as it had been in the Mesolithic for several millennia (Cowell & Innes 1994), although there is some quickening of the pace of clearance and a probable expansion in land-use in the 4th millennium BP (early Bronze Age).

Although the pattern of small woodland disturbances becomes more widespread in the Merseyside part of the Basin in the Neolithic, the nature of each disturbance episode is still limited in extent. Each episode is also succeeded by reasonably long periods of forest regeneration. This is also the pattern in the uplands with only small, occasional breaks in woodland cover (Barnes 1982).

An 'Elm Decline' is present in several dated pollen diagrams from the Basin towards the end of the 6th millennium BP (Cowell & Innes 1994; Howard-Davis *et al.* 1988). In other areas of the country, this often marks the beginning of new trends of woodland clearance associated with agriculture. In much of the Basin this is not the case and the trend may be natural, although at Holcroft Moss and Lindow Moss in the Mersey valley and Hatchmere, Cheshire potentially significant clearance activity is present after the 'Elm Decline'

(Birks 1965; Howard-Davis *et al.* 1988). Other natural changes were also taking place. Woodland cover was still prevalent up to *c.*350m in the Pennines but blanket peat continued to spread, particularly in areas with poor drainage (Barnes 1982). In some localities in the lowlands, wetter conditions may also have become more prevalent from the incidence of pool peats in some of the Greater Manchester peat bogs (Hall *et al.* 1995, p. 117).

The archaeological evidence for the late-6th to late-4th millennium BP largely mirrors the pollen evidence. Neolithic settlements are found in the same localities as in the Mesolithic and of a similar form, suggesting exploitation of the landscape had changed little. The recent discovery by National Museums & Galleries on Merseyside of a wooden trackway of *c.*4,900 BP on the beach at Hightown near Formby, Merseyside highlights the continuing importance of the coast. The incidence of Neolithic stone axes, some of which may have a link with woodland clearance, tends to reinforce this pattern (Figure 4.2). The axes from the uplands are, however, found mainly along the lower fringes, particularly in the river valleys, in areas where little Mesolithic material is known. A number of Mesolithic sites at higher altitudes, particularly in the Saddleworth/Marsden area do though include Neolithic flintwork, especially arrowheads.

No major changes took place during the next thousand years, covering the earlier Bronze Age, as the inland forest remained relatively dense and damp. In the lowlands, small, infrequent woodland disturbances are recorded between *c.*4,000–3,400 BP in Merseyside, similar to those in the Neolithic (Cowell & Innes 1994). These are quite low intensity occurrences, mainly recognised by the appearance of weeds, plantains (*Plantago*), Bracken (*Pteridium*) and grasses, with only very limited reductions in woodland cover. Settlement evidence for this period is limited, with few core areas recognised although scattered chance finds are more numerous than in the Neolithic, suggesting that Bronze Age communities were still mobile to some degree. Upland areas provide a similar pattern, although the clearings become more widespread, which with the increased number of finds, suggests they and their fringes were being used more extensively than in the Neolithic (Barnes 1982). Flint arrowheads are common from the higher parts of the uplands suggesting that hunting was still important in these landscapes.

Elements of a more visible social cohesion are found in the Basin from the distribution of burial sites during this time (Figure 4.2). Neolithic examples are found along the upland fringes in Cheshire (Longley 1987) and Lancashire (Bu'lock 1959), and in the lowlands in Merseyside (Cowell & Warhurst 1984). In the early Bronze Age, earthen burial mounds (barrows) are common in the uplands and major river valleys. These remained as fixed points over many centuries, as witnessed at Winwick in the Mersey valley (Freke & Holgate 1990). Their existence presupposes some signif-

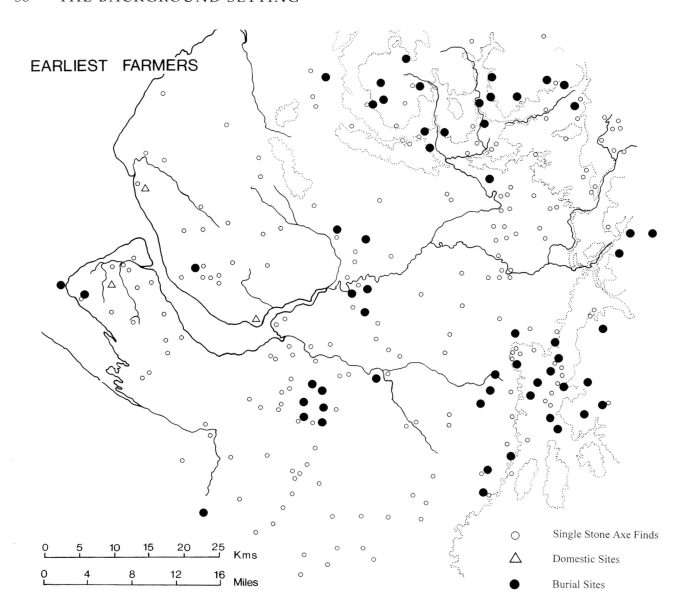

EARLIEST FARMERS

○	Single Stone Axe Finds
△	Domestic Sites
●	Burial Sites

Figure 4.2. Sites and findspots belonging to the first farmers of the Neolithic and Bronze Age periods
in the Mersey Basin, from c.3,500–550 BP.

icant reduction in woodland by c.3,800 BP, as they must have acted as visible markers in the landscape. In the uplands, soil deterioration was taking place, as barrows were erected over soils with a developing podsol structure with local heathland development within Birch and Hazel woodland (Tallis & McGuire 1972). Some areas of the lowlands may also have become heathland during this period with Heather and Birch becoming more common at the margins of the wetland (chapter three, this volume).

The first settled farming communities c.3,200 BP–c.AD 500

At the beginning of the 3rd millennium BP increased rainfall and a fall in temperature of c.2°C, to a summer average c.0.5°C lower than that of today (Lamb 1981) may have contributed to changes in the archaeological

pattern. Raised bog became prevalent in the major lowland valleys of the Basin, particularly the middle Mersey and in the uplands (Tallis & Switsur 1973), and in inland mires such as at Simonswood and Parr Moss, Burtonwood, during the middle to later part of the millennium (Cowell & Innes 1994), leading to areas of low agricultural productivity. Recurrence surfaces in local bogs imply two horizons of particular deterioration, typically dated at Chat Moss, Greater Manchester to the end of the 4th millennium BP and to c.2,600 BP (Nevell 1992). Nationally, this climatic deterioration is seen as being a possible cause for the archaeological changes seen at the end of the earlier Bronze Age at c.3,200 BP (Burgess 1974).

The main artefactual evidence in the region for the period after c.3,000 BP comes from metalwork of late Bronze Age date. Nationally, this is commonly found around wetland areas and rivers, particularly in the form

Figure 4.3. Early Neolithic (*c*.4,900 BP) wooden trackway under excavation on the beach at Hightown, near Formby, Merseyside.

of hoards (Bradley 1984). In the north-west, hoards are rare, the pattern being dominated by single finds with a trend for them to be located in the middle to upper reaches of the main rivers in the region, contrasting with the pattern in the early Bronze Age. This dislocation of the pattern of metalwork finds from the lower Mersey to the upper reaches of the rivers in the later Bronze Age is interpreted as a response to the worsening of conditions on the lower ground (Davey 1976).

It is during this period of the late Bronze Age, however, that the pattern of small, fairly widespread, but infrequent woodland disturbances alters in the western part of the Basin. The areas around the Merseyside central mosslands were for the first time the focus of more concerted farming activity during the early to mid-3rd millennium BP. This represents the first relatively substantial clearance of woodland in these areas and the best indications of the adoption of mixed agriculture (Cowell & Innes 1994). In the east of the Mersey Basin, however, such activity is not noticed until nearer the end of the millennium (Howard-Davis *et al.* 1988), although small scale, low impact, short lived activity is still seen

in some areas of the Pennine fringes preceding this (Tallis & Switsur 1973).

The first substantial farm settlements became established during the 3rd millennium BP, although close dating for them is poor at the moment. They are in the form of oval or sub-rectangular ditched enclosures, mainly confined to the Triassic sandstone belt in the Wirral and southern half of Merseyside (Philpott 1994), extending to the middle reaches of the Mersey valley (Nevell 1989a), and across central Cheshire (R. Philpott pers comm., Figure 4.4). They may be several centuries later (later Iron Age) than the early to mid-3rd millennium BP (late-Bronze Age/early-Iron Age) clearance horizon in the pollen diagrams of the western part of the Basin. The nature of the environmental changes seen at this horizon, the presence of contemporary metalwork and of sites such as the late-Bronze Age hill settlement at Beeston, Cheshire (Keen & Hough 1993) in the western part of the Basin, however, provide a context that hints that some ostensibly late Iron Age sites could be earlier. This would not accord with the argument for settlement dislocation towards the upper reaches of the main valleys in the Basin for climatic reasons.

Until, and if, part of the lowland settlement pattern of the local Iron Age can be shown to have its general origins in the period of worsening climate in the late-Bronze Age/early-Iron Age, the first identifiable archaeology of settled farmsteads in the lowlands of the Basin dates to the period towards the end of the 3rd millennium BP (late-Iron Age). Three main farmstead enclosures have been excavated in the Basin, at Great Woolden, Halewood, and Irby, all of which suggest that late-Iron Age settlement was, to differing degrees, succeeded by Romano-British occupation on the same site (Philpott 1993; Cowell & Philpott 1994; Nevell 1989b). This suggests continuity of settlement into the Romano-British period may have been a common feature of the area. It is at this time, beginning in the second half of the millennium, that the first concerted clearances associated with cereals are found in the eastern part of the Basin, as at Chat Moss and Lindow Moss (Nevell 1992) and on the fringes of the uplands (Tallis & Switsur 1973). This coincided with an improvement in climate, becoming warmer and drier (Lamb 1981). The pollen sites from the western part of the Basin also show clearance activity with some cereal evidence subsequent to the mid-3rd millennium BP, but none are dated absolutely.

The impact of the Roman conquest of Britain

The impact of the Roman legions on the rural landscape in the 1st century AD was directly limited to the network of roads through the region (Margary 1967) linking the major forts, towns and industrial settlements such as Wilderspool, Warrington , and other settlements such as at Wigan. A network of farmsteads existed across southern parts of the Basin, probably representing an increase in the density of the settlement pattern from the

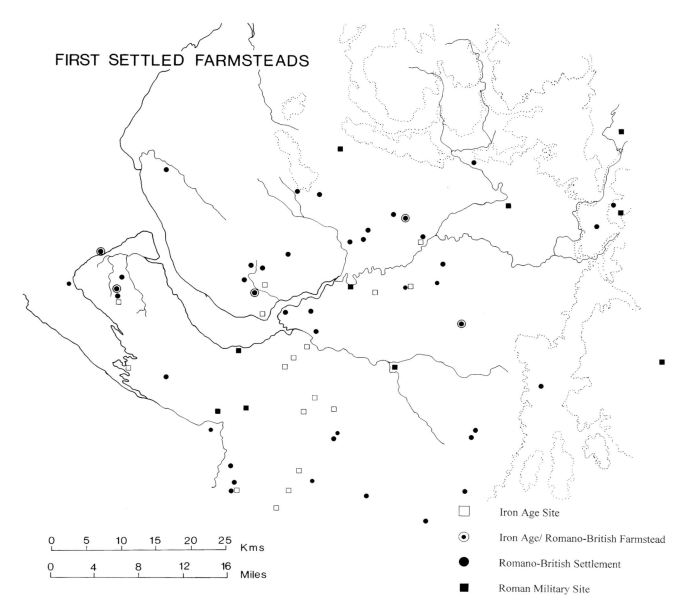

FIRST SETTLED FARMSTEADS

□   Iron Age Site

⊙   Iron Age/ Romano-British Farmstead

●   Romano-British Settlement

■   Roman Military Site

Figure 4.4. Settlements of the late-prehistoric and Romano-British periods in the Mersey Basin, from c.3,000–1,500 BP.

Iron Age. The important coastal settlement of Meols, at the mouth of the Dee, may have acted as a focus for the distribution of a series of scattered farmsteads around the sandstone ridges in central Wirral (Philpott 1993).

The pollen evidence for this period is very limited but the Domesday Survey suggests that by the late-10th century AD woodland still covered large areas of the Basin. Cropmark enclosures are now recognised, however, on the heavier soils in the south-east of the Basin through programmes of aerial photography (Collens 1994; Philpott 1994; Nevell 1989b) and as earthworks in some foothill locations (Nevell 1992) which imply scattered clearings in the woodland were relatively common. Recent excavations have shown that even this distribution may be a great underestimate of the extent of Romano-British rural settlement in the area (Cowell & Philpott 1994).

The scale of clearance around each farmstead is not clear for many sites. At Featherbed Moss in the eastern foothills (Nevell 1992; Tallis & Switsur 1973) relatively substantial clearance associated with cereal farming, sustained over several centuries, is attested.

In the coastal, and sandy areas in the north and north-west of the Basin such sites are proving more difficult to locate, suggesting that areas formerly attractive to settlement had now become more marginal. The fact that some of the mosslands were acid raised bog at this time may have made some areas of the north central part of the Basin less attractive for mixed farming. The pollen diagram, however, from Knowsley Park Moss suggests clearance was taking place on an increased scale to that of the late-Bronze Age/early-Iron Age, with mixed farming being carried out somewhere in the vicinity at c.AD 300. Although the activity appears to be fairly intense, the extent of the clearance was probably limited (Cowell & Innes 1994, p. 129). Other sites may also have been placed adjacent to mosslands (Cowell & Innes 1994; Nevell 1989b). This suggests that mossland resources, perhaps unconnected with agriculture, were still being exploited but the reason for settlement location would seem to be the conjunction of a number of complementary resources, with sandstone and clay areas being more favoured for settlement than the lighter, previously attractive sandy soils. With the trend in the region for late prehistoric sites to be on the same locations as the Roman ones, this pattern may have much earlier origins.

The emergence of new settlement patterns *c*.AD 500–1,000

After the withdrawal of the Roman army from Britain in the early 5th century AD the period up to the Norman Conquest is often known as the Dark Ages. Direct evidence for settlement and landuse becomes very scanty, although it is a period when many important developments, visible in the archaeology of the post-Conquest period became established (chapter five, this volume). The details of these developments are, however, not well understood in the region. The best evidence is the Domesday Survey from which it is possible to extrapolate backwards to identify trends and developments.

By the late medieval period (11th–15th century AD) the landscape witnessed several major changes. Some areas, particularly where sandstone dominates the local geology, had developed what is regarded as the typical medieval landscape of townships (territories made up of several estates), large communal arable fields, and smaller, privately owned estates, nucleated hamlets or villages alongside isolated settlements, increasing clearance of woodland, and the growth of scattered towns (chapter five, this volume). One of the main problems of the pre-Conquest period is to identify to what extent these major developments had originated during this period.

The earliest Saxon (pre-Conquest) settlers may have reached the area during the 7th century from Cheshire (Thacker 1987) with many of the place names belonging to the 'tun' form e.g. Huyton, Denton, etc., which is regarded as a possible later phase of settlement than the earliest post-Roman phase. The 7th and early 8th centuries also marked a fall in tree cover in parts of the south-east of the Basin (Nevell 1992) which may be seen as an expression of this expansion of settlement.

The densest pattern of Saxon place names, which probably include many pre-Conquest settlements, is found in the same areas where most of the Romano-British farmsteads are known. A pattern of land ownership and landuse based on large agricultural estates is generally associated with the Saxon period (Sawyer & Thacker 1987). Large areas were still heavily wooded, particularly in the north and the east of the Basin, and clearance and settlement of many of these areas only properly started a century or so after the Conquest (Cowell 1982; Lewis 1982), so that the landscape of many

Saxon estates would have included much woodland. Some areas, e.g., the large township of West Derby, probably retained their wooded status to function as royal late-Saxon estates which may have been retained for hunting (Shaw 1956). There are grounds for thinking that some Saxon estates may be related to Romano-British ones and that a degree of conservatism may have held in landuse and settlement pattern (Cowell & Philpott 1994), suggesting a degree of continuity in site location and perhaps landuse and land tenure in some locations. The only pollen diagram which covers this period, however, at Featherbed Moss, shows that regeneration of woodland took place during the 6th century AD after a period of Romano-British farming (Tallis & Switsur 1973). This was also a period when the climate deteriorated, with increasing rainfall and a decline in average temperatures between the 5th and 7th centuries AD.

For those townships in the medieval period which had developed a mixed landscape including settlement nucleation and communal resources, the major problem is to define what social, economic or even political conditions lay behind these changes and at what rate the process took place. Centres of population with parish churches such as Huyton, Childwall or Prescot, in Merseyside may be examples of a relatively widespread trend, which is likely to be pre-Conquest in date associated with the introduction of Christianity into the area after the 6th or 7th centuries AD (Cowell 1982). Small townships on the Wirral suggest that by the time township boundaries came to be defined in the landscape, certainly by the late medieval period (11th–15th century AD), there was greater competition for land between communities here than to the east of the River Mersey, but there is no evidence that this had led to earlier general nucleation in the Wirral. Townships with present-day villages with Scandinavian names, such as Irby, Greasby, or Frankby, are likely to have received an influx of settlers by way of Ireland in the 10th century (Chitty 1978). Again there is no evidence to show whether this influx was a contributory factor to the growth of nucleation or whether it was assimilated into a pre-existing dispersed or nucleated pattern.

Although a number of townships in the Mersey Basin retained a pattern of dispersed settlement during the late-medieval period, which might reflect land organisation from a much earlier period in some cases, many more developed a form of common field system which would have transformed the appearance of the landscape. In its classic form this was a late-Saxon feature of midland and eastern England, but to what extent it developed in a pre-Conquest context in north-western England is unclear. There is evidence, though, that some common systems may have developed quite late in the late-medieval period (chapter five, this volume).

Away from the belt of potential early settlement, in the uplands and in large areas of the lowlands, particularly around the mossland in the north and east of the Mersey Basin, land remained largely undeveloped and marginal into the medieval period. This contrast conditioned the appearance of parts of the landscape well into the post-medieval period, in a way retaining some small echo of its prehistoric past.

Thus, the landscape pattern for approximately 9,000 years before the Domesday Survey was one rooted in woodland, fen, swamp, peat bog, and long sweeps of coast. Early human intervention in this environment, due to low population pressure and the sustainable nature of the human activity, meant that the effects were limited both in scale and distribution. The vegetation in some areas, such as the coasts or the uplands, may have been more seriously affected during this time, but this is often likely to have been the result of the broad natural changes taking place with human interference contributing either to speed up or extend the process. Even when the nature and density of settlement changed, c.3,000 years ago, for the first half of this period the natural landscape would not have been unfamiliar to a hunter of the Mesolithic. It is not until the post-Roman period that the pattern of settlement and landuse recognisable today probably started to be defined, but those links are still very obscure and many areas of the Mersey Basin would still have been dominated by woodland and moss. It is only with the population rise of the late medieval period that many areas of the Mersey Basin were developed in a way that still has an impact on the nature of today's landscape.

References

Birks, H.J.B. (1964). Chat Moss, Lancashire. *Memoirs and Proceedings of the Manchester Literary and Philosophical Society*, **106**, 22–45.

Birks, H.J.B. (1965). Pollen Analytical Investigations at Holcroft Moss, Lancashire and Lindow Moss, Cheshire. *Journal of Ecology*, **53**, 299–314.

Barnes, B. (1982). *Man and the Changing Landscape*. Merseyside County Museums, University of Liverpool Department of Prehistoric Archaeology, Liverpool. Work Notes, **3**. Merseyside County Council.

Bradley, R. (1984). *The Social Foundations of Prehistoric Britain*. Longman, London.

Bu'lock, J.D. (1959). The Pikestones: A Chambered Long Cairn of Neolithic Type on Anglezarke Moor, Lancashire. *Transactions of the Lancashire & Cheshire Antiquarian Society*, **68**, 143–45.

Burgess, C. (1974). The Bronze Age. *British Prehistory* (ed. C. Renfrew), pp. 165–233. Duckworth, London.

Chitty, G.S. (1978). Wirral Rural Fringes Survey Report. *Journal of the Merseyside Archaeological Society*, **2**, 1–25.

Collens, J. (1994). Recent Discoveries from the Air in Cheshire. *From Flints to Flower Pots, Current Research in the Dee–Mersey Region* (ed. P. Carrington), pp. 19–25. Chester Archaeological Service Occasional Paper **2**, Chester.

Cowell, R.W. (1982). *Liverpool Urban Fringe Survey*. Unpublished report at Liverpool Museum, National Museums & Galleries on Merseyside.

Cowell, R.W. (1991). The Prehistory of Merseyside. *Journal of the Merseyside Archaeological Society*, **7**, 21–61.

Cowell, R.W. (1992). Prehistoric Survey in North Cheshire. *Cheshire Past*, **1**, 6–7.

Cowell, R.W. & Innes, J.B. (1994). *The Wetlands of Merseyside*. North West Wetlands Survey **1**, Lancaster Imprints 2, Lancaster.

Cowell, R.W. & Philpott, R.A. (1994). Excavations along the route of the M57–A562 Link Road, Merseyside, in 1993. Unpublished report at Liverpool Museum, National Museums & Galleries on Merseyside.

Cowell, R.W. & Warhurst, M.H. (1984). *The Calderstones: a Prehistoric Tomb on Merseyside*. Merseyside Archaeological Society, Liverpool.

Davey, P.J. (1976). The Distribution of Bronze Age Metalwork from Lancashire and Cheshire. *Journal of the Chester Archaeological Society*, **59**, 1–13.

Freke, D.J. & Holgate, R. (1990). Excavations at Winwick, Cheshire in 1980: 1. Excavation of two 2nd millennium BC mounds. *Journal of the Chester Archaeological Society*, **70** (for 1987–8), 9–30.

Hall, D., Wells, C., Huckerby, E., Meyer, A. & Cox, C. (1995). *The Wetlands of Greater Manchester*. North West Wetlands Survey **2**, Lancaster Imprints 3, Lancaster.

Hibbert, F.A., Switsur, V.R. & West, R.G. (1971). Radiocarbon dating of Flandrian zones at Red Moss, Lancashire. *Proceedings of the Royal Society of London B*, **177**, 161–76.

Howard-Davis, C., Stocks, C. & Innes, J. (1988). *Peat and the Past*. Lancaster University, Lancaster.

Jacobi, R.M. (1980). The Early Holocene Settlement of Wales. *Culture and Environment in Prehistoric Wales* (ed. A.J. Taylor), pp. 131–206. British Archaeological Reports (British Series) **76**, Oxford.

Jacobi, R.M., Tallis, J.H. & Mellars, P. (1976). The Southern Pennine Mesolithic and the Ecological Record. *Journal of Archaeological Science*, **3**, 307–320.

Keen, L. & Hough, P. (1993). *Beeston Castle, Cheshire, a report on the excavations 1968–85*. Archaeological Report no. **23**. Historic Buildings and Monuments Commission, London.

Lamb, H.H. (1981). Climate from 1000 BC to 1000 AD. *The Environment of Man: the Iron Age to the Anglo Saxon Period* (eds M. Jones & G. Dimbleby), pp. 53–65. British Archaeological Reports (British Series) **87**, Oxford.

Lewis, J.M. (1982). *Sefton Rural Fringes Survey Report*. Unpublished report at Liverpool Museum, National Museums & Galleries on Merseyside.

Longley, D.M.T. (1987). Prehistory. *A History of the County of Chester*, Vol. I (eds B.E. Harris & A.T. Thacker), pp. 36–114. The Victoria History of the Counties of England, published for the Institute of Historical Reseach by Oxford University Press, Oxford.

Margary, I.D. (1967). *Roman Roads in Britain* (revised edn). John Baker, London.

Mellars, P. (1976). Fire Ecology, Animal Populations and Man: a Study of Some Ecological Relationships in Prehistory. *Proceedings of the Prehistoric Society*, **42**, 15–45.

Nevell, M.D. (1989a). An Aerial Survey of Southern Trafford and Northern Cheshire. *Greater Manchester Archaeological Journal*, **3** (for 1987–8), 27–34.

Nevell, M.D. (1989b). Great Woolden Hall Farm: Excavations on a Late Prehistoric/Romano-British Native Site. *Greater Manchester Archaeological Journal*, **3** (for 1987–8), 35–44.

Nevell, M. D. (1992). *Tameside Before 1066*. Tameside Metropolitan Borough Council, Manchester.

Philpott, R.A. (1993). A Romano-British Farmstead at Irby, Wirral, and its Place in the Landscape: An Interim Statement. *Archaeology North West: Bulletin of Council for British Archaeology North West*, **5**, 18–24.

Philpott, R. A. (1994). New Light on Roman Settlement: Recent Aerial photography in Cheshire. *Cheshire Past*, **3**, 6–7.

Sawyer, P. H. & Thacker, A.T. (1987). The Cheshire Domesday. *A History of the County of Chester*, Vol. I (eds B.E. Harris & A.T. Thacker), pp. 293–370. The Victoria History of the Counties of England, published for the Institute of Historical Reseach by Oxford University Press, Oxford.

Shaw, R. C. (1956). *The Royal Forest of Lancaster*. The Guardian Press, Preston.

Smith, C. (1992). *Late Stone Age Hunters of the British Isles*. Routledge, London.

Stonehouse, P. (1989). Mesolithic Sites on the Pennine Watershed. *Greater Manchester Archaeological Journal*, **3** (for 1987–8), 5–17.

Stonehouse, P. (1994). Mesolithic Sites on the Pennine Watershed Part II. *Archaeology North West: Bulletin Council for British Archaeology North West*, **8** (Vol. 2, Part II), 38–47.

Thacker, A. T. (1987). Anglo Saxon Cheshire. *A History of the County of Chester*, Vol. I (eds B.E. Harris & A.T. Thacker), pp. 237–292. The Victoria History of the Counties of England, published for the Institute of Historical Reseach by Oxford University Press, Oxford.

Tallis, J. H. & McGuire, J. (1972). Central Rossendale: the Evolution of an Upland Vegetation. *Journal of Ecology*, **60**, 721–51.

Tallis, J. H. & Switsur, V.R. (1973). Studies on southern Pennine Peats VI. A radiocarbon dated pollen diagram from Featherbed Moss, Derbyshire. *Journal of Ecology*, **61**, 743–51.

Williams, C. T. (1985) *Mesolithic Exploitation Patterns in the Central Pennines, A Palynological Study of Soyland Moor.* British Archaeological Reports (British Series), 139, Oxford.

Wymer, J.J. & Bonsall, C. J. (1977). *Gazetteer of Mesolithic Sites in England and Wales.* Council for British Archaeology: Research Report, **20**, London.

The Tide of Change

J.F. HANDLEY

The first section of this volume concluded that, for about 9,000 years before Domesday, the landscape pattern of the Mersey Basin was 'one rooted in woodland, fen, swamp, peat bog and long sweeps of coast'. Human influence is there to see but these landscapes were essentially shaped by natural processes. This section shows that the tide of change was to quicken dramatically during the next millennium when landscape change was increasingly driven by cultural influences.

Chapter five documents the influence of agriculture on the landscape beginning with widespread forest clearance to feed a steadily growing population. Climate change and disease in the 14th century caused social and economic dislocation and with it a switch in land-use from arable to pastoral. As population growth resumed urban centres began to take shape within an increasingly 'enclosed' landscape of hedgerows and dikes.

The 18th century witnessed further profound change with the coming of the industrial revolution and the emergence of a modern economy powered by fossil fuel rather than wind, water and biomass. The new industrial prosperity brought with it major environmental impacts. The consequences of this quickening 'tide of change' are documented in contrasting accounts of what remains today of the original natural habitats and what new opportunities for wildlife were created by industrialisation. The balance sheet shows significant losses but also some surprising gains.

The final contribution analyses the most recent evidence for land-use change and suggests that the period since the 1970s has been one of relative stability. However, what is striking is the paucity of systematically gathered information, which is geographically specific and sufficiently fine-grained to illustrate landscape dynamics in the Mersey Basin today. At the end of a millennium which began with the Domesday survey there is an urgent need to remedy this deficiency.

CHAPTER FIVE

The human influence: the Norman Conquest – Industrial Revolution

R.A.PHILPOTT AND J.M.LEWIS

Introduction

In the mid-17th century Lancashire was described as a 'close county full of ditches and hedges' (Walker 1939, p.72), a description which might equally well have been applied to Cheshire. The landscape by that time was an intensely partitioned and virtually entirely man-made one. The process by which such a landscape developed across these two counties by 1700 involved a combination of factors, social, demographic, climatic, and economic, through the preceding 600 years.

The landscape at Domesday (AD 1086)

The pattern of human settlement in the Mersey Basin by the late Anglo-Saxon period consisted largely of single farms and small hamlets. At Domesday the region had only one town, Chester, although the Cheshire salt 'wiches' should perhaps qualify as urban, and there appear to have been few villages in the classic Midland sense of a nucleated settlement with parish church and manor house. Many places which are mentioned in the Domesday Book and which had become villages by the 16th or 17th century when the earliest maps become available were probably no more than single farms or small clusters of dwellings in 1086: Domesday surveyed resources and estates not villages (Sawyer & Thacker 1987). Here, as elsewhere in northern England, the majority of villages may well have developed in the post-Conquest period but nucleated settlements certainly did become established at some places which were settled early, often because they were locally important as parish or administrative centres. They are often dry-point sites set on sandstone rises, with good potential for arable land in the vicinity, and their place-names often contain classic Saxon or Norse habitative elements, such as -tūn (Figure 5.1), -ham, -bury, or -by (Gelling 1978, p. 143).

The distribution of settlement in the early period is broadly indicated by the location of estates and their inhabitants in the Domesday Book. Domesday refers to, without necessarily naming, nearly 450 places in southern Lancashire and Cheshire (Figure 5.2), although some places contained more than one estate. The Domesday population of both Cheshire and Lancashire was low with perhaps under 10,000 in each county. Overall, Domesday records a low population of 1,524 individuals for Cheshire in 1086 (Terrett 1962a, p. 350) – to be multiplied by a factor of four or five for actual population (i.e., approximately 6,000–7,500) and it has been claimed that the county was the poorest of the Marcher Shires of England competing only with Derbyshire for the lowest population density in the region (Higham 1993, p. 203). The most densely occupied areas of Cheshire were Wirral and the Dee valley with perhaps three to four persons per square mile (1 square mile = 2.59 square kilometres); by contrast, the Pennine slopes of east Cheshire were very sparsely populated with only one person per square mile and some uninhabited vills. There are also significant gaps such as the Kingsley area in what was later to become the Royal Forest of Delamere and Carrington Moss in northern Cheshire where woodland, poor soil or mossland were unfavourable to agriculturally-based settlement. The information for Lancashire is much less detailed but the estimated population of 1,780 individuals for the region between the River Ribble and the River Mersey suggests a density of no more than two people per square mile and a total of approximately 7,000–8,700 once multiplied (Terrett 1962b, p. 407). Here the exceptional size of the ecclesiastical parishes and of their component townships demonstrates both the low population and the poor quality of the land, particularly where they embraced tracts of uninhabited woodland or mossland.

Domesday allows us to observe the effect of one major historical event which had a serious, if temporary, impact on the landscape. The 'harrying of the North', the campaigns of 1069–70 when William the Conqueror's army brought the Midlands and the North under the full control of the king, seems to have been deliberate devastation as reprisal for resistance to Norman rule (Sawyer & Thacker 1987, pp. 336–37; Higham 1982, p. 20). The result can be seen in the large number of vills which are still recorded in 1086, some seventeen years later, as 'waste', i.e., land which had gone out of cultivation. Eastern Cheshire appears to have been particularly hard-hit, with numerous underpopulated or deserted settlements, the west of the county recovered quickly, while

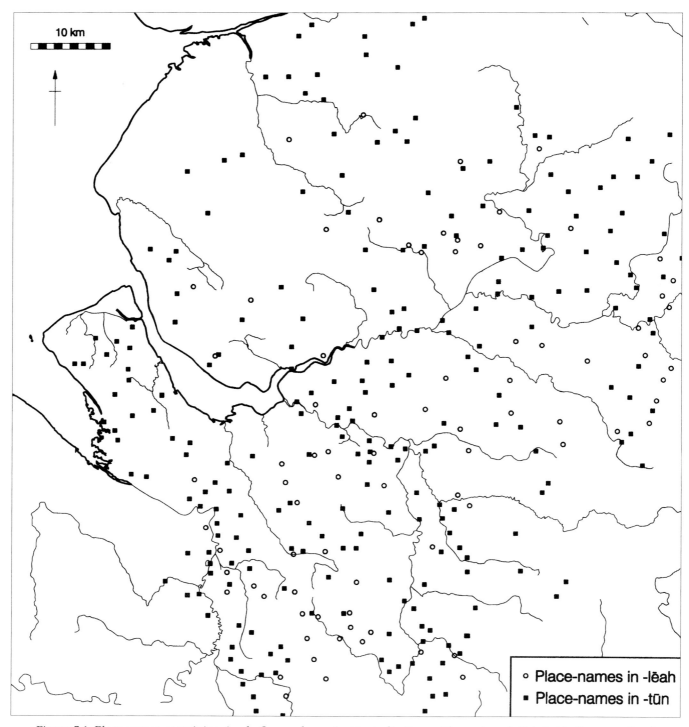

Figure 5.1. Place-names containing Anglo-Saxon elements *-tūn*, indicating settlement, and *-lēah*, indicating woodland clearance (after Kenyon 1989).

southern Lancashire seems to have escaped the worst effects of the destruction of 1070.

Already by Domesday the region had developed a complex subdivision of estates and landholdings and it is the township which provides the physical and administrative framework for the organisation of the landscape. Townships had developed in the late Anglo-Saxon period and are often, although by no means always, identical with the manor. The township was the 'economic area' capable of supporting a settlement or group of hamlets (Roberts 1979, p. 77). Each township had a variety of resources, managed for the benefit of the lord or lords and his tenants, usually consisting of variable proportions of waste, woodland, meadow and arable. Regulation by the manorial court ensured the equitable distribution of different types of land or access to it and defined the rights and obligations of the inhabitants. Neighbouring townships could share resources on their mutual margins such as mossland and woodland.

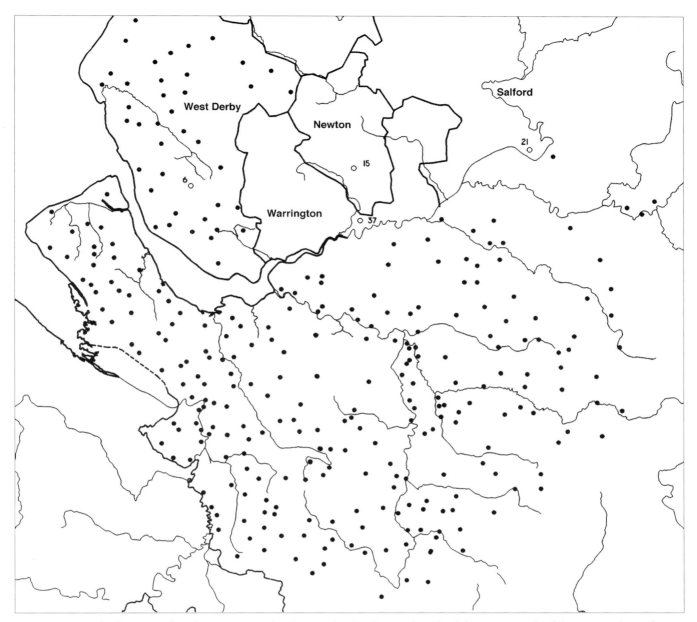

Figure 5.2. The location of settlements named in Domesday Book 1086; hundredal centres north of the Mersey have the total of unnamed places (after Terrett 1962).

The agricultural systems like the settlements themselves have a distinctive regional character. Discrete estates farming their own land in severalty from a single farmstead were common, and in this fairly conservative area with low population pressure they probably represent the descendants of an ancient form of land organisation and settlement pattern which may trace its ancestry from Romano-British enclosed farmsteads. In many places at Domesday it is likely that the population was too small and draught animals too scarce to allow the development or introduction of two- or three-field common arable rotation on a strip basis (Higham 1993, p. 203). Such a system may have come in with increasing population from the later 11th century onwards, but it was by no means universal, and even neighbouring townships might develop very different agricultural systems through circumstances of ownership or early

land-use (Figure 5.3). In form the Mersey Basin open field developed elements quite distinct from the well-known Midland-type system (Sylvester 1950, 1957, 1959; Chapman 1953; White 1983, 1995; Youd 1962; Chitty 1978; Cowell 1982; Lewis 1982, 1991). In Cheshire and Lancashire common arable, for example, did not necessarily have equal shares for all tenants in all fields, but fields could be intermixed between small numbers of tenants. Labour services too were light by comparison with the Midlands and were frequently and early commuted to cash payments. In aspect, a township might contain a diverse range of open fields, enclosed crofts farmed in strips, and crofts held in severalty in proportions that varied from township to township.

The location of townships with an open field system is closely matched by the distribution of early settlement. The settlement pattern was itself determined in part by

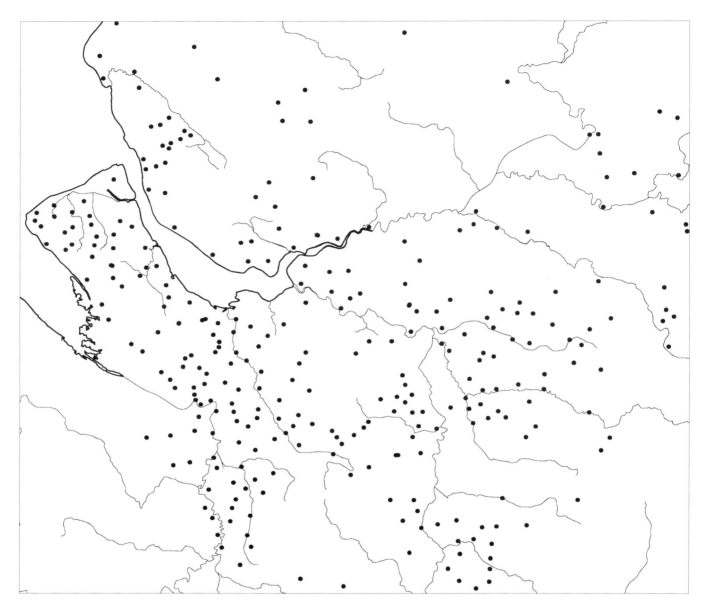

Figure 5.3. The location of open field systems, indicating organised common agriculture
(after Sylvester 1963; Morris 1983, and unpublished sources).

the presence of favourable soils, some derived from Shirdley Hill Sands, but also over sandstone and boulder clay (Shaw 1956, p. 296; Youd 1962, p. 5). In Cheshire, at Domesday, the land was understocked with ploughteams, with on average only half the teams that the land could have supported being used, but there are marked differences between the west and east. The density of teams in 1086 is ten times higher in Wirral and the Dee valley than the east and north-east of the county, with a belt of intermediate density in central and northern Cheshire. There is a striking correlation between those areas where Domesday has a high density of ploughteams and those which subsequently show some evidence of open arable cultivation. West Cheshire, the anciently-settled Dee valley and Wirral, were largely dominated by open field agriculture while in central Cheshire a belt of common arable field townships was bordered to east and west by the forests of Macclesfield and Delamere 'in which pastoralism predominated and individual assarts were more numerous than common field strips' (Elliott 1973, p. 50).

North of the River Mersey, the western and central part of West Derby hundred consisted of an extensive arable belt in which nucleated settlements farmed open fields. Usually on the margins of the townships were areas of carr or marshes for meadow and grazing (Shaw 1956, p. 345). Inland from the coastal arable belt was an extensive woodland region extending south from Burscough to West Derby, Upholland, to the Prescot area. In the east of Lancashire open fields occur mostly in river valleys (Youd 1962) while few of the mossland townships of Halsall, Kirkby and Simonswood, had common arable fields (Tables 5.1 and 5.2).

In the early post-conquest period many communities practised a mixed agricultural regime but the precise balance depended on local circumstances and condi-

Township	Arable	Oxen/cows	Sheep	Goats	Horses	Pasture	Pigs	Wood	Meadow	Marsh	Fishery
Great Crosby	•									•	
Formby	•	•									•
Hale/Halewood	•	•			•		•	•	•		•
West Derby	•							•	•		
Toxteth					•	•		•			•
Downlitherland	•										
Widnes		•			•				•		
Little Crosby	•										
Poulton with Fearnhead	•	•				•		•	•		•
Woolston with Martinscroft		•				•	•				•
Altcar	•	•	•		•	•		•	•		
Aigburth	•					•			•		
Kirkdale	•								•		•
Speke	•		•				•	•			
Ravenmeols	•	•	•		•	•	•				•
Ainsdale	•		•			•			•	•	•
Garston	•	•	•								•
Bootle	•					•			•		
Ince Blundell	•	•	•							•	
Rixton with Glazebrook	•										•

Table 5.1. Summary of medieval land-use (coastal and riverine settlements north of the River Mersey).

tions. Livestock were needed for various purposes, as draught or riding animals, for meat or wool. Some areas through their particular geographical or climatic situation were ideally suited to animal husbandry. The south Lancashire coastal belt has a strong emphasis on sheep farming in the monastic grants of the 13th century, while the woodland belt including Melling in Merseyside and the forests of Delamere and Macclesfield in Cheshire have frequent mention of pannage for pigs and a wider range of stock.

Clearance and the expansion of agriculture

Any expansion of arable land took place at the expense of the waste and woodland. Woodland is considered in more detail elsewhere in this volume (chapter ten) but some points with a direct bearing on the landscape development are discussed briefly. At Domesday, woodland was extensive in the Mersey Basin although it is not recorded consistently. Well-wooded areas included that east of St Helens (Newton hundred with its measure of woodland larger than the hundred itself and probably including Warrington's assessment), the Melling/Lydiate area, Delamere and in eastern Cheshire, in Macclesfield Forest. Place-names, often dating to the later Saxon period, confirm their generally wooded nature (Figure 5.1). However, much woodland had probably been cleared already. In some areas, notably the west of Cheshire, very little is mentioned and early clearance names are scarce. By the Norman Conquest, forest is already recorded in West Derby, and in the later 11th

century extensive areas of land in both Lancashire and Cheshire (forests of Lancaster, Wirral, Macclesfield and Delamere) were designated as Forest and reserved for royal hunting. They were subject initially to draconian forest law, which imposed severe restrictions on clearances, but once these were relaxed by the 13th-century arable expansion and settlement do not seem to have been unduly impeded.

Progressive clearance eroded the extent of woodland, and by the 16th century commentators lament the scarcity of timber. Replanting took place under the initiative of individual landowners in the 17th and 18th centuries, but much of the woodland which can be seen on the 18th- and 19th-century maps of the region is post-medieval plantation.

The clearance that made such inroads into the woodland and waste of the Mersey Basin continued a process which was under way in the late Saxon period. Through the late 11th to mid-14th century the landscape saw a series of major developments. The main factor was the rapid growth in the population. England's population is thought to have increased from 1.1 million in 1086 to 3.3 million just before the Black Death in the mid-14th century (Beresford & Hurst 1989, p. 7), but there are no means of calculating accurately population growth either in Lancashire or in Cheshire. The rise of 360% at Burton in Wirral between 1086 and the early 14th century suggests the national pattern was mirrored here (Booth 1981, pp. 2–3). The population growth led to increased demand for agricultural land. This was met in two main ways, expanding the open arable fields at the expense of the waste or marsh lying immediately around them, or

Township	Arable	Oxen/cows	Sheep	Goats	Horses	Pasture	Pigs	Wood	Meadow
Burtonwood	•	•	•		•		•	•	•
Rainford							•		
Fazakerley	•								
Aughton/Litherland						•			
Walton-on-the-Hill	•	•	•			•	•	•	•
Knowsley	•					•			•
Huyton	•					•		•	
Kirkby	•							•	
Little Woolton	•	•	•	•	•		•	•	
Roby	•								
Sutton	•						•		
Maghull							•	•	
Tarbock							•		
Eccleston	•	•				•		•	
Cronton	•								
Newton	•								•
Dalton	•						•	•	
Allerton	•	•	•						
Sefton, Netherton, Lunt	•								•
Thornton	•								•
Whiston	•								
Billinge	•						•	•	
Bickerstaffe	•							•	
Upholland							•	•	
Haydock	•						•		•
Lathom	•						•	•	
Melling	•						•	•	
Bold	•					•	•	•	•
Hurlston	•					•			•
Great Sankey	•					•		•	•
Lydiate			•	•	•		•	•	
Windle							•		

Table 5.2. Summary of medieval land-use (inland settlements north of the River Mersey).

clearance of more extensive pockets of woodland or waste around the margins of the townships. Large areas were still being cleared into the early 14th century, with monastic houses who were amongst the largest landowners in the counties active in the forefront of the movement. The cleared land might be added to the open fields or farmed in severalty as private estates. Numerous separate estates were created during the 12th–14th centuries, often on the edge of townships, as a reward for services to overlords, or for the younger sons of manorial families. Common arable field systems probably developed for the first time in many areas during this period, although they are found by no means everywhere (Figure 5.3). In addition, areas of the region, which were uninhabited or sparsely populated were colonised; eastern Cheshire may have been settled partly through an act of policy by Norman earls of Chester.

The impact on settlement too was marked. Existing rural settlements increased in size and population but new subsidiary settlements were established on the margin of existing townships. New chapels of ease were created to serve distant areas of large parishes. During the 13th and earlier 14th centuries the increasing need for cash by peasants to pay rents and rise in cash- rather than service-based transactions stimulated trade and exchange, which led to the development of towns (Philpott 1988). Market and borough charters were granted to a network of places, often parish or administrative centres, where a scattered population took the opportunity to trade, but in a few cases, such as Tarbock, centrally within a dispersed non-nucleated settlement. During the late medieval period economic downturn and decline in trade ended the burghal status of a number of small market towns, some failing altogether like Hale or Roby, but population increase in the more favourably located and larger towns ensured their survival through the post-medieval period. The influx of rural poor in the 16th and 17th centuries who suffered hardship from static wages and rising prices swelled the local populations of specialist craftsmen and artisans, whose dependence on agriculture was diminished if not completely broken.

Throughout most of the medieval and early post-medieval period, towns played a minor role in the development of the landscape. They were small in extent, Liverpool by the 1660s having no more than seven streets, and in many cases retained a strong agricultural component until well into the post-medieval period. Early importance was no guarantee of continued success. A hundredal centre at Domesday such as West Derby might be overshadowed as early as the 13th century by a more prosperous or better situated neighbour (Liverpool). Conversely, in the industrial and commercial expansion of the 18th or 19th centuries minor agricultural settlements could grow into major modern towns such as Birkenhead or St Helens.

During the 13th–14th centuries there was a rise in the conspicuous marks of status within the landscape such as construction of moated houses and the creation of hunting parks for manorial use. The park was the preserve of the local landowners, and the region follows the national pattern in seeing an upsurge in their creation in the period 1200–1350. In the later medieval period, the expense of upkeep proved too great for many landowners and parks were often turned over to pasture (Cantor 1983, p. 3). During the 16th to mid-17th centuries many parks were enclosed and farms created within their bounds (Cantor & Hatherly 1979, p. 79). However, in some cases existing medieval parks were greatly expanded in the late medieval period and hunting parks became more ornamental and recreational by the 17th century. Large landowners often landscaped parks with follies and pools. Many parks were declining in the later medieval period and were often converted to grazing or even arable and sold off. Others such as Knowsley survived into the post-medieval period to become amenity parks, landscaped as the graceful setting for large country houses.

The limits of arable expansion

Settlement expansion and population growth probably reached its height in the late 13th century and continued into the early 14th century. However, the population growth began to slow down early in the 14th century as a result of a combination of sudden climatic downturn, a series of disastrous harvests, outbreaks of disease amongst livestock, and social unrest. A more severe blow was to follow with the devastation of the bubonic plague in 1348/9, and further outbreaks later in the same century. The impact of the Black Death is hard to gauge accurately but nationally the population fell by an estimated 25–40% (Smith 1992, p. 209). Labour became scarce and land plentiful. Prices declined, arable cultivation became less profitable, and demesnes were leased out by lords of the manor. Pastoral farming which was less labour-intensive gained ground rapidly, although it

had always been strong in certain areas, and a new emphasis in documents can be traced on the values for pasture land and herbage where previously arable commanded high prices.

Climatic change had an impact on low-lying coastal regions. Locally-experienced storms and periods of sea-level change had some effect on settlement patterns and farming practices in the coastal and riverine areas. Periods of dune instability at a time of low sea-level contrast with those of high sea-level and a consequent increase in the water table; in general terms each would affect the local community, the former by impoverishing if not obscuring cultivable soils and the latter by reducing hard-won reclaimed mosslands and marshlands to wet, summer pasture. In the early 13th century land was lost to the sea on Wirral and at Ince on the Mersey Estuary (Hewitt 1929, p. 5), and the ancient coastal settlement at Meols may also have been a consequence of inundation rather than long-term depopulation (Chitty 1978, p. 21). On the south Lancashire coast Argarmeols (Birkdale), had disappeared due to inundation by 1346 and the amount of arable land in Ravenmeols, a little further south, had been reduced by 1289 (Lewis 1982, pp. 61–62). The Cistercian abbey at Stanlow, founded on the Mersey marshes in 1178, was eventually moved to Whalley, in Lancashire, in 1296 after several inundations. Further episodes of severe flooding and encroachment were recorded along the Mersey marshes and Formby coast during the 14th and 15th centuries (Greene 1989, p. 31; Hewitt 1929, p. 5 note 11; Lewis 1982, p. 62).

Depopulation resulting from the Black Death hastened rather than initiated a process which was under way by the early 14th century towards enclosing the landscape by hedges and ditches. Enclosures were versatile; they could be used for both arable cultivation and control of livestock. Assarts farmed in severalty were often enclosed from the outset, but increasingly too there was a move towards the exchange of strips in outlying fields in a township to create consolidated blocks. The limited numbers of owners or tenants in the Lancashire and Cheshire fields and the low degree of intermixing within individual fields meant that agreement was easily reached. The process in the region was largely achieved by the 16th century, without the need for Parliamentary Enclosure Acts found in the Midlands. Nor was there the misery of clearance from the land of the poor which caused such hardship and desertion of settlements elsewhere.

The post-medieval landscape

By the 16th century, much of the region was under grass, and arable cultivation was practised only as required to feed the family and animals. In the north of Cheshire, cattle rearing and fattening dominated whilst the south and west of the county, with the exception of Wirral, was given over to dairy farming. The hinterland of the post-medieval towns were increasingly dominated by pasture set aside to supply animals within them.

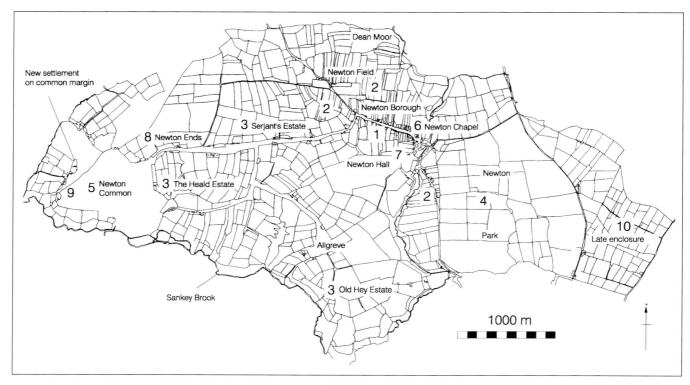

Figure 5.4. Newton-in-Makerfield (now Newton-le-Willows) in 1745.

In 1745 the township retained fossilised elements of the medieval landscape.
1. Decayed nucleated settlement (the borough, with market charter of 1257).
2. Relict open fields, including a townfield.
3. Three medieval estates recorded in the 14th century (two discrete, one scattered).

4. Former hunting park, in existence by 1322.
5. Unenclosed common.
6. Chapel, recorded by 1284.
7. Manor house, recorded by 1465.
8. Subsidiary hamlet, Newton Ends.
9. New settlement on the margin of the common.
10. Late rectilinear enclosure of mossland.

Throughout the late medieval period the exchange and consolidation continued so that by the 16th century the landscape of the Mersey Basin had acquired its 'closed' aspect (Figure 5.4). New farmsteads were constructed in the blocked holdings and a new tendency developed towards dispersal of farms around the margins of townships. This was strengthened by the population rises of the 16th and 17th centuries: with the first reliable figures in the 1560s Cheshire and southern Lancashire together numbered 112,000, but over the next century grew rapidly at near the national average rate to 182,000 (Phillips & Smith 1994, p. 5). By 1500 the landscape still contained much unused or under-used land, with one estimate of extent of waste at the end the medieval period at nearly 50% (Rodgers 1955, p. 88). This came under renewed pressure from the rising population, leading to the taking into cultivation of increasingly marginal land – the moor, waste, moss and forest – and the creation of cottages on the edges of the much-eroded common land.

Alongside the change in the physical disposition of the landscape came agricultural improvements in the drainage and reclamation of land, in its fertilisation and in the increasing specialisation of production. The post-medieval period saw the continued reclamation and cultivation of the mosslands, which had their beginnings in initiatives of the monastic houses in the Sefton area as early as the 14th century. The main efforts in the low-lying marshy western portion of the south Lancashire plain required large-scale engineering works of the 18th century, when Martin Mere was finally drained and the seasonal flooding of the Alt was improved by the Alt Drainage Act of 1779 (19 Geo III, Cap. 33). It was only in the 19th century that arable management of these poorly-drained lands behind the coastal sand dunes became economically viable. Other small wetland areas in Cheshire and Lancashire such as Newton Carr in Wirral, were drained, surveyed and partitioned with character-istic straight boundaries in the 18th and 19th centuries. The creation of long narrow strips called 'moss rooms' for turbary demonstrates the increasingly tight management of the resource, while drainage provided valuable additional arable land to help sustain the continuing population increase of the later 17th-18th centuries. However, some mosses, notably those of northern Merseyside, remained unreclaimed by the mid-19th century (Figure 5.5).

The use of marling to improve soil fertility on

Figure 5.5. Yates' map of Lancashire 1786, showing the developed post-medieval landscape, with a network of isolated farms, small nucleated villages, parks and extensive mosses surviving in the Simonswood-Kirkby area. Liverpool is rapidly expanding but remains distinct from Everton.

cultivable lands and to bring less tractable lands into production is recorded at least as early as the 13th century, and it became important for improvement of reclaimed mosslands soils in the 18th century (Hewitt 1920, pp. 22–23; Elliott 1973, p. 60). The extraction has left its mark in the form of pits, often grouped together in boulder clay regions.

The industries which proved so important in the region in the 18th and 19th centuries had their origins in the post-medieval or medieval periods, but their impact on the landscape was minor and localised (Morris 1983, pp. 19–21). Extractive industries in the countryside such as coal-mining or clay digging for pottery production had begun in the medieval period, but are documented increasingly commonly from the 16th century. Like textile production, these industries initially appear to be a part-time activity for smallholders with a few livestock, but began to attract capital investment during the 17th century. Salt, which had been exploited from the Iron Age in Cheshire, during the period discussed here was always an urban industry with far-reaching trade networks. During the 17th century production was stimulated by demands of dairying and provision of salt food for shipping. The textile industry, too, is recorded from the medieval period but by the 17th century wool, cotton and linen trades were strongly represented in south-east Lancashire. The development of burgeoning industries, notably coal and cloth in southern Lancashire and Cheshire salt, was hampered by poor communications, although turnpike trusts and canals early in the 18th century (Phillips & Smith 1994, p. 85) began to make improvements to major routes.

By the beginning of the 18th century the landscape was heavily enclosed, pasture was dominant and Cheshire's dairying reputation was already firmly established. Many new farms were created on blocks of land amalgamated out of scattered medieval holdings. Part of the rapid population increase was accommodated in cottages encroaching on the reduced common land, the others in enlarged villages and towns, but the majority of the population continued to depend on agriculture for their livelihood.

Conclusions

At the outset of the period the Domesday Book demonstrates that the Mersey Basin had a low dispersed population living in individual farms or small hamlets, with few truly nucleated settlements, and a great underexploitation of the agricultural potential. Three centuries of population increase resulted in colonisation of woodland and waste, and an expansion of the arable land by clearance. Disease exacerbated by climatic deterioration proved decisive in halting the population increase. The resulting social and economic disruption led to the demise of the feudal system and hastened incipient landscape changes. The distinctive regional variant of the open field system, which however was never universally adopted, began to decay and a shift in balance can be detected in the late medieval period from arable towards pastoral farming, which was less labour-intensive and favoured enclosed landscapes. Enclosure and consolidation by exchange was common throughout the later medieval period so that much of the landscape by 1700 was held in separate holdings, although some towns and villages retained shrunken open fields. In some places, notably the towns where ownership was most complex, the fossilised relic of the medieval open fields, the townfield, survived long enough to be recorded in a growing number of estate maps. Major landowners at all stages could retard or instigate change but the region was characterised by a high proportion of freemen, often farming discrete estates, and in the post-medieval period by a rising yeoman class. Despite technical advances in both agriculture and industry, the impact on the landscape remained relatively localised and superficial throughout the period. The towns failed to make a serious effect on the agricultural landscape until the post-medieval period, when they stimulated demand for fodder and other produce, whilst preserving by extreme subdivision the common arable fields in their immediate environs. The region continued to depend heavily on agriculture for its livelihood but by 1700 the stage was set for the major changes of the Industrial Revolution which were to see an intensification of agricultural production to supply the markets of the expanding towns.

References

Beresford, M.W. & Hurst, J.G. (1989). *Deserted Medieval Villages.* Lutterworth, Guildford/London.

Booth, P.H.W. (1981). *The financial administration of the lordship and county of Chester 1272–1377.* Chetham Society, Manchester.

Cantor, L.M. (1983). *The Medieval Parks of England: A Gazetteer.* Loughborough University of Technology, Loughborough.

Cantor, L.M. & Hatherly, J. (1979). The Medieval Parks of England. *Geography*, **64**, 71–85.

Chapman, V. (1953). Open Fields in West Cheshire. *Transactions of the Historic Society of Lancashire and Cheshire*, **104**, 35–59.

Chitty, G. (1978). Wirral Rural Fringes Survey. *Journal of the Merseyside Archaeological Society*, **2**, 1–25.

Cowell, R.W. (1982). *Knowsley Rural Fringes Report.* Merseyside County Museums, Liverpool (unpublished report deposited in the Department of Archaeology and Ethnology, Liverpool Museum, National Museums & Galleries on Merseyside).

Elliott, G. (1973). Field Systems of North West England. *Studies of Field Systems in the British Isles* (eds A. Baker & R. Butlin), pp. 41–81. Cambridge University Press, Cambridge.

Gelling, M. (1978). *Signposts to the Past: Place-names and the history of England.* J.M. Dent and Sons, London.

Greene, P. (1989). *Norton Priory.* Cambridge University Press, Cambridge.

Hewitt, W. (1920). Marl and Marling in Cheshire. *Proceedings of the Liverpool Geological Society* Part 1, **13** (for 1919–20), 24–8.

Hewitt, H.J. (1929). *Medieval Cheshire – An Economic and Social History.* The Chetham Society, New Series, 88. Manchester.

Higham, N.J. (1982). Bucklow Hundred: the Domesday Survey and the Rural Community. *Cheshire Archaeological Bulletin*, **8**, 15–21.

Higham, N.J. (1993). *The Origins of Cheshire.* Manchester University Press, Manchester.

Kenyon, D. (1989). Notes on Lancashire Place-Names 2; the Later Names. *English Place-Names Society Journal*, **21**, 23–53.

Lewis, J. (1982). *Sefton Rural Fringes Survey*. Merseyside County Museums, Liverpool, (unpublished report deposited in the Department of Archaeology and Ethnology, Liverpool Museum, National Museums & Galleries on Merseyside).

Lewis, J.M. (1991). Medieval Landscapes and Estates. *Journal of the Merseyside Archaeological Society*, **7**, (for 1986–7), 87–104.

Morris, M.G. (1983). *The Archaeology of Greater Manchester. Volume I: Medieval Manchester: A Regional Study*. Greater Manchester Archaeological Unit, Manchester.

Phillips, C.B. & Smith, J.H. (1994). *Lancashire and Cheshire from AD 1540*. Longman, London and New York.

Philpott, R.A. (1988). *Historic Towns of the Merseyside Area: a study of urban settlement to c.1800*. Liverpool Museum Occasional Paper 3. National Museums & Galleries on Merseyside, Liverpool.

Roberts, B.K. (1979). *Rural Settlement in Britain*. Hutchinson, London.

Rodgers, H.B. (1955). Land Use in Tudor Lancashire: The Evidence of the Final Concords, 1450–1558. *Transactions of the Institute of British Geographers*, **21** (1955), 79–97.

Sawyer, P.H. & Thacker, A.T. (1987). The Cheshire Domesday. *A History of the County of Chester* Vol. I (eds B.E. Harris & A.T. Thacker), pp. 293–341. The Victoria History of the Counties of England. Published for the Institute of Historical Research by Oxford University Press, Oxford.

Shaw, R.C. (1956). *The Royal Forest of Lancaster*. Guardian Press, Preston.

Smith, R. (1992). Human Resources. *The Countryside of Medieval England* (eds G. Astill A. Grant), pp. 188–212. Blackwell, Oxford.

Sylvester, D. (1950). Rural Settlement in Cheshire: Some Problems of Origin and Classification. *Transactions of the Historic Society of Lancashire and Cheshire*, **101**, 1–37.

Sylvester, D. (1957). The Open Fields of Cheshire. *Transactions of the Historic Society of Lancashire and Cheshire*, **108** (for 1956), 1–33.

Sylvester, D. (1959). A Note on Medieval Three-Course Arable Systems in Cheshire. *Transactions of the Historic Society of Lancashire and Cheshire*, **110**, 183–86.

Terrett, I.B. (1962a). Cheshire. *The Domesday Geography of Northern England* (eds H.C. Darby & I.S. Maxwell), pp. 330–91. Cambridge University Press, Cambridge.

Terrett, I.B. (1962b). Lancashire. *The Domesday Geography of Northern England* (eds H.C. Darby & I.S. Maxwell) pp. 392–418. Cambridge University Press, Cambridge.

Walker, F. (1939). *Historical Geography of South West Lancashire before the Industrial Revolution*. The Chetham Society, New Series, 103, Manchester.

White, G. (1983). On Dating of Ridge-and-Furrow in Cheshire. *Cheshire History*, **12**, (Autumn 1983), 20–23.

White, G. (1995). Open fields and rural settlement in medieval west Cheshire. *The Middle Ages in the North-West* (eds T. Scott & P. Starkey), pp. 15–35. Leopard's Head Press, Oxford.

Youd, G. (1962). The Common Fields of Lancashire *Transactions of the Historic Society of Lancashire and Cheshire*, **113**, 1–41.

Where there's brass there's muck: the impact of industry in the Mersey Basin c.1700–1900.

A.E. JARVIS AND P.N. REED

Introduction

The presentation of even a narrative, *a fortiori* an explanation, of the industrialisation of the Mersey Basin would be far too lengthy to include in this chapter. What is offered instead is a sketch of the connections between different developments to form the background to an explanation of some of the effects of 'The Industrial Revolution'.

That expression is enclosed in quotes because there is now a fair measure of debate whether the events to which it has been applied were actually revolutionary, or whether the term arose only from a perceived discontinuity of development which in turn arose only from our former ignorance of the connections. That is a debate for another place: for present purposes we may leave it aside and simply note that developments in such fields as the application of water power to processes other than flour milling increased both in rate of change and extent of application. The availability of water-power on the River Derwent was a significant factor in the location of the Lombe brothers' silk mill in Derby, an enterprise which can be argued to constitute a 'factory' and thus to oust Arkwright from his place as the supposed inventor of the factory system. The River Goyt provided the power for the important silk mills of Macclesfield, and water continued to be the main prime mover for factory driving well into the 19th century. For further details and extensive bibliographies see Hudson (1992) and Reynolds (1981).

Cheshire silk and Lancashire cotton are the prototype factory industries in which the production process is broken down into stages, each carried out by specialised machinery. Because the machinery is expensive, the unit of production must grow in size, which both demands and enables the de-skilling of the individual steps of the process. That simplifies the recruitment and training of workers, which enables a further increase in size of operation. There is, however, only a finite number of foot-pounds of work in an entire river system, which means that further growth may be constrained by either the size or the number of mills on any particular part of it. The remedy already existed, namely the rotative steam engine: more expensive than water-power, it was gradually adopted as and when continued expansion made it profitable. The mere availability of technology did not guarantee its adoption – the Newcomen engine continued with remarkable tenacity long after Watt had quadrupled its thermal efficiency (Hills 1989).

The nature of industrialisation

The steam engine changed the rules. It was now possible to employ almost any amount of power in any location where coal was obtainable at an acceptable price. Again, the necessary technology (for obtaining coal) was already in existence. The raw materials – cotton and silk – which dominated this phase of industrial development could not be produced in any meaningful quantity in this country. At least as important was the fact that the large amounts of homogeneous products of the cotton mills very soon exceeded local consumption and became dependent on export markets before the installed horse-power of steam engines came to exceed that of water-wheels. Whatever the parentage of invention, necessity is undoubtedly the mother of investment, and the second half of the 18th century saw widespread road improvements whose importance is often under-rated (Bird 1969) and the building of most of the principal canals of the country. Needless to say, several of these were geared to meeting the industrial needs of southern Lancashire and northern Cheshire, and the first industrial canal, the first canal to cross a river valley and the first to cross a watershed (the two latter 'firsts' extending only to England), connected with the River Mersey (Hadfield & Biddle 1971). The Trent & Mersey canal may well have been the first to establish a 'linear habitat' along which characteristic canalside plants and animals proliferated, though it must be remembered that both the water and the margins soon became heavily polluted for reasons given below.

The greatest transport need was for a port. This was in part to serve coastal shipping, whose importance tends to be underestimated, but principally to provide overseas raw materials and serve export markets. During the 18th century, the Port of Liverpool grew at an increasing rate: between 1757 and 1857 the number of vessels using the port rose sixteenfold and the revenue rose one hundred and sixtyfold, despite cuts in the rates of dues. In 1757 the physical extent of the docks was under 8 acres (3.24ha), while by 1857 it was 290 acres (117.45ha) – with another 160 acres (64.8ha) in Birkenhead. Round it there grew up a series of satellite ports – Runcorn, Widnes, Ellesmere Port, Tarleton to name but a few, which linked the canal hinterland with Liverpool through the medium of the ubiquitous Mersey Flats. All these developments were interdependent, and the best general guide to them is still Hyde (1971), with more specialised contributions from Hadfield & Biddle (1971), Porteous (1977), Stammers (1993) and Jarvis (1996).

There were further links. Textile industries have many ancillary processes which, traditionally, were not integrated with spinning or weaving. These include bleaching, dyeing and printing, and the demand for these services naturally increased in proportion to the growth of output of yarns and textiles. Dyeing did not change as early as the others, but the adoption of chlorine-based 'bleaching powder' and the rapidly increasing demand for alum as a mordant probably affected the chemical industry as much as the textile industries (Clow 1952). The adoption of steam printing of *The Times* in 1814 opened the way for bulk printing of textiles (and other products like wallpaper).

These changes required increasingly large and complex items of plant. Down to perhaps 1830, we find that top-flight craftsmen, especially millwrights, retained a good deal of control in the design and construction of plant. Where they were subordinated to people who might already be termed professional engineers, those engineers had often risen from the ranks of millwrighting or allied occupations. A rapidly-increasing application of scientific theory and predictive methods, especially in thermo-dynamics and strength of materials, brought about a growing separation of design and construction and more particularly a growing specialisation. Lancashire became a major centre of the manufacture of factory machinery, the boilers and engines to drive it and the machine tools to make it. The enhanced design and precision of execution made machinery faster and more reliable, but more expensive too. These issues have been the subject of long-running historical debate, to which the latest contribution is made by Jarvis (1997).

There used to be a romantic view that gas lighting was introduced as a paternalist benefit to enable thrifty housewives to spend their evenings sewing and self-helping intelligent artisans to read Plato. Those were side-effects: the real purpose of gas lighting was to enable more efficient mills to become more efficient still by means of shift working, and it should come as no surprise that the most rapid spread of the gas industry follows shortly after the 'ten hours act' of 1847, encouraging the employment of two shorter shifts in place of one longer one. Gas, with its large and constant demand for coal and its enabling of greatly enhanced return on invested capital, can be seen as a significant catalyst in what some

1715	Liverpool's first dock.
1718	The Lombe brothers' silk mill, Derby.
1733	The flying shuttle.
1737	Sulphuric acid.
1757	Sankey navigation.
1761	Bridgewater Canal.
1764	The spinning jenny.
1771	Arkwright's mill at Cromford.
1777	Trent & Mersey Canal.
1779	Crompton's mule.
1781	Boulton & Watt's rotative steam engine.
1787	Cartwright's power loom.
1789	Arkwright's water frame.
1799	Bleaching powder.
1802	Gas lighting introduced at Watt's Soho Works.
1814	Steam printing.
1816	Leeds & Liverpool Canal completed. (at last!)
1817	The Jaquard loom.
1818	Liverpool Gas Light Company.
1828	Muspratt's 70.43m. chimney (for HCl).
1830	Liverpool & Manchester Railway.
1832	First cholera pandemic.
1847	Liverpool appoints James Newlands Borough Engineer.

Table 6.1. Chronological summary of the major events in the industrialisation of the Mersey Basin.

have termed the 'Second Industrial Revolution'. Williams (1981) provides a general history of the gas industry, while Griffiths (1992) considers the origins in greater detail.

All of these changes fed back into each other, and into others as yet unmentioned. Warrington was a traditional centre of hand wire-drawing, but its position in relation to the most productive parts of the Lancashire coalfield assured it a major role in the large-scale manufacture of iron (later steel) winding cables for the new deep mines which were enabled by better pumping, ventilating and winding machinery.

The Mersey Basin also played a key role in the development of railways, especially through the building of the first real main-line railway, the Liverpool & Manchester (L&MR). Railways eventually interacted with the supplies and the produce of practically every local industry, but their initial impact was mainly in passenger carriage (Lardner 1850). The L&MR made it possible to do business in person on a daily basis and to dispatch trade samples in the knowledge that they would arrive within a day. Before the introduction of the penny post and the electric telegraph, this was an innovation of the utmost importance to all the wheelers and dealers on whom every industry, then as now, depended for both purchases and sales. Railways, through their consumption of coal, were a major pollutant but they were also a major provider of linear habitats.

Virtually all the changes mentioned implied a growth of towns. The steam engine enabled, probably eventually required, the appearance of places like Oldham which were entirely dominated by mills and factories. The engineering industry is necessarily gregarious, as machinists need suppliers of castings, materials and tools nearby. It is all too easy to forget the merchants and brokers: they needed market places in Liverpool and Manchester, and they needed extensive wholesaling infrastructures. Ellison (1886) gives an idea of the intricacies of the 'networking' system. The results of these needs, coupled with rapid population increase, are well known: rapid urbanisation leading to over-populated squalor and assisting in the spread of epidemic diseases on a scale unknown since the last visitation of the Black Death – see chapter five, this volume.

There is one consequence which was inevitable. Every industrial development mentioned together with many others affected the natural environment to a greater or lesser extent. Even comparatively clean industries like machine tool manufacture produced smoke, and the obstruction of watercourses by ash and cinders was a long-term problem in the Manchester area (Report of the Royal Commission 1870). Mining caused subsidence, polluted underground watercourses and shifted water-tables, as did the use of wells for municipal water supplies and industrial process or cooling water. Perhaps the greatest disruption of this kind was caused by brine pumping in the Cheshire saltfield, damaging buildings and bringing about significant landscape and habitat changes through the formation of flashes (Report of the Select Committee 1890–91). Brine evaporation was particularly messy because it required a low sustained heat, which was most economically achieved by the fairly slow combustion of the worst grades of Lancashire coal. These coals could produce appalling smoke even when burned in relatively 'high-tech' boilers – and in *Hard Times* Dickens remarks on the way this was viewed as a symbol and an indicator of prosperity in Coketown.

Because early process industries were relatively inefficient, large amounts of waste were simply piled up or quietly released to atmosphere or into rivers. These were the direct results of industrialisation, but the indirect effects were possibly worse. Millions of households burned local soft coal in highly inefficient grates, but the largest pollutant of all was sewage. There is a perceived image of the Victorians as being 'hung up' about sex: perhaps they were, but they still bred like 'bunny-rabbits' (see Table 6.2). Concentrate millions of people in a relatively small river system and the millions of tons of sewage they produce each year substantiates the title of this paper. Before the construction of the Manchester Ship Canal, the natural channel of the River Irwell and the artificial one of the Mersey & Irwell Navigation were so full of 'solids' that Salford regularly got what it deserved by being flooded feet deep in sewage. (Though Salford naturally, and possibly defensibly, claimed that the Mancunians were to blame, owing to the fact that the river flowed more swiftly on the Manchester bank, resulting in the deposition of solids – of whatever provenance – on the Salford side.)

The Ship Canal had many and various other effects. It effectively severed the area known as Moss Side (between Warrington and Runcorn) from the rest of the world, thereby creating an entirely new habitat for present day bird watchers. The downside of its improvements to the drainage of Salford was that it needed constant dredging, which resulted in the creation of a small desert of sludge lagoons at Weston Marsh. Dredging of the Mersey approaches to allow access across the Bar for larger vessels and over a longer period of the tide began in 1890, and just before the Great War involved the constant employment of all of the four largest dredgers in the world. The impact of their work has yet to be understood.

Population: (thousands)

	British Isles	Lancashire
1751	6,467 (est)	
1801	8,893	673
1851	17,928	2,301
1901	32,528	4,373
	Liverpool	Manchester
1801	82	75
1851	376	303
1901	685	544
	Oldham	Bolton
1801	12	18
1851	53	61
1901	137	168

Estimated Coal Production: Lancashire and Cheshire (thousand tons)

1700	80	1750	350
1800	1,400	1850	9,600
1900	28,700 (Lancashire only)		

Coal Consumption: UK manufacturing (million tons)

1816	4.9	1855	18
1887	46	1903	62

Soap Duties: amount of soap charged on (million lbs)

1713	24.4	1750	28.4
1800	46.9	1850	164.2

Paper Duties: England and Wales (tons)

1713	2,583	1750	4,115
1800	12,394	1850	44,159

Exports of cotton goods: UK totals (£ thousands)

1700	28	1750	20
1800	5,851	1850	28,300
1900	69,800		

Table 6.2. The industrialisation of the Mersey Basin: a few key statistics taken from Mitchell (1988).

Pollutants and the environment

Later in the 19th century the beginnings of what is now the environmental lobby could be identified. It was mostly ineffectual despite the movement towards pollution control which is described below. What really made the difference was the realisation that pollution was waste: black smoke was unburned calories; sulphur dioxide from copper smelting could be reduced and sold as flowers of sulphur; sewage could be de-watered and sold as fertiliser.

Nevertheless, the effects of industrialisation on the natural environment changed over the period 1700–1900 and were mitigated by the ever increasing sophistication of the chemicals and materials being produced and the terms of controlling legislation.

Table 6.3 shows some of the major industrial sectors of the Mersey Basin together with some illustrative examples of the pollutants associated with each sector. The range of industrial activity was high as would be expected from an area so closely involved with the Industrial Revolution but also, the 'cocktail' of chemicals/materials impacting on the natural environment was very considerable. At certain times over this period, e.g., the early years of the 19th century, the mixture of pollutants was remarkably varied. Through the 19th century as a whole the impact of industrial activity on the environment was probably at its greatest and industry, local government and central government struggled to provide a legislative framework to reduce the effects of these pollutants.

The chemical industry

In this context it is useful to consider the chemical industry in more detail. Today the economic viability of a chemical process is paramount, and this will be determined by a number of factors including the choice of process, the costs of raw materials, the cost of energy and the recycling of chemicals from one process to another to provide value for money for the plant overall. However, before 1850 little or no attempt was made to recycle waste products from one process as raw materials for another process. Any products surplus to needs were dumped on the surrounding land if they were solids, fed into rivers or streams if they were liquids or released into the atmosphere if they were gases. It does not take a very creative imagination to picture the kind of natural environment that resulted. Without some kind of intervention the situation was only going to get steadily worse.

A good example to illustrate these issues is the Leblanc process introduced into the UK in the early years of the 19th century for the production of alkali (in the form of sodium carbonate) from salt. Before this process alkali was produced from natural sources – usually from the ashes of kelp or from barilla derived from a Mediterranean plant. When the Peninsular War prevented supplies of barilla reaching the UK, other

Source/Industry	Pollutants
Households	Sewage
	Coal Smoke
Chemical	Hydrogen chloride
	Hydrochloric acid
	Sulphur waste
	Ammonia
	Oxides of nitrogen
	Nitric acid
	Sulphur dioxide
	Sulphuric acid
	Organic residues
Bleaching	Bleaching powder
	Hydrochloric acid
	Sulphuric acid
Paper	Alkali liquors
	Rags
Tanneries	Spent tan liquor
	Lime liquor
Cotton	Bleaching powder
	Lime
Dyeworks	Organic residues
	Cyanides
Gas works	Tar residues
Agriculture	Fertilisers
	Pesticides
Engineering	Acids
	Coal smoke
	Oils
Metal refining	Arsenic
	Cadmium
Petrochemicals	Various organic compounds
Woollen works	Vat liquors for printing
	Nitrogenous organic waste
	Soap suds
Nuclear related	Radioactive radiation
	Radioactive waste

Table 6.3. Major industries of the Mersey Basin and their pollutants

sources had to be found urgently because so many parts of industry at that time depended on the availability of cheap alkali, e.g., textiles, soap and glass.

The Leblanc process required coal, salt and limestone. All these were readily available in the Mersey Basin or in the case of limestone, brought in from the surrounding areas. From about 1820 until the 1880s the Mersey Basin was a centre for the alkali industry using the Leblanc process with the main production being centred at various times in Liverpool, St Helens, Newton le Willows, Runcorn and Widnes. When James Muspratt, a Dublin chemical manufacturer, moved to Liverpool in 1822 to take advantage of the opportunities for the Leblanc process, it marked a new phase of the development of the chemical industry with the changeover from a small scale trade to the large tonnage alkali production. The dramatic increase in production brought increased threats to the natural environment.

An outline of the process is given in Figure 6.1. For every tonne of salt decomposed half a tonne of hydrogen chloride gas (a very pungent gas known as muriatic acid gas in the alkali trade) was produced with about two tonnes of alkali waste. In the Merseyside area in the 1840s it is estimated that over 100,000 tonnes of salt were converted into alkali yielding about 60,000 tonnes of hydrogen chloride gas. There were limited attempts to disperse the gas with most manufacturers releasing the gas from tall chimneys (the chimney of Muspratt's works in Vauxhall Road, Liverpool was reputed to be over 70m high), and the number of such chimneys (Figure 6.2) in an area became a barometer of industrial activity. Probably they should have been seen as 'ominous land-marks' for the damage their gases were causing.

In 1836 William Gossage developed a method of condensing the muriatic acid gas using a derelict wind-mill packed with bracken and twigs through which he ran water. The water was brought into maximum contact with the gas (which is very soluble in water) producing hydrochloric acid. Unfortunately, until the 1860s this supply of acid far exceeded the demand, and the acid was run off into surrounding rivers and streams with debilitating effect. In the 1860s the hydrochloric acid was used as a source of chlorine in the bleaching of esparto grass during the manufacture of paper. This is an early example of the by-products of one process being used as the raw materials for another, and as chemical under-standing of the processes increased and the competitive nature of the industry grew, so the routing of materials for as many purposes as possible was more widely adopted.

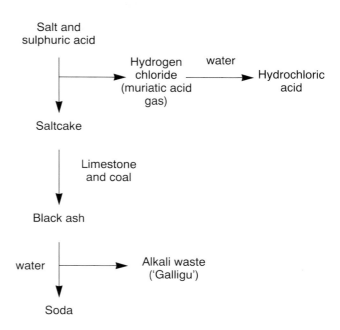

Figure 6.1. Leblanc process for the production of soda.

Even after Gossage's invention few manufacturers adopted his 'acid tower' with which to condense their muriatic acid gas. Many did not understand the princi-ples involved as very few chemical works had qualified chemists before the 1880s. The manufacturers were content to release the gas into the atmosphere and were not concerned about the social or environmental aspects.

Figure 6.2. The smoke environment in Widnes during Leblanc period.

Few saw the need to invest in the towers. After all, they were not required by law to do so, and the extra cost might put them at an economic disadvantage against other manufacturers.

While the ever-increasing amounts of gas released into the atmosphere in the Mersey Basin exacerbated the already poor environmental conditions, the law did try to intervene. Muspratt found himself in court on a number of occasions to face charges of causing a nuisance. In one case in 1838 he escaped with a fine of one shilling having 'proved' that muriatic acid gas possessed beneficial properties. He also prevented most prosecution witnesses from giving evidence. More worrying was the difficulty both the judge and jury had in admitting scientific evidence into the proceedings when the evidence from defence and prosecution was directly conflicting. In many court cases of the period this evidence was eliminated from the proceedings. Another difficulty was attributing responsibility for damage to particular factories or works, especially where a number of such works were grouped together as was the case in most towns.

By the early 1860s the weight of opinion from landowners, farmers, doctors and the public (very much centred on the Mersey Basin area where the damage from the Leblanc process was at its greatest) forced the government to intervene and move away from their previous *laissez-faire* approach. The lobby achieved such a momentum that in 1862 Lord Derby moved for an inquiry in the House of Lords. A Committee was set up and moved quickly, hearing evidence from over 45 witnesses including eminent scientists, farmers, local authorities, doctors and manufacturers. The *Report from the Select Committee of the House of Lords on the Injury from Noxious Vapours* was published in August 1862, and in March 1863 a private bill was brought by Lord Stanley of Alderley which was passed in July 1863 as the Alkali Works Act for an initial five-year period. The provision of the legislation included the requirement for all alkali works to condense at least 95% of their muriatic acid gas, the appointment of an Inspector and a team of sub-inspectors and the recovery of damages by civil action brought by the Inspector in the County Court.

Evidence before the Select Committee confirmed that while manufacturers were aware of the Gossage tower and the inherent benefits, few had made use of it. Yet Robert Angus Smith (the first Inspector under the Alkali Works Act) was able to show in his First Annual Report in 1865 that the provision of Gossage towers was a sound investment when compared with the cost of fines for causing a nuisance. By this stage (and even before enforcement of the legislation) the manufacturers had changed their stance, most had built towers and most were achieving levels of condensation of the gas in excess of the legal requirements of 95%.

The relationship between Smith and his inspectors on the one hand and the manufacturers on the other, was key to the successful enforcement of the Act. The Alkali Inspectorate under Smith's leadership and direction showed sensitivity in dealing with the manufacturers and developing a mutually beneficial partnership. The inspectors were providing a peripatetic service for the manufacturers and assisting them in being more efficient in the operation of their works without providing necessarily an economic advantage to one of them – a very difficult tightrope to walk. At an early stage Smith dismissed as unscientific and unsystematic the suggestion that some people were sufficiently skilled as observers to enable them to differentiate between a 5% escape of gas and a 6% escape; instead he saw the need for rigorous chemical analysis of the gases released from the chimneys of chemical works. Sophisticated self-acting aspirators were designed and built so that collecting and analysing the gases could continue at regular intervals throughout the day and night under 'sealed' conditions, where the manufacturers and their staff were unable to interfere and falsify results. This greatly aided the inspection process where there were only four inspectors plus Smith to cover the whole country.

In 1868 the Alkali Works Act legislation was reviewed and an assessment made of its effective enforcement. The levels of muriatic acid gas had been greatly reduced with the accompanying reduction in the environmental effects. In July 1868 a new Bill was introduced to extend the 1863 legislation. This gave Smith's work new momentum and even greater commitment to applying effective legislation to other sectors of the chemical industry. There were two immediate concerns: a percentage measure was outdated (5% of several 100,000 tonnes is a considerable quantity) and a volumetric measure was required; as the Leblanc process was being replaced by the ammonia-soda process, the nuisance from alkali works was from sulphurous and nitric acids and ammonia, and the terms of any legislation needed to reflect these changes. Because of the success Smith had in enforcing the earlier legislation, Parliament felt able to adopt measures to take account of the developing situation. As the chemical industry changed (as with other industry sectors), so it was necessary for the terms of any legislation to change to provide the inspectors with the necessary powers to reduce damage to the natural environment, while enabling these important industries to function within an increasingly competitive and international market.

Table 6.4 illustrates how legislation changed over the period to provide better protection of the natural environment and improve the conditions for day-to-day living. It is interesting to note that running parallel to these chemical pollutants in this period was the damage from black coal smoke which predates most of these chemical pollutants and was not really satisfactorily controlled until 1956 when the Clean Air legislation was put into effect. Fortunately, smogs are now a phenomenon of the past in the UK.

Pollutants were not confined to the air. As with the case of muriatic gas there was frequently a link between air and water pollution. While people were generally

1770	Charles Roe and Company prosecuted by Liverpool Corporation for causing nuisance, and copper works in Liverpool closed down.
1831	James Muspratt prosecuted by Liverpool Corporation for causing nuisance, and 1838 alkali works effectively closed down, but moved works to St Helens, Newton-le-Willows and Widnes.
1853	Liverpool Corporation formed Smoke Prevention Committee to control smoke from coal burning.
1863	Alkali Works Act to control emission of hydrogen chloride gas from alkali works; setting up of Alkali Inspectorate.
1874	Alkali Works Amendment Act: additional constraint on amount of hydrogen chloride emissions.
1881	Alkali, etc., Works Regulation Act: extended to manufacture of sulphuric acid, chemical manures, gas liquors, nitric acid, sulphate of ammonia and chlorine and bleaching powder.
1892	Alkali, etc., Works Regulation Act: further extension to include extraction of zinc ore, tar distilling and recovery of alkali waste.
1956	Clean Air Act: prohibited black smoke, regulated grit and dust, prescribed the design of new furnaces, introduced smokeless zones and smoke-control areas.
1996	The Environment Agency established.

Table 6.4. Major events in the control of air pollution.

more aware of air pollution because of breathing the obnoxious fumes and the associated smell or taste, water pollution was not so immediately evident, except if you were fishing in a local river or stream (Jarvis 1995). Nevertheless, as with the air so there was an increasingly complex 'cocktail' of pollutants being dispersed through the water system. It is, however, important to put the impact of industrialisation into perspective. Household sewage had been the main source of water pollution since the early part of the 19th century, coinciding with the greatly increased population of towns. The effective disposal of sewage waste then began to run parallel to the need to provide safe drinking water. Although improvements in sewage disposal have and continue to be made it is still a major source of pollution.

Table 6.5 shows some of the key pieces of legislation in the control of water pollution and improved drinking water supplies. Although the control of air pollution led the way as it was demonstrated that air quality could be improved by legislation and the appointment of inspectors, so the emphasis began to focus on the control of water quality. As with air pollution, there was a gradual tightening of the terms of the legislation to meet ever-more stringent requirements of water quality. With the Rivers Pollution Act of 1876 it was almost certain, even before the legislation was passed, that Smith would be asked to take responsibility for enforcing the legislation in parallel with his work on air pollution. Smith brought the same rigor to the enforcement of this legislation that he had brought to the Alkali Works Act, and achieved similar improvements.

Conclusions

Pollution from industrial activity is often naïvely thought to be a post-Second World War phenomenon, and while the sophistication of the chemical and materials waste has grown, the origins are very much part of the activities associated with the Industrial Revolution. The waste products from industrialisation are varied in their potential danger and in their quantity and control of them is even more important now than at the start of the Industrial Revolution. The legislation adopted in the middle of the 19th century and the subsequent extensions, together with the methodology set in place by Robert Angus Smith, have carried through during the 20th century to the Alkali Inspectorate and more recently to the Health and Safety Executive, the Environment Agency and other government agencies with responsibility for the natural environment. Nevertheless, the effects of the pollution (together with the use of land for a variety of industrial activities) from earlier phases of industrial development have left a legacy which is evident in the diverse habitats within the Mersey Basin area. This legacy has left its mark in the effect of air and water pollution, the development of large urban and industrial areas, derelict land often involving heaps of waste material, creation of subsidence lakes (flashes) and linear transport routes of canals, railways and roads, some of which, e.g., motorways, are still being created.

Today the de-industrialisation of the Mersey Basin provides the opportunity to take stock. Industrialisation has produced some hideous results. But man is not unique in altering the environment, e.g., Beavers (*Castor* spp.), can make major changes to medium sized river systems. However, the speed with which 'nature'

1786	*From Improvement Acts –*	
	1786	Liverpool
	1813	Warrington
	1833	Birkenhead
	1845	St Helens
	1852	Runcorn
1846	Liverpool Sanitary Act	
1847	Liverpool appoints first full-time Borough Engineer (James Newlands) at same time as first Medical Officer of Health.	
1848	Public Health Act.	
1848	Liverpool Corporation buy out two local water companies and extend supply.	
1876	Rivers Pollution Act.	
1876	Local Government Board was allowed to set up Mersey and Irwell Joint Committee.	
1885	Rivers Pollution Prevention Act	
1887	Rivers Pollution Prevention Act Amendment: allowed for an inspector to be appointed by the Local Government Board.	
1892	Mersey and Irwell Prevention of Pollution Act.	
1996	The Environment Agency.	

Table 6.5. Major events in the control of water pollution

recovers from all but the most toxic remains of industrialisation suggests that in the long term there may not be too much to worry about.

References

Bird, A. (1969). *Roads and Vehicles.* David & Charles, Newton Abbot.

Clow, A. & N. (1952). *The Chemical Revolution.* Batchworth, London.

Ellison, T. (1886). *The Cotton Trade of Great Britain.* Reprinted by Cass, London, 1968.

Griffiths, J. (1992). *The Third Man.* Deutsch, London.

Hadfield, C. & Biddle, G. (1971). *Canals of the North West.* David & Charles, Newton Abbot.

Hills, R.L. (1989). *Power from Steam.* Cambridge University Press, Cambridge.

Hudson, P. (1992). *The Industrial Revolution.* Arnold, London.

Hyde, F.E. (1971). *Liverpool and the Mersey.* David & Charles, Newton Abbot.

Jarvis, A. (1995). An historical backwater : the fishing and fish trading of Liverpool. *Northern Seas Yearbook,* **1995**, 51–76.

Jarvis, A. (1996). *The Liverpool Dock Engineers.* Sutton Publishing, Stroud.

Jarvis, A. (1997). 'Theory versus Practice in Dock Engineering'. *Transactions of the Newcomen Society,* **69**, 57–68.

Lardner, D. (1850). *Railway Economy.* Taylor, London.

Mitchell, B.R. (1988). *British Historical Statistics.* Cambridge University Press, Cambridge.

Porteous, J.D. (1977). *Canal Ports,* Academic Press, London.

Report of the Royal Commission on The Best Means of Preventing Pollution of Rivers, British Parliamentary Papers 1870 (37) XLI.

Report of the Select Committee on Brine Pumping, British Parliamentary Papers 1890–91 (206) XI. 219.

Reynolds, T.S. (1981). *Stronger than a Hundred Men: the History of the Vertical Water Wheel.* Johns Hopkins University Press, Baltimore.

Stammers, M.K. (1993). *Mersey Flats and Flatmen.* Dalton, Lavenham.

Williams, T.I. (1981). *History of the Gas Industry.* Clarendon Press, Oxford.

CHAPTER SEVEN

Natural habitats of the Mersey Basin: what is left?

L. WEEKES, T. MITCHAM, G. MORRIES AND G. BUTTERILL

Introduction

This chapter reviews the status of the remaining semi-natural habitats of the Mersey Basin. By the middle of the last century, the wildlife and habitats of the Mersey Basin were as thoroughly explored as any area of comparable size in the world. By contrast, they are relatively poorly known and documented today. This must be due, in part at least, to the great loss of semi-natural habitats in the area over the last 150 years. Interest started to revive with the general growth of environmental awareness in the 1960s and 70s, but it was not until the late 1980s that any systematic surveys of habitat distribution were undertaken. The information presented here regarding what semi-natural habitats remain is largely based on this survey work.

Mossland

Intact lowland raised bogs are one of Europe's rarest and most threatened habitats. The importance of the lowland mosslands of the Mersey Basin can be appreciated as, after the great expanse of fenland peat surrounding the Wash, the central Lancashire and Greater Manchester area is home to the most extensive lowland peat deposits in Britain. These once extensive areas of mossland have been considerably affected by man, and the majority lost. What remains should be a high priority for conservation effort.

The Pennine uplands once had extensive areas of blanket bog, which have also been considerably altered by human activities. This topic has been dealt with else-

where in this volume (chapter eleven) and so this chapter concentrates on lowland bogs.

Serious exploitation of the mosslands began with the rapid population rise of Manchester and Liverpool. Large-scale drainage of mosslands for agriculture in the area was first attempted in 1692 by Thomas Fleetwood at Martin Mere. An intensive phase of drainage, exploitation and development ensued. Landfill is still a major issue on the mosses; urbanisation and infrastructure development are a constant threat and the industrial extraction of peat for the horticultural industry is a major pressure on this delicate ecosystem.

Today, the lowland raised bogs of the Mersey Basin have all but disappeared. The mosslands now largely comprise a complex patchwork of agricultural land with drainage networks and a relatively small number of remnant bogs (Table 7.1). All of these bog remnants are highly disturbed and occur in a range of shapes and sizes; few are capable of supporting stable populations of characteristic mossland plants and animals.

The degree of loss of the Mersey Basin's mossland can be illustrated by the fact that in Lancashire, Merseyside and Greater Manchester there were 10,728ha of untouched wet mossland remaining in the mid-19th century. By the mid-20th century just 2,804ha of greatly modified mossland remained (Greater Manchester Countryside Unit 1989).

Soil survey records indicate that Chat Moss originally occupied 2,650ha (English Nature 1992) (Figure 7.1). It has rapidly declined over recent years with 800ha of raw mossland surviving in 1958, which had reduced to 440ha in 1984 and to 233ha in 1989. Only 68ha of remnant moss-

	Altcar deposit	Chat Moss deposit	Risley Peat deposit	Simonswood complex
Area of peat deposit	1,470	2,650	810	2,140
Area of SSSI	0	230	100	0
Extract peat for horticulture	0	310	0	135
Area under agriculture	1,440	1,900	660	1,700

After English Nature (1992).

Table 7.1. Estimates of area (ha) for the dominant land-uses on the four major peat deposits of the Mersey Basin.

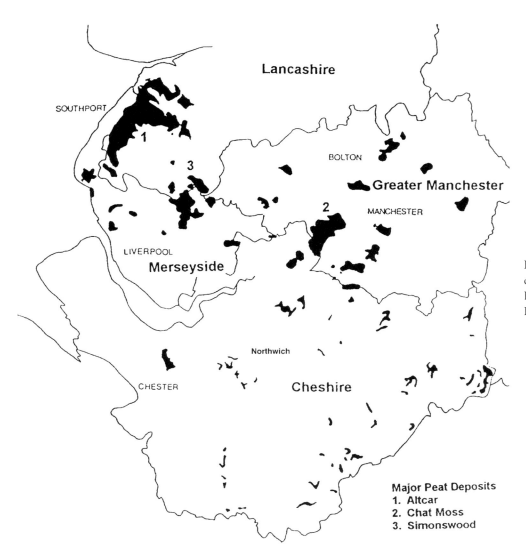

Figure 7.1. Extent of peat development in the Mersey Basin (after Fairhurst 1992 and English Nature 1992).

Major Peat Deposits
1. Altcar
2. Chat Moss
3. Simonswood

land occurs in Greater Manchester County outside the Chat Moss complex (Greater Manchester Countryside Unit 1989), of which 44.5ha of Red Moss, near Bolton, is threatened by landfill.

The situation in Cheshire is also reaching critical levels. The 1983/84 survey of semi-natural habitats (English Nature 1983/4), indicated that only 159.2ha of lowland raised mire and 20.4ha of basin mire remained relatively intact.

However, many of the remnant mosses now enjoy protection in unitary/local plans or as Sites of Special Scientific Interest (SSSI). Many sites could, with appropriate management, be made wetter and significant *Sphagnum* cover re-established.

Meres

The meres of the Mersey Basin are an internationally important feature of the lowland glaciated landscape, which extends into Lancashire, Merseyside, Greater Manchester, Clwyd, Shropshire and Staffordshire. The sites in Cheshire, form part of the North West Midland Meres, a group of generally fertile lakes, occupying hollows in the glacial drift surface which cover most of

Figure 7.2. Birch clearance on Abbots Moss, Cheshire.

the Shropshire and Cheshire plain. There are more than 60 open water bodies known as meres or pools, 32 of which lie within the Cheshire area of the Mersey Basin.

Meres originated from several causes. Many of the basins in which they occur may be kettleholes, created by ice blocks, which became separated from the retreating ice face, or were buried in the glacial outwash of clays and sands, some 12,000 years ago. More recently, subsidence of the underlying salt beds as a consequence of brine extraction, caused their formation. This is believed to be a factor in the creation of Rostherne Mere and Oakmere.

Most of the meres are to a greater or lesser extent fed and maintained by mineral rich ground water, with long retention times being typical. They vary in depth (1m–27 m), area (<1ha to 70ha) and water chemistry. The pools typically shelve steeply and are fringed with Reed swamp and Alder carr which provide additional habitats for wildlife.

Since their formation, they have been vulnerable to fluctuations in ground water level and supply, brought about by climatic variations and changes to trophic status. Good examples of hydroseral succession are also found, e.g., Quoisley Meres. However, some meres have probably changed little since the 13th century, as past records of fishing rights at Oakmere and Budworth Mere demonstrate. Alternatively, some mosses are shown as meres on early maps, so that the time taken to change from open water to peatland has varied enormously from one site to another. It is believed that most of these changes have occurred naturally.

Since the development of agricultural improvements in the 18th and 19th centuries, however, substantial changes have occurred. Land drainage has reclaimed many of the peat mosses, marshes and fens adjacent to the meres. This has greatly reduced the area of wetlands surrounding the meres and thus the later stages of hydroseral succession, e.g., fen pools with Alder carr, are particularly rare in the area.

There has also been an increase in the overall nutrient load to meres through changes in agricultural practice over the years, e.g., increases in cattle keeping and a switch from pasture to arable farming (see chapter thirteen, this volume for a more detailed account of factors affecting the meres). Beyond this, some meres have suffered further eutrophication due to pollution of the streams entering them, usually by farm wastes. The meres are, however, claimed as Britain's naturally eutrophic lakes, with evidence of blue-green algal blooms dating back to the last century and earlier. Nevertheless, there has been considerable anthropogenic eutrophication in recent decades. Trampling by cattle also inhibits the normal succession of vegetation, and there is evidence that the plants and animals surrounding the meres have been greatly affected. Nutrient control is urgently required on a number of meres within the Mersey Basin, but to do so requires an understanding of the complex factors involved and could be difficult to implement. Additionally, because zooplankton grazing is an important control of algae in some meres, reduction of the existing fish stock to discourage zooplankton feeding fish may be necessary.

In conclusion, the meres are suffering from a variety of anthropogenic effects. The recent designation of a number of the midland meres as Ramsar sites in addition to their status as SSSIs and National Nature Reserves (NNR) may help emphasise the importance of this series of freshwater pools and encourage people to look after this valuable asset.

Lowland heath

Heathland is characterised by a pioneer community of limited diversity, in which the vegetation is dominated by ericaceous species. The Nature Conservancy Council (1990) defined it as vegetation dominated by dwarf shrubs, notably Heather (*Calluna vulgaris*), Cross-leaved Heath (*Erica tetralix*), Bell Heather (*Erica cinerea*), Bilberry (*Vaccinum myrtillus*) and Western and Dwarf Gorse (*Ulex gallii* and *U. minor*).

Although some heaths may have an ancient, natural origin much of what is now lowland heath was probably broadleaved woodland (Webb 1986). The trees were cleared by man for crop growing and grazing about 4,000 years ago (chapter four, this volume). Gradually and largely because there were no trees to bring up nutrients from deeper layers, the sandy soils became leached and nutrient poor under the more open conditions, and heathland became established. For example, the Royal Forest of Macclesfield was established in the 12th century, but where land was subsequently cleared heathland dominated the area, which was used for pastural purposes until the introduction of agrochemicals in the last 50 years improved soil fertility.

Despite its largely man-made origin (see also chapter eight, this volume) lowland heathland is a significant wildlife habitat and landscape feature. The location of heathland vegetation today reflects not so much its natural biogeographical range, but where it has survived through human activities or where newly created sites have been formed, e.g., the sand quarries. Thus, many of the remaining sites are where grazing is light, the soil too shallow for trees and the land too steep for arable agriculture. They do not necessarily represent in extent or location the nature of the former heathland of the Mersey Basin and those that do survive often have a depauperate flora to that known 100 years ago (de Tabley 1899) and despite active conservation measures, e.g., at Thurstaston on Wirral, species continue to be lost. The total area of heathland types in the Mersey Basin as recorded in 1993 is noted in Table 7.2.

In Cheshire, lowland heath is associated with the sandy soils in the Delamere and Goostrey areas and the sandstone outcrops of Thurstaston, Runcorn Hill and the mid-Cheshire ridge. According to the Cheshire Heathland Inventory (Clarke 1995), lowland dry heath covers 49ha of the county and lowland wet heath covers 10.85ha, a total of 59.85ha, distributed over 45 sites.

The table refers only to the areas of open heathland currently recorded on sites and not their total areas which may include other habitats.

Heathland type	Greater Manchester	Lancashire	Cheshire	Derbyshire	Merseyside
Dry heath	50.1	30.05	54.9	1.6	262.2
Wet heath	15.3	7.5	10.9	0	1
Total	65.4	37.55	65.8	1.6	263.2

Figures taken from the Lowland Heathland Inventory (English Nature 1993).

Table 7.2. The Total area (ha) of heathland types in the Mersey Basin.

22.7ha (14.5%) of the heathland area (both upland and lowland) lies within the boundaries of nine SSSIs and 115.15ha (73.8%) within 34 Sites of Biological Interest (SBI).

More detailed consideration of uplands is given elsewhere in this volume (chapter eleven). However, upland dry heathland was recorded in the 1983/84 survey (English Nature 1983/4) mainly in the eastern fringe of Cheshire, together with a small amount at the southern end of the mid-Cheshire ridge. Figures taken from the Cheshire Heathland Inventory (Clarke 1995), suggest that upland dry heath covers 86.1ha of the county, whereas wet heath covers 10.0ha, a total of 96.1ha, distributed over 26 sites.

In general, heathland has been lost through agricultural improvements, especially following the Enclosure Acts in the period from the 16th century. However, heathlands were still traditionally widespread in Europe until the early years of this century, often being used for common grazing. Since 1949, 40% of lowland British heath on acid soil has been lost by conversion to arable or intensive grazing, afforestation and building or succession to scrub, due to a lack of management (Nature Conservancy Council 1984). Additional pressures include those from recreation, uncontrolled fires, forestry and increased fertility from agricultural runoff.

Recognition of the problems associated with the conservation of heathland can only improve the chances of its survival and of its associated wildlife. Changes in agricultural policy and improvements in habitat creation, management and protection will go some way towards conserving this habitat for the future.

Ancient woodland

Forest once covered large areas of the Mersey Basin. In Roman and Saxon times the area remained extensively wooded, but by late medieval times woods were fragmented through deforestation for agriculture, construction and fuel, largely restricting them to river valleys.

The sites that have been continuously wooded since 1600 and are present today, may be fragments of this original 'wildwood' (ancient woodland), or they may have had their structure modified by past management (ancient semi-natural). The management undertaken, the relatively undisturbed soils and the length of time these sites have been continuously wooded has enabled rich communities of flora and fauna to develop and persist. However, the decline in this habitat continues today. Table 7.3 illustrates the overall trend in the change in area of ancient semi-natural woodland, throughout and beyond the boundaries of the Mersey Basin.

In Cheshire, ancient woodlands are mainly found on the steep-sided cloughs of the river valleys, especially those of the River Dane, River Bollin and River Weaver and their tributaries, and along the mid-Cheshire ridge in the vicinity of Peckforton. The other large areas of remaining woodland are found principally on private estates. Cheshire is deficient in woodland by national standards. Only 3.8% (8,640ha) of the county is covered

	Cheshire	Derbyshire	Lancashire	Manchester	Merseyside
Area of county	232,842	263,098	306,951	128,674	65,202
Area of ancient woodland	1,681	4,392	2,764	783	111
Area of semi-natural woodland	1,263	2,583	2,314	769	111
Area cleared since 1920	102	651	116	24	18

Figures taken from English Nature Research Report 177: amendments to the Ancient Woodland Inventory (July 1994 – February 1996).

Table 7.3. Area (ha) of ancient and semi-natural woodland of the counties of the Mersey Basin.

by woodland, although the area of woodland has remained broadly the same since the Second World War. The majority of remaining ancient woodlands are less than 11ha in area and 65% of them are less than 5ha.

In Rossendale and Blackburn, the two districts of Lancashire within the Mersey Basin, present woodland cover is 0.9% and 4.1% respectively. The loss of ancient woodland is probably more complete here than anywhere else in the county, a mere 19ha remain in Rossendale. There is little evidence that the remaining ancient woodland was systematically managed in the past and only a small minority of the woods in eastern Lancashire are now stockproof. The gradual attrition of woodland through grazing, can be seen perhaps most clearly in Rossendale.

In the Greater Manchester/Merseyside area of the Mersey Basin, most of the ancient semi-natural woodland lies on the acidic and neutral soils of the underlying coal measures and bunter sandstone. Very few are on the more calcareous soils of the keuper marls to the south, largely because these were reclaimed for agriculture. 29.5% of the woodland in Manchester and 6.6% of the woodland in Merseyside, is thought to be of ancient origin. Of this, some 98% is presently considered to be semi-natural. 62% of the woodlands are less than 5ha in size and only four are larger than 10ha. Unlike other areas, however, only a small proportion of ancient woodland found scattered in these urbanised counties, has been converted into plantation. This is because of their small size, their poor degree of accessibility and their urban setting.

Ancient woodland in blocks of 2ha constitutes about 2% of Derbyshire's area, although little of this is actually present in the part of the county covered by the Mersey Basin. The size and distribution of woodlands in the county is much the same as the rest of the Mersey Basin, and similarly there have been significant changes in the ancient woodland cover over the last 90 years. Clearance for agriculture has accounted for 75% of ancient woodland loss in Derbyshire, both as a result of over-grazing, the resulting lack of regeneration and direct grubbing out of sites.

The importance of semi-natural ancient woodlands is now widely acknowledged although despite this, the resource is declining rapidly. It is now a major priority to prevent any further reduction in the area or in the nature conservation value of remaining ancient woodland.

In addition to site protection changes in the policies of the Forestry Commission, improved grant schemes, initiatives such as the planting of New Native Woodlands and improved links between woodland owners and timber using bodies, will hopefully prove beneficial for the conservation of woodlands. However, financial incentives remain low when compared with agricultural incentives and potential climatic change may further influence the development of woodlands. A more detailed account of woodlands in the region is given elsewhere in this volume (chapter ten).

Rivers and riverine features

The Mersey Basin consists of a network of rivers and streams, draining 5,000km^2 of Merseyside, Greater Manchester, Cheshire, Derbyshire and Lancashire (Figure 7.3). All waters within the catchment eventually enter the Mersey Estuary and finally the Irish Sea. The Basin is made up of 1,725km of rivers and streams.

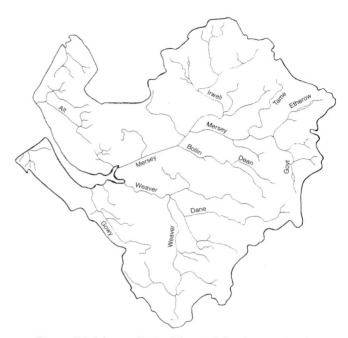

Figure 7.3. Mersey Basin (Physical Catchment Area).

Riverine systems exhibit an extremely diverse range of habitats. In a natural system, such habitats are found in a continuum and are constantly changing. Upland streams, e.g., the upper reaches of the River Goyt and River Etherow, are characteristically fast flowing bedrock streams. Both these rivers flow through an Environmentally Sensitive Area (ESA) designated for its 'high landscape, wildlife and historical value', containing two Special Protection Areas (SPA), as well as several SSSIs. In contrast, lowland rivers such as the River Dane, are often meandering systems with areas of erosion and deposition. 295.2ha of the River Dane have been designated SSSI, due to its important fluvial geomorphology, which includes clearly visible river terraces.

In-channel features, e.g., gravel bars, offer refuges for invertebrates and riffles provide spawning areas for fish. The River Medlock, although highly modified in parts, retains some areas of natural in-channel features, e.g., stony substrates, marginal gravel and some riffles. Eroding bankside cliffs found by the River Bollin and River Dane provide nesting sites for Kingfishers (*Alcedo atthis*) and Sand Martins (*Riparia riparia*).

A variety of natural habitats can also be found within the river flood plains. Backwaters, whether connected to the main channel or in the form of ox-bow lakes, offer refuges for wetland wildlife during periods of flooding and pollution. An excellent example of this feature can be found at Castle Hill on the River Bollin, where a 250m ox-bow lake is present. The ponds and ox-bows often have a diverse marginal flora, offering ideal sites for Warty or Great Crested Newt (*Triturus critatus*), a species protected under the Wildlife & Countryside Act (Department of the Environment 1981). Backwaters are also important spawning areas for fish. Additional significant wildlife habitats associated with these riverine systems, are the clough woodlands, Alder/Willow carr and flushes.

Unmodified rivers occasionally flood adjacent areas. In low lying river systems this can result in the formation of flood meadows, which have continuously high water tables and support a richly diverse flora and fauna. Flood meadows are no longer a common feature of the Mersey Basin, due mainly to agricultural changes, land drainage and flood defence measures. Less than 0.2% of unimproved, species rich wet grassland remains in Cheshire. The River Gowy drains a large and diverse ditch system, with associated unimproved acidic grassland over alluvial soils and deep acidic peat, which has formed under estuarine conditions, 90ha of which are a Site of Biological Importance (SBI). Stanley Bank Meadows SSSI covers 14.9ha of damp unimproved neutral grassland, which is now an extremely rare habitat in Merseyside.

A large majority of water courses within the Mersey Basin have been artificially straightened. The downstream section of the River Weaver, for example, was canalised for navigation purposes, resulting in extensive losses to the natural riverine features. The few remaining un-engineered stretches of this river offer a good insight into its natural course. Extensive areas of the flood plains have been modified to increase the area available for agriculture and to limit the risk of flooding.

In urban areas the land next to water courses has been developed to the bank top. The River Mersey itself has also been subject to increasing urban development pressure. Substantial flood bank protection has occurred, to form a fairly uniform area with little wildlife interest. Banks have also been reinforced by various means to limit natural erosion and the meandering nature of the river or stream.

Straightening, widening, deepening and embanking of rivers with low flow rates means that it is extremely difficult for these low energy systems to reassert their natural channel structure, after such engineering. Similarly, upland rivers have been subject to constraint, by the damming of the upper reaches to form reservoirs, e.g., River Croal and River Roach.

Very few waterways have suffered little or no human influence. Pollution, domestic and industrial, also puts pressure on the flora and fauna of the river and its associated river corridor. For example, leaching spoil heaps and direct discharges from extensive mining operations have left a legacy of water quality problems in the River Sankey/River Glaze catchment area. Urban run off via storm drains and surface water run off, contribute further to the pollution problems. If the wildlife of the riverine systems in the Mersey Basin is to be conserved in the long term, such problems need to be and indeed are being addressed.

Sand dunes/saltmarsh systems and mudflats

The coastal habitats of the Mersey Basin include the sand dunes of the Sefton coast and the saltmarshes and intertidal flats of the Mersey Estuary. These coastal ecosystems are valuable wildlife habitats, but as they are considered elsewhere (chapter sixteen, this volume) only a brief mention will be given here.

Only the southern half of the Sefton coast lies within the Mersey Basin area. However, it is impossible not to consider the system as a whole even though it extends beyond the Basin boundary. Approximately 2,100ha of dune survives, out of a total area of blown sand, which was probably once in excess of 3,000ha. In 1991 the dunes were estimated to extend for 17km and have an average breadth of 1.5km.

The dune vegetation on the Sefton coast currently stretches in a shallow crescent, from the north of Seaforth Dock to the north of Southport. At both the southern and northern ends of this area, building development and alteration of the natural landscape have confined the surviving dune vegetation to a very narrow strip at the top of the beach. Despite the loss of over 35% of the original dune area to development (Jackson 1979), the dunes are still a good example of a west-coast calcareous dune type, important on a European, national and local level, forming part of a complex of dune sites on the east Irish Sea Coast. It is the home of many rare and scarce species.

The importance of the Sefton coast for nature conservation is recognised by the designation of nearly the whole dune system as SSSI. This recognition is further strengthened by the presence of two National Nature Reserves, two Local Nature Reserves and National Trust land (Doody 1991).

The dunes of the Wirral Coast including Red Rocks SSSI (11.38 ha) and Wallasey dunes, also deserve a mention. Red Rocks Marsh lies between two parallel ridges of sand dune and until recently held a breeding colony of Natterjack Toads (*Bufo calamita*). A reintroduction programme is underway to re-establish these amphibians.

Within the Mersey Basin there are two estuaries, the Mersey Estuary and the much smaller Alt Estuary. The Mersey Estuary is 8,914ha, with an intertidal area of 5,607ha and a shore length of 102.6km. It comprises a number of valuable estuarine habitats including saltmarshes and intertidal mud flats, supporting a variety of associated species. Because of the importance of this area for wildlife, 24 SBIs have been designated, along with one NNR, three SSSIs, two SPAs and two Ramsar sites.

The Mersey catchment and its estuary continues to suffer, serious environmental degradation, receiving effluent from the major industrial sites and conurbations. The heavy pollution levels, have had a major impact on the wildlife, in addition to the effects of disturbance and loss of habitat. The Mersey Estuary Conservation Group and the Mersey Basin Campaign were established to promote the importance of the area and to safeguard and improve the environment. Following substantial investment, improvements in water quality and reduction in the pollution entering the estuaries are helping them recover from neglect and consequently support more wildlife (chapter fifteen, this volume).

Over the last 25 years, the importance of the Mersey Estuary for wildlife has increased substantially despite its pollution load. A key factor contributing to this was the increasing loss of the traditional European wintering grounds so that flocks of birds moved to the Mersey Estuary, as the best alternative site. During the mid-1960s, the treatment of effluent improved water quality with a consequent return of planktonic and benthic life. The high organic load of the estuary ensured maximum invertebrate productivity, which may be part of the reason why the Mersey Estuary continues to support higher densities of wildfowl and waders than neighbouring estuaries. Finally, there have been changes in the hydraulic regime which has allowed the return of a more dynamic system, making invertebrate food sources more available for some bird species. The area of saltmarsh available for feeding and roosting also seems to have increased around the same time. Hopefully, such positive changes will continue.

Wet flushes

The extent of wet flushes in the Mersey Basin is poorly documented. However, the majority of such sites are found in the upper reaches of the catchment. The surrounds of the River Goyt are typified by wet and dry heather moorland and acidic grassland with associated flushes, mires and blanket bogs. Flushes may be acidic or calcareous, both being found in the Mersey Basin, although the former type is more common.

The flushes are important in the way they alter the physical conditions of a site, allowing species with different ecological requirements to survive, increasing the diversity of the area. Longworth Clough SSSI exemplifies the complex transitions between vegetation communities related to drainage patterns and soil water conditions, which exist because of the base-poor flushes.

Lower Red Lees Pasture SSSI in south eastern Lancashire, is one of the few remaining examples of a herb-rich, unimproved neutral to slightly acidic pasture. Water seepages along a shallow tree- and scrub-invaded clough on the northern boundary of the site give rise to base-rich flush communities and areas of marshy grassland. Rushes, sedges and Yorkshire-fog (*Holcus lanatus*) dominate the flora, along with species such as Wild Angelica (*Angelica sylvestris*), Marsh Thistle (*Cirsium palustre*), Ragged Robin (*Lychnis flos-cuculi*) and Cuckooflower (*Cardamine pratensis*).

In Cheshire, many of the flushes are associated with the river valleys. Dane-in-Shaw Pasture (SBI) is one of the largest, most botanically diverse areas of flushed neutral grassland remaining in lowland Cheshire, with springs which issue from the north-facing slopes.

Where calcareous springs create base-rich flushes, carpets of lime-loving bryophytes in which the moss *Cratoneuron commutatum* (Hedw.) Roth. is characteristic, occur. Greater Tussock sedge (*Carex paniculata*), often associated with calcareous fens, is also a feature.

This type of habitat was probably once more widespread, however, due to falling ground water levels, drainage and improvement of the land for agricultural purposes, it is becoming increasingly scarce. Current conservation measures are limited to the designation as SSSIs or SBIs of a few sites.

Conclusion

It was clear from our research that a considerable amount of information exists on the semi-natural habitats of the Mersey Basin. It is however, dispersed, mostly botanical, of variable age and in a variety of formats and therefore, not easily comparable. The information, when pieced together, forms a depressing picture of high quality habitat loss. However, several trends within the Basin, give cause for optimism:

1. the rapid increase of awareness within local government of the need to integrate environmental thinking within all policy areas;

2. national government's commitment to safeguarding biodiversity, through its endorsement of *Biodiversity: The UK Steering Group Report* (Department of the Environment 1995);

3. the increase in partnership solutions to wildlife conservation problems;

4. the protection received through national and international wildlife related designations and the development and implementation of agri-environment schemes, e.g., Countryside Stewardship.

However, there is no room for complacency. Statutory designations are not enough to safeguard the Basin's biodiversity, the network of non-statutory wildlife sites also need protection to allow them to provide for the enriching of the wider countryside and urban areas.

The challenge for us all is to work together and through the process of producing and implementing Local Biodiversity Action Plans commit ourselves to a programme of actions, which will help to develop a more sustainable future for the wildlife and natural habitats of the Basin and beyond.

References

Included here are many unpublished documents and publications used in compiling this chapter but not necessarily cited in the text.

Bevan, J.M.S., Robinson, D.P., Spencer, J.W. & Whitbread, A. (1992). *Derbyshire Inventory of Ancient Woodland*, NCC, Peterborough.

Carter, A. & Spencer, J. (1988). *Greater Manchester and Merseyside Inventory of Ancient Woodland (Provisional)*. NCC, Peterborough.

Cheshire Wildlife Trust and Cheshire County Council (1995). *Sites of Biological Importance Register*. Deposited at Cheshire Wildlife Trust, Grebe House, Reaseheath, Nantwich, Cheshire, CW5 6DG.

Clarke, S. A. (1995). *Cheshire Heathland Inventory*. Deposited at Cheshire Wildlife Trust, Grebe House, Reaseheath, Nantwich, Cheshire, CW5 6DG.

de Tabley, Lord (1899). *The Flora of Cheshire*. Longmans, Green and Co., London.

Department of the Environment (1981). *Wildlife & Countryside Act*. HMSO, London.

Department of the Environment (1995) *Biodiversity: The UK Steering Group Report*. HMSO, London.

Doody, J. P. (1991). Foreword. *The Sand Dunes of the Sefton Coast* (eds D. Atkinson & J. Houston), pp. v–vi. National Museums & Galleries on Merseyside in association with Sefton Borough Council, Liverpool.

English Nature (1983/4). *Cheshire Survey of Semi-natural Habitats*. Deposited at English Nature, Attingham Park, Shrewsbury, SY4 4TW.

English Nature (1992). *Distribution and Status of Lowland Peat in the Mersey Basin Area*. Deposited at English Nature, Attingham Park, Shrewsbury, SY4 4TW.

English Nature, RSPB (1993). *The Lowland Heathland Inventory*, English Nature, Peterborough.

English Nature. *Site of Special Scientific Interest Schedules, Cheshire, Derbyshire, Greater Manchester, Lancashire and Merseyside*. Deposited at English Nature, Attingham Park, Shrewsbury, SY4 4TW.

Environment Agency (1996). *Alt/Crossens Catchment Management Plan Consultation Report*. Deposited at Environment Agency, Richard Fairclough House, Knutsford Road, Warrington, WA4 1HG.

Environment Agency (1996). *Bollin Sub-Catchment Report*. Deposited at Environment Agency (as above).

Environment Agency (1996). *Goyt/Etherow Sub-Catchment Report*. Deposited at Environment Agency (as above).

Environment Agency (1996). *River Habitats in England and Wales: A National Overview*. Deposited at Environment Agency (as above).

Environment Agency (1996). *Sankey/Glaze Local Management Plan Consultation Report 2nd Draft*. Deposited at Environment Agency (as above).

Environment Agency (1996). *Upper Mersey Catchment Management Plan Consultation Report*. Deposited at Environment Agency (as above).

Fairhurst, J. (1992). *Cheshire State of the Environment Project: Technical Report Number 3, Habitats and Wildlife*. Cheshire County Council, Chester

Fairhurst, J. (1992). *Cheshire State of the Environment Project: Technical Report Number 4, Economic Landuse*. Cheshire County Council, Chester.

Greater Manchester Countryside Unit (1989). *The Mosslands Strategy: A Strategy for the Future of Chat Moss, Greater Manchester*. Greater Manchester Countryside Unit, Manchester

Isaac, D. & Reid, C. (1991). *Amendments to the Ancient Woodland Inventory for England, July 1994 – February 1996*. English Nature Research Reports, No. 177. English Nature, Peterborough.

Jackson, H.C. (1979). The decline of the sand lizard, *Lacerta agilis* L., population on the sand dunes of the Merseyside coast, England. *Biological Conservation*, **16**, 177–193.

Mersey Basin Campaign (1994). *Mersey Estuary Management Plan, Draft*. Deposited at Mersey Basin Campaign, Voluntary Sector Network, 111 The Piazza, Piccadilly Plaza, Manchester. M1 4AN.

Morries, G. (1986). *Lancashire's Woodland Heritage*. Lancashire County Council, Preston.

Moss, B., McGowan, S., Kilinc, S. & Carvalho, L. (1992). *Current Limnological Condition of a Group of the West Midland Meres that Bear SSSI Status*. Final Report of English Nature Research Contract Number F72-06-14, Department of Environmental and Evolutionary Biology, University of Liverpool.

National Rivers Authority (1994). *River Irwell Catchment Management Plan: Consultation Report, Chapter one – River Irwell introduction*. Deposited at Environment Agency (as above).

National Rivers Authority (1994). *River Irwell Catchment Management Plan: Water Quality Supplement*. Deposited at Environment Agency (as above).

National Rivers Authority (1995). *River Gowy Rapid Corridor Survey*. Deposited at Environment Agency (as above).

National Rivers Authority (1995). *River Irwell Catchment Management Plan: Action Plan*. Deposited at Environment Agency (as above).

National Rivers Authority (1995). *The Mersey Estuary A Report on Environmental Quality*. Water quality series, **No 23**. HMSO, London. Deposited at Environment Agency (as above).

National Rivers Authority North West (1995). *Stillwaters Project Summary*. Deposited at Environment Agency (as above).

Nature Conservancy Council (1984). *Nature Conservation in Britain*. NCC, Peterborough.

Nature Conservancy Council (1990). *Handbook for Phase 1 Habitat Survey*. NCC, Peterborough.

Newton, A. (1971). *Flora of Cheshire*. Cheshire Community Council, Chester.

Phase 1 Habitat Survey of Greater Manchester (1990/1992). Greater Manchester Ecology Unit. Deposited at GMEU, Council Offices, Wellington Road, Ashton-under-Lyne, Tameside, OL6 6DL.

Phillips, P.M. (1994). *Lancashire Inventory of Ancient Woodlands (Provisional)*. English Nature, Peterborough.

Robinson, D.P. & Whitbread, A. (1988). *Cheshire Inventory of Ancient Woodland (Provisional)*. NCC, Peterborough.

Ward, D., Holmes, H. & José, P. (eds) (1994). *The New Rivers and Wildlife Handbook*. RSPB, Sandy.

Savage, A.A. (1976). *The Nature and History of the Cheshire Meres*. News Bulletin of the Cheshire Conservation Trust, **2 (9)**, 1–2.

Webb, N. (1986). *Heathlands*. The New Naturalist. Collins, London.

CHAPTER EIGHT

Man-made habitats of the Mersey Basin: what is new?

H.J. ASH

Introduction

Mankind's activities in the Mersey Basin have destroyed much wildlife habitat. However, they have also created new opportunities, often accidentally. Looking at the Basin's areas, it is easy to be depressed by the lack of opportunity for species other than humans. A few forms have prospered at the expense of many others. In urban areas such as Knowsley and St Helens, half the urban greenspace (20% total urban area) is devoted to amenity grassland, dominated by Perennial Rye-grass (*Lolium perenne*) and a handful of other grasses and rosette species (Gilbert 1989; St Helens Wildlife Advisory Group 1986). This supports such a limited range of organisms, it has been dubbed 'green desert'. Another quarter of the greenspace (10% urban area) is occupied by rough, unmanaged grassland, dominated by False Oat-grass (*Arrhenatherum elatius*) and Cock's-foot (*Dactylis glomerata*) with a handful of tall herbs such as thistles (*Cirsium arvense, C. vulgare*), docks (*Rumex* spp.) and Rosebay Willow-herb (*Chamerion angustifolium*). This is floristically poor, but has some value to small mammals, including children, who are often short of informal play space close to home. However, hidden away among the debris of past industrial activity, there are sites supporting a surprising range of wildlife; not replacements for what has been lost, but different communities which would not be here without man's intervention.

Calcareous sites

The Mersey Basin has few naturally-occurring calcareous areas; just the coastal dunes and Pennine fringe. However, limestone is used in a range of industrial processes, in the chemicals and glass industries particularly, and forms the basis of a number of waste deposits:

1. blast furnace slag, e.g., Kirkless Lane, Wigan;

2. Leblanc waste from 19th-century manufacture of sodium carbonate and bleaching powder, e.g., Nob End, Bolton; St Helens; Bury; Widnes;

3. calcium sulphate from hydrofluoric acid production, e.g., Runcorn.

Examples of each of these have been left untreated since tipping ceased, often decades ago, so that although the substrate is unnatural, the colonisation is a natural primary succession. Such calcareous sites start with a pH of 8–10, weathering to a level not dissimilar to a limestone grassland (Ash 1983, 1991). Nutrient levels, especially nitrogen and phosphorus, are very low, with phosphorus fixed in insoluble forms by the calcium. Drought, extreme surface temperatures and, on blast furnace slag, very stony texture add to the problems of colonising plants. The nearest natural calcareous habitats are 30–40kms away, so these areas are 'islands' in a sea of acidic/neutral substrates. The colonising flora is a mixture of such widespread species as can cope with the edaphic conditions, e.g., Red Fescue (*Festuca rubra*), Cock's-foot, Colt's-foot (*Tussilago farfara*), and species which have succeeded in spreading from calcareous habitats, primarily the sand dunes (Ash, Gemmell & Bradshaw 1994). Prominent among the latter are the marsh and spotted orchids (*Dactylorhiza praetermissa, D. fuchsii* and hybrids, and *D. incarnata*) and sometimes Fragrant Orchid (*Gymnadenia conopsea*), but others include Common Centaury (*Centaurium erythraea*), Blue Fleabane (*Erigeron acer*) and Creeping Willow (*Salix repens*). One site, Nob End near Bolton, is now a Site of Special Scientific Interest (SSSI) for its flora (Table 8.1), and is a country park. Most of these long-distance colonisers have good dispersal mechanisms, e.g., wind-blown seeds. Other species from equivalent habitats will succeed if introduced artificially, e.g., Yellow-wort (*Blackstonia perfoliata*) and Autumn Gentian (*Gentianella amarella*) on Leblanc waste (Ash *et al.* 1994). On very infertile sites such as these the succession does not start with annuals – probably there are just not enough nutrients to complete a life cycle in one season. The primary colonisers are perennial herbs and grasses, and the succession proceeds from open grassland with herbs and bare ground, to a closed, usually species-rich, grassland community. The usual tree colonists of derelict land, Silver Birch (*Betula pendula*) and willows (*Salix caprea, and S. cinerea*) do not succeed on these calcareous wastes, but Hawthorn (*Crataegus monogyna*) will gradually invade if seed sources are available and grazing animals are absent. Growth rates are very slow, but some 115

Acer pseudoplatanus	+	Dactylorhiza praetermissa	3	Plantago lanceolata	4
Achillea millefolium	2	Dactylorhiza purpurella	3	Plantago major	+
Achillea ptarmica	+	Equisetum arvense	2	Pohlia nutans	1
Agrostis capillaris	1	Euphrasia nemorosa	1	Potentilla anglica	1
Agrostis stolonifera	3	Festuca arundinacea	2	Potentilla reptans	+
Angelica sylvestris	2	Festuca ovina	2	Ranunculus acris	+
Anthoxanthum odoratum	1	Festuca rubra	5	Ranunculus repens	1
Arabidopsis thaliana	+	Gymnadenia conopsea	4	Rubus fruticosus	3
Arrhenatherum elatius	1	Heracleum sphondylium	3	Rumex acetosa	+
Bellis perennis	4	Hieracium sabaudum	1	Sambucus nigra	+
Carex flacca	2	Hieracium vulgatum	2	Senecio jacobaea	1
Carlina vulgaris	2	Holus lanatus	1	Sisyrinchium bermudiana	2
Centaurea nigra	6	Hypochoeris radicata	2	Solidago canadensis	1
Centaurium erythraea	1	Lathyrus pratensis	2	Succisa pratensis	5
Cerastium fontanum	1	Leontodon autumnalis	+	Taraxacum agg.	1
Cirsium arvense	2	Linum catharticum	4	Tragopogon pratensis	4
Cirsium vulgare	+	Lolium perenne	1	Trifolium pratense	4
Crataegus monogyna	4	Lotus corniculatus	7	Trifolium repens	1
Dactylis glomerata	4	Molinia caerulea	1	Tussilago farfara	2
Dactylorhiza fuchsii	2	Ophioglossum vulgatum	1	Urtica dioica	+
Dactylorhiza fuschii x D.praetermissa	2	Orobanche minor	2	Orchis morio recorded 1970s, but not since.	
Dactylorhiza incarnata	3	Pilosella officinarum	3		

Table 8.1. Plant species list for Leblanc waste area of Nob End SSSI, near Bolton. 7.5ha, pH 7.9–8.2. Waste tipping ceased 1881. Large orchid populations noted by 1954. Estimated DOMIN cover values.

years after abandonment, Nob End is having to be managed to control scrub and maintain the species-rich grassland.

Acidic sites

Man has been unintentionally creating habitats on acidic substrates in Merseyside for centuries. Wirral still has considerable areas of lowland heath at Thurstaston Common, Heswall Dales, Caldy Hill and several smaller sites. Although most heaths have been created by human activity (Webb 1986) it is likely that at least some have an ancient and natural origin. Thus, some of the coast-facing slopes of Wirral heaths may be truly 'natural', but most are the product of the activities of man and his animals on thin, acid sandy soils and Cowell (chapter four, this volume) shows that humans have lived in the area continuously since Mesolithic times. Most of the areas are dry maritime heath, with Western Gorse (*Ulex gallii*) and Bell Heather (*Erica cinerea*) abundant among the Heather (*Calluna vulgaris*). Small damp areas support Cross-leaved Heath (*Erica tetralix*), Deergrass (*Trichophorum cespitosum*), Bog Asphodel (*Narthecium ossifragum*) and even relict populations of Round-leaved Sundew (*Drosera rotundifolia*) and Marsh Gentian (*Gentiana pneumonanthe*). Grazing and controlled burning faded from these heaths in the first half of this century, as development reduced and fragmented them. Birch, Scots Pine (*Pinus sylvestris*) and Oak (*Quercus* spp.) have invaded, converting some sites, e.g. Irby Common,

to secondary woodland. Considerable conservation effort has been expended on the larger sites in recent years, removing scrub and controlling Bracken (*Pteridium aquilinum*). On Thurstaston Common, the National Trust has re-instated grazing in three large paddocks, using a small flock of Herdwick wethers (sheep). Once initial problems with some dogs and their owners had been overcome, these have proved successful managers.

Man's activities have also served to change the nature of existing soils, especially through the effects of acid rain. In the early 19th century a Leblanc works was established in Liverpool (Jarvis & Reed, chapter six, this volume), the hydrochloric acid from whose chimney had such devastating effects on the farmers of Everton that the owner was forced to move to Earlestown (where his waste heap, known as Mucky Mountains, is extant adjacent to the Sankey Canal, supporting an interesting flora including Pyramidal Orchid (*Anacamptis pyramidalis*) and Quaking-grass (*Briza media*)). More generally, the acidity from coal-burning has lowered the pH of the soils of the older parks such as Sefton Park, Liverpool, especially where soils were thin or sandy, rather than clay. Common Bent (*Agrostis capillaris*) and Red Fescue dominate in such grasslands, with Common Bird's-foot-trefoil (*Lotus corniculatus*), Autumn Hawkbit (*Leontodon autumnalis*) and Heath Bedstraw (*Galium saxatile*). Where limewash was used to line out the sports pitches, a narrow band of less calcifuge plants provides more permanent markings: better grass growth and the presence of species such as Creeping Buttercup (*Ranunculus repens*) and Daisy (*Bellis perennis*) (Bradshaw 1980).

Coal fuelled industry in the Mersey Basin for around 200 years. Its extraction left many waste deposits, which have been the major target of four decades of reclamation programmes. The shales associated with the Lancashire coalfield usually have a high pyrites content, which under natural weathering releases acids (Bradshaw & Chadwick 1980). As a consequence most of the Basin's colliery wastes are acidic (pH 3–5), and reclamation techniques have centred on treatment with large quantities of limestone, followed by grass and tree establishment. However, there remain sufficient examples of colliery shale, and other acidic wastes such as clinker, cinders and sandstone, to illustrate the succession.

When new, these materials are severely deficient in nutrients, especially nitrogen (at least in available form) and phosphate. They are subject to extreme temperatures, drought, poor physical structure, erosion, and, on recent deposits, compaction by heavy machinery. Whereas calcareous wastes weather to a neutral or slightly alkaline substrate, acidic ones only ameliorate as an organic layer accumulates on the surface. However, they are somewhat less isolated from potential colonisers.

As with calcareous wastes, the first colonisers are perennials: Common Bent, Yorkshire-fog (*Holcus lanatus*), Rosebay Willow-herb, Colt's-foot and hawkweeds (*Hieracium* section *Sabauda*). Pioneer trees (*Betula* spp. and *Salix* spp.) often colonise at this early stage of very open vegetation, especially if seed sources are close, but grow very slowly (Curtis 1977). Usually the vegetation slowly closes over 50 years or more, becoming grassland with scrub and eventually Birch/Willow woodland with a species-poor, grassy understorey. If oaks (usually *Quercus robur*) are nearby, and carriers for their acorns such as Jays (*Garrulus glandarius*) or people, they will establish at the grassland stage and eventually dominate the woodland. On some less hostile spoils Sycamore (*Acer pseudoplatanus*) also invades as the organic layer accumulates.

Sometimes the succession takes other routes (Figure 8.2). On very acid spoils Wavy Hair-grass (*Deschampsia flexuosa*) can dominate to the virtual exclusion of other species. Elsewhere, especially on small rural heaps, various species characteristic of moorland occur: Matgrass (*Nardus stricta*), Purple Moor-grass (*Molinia caerulea*), Heather and Crowberry (*Empetrum nigrum*). Other acidic wastes develop similarly, but sometimes become colonised by Gorse (*Ulex europaeus*), which may form impenetrable stands; Gorse is rare on colliery shales. The ecology of these different routes is little understood, although seed sources and (for Gorse) phosphate levels may be presumed to play a part. A better understanding would be worthwhile, not least to help those trying to develop alternative reclamation techniques, which do not involve digging up environmentally sensitive limestone areas to reclaim wastes!

Figure 8.1. Nob End Country Park, Bolton. SSSI on Leblanc waste (*Photo: H. Ash*).

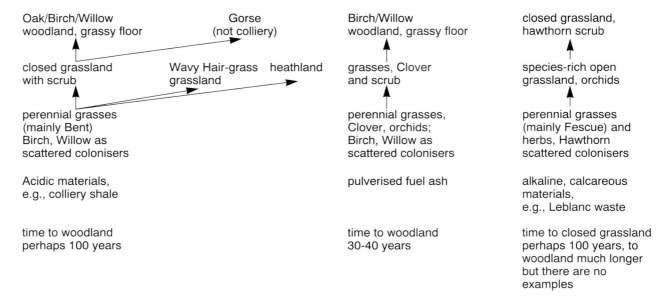

Figure 8.2. Typical plant successions on industrial wastes in the Mersey Basin.

Other unusual substrates

Calcareous wastes bear some resemblance to limestone soils, and colliery wastes to natural acidic substrates, but not all man-made substrates have such analogues. One of the few industrial wastes still to be deposited in large amounts is pulverised fuel ash (PFA), from coal-burning power stations. Unlike colliery shale or chemical wastes, it is fairly benign, with a silty texture, some phosphate (though no nitrogen) and a pH just above neutral, gradually reducing under weathering (Ash 1983). However, it is liable to form cemented layers which impede root growth, and when fresh it has toxic levels of boron. These leach sufficiently to allow plant growth within 5–10 years (less if the ash is lagooned). Some sites are initially saline and are colonised by plants tolerant of brackish conditions: Spear-leaved Orache (*Atriplex prostrata*) and Red Goosefoot (*Chenopodium rubrum*). On less saline sites, or as the salts leach out, perennial grasses and herbs establish, often the same suite of species, capable of survival on very low nutrients, that appear on other wastes: Yorkshire-fog, bents, Red Fescue, Colt's-foot and Field Horsetail (*Equisetum arvense*). Clovers (*Trifolium* spp.) are at a double advantage, being boron-tolerant as well as nitrogen-fixing, and can dominate a site in early years. Frequently there are swarms of marsh and spotted orchids with spectacular hybrids. Birch and Willow also colonise while the vegetation remains open, and proceed to turn the area into woodland. This succession can be relatively swift; PFA tipped into a subsidence flash at Wigan Power Station took 20 years to develop spectacular marsh orchid colonies, and within another 10 years was dense Willow/Birch woodland, very good for birds especially Short-eared Owls (*Asio flammeus*), but needing management to retain an interesting ground flora. With such management Marsh Helleborine (*Epipactis palustris*) and Round-leaved Wintergreen (*Pyrola rotundifolia*)

have flourished and some marsh orchids have been retained (S. Crombie pers. comm.).

Often industries are or were associated with a particular area. St Helens' glass production resulted in several large heaps of Burgy waste, a mixture of sand and jeweller's rouge once used for polishing plate glass. It is rarely found elsewhere in the country. Similarly Leblanc waste is almost confined to north-western England, and Prescot has an area of copper-contaminated soils. Burgy waste was tipped behind bunds, rising to 15m and

Figure 8.3. Marsh Helleborine on PFA, Wigan (*Photo: H. Ash*).

covering several hectares. It is largely dominated by Tall Fescue (*Festuca arundinacea*), a species frequently found on alkaline soils of industrial origin. One heap, topped with sand washings and war-time sandbags as well as Burgy, supports sand dune species and well developed Willow scrub with many birds, and is listed as of major ecological importance to the town: that did not stop it being given permission on appeal for housing. It had not been built on by July 1996, but the planning permission remained in force. Such industrial wastes have links to local history, and are often the only remaining relics of the industry on which the development of the community was based, and thence have cultural as well as biological significance. These sites are valuable to wildlife and to people. They often include some of the best sites for wildlife in urban areas, and the most available opportunities for recreation in semi-natural surroundings. The problem is that it is still difficult to defend them from proposals for redevelopment or even reclamation. I believe they must be defended, just as much as ancient woodlands and grasslands, if they and the plants and animals they support are to survive.

Another common substrate in urban areas, especially where demolition occurs, is brick rubble. However, the issues associated with this substrate are considered by Bradshaw (chapter twelve, this volume).

Wetlands

Such considerations do not just apply to dry land. Man's activities have decimated the region's natural wetlands, but created a variety of new ones; canals, starting with the Sankey Navigation in 1757, reservoirs, subsidence flashes and many small marshes where drainage has been impeded. Ponds are treated in detail by Boothby & Hull (chapter fourteen, this volume). In water bodies isolated from land drainage, such as some industrial reservoirs and canals, water quality can be good and a range of aquatic species flourish – duckweeds (*Lemna* spp.), pondweeds (*Potamogeton natans, P. crispus, P. pectinatus*), waterweeds (*Elodea* spp.), water-starworts (*Calitriche* spp.), but also unusual plants. Fringed Water-lily (*Nymphoides peltata*) grows along considerable stretches of the Leeds-Liverpool Canal in Liverpool, Floating Water-plantain (*Luronium natans*) in Manchester, White Water-lily (*Nymphaea alba*) at Top Dam, Eccleston, and Water-soldier (*Stratiotes aloides*) is embarrassingly successful since introduction to a number of Wirral marl pits. Many such sites are popular with anglers, whilst the large area of subsidence flashes south of Wigan are a major locality for migrating and resident birds.

Marshes colonise quickly, and can become valuable wildlife habitats in a few decades. Kraft Fields at Knowsley Industrial Estate was stripped of topsoil in the 1960s. Within 20 years it had a plant list of over 100 species (Table 8.2), including Common Cottongrass (*Eriophorum angustifolium*), Common Club-rush (*Schoenoplectus lacustris*), marsh orchids and large areas

Achillea millefolium	R	*Juncus conglomeratus*	O
Achillea ptarmica	O	*Juncus effusus*	O
Agrostis capillaris	R	*Juncus inflexus*	R
Agrostis stolonifera	O	*Lapsana communis*	R
Alchemilla xanthochlora	R	*Lathyrus pratensis*	O
Angelica sylvestris	F	*Lathyrus sylvestris*	R
Anthoxanthum odoratum	R	*Lemna minor*	R
Apium nodiflorum	R	*Leontodon autumnalis*	O
Arrhenatherum elatius	F	*Leucanthemum vulgare*	O
Artemisia vulgaris	R	*Listera ovata*	R
Aster novi-belgii	O	*Lotus corniculatus*	O
Bellis perennis	R	*Lotus pedunculatus*	O
Calystegia sepium	R	*Melilotus officinalis*	R
Carex demissa	R	*Mentha arvensis*	R
Carex flacca	F	*Oenanthe crocata*	R
Carex hirta	O	*Ononis repens*	R
Carex ovalis	R	*Ophrys apifera*	R
Carex pseudocyperus	R	*Phalaris arundinacea*	F
Carex remota	R	*Phleum pratense*	R
Centaurea nigra	R	*Plantago lanceolata*	O
Centaurium erythraea	R	*Plantago major*	R
Cerastium fontanum	R	*Potentilla anserina*	F
Chamerion angustifolium	F	*Potentilla reptans*	F
Cirsium arvense	R	*Prunella vulgaris*	O
Cirsium vulgare	R	*Pulicaria dysenterica*	R
Convolvulus arvensis	R	*Quercus robur*	R
Crataegus monogyna	R	*Ranunculus repens*	F
Cynosurus cristatus	O	*Rubus caesius*	R
Cytisus scoparius	R	*Rubus fruticosus*	O
Dactylis glomerata	F	*Rumex acetosella*	R
Dactylorhiza fuchsii	O	*Rumex crispus*	R
Dactylorhiza fuschii x *praetermissa*	O	*Rumex obtusifolius*	R
Dactylorhiza incarnata	R	*Salix cinerea*	R
Dactylorhiza praetermissa	O	*Salix repens*	R
Deschampsia flexuosa	R	*Salix viminalis*	R
Dipsacus fullonum	R	*Schoenoplectus lacustris*	R
Eleocharis palustris	F	*Senecio erucifolius*	R
Elytrigia repens	O	*Senecio jacobaea*	R
Epilobium hirsutum	F	*Sisyrinchium bermudiana*	R
Epilobium montanum	R	*Solidago canadensis*	R
Epilobium palustre	O	*Sonchus arvensis*	R
Epilobium parviflorum	O	*Stachys palustris*	O
Equisetum arvense	O	*Stachys sylvatica*	R
Equisetum palustre	O	*Tragopogon pratensis*	R
Eriophorum angustifolium	R	*Trifolium hybridum*	R
Fallopia japonica	R	*Trifolium medium*	O
Festuca rubra	R	*Trifolium pratense*	O
Galium palustre	R	*Trifolium repens*	O
Geranium dissectum	R	*Tussilago farfara*	O
Glyceria fluitans	R	*Typha latifolia*	F
Glyceria notata	R	*Ulex europaeus*	R
Heracleum sphondylium	O	*Vicia cracca*	O
Hieracium sabaudum	R	*Vicia hirsuta*	R
Holcus mollis	O	*Vicia sativa*	R
Holus lanatus	F	*Vicia sepium*	R
Hypochoeris radicata	O	*Viola arvensis*	R
Juncus acutiflorus	R		
Juncus articulatus	F		

Table 8.2. Flora of Kraft Fields, Knowsley Industrial Estate, Merseyside. Former farmland, topsoil stripped 1960s leaving sands and clays. 10ha. pH 6.5–7.3. DAFOR abundances.

of rushes (*Juncus* spp.), Bulrush (*Typha latifolia*) and Great Willowherb (*Epilobium hirsutum*). A boardwalk was installed and the site used for education. At Dibbinsdale in Wirral, a dam installed on the River Dibbin in the 1860s appears to have caused the formation of a large reed-marsh (*Phragmites australis*) on the flood plain upstream, which now has breeding Sedge Warbler (*Acrocephalus schoenobaenus*) and Reed Warblers (*A.scirpaceus*) and is an important part of its SSSI. Marshes can be attractive communities to people, especially where tall herbs give good floral displays, e.g., an area at Eastham, Wirral, which has suffered impeded drainage since the M53 was built, where Southern Marsh-orchid (*Dactyloriza praeter-missa*) and Common Fleabane (*Pulicaria dysenterica*) flourish, or the bright fringe to many polluted waterways provided by Indian or Himalayan Balsam (*Impatiens glandulifera*). Leachate from tipped waste can have interesting effects; the alkaline leachate from a tip at Runcorn supports Sea Club-rush (*Bolboschoenus maritimus*), while saltmarsh has come as far inland as St Helens where Reflexed Saltmarsh-grass (*Puccinellia distans*) has colonised the leachate from the Burgy banks.

More saline-tolerant plants may become obvious in future. The effects of spreading salt on our roads are now visible every spring as a band of pale lilac along the very edge of main road verges. The plant responsible is Danish Scurvygrass (*Cochlearia danica*), a common species around the coasts on walls, banks, sand and rock

(chapter nineteen, this volume). Countrywide a number of other maritime species have been reported from road-sides (Scott 1985), such as saltmarsh-grasses (*Puccinellia* spp.) and Lesser Sea-spurrey (*Spergularia marina*).

Urban wetlands are just as vulnerable to drainage and natural succession as their traditional counterparts. They are unlikely to be drained for agriculture, but changing industrial needs, new development and failure of old dams can all change water levels. Once again, decisions have to be made over what is to be retained and how to do it.

Management

There is another problem in relation to wildlife on derelict land. All these sites are undergoing succession, either primary or secondary. Some of them have reached a stage which is particularly valuable to wildlife, such as species-rich grassland, of which semi-natural versions have suffered drastic declines in recent decades. Or they may be particularly attractive to people, like the orchids on PFA. If such sites are to be kept in a desired state, they will need management, just as semi-natural sites do, and this will require time and resources. Most of these sites have been totally neglected since they were formed, so no-one is in the habit of taking care of them. It has been suggested for PFA that new sites should be created to replace existing ones as they follow their natural succes-

Figure 8.4. New Ferry Butterfly Park, Wirral: school visit to former railway goods yard, now community nature reserve
(*Photo: H. Ash*).

sion (Shaw 1994); that may be extreme, but thought is needed as to whether the best waste sites should be conserved, and how, and we should be prepared to take action where necessary. Many such sites are irreplaceable, since industries have changed, and fortunately modern pollution legislation does not allow some past practices. Even if new sites are created, and people are prepared to live with an ugly view for decades while succession proceeds, new sites may never become as rich as the older ones, because in the modern, depauperate landscape the seed sources are much sparser and poorer in species than 50 or 100 years ago.

One way to address both these problems is to get the local community involved. At Bebington railway station on Wirral, the goods yard became derelict in the 1960s, and in 1993 was turned into 'New Ferry Butterfly Park'. It has a variety of soils – coal from the staithes, lime from a water treatment works which softened water for steam engines, ballast from old sidings, building rubble and clay. Over the years a wide variety of plants and invertebrates moved in; 23 species of butterfly have been recorded, at least 12 breeding. None is rare, but the variety is remarkable for a small area of 1.4ha in a densely-built, urban area. A local resident tried for 20 years to get recognition and protection for the site. The railway company, who owned the site, had planning permissions, but failed to attract a buyer, because of poor ground conditions and inadequate road access. Eventually the last planning permission lapsed and Cheshire Wildlife Trust were able to lease the site and now help a group of local people to run it. Extensive management work was needed, to erect fencing, lay paths, clear mounds of rubbish, thin scrub, dig a pond, control bramble, start grassland management; all done by volunteers and grants to maintain and enhance its wildlife value. The Park was officially opened in July 1995 by Lyndon Harrison, MEP for the area and since then local schools have used it for field studies. All this has not stopped the railway company from applying to have part of the site zoned for housing in Wirral's Unitary Development Plan: needless to say there have been vociferous objections, and in July 1996 the results of a public inquiry were awaited hopefully! [In August 1997 the Inspector refused the zoning for housing.]

If such 'man-made', or at least 'man-started' sites are considered valuable to our wildlife and culture, the community will have to work to maintain and defend such areas, just as much as traditional wildlife sites.

New-made communities

Most of the habitats so far considered have arisen by natural processes on man-made sites, with little or no interference in their successions. In recent years conscious 'habitat creation' has begun to make an impact on the towns of the Mersey Basin, with deliberately planned landscapes, intended primarily to improve the amenity value of urban areas, but also increasing the opportunities for wildlife. Knowsley Borough Council,

among other efforts to improve the Borough's image, has worked with the Groundwork Trust and Landlife over a decade, on both practical projects and research into effective techniques. At Tobruk Road, Huyton, the Alt valley used to be a canalised stream bordered by mown grassland. The stream still runs in its canal, but the banks have been landscaped with tree and shrub plantings, in substantial blocks, and areas of wild flower grassland (Luscombe & Scott 1994). Management is something of a problem; mowing gangs do not always get the boundaries to the wildflower areas correct, leaving areas of amenity grassland unmown which become unsightly as the season progresses. This is at least better than the problem at Tower Hill, Kirkby, where wildflower areas were mown early in 1995 instead of being left to flower. Disposal of long cuttings after the autumn cut is a problem, until large-scale composting schemes are established. Stadtmoers Country Park, Whiston is a large area established on former derelict land – claypits and collieries, some subsequently filled with domestic refuse. A wildflower grassland sown on sandy subsoil in 1983 shows that this habitat can be sustained, given the correct soil conditions and management. Other parts of the Park have extensive grasslands and experimental areas, used to test methods for enriching both managed and unmanaged grasslands (Ash, Bennett & Scott 1992). The improvements of these plantings to the visual landscape are obvious; systematic work on their effects on wildlife are still lacking, although casual observation indicates that insect life certainly increases in the short term, and sustainable bird populations would be expected to increase as time goes on. Usually these landscapes replace mown amenity grassland or newly-demolished buildings, and can only increase the local opportunities for wildlife, and for human contact with that wildlife. Re-creation of lost natural habitats, such as ancient woodlands and meadows, is not possible, but these new habitats can enrich urban areas, offer new homes for some species, and by allowing urban people contact with nature, improve their lives and the value placed on the other species with which we share our planet. Landlife's wildflower seed production grounds in Knowsley are visually spectacular in flower; they also allow Skylarks (*Alauda arvensis*) to breed.

Conclusion

Man's activities in the Mersey Basin have left a range of habitats of wildlife interest. They demonstrate plant succession, offer homes to a wide range of species and can be attractive to people. If the best are to be retained, they will need active protection and management, just as much as more natural habitats. Many are in urban areas and, along with deliberately-created habitats, can improve people's lives and contribute to persuading them to value the natural world in which we all live.

References

Ash, H.J. (1983). *The Natural Colonisation of Derelict Industrial Land*. PhD thesis, University of Liverpool.

Ash, H. J. (1991). Soils and vegetation in urban areas. *Soils in the Urban Environment* (eds P. Bullock & P.J. Gregory), pp. 153–172. Blackwell Scientific Publications, Oxford.

Ash, H.J., Bennett, R. & Scott, R. (1992). *Flowers in the Grass*. English Nature, Peterborough.

Ash, H.J, Gemmell, R.P. & Bradshaw, A.D. (1994). The introduction of native plant species on industrial waste heaps: a test of immigration and other factors affecting primary succession. *Journal of Applied Ecology*, **31**, 74–84.

Bradshaw, A.D. (1980). Mineral Nutrition. *Amenity Grassland: An Ecological Perspective* (eds I.H. Rorison & R. Hunt), pp. 101–18. Wiley, London.

Bradshaw, A.D. & Chadwick, M.J. (1980). *The Restoration of Land*. Blackwell Scientific Publications, Oxford.

Curtis, M. (1977). *Trees on Tips*. MSc dissertation, University of Salford.

Gilbert, O.L. (1989). *The Ecology of Urban Habitats*. Chapman & Hall, London.

Luscombe, G. & Scott, R. (1994). *Wildflowers Work*. Landlife, Liverpool.

Shaw, P. (1994). Orchid Woods and Floating Islands – the Ecology of Fly Ash. *British Wildlife* **5**, 149–57.

Scott, N.E. (1985). The updated distribution of maritime species on British roadsides. *Watsonia*, **15**, 381–86.

St Helens Wildlife Advisory Group (1986). *A Policy for Nature*. Available from: The Land Manager, Community Leisure Department, Century House, Hardshaw Street, St Helens, Merseyside.

Webb, N. (1986). *Heathlands*. The New Naturalist. Collins, London.

CHAPTER NINE

Recent landscape changes: an analysis post-1970

C.J. BARR AND G.J. STARK

Introduction to landscape change

Landscape change means different things to different people and good, consistent definitions are needed so that the statistics of change may be properly understood. Landscape change may represent changes in land use from, say, food production to housing, shifts which are driven by the changing needs and priorities of an ever more affluent society. Some changes are permanent and irreversible, such as the conversion of permanent pasture to arable crops, while others represent part of a normal agricultural rotation. While landscape change is often measured quantitatively (e.g., the length of hedgerow lost), it is important to note that more subtle, qualitative changes may also be taking place, e.g., in the species composition of grasslands.

In the natural sciences, landscape change may be analysed in terms of (in descending order of spatial organisation): land cover (e.g., crops, woodland, and urban land); landscape elements and habitats (e.g., trees, hedges and ponds); and flora and fauna, often represented by populations which fluctuate over a long time-scale. Other interest groups might be concerned with visual amenity (e.g., changing seasonal patterns); cultural changes (which are often irreversible); and socio-economic aspects (clear driving forces behind both urban and rural change). While landscape change is very important in terms of its consequential effects on the flora and fauna, it is a large, complex, and involved area for study and not one which the biologist should tackle in isolation.

Scale and definitions

Analysis of change at the regional scale, and its relationship to the national picture, is an important task for a wide range of organisations with responsibilities for planning and resource assessment. Care must be taken, however, in the interpretation of regional data and especially when analysing change. Differences in the definitions of categories used by different data gatherers, or differences in the geographical extent of an area, may be far more significant than any 'real' changes detected by comparison of data sets. For example, the Forestry

Commission North West Conservancy stretches from Cumbria to Warwickshire (inclusive), while the Department of the Environment (DOE) 'Standard Region' classification considers the North West to comprise Lancashire, Greater Manchester, Merseyside and Cheshire only. For the best estimates of change, landscape surveys must be undertaken in the same geographical region, using identical methods and definitions. The results of such surveys are rare indeed, and so compromises have to be made and the relationships between different surveys properly understood.

Sources of information

Many sources of information are available from different agencies to describe landscapes in the Mersey Basin. Statistics published by the Forestry Commission (FC) and based on their 1980 woodland census, estimate that there was a total of 1,677ha of woodland in the county of Merseyside and a woodland cover density of 2.1% for the county of Greater Manchester (Locke 1987). The Ministry of Agriculture, Fisheries and Food (MAFF) Digest of Agricultural Census Statistics for 1994 indicates the area of grassland in Cheshire to have been 132,000ha, 79% of agricultural land in the county (MAFF 1991 to 94). According to the 1990 Land Cover Map of Great Britain, created from an analysis of satellite imagery (e.g., Fuller & Parsell 1990), there was a mean density of 21.6ha per km square of urban and suburban land in the Mersey Basin in that year. From these and other statistics we can describe the landscape of the Mersey Basin as one with a high density of urban areas, little woodland and the majority of agricultural land being under grass.

However, many of these sources do not adequately convey landscape change. Although there were relatively early surveys on land use, e.g., the First and Second Land Utilisation Surveys (Stamp 1937–47; Coleman 1961), consistent information on change at the national or regional level has not become available until relatively recently. There are several examples of regional change statistics in both the published and the unpublished literature. Data on agricultural crops and uses are published annually (e.g., MAFF. 1992) showing, for example, a 25%

Greater Manchester

	1974	%	1979	%	1984	%	1989	%	1994	%
Total Agr. land (major)	**48777**	%	**45604**	%	**43321**	%	**42158**	%	**40647**	%
Arable	**8198**	17	**7674**	17	**7299**	17	**7841**	18	**6238**	15
Wheat	632	1	566	1	850	2	1674	4	2094	5
Barley	5971	12	5834	13	4986	12	4231	10	2654	7
Crops for stockfeed	195	0	155	0	212	0	233	1	389	1
Potatoes	703	1	720	2	807	2	668	2	523	1
Rape	0	0	38	0	277	1	428	1	323	1
Sugar beet	0	0	45	0	42	0	44	0	41	0
Other arable crops	697	1	316	1	125	0	203	0	214	0
Horticulture	**992**	2	**987**	2	**966**	2	**915**	2	**752**	2
Vegetables	858	2	890	2	844	2	797	2	642	2
Orchards and small fruit	8	0	5	0	26	0	22	0	15	0
Glass	57	0	17	0	17	0	18	0	19	0
Bulbs, flowers and HNS	69	0	75	0	79	0	78	0	76	0
Grass and other land	**39630**	81	**36940**	81	**35056**	81	**33762**	80	**33720**	83
Under 5 yrs	3828	8	2757	6	3553	8	3387	8	3252	8
Over 5 yrs and other land	35801	73	34183	75	31503	73	30375	72	30468	75

Year — column headers: 1974, 1979, 1984, 1989, 1994

Cheshire

	1974	%	1979	%	1984	%	1989	%	1994	%
Total Agr. land (major)	**175326**	%	**174810**	%	**175166**	%	**173298**	%	**167468**	%
Arable	**37312**	21	**37242**	21	**34402**	20	**35849**	21	**33941**	20
Wheat	3753	2	4351	2	7121	4	9830	6	9416	6
Barley	24684	14	24807	14	19446	11	17089	10	11764	7
Crops for stockfeed	1636	1	2302	1	1085	1	2009	1	5995	4
Potatoes	3944	2	4325	2	4599	3	4235	2	4148	2
Rape	8	0	55	0	1158	1	1626	1	1512	1
Sugar beet	34	0	310	0	121	0	154	0	161	0
Other arable crops	3253	2	1902	1	872	0	906	1	945	1
Horticulture	**1458**	1	**1648**	1	**1512**	1	**1299**	1	**1076**	1
Vegetables	873	0	981	1	714	0	574	0	536	0
Orchards and small fruit	279	0	351	0	423	0	345	0	168	0
Glass	26	0	30	0	35	0	43	0	42	0
Bulbs, flowers and HNS	280	0	286	0	340	0	337	0	330	0
Grass and other land	**136558**	78	**135920**	78	**139252**	79	**136150**	79	**132408**	79
Under 5 yrs	39967	23	32741	19	31961	18	28158	16	29008	17
Over 5 yrs and other land	96591	55	103179	59	107291	61	107992	62	103400	62

Table 9.1. Agricultural statistics for the counties of Greater Manchester, Merseyside, Cheshire and Lancashire for the period 1974 to 1994. Areas are in hectares (Source: MAFF 1973 to 79; MAFF 1980 to 89 and MAFF 1991 to 94).

increase in the planted area of oilseed rape between 1989 and 1990. County figures are available although not published routinely. Similarly, the Forestry Commission (e.g., Forestry Commission 1983) publishes data at intervals, but with regional summaries; for example non-woodland trees increased in volume by about 57% in the North West Conservancy between 1951 and 1980.

Other sources of information on landscape change include: the 'Monitoring Landscape Change' project funded by the DOE and the Countryside Commission (Hunting Surveys and Consultants Ltd 1986); the former Nature Conservancy Council's 'National Countryside Monitoring Scheme', completed for only a few counties in England, but including Cumbria (Budd 1989); the National Park Monitoring project (Countryside Commission 1991); the Phase I and Phase II habitat surveys of the national conservation agencies (e.g., Moreau 1990); and the monitoring undertaken by the Ordnance Survey on behalf of the DOE (Department of the Environment 1992). The County Councils in the North West are in the process of producing Green Audits (e.g., Lancashire County Council 1991), and further new initiatives include the Countryside Commission's 'New Map of England'. It is unclear how these initiatives will contribute to landscape change statistics in the future.

The Institute of Terrestrial Ecology (ITE) has carried out a series of national surveys of land cover, landscape features, and vegetation, using a sampling approach. Since the methods and definitions are constant between surveys, reliable estimates of change (together with statistical error terms) can be generated. The latest of these surveys was 'Countryside Survey 1990' (CS1990) which involved not only a detailed field survey of 508 representative 1km squares in Great Britain (GB), but also the construction of a Land Cover Map of the whole land surface, from remotely-sensed data (Barr *et al.* 1993).

To find out what other information would be avail-

Merseyside

	1974	%	1979	%	1984	%	1989	%	1994	%
Total Agr. land (major)	**21094**	%	**20345**	%	**20002**	%	**20606**	%	**19528**	%
Arable	**12112**	57	**11483**	56	**11702**	59	**12383**	60	**10111**	52
Wheat	1225	6	836	4	1688	8	3528	17	3453	18
Barley	7874	37	8676	43	7668	38	6012	29	3543	18
Crops for stockfeed	119	1	166	1	314	2	895	4	991	5
Potatoes	1291	6	1228	6	1251	6	925	4	776	4
Rape	0	0	24	0	312	2	505	2	740	4
Sugar beet	111	1	290	1	219	1	202	1	224	1
Other arable crops	1492	7	263	1	250	1	316	2	384	2
Horticulture	**1634**	8	**1616**	8	**1945**	10	**1335**	6	**929**	5
Vegetables	1556	7	1508	7	1736	9	1160	6	822	4
Orchards and small fruit	23	0	39	0	127	1	98	0	27	0
Glass	13	0	15	0	12	0	16	0	15	0
Bulbs, flowers and HNS	42	0	54	0	70	0	61	0	65	0
Grass and other land	**7348**	35	**7246**	36	**6355**	32	**6888**	33	**8488**	43
Under 5 yrs	2662	13	1811	9	1615	8	1344	7	1507	8
Over 5 yrs and other land	4686	22	5435	27	4740	24	5544	27	6981	36

Lancashire

	1974	%	1979	%	1984	%	1989	%	1994	%
Total Agr. land (major)	**239887**	%	**235570**	%	**223997**	%	**222841**	%	**220441**	%
Arable	**24434**	10	**27439**	12	**24487**	11	**24620**	11	**2118**	10
Wheat	3266	1	2411	1	4147	2	6821	3	7910	4
Barley	16769	7	18117	8	15147	7	11616	5	6232	3
Crops for stockfeed	893	0	815	0	846	0	1862	1	2366	1
Potatoes	3009	1	3031	1	3207	1	2657	1	2683	1
Rape	0	0	24	0	456	0	834	0	827	0
Sugar beet	64	0	338	0	296	0	307	0	338	0
Other arable crops	432	0	2703	1	388	0	523	0	824	0
Horticulture	**4844**	2	**5625**	2	**6058**	3	**5192**	2	**5367**	2
Vegetables	4493	2	5322	2	5679	3	4828	2	4935	2
Orchards and small fruit	58	0	34	0	103	0	72	0	26	0
Glass	158	0	178	0	169	0	184	0	184	0
Bulbs, flowers and HNS	134	0	91	0	107	0	108	0	222	0
Grass and other land	**210609**	88	**202506**	86	**193452**	86	**193029**	87	**193895**	88
Under 5 yrs	10668	4	12704	5	15019	7	13821	6	16169	7
Over 5 yrs and other land	199941	83	189802	81	178433	80	179208	80	177726	81

able to study recent landscape change in the Mersey Basin, the authors consulted local organisations such as County Councils and Universities. The response demonstrated that whilst some local information might be available, e.g., as a set of records or aerial photographs, it would be difficult to compile consistent data sets for the Mersey Basin as a whole and almost impossible to draw conclusions about change from these.

Using county-based data

For information on the Mersey Basin, it is possible to extract data from sources of national statistics published by county. The counties of Cheshire, Merseyside and Greater Manchester are almost exclusively in the Mersey Basin, accounting for approximately 50%, 15% and 30% of the region respectively. Lancashire occupies a further 5% of the northern part of the Basin.

June agricultural census returns are published annually by MAFF and county figures are included for some topics (MAFF 1973 to 79; MAFF 1980 to 89; MAFF 1990; MAFF 1991 to 94). County figures for Cheshire,

Merseyside, Greater Manchester and Lancashire during the period 1974 and 1994 are shown in Table 9.1. The chosen categories are those which have more or less constant definitions over the period.

Using the countryside information system

The Countryside Information System (CIS) is a computer-based package which gives a user the ability to define particular areas of GB (e.g., Scotland, National Parks, land over 100m, Bedfordshire, or the Mersey Basin) and to compute countryside data for the specified region. Where change data exist, then changes can be computed for the same areas. Information can be overlaid so that the area of coniferous woodland on land over 150m in Wales could be calculated simply. The CIS was developed as a tool for analysing, interrogating and presenting data about the countryside in a way which was responsive to policy questions (Haines-Young, Bunce & Parr 1994) and, although developed originally to present Countryside Survey data to a wide user community, it is not limited to the use of such data and allows any spatially referenced database to be incorporated.

The initial development was through extensive evaluation and testing of prototype systems by users in government departments and agencies (Howard *et al.* 1994). CIS is able to provide access to a wide range of information about the British countryside by adopting the 1km squares of the National Grid as a standard by which to summarise data. Many kinds of information about the countryside can be presented as either 'presence/absence in', or 'area occupied within', a 1km square. In CIS terminology 'presence/absence' datasets are called region files (an example would be all 1km squares which contain part of the Mersey Basin) and 'area occupied' datasets are known as census files (for example, the number of hectares of woodland in all 1km squares).

An additional feature of CIS is the ability to view data collected on a sample basis. CIS integrates sample data with other data sources through the ITE Land Classification (Bunce *et al.* 1996). This is a classification of all 1km squares in GB into 32 Land Classes, based on a multivariate analysis of a range of environmental parameters (such as geology, climate and physiography). A sample dataset in CIS consists of a mean and associated variance for each Land Class. These values can be used to estimate the amount of a feature for any region defined by the user, based on the occurrence of the ITE Land Classes. Sample data for change of land use are available for the period between CS1990 and an earlier ITE survey of land use conducted using the same methodology in 1984. These data can be used to make estimates for the Mersey Basin region, though the CS1990 field survey was designed for calculation of national statistics and estimates for small regions should be treated with caution. Estimates of statistical error are given and areas such as the Mersey Basin are at the lower end of the acceptable range. However, in the absence of any other data, the CIS does provide consistent estimates of the stock and change of landscape features in the Mersey Basin.

Some specific examples of landscape change in the Mersey Basin

Agriculture

Between 1974 and 1994, MAFF data show that there was an overall decline in the total area of agricultural land in the four counties of 37,000ha, amounting to 8% of the total area of agricultural land (Figure 9.1). Considerable fluctuations in the number of agricultural holdings in the four counties were recorded over the period (Figure 9.2). At least part of the explanation for this is likely to be the periodic reassessment of holdings included in the census. Overall there were 874 fewer holdings at the end of the period. Figure 9.3 contrasts land use on agricultural holdings at the beginning and end of the period for each county. Change has been slight with the most

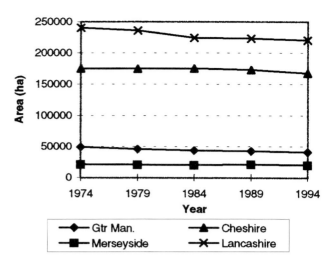

Figure 9.1. The total area of agricultural land in the counties of Cheshire, Merseyside, Greater Manchester and Lancashire between 1974 and 1994 (Source: MAFF 1973 to 79; MAFF 1980 to 89 and MAFF 1991 to 94).

noticeable change being from arable land to grass and other land uses, in all four counties.

Changes in land use are recorded for the DOE by the Ordnance Survey (OS) as map revisions are undertaken. Statistics are published by DOE as the 'Land Use Change in England' series and county figures for change of land use to urban and residential are available for the period

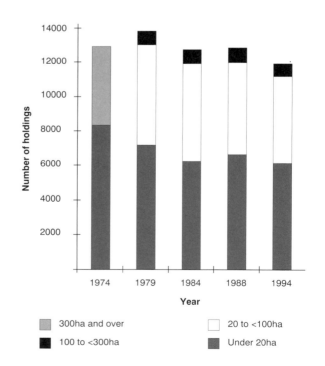

Figure 9.2. The number of agricultural holdings in Cheshire, Merseyside, Greater Manchester and Lancashire between 1974 and 1994 (Source: MAFF 1973 to 79; MAFF 1980 to 89 and MAFF 1991 to 94). Figures for the larger size classes in 1974 are not available, since earlier farm size ranges quoted in acres have no equivalent in the current hectare ranges.

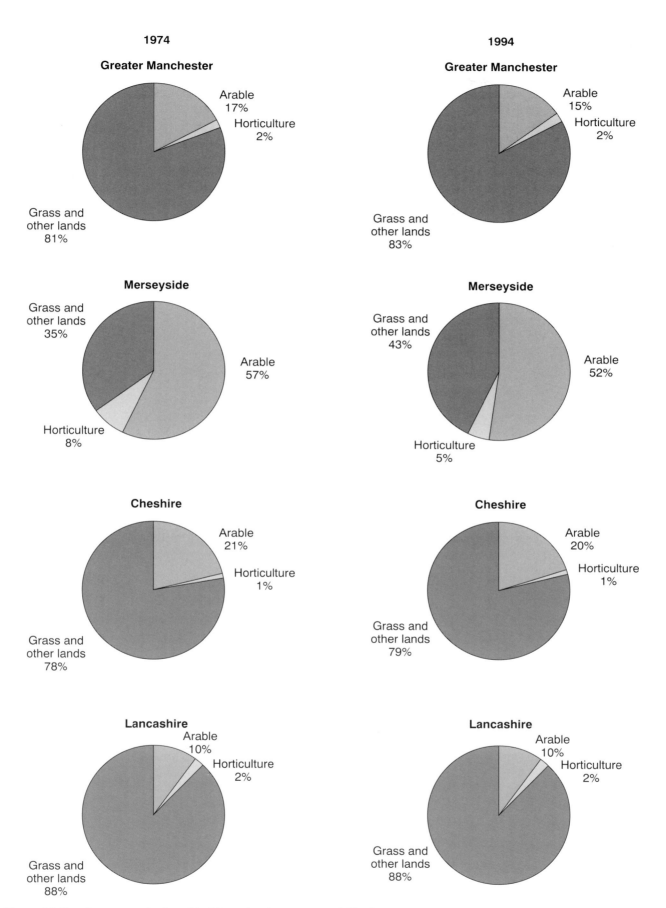

Figure 9.3. Land use on agricultural holdings for the counties of Cheshire, Merseyside, Greater Manchester and Lancashire for 1974 and 1994 (Source: MAFF 1973 to 79 and MAFF 1991 to 94).

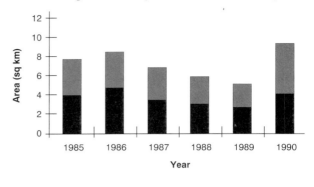

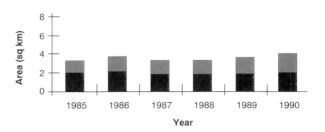

Figure 9.4. Changes in land use to urban and residential for the counties of Cheshire/Lancashire and Merseyside/Greater Manchester between 1985 and 1990 (Source: DOE 1992 to 95).

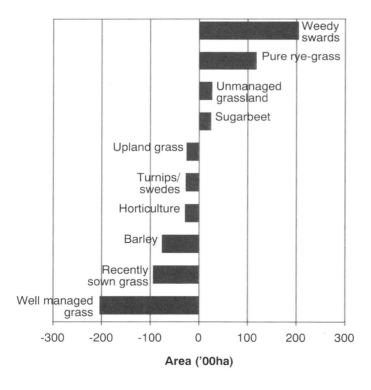

Figure 9.5. Estimated land cover changes in the Mersey Basin region between 1984 and 1990. Figures were calculated in CIS using data from CS1990. Only land covers with over 2,000ha of change have been included.

1985 to 1990 (Department of the Environment 1992 to 95). Figure 9.4 shows the area of land which was recorded as changing to urban or residential for each year, apportioned according to whether the previous land use had been rural or urban. Over the six-year period for which statistics are available, 32ha of land previously classed as rural was recorded as converted to urban and 17ha to residential, in the four Mersey Basin counties. These figures demonstrate a gradual conversion from rural to urban land use, though they do not account for the larger losses of agricultural land indicated by the MAFF statistics.

CS1990 results for land cover are summarised under 58 categories. Land cover categories for which a change of greater than 2,000ha is estimated are shown in Figure 9.5. The largest changes are increases of 11,600ha of pure Rye-grass and 20,300ha of weedy swards and decreases of 20,100ha of well managed grass and 9,400ha of recently sown grass. These shifts mirror those seen nationally and are a result of changing grassland management practices towards less frequent re-seeding. The consequences of these changes are the more frequent occurrence of weedy swards and the use of non-seeding Rye-grass species.

The landscape impact of these changes to grassland management may be slight. More significant for the landscape of the Mersey Basin may be the shift away from arable crops. Barley in particular has declined over this period, an estimated 7,400ha for the Mersey Basin between 1984 and 1990 according to the CS1990, and a recorded 8,299ha for the counties of Cheshire, Merseyside, Greater Manchester and Lancashire between 1984 and 1989 according to MAFF statistics (MAFF 1980–89).

Woodland and forests

Figures from the 1980 FC woodland census are available by county (Locke 1987). The density of woodland in all four counties (Cheshire 3.8%, Greater Manchester 2.1%, Merseyside 2.6% and Lancashire 3.7%) is low by comparison with other counties in England. There is a lack of comparable data at the beginning and end of the period under consideration and, anyway, changes in the method of recording woodlands have made the detection of real change difficult (Peterken 1983).

Figures for the area of woodland on agricultural holdings are available by county for the period 1973 to 1979 and then 1990 from the MAFF statistics (MAFF 1973–79

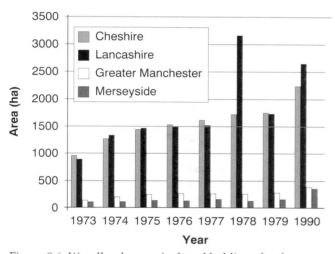

Figure 9.6. Woodland on agricultural holdings for the counties of Cheshire, Merseyside, Greater Manchester and Lancashire for the period 1973 to 1979 and 1990 (Source: MAFF 1973 to 79 and MAFF 1990).

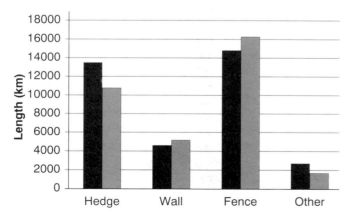

Figure 9.7. Changes to boundary features in the Mersey Basin region between 1984 and 1990. Figures were calculated in CIS using data from CS1990. Where several boundary types were present in a single boundary preference was given in the order: hedge, wall, fence then other.

and MAFF 1990). The amount of woodland increased by 1,908ha between 1973 and 1979 and had increased by a further 1,712ha by 1990 (Figure 9.6).

Landscape features

CS1990 included the recording of landscape features such as field boundaries. Figure 9.7 shows changes to field boundaries between the 1984 and 1990 surveys within the region. Overall there has been a decrease of 1,730km (5%) in the length of boundaries in the region. Within this total the length of hedgerow has declined by 20% which is comparable with the national estimate of 23%. In GB as a whole, it has been shown that much of this change is due to lack of hedgerow management leading to hedges growing into lines of trees, or degenerating into scattered shrubs, rather than outright removal (Barr, Gillespie & Howard 1994).

General trends in the landscape, post-1970

This cursory analysis of available statistics points to a period of relative stability in the landscape of the Mersey Basin since 1970. There was an overall reduction in the area of agricultural land and a commensurate loss in the number of agricultural holdings. Within these holdings there have been few changes in the use of the land although there is a reduction in the area of arable crops. There have been modest increases in the area of woodland on farmland and, as elsewhere in GB, hedgerows have been lost, probably due to a lack of management.

The apparent general stability in landscape change, post-1970, may however disguise changes in the quality of landscape elements, as indicated by the subtle changes in grassland types detected within CS1990. These might be due to intensification of land use in some areas and relaxation of management (or even set aside) in other parts of the region. Current work at ITE is looking at changes, and causes of change, in the botanical composition of landscape elements.

Conclusions

In gathering information for this paper on landscape change, it has become clear that it is difficult to find relevant data which have been collected in a consistent way for the Mersey Basin as a whole, and therefore it is difficult to compute change statistics with confidence. Potentially, the CIS is a useful tool in this respect as it allows data from different sources to be compared for any specified region.

Overall, there appears to be little net change in land use and landscape features in the basin in the period post-1970. It remains predominantly an agricultural area, mostly under grassland systems, but also with a relatively large proportion of urban land. However, some results suggest that there may be changes in the quality of the landscape and this provides scope for more research.

References

Barr, C.J., Bunce, R.G.H., Clarke, R.T., Fuller, R.M., Furse, M.T., Gillespie, M.K., Groom, G.B., Hallam, C.J., Hornung, M., Howard, D.C. & Ness, M.J. (1993). *Countryside Survey 1990 Main Report.* Volume 2 in the Countryside 1990 series. Department of the Environment, London.

Barr, C.J., Gillespie, M.K. & Howard, D. (1994). *Hedgerow Survey 1993 stock and change estimates of hedgerow lengths in England and Wales, 1990–1993.* Department of the Environment, Bristol.

Budd, J.T.C. (1989). National Countryside Monitoring Scheme. *Rural Information for forward planning* (ITE symposium no. 21) (eds R.G.H. Bunce & C.J. Barr). Institute of Terrestrial Ecology, Grange-over-Sands.

Bunce, R.G.H., Barr, C.J., Clarke, R.T., Howard, D.C. & Lane A.M.J. (1996). Land classification for strategic ecological survey. *Journal of Environmental Management,* **47**, 37–60.

Coleman, A. (1961). The second land use survey: progress and prospect. *Geographical Journal,* **127**, 168–86.

Countryside Commission. (1991). *Landscape change in the national parks*: summary report of a research project carried out by Silsoe College. Countryside Commission, Cheltenham.

Department of the Environment. (1992). *Land Use Change in England.* DOE Statistical Bulletin (92)3. DOE, London.

Department of the Environment. (1992 to 95). *Land Use Change in England* No. 7 to 10. DOE Statistical Bulletin, London.

Forestry Commission. (1983). *Census of Woodlands and Trees 1979–82 (North West England).* Forestry Commission, Edinburgh.

Fuller, R.M. & Parsell, R.J. (1990). Classification of TM imagery in the study of land use in lowland Britain: practical considerations for operational use. *International Journal of Remote Sensing,* **11**, 1901–17.

Haines-Young, R.H., Bunce, R.G.H. & Parr, T.W. (1994). Countryside Information System: an information system for environmental policy development and appraisal. *Geographical Systems,* **1**, 329–45.

Howard, D.C., Bunce, R.G.H., Jones, M. & Haines-Young, R.H. (1994). *Development of the Countryside Information System.* Volume 4 in the Countryside 1990 series. Department of the Environment, London.

Hunting Surveys and Consultants Ltd. (1986). *Monitoring Landscape Change.* Huntings, Borehamwood.

Lancashire County Council. [1991]. *Lancashire – a green audit: summary.* Lancashire County Council, Preston.

Locke, G.M.L. (1987). *Census of Woodlands and Trees 1979–82.* Forestry Commission Bulletin 63. Forestry Commission, Edinburgh.

MAFF. (1973 to 79). *Agricultural Statistics England and Wales.* Volumes 1973 to 1978/1979. HMSO, London.

MAFF. (1980 to 89). *Agricultural Statistics United Kingdom.* Volumes 1980 and 1981 to 1989. HMSO, London.

MAFF. (1990). *Final Results of the June 1990 Agricultural and Horticultural Census: England and Wales, Regions and Counties.* MAFF, London.

MAFF. (1991 to 94). *The Digest of Agricultural Census Statistics: Volumes 1991 to 1994.* HMSO, London.

MAFF. (1992). *Agriculture in the United Kingdom: 1991.* HMSO, London.

Moreau, M. (1990). *The Phase I Habitat Survey in Bedfordshire.* Nature Conservancy Council, Letchworth.

Peterken, G. (1983). Woodland surveys can mislead. *New Scientist,* **100** (1388), 802–03.

Stamp, L.D. (1937–47). *The Land of Britain: The Final Report of the Land Utilisation Survey of Britain.* Geographical Publications, London.

Changing Habitats 1

E.F. GREENWOOD

In the previous two sections the changing landscape of the Mersey Basin since the retreat of the last glaciation, which began some 15,000 years ago, has been described and the increasing effect of human impact noted.

In this and subsequent sections a more detailed look is taken at selected habitats, plants and animals that live or have lived in the region. In the first section, on changing habitats, an analysis of three of the most important terrestrial ones is undertaken. Chapter ten shows what happened to the woodland that covered so much of the Mersey Basin. At the time of Doomsday over a thousand years ago there was plenty of woodland, but even then less than 30% of Cheshire was woodland. In the following centuries much of this woodland was lost through human impact, but from about the end of the 18th century plantations and parkland trees were planted. Nevertheless, the Mersey Basin is today one of the least woodland areas in Europe with only 4% cover or less. A determined effort is now being made to increase the amount of woodland with the creation of the Mersey and Red Rose Forests.

Much of the east of the Mersey Basin is upland and even here woodlands once covered a large part of the area (chapter eleven). From the earliest times human intervention has reduced this woodland to remnants. In many places bogs developed with *Sphagnum* spp. being a major component of the vegetation. But the effects of the industrial revolution were highly damaging and most of the *Sphagnum* was killed off. Today the uplands continue to endure severe human impact, especially from overgrazing by sheep, resulting in a degraded landscape with erosion in many places.

Chapter twelve demonstrates what is happening to plants and animals in the large urban habitats created by human intervention. Here chance and the adaptability of plants and animals to changed and sometimes hostile environments is shown. These positive reactions, if allowed, result in the development of woodland once again.

These three chapters all show the considerable and sometimes alarming deleterious effect of human intervention over not hundreds, but thousands of years. Yet they also show hope and promise through a combination of the considerable resilience and adaptability of many plants and animals to changed circumstances, and more recently efforts by humans themselves to improve the environment, so creating new opportunities for wildlife to flourish.

CHAPTER TEN

A history of woodland in the Mersey Basin

D. ATKINSON, R.A. SMART, J. FAIRHURST, P. OLDFIELD AND J.G.A. LAGEARD

Introduction

From prehistoric times to the present day, the history of woodland in the Mersey Basin, like that in much of industrial north-west Europe, has been dominated by deforestation and damage with relatively modest re-planting. The present-day counties of Cheshire, Greater Manchester and Merseyside, whose boundaries define the geographical limits of this review, are among the least wooded in Europe; each with 4% woodland cover or less (see chapter nine, this volume). This compares unfavourably with the *c.*10% cover in Britain as a whole (Forestry Commission 1997). Woodland appears always to have provided a resource. But how people have viewed it and therefore exploited or managed it has changed many times and often quite dramatically, even in recent decades. Details of these changes since the Norman Conquest, and their effects especially on the landscape contained within the present-day boundaries of Cheshire and Merseyside, form the subject of this chapter. We conclude with an assessment of the wood-land resource for the 21st century: this provides some hope for the future, but also points to problems that need to be addressed if ecological and economic sustainability are to be achieved.

Domesday woodland and the medieval Royal Forests

Despite the difficulties in assessing the extent of wood-land cover at the time of Domesday, two estimates for Cheshire based on a variety of evidence suggest that the county was well-wooded with perhaps 25–27% cover (Rackham 1986, p. 78; Yalden 1987). Since much more land was capable of supporting woodland, it appears that the majority had been cleared for agriculture before Domesday. Administrative areas (hundreds) in the west of the county, including Wirral, which was both densely populated (Table 10.1) and adjacent to two navigable river estuaries, contained little taxable woodland. Yet to the south and south-east (e.g., in the Macclesfield hundred) woodland cover was extensive (Table 10.1, Figure 10.2). In the hundred of West Derby to the north of the River Mersey, it seems that except for pre-

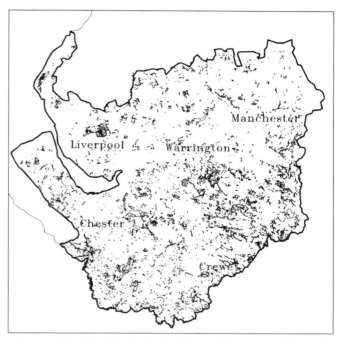

Figure 10.1. Woodlands in the Mersey Basin. Woodland of more than 2ha area in the counties of Cheshire, Greater Manchester and Merseyside. Data obtained from aerial surveys flown in 1993.

Hundred	Woodland (km²)	Population (per km²)
Wirral	5.78	1.43
Bucklow West	21.44	0.66
Bucklow East	37.05	0.23-0.27
Broxton	39.02	0.39–1.24
Eddisbury North	25.50	1.0
Eddisbury South	35.01	0.27–1.27
Nantwich	129.08	0.39–0.69
Northwich	86.95	0.39–0.58
Macclesfield	579.93	0.15
	959.76	

(Calculated from Yalden 1987)

Table 10.1. Cheshire Domesday woodland recorded by Hundreds.

Forest	Boundaries	Earliest reference	Changes in extent	Year of disafforestation
Delamere	Rivers Mersey (N), Gowy (W), Weaver (E) and Weaver tributary (S). Precise boundaries unclear (Green 1979, p. 172).	Indirectly in Domesday. By name in about 1129 (Green 1979, p. 172).	By 1600 almost all of old forest of Mondrem excluded (Green 1979, p. 172).	1812
Macclesfield	Rivers Mersey (N), Goyt (E), and Dane (S). Western boundary not clearly defined (Green 1979, p. 179).	Indirectly in Domesday (Morris 1978 1:25, 1:26). By name in a Charter of 1153–60 (Green 1979, p. 178).	The forest of Leek detached in the 13thC (Green 1979, p. 178).	1684 (Green 1979, p. 184).
Wirral	The Wirral peninsula (Green 1979, p. 184).	1194–1228 Charter (Green 1979, p. 185).	Stanney Grange disafforested by Ranulph III (1181–1232) (Green 1979, p. 187).	1376 (Green 1979, p. 187).
West Derby	West Derby Hundred south west of a line running approximately from Southport to Warrington (James 1981, p. 76).	By 1199 (Farrer & Brownhill 1990, pp. 1–2).	Toxteth disafforested about 1593 (Shaw 1956, p. 466).	Uncertain. A 1716 survey omits any mention of West Derby Forest (Shaw 1956, p. 466).
Rossendale (area between Accrington and Bacup only)	Southern and eastern boundary the River Irwell as far as its source on Thieveley Pike (James 1981, p. 76).			About the beginning of the 16thC (James 1981, p. 76).

Table 10.2. Medieval Royal Forests in the Mersey Basin (disafforestation refers to the removal of Forest Law).

Conquest nucleated settlements, such as at Kirkby and Eccleston, much of the area was wooded including considerable tracts of mossland and heath (Cowell & Innes 1994, p. 133). Studies of place names in West Derby have given an indication of past woodland cover and landscape. For instance, the derivation of Akenheaved, a minor name in Aintree township, suggests the top of an oak headland (Russell 1987, pp. 173–74).

The Royal Forests of Delamere and Mondrem, Macclesfield, Wirral, West Derby, and part of Rossendale were extensive tracts of unenclosed land in the region designated as royal hunting reserve in the 11th century. They contained not just woodlands, but also villages and areas of cultivation, pasture, and wasteland owned partly by the king as demesne and partly by his subjects (James 1981, Chapters 1–3). The Forest Law, which helped to preserve the woodland, including wood-pasture, probably helped to conserve biodiversity for up to several hundred years before disafforestation (Table 10.2).

Imparkment or enclosure of land, woodland or forest for sporting purposes occurred on an increasing scale from the 13th century onwards (e.g., Aston Wood, Cheshire (Warburton Muniments); see also Table 10.3). Medieval parks were often compartmented in order that deer, pannage and woods could be managed efficiently (Lasdun 1991, p. 7; Ives 1976, p. 51).

Woods regenerated naturally and were managed as coppice or woodpasture in which occasional trees were left to grow on for timber. Coppice mainly of Oak

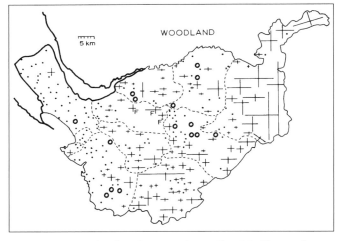

Figure 10.2. The distribution of woodland in Domesday Cheshire. The lines indicate the length and breadth of woodland. Places named in Domesday but with no mention of woodland are indicated by dots. Places with small amounts of woodland – less than 144ha (½ league × ½ league) – are shown as hollow circles. Manors associated with Delamere Forest are marked F (after Yalden 1987).

(*Quercus* sp.), Ash (*Fraxinus excelsior*), Alder (*Alnus glutinosa*), Willow (*Salix* spp.), Hazel (*Corylus avellana*), and Wych Elm (*Ulmus glabra*) provided the basic needs of fuel, fencewood and poles (Rackham 1990, pp. 55, 65). Pollards in wood pastures provided similar material.

Of the indigenous British trees, Beech (*Fagus sylvatica*),

Location	Year	Reference
Neston	1258	Tait 1923, p. 302.
Knowsley	1292	Farrer & Brownhill 1990, p. 158.
Tarvin	1299	Green 1979, p. 178.
Shotwick	1327	Stewart-Brown 1912, p. 100.
Arley	by 1383	Arley Charters 1866. Lease of 11th Nov, 7. Ric II 1302, Peter de Werbeton to Wm.de.Wermyncham.
Lyme	after 1388	Elizabeth Banks Associates (1993) Restoration Management Plan 2.2.
Adlington	1462	Green 1979, p. 179.

Table 10.3. Some examples of medieval imparkment

Hornbeam (*Carpinus betulus*) and Scots Pine (*Pinus sylvestris*) were probably not present in Mersey Basin woodlands in 1086, though Scots Pine had been a dominant species in the distant past (chapter three, this volume). An introduced tree, the English Elm (*Ulmus procera*) was almost certainly present while it is possible that the Romans had brought Sweet Chestnut (*Castanea sativa*) and Walnut (*Juglans regia*) to the area, but these trees were most likely to have been planted round settlements rather than in woodlands (Evans 1984, pp. 168, 204, 208; Mitchell 1984).

Woodland losses

Domesday to the Industrial Revolution
Pressures on the forest increased with the rise in population until the mid-14th century and many assarts or woodland clearances took place (Green 1979; Farrer & Brownhill 1990; Newbigging 1868; Shaw 1956; Cowell & Innes 1994, also Table 10.2). This was seen in West Derby, for instance, in the 13th century where agricultural expansion was also associated with a large increase in rectorial corn tithes and manorial grants (Berry 1980, p. 8). By the early 16th century about half of the forest of Macclesfield was occupied by settlers with farms (Davies 1961, p. 44).

Dwindling wood supplies prompted a 1482 Act to protect coppice regrowth (22 Edw. IV, Cap. 7), and later the 1543 Preservation of Woods Act (35 Henry VIII, Cap. 15). Tudor alterations to Bramall Hall were one victim of the shortage of good oaks, and had to be carried out using old timbers.

The Civil War also affected the woodland resource. Overcutting and devastation of the Deer populations during that war altered the forest composition, and by 1661 many of the 2,200 oaks that were estimated to be present in Delamere Forest at the start of the war had been lost. Only enough trees for fuel remained (Green 1979, p. 176). During that period the forest areas at Delamere became predominantly heathland grazed by 20,000 sheep (Palin 1843, p. 19).

Wood demands increased and shortages occurred as industries developed. Tree-ring evidence suggests that Oak was used from the 12th century in the salt industry infrastructure (Leggett 1980; see also Table 10.9). Wood or charcoal provided fuel for the salt, glassmaking, iron and copper industries, but were gradually replaced by coal in the 17th and 18th centuries (King 1656; Awty 1957; Vose 1977; Carlon 1979, 1981; see Table 10.4). Until the 17th century, supplies of fuelwood for the salt industry in Nantwich were partly met from woods at Awsterton, Cheshire, which were managed on twenty-year coppice rotations (King 1656, p. 66). A fivefold increase in Lancashire's coal production between the time of Elizabeth I (1558–1603) and 1700 was partly attributed to an increasing shortage of timber which pushed up wood prices and caused people to search for a substitute (Challinor 1972, pp. 10–11). But coal-mining in Lancashire and Cheshire also required ever-increasing supplies of pit timber as production rose further in the 18th century and mines became deeper.

Large quantities of bark, especially Oak, were required for tanning hides (Table 10.4), and often generated more income than the timber beneath it. Early in the 18th century bark was being exported to Ireland (Davies 1960, p. 12), but by the beginning of the 19th century Cheshire tanners were having great difficulty finding sufficient supplies of bark (Holland 1808, p. 197).

Many wooden naval, as well as other ships, were built in Liverpool after 1739 (Northcote Parkinson 1952, p. 105). Woodland exploitation was preferentially near to supply routes, where shortages were therefore most acutely felt, as John O'Kill indicated in 1763: 'as to the decrease of timber fitting for His Majesty's use in Lancashire, Cheshire, and North Wales I believe fifteen parts out of twenty are exhausted within these fifty years. I mean what was growing near any navigable river' (Fisher 1763, pp. 46–47). Indeed, it was the need for Oak for shipbuilding which was the driving force behind forest development until the change from wooden ships to ironclads in the mid-19th century (James 1981, p. 189).

The Industrial Revolution and two World Wars
The effects of industrialisation are illustrated by the Garston Hall estate, south Liverpool. All the 40 woods and shelter belts planted between 1800 and 1840 had been destroyed by about 1930 following the development of railway marshalling yards associated with Garston Docks and subsequent residential development (Berry & Pullan 1982). Other examples are listed by Handley (1982).

Timber imports increased considerably following industrialisation and the development of the railways in the 19th century (Forestry Commission 1921). At the start of the First World War home-grown timber barely met 10% of the nation's requirements and extensive fellings were made during the war to make up for the deficit in imports (Forestry Commission 1921). In Cheshire 1,310ha were felled (Forestry Commission 1928). The Forestry Commission was established in 1919 partly in response to these national shortages (James 1981). Grants

Species		Uses	Period	Reference
Oak				
	25–100 yrs	Building timber	Medieval – 19thC	Rackham (1991)
	Larger trees	Bridge bearers, mill posts	Medieval – 19thC	Bagley (1968)
	Unspecified	Shipbuilding	Particularly from 17thC	Smart (1992)
		Fencing, furniture, gates, wooden pipes.	Medieval – 13thC	Leggett (1980)
	Bark	Tanning, the most favoured species.	Medieval largely until early 20thC	Edlin (1949, p.87) Hodson (1978, p.138)
Ash		Shafts, tools, handles, carts, rails, wheels, bentware.		Smart (1992, p.116)
		Cooper timber	18thC	Bagley (1968)
Elm		Wheelwrights timber. Furniture, coffins, wooden pipes, vessels and storage ships. Underwater work. Keels and bottoms of flats.		Smart (1992, p.116).
Poplar		Flooring, boarding in carts and boxes, low-grade furniture and fittings.		Smart (1992, p.116). Holland (1808, p.206)
		Rebuilding bridge over Mersey at Stretford.	1745	Jarvis (1944).
Alder		Turnery, clogs		Edlin (1949, p.23–24)
	Poles	Drying cotton yarn	18thC	Holt (1795, p.85)
	Bark	Tanning		Edlin (1949, p.87)
	Bark	Dyes	18thC, 19thC	Holland (1808, p.206)
Birch		Turnery		Edlin (1949, p.42)
		Bobbins, spools, reels	19thC	Edlin (1949, p.42)
		Lancashire cotton industry		
	Twigs	Besoms	Medieval onwards, 1713	Bagley (1968) Edlin (1949, p.42)
	Bark	Tanning	Medieval on	Edlin (1949, p.87)
Willow		Basket work		Holt (1795, p.85)
		Baskets for salt	18thC	Holland (1808, p.206)
	Bark	Tanning		Edlin (1949, p.87)
Unspecified		Mining timber	Mainly from late 17thC	Shercliff, Kitching & Ryan (1983)
		Fuel for salt industry	Medieval to 1690	King (1656)
		Fuel for glassmaking		
		in Vale Royal	1284–1309	Vose (1977)
		in West Derby	c.1600	Vose (1995)
		Charcoal – iron forges	From 1619 at Tib Green, Doddington to the 18thC	Awty (1957)
		Copper smelting (e.g., Alderley Edge and Gallantry Bank, Cheshire (small scale)	Up to 18thC	Carlon (1979)

Table 10.4. Some historical uses of timber prior to the 20th Century

were made available to encourage planting and restocking of both conifers and hardwoods, but take-up was slow. By 1930 there had been little success in either arresting the deterioration of the home woodlands in private ownership or restoring the pre-war position (James 1981). However, locally there was more activity. On the Peckforton Estate in Cheshire, for example, where there were widespread war-time fellings, 86ha were reforested between 1922 and 1927 (Peckforton Estate Papers). Of the extensive fellings during the Second World War in the Mersey Basin, 960ha were from Cheshire of which 138ha were in Delamere Forest (Forestry Commission 1952; Forestry Commission Delamere Records). On the Sefton coast, net losses from all causes were estimated at about 20% for the period 1925–45 (Joint Countryside Advisory Service 1990).

Post-war losses

From about 1960 to 1982 Cheshire lost an estimated 660ha of woodland, Greater Manchester 190ha, and Merseyside 60ha – a total of 910ha due mainly to urban development and associated land use and agriculture (Forestry Commission 1984). There was some compensation by planting along motorways and trunk roads, and the natural colonisation of disused railway tracks.

Areas of coppice have constantly declined. In the 1924 census Cheshire had 134ha of coppice and 157ha of coppice-with-standards. By the time of the 1947–49 census there were 21ha of coppice and no coppice-with-standards, and in the 1979–82 census just 13ha of coppice-with-standards. At that time there was only 1ha of coppice recorded in Greater Manchester and none in Merseyside. It should be noted that Cheshire county boundaries changed in 1974 and the figures are not strictly comparable.

Pathogens and pollution

Pathogens have always played an important role in tree health, but their impact will have been altered by the widespread importation of timber; the development of near-monoculture plantations; improved control measures for pests and pathogens; and the increase in other stress-factors, especially pollutants which may alter the balance of the relationship between a tree and its pathogens (e.g., Innes 1987). The most catastrophic effect of a pathogen in recent decades was the outbreak of Dutch Elm disease which spread through the area during the 1970s and 1980s. The first official record of Dutch Elm disease in Merseyside was from Birkenhead in 1973. Whether or not this arrived as a direct import from Canada, as suggested by Marshall & Dawkins (1981), or was simply part of the general northward spread of the disease is not clear. By 1975 the disease was a major problem. However, a lack of political and financial commitment resulted in many diseased trees being left standing for well over a year (Greig & Gibbs 1983). The consequences of this were substantial. Of an estimated 76,000 highway trees in Merseyside in the mid-1970s about 18,600 were elms. Between 1975 and 1981 an estimated 10,800 of these elms were felled. Since highway trees may comprise only about a third of total trees in the county (Marshall & Dawkins 1981) and since the disease continued well into the 1980s, the total number of elms lost in the county is likely to have been several tens of thousands. The argument that pollutants or other stressors were necessary before the disease could overcome the defences of the trees was countered by Heybroek, Elgersma & Scheffer (1982) who noted that it was the trees showing strong growth that were the first to fall prey, while trees that had practically stopped growing suffered less. Instead, they said the disease could be regarded simply as an ecological accident resulting from the importation of an aggressive form of a fungal pathogen from one continent (North America) to another (Europe). A further impression of the impact of this 'accident' in the Mersey Basin area can be seen from the proportion of dead trees noted in the 1979–82 census that were Elms. In Merseyside, 55% of dead trees were elms; in Cheshire, 52%; and in Greater Manchester, 10% (Forestry Commission 1984). Given the history of this 'accident' it is appropriate to ask if lessons can be learned that are relevant for other potential pathogens, e.g., Oak Wilt and Ash Dieback?

Dramatic losses of trees caused by pollution were observed in the 1880s when emissions from chemical factories at Weston near Runcorn killed trees within a distance of 13km (8 miles), including 5,000 trees on the Norton estate (Dodd 1987). It was also suggested (Farrar, Relton & Rutter 1977) that the distribution of Scots Pine in the industrial Pennines is limited by concentrations of sulphur dioxide in the air.

Impacts of pollutants are sometimes more subtle, as was observed in a wood in Prescot, Merseyside, following a hundred years of metal processing in the town (Dickinson *et al.* 1996). Despite the uptake of the metals by the trees, which were mainly Sycamore (*Acer pseudoplatanus*), only a very limited effect was observed on tree growth before 1970. With emissions declining, this effect became even less after 1970. However, toxicity symptoms were observed in tree seedlings and the decay of leaf litter was inhibited at the site.

Other sub-lethal effects of pollutants were observed at Delamere Forest, where the goldening of Pine needles and needle loss in year three were associated with high levels of sulphur in the foliage which may be related to high levels of sulphur dioxide in combination with other pollutants (Inman & Reynolds 1995).

Development of plantations

Landscape, timber and game cover

Most of the present-day woodland cover comprises plantations dating from the 18th and later centuries. However, woodlands are known to have been planted since at least the first part of the 17th century (e.g., close to Simonswood; Shaw 1956, p. 468).

The great Halls were being landscaped in the 17th century, e.g., at Knowsley during the period 1651–72 (Sholl 1985, p. 14) and Dunham Massey, where a Kip engraving of 1697 shows established avenues and trees in formal gardens.

At the Royal Society in 1662, when there was great concern at the depletion of Britain's timber stocks, particularly shipbuilding Oak, John Evelyn presented his paper 'Sylva' which encouraged the planting of trees and care of woodlands. By the beginning of the 18th century trees were being planted for timber and underwood to meet estate needs (Table 10.5). At the beginning of the 19th century, Dunham Massey was considered to hold the largest stock of Oak timber in Cheshire (Holland 1808, p. 197).

Following the 1756 Enclosure Act opportunities arose for areas of moss and common to be planted as at Hill Top, Appleton which was fenced, drained and planted in 1765 (Warburton Muniments 1758–70). The Royal Society for the Arts gave awards to encourage the establishment of plantations from 1757 until 1835, e.g., the planting of 54ha of waste moorland near Delamere in 1795, and 847,650 trees at Taxall, Cheshire in 1796 (Royal Society of Arts 1801–02).

An indication of land use and extent of woodland, including new plantations can be seen on the first reasonably accurate maps of Lancashire (by Yates in 1787) and Cheshire (by Burdett in 1777). Though mixed plantations were favoured a 1792 report stated that Oak was still much planted in Cheshire and other species were cut to make way for it. By contrast the Lancashire report stated that fewer Oak were planted than any other timber (Commissioners 11th Report 1792), and Holt (1795, p. 84) described the woods and plantations in Lancashire as 'embellishments for gentlemen's seats, cover for game, or shelter from the blast rather than with a view to supplying the country with timber, and preventing importation'.

The Act of Enclosure for Delamere in 1812 was part of a parliamentary programme to use Crown lands for much-needed timber production. Although half of the land was set out in allotments in four new townships, some 1,557ha was to be planted as Crown forest (Simpson 1967) which is by far the largest planting scheme carried out in the Mersey Basin area (Smart 1992, pp. 73–86 and Fairhurst 1988). By 1823 all but 81ha of this land had been planted with Pedunculate Oak (*Quercus robur*), although initial difficulties led also to the planting of Scots Pine and European Larch (*Larix decidua*) as nurse species (Palin 1848; Simpson 1967, p. 270). Interestingly, Sessile Oak (*Q. petraea*), rather than Pedunculate Oak had probably been the main Oak constituent of the natural woodland (Smart 1992, p. 74). Extensive marling was undertaken between 1856 and 1864 (Grantham 1864) to reclaim 498ha of forest for agriculture leaving the Crown woods to be converted into predominantly coniferous plantation at the beginning of the 20th century (Popert 1908).

Game cover shrubs, including Rhododendron (*Rhododendron ponticum*), were included in many of the plantations established at Knowsley by the 12th Earl of Derby (1770–1830), and coverts became widely established on the estates in the 19th century, e.g., Fox Covert, (Lower Peover, 1832, Smart 1992, p. 62; Table 10.5). Later in the century pheasant shooting became an important country pursuit and mixed planting of broadleaves and conifers predominated, the latter providing shelter and cover.

Between 1840 and 1910 at a time of increasing prosperity, 246 new woods larger than 0.2ha were planted on private estates in what is now Merseyside, e.g., Halsnead in St Helens and in new public parks, e.g., Birkenhead and Sefton (Berry & Pullan 1982). But at the same time urban, industrial and agricultural activity led to the destruction of 156 Merseyside woods: the net change was an increase from 1,371ha to 1,651ha (Berry & Pullan 1982).

The choice of tree species planted changed with time (Table 10.5). The European Larch was planted in great quantity at Tatton and other estates in the early 19th century (Caldwell archives 1828-34). Later in the century western American conifer species were introduced including Sitka Spruce (*Picea sitchensis*), (Smart 1992, p. 61). Another successful introduction, Corsican Pine (*Pinus nigra* ssp. *laricio*) first used in Delamere in 1894 is now the main species planted there. Widely used on the estates, it has also proved invaluable in sand dune stabilisation on the Sefton coast. Oak was (and remains) the most planted hardwood in the mixed stands favoured on most estates and Beech has been widely planted on the lighter soils on which it is most successful.

Protection woodlands
Coastal plantations
Trees have been planted adjacent to the coast between Liverpool and Southport since at least the early 18th century, and probably much earlier, to protect sensitive

Figure 10.3. Austrian Pine woods planted on sand dunes at Ainsdale, Merseyside (*Photo: D. Atkinson*).

areas immediately inland of the dunes. In February and March 1712, for instance, Nicholas Blundell planted Horse-Chestnut (*Aesculus hippocastanum*), willows and poplars (*Populus* spp.), as well as a variety of shrubs adjacent to his ditches to protect them from encroachment by sand (Bagley 1968, 1970). Conifer plantations behind areas of planted Marram (*Ammophila arenaria*) on the most seaward dunes can stabilise further the partly vegetated surfaces (Macdonald 1954) and help to reduce erosion by wind and blown sand (Lehotsky 1941). By the end of the 19th century no technical barriers remained to the creation of large pine plantations – both techniques and species from continental Europe had been employed

Table 10.5. (right) History of plantations 1650–1900

Species used

A = *Alnus glutinosa*	N = *Castanea sativa*
B = *Fraxinus excelsior*	O = *Acer pseudoplatanus*
C = *Fagus sylvatica*	P = *Juglans regia*
D = *Betula* spp.	Q = *Salix* spp.
E = *Ulmus* spp.	R = Broadleaved species
F = *Carpinus betulus*	S = *Abies alba*
G = *Aesculus hippocastanum*	T = *Populus balsamifera*
H = *Tilia* spp.	U = *Larix decidua*
I = *Quercus* spp.	V = *Pinus nigra* spp. *laricio*
J = *Quercus ilex*	W = *Pinus sylvestris*
K = *Platanus* spp.	X = *Pinus strobus*
L = *Populus tremula*	Y = *Picea abies*
M = *Populus nigra, P.alba*	Z = Conifer species

Species used with mixture percentages when known (see Key opposite)

Date	Location	A	B	C	D	E	F	G	H	I	J	K	L	M	N	O	P	Q	R	S	T	U	V	W	X	Y	Z	Note	Reference
1650s	The Mere, Alderley			X																								Seed source Worcestershire	Ormerod 1882, pp. 305–06
1702–28	Little Crosby	X	X	X	X	X	X	X	X	X	X	X	X	X	X	X	X	X	X	X	X			X				Nursery and plantations	Bagley 1968, 1970, 1972
1710–50	The Park, Dunham Massey			X		X				X																		100,000 trees for landscape and timber	National Trust, 1991, Dunham Massey archives
1748	Tatton Plantation													X															Tatton Muniments
1749–56	Peover – Nursery		X	X		X	X		X	X	X	X			X	X				X	X	X		X		X			Mainwaring Collection
1756	– Circular Plantation			14		13	14	3							14					1		18		18		5			Mainwaring Collection
1759	– Plantations													X				X										Farm poplar and willow plantations	Mainwaring Collection
1792	Higmere					15								15								30		31					Caldwell Archives
1795	Near Delamere		1	4		1	9			3	3					3			1			37		50				133 acres heathland site	RSA 1801–02
1796	Taxall	7	14	4		18	14	3		3						11			2			35		4			2	Upland site 847,650 trees	RSA 1801–02
1797	Alderley Edge			26		5								5								12			26	26			Caldwell Archives
1813	Delamere Forest									X																		First Delamere planting 100% Oak	Smart 1992
1820	Delamere Forest									X					X									X				Oak with Sweet Chestnut and Scots Pine	Smart 1992
1822	Delamere Forest									X					X							X		X				Larch introduced	Smart 1992
1825	Howies Plantation, Knowsley		2							2					2	8						44		25		17			Sholl 1985
1828	Arley – Covert		10							10												40		20		20			Caldwell Archives
1828–34	Tatton Plantations		1																2	2	1	84		6		6		May have included hardwoods from other sources	Caldwell Archives
1829	Adlington									45												22		19		14			Caldwell Archives
1832	Lower Peover		10							9												41	X	30		10			Caldwell Archives
1894	Delamere Forest				X																	X	X	X					Smart 1992
1900	Delamere Forest																						X	X	X				Smart 1992

1707: Nicholas Blundell plants 'witherns' [willows] and other [unspecified] species on the dunes.	Bagley (1968)
By 1795: Rev. Formby successfully established Sycamore, Ash, Alder, 'platanus' [Plane] and 'fir' [probably Scots Pine] at Firwood, Formby.	Holt (1795)
From 1837: Large-scale planting of mainly Scots Pine and Larch at Culbin Sands, north-east Scotland, using techniques which had been employed as early as 1789 along the Gulf of Gascony, France.	Ross (1992)
From c.1850: Large-scale Pine planting at Holkham, Norfolk and the first extensive use of Corsican Pines on British dunes.	Macdonald (1954)
1887: Experimental tree-planting on Sefton coast by Charles Weld Blundell.	Jones, Houston & Bateman (1993)

Table 10.6. Events preceding the large-scale tree planting on the Sefton coast between 1894 and 1925

successfully in the creation of plantations on other British dunes (Table 10.6). Afforestation was also possible on a large scale at this time because all the coastal land between Ainsdale and Ravenmeols (at the southern edge of Formby) was effectively under the ownership of just two estates. A major programme of planting was therefore carried out between 1894 and 1925 by these estates – mainly of Austrian (*Pinus nigra* ssp. *nigra*) and Corsican Pines. Before this there had been only small-scale planting (Table 10.6). The development of these plantations is described by Ashton (1920), Gresswell (1953), Joint Countryside Advisory Service (1990), Jones, Houston & Bateman (1993) and Wheeler, Simpson & Houston (1993). By 1925 the basic pattern of woodland that is seen today on the coast was in place.

Even by 1925 some of the more seaward planting had been overwhelmed by sand or eroded by the sea (Joint Countryside Advisory Service 1990), and Sea-buckthorn (*Hippophae rhamnoides*) was introduced to protect the seaward edge of the plantations (Clements & Lutley 1987). Nonetheless losses of seaward plantations continue to the present day.

Since 1965 a greater variety of landowners have provided more varied management (Table 10.7). Although these plantations now serve many purposes (Wheeler *et al.* 1993), their role as protection woodlands – providing a valuable shelterbelt for Freshfield and Formby – remains paramount. Even the ongoing phased clear-felling of up to 40ha of frontal woodland at Ainsdale Sand Dunes National Nature Reserve is seaward of a large area of rear dune woodlands which is managed for continuity of cover, and forms an important shelter belt. This bold approach to dune management aims to restore and rejuvenate a dynamic semi-natural sand-dune system following the deterioration in nature conservation value caused at least partly by the dense plantations of non-native pines and a reduction in grazing following myxomatosis in the mid-1950s (Sturgess 1993, Sturgess & Atkinson 1993; Wheeler *et al.* 1993). In 1991 the total estimated area under tree-cover on the Sefton dune coast was 289ha; this represents about 14% of all the woodland in Merseyside (Wheeler *et al.* 1993). Pines still dominate these areas. The amount of deciduous tree-cover has also increased since the original period of conifer planting, but still accounts for less than 5% of the coastal woodland (Wheeler *et al.* 1993).

Catchment plantations

By far the largest plantation in a reservoir catchment in the Mersey Basin is Macclesfield forest. The 390ha of woodland comprises mainly Japanese Larch (*Larix kaempferi*) and Sitka Spruce with smaller amounts of other softwoods and some hardwoods including Beech and Sycamore. Its origin is intimately associated with the increasing demand for water, and the construction of reservoirs since the Industrial Revolution. The population of Macclesfield increased rapidly from about 1850 to its peak in 1881 when there were nearly 4,000 more

ACTIVITY	EXAMPLES
Felling and re-planting of small pockets of trees to regenerate Pine woods.	National Trust, Formby Point.
New planting on exposed western edge of plantation.	Sefton MBC, Lifeboat Road, Formby.
Thinning of mature stands of Pine to obtain advanced natural regeneration before felling.	Formby Golf Club (R.A. Smart, pers. obs.).
Thinning of pines and underplanting with deciduous species such as Beech and Oak rear woodlands.	National Trust, Formby and English Nature, Ainsdale NNR.
Coppicing of Alder, Sycamore and Birch to yield timber for brushwood or poles.	National Trust, Formby.
Clear-felling: (a) to create fire-breaks (b) to remove frontal woodland	Ainsdale NNR.
No management; natural regeneration of pines and other species.	Some private land.

Table 10.7. Some woodland management activities on the Sefton coast since the late 1970s (from Wheeler, Simpson & Houston 1993 and R.A. Smart, personal observations)

people than there are today. The demand for water led to the construction of the three Langley reservoirs, yet domestic demand continued to increase, prompting Macclesfield Corporation to construct the Trentabank Reservoir in 1929. After completion in 1930, trees were planted in its catchment to protect the water supply from pollution and to produce marketable timber (Smart 1992, p. 86).

Post-war forestry

A report on post-war forest policy (Forestry Commission 1943) set a national target of 5 million acres (*c*.2 million ha) of managed and developed forest, and proposed that private woodlands should be managed primarily for timber production. The 1947–49 census of woodlands of 2ha and over established the current situation in both Cheshire and Lancashire (Forestry Commission 1952). A Dedication Scheme announced in 1943, which became the main subject of the 1947 Forestry Act, was finally accepted by woodland owners in 1950. It gave them long-term confidence and provided incentives in the form of grants to regenerate, manage, and extend woodlands (James 1981). Other schemes and grants were also introduced to encourage management and timber production (Table 10.8).

In 1974 a new Dedication Scheme, Basis III, was introduced because Government took the view that the provision of employment and environmental gain should be the primary purpose of grant aid rather than the encouragement of timber production. Subsequent grant schemes swung the emphasis further from the needs of a strategic timber reserve and reduction of imports, towards multi-purpose forestry and environmental benefits. However, the many changes in grant scheme (Table 10.8), and conditions attached, combined with changes in taxation served as a disincentive to some estate and woodland owners.

A woodland resource for the 21st century

The woodland and timber resource comprises not just the present and planned areas of tree cover, but also ancient tree and pollen grains preserved by peat accumulation, which provides a valuable resource for research (for environmental and climatic reconstructions). This lends further argument for the conservation of wetlands which enable these woodland relics to be preserved. Table 10.9 and Figure 10.5 list and locate prehistoric and historic tree-ring

1943	Post-war Forestry Policy and Dedication Scheme announced.
1945	Forestry Act passed.
1947	Forestry Act to deal with matters arising from the Dedication Scheme.
1947	Town and Country Planning Act giving local authorities powers to make Tree Preservation Orders.
1949–55	Thinning grants available.
1950	Dedication Scheme finally accepted by woodland owners.
1950	Small Woods Scheme announced.
1950–55	Poplar planting grants available.
1951	Forestry Act included a replanting commitment as a condition of granting a felling licence.
1953	Approved woodland scheme planting grants introduced.
1953–62	Scrub clearance grants available.
1967	Forestry Act.
1972	Review of forest policy following cost-benefit analysis.
1973	A new Dedication Scheme announced which would replace existing dedication, approved, and smallwoods schemes.
1974–81	The new Dedication Scheme, Basis III, contained incentives to plant hardwoods and improve the environment.
1981–88	Forestry Grant Scheme with further incentives for hardwood planting.
1985–88	Broadleaved Woodland Grant Scheme gave added protection to semi-natural ancient woodland.
1988 on	Woodland Grant Scheme with subsequent changes.
1988 on	Farm Woodland Scheme to encourage diversification into forestry followed in 1992 by Farm Woodland Premium Scheme.
1988–89	Provisional County Inventories of ancient woodlands published by the Nature Conservancy Council.
1991	Mersey Forest establishment started.
1992	Red Rose Forest establishment started.
1994	Government statement 'The UK Programme and Sustainable Forestry', a follow up of the Earth Summit in Rio. Government's proposals for forestry put forward in 'Our Forests – The Way Ahead'. Further changes to the Woodland Grant Scheme which included considerable cuts in restocking grants.
1995	EU Agricultural Council agreed that tree planting including short rotation coppice, would be allowed on set-aside land.

Table 10.8. Some post-war Forestry Policies, Acts, Grants and Schemes
Compiled from: James (1981); Forestry Commission Scheme Leaflets; Institute of Chartered Foresters News

Table 10.9. Tree-ring chronologies from in and surrounding the Mersey Basin region.

PREHISTORIC PINE

	Site	Chronology Name/code	Radiocarbon years before present (BP)	NGR	Source
1.	Church Moss, Davenham (date from one tree)	–	7810±40 (B-82584)	SJ 665 714	University of Manchester Archaeological Unit 1995
2.	Lindow Moss, Wilmslow	LM1	5190±50 (GU-5567)	SJ 822 807	Lageard, Chambers & Thomas 1999
	Lindow Moss	LM2	5260±70 (GU-5568)	"	"
	Lindow Moss	LM3	5150±50 (GU-5569)	"	"
	Lindow Moss	LM4	5330±80 (GU-5570)	"	"
3.	White Moss, Alsager	Chron 1	4505±40 (SRR-4500)	SJ 774 552	Lageard 1992; et al. 1999
			4335±40 (SRR-4501)	"	
	White Moss	WM4	4160±40 (SRR-3941)	SJ 774 552	Calendar age see Chambers et al. 1999
			4125±50 (SRR-3942)	"	
			4115±40 (SRR-3943)	"	
			4090±50 (SRR-3944)	"	
			4015±45 (SRR-3945)	"	
			4055±45 (SRR-3946)	"	
4.	Day Green Farm		–	SJ 781 573	Lageard, samples collected

PREHISTORIC OAK

	Site	Chronology Name/code	Calendar age	NGR	Source
5.	Meols, Liverpool	–	Undated	SJ 238 909	Hillam unpub.
6.	White Moss	WM1	2190–1891 BC	SJ 777 552	Lageard et al. 1999.
	White Moss	WM2	3228–2898 BC	"	Lageard et al. 1999.
7.	Ashton Lane		4465–3929 BC	SD 412 436	Brown pers. comm. for all subsequent prehistoric oak chronologies.
					Sources for these include: Pilcher et al. 1984 Baillie and Brown 1988 Hillam et al. 1990 Baillie 1995
8.	Balls Farm		4433–4165 BC	SD 408 220	
9.	Berry House Farm		4922–4623 BC	SD 425 158	
10.	Broad Lane		3516–2986 BC	SD 405 444	
11.	Clay Brow Farm		4770–4601 BC	SD 426 149	
12.	Croston Moss 1		3198–1682 BC	SD 472 170	
	Croston Moss 2		1584–970 BC	SD 472 170	
13.	Curlew Lane		Undated	SJ 441 141	
14.	Eskham House Farm 1		3601–3109 BC	SD 440 440	
	Eskham House Farm 2		5012–4604 BC	SD 440 440	
15.	Hill Farm 1		3807–3494 BC	SD 314 018	
	Hill Farm 2		3519–3282 BC	SD 314 018	
16.	Leyland		1553–1032 BC	SD 523 236	
17.	Lower House Farm		4433–4224 BC	SD 3512	
18.	Meanygate Farm		2976–2698 BC	SD 404 173	
19.	New Eskham House Farm		3199–3006 BC	SD 418 437	
20.	New House Farm		Undated	SD 450 136	
21.	New Lane Farm		4940–4748 BC	SD 4213	
22.	North Wood's Hill Farm 1		4800–4647 BC	SD 449 457	
	North Wood's Hill Farm 2		3516–2986 BC	SD 449 457	
23.	Rougholm Farm		3445–3135 BC	Unknown	

24.	South Wood's Hill Farm 1	3931–3238 BC	SD 450 455
	South Wood's Hill Farm 3	4371–4113 BC	SD 450 455
	South Wood's Hill Farm 4	3145–2717 BC	SD 450 455
25.	Tinsley's Lane 1	4286–3862 BC	SD 406 437
	Tinsley's Lane 2	3851–3572 BC	SD 406 437
	Tinsley's Lane 3	3489–3160 BC	SD 406 437
26.	Whams Farm	Undated	SD 412 162
27.	Wild Goose Slack Farm	4935–4569 BC	SD 449 008
28.	Wood Moss Lane	Undated	SD 388 143

HISTORIC OAK

	Site	Chronology Name/code	Calendar age	NGR	Source
29.	Baguley Hall		AD 1037–1290	SJ 817 887	Leggett 1980
30.	Nantwich		AD 930–1330	SJ 650 523	"
31.	Peel Hall		AD 1378–1481	SJ 833 873	"
32.	Staley Hall		AD 1365–1554	SJ 975 997	"
33.	Eccleston Hall		AD 1121–1301	SJ 488 950	Groves unpub.
34.	The Falcon Inn, Chester		AD 991–1234	–	Groves & Hillam forthcoming
35.	36 Bridge Street, Chester		AD 1073–1317	SJ 405 662	Groves & Hillam forthcoming
36.	Bowers Row Car Park, Nantwich		AD 920–1208	–	Hillam unpub.
37.	Lightshaw Hall, nr. Wigan		AD 1106–1270 AD 1414–1552	SJ 614 996 "	Groves forthcoming "
38.	Sefton Fold, nr. Manchester		AD 1507–1601	SD 648 097	Groves & Hillam unpub.
39.	Willaston, nr. Nantwich		AD 917–1205	SJ 671 525	Groves 1990
40.	Wigan – 2 timber posts		AD 1029–1205		Groves 1987
41.	Lydiate Hall		AD 1369–1541	SD 364 049	Leggett 1984–85
42.	The Scotch Piper Inn, Lydiate		AD 1366–1531	SD 365 048	Leggett 1984–85
43.	21–23 Eccleston Road, Prescott (one timber, date for latest tree-ring)		AD 1513	–	Leggett pers. comm. in Cowell & Chitty 1982–83
44.	Old Abbey Farm, Risley		–	SJ 662 935	Dendrochronological analyses pending 1996, Lancaster University Archaeology Unit
45.	Kersall Cell, Salford		AD 1367–1510	SD 810 955	Howard pers. comm.
46.	Staircase Café, Stockport		AD 1389–1458	SJ 898 904	ibid
47.	Speke Hall		AD 1387–1598	SJ 410 820	ibid
48.	Brook Farm, nr Knutsford		AD 1402–1585	SJ 791 764	ibid
49.	Little Moreton Hall, nr Congleton		AD 1393–1538	SJ 833 589	ibid
50.	Ordsall Hall, Salford		AD 1385–1512 AD 1076–1345	SJ 815 973	ibid
51.	Morleys Hall, nr Leigh		AD 1386–1463	SJ 689 992	ibid

MODERN OAK

	Site	Chronology Name/code	Calendar age	NGR	Source
52 and 53.	Peckforton		AD 1780–1976	SJ 533 582 SJ 536 578	Leggett 1980

DENDROCHRONOLOGY LABORATORIES

Dendrochronology Laboratory, Palaeoecology Centre, Queen's University of Belfast, BT7 1NN. (Mr D. Brown.)
Tree Ring Dating Laboratory, Department of Archaeology, University of Nottingham, NG7 2RD. (Mr R. Howard.)
Dendrochronology Laboratory, Archaeology Research School, University of Sheffield, West Court, 2 Mappin Street, Sheffield, S1 4DT. (Dr J. Hillam & Ms C. Groves.)

Figure 10.4. Aerial view of planted Pine woods on the sand dunes of the Sefton Coast (*Photo: J. Houston*).

chronologies in and adjacent to the Mersey Basin.

The development of the Mersey Forest and Red Rose Forest provide important mechanisms to increase significantly the extent of woodland in the 21st century and involve local people in its use and management (the Mersey Forest Plan 1994 and Red Rose Forest Plan 1994; Table 10.9). Some 50 woods in the Mersey Forest area, covering 220ha, are now managed for public access, landscape and wildlife by the Woodland Trust. Whilst this includes outstanding sites such as Floodbrook Clough SSSI, in Runcorn, (which suffered particularly loss of canopy through Dutch Elm disease) many of the sites are secondary woodland and indeed the Trust seeks to acquire land for new woodland planting. The significance of both existing and projected Mersey Basin woodlands (Figure 10.1) can be considered against both global and local needs, which have been summarised in four major international agreements made at the United Nations Conference on Environment and Development 1992 (The Earth Summit, Rio) (Quarrie 1992, see Table 10.11). In addition to supporting landscape and recreational amenity three major functions of woodland for the future are:

1. A source of biological diversity (biodiversity)
The distribution of the significant number of ancient woodland fragments (continuously wooded since AD 1600) across the Mersey Basin is displayed in Figure 10.6, and can be compared with that for total woodland in

Figure 10.1 (see also chapter seven, this volume). Whilst more recent plantations are often associated with poorer agricultural soils, ancient woodland tends to be confined to areas where access for management has long been difficult, particularly in the incised cloughs of river valleys (Figure 10.7).

Since most of the woodland across the region has been planted or replanted since the 18th century, many sites have few plant species. Thus, 70% of woods surveyed in north Merseyside contained fewer than 21 species of flowering plant (Berry & Pullan 1982). In addition most of the extant woodlands shown in Figure 10.1 are small with 74% of the 679 woodland sites in Merseyside extending to less than 2ha. Moreover, Rhododendron was present in about 60% of woods and Sycamore was regenerating in half of them, altering their composition (Berry & Pullan 1982; see also Roberts 1974).

The proposed national Biodiversity Action Plans include the requirement to sustain ancient semi-natural woodland. The first local Biodiversity Action Plans for woodlands in the Mersey Basin were formulated in 1996/7 as a component of Local Agenda 21.

2. A component in the carbon cycle
Increasingly, woodland is recognised as a way of offsetting the effects of practices that produce carbon dioxide (CO_2).

In addition to restocking, an average area of 90.4ha per year was newly planted in the Mersey Basin in the

Figure 10.5. Location of tree-ring chronologies in and surrounding the Mersey Basin. Numbers refer to Table 10.9 which gives further information of chronologies.

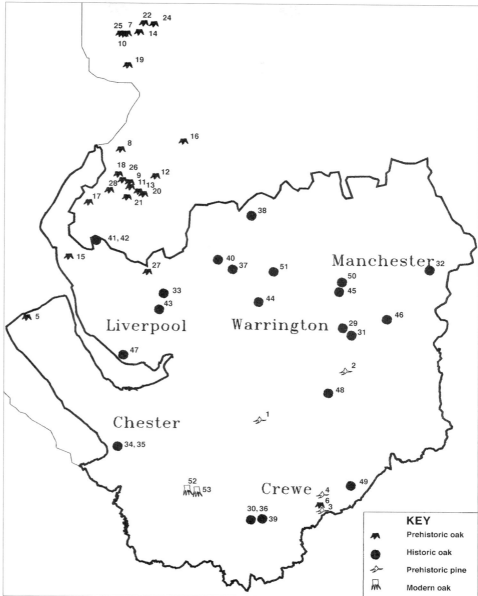

Figure 10.6. Ancient woodland sites in the Mersey Basin. These sites have been continuously wooded since at least AD 1600. Data from ancient woodland inventories for Cheshire, Greater Manchester and Merseyside (English Nature), and selected background sources.

period 1992–95 (average block size, 2.2ha), 92% of which was with broad-leaved species. Also, new temporary plantations, including coppices, have been established: these include *c*.70ha that were planted on vacant industrial land in Knowsley Metropolitan Borough in the 10-year period to April 1996.

3. A sustainable source of timber

In 1980 the region had only about 12,622ha of high forest (Forestry Commission 1984). The current low restocking rates (29.3ha per year across the region) are cause for considerable concern. On an assumed rotation of 100 years 126ha would be regenerated annually in a normal forest. The considerable reduction in restocking grants in 1994 could lead to even lower restocking, woodland neglect and hence reduced sustainability.

The sustainable timber resource must also include the important non-woodland trees (isolated trees, clumps and linear features, e.g., in hedgerows and parks). The 1980 census demonstrated an ageing population

Figure 10.7. Aerial view of woodlands in the Weaver valley east of Calton Hall, Kingsley, Cheshire (*Photo: R.A. Philpott*).

Guiding principles

improve the landscape and protect high quality areas

increase opportunities for access, sport and recreation

protect the best agricultural land from irreversible development

regenerate the environment within green belt and equivalent areas

protect sites of nature conservation

ensure community forests can be used for environmental education

improve the economic well-being of towns

encourage a high level of community involvement

seek private sector support to implement the forests

Six central themes for the Mersey Forest

convert wasteland to woodland

create networks of wooded greenways

green key transport routes

return farmland to forestry

weave woodland into new development

capitalise on the existing woodland assets

(The Mersey Forest Team 1994 and Red Rose Forest Team 1994)

Table 10.10. The Mersey and Red Rose Forests

---

numbering about 4,627,400 (Forestry Commission 1984, Table 10.12). The maintenance of non-woodland trees was seen to be no longer integrated into economic land use at a time when agricultural productivity was at a premium, and that retention and restoration of hedgerows with trees can only be achieved through financial incentives. Given an assumed average life span of 100 years, a minimum planting programme of some 46,000 trees per annum is required.

More encouragingly, United Utilities (formerly North West Water) which manages most of the water supply catchment plantations in north-west England, including Macclesfield, propose to maintain a sustained timber yield. They intend also, in the five years from 1995, to increase their planting and replanting programme in north-west England about threefold to a million trees a year, and to adopt a policy of maintaining continuous woodland cover (North West Water 1995).

The Sustainable Development Panel, set up by UK government as part of its commitment to Agenda 21 (Table 10.11), recommends that a national strategy should integrate forestry with other land uses recognising that the distinction between forestry and agricultural products is now becoming blurred. Such a National Forestry Strategy supported by regional strategies such as those for the Mersey Basin, which include the Mersey Forest and Red Rose Forest, should identify the incentives needed to meet specific agreed targets.

The Convention on Biological Diversity requires an audit of the biological resource with a commitment to sustaining the diversity of species. In the woodland context this dramatically changes the status of the largely neglected Ancient Woodlands.

The Convention on Climate Change requires particular consideration of the forest/woodland ecosystems in maintaining carbon sinks and climatic stability.

The Declaration of Forest Principles requires a fundamental review of our consumption of timber-based products to ensure the sustainable management of forests world wide.

Agenda 21 is the global strategy engaging all levels of society, including scientists, educationalists, local authorities and local communities to each play their part in shifting from an exploitative culture to a sustainable culture which respects both human needs and life supporting ecosystems.

Table 10.11. Four international agreements from the Earth Summit (1992) with direct relevance to the Woodland Resource of the Mersey Basin (Quarrie 1992)

Economic sustainability now needs to be integrated with ecological sustainability.

Acknowledgements

David Brown, Cathy Groves, Jennifer Hillam and Robert Howard kindly provided details of tree-ring chronologies. Other information was generously provided by I. Briscoe, S. Freeman, G. Heddon, C.J. Henratty, Dr D.P. O'Callaghan, P. Rawlinson and P. Russell. Hayley Atkinson cheerfully helped to extract all references to trees and woodland from the Great Diurnal of Nicholas Blundell. JGAL acknowledges the support of a NERC research studentship, grants from Cheshire County Council and the British Ecological Society (Small Ecological Project Grant No. 1145). Finally to the Word Processing Centre, Cheshire County Council for the table layouts and deciphering varying degrees of scrawl.

References

The location of archives and unpublished sources is given in parenthesis at the end of the reference citation. These locations include Cheshire Record Office (Cheshire CRO); Joint Countryside Advisory Service (JCAS) at Bryant House, Liverpool Road, Maghull and the John Rylands Library, Manchester (JRULM). To help find the documents, reference numbers are also often given.

Arley Charters, (1866). Calendar p. 11. (Cheshire CRO).

Ashton, W. (1920). *The Evolution of a Coast-line*. Stanford Ltd, London.

Awty, B.G. (1957). Charcoal ironmasters of Cheshire and Lancashire. *Transactions of the Historical Society of Lancashire and Cheshire*, **109**, 71–124.

Bagley, J.J. (1968). *The Great Diurnal of Nicholas Blundell of Little Crosby, Lancashire, Volume One, 1702–1711*. The Record Society of Lancashire and Cheshire, Manchester.

Bagley, J.J. (1970). *The Great Diurnal of Nicholas Blundell of Little Crosby, Lancashire, Volume Two, 1712–1719*. The Record Society of Lancashire and Cheshire, Manchester.

	Density per sq km			Total Non-Woodland Tree Population
	Isolated Trees	*Clumps*	*Linear Features*	
Cheshire	207	46	1.47km	2,030,450
Greater Manchester	399	85	0.9km	1,876,510
Merseyside	267	49	0.8km	720,440
Total				4,627,400

All figures from 1979–92 census Forestry Commission.
Clumps – small woods less than 0.25ha
Linear features – strips less than 20m mean width and more than 25m length.

Table 10.12. Non-woodland Tree Census (1979–82)

Bagley, J.J. (1972). *The Great Diurnal of Nicholas Blundell of Little Crosby, Lancashire, Volume Three, 1720–1728*. The Record Society of Lancashire and Cheshire, Manchester.

Baillie, M.G.L. (1995). *A Slice through Time, Dendrochronology and Precision Dating*. Batsford, London.

Baillie, M.G.L. & Brown, D. (1988). An overview of oak chronologies. *British Archaeological Reports, British Series*, **196**, 543–48.

Beck, H. (1969). *Tudor Cheshire*. Cheshire Community Council, Chester.

Berry, P.M. (1980). *An Evaluation of Woodlands on North Merseyside*. PhD thesis, University of Liverpool.

Berry, P.M. & Pullan, R.A. (1982). The woodland resource: management and use. *The Resources of Merseyside* (eds W.T.S. Gould & A.G. Hodgkiss), pp.101–18. Liverpool University Press, Liverpool.

Caldwell Archives. (Cheshire CRO DDX 363).

Carlon, C.J. (1979). *Alderley Edge Mines*. John Sherratt & Son Ltd, Altrincham.

Carlon, C.J. (1981). *The Gallantry Bank Copper Mine, Bickerton, Cheshire*. British Mining No. 16, Northern Mine Research Society, Sheffield.

Challinor, R. (1972). *The Lancashire and Cheshire Mines*. Frank Graham.

Chambers, F.M., Lageard, J.G.A., Boswijk, G., Thomas, P.A., Edwards, K.J. & Hillam, J. (1997). Dating prehistoric fires in northern England to calendar years by long-distance cross-matching of pine chronologies. *Journal of Quaternary Science*. **12**, 253–256.

Clements, D. & Lutley, W. (1987). *National Trust Biological Survey: Formby*. Report of the NT Biological Team. Unpublished report. The National Trust, Cirencester. (JCAS database).

Commissioners 11th Report (1792). Enquiring Into the State of The Woods and forests of the Crown, Appendix 11, Question 13. J. Debrett, London. (Forestry Commission Library, Alice Holt, Hants).

Cowell, R.W. & Chitty, G.S. (1982–83). A timber framed building at 21–23 Eccleston Street, Prescot (site 30). *Journal of the Merseyside Archaeological Society*, **5**, 23–33.

Cowell, R.W. & Innes, J.B. (1994). *The Wetlands of Merseyside*. Lancaster Imprints, Lancaster.

Davies, C.S. (1960). *The Agricultural History of Cheshire 1750–1850*. The Chetham Society 3rd Series, 10, Manchester.

Davies, C.S. (1961). *History of Macclesfield*. Manchester University Press, Manchester.

Dickinson, N.M., Watmough, S.A. & Turner, A.P. (1996).

Ecological impact of 100 years of metal processing at Prescot, N.W. England. *Environmental Reviews*, **4**, 8–24.

Dodd, J.P. (1987). *A History of Frodsham and Helsby*. Privately published (J.P. Dodd), Frodsham.

Dunham Massey. Accession List Records, Windblown Trees in Dunham Massey Park, Box, 15. (JRULM.)

Earwaker Collection, City Record Office, Chester. (CR 6311–2.)

Edlin, J.T. (1949). *Woodland Crafts in Great Britain*. Batsford, London.

Elizabeth Banks Associates (1993). *Lyme Park Restoration Management Plan 2.2*. Unpublished report. (Stamford Estate Office, Altrincham.)

Evans, J. (1984). *Silviculture of Broadleaved Woodland*. Forestry Commission Bulletin No. 62, HMSO, London.

Fairhurst, J.H. (1988). *A Landscape Interpretation of Delamere Forest*. Unpublished dissertation, University of Liverpool (Continued Education Library, University of Liverpool).

Farrar, J.F., Relton, J. & Rutter, A.J. (1977). Sulphur dioxide and the scarcity of *Pinus sylvestris* in the Industrial Pennines. *Environmental Pollution*, **14**, 63–68.

Farrer, W. & Brownhill, J. (1990). West Derby. Vol. 3 *The Victoria History of the Counties of England. A History of Lancaster* (eds W. Farrer & J. Brownhill). Published by Archibald Constable & Co. 1907, and reprinted photographically by William Dawson & Sons, Folkestone.

Fisher, R. (1763). *Heart of Oak, The British Bulwark*. Johnson, London.

Forestry Commission (1921). *The First Annual Report of the Forestry Commissioners, Year ending September 1920*. HMSO, London.

Forestry Commission (1928). *Report on Census of Woodlands and Census of Home Grown Timber 1924*. HMSO, London.

Forestry Commission (1943). *Post War Forestry Policy*. HMSO, London.

Forestry Commission (1952). *Census of Woodland 1947–49: Woodlands of 5 acres and over*. HMSO, London.

Forestry Commission (1984). *Census of Woodland and Trees 1979–82, Counties of Cheshire, Greater Manchester and Merseyside*. Forestry Commission, Edinburgh.

Forestry Commission (1997). *Forestry Commission: Facts and Figures 1996–97*. Forestry Commission, Edinburgh.

Grantham, R.B. (1864). A description of the works for reclaiming and making parts of the late forest of Delamere in the County of Cheshire. *Journal of the Royal Agricultural Society*, **35**, 369–80.

Green, J.A. (1979). Forests. *A History of Chester*, Vol. II *The Victoria History of the Counties of England* (ed. B.E. Harris). Published for the Institute of Historical Research by Oxford University Press, Oxford.

Greig, B.J.W. & Gibbs, J.N. (1983). Control of Dutch Elm Disease in Britain. *Research on Dutch Elm Disease in Europe* (ed. D.A. Burdekin), pp. 10–16. HMSO, London.

Gresswell, R.K. (1953). *Sandy Shores in South Lancashire; the Geomorphology of South-West Lancashire*. Liverpool University Press, Liverpool.

Groves, C. (1987). *Tree-ring dating of two timber posts from Wigan, 1984*. Ancient Monuments Laboratory Report Series 133/87. (Ancient Monuments Laboratory, English Heritage, London.)

Groves, C. (1990). *Tree-ring analysis of medieval bridge timbers from Willaston moated site, near Nantwich, Cheshire*. Ancient Monuments Laboratory Report Series 29/90. (Ancient Monuments Laboratory, English Heritage, London.)

Handley, J. (1982). The land of Merseyside. *The Resources of Merseyside* (eds W.T.S. Gould & A.G. Hodgkiss), pp. 83–100. Liverpool University Press, Liverpool.

Heybroek, H.M., Elgersma, D.M. & Scheffer, R.J. (1982). Dutch elm disease: an ecological accident. *Outlook on Agriculture*, **11**, 1–19.

Hillam, J., Groves, C.M., Brown, D.M., Baillie, M.G.L., Coles, J.M. & Coles, B.J. (1990). Dendrochronology of the English

Neolithic. *Antiquity*, **64**, 210–20.

Hodson, J.L. (1978). *Cheshire 1660–1760*. Cheshire Community Council, Chester.

Holland, W.B. (1808). *General View of the Agriculture of Cheshire*. Phillips, London.

Holt, J. (1795). *General View of the Agriculture of the County of Lancaster*. G. Nicol, London.

Inman, M. & Reynolds, S. (1995). *Physiological health check monitoring of (Pinus sp.) in Delamere*. Unpublished report. University of Wolverhampton. (Planning Department, Cheshire County Council, file reference 4143.)

Innes, J.L. (1987). *Air Pollution and Forestry*. Forestry Commission Bulletin 70. HMSO, London.

Ives, E.W. (1976). Letters and Account of William Brereton 1490–1536. *Record Society of Lancashire and Cheshire*, **116**, 51.

James, N.D.G. (1981). *A History of English Forestry*. Blackwell, Oxford.

Jarvis, R.C. (1944). The rebellion of 1745: the turmoil in Cheshire. *Transactions of the Lancashire and Cheshire Antiquarian Society*, **57**, 43–70.

Joint Countryside Advisory Service (1990). *A Working Plan for Woodlands on the Sefton Coast*. (JCAS database 080 Me 006.)

Jones, C.R., Houston, J.A. & Bateman, D. (1993). A history of human influence on the coastal landscape. *The Sand Dunes of the Sefton Coast* (eds D. Atkinson & J. Houston), pp. 3–18. National Museums & Galleries on Merseyside in association with Sefton Metropolitan Borough Council, Liverpool.

King, D. (1656). *Vale Royal of England*. Daniel Webb, London.

Lageard, J.G.A. (1992). *Vegetational history and palaeoforest reconstruction at White Moss, south Cheshire, UK*. PhD thesis, Keele University.

Lageard, J.G.A. (1998). Dendrochronological analysis and dating of subfossil *Pinus sylvestris* L. at Lindow Moss, Cheshire. *Bulletin of the British Ecological Society*, **29 (2)**, 31–32.

Lageard, J.G.A., Chambers, F.M. & Thomas, P.A. (1999). Climatic significance of the marginalisation of Scots Pine (*Pinus sylvestris* L.) circa 2500 BC at White Moss, south Cheshire, UK. *The Holocene*. (In press.)

Lasdun, S. (1991). *The English Park*. André Deutsch, London.

Leggett, P.A. (1980). *The use of tree-ring analyses in the absolute dating of historic sites and their use in the interpretation of past climatic trends*. PhD thesis, Liverpool Polytechnic.

Leggett, P.A. (1984–85). Dendrochronological study of timbers from the Scotch Piper Inn. *Journal of the Merseyside Archaeological Society*, **6**, 69–73.

Lehotsky, K. (1941). Sand dune fixation in Michigan. *Journal of Forestry*, **39**, 998–1004.

Macdonald, J. (1954). Tree planting on coastal sands in Great Britain. *Advances in Science*, **11**, 33–37.

Mainwaring Collection, Box 42. Foresters Notebook 1749–1768. (JRULM).

Marshall, S.A. & Dawkins, R.D.H. (1981). The financial impact of the Dutch Elm Disease on a local authority. *Arboricultural Journal*, **5**, 256–62.

Mersey Forest (1994). *Mersey Forest Plan*. (Mersey Forest Project Office, Risley Moss, Warrington.)

Mitchell, A.F. (1984). Native British Trees. *Research Information Note 53.80.SILS*, Forestry Commission.

National Trust (1991). *Dunham Massey Guide*. National Trust, London.

Newbigging, T. (1868). *History of the Forest of Rossendale*. Simpkin Marshall, Bacup.

North West Water, (1995). *North West Water woodland strategy statement*. North West Water, Warrington.

Northcote Parkinson, C. (1952). *The Rise of the Port of Liverpool*. Liverpool University Press, Liverpool.

Ormerod, G. (1882). *History of Cheshire*. Routledge and Son, London.

Palin, W. (1843). The Farming of Cheshire. (Cheshire CRO X630.)

Peckforton Estate Papers. Reafforestation. (Cheshire CRO

DTW 2477/E/4.)

Pilcher, J.R., Baillie, M.G.L., Schmidt, B. & Becker, B. (1984). A 7,272 year tree-ring chronology from W. Europe. *Nature,* **312**, 150–52.

Popert, E.H. (1908). *Report on the Crown Woods at Delamere, Cheshire.* HMSO, London.

Quarrie, J. (ed.) (1992). *Earth Summit '92. The United Nations Conference on Environment and Development, Rio de Janeiro 1992.* Regency Press, London.

Rackham, O. (1986). *The History of the Countryside.* Dent, London.

Rackham, O. (1990). *Trees and Woodland in the British Landscape.* Revised Edition. Dent, London.

Red Rose Forest Team (1994). *Red Rose Forest Plan.* (Community Forest Centre, Salford Quays.)

Roberts, J. (1974). *The Distribution and Vegetation Composition of Woodland on the Wirral Peninsula, Cheshire.* PhD thesis, University of Liverpool.

Ross, S. (1992). *The Culbin Sands – Fact and Fiction.* Centre for Scottish Studies, University of Aberdeen.

Royal Society of the Arts (1801–02). Agricultural Minutes C10/60/F2 and C10/154/F2.

Russell, P. (1987). *The Nomenclature of the West Derby Hundred.* MPhil thesis, University of Liverpool.

Shaw, R.C. (1956). *The Royal Forest of Lancaster.* The Guardian Press, Preston.

Shercliff, W., Kitching, D. & Ryan, J. (1983). *Poynton A Coal Mining Village.* Publisher and place not stated. (Chester CRO.)

Sholl, A. (1985). *Historical Development of Knowsley Park.* Compilation of source material and historical notes. Groundwork Trust for St Helens and Knowsley. (Earl of Derby's Library, Knowsley.)

Simpson, E.S. (1967). The reclamation of the Royal Forest of Delamere. *Liverpool Essays in Geography – a Jubilee Collection* (eds R.W. Steel & R. Lawton), pp. 271–91. Longmans, London.

Smart, R.A. (1992). *Trees and Woodlands of Cheshire.* Cheshire Landscape Trust, Chester.

Stewart-Brown, R. (1912). Royal Manor and Park of Shotwick. *Historical Society of Lancashire and Cheshire,* **64**, 104.

Sturgess, P. (1993). Clear-felling dune plantations: studies in vegetation recovery on the Sefton coast. *The Sand Dunes of the Sefton Coast* (eds D. Atkinson & J. Houston), pp. 85–93. National Museums & Galleries on Merseyside in association with Sefton Metropolitan Borough Council, Liverpool.

Sturgess, P. & Atkinson, D. (1993). The clear-felling of sand-dune plantations: soil and vegetational processes in habitat restoration. *Biological Conservation,* **66**, 171–83.

Tait, J. (1923). *Chartulary of Register of the Abbey of St Werburgh, Chester.* The Chetham Society, New Series, 82, Manchester.

Tatton Muniments. Egerton Family Correspondence 2/1/41. (JRULM.)

University of Manchester Archaeological Unit (1995). Davenham Bypass: Archaeological evaluation. Unpublished report. (University of Manchester Archaeological Unit.)

Vose, R.H. (1977). *Glassmaking at Kingswood, Delamere, Cheshire.* Winsford Local History Society and the Michaelmas Trust, Winsford.

Vose, R.H. (1995). Excavations at the *c.*1600 Bickerstaffe glasshouse, Lancashire. *Journal of the Merseyside Archaeological Society,* **9**, 1–24.

Warburton Muniments (1758–1770). Peter Harpers Account Books, 1758–1770 and 1302 Lease. (JRULM), Box 26 Folder 3.

Wheeler, D.J., Simpson, D.E. & Houston, J.A. (1993). Dune use and management. *The Sand Dunes of the Sefton Coast* (eds D. Atkinson & J. Houston), pp. 129–50. National Museums & Galleries on Merseyside in association with Sefton Metropolitan Borough Council, Liverpool.

Yalden, D.W. (1987). The natural history of Domesday Cheshire. *Naturalist,* **112**, 125–31.

CHAPTER ELEVEN

The uplands: human influences on the plant cover

J.H. TALLIS

Introduction

Geologically and geographically, the Mersey Basin uplands are part of 'highland Britain' (Figure 11.1). Consequently, the plant and animal life there is exposed to the harsh environmental conditions characteristic of all the highland zone: a cold wet climate, a prevalence of shallow and infertile soils, and a high proportion of steeply sloping and often rocky ground (McEwen & Sinclair 1983). Only the most hardy plants and animals can survive. The same hostile combination of climate and geology normally deters human settlement. However, if humans do invade the uplands, either as visitors or as settlers, then additional pressure is placed on a plant cover that is already stressed by the intrinsic harshness of the upland environment. Irremediable damage to that fragile cover can result. Nowhere in Britain is this more apparent than in the Mersey Basin uplands. Here there is a record of human presence extending back over 8,000 years, and a current population in the surrounding lowlands of more than 5 million people who have easy access (< 30km distance) to the uplands (Figure 11.1). For many of those people who visit the uplands for recreation and pleasure (at least 100,000 each week in summer – Shimwell 1981), the bleak peat-covered moorlands, the poor-quality pastures and the open treeless vistas of the Mersey Basin uplands may appear an epitome of 'highland Britain' – a landscape perhaps as Nature intended. The reality is probably closer to 'a man-made desert', with 'the creation of the moorland environment... as much a social failure as a natural phenomenon' (Spratt 1981).

The distinctive character of the Mersey Basin uplands

At least three characteristics of the plant cover of the Mersey Basin uplands can be highlighted which are not typical of other upland areas of Britain, and which in combination make it unique. These are:

1. A notable scarcity of particular plant groups in the vegetation:

(a) mosses (and particularly bog moss, *Sphagnum*);

(b) upland pasture grasses such as the fescues and bents (*Festuca* and *Agrostis* spp.);

(c) grassland herbs such as Daisy (*Bellis perennis*) and Tormentil (*Potentilla erecta*); and

(d) bog plants such as Bog-rosemary (*Andromeda polifolia*), Cranberry (*Vaccinium oxycoccos*) and Round-leaved Sundew (*Drosera rotundifolia*).

As a result there are extensive areas of species-poor grassland dominated by Wavy Hair-grass (*Deschampsia flexuosa*) or Mat-grass (*Nardus stricta*), and species-poor moorland dominated by cotton-grasses (*Eriophorum* spp.) or Purple Moor-grass (*Molinia caerulea*).

2. A lower-than-average representation of Heather (*Calluna*) moorland, and a higher-than-average representation of either *Molinia* grassland or *Eriophorum* moorland. This feature is apparent if comparison is made with the overall vegetation cover of the twelve upland parishes in England and Wales surveyed for the 'Upland Landscapes Study' in the early 1980s. The results of that survey (Allaby 1983) are given in Table 11.1, together with equivalent data for the Anglezarke Moors of Rossendale, and for the four large Mersey Basin parishes of the North Peak (Charlesworth, Hayfield, Saddleworth

	A	B	C
Smooth grassland (fescues, bents)	17.1	0	
Coarse grassland (*Molinia*)	11.1	**46.7**	35.8
Coarse grassland (*Nardus, Deschampsia*)	13.3	19.1	
Bracken	8.5	0.2	1.9
Dwarf shrubs : *Calluna*, etc.	32.6	**7.3**	**16.7**
Sedge & rush moorland	16.6	**26.7**	**41.8**

Table 11.1. The plant cover (as % total area) of (A) twelve upland parishes of England and Wales (combined results of Allaby 1983); (B) the Anglezarke moorlands, Rossendale (data of Bain 1991); (C) the combined parishes of Charlesworth, Hayfield, Saddleworth and Tintwistle (data of Phillips, Yalden & Tallis 1981). Noteworthy differences in columns B and C as compared with column A are shown in bold.

(a)

Figure 11.1. (a) The position of the Mersey Basin uplands in relation to upland areas of England and Wales as a whole; ground above 244m altitude is shown black. (b) The Mersey Basin Uplands, and location of sites mentioned in the text. The upland areas are shaded above the 244m and 427m contours – the notional lower limits of the uplands and of deeper blanket peat, respectively. Urban centres are shown in black, with populations in thousands superimposed.

(b)

and Tintwistle – total area 130km²). The lower-than-national representation of Heather moorland and the higher-than-national representation of *Molinia* grassland and *Eriophorum* (sedge) moorland in both these areas is clearly shown.

3. Widespread erosion of the plant cover, with patches or larger areas of bare soil and peat exposed. The peat cover that blankets the flatter ground above 450m altitude, in particular, is often massively eroded. In the four parishes of Charlesworth, Hayfield, Saddleworth and Tintwistle, about 12% of the land (15.8km²) was bare or partly bare in 1981 (Phillips, Yalden & Tallis 1981). Here there are probably 'greater expanses of deep and heavily eroded peat than can be found in any other mountain region of the British Isles' (Conway 1954). This eroded peat landscape has been aptly called a 'wet desert'.

The record of human presence

Human presence in the Mersey Basin uplands is documented in a number of ways. Settlement features (farm buildings, enclosed fields, etc.) from both the historic and prehistoric periods afford direct evidence of presence, as do written records from more recent centuries (maps, stock numbers, litigation proceedings, etc.). Burial mounds and various components of the hunting or farming 'tool-kit' (flint arrowheads, pottery vessels, etc.) afford further evidence of prehistoric presence. The growth of industrial towns and cities in the surrounding lowlands is documented directly in population censuses, and indirectly in the soot and heavy metal deposits on the upland vegetation (Livett, Lee & Tallis 1979).

These varied lines of evidence highlight five major periods of heightened human impact on the Mersey

Basin uplands:

1. from *c*.8,600 to 5,300 BP (the Mesolithic period) – when parts of the uplands were probably used as summer hunting grounds (Wymer 1977; Barnes 1982; Williams 1985);

2. from *c*.3,900 to 3,200 BP (the Early Bronze Age) – when the first upland farms were established (Barnes 1982; Vine 1982; Bain 1991);

3. from *c*.AD 1250 to 1507 (the Medieval period) – when local cattle and sheep ranches were set up as Forest Law was relaxed (Montgomery & Shimwell 1985; Bain 1991);

4. from AD 1507 to 1675 – the expansion of upland farming in the post-disafforestation period (Montgomery & Shimwell 1985); and

5. from AD 1675 to present – agricultural intensification and industrial expansion (Montgomery & Shimwell 1985).

The different upland resources utilised in these five impact-periods are summarised in Table 11.2.

A model of vegetation change

The cold wet climate of all upland areas of Britain results almost inevitably in long-term deleterious soil changes. The prevailing downward movement of water in the soil

	1	2	3	4	5
Food materials:					
Wild animals and plants	+	+			
Domesticated animals & plants		+	+	+	+
Raw materials:					
Wood		+	+	+	
Peat			+	+	
Stone				+	+
Water					+
Recreation:					
Sport			+		+
Walking					+
Tourism					+

Table 11.2. The upland resource and its utilisation; 1–5 are the human impact-episodes mentioned in the text.

produced by the annual excess of precipitation over evaporation leads inexorably to leaching, acidification and podsolisation. On flatter ground, where drainage is impeded, water ponds up in the soil, resulting in water-logging and ultimately the accumulation of peat. The potential productivity of the ecosystem is thus inevitably reduced, as indicated schematically by the line AB in Figure 11.2. Additional environmental stress (which could be climate change, but is more likely to be human-induced) is represented in Figure 11.2 by the displacements S_1, S_2 and S_3. These give successively lower

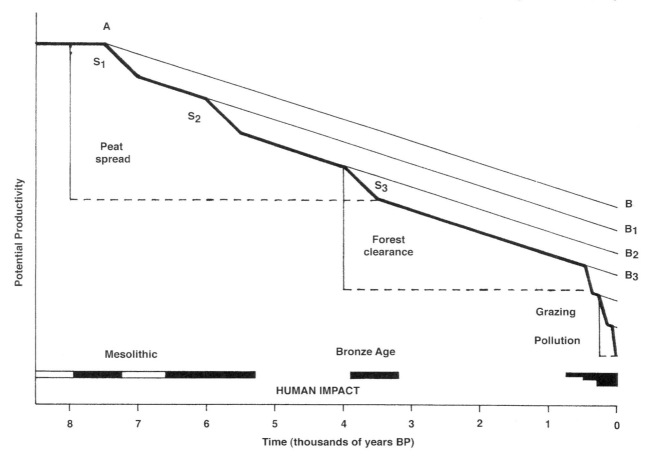

Figure 11.2. Schematic chart of major impacts on the Mersey Basin uplands.

positions of the overall trend line – to AB₁, AB₂ and AB₃ – and hence a less productive vegetation cover.

Six such displacements, representing responses to periods of accentuated environmental stress, can in fact be recognised in the documented history of the plant cover of the Mersey Basin uplands. Recognition is based on lines of evidence derived solely from the plant cover itself, without recourse to the evidence on human impact summarised above. These lines of evidence are considered in the following Sections.

The long-term perspective

Twenty thousand years ago, at the height of the last cold stage, the Mersey Basin uplands were a wasteland of snow and ice – a wind-blasted polar desert overlooking the ice sheets of the Lancashire and Cheshire lowlands. A single pollen diagram from an upland site just outside the Mersey Basin catchment (Middle Seal Clough, below the north face of Kinder Scout at 490m altitude), records the early stages of vegetation recovery between 9,800 and 8,900 years ago. During that period, scrub of Willow (*Salix*) and Birch (*Betula*), and later Hazel (*Corylus avellana*), spread rapidly upwards (Johnson, Tallis & Wilson 1990). By 8,600 years ago, Hazel was widespread over a considerable altitudinal range, as witnessed by the pollen diagrams at two further sites within the Mersey Basin catchment itself: Robinson's Moss (Tallis & Switsur 1990), and Soyland Moor (Williams 1985). These two sites also record the subsequent spread of forest trees, such that by 7,500 years ago the hillslopes were forested up to about 525m altitude (Figure 11.3); above

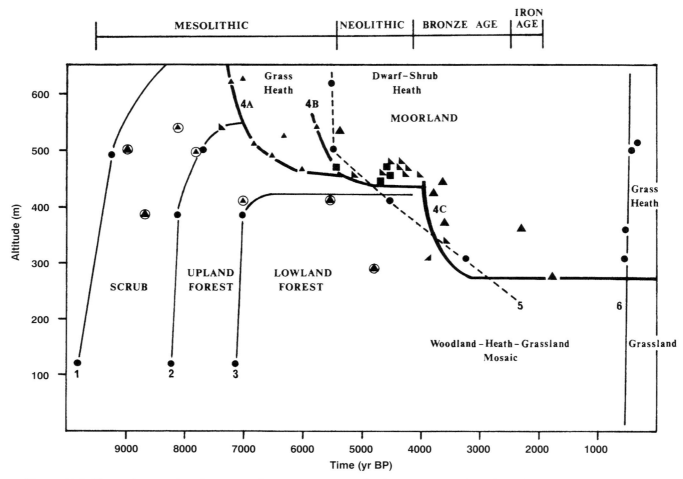

Figure 11.3. Chart of vegetation changes in the Mersey Basin uplands, based on radiocarbon dates and pollen analyses at various sites (see Appendix for details). The following codings are used for datings at individual sites:

▲ radiocarbon date of the basal peat
◢ radiocarbon date of tree remains below the peat
● other radiocarbon dates
○ sites with early peat formation

■ radiocarbon date of tree remains at the peat base
◣ radiocarbon date of tree remains above the peat base
▲ pollen-analytical date for the basal peat.

Lines 1–6 show particular features of the vegetation history:
1, the upper limit of scrub (marked by a rise in birch pollen and a fall in juniper pollen);
2, the upper limit of upland forest (marked by a rise in pine pollen);

3, the upper limit of lowland forest (marked by a rise in alder pollen);
4, the onset of peat formation;
5, soil podsolisation (marked by a rise in Ericaceae pollen);
6, spread of grassland (marked by a rise in grass pollen).

that level, scrub covered all but the most exposed ground. The pollen influx to Robinson's Moss then consisted of 80 – 90% tree and shrub pollen, as compared with < 20% at the present day.

Evidence of this former more extensive forest cover over the southern Pennines and Rossendale is also provided by the numerous roots, trunks and branches of trees embedded and preserved at the base of the upland peats (Tallis & Switsur 1983; Bain 1991). These tree remains date variously from about 7,500 to 3,500 years ago (Appendix). They show that Pine and Oak were common components of the forest up to 525m altitude, but at higher altitudes a scrub of Birch and Willow (and also Hazel, on the basis of the pollen evidence) was predominant (Table 11.3).

The upland forest and scrub established itself initially at these higher altitudes in a warm, dry and relatively benign climate. Beginning about 7,500 years ago, however, the climate became substantially wetter. That change led gradually but inexorably to waterlogging of the soils on the flatter ground, and to leaching and acidification of the soils on the hillslopes. As a result, the uplands became increasingly less favourable for tree and shrub growth. The progress of these soil changes is charted in Figure 11.3, where the initiation and spread

Altitudinal interval (m)	Total number of sites	Number of sites with:			
		Pine	Birch	Oak	Willow
<375	9	5	3	4	
380–425	10	8	4	1	2
430–475	15	7	8	5	3
480–525	16	7	7	5	6
530–575	1	1	1		1
580–625	2		1		2

Table 11.3. The distribution of peat-preserved tree remains in relation to altitude in the Southern Pennines (data of Tallis & Switsur 1983).

of blanket peat and the expansion of Heather are used as recognisable consequences of soil waterlogging and of soil acidification, respectively. Peat initiation and spread occurred between *c.*7,500 and 3,500 years ago, and expansion of Heather between *c.*5,500 and 3,500 years ago.

In the face of these changes, the forest and scrub receded – first from the higher flatter ground, where its former presence is recorded in the preserved tree remains, and later from the hillslopes. Its retreat from the hillslopes is shown in the five pollen diagrams summarised in Figure 11.4, from sites within, or close to,

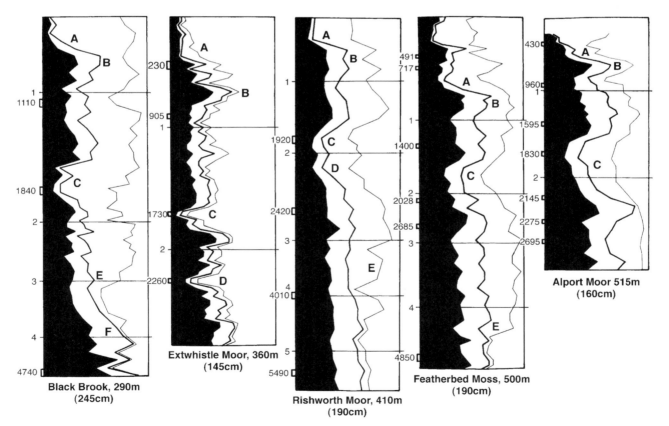

Figure 11.4. Summary pollen diagrams from: Black Brook, Rossendale (Bain 1991); Extwistle Moor (Bartley & Chambers 1992); Rishworth Moor (Bartley 1975); Featherbed Moss (Tallis & Switsur 1973); and Alport Moor (Tallis & Livett 1994). Components of each diagram, from left to right, are: total tree pollen, shrub pollen, Ericaceae, and other non-arboreal pollen (all as % total land pollen, TLP). Dates of radiocarbon-dated peat samples (yrs BP) are shown at the left of each diagram. The horizontal lines show approximate dates at 1 ka (thousand year) intervals. A, B, C, D, E and F are pollen features referred to in the text. Depths of the peat column analysed are shown below each site name.

the Mersey Basin uplands ranging in altitude from 290m to 515m. What is very apparent in Figures 11.3 and 11.4 is the discontinuous nature of the forest retreat. Three major episodes of peat spread are highlighted in Figure 11.3: at c.7,500–7,000, 6,000–5,500 and 4,000–3,500 BP. Marked reductions in tree and shrub pollen (APC) occur in some or all of the pollen diagrams in Figure 11.4 at the levels labelled F, D, C and A: at c.4,000 BP, c.2,260 BP, c.2,000–1,600 BP and c.500–400 BP. In between are periods of forest recovery.

The spread of peat

Numerous finds of small worked flints (microliths) buried below the peat (Wymer 1977; Barnes 1982; Williams 1985) testify to a regular summer population of Mesolithic hunters in the Mersey Basin uplands during the early stages of peat spread (7,500–5,500 BP). The pollen evidence for this timespan suggests a complex vegetation mosaic, of high forest, scrub, grassland, heath and bog, with the emphasis shifting perceptibly from forest towards bog through time. Long-continued episodes of reduced Hazel pollen values, accompanied by increased values of herbaceous and ericaceous plants, are recorded in both the Soyland Moor and Robinson's Moss pollen diagrams: from 7,900 to 7,250 and 6,600 to 4,965 BP at Soyland Moor (Williams 1985), and from 9,000 to 8,500, 7,700 to 7,500 and 5,500 to 4,900 BP at Robinson's Moss (Tallis & Switsur 1990). All the episodes at Robinson's Moss are accompanied by high concentrations of carbonised plant material in the peat (Figure 11.5). Accordingly it has been suggested that

these episodes record phases of repeated burning (either accidental or deliberate) of the high-altitude scrub (Tallis & Switsur 1990). At Holme Moss, the pollen evidence indicates that Hazel scrub occupied the plateau up to 5,400 BP, and was then destroyed by fire immediately before the onset of peat accumulation (Livett & Tallis 1994).

A plausible pattern of land-use (Jacobi, Tallis & Mellars 1976; Williams 1985) is of long-continued exploitation of the higher moorlands for wild game (perhaps Red Deer), through regular burning of the encroaching Hazel and Birch scrub, to provide more nutritious regrowth. This practice led eventually to soil impoverishment and also to the spread of peat, as removal of the tree cover could have been sufficient to raise the water balance of the soil to a level where waterlogging and the accumulation of peat occurred inevitably (Moore 1975, 1993).

It is likely that the Mesolithic hunters utilised only the zone of scrub and grassland/heath above the forests. Before 8,000 BP a range of altitudes could have been exploited, and at lower-altitude sites (such as Soyland Moor, and others in the Saddleworth – Marsden area) regular annual visits would have kept back the encroaching forest for many centuries. Less heavily-exploited, lower-altitude sites would eventually have been abandoned to the forest, however, so that from 8,000 to 7,000 BP perhaps only the highest ground was being visited regularly. As the climate became wetter after 7,500 BP, peat spread would eventually have led to the abandonment of these sites also. Progressive soil deterioration might then have resulted in an opening up

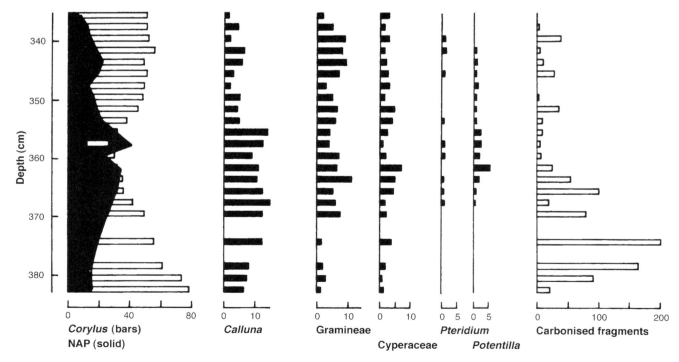

Figure 11.5. Changes in selected pollen and spore components at Robinson's Moss between c.7,700 and 7,500 BP; all values are expressed as % total land pollen, except for Corylus, which is shown as % total tree + shrub pollen. The frequency of burning is shown as number of carbonised fragments per slide-traverse. Re-drawn from Tallis & Switsur (1990).

of the uppermost levels of the forest below the peat blanket, and an extension of scrub, so that by 6,000 BP new hunting grounds at slightly lower altitudes were becoming available and being exploited. These, too, were eventually abandoned as peat continued to spread. On the lower-altitude Rossendale uplands, forest and scrub probably persisted until at least 4,000 BP (Bain 1991), but was then cleared, almost certainly as a result of Bronze Age activity in the uplands (level F in the Black Brook pollen diagram, Figure 11.4). Again, peat formation ensued.

In the southern Pennines peat formation began at a much earlier date than in most other upland regions of Britain. Thus in south-west, central and northern Scotland and the Outer Hebrides, the major period of peat spread was after 5,500 BP; in Orkney and Shetland, the Inner Hebrides, western and northern Ireland, mid- and north Wales and the northern Pennines, it was delayed until after 4,500 BP (Tallis 1995a). By this time, the present-day extent of blanket peat in the southern Pennines had nearly been achieved. In all these regions of Britain, much of the peat spread was over ground that was previously covered by forest and scrub (Birks 1988). The differences in timing of peat initiation between regions can conceivably be related to differing levels of prehistoric activity, and associated scrub clearance, in the uplands.

The clearance of the hillslope forests

Limited episodes of clearance of the forest cover from the Mersey Basin hillslopes over the time-period from 3,000 to 700 BP are recorded in all five of the pollen diagrams in Figure 11.4. In between the clearance episodes the forest returned to varying degrees. As the values for tree and shrub pollen at level B (*c*.700 years ago) were substantially the same as those at 3,000 BP, however, these forest clearance episodes can have had little long-term effect on the upland environment.

The forest regeneration episode at level B is almost certainly associated with the emplacement of large parts of the Mersey Basin uplands under Forest Law in the early Medieval period. The pollen evidence indicates that the composition of the upland forest then differed in detail from that of earlier forests (more Oak and Birch, less Hazel, for example), but that forest and scrub was nonetheless extensive. Subsequent clearance, in contrast to earlier episodes, was effectively permanent. Where documentary evidence exists, it indicates that substantial inroads were being made into the upland forests by AD 1300 (Tallis & McGuire 1972). The pace of clearance quickened after disafforestation in AD 1507, and in parts of Rossendale at least, clearance was almost complete by AD 1600 (Tallis & McGuire 1972). The uplands were then given over almost entirely to management for sheep and cattle, and locally later (post-AD 1800) for Red Grouse (*Lagopus lagopus*) and water catchment.

The grazing factor

A detailed picture of the upland landscape at the beginning of the 20th century can be derived from the maps of the Peak District by Smith and Moss (1903) and Moss (1913). In that landscape, Heather moor was more widespread than it is today and grassland less extensive. Table 11.4 summarises the differences for the four parishes of Charlesworth, Hayfield, Saddleworth and Tintwistle.

	1913	1979
Dwarf-shrub moorland (*Calluna* or *Vaccinium* dominant or co-dominant)	25.2	16.7
Eriophorum and eroding blanket bog	45.5	41.8
Grassland and bracken	29.3	37.7

Table 11.4. The extent of three major vegetation types (as % total area) in the four upland parishes of Charlesworth, Hayfield, Saddleworth and Tintwistle in 1913 and 1979 (data of Anderson & Yalden 1981).

The balance between Heather moor and grassland in upland areas is known to be influenced by grazing (Yalden 1981a). The western slopes of Kinder Scout were covered by Heather (*Calluna vulgaris*) and Bilberry (*Vaccinium myrtillus*) in the early 1900s (Moss 1913), but by 1982 the plant cover had degenerated to a discontinuous turf of Wavy Hair-grass interspersed with patches of Mat-grass, Bilberry and bare ground; Heather was virtually absent. Under National Trust management, sheep numbers were progressively reduced over the next 10 years by active shepherding, from 2.5 sheep to 0.18 sheep per hectare. By 1992, with lowering of the grazing pressure, Heather and Bilberry were spreading and most of the bare ground was revegetated (Table 11.5).

	1983	1992
Deschampsia flexuosa	41	83
Calluna vulgaris	0	25
Vaccinium myrtillus	1	16
Bare ground	51	6

Table 11.5. The plant cover (% cover) along 12 permanent transects on the west slopes of Kinder Scout at 450–530m altitude in 1983 and 1992 (data of Anderson 1997).

Sheep numbers on the moorlands of the Peak District are known to have risen steadily over the period from 1950 to 1989, with a fourfold increase in some areas (Figure 11.6). Before that, numbers had remained fairly stable back to at least 1914 (Yalden 1981b) – and indeed may not have been very different in 1690 (Shimwell 1974). The high stocking rates over the last 45 years have

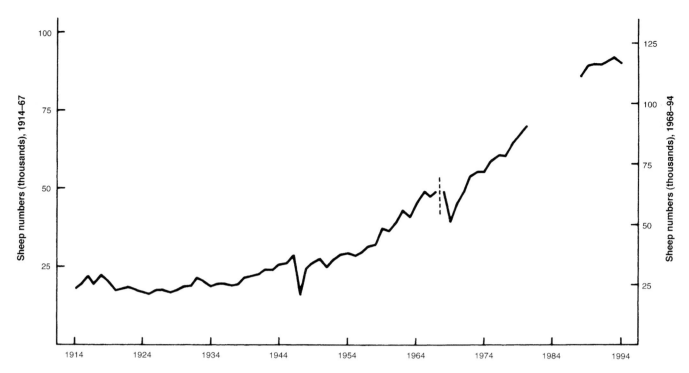

Figure 11.6. Trends in sheep numbers on the moorlands of the Peak District, 1914–1994. Because of differences in the way MAFF sheep statistics have been collected, the graph utilises two overlapping sets of data (with different vertical axes): 1914–1977: combined parishes of Hope Woodlands, Derwent, Edale, Charlesworth, Hayfield and Chinley/Buxworth/Brownside; 1968–1994: above parishes, plus Aston, Bamford, Brough and Shatton, Castleton, Hope, Thornhill, Chisworth, Glossop, Tintwistle, Whaley Bridge and New Mills. For problems in the collation of the data, see Yalden (1981b) and Anderson, Tallis & Yalden (1997).

undoubtedly been a major factor in the decline of Heather and the spread of grasses – though recent work in the Netherlands suggests that in the future the increased nitrogen concentrations in acid rain (see below) could further favour the spread of Wavy Hair-grass and Purple Moor-grass at the expense of Heather (de Smidt 1995).

The blighted landscape

A record of the rampant industrial growth (and concomitant population increase) that has occurred in the Mersey Basin lowlands over the last 250 years is preserved in the soot-blackened uppermost layers of the upland peats, and their associated higher concentrations of lead, zinc, copper and nickel (Figure 11.7). The upland peats and soils have also been watered over this time-period by acid rain, so that their pH may be as much as one unit lower than that of soils and peats in other, cleaner, upland areas. The upland plants are inevitably also affected, with higher internal concentrations of potentially toxic heavy metals (Livett, Lee & Tallis 1979) and of nitrogen (Press, Woodin & Lee 1986).

It is tempting to ascribe the scarcity of certain plant groups in the Mersey Basin uplands to this pollution. There is certainly direct experimental evidence that some *Sphagnum* spp. are deleteriously affected by acid rain (Lee 1981; Ferguson & Lee 1983; Lee, Tallis & Woodin

1988). The peat stratigraphy shows that over large areas of the higher moorlands of the Mersey Basin *Sphagnum* was a major component of the bog vegetation from early Medieval times through to about AD 1750 (Tallis 1965, 1987). Its remains disappear from the peat at the level when soot contamination first becomes apparent and heavy metal concentrations rise. The implication is clear: that *Sphagnum* was killed off by the products of the Industrial Revolution.

The growth of at least two other common moorland plants – Heather and Common Cotton-grass (*Eriophorum angustifolium*) – has also been shown to be adversely affected at pH values below about 3.3 (Richards 1990; Caporn 1997). Some southern Pennine peats are as acid as pH 2.8 (Anderson, Tallis & Yalden 1997). There is thus good reason to believe that the Mersey Basin uplands are indeed a blighted landscape, caused by pollution from the surrounding lowlands.

It would be a mistake, however, to ascribe all the peculiarities of the upland plant cover to pollution. Thus the *species-poverty* of the vegetation is the result of at least three processes acting in combination:

1. the intrinsic infertility of many of the upland soils (especially those overlying Millstone Grit);

2. the selective action of several centuries of grazing and burning (allowing only the more resistant plant species to survive); and

3. air pollution (damaging the bryophytes and lichens in particular).

Even though large areas of *Sphagnum* were undoubtedly killed off by pollution in the 18th and 19th centuries, its abundance had already been reduced in many places long before that. The peat stratigraphy of deeply-gullied sites shows that *Sphagnum* had disappeared at these sites by the 16th century, if not earlier (Tallis 1985, 1987; Montgomery & Shimwell 1985). The *scarcity of dwarf-shrub heath* (and particularly Heather moorland), and the prevalence of grassland and sedge moorland, is again the product of several centuries of grazing and burning, with the effects already noticeable probably by the late 17th century. Thus, pollen analysis of sites currently in uneroded moorland (where the patterns of vegetation change have not been influenced by erosion) show that Heather pollen was predominant until about AD 1500, but that subsequently grass pollen rose steadily, most notably after *c.*AD 1650 (Figure 11.8). This is when hill farming became widely established in the Mersey Basin uplands (human impact episodes 4 and 5), with the plant cover increasingly exposed to the debilitating and selective action of sheep grazing.

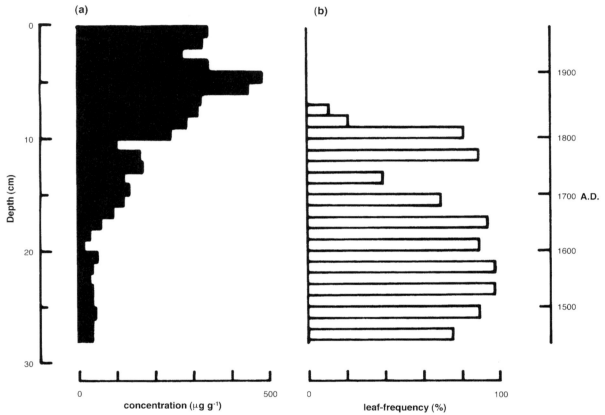

Figure 11.7. Concentration of lead (a) and frequency of *Sphagnum* leaves (b) in the upper layers of a peat profile from Featherbed Moss, Snake Pass (data of Livett (1982) and unpublished).

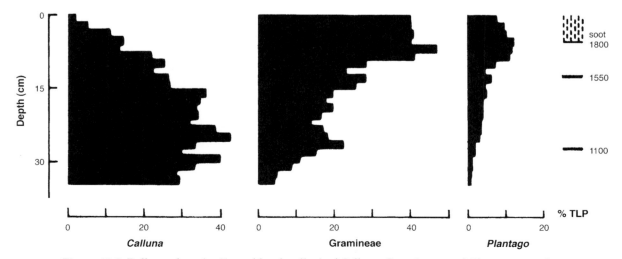

Figure 11.8. Pollen values (as % total land pollen) of *Calluna*, Gramineae and *Plantago* over the last 1,000 years at Featherbed Moss, Southern Pennines (Site 2 of Tallis 1965).

The scars of battle

The prevalent erosion of the plant cover at the present day in the Mersey Basin uplands is a more complex issue. The landscape is stressed and scarred as a result of a succession of human impacts (Figure 11.2), with erosion of different types, and resulting from different processes, often superimposed one upon another. The erosion is very much a feature of the higher ground, so that it is far more prevalent in the southern Pennines than in Rossendale. Three different sets of *processes* contribute to it:

1. disruption or destruction of the plant cover and exposure of bare peat or soil;

2. prevention of recolonisation of these bare areas, once formed, by plants; and

3. physical and chemical removal of the unstabilised bare peat and soil.

Physical and chemical removal (by water, wind and biochemical oxidation) affects only the surface peat/soil layers that have been loosened by frost and drought (Burt & Gardiner 1984; Francis 1990; Labadz, Burt & Potter 1991), and operates in all upland regions. It is a consequence of the harsh climatic conditions there. The initial disruption of the vegetation cover, and subsequent prevention of recolonisation, on the other hand, results from the action of largely extrinsic *agents* of erosion. Those that can be identified for the Mersey Basin uplands include pollution, grazing, fire, trampling, peat cutting and cloudbursts.

In non-polluted upland areas of Britain, mosses and liverworts 'fill in' the spaces between the individual higher plants in the vegetation, and cover over any unprotected soil and peat; *Sphagnum* is particularly characteristic of the wetter places. In the Mersey Basin uplands this group of plants has been killed off by pollution (and, to a lesser extent, by burning), exposing unprotected soil and peat. The ability of the higher plants subsequently to grow together, and minimise the damage caused by the death of the bryophytes, has been hampered by sheep grazing and intermittent burning. Heavy sheep grazing, particularly on steeper slopes, may even exacerbate the vegetation break-up. The recovery of the plant cover when sheep grazing is removed has been demonstrated in a variety of experimental trials in the Peak District National Park (Tallis & Yalden 1983; Pigott 1983; Anderson, Tallis & Yalden 1997).

Another widespread cause of erosion is damage from accidentally-started moorland fires ('wildfires') during dry weather. More than 300 wildfires were recorded on the moorlands of the Peak District National Park in the period from 1970 to 1995, mostly in years with prolonged dry weather in spring or summer (notably 1976). In total, about 42km² of the moorland was burnt (some 8% of the total moorland area – Anderson, Tallis & Yalden 1997). Some 45% of the fires are known to have started next to roads and close to the Pennine Way and other footpaths, so that much fire damage is clearly a product of the increasing accessibility of the uplands over the last 30 years. The larger and more severe fires have contributed substantially to the bare and eroding ground visible today, because recolonisation by plants has often been slow. Extensive bare areas still persist from major fires in 1976, 1959 and 1947 (Radley 1965; Tallis 1981). Up to 15–20% of the bare ground present in the Peak District National Park could have originated from wildfires (Tallis 1982), some of it from fires that occurred more than 200 years ago (Tallis 1987).

The periodic high concentrations of carbonised plant material down the peat profile at many sites suggest that wildfires have always been a hazard on the moorlands. At Alport Moor there are at least 15 such 'burning peaks' within the peat formed over the last 2,500 years (Tallis & Livett 1994). In addition, frequent, if rather haphazard, rotational burning of the vegetation has been carried out deliberately over the last few centuries, to encourage regrowth of either the coarse moorland grasses (at burning intervals of 5–7 years) or of Heather (at intervals of 10–15 years; Hobbs & Gimingham 1987).

Trampling, peat cutting and cloudbursts result in more localised erosion. The southern section of the Pennine Way was described in 1989 as 'a man-made quagmire in wet conditions' (Porter 1989). Nevertheless, the total contribution of trampling is small in the context of the whole landscape: no more than 56ha of eroded ground along moorland footpaths in the Peak District National Park (total area 52,000ha – Yalden 1981c). Nevertheless, more than £200,000 has already been spent in restoration work (Anderson, Tallis & Yalden, 1997). Peat cutting on the moorlands may have been more extensive in the past than is generally realised (P. Ardron, personal communication), but much of it occurred in the Middle Ages and the cut-over areas are now stabilised. Two sites of severe erosion in the Mersey Basin uplands have been attributed to storm damage: Cabin Clough, near Glossop, is known to have been devastated by a cloudburst on 30 July 1834 (Montgomery & Shimwell 1985), whilst the products of a peatslide, perhaps around AD 1770, are still visible on the north-eastern side of Holme Moss (Tallis 1987). Other sites may well exist that have not yet been documented.

Sheep play a further role in the erosion process. Heavy grazing limits the supply of native seed available to recolonise bare ground, and damages the new plant cover as it attempts to get established. Sheep thus reinforce the inherent harshness of the upland environment, which restricts seedling establishment by promoting surface instability of the bare peat and soil. A further constraint derives from the additional acidity produced by acid rain. Even native moorland plants now find it difficult to germinate and establish on the most acid peats (Richards 1990; Richards, Wheeler & Willis 1995).

The Badlands of Britain

The oldest, and also the most widespread, erosion features on the moorlands are the gully systems, which are found particularly in the deeper peats above 450m altitude. The most intense erosion, by close-set reticulate gullying, normally occurs only above about 550m altitude (Bower 1960; Anderson & Tallis 1981). The development of the gullies appears to have coincided with periods of increased environmental stress on the Mersey Basin uplands in the last 450 years. Thus three phases of gullying have been distinguished. The deepest gullies, incised through 2m depth of peat or more into the underlying mineral substrate, probably started to form 400–500 years ago (Tallis 1995b). The shallower gullies, still contained entirely within the peat mass, represent a second phase of extension beginning 200–250 years ago (Tallis 1965). Very recent gully systems can also be observed, forming on peat areas bared by wildfires (Turtle 1984).

These three phases of gullying certainly match in time with episodes of perturbation of the bog surface (by post-disafforestation sheep farming, air pollution and wildfires, respectively). However, it is possible that the initial damage that led to the gullying occurred naturally, by extreme desiccation of the peat mass during the drier conditions of the so-called Early Medieval Warm Period of *c*.AD 1050–1200 (Tallis 1995b). The colder wetter conditions of the Little Ice Age, from *c*.AD 1550 to 1800, also led to an increased abundance of *Sphagnum* on as yet uneroded areas of the moorlands (Tallis 1987), so that the subsequent effects of pollution could have been enhanced by this natural climatic change.

Postscript

Gully erosion in the southern Pennines is exceptionally severe as compared with other upland areas of Britain. Gullying is most marked in the deeper peats, and deep peat is unusually widespread in the southern Pennines. This could be a consequence of the long time-period over which peat has accumulated there (see above). The early onset of peat formation could conceivably be linked to human perturbation also (burning of the upland scrub by Mesolithic hunters – Tallis 1991). If so, then the upland landscapes of the Mersey Basin are a product of human-induced environmental stress extending back not hundreds but thousands of years.

Acknowledgements

The following colleagues contributed substantially to the ideas in this chapter, through discussions and the provision of data: Mrs Penny Anderson, Dr Malcolm Bain, Ms Daryl Garton, Dr David Shimwell and Dr Derek Yalden.

Appendix

Sources of data used in the compilation of Figure 11.3.

Site	Altitude (m)	Date (yrs BP)	Code	Source*
A. Initial rise in Birch pollen, decline in Juniper pollen				
Red Moss	120	9798	Q-924	1
Middle Seal Clough	490	9230	SRR-336	2
Robinson's Moss	500	8950	Q-2320	3
B. Increase in Pine pollen, initial rise in Oak pollen				
Red Moss	120	8196	Q-918	1
Soyland Moor	385	8110	Q-2931	4
Robinson's Moss	500	7675	Q-2273	3
C. Initial rise in Alder pollen				
Red Moss	120	7107	Q-916	1
Soyland Moor	385	7640	Q-2390	4
D. Basal peat, radiocarbon date				
Robinson's Moss	500	8950	Q-2320	3
Soyland Moor	385	8650	Q-2392	4
Holme Moss	535	5370	GU-5376	5
Arnfield Moor	445	3610	GU-5378	5
Ogden Clough	370	3560	GU-5380	5
Black Brook	290	4740	HAR-6210	6
Round Loaf	305	3880	BIRM-1161	6
Winter Hill	427	3750	BIRM-1162	6
Pikestones	275	1710	HAR-6209	6
Rishworth Moor	410	5490	GAK-2822	7
Extwistle Moor	360	2260	BIRM-689	8
E. Basal peat, pollen-analytical estimated date				
Alport Moor	540	8100		9
Robinson's Moss B	495	7800		9
Bleaklow	622	7200		9
Ringinglow C	410	7000		9
Kinder	625	7000		9
Featherbed Moss	510	6800		9
Featherbed Moss	490	6500		9
Salvin Ridge	525	6300		9
Featherbed Top	540	5500		9
Tintwistle High Moor	467	6000		9
F. Tree remains at peat base				
Lady Clough Moor	470	5410	Q-1349	10
Coldharbour Moor	450	4670	Q-1407	10
Featherbed Moss	475	4570	Q-1346	10
Tintwistle Knarr	470	4475	Q-2314	10
G. Tree remains within peat				
Deep Clough	340	3540	BIRM-147	11
Over Wood Moss	540	7350	Q-1404	10
Laund Clough	455	5110	Q-1402	10
Rawkin's Brook	465	4620	Q-1408	10
Lady Clough Moor	480	4340	Q-1350	10
Lady Clough Moor	480	4495	Q-1348	10
Featherbed Moss	475	4320	Q-1347	10
Laund Clough	455	4250	Q-1401	10
Tintwistle Knarr	470	4210	Q-1405	10

Continued overleaf

* 1 = Hibbert, Switsur & West 1973
2 = Johnson, Tallis & Wilson 1990
3 = Tallis & Switsur 1990
4 = Williams 1985
5 = Unpublished data
6 = Bain 1991
7 = Bartley 1975
8 = Bartley & Chambers 1992
9 = Tallis 1991
10 = Tallis & Switsur 1983
11 = Tallis & McGuire 1972
12 = Conway 1954
13 = Tallis & Switsur 1973
14 = Tallis & Livett 1994.

| Far Back Clough | 400 | 3995 | Q-1406 | 10 |
| Tintwistle Knarr | 470 | 4000 | Q-2315 | 10 |

H. Rise in Ericaceae pollen

Bleaklow	622	5500		12
Robinson's Moss	500	5470	Q-2434	3
Alport Moor	540	>4900	Q-2431	3
Rishworth Moor	410	4010		7
Round Loaf	305	3200		6

I. Rise in Gramineae pollen

Featherbed Moss	500	491	Q-849	13
Alport Moor	515	430	SRR-4783	14
Extwistle Moor	360	1460AD		8

References

Allaby, M. (1983). *The Changing Uplands*. Countryside Commission, Cheltenham.

Anderson, P. (1997). Changes following the reduction in grazing pressure on the west face of Kinder Scout. *Restoring Moorland. Peak District Moorland Management Project, Phase 3 Report* (eds P. Anderson, J.H. Tallis & D.W. Yalden). Peak Park Joint Planning Board, Bakewell, Derbyshire.

Anderson P. & Tallis, J. (1981). The nature and extent of soil and peat erosion in the Peak District – field survey. *Moorland Erosion Study. Phase 1 Report* (eds J. Phillips, D. Yalden & J. Tallis), pp. 52–64. Peak Park Joint Planning Board, Bakewell, Derbyshire.

Anderson, P., Tallis, J.H. & Yalden, D.W. (eds) (1997). *Restoring Moorland. Peak District Moorland Management Project, Phase 3 Report*. Peak Park Joint Planning Board, Bakewell, Derbyshire.

Anderson, P. & Yalden, D.W. (1981). Increased sheep numbers and the loss of heather moorland in the Peak District, England. *Biological Conservation*, **20**, 195–213.

Bain, M.G. (1991). *Palaeoecological Studies in the Rivington Anglezarke Uplands, Lancashire*. PhD thesis, University of Salford.

Barnes, B. (1982). *Man and the Changing Landscape*. Merseyside County Museums, Liverpool.

Bartley, D.D. (1975). Pollen analytical evidence for prehistoric forest clearance in the upland area west of Rishworth, West Yorkshire. *New Phytologist*, **74**, 375–81.

Bartley, D.D. & Chambers, C. (1992). A pollen diagram, radio-carbon ages and evidence of agriculture on Extwistle Moor, Lancashire. *New Phytologist*, **121**, 311–20.

Birks, H.J.B. (1988). Long-term ecological change in the British uplands. *Ecological Change in the Uplands* (eds M.B. Usher & D.B.A. Thompson), pp. 37–56. Blackwell, Oxford.

Bower, M.M. (1960). Peat erosion in the Pennines. *Advancement of Science, London*, **64**, 323–31.

Burt, T.P. & Gardiner, A.T. (1984). Runoff and sediment production in a small peat-covered catchment: some preliminary results. *Catchment Experiments in Fluvial Geomorphology* (eds T.P. Burt & D.E. Walling), pp. 133–51. Geo Books, Norwich.

Caporn, S.M. (1997). Air pollution and its effects on vegetation. *Restoring Moorlands. Peak District Moorland Management Project, Phase 3 Report* (eds P. Anderson, J.H. Tallis & D.W. Yalden), pp. 28–35. Peak Park Joint Planning Board, Bakewell, Derbyshire.

Conway, V.M. (1954). The stratigraphy and pollen analysis of southern Pennine blanket peats. *Journal of Ecology*, **42**, 117–47.

de Smidt, J.T. (1995). The imminent destruction of north-west European heaths due to atmospheric nitrogen deposition. *Heaths and Moorland: Cultural Landscapes* (eds D.B.A. Thompson, A.J. Hester & M.B. Usher), pp. 206–17. Scottish Natural Heritage, Edinburgh.

Ferguson, P. & Lee, J.A. (1983). Past and present sulphur pollution in the Southern Pennines. *Atmospheric Environment*, **17**, 1131–37.

Francis, I.S. (1990). Blanket peat erosion in a mid-Wales catchment during two drought years. *Earth Surface Processes and Landforms*, **15**, 445–56.

Hibbert, F.A., Switsur, V.R. & West, R.G. (1973). Radiocarbon dating of Flandrian pollen zones at Red Moss, Lancashire. *Proceedings of the Royal Society, Series B*, **177**, 161–76.

Hobbs, R.J. & Gimingham, C.H. (1987). Vegetation, fire and herbivore interactions in heathland. *Advances in Ecological Research*, **16**, 87–173.

Jacobi, R.M., Tallis, J.H. & Mellars, P.A. (1976). The Southern Pennine Mesolithic and the ecological record. *Journal of Archaeological Science*, **3**, 307–20.

Johnson, R.H., Tallis, J.H. & Wilson, P. (1990). The Seal Edge Coombes, Derbyshire – a study of their erosional and depositional history. *Journal of Quaternary Science*, **5**, 83–94.

Labadz, J.C., Burt, T.P. & Potter, A.W.R. (1991). Sediment yield and delivery in the blanket peat moorlands of the Southern Pennines. *Earth Surface Processes and Landforms*, **16**, 255–71.

Lee, J. (1981). Atmospheric pollution and the Peak District blanket bogs. *Moorland Erosion Study. Phase 1 Report* (eds J. Phillips, D. Yalden & J. Tallis), pp. 104–08. Peak Park Joint Planning Board, Bakewell, Derbyshire.

Lee, J.A., Tallis, J.H. & Woodin, S.J. (1988). Acidic deposition and British upland vegetation. *Ecological Change in the Uplands* (eds M.B. Usher & D.B.A. Thompson), pp. 151–62. Blackwell, Oxford.

Livett, E.A. (1982). *The Interaction of Heavy Metals with the Peat and Vegetation of Blanket Bogs in Britain*. PhD thesis, University of Manchester.

Livett, E.A., Lee, J.A. & Tallis, J.H. (1979). Lead, zinc and copper analyses of British blanket peats. *Journal of Ecology*, **67**, 865–91.

Livett, E. & Tallis, J. (1994). *North Peak ESA: Pollen and Charcoal Analyses from Tintwistle Moor and Holme Moss*. Internal Report to the Peak Park Joint Planning Board, Bakewell, Derbyshire.

McEwen, M. & Sinclair, G. (1983). *New Life for the Hills*. Council for National Parks, London.

Montgomery, T. & Shimwell, D. (1985). *Changes in the environment and vegetation of the Kinder–Bleaklow SSSI, 1750–1840: historical perspectives and future conservation policies*. Internal Report to the Peak Park Joint Planning Board, Bakewell, Derbyshire.

Moore, P.D. (1975). Origin of blanket mires. *Nature, London*, **256**, 267–69.

Moore, P.D. (1993). The origin of blanket mire, revisited. *Climate Change and Human Impact on the Landscape* (ed. F. Chambers), pp. 217–24. Chapman & Hall, London.

Moss, C.E. (1913). *The Vegetation of the Peak District*. Cambridge University Press, Cambridge.

Phillips, J., Yalden, D. & Tallis, J. (1981). *Moorland Erosion Project. Phase 1 Report*. Peak Park Joint Planning Board, Bakewell, Derbyshire.

Pigott, C.D. (1983). Regeneration of oak–birch woodland following exclusion of sheep. *Journal of Ecology*, **71**, 629–46.

Porter, M. (1989). *Pennine Way Management Project. Second Annual Report 1988–89*. Countryside Commission, Cheltenham.

Press, M.C., Woodin, S.J. & Lee, J.A. (1986). The potential importance of an increased atmospheric nitrogen supply to the growth of ombrotrophic *Sphagnum* species. *New Phytologist*, **103**, 45–55.

Radley, J. (1965). Significance of major moorland fires. *Nature, London*, **205**, 1254–59.

Richards, J.R.A. (1990). *The Potential Use of Eriophorum angustifolium in the Revegetation of Blanket Peat*. PhD thesis, University of Sheffield.

Richards, J.R.A., Wheeler, B.D. & Willis, A.J. (1995). The growth and value of *Eriophorum angustifolium* Honck. in relation to the revegetation of eroding blanket peat. *Restoration of Temperate Wetlands* (eds B.D. Wheeler, S.C. Shaw, W.J. Fojt & R.A. Robertson), pp. 509–21. Wiley, Chichester.

Shimwell, D. (1974). Sheep grazing intensity in Edale, 1692–1747, and its effect on blanket peat erosion. *Derbyshire Archaeological Journal*, **94**, 35–40.

Shimwell, D. (1981). People pressure. *Moorland Erosion Study. Phase 1 Report* (eds J. Phillips, D. Yalden & J. Tallis), pp. 148–59. Peak Park Joint Planning Board, Bakewell, Derbyshire.

Smith, W.G. & Moss, C.E. (1903). Geographical distribution of vegetation in Yorkshire. *Geographical Journal*, **21**, 375–401.

Spratt, D.A. (1981). Prehistoric boundaries on the North Yorkshire Moors. *Prehistoric Communities in Northern England: Essays in Economic and Social Reconstruction* (ed. G. Barker), pp. 87–104. Dept. of Prehistory and Archaeology, University of Sheffield.

Tallis, J.H. (1965). Studies on southern Pennine peats. IV. Evidence of recent erosion. *Journal of Ecology*, **53**, 509–20.

Tallis, J. (1981). Uncontrolled fires. *Moorland Erosion Study. Phase 1 Report* (eds J. Phillips, D. Yalden & J. Tallis), pp. 176–82. Peak Park Joint Planning Board, Bakewell, Derbyshire.

Tallis, J.H. (1982). The Moorland Erosion Project in the Peak Park. *Recreation Ecology Research Group Report*, **8**, 27–36.

Tallis, J.H. (1985). Mass movement and erosion of a southern Pennine blanket peat. *Journal of Ecology*, **73**, 283–315.

Tallis, J.H. (1987). Fire and flood at Holme Moss: erosion processes in an upland blanket mire. *Journal of Ecology*, **75**, 1099–129.

Tallis, J.H. (1991). Forest and moorland in the South Pennine uplands in the mid-Flandrian period. III. The spread of moorland – local, regional and national. *Journal of Ecology*, **79**, 401–15.

Tallis, J.H. (1995a). Blanket mires in the upland landscape. *Restoration of Temperate Wetlands* (eds B.D. Wheeler, S.C. Shaw, W.J. Fojt & R.A. Robertson), pp. 495–508. Wiley, Chichester.

Tallis, J.H. (1995b). Climate and erosion signals in British blanket peats: the significance of *Racomitrium lanuginosum* remains. *Journal of Ecology*, **83**, 1021–30.

Tallis, J.H. & Livett, E.A. (1994). Pool-and-hummock patterning in a southern Pennine blanket mire I. Stratigraphic profiles for the last 2800 years. *Journal of Ecology*, **82**, 775–88.

Tallis, J.H. & McGuire, J. (1972). Central Rossendale: the evolution of an upland vegetation. I. The clearance of woodland. *Journal of Ecology*, **60**, 721–37.

Tallis, J.H. & Switsur, V.R. (1973). Studies on southern Pennine peats. VI. A radiocarbon-dated pollen diagram from Featherbed Moss, Derbyshire. *Journal of Ecology*, **61**, 743–51.

Tallis, J.H. & Switsur, V.R. (1983). Forest and moorland in the South Pennine uplands in the mid-Flandrian period. I. Macrofossil evidence of the former forest cover. *Journal of Ecology*, **71**, 585–600.

Tallis, J.H. & Switsur, V.R. (1990). Forest and moorland in the South Pennine uplands in the mid-Flandrian period. II. The hillslope forests. *Journal of Ecology*, **78**, 857–83.

Tallis, J.H. & Yalden, D.W. (1983). *Peak District Moorland Restoration Project, Phase 2 Report*. Peak Park Joint Planning Board, Bakewell, Derbyshire.

Turtle, C.E. (1984). *Peat Erosion and Reclamation in the Southern Pennines*. PhD thesis, University of Manchester.

Vine, P.M. (1982). The Neolithic and Bronze Age Cultures of the Middle and Upper Trent Basin. *British Archaeological Reports, British Series*, **105**, 1–410.

Williams, C.T. (1985). Mesolithic exploitation patterns in the Central Pennines. A palynological study of Soyland Moor. *British Archaeological Reports, British Series*, **139**, 1–179.

Wymer, J.J. (1977). *Gazetteer of Mesolithic Sites in England and Wales*. Council for British Archaeology, London.

Yalden, D. (1981a). Sheep and moorland vegetation – a literature review. *Moorland Erosion Study. Phase 1 Report* (eds J. Phillips, D. Yalden & J. Tallis), pp. 132–41. Peak Park Joint Planning Board, Bakewell, Derbyshire.

Yalden, D. (1981b). Sheep numbers in the Peak District. *Moorland Erosion Study. Phase 1 Report* (eds J. Phillips, D. Yalden & J. Tallis), pp. 116–24. Peak Park Joint Planning Board, Bakewell, Derbyshire.

Yalden, D. (1981c). Loss of grouse moors. *Moorland Erosion Study. Phase 1 Report* (eds J. Phillips, D. Yalden & J. Tallis), pp. 200–03. Peak Park Joint Planning Board, Bakewell, Derbyshire.

CHAPTER TWELVE

Urban wastelands – new niches and primary succession

A.D. BRADSHAW

Introduction

In most of Great Britain plant and animal communities are old – old in relation to our own life span at least. Indeed, except in special industrial habitats, such as those discussed by Ash (chapter eight, this volume), they have been in existence for several millennia, usually since the last glacial period. They may have changed under the influence of climate or human activity, but some sort of integrated plant and animal community has been present for a very long time.

This means that there has been a cover of plants which has accumulated nutrients and generated organic matter. The organic matter has become incorporated into the soil and then decomposed in the soil material by the combined effects of different soil organisms. As a result, relatively benign environments with fertile soils have been produced, which because of the time available have become colonised by many different species. There have been time and opportunity for full development of the features of structure and function that make up a complete and viable ecosystem.

The environments within the middle of cities are very different. Firstly, they are very recent; they have only been in existence since disturbance last occurred – due to road work, housing clearance, building construction, or waste disposal. Secondly, they are often ephemeral; they may exist for two or three years between the clearance of one building and the start of another. Thirdly, the soils are mostly inorganic, best described as skeletal; there has been no time for organic matter development and incorporation, only sand or gravel or mortar and broken concrete. Fourthly, they are likely to be physically and chemically stressful to plants; the surface of brick wastes can be hot and dry, and high in alkaline substances such as lime.

The plants which grow under these conditions might be considered to be of little interest. The situations themselves could be considered of little interest too, because they are so unlike normal habitats. But what occurs in them is what has occurred in the early development of the mature ecosystems to which we usually pay attention. The development is called primary succession, because of the succession of species which appear as time progresses and the environment changes.

It is an important process because it is what is involved in the origin of all ecosystems. It is obvious that early succession species are mostly annuals and biennials and that late succession species are perennials and woody species. There are, however, three different models of the processes involved (Connell & Slatyer 1977). In the first, species arrive as they can and their appearance is related solely to their life history characteristics; those remaining at the end are those which can tolerate the changing environmental conditions that develop – the *tolerance* model. In the second, the early species modify the environment so it is more suitable for the later species – the *facilitation* model. In the third model, once the early species have developed, they prevent the later species from developing until they have died and vacated the space they occupy – the *inhibition* model.

It is usually difficult to see succession in progress, because it took place a long time ago. Because of their history of change and clearance, however, the inner urban areas of the Mersey Basin provide excellent examples of primary succession in progress. The areas are scattered throughout the region and are easy to find; some are very spectacular, and there are many different types of site and environment. What is very clear is that there are a large number of species to be found in all of them and that these species change with time. So what processes are involved? I will take just two, urban clearance areas and disused railway lines, of which there are plenty in the Mersey Basin, to show what there is to discover – how new niches for plants, and for whole ecosystems, develop. For what happens more generally the reader is recommended to consult the excellent account by Gilbert (1989).

Site characteristics

Urban clearance areas and railway lands are both physically extreme. The soils are skeletal; when buildings have been cleared very stony substrates are left, pieces of brick and concrete with rather sandy material (commonly > 50% sand) in the cracks between. Sometimes the surfaces are hard and compacted. Railway lands are similar; coarse stony ballast was brought in to make the foundations for the sleepers. Both can be very dry at the surface, although there may be moisture underneath.

Chemically, both are bound to be deficient in nitrogen, since this element, which is the nutrient required in the greatest amount by plants (Bradshaw 1983), is accumulated almost entirely by biological processes and held in organic matter. This will not have had time to occur in skeletal soils. Other nutrients can vary. Calcium is always high in brick wastes, from mortar and cement; potassium and phosphate are present in the clays from which the bricks were made and become available as the bricks weather (Dutton & Bradshaw 1982) (Table 12.1). The railway ballast was commonly just crushed limestone rock from Derbyshire and North Wales, containing little but calcium; but in some places it was cinders and boiler ash, low in calcium and most other important elements. Underneath the ballast however there may be a quite fertile subsoil.

There are a number of places in the Mersey Basin where there are special toxicities due to past industry, especially chromates from tanning, and cyanides and phenols from gasworks wastes. But this sort of toxicity is unusual in brick wastes and railway land, and at the same time these areas are mostly nearly neutral in soil pH. However where ash has been used as ballast for rail tracks, there can be considerable acidity, giving pH 4–4.5, as low as in heathlands.

The sites are therefore not necessarily impossible for plant growth, and this applies even to very small areas such as in the spaces between bricks and lumps of concrete, which may be filled with sandy-loam material. So what actually happens?

Colonisation and chance

When these areas are first formed it is unusual for them to be quickly covered by plants, although a wide range of species may be represented. If the site characteristics suggest that conditions are not hopeless, what is restricting an immediate outburst of plants? The first problem is the availability of suitable colonists. This is partly a matter of chance, but partly a matter of biological logic. There are several reasons why a species does not arrive at a particular site.

Distribution characteristics

Species with light, easily dispersed seeds such as Oxford Ragwort (*Senecio squalidus*), Mugwort (*Artemisia*

vulgaris) and Annual Meadow-grass (*Poa annua*) occur on every urban clearance site in Liverpool, but Fat-hen (*Chenopodium album*) and clovers (*Trifolium* spp.), with much heavier seeds do not. Among trees and shrubs, it is conspicuous that Willow species, especially Goat Willow (*Salix caprea*) and Sallow (*S.cinerea*), will turn up everywhere; their minute seeds with a bundle of delicate hairs, the pappus, can be carried many kilometres. By contrast, despite its visible local successes, Sycamore (*Acer pseudoplatanus*) only appears in the vicinity of a suitable parent. Ash (*Fraxinus exelsior*) is similar. Both may have wings, but the seeds are relatively heavy. Birch (*Betula* spp.) is intermediate; its light seeds with wings mean it can spread widely over an area, such as in the derelict railway land at Garston docks, but only because seed parents exist in the vicinity.

It is obvious that a species which can produce many seeds is likely to be more successful than one which produces few. But in colonising situations a species that produces seeds within the first year can multiply much more quickly than one producing seeds only after two years – 100 seeds produced by a plant of annual meadow grass can produce 100 x 100 seeds, i.e., 10,000, by the end of the second year. Little wonder that many of early colonists are annuals. There is even evidence from local evolution of this pressure to produce seed. The inner city populations of Annual Meadow-grass from Liverpool have been shown to flower earlier and more freely than populations from pastures (Figure 12.1).

A perennial species has, however, the advantage that once it has arrived it has the potential to hold on to its living space. If it can then spread vegetatively, by rhizomes or stolons, it can expand its position without going through the risks of a seed and seedling stage. In this category are species which are very successful on many different sites, such as Yorkshire Fog (*Holcus lanatus*) and Creeping Bent (*Agrostis stolonifera*); they tend to become dominant after the annuals. False Oat-grass (*Arrhenatherum elatius*) and Bramble (*Rubus* spp.) are slower to establish and tend to be become common later. The long stolons of Creeping Bent allow it to spread over hard surfaces and root where conditions are more favourable; Colt's-foot (*Tussilago farfara*) spreads underground and Bramble, of course, above the ground.

Opportunity

Whatever its distribution characteristics, a species can only spread into a new area if it is already present some-

Site	Nitrogen[1]	Phosphorus[2]	Potassium[2]	Magnesium[2]
Good garden soil	1027(119)	30	83	66
Urban site 1	480 (3)	12	81	72
Urban site 2	480 (-9)	22	173	145
Urban site 3	405 (-6)	5	77	323
Urban site 4	870 (-4)	65	94	393

Table 12.1. Chemical characteristics of soils in urban clearance areas in Liverpool (from Dutton & Bradshaw 1982) .

[1] total (mineralisable in brackets) (ppm)   [2] available (ppm)

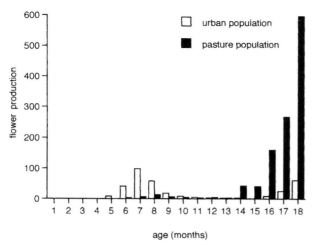

Figure 12.1. Evidence for natural selection for colonisation; much earlier flower production in an urban, Liverpool, population of *Poa annua* than in a pasture population from Cheshire (Law *et al.* 1977).

Calcareous wastes	Acid wastes
early stages	
Poa annua	*Agrostis capillaris*
Senecio squalidus	*Polytrichum* sp.
Holcus lanatus	*Aira praecox*
Agrostis stolonifera	*Hieracium sp.*
Trifolium repens (L)	*Lotus corniculatus* (L)
Sagina procumbens	*Rumex acetosella*
Matricaria recutita	*Vulpia bromoides*
Reseda luteola	*Campylopus inflexus*
Trifolium dubium (L)	*Aulacomium palustre*
	Cladonia sp.
middle stages	
Plantago lanceolata	*Lotus corniculatus* (L)
Dactylis glomerata	*Luzula campestris*
Buddleja davidii	*Deschampsia flexuosa*
Arrhenatherum elatius	*Carex ovalis*
Juncus effusus	*Festuca rubra*
Artemisia vulgaris	*Chamerion angustifolium*
Lotus corniculatus (L)	
Trifolium pratense (L)	
Rubus spp.	
Erysimum cheiranthoides	
Vicia angustifolia (L)	
late stages	
Salix cinerea	*Betula pubescens/pendula*
Salix caprea	*Calluna vulgaris*
Betula pubescens/pendula	*Hedera helix*
Quercus robur	*Lonicera periclymenum*
Alnus glutinosa	*Quercus robur*
Acer pseudoplatanus	*Salix caprea*
Fraxinus excelsior	*Salix cinerea*
Crataegus monogyna	

Table 12.2. Plant species particularly characteristic of primary successions on wasteland in the Mersey Basin, arranged in order of usual commonness, legumes indicated by (L); in many sites species indicated as belonging to early, middle or late stages may occur together, and because of the effects of chance there are likely to be considerable other deviations from this list.

where in the neighbourhood. Species such as Yellow-wort (*Blackstonia perfoliata*) and Blue Fleabane (*Erigeron acer*) that occur 30 kilometres away clearly find it difficult to immigrate into sites in the Mersey Basin however suitable these might be (Ash, chapter eight, this volume). But it is almost as important whether the species is available in the immediate vicinity, within a few hundred metres. In cities such as Liverpool and Birkenhead there have been always a number of urban clearance areas in existence at any one time which can be colonised by a range of species (Table 12.2). But as colonisation of different sites takes place, quite startling differences in species occurrence can develop. This is particularly obvious with the Butterfly-bush or Buddleia (*Buddleja davidii*). It is an introduced shrub well adapted to the growth on brick waste. Yet it is only found on certain sites, related to its presence in a neighbouring area, usually upwind, where it may often have been planted for ornamental purposes. White and Red Clover (*Trifolium repens* and *T.pratense*), species which have an important role in soil development on brick wastes, will nearly always eventually be found on urban sites, but their initial appearance is strongly influenced by the occurrence of seeding plants in the immediate vicinity. The same applies to other more ubiquitous species such as mayweeds and Rosebay Willowherb (*Chamerion angustifolium*).

Establishment and ecological adaptation

It is not enough for propagules to arrive at a site. They have to be able to establish and grow. To do this the individual plants must firstly possess specific adaptations to overcome the substrate conditions. These adaptations are innumerable and their significances are well discussed elsewhere (Harper 1977), but evidence for their influence can readily be seen in the urban areas of the Mersey Basin.

Adaptation to soil physical characteristics

On urban brick wastes surfaces are usually hard and covered with fine textured material. On this only small seeds can grow because they can make good physical contact over a relatively large area of their seed coat and can therefore absorb water easily; large seeds can make contact only over a small part. It is therefore not surprising to find on brick wastes that it is small seeded species such as grasses that are initially successful. When, by contrast, a vegetation cover has begun to develop, the whole situation changes. Now the seedlings have to be able to compete with this cover, by having enough reserves to grow through it, and at the same time the surface of the ground is more moist. So species with bigger seeds are usually more successful. This includes such species as White Clover, Treacle Mustard (*Erysimum cheiranthoides*) and plantains (*Plantago* spp.).

Smooth surfaces, however, offer only rather exposed conditions, difficult for any seeds. A rough surface due to gravel or other coarse material provides protected microsites in which germinating seeds can prosper. This is well known in the colonisation of areas destroyed by volcanic eruptions such as Mount St Helens (del Moral 1993). The stony surfaces of old railway lines such as the Halewood Triangle of the Cheshire Lines, disused since 1964, have been spectacularly colonised by seedlings from the very small wind blown seeds of Sallow and Birch. This colonisation is helped by the initial absence of vegetation, which allows the seedlings to grow without interference. Stony brick wastes can be similar. By contrast, in the grass covered areas in the middle of the Halewood Triangle there is no sign of such colonisation. Instead the main woody colonists have been Hawthorn (*Crataegus monogyna*) and Oak (*Quercus* sp.), both species with large seeds.

Adaptation to soil chemical characteristics

There is a danger of assuming that the chemical conditions of urban areas are all similar or, if they are different, have no influence on primary succession. Since the urban site materials are mostly poor and calcareous there tends to be a common range of species. But the ballast of some railway lines was ash and cinders, not only poor in many nutrients but also very acid, with a pH of about 4. On such material a different range of species is to be found, since very few of the herbaceous species mentioned so far can survive. The early colonists are restricted to acid tolerant mosses such as *Polytrichum* spp. and annuals such as Early Hair-grass (*Aira praecox*). The main grass is Common Bent (*Agrostis capillaris*), normally to be found on heathland (Table 12.2). Then as a great surprise, in some places, such as the disused marshalling yards serving Garston Docks, Heather (*Calluna vulgaris*) appears, with Wavy Hair-grass (*Deschampia flexuosa*) and Oval Sedge (*Carex ovalis*). Where these have come from is unknown, but there is now so much Heather that the planners have given the area the name Cressington Heath, and it has been recognised as a potential local nature reserve. A number of other species typical of local heathland, however, such as Sheep's-fescue (*Festuca ovina*), Heath Bedstraw (*Galium saxatile*), Tormentil (*Potentilla erecta*) and Bell Heather (*Erica cinerea*), are missing, giving support to the idea that chance and opportunity are as important factors as ecological adaptation.

In damp or wet areas, in poorly drained railway tracks or where there have been excavations, such as in the old Garston gasworks site, moisture-loving species can occur. Typical are Hard and Soft Rush (*Juncus inflexus* and *J. effusus*). However, these are uncommon in most urban areas and therefore will not always be available for colonisation. Other examples of differentiation in the type of primary succession in relation to soil characteristics occur, but too few studies have been undertaken so far to distinguish them properly.

Growth and development

In a skeletal habitat growth may be able to start, but can it be sustained? This depends on adequate continuing supplies of the materials provided by the soil – water and nutrients. In primary successions failure or poor growth is easy to see; it is less easy to discover what are its critical causes.

Importance of water

A stony soil such as brick waste, containing no organic matter, can hold very little water; less than a third that of a normal soil. Although it may be moist over the winter, once drying conditions occur in the spring there can be little moisture left in the surface layers. For this reason many of the early colonists such as Annual Meadow-grass are annuals which germinate in the winter or early spring, and die, having set seed, by the early summer.

There is an alternative strategy, however. In all such situations there is always water lower in the soil profile. This will be available to any plant that can develop a large root system. This essentially requires the plant to be able to grow longer, even to be perennial. Woody plants and perennials with deep root systems, such as False Oat-grass and Mugwort, colonising urban areas, show no signs of water shortage. But this more substantial growth requires a supply of nutrients.

Importance of nutrients

A prime requisite for substantial growth is therefore an adequate supply of nutrients. From what was said earlier, the nutrient most likely to be deficient is nitrogen, without which little or no growth is possible. For good growth a continuous vegetation cover requires an annual supply of about 100kg N ha^{-1}. The over-riding importance of nitrogen has been demonstrated in fertiliser experiments exploring the problems facing vegetation artificially established on Liverpool brick wastes (Figure 12.2). It is significant that where nitrogen is applied once, growth falls off in the second year unless further nitrogen is applied. A continuing supply is needed. Similar experiments have not been carried out on a natural urban primary succession, but conspicuous green patches of better growth can be seen in naturally colonised urban areas where dogs have urinated or rabbits have left a patch of droppings.

How is this nitrogen to become available? It normally comes from the release of mineral nitrogen by the decay of organic matter. Some nitrogen is bound to be present in the small amount of organic matter in the skeletal soil, but it will only be enough to allow very limited growth. A second source is the nitrogen contained in rain. In country areas this contributes no more than 10kg N ha^{-1} yr^{-1}; in urban areas of the Mersey Basin this figure can be doubled or trebled by aerial pollution. A prime requisite of plants is therefore to have an extensive root system to scavenge for this and other nutrients. Woody plants such as Goat Willow and Buddleia particularly can achieve

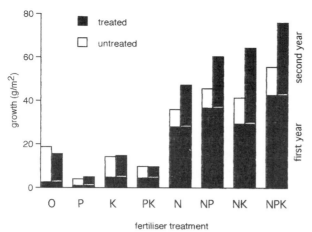

Figure 12.2. The effects of addition of fertilisers to grassland newly established on brick waste; the main effect is from nitrogen, but the need to repeat the addition in a subsequent year indicates the serious lack of nitrogen capital (Bloomfield *et al.* 1982).

Figure 12.3. Excellent growth of Buddleia where everything else is rather moribund; the extensive root system of the Buddleia allows it to scavenge successfully for nutrients (*Photo: A.D. Bradshaw*).

this, and can be very successful in nutrient poor sites when herbaceous species are doing badly (Figure 12.3). In consequence they are often termed scavengers.

The most successful strategy is, however, that adopted by legumes. They are able to make use of the limitless supplies of nitrogen in the air by the activities of nitrogen-fixing bacteria living in nodules on their roots. The plant provides protection and energy to the bacteria, and the bacteria provides fixed nitrogen which can be used immediately by the plant, making it independent of external supplies of nitrogen. If therefore a species such as White Clover arrives in an area of brick waste in Liverpool it immediately grows and spreads (Figure 12.4). It can fix over 100kg N ha^{-1} yr^{-1}, quite enough for its own growth and even for accompanying plants. After one or two years the latter begin to go green and grow vigorously. The whole succession takes on a new lease of life.

There are a number of legumes adapted to the poor calcareous conditions of brick wastes, notably White and Red Clovers and Common Bird's-foot-trefoil (Table 12.2). Which are to be found on a particular site seems to depend very much on chance immigration. The arrival of legumes in a succession means that there is an immediate improvement in plant cover due to their own growth, but because of their contribution to the overall nitrogen of the site there is a marked increase in the growth of all species.

Development of ecoystem processes

The effect of the developing vegetation is to contribute organic matter to the soil and visibly alter its texture and structure. This is visible on many sites. At the same time the nitrogen content of the soil is increased and the carbon/nitrogen ratio decreased. All this favours an increase in the biological activity of the soil, in particular

Figure 12.4. A single plant of White Clover; because it is a nitrogen-fixer it is itself growing excellently and will soon encourage the growth of associated species (*Photo: A.D. Bradshaw*).

	reclaimed brick wastes			normal soil
	raw brick waste	*grass only*	*grass and clover*	*good lawn*
nitrogen – total (ppm)	500	850	1600	2440
– mineralisable (ppm)	32	12	84	165
C/N ratio	38	46	29	21
yield of bioassay (g/m²)	510	450	940	950

Table 12.3. Changes occurring in nitrogen levels and availability in urban brick waste sites: a comparison of sites with raw brick waste with a) sites with grass only, b) sites with grass with good clover, and c) a long established ornamental lawn (means of at least nine sites in each category): bioassay is yield after 29 weeks of Rye-grass sown on soil samples in pots (from Marxen-Drewes 1983).

the organic matter turn over. This is best revealed by measurements of soil respiration – the amount of carbon dioxide being produced – but these are not available. However values for mineralisable nitrogen, the mineral nitrogen released by microbial processes when the soil is incubated, are perhaps the real key, since this fraction indicates what nitrogen the soil is able to offer growing plants on a continuous basis. The sort of changes that occur are illustrated in Table 12.3 by results for a set of soils under artificial grasslands established on brick waste in Liverpool compared with a garden soil as control.

A more direct measure of the improved fertility can be obtained by a bioassay in which plants are grown on the soils; this is included in Table 12.3. This confirms the poverty of the raw brick waste and the startling improvements that can occur once Clover has taken hold, improvements which make the Clover-rich site soil as good as soil from a long-established grass lawn. It is interesting that the site on which a poor grass sward was established behaves worse than the raw brick waste. This is probably because the grass has taken up all the available nitrogen and rendered it unavailable to other species. On this site the C/N ratio is higher, which would make the nitrogen less readily released by microbial activity.

The same processes of ecosystem development can be seen in the areas of disused railway lines. However where cinders were used as a ballast the process of nitrogen accumulation can be upset because the acid soil conditions do not permit the establishment of legumes. As a result nitrogen accumulation is slowed to what the vegetation can trap from the rain, and development is much slower.

Increasing competition

The soil studies show the way in which conditions progressively improve. This brings into importance a new factor, competition, which although it may have been present earlier, comes into play particularly once a vigorous vegetation has developed. This vegetation can interfere with establishment and growth of other species.

Its most obvious effects are in the disappearance of the annuals. The solid swards of perennial grasses such as Yorkshire-fog and Cock's-foot (*Dactylis glomerata*) make it difficult for new generations of seedlings of annuals to establish. The succession may appear to reach a standstill.

But it is at this stage that the final major act of the succession occurs – woody species begin to become visible, although they have very often been present earlier. It is unfortunate for a student of primary succession that at this stage someone often notices the incursions of taller plants and orders a 'tidying up'. But if this does not occur, then the changes to scrub and woodland are most interesting.

Obviously once established, with their taller growth and more extensive root systems, woody plants should be able to win in the competition battle. But establishment may be a problem, depending on a chance gap, or safe site. As a result the establishment of woody vegetation may be delayed or only sporadic in well developed grassy areas. However, where conditions for establishment are favourable early on, and seed parents exist in the vicinity, woody vegetation can get a hold early and hasten the whole course of succession in a spectacular fashion, as on the rail tracks at Halewood.

The woody endpoint

If the areas remain untouched there is nothing to stop them developing into woodland. In areas where Buddleia gets a hold there can be a rather scruffy stage after about twenty years when it starts to die back, before more permanent species develop. On most sites in the Mersey Basin, however, because of their powers of immigration, dense Sallow or Birch woodland develops; for a decade or more this can be completely impassable, but then natural thinning processes start to occur and tree numbers drop from about 10m⁻² to less than 1m⁻².

In such woodland there is little scope for other species, and perhaps invasion by Oak and other species may have to wait until space appears. But in many of these dense woodlands, such as at Halewood, small numbers of Pedunculate Oak, Sycamore and sometimes Alder (*Alnus glutinosa*) are already present, which will be able to outlast the shorter lived species. Very few woodland herb species occur. This could be due to the density of the trees, but it is equally likely that

Figure 12.5. Nearly the end of the process – woodland over 100 years old on disused railway land; but a number of typical woodland species are missing – they have not yet arrived (*Photo: A.D. Bradshaw*).

suitable species are not available in the vicinity.

There is one wood on railway land of considerable age. This is between the converging tracks at the tip of the Halewood Triangle. It was allowed to start its succession when the railway was first built through farmland in 1879, and it is now a fine Oak–Birch wood (Figure 12.5). However a simple survey shows that the succession is not complete even after 100 years. There is a strange absence of a typical woodland ground flora, species such as Dog's Mercury (*Mercurialis perennis*) and even Bluebell (*Hyacinthoides non-scripta*) – although the latter is present at the entrance, obviously planted. A similar absence is found in the planted woodlands of the Mersey Basin. It is well know that the species of ancient woodland have very limited powers of dispersal (Peterken 1974) and there are no sources of these species in the vicinity. Perhaps under modern conditions the final stages of the succession can only be achieved with human assistance.

Animals

Animals depend on plants for their food and energy, so in many ways they play a secondary role in successions. They are important in the cycling processes, none more so than the earthworms which rapidly colonise brick wastes, finding the calcareous soil very much to their liking. In making burrows they loosen the soil and

reduce its density. The fine soil they cast onto the surface rapidly covers the brick waste, at a rate of about 4mm per year, so that after 10 years or so brick waste sites in Liverpool can be found to be covered with over 4cm of excellent material (Figure 12.6). This matches what over 100 years ago Darwin (1881) reported occurring in normal soils. At the same time the earthworms take down into their burrows large amounts of leaf material which becomes incorporated into the soil. Their contribution to the succession is therefore very important.

The animals in the Mersey Basin have not been extensively studied; however, good descriptions exist for other areas (Gilbert 1989). It must be remembered that there are many animal species waiting to take advantage of the improving conditions. If the vegetation of any well colonised grassy site is parted to ground level, it will reveal a network of trackways formed by small mammals such as voles and shrews, living off either the vegetation itself or the substantial developing insect populations. Overhead somewhere will be a kestrel, roosting in an old building but feeding off the small mammals.

The areas with shrubs begin to support excellent populations of Blackbirds (*Turdus merula*), Wrens

Figure 12.6. The contribution of earthworms; after 18 years this grassed brick waste is covered with over 5 cm of fine soil due to the earth brought to the surface by the well-developed earthworm population (*Photo: A.D. Bradshaw*).

(*Troglodytes troglodytes*), Robins (*Erithacus rubecula*) and tits (*Parus* spp.). Perhaps what is most outstanding, however, is to hear, every spring, the soft falling song of Willow Warblers (*Phylloscopus trochilus*) which have migrated from Africa to take up residence in the new Sallow woodlands in the Mersey Basin which they find much to their liking.

The succession telescoped

On some sites many of the late succession species can be found appearing early. This suggests that the constraints on growth which have been discussed may not always be operating. Species of relatively fertile soils, such as Perennial Rye-grass (*Lolium perenne*), Meadow Fescue (*Festuca pratensis*), Common Nettle (*Urtica dioica*), typically associated with human habitation and buttercups (*Rununculus* spp.), as well as many of the woody species, can be found on rather young inner city wasteland, growing vigorously.

There are two possible explanations. The first is that the soils in these sites are not actually as poor as they appear at first sight. In many situations the site may have been formed from the clearance of old housing and contain a considerable amount of garden soil, albeit mixed with bricks and other stony material. This sort of soil can be very fertile. In these circumstances the succession that is occurring is more like that found in situations where, although the vegetation has been destroyed, the soil has not. This type of succession is described as secondary and is typical where arable fields have gone out of cultivation. The main constraints in these situations are the availability and colonising power of the individual species. In urban areas there is always the possibility that several species may have come through from previously existing gardens, in soil and other materials, something which does not usually occur in normal secondary successions, from arable fields for instance.

The second possible explanation is that the idea that the occurrence and growth of species in primary successions are always limited by fertility does not always apply. Many species characteristic of the more fertile soils found in the middle stages of the succession can grow relatively well on infertile soils. In the list given in Table 12.2 this could certainly apply to Ribwort Plantain (*Plantago lanceolata*), Cock's-foot, Buddleia and Sallow, and perhaps to some of the other species too. Unfortunately there is little critical evidence about this. It is one more of the ecological and intellectual challenges of urban sites and of succession in general.

Conclusions

The new habitats of the Mersey Basin may look unprepossessing. But they provide good evidence not only of the way plants and animals colonise, and of the ways in which ecosystems are formed, but also of the different models, already mentioned, suggested to be operating in primary succession (Connell & Slatyer 1977). In all models the early species cannot grow once the site is occupied by the later species. But the long held view is that succession is controlled and driven by the processes of environmental improvement, particularly by the improvements arising from the growth of the early species allowing subsequent species to colonise and grow – the *facilitation* model. This is the way in which most of the evidence presented here would seem to argue. But since it is perfectly possible for late species to arrive and grow early on, it is possible to argue that the observed changes occurring in succession are driven more by accident of arrival combined with speed of growth – the *tolerance* model. There are also signs that later species may not be able to invade because the site is already occupied – the *inhibition* model.

If the evidence is taken at its face value it would appear that all these processes are operating in urban areas, and that no one process has overall control. It would be of great value to study what is going on in more detail, and with experimental interventions to test the significance of individual factors. The advantage of urban areas is that this can be done with little expense. There is also the advantage that changes can be watched and followed as they occur week by week without having to try to guess from an annual visit what has happened. All that occurs in an urban succession has a reason and a cause that ought to be definable, if one can only look closely enough.

At the same time it must not be forgotten that these same processes can produce plant communities of considerable attraction and landscape value, at little or no cost. It is too easy to sweep them away in their younger stages in the causes of tidiness or development. We should learn to cherish them.

References

Bloomfield, H.E., Handley, J.F. & Bradshaw, A.D. (1982). Nutrient deficiencies and the aftercare of reclaimed derelict land. *Journal of Applied Ecology*, **19**, 151–58.

Bradshaw, A.D. (1983). The reconstruction of ecosystems. *Journal of Applied Ecology*, **20**, 1–17.

Connell, J.H. & Slatyer, R.O. (1977). Mechanisms of succession in natural communities and their role in community stability and organisation. *American Naturalist*, **111**, 1119–44.

Darwin, C. (1881). *The Formation of Vegetable Mould through the Action of Earthworms*. John Murray, London.

Dutton, R.A. & Bradshaw, A.D. (1982). *Land Reclamation in Cities*. HMSO, London.

Gilbert, O.L. (1989). *The Ecology of Urban Habitats*. Chapman & Hall, London.

Harper, J. (1977). *Population Biology of Plants*. Academic Press, London.

Law, R., Putwain, P.D.P., & Bradshaw, A.D. (1977). Life history variation in *Poa annua*. *Evolution*, **6**, 233–46.

Marxen-Drewes, H. (1983). *Nitrogen in Urban Ecosystems*. MSc thesis, University of Liverpool.

del Moral, R. (1993). Mechanisms of primary succession on volcanoes: a view from Mount St Helens. *Primary Succession on Land* (eds J. Miles & D.W.H. Walton), pp. 79–100. Blackwell, Oxford.

Peterken, G.F. (1974). A method for assessing woodland flora for conservation using indicator species. *Biological Conservation*, **6**, 239–45.

Changing Habitats 2

S. WALKER

Most will be aware that the Environment Agency was formed on 1 April 1996 from the amalgamation of the National Rivers Authority, Her Majesty's Inspectorate of Pollution and staff from the Metropolitan and County Councils responsible for Waste Regulation. The Agency's vision is to provide a better environment in England and Wales for present and future generations. It aims to protect and improve the environment as a whole by effective regulation, by its own actions and by working in partnership with others.

This section continues the theme on changing habitats with the focus now shifting to the water and waterside environments.

In introducing the topic I would like to draw your attention to the increasingly 'good news' story of the Mersey Estuary and the improvements in quality that have been seen in recent years. These improvements are well described in the National Rivers Authority report of 1995 entitled *The Mersey Estuary : A Report on Environmental Quality* (NRA Water Quality Series No. 23). The document describes the physical and biological processes and the ecological and chemical quality of the estuary. It describes the potential for the future in the context of the regulatory framework. Though the quality of the Mersey Estuary has significantly improved in recent times, there is still much more to be achieved.

This section gives an insight into the potential, not just for the estuary but for the Mersey Basin as a whole. Chapters thirteen and fourteen describe the habitats and the changes that have taken place to the freshwaters of the Mersey Basin. These have been largely man induced and have been considerable with heavy pollution of many rivers. The authors consider that future prospects are mixed and depend upon long-term developments and management policies.

Chapters fifteen and sixteen continue with an assessment of estuarine and coastal habitats. Again the massive impact of human intervention and pollution is recorded even in the supposedly more natural sand dunes and saltmarshes. However, recent measures to remove pollution and restore habitats in the Mersey Estuary are being rewarded by an increase in biodiversity and a more optimistic future is foreseen. The coastal sand dunes and saltmarshes are dynamic habitats influenced by human activities but there are opportunities to influence the changes to provide more 'natural' and self sustaining systems than at present.

CHAPTER THIRTEEN

Biological change in the freshwaters of the Mersey Basin

J.W. EATON, D.G. HOLLAND, B. MOSS AND P. NOLAN

Introduction

The Mersey Basin offers a diversity of freshwater habitats. Fast-flowing stony and peaty upland headwaters of the River Mersey contrast with slower, silty channels in lowland areas. The Cheshire meres to the south of the river are a group of standing waters of various sizes and depths; some are connected to the river system, others are isolated. To the north as well as the south, former lake basins have succeeded to raised bogs, or mosses, many of them now drained and degraded. Man has added to this diversity by creating many artificial water-

bodies within the Mersey Basin. These include reservoirs, ornamental lakes, navigation canals, ditches and ponds.

The biology of most of these freshwaters only began to be recorded in any detail in the second half of the 20th century and then only to a limited extent. Before this a systematic search of the copious but scattered records left by 19th-century natural historians would almost certainly provide historic information. Nevertheless, knowing the enormous changes in land- and water-use which have occurred in areas such as the Mersey Basin since the start of the Industrial Revolution (Eaton 1989),

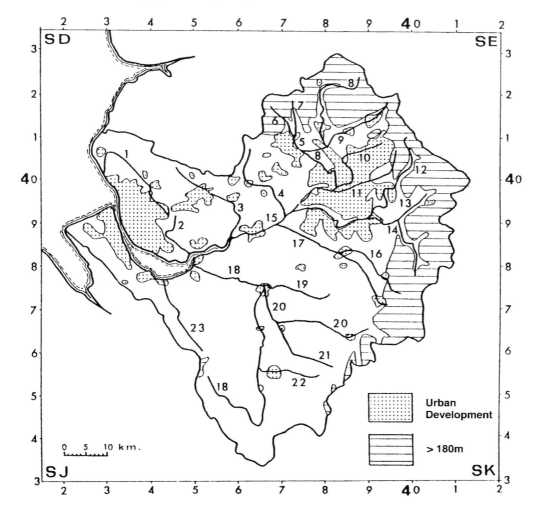

Figure 13.1. Rivers of the Mersey Basin, with topography and urban development.

1. River Alt
2. Ditton Brook
3. Sankey Brook
4. River Glaze
5. River Croal
6. Eagley Brook
7. Bradshaw Brook
8. River Irwell
9. River Roch
10. River Irk
11. River Medlock
12. River Tame
13. River Etherow
14. River Goyt
15. River Mersey
16. River Dean
17. River Bollin
18. River Weaver
19. Peover Eye
20. River Dane
21. River Wheelock
22. Valley Brook
23. River Gowy.

it is possible to deduce some of the corresponding biological changes which have probably occurred in the water-bodies involved.

This chapter outlines and interprets changes in fresh-water habitats and their biota in the Mersey Basin, before giving a view of likely future trends, where these can be surmised.

Rivers

Habitats

Physical change

The rivers of the Mersey Basin (Figure 13.1) have been extensively modified during agricultural, industrial and residential developments in the catchment. This has been partly to exploit their value as water sources, effluent receptors and transport routes, but partly also to control their erosive energy and periodic flooding, so that their flood plains could be developed.

Intensive urban development in the Mersey Basin began at the start of the Industrial Revolution, when river management increasingly created walled channels, weirs, mill pools and leats as common features. Many of the rivers of the northern part of the Mersey Basin are now regulated by reservoirs, with resultant long-term changes in river flow, velocities and sediment transfers. Communities in the rivers have adjusted to these physical changes. Flow regimes vary according to the season and the drought which began in the 1994/95 winter resulted in compensation flows to some rivers being reduced in 1995 and 1996 (National Rivers Authority 1996a).

The lower sections of the River Weaver were extensively modified by the construction of the Weaver Navigation Channel. Remnants of the former mean-dering channel can be seen in the flood plain between Frodsham and Winsford, and provide habitats which are now valuable wildlife havens for wetland plants and insects such as dragonflies. The River Mersey itself was greatly altered by the construction of the Manchester Ship Canal, and impact on the river can still be seen today.

A systematic programme of 'river improvements' and land drainage continued here until the early 1980s. Especially during the 1960s and 1970s, considerable lengths of river were deepened, widened and straight-ened. Whilst this enabled intensified use of the flood plain, the natural storage capacity for flood waters was lost, requiring the construction of additional urban and agricultural flood defences to protect infrastructures such as roads and railways, industrial complexes and agricultural land.

Some stretches of rivers and streams in Manchester, Merseyside and urban areas elsewhere in the Mersey Basin are now hidden in pipes and tunnels. A culverted river is virtually uninhabitable to wildlife, and a canalised open concrete channel is little better. Uniform, featureless channels can support only the commonest and most tenacious river plants and animals, particu-

Figure 13.2. Bedford Brook managed for flood control 'improvements' (*Photo: D.G. Holland*).

larly when this habitat simplification is combined with poor water quality. Such uniformity, together with destruction of the natural, diverse bankside vegetation by the engineering construction works and subsequent intensive management, has helped spread aggressive alien species such as Indian or Himalayan Balsam (*Impatiens glandulifera*) and Japanese Knotweed (*Fallopia japonica*) which are widespread throughout the catch-ment.

By contrast, rivers such as the Dane and Dean in Cheshire, which have received little or no management in the past, retain physical diversity. Riffles and pools, together with varied banks, shoals, cliffs and wetland margins support diverse channel vegetation and a range of bankside trees and shrubs. Good examples of river cliffs, which provide valuable habitats for birds, e.g., Sand Martin (*Riparia riparia*) and Kingfisher (*Alcedo atthis*) and insects, e.g., solitary wasps and bees, survive on unconstrained stretches of the Rivers Mersey (between Ashton and Carrington), Bollin and Tame. On the flood plains, marshes, herb-rich pastures, wet wood-lands, river terraces and ox-bow lakes can be found. Good examples of flood plain features can be seen on the River Dane and on the River Bollin upstream of Manchester Airport and Wilmslow.

In recent years river management policies have changed. The Environment Agency and its predecessor the National Rivers Authority, have been given conser-vation responsibilities in respect of wildlife, landscape and heritage. These statutory duties and obligations are currently detailed in Sections 6(1), 7(1), 8 and 9 of the Environment Act 1995. Under this Act, and earlier Acts relevant to the water environment, e.g., Wildlife and Countryside Act 1981, Water Resources Act 1991, management is increasingly focusing on techniques sympathetic to the protection and enhancement of wildlife. Conservationists and river engineers work together to ensure all capital construction schemes and routine maintenance programmes are designed to do minimal damage to the natural environment. In addition, the Agency is actively involved in recreating more natural conditions out of existing heavily engineered watercourses (Royal Society for the Protection of Birds, National Rivers Authority and Society for Nature Conservation 1994), e.g., restoration projects on Padgate and Whittle Brooks in Warrington and deculverting of sections of the River Alt (Nolan & Guthrie in press). Furthermore, the Agency comments on applications by third parties for new developments and has policies which seek to retain river corridors as features of such developments. To provide a basis for more sustainable management of the rivers, Local Environment Agency Plans have been prepared to identify issues which it is feasible to resolve, in a more balanced approach to new management (National Rivers Authority 1994, 1996c; Environment Agency 1996).

Water quality influences

The water quality in a river greatly influences which plant and animal species occur in it. Holland and Harding (1984) describe the appalling conditions created by the Industrial Revolution in the Mersey Basin and show how gradual recovery started in the 1950s. Figure 13.3, recording the oxygen conditions at three sites, illustrates the substantial improvements which have been made in the last 40 years in the more industrial part of the Mersey Basin. Aquatic plant and invertebrate communities are key indicators of water quality, and the following section shows how plants, invertebrates and fish have responded to changes during this period.

Life in the rivers
Plants
As is the case with many British rivers, the River Mersey and its tributaries have received little systematic survey from botanists, and historical documentation of plants is limited. River Corridor Surveys (National Rivers Authority 1992) and River Habitat Surveys (National Rivers Authority 1996b) provide useful information on the distribution of aquatic and marginal plants and their habitats, but they have not been collated into any systematic database. Most information on the Mersey system comes from data collected after 1978 by Harding (1981) and Holland & Harding (1984).

In prehistoric times many parts of the Mersey Basin were densely wooded and growth of riverine plants was restricted by dense shading. As woodland clearance and increased nutrient run-off from the land occurred, there was probably a marked increase in submerged plant growth. A few clues to the nature of these plant communities can be seen in present vegetation in, for example, the upper reaches of the River Etherow and River Goyt which have not been subject to the kind of pollution affecting the rivers downstream. Here the bed is rocky and the vegetation is dominated by mosses and liver-

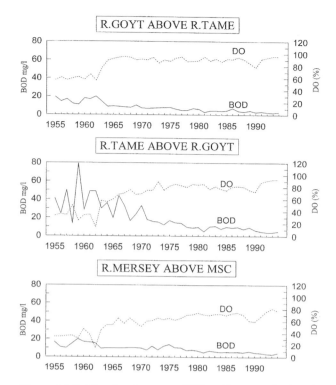

Figure 13.3. Dissolved oxygen (DO as % saturation) and biochemical oxygen demand (BOD as mg/l) in three rivers of the Mersey Basin. MSC – Manchester Ship Canal.

worts with four species, *Hygrohypnum ochraceum,* (Wils.) Loeske, *Fontinalis squamosa* Hedw., *Racomitriun aciculare* (Hedw.) Brid. and *Scapania undulata* (L.), being especially characteristic of these acidic upland rivers.

Although many of the rivers have probably always contained areas of sand, gravel and mud suitable for the establishment of rooted plants, none has remained unaffected by pollution or artificial channel management. Surveys of the distribution of River Water-crowfoot (*Ranunculus fluitans*) in the Mersey catchment (Harding 1981), indicated that although the species is unable to form large beds in rivers affected by severe organic pollution, occasional plants may survive for long periods in such situations. This can happen even in competition with dense growths of pollution tolerant plants such as Fennel Pondweed (*Potamogeton pectinatus*) which has become widespread in the Mersey Basin as organic pollution has decreased. Since Harding's survey in 1978/80, Fennel Pondweed, present then in the Rivers Bollin, Dane and Dean, has now been displaced there by River Water-crowfoot.

Improving water quality in the Mersey Basin generally has been associated with an increase in abundance and diversity of channel and marginal vegetation. The largely sandy/silty nature of the lowland rivers favours colonisation by plants such as Branched Bur-reed (*Sparganium erectum*), Reed Canary-grass (*Phalaris arundinacea*) both common throughout; Common Reed (*Phragmites australis*), e.g., River Mersey in Warrington; Reed Sweet-grass (*Glyceria maxima*), e.g., Rivers Gowy,

Figure 13.4. River Dane, Congleton showing natural river processes of erosion and deposition (*Photo: D.G. Holland*).

Figure 13.5. River Rehabilitation Scheme on Whittle Brook, Great Sankey. Low-level shelf for wet habit and bank slope reduced with grass mat to re-stablish flora (*Photo: D.G. Holland*).

Birket and Weaver; Yellow Iris (*Iris pseudacorus*), Water Forget-me-not (*Myosotis scorpioides*), Brooklime (*Veronica beccabunga*) and aquatics such as water-starworts (*Callitriche* spp.), Fool's Water-cress (*Apium nodiflorum*), Fennel Pondweed, Curled Pondweed (*Potamogeton crispus*) and Broad-leaved Pondweed (*P. natans*).

In Cheshire, the River Gowy and River Weaver receive nutrients from treated sewage effluents and agricultural run off, creating eutrophic conditions in which Yellow Water-lily (*Nuphar lutea*) and Flowering-rush (*Butomus umbellatus*) are common in slow-flowing sections, and Celery-leaved Buttercup (*Ranunculus sceleratus*) and the sweet-grasses *Glyceria fluitans*, *G. declinata* and *G. notata* are frequent on cattle-poached margins.

Ditch communities of regional conservation importance are found on drained wetlands of the Frodsham and Ince Marshes and Gowy Meadows, where the pond-like conditions have enabled uncommon plants such as Bladderwort (*Utricularia* spp.), Small Pondweed (*Potamogeton berchtoldii*) and Water-violet (*Hottonia palustris*) to survive, though they are now under threat from intensive agriculture.

In addition to the effects of changes in water and river maintenance practices, plant distribution has also been influenced by the introduction of alien species. These include Indian Balsam, Japanese Knotweed and Giant Hogweed (*Heracleum mantegazzianum*), which has increased dramatically in the last 10 years in the river systems of the Bollin and the Croal–Irwell. Aquatics such as New Zealand Pigmyweed (*Crassula helmsii*) and Water Fern (*Azolla filiculoides*) are currently invading some standing waters in the Mersey Basin. Canadian Waterweed (*Elodea canadensis*) became established widely during the 19th century, but in the last 30 years it has been displaced in many places by Nuttall's Waterweed (*E. nuttallii*).

Invertebrates

Holland (1976a) reported the distribution of *Asellus aquaticus* L. and *Gammarus pulex* L. in the rivers of the Mersey Basin during 1971 and related their presence to water quality. With the accumulation of a further 24 years of data collection (surveys of rivers two or three times each year), it is now possible to see how water quality improvements have altered the distribution of invertebrate animals. The 1971–72 results are compared with those from a much larger number of survey sites used in 1994–95 in Figures 13.6–13.9. The distributions of four groups are compared: *Asellus* Geoffrey, *Gammarus* Fabricius, *Baetis* Leach and Ephemeroptera (excluding *Baetis* spp.)/Plecoptera, which have been selected to cover the whole range of water quality from badly polluted to unpolluted. *Gammarus* includes the

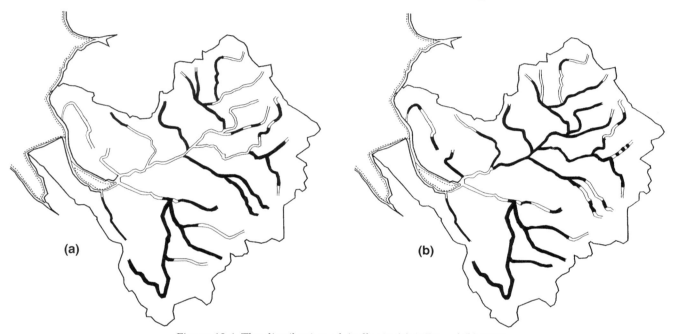

Figure 13.6. The distribution of *Asellus* in (a) 1970 and (b) 1994.

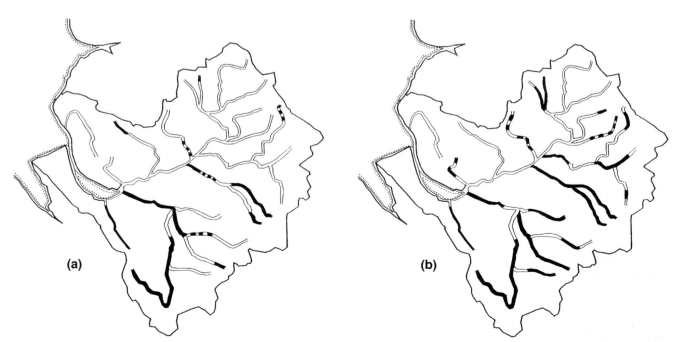

Figure 13.7. The distribution of *Gammarus* in (a) 1970 and (b) 1994.

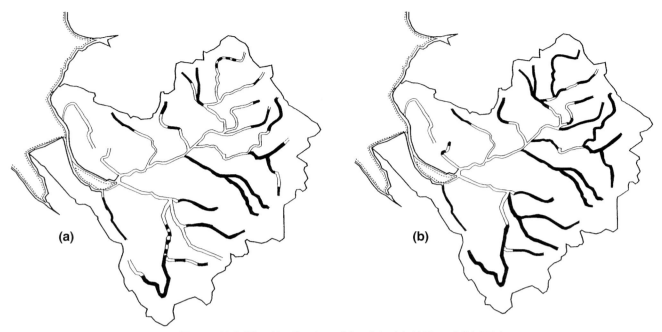

Figure 13.8. The distribution of *Baetis* in (a) 1970 and (b) 1994.

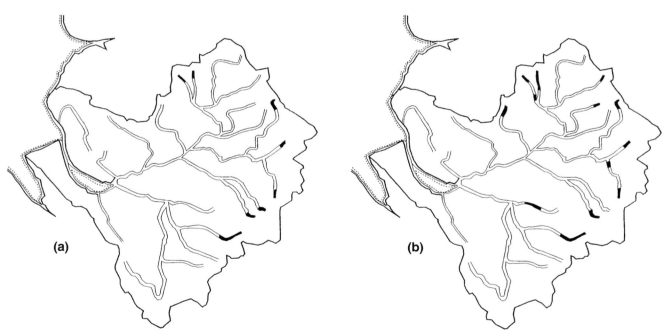

Figure 13.9. The distribution of Ephemeroptera (excluding *Baetis*)/Plecoptera in (a) 1970 and (b) 1994).

brackish-water species referred to below.

Comparisons show changes over the 24-year period which reflect the water quality improvements known to have taken place throughout the Mersey Basin. *Asellus* established itself in many stretches where previously it was absent, and it has disappeared in other lengths where it was once recorded. Appearances generally correspond with known water quality improvements from poor to moderate; disappearances are often displacements by clean water species where previously moderate quality water has been upgraded.

Freshwater species of *Gammarus* show a similar

advance into cleaner waters, mostly into the rivers of the upper Mersey, where in the early 1970s it was notably scarce. The spread of *Baetis* into many new river stretches provides a vivid biological statement of water quality improvements in the catchment. The poor distributions of clean-water Ephemeroptera and Plecoptera reflect pollution problems that still exist. Indeed this confirms what is widely acknowledged, that despite improvements, the River Mersey remains one of the most polluted rivers in Britain today

The Environment Agency has now adopted a more detailed form of invertebrate survey. Data from 1990 and

1995 are still being collated but should provide valuable information.

Holland (1976b) linked the distribution of the three species *G. duebeni*, *G. tigrinus* and *G. zaddachi* to the various inputs of saline water from direct discharges and the water-table. Conditions have altered markedly since then, but although detailed current records are not available, some notable changes can be described. The salt discharge to the Trent and Mersey Canal, which took the salinity to above 50% of sea water, ceased and in the fresh-water conditions now prevailing, the three species have probably been lost. However, *G. zaddachi* has firmly established itself in the River Weaver from Northwich to Frodsham, where a range of inorganic salts continues to be discharged to the river by chemical industries.

A notable 50-year series of papers reports the work of McMillan on the Mollusca of rivers and other freshwater habitats in the region. The accumulated record shows various changes in distribution of individual species, especially the spread of aliens via interconnected waterways. This literature is listed in the references under Fisher & Jackson (1936) and McMillan, with others, 1942 to 1991.

Fish

In the early 1970s, the River Mersey was widely regarded as an area devoid of river fisheries (Figure 13.10(a)). Futile attempts were made at various times in the 1970s to introduce fish into several stretches of river, but organic and toxic pollution were always too great for fish survival. Zinc in the River Etherow and other toxic metals in the River Tame provided particularly adverse conditions.

The successive agencies responsible for the management of the river system have always looked for the bene-fits of success in improving water quality in terms of fishery development. In 1976 the North West Water Authority established a fisheries department to serve the area, and since then, a policy of fish stocking has been pursued as environmental conditions have allowed. From time to time, the existence of unknown fish populations has emerged, either through the occurrence of fish mortalities in pollution events, or from local anglers pursuing their sport on stretches hitherto believed to be fishless.

The situation today is summed up in Figure 13.10(b). A significant reduction in the number of completely fishless rivers has taken place. Whilst the total of viable fisheries has not increased much, encouragement can be taken from the large number of rivers where minor fish such as Three-spined Stickleback (*Gasterosteus aculeatus*) and Stone Loach (*Noemacheilus barbatulus*) now exist, and where coarse fish populations are surviving.

Lakes

Natural standing waters in the Mersey Basin consist largely of a group of relatively deep lakes, known as the meres (Gorham 1957a & b; Reynolds & Sinker 1976; Savage & Pratt 1976; Reynolds 1979; Savage 1990; Savage, Bradburne & Macpherson 1992; Moss *et al.* 1992; Moss, McGowan & Carvalho 1994), situated in Cheshire and formed by the melting of icebergs buried in glacial drift, some ten thousand years ago. Also grouped as 'meres' are some small, shallow lakes formed by a variety of means. Although many were man-made in the last two centuries and are to be found on former great estates, some are probably natural. Of these there were originally many more, but they have naturally filled in with vegetation to form the raised bogs, or mosses (Sinker 1962;

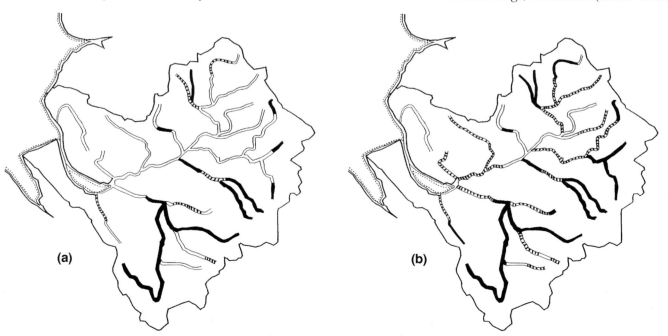

Figure 13.10. The distribution of fisheries in (a) 1972 and (b) 1995. Solid lines are established fisheries, hatched lengths are minor or emerging fisheries.

Figure 13.11. Mere Mere is a classic west midlands mere, with summer stratification, blue-green algal blooms and a rich littoral macrophyte community. Its use as a driving practice range for the local golf club poses no hazard to the lake, but makes sampling it occasionally exciting (*Photo: B. Moss*).

Tallis 1973), many of which have now been drained for agriculture or peat extraction.

The meres, with other similar lakes in adjoining river catchments, form a natural grouping from a limnological point of view. The deeper ones (operationally defined as >3m maximum depth and descending to 31m in Rostherne Mere) stratify in summer to form a distinct epilimnion and hypolimnion. The latter may often become anaerobic. The rate of water replacement is comparatively low because the meres are dominated by ground water supplies in many cases.

Following earlier suggestions by Reynolds (1979), recent surveys show that phytoplankton production is controlled by nitrogen supply (Moss *et al.* 1992; 1994) rather than the phosphorus supply that controls production in many, if not most lakes. The reason for this is not that the rate of input of nitrogen is necessarily very low, nor that that of phosphorus is particularly high. The lakes lie in agricultural catchments from which substantial amounts of nitrogen leach to the basins, and the nitrogen to phosphorus ratios of the inflowing or percolating waters are high, as is usual elsewhere.

However, denitrification in the wet meadows and reed fringes of the lakes may cause substantial loss of nitrogen, whilst other mechanisms, unusually, lead to retention of phosphorus in the water (Moss *et al.* 1997). In most lakes phosphorus is rapidly lost to the overflow or the sediments. In the deeper meres, the rate of flushing

is low, such that the main sink for phosphorus has been the sediments. Over many years, these sediments may have become saturated and can no longer absorb the incoming supplies of phosphorus, however small, from the catchment, so these accumulate in the water (Kilinc 1995).

The water itself thus has a low nitrogen to phosphorus ratio, a condition associated, together with thermal stratification and a base-rich water supply, with production of blue-green algae (properly called cyanoprokaryotes). These may sometimes float to the surface to form a bloom, a phenomenon known in the Shropshire meres as the 'breaking of the meres' (Griffiths 1925) by analogy with the scums of yeast that used to form in brewing vats. In recent years such blooms have come to be associated with eutrophication, the artificial enrichment of surface waters with nutrients from agricultural and domestic effluents.

Blooms in the meres are clearly an ancient phenomenon. They are referred to by Phillips (1884), and figure earlier in the folklore consciousness of the area (Webb 1924). Recent analyses of sediments from Whitemere and Colemere for pigments specific to particular algal groups, suggest that cyanoprokaryotes have been common in at least one mere for at least 6,000 years (McGowan 1996). There has nonetheless also been some recent eutrophication, superimposed on this ancient phenomenon and presumably driven by increased nitrogen run-off as agriculture has intensified in the post-war years (Brinkhurst & Walsh 1967; Grimshaw & Hudson 1970; Livingstone 1979; Nelms 1984; Reynolds & Bellinger 1992; Carvalho 1993; McGowan 1996).

Rostherne Mere, a National Nature Reserve, is one of the best-known of these lakes, with a lengthy record of scientific investigations (Banks 1970; Grimshaw & Hudson 1970; Goldspink 1978, 1981, 1983; Goldspink & Goodwin 1979; Carvalho 1993; Carvalho, Beklioglu & Moss 1995; Moss *et al.* 1997). It too is nitrogen limited and has extensive blue-green algal growths. The accumulations of blue-green algae, which may sometimes be highly toxic, have caused problems for local cattle. A combination of a desire to reduce these blooms, a conventional belief, based on a wealth of evidence from elsewhere, in the efficacy of phosphorus control in controlling eutrophication, and the overloading of a sewage treatment works designed for considerably fewer people than it now serves, led North West Water to divert the treated sewage effluent from the mere's inflow in 1991.

This discontinued the main (and considerable) source of phosphorus to the lake and there has been a modest decrease in the concentrations of phosphorus in the water (Carvalho 1993; Carvalho *et al.* 1995; Beklioglu 1995; Moss *et al.* 1997). There has been little change in the phytoplankton populations however, which, for the reasons adduced above, are nitrogen-controlled and are likely to remain so for the immediate future and probably much longer. Rostherne Mere has a greater flushing rate than the groundwater-fed meres and may, theoretically, reach a phase of phosphorus limitation eventually as the present stores are displaced and not replaced. For this reason it is a particularly interesting site. Deep, well-flushed lakes are usually readily restorable by phosphorus control.

Rostherne Mere is also of interest in having been among the first lakes to be designated 'guanotrophic' (Brinkhurst & Walsh 1967). Its nutrient supply was thought to have been dominated by the excreta of the birds roosting on it. There are genuinely guanotrophic lakes (Moss & Leah 1982), but quantitative studies have shown that Rostherne Mere is not one of them, and probably never was! Birds provide 1–2% of its phosphorus and nitrogen supplies (Carvalho *et al.* 1995).

Upstream of Rostherne Mere, and also originally a recipient of the sewage effluent, is Little Mere, an example of one of the group of shallow meres. Like many of the group, it was formed by the damming of a stream which emerged from the deeper Mere Mere (itself of interest, not least for its name), passed through Little Mere and then flowed down to Rostherne Mere. The shallow meres potentially contain ecosystems dominated by submerged and floating-leaved aquatic plants, but several have lost these as a result of changes consequent on eutrophication and other influences (Scheffer *et al.* 1993; Moss, Madgwick & Phillips 1996).

The plant communities are very resistant to increases in nutrients because of a suite of stabilising mechanisms that prevent phytoplankton from taking advantage of the nutrients and competitively displacing the plants. These include the provision of refuges against fish predation for invertebrates such as water fleas (particularly *Daphnia* spp.) which graze the algae growing suspended in the water, and snails which feed upon the algae coating submerged plants, thereby limiting the increase of the algae and keeping the water clear and leaf surfaces open to incoming light. The plants are therefore able to photosynthesise and grow without undue interference from the algae.

If the plants are damaged (for example by overcutting, boat propellers, grazing by carp, swans or geese), if the grazers are poisoned by pesticide run-off or other toxins, or if the balance of the fish community changes in favour of zooplankton-eating fish, the stabilising mechanisms break down and the algae can rapidly take over. The clear water plant-dominated state can then become a turbid phytoplankton-dominated one. Studies of the shallow meres have shown an inverse relationship between the crop of algae and the number of *Daphnia,* the main algal grazers, in the water (Moss *et al.* 1994). Where the *Daphnia* are few and the water is turbid with algae, the plants have been lost. In general the switch to turbid water is more likely to occur when the nutrient input is high, though one of the additional agents of change must also be operating.

Little Mere is of considerable theoretical interest among these shallow lakes because, before 1991, when the sewage effluent was diverted, it had huge concentrations of nutrients, yet clear water and a reasonable abundance of aquatic plants. The usual stabilising mechanisms of the plant community were fortified by a considerable population of bright cherry-red coloured *Daphnia magna* Sars (Carvalho 1994). This is an efficient grazer, but so large (up to 4mm) that it is a preferred prey of many fish, with which it cannot easily co-exist.

In Little Mere, however, the sewage effluent was not of high quality. It de-oxygenated the water, preventing sustainable populations of fish, but allowed the haemoglobin-rich *Daphnia magna* to survive and graze. Diversion of the effluent allowed fish to recolonise. The *Daphnia magna* was then replaced by less conspicuous *Daphnia* species, the stabilising mechanisms of the plant communities persisted and plant dominance continued and even extended in the mere (Beklioglu 1995; Beklioglu & Moss 1995, 1996).

Because there is considerable interest in the restoration (Moss *et al.* 1996) of the huge numbers of shallow lakes that have lost their plant communities in lowland Europe, particularly in Denmark, Sweden and the Netherlands, as well as in such well-known areas in England as the Norfolk Broads, the information still emerging from studies of Little Mere, no less than that from Rostherne and the other deep meres, is of considerable international interest.

Artificial standing waters

There are over 30 substantial reservoirs on upland tributaries in the Mersey catchment (Holland & Harding 1984). These are relatively acid for the most part, because of anthropogenic acidification of their gathering grounds. There is little published work on their biology, although unpublished data may well exist. Where they function with considerable drawdown of water level, their littoral communities are likely to be impoverished, although further north, e.g., at Grizedale Reservoir in Lancashire, a highly specialised flora, with Water-purslane (*Peplis portula*) and Shoreweed (*Littorella uniflora*) both rare in the region, may be found. More generally, they might be expected to be depauperate in their plankton and profundal benthos, because of acidity and low nutrient status, though the shaley catchments probably buffer the acidification to some extent.

In addition, numerous small reservoirs ('lodges') and holding lagoons were constructed for, and often within the premises of, factories and collieries. Where they received heated water from industrial processes, they sometimes supported exotic tropical waterplants (Fox 1963) presumably introduced by aquarists. De-industrialisation and the improved availability of public mains water supplies have been followed by the draining and infill of some of these waterbodies. Many do, however, survive. Some have been stocked with fish and are used for recreational angling. They represent a currently uninvestigated but potentially rich biological resource within the Mersey Basin.

The salt industry is responsible for having created a number of shallow, saline waterbodies or flashes caused partly by land subsidence over extraction workings, and these are used to accommodate saline wastes from the processes. The natural history of the flashes has been studied because of the importance of these waters to wading birds and also because of the unusualness of inland saline habitats and their associated faunas in a wet country like Britain (Holland 1976; Savage 1971, 1979, 1981, 1985).

Finally, there is a myriad of small agricultural ponds, usually groundwater fed, throughout the area, but especially in the lowlands south of the River Mersey. Their biology and future prospects are described by Boothby *et al.* (1995) and Boothby & Hull (chapter fourteen, this volume).

Canals

The Industrial Revolution created a demand for inland bulk transport which could only be satisfied to a small extent by navigation on the Rivers Mersey, Irwell and Weaver.

In response, the construction of artificial canals began with the Sankey Navigation, opened in 1757, followed by the Bridgewater Canal between the River Mersey at Runcorn and central Manchester in 1776. Most of the network shown in Figure 13.12 was completed over the next few decades, making the region second only to the Black Country in its density of navigations. Three trans-Pennine lines and links to the midlands and to the south were supplemented by internal routes, all constructed to small dimensions as compared with main rivers, to keep down excavation costs and subsequent water requirements for locks. Typically the channels are

Figure 13.13. Leeds & Liverpool Canal, Litherland. 1950s – coal barge approaching Liverpool (*Photo: British Waterways*).

10–15m wide and have maximum design depths in the range 1.0–1.7m.

Railway competition, beginning with the opening of the Liverpool & Manchester Railway in 1830, ended construction of small canals, but a final major addition came in 1894 with the opening of the Manchester Ship Canal. Designed for large, sea-going craft, this has minimum dimensions of 27m wide x 8.5m deep.

The early colonisation of these new freshwater habitats by flora and fauna is unrecorded, but it is clear from old illustrations and a few herbarium records that, in the cleanwater sections, pond-like species assemblages were present during the era of horse-drawn and sailed craft. Sedges (*Carex* spp.) were often planted to stabilise banks and mention of fisheries implied the presence of functioning food webs in the channels. Pollution affected some sections and probably intensified and spread as transport-requiring industries grew up in waterside locations and also used the canals for effluent disposal. River Board reports show that the Leeds & Liverpool Canal in Liverpool was still so grossly polluted by a range of city industries until the end of the 1960s that it was often black and anaerobic, with gas eruptions of hydrogen sulphide and methane.

The change from horse and sail to propeller-driven movement began on a large scale in the 1870s and led to greatly increased disturbance by each boat passage. Bank erosion became a problem and vegetation-based protection was replaced by stone, brick, concrete and metal hardening with associated loss of marginal plants and their fauna.

Rail and later road competition gradually reduced traffic on the canals. Whilst the main routes retained some freight until the middle of the 20th century, others declined into low activity. Some were filled in, but many were retained for their water supply and drainage func-

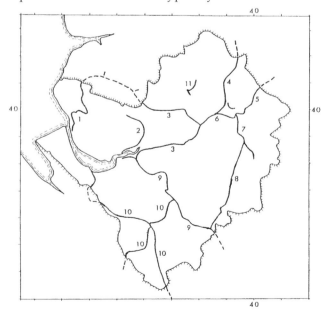

Figure 13.12. Canals of the Mersey Basin. 1. Leeds & Liverpool. 2. St Helens. 3. Bridgewater. 4. Rochdale. 5. Huddersfield Narrow. 6. Ashton. 7. Peak Forest. 8. Macclesfield. 9. Trent & Mersey. 10. Shropshire Union. 11. Manchester, Bolton and Bury.

tions. Reports of difficulties with weeds obstructing channels increased through the first half of the century (Murphy, Eaton & Hyde 1982), as boat traffic ceased to restrain their growth.

Nationally, the mid-20th century was the peak time for colonisation of the waterways by flora and fauna (Murphy, Eaton & Hyde 1982) and in the Mersey Basin network some diverse and conservationally important assemblages developed and, in some case, persisted. Shimwell (1984) and Bignall (1992) describe rich floras and faunas in some Manchester canals, but overall the second half of the century has been marked by a decline in species diversity and conservation interest. This has been caused by quite different circumstances in different canals.

Increasing use by recreational boat traffic is one factor, particularly in scenically attractive rural lengths, e.g., Shropshire Union and Macclesfield Canals (Murphy & Eaton 1983). Changing management is another factor. When gross pollution ceased in 1969 in the Liverpool section of the Leeds & Liverpool Canal submerged vegetation became abundant and by 1979 a total 24 species of aquatic angiosperms, bryophytes and charophytes was present, together with a rich invertebrate fauna (Eaton & Freeman 1982; Murphy & Eaton 1981; Murphy, Hanbury & Eaton 1981; Hanbury, Murphy & Eaton 1981). Further species colonised over the next 15 years, bringing the total to over 30 aquatic plant species (Eaton, personal observation). Then in 1994 a breach caused water loss and drying out. The length was refilled with brackish water from Liverpool Docks; the section nearest the terminus was then emptied again and deep-dredged before being re-watered in 1995. Six of the former species re-established during 1996.

A third factor has been the decrease in thermal pollution. Formerly, industrial discharges of hot water into the Stockport Branch of the Ashton Canal, combined presumably with aquarists' introductions, led to establishment of tropical vegetation, e.g., Large-flowered Waterweed (*Egeria densa*), Curly Waterweed (*Lagarosiphon major*) and *Najas graminea* (Bailey 1884; Weiss & Murray 1909; Kent 1955a, b; Shaw 1963). Another branch at Hollinwood sustained Tapegrass (*Vallisneria spiralis*) and Hampshire-purslane (*Ludwigia palustris*) in a heated section (Shaw 1963). The Pocket Nook Branch of the St Helens Canal received waste heat from the Ravenhead Glassworks and Large-flowered Waterweed and Curly Waterweed, one of the earliest northern populations of Water Fern and a range of tropical fish including large *Tilapia* spp., were present (Eaton, personal observation). All of these unusual species assemblages subsequently disappeared. The Stockport and Hollinwood sites are now filled in and at St Helens the main heating ceased in 1980, leading to the death of the tropical fish and their replacement by stocked cold water species. During the 1990s channel clearance as part of an environmental improvement project eliminated surviving unusual flora.

The final factor causing decline in species diversity

Figure 13.14. Rochdale Canal, Failsworth. Derelict: reeds and abundant Floating Water-plantain 1991
(*Photo: N.J. Willby*).

was natural vegetation succession and competitive exclusion of species, where no weed control took place on unnavigated canals (Murphy, Eaton and Hyde 1980). Murphy and Eaton (1981) showed how in the shallow water of the Huddersfield Narrow Canal succession to monocultures of Branched Bur-reed or Reed Sweet-grass could be reversed by clearance, but quickly resumed and returned to monoculture within a few years. The upper part of the remaining isolated length of the Hollinwood Branch developed into a Reed Sweet-grass swamp, but the lower part is kept open by conservationists using manual clearance, and 32 aquatic plant species and a further 19 associated wetland and riparian species were listed in the Nature Conservancy Council's 1981 survey which led to its designation as a Site of Special Scientific Interest. The Prestolee section of the Manchester, Bolton and Bury Canal, is cleared regularly for angling and is a locality for the rare introduced freshwater jellyfish *Craspedacusta sowerbyii* Lankester (Shimwell 1984).

The connections which canals have established with catchments outside the Mersey Basin seem to have been the means of species migrations across watersheds. Thus, Willby & Eaton (1993) provide evidence that Floating Water-plantain (*Luronium natans*) reached canals in the region via the Shropshire Union link from the Welsh catchment of the River Dee, whilst the eastern European amphipod *Corophium curvispinum* Sars. var. *devium* Wundsch spread northwards from its original site of introduction on the Avon Navigation at Tewkesbury via the Shropshire Union Canal to the Mersey Basin (Holland 1976; Pygott & Douglas 1989; the few Mersey Basin locations in their Figure 1 have since been supplemented and the species appears to be continuing its spread). The small freshwater snail, *Marstoninopsis scholtzi* Schmidt, is present in a few canals in the Manchester area. However, the origin of this stable population is unknown but its native population in East Anglia is declining (Bratton 1991).

The future

Man-induced change has been a major factor in all types of freshwaters of the Mersey Basin for at least the past 200 years and seems likely to continue in the future. In the case of rivers, whilst further local regulation and channelisation projects are inevitable adjuncts to catchment development, these are likely to be undertaken in a sensitive way to allow some return to richer floras and faunas, supported by further reductions in pollution.

For standing waters, control of the quantities and qualities of their water sources and the demands made upon them for water supply, fishing and other recreational uses will determine their future ecosystems. There is a strong argument for making conservation a high priority in the case of the meres, on account of their intrinsic scientific interest, and their proposed designation as an EU Special Area of Conservation under the Habitats Directive 1992.

Canal ecosystems have lost some features of interest in the past few decades and there are currently pressures which may continue this decline, notably complete clearances during urban regeneration projects and increasing use for recreational boating and fisheries.

Overall therefore, the freshwaters of the Mersey Basin have mixed prospects, the outcome of which depends upon long-term development and management policies within the catchments. Climatic change adds further uncertainty, especially since freshwaters seem peculiarly susceptible to colonisation by introduced species, and the range of those potentially able to establish could be greatly expanded at higher temperatures.

Acknowledgements

We are grateful to the Environment Agency and Mrs N. McMillan for information supplied for this paper and to Gill Haynes for technical assistance. The views expressed by the authors are their own and do not necessarily reflect those of the Environment Agency or any other organisation.

References

Bailey, C. (1884). Notes on the structure, the occurrence in Lancashire, and the source of origin, of *Naias graminea Delile*, var. *Delilei Magnus*. *Journal of Botany*, **22**, 305–33.

Banks, J.W. (1970). Observations on the fish population structure of Rostherne Mere, Cheshire. *Field Studies*, **3**, 357–79.

Beklioglu, M. (1995). *Whole lake and mesocosm studies on the roles of nutrients and grazing in determining phytoplankton crops in a system of shallow and deep lakes*. PhD thesis, University of Liverpool.

Beklioglu, M. & Moss, B. (1995). The impact of pH on interactions among phytoplankton algae, zooplankton and perch (*Perca fluviatilis*) in a shallow, fertile lake. *Freshwater Biology*, **33**, 497–509.

Beklioglu, M. & Moss, B. (1996). Mesocosm experiments on the interaction of sediment influence, fish predation, and aquatic plants with the structure of phytoplankton and zooplankton communities. *Freshwater Biology*, **36**, 315–25.

Bignall, M.R., (1992). *Rare Plants in the Canals of the Metropolitan Counties of NW England*. Report for English Nature, January 1992.

Boothby, J., Hull, A.P., Jeffreys, D.A. & Small, R.W. (1995). Wetland loss in North-West England: the conservation and management of ponds in Cheshire. *Hydrology and Hydrochemistry of British Wetlands* (eds J.M.R. Hughes & A.L. Heathwaite), pp.432–44. Wiley, Chichester.

Bratton, J.H. (1991). *British Red Data Books: 3. Invertebrates other than Insects*, pp.47–48. Joint Nature Conservation Committee, Peterborough.

Brinkhurst, R.O. & Walsh, B. (1967). Rostherne Mere, England: a further instance of guanotrophy. *Journal of the Fisheries Research Board of Canada*, **24**,1299–1309.

Carvalho, L.R. (1993). *Experimental limnology on four Cheshire meres*. PhD thesis, University of Liverpool.

Carvalho, L.R. (1994). Top-down control of phytoplankton in a shallow, hypertrophic lake: Little Mere, England. *Hydrobiologia*, **275/276**, 53–63.

Carvalho, L.R., Beklioglu, M. & Moss, B. (1995). Changes in a deep lake following sewage diversion – a challenge to the orthodoxy of external phosphorus control as a restoration strategy. *Freshwater Biology*, **34**, 399–410.

Eaton, J.W. (1989). Ecological Aspects of Water Management in Britain. *Journal of Applied Ecology*, **26**, 835–49.

Eaton, J.W. & Freeman, J. (1982). Ten Years' Experience of Weed Control in the Leeds & Liverpool Canal. *Proceedings EWRS 6th Symposium on Aquatic Weeds, 1982*, 96–104. Novi Sad, Jugoslavia.

Environment Agency (1996). *Alt Crossen Catchment Management Plan*. Environment Agency, N.W. Region, Preston.

Fisher, N. & Jackson, J.W. (1936). Early records of Lancashire and Cheshire non-marine Mollusca by James Wright Whitehead. *Journal of Conchology*, **20**, 275–81.

Fox, B.W. (1963). Plants of industrial tips and waste land. *Travis's Flora of South Lancashire* (eds J.P. Savidge, V.H. Heywood & V. Gordon), pp. 73–76. Liverpool Botanical Society, Liverpool.

Goldspink, C.R. (1978). Comparative observations on the growth rate and year class strength of roach *Rutilus rutilus* L. in two Cheshire lakes, England. *Journal of Fish Biology*, **12**, 421–33.

Goldspink, C.R. (1981). A note on the growth rate and year class strength of bream, *Abramis brama* L. in three eutrophic lakes, England. *Journal of Fish Biology*, **19** , 665–73.

Goldspink, C.R. (1983). Observations on the fish populations of the Shropshire–Cheshire meres with particular reference to angling. *Proceedings 3rd British Freshwater Fisheries Conference*, University of Liverpool, Liverpool.

Goldspink, C.R. & Goodwin, D.A. (1979). A note on the age composition, growth rate and food of perch *Perca fluviatilis* L., in four eutrophic lakes, England. *Journal of Fish Biology*, **14**, 489–505.

Gorham, E. (1957a). The chemical composition of some waters from lowland lakes in Shropshire, England. *Tellus*, **9**, 174–79.

Gorham, E. (1957b). The ionic composition of some lowland lakes from Cheshire, England. *Limnology and Oceanography*, **2**, 22–27.

Griffiths, B.M. (1925). Studies on the phytoplankton of the lowland waters of Great Britain. III. The phytoplankton of Shropshire, Cheshire and Staffordshire. *Botanical Journal of the Linnean Society of London*, **47**, 75–92.

Grimshaw, H.M. & Hudson, M.J. (1970). Some mineral nutrient studies of a lowland mere in Cheshire, England. *Hydrobiologia*, **36**, 329–41.

Hanbury, R.G., Murphy, K.J. & Eaton, J.W. (1981). The ecological effects of 2-methylthiotriazine herbicides used for aquatic weed control in navigable canals. II. Effects on macroinvertebrate fauna and general discussion. *Archiv für Hydrobiologie*, **91**, 408–26.

Harding, J.P.C. (1981). *Macrophytes as Monitors of River Water Quality in the Southern NWWA Area*. North West Water Authority Rivers Division Ref. No. TSBS-81-2. British Lending Library Loan Collection.

Holland, D.G. (1976a). The distribution of the freshwater Malacostraca in the area of the Mersey and Weaver River Authority. *Freshwater Biology*, **6**, 265–76.

Holland, D.G. (1976b). The inland distribution of brackish-water *Gammarus* species in the area of the Mersey and Weaver River Authority. *Freshwater Biology*, **6**, 277–85.

Holland, D.G. & Harding, J.P.C. (1984). The Mersey. *Ecology of European Rivers* (ed. B.A. Whitton), pp. 113–44. Blackwell Scientific Publications, Oxford.

Kent, D.H. (1955a). *Egeria densa* Planch. *Proceedings of the Botanical Society of the British Isles*, **1**, 322.

Kent, D.H. (1955b). *Lagarosiphon major* (Ridley) C.E. Moss. *Proceedings of the Botanical Society of the British Isles*, **1**, 322–23.

Kilinc, S. (1995). *Limnological studies on the North West Midland meres, with special reference to Whitemere*. PhD thesis, University of Liverpool.

Livingstone, D. (1979). *Algal remains in recent lake sediment*. PhD thesis, University of Leicester.

McGowan, S. (1996). *Ancient cyanophyte blooms. Studies on the palaeolimnology of White Mere and Colemere*. PhD thesis, University of Liverpool.

McMillan, N. (1942). Cheshire conchological notes. *North-Western Naturalist*, **16**, 328.

McMillan, N. (1944). *Planorbis corneus* (L.) in Wirral. *Journal of Conchology*, **22**, 103.

McMillan, N. (1947). Cheshire conchological notes no. 2. *North-Western Naturalist*, **21**, 103–04.

McMillan, N. (1947). Further notes on *Planorbis corneus* (L.) in Wirral. *Journal of Conchology*, **22**, 248.

McMillan, N. (1947). The land and freshwater Mollusca of the Wirral peninsula of Cheshire. *Report and Proceedings of the Chester Society of Natural Science, Literature and Art: Robert Newstead Memorial Volume*, pp. 83–93.

McMillan, N. (1948). *Bithynia tentaculata* (L.) in "closed" ponds. *Journal of Conchology*, **23**, 22.

McMillan, N. (1953). Cheshire conchological notes no. 3. *North-Western Naturalist*, New Series, **1**, 96.

McMillan, N. (1955). Notes on local non-marine Mollusca. *Proceedings of the Liverpool Naturalists' Field Club for 1954*, 19–20.

McMillan, N. (1955). The range of *Planorbarius* in the British Isles. *Journal of Conchology*, **24**, 63–65.

McMillan, N. (1956). Notes on local Mollusca. *Proceedings of the Liverpool Naturalists' Field Club for 1955*, 13–15.

McMillan, N. (1959). Notes on the land and freshwater Mollusca of Wirral, Cheshire 1948–1958. *Proceedings of the Liverpool Naturalists' Field Club for 1958*, 10–21.

McMillan, N. (1959). The Mollusca of some Cheshire marl-pits: a study in colonization. *Journal of Conchology*, **24**, 299–315.

McMillan, N. (1962). *Pisidium pseudosphaerium* Favre in Cheshire. *Journal of Conchology*, **25**, 63.

McMillan, N. (1963). Non-marine Mollusca. *Lancashire and Cheshire Fauna Committee* 33rd. Reports, pp. 48–50.

McMillan, N. (1963). The *Pisidium*-fauna of Bromborough, Cheshire. *Journal of Conchology*, **25**, 183–88.

McMillan, N. (1964). Report of Field Meeting held 1st May at Guide Bridge, Lancashire. *Conchologists' Newsletter* no. **14**, 93–94.

McMillan, N. (1967). A Cheshire locality for *Anodonta complanata* Rossmassler. *Conchologists' Newsletter* no. **20**, 142.

McMillan, N. (1967). Field Meeting to Leeds and Liverpool Canal, Lancashire. *Conchologists' Newsletter* no. **21**, 8–9 .

McMillan, N. (1967). Field Meeting to Plumley Nature Reserve,

Cheshire, 30th April 1966. *Conchologists' Newsletter* no. **20**, 142–43.

McMillan, N. (1969). The effect of the exceptionally severe winter of 1962/63 on the Mollusca of a Cheshire pond. *Conchologists' Newsletter* no. **33**, 155–56.

McMillan, N. (1970). Report on the Mollusca, 1968 and 1969. *Lancashire and Cheshire Fauna Society Publication*, **57**, 12–13.

McMillan, N. (1977). Records of Cheshire non-marine Mollusca, mainly from the Wirral peninsula. *Lancashire and Cheshire Fauna Society Publication*, **71**, 5–6.

McMillan, N. (1989). Observations on the freshwater Mollusca of some Cheshire marl-pits over forty-four years. *Conchologists' Newsletter* no. **108**, 157–65.

McMillan, N. (1991). The history of alien freshwater Mollusca in North-West England. *Naturalist*, **115**, 123–32. (Cover dated 1990.)

McMillan, N. & Ellison, N.F. (1944). Some habitats of *Hydrobia jenkinsi* (Smith) in Wirral, Cheshire. *North-Western Naturalist*, **18**, 320–22.

McMillan, N. & Fogan, M. (1967). Non-marine Mollusca: some noteworthy records and a note on 'garden' species. *Lancashire & Cheshire Fauna Committee 37th Report*, pp. 39–40.

McMillan, N. & Fogan, M. (1969). Field Meetings at Huyton and Knowsley Park, South Lancashire, October and November 1968. *Conchologists' Newsletter* no. **29**, 98–99.

McMillan, N. & Greenwood, E.F. (1969). The giant *Anodonta cygnea* of Claughton, West Lancashire. *Conchologists' Newsletter* no. **29**, 102–03.

McMillan, N. & Millott, J.O'N. (1950). Records of non-marine Mollusca from Cheshire, Flintshire and Denbighshire. Cheshire and North Wales Natural History vol. III. *Proceedings of the Chester Society of Natural Science, Literature and Art for 1949*, pp. 165–72.

McMillan, N. & Millott, J.O'N. (1954). Notes on the non-marine Mollusca of Cheshire and North Wales. Cheshire and North Wales Natural History vol. V. *Proceedings of the Chester Society of Natural Science, Literature and Art for 1951, 1952 & 1953*, pp. 109–13.

McMillan, N. & Wallace, I.D. (1979). Non-marine Mollusca in the Wirral peninsula, Cheshire: records and notes. *Lancashire and Cheshire Fauna Society Publication*, **75**, 5–8.

McMillan, N., Edwards, W.F., Fogan, M. & Millott, J.O'N. (1966). The Mollusca of canals in Lancashire and Cheshire. *Lancashire & Cheshire Fauna Committee 36th Report*, pp. 36–41.

Moss, B., Beklioglu, M., Carvalho, L.R., Kilinc, S., McGowan, S. & Stephen, D. (1997). Vertically-challenged limnology; contrasts between deep and shallow lakes. *Hydrobiologia*, **342/343**, 257–67.

Moss, B. & Leah, R.T. (1982). Changes in the ecosystem of a guanotrophic and brackish shallow lake in eastern England: potential problems in its restoration. *Internationale Revue der gesamten Hydrobiologie*, **67**, 635–59.

Moss, B., Madgwick, J. & Phillips, G. (1996). *A Guide to the Restoration of Nutrient-Enriched Shallow Lakes*. Broads Authority and Environment Agency, Norwich.

Moss, B., McGowan, S. & Carvalho, L.R. (1994). Determination of phytoplankton crops by top-down and bottom-up mechanisms in a group of English lakes, the West Midland Meres. *Limnology and Oceanography*, **39**, 1020–29.

Moss, B., McGowan, S., Kilinc, S. & Carvalho, L.R. (1992). *Current limnological condition of a group of the West Midland Meres that bear SSSI status*. Final Report, English Nature Contract F72-06-14.

Murphy, K.J. & Eaton, J.W. (1981). Ecological effects of four herbicides and two mechanical clearance methods used for aquatic weed control in canals. *Proceedings of a Conference on Aquatic Weeds and their Control, Association of Applied Biologists*, pp. 201–17. Christ Church, Oxford.

Murphy, K.J. & Eaton, J.W. (1983). Effects of pleasure-boat traffic on macrophyte growth in canals. *Journal of Applied Ecology*, **20**, 713–29.

Murphy, K.J., Eaton, J.W. & Hyde, T.M. (1980). A Survey of Aquatic Weed Growth and Control in the Canals and River Navigations of The British Waterways Board. *Proceedings 1980 British Crop Protection Conference – Weeds*, **2**, 707–14.

Murphy, K.J., Eaton, J.W. & Hyde, T.M. (1982). The Management of Aquatic Plants in a Navigable Canal System used for Amenity and Recreation. *Proceedings EWRS 6th Symposium on Aquatic Weeds*, **1982**, 141–51. Novi Sad, Jugoslavia.

Murphy, K.J., Hanbury, R.G. & Eaton, J.W. (1981). The ecological effects of 2-methylthiotriazine herbicides used for aquatic weed control in navigable canals. I. Effects on aquatic flora and water chemistry. *Archiv für Hydrobiologie*, **91**, 204–331.

National Rivers Authority (1992). *River Corridor Surveys, Methods and Procedures*. Conservation Technical Handbook No. 1., National Rivers Authority, Bristol.

National Rivers Authority (1994). *River Irwell Catchment Management Plan*. National Rivers Authority, N.W. Region, Warrington.

National Rivers Authority (1996a). *An Initial Review of the 1995 Drought*. Internal Report, National Rivers Authority, N.W. Region, Warrington.

National Rivers Authority (1996b). *River Habitat Survey*. National Rivers Authority, Bristol.

National Rivers Authority (1996c). *Upper Mersey Catchment Management Plan*. National Rivers Authority, N.W. Region, Warrington.

Nelms, R. (1984). *Palaeolimnological studies of Rostherne Mere (Cheshire) and Ellesmere (Shropshire)*. PhD thesis, Liverpool Polytechnic.

Nolan, P.A. & Guthrie, N. (in press). River rehabilitation in an urban environment: examples from the Mersey Basin, NW England. *Proceedings of an International Conference on River Restoration, 1996*. European Centre for River Restoration – National Environment Research Unit, Silkeborg, Denmark.

Phillips, W. (1884). The breaking of the Shropshire meres. *Transactions of the Shropshire Archaeological and Natural History Society*, **7**, 277–300.

Pygott, J.R. & Douglas, S. (1989). Current distribution of *Corophium curvispinum* Sars. var. *devium* Wundsch (Crustacea: Amphipoda) in Britain with notes on its Ecology in the Shropshire Union Canal. *Naturalist*, **114**, 15–17.

Reynolds, C.S. (1979). The limnology of the eutrophic meres of the Shropshire–Cheshire plain. *Field Studies*, **5**, 93–173.

Reynolds, C. S. & Bellinger, E.G. (1992). Patterns of abundance and dominance of the phytoplankton of Rostherne Mere, England: evidence from an 18-year data set. *Aquatic Sciences*, **54**, 10–36.

Reynolds, C.S. & Sinker, C.A. (1976). The meres: Britain's eutrophic lakes. *New Scientist*, **71**, 10–12.

Royal Society for the Protection of Birds, National Rivers Authority & Royal Society for Nature Conservation (1994). *The New Rivers and Wildlife Handbook*. RSPB, The Lodge, Sandy, Bedfordshire, England.

Savage, A.A. (1971). The Corixidae of some inland saline lakes in Cheshire, England. *Entomologist*, **104**, 331–44.

Savage, A.A. (1979). The Corixidae of an inland saline lake from 1970 to 1975. *Archiv für Hydrobiologie*, **86**, 355–70.

Savage, A.A. (1981). The Gammaridae and Corixidae of an inland saline lake from 1975 to 1978. *Hydrobiologia*, **76**, 33–44.

Savage, A.A. (1985). The biology and management of an inland saline lake. *Biological Conservation*, **31**, 107–23.

Savage, A.A. (1990). The distribution of Corixidae in lakes and the ecological status of the North West Midland meres. *Field Studies*, **7**, 516–30.

Savage, A.A. & Pratt, M.M. (1976). Corixidae (water boatmen) of the Northwest midland meres. *Field Studies*, **4**, 465–76.

Savage, A.A., Bradburne, S.J.A. & Macpherson, A.A. (1992). The morphometry and hydrology of Oak Mere, a lowland, kataglacial lake in the north-west midlands, England. *Freshwater Biology*, **28**, 369–82.

Scheffer, M., Hosper, S.H., Meijer, M-L., Moss, B. & Jeppesen, E. (1993). Alternative equilibria in shallow lakes. *Trends in Ecology and Evolution*, **8**, 275–79.

Shaw, C.E. (1963). Canals. *Travis's Flora of South Lancashire* (eds J.P. Savidge, V.H. Heywood & V. Gordon), pp. 71–73. Liverpool Botanical Society, Liverpool.

Shimwell, D. (1984). *The wildlife conservation potential of the canals of Greater Manchester County*. Countryside Commission and Groundwork North West, Manchester.

Sinker, C.A. (1962). The North Shropshire Meres and Mosses; a background for ecologists. *Field Studies*, **1**, 101–38.

Tallis, J.H. (1973). The terrestrialisation of lake basins in North Cheshire, with special reference to the development of a 'Schwingmoor' structure. *Journal of Ecology*, **61**, 537–67.

Webb, M. (1924). *Precious Bane*. Jonathan Cape, London

Weiss, F.E. & Murray, H. (1909). Alien Plants of the Reddish Canal. *Manchester Memoirs*, **53**, no. 14.

Willby, N.J. & Eaton, J.W. (1993). The Distribution, Ecology and Conservation of *Luronium natans* (L.) Raf. in Britain. *Journal of Aquatic Plant Management*, **31**, 70–76.

CHAPTER FOURTEEN

Ponds of the Mersey Basin: habitat, status and future

J. BOOTHBY AND A. HULL

Introduction – a brief history of ponds

Within the Mersey Basin there are several thousand small water bodies including lakes, meres, moats, flashes, pits and ponds. Though some of these may be natural features, remnants of glacial and periglacial conditions, a man-made origin for most small water bodies seems very likely. Ponds in north-west England (Cheshire, Greater Manchester, Lancashire and Merseyside), as elsewhere in lowland Britain, have been dug in considerable numbers for many centuries, but unlike elsewhere many remain visible in the rural landscape. Today, the Mersey Basin is at the heart of the greatest concentration of lowland ponds remaining in the British Isles, or, indeed, in Europe.

Though brick-clay extraction and sand-and-gravel working helped to create this resource, overwhelmingly the ponds were created by the ancient practice of marling, a practice which was certainly recorded during the 13th century, and which reached its peak in the mid- to late 18th century (Hewitt 1919; Hewitt 1929; Porteous 1933). Many pits were dug in close proximity to each other – sometimes as many as ten ponds or more in a cluster – in order to exploit a particularly rich lode of this mineral manure. Following excavation, the clayey-marls were often subjected to a number of treatments (e.g., frost-weathering, baking) and then spread on the land to improve fertility. Typically small-scale workings (say 30m in diameter) would use a horse and cart or horse-driven gin (Middleton 1949; Prince 1964), though there are later records of more substantial mechanised workings (Grantham 1864; Ferro & Middleton 1949). The application of marl was fairly heavy, changing the soil composition and playing a significant role in increased agricultural productivity.

There is evidence to suggest that the benefits of marling were not only substantial but also reasonably persistent, and many land leases of the late 17th and early 18th centuries permitted (and later required) marl to be exploited. In time, farmers came to use a variety of fertilisers and nitrogen-fixing crops – vetch, clover, trefoils – in their search for higher productivity. By the 1830s, marl was almost completely displaced by some of the new manures (e.g., guano and sodium nitrate) distributed by a growing transport infrastructure. On the dairying lands much use was made both of bone-dust fertiliser 're-exported' from the towns, and of stable and other manure transported by canal barge (Fussell 1954); Manchester alone produced 63,000 tons of night-soil annually in the 1840s (Davies 1960). The rapid regional growth of urban areas forced more land into agricultural production; many fields were levelled out, drained and ponds filled in, a process which has continued to the present.

The pond habitat is one of continuous change and this discussion considers the nature of the pond habitat in the region, identifies changes in its status, and reviews the future for this distinctive regional landscape.

The pond habitat

What constitutes the pond habitat?

The pond habitat can be variously interpreted as 1. the stock of the pond resource; 2. the individual ponds; and 3. the pondscape. Each is now explored in turn:

1. The stock of the resource

We estimate the number of pond sites in north-west England in 1996 at no more than 36,000, compared with perhaps 125,000 in the late 19th century. In the Mersey Basin area the total would be approximately 18,000. Based largely upon estimates made for Cheshire (Boothby, Hull & Jeffreys 1995a) the number of 'wet' sites is probably only 11,000; many other formerly wet sites are in advanced vegetational succession. Figure 14.1 shows the current pond sites, located mostly in the lowlands.

2. Individual ponds

The individual pond and its surrounding terrestrial buffer zone constitute a habitat for many animals and plants. For some, e.g., fish, aquatic plants and certain invertebrates, the habitat requirements depend upon such physiographical variables as hydrochemistry, water depth, degree of overshading, interspecific predation, pollution events, rainfall levels, temperature, and elevation. Though there is significant variation in these elements across the region, the bulk of ponds are in

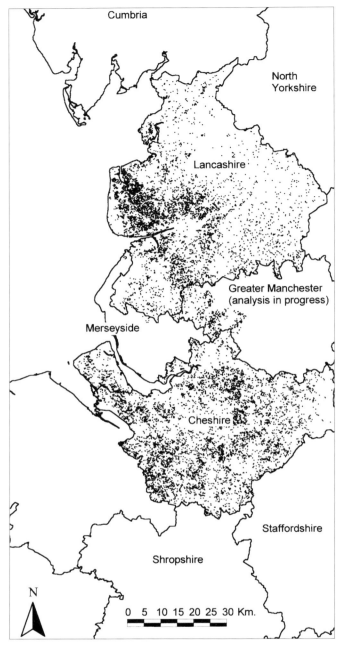

Figure 14.1. The ponds of north-west England.

3. From pond cluster to pondscape

For some species, a congregation of ponds is probably necessary for their persistence. Amphibians in particular exhibit marked mobility around the congregation in both foraging and colonisation behaviours. Indeed, many amphibians exist in metapopulations, in which 'sub-populations', with a varying home territory, interchange genetic material with nearby groups on a year-by-year basis, thus helping to ensure survival (Fahrig & Merriam 1993; Ebenhard 1991; Reading, Loman & Madsen 1991).

Seasonal mobility of amphibians could be 1,000m or more, but a more conservative estimate would be around 300m (Macgregor 1995). Individual ponds isolated at greater distances may have populations which are at risk from local extinction and which may not then be recouped by recolonisation (Sjögren 1991). It is thus safe to assume that a 'healthy' congregation of ponds contains not only suitable pond sites, but has a spatial arrangement of ponds which is also optimal. In this context, 'optimal' also includes the nature of the landscape matrix found between ponds (Ebenhard 1991). Grazed land is near to optimal in terms of its permeability to amphibians, ploughed land less optimal, and urban infrastructure may be an almost total impedance.

Ponds in clusters offer the 'safest' landscape for maintaining biodiversity. We may expect 'safe' landscapes to exhibit minimal spatial fragmentation, and that local clusters should be part of a wider 'pondscape'.

Biological status and change

Pond status

With some 18,000 individual pond sites within the Basin, it is perhaps unrealistic to suppose that we shall ever have complete, up-to-date biological records for each pond site, though this is already possible in some localities. However, sample information is becoming available on the overall status of ponds, and is forming a bench-mark for regional pond data (Pond *Life* Project 1996). This analysis shows only the broadest details of species composition, though inspection of the underlying statistical structure of the faunal, floral, and physiographical variables is expected to reveal more substantial patterns.

1. Plants

Of the 271 ponds surveyed throughout Lancashire and Cheshire in 1995, the maximum number of plant taxa recorded in any one pond was 45. Some 24% of ponds held 13 species or fewer, many of these sites being overshaded. Ponds with 29 or more plant species were, by this simple definition, in the top 10% of those surveyed (Table 14.1). Within this pattern, 26 ponds held between 5 and 10 taxa of submerged and floating species, and 39 ponds (14%) contained no aquatic plant species at all. Though aquatic vegetation was often to be found in small isolated patches, floating vegetation was often more extensively developed. Emergent vegetation was particularly prominent in the region's ponds; at 74 ponds,

lowland agricultural settings. Given their historical origins as marl pits, many have high pH values (Day, Greenwood & Greenwood 1982; Boothby *et al.* 1995b). Many pond species have specific requirements or tolerances, e.g., the necessity of emergent vegetation for dragonflies, gentle pond banks for amphibians, shaded ponds for certain invertebrates; there may be no such thing as an 'average pond', and all provide valuable habitats (Biggs *et al.* 1994).

Overall, the presence of some floral species seems to be fortuitous from pond to pond, and certainly the presence of a particular species cannot usually be inferred from a knowledge of its presence at a nearby pond; any individual pond could contain locally or regionally rare species.

Taxa recorded	<10	11–20	21–30	31–35	36–40	>40
Number of ponds in:						
Cheshire	21	81	43	4	1	2
Lancashire & Wigan	20	46	42	8	2	1
Full survey	41	127	85	12	3	3

Table 14.1. Distribution of abundance of aquatic plant taxa in surveyed ponds.
Adapted from Table 2.1, Pond *Life* Project (1996).

Bulrush (*Typha latifolia*) was often found as floating beds and is a rapid coloniser of ponds. Substantial numbers of ponds were found with stands of Branched Bur-reed (*Sparganium erectum*), Floating Sweet-grass (*Glyceria fluitans*) and Cyperus Sedge (*Carex pseudocyperus*) (Table 14.2); six 'rare' plant species were encountered in the survey: Soft Hornwort (*Ceratophyllum submersum*), Fringed Water-lily (*Nymphoides peltata*), Water Soldier (*Stratiodes aloides*), Tufted-sedge (*Carex elata*), Cowbane (*Cicuta virosa*) and Galingale (*Cyperus longus*). Of these Cowbane, Water Soldier, Fringed Water-lily and Galingale are nationally scarce (Stewart, Pearman & Preston 1993).

Acorus calamus	4
Bolboschoenus maritimus	1
Carex elata	1
Carex paniculata	13
Carex vesicaria	1
Carex acutiformis	9
Carex otrubae	17
Carex pseudocyperus	62
Carex rostrata	10
Eleocharis palustris	52
Equisetum fluviatile	56
Glyceria fluitans	106
Glyceria maxima	4
Phalaris arundinacea	87
Phragmites australis	12
Schoenoplectus lacustris	7
Sparganium erectum	142
Typha angustifolia	15
Typha latifolia	74

Table 14.2 . Potential dominants of swamp communities: total occurrences in the 271 ponds surveyed.
Note: from Table 2.10; Pond *Life* Project (1996).

2. Invertebrates
Across the 271 surveyed ponds, invertebrate species were found in all but 8 ponds; one pond held 59 species, but the majority held between 16 and 33 species. Whilst many species were common, several regionally or locally notable species were found, and 25 species with official

Joint Nature Conservation Committee (JNCC) scarcity status were found – these include one of the country's rarest beetles (Red Data Book (RDB) 1 Endangered), Lesser Silver Water Beetle (*Hydrochara caraboides*), until recently not encountered outside of the Somerset Levels. Specimens of scarce species were found in 102 ponds, some holding more than one such species. The JNCC's Invertebrate Sites Register Invertebrate Index (ISRII) allows any pond to be scored for its invertebrate interest. Of the 76 pond-clusters forming the focus of the survey, 41 score at least 20 points (significant) with a top-score of 350: this last is at a site in Wigan where opencast coal is to be extracted. Figure 14.2 shows the distribution of 'significant' invertebrate sites to be a region-wide phenomenon and not restricted solely to the remoter, more-rural environments.

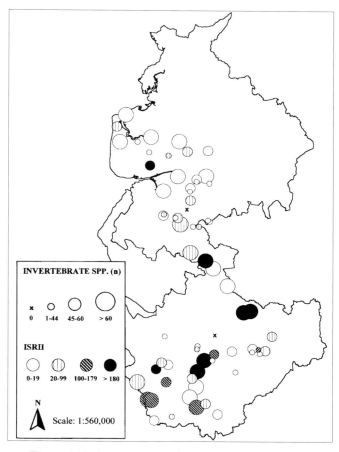

Figure 14.2. Aquatic invertebrate species at surveyed ponds/pond clusters. Symbol size denotes number of species; shading indicates ISRII value (see legend).

3. Amphibians
Amphibians are currently under considerable stress throughout the world (Wake 1991; Blaustein, Wake & Sousa 1994). The region contains all six of the recognised native British species, though the Natterjack (*Bufo calamita*) is found only on the coastal margins. In the survey, the number of species found at any one pond was very variable. One pond surveyed held 5 amphibian

species and 3 other ponds held 4 species; about one third of ponds (31.2%) showed no evidence of amphibians at all, though this cannot be interpreted as permanent absence.

The Common Frog (*Rana temporaria*) is widely found in 41% of ponds, and the Common Toad (*Bufo bufo*) is found in over 17% of ponds. The protected species Warty or Great Crested Newt (*Triturus cristatus*) was found in 23% ponds, though it was much more common in Cheshire (35% of ponds); Palmate (*T. helveticus*) and/or Smooth Newts (*T. vulgaris*) were found in 18% of ponds. These data confirm the significance of the region and its ponds as substantial amphibian habitats, a picture which is not always accurately recorded (Hilton-Brown & Oldham 1991). Most importantly, the persistence of amphibians has widely been seen to be related to the integrity of the *pondscape* and not simply to the survival of *individual* ponds: it is to this wider context that we now turn.

The changing status of the pondscape

Since the cessation of agricultural pond excavation in the early 19th century:

1. many ponds have been lost; comparatively few new ponds have been added, perhaps fewer than 1000 across the region, principally for fishing;

2. vegetational succession has been marked;

3. pond-densities have declined (from $c.17\text{km}^{-2}$ to $c.3\text{km}^{-2}$);

4. the spatial extent of the pondscape has been much reduced; and

5. the fragmentation of the remaining pond landscape has greatly increased.

The fragmentation of the pondscape can be visualised using a procedure of distance-counting (Unwin 1979). In

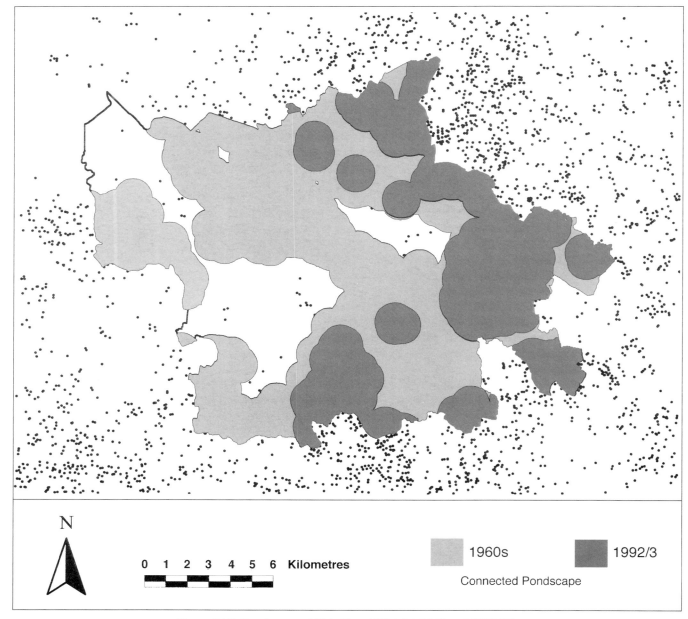

Figure 14.3. Pondscape of Vale Royal District, 1969 and 1992/93.

	1960s	*1992–93*
Total area of connected pondscape		
– (km²)	310	121
– as % District area	[81%]	[31.6%]
Number of fragments	3	10
Area of largest fragment (km²)	288	68
Area of second-largest fragment (km²)	23	23

Table 14.3. Pondscape change in Vale Royal District: summary statistics.

this, for each pond, the procedure counts the numbers of ponds within a specific search-radius, giving, for each pond, a value for connectedness. Mapping this connectedness shows the spatial extent of the pondscape and the increase of fragmentation. An example of this has been prepared for the District of Vale Royal in Cheshire.

In Figure 14.3, the pondscape is defined for the ponds of *c*.1969 (in light grey). The limit of the pondscape is defined as a line enclosing those ponds with the same value of connectedness (for Vale Royal – 19 ponds within 1,000m of any given pond). Other ponds lie outside this defined pondscape, but they are relatively isolated; there is almost uninterrupted coverage of the District by a connected pondscape. The configuration of the pondscape for 1992/93 is also shown (in darker grey) and the changes from the earlier map are clear to see: the pondscape now covers less than one quarter of the original area; it is fragmented into ten pieces, and the largest occupies only 68km² compared to 288km² (see Table 14.3). Figure 14.4 shows an attempt, using a similar approach, to map the pondscape for north-west England as a whole. Analysis for areas between Cheshire and Lancashire is incomplete at this time, but the connected pondscape certainly extends through Wigan, into Liverpool, Wirral and Knowsley / St Helens to the south and west, and into the fringes of Greater Manchester (see Figure 14.1).

Loss mechanisms

The era represented by the map of changing pondscape is a significant one both for the Mersey Basin and for elsewhere across England. Amongst the most significant features are: the intensification of agriculture, involving increased use of agri-chemicals; the growth of the transport infrastructure, including motorways; the spread of suburbs; and the ruralisation of manufacturing.

Though much of the farmland of the region has remained in pastoral use, helping ponds to survive, the search for increased profitability by farmers has meant that ponds, like hedgerows and trees, are often seen as archaic and therefore expendable landscape features. Perceived in this light, they are sometimes used for dumping farm waste, and some have been ploughed out or drained. As a generalisation, 'benign neglect' plays the most significant role in pond loss on agricultural land (Boothby *et al*. 1995b). With the loss of a purpose for most ponds, vegetational succession will often run

unchecked, aided by nitrate-rich run-off from agricultural fertilisers. This run-off would formerly have been intercepted by the soil and vegetation of the immediate pond buffer-zone, but many such areas have been incorporated into used agricultural land, allowing agri-chemicals to reach ponds. Given the origin of many of the ponds as sources of marl fertiliser, this is indeed ironic.

Across the region, urban spread and its associated infrastructural development has removed many pond sites. Only recently have building developers begun to incorporate existing ponds within new estates; only recently have new roads or other developments begun to incorporate substantial development mitigation packages within their proposals; only recently have golf-course architects realised that ponds can be

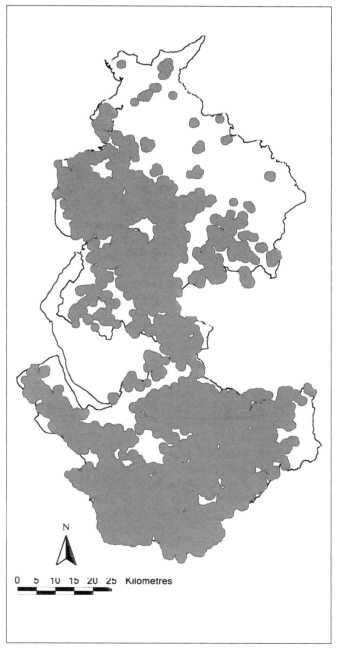

Figure 14.4. The pondscape of north-west England.

accommodated within their boundaries. Table 14.4 summarises the mechanisms of pond loss in Cheshire; only limited analysis is as yet available for Lancashire and other parts of the region (Boothby *et al.* 1995a), but research elsewhere (Heath & Whitehead 1992) suggests that similar forces will have been at work.

Looking to the future – threats and opportunities

We can evaluate the future for ponds using the concepts contained in Table 14.5. The *strengths* of the pondscape of the region lie in its diversity of animals and plants, which is considerable. For some substantial parts of the area, there is still sufficient congregation of ponds to afford habitats for those species which require 'connected' multi-patch habitats. Though evidence is sporadic, the waters of ponds are not known to be grossly or widely polluted (Boothby *et al.* 1995b). They are widely used for coarse fishing, they have provided generations of children with an educational and recreational resource, and, with their surrounding tree cover, they often provide prominent local landmarks. Where they are not over-managed, they provide local wilderness – or, at least, wild corners of nature and all this in the context of an historical landscape feature which represents once-widespread farming practices.

But there are *weaknesses* too. Earlier surveys notwithstanding (Day *et al.* 1982), our knowledge base for ponds is woefully thin; even counting the ponds accurately represents a major leap forward. Most ponds are on inaccessible farmland where, as a result of benign neglect, they are disappearing; their former economic functions have been lost and, with a few exceptions, new uses have not been found. The cost of surveying, monitoring, or actively managing the remaining stock could be prohibitive. Ponds stand relatively unprotected by legal designation other than for a relatively small and select(ed) number which have biological or archaeological interest.

The *threats* to ponds come, as we have seen, from a

| | Ponds lost (%) to: | | | Ponds in advanced |
	agriculture	*building and infrastructure*	*recreation*	*vegetational succession (%)*
Cheshire	19.1	7.5	2.2	40.0
Districts				
minimum	13.1	1.4	< 0.1	22.0
maximum	23.7	33.1	10.9	48.6

Table 14.4. Mechanisms of pond loss, *c.*1969–1992/93: Cheshire County.

variety of sources, but perhaps 'benign neglect' will continue to threaten; this is, in part, a perceptual problem, sometimes seen in the dumping of farm waste in a convenient 'damp hole in the ground'. This neglect will also be recognised in advanced vegetational succession, drying-out, and, ultimately, reversion to terrestrial habitat. As many ponds are in or are entering this phase, we may justifiably be concerned about the biodiversity of the stock of ponds in the region, especially as so few new ponds are being dug. At individual ponds, localised pollution events may render the site inhospitable, and those who walked the countryside in the mid-1990s will have had no difficulty in recognising the scale and criticality of the extended drought at that time. The implications of this 'catastrophic' event for species and habitat survival have yet to be quantified.

Lest all this sounds too negative, we must conclude by considering the *opportunities*. These arise from a popular concern to protect pond landscapes, and call into consideration a range of initiatives from new agricultural policies to the instigation of new planning policy potentialities.

We consider that, at the farm level, there may be some value in considering afresh the economic value of ponds, whether this be for the leasing of fishing rights, the exploration of new food sources, or the exploitation for scien-

Strengths	Weaknesses
high biodiversity	meagre knowledge-base
low incidence of pollution	often on inaccessible farmland
educational potential	loss of main economic function
recreational uses, especially angling	high costs of survey and management
significant landscape feature	general lack of legal protection
'wilderness' remnant	weak image amongst some farmers and land managers
historical/ archaeological continuity	
Opportunities	**Threats**
new economic value	benign neglect
changing agricultural policies	loss to other uses
strengthening of Countryside Stewardship	vegetational succession / drying-out
planning mitigation	lowering of biodiversity
pond-friendly planning policies	local pollution events
local enthusiasm and organisation	sustained drought
developing knowledge-base	fragmentation
	agricultural intensification

Table 14.5. Ponds: strengths, weaknesses, opportunities, threats.

tific and research purposes. We firmly believe that most farmers do not set out to delete ponds from their land: they simply fail to see an alternative which makes any economic sense. In this context, we now feel that the changing emphases of both agricultural policy and of nature conservation policies may be coinciding. The Countryside Stewardship initiative is now (1996) replacing the largely discredited Set Aside scheme as the appropriate vehicle for delivering nature conservation on farmland. For the first time this should allow some farmers to conserve ponds and small wetlands, and to be compensated for doing so. In this region, it may be possible to give the Countryside Stewardship a 'pondy' flavour in recognition of the distinctiveness of the regional landscape.

At other policy levels, there are opportunities to be seized. Though planning policy and practice is now required to consider explicitly the value of development, local planning authorities are also empowered to seek mitigation for any deleterious effects on landscape and habitat. That this can work to the benefit of ponds can be seen in the proposed mitigation package for the second runway at Manchester Airport: the developers are to provide 97 new or re-created ponds to re-establish habitat, both aquatic and terrestrial, for the important newt colony at that site. In all, 43 ponds will be destroyed, and the surrounding landscape changed significantly, if, in part, temporarily. This significant legal agreement is possible because of the principle of 'no net loss of environmental value' incorporated in the appropriate Structure Plan, and thence into Cheshire County Council policy (Cheshire County Council 1990). Whilst the proposed scale of environmental and landscape change at the airport creates concern in many people, the availability of mitigation should not be minimised in its importance.

Finally, opportunities also lie in local people and organisations. There is a massive will to undertake environmental conservation as witnessed by the size and scope of membership in voluntary bodies such as the Wildlife Trusts, BTCV, and others (Hull & Boothby 1996). In such a context, the Pond *Life* Project (Boothby *et al.* 1995a) plays a role in helping to co-ordinate volunteer attempts to survey, analyse and manage the ponds of the region. Operating through a 'pond warden' system we are attempting to focus enthusiasm, research capability, and practical experience towards sustaining and, where possible, increasing the stock of ponds, to reducing fragmentation of the pondscape, and to building a sustainable network of individuals, voluntary organisations, and planning authorities for the future.

In all of these opportunities, we are convinced of the necessity to focus not just on the individual pond, or even on several hundred individual ponds, but to stress the importance of the cohesion of the landscape, and to inform management actions accordingly.

Acknowledgements

The Pond *Life* Project is financially supported by the *Life* Programme of the European Union, by Liverpool John Moores University, and by co-operating partners in north-west England, the Netherlands, Belgium, and Denmark.

Surveys for the Project summarised here have been carried out by Jonathan Guest Ecological Survey; maps have been prepared by Jon M. Bloor.

References

Biggs, J., Corfield, A., Walker, D., Whitfield, M. & Williams, T. (1994). New approaches to the management of ponds. *British Wildlife*, **5(5)**, 273–87.

Blaustein, A.R., Wake, D.B. & Sousa, W.P. (1994). Amphibian declines: judging stability, persistence and susceptibility of populations to local and global extinctions. *Conservation Biology*, **8(1)**, 60–71.

Boothby, J., Hull, A.P. & Jeffreys, D.A. (1995a). Sustaining a threatened landscape: farmland ponds in Cheshire. *Journal of Environmental Planning and Management*, **38(4)**, 561–68.

Boothby, J., Hull, A.P., Jeffreys, D.A. & Small, R.W. (1995b). Wetland loss in North-West England: the conservation and management of ponds in Cheshire. *Hydrology and hydrochemistry of wetlands* (eds J. Hughes, & A.L. Heathwaite), Ch. 27. Wiley, London.

Cheshire County Council (1990). *County Structure Plan Review*. CCC, Chester.

Davies, C.S. (1960). *The Agricultural History of Cheshire, 1750–1850*. The Chetham Society, 3rd Series, 10, Manchester.

Day, P., Deadman, A.J., Greenwood, B.D. & Greenwood, E.F. (1982). A floristic appraisal of marl pits in parts of north-western England and northern Wales. *Watsonia*, **14**, 153–65.

Ebenhard, T. (1991). Colonisation in metapopulations: a review of theory and observations. *Biological Journal of the Linnean Society*, **42**, 105–21.

Fahrig, L. & Merriam, G. (1993). Conservation of fragmented populations. *Conservation Biology*, **8(1)**, 50–59.

Ferro, R.B. & Middleton, A.C. (1949). Clay marling: mechanised methods. *Agriculture*, **56**, 123–28.

Fussell, G.E. (1954). Four centuries of Cheshire farming systems, 1500–1900. *Transactions of the Historic Society of Lancashire and Cheshire*, **106**, 57–79.

Grantham, R.B. (1864). A description of the works for reclaiming and marling parts of the late Delamere Forest. *Journal of the Royal Agricultural Society of England, I*, **25**, 369–80.

Heath, D.J. & Whitehead, A. (1992). A survey of pond-loss in Essex, South-east England. *Aquatic Conservation: Marine and Freshwater Ecosystems*, **2**, 267–73.

Hewitt, E. (1929). *Medieval Cheshire*. Manchester University Press, Manchester.

Hewitt, W. (1919). Marl and marling in Cheshire. *Proceedings of Liverpool Geological Society*, **13**, 24–28.

Hilton-Brown, D. & Oldham, R.S. (1991). *The status of widespread amphibians and reptiles in Britain 1990, and changes during the 1980s*. Nature Conservancy Council, Peterborough.

Hull, A.P. & Boothby, J. (1996). Networking, partnership and community conservation in North West England. *Nature Conservation 4: The role of networks* (eds D.A. Saunders, J.L. Craig & E.M. Mattiske), pp. 341–55. Surrey-Beatty, Chipping Norton, NSW, Australia.

Macgregor, H. (1995). Crested newts – ancient survivors. *British Wildlife*, **7(1)**, 1–8.

Middleton, A.C. (1949). Clay marling: some historical notes. *Agriculture*, **56**, 80–84.

Pond *Life* Project (1996). *Critical pond biodiversity survey, 1995.* Pond *Life* Project, John Moores University, Liverpool.

Porteus, T.C. (1933). *Calendar of the Standish Deeds 1230–1575.* Public Library Committee, Wigan.

Prince, H.C. (1964). The origins of pits and depressions in Norfolk. *Geography,* **40,** 15–32.

Reading, C.J., Loman, J. & Madsen, T. (1991). Breeding pond fidelity in the common toad *Bufo bufo. Journal of the Zoological Society of London,* **225,** 201–11.

Sjögren, P. (1991). Extinction and isolation gradients in metapopulations: the case of the pool frog (*Rana lessonae*). *Biological Journal of the Linnean Society,* **42,** 135–47.

Stewart, A., Pearman, D.A. & Preston, C.D. (1993). *Scarce Plants in Britain.* JNCC, Peterborough.

Unwin, D.J. (1981). *Introductory spatial analysis.* Methuen, London.

Wake, D.B. (1991). Declining amphibian populations. *Science,* **253,** 860.

Map copyright

Boundaries for the Figures in this chapter are derived from OS Strategi data sets provided by Ordnance Survey under the terms of the CHEST Licensing Agreement.

CHAPTER FIFTEEN

Liverpool Bay and the estuaries: human impact, recent recovery and restoration

S.J. HAWKINS, J.R. ALLEN, N.J. FIELDING, S.B. WILKINSON
AND I.D. WALLACE

Introduction

Liverpool Bay and the estuaries that empty into it can be viewed as one interconnected ecosystem. The ecology of the estuaries and the Bay cannot be separated: considerable freshwater run-off enters the Bay via the estuaries from the notoriously wet north-western catchment; the large tidal range (10m) means high salinity water penetrates far up the estuaries on every tide. In order to be manageable, however, this chapter restricts attention to the Rivers Dee, Mersey and Ribble and the adjacent portion of Liverpool Bay (see Figure 15.1), focusing largely on the Mersey Estuary.

It is also impossible to separate the natural and anthropogenic factors acting on Liverpool Bay and its estuaries. Human activity has influenced the catchment and estuaries since earliest times (e.g., Chester was a Roman port). Human impacts have also been a major factor since industrialisation began in the 18th century. Indus-

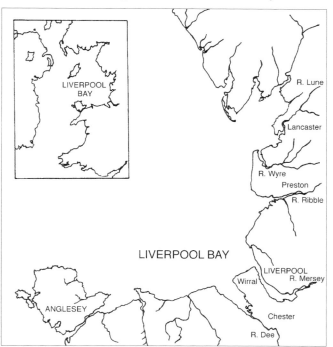

Figure 15.1. The region under study showing the Mersey Estuary.

trialisation and the development of the Port of Liverpool have led to considerable modification of the lower estuary, including an extensive series of walls first built in the last century to train the shifting sandbanks of the Bay to maintain navigation channels into the Narrows. The construction of the Manchester Ship Canal (opened 1894) changed the morphology of the upper Mersey Estuary and the normal cyclical channel migration (Bennett, Curtis & Fairhurst 1995). The River Ribble was also trained within levees when the docks were built in late 19th century. The upper Dee Estuary was subject to similar canalisation coupled with extensive land reclamation (see chapter sixteen, this volume).

As well as physical deformation there has been considerable input of waste via the rivers, directly to the estuaries and by dumping into the Bay itself. A variety of industrial and a huge quantity of domestic wastes, as well as dredging spoil have been discharged or dumped over the years. The River Mersey with its highly industrialised catchment has particularly suffered, earning the reputation of being the most polluted estuary in Europe (Clark 1989). In contrast the River Dee and River Ribble have been impacted to a much lesser extent, although point sources of pollution have had and continue to have some local effects.

We wish to highlight the lack of published work on the River Mersey; much of our review is derived from the 'grey' literature of reports, workshop proceedings and student theses. Early work on the region included floristic (e.g., Harvey-Gibson, 1890, 1891) and faunistic catalogues (e.g., Byerley, 1854; the work of Liverpool Marine Biology Committee edited by Herdman, 1886–92 summarised in Herdman, 1920). The story of the River Mersey up to the early 1970s is well told by Porter (1973). A wealth of anecdotal information and firsthand experience by local naturalists as well as professional investigations of the Mersey Estuary was summarised at a meeting of the Mersey Estuary Conservation Group in November 1988 (Curtis, Norman & Wallace 1995). An excellent recent summary on the water quality, pollution and ecology of the Mersey is the 'Mersey Estuary', a report on environmental quality (National Rivers Authority 1995).

Recent hydrocarbon exploitation has prompted

summaries of the environment and ecology of Liverpool Bay (Rice & Putwain 1987; Taylor & Parker 1993; Darby *et al.* 1994). There is also much relevant information in the various volumes of The Irish Sea Study Group (1990). Perhaps the most comprehensive recent study in the region was made to provide a baseline for the proposed construction of the Mersey Barrage which unfortunately is not in the public domain (Environmental Resources Limited report to Mersey Barrage Company 1993, copy in Zoology Department, Liverpool Museum). This work covered all aspects of the ecology of the River Mersey including a much needed recent survey of the benthos (Jemmett pers. comm.). These recent studies aside there has been surprisingly little published on the ecology of the various estuaries since the classic studies either side of the Second World War (Fraser 1931, 1932, 1935, 1938; Bassindale 1938; Pierce 1941; Corlett 1948; Popham 1966).

In the rest of this chapter background ecological information on Liverpool Bay, River Ribble and River Dee is briefly summarised. We then focus on the River Mersey, summarising what is known about its ecology before major impact and its subsequent recovery as a consequence of de-industrialisation and depopulation, tighter environmental controls and amelioration initiatives such as the Mersey Basin Campaign. Finally we describe pioneering work on restoration ecology of the former Merseyside docks. This is work that started in Liverpool and has been applied successfully elsewhere in the UK. It has shown what can be achieved in terms of water quality improvements as part of inner city renewal schemes. We finish with an appraisal of the current status of the region and its international importance for conservation.

Background information: Liverpool Bay, River Dee and River Ribble

Research on Liverpool Bay intensified in response to the dumping of sewage sludge, dredge aggregate and industrial waste in the 1970s (e.g., Department of the Environment 1972; Rees 1975). Elevations of organic matter, inorganic nutrients (nitrogen and phosphorus), heavy metals and resistant organics were detected in the areas near the sludge dumping grounds. Impacts on the benthos were less clear-cut due to the spatial and temporal variability of the highly unstable sediments (Rees *et al.* 1992). In particular there are highly localised pockets of muddy sediment which can support very dense communities of benthic animals* (Rees, Nicholaidou & Laskaridou 1977). The area is also notorious for wrecks of shellfish (Common Cockle, *Cerastoderma edule* and Rayed Trough Shell, *Mactra corallina*) in which large numbers of bivalves are washed up on the coast; these occur frequently and are natural

events caused by storms and very cold weather (McMillan 1975).

The inshore and intertidal communities are dominated by sandy or muddy sediments flanked at their terrestrial margins by extensive saltmarshes. The only significant area of natural rocky shore is at New Brighton and at Hilbre Island (reviewed in Craggs 1982) which supports an interesting rocky shore community truncated at its seaweed border by sand (Russell 1972, 1973, 1982). Limpets (*Patella vulgata*), the dominant grazer in north-eastern Atlantic rocky shore (Hawkins *et al.* 1992) communities, are scarce. Their numbers are reduced by cold winters, e.g., 1947 (Burd 1947) and 1962–63 (B. Bailey pers. comm.). They are also vulnerable to siltation, and their numbers are probably low even where suitable habitat exists presumably due to poor larval supply from the nearest extensive breeding population on the Great Orme. Common Winkle (*Littorina littorea*), however, are plentiful and assume the role of major grazer. Silt is probably also the reason for the absence from the rocky littoral of chitons, top shells, sea-squirts and the scarcity of sponges. Rising sediment levels have greatly reduced the sub-littoral and as early as 1854 were blamed for the disappearance of Lobsters (*Homanus gammarus*) at Hilbre (Byerley 1854).

Artificial hard substrata abound in Liverpool Bay and the estuaries. The docks are considered in detail later. Pilings, sea-walls and sea defences, (e.g., the fish tail groynes on Wirral) all support impoverished rocky shore communities dominated by wrack seaweeds (*Fucus* spp.), barnacles (*Semibalanus balanoides* and *Elminius modestus*), Common Mussel (*Mytilus edulus*) and Common Winkle, plus plenty of ephemeral algae such as *Enteromorpha*. Limpets have appeared recently on the sea-wall at New Brighton and on the new defences along with Beadlet Anemone (*Actinia equina*). Offshore, various wrecks act as artificial reefs and are colonised by diverse assemblages of subtidal fouling organisms (see Hartnoll 1993 for review).

Coastal sediment communities are productive but of generally low diversity in part due to the very homogeneous nature of their habitats. Sedimentary substrates dominate in both the intertidal and immediate subtidal zones in the Liverpool Bay area (Mills 1991).

The relatively few studies made over the years (Bassindale 1938: Gardiner 1950; Stopford 1951; Perkins 1956; Popham 1966; Gilham 1978; Bamber 1988; Al-Masnad 1991; Davies 1991; Garwood & Foster-Smith 1991; and see Mills 1991; Davies 1992; Hawkins 1993; Darby *et al.* 1994 for reviews) have revealed typical communities whose composition reflects particle size and depth. Lowshore and shallow areas of muddy sand have a rich fauna with bivalves, e.g., Common Cockle, Banded Wedge Shell (*Donax vittatus*) and echinoderms, Brittlestar (*Ophiura ophiura*) and Heart Urchin (*Echinocardium cordatum*), being prominent. Coarser, more mobile areas have a more impoverished fauna dominated by Striped Venus Shell (*Chameiea gallina*) and Sand Mason Worm (*Lanice conchilega*). Coarse intertidal

---

* Names of invertebrate animals follow as far as possible Hayward & Ryland (1995).

sediments support amphipods (*Bathyporeia* spp., *Haustorius arenarius*), polychaetes (*Nepthys* spp, *Nerine cirratulus*) and low down the Thin Tellin bivalve (*Angulus tenuis*). In clean sand at the mouth of the River Dee, the worm, *Spio filicornis,* dominates along with Lug Worm (*Arenicola marina*) and Sand Mason Worm; in more sheltered and hence slightly muddier areas Baltic Tellin (*Macoma balthica*), the polychaete (*Pygospio elegans*) and higher densities of Lug Worm occur. At the seaward end of the Great Burbo Bank a patch of coarser sand, gravel and cobble occurs and here Dahlia and Cave Anemones (*Urticina felina* and *Sagartia trogloddytes*) and the King Rag Worm (*Neanthes virens*) have all been recorded (Bassindale 1938).

The large expanses of intertidal flats from Crosby to Fleetwood support a typical low biomass crustacean and small polychaete dominated community over much of their extent, giving way to a richer community supporting bivalves in the stabler sand of the lower shore of the Sefton coast. The finer, muddier sediments of the River Ribble (Popham 1966; Davies 1991) support typical estuary species, e.g., Baltic Tellin, Common Cockle, the crustacean *Corophium volutator* and Common Ragworm (*Hediste diversicolor*).

Changes are occurring in the River Ribble as the channel to the former port of Preston is no longer dredged and maintained (H.D. Jones pers. comm.). At Preston Docks, Conlan *et al.* (1988, 1992) showed the

benthic communities to be very impoverished, an observation typical of a low salinity basin.

The effects of the extensive colonisation by Common Cord-grass (*Spartina anglica*), in both the Ribble and Mersey estuaries were reviewed by Doody (1984); Common Cord-grass has also covered large areas of the Dee Estuary. The spread of this species is of concern because it can result in the loss of intertidal feeding areas for wildfowl, and accelerates sediment accretion.

The Mersey Estuary

Historically, the Mersey Estuary contained sufficient Salmon (*Salmo salar*), Thick-lipped Grey Mullet (*Chelon labrosus*), Sturgeon (*Acipenser sturio*), Eels (*Anguilla anguilla*) and Smelt (*Osmerus eparlanus*) to support local fisheries for these species. Shrimp (*Crangon crangon*) and Flounder (*Pleuronectes flesus*) were also caught in the upper estuary (Cunningham 1898; Dunlop 1927). Thus it is safe to assume that human impact on the estuary was probably negligible until the Industrial Revolution. Although over 100 years of biological and chemical data are available for the River Mersey, differences in objectives, site selection, collection techniques, taxonomic expertise and analytical techniques between surveys mean that comparisons are exceptionally difficult to make. Furthermore, by the time surveys started the River Mersey was by no means pristine! Nevertheless,

Figure 15.2. Victoria Promenade, Widnes and the Mersey Estuary 1986 (*Photo: John Davies*).

Bassindale's 100 sampling site survey in 1933 (Bassindale 1938) provides a useful reference point for the River Mersey at the onset of the worst water quality conditions which probably occurred during the period 1940 to 1970 (Porter 1973). Another approach is the analysis of core samples coupled with radiometric dating. This work shows that the estuary was probably badly affected by pollution by the early years of the 20th century (National Rivers Authority 1995). Highest levels occurred for most heavy metals from the 1920s onwards, with decline starting in some cases as early as the 1930s (zinc, copper), but in others (e.g. mercury) only in recent years (see Figures 4.11 and 4.12 in National Rivers Authority 1995, based on Leah and co-workers, unpublished).

The major problem for the River Mersey has always been organic input rather than toxic chemicals. With the growing population and industry on the banks of the River Mersey, increased quantities of mainly domestic sewage and some industrial organic effluent introduced to the river reduced water quality considerably, so that anoxic conditions persisted for prolonged periods from the 1930s onwards (Bassindale 1938; Fraser 1938; Porter 1973 for review). In the upper estuary, a pronounced oxygen sag occurred regularly during summer low tide periods, causing anaerobic conditions and an associated offensive smell (Mersey & Weaver River Authority 1972; Irish Sea Study Group 1990). From the 1930s onwards, the general trend was one of reducing species abundance and diversity (Bassindale 1938; Holland & Harding 1984; Readman, Preston & Montoura 1986; Wilson, D'arcy & Taylor 1988; Environmental Advisory Unit of Liverpool University Ltd 1991). Salmon were effectively eradicated and the fisheries in the upper estuary severely limited (Liverpool Bay Study Group 1975; Wilson, D'arcy & Taylor 1988; Dempsey 1989). The loss of invertebrates due to anoxic bottom conditions, notably during the 1960s was considered a major factor in the decline of resident fisheries (Burt 1989). Around 1960 all but a few transient pelagic fish were absent from the inner and middle reaches of the estuary, and these did not penetrate much beyond the narrows (Porter 1973).

A number of heavy metals such as lead, mercury and arsenic and other persistent organic contaminants were, and still are, found in the water, sediments and marine organisms within the region at elevated concentrations, relative to other UK waters (Bull et al. 1983; Russell et al. 1983; Riley & Towner 1984; Norton, Rowlatt & Nunny 1984; Dickson & Boelens 1988; Jones & Head 1991; Law et al. 1992; Leah et al. 1992; Thompson et al. 1996). These concentrations tend to be highest close to the mouth of the River Mersey and to decrease with increasing distance offshore. There have also been acute incidents of lead poisoning of waders and wildfowl (Head, D'arcy & Osbaldeston 1980; Bull et al. 1983; Osborn, Every & Bull 1983). A study of the fauna and heavy metals present in the mud in Collingwood Dock found very high levels of lead and zinc with the polychaete, *Capitella capitata*, the dominant infaunal species (James & Gibson 1980).

In addition, the predominance of petrochemical and chemical industries led to chronic and acute pollution incidents, probably at their worst during the Second World War when pollution controls were relaxed (Hardy 1995). The most significant pollution incident in recent years involved a breakage in the pipeline, running from the Tranmere oil jetty to the refinery in 1989 (Hall-Spencer 1989; Taylor 1991). In addition to the 1989 pipeline spill, a series of smaller incidents involving the Stanlow refinery and other industrial plants in the Mersey Basin have continued to cause problems, with a number of prosecutions following.

The morphology of the Mersey Basin and estuary worsens the effects of pollution. The narrow mouth of the estuary and its rather long flushing time (1–3 weeks) hinders dispersal of pollutants. The freshwater reaches of the River Mersey and the Manchester Ship Canal have been efficient conveyers of the accumulated wastes of much of industrial Lancashire and Cheshire, which are then discharged into the upper estuary (see National Rivers Authority 1995 for review).

Pollution problems in the Mersey Estuary have decreased since the 1960s (Wilson, D'arcy & Taylor 1988; Irish Sea Study Group 1990). In the 1970s Liverpool Corporation (see Porter 1973) initiated water quality improvements, and in 1985 the Department of the Environment launched the Mersey Basin Campaign. In addition to maintaining dissolved oxygen levels in the estuary and preventing the fouling of beaches by gross solids, the Mersey Basin Campaign aims to ensure that all rivers in the region meet class 2 classification requirements by 2010 (Codling, Nixon & Platt 1991; Wood-Griffiths 1993). The completion of the major interceptor pipeline leading to the Sandon Dock sewage treatment system will have a major impact on water quality in the Mersey Estuary (Taylor & Parker 1993) as will secondary treatment at Sandon, Wirral and Widnes works.

A comparison between the findings of early studies (e.g., Herdman 1920 for summary; Dunlop 1927; Fraser 1935, 1938; Bassindale 1938; Hardy 1995) and more recent surveys (Carter 1985; Wilson, D'arcy & Taylor 1988; Environmental Advisory Unit 1991; Environmental Resources Limited 1993) provides an indication of biological recovery in the River Mersey. Recently there has been an increase in species diversity recorded within the Mersey Estuary including both marine invertebrates and fish. Carter (1985) recorded a more diverse fauna than in previous studies, and suggested that this apparent improvement had occurred since the clean up campaign was initiated. That fish are being caught by anglers in the upper estuary (Wilson, D'arcy & Taylor 1988), is encouraging, as is the indication of a return of salmonids to the estuary (Zheng 1995; Fielding 1997). The increasing abundance and diversity of fish observed by anglers probably reflects similar changes in the state of an important estuarine food resource, the benthic fauna (Environmental Advisory Unit 1991). In 1987, a total of 40 fish species were recorded, ten of which were freshwater. The species dominating the fish communities were Sprat (*Sprattus sprattus*), Herring (*Clupea*

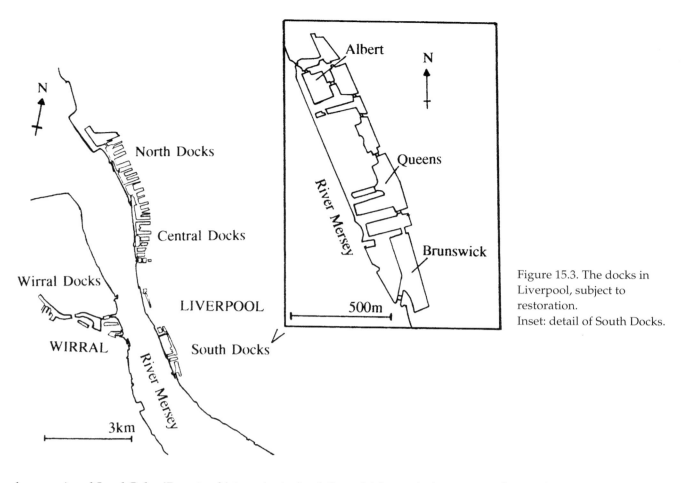

Figure 15.3. The docks in Liverpool, subject to restoration. Inset: detail of South Docks.

harengus) and Sand Goby (*Pomatoschistus minutus*), while flatfish, Whiting (*Merlangius merlangus*) and Eels were also abundant (Henderson 1988). Increases in fish eating birds have also occurred since the early 1970s, with Cormorant (*Phalacrocorax carbe*), Grebe and Grey Heron (*Ardea cincerea*) all rising in numbers as the abundance of their food increased (Thomason & Norman 1995). Unfortunately, heavy metals and other contaminants present risks for the human consumption of fish, particularly bottom dwelling species such as Plaice (*Pleuronectes platessa*) and Flounder, which have greater contact with the contaminated sediments (see Henderson 1988; Collings, Johnson & Leah 1996; Leah *et al.* 1997).

The maintenance of a dense population of Common Cockles and Baltic Tellin recorded in 1985 at Dingle after a long absence, and the sporadic appearance of mussels at four middle zone sites point to long-term water quality improvement in recent years. A highly significant improvement in the freshwater fauna noted at Warrington in 1987 also provides biological evidence for an overall improvement in water quality in the inner zone in the last few years (Holland 1989). There are still some puzzles; Laver Spire Shell (*Hydrobia ulvae)* and *Corophium volutator* (which should be found on suitable muddy shores) were apparently absent or scarce (Ghose 1979) but have been found again in recent years (Environment Resources Ltd 1993) with *Corophium* occurring in large numbers. At the time of writing a fairly typical estuarine fauna dominated by the Baltic Tellin, Common Cockle and Common Ragworm was present.

Restoration of the Docks on Merseyside

History of the Docks

Liverpool was well situated for the growing trade with Africa and the colonies of the Americas at the end of the 17th century. However, the waters of the Mersey Estuary presented a major restriction to the growth of shipping trade, with strong tides, large tidal range and shifting shoals. In response to this pressure, construction of the first commercial maritime dock in the world began in 1710 (Ritchie-Noakes 1984) within the confines of a shallow creek (known as 'The Pool'), which had previously provided some shelter for ships. This dock (Old Dock) retained water at all states of the tide and allowed unrestricted loading and unloading of ships directly into warehouses on the quayside. The construction of this dock sparked off a spurt of trade centred on Liverpool which was sustained by the continual construction of new docks and industrialisation of the hinterland of the Mersey Basin. The docks expanded in a narrow ribbon along the north-eastern bank of the River Mersey, finally forming two main connected series of docks, known respectively as the North Docks and the South Docks (Figure 15.3). A third major area of dock basins was constructed on the south-western bank of the river, stretching inland from Birkenhead. At its peak Liverpool boasted over 100 docks stretching 10km upstream from the river mouth. The construction of docks and other structures along the banks of the River Mersey constituted a major modification of the shoreline habitats. Intertidal areas of soft sediment and a natural seawater pool were replaced by the hard substrate of retaining walls, permanently submerged sediment and extensive areas of standing water.

With the gradual change to larger ships, containerised shipping and road haulage, the older commercial docks throughout the UK suffered a serious decline in trade in the second half of this century, many falling into complete disuse and decay. These docks were often situated on prime land close to the centre of major cities and were targeted for redevelopment as part of the urban regeneration schemes of the early 1980s. In the majority of cases the water-space of the docks was retained as a central feature. Such development schemes have been carried out for the whole of the South Docks and, more recently, smaller areas of Wirral and the North Docks.

The Mersey Estuary provides the source of water for all docks on Merseyside and consequently water quality has often been poor. This is not a problem for docks used for shipping, but redevelopment schemes rely on the appeal of a waterside location. The problems encountered have proved similar throughout the redeveloped docks on Merseyside. Essentially, they are caused by the silty, nutrient rich and often sewage contaminated water from the River Mersey, and are of four main types: (1) phytoplankton blooms, resulting in turbid or brightly coloured water; (2) periods of low oxygen concentration in deeper water, with associated release of foul smelling hydrogen sulphide gas and mortality of fauna; (3) contamination of water with faecal indicator organisms and hence possibly pathogens; (4) fine silt forming a thick layer on the dock bottom containing high organic matter and pollutants such as heavy metals and persistent organics. These water quality problems are typical of many redeveloped docks throughout the UK (Hendry *et al.* 1988; Conlan, White & Hawkins 1992; Hawkins *et al.* 1992).

Redevelopment, water quality and ecology of the South Docks – a case study

The decline of the South Docks began after the Second World War, and by 1972 the docks were closed to commercial shipping. Subsequently the gates of the docks were left open, and silt deposited by the tides quickly built up to 10m deep in places. In 1981 the Merseyside Development Corporation was formed with a responsibility to develop the docks as a commercial project with funding from both public and private sectors. Dredging of the docks began in 1981, water was gradually replaced as dredging progressed, finishing in 1985 with replacement of the double lock gates at Brunswick river entrance. Thus, the South Docks became an interconnected chain of docks varying in depth from

3.5m to 6m (Figure 15.2). The water is brackish with salinity between 24‰ and 28‰; about three-quarters the salinity of the open Irish Sea. The South Dock area was redeveloped for a variety of uses. The historic warehouses hold offices, residential accommodation, the Tate Gallery North, the Merseyside Maritime Museum and shops. The Albert Dock is a major tourist attraction; there is a watersports centre in Queen's Dock and a marina in Coburg Dock. A new Customs and Excise building spans the Graving Dock at Queen's Dock. Developments are continuing with further recreational and housing projects planned in the vicinity of Princes Dock.

Severe water quality problems were recorded in the South Docks in the years following redevelopment, despite limited exchange of water with the Mersey Estuary. A series of projects supervised from the Universities of Liverpool and Manchester began in 1988 (Mincher 1988; Lonsdale 1990; Allen 1992; Wilkinson 1995; Zheng 1995; Fielding 1997). Throughout the first summer of monitoring severe problems were evident, similar to those recorded in previous years by the Merseyside Development Corporation (Allen 1992). Persistent dinoflagellate blooms coloured the water orange-brown and caused poor water clarity. The dominant species was *Prorocentrum minimum* which has been linked to paralytic shellfish poisoning outbreaks in other areas. Water clarity was found to be a good indicator of phytoplankton density as suspended sediment loads were very low due to conditions of little water movement (Figure 15.3). Dissolved oxygen levels above the sediment were often very low in deeper docks. The associated foul odours and occasional dying fish detracted from the appeal of the area. Oxygen depletion was attributed to decay of phytoplankton cells and a high demand from the organically rich sediments, coupled with a tendency for thermal stratification (Hawkins *et al.* 1992; Allen *et al.* 1992).

Remedial measures to improve water quality were attempted, based on previous experience at Sandon Dock, a north Liverpool dock used for a while as a fish and shellfish farm established by the Mersey Dock & Harbour Company (with advice from the Department of Zoology of the University of Liverpool). Here, between 1978 and 1983, artificial mixing was used successfully to eliminate anoxic conditions, and improvements in water clarity were attributed to the filtering effect of the large Common Mussel population growing on ropes and walls in the dock (Russell *et al.* 1983). In the South Docks, the Queen's Graving Dock was selected as an experimental site due to its semi-isolated nature. A helical type air lift mixer was deployed in this dock by Parkman Engineering to which we added a large population of mussels in mesh tubing suspended from a buoyed longline (Allen *et al.* 1992; Allen & Hawkins 1993). Preliminary investigations of the walls and sediment throughout the South Docks at this time indicated that benthic communities were very poorly developed. However, in late summer and Autumn 1988, four months after the start of our project, a large natural settle-

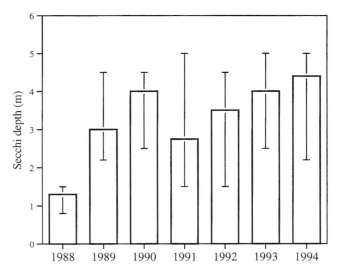

Figure 15.4. Improvements in water quality in the docks in Liverpool, as measured by Secchi disc extinction (i.e., depths at which a white disc lowered into the water disappears from view). Median ± ranges.

ment of mussels occurred in the South Docks. This may have been linked to much locking in and out of ships during the 'Tall Ships' race. Settlement was particularly dense in the Albert Dock, with mussels almost completely covering the dock wall. In the summers immediately following the introduction or settlement of mussels, marked improvements in water clarity were observed in both the Queen's Graving and Albert Docks (Figure 15.4). Bottom oxygen levels improved even in the Albert Dock, where no artificial mixing was initially used: with saturations of less than 20% being recorded for a maximum duration of almost three months in the summer of 1988, reducing to two to three weeks in 1989 and not occurring at all in 1990. Subsequently only very short periods of low bottom oxygen were recorded (e.g., in 1994) but oxygen levels were quickly raised using the simple mixing device installed in 1992 (Allen 1992; Zheng 1995; Wilkinson *et al.* 1996).

Water quality improvements were linked to a decline in the frequency and persistence of phytoplankton blooms, primarily of euglenoid and dinoflagellate species. The decline in phytoplankton blooms could not be explained by changes in nutrient availability, weather conditions or zooplankton grazing observed over the same period. Calculations of weight specific filtration rates for the mussel populations were made from published figures and from preliminary *in situ* measurements. It was estimated that the time taken for the Albert Dock mussels to filter a volume of water equal to that contained in the dock was in the order of one to three days (Allen & Hawkins 1993). It is thought likely, therefore, that the observed improvements in water quality were due, at least in part, to control of the phytoplankton populations by mussel filtration. Continued monitoring of water quality showed that improvements were sustained over a seven year period. During this time,

however, new recruitment of mussels on the walls was poor, and other filter feeding species became increasingly important, in particular a sea squirt *Ciona intestinalis*. In 1996 a new recruitment of mussels, which probably occurred in late 1995, became apparent (Fielding 1997). Therefore, while the relative abundance of species may fluctuate, the system appears to be sustainable with large numbers of filter feeders and good water quality.

The redevelopment of the South Docks and subsequent improvements in water quality have allowed colonisation by a relatively diverse estuarine/marine fauna. Once initial dredging of the South Docks was finished it is likely that the walls were affected by sediment, and the newly dredged bottom was devoid of benthic organisms. Since that time a gradual increase in the number of species recorded in the South Docks has been seen. By June 1988, one to five years after dredging was completed depending on the dock basin, encrusting bryozoans had become the major occupier of space on the walls with practically no other attached macrofauna present. The dense mussel settlement in Autumn 1988 provided a secondary substratum for a rich associated fauna (Allen, Wilkinson & Hawkins 1995). The Common Mussel very quickly became the dominant species and has remained so ever since. Recently, there has been an increase in the diversity and importance of other filter feeding species, particularly sea squirts (*Molgula manhattensis, Styela clava* and *Ciona intestinalis*) and the sponge *Halichondria bowerbanki*. The ephemeral nature of all the algal species so far recorded from the South Docks means that there has been no long-term dominance by this group (see chapter seventeen, this volume for details). Benthic fauna and flora are still largely confined to the wall. The majority of the species recorded from the sediment covered floor of the docks are short lived, and while longer lived species do colonise they apparently do not persist. Seventeen species of fish have been recorded from the South Docks to date, including a sea trout, *Salmo trutta* (Heaps 1988; Hawkins *et al.* 1993; Zheng 1995; Fielding 1997). The increased species diversity of the docks is reflected in the total species list which included over 90 species of macroflora and fauna by early 1994 (Allen, Wilkinson & Hawkins 1995).

New species are still being added to the list. Three of the species found in the South Docks may be regarded as lagoonal specialists (Barnes 1989). These are an amphipod *Corophium insidiosum*, the prawn *Palaemonetes varians* and a bryozoan *Conopeum seurati*. The potential of redeveloped docks as a resource in conservation of lagoonal and other species is an area warranting further investigation (Hawkins *et al.* 1993; Allen, Wilkinson & Hawkins 1995). The dockland areas on Merseyside represent a major habitat in the lower estuary, with the South Docks alone containing almost 30 hectares of water space.

Future prospects

Although Liverpool Bay and its estuaries are often considered as a highly polluted region, this chapter highlights the abundance of their marine life. Whilst not particularly diverse, in part due to a lack of habitat variety, the productivity of Liverpool Bay and its estuaries is high. They perform an important role as a nursery ground for Irish Sea juvenile fish and a winter feeding ground for birds from as far apart as Greenland and northern Russia. Various conservation designations testify to the recognition of the international importance of these feeding grounds (Taylor & Parker 1993; National Rivers Authority 1995; chapter seven, this volume).

In summary, following a concerted effort to improve the water quality there is a continuing recovery of the plant and animal populations which is reflected in an increasing biodiversity of the Mersey Estuary. Marine life *is* returning to the River Mersey. Broadscale and long term (20–30 years) improvements are, in part, an accidental by-product of de-industrialisation and depopulation of north-western England. They are also a response to environmental improvements throughout the region as part of the Mersey Basin Campaign. The neglect of the River Mersey since the Industrial Revolution was so extensive that a considerable time period seems likely before major recovery is evident. Complete recovery may never occur because of the amount of toxic material stored in waste tips and dumps lining the River Mersey and in the sediments themselves. The extensive reconfiguration of the estuary by engineering during development has inevitably led to irreversible change; but many of the newly created habitats provide opportunities for colonisation by a variety of species.

Locally, and on shorter timescales (<10 years), deliberate restoration of habitats is playing a role, coupled with natural advection of larvae and algal propagules from Liverpool Bay. Redevelopment of disused docks is ongoing in both Wirral and the North Docks. Experience from Sandon, the South Docks and Wirral waterfront has shown that water quality problems of severe phytoplankton blooms and anoxia are to be expected in newly redeveloped docks although remedial techniques are available (summarised in Allen & Hawkins 1993). Studies at Sandon and the South Docks have shown that a relatively diverse estuarine/marine flora and fauna can develop with time. Both the potential for biological diversity and good water quality could be increased if appropriate designs were considered at the planning stage. Such measures might include an increase in habitat diversity and the provision of suitable surfaces for colonisation by filter feeders, along with the use of water mixers where necessary.

Organisms can now live in the River Mersey and are not periodically killed by low oxygen. Ironically, organisms such as marine benthos and fish now survive long enough to accumulate pollutants: not only heavy metals (Leah *et al*. 1991; Leah, Evans & Johnson 1992) but also persistent organics (Thompson *et al*. 1996). Despite a possible risk to human health, the influence of these compounds on populations and communities is likely to be small. With tightening regulations, it is also unlikely that a major bird kill could occur again due to accumulation of pollutants, which pass unchanged up the food chain. Though by no means pristine, the River Mersey is recovering and beginning to match the biodiversity of the adjacent estuaries. The ecosystem is remarkably robust and has been enhanced by human provision of new habitats: coastal defences, forming artificial rocky shores and the 'lagoonoids' of the docks (Allen *et al*. 1995).

Acknowledgements

This work was mainly funded by the Merseyside Development Corporation with additional funding by the Department of Education Northern Ireland (SBW), NERC (NJF) and NMGM (IDW). Dr K.N. White, Dr H.D. Jones (University of Manchester) and Dr G. Russell (University of Liverpool) are thanked for their various inputs into the 'docks' project. Tony Tollitt, Jimmy McGill, Vanessa Wanstall, Wei Zhong Zheng and Gill Heyes are thanked for their help in the field.

References

Al-Masnad, F. (1991). *An assessment of the biological status of the Dee Estuary*. PhD thesis, University of Manchester.

Allen, J.R. (1992). *Hydrography, ecology and water quality management of the South Docks, Liverpool*. PhD thesis, University of Liverpool.

Allen, J.R., Hawkins, S.J., Russell, G.R. & White, K.N. (1992). Eutrophication and urban renewal: problems and perspectives for the management of disused docks. *Science of the Total Environment, Supplement 1992*, pp. 1283–95, Elsevier Science Publishers B.V., Amsterdam, Netherlands.

Allen J.R. & Hawkins S.J. (1993). Can biological filtration be used to improve water quality? *Urban Waterside Regeneration, problems and prospects* (eds K.N. White, E.G. Bellinger, A.J. Saul, M. Symer & K. Hendry), pp. 377–85. Ellis Horwood series in Environmental Management, Science and Technology, Ellis Horwood Press, Hemel Hempstead.

Allen, J.R., Wilkinson, S.B. & Hawkins, S.J. (1995). Redeveloped docks as artificial lagoons: the development of brackish-water communities and potential for conservation of lagoonal species. *Aquatic Conservation: Marine and Freshwater Ecosystems*, **168**, 299–309.

Bamber, R.N. (1988). *A survey of the intertidal soft-bottomed fauna of the Mersey Estuary*. March 1988, CEGB.

Barnes, R.S.K. (1989). The coastal lagoons of Britain: an overview and conservation appraisal. *Biological Conservation*, **49**, 295–313.

Bassindale, R. (1938). The intertidal fauna of the Mersey Estuary. *Journal of the Marine Biological Association of the U.K.*, **23**, 83–98.

Bennett, C., Curtis, M. & Fairhurst, C. (1995). Recent changes in the Mersey Estuary 1958–1988. *The Mersey Estuary – Naturally Ours* (eds M.S. Curtis, D. Norman & I.D. Wallace), pp. 12–23. Mersey Estuary Conservation Group, Warrington.

Bull, K.R., Every, W.J., Freestone, P., Hall, J.R. & Osborn, D. (1983). Alkyl lead pollution and bird mortalities on the Mersey Estuary 1979–1981. *Environmental Pollution*, **31 (Series A)**, 239–59.

Burd, A.C. (1947). Faunal notes on Hilbre. *Proceedings of the Liverpool Naturalists' Field Club for 1946*, **1946**, 29–30.

Burt, A.J. (1989). An ecosystem approach to the Mersey barrage, Liverpool. *The Proceedings of the Mersey Barrage Symposium* (eds B. Jones & B. Norgain), pp. 17–26. The North of England Zoological Society, Chester.

Byerley, I. (1854). The fauna of Liverpool. *Proceedings of the Literary and Philosophical Society of Liverpool*, **8**, Appendix.

Carter, J.J. (1985). *The influence of environmental contamination on the fauna of the Mersey Estuary*. MSc thesis, University of Manchester.

Clark, R.B. (1989). *Marine Pollution*. (2nd edn). Clarenden Press, Oxford.

Codling, I.D., Nixon, S.C. & Platt, H.M. (1991). *The Mersey Estuary. An assessment of the biological status of intertidal sediments.* Report to the National Rivers Authority. WRC report No. NR 2757, April 1991, 54 pp. Water Research Centre, Medmenham, Buckinghamshire.

Conlan, K., Hendry, K., White, K.N. & Hawkins, S.J. (1988). Disused docks as habitats for estuarine fish: a case study of Preston dock. *Journal of Fish Biology*, **33 (Supplement A)**, 85–91.

Conlan, K., White, K.N. & Hawkins, S.J. (1992). The hydrography and ecology of a re-developed brackish-water dock. *Estuarine, Coastal and Shelf Science*, **35**, 435–52.

Corlett, J. (1948). Rates of settlement and growth of the 'pile' fauna of the Mersey Estuary. *Proceedings and Transactions of the Liverpool Biological Society*, **56**, 2–25.

Collings, S.E., Johnson, M.S. & Leah, R.T. (1996). Metal contamination of angler-caught fish from the Mersey Estuary. *Marine Environmental Research*, **41**, 281–97.

Craggs, J.D. (ed.) (1982). *Hilbre the Cheshire Island its history and natural history*. Liverpool University Press, Liverpool.

Cunningham, J.T. (1898). *The natural history of the marketable marine fishes of the British Isles*. Macmillan and Co., London.

Curtis, M.S., Norman, D. & Wallace, I.D. (eds) (1995). *The Mersey Estuary – Naturally Ours*. Mersey Estuary Conservation Group, Warrington.

Darby, D., Lawrence, S., Wolff, G. & Hawkins, S. (1994). *Environmental Assessment for blocks 110/13 and 110/15, Liverpool Bay*. Report commissioned by Hamilton Oil Company, London.

Davies, J. (1992). *Littoral survey of the Ribble, Duddon and Ravenglass Estuary systems, east basin of the Irish Sea*. Joint Nature Conservation Committee report, No. 37. (Marine Nature Conservation Review Report, No. MNCR/SR/21.)

Davies, L.M. (1991). *Littoral survey of the coast from Crosby to Fleetwood*. Nature Conservancy Council, CSD report No. MNCR/SR/17.

Dempsey, C.H. (1989). Implications of a barrage for present and future fisheries in the Mersey Estuary. *The Mersey Barrage. The Proceedings of the Mersey Barrage Symposium* (eds B. Jones & B. Norgain), pp. 72–91 The North of England Zoological Society, Chester.

Dent, D. (1986). *A survey of the mussel beds on the Ribble Estuary at Lytham*. BSc thesis, Department of Zoology, University of Manchester. (Copy at Department of Zoology, Liverpool Museum.)

Department of the Environment (1972). *Out of Sight, Out of Mind. Report of the Department of the Environment Working Party on sludge disposal in Liverpool Bay*. HMSO, London.

Dickson, R.R. & Boelens, R.G.V. (1988). *The status of current knowledge on anthropogenic influences in the Irish Sea*. I.C.E.S. Co-op Rep. No. 155, International Council for Exploration of the Sea, Copenhagen, Denmark.

Doody, J.P. (ed.) (1984). *Spartina anglica in Great Britain. A report of a meeting held at Liverpool University on 10th November 1982*. NCC. (Focus on marine nature conservation, No. 5), Peterborough.

Dunlop, G.A. (1927). Early Warrington fisheries: an historical sketch. *Proceedings of the Warrington Literary and Philosophical Society*, **1927–1929**, 7–20.

Environmental Advisory Unit of Liverpool University Ltd (1991). *The Mersey oil spill project 1989–90. A summary report of the studies undertaken into the long term environmental impacts of the August 1989 oil-spill into the Mersey Estuary.* Mersey Oil Spill Advisory Group, Liverpool.

Environmental Resources Limited (1993). *Hamilton and Hamilton oil north gas platforms, block 110/13 Liverpool Bay: environmental assessment*. ERL, London.

Fielding, N.J. (1997). *Fish and benthos communities in regenerated dock systems on Merseyside*. PhD thesis, University of Liverpool.

Fraser, J.H. (1931). *The fauna and flora of the Mersey Estuary with special reference to pollution and sedimentary deposits*. MSc thesis, University of Liverpool.

Fraser, J.H. (1932). Observations on the fauna and constituents of an estuarine mud in a polluted area. *Journal of the Marine Biological Association of the UK.*, **18**, 69–85.

Fraser, J.H. (1935). The fauna of the Liverpool Bay shrimping grounds and the Morecambe Bay spawning grounds as revealed by the use of a beam-trawl. *Proceedings and Transactions of the Liverpool Biological Society*, **48**, 65–78.

Fraser, J.H. (1938). The fauna of fixed and floating structures in the Mersey Estuary and Liverpool Bay. *Proceedings and Transactions of the Liverpool Biological Society*, **51**, 1–21.

Gardiner, A.P. (1950). Recorder's report: marine Mollusca. *Journal of Conchology*, **23**, 124–26.

Garwood, P. & Foster-Smith, R. (1991). *Intertidal from Rhos Point to New Brighton*. Report contracted by the University of Newcastle and Dove Marine Laboratory, Cullercoats. Nature Conservancy Council, CSD Report No. 1194.

Gillham, R.M. (1978). *An ecological investigation of the intertidal benthic invertebrates of the Dee Estuary*. PhD thesis, University of Salford.

Ghose, R.B. (1979). *An ecological investigation into the invertebrates of the Mersey Estuary*. PhD thesis, University of Salford.

Hall-Spencer, J. (1989). Pipeline leak into the Mersey. *Marine Pollution Bulletin*, **20**, 480.

Hardy, E. (1995). An introduction to the natural history of the Mersey Estuary. *The Mersey Estuary – Naturally Ours* (eds M.S. Curtis, D. Norman & I.D. Wallace), pp. 24–32. Mersey Estuary Conservation Group, Warrington.

Hartnoll, R.G. (1993). Shallow subtidal hard substrata. *The coast of North Wales and North West England, an environmental appraisal* (eds P.M. Taylor & J.G. Parker), pp. 42–43. Hamilton Oil Company, London.

Harvey-Gibson, R.J. (1890). Report on the marine algae of the LMBC district. *Proceedings and Transactions of the Liverpool Biological Society*, **3**, 128–54.

Harvey-Gibson, R.J. (1891). A revised list of the marine algae of the LMBC district. *Proceedings and Transactions of the Liverpool Biological Society*, **5**, 83–142.

Hawkins, S.J. (1993). Coastal habitats, communities and species. *The coast of North Wales and North West England: an environmental appraisal* (eds P.M. Taylor & J.G. Parker), pp. 19–24, Hamilton Oil Company, London.

Hawkins, S.J., Allen, J.R., Russell, G., White, K.N., Conlan, K., Hendry, K. & Jones, H.D. (1992). Restoring and managing disused docks in inner city areas. *Restoring the Nation's Marine Environment* (ed. G.W. Thayer), pp. 473–542. National Oceanic and Atmospheric Administration, Maryland Sea Grant College publication, Maryland, USA.

Hawkins, S.J., Allen, J.R., Russell, G., Eaton, J.W., Wallace, I., Jones, H.D., White, K.N. & Hendry, K. (1993). Former commercial docks as a resource in urban conservation and education. *Urban Waterside Regeneration, problems and prospects* (eds K.N. White, E.G. Bellinger, A.J. Saul, M. Symer & K. Hendry), pp. 386–99. Ellis Horwood series in Environmental Management, Science and Technology, Ellis Horwood, Press, Hemel Hempstead.

Hayward, P.J. & Ryland, J.S. (1995). *Handbook of the Marine*

Fauna of North-West Europe. Oxford University Press, Oxford.

Head, P.C., D'arcy, B.J. & Osbaldeston, P.J. (1980). *The Mersey Estuary bird mortality.* Autumn-winter 1979, preliminary report. Scientific Report DSS-EST-80-1, North West Water.

Heaps, L. (1988). *The fish populations of the South Docks, Liverpool.* BSc. Honours project, Department of Environmental Biology, University of Manchester. (Copy at University of Manchester Library.)

Henderson, P.A. (1988). The structure of estuarine fish communities. *Journal of Fish Biology,* 33 (Supplement A), 223–25.

Herdman, W.A. (1920). Summary of the history and work of the Liverpool Marine Biology committee. *Proceedings and Transactions of the Liverpool Biological Society,* 34, 23–74.

Hendry, K. (1993). Former commercial docks as a resource in urban conservation and education. *Urban Waterside Regeneration, problems and prospects* (eds K.N. White, E.G. Bellinger, A.J. Saul, M. Symer & K. Hendry), pp. 386–99. Ellis Horwood series in Environmental Management, Science and Technology, Ellis Horwood Press, Hemel Hempstead.

Hendry, K., White, K.N., Conlan, K., Jones, H.D., Bewsher, A.D., Proudlove, G.S., Porteous, G., Bellinger, E.G. & Hawkins, S.J. (1988). *Investigations into the ecology and potential use for nature conservation of disused docks.* (Contractor: Department of Environmental Biology, University of Manchester.) Nature Conservancy Council, CSD Report No. 848.

Holland, D. (1989). 'Alive and Kicking'. The fish and invertebrates of the Mersey Estuary. *Proceedings of the Mersey Barrage Symposium* (eds B. Jones & B. Norgain), pp. 42–63. North of England Zoological Society, Chester.

Holland, D.G. & Harding, J.P.C. (1984). (ed. B.A. Whitton), pp. 113–44, *Ecology of European Rivers.*

The Irish Sea Study Group (1990). *The Irish Sea. An Environmental Review. Introduction and Overview.* Liverpool University Press, Liverpool.

James, C.J. & Gibson, R. (1980). The distribution of the polychaete *Capitella capitata* (Fabricus) in dock sediments. *Estuarine and Coastal Marine Science,* 10, 671–83.

Jones, P.G.W. & Head, P.C. (1991). Turning the tide on pollution – the Mersey Estuary. *Proceedings of the International conference on environmental pollution (1),* Lisbon, Portugal.

Law, R.J., Jones, B.R., Baker, J.R., Kennedy, S., Milne, R. & Morris, R.J. (1992). Trace metals in the livers of marine mammals from the Welsh coast and Irish Sea. *Marine Pollution Bulletin,* 24, 296–304.

Leah, R.T., Evans, S.T., Johnson, M.S. & Collings, R.T. (1991). Spatial patterns in accumulation of Hg by fish from the north-east Irish Sea. *Marine Pollution Bulletin,* 22, 172–75.

Leah, R.T., Evans, S.J. & Johnson, M.S. (1992). Arsenic in plaice (*Pleuronectes platessa*) and whiting (*Merlangius merlangus*) from the north east Irish Sea. *Marine Pollution Bulletin,* 24, 544–49.

Leah, R.T., Johnson, M.S., Connor, L. & Levence, C. (1997). Polychlorinated biphenyls in fish and shellfish from the Mersey Estuary and Liverpool Bay. *Marine Environmental Research,* 43, 345–58.

Liverpool Bay Study Group (1975). *Liverpool Bay. An assessment of present knowledge.* The Natural Environment Research Council publications series 'C' No. 14.

Lonsdale, K. (1990). *The hydrology and ecology of the Albert Dock complex, Liverpool with particular reference to fish populations.* MSc thesis, Department of Environmental Biology, University of Manchester.

McMillan, N.F. (1975). "Wrecks" of marine invertebrates in the Liverpool Area 1946–1975. *Lancashire and Cheshire Fauna Society Publication,* 67, 21–22.

Meng, F.H. (1976). *A pollution study of River Mersey by using natural algal communities and laboratory bioassay.* MSc thesis, University of Liverpool.

Mersey & Weaver River Authority (1972). *Seventh Annual Report.*

Mills, D.J.L. (1991). *Marine Nature Conservation Review. Benthic marine ecosystems in Great Britain: a review of current knowledge. Cardigan Bay, North Wales, Liverpool Bay and the Solway (MNCR coastal sectors 10 and 11).* Nature Conservancy Council, Peterborough.

Mincher, P.T. (1988). *The hydrography and ecology of the Liverpool docks.* MSc thesis, University of Manchester.

Moore, D.M. (1978). Seasonal changes in distribution of intertidal macrofauna in the lower Mersey Estuary. *Estuarine and Coastal Marine Science,* 7, 117–25.

National Rivers Authority (1995). *The Mersey Estuary. A report on environmental quality.* Water quality series No. 23. HMSO, London.

Norton, M.G., Rowlatt, S.M. & Nunny, R.S. (1984). Sewage sludge dumping and contamination of Liverpool Bay sediments. *Estuarine, Coastal and Shelf Science,* 19, 69–87.

Osborn, D., Every, W.J. & Bull, K.R. (1983). The toxicity of trialkyl lead compounds to birds. *Environmental Pollution,* 31 (Series A), 261–75.

Perkins, E.J. (1956). The fauna of a sandbank in the mouth of the Dee Estuary. *Annals and Magazine of Natural History.* 9, Series 12, 112–28.

Pierce, E.L. (1941). The occurrence and breeding of *Sagitta elegans* Verill and *Sagitta setosa* J.Muller in parts of the Irish Sea. *Journal of the Marine Biological Association of the U.K.,* 25, 113–24.

Popham, E.J. (1966). The littoral fauna of the Ribble Estuary, Lancashire, England. *Oikos,* 17, 19–32.

Porter, E. (1973). *Pollution in four industrial estuaries. Four case studies for the Royal Commission on Environmental Pollution.* HMSO, London.

Readman, J.W., Preston, M.R. & Montoura, R.F.C. (1986). An investigated technique to quantify sewage, oil and PAH pollution in estuaries and coastal environments. *Marine Pollution Bulletin,* 17(7), 298–308.

Rees, E.I.S. (1975). Benthic and littoral fauna of Liverpool Bay. *Liverpool Bay An assessment of present knowledge.* (Compiled by members of the Liverpool Bay study group.) The Natural Environment Research Council publications series 'C' No. 14.

Rees, E.I.S., Nicholaidou, A. & Laskaridou, P. (1977). The effects of storms on the dynamics of shallow water benthic associations. *Proceedings of the 11th European Marine Biology Symposium* (eds B.F. Keegan, P. O'Ceidigh & P.J.S. Boaden), pp. 265–474. Pergamon Press, London.

Rees H.L., Rowlatt, S.M., Limpenny, D.S., Rees, E.I.S. & Rolfe, M.S. (1992). *Benthic studies at dredged material sites in Liverpool Bay.* Ministry of Agriculture, Fisheries and Food Directorate of Fisheries Research. Aquatic Environment Monitoring report, Number 28.

Rice, K.A. & Putwain, P.D. (1987). *The Dee and Mersey Estuaries: environmental background.* Shell UK Limited, London.

Riley, J.P. & Towner, J.V. (1984). The distribution of alkyl lead species in the Mersey Estuary. *Marine Pollution Bulletin,* 15, (4), 153–58.

Ritchie-Noakes, N. (1984). *Liverpool's historic waterfront – The world's first mercantile dock system.* HMSO, London.

Russell, G. (1972). Phytosociological studies on a two-zone shore. I. Basic pattern. *Journal of Ecology,* 60, 539–45.

Russell, G. (1973). Phytosociological studies on a two-zone shore. II. Community structure. *Journal of Ecology,* 61, 525–36.

Russell, G. (1982). The Marine Algae. *Hilbre. The Cheshire Island: its history and natural history* (ed. J.D. Craggs), pp. 65–74. Liverpool University Press, Liverpool.

Russell, G., Hawkins, S.J., Evans, L.C., Jones, H.D. & Holmes, G.D. (1983). Restoration of a disused dock basin as a habitat for marine benthos and fish. *Journal of Applied Ecology* 20, 43–58.

Stopford, S.C. (1951). An ecological survey of the Cheshire foreshore of the Dee Estuary. *Journal of Animal Ecology*, **20**, 103–22.

Taylor, P.M. (1991). A pipeline spill into the Mersey Estuary, England. *Proceedings 1991 International Oil Spill Conference*, pp. 399–405. American Petroleum Institute, Washington DC, USA.

Taylor, P.M. & Parker, J.G. (1993). *The Coast of North Wales & North West England. An Environmental Appraisal.* Hamilton Oil Company Ltd., London.

Thomason, G. & Norman, D. (1995). Wildfowl and waders of the Mersey Estuary. *The Mersey Estuary – Naturally Ours* (eds M.S. Curtis, D. Norman & I.D. Wallace), pp. 33–59. Mersey Estuary Conservation Group, Warrington.

Thompson, A., Allen, J.R., Dodoo, D., Hunter, J., Hawkins, S.J. & Wolff, G.A. (1996). Distributions of chlorinated biphenyls in mussels and sediments from Great Britain and the Irish Sea Coast. *Marine Pollution Bulletin*, **32(2)**, 232–37.

Wilkinson, S.B. (1995). *The ecology of benthos in Liverpool Docks.* PhD thesis, University of Liverpool.

Wilkinson, S.B., Zheng, W., Allen, J.R., Fielding, N.J., Wanstall, V.C., Russell, G. & Hawkins, S.J. (1996). Water quality improvements in Liverpool Docks: the role of filter feeders in algal and nutrient dynamics. *P.S.Z.N.I. Marine Ecology*, **17(1–3)**, 197–211.

Wilson, K.W., D'arcy, B.J. & Taylor, S. (1988). The return of fish to the Mersey Estuary. *Journal of Fish Biology*, **33 (Supplement A)**, 235–38.

Wood-Griffiths, L. (1993). *Mersey Estuary management plan. Report on nature conservation and water pollution.* Department of Civic Design, University of Liverpool, Liverpool.

Zheng, W. (1995). *Water quality problems of the Liverpool docks system in relation to the adjacent estuary.* PhD thesis, University of Liverpool.

CHAPTER SIXTEEN

Saltmarshes and sand dunes – natural or not

J.P. DOODY

Introduction

Saltmarshes and sand dunes are described in most ecological text books as exhibiting primary succession. Coastal habitats are also often described as being amongst the most natural, and saltmarshes and sand dunes are the most frequently quoted examples. The classic studies of the saltmarshes and sand dunes on the north Norfolk coast (for example Chapman 1938, 1941, 1959; Steers 1960) or the Dovey Estuary in western Wales (Yapp, Johns & Jones 1917) emphasised the natural status of the vegetation. Indeed these studies looked at systems where the ecological processes appeared to have been virtually free from direct human influence.

The results of these and other studies often describe the vegetation as a series of types progressing from the early pioneer stages to more complex forms, which are related to the physical parameters affecting their development. In the case of saltmarshes and sand dunes this includes tides, waves and winds, sediment and soil characteristics. This has led to the impression that the process of succession takes place in a sequence which is determined exclusively by natural forces. Selection of areas for conservation designation frequently uses the existence of recognised vegetation patterns based on the understanding of this 'ecological succession'. Subsequent management often seeks to maintain this pattern in the face of change. This chapter examines the evidence from the natural world for the existence of natural habitats and asks if the influence of man has reached such a point that natural habitats (and nature reserves) in north-western Europe can only be sustained with direct human intervention.

Saltmarshes and sand dunes – as ecological systems

That there are zonations which can be attributed to environmental gradients in coastal vegetation is not in dispute. There are numerous examples of primary succession where specialised plant species adapted to the rigors of their environment, provide the main agents in stabilisation. Anyone looking at the early stages in saltmarsh or sand dune growth will need little convincing that there is a natural pattern to the mosaic of vegetation, which can be related to the sequence of development.

Accretion of sediment on the tidal flat surface occurs around primary colonisers of mudflats such as Common Glasswort (*Salicornia europea*) or Annual Sea-blite (*Suaeda maritima*) in north-western Europe. In saltmarshes these pioneers, in addition to being tolerant of immersion in sea water, depend on periods during the early stages in plant establishment when they are free from tidal movement. As sediment height increases the marsh is subject to progressively fewer tidal inundations, less sediment is deposited and a richer complement of plants and animals replaces the specialist salt tolerant species (Ranwell 1972a). Thus from an ecological point of view saltmarshes exhibit primary succession and a parallel spatial zonation related to tidal inundation, 'largely without human interference' which makes them ideal for studying the processes associated with 'natural' vegetation development (Gray 1992).

In the early stages of dune growth there are similarly a few species which can tolerate inundation with sea water or spray, rapid changes in rates of sand deposition, desiccation and exposure. The sometimes spectacular development of foredunes is directly related to the ability of plants such as Sand Couch (*Elytrigia juncea*) and Marram (*Ammophila arenaria*) to withstand burial by sand, together with the other stresses present in this unstable and inhospitable environment (Ranwell 1972a). In both cases the resulting succession is often described as a zonation which reflects the physical parameters influencing its development and shown in text books as a linear profile through the saltmarsh or sand dune.

Saltmarshes and sand dunes – as complex systems

Saltmarshes are much more complex systems than the straightforward succession described above appears to suggest. Accretion does result in more diverse forms of vegetation and associated animal species, and transitions to terrestrial vegetation can be the most complex. However, this apparently simple picture hides a complex relationship. Sea-level change may introduce long-term patterns which are difficult to separate from sequences of erosion and regrowth as estuary channels move. A series of steps can form as new saltmarsh develops to seaward of the eroding cliffed saltmarsh edge, as occurred in the Mersey Estuary before the building of the Manchester Ship Canal (Bennett, Curtis & Fairhurst 1995) or on the Solway in south-western Scotland (Marshall 1962). Salt-pans represent another element in the complex mosaic, and deposits of seaweed on the tide-line may smother the surface vegetation creating further spatial variation as the strandline deposits rot.

Sand dunes also show forms of successional development in the early stages of growth by the accretion of sand, aided by specialist plants. However, once the main body of the dune is formed, other processes come into play and the change from mobile foredunes and yellow dunes to grassland, heath, scrub and woodland is rarely a straightforward progression. Blowouts occur with or without the intervention of man and can be the precursors of dune slacks (Ranwell 1972a). Similarly the reprofiling of dune ridges under the influence of changing wind patterns brings an infinitely variable topography, the origins of which may be difficult or impossible to unravel.

Against this background of change associated with the physical characteristics of the habitat, the most common use of both saltmarshes and dunes is by grazing animals. Herbivores such as ducks and geese, on saltmarsh, and Rabbits (*Oryctolagus cuniculus*) on sand dunes, probably grazed both habitats before their extensive use by domestic stock. In addition to the direct effect on the nature of the vegetation, they also introduce structural change in the habitat through physical impacts such as trampling and burrowing.

Grazing occurs extensively on saltmarshes in Great Britain (especially in the west and north) and throughout the rest of north-western Europe (Dijkema 1984). It has a major effect on the structure and species composition of the marsh. In general, as grazing intensity increases, there is a loss of structural diversity as the standing crop is removed. At the same time grazing-sensitive species are removed from the sward, reducing species diversity. The loss of structural diversity also reduces the range and diversity of invertebrates and breeding bird populations (Figure 16.1). However, as the sward becomes shorter and dominated by tillering grasses (*Puccinellia maritima* and *Festuca rubra*), it is favoured by grazing ducks and geese. These effects are more pronounced as other, human activities associated with 'improving' grazing may cause further change. On saltmarshes these may include drainage and erection of summer dykes or banks.

On calcareous sand dunes grazing has helped to create a rich flora and fauna similar to that of calcareous grasslands. Continued grazing is necessary for the survival of the rich plant communities and helps prevent the growth of course grasses and scrub. On acid dunes, where heath is dominated by Heather (*Calluna vulgaris*), Crowberry (*Empetrum nigrum*) or other heathers, lower levels of grazing may also be important for maintaining the status quo, and preventing scrub development at the expense of the heath. In the past overgrazing on the dunes by cattle and sheep, particularly when combined with burrowing Rabbits, can lead to unstable conditions and eventually, large-scale erosion. Although this has resulted in many dunes where erosion control is a major consideration (Ranwell & Boar 1986) it can introduce further patterns into the vegetation as recolonisation takes place following removal of the destabilising vector.

Other human influences – the history of intervention in UK and Europe

As has already been intimated above, coastal habitats are

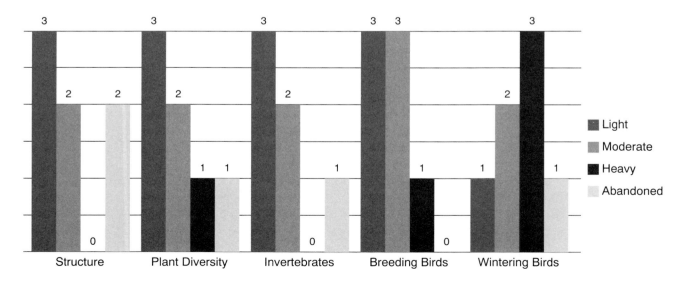

Figure 16.1. Summary of nature conservation interest in relation to grazing levels on saltmarshes in north-west Europe.

0–3 indicates level of nature conservation interest for each component of the system in relation to grazing pressure:
0 – little or no interest; 1 – minor interest; 2 – moderate interest; 3 – major and significant interest.

often considered amongst the most natural ecosystems. However, in addition to their extensive use by grazing animals, they have also been directly modified by human activities over many years. On the sedimentary shorelines of the Wash, artificial embankments to enable salt making, were present in some numbers in Roman times (Simmons 1980). Hay making, oyster cultivation, turf and reed cutting, and samphire gathering all take place or have taken place on upper marshes throughout Europe (Dijkema 1984). The deliberate planting of Common Cord-grass (*Spartina anglica*) – itself a hybrid fashioned from the interaction of a native and an introduced species – (Marchant 1967) has also been a major influence.

Occupation of sand dunes probably dates back several thousand years, and many sites have examples of middens with the remains of shellfish on them. An analysis of flint tools suggests that settlers of Torrs Warren, in south-western Scotland, may have appeared between 5,500–7,000 years ago (Coles 1964). It seems that cultivation has taken place since then, and in 1572 three farm houses were recorded on the Warren. As long as 4,500 years ago a small settlement existed on the shore of Skaill Bay in Orkney. The Neolithic people who inhabited the site, known today as 'Skara Brae', seem to have been agriculturists as well as hunter/gatherers (Ritchie & Ritchie 1978) until their village was overwhelmed by a sand storm. Since Medieval times dunes were used extensively as rabbit warrens (Thompson & Worden 1956), and are grazed by domestic stock to the present day.

More recent human activity has included major direct loss of habitat and the impact of this is considered in more detail in relation to the saltmarshes and sand dunes of the Mersey Basin.

The Dee, Mersey and Ribble Estuaries

Enclosure of the upper Dee Estuary began around 1730 and continued up to 1986 (Figure 16.2a). Much of the land gained was at the expense of the saltmarsh and was subsequently developed for industry, housing, roads and agriculture including grazing marsh. It is estimated that approximately 4,600ha were enclosed between 1737 and 1877 (Rice & Putwain 1987) for residential land, agriculture and industry. This gradual reduction of the size of the estuary was followed by an extension of saltmarsh. This is thought to be partly due to the reduction in tidal volume, which in turn has reduced scour and helped accelerate the natural sedimentation tendency within the estuary. This process was aided by the introduction of Common Cord-grass around 1930, and since then some 1500ha of intertidal mud was naturally 'reclaimed'. Marker (1962) estimated that at Parkgate between 1947 and 1963 vertical accretion of the *Spartina* marsh took place at a rate of approximately 25mm per year.

In the Mersey Estuary much of the tidal land around Frodsham was cut off from the main river by the building of the Manchester Ship Canal between 1887 and 1893. The land is now used for industry and agriculture. This not only had a profound effect on the shoreline of the south side of the estuary, but it also influenced the way in which the estuary channels behaved and their effect on the balance between erosion and accretion of saltmarsh (Bennett *et al.* 1995). When taken together with the major port and other infrastructure developments, the shoreline of the estuary has a high proportion of its waterfront composed of vertical sea-walls. Transitions to non-tidal habitats are virtually non-existent.

Land claim on the Ribble Estuary is less well documented, though the progress of the more recent loss of tidal land for agricultural use has been studied (Figure 16.3). Enclosure for industry and agriculture took place

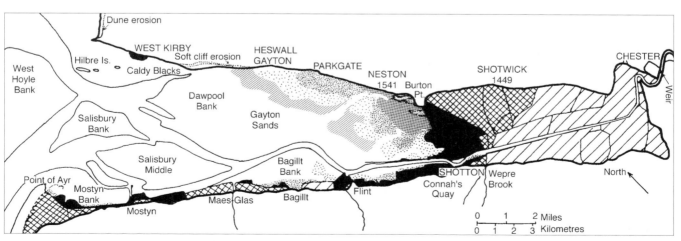

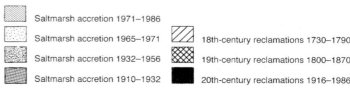

Figure 16.2. (a) Enclosure of the Dee Estuary 1730–1986;
(b) saltmarsh accretion 1910–1986.

Saltmarsh accretion 1971–1986

Saltmarsh accretion 1965–1971

Saltmarsh accretion 1932–1956

Saltmarsh accretion 1910–1932

18th-century reclamations 1730–1790

19th-century reclamations 1800–1870

20th-century reclamations 1916–1986

during the last century. An increase in siltation and salt-marsh growth is attributed to the development of industry and associated control of the river flows including the training of the Ribble Channel in the 1840s (Berry 1967; Robinson 1984). As in the Dee Estuary the growth of the saltmarsh appears to have been aided by the planting of Common Cord-grass, in this case in 1932. Not only did this fundamentally change the nature of the saltmarsh vegetation, but it also created concerns for amenity interests, as the grass expanded onto the Southport beaches (Truscott 1984). The extent of salt-marsh loss in the major estuaries of the north-west before 1911 is shown in Table 16.1.

Further enclosures have taken place since then including 320ha within the Ribble Estuary in the 1980s. Although not dealt with in detail here, other human uses of these estuaries have had a further effect on their status for both economic and cultural use, and nature conservation. Pollution, by a variety of heavy metals, sewage and radioactive discharges together with oxygen depletion, has affected fisheries and been linked to the death of bird populations in the past, particularly in the Mersey Estuary.

The Sefton coast

The original area of blown sand along the Sefton coast is amongst the most extensive in Great Britain. The original dune landscape may have extended for approxi-

Site name	Area (ha) enclosed	Source
Dee Estuary	3,160 (by 1857)	(Royal Commission on Coastal Erosion and Afforestation 1911)
	4,600 (1737–1877)	(Rice & Putwain 1987)
Mersey	492 (19th century)	(Royal Commission on Coastal Erosion and Afforestation 1911)
The Ribble	1,960 (19th century)	(Buck 1993)

Table 16.1. Loss of estuarine habitat.

mately 3,000ha, though today the area of vegetated dune is much smaller, probably about 2,113ha (all dunes in Merseyside). In Medieval times uncontrolled use of the dunes for grazing, use of Marram for thatch and cattle bedding lead to massive dune erosion. Greater control of the use of the dune, including prohibition of Marram cutting and the requirement for tenants to spend up to 6 days per year planting the species helped reinstate a more stable dune. By the early 1800s what was considered to be a more acceptable dune landscape had been created which, on the face of it, appeared largely unaffected by human activity. Things began to change again, and in the early 1900s further dune stabilisation, Asparagus (*Asparagus officinalis* ssp. *officinalis*) planting and afforestation all influenced the development of the

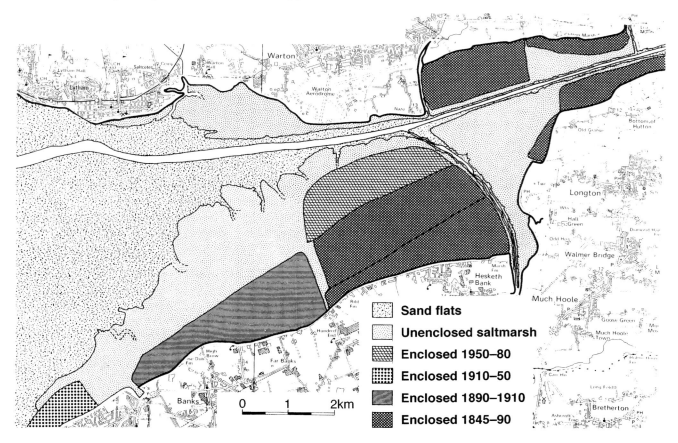

Sand flats
Unenclosed saltmarsh
Enclosed 1950–80
Enclosed 1910–50
Enclosed 1890–1910
Enclosed 1845–90

0   1   2km

Figure 16.3. Saltmarsh enclosure in the Ribble Estuary, 1845–1980.

dune. It was during this period that Formby Point began to erode, following a period between 1845 and 1906 when it grew seawards under the influence of active management. The advent of tourism, promoted further stabilisation, including the introduction of Sea-buckthorn (*Hippophae rhamnoides*), and these and other influences such as the building of a golf course, rifle range and sand extraction reduced the area of open dune (Atkinson & Houston 1993).

The evidence, therefore, from the Mersey Basin and elsewhere shows that both saltmarshes and sand dunes have been influenced by human activity for centuries. This has ranged from total destruction of the habitat, to modification of natural forms and the creation of areas which appear natural but are largely the result of human intervention. Understanding the extent of human influence is a key element in assessing the value of habitats and sites for conservation purposes, and is crucial to management decisions.

Nature conservation and human activity

The identification of saltmarsh and sand dunes as important examples of particular types of habitats is based on the notion that there is a classification which can be recognised in the field, and that this can provide a basis for assessment. In Britain the early pioneers of the conservation movement, notably Tansley, described the vegetation of the British Isles in terms of zonations which for saltmarshes at least 'correspond, in a general way, with the saltmarsh succession' (Tansley 1953). His exposition of the conservation needs as expressed in 'Our heritage of wild nature' (Tansley 1945) continued the tradition of viewing the special habitat and species of importance to conservation to equate with those which the ecologist considered 'natural' or 'semi-natural'. In themselves these terms have come to mean something which suggests little or no human influence. Ratcliffe (1977) in his description of the assessment of the key conservation areas in Great Britain ascribes great importance to 'naturalness' and 'typicalness' as primary criteria for site selection. However this publication and the subsequent *Guidelines* for the selection of biological SSSIs (Nature Conservancy Council 1989) stress the fact that few if any habitats are really natural. Those which may be 'most natural' are confined to 'high mountains… and certain coastal features' and that up to 30% of the total is modified in some way and classed as '*semi-natural*'. However the selection of sites must 'satisfy a certain level of quality marked by lack of features which indicate gross or recent human modification'.

Thus, whilst recognising the influence of human activity on most habitats and species, the selection and subsequent management of many sites, particularly saltmarshes and sand dunes, has been concerned primarily with the conservation of the classic sequence of vegetation and the associated animals. Much activity has centred around the protection of the features for which

the sites, including nature reserves, were established. This is manifested in the importance attached to arresting succession particularly where the invasion of 'non-native' species such as Common Cord-grass (Doody 1984; Gray & Benham 1990) on mudflats and Sea-buckthorn (Ranwell 1972b) on dunes. In certain situations, notably on sand dunes, this approach may result in other potentially more damaging losses as, for example, when scrub invades open species rich dune vegetation (Doody 1989). This approach, which is based on the relatively narrow view of succession may also reduce the number of options considered by the conservation manager for the site (Doody 1993).

A key question from a nature conservation point of view therefore relates to whether saltmarshes and sand dunes are really 'natural' systems exhibiting inherent characteristics which can be used as a basis for determining management options. In particular does the spatial mosaic of vegetation used to assess the site for conservation purposes give an adequate representation of a successional sequence? In the situations where invasive, non-native plants and animals threaten the survival of existing habitats, such as the two cases mentioned above the answer may be obvious. However, most examples of saltmarsh and sand dune successions do not proceed in an orderly fashion from one stage to the next, and it is not possible to infer a successional relationship from the spatial zonation. Thus, in defining management options, much more complex patterns of change may need to be interpreted. At the same time, adhering to the notion that these systems have some inherent naturalness which can be considered in isolation from human influence, is clearly not sustainable.

Conclusion – are saltmarshes and sand dunes natural or man-made?

The view that the ecological or geomorphological development of coastal habitats is 'natural' must be tempered by the recognition that most, if not all examples, have been modified in some way by human activity. Not only are most coastal systems influenced by activities taking place in the hinterland which affect water quality and sediment movement, but also other habitats (salinas, in the Mediterranean and coastal grazing marsh, in southeastern England, for example) have been created by past human use. Throughout Europe individual habitats have been modified by different levels of human activity. It is almost certain that the open areas of upper saltmarsh would have provided rich pasturage in the winter months, and the early settlers in America cut hay on saltmarshes, a practice borrowed from north-western Europe. Grazing and turf cutting continue to be practised today, especially in north-western England, and reed cutting for thatch occurs in the Tay Estuary in eastern Scotland. Almost all dunes have been used to graze domestic stock, and about 8,000 years BP sheep herding was prevalent in many areas of the Mediterranean. Sheep and goats continue to influence some of the remaining undeveloped dunes in the eastern Mediterranean, notably in Turkey. Historically there are also numerous examples of large-scale destabilisation due to overuse from other activities such as over-grazing and burning, and Marram grass cutting for bedding and thatch, which have resulted in major sand movement, e.g., in the Outer Hebrides (Angus & Elliot 1992), Denmark (Skarregaard 1989) and the National Park of Doñana (Garcia Nova 1979).

In considering, therefore, whether saltmarshes and sand dunes are really natural systems it is important to understand the extent of man's impact upon their development. In one sense, as has been described above, there are probably no saltmarshes or sand dunes in Europe which are entirely 'natural', i.e., have not in some way been influenced by human activity. Even the extensive unmodified lagoons and deltas with their apparently natural saltmarshes and sand dunes in Albania and eastern Turkey, grow rapidly today because of deforestation in the hinterland. Even here drainage and land 'improvement' for agriculture has destroyed large areas of transitional vegetation, and pollution is a major consideration. On closer inspection even the most 'natural' examples of succession may have been initiated by human activity. The growth of the 5km-long dune spit of Bull Island, Dublin Bay is directly attributable to the construction of a breakwater into the Bay between 1819 and 1823 (Jeffrey 1977). *Perhaps the best that can be said is that in the early stages of development saltmarshes and sand dunes exhibit characteristics of natural succession.*

This conclusion may have important consequences both for the development of conservation policy and the ecological principles upon which it has been based. Agenda 21, a programme for action agreed at the United Nations, Earth Summit in Rio in 1992 aims to help achieve the twin goals of sustainable human development and the maintenance of biodiversity. The statements clearly point the way towards recognition of the interrelationship between the so-called 'natural environment' and human economic and cultural activity. If policies are to be developed which fulfil the aspirations both of the politicians and the traditional conservationist, future studies of saltmarshes and sand dunes and their management for conservation must include human use as a key component of the 'natural' system.

The description of the coastal habitats of the Mersey Basin and human influence upon them suggests that the extent of modification, even of the apparently most natural areas, is such that continued human intervention is required for their conservation. This is almost certainly true if the aim of the conservation policy is to maintain the *status quo* for the habitats, identified as being of importance when the site was first assessed. However, the traditional approach which seeks to arrest succession may not be adequate, partly because of the resource implications. Too often other options may be overlooked because saltmarsh or sand dune erosion, especially when apparently caused by human use, are viewed as indicating the vulnerable and sensitive nature of the

habitats which as a consequence, require protection. It is not unusual to find rocks placed along the eroding edge of saltmarshes, e.g., in the Severn Estuary, and almost all major sand dune systems in north-western Europe have been 'protected' by chestnut paling fencing and/or Marram planting. If a longer view is taken, and it is accepted that past human use has played a significant part in the evolution of the current interest, we may decide on a different approach to management.

Change is an important component of coastal systems, and saltmarshes and sand dunes are particularly well adapted to accommodate environmental perturbations, whether due to natural processes or human intervention. Saltmarsh erosion and accretion are natural phenomena, taking place in response to changes, for example, in the location of the tidal channels or, over a longer time period, in sea-level. Mobile sand driven by wind is required for dune development, and erosion is essential for the development of dune slacks. Initiating change may provide an important opportunity for the rejuvenation of degraded habitats. In this context the alliance between the ecologist, geomorphologist and coastal engineer in recreating saltmarshes on the Essex coast as part of a new approach to sea defence, may yet instil a more pro-active approach to conservation than has hitherto been considered appropriate. Perhaps ultimately we will emulate our ancestors, and in some areas initiate major change and then step back and let nature take its course. They did it by accident; we can do it by design! In so doing we may not have the same nature conservation features as before, but if the area over which the processes are allowed to develop is large enough, the resulting system may be more 'natural' and self-sustaining than at present.

In this context the Mersey Basin and its coastal areas are no exception. The Dee Estuary will continue to accrete as the saltmarsh (mainly Common Cord-grass) expands onto the mudflats. This, in its turn, will reduce the available feeding habitat for the internationally important wintering populations of waterfowl. Whether control will become necessary, as has happened at other conservation sites in the UK and elsewhere around the world (Doody 1984; Gray & Benham 1990), to prevent significant habitat loss and threats to the wintering bird populations feeding on the mudflats, will need to be constantly assessed. What is clear is that the recent decision to allow the extension of the Mostyn dock on the Welsh shore must add to the pressures which enhance siltation. Both here and in the Mersey Estuary, where Common Cord-grass appears to be expanding, the spread of the species should be carefully monitored. In this context it will be important to understand the nature of the forces which may have helped stimulate its growth. Is there a fundamental change in the nature of the sediments? What is the impact of sand dredging in the outer Ribble Estuary? Has it shifted the balance of the sediment type from a sandy matrix to a smaller, muddy substrate more suitable for Common Cord-grass growth along the Sefton shore?

The situation in Albania, where new coastal habitats are formed from sediment released as a result of deforestation in the mountains, also reminds us that human activities can influence coastal developments far away from the activity itself. In looking, therefore, at the future of the coastal habitats of the Mersey Basin, the whole area, from the nearshore marine environment to the active intermediate coastal zone and the hinterland as far inland as the catchment of the three main rivers, must be considered. Integrating planning and management in this zone will help to ensure decisions are taken which help to prevent one sectoral activity damaging the interests of another.

References

Angus, S. & Elliot, M.M. (1992). Erosion in Scottish machair with particular reference to the Outer Hebrides. *Coastal dunes, geomorphology, ecology and management for conservation* (eds R.W.B. Carter, T.G.F. Curtis & M.J. Sheehy-Skeffington), pp. 93–112. A.A Balkema, Rotterdam, Netherlands.

Atkinson, D. & Houston, J. (eds) (1993). *The Sand Dunes of the Sefton Coast*. National Museums & Galleries on Merseyside in association with Sefton Metropolitan Borough Council, Liverpool.

Bennett, C., Curtis, S. & Fairhurst, C. (1995). Recent changes in the Mersey Estuary 1958–1988. *The Mersey Estuary – Naturally Ours* (eds M.S. Curtis, D. Norman & I.D. Wallace), pp. 12–23. Mersey Estuary Conservation Group, Warrington.

Berry, W.G. (1967). Saltmarsh development in the Ribble Estuary. *Liverpool essays in geography – A Jubilee Collection* (eds R.W. Steel & R. Lawton), pp. 121–35. Longmans, London.

Buck, A.L. (1993). *An inventory of UK estuaries, 3. North-west Britain*. Joint Nature Conservation Committee, Peterborough.

Chapman, V.J. (1938). Studies in saltmarsh ecology, I–III. *Journal of Ecology*, **26**. 144–79.

Chapman, V.J. (1941). Studies in saltmarsh ecology, IV. *Journal of Ecology*, **29**. 69–82.

Chapman, V.J. (1959). Studies in saltmarsh Ecology, IX. Changes in saltmarsh vegetation at Scolt Head Island. *Journal of Ecology*, **47**, 619–39.

Coles, J.M. (1964). New aspects of Mesolithic settlement of south-west Scotland. *Transactions of the Dumfries and Galloway Natural History and Antiquarian Society*, **XL**, 67–98.

Dijkema, K.S. (ed.) (1984). *Salt marshes in Europe*. Nature and environment series, No. 30. Council of Europe, Strasbourg, France.

Doody, J.P. (ed.) (1984). *Spartina anglica in Great Britain*. Focus on nature conservation, **No. 5**. Nature Conservancy Council, Attingham.

Doody, J.P. (1989). Management for nature conservation. *Coastal Sand Dunes* (eds C.H. Gimmingham, W. Ritchie, B.B. Willetts & A.J. Willis), pp. 247–65. *Proceedings of the Royal Society of Edinburgh*, **96B**.

Doody, J.P. (1993). Changing attitudes to coastal conservation. *ENact*, English Nature, Peterborough.

Garcia Nova, F. (1979). The ecology of vegetation of the dunes in Doñana National Park (south-west Spain). *Ecological*

Processes in Coastal Environments (eds R.L. Jefferies, & A.J. Davy), pp. 571–92. (British Ecological Society Symposium) Blackwell Scientific Publications, Oxford.

Gray, A.J. (1992). Saltmarsh plant ecology: zonation and succession revisited. *Saltmarshes – Morphodynamics, conservation and engineering significance* (eds J.R.L. Allen & K. Pye), pp. 63–79. Cambridge University Press, Cambridge.

Gray, A.J. & Benham, P.E.M. (1990). *Spartina anglica – a research review*. ITE research publication, No 2. HMSO, London.

Jeffrey, D.W. (1977). *North Bull Island, Dublin Bay – a modern coastal natural history*. The Royal Dublin Society, Dublin.

Marchant, C.J. (1967). Evolution of *Spartina* (Gramineae). 1. The history and morphology of the genus in Britain today. *Journal of the Linnean Society, Botany*, **60**, 1–24.

Marker, M.E. (1962). The Dee Estuary: its progressive silting and saltmarsh development. *Transactions of the Institute of British Geographers*, **211**, 65.

Marshall, J.R. (1962). The physiographic development of Caerlaverock merse. *Transactions of the Dumfries and Galloway Natural History and Antiquarian Society*, **39**, 102.

Nature Conservancy Council (1989). *Guidelines for the selection of biological SSSIs*. Nature Conservancy Council, Peterborough.

Ranwell, D.S. & Boar, R. (1986). *The coast dune management guide*. Institute of Terrestrial Ecology, Monks Wood, Huntingdon.

Ranwell, D.S. (1972a). *Ecology of Saltmarshes and Sand Dunes*. Chapman & Hall, London.

Ranwell, D.S. (1972b). *The management of sea buckthorn Hippophae rhamnoides L. on selected sites in Great Britain*. Report of the Hippophae Study Group. Nature Conservancy (NERC).

Ratcliffe, D.A. (1977). *A nature conservation review*. Cambridge University Press, Cambridge.

Rice, K.A. & Putwain, P.D. (1987). *The Dee and Mersey Estuaries: environmental background*. Shell UK Limited, London.

Ritchie, A. & Ritchie, G. (1978). *The ancient monuments of Orkney*. HMSO, Edinburgh.

Robinson, N.A. (1984). The history of *Spartina* in the Ribble estuary. *Spartina anglica in Great Britain* (ed. P. Doody). Focus on nature conservation, No. 5, pp. 27–29. Nature Conservancy Council, Attingham Park.

Royal Commission on Coastal Erosion and Afforestation (1911). *The reclamation of Tidal lands*. Third (and final) Report Vol. III, Pt V, HMSO, London.

Simmons, I. (1980). Iron Age and Roman coast around the Wash. *Archaeology and coastal change* (ed. F.H. Thompson). Occasional Paper No. 1. The Society of Antiquities, London.

Skarregaard, P. (1989). Stabilisation of coastal dunes in Denmark. *Perspectives in coastal dune management* (eds F. van der Meulen, P.D. Jungerius and J.H. Visser), pp. 151–61. SPB Academic Publishing, The Hague, Netherlands.

Steers, J.A. (ed.) (1960). *Scolt Head Island*. Heffer, Cambridge.

Tansley, A.G. (1945). *Our heritage of wild nature*. Cambridge University Press, Cambridge.

Tansley, A.G. (1953). *The British Islands and their vegetation, volume II*. Cambridge University Press, Cambridge.

Thompson, H.V. & Worden, A.N. (1956). *The rabbit*. New Naturalist. Collins, London.

Truscott, A. (1984). Control of *Spartina anglica* on the amenity beaches of Southport. *Spartina anglica in Great Britain* (ed. P. Doody). Focus on nature conservation, No. 5, pp. 64–69. Nature Conservancy Council, Attingham Park.

Yapp, R.H., Johns, D. & Jones, O.T. (1917). The saltmarshes of the Dovey Estuary. II, The saltmarshes. *Journal of Ecology*, **5**, 65–103.

SECTION FIVE

The Changing Flora

A.D. BRADSHAW

At first sight it might appear that the only lesson to be learnt from a complex urban area such as the Mersey Basin is that whenever conditions become difficult for them, plants and species disappear, and as a result the flora becomes more and more impoverished. This is indeed clear from the following chapters, and emphasises a serious message for all those caring for our environment.

Yet three notable principles are also apparent. The first is that if and when environmental damage abates there can be rapid recolonisation by the affected species. Yet this colonisation can be a fickle process, some species not showing the same ability to return as others, for reasons not yet always understood.

The second is that industrial activity creates new environments that may be suitable for species which did not find a suitable habitat previously. The third principle is that where there is so much human activity, there is a continuous in-flow of species which may be able to take advantage of the new habitats available.

From all this comes the not necessarily expected fact that the history of an industrialised region such as the Mersey Basin is not one of a downward spiral towards loss of diversity, but even an increase. There has been a remarkable process of change and adjustment as different species either lose or gain in relation to the complex environmental changes occurring, just as they have naturally over the past aeons of time.

CHAPTER SEVENTEEN

Marine algae: diversity and habitat exploitation

G. RUSSELL, A.W.L. JEMMETT AND S.B. WILKINSON

Introduction

The historical record of marine algae in the Mersey Basin starts in the second half of the 19th century. It therefore covers a period of considerable change both in the size of the human population and in the industrial activity of the region. Most of the information available has been obtained from studies of the estuaries of the Rivers Mersey and Dee, and it is on these that this paper will concentrate (Figure 17.1).

It is scarcely possible to investigate the marine vegetation of any major estuary in the UK without taking some account of the effects of industrial, agricultural or domestic pollution and, in that respect, the two estuaries offer an interesting contrast. The Dee catchment area includes the sparsely populated mountains of Snowdonia, and its water enters the tidal reaches in a condition that is generally Good or Very Good, although some of the smaller tributaries may be affected by agricultural and sewage pollution (NRA 1996). Industrial pollution (copper, zinc and organo-tins) may on occasion reach unacceptable levels in the Estuary. Sewage contamination of the tidal reaches has also reduced water quality and, at West Kirby, the water now (1996) fails to meet the EC Bathing Waters Directive. However, of the 65.5km of estuary, 63.0km is still classified as Good and the remaining 2.5km as Fair (NRA 1996).

The River Mersey and its tributaries, on the other hand, flow through large centres of population before becoming tidal, and water quality has been Poor or Bad over much of its length throughout this period (NRA 1995). Indeed, its pollution history can be traced back to the late 18th century, when the industrialisation of northwest England began, and quite recently the estuary was considered the worst polluted in Europe (Head & Jones 1991). This raises a rather obvious question: have the differences between the River Dee and River Mersey been expressed in the character of the marine algal vegetation? As with many simple questions, the answer has proved to be elusive and incomplete.

Macroalgae

Hilbre Island (Figure 17.1), at the mouth of the River Dee, has been visited for its seaweeds, certainly since the 1860s. F.P. Marrat (Marrat 1863–64), who worked in Liverpool City Museum, made several excursions at that time and the results of his observations were later incorporated into species lists by Gibson (1889, 1891). E.A.L. Batters, possibly the most eminent of late-Victorian phycologists in the UK, also came to the Island on at least one occasion (Batters 1902). His interest in Hilbre was probably occasioned by the fact that it is almost the only example of natural rocky shore in the long stretch of coastline between Cumbria and the Great Orme. It must have been seen therefore as important in the compilation of regional seaweed floras for the UK (Holmes & Batters 1890). However, these late-19th-century lists have since proved to be much more interesting as evidence of floristic change. Drawing from these and from personal records, Russell (1982) listed 151 species of macroalgae for Hilbre (Table 17.1) of which 38 had not been seen in recent years, while a further 33 species were considered to be definitely absent. Prominent among the latter were the kelps (*Alaria, Chorda, Laminaria* spp.) together with their common understorey species (*Delesseria, Membranoptera, Odonthalia, Palmaria, Phycodrys, Ptilota* spp.). Thus, an entire zone of vegetation has disappeared from an estuary that has been relatively unpolluted throughout its history. The build-up of sand and other sediments in the estuary seems likely to have buried some of the sublittoral reefs, but areas of lower-shore rock, potentially suitable for a kelp forest,

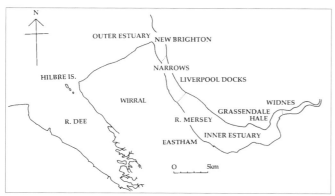

Figure 17.1. Outline map of estuaries of the Rivers Dee and Mersey showing locations of sites referred to in text.

NOSTOCOPHYCEAE
+ *Calothrix crustacea*
+ *Entophysalis conferta*
+ *E. deusta*
+ *Microcoleus lyngbyaceus*
+ *Oscillatoria lutea*
+ *Schizothrix calcicola*
+ *S. tenerrima*
+ *Spirulina subsalsa*

BANGIOPHYCEAE
? *Antithamnion cruciatum*
− *Ahnfeltia plicata*
+ *Audouinella daviesii*
? *A. floridula*
? *A. membranacea*
+ *A. purpurea*
+ *A. secundata*
+ *A. thuretii*
? *A. virgatula*
+ *Bangia atropurpurea*
? *Callithamnion corymbosum*
+ *C. hookeri*
+ *C. roseum*
+ *Catenella caespitosa*
? *Calliblepharis ciliata*
? *Ceramium circinnatum*
+ *C. deslongchampii*
? *C. fastigiatum*
+ *C. rubrum*
? *C. shuttleworthianum*
? *C. strictum*
? *C. tenuissimum*
+ *Chondrus crispus*
+ *Corallina officinalis*
− *Cryptopleura ramosa*
? *Cystoclonium purpureum*
− *Delesseria sanguinea*
+ *Dumontia contorta*
+ *Erythrotrichia carnea*
+ *Furcellaria lumbricalis*
+ *Gelidium pusillum*
? *G. sesquipedale*
+ *Gracilaria verrucosa*
− *Griffithsia flosculosa*
− *Gymnogongrus crenulatus*
− *Heterosiphonia plumosa*
+ *Hildenbrandia rubra*
− *Laurencia pinnatifida*
− *Lomentaria articulata*
− *Mastocarpus stellatus*
− *Membranoptera alata*
? *Monosporus pedicellatus*
− *Nemalion helminthoides*

− *Odonthalia dentata*
− *Palmaria palmata*
− *Petrocelis cruenta* (probably = *Mastocarpus stellatus*)
− *Phycodrys rubens*
− *Phyllophora crispa*
− *P. pseudoceranoides*
+ *Phymatolithon lenormandii*
? *Pleonosporium borreri*
− *Plocamium cartilagineum*
− *Plumaria elegans*
? *Polysiphonia fibrata*
? *P. fruticulosa*
d *P. lanosa*
+ *P. atlantica*
? *P. nigrescens*
+ *P. urceolata*
+ *Porphyra linearis*
+ *P. leucosticta*
+ *P. purpurea*
− *Pterosiphonia thuyoides*
− *Ptilota plumosa*
? *Rhodomela confervoides*
? *R. lycopodioides*
? *Spermothamnion repens*

FUCOPHYCEAE
− *Alaria esculenta*
+ *Ascophyllum nodosum*
? *Asperococcus fistulosus*
? *Chilionema ocellatum*
− *Chorda filum*
− *Chordaria flagelliformis*
+ *Cladostephus spongiosus*
− *Cutleria multifida*
d *Desmarestia aculeata*
? *Ectocarpus fasciculatus*
+ *E. siliculosus*
? *Dictyosiphon foeniculaceus*
+ *Elachista fucicola*
− *Fucus ceranoides*
+ *F. serratus*
+ *F. spiralis*
+ *F. vesiculosus*
+ *Giffordia granulosa*
+ *G. ovata*
? *Halopteris scoparia*
d *Halidrys siliquosa*
+ *Hecatonema maculans* (probably = *Punctaria* sp.)
+ *Isthmoplea sphaerophora*
− *Laminaria digitata*
− *L. hyperborea*
− *Leathesia difformis*

− *Litosiphon pusillus*
− *Mesogloia vermiculata*
+ *Myrionema strangulans*
? *Myriotrichia clavaeformis*
+ *Pelvetia canaliculata*
+ *Petalonia fascia*
? *P. zosterifolia*
+ *Petroderma maculiforme*
? *Punctaria latifolia*
+ *P. tenuissima*
+ *Ralfsia verrucosa*
+ *Scytosiphon lomentaria*
+ *Sphacelaria fusca*
? *S. cirrosa*
? *S. plumosa*
+ *S. radicans*
+ *Spongonema tomentosum*
+ *Stictyosiphon tortilis*
+ *Waerniella lucifuga*

CHLOROPHYCEAE
+ *Blidingia marginata*
+ *B. minima* (= *B. ramifera*)
? *Bryopsis plumosa*
? *B. hypnoides*
+ *Chaetomorpha linum*
+ *Chlorococcum submarinum*
? *Cladophora hutchinsiae*
+ *C. pellucida* (1 record since 1982)
+ *C. rupestris*
+ *C. sericea*
? *Epicladia flustrae*
+ *E. perforans*
? *Enteromorpha clathrata*
+ *E. compressa*
+ *E. intestinalis*
? *E. linza*
+ *E. prolifera*
+ *E. ralfsii*
? *E. ramulosa*
+ *Eugomontia sacculata*
+ *Percursaria percursa*
+ *Pringsheimiella scutata*
+ *Prasiola stipitata*
+ *Pseudococcomyxa adhaerens*
+ *Rhizoclonium riparium*
+ *Ulva lactuca*
+ *Ulothrix flacca*
+ *U. subflaccida*
+ *U. speciosa*
+ *Urospora penicilliformis*
− *Spongomorpha arcta*

Table 17.1. Benthic macroalgae of Hilbre Island (from Russell 1982). Species names, as far as possible, follow South & Tittley (1986), and readers are referred to that publication for the species authorities.

+ = species seen in recent years and probably still present
? = formerly recorded and possibly still present
− = formerly recorded but now considered definitely absent
d = present only as drift plants.

remain at the seaward end of Hilbre (Russell 1972). A possible explanation for the loss of these species is provided by Marrat (1863–64) who, in one of his reports, writes enthusiastically about the clear rock pools of Hilbre. Dee Estuary water is now very turbid as a result of suspended clay minerals, and light transmission is consequently poor. The similarly turbid water of the

Bristol Channel was investigated by Dring (1987), who concluded that the lower 1–2m of the intertidal zone at Avonmouth receives insufficient light for the sustained growth of *Fucus serratus*. So, the absence of light necessary for the formation of a kelp forest may have been the crucial factor in its disappearance. The importance of light in the zonation of Hilbre seaweeds can also be inferred from the fact that the zone of maximum species diversity is the upper and not the lower eulittoral, as might be expected on most UK rocky shores (Russell 1973). Algae are adaptable plants, however, and the low-lying rock at Hilbre has been exploited, in summer especially, by ephemerals such as *Ulva*, *Enteromorpha* and *Pilayella* species (Russell 1973, 1982).

Clay minerals do not only reduce light transmission, however. During periods of calm weather, the sea conditions may permit sediments to settle out on rock surfaces, forming a thick blanket. This can be lethal to small algae and to barnacles and is, at the same time, an unsuitable surface for fresh algal colonisation.

Documentary evidence for floristic change in the River Mersey is less complete than that for Hilbre. Gibson (1891) chose, inexplicably, to combine algal records from the River Dee and River Mersey in a single list, while keeping those of Hilbre separate. While some of the records in his earlier list (Gibson 1889) clearly refer to locations in the River Mersey, the detail is insufficient to allow compilation of a flora comparable with that of Hilbre. However, Gibson (1889) quotes an observation by Marrat that many Mersey seaweeds had been more healthy in appearance in 1860, and it is certainly the case that numerous Mersey species recorded in this publication are now absent. According to Gibson, the deterioration noted by Marrat was due, without a shadow of doubt, to the impact of increased industrial effluent, and chemical pollution of the River Mersey has certainly been serious and continuous. Analyses of arsenic, chromium, copper, lead, mercury and zinc in mud cores at Widnes (Figure 17.1) show increases in all by 1890, but to levels that are very low in comparison with those reached in the mid-20th century (NRA 1995). Either the algae in 1889 were unexpectedly sensitive to industrial pollution or some other factor(s) had also been involved in their demise. The natural sandstone reefs of the Mersey Estuary at New Brighton and upstream at Grassendale and Eastham (Figure 17.1) remain poor in species.

Artificial substrates such as promenade walls and the more recently constructed coastal defences at New Brighton and along the north Wirral shore (Davies 1989) are also uninteresting floristically. Perhaps the most successful intertidal taxa are *Fucus vesiculosus* and several species of *Enteromorpha*. These are notoriously variable genetically, phenotypically plastic and with broad niche ranges. For example, it has been found that *F. vesiculosus* from strongly wave-exposed shores has a lower intrinsic growth rate than conspecific populations living in shelter (Bäck, Collins & Russell 1992a). Also, Baltic *F. vesiculosus* is more tolerant of greatly reduced water salinity, and less tolerant of high salinities, than populations from Atlantic coasts (Bäck *et al*, 1992a). The inability of Baltic plants to survive high salinities is now known to be due to their rather weak capacity for the biosynthesis of mannitol, an important osmolyte of brown algae (Bäck, Collins & Russell 1992b). In the case of the Dee and Mersey populations, the natural vari-

ability of *F. vesiculosus* has been further increased by introgression (Burrows & Lodge 1951; Russell 1995).

Enteromorpha intestinalis on Irish Sea coasts has been found to possess at least three different salinity ecotypes (Reed & Russell 1979). Estuarine populations are analogous to Baltic *Fucus* in being tolerant to low and intolerant to high salinities. Low-shore marine ecotypes lack tolerance to reduced salinities, but grow well in fully saline media. The third group comprises plants from high-shore marine rock pools. These pools experience major fluctuations in salinity arising from dilution (rainfall) and concentration (evaporation), and the *Enteromorpha* from such habitats has the broadest tolerance range of all (Reed & Russell 1979). Salinity has also been found to trigger plastic responses resulting in branch proliferation in this species (Reed & Russell 1978).

The success of these taxa in the River Mersey echoes an observation by Nevo *et al.* (1986) that narrow-niche gastropods with low genetic diversity are less able to survive treatment with marine pollutants than broad-niche species with greater variability.

Apart from *Fucus vesiculosus*, the only large brown seaweed in the River Mersey is *Ascophyllum nodosum*. At present, this species is confined to a small area of shore at Eastham (Figure 17.1) where it forms a narrow belt in the upper eulittoral zone. The fronds of these plants are of interest because they fail to branch until they reach an age of about 6 years and, consequently, they have a curiously linear appearance (Figure 17.2). It seems likely that the fronds have responded in an adaptive way to the poor light conditions in the Mersey water. Thus, the early linear development should enable fronds to maximise their rate of entry into the better-lit surface waters, where improved irradiance will permit branching, and hence increased tissue production, to occur.

It is the restored disued Liverpool Docks (Figure 17.1) which provide most information on the potential ability of seaweed species to colonise Mersey Estuary water. The restoration of Sandon Dock (Russell *et al.* 1983) and the South Docks (Allen, Wilkinson & Hawkins 1995) has created environments in which water clarity has been greatly improved, partly through settling of mud particles, and partly through filtration by mussels. In spite of the fact that the docks were filled, and are still topped up, with polluted Mersey water, their seaweed floras already include a number of species that are absent from the intertidal reefs of the estuaries (Allen *et al.* 1995; Wilkinson 1995); see also Table 17.2. Some are likely to have been recruited from relatively distant sites, such as Anglesey or possibly the Isle of Man (e.g., *Palmaria palmata*, *Giffordia sandriana*, *Sorocarpus micromorus*, *Desmarestia viridis*, *Cladophora vagabunda*).

A surprising feature of the dock floras is the continued absence of large perennial brown algae. An experimental introduction of *Laminaria saccharina* to Sandon Dock resulted in rapid losses of plants and, by the end of the experiment, the few survivors were overgrown by epiphytic ephemeral algae and sessile animals (Russell *et al.* 1983). A similar introduction of *Fucus vesiculosus* to

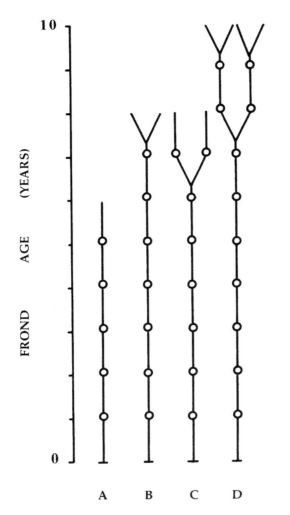

Figure 17.2. Diagrams of four fronds of Mersey *Ascophyllum nodosum* with small circles denoting gas bladders. After year 1, this species normally produces one bladder and one dichotomy from every tip each year. Frond A is therefore 6 years old, fronds B and C are 8 years old, while D is 10. Note absence of branching until approximately year 6.

NOSTOCACEAE
Oscillatoria margaritifera

BANGIOPHYCEAE
Audouinella secundata
Ceramium rubrum
C. strictum
Erythrotrichia carnea
Palmaria palmata
Polysiphonia urceolata
Pterothamnion plumula

FUCOPHYCEAE
Ectocarpus siliculosus
Giffordia granulosa
G. ovata
G. sandriana
Leptonematella fasciculata
Pilayella littoralis
Punctaria latifolia

Scytosiphon dotyi
Sorocarpus micromorus
Stictyosiphon soriferus

CHLOROPHYCEAE
Bryopsis hypnoides
B. plumosa
Cladophora vagabunda
Enteromorpha compressa
E. intestinalis
E. linza
Monostroma grevillei
Ulothrix speciosa
U. subflaccida
Urospora penicilliformis
Ulva lactuca

TRIBOPHYCEAE
Vaucheria litorea

Table 17.2. Benthic macroalgae found in Liverpool South Docks since their restoration in 1985. Princes Dock, which lies seaward of the South Docks, contains also *Desmarestia viridis* and occasional depauperate *Fucus* of uncertain species.

may be closed during periods of gross pollution in the estuary provides an additional element of protection. This proved to be the case during an episode of oil pollution in the River Mersey in August 1989 (Environmental Advisory Unit 1991) when the gates to the South Docks were kept shut.

Microalgae

The written history of microalgae in the estuaries is too fragmentary to give reliable evidence of historical change. The subfossil diatom record, used extensively in constructing lake histories, is unlikely to be reliable in most estuaries where water movement can disturb sediments. However, at Hale (Figure 17.1) on the Liverpool bank of the inner estuary, a small area of *Phragmites* (Common Reed) marsh has been cut into by a landward shift in the River channel. As a result, a face *c.*1.5m in height has been exposed, revealing alternating bands of leaf litter and estuarine mud (Figure 17.4). Radionuclide dating has confirmed that these are annual deposits, and that the marsh came into being at about 1912 (Jemmett 1991). The process of marsh development is essentially one of build-up of mud around the bases of Common Reed stems, which collapse during winter and are replaced in spring by a further crop of new shoots. Altogether, 88 species of diatom were identified in a monolith cut from the marsh face in November 1988, but, for the sake of simplicity, these have been reduced to three broad categories: *epiphyton* (diatoms usually found attached to surfaces of algal or flowering plant macrophytes), *epipelon* (diatoms usually found living on the surface of or in the interstices of mud), and *plankton* (diatoms usually found free-floating in the water column). The relative abundances of these are shown in Figure 17.5, and it is clear from this that plankton forms

the South Docks in February 1994 was terminated three months later when the plants were visibly disintegrating under a dense growth of epiphytic algae (Figure 17.3). This overgrowth could not be attributed to excessive nutrient concentrations in the dock, for phytoplankton production had reduced these to levels similar to those in coastal waters outside the estuaries throughout the period of the experiment (Dr J.W. Eaton, pers. comm.). The factor limiting the development of a macrophyte forest in the docks may well be the absence of turbulence. On intertidal rocky shores, wave action causes brown algal macrophytes to whip-lash, and this movement is likely to enhance the self-cleaning mechanisms of the plants (skin shedding). It would be interesting to see if perennial seaweeds, whose defences against epiphytes are chemical rather than physical (*Desmarestia* spp.?), could prove more successful in docks. Even without perennial species, docks have obvious potential as refuges for benthic algae, and the fact that dock gates

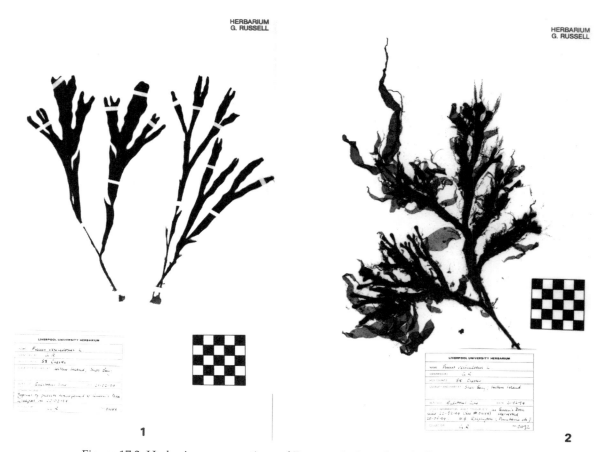

Figure 17.3. Herbarium preparations of *Fucus vesiculosus* from Hilbre Island.
1: plants from sample collected in February 1994 for introduction into Liverpool South Docks, and
2: heavily epiphytised plant after three months immersion. Scale grid = 5 x 5cm.

the most abundant group for much of the 80-year history of the marsh. It is evident also that there is considerable variation from year to year in all groups. Nevertheless, there is a significant change (p< 0.05) in all three after 1960, at which date there is a reduction in plankton and increases in both epiphyton and epipelon. While it might be tempting to ascribe this pattern to some change in water quality, the likeliest explanation is simply that the height of the marsh had reached a critical level at which tidal inundations became less frequent and of shorter duration. This would have reduced the incidence of plankton while the more stable conditions presumably proved more favourable for the development of epiphyton and epipelon.

The most abundant planktonic diatom in the monolith was *Skeletonema costatum* (Grev.) Clev. and its record of changing frequency is shown Figure 17.6. This species was also significantly less abundant after 1960 (p< 0.05), though varying from year to year throughout the period. This irregularity seems likely to be a natural phenomenon, rather than a sampling artefact, as numbers of *Skeletonema* in recent water samples are variable through time and from site to site in the same year (Figure 17.7). Figure 17.7 shows also that *Skeletonema* has a single annual peak of rather short duration from April to May. None of the important nutrients for diatom metabolism

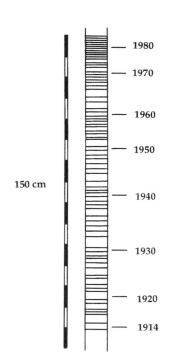

Figure 17.4. Diagram of exposed face of *Phragmites* marsh at Hale in November 1988. Transverse lines denote horizontal bands of leaf litter alternating with mud layers of different thickness. Redrawn from Jemmett (1991).

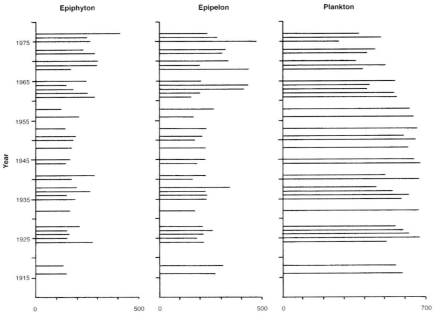

Epiphyton   Epipelon   Plankton

Figure 17. 5 (left) Mean abundances of subfossil diatoms in a Hale marsh monolith; epiphytic, epipelic and planktonic diatoms are treated separately. Drawn from raw data obtained by A.W.L. Jemmett. Mean values were calculated from three replicate samples from each year investigated. The numbers of frustules counted in each sample ranged from 956 to 1,114 but the final numbers were all adjusted to 1,000.

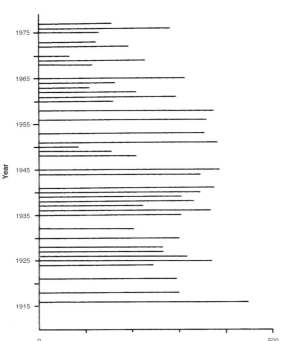

Figure 17.6 (above) Mean abundances of *Skeletonema costatum* in Hale marsh monolith. Drawn from raw data obtained by A.W.L. Jemmett.

Figure 17.7 (right) Annual abundances of *Skeletonema costatum* in water samples taken from three sites in the Mersey Estuary: Pier Head (Narrows), Eastham Channel (Inner Estuary) and New Brighton (Outer Estuary). Note variation in sizes of spring peaks from year to year and at different sites in the same year. Note also consistent absence of autumn bloom. 1983 data obtained by G.R. 1991 graphs redrawn from Environmental Resources Ltd (1993).

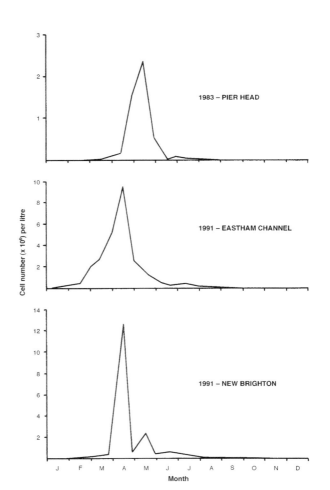

follows this pattern (NRA 1995). The best fit is provided by silicate, levels of which fall away markedly in the inner estuary in late spring. However, silicate concentrations return to higher values in autumn when no corresponding *Skeletonema* bloom occurs. It is possible that zooplankton grazing prevents an autumn bloom, but a likelier explanation is that light is then insufficient to sustain growth. The turbidity of Mersey Estuary water has been quantified by Russell *et al.* (1983), who recorded Secchi disc extinction depths (i.e., depths at which a white disc lowered into the water disappears from view) that seldom exceeded 10cm.

Skeletonema is a common estuarine diatom and its abundance has been high throughout the period of marsh development. There is no evidence of any adverse effects of the increasing heavy-metal pollution at that time. A possible explanation of its resilience has been provided recently by Medlin *et al.* (1991) who compared four geographically isolated strains on the basis of morphology and by means of their ribosomal DNA nucleotide sequences. The strains proved to be diverse genetically and two were considered sufficiently distinct to belong to a new species. Thus, the success of *Skeletonema* in a polluted environment can be linked once again with genetic variability and with a broad-niche range.

Discussion

There is little doubt that the number of species of macroalgae at Hilbre has been in decline over the past 100 years, despite the fact that the Dee Estuary has not been and is not heavily polluted. Although there is always a danger in proposing single factor explanations of events of this kind, light reduction caused by an increase in suspended fine sediments seems likely to have been a major agent of change. Jemmett (1996) has emphasised that the cloudiness of Dee Estuary water is due to suspended silt and clay particles, and is a natural feature, which should not be misconstrued as evidence of poor water quality. However, a connection is possible in that the suspended material also includes a proportion of organic matter, some of which may well originate in domestic effluent.

In the River Mersey, where a definite but unquantifiable decrease in macroalgal diversity has also occurred, pollution has been on an altogether different scale. In 1982, the Secretary of State for the Environment referred to the river as '… an affront to the standards a civilised society should demand of its environment …' (Head & Jones 1991). Yet it has proved possible for some naturally variable taxa to exploit even these demanding conditions and to achieve some success in vegetating the available intertidal substrate. As in the River Dee, turbidity has certainly been involved in the species losses, for clarification of impounded Mersey water in Liverpool docks has been followed quite rapidly by the appearance of several unexpected species of macroalgae. However, pollution and turbidity are again inextricably linked, for many of the chemical pollutants may be bound to the sediments as well as dissolved in the water.

Signs of amelioration of Mersey water have been detected beyond the confines of the restored docks. Concentrations of lead and mercury in the tissues of *Fucus vesiculosus* have declined since 1980 (Head & Jones 1991), reflecting a general reduction of most metals in the estuarine sediments (Mersey Basin Campaign 1995; Head & Jones 1991). Since 1981, North West Water has been engaged upon an ambitious programme to reduce domestic effluent in the River Mersey and its tributaries, with the aim of achieving a minimum quality of Fair throughout by the year 2000 (Head & Jones 1991). It has also been reported that Welsh Water (Hyder plc) have plans for improved sewage treatment, which ought to lead to better water quality in the Dee Estuary (Jemmett 1996).

There is considerable public concern about the quality of the two estuaries and good evidence that improvements are under way. Management plans have been published (Mersey Basin Campaign 1995; Jemmett 1996) detailing proposals for further environmental enhancement. It is difficult to guess what the impact of these on the macro- and microalgal vegetation might be, but the adaptability of algae should ensure that any new niches will be filled rather rapidly.

Acknowledgements

We are grateful to Gill Haynes for technical help over the years and to Peter Head for up-to-date advice on the state of the Mersey Estuary.

References

Allen, J.R., Wilkinson, S.B. & Hawkins, S.J. (1995). Redeveloped docks as artificial lagoons: The development of brackish-water communities and potential for conservation of lagoonal species. *Aquatic Conservation: Marine and Freshwater Ecosystems*, **5**, 299–309.

Bäck, S., Collins, J.C. & Russell, G. (1992a). Effects of salinity on growth of Baltic and Atlantic *Fucus vesiculosus*. *British Phycological Journal*, **27**, 39–47.

Bäck, S., Collins, J.C. & Russell, G. (1992b). Comparative ecophysiology of Baltic and Atlantic *Fucus vesiculosus*. *Marine Ecology Progress Series*, **84**, 71–82.

Batters, E.A.L. (1902). A catalogue of the British marine algae. *Journal of Botany, London*, **40** suppl., 1–107.

Burrows, E.M. & Lodge, S. (1951). Autecology and the species problem in *Fucus. Journal of the Marine Biological Association of the United Kingdom*, **30**, 161–76.

Davies, C.D. (1989). Wirral scheme. *Coastal Management* (Institute of Civil Engineering – Maritime Engineering Board), pp. 293–307. Thomas Telford, London.

Dring, M.J. (1987). Light climate in intertidal and subtidal zones in relation to photosynthesis and growth of benthic algae: a theoretical model. *Plant Life in Aquatic and Amphibious Habitats* (ed. R.M.M. Crawford), pp. 23–34. Blackwell Scientific Publications, Oxford.

Environmental Advisory Unit of Liverpool University Ltd. (1991). *The Mersey Oil Spill Project 1989–90*. Mersey Oil Spill Advisory Group, Liverpool.

Environmental Resources Ltd. (1993). *Stage IIIa Environmental Studies: E1 Plankton Studies in the Mersey Estuary*. Final

Report to Mersey Barrage Company.

Gibson, R.J.H. (1889). Report on the marine algae of the L.M.B.C. district. *Proceedings and Transactions of the Liverpool Biological Society*, **3**, 128–54.

Gibson, R.J.H. (1891). A revised list of the marine algae of the L.M.B.C. district. *Proceedings and Transactions of the Liverpool Biological Society*, **5**, 83–43.

Head, P.C. & Jones, P.D. (1991). The Mersey estuary: turning the tide of Pollution. *Environmental Pollution*, **1**, 517–28.

Holmes, E.M. & Batters, E.A.L. (1890). A revised list of the British marine algae. *Annals of Botany*, **5**, 63–107.

Jemmett, A.W.L. (1991). *An investigation into the heavy metals, sediment and vegetation of a Mersey estuary saltmarsh*. PhD thesis, University of Liverpool.

Jemmett, A.W.L. (1996). *The Dee Estuary Strategy Final Report: January 1996.* Dee Estuary Strategy, Metropolitan Borough of Wirral, Birkenhead.

Marrat, F.P. (1863–64). Several short hand-written lists in issues of the *Liverpool Naturalists' Scrap Book* for these years. Liverpool City Library, H580LIV.

Medlin, L.K., Elwood, H.J., Stickel, S. & Sogin, M.L. (1991). Morphological and genetic variation within the diatom *Skeletonema costatum* (Bacillariophyta): Evidence for a new species *Skeletonema pseudocostatum. Journal of Phycology*, **27**, 514–24.

Mersey Basin Campaign (1995). *Mersey Estuary Management Plan: A Strategic Policy Framework.* Liverpool University Press, Liverpool.

Nevo, E., Noy, R., Lavie, B., Beiles, A. & Muchtar, S. (1986). Genetic diversity and resistance to marine pollution. *Biological Journal of the Linnean Society*, **29**, 139–44.

NRA (1995). *The Mersey Estuary: A Report on Environmental Quality.* HMSO, London.

NRA (1996). *The River Dee Catchment Management Plan Action Plan:* 1996. National Rivers Authority, Bangor.

Reed, R.H. & Russell, G. (1978). Salinity fluctuations and their influence on 'bottle brush' morphogenesis in *Enteromorpha intestinalis* (L.) Link. *British Phycological Journal*, **13**, 149–53.

Reed, R.H. & Russell, G. (1979). Adaptation to salinity stress in populations of *Enteromorpha intestinalis* (L.) Link. *Estuarine and Coastal Marine Science*, **8**, 251–58.

Russell, G. (1972). Phytosociological studies on a two-zone shore. I Basic pattern. *Journal of Ecology*, **60**, 539–45.

Russell, G. (1973). Phytosociological studies on a two-zone shore. II Community structure. *Journal of Ecology*, **61**, 525–36.

Russell, G. (1982). The marine algae. *Hilbre the Cheshire Island: its history and natural history.* (ed. J.D. Craggs), pp. 65–74, Liverpool University Press, Liverpool.

Russell, G. (1995). Pyrolysis mass spectrometry: a fresh approach to old problems in brown algal systematics? *Marine Biology*, **123**, 153-157.

Russell, G., Hawkins, S.J., Evans, L.C., Jones, H.D. & Holmes, G.D. (1983). Restoration of a disused dock basin as a habitat for marine benthos and fish. *Journal of Applied Ecology*, **20**, 43–58.

South, G.R. & Tittley, I. (1986). *A Checklist and Distributional Index of the Benthic Marine Algae of the North Atlantic Ocean.* Huntsman Marine Laboratory and British Museum (Natural History), St Andrews and London.

Wilkinson, S.B. (1995). *The ecology of the benthos in Liverpool docks.* PhD thesis, University of Liverpool.

CHAPTER EIGHTEEN

The influence of atmospheric pollution on the lichen flora of Cheshire

B.W. FOX

Introduction

The earliest known records of lichens in Cheshire are probably contained in Dawson Turner and L.W. Dillwyn's account in *The Botanists Guide through England and Wales* printed in 1805, in which 26 species were recorded. Based on my own work in preparing *The Lichen Flora of Cheshire*, this total is much lower than is known today (over 260 species) in the county, but it includes large, very pollution sensitive species such as Lichen pulmonarius (*Lobaria pulmonaria*), Lichen scrobiculatus (*Lobaria scrobiculata*), found by John Bradbury (1768–1823) of Stalybridge, Cheshire on old oak trees in Stayley Rushes. (Lichen names in italics are those currently used in Purvis *et al.* 1992.)

Other species collected by Bradbury were Lobaria laetevirens (*Lobaria virens*), Parmeliella plumbea (*Degelia plumbea*) and Cornicularia triste (*Cornicularia normoerica*), all of which are long since extinct from Cheshire and from this locality. Even the ultra sensitive *Usnea articulata* was recorded by him 'in plenty' in Lyme Hall parkland, in Cheshire.

Since some of the sites at which these were recorded were down-wind of the Manchester conurbation, one can conclude that any influence of aerial pollution originating from this source had not yet started to affect the lichen population at this time.

We also know that on the red sandstone rocks of the Bidston lighthouse area, on the west coast of the Wirral peninsula, Umbilicaria pustulata (*Lasallia pustulata*) was found in 'plenty' by Bradbury in 1805, together with *Umbilicaria deusta*. They were still present when Frederick Price Marrat (1820–1904) visited the site (Marrat 1860), and an excellent herbarium specimen, that was obviously growing well, is housed in the herbarium at Liverpool Museum.

In 1859, Leo Grindon in *The Manchester Flora* wrote of lichens.

Many pretty species [lichens] are to be found on the moors, and in the neighbouring woods and cloughs and in parks and old orchards in Cheshire; but the majority of those enumerated are not obtainable nearer [to Manchester] than on the high hills beyond Disley, Ramsbottom, Stalybridge and Rochdale, and even there a quantity has been lessened of late years, through the cutting down of old woods and the influx of factory smoke, which appears to be singularly prejudicial to these lovers of pure atmosphere.

It was thus reasonable to assume that the plume of pollution originating from the Manchester area had not yet penetrated much further than its outskirts represented by these towns.

A century ago, Wheldon recorded *Ochrolechia tartarea* in Eastham Wood, Wirral (Travis 1922), a species now apparently absent from Cheshire. It was not found on my visit to these woods in 1991, and judging from the present change in the surrounding environment, it is unlikely to be found there in the near future. The pollution pressure on this woodland is almost certainly due to surrounding encroaching urbanization and the consequent pollution from that source.

The overall impression gained therefore is that there has been a marked increase in the damaging effects of atmospheric pollution over the last century and that judging from sites like this one, no improvement has taken place in recent years.

Wheldon and Travis, in their *Lichen Flora of South Lancashire*, deal at length with the depredation of smoke pollution in these areas next to Cheshire. They suggested that maximum possible damage had occurred. Judging from Travis's collections in the Liverpool Museum, considerable decimation of *Umbilicarias* in the Bidston lighthouse area had also occurred. In *The Lichens of the Wirral* (1922) and later in his additions (1925), Travis noted this degradation, and that *Lasallia pustulata* only occurred in two places in a very stunted state. I visited the site in 1980, and found several plants of *Umbilicaria polyphylla*, apparently growing reasonably well, but no evidence of either *U. deusta* or *L. pustulata*. I visited the site again in 1991 and found only two specimens of *U. polyphylla*, growing reasonably well. However, the site is subject to a high level of public pressure, and this in addition to any influence of atmospheric pollution could cause the decrease in the species diversity of the lichen flora (Table 18.1).

Apart from sulphur dioxide, the effects of carbon

1805	*Lobarion* community recorded as well established.
1859	Leo Grindon noted influence of pollution on lichens in the Manchester area, *Lobarion* still present East of Manchester.
1860	Marrat collects fine specimens of *L. pustulata* at Bidston.
1897	*Ochrolechia tartarea* collected by Wheldon in Eastham woods.
1915	From Travis's collection of *Umbilicarias* in Liverpool herbarium, pollution had set in having considerable effect.
1922	*Lasallia pustulata* recorded by Travis at Bidston, but very depauperate, hardly recognisable. *Umbilicaria deusta* still present but damaged.
1977	The first record in Cheshire of *Usnea subfloridana* at Rostherne Mere, by G.M.A. Barker.
1980	Both *L. pustulata* and *U. deusta* gone from Bidston. Several specimens of *U. polyphylla* present. (B.W. Fox)
1983	*Usnea* spp. found at Foden's Flash by J. Guest.
1991	Only two small plants of *U. polyphylla* could be found by B.W. Fox at Bidston. *Usnea* spp. becoming widespread in Willow Carrs.

Table 18.1. The chronology of lichen observations in Cheshire.

pollution are less well known from a lichen point of view. This may be more important for monitoring other plants and animals however, and the excellent surveys of melanic forms of the Scalloped Hazel moth (*Gonodontis bidentata*) conducted during the early 1970s by J.B. Bishop and his co-workers may reflect this (Bishop & Cook 1975).

Sulphur dioxide pollution levels in Cheshire

Following the fateful smog of London in 1952, when over 4,000 people died as a direct result, the Clean Air Act of 1956 became law. It was not until the early sixties that this Act developed its teeth, and by the Clean Air Act 1968 and later Control of Pollution Act in 1974, the effect of pollution decrease was becoming obvious. No more dense smogs have been seen during climatic inversions

in autumn. One of the earliest systematic records of the sulphur dioxide levels of the county of Cheshire was prepared in 1961 by the Warren Springs Pollution Laboratories in Stevenage. Some 90 sites were established throughout Cheshire and the sulphur dioxide levels were monitored for varying lengths of time in each of the sites. Some were monitored from 1961, and at a few places there has been a continuous record of the mean winter levels until the mid eighties. Four of the sites for which long records are available are included in Figure 18.1, and it can be seen that the values have fallen from 300–400 micrograms per cubic metre to less than 20 in the mid 1980s when recordings ceased. Levels of over 2,000 micrograms per cubic metre occurred in the Widnes area in 1961 and Ellesmere Port in 1966. Even these very high levels were probably lower than those which may have occurred before systematic recording began. It is also interesting to note that for some reason a second peak occurred during the early seventies, especially in the Warrington area. The most recently recorded levels in 1985 averaged between 20 and 40 micrograms per cubic metre for most of these areas.

The effect of sulphur dioxide pollution on Lichens

Sulphur dioxide is a major component of industrial and urban emissions, and has been shown to be very toxic to lichens. *In vitro* work by Ferry & Baddeley in 1976 showed that the gas was very disruptive to the photosynthetic biochemistry of the plant. It is water soluble and forms sulphurous acid when combined with terrestrial water or rain. The main effect of this sulphurous acid is, at high concentrations, to disrupt photosynthesis itself, as well as nitrogen fixation. Recent work (Lange *et al.* 1989) shows that an even more sensitive effect of sulphur dioxide toxicity is on the transfer of carbohydrates from the algal to the fungal partner in the symbiont. Other unknown pollutants from traffic emissions seem to increase the level of chlorophyll present, thought to be caused by the stimulatory effects on the

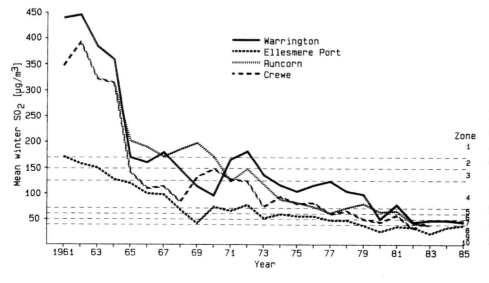

Figure 18.1. Mean winter sulphur dioxide levels (in micrograms per cubic metre) for four key sites in Cheshire. Adapted from data from the Warren Springs Pollution Laboratory, Stevenage. Superimposed are lines corresponding to Hawksworth & Rose's zone scales of pollution.

Zone	Sulphur dioxide levels μgm⁻³	Tree bark distribution	Zone	Sulphur dioxide levels μgm⁻³	Tree bark distribution
0	???	Nil	6	~50	*Parmelia caperata* (r)
1	>170	[*Pleurococcus*] base only			**Pertusaria albescens** (r)
2	~150	*Lecanora conizeoides* base only			*Pertusarias* (r)
3	~125	*Lepraria incana* base only			*Parmelia revoluta* (r)
		Buellia punctata			*Graphis* spp. (vr)
4	~70	*Parmelia sulcata*			*Pseuderv furfuracea.*
		Hypogymnea physodes			*Bryoria fuscescens*
		Lecanora expallens			*Parmelia revoluta* (r)
		Chaenotheca ferrug.(r)			**Parmelia easperatula** (r)
		Buellia canescens	7	~40	**Usnea subfloridana**
		Physcia adscendens			*Pertusaria hemisphaerica*
		Xanthoria parietina	8	~35	*Usnea ceratina*
5	~60	*Evernia prunastrii*			**Parmelia perlata** (vr)
		Ramalina farinacea			*Normandina pulchella*
		Physconia grisea (r)	9	<30	*Lobarias*
		Phaeophyscia orbicularis			*Dimerella lutea*
		Schismatomma decolorans			*Pachyphiale cornea*
		Xanthoria candelaria			*Usnea florida*
		Opegrapha spp.	10	0	All species.

Table 18.2. A brief listing of lichens employed in Hawksworth & Rose scale of pollution zones. Only bark species are used. Those in bold print are at present known to be rare in Cheshire.

nitrogen metabolism, which in turn stimulates chlorophyll synthesis (von Arb & Brunold 1989). It is not known how these possible pollutants modify lichen growth and survival.

One of the well known scales relating the frequency of lichens to the levels of sulphur dioxide in the environment was published by Hawksworth & Rose in 1970 (Table 18.2), and has been adapted in a number of different forms by authors throughout the world to provide a biological monitor for the study of this particular pollutant in the environment. In it, the authors defined a number of scales or zones from 0 (most polluted) to 10 (no pollution) which different species of lichens can tolerate, and by observing the mode of growth of these species on different substrates, some estimate of the prevailing sulphur dioxide concentrations can be determined. A 'mucky air map' was derived from information received from 15,000 schoolchildren as a result of the skilful application of a simplified version of this monitor by Gilbert in 1971 and reproduced by Richardson in his book *The Vanishing Lichens*.

Between 1958 and 1971 there was a 54% reduction in the ambient sulphur dioxide levels in the north-west region (North West Economic Planning Council 1974). These were still regarded, however, as the highest in the country outside the Greater London area. R. Bevan of the University of Liverpool was commissioned by Merseyside County Council to complete a biological survey of the Merseyside area, using lichens and a fungus, the well known Tar Spot (*Rhytisma acerinum*), which grows conspicuously on Sycamore (*Acer pseudocampestris*) and can be readily observed, and to some degree quantified.

In this study, the scale of indicators used was to cover the upper range of atmospheric pollution from 40 to 170 micrograms per cubic metre of sulphur dioxide. *Rhytisma* does not grow above an average pollution level of 90 micrograms per cubic metre, and is thus a good median indicator for the range chosen for study. Three lichens occurring on specific habitats were chosen. It is important that the habitats were consistent throughout the survey, and these were sensibly defined at an early stage: *Lecanora conizeoides* on the lower two metres of tree trunks (representing an upper limit of 170 micrograms per cubic metre), *Xanthoria parietina* on asbestos roofs (representing an upper limit of 125 micrograms per cubic metre), and *Parmelia saxatilis* on acid sandstone (an upper limit of 60 micrograms per cubic metre). These were a good choice for this type of survey as they were easy to identify and record. However, one must bear in mind that the latter two lichens can locally be strongly influenced by the presence of eutrophication derived from bird activity and the proximity of sewerage farms generating ammoniacal gases. The result was an interesting and informative map based on this data (Figure 18.2a/b) showing the expected high concentrations centred around the principal towns in the area. The results were subsequently published by Vick & Bevan (1976).

A further similar survey, commissioned by the Merseyside County Council, was undertaken by Alexander and Henderson Sellers of the University of Liverpool Geography Department in 1980 (Alexander 1982). These results confirmed that the levels of pollution were decreasing over the intervening period and could be observed by the general movement of the inner limits of the zones into the town areas (Figure 18.2a/b).

In 1986, a further survey was undertaken, by Sewell and Ashton on behalf of Landlife,* using three 'indicator' species, viz., *Lecanora muralis*, based on a biological scale devised by Seaward (1976), *Xanthoria parietina* and *Parmelia saxatilis* on the same substrates. This system is

* Copy at Joint Countryside Advisory Service, Bryant House, Liverpool Road North, Maghull, Merseyside, L31 2PA.

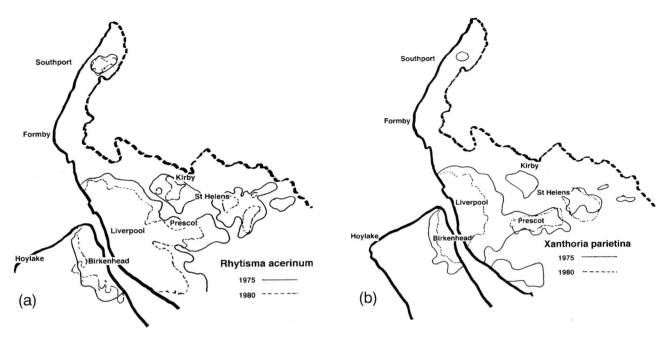

Figure 18.2. An approximate contour plot of the inner range of *Rhytisma acerinum (a)* and *Xanthoria parietina (b)*, derived from the work of Vick & Bevan (1975, solid line) and from Alexander (1980, dashed line).

based on absence or presence on substrates ranging from cement tile roofs to siliceous wall capstones, loosely based on relative pHs ranging from 9.6 to 5.25. This appears to work well for *L. muralis,* but has not been proven for *X. paretina* and *P. saxatilis.* Lack of substrate availability in the region, and the lack of attention to the age of the substrate exposure also reduced the value of this survey. The authors did indicate that some further improvement had occurred in the six years and correctly surmised that this type of study may have reached the limits of its usefulness. However, I strongly disagree with their conclusion that in general 'lichens as bioindicators of ameliorating conditions may be approaching the end of its viability as a survey method'. In my view, the subtlety of the changes occurring over a greater range of pollution sensitive species has only just begun to be appreciated. These taxa will, I am sure, provide a potentially powerful tool to recognise new pollutants in the future, when their subtle effects on lichens are more fully understood.

The lichens of Crack-willow (*Salix fragilis*) carrs in Cheshire

In 1977, G.M.A. Barker collected a small specimen of *Usnea subfloridana* in Shaw Green Willows in Rostherne Mere. This appears to be the first voucher-supported specimen of *Usnea* in Cheshire this century. In 1983 Mr Jonathen Guest drew my attention to further small specimens in Foden's Flash, a bird reserve. Since then there have been many reports of small plants of this species in many willow carrs, accompanied by a characteristic group of other lichens that appear to precede and succeed this species in this type of habitat.

This small community of species is characterised by a dominance of *Parmelia sulcata*, almost invariably associated with some *Parmelia subaurifera*, and/or *Parmelia glabratula, Hypogymnia physodes, Evernia prunastrii,* and more rarely by *Ramalina farinacea, Parmelia revoluta, Parmelia subrudecta, Parmelia caperata* and *Physcia aipolia.* It appears to be characteristic of Crack-willow (*Salix fragilis* – as distinct from other waterside *Salix* species) bark, and the community does not fit comfortably into any of the phytosociological groups described by James, Hawksworth & Rose in 1977. This community of lichens appears to be part of a pattern of recolonisation which has occurred over this period within many of the central industrial areas of England. The best site for observing this re-entry in most cases has been old Crack-willow overhanging standing water in partial shade. The preference for this habitat is almost certainly related, in part, to the favourable pH of this type of bark and the relatively constant high humidity content of the atmosphere surrounding it.

Their colonisation in Cheshire has also been observed on other substrates, such as boles of Sycamore trees, and was summarised by Guest in 1989. Several of the species have been observed as near as 15km from the centre of Manchester.

Dynamic patterns of lichen recolonisation

By observing a number of willow carrs in different parts of Cheshire, I was able to indicate (Fox 1988) that if their frequency within these habitats were compared, an order of entry could perhaps be established. The suggested sequence has been modified slightly following incorporation of further records from these areas. A more detailed study of the lichen population has

Figure 18.3. Typical Crack-willow carr, 1997. (*Photo: B.W. Fox*).

now been undertaken in readiness for the preparation of a full flora of all lichen species in Cheshire. Some indication of the present (*c.*1992) status of the *Parmelia sulcata* community can be deduced by studying the frequency of occurrence of different members of the *Parmelia sulcata* alliance in a selected number of 32 willow carr sites in Cheshire (Figure 18.5). This histogram gives some indication of the order of recolonisation of the different species of this community into these sites. It can be seen that *P. sulcata*, being present in almost all the sites, is a good indicator of the presence of this community at willow carr sites and appears to be the first coloniser of them. It would be valuable to survey these sites again now, some eight years later, to discover any further improvements in their status.

It is now well over a decade since levels of sulphur dioxide reached low winter mean levels of around 20–30 micrograms per cubic metre. Why therefore have we not seen the re-entry of *Graphis* species *Phlyctis argena*, more *Parmelia* species, *Nephromas*, and even some of the *Lobarion* species? There have been several accounts of small healthy looking tufts of *Usnea* species, which on later re-inspection have disappeared or degenerated, or at best halted in growth. In addition, the Hawksworth and Rose scale originally appeared to indicate that pollution levels corresponded with the more severe end, Zones 0 to 3, representing a severe level of pollution throughout the county, with sulphur dioxide levels in

Figure 18.4. Fallen branch of Crack-willow covered with *Parmelia saxatilis* and *Parmelia subaurifera*, in a Cheshire willow carr. (*Photo: B.W. Fox*).

excess of 125 micrograms per cubic metre (approximately .044 parts per million). The more recent appearance of such species as *Usnea subfloridana* and *Physcia aipolia* appear to be examples of the so-called zone skipping phenomenon, described by Hawksworth & McManus in 1989. This is considered to be due to the

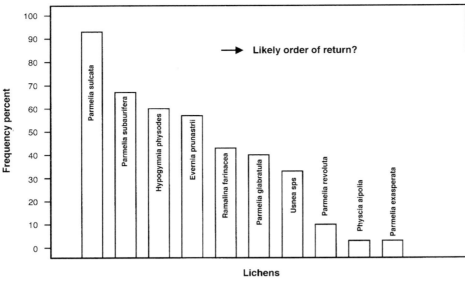

Figure 18.5. Relative abundance of different species derived from 32 Crack-willow carr sites, around 1992. The plot consists of the relative number of sites containing the species, and may represent the order of re-entry into these sites. The pattern refers to the situation around 1992, and a present-day survey would also include other species such as *Parmelia caperata* and *Parmelia perlata*.

preferential colonisation of some zone 6 and 7 species in the rapidly reducing sulphur dioxide environment, implying that the remaining species expected within these zones will appear in good time.

One can propose several other possible reasons which cause this impedance of the establishment of further new and more interesting species:

1. the levels of atmospheric sulphur dioxide may be rising again;

2. there may be some other lichen damaging contaminants from other sources, such as car emissions, oil and gas central heating systems, new industrial processes that may have caused new contaminants to enter the atmosphere which may be presently rising and are unmonitored;

3. there may be a greater influence of transient spikes of higher sulphur dioxide level caused by local climatic factors or occasional pollution accident.

This latter condition may be important as the figures for

Warrington (Figure 18.6), for example, show. The levels of sulphur dioxide rise episodically to high levels, and these could be highly damaging even for the short periods of exposure experienced. This kind of atmospheric pollution pressure could be responsible for the rise and fall observed in *Usnea* spp.

The monitoring of local spikes of pollution is not possible with the present distribution and numbers of monitoring equipment, and indeed to undertake this type of measurement may be too costly to apply generally. It would however be useful to be able to install monitors in those areas where intermittent growth of these species has been observed to see if any of these pollution spikes can still be detected.

I would like to propose that the factors favouring the successful return of the more sensitive species may be by establishing conditions which ensure that:

1. the development of the soredium on the substrate is largely unaffected by the atmospheric concentration of Establishment Hindering Chemicals (EHCs); and

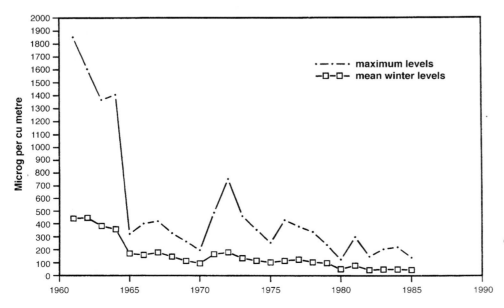

Figure 18.6. The maximum recorded sulphur dioxide levels for the Warrington area, compared with the annual means during the same years as in Figure 18.1. Note the enhanced ordinate scale.

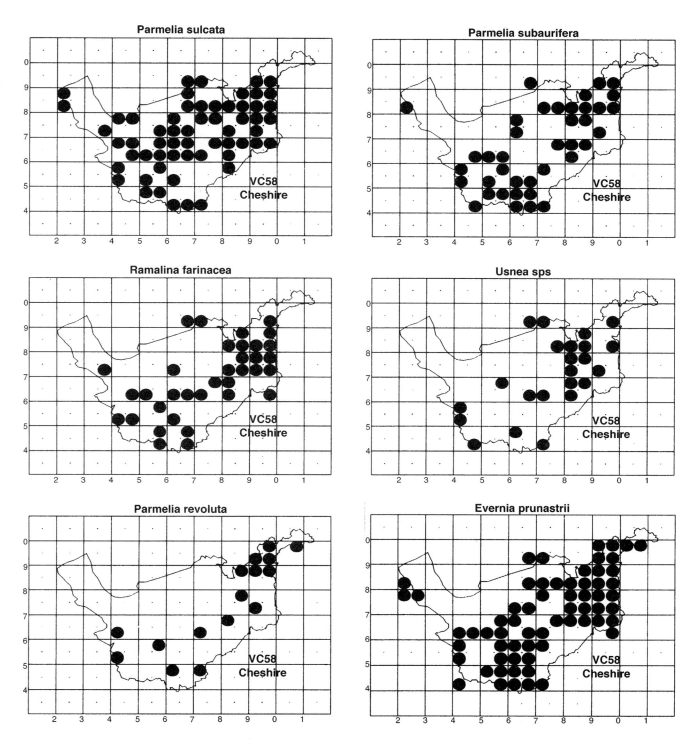

Figure 18.7. The distribution of six of the species used in the coincidence map, Figure 18.8. (Map prepared using software supplied by Dr Alan Morton, Imperial College, University of London, UK).

2. continuous growth of lichens once established on their substrate are not hindered by Continuous Growth Inhibiting Chemicals (CGICs). It may be the selective influence of these, as yet hypothetical pollutants on the different sensitivities of lichen species which is creating the zone skipping phenomenon. I would not be surprised to learn that the chemical nature of these two groups of pollutants will be found to be different, and will require detailed studies to determine their nature.

Using Alan Morton's DMAP software,* a coincidence map (Figure 18.8) of six members of this community can be plotted over Cheshire, and assuming that willow carrs can be found almost everywhere in the county, some indication of the geographical distribution of this

* Dr A. Morton, Department of Biology, Imperial College, University of London, Berks, UK

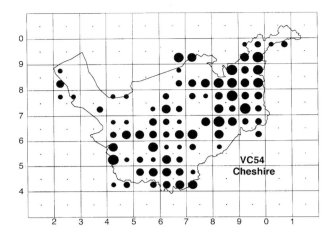

Figure 18.8. The coincidence distribution of the six species illustrated in Figure 18.7. Symbol size is directly related to the number of the species found together in the quadrant. It can be seen that clusters of enriched sites occur in the north-east and south-central areas of the county. A band of low frequency occurs from the industrial areas in the north-west to the south-eastern side of the county and could represent a plume of episodic pollution down-wind of the industrial areas in the north-west. The data applies to that observed in and around 1992. By 1996 this situation had almost certainly improved. (Dr Alan Morton's, DMAP software).

returning population can be deduced. It can be seen that the highest values occupy three broad areas, the north-eastern corner, the south and western corner, and a small area in the north-central region. This map was constructed from data up to 1991–92 and is likely to represent a transient status at that time. There appears to be a plume of slower recovery occurring across the county, down-wind of the industrial conurbations of Ellesmere Port and northern Wirral, which could lead to a quite different distribution following the recovery of lower pollution levels throughout the county. Only time will tell.

Conclusions

Since the pollution control measures of the 1960s, there has been a steady increase in the numbers and variety of lichens in all areas of Merseyside. More and more foliose and fruticose species are entering town parks in suitable sites and once established, an increasing proportion of young plants survive and continue to grow to larger, more visible lichens. Surveys undertaken in the 1970s and 1980s are reviewed and compared, and it is time to ask if the rapid changes occurring in the distribution of the taxa surveyed can provide new information about the changing quality of our atmosphere.

Of particular interest is the re-entry of a characteristic group of lichens dominated by *Parmelia sulcata* appearing on Crack-willow trees, usually overhanging wet areas in Cheshire. This data confirms that the consid-

erable decrease in the sulphur dioxide pollution of the atmosphere of Cheshire is reflected in a marked improvement in the quality of the lichen flora. There is evidence of 'zone skipping', considered to be the effect of a rapidly reducing sulphur dioxide level allowing selective growth of certain zone 6 and 7 species. What is inhibiting the more pollution sensitive species from appearing? Transient spikes of sulphur dioxide pollution occurring as a result of local climatic disturbance or occasional industrial problems is considered a possible cause. However, there is also the possibility that a further unknown series of pollutants may be affecting the establishment and continuing growth of certain species which would otherwise have started colonising selected sites without their influence. The need for more localised and selective sulphur dioxide monitoring sites is suggested, and further work to establish the possible nature of growth Inhibiting Chemicals (EICs and CGICs) is strongly recommended.

References

Alexander, R.W. (1982). The interpretation of lichen and fungal response to decreasing sulphur dioxide levels on Merseyside. *Environmental Education and Information*, **2 & 3**, 193–202.

Bishop, J.A. & Cook, L.M. (1975) Moths, melanism and clean air. *Scientific American*, **232(1)**, 90–99.

Ferry, B.W. & Baddeley, M.S. (1976). Sulphur Dioxide Uptake in Lichens. *Lichenology: Progress and Problems* (eds D.H. Brown, D.L. Hawksworth & R.H. Bailey), pp. 407–18. Academic Press, London.

Fox, B.W. (1988). Improvements in the lichen flora of a midland county. Abstract of AGM symposium. *Bulletin of the British Lichen Society*, **62**, 7.

Grindon, L.H. (1859). *The Manchester Flora*. William White, London.

Guest, J. (1989). Further colonization of Cheshire by epiphytic lichens. *Bulletin of the British Lichen Society*, **64**, 29–31.

Hawksworth, D.L. & McManus, P.M. (1989). Lichen colonization in London under conditions of rapidly falling sulphur dioxide levels, and the concept of zone skipping. *Botanical Journal of the Linnean Society*, **100**, 99–109.

Hawksworth, D.L. & Rose, F. (1970). Qualitative scale for estimating sulphur dioxide air pollution in England and Wales using Epiphytic Lichens. *Nature*, **227**, 145–48.

James, P.W., Hawksworth, D.L. & Rose, F. (1977). Lichen Communities in the British Isles: A preliminary conspectus. *Lichen Ecology* (ed. M.R.D. Seaward), pp. 296–413. Academic Press, London.

Lange, O.L., Herber, U., Schulze, E.D. & Ziegler, H. (1989). Atmospheric pollutants and plant metabolism. *Ecological Studies*, **7**, 238–73.

Marrat, F.P. (1860). Hepatics and Lichens of Liverpool and its vicinity. *Proceedings of the Literary and Philosophical Society of Liverpool*, **14**, (Appendix), 3–14.

North West Economic Planning Council (1974). *Strategic Plan for the North West*. HMSO, London.

Purvis, O.W., Coppins, B.J., Hawksworth, D.L., James, P.W. & Moore, D.M. (eds) (1992). *The Lichen Flora of Great Britain and Ireland*. The British Lichen Society, The Natural History Museum, London.

Richardson, D. (1975). *The Vanishing Lichens*. Douglas David and Charles Ltd, Canada.

Seaward, M.R.D. (1976). Performance of *Lecanora muralis* in an urban environment. *Lichenology: Progress and Problems*, (eds

D.H. Brown, D.L. Hawksworth & R.H. Bailey), pp. 323–57. Academic Press, London.

Travis, W.G. (1922). The Lichens of the Wirral. *Lancashire and Cheshire Naturalist*, **14**, 177–90.

Travis, W.G. (1925). Additions to the Lichen Flora of the Wirral. *Lancashire and Cheshire Naturalist*, **17**, 152–54.

Turner, D. & Dillwyn, L.W. (1805). *The Botanists' Guide through England and Wales.* Philips and Farndon, London.

Vick, C.M. & Bevan, R. (1976). Lichens and Tar Spot Fungus (*Rhytisma acerinum*) as indicators of sulphur dioxide pollution on Merseyside. *Environmental Pollution*, **11**, 203–16.

von Arb, C. & Brunold, C. (1989). Lichen physiology and air pollution. 1 Physiological responses in situ *Parmelia sulcata* among air pollution zones within Biel, Switzerland. *Canadian Journal of Botany*, **68**, 35–42.

Wheldon, J.A. & Travis, W.G. (1915). The lichens of South Lancashire. *Linnean Society Journal of Botany*, **43**, 87–136.

CHAPTER NINETEEN

Vascular plants: a game of chance?

E.F. GREENWOOD

Introduction

The Mersey Basin region is a varied one, made up of extensive coastal areas, mainly of saltmarsh and sand dune, but with some clay cliffs, intensive arable and pastoral agricultural areas, and on the eastern margins large upland areas over 500m altitude. Formerly important habitats, such as the many lowland raised bogs, shallow meres and sandstone headlands on the tidal River Mersey, have largely gone through developments of various kinds. Perhaps the most significant feature today is the presence of the large urban and industrial conurbations of Greater Manchester and Merseyside – a powerhouse of the industrial revolution for over 200 years. Human intervention in the area has been massive and nothing of the truly natural habitats remains. Nevertheless, large areas of wildscape and semi-natural areas survive or have been created in the last 200 years as a consequence of human intervention.

What has been happening to the flowering plants and ferns which, with other plant and animal species including humans, inhabit this area? The changes that have occurred may look as if it is all a matter of chance, but is it? Unfortunately the poor quality of the available data limits precise conclusions, but interesting generalisations are certainly possible.

The Mersey Basin area is defined as the catchment area of the River Mersey. (The Mersey Basin Campaign area also includes the Leeds & Liverpool Canal corridor.) It includes parts of the modern administrative areas of Cheshire, Derbyshire, Greater Manchester, Lancashire and Merseyside. However, botanical recording is based on Watsonian vice-counties, which are sub-divisions of the administrative counties of the late 19th century. Most of VC58 and 59 (Cheshire and South Lancaster) contain substantial parts of the Mersey Basin of which only a small upland area falls outside (in Derbyshire VC57) these vice-counties. This chapter relates primarily to vice-counties 58 and 59 (the Mersey Basin region) together with vice-county 60 (West Lancaster or most of Lancashire north of the River Ribble) where detailed recording has taken place over the last 30 years.

The first local floras (Hall 1839; Buxton 1849) are really no more than rough indications of what grew in the region 150 or so years ago. Since then a succession of local floras has been published, but it was not until the advent of the 'Atlas' (Perring & Walters 1962) that a quantitative approach to recording was developed at a 10 x 10km square level. Unfortunately, in the Mersey Basin only Cheshire, at a 5 x 5km square level, was recorded systematically (Newton 1971). Further north, in VC60, systematic recording on a 2 x 2km square basis was undertaken over the last 30 years, giving a much more detailed analysis than is available further south. However thorough, recording the presence or absence of species in an area as large as a 2 x 2km square is a somewhat chancy affair. The Botanical Society of the British Isles (BSBI) monitoring exercise in 1987–89 (Rich & Woodruff 1990) demonstrated the difficulties of trying to make assessments of change since 1962 on a quantitative basis. Despite these difficulties it is believed that over 100 years, at least, it is possible to make some valid generalisations. In compiling this account the main works used were those by de Tabley (1899), Newton (1971, 1990) (for Cheshire), Savidge, Gordon & Heywood (1963) (for South Lancaster) and Wheldon & Wilson (1907), and results of survey work compiled in the last 30 years (for West Lancaster). Where possible the results of recent recordings have been included.

Changes to the vascular flora over 200 years

Native species

These are defined as those which are present without intervention by humans, whether intentional or unintentional, having come from an area in which they are native. In practice it is impossible to determine the status of some species, and in this account all species which are known to have been established in the area for 500 or more years are regarded as native. This still leaves a few species whose status is uncertain and inevitably, in the absence of definitive information, decisions regarding the status of individual species are subjective.

Table 19.1 analyses the composition of the flora of the Mersey Basin region (VC58 and 59) along with floras of West Lancaster (60), Durham (66) and Northumberland (67 and 68), all of which contain large conurbations,

	*Total no. of species and hybrids (incl. aliens)	Total no. of native species and hybrids	Total no. of all aliens		Total no. of casual aliens		Total no. of extinct native species	
			No.	% of total no. of species and hybrids	No.	% of aliens	No.	% of total of native species
VC58 Cheshire	1,231	868	363	30	138	38	82	9.5
VC59 S. Lancaster	1,516	831	685	45	419	61	100	12.0
VC60 W. Lancaster	1,579	922	657	42	428	65	38	4.0
VC66 Durham[1]	1,656	1,000	656	40	226	34.5	96	9.6
VC67 & 68 Northumberland[2]	1,575	949	626	40	347	55	23	2.4

*Excluding critical micro species of *Rubus, Hieracium* and *Taraxacum*   [1] Graham (1988)   [2] Swann (1993)

Table 19.1. Analysis of the flora of five northern vice-counties in England.

upland and coastal regions, and compares them in terms of native, established and casual alien and extinct species. Extinct species are those which have not been recorded for a substantial time (say 30 years) or where the last established locality for a species is known to have been lost. Caution should be exercised when considering if a species is extinct, as some have only occurred at a few sites and then irregularly over long periods of time, e.g., Lesser Twayblade (*Listera cordata*). Those consid-

ered extinct in VCs 58–60 are listed in Table 19.2.

Table 19.1 shows that in the Mersey Basin region approximately 844 native species have been recorded (average for the five areas listed in the table: 913). This may be too low, and with more intensive fieldwork it should be possible to increase this number substantially – say by 30 species.

Of those native species recorded approximately 10.8% (or 91 species) have become extinct (listed in Table 19.2).

Table 19.2. Extinct native species in Cheshire and Lancashire (VC58-60) with dates of last known occurrence when known.

Species	VC58	VC59	VC60	BSBI *
Agrostemma githago	×	1964	✓	−49 S
Alopecurus bulbosus	×	1864	−	+91 I
Anagallis minima	×	1859	✓	−73 S
Antennaria dioica	−	1954	1909	−5 I
Anthriscus caucalis	✓	✓	1905	−21 I
Asplenium marinum	✓	1908	✓	−10 I
Asplenium viride	−	1915	−	−22 I
Bupleurum tenuissimum	×	−	−	−42 S
Calamagrostis canescens	✓	1892	−	4 I
Calystegia soldanella	×	✓	✓	−37 S
Carduus tenuiflorus	✓	1907	✓	−32 S
Carex diandra	×	1850	✓	−33 I
Carex dioica	×	✓	✓	−11 I
Carex divulsa	×	−	−	+28
Carex elata	✓	1880	✓	−20 I
Carex elongata	✓	1900	−	+35 I
Carex filiformis	1867	1859	−	−
Carex lasiocarpa	×	×	✓	−28 I
Carex limosa	✓	−	1912	−26 I

Species	VC58	VC59	VC60	BSBI *
Carex strigosa	✓	1927	✓	+10 I
Carex viridula ssp. *brachyrrhyncha*	×	1964	✓	−2 I
Carex viridula ssp. *viridula*	×	✓	✓	−32 ?
Catapodium rigidum	×	1939	✓	−1 I
Centaurium latifolium	−	1872	−	−
Centaurium littorale	×	✓	✓	−100 S
Cephalanthera longifolia	−	−	1898	−
Ceratophyllum submersum	✓	1870	✓	+17 I
Cicuta virosa	✓	1861	−	−5 I
Clinopodium acinos	×	1859	✓	−21 I
Cochlearia officinalis	✓	1868	✓	−17 ?
Coeloglossum viride	×	1914	✓	−40 S
Cryptogramma crispa	×	×	✓	−12 I
Cuscuta spp. and *C.epithymum*	×	✓	−	−32 S
Daphne laureola	✓	1866	✓	−13 I
Descurainea sophia	×	✓	✓	+4 I
Dianthus deltoides	×	1887	−	−41 I
Diphasiastrum alpinum	−	1850	1907	−57 I
Draba muralis	−	1851	✓	+17 I
Drosera intermedia	1980s	1965	1858	−4 I
Drosera longifolia	×	1868	1902	−33 I
Dryopteris oreades	−	1957	−	+100 S
Dryopteris cristata	×	1851	−	−3 ?

* BSBI Monitoring Scheme changes (%) 1962–1987/88 based on sample 10 × 10km squares of the UK National Grid

Species				
Eleocharis multicaulis	✓	1885	✓	−11 I
Eleogiton fluitans	✓	1917	1925	−4 I
Elytrigia atherica	✓	1891	✓	0 I
Epipactis phyllanthes	×	✓	✓	+35 I
Erodium moschatum	1962	1929	1931	−32 I
Euphorbia exigua	×	✓	✓	−17 S
Euphrasia micrantha	−	−	1907	+5 ?
Filago minima	×	1914	✓	−29 S
Filago vulgaris	×	1930	✓	−33 S
Galeopsis angustifolia	×	1907	✓	−51 S
Genista anglica	×	✓	✓	−40 S
Gentiana pneumonanthe	✓	✓	1941	−17 I
Gentianella campestris	×	✓	✓	−28 I
Geranium columbinum	×	1913	✓	−13 I
Gnaphalium sylvaticum	×	1928	✓	−61 S
Groenlandia densa	×	1918	✓	−24 S
Gymnocarpium robertianum	−	1860	✓	+10 I
Gymnocarpium dryopteris	×	1964	✓	−43 S
Hammarbya paludosa	×	1878	−	+65 I
Helleborus viridis	−	1963	✓	−18 I
Huperzia selago	×	1880	✓	−32 I
Hymenophyllum tunbrigense	−	1840	1907	+100 I
Hymenophyllum wilsonii	−	1860	✓	−5 I
Hypericum elodes	✓	1873	1931	−4 I
Hypochaeris glabra	×	1928	−	−47 S
Impatiens noli-tangere	×	1903	✓	−22 I
Isoetes sp.	−	−	Pre-historic	−
Juncus balticus	−	✓	Early 1960s	−
Lamium confertum	−	1899	1907	−26 I
Lathyrus sylvestris	×	✓	−	−25 I
Lepidium ruderale	×	1959	−	−4 I
Limonium vulgare	×	1860	✓	−22 ?
Limosella aquatica	✓	✓	1964	−5 I
Listera cordata	×	✓	✓	−45 I
Lithospermum arvense	×	1936	✓	−26 S
Lycopodiella inundata	×	1880	−	−17 I
Lycopodium clavatum	×	✓	✓	−45 S
Maianthemum bifolium	−	1597	−	−
Marrubium vulgare	×	1926	−	−54 S
Mentha pulegium	×	✓	−	−33 I
Mertensia maritima	−	−	1941	−100 S
Meum athamanticum	−	1914	−	−33 I
Moenchia erecta	×	1915	−	−18 I
Monotropa hypopitys	×	✓	✓	−13 I
Myosurus minimus	✓	−	1857	−12 I
Ophrys insectifera	−	1850	✓	−29 I
Orchis ustulata	−	−	1930s	−66 S
Orobanche rapum-genistae	×	1850	−	−100 S
Papaver argemone	×	×	✓	−30 S
Peucedanum palustre	−	1870	−	−
Peucedanum ostruthium	×	1908	−	−22 I
Phegopteris connectilis	×	✓	✓	−18 I
Pilularia globulifera	×	1874	−	−5 I
Poa palustris	×	✓	−	−100 I
Polystichum setiferum	✓	1850	✓	+30 S
Potamogeton coloratus	×	1827	✓	−15 I
Potamogeton gramineus	✓	✓	1881	−28 I
Potamogeton praelongus	×	×	−	−100 S
Pseudorchis albida	×	1900	Early 20thC	−100 I
Puccinellia rupestris	×	1888	−	−4 I
Pyrola media	×	1860	−	+1 I
Pyrola minor	×	✓	−	−45 I
Radiola linoides	×	1915	1949	−35 S
Ranunculus arvensis	×	1934	1963	−52 S
Ranunculus parviflorus	×	×	−	−32 I
Ranunculus sardous	×	✓	✓	+13 I
Ranunculus x *bachii*	−	1914	1914	−
Rhynchospora alba	✓	1900	✓	−22 I
Ribes spicatum	−	1903	−	−45 I
Ruppia cirrhosa	−	1863	−	−45 I
Sagina subulata	×	−	−	−4 I
Salix phylicifolia	−	1888	✓	−19 I
Salvia verbenaca	✓	×	1901	+35 I
Saxifraga hirculus	×	−	−	−
Scandix pecten-veneris	×	×	✓	−72 S
Scheuchzeria palustris	×	Pre-historic	Pre-historic	−
Schoenus nigricans	×	✓	✓	−18 I
Sedum anglicum	✓	−	1885	−6 I
Selaginella selaginoides	×	1942	✓	−26 I
Seriphidium maritimum	1974	1859	✓	−23 I
Serratula tinctoria	✓	×	✓	−14 I
Silaum silaus	−	1888	1901	−8 I
Sparganium natans	×	−	✓	−45 I
Spergularia rupicola	✓	1927	1925	+6 I
Spiranthes spiralis	×	1905	✓	−50 S
Stellaria palustris	−	1926	1974	−9 I
Tephroseris palustris	−	−	1858	−
Torilis nodosa	×	1963	✓	−24 S
Trifolium micranthum	✓	1956	✓	−9 I
Trifolium squamosum	−	1811	−	−24 I
Trifolium subterraneum	×	1948	−	+17 I
Trifolium suffocatum	−	1964	1860	+91 I
Trollius europaeus	×	✓	✓	−16 I
Utricularia intermedia	−	1838	−	−100 I
Utricularia minor	✓	1956	1944	−37 I
Valerianella dentata	×	1903	1957	−39 S
Veronica spicata ssp. *hybrida*	−	−	1863	−
Vicia lutea	×	✓	−	+91 I
Viola tricolor ssp. *curtisii*	×	✓	✓	−
Wahlenbergia hederacea	✓	1908	1880	−38 S
Zostera marina	1851	1900	−	−57 I
Total	82	100	38	

S = Significant
I = Insignificant
− = No record
✓ = Not extinct
× = Believed extinct (no date)

The average for the five areas analysed in Table 19.1 suggests the loss should only be 7.5% (or 68 species). More intensive field survey might reveal that some supposedly extinct native species are still growing in the area. Nevertheless, it is likely that human intervention has adversely affected the survival of native species in the more urbanised areas. It is also interesting that the lists of extinct species for the three Cheshire and Lancashire vice-counties vary considerably. Often this is because the species which have become extinct were always rare and therefore vulnerable, being known to occur in only a few localities. Whilst reasons for extinction can be readily related to the destruction of habitats through urbanisation and agricultural improvements, habitat changes may be more indirectly caused by eutrophication of soils. However, climatic changes and other factors may be involved.

In an effort to obtain a better understanding of what might be happening, a more detailed analysis of changes to the native flora was undertaken in West Lancaster, which is better known to the author. In VC60 extinction of the native flora accounts for only 4.0% (38) of the total, but new native species discovered in the last 30 years accounted for 4.7% (43) of the flora, Table 19.3. Of these, 11 species or 1.2% of the native species were added as a consequence of a better understanding of more difficult

or critical groups. At least seven of the species have spread into the area (colonist) during the last 100 years whilst the remainder were probably overlooked by earlier recorders.

Wheldon & Wilson's *Flora* (1907) is a model for its time and reflects careful study and extensive fieldwork over 30 years at the end of the 19th century. With this in mind, an attempt was made to identify species that might be becoming more common (114 species) or less common (48 species), Tables 19.4 and 19.5. The figure for decreasing species is likely to be fairly accurate, but the much larger number of increasing species is due at least in part to the more thorough recording in the last 30 years.

In Table 19.6 the changes to the native flora of VC60 are summarised. This suggests that the numbers of new and extinct taxa are roughly equal, but that more native species are extending their range than are becoming more restricted.

This is perhaps a surprising conclusion. However, it is likely that the more thorough surveys of the last 30 years account for the present apparently optimistic picture. Unfortunately, not many attempts have been made either nationally or locally to assess change in this way. Nevertheless Braithwaite (1992), examining the largely rural county of Berwickshire on the east coast and

| Species | Distribution preferences | | BSBI† |
	Geographical	Habitat	
Alisma lanceolatum	General	Aquatic	+1 I
Anthemis arvensis	General	Ruderal	–28 S
Atriplex longipes	Northern	Coastal	–
Bromopsis benekenii	General	Woodland	–
Bromopsis erecta	Southern	Grassland	–1 I
Bromus lepidus	General	Ruderal	–49 S
Callitriche brutia	Southern	Aquatic	+100 ?
Carex ericetorum	Continental	Grassland	–
Carex lasiocarpa	Northern	Heath	–28 I
Carex strigosa	Southern	Woodland	+10 I
Ceratophyllum demersum	General	Aquatic	+16 I
Ceratophyllum submersum	Southern	Aquatic	+17 I
Crepis biennis	Northern	Woodland	–20 ?
Dactylorhiza praetermissa	Southern	Grassland	+22 S
Daphne mezereum	General	Woodland	–
Deschampsia cespitosa ssp. *parviflora*	General	Woodland	–
Dryopteris aemula	Western	Woodland	–12 I
Epilobium alsinifolium	Northern	Aquatic	–22 I
Epipactis leptochila var. *dunensis*	Endemic	Coastal	–
Epipactis phyllanthes	Western	Coastal	+35 I
Eriophorum latifolium	General	Aquatic	+13 I
Festuca filiformis	Western	Heath	–11 ?
Filago minima	General	Ruderal	–29 S
Galeopsis bifida	General	Ruderal	–
Galium palustre ssp. *elongatum*	General	Aquatic	+99 ?
Glyceria declinata	Western	Aquatic	+20 S
Hordelymus europaeus	Southern	Woodland	–49 I
Hordeum secalinum	Southern	Grassland	–6 I
Ledum palustre ssp. *groenlandicum*	American	Heath	–
Lotus glaber	Southern	Grassland	–4 I
Myosotis stolonifera	Western	Aquatic	+65 S
Persicaria laxiflora	Southern	Aquatic	–16 I
Persicaria minor	General	Aquatic	–13 I
Poa angustifolia	General	Grassland	–
Poa humilis	Northern	Grassland	–
Potamogeton coloratus	General	Aquatic	–15 I
Puccinellia distans	General	Coastal	+40 S
Sorbus torminalis	Southern	Woodland	+35 S
Spartina anglica	General	Coastal	+3 I
Stellaria pallida	Continental	Coastal	–34 S
Trifolium micranthum	Southern	Grassland	–9 I
Veronica catenata	General	Aquatic	+16 ?
Vulpia myuros	Southern	Ruderal	+28 S

* Critical species
S = Significant
I = Insignificant
† BSBI Monitoring Scheme changes (%) 1962–1987/88 based on sample 10 × 10km squares of the UK National Grid

Table 19.3. Native species discovered in VC60, in the period 1907–1995.

Species	Distribution preferences — Geographical	Distribution preferences — Habitat	BSBI†
Acer campestre	Continental	Marginal	+4 I
Agrostis gigantea	General	Ruderal	+33 S
Aira caryophyllea	Southern	Ruderal	−15 S
Anchusa arvensis	General	Ruderal	−8 I
Atriplex littoralis	General	Coastal	−6 I
Berula erecta	General	Aquatic	0 I
Beta vulgaris ssp. *maritima*	Western	Coastal	+282 ?
Bidens cernua	General	Aquatic	−18 I
Bidens tripartita	General	Aquatic	−5 I
Blysmus rufus	Northern	Coastal	−5 I
Brassica nigra	Southern	Ruderal	−1 I
Cakile maritima	Western	Coastal	−18 I
Calamagrostis epigejos	General	Marginal	+4 I
Callitriche hamulata	Northern	Aquatic	−11 ?
Carex curta	General	Aquatic	−4 I
Carex distans	General	Coastal	−23 I
Carex elata	General	Aquatic	−20 I
Carex pilulifera	General	Heath	−16 S
Catabrosia aquatica	General	Aquatic	−13 I
Catapodium rigidum	Southern	Ruderal	−1 I
Centaurium pulchellum	General	Coastal	−7 I
Cerastium arvense	General	Marginal	−18 S
Chaenorhinum minus	General	Ruderal	+2 I
Chamerion angustifolium	General	Ruderal	+1 I
Coincya monensis ssp. *monensis*	Endemic	Coastal	−22 I
Conium maculatum	General	Ruderal	−1 I
Coronopus squamatus	General	Ruderal	+6 I
Crambe maritima	Western	Coastal	−23 I
Dipsacus fullonum	Southern	Marginal	+8 S
Echium vulgare	General	Ruderal	−19 S
Eleocharis quinqueflora	General	Aquatic	−12 I
Eleocharis uniglumis	General	Aquatic	−4 I
Elytrigia atherica	Western	Coastal	0 I
Epilobium roseum	General	Aquatic	+4 ?
Equisetum variegatum	Northern	Coastal	−22 I
Erodium cicutarium	General	Ruderal	−12 S
Festuca altissima	Northern	Woodland	+51 I
Festuca arundinacea	General	Marginal	+23 ?
Fumaria purpurea	Endemic	Ruderal	−33 I
Gagea lutea	General	Woodland	−17 I
Galium uliginosum	General	Aquatic	−18 S
Glyceria maxima	General	Aquatic	+4 I
Glyceria notata	General	Aquatic	+16 S
Helictotrichon pubescens	Northern	Grassland	+8 I
Hordeum murinum	Southern	Ruderal	+1 I
Juncus subnodulosus	General	Aquatic	+17 ?
Lamium album	General	Marginal	−3 I
Lamium amplexicaule	General	Ruderal	+2 I
Lamium hybridum	General	Ruderal	+25 S
Lathraea squamaria	General	Woodland	−23 I
Lemna gibba	General	Aquatic	−13 I
Lepidium campestre	General	Ruderal	−28 S
Lepidium heterophyllum	Western	Ruderal	−31 S
Leymus arenarius	Western	Coastal	+8 I
Limonium humile	Western	Coastal	−22 ?
Limonium vulgare	Western	Coastal	−22 ?
Milium effusum	General	Woodland	−1 I
Myosotis ramosissima	General	Coastal	−20 S
Myosotis secunda	Western	Aquatic	+16 I
Myosotis sylvatica	General	Marginal	+62 S
Myriophyllum alterniflorum	General	Aquatic	−15 I
Ophrys apifera	Southern	Marginal	0 I
Ornithogalum umbellatum	Southern	Marginal	+14 I
Ornithopus perpusillus	Western	Grassland	−25 I
Orobanche minor	Southern	Ruderal	−20 S
Parapholis strigosa	Western	Coastal	−1 I
Phleum arenarium	Southern	Coastal	−16 I
Picris echioides	Southern	Marginal	+4 I
Plantago coronopus	Southern	Coastal	−9 I
Poa compressa	General	Ruderal	+27 S
Polygonum oxyspermum ssp. *raii*	Western	Coastal	−24 ?
Polystichum setiferum	Southern	Woodland	+30 S
Potamogeton alpinus	General	Aquatic	−49 I
Potamogeton pectinatus	General	Aquatic	+42 S
Potentilla palustris	General	Aquatic	−16 I
Ranunculus lingua	General	Aquatic	+40 S
Ranunculus sardous	General	Ruderal	+13 I
Ranunculus sceleratus	General	Aquatic	+2 I
Raphanus raphanistrum ssp. *maritimus*	Western	Coastal	−11 I
Raphanus raphanistrum ssp. *raphanistrum*	General	Ruderal	−7 I
Ribes nigrum	General	Marginal	+22 S
Ribes rubrum	General	Marginal	+21 ?
Rorippa palustris	General	Aquatic	+12 I
Rorippa sylvestris	General	Aquatic	+3 I
Rumex hydrolapathum	General	Aquatic	−7 I
Sagina maritima	Western	Coastal	−28 I
Salix viminalis	General	Aquatic	+10 S
Samolus valerandi	General	Coastal	−15 I
Saxifraga granulata	General	Marginal	−15 I
Schoenoplectus tabernaemontani	General	Aquatic	+11 I
Scrophularia auriculata	Southern	Aquatic	−2 I
Senecio erucifolius	Continental	Marginal	+3 I
Senecio viscosus	General	Ruderal	+8 I
Seriphidium maritimum	Western	Coastal	−23 I
Solanum nigrum	General	Ruderal	+4 I
Spirodela polyrhiza	General	Aquatic	−11 I
Stachys arvensis	Southern	Ruderal	−15 S
Stellaria neglecta	General	Woodland	+23 I
Tanacetum vulgare	General	Marginal	+1 I
Thalictrum flavum	General	Aquatic	−14 I
Thlaspi arvense	General	Ruderal	−1 I
Tilia cordata	Continental	Woodland	+19 I
Trifolium fragiferum	Western	Coastal	−15 I
Typha angustifolia	General	Aquatic	+14 I
Valerianella locusta	General	Ruderal	−16 S
Veronica anagallis-aquatica	General	Aquatic	−8 ?
Veronica hederifolia	General	Ruderal	+6 I
Veronica scutellata	General	Aquatic	−18 S
Vicia hirsuta	General	Ruderal	+1 I
Vicia lathyroides	General	Coastal	+26 I
Vicia tetrasperma	General	Ruderal	+10 I
Viola palustris	General	Aquatic	−5 I
Viola reichenbachiana	Southern	Woodland	−2 I
Vulpia bromoides	Southern	Ruderal	−5 I

S = Significant
I = Insignificant
† BSBI Monitoring Scheme changes (%) 1962–1987/88 based on sample 10 × 10km squares of the UK National Grid

Table 19.4. Species showing an apparently increasing frequency of occurrence in VC60, 1907–1992.

Species	Distribution preferences Geographical Habitat		BSBI†
Actaea spicata	General	Marginal	–
*Agrostemma githago	Southern	Ruderal	–49 S
Asplenium marinum	Western	Coastal	–10 I
Asplenium viride	Northern	Rocks	–22 I
Baldellia ranunculoides	General	Aquatic	–37 S
Botrychium lunaria	General	Grassland	–19 I
Cirsium heterophyllum	Northern	Marginal	–22 I
Coeloglossum viride	General	Grassland	–40 S
Cryptogramma crispa	Northern	Rocks	–12 I
Cynoglossum officinale	General	Marginal	–34 S
Drosera rotundifolia	General	Heath	–13 I
Filago vulgaris	Continental	Ruderal	–33 S
Gentianella campestris	General	Grassland	–28 I
Gnaphalium sylvaticum	General	Grassland	–61 S
Groenlandea densa	General	Aquatic	–24 S
Helleborus viridis	General	Woodland	–18 I
Huperzia selago	General	Rocks	–32 I
Hymenophyllum wilsonii	Western	Rocks	–5 I
Jasione montana	General	Heath	–22 S
Juniperus communis	General	Marginal	–11 ?
Limonium britannicum ssp. *celticum*	Endemic	Coastal	–11 ? (for agg).
Listera cordata	Northern	Heath	–45 I
Lithospermum arvense	General	Ruderal	–26 S
Lycopodium clavatum	General	Heath	–45 S

Species			
Malva neglecta	General	Ruderal	–3 I
Ophrys insectifera	General	Marginal	–29 I
Orchis morio	General	Grassland	–32 S
Osmunda regalis	Western	Aquatic	+23 I
Paris quadrifolia	General	Woodland	–24 S
Pedicularis palustris	General	Aquatic	–25 S
Pinguicula vulgaris	General	Aquatic	–14 I
Platanthera bifolia	General	Grassland	–34 S
Platanthera chlorantha	General	Grassland	–13 I
Primula farinosa	General	Aquatic	–5 I
Pyrola rotundifolia	Western	Coastal	+100 ?
Ranunculus baudottii	Western	Coastal	–4 I
Ranunculus circinatus	General	Aquatic	–27 S
Ranunculus peltatus	Western	Aquatic	+41 ?
Salix myrsinifolia	Northern	Marginal	–17 ?
Salix phylicifolia	Northern	Marginal	–19 I
Selaginella selaginoides	Northern	Aquatic	–26 I
Sherardia arvensis	General	Ruderal	–13 S
Sparganium natans	General	Aquatic	–45 I
Trollius europaeus	Northern	Marginal	–16 I
Utricularia vulgaris	General	Aquatic	–16 I
Verbena officinalis	General	Marginal	–15 I
Veronica agrestis	General	Ruderal	+7 I
Veronica polita	General	Ruderal	+4 I

S = Significant
I = Insignificant
† BSBI Monitoring Scheme changes (%) 1962–1987/88 based on sample 10 × 10km squares of the UK National Grid
* Probably of ancient introduction

Table 19.5. Species showing an apparently decreasing frequency of occurrence in VC60, 1907–1997.

	Numbers	% of native VC60 flora	National changes to VC60 species			
			Decreasing		Increasing	
			No	% of VC60 species	No	% of VC60 species
New taxa	43	4.7	17	40	16	37
Increasing taxa	114	12.4	65	57	46	40
Total	157	17.1	82	52	62	40
Extinct taxa	37	4.0	25	68	5	14
Decreasing taxa	48	5.2	42	88	5	10
Total	85	9.2	67	79	10	12

Table 19.6. Summary of changes in the native flora of VC60, 1907–1995 compared with possible changes observed nationally 1962–1988.

over a much shorter time period, concluded that 11.5% of the flora was declining and that only 5.5% was showing any increase – almost the exact reverse of the results reported here.

At a national level the BSBI instigated a sample survey, or monitoring scheme, of which one of the objectives was to assess the change in frequency of species in the British Isles between the publication of the 'Atlas' (Perring & Walters 1962) and their survey period of 1987/88. A report was produced (Rich & Woodruff 1990)

which described the project and presented the results. In doing so the authors described the difficulties of making any accurate conclusions. In particular the problems of comparing like with like proved largely insuperable. As a consequence in only a few cases was it possible to determine change in frequency with any confidence. Nevertheless the report (although not reproduced in Palmer & Bratton 1995) does indicate the percentage changes noted for each species and, using the data for England, included in Tables 19.4 and 19.5. Table 19.6

summarises the changes nationally for VC60 species. This shows that, for both extinct/decreasing species and new/increasing species, most appear to be declining in frequency nationally, but there is a difference between the two groups. In the new/increasing group 40% are increasing nationally whilst 52% are decreasing. However, in the extinct/decreasing group only 12% are increasing whilst 79% are decreasing nationally. However, the BSBI survey was assessing change over only the last 30 years or so, rather than the last 90 years for VC60. Nevertheless, despite the inadequacies of the data and difficulties of comparing like with like, it may be that the trends reported here for VC60 are reflected, on a shorter time-scale, nationally.

In Tables 19.7 and 19.8 an attempt is made to reflect those species showing change in terms of broad European phytogeographical affinities and habitat preferences. These tables show that generally distributed species or species with a southern distribution tend to be increasing, whilst northern species are declining. In terms of habitat preferences aquatic, ruderal and coastal species are all increasing, but heath and grassland species appear particularly vulnerable to change.

	Decreasing and extinct	Increasing and new	Net loss (-) or gain (+)
Northern	18	10	-8
Southern	5	28	+23
Western	14	21	+7
Continental	2	5	+3
General	46	89	+43
American	0	1	+1
Endemic	0	3	+3
Total	**85**	**157**	

Table 19.7. Changing numbers of native species in VC60, 1907–1992 according to European phytogeographical preferences (number of species).

	Decreasing and extinct	Increasing and new	Net loss (-) or gain (+)
Heath	13	4	-9
Aquatic	19	46	+27
Rock	6	0	-6
Ruderal	11	37	+26
Coastal	7	30	+23
Grass	16	9	-7
Wood	4	16	+12
Marginal	9	15	+6
Total	85	157	

Table 19.8. Changing numbers of native species in VC60, 1907–1992 according to broad habitat preferences (number of species).

These changes accord well with observed changes in environmental data where available. In 1991 Lancashire County Council published 'A Green Audit' (Anon 1991) which summarised these changes. In terms of climatic change over a period of 210 years, 1750–1960, summer temperatures have remained more or less unchanged but in winter January temperatures have risen 1.7°C, in February 0.5°C, in November 0.8°C and in December 1.1°C. Thus, winters have become warmer, but it should be noted that this warming started before the full onset of the industrialisation of the Mersey Basin region in the 19th century. Figures were not calculated for the years since 1960, but they include some of the coldest and mildest winters on record as well as some of the warmest summers. There is no doubt that there has been an overall warming of the climate, (Figure 19.1), which favours species of a more southerly distribution, whilst northern species are disadvantaged. Whether the warming is caused or influenced by human intervention is still uncertain, but recent evidence suggests that it is (see chapter one, this volume).

Rainfall data is available for Preston covering the 140 years from 1850 (Figure 19.2). Rainfall is highly variable,

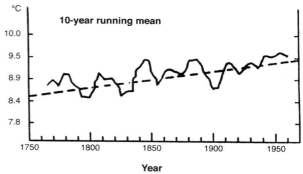

Figure 19.1. Long-term temperature trends on the Lancashire plain, 1750–1960.
(Source: Savidge, Heywood & Gordon 1963, and reproduced by permission of Liverpool Botanical Society.)

but overall the trend is for the climate to get wetter – by perhaps 100mm over the period of 140 years. This would favour wetland species where drainage has not taken place. However, the dry period starting in 1995 is exceptional, but it is still too early to determine its significance.

Data for habitat changes are poor. Woodland has probably changed little in extent, but over the last 200 years mainly broad-leaved plantations were planted in the Fylde (and in South Lancaster), and in the last 50 years conifer woods were planted more widely. Overall there is probably more woodland today than at any time in recent history, but this masks the destruction of old, more natural and therefore species rich woodland.

Hedgerows can be described as woodland edge habitats and can form important linear habitats. In the lowland areas in the west of Lancashire (and in

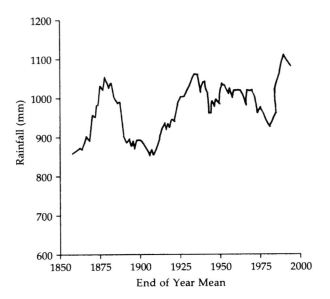

Figure 19.2. Rainfall at Preston, 1849–1989. (Source: Lancashire Polytechnic 1989, and reproduced by persmission of Liverpool Botanical Society).

Merseyside) most of the hedges were planted in the last 200 years. Nevertheless, it is estimated that 10% of the county's hedges are species rich. In a comparative survey between 1963 and 1988 about 25% of the hedges seem to have been lost, but often in localised areas in the west where few and comparatively recently planted hedges existed. In Cheshire 60% of hedges seem to have been lost in the period 1850–1987 (Anon 1993).

Upland heaths have probably not changed greatly in extent but moor burning is a characteristic feature of land management; occasionally more devastating fires have occurred, e.g., in 1947 in Bowland. However, moor burning, increased grazing and atmospheric pollution, especially of nitrogen, have probably changed the nature of the upland areas, reducing the extent of dwarf shrub communities and favouring the spread of grasslands (chapter eleven, this volume; de Smidt 1995). In lowland areas 98% of the Lancashire peat mosslands have been lost, a situation certainly reflected further south in the Mersey Basin. There were probably only a few lowland dry heaths in Lancashire and they have largely been lost, but a few persist south of the River Mersey, especially in Wirral. However, these have seen a considerable loss of species diversity during the last 100 years or so.

There have been major changes to aquatic habitats, but it is possible that overall there has been an increase in area. In the north of West Lancaster (VC60) the extensive swamps and fens at Leighton Moss containing 80ha of reedbed are entirely new, having been formed in the last 80 years or so. Similarly, numerous gravel pits, salt subsidence pools and reservoirs have greatly added to the extent of aquatic habitats over the last 100 years. On the other hand, marl pits have been reduced by some 63% (10,758 ponds) between 1845 and 1988 in Lancashire as a whole. However, half of this loss was between 1965

and 1988. In Cheshire (Anon 1993) the loss in a similar period was also 63% (29,500 out of 47,000).

In Lancashire there have been major changes in coastal habitats. Destruction of cliffs, saltmarshes and sand dunes occurred through urbanisation, industrialisation and land reclamation. Natural accretion (and erosion) has also taken place, so that overall there is perhaps an increase in the extent of coastal habitats with perhaps larger areas of saltmarshes (Berry 1967; Pringle 1987; Gray & Scott 1987), but smaller areas of sand dunes. However, change in the extent of coastal habitats may be cyclical as the relatively recently formed saltmarshes at Silverdale are now (1996) eroding (Peter 1994).

No figures exist for changes in Lancashire grasslands, but nationally it is estimated that 95% of species rich lowland, neutral grassland has been lost. It is believed that the local situation in the Mersey Basin region and in West Lancaster reflects the national position.

Comparable water quality data for Lancashire is not available, but it is clear that in recent years there has been considerable nutrient enrichment affecting in particular aquatic, heath and grassland habitats. Indeed it is known that in Lancashire EC standards are frequently exceeded, especially with high levels of nitrogen. During the last 20 years or so there have been heavy applications of nitrogenous fertilisers to agricultural land, and enrichment has also been caused by higher levels of atmospheric nitrogen (de Smidt 1995).

Rocky habitats in Lancashire have always been limited. However, the development of Heysham Harbour and public pressure at Silverdale removed or severely degraded this habitat. Similar habitats on the Mersey Estuary were also lost through urbanisation in the 19th century. Inland, peat erosion has revealed new areas of rock and scree in upland areas but they are nutrient poor and inhospitable to plant growth. Any plants that do colonise these areas are also liable to be eaten, as they are within heavily grazed areas the intensity of which has increased considerably in recent years.

Data for urbanisation of the landscape has not been compiled. However, by the beginning of the 19th century the population of Lancashire had already increased from a mainly rural (85%) population of 196,100 in 1690 to 672,700 in 1801. By 1994 the largely urban (75%) population of 1,424,000 was found in greatly enlarged conurbations. Much larger increases in population occurred in Greater Manchester and Merseyside with a population in 1994 of 2,578,000 and 1,434,400 respectively (Church 1996).

To accommodate this enlarged population and its associated industries considerable areas of agricultural land and semi-natural habitats were used by extending existing towns and cities, and in some areas by creating new ones (Freeman 1962; Lawton 1982).

Despite the quality of the available data, it would appear that the floristic changes observed in West Lancaster (VC60) are consistent with the habitat changes described above for a wider area.

The marked increase in aquatic species is consistent

with a wetter climate and the general increase in fens and man-made habitats of gravel pits and reservoirs, etc., despite the loss of marl pits and some drainage. However, closer examination shows that losses are of species requiring nutrient poor water, e.g., Lesser Bladderwort *(Utricularia minor),* whilst the increasing ones favour nutrient rich waters, e.g., Celery-leaved Buttercup *(Ranunculus sceleratus),* Bur-marigolds *(Bidens* spp.), etc., which is consistent with increased eutrophication.

Similarly, the increase in ruderal species reflects the general increase in the size of the urban habitat and the creation of open habitats through man-made activities. The significance of urban habitats will be discussed further in relation to alien species. Some reduction in arable farmland weeds might be expected, but this was scarcely if at all detected.

The increasing spread of coastal species is consistent with the developing saltmarshes and although the extent of the sand dunes is reduced, developing dunes are still found on the Fylde coast.

There seems to be a slight, perhaps insignificant, increase in species favouring woodland and marginal habitats. This is difficult to explain as there has been a reduction of older more natural and species rich woodlands.

The decrease in species favouring heaths, grasslands and rocky places correlates well with the known decrease in the extent of these habitats and with increasing soil nitrogen levels.

Tables 19.4–8 inclusive, which form the basis of this analysis, were compiled by comparing data for 1907 with data for 1992. Those species which have had short-term changes in abundance or where localities were not listed

Figure 19.3. Danish Scurvygrass on a Merseyside roadside
(Photo: H. Ash).

by Wheldon & Wilson (1907) do not appear in the tables and yet can be very interesting. There has been an explosive spread of Danish Scurvygrass *(Cochlearia danica)* along motorways and A class roads in the Mersey Basin since 1992. In West Lancaster this spread was not noted until 1995 when the central reservation of the M6 suddenly became carpeted with this species from its junction with the M55 north of Preston to Carnforth and along the M55 itself towards Blackpool. The spread of this plant has been noted throughout England, and several notes have appeared in *BSBI News* (e.g., Allen 1996; Pinkiss 1996) reporting its spread and postulating reasons why this might have occurred. The most favoured reason is that the use of rock salt as a winter de-icing agent produces open habitats with saline conditions favoured by this species. However, it has also been noted to colonise non-saline but open habitats, and in Wirral it has colonised bare ground following roadside herbicide treatments.

Less easy to document has been the apparent spread of Sticky Mouse-ear *(Cerastium glomeratum).* In 1907 it was too common for localities to be listed by Wheldon & Wilson (1907), but qualitatively it seems to have increased in abundance not only in West Lancaster but generally; this was one of the few species where Rich & Woodruff (1990) noted a significant increase. It is a ruderal and grassland species favouring nitrogen enriched soils.

Western Gorse *(Ulex gallii)* is also not included in the tables, although for a period of several years in the 1970s it became particularly abundant for several miles on the roadside banks of the M6 near Lancaster. Heathland habitats, which it favours, are rare in VC60, but a suitable nearby seed source occurred at Galgate and the newly built motorway provided a suitable habitat. However, by 1996 it had disappeared.

These changes suggest that complex forces are at work in determining the changing abundance and distribution of species. Some of the changes are very short-term, but others appear long-lasting. Whilst the causes of change for some species may be clearly indicated, e.g., loss of habitat, for many species the reasons remain unknown.

The climatic and habit changes described are appropriate to most of the Mersey Basin region, with perhaps a greater emphasis there on habitat destruction through urbanisation. There is no reason to believe that, whilst this analysis is based largely on West Lancaster data, similar floristic changes and the processes involving change are not also taking place in the region as a whole.

Alien species

If the analysis of change to the native flora is somewhat inconclusive, an analysis of alien species presents further problems. Alien species are defined as those which are brought into the area by humans either intentionally or unintentionally, but which may be native in some other parts of the British Isles; or have come to the area without human intervention, but from an area in which it is alien.

As was discussed earlier, applying this definition in practice often causes difficulties which are compounded by trying to determine if a species is naturalised or not. A naturalised (or established) species is one which has been present at a site in the wild (i.e., without human intervention) for at least five years, and is spreading vegetatively or is effectively reproducing by seed. This definition also includes persistent species which are present in the wild for at least five years, but are neither spreading significantly vegetatively nor by seed. An attempt was made to apply these definitions to the flora of the Mersey Basin region and VC60. Using Newton (1971, 1990); Savidge, Heywood & Gordon (1963) and recent data, especially for VC59 and VC60, an attempt was made to determine the status of alien species on an individual basis. In making this analysis personal judgement was used, and as such the results might well vary if other individuals or a committee approach were taken to assess status.

Nevertheless, Table 19.1 shows that alien species form an important component of the total flora ranging from 30% in Cheshire to 45% in South Lancaster. In Cheshire the low figure is probably due to recorders not noting many clearly introduced species of casual occurrence or not considering species were 'wild'. However, if the number of naturalised species is considered, the numbers show much less variation ranging from 15% in West Lancaster to 18% in Cheshire (Table 19.1 and 19.9).

There is no doubt that, whilst there may be a small net loss of native species to the region, the total number of established taxa growing in the area is now greater than at any time in recent history. At any one time this total is further increased by a large number of casual species. This increase is due almost entirely to human intervention of some kind.

In order to understand further when and how the naturalised aliens came to be established, an analysis of the local floras of the region was undertaken. Table 19.10 lists the established alien species for Cheshire and Lancashire (VC58, 59 and 60) with an approximate date of when a species was first recorded or noted. No data is given where a species is not considered naturalised, even though it may occur in the vice-county.

Table 19.11 groups the date of first record into 50 year categories (chosen on the basis of the dates of local flora publications). This demonstrates that the numbers of species becoming established on an annual basis remains remarkably constant over nearly 170 years, averaging one to two species per annum, but the figures also suggest that during the present century the rate of naturalisation has increased.

Using local floras and Clement & Foster (1994), the main means of introduction for each species can be assessed (Table 19.12). Despite the influence of the major ports on the River Mersey, most species naturalised in the region are garden escapes, which, together with medicinal and culinary herbs and plants grown in aquaria, account for some 68% of naturalised alien species. Much less important are species introduced with crops or escaped crop and amenity plantings and accidental introductions. Also amongst the new taxa are a small number that are new to science. Examples include Common Cord-grass (*Spartina anglica*) and Montbretia (*Crocosmia* x *crocosmiflora*).

It may seem surprising that the horticultural industry should be so important, but the region has a long history of horticultural endeavour extending well over 200 years. This involved all classes of society from the 18th century (Secord 1994a & b). It also saw the establishment of the Liverpool Botanic Garden in 1802, the University

	Total no. Aliens	Casual		Naturalised	
		No.	% of total aliens	No.	% of total aliens
VC58	363	138	38	225	62
VC59	685	419	61	266	39
VC60	657	428	65	229	35

Table 19.9. Number of casual and alien species in Lancashire and Cheshire VC58–60.

Date Class Vice-county	Before 1830 (50 years)	1830–1879 (50 years)	1880–1929 (50 years)	1930–1979 (50 years)	After 1980
Cheshire 58	8%	32%	12.5%	35%	13%
S. Lancs 59	8%	25%	25%	35%	7%
W. Lancs 60	5%	14%	28%	44%	9%
Average	7%	23%	22%	38%	10%
Equivalent no. of species	17	57	53	91	24 (80 extrapolated over 50 years)
No. per year (approx.)	–	1	1	2	2

Table 19.11. Date of first record of naturalised aliens in Cheshire and Lancashire (VC58–60) (% of total naturalised aliens).

Table 19.10. Naturalised alien species in Cheshire and Lancashire (VC58–60)

Name of Plant	VC58	VC59	VC60	Means of Introduction	Region of Origin
Acer platanoides	1971	Post 1963	1964	Amenity	Eurasia
Acer pseudoplatanus	Before 1830?	15th Century	Before 1830?	Amenity	Eurasia
Aconitum napellus	–	1963	–	Garden	Europe
Acorus calamus	1670	1872	1837	Garden	E.Asia
Adiantum capillus-veneris	1971	–	–	Unknown	BI. World-wide
Aesculus hippocastanum	Before 1830?	Before 1830?	Before 1830?	Amenity	Europe
Agrostemma githago	1868	1839	1775	Grain	Mediterranean
Agrostis scabra	–	1966	–	Grain	Europe
Allium carinatum	1976	1995	1948	Garden	Europe, Asia
Allium oleraceum	1899	1865	1901	Accidental	Eurasia
Allium paradoxum	–	1983	1989	Garden	C.Asia
Allium scorodoprasum	1899	1899	1908	Accidental	Eurasia
Alnus incana	–	1960	1987	Amenity	Eurasia
Alopecurus myosuroides	1835	1838	1883	Accidental/Natural Spread?	Eurasia, Africa
Althaea officinalis	–	1826	–	Accidental?	Eurasia, Africa
Ambrosia psilostachya	–	1903	1902	Grain	N.America
Anaphalis margaritacea	1971	1907	1907	Garden	Eurasia, N.America
Angelica archangelica	1899-1933	1887	1982	Medicinal	Eurasia
Antirrhinum majus	1933	1807	1901	Garden	Mediterranean
Aponogeton distachyos	–	1976	–	Aquarium	S.Africa
Aquilegia vulgaris	1859	Native?	Native	Garden or natural spread	Eurasia, Africa
Arenaria balearica	1931	1933	1942	Garden	Mediterranean
Armoracia rusticana	1597	1933	1891	Medicinal	Eurasia, Africa
Arum italicum	–	1994	–	Garden	Europe
Asparagus officinalis ssp. *officinalis*	1838	1933	1829	Agriculture	Eurasia
Aster novi-belgii s.l.	1880	1837	1964	Garden	N.America
Astrantia major	–	1960	1987	Garden	Europe
Avena fatua	1805	1840	1900	Grain	Europe
Azolla filiculoides	1939	1976	1985	Aquarium	Americas
Barbarea intermedia	1859	1862	1967	Accidental	Europe, Africa
Berberis vulgaris	1808	1851	1858	Garden	Europe
Bidens frondosa	1989	1913	–	Garden	N. & S.America
Borago officinalis	–	1910	–	Garden	Europe
Brassica napus	1860s	1962	1962	Agriculture	?
Brassica rapa ssp. *campestris*	1850s	1963	1874	Agriculture	Europe
Bromopsis inermis	1990	1940–49	1948	Agriculture	Europe
Buddleja davidii	1971	Post 1963	1966	Garden	China
Calla palustris	1970	1994	–	Garden	Eurasia & N.America
Calystegia pulchra	1968	1951. 1st British	1964	Garden	N.E.Asia
Calystegia silvatica	1962	1863. 1st British	1952	Garden	S.W.Asia
Campanula persicifolia	–	1939	–	Garden	Eurasia
Campanula rapunculoides	1859	1871-1900	1881	Garden	Eurasia
Carpinus betulus	1859	1851	1907	Amenity	Eurasia
Castanea sativa	1851	1851	1907	Amenity	Eurasia, Africa
Centaurea montana	1990	1918	1966	Garden	Europe
Centranthus ruber	1851	1851	1962	Garden	Mediterranean, Asia
Cerastium tomentosum	1933	1933	1931	Garden	Europe
Ceratochloa carinata	1970	1958	1989	Accidental	N.America
Chamaecyparis lawsoniana	c.1990	–	–	Garden	N.America
Chelidonium majus	1839	1839	1858	Medicinal	Eurasia
Chenopodium bonus-henricus	1839	1839	1874	Medicinal	Eurasia
Chenopodium murale	1839	1839	1900	Accidental	Eurasia, Africa
Cicerbita macrophylla	1971	1960	1942	Garden	Eurasia
Cichorium intybus	1839	1914	1860	Garden	Eurasia
Claytonia perfoliata	1860s	1916	1946	Garden	N.America
Claytonia sibirica	1962	1876	1902	Garden	N.America
Clematis vitalba	1801	1850	1899	Garden or natural spread	Eurasia, Africa
Conyza canadensis	1925	1913	1962	Accidental	N.America

Name of Plant	VC58	VC59	VC60	Means of Introduction	Region of Origin
Cornus sericea	1990	1940	1986	Amenity	N.America
Coronopus didymus	1847–59	1880	1915	Accidental	S.America
Corrigiola litoralis	–	1928	1965	Accidental	Eurasia, Africa
Cotoneaster horizontalis	1990	1955	1967	Garden	W.China
Cotoneaster microphyllus/ integrifolius	–	–	1902	Garden	Himalayas, W.China
Cotoneaster salicifolius	–	1991	–	Garden	China
Cotoneaster simonsii	–	1961	1967	Garden	Himalayas
Cotula coronopifolia	1880	1970s	–	Garden	S.Africa, Australasia
Cotula squalida	–	1960	–	Garden	New Zealand
Crambe cordifolia	–	1988	–	Garden	S.E.Asia
Crassula helmsii	1990	1976	1984	Aquarium	Australasia
Crataegus laciniata	–	1964	–	Garden	Europe, Asia
Crepis vesicaria	1941	1930	1979	Accidental	Mediterranean, Asia
Crocosmia x *crocosmiiflora*	1970	1963	1964	Garden	Cultivated
Crocus nudiflorus	1830	1830	1907	Garden	Europe
Crocus tommasinianus	*c.*1990	–	–	Garden	Europe
Crocus vernus	1859	1808	1885	Garden	Europe
Cymbalaria muralis	1851	1851	1874	Garden	Europe
Cymbalaria pallida	1990	1962	1948	Garden	Europe
Cyperus longus	–	1952	–	Garden	Europe
Descurainia sophia	1838	1838	1837	Accidental	Widespread
Diplotaxis muralis	1860	1872	1899	Grain, ballast	Mediterranean
Diplotaxis tenuifolia	1670	1927	1920s	Grain	Europe
Doronicum pardalianches	1855	1930	1941	Medicinal	Europe
Doronicum plantagineum	1989	–	–	Garden	Europe
Egeria densa	–	1955	–	Aquarium	S.America
Elodea canadensis	1859	1859	1864	Aquarium	N.America
Elodea nuttallii	1987	1979	1976	Aquarium	N.America
Epilobium brunnescens	1933	1937	1931	Garden	New Zealand
Epilobium ciliatum	1965	1970s?	1964	Timber	N.America
Epilobium pedunculare	1938	–	–	Garden	New Zealand
Erinus alpinus	–	1872	1942	Garden	Europe
Erysimum cheiranthoides	1851	1851	1875	Accidental	Widespread
Erysimum cheiri	1850s	1851	1864	Garden	Europe
Euphorbia cyparissias	1895	1941	1897	Garden	Europe
Euphorbia esula and *Euphorbia* x *pseudovirgata*	–	1946	1966	Grain	Eurasia
Fagus sylvatica	Before 1830	15th Century	18th Century	Amenity	Eurasia
Fallopia baldschuanica	–	1939	1962	Garden	Japan
Fallopia japonica	1962	1933	1933	Garden	Japan
Fallopia japonica x *sachalinensis* = *F.* x *bohemica*	–	1992	1985	Accidental	Unknown
Fallopia sachalinensis	1962	1953	1963	Garden	Japan
Festuca heterophylla	1968	–	1987	Garden	Europe
Ficus carica	1979	1913	1968	Accidental, garden	S.W.Asia
Foeniculum vulgare	1851	1838	1907	Medicinal	Widespread
Fragaria x *ananassa*	1971	19th Century	1965	Garden	Cultivation
Galanthus nivalis	1851	1887	1858	Garden	Eurasia
Galega officinalis	1971	1912	–	Garden	Eurasia
Galinsoga parviflora	1928	1874	1964	Garden	S.America
Galinsoga quadriradiata	1940	1948	1962	Horticultural seed	Tropical America
Gaultheria mucronata	–	1956	1966	Garden	S.America
Gaultheria shallon	1971	Post 1963	–	Amenity	N.America
Geranium endressii	1971	1963	1964	Garden	Europe
Geranium phaeum	1839	1851	1858	Garden	Europe
Geranium pyrenaicum	1873	1885	1882	Garden	Eurasia, Africa
Geranium x *magnificum*	–	–	1966	Garden	Cultivation
Gunnera tinctoria	1970	–	–	Garden	S.America
Hebe sp.	*c.*1990	–	–	Garden	Australasia
Heracleum mantegazzianum	1962	1952	1962	Garden	S.W.Asia
Hesperis matronalis	1801	1851	1837	Garden	Eurasia

Name of Plant	VC58	VC59	VC60	Means of Introduction	Region of Origin
Hieracium grandidens	1971	1948	1966	Accidental	Europe
Hippophae rhamnoides	1872	1899	1905	Amenity	Eurasia
Hirschfeldia incana	1920	1939	1966	Grain	Mediterranean
Hyacinthoides hispanica and hybrids	1971	1928	1965	Garden	Europe
Hypericum calycinum	1971	–	1965	Garden	Eurasia
Illecebrum verticillatum	–	1976	–	Accidental	Europe
Impatiens capensis	1938	1905	–	Garden	N.America
Impatiens glandulifera	1932	1913	1938	Garden	Asia
Impatiens parviflora	1917	1855-63	1966	Timber	Asia
Inula helenium	1805	1963	1805	Garden	Eurasia
Iris foetidissima	1990	–	–	Garden	Europe
Juncus tenuis	1927	1903	1925	Grain	N.America
Kniphofia uvaria	–	1990s	1987	Garden	S.Africa
Lagarosiphon major	1971	1953	–	Aquarium	S.Africa
Lamiastrum galeobdolon ssp. *argentatum*	1990	Post 1963	1987	Garden	?
Lamium maculatum	1859	1838	1858	Garden	Eurasia
Larix decidua	Before 1830?	Before 1830?	Before 1830?	Forestry	Europe
Lathyrus aphaca	–	1854	–	Impurity	Eurasia
Lathyrus latifolius	1971	1902	1965	Garden	Europe, Africa
Lathyrus tuberosus	–	1914	–	Grass, bird seed	Eurasia
Ledum palustre ssp. *groenlandicum*	1971	1917	1972	Accidental or natural	N.America
Lemna minuta	1989	1995	–	Aquarium	N. & S.America
Lepidium draba ssp. *draba*	1899	1929	1899	Grain	Eurasia
Lepidium latifolium	1840	1633	1994	Medicinal	Eurasia, Africa
Leucanthemum maximum					
and *L.* x *superbum*	1971	1963	1964	Garden	Cultivated
Ligustrum ovalifolium	1971	1963	1964	Garden	Eurasia
Lilium martagon	1965	1964	1949	Garden	Eurasia
Lilium pyrenaicum	–	1986	1965	Garden	Europe
Linaria purpurea	1930	1976	1964	Garden	Mediterranean
Linaria repens	–	1934	1907	Accidental	Europe
Linaria vulgaris x *L. repens* = *L.* x *sepium*	–	1979	–	Accidental	Europe
Lobularia maritima	1962	1872	1903	Garden	Mediterranean, Asia
Lolium multiflorum	1861	1933	1893	Agriculture	Europe
Lolium temulentum	1858	1849	1899	Grain	Eurasia
Lonicera involucrata	–	–	1965	Garden	N.America
Lonicera xylosteum	1870	1838	1900	Garden	Eurasia
Ludwigia palustris	–	1927		Accidental	Eurasia, Africa
Lunaria annua	–	1991	1931	Garden	Europe
Lupinus arboreus	1971	1926	1966	Garden	N.America
Lupinus nootkatensis, L. x *regalis*	1933		1899	Garden	N.America
and *L. polyphyllus*	–	19th Century	–		
Luzula luzuloides	–	1920	–	Garden	Europe
Lychnis coronaria	*c*.1990	–	–	Garden	Eurasia
Lycium barbarum and *L. chinense.*	1899	1929	1907	Garden	China
Lysimachia punctata	1971	1962	1966	Garden	Eurasia
Mahonia aquifolium	1970	1948	1967	Garden	N.America
Matricaria discoidea	1904	1902	1901	Grain	N.E.Asia
Meconopsis cambrica	–	1963	1863	Garden	Europe
Medicago arabica	1851	1854	–	Grass	Europe, Africa
Medicago polymorpha	1857	1850s	1887	Grass	Eurasia, Africa
Medicago sativa	1845	1851	1901	Grass	Eurasia, Africa
Melilotus altissimus	1851	1828	1858	Accidental	Europe
Melilotus officinalis	1861	1903	1904	Bird Seed	Eurasia
Melitotus albus	1863	1828	1903	Accidental	Eurasia
Mentha spicata	1971	1926	1900	Herb	?
Mentha spicata x *M. longifolia*					
= x *villosonervata*	1971	–	1982	Herb	?
Mentha spicata x *M. suaveolens*					
= *Mentha* x *villosa*	1971	–	1960	Herb	?
Mimulus guttatus s.l.	1808	1871	1887	Garden	N.America

Name of Plant	VC58	VC59	VC60	Means of Introduction	Region of Origin
Mimulus moschatus	1970	1933	1959	Garden	N.America
Myrrhis odorata	1825	1828	1858	Medicinal	Europe
Narcissus pseudonarcissus (and horticultural forms)	*c.*1990	–	1960s	Garden	Cultural
Nectaroscordum siculum	1990	–	–	Garden	Europe, Asia
Nepeta x *faassenii*	1990	–	–	Garden	Cultivation
Nymphoides peltata	1810	1844	1985	Garden	Eurasia
Oenothera biennis	1851	1801	1898	Garden	N.America?
Oenothera x *fallax*	–	1892	1907	Garden	Local
Oenothera glazioviana	1893	1881	1902	Garden	N.America
Onobrychis viciifolia	1990	1845	1966	Agriculture	Europe
Onopordum acanthium	–	1903	–	Garden	Eurasia
Ornithogalum angustifolium	1859	1864	1775	Garden	Europe
Oxalis articulata	–	1963	1966	Garden	S.America
Oxalis corniculata	1840	–	1922	Garden	Widespread
Oxalis stricta	–	1848	1964	Garden	N.America
Papaver somniferum ssp. *somniferum*	1899	1962	1941	Garden	W.Asia
Parthenocissus tricuspidata	–	Post 1963	1965	Garden	E.Asia
Pentaglottis sempervirens	1849	1838	1858	Garden	Europe
Persicaria campanulata	1971	1980	–	Garden	Himalayas
Persicaria wallichii	1990	1953	1965	Garden	Himalayas
Petasites albus	1962	1910	1945	Garden	Eurasia
Petasites fragans	1872	1887	1900	Garden	Mediterranean
Petasites japonicus	1940	1988	–	Garden	E.Asia
Peucedanum ostruthium	1918	1806	1888	Medicinal	Europe
Pilosella aurantiaca ssp. carpathicola	1899	*c.*1900	1903	Garden	Europe
Pinus nigra	–	1890s	–	Forestry	Europe
Pinus sylvestris	Before 1830?	Before 1830?	Before 1830?	Forestry	Eurasia
Poa chaixii	1970	–	–	Garden	Europe
Populus alba	1838	1838	1907	Garden	Europe
Populus candicans group	1971	1933	1964	Amenity	?
Populus nigra hybrids	1838	1838	1893	Garden	Cultivation
Populus x *canescens*	1899	1849	1963	Garden	Europe
Potamogeton epihydrus	–	1959	–	Aquarium	Europe/N.America
Potentilla argentea	1861 (Native?)	1902 (Native?)	1987	Accidental/Natural	Widespread
Potentilla norvegica	1971	1898	1941	Garden, bird seed	Widespread
Potentilla recta	1971	1972	1962	Garden, bird seed	Eurasia, Africa
Prunus cerasifera	1990	–	1965	Garden	Eurasia
Prunus cerasus	1838	1865	1965	Garden	Eurasia
Prunus domestica ssp. *domestica* & ssp. *institia*	1838	1838	1962	Garden	Eurasia?
Prunus laurocerasus	1971	1963	1975	Garden	Eurasia
Pseudofumaria lutea	1805	1858–65	1860	Garden	Europe
Pyrus communis and *P. pyraster*	1851	1851	1860	Garden	Eurasia
Quercus cerris	1971	1962	1964	Amenity	Eurasia
Quercus ilex	1971	1962	1964	Garden	Mediterranean
Reseda alba	1980	1861	–	Garden	Mediterranean, Asia
Rheum officinale and *R.* x *hybridum*	–	1954	1987	Garden	Asia & Cultivation
Rhododendron ponticum	1874	1962	1962	Amenity	Eurasia
Ribes rubrum	1846	1842	1858	Garden	Europe
Ribes sanguineum	1990 Self sown ?	19th Century	1964	Garden	N.America
Rosa rubiginosa	1899	1851	1906	Amenity	Eurasia
Rosa rugosa	1995	1927	1946	Amenity	E.Asia
Rubus armeniacus	–	1963?	–	Garden	Eurasia
Rubus tricolor	–	Post 1970	1989	Garden	China
Rumex pseudoalpinus	–	1859	–	Garden	Eurasia
Rumex scutatus	–	1907	1972	Garden	Eurasia, Africa
Ruscus aculeatus	1971	1963	1967	Garden	Mediterranean
Sagittaria sagittifolia	1859	1923	1875	Accidental/Natural Spread	Eurasia
Salix daphnoides	–	1951	1967	Amenity	Europe
Salix x *rubens* and *Salix* x *rubra*	1971	?	1986	Amenity	Europe

Name of Plant	VC58	VC59	VC60	Means of Introduction	Region of Origin
Sambucus ebulus	1838	1838	1946	Garden	Eurasia
Sambucus racemosa	1970	1949	–	Garden	Eurasia
Sanguisorba minor ssp. *muricata*	1971	1907	1989	Agriculture	Europe
Saponaria officinalis	1839	1801	1718	Garden	Eurasia
Saxifraga x *polita*	–	1985	1857	Garden	?
Saxifraga x *urbium*	1836	1801	1899	Garden	Cultivation
Securigera varia	1855	1876	1910	Garden	Eurasia
Sedum album	1928	1881	1891	Garden	Eurasia, Africa
Sedum spurium	–	1959	1968	Garden	C.Asia
Sempervivum tectorum	1839	1839	1837	Garden	Europe
Senecio fluviatilis	1810	1849	1858	Garden	Europe
Senecio ovatus	–	1963	1966	Garden	Eurasia
Senecio squalidus	1926	1931	1948	Garden	Europe
Senecio viscosus	1867	1858	1688	Accidental	Eurasia
Senecio x *albescens*	1995	1993	1985	Garden	?
Sigesbeckia serrata	–	1928	–	Grain	C. & S.America
Sinapis alba	1839	1963	1874	Agriculture	Eurasia
Sisymbrium altissimum	1903	1923	1901	Grain	Eurasia
Sisymbrium orientale	1962	1909	1910	Grain	Mediterranean
Sisymbrium strictissimum	–	1890	Unknown	?	Europe
Sisyrinchium bermudiana/ S. montanum?	1985	1911	1900	Garden	N.America
Smyrnium olusatrum	1837	1903	1858	Medicinal	Widespread
Soleirolia soleirolii	1971	–	1965	Garden	Mediterranean
Solidago canadensis	1925	1963	1964	Garden	N.America
Solidago gigantea	1988	1927	1971	Garden	N.America
Sorbus aria s.l.	1851	1851	Native	Garden	Europe
Sorbus croceocarpa	–	–	1990	Garden	?
Sorbus intermedia	1968	1926	1964	Garden	Europe
Spartina anglica	1925	1930	1932	Amenity/natural spread	Accidental
Spiraea salicifolia and spp.	1930	1908	1963	Garden	N.America & cultivated
Stratiotes aloides	1858	1805	1858	Garden/accidental	Eurasia
Symphoricarpos albus	1933	1933	1933	Amenity	N. America
Symphytum x *uplandicum*	1968	1901	1968	Agriculture	Cultivated
Syringa vulgaris	–	Post 1963	1964	Garden	Europe
Tanacetum balsamita	–	1801	–	Garden	S.W.Asia
Tanacetum parthenium	1851	1938	1907?	Medicinal	Eurasia
Taxus baccata	1844	Native?	Native	Amenity	Eurasia, Africa
Tellima grandiflora	1941	–	1975	Garden	N.America
Thlaspi arvense	1867	1872	1883	Grain	Eurasia, Africa
		Possibly native			
Tilia x *vulgaris*	1851	1851	1907	Amenity	Europe
Tolmiea menziesii	1971	1928	1964	Garden	N.America
Tragopogon porrifolius	–	1597	–	Garden	Europe
Trifolum hybridum	1860	1859	1887	Agriculture	Eurasia
Trifolium pannonicum	–	1916	–	Impurity	Europe
Tulipa sylvestris	1836	–	1870	Garden	Mediterranean
Valeriana pyrenaica	1970	1963	–	Garden	Europe
Vallisneria spiralis	–	1940	–	Aquarium	Tropics
Verbascum densiflorum	–	1985	–	Garden	Eurasia
Verbascum nigrum	1890	1913	1960	Accidental or natural	Eurasia
Verbascum virgatum	–	1988	–	Accidental	Europe
Veronica filiformis	1950	1950s	1944	Garden	C.Asia
Veronica peregrina	1870	1865	1909	Horticultural seed	N. & S.America
Veronica persica	1847	1872	1907	Agricultural seed	S.W.Asia
Vinca major	1962	1946	1837	Garden	Eurasia
Vinca minor	1962	1812	1858	Garden	Eurasia
Viscum album	1983	1877	1950s	Garden	Europe
Vitis vinifera	–	1942	–	Accidental	Europe
Vulpia myuros	1898	1933	1969	Grain/natural spread	Widespread

Accidental		Crop, Amenity Introductions, etc.				Garden		
Unknown or accidental	*Impurity with timber, bird seed, grain, agricultural seed, ballast, etc.*	*Amenity*	*Forestry*	*General Agriculture*	*Grassland*	*Garden*	*Medicinal and culinary herbs*	*Aquarium*
10%	9%	7%	1%	3%	1%	60%	5%	3%
Total 19%		Total 12%				Total 68%		

Table 19.12. Means of introduction for naturalised alien species in Cheshire and Lancashire (VC58-60).

Region of Origin / Vice-county	*Cultivated Accidental Unknown*	*Widespread Europe, N.Africa, W. & C.Asia, India*	*N. & S.America*	*S.Africa Australasia*	*E.Asia China Japan*
A. *Naturalised aliens* (VC58–60	8%	68%	15%	3%	6%
B. *All aliens* Ex. Travis' Flora S.Lancs VC59	15%	71%	11%	2%	1%

Table 19.13. Origin of naturalised alien species in Cheshire and Lancashire (VC58–60).

of Liverpool Botanic Garden started by A.K. Bulley in the early 20th century (McLean 1997), and in the last 30 years the development of numerous garden centres and water gardens throughout the region.

Table 19.13 attempts to show the geographical origination of naturalised species. Botanists and horticulturists have explored the globe in search of suitable species for cultivation, but to prosper they must be suitable for the climatic conditions of the region. Not surprisingly some 68% of the taxa have a widespread European, Mediterranean or West Asian distribution. However, a significant number originate in the Americas.

Conclusion

The title of this paper refers to a 'game of chance'. Whilst the element of chance is present, what has and is happening to the floristic composition of the flora is not particularly chancy. Indeed there seems to be a great deal of logic about it.

Human intervention through urbanisation, industrialisation and agriculture has reduced, and in some cases almost to extinction, many natural and semi-natural habitats. Where the loss is total or almost so, then the native species have suffered badly. However, the same processes have created many new habitats and, if suitable, the native flora is not slow to take advantage of these man-made habitats (Greenwood & Gemmell 1978; Day *et al.* 1982). It is also suggested that at least some southern species are extending their range northwards, a good example being Southern Marsh-orchid

(*Dactylorhiza praetermissa*), probably as a consequence of climatic amelioration.

However, by far the most important factor influencing the composition of the flora of the region was, and continues to be, the horticultural industry. This industry flourished at least as early as the 18th century, and as the population grew and urbanisation of the region took place people of all social groupings had a desire to cultivate plants. These plants were grown for different reasons, but something like 197 of the 290 or so naturalised aliens owe their introduction to this industry. Yet it is an industry that directly leaves little noticeable mark on the landscape unlike that left by modern agriculture, extractive industries, communications systems and the built landscape itself.

Overall, therefore, human intervention has been a major cause of change to the floristic composition of the region's flora so that it is now more diverse than at any time in post-glacial history. Globally, human intervention reduces species diversity catastrophically, but the findings reported here confirm that in certain circumstances and over limited areas the reverse is true, and species diversity is increased (McNeeley *et al.* 1995). Whilst chance plays its part, change is perhaps more predictable than chancy. Furthermore, it may well be possible to predict changes more accurately in the future, given a knowledge of climatic and habitat changes and a knowledge of the species being introduced to gardens, for amenity plantings and agriculture. It is likely that the trends noted here will continue except that, as global and therefore local warming continues (United Kingdom

Climates Change Impacts Review Group 1996), coastal communities may be subject to increased erosion.

Acknowledgements

In compiling the data for this paper I am grateful to all the botanists who have sent me information over the years. However, I am especially grateful to Peter Gateley (BSBI recorder for VC59, South Lancaster) for providing recent data, for South Lancaster and commenting on an early draft, and to Professor A.D. Bradshaw for his comments and encouragement.

References

Allen, D. (1996). The earliest records of Danish Scurvy-grass, *Cochlearia danica*, on inland railway tracks. *BSBI News*, **72**, 24.

Anon. [1991]. *Lancashire, A Green Audit*. Lancashire County Council, Preston.

Anon. [1993]. *The State of Cheshire's Environment*. A broadsheet published by Cheshire County Council, Chester.

Berry, W.G. (1967). Saltmarsh development in the Ribble Estuary. *Liverpool Essays in Geography, A Jubilee Collection* (eds R.W. Steel & R. Lawton), pp. 121–35. Longmans, London.

Braithwaite, M. (1992). BSBI Monitoring Scheme 1987–88. Change at a local level – VC81, Berwickshire. *BSBI News*, **61**, 16–19.

Buxton, R. (1849). *Botanical Guide to the Flowering-Plants, etc. found indigenous within 16 miles of Manchester*. London.

Church, J. (ed.) (1996). *Regional Trends*. Office for National Statistics, HMSO, London.

Clement, E.J. & Foster, M.C. (1994). *Alien Plants of the British Isles*. Botanical Society of the British Isles, London.

Day, P., Deadman, A.J., Greenwood, B.D. & Greenwood, E.F. (1982). A floristic appraisal of marl pits in parts of north-western England and northern Wales. *Watsonia*, **14**, 153–65.

de Smidt, J.T. (1995). The imminent destruction of north west European heaths due to atmospheric nitrogen deposition. *Heaths and Moorland: Cultural Landscapes* (eds D.B.A. Thompson, A.J. Hester & M.B. Usher), pp. 206–17. Scottish National Heritage, HMSO, London.

de Tabley, Lord (1899). *The Flora of Cheshire*. Longmans, Green and Co., London.

Freeman, T.W. (1962). The Manchester Conurbation. *Manchester and its Region* (ed. C.F. Carter), pp. 47–60. Manchester University Press, Manchester.

Graham, G.G. (1988). *The Flora and Vegetation of County Durham*. The Durham Flora Committee and the Durham County Conservation Trust, Wallsend.

Gray, A.J. & Scott, R. (1987). Saltmarshes. *Morecambe Bay, An Assessment of Present Ecological Knowledge* (eds N.A.

Robinson & D.W. Pringle), pp. 97–117. Centre for North-West Regional Studies in conjunction with the Morecambe Bay Study Group, Lancaster.

Greenwood, E.F. & Gemmell, R.P. (1978). Derelict industrial land as a habitat for rare plants in S. Lancs. (VC59) and W. Lancs. (VC60). *Watsonia*, **12**, 33–40.

Hall, T.B. [1839]. *A Flora of Liverpool*, Whitaker & Co., London.

Lancashire Polytechnic (1989). *Annual Report of the Director of the Observatories*. Lancashire Polytechnic, Preston.

Lawton, R. (1982). From the Port of Liverpool to the Conurbation of Merseyside. *The Resources of Merseyside* (eds W.T.S. Gould & A.G. Hodgkiss), pp. 1–13. Liverpool University Press, Liverpool.

McLean, B. (1997). *A pioneering plantsman A.K. Bulley and the great plant hunters*. The Stationery Office, London.

McNeeley, J.A., Gadgil, M., Leveque, C., Padoch, C. & Redford, K. (1995). Human Influences on Biodiversity. *Global Biodiversity Assessment* (ed. V.H. Heywood), pp. 711–821. Cambridge University Press, Cambridge.

Newton, A. (1971). *Flora of Cheshire*, Cheshire Community Council, Chester.

Newton, A. (1990). *Supplement to Flora of Cheshire*. A. Newton, Leamington Spa.

Palmer, M.A. & Bratton, J.H. (eds) (1995). *A sample survey of the flora of Britain and Ireland*. U.K. Nature Conservation No. 8, Joint Nature Conservation Committee, Peterborough.

Perring, F.H. & Walters, S.M. (1962). *Atlas of the British Flora*. Botanical Society of the British Isles, London.

Peter, D. (1994). *In and around Silverdale*. Barry Ayre, Carnforth.

Pinkess, L.H. (1996). Danish Scurvy grass on a Worcestershire road. *BSBI News*, **72**, 25.

Pringle, W.A. (1987). Physical processes shaping the intertidal and subtidal zones. *Morecambe Bay, an assessment of present ecological knowledge* (eds N.A. Robinson & D.W. Pringle), pp. 51–73. Centre for North-West Regional Studies in conjunction with the Morecambe Bay Study Group, Lancaster.

Rich, T.C.G. & Woodruff, E.R. (1990), *BSBI Monitoring Scheme 1987–1988*. 2 vols. A report for the Nature Conservancy Council.

Savidge, J.P., Heywood, V.H. & Gordon, V. (1963). *Travis's Flora of South Lancashire*. Liverpool Botanical Society, Liverpool.

Secord, A. (1994a). Corresponding interests: artisan and gentlemen in nineteenth-century natural history, *The British Journal for the History of Science*, **27**, 383–408.

Secord, A. (1994b). Science in the pub: artisan botanists in early nineteenth-century Lancashire, *History of Science*, **32**, 269–315.

Swann, G.A. (1993). *Flora of Northumberland*. The Natural History Society of Northumbria, Newcastle upon Tyne.

United Kingdom Climate Change Impacts Review Group (1996). *Review of the Potential Effects of Climate Change in the United Kingdom. Second Report*. Prepared at the request of the Department of the Environment. HMSO, London.

Wheldon, J.A. & Wilson, A (1907). *The Flora of West Lancashire*, Liverpool.

The Changing Fauna

B.N.K. DAVIS

This last group of three chapters covers changes in the records of invertebrates, amphibians, lizards, mammals and birds in north-west England over the past 15,000 years. At the start of this period, Britain contained species characteristic of the last glacial period such as Woolly Mammoth and Giant Deer, which have since become totally extinct, while others such as Lemmings and Reindeer have retreated to Scandinavia and Siberia. Before the Industrial Revolution the wilder north of England became a haven for the larger mammals, such as Wolves and Bears, when such species had been driven out of southern and eastern England at a much earlier date. Other groups of animals have enterprisingly exploited the new range of habitats created through forest clearance, land drainage and agriculture, and the even more disturbed urban-industrial landscape. In this century, however, there has been a retraction again, particularly among the birds, butterflies and other well recorded groups as woodlands and wetlands have shrunk in extent, and land management has intensified. Forecasts of global warming over the next 50 years suggest changes as rapid as those that took place around 10,000 BP. Already there are suggestions that some invertebrates are responding to the warmer conditions. These records of past faunistic changes and present status, therefore, are not just of local significance, but may serve as markers for determining and analysing future changes at a regional and national scale.

CHAPTER TWENTY

Changes in the land and freshwater invertebrate fauna

S. JUDD

Introduction

The distribution of invertebrate animals has fluctuated continually since the retreat of the ice age from north-western England some 12,000 years ago. Post-glacial changes have been driven by changes in climate and increasingly by human influence.

There are four main categories into which the changes shown by invertebrates can be grouped: extinctions, additions, changes in distribution and changes in diversity (Foster 1992), all of which will be discussed in this chapter. Together these can indicate general trends and illustrate major changes in the fauna as a whole. Long-term monitoring work suggests that there are both short- and long-term fluctuations in insect diversity, and in the distribution and abundance of individual species. However, the features influencing change are complex, and separating the effects of climate, land-use and natural population variability are not fully understood (Luff & Woiwod 1995).

This account provides a synthesis of information for Watsonian vice-counties 58 and 59, Cheshire and South Lancaster. Examples are drawn from a wide variety of invertebrate taxa. Nomenclature and national categories for species status are taken from Ball (1992).

Invertebrate faunal studies

The strong tradition of invertebrate faunal studies in north-west England began with the publication of Byerley's *Fauna of Liverpool* in 1854. It was assisted by the foundation of the Lancashire and Cheshire Entomological Society in 1877. Initial studies, mainly on the Coleoptera and Lepidoptera (Ellis 1889, 1890; Sharp 1908), culminated in the first, and unfortunately, the only full faunal check-list for Lancashire and Cheshire, to be published by the influential Fauna Committee (Lawson 1930). This was prefaced with the proud boast that 'the fauna had been more systematically investigated and was more completely known than that of any other two counties in the whole of the British Isles'.

Subsequent notable regional contributions included work on Coleoptera, Diptera, Lepidoptera and Odonata (Mansbridge 1940; Smith 1948; Ford 1953; Kidd &

Brindle 1959; Johnson 1962; Rutherford 1983, 1994; Sumner 1985), whilst the innovative study of Cheshire dragonflies by Gabb & Kitching (1992) provided, for the first time, distribution maps, location and habitat data, and information on behaviour and developmental stages. A limited number of check-lists for orders and families have also been published in the last 10 years (Hull 1987, 1990; Judd 1987; Cross 1989; Chandler 1991; Felton 1991; Garland & Appleton 1994). These indicate that 50–60% of the British invertebrate fauna of *c*.28,000 species are present in Lancashire and Cheshire.

Sites of importance for the conservation of invertebrates in Cheshire, Lancashire, Merseyside and Greater Manchester were evaluated by Parsons (1987 a,b,c). Examples of detailed site surveys include those for Dunham Park (Johnson, Robinson & Stubbs 1977) and Hilbre Island (Wallace & Wallace 1982). Subsequently, Atkinson & Houston (1993) collated information for the Sefton Coast.

Relic faunas

The quaternary migrations of many species of insects in response to complex, and often rapid glacial/interglacial climatic oscillations, bear witness to the astonishing capacity of insect populations to track changing environments (Lawton 1995). Nevertheless, some populations became trapped in one, or a few locations in the British Isles, and are likely to have been isolated from continental populations for at least 10,000 years. These represent important biological capital in the context of conservation (Hammond 1974) and may be important during a northerly spread of species resulting from temperature increase. However, southern species with northern refugia must be distinguished from thermophilous species that make frequent sorties into northern Britain (Foster 1992).

Four relic species are recorded from single sites in the region and nowhere else in Britain. The most intriguing of these is the distinctive and flightless, parthenogenetic, Red Data Book 1 (*RDB1*) leaf beetle *Bromius obscurus*, which is associated with willow-herbs, especially Rosebay Willowherb (*Chamerion angustifolium*). It was rediscovered in 1979 on a disused railway line adjacent to the River Dane at Hugbridge, Cheshire (Kendall 1982). Its prior absence had been puzzling, because it is a common Scandinavian insect and was common in Britain during the climatic mild phase *c*.12,000-11,000 BP.

Two others, both spiders, are restricted to the small, isolated 'schwingmoor' at Wybunbury Moss National Nature Reserve (Felton & Judd 1997). The fourth, another relic mossland species, is the pselaphid beetle *Plectophloeus erichsoni*, which occurs on what remains of Chat Moss (Johnson & Eccles 1983).

The presence of the money spider *Carorita limnaea* and the gnaphosid spider *Gnaphosa nigerrima* at Wybunbury Moss, is a biogeographical mystery. Both must have been present in Britain, though not necessarily at Wybunbury, during the Boreal period, before the severance of the land connection with continental Europe (*c*.8,300 BP). It is most unlikely that they originate from re-immigrant stock. They could have been widely distributed throughout Britain during the extension of ombrogenous mires in the Atlantic Period (*c*.6,000 BP), their distributions then contracting due to subsequent destruction and fragmentation of this habitat. Interestingly, the Arctic-Alpine, nationally scarce Manchester Treble Bar moth (*Carsia sororiata*), is also recorded from Wybunbury.

Other rare invertebrates, once more widely distributed but now restricted to favourable sites, include the coastal *RDB* moths the Sandhill Rustic (*Luperina nickerlii*) and the Belted Beauty (*Lycia zonaria*), which are both possibly glacial-phase survivors. However, most are saproxylic species which include relic elements of a fauna associated with unmanaged forest cover in the first half of the Holocene (Harding & Alexander 1993).

Today it is almost only in pasture woodlands that the overmature tree/dead wood component of the primeval forest ecosystem survive, in lowland Britain (Harding 1979). Surprisingly, in a region with under half the national average area of woodland (chapter ten, this volume), three sites in the Mersey Basin are considered nationally important for their saproxylic fauna (Harding & Alexander 1993). They are the pasture woodland of the 16th-century Deer Park at Dunham Massey, Greater Manchester; the 18th-century Stockton's Wood, a plantation on former pasture woodland on the National Trust's Speke Hall estate, Merseyside and the ancient woodland of the lower River Weaver woodlands in Cheshire.

Dunham Park has attracted coleopterists since the 1860s. It is the only site in north-western England with an appreciable number of old trees, and supports 34 indicator species of ancient woodland (Johnson, Robinson & Stubbs 1977). Three *RDB* beetles and one *RDB* fly are recorded, together with nearly 100 nationally scarce species. It is also the only known north western site for 27 species, and the northernmost site for 12 species.

Pollution from an adjacent factory and fire damage killed many trees at Stockton's Wood in the 1980s. These dead trees have yielded a remarkable assemblage of beetles, of which 23 are indicators of ancient woodland (Eccles 1987). They are probably present throughout the wood, but the burnt trees sustain an abnormally high population. Their presence, in a secondary woodland, is something of an enigma, but it is thought that they transferred from earlier pasture woodland on this site. Alternatively, they might have originated from ancient woodland along the edge of the Mersey Estuary, which probably supported a fauna similar to the contiguous Weaver Valley, 16km distant.

Cyclical changes

Stability is the exception rather than the rule in the natural environment, and change is a normal condition in ecological ecosystems (Wyatt 1992). Four butterfly species (Table 20.1) became extinct in Merseyside and Cheshire during contractions in range, only to reappear during an expansive phase. The fluctuating presence of species at particular sites is illustrated by a study of butterflies along the Heald Green Railway Cutting in Cheshire between 1984 and 1993. Of the 21 species recorded during this period, two became established, four were seen with greater regularity and two were lost (Shaw 1993).

Britain's largest dragonfly, the Emperor (*Anax imperator*), was first recorded at Ainsdale, in the hot summer of 1976, 130km from its nearest regular breeding colony in the West Midlands. Its population peaked in 1983, when 40 were seen. Subsequently, numbers declined markedly and the loss of this isolated population must be a distinct possibility, unless more hot summers like that of 1995 re-occur (Hall & Smith 1991).

Long-term decline and extinction

Species hardly ever occupy their full ranges. Outlying records for many predominantly southern species, such as the nettle feeding seedbug *Heterogaster urticae*, indicate that they probably occurred further north than now when temperatures were 2–3°C higher. Local extinctions of species are most likely to occur at the limits of their ranges; with a few notable exceptions, most of the native terrestrial biota of the British Isles have suffered range contraction and fragmentation due to habitat loss (Vincent 1990).

Unlike the native regional flora, which has declined by 10% (chapter nineteen, this volume), extinction rates for most invertebrates are unknown. However, 18 of the 65 scarab species have been lost in Lancashire and Cheshire since 1908, and only two gained – a decline of 22% (Johnson 1962). For eight of these extinct species Lancashire and Cheshire are near the limit of their northern distribution, and it is quite possible that industrialisation has tipped the balance against their survival. Another six are coastal, where their habitat has been restricted by urban development.

The decline of Britain's butterflies has been particularly severe (Thomas 1991). Nationally, nearly half of the 59 resident species have experienced major contractions in range (Warren 1992), while ten species have disap-

Extinctions (Last record)	Cyclical extinctions & re-colonisation	Major contraction	Fluctuating	Relatively stable	Extending
Grizzled Skipper (1971)	Small Skipper	Small Pearl Bordered Fritillary	Large Skipper	Large White	Brimstone
Wood White (1850s)	Comma	Dark Green Fritillary	Dingy Skipper	Small White	
Small Blue (1850s)	Ringlet	Small Heath	Orange Tip	Green-veined White	
Silver-studded Blue (1920s)*			White-letter Hairstreak?	Green Hairstreak	
Duke of Burgundy (1850s)			Holly Blue	Purple Hairstreak	
Large Tortoiseshell (1876)			Peacock	Small Copper	
Pearl-bordered Fritillary (1941)			Speckled Wood	Common Blue?	
High Brown Fritillary (1922)			Wall Brown	Small Tortoiseshell	
Marsh Fritillary (1882)			Gatekeeper	Grayling	
Large Heath (1929)			Meadow Brown		

Vagrants: Silver-washed Fritillary, Marbled White
Migrants: Clouded Yellow, Pale Clouded Yellow, Long-tailed Blue, Red Admiral, Painted Lady, Camberwell Beauty
* Re-introduced in 1994

Table 20.1. The changing butterfly fauna of Cheshire and Merseyside since 1854. Based on Rutherford (1983), Anon (1991), Creaser (1992), Shaw (1994, 1995).

peared from Cheshire and Merseyside (Table 20.1). Excluding vagrants and migrants, this gives a local extinction rate, since 1854, of 28%, all but one before 1946.

For the well-studied macro-Lepidoptera, 62 of the 568 Cheshire species, have not been recorded since 1960 (Rutherford 1994). However, over half are either immigrants, vagrants or of dubious veracity which would suggest that no more than 5% have become extinct in the last 30 years. This is similar to the less well studied spiders, which have shown a 7% decline (25/367 species) in Lancashire and Cheshire since 1930 (Felton 1991). In contrast, a surprisingly high proportion (28/82) of ants and solitary wasps listed by Garland & Appleton (1994) have not been recorded in the last 30 years. This 34% decline contrasts with the national extinction rate for aculeates of 5% (Falk 1991), and may reflect a lack of recording as well as habitat loss.

At least 10 species recorded from the region have become extinct nationally. Of these, the strange story of the Manchester Tinea moth (*Euclemensia woodiella*) is worthy of repetition. This was discovered new to science by Robert Cribb in 1829 when *c.*30 specimens were taken from a hollow tree on Kersall Moor, Greater Manchester. It has never been recorded here, or anywhere else since, but there are three surviving museum specimens (Brindle 1952).

The heathland habitat of the Silver-studded Blue butterfly (*Plebejus argus*) at Bidston Hill, Merseyside, where this species was abundant in the 1850s, was planted as woodland during the latter half of the 19th

century, and this species was last recorded here around 1885 and at Delamere Forest in 1921. The Marsh Fritillary butterfly (*Eurodryas aurinia*) has declined nationally due to the 'improvement' and drainage of damp grassland. It was evidently abundant in the middle of the last century in Cheshire, but had disappeared from the county by 1882. The Large Heath butterfly (*Coenonympha tullia*) occurred in profusion on Simonswood Moss in the 1850s. Forty years later it was still common on all Lancashire mosses (now mostly in the counties of Greater Manchester and Merseyside), but by 1913 it was scarce or extinct in Lancashire. The major cause of its decline was the drainage of its habitat for the development of industry and agriculture (Emmet & Heath 1989). Similarly, the nationally scarce Variable Damselfly (*Coenagrion pulchellum*) disappeared from Wirral with the infilling of ponds (Judd 1986).

Such gross changes in land-use clearly affect the structure and composition of invertebrate communities, but relatively minor changes in land use occur more often and can also have marked effects (Usher 1995). For instance, four of the extinct butterfly species in Merseyside and Cheshire – the Wood White (*Leptidea sinapis*), Duke of Burgundy Fritillary (*Hamearis lucina*), Pearl-bordered Fritillary (*Boloria euphrosyne*) and High Brown Fritillary (*Argynnis adippe*) and one declining species, the Small Pearl-bordered Fritillary (*Boloria selene*), are all woodland species whose declines are linked nationally to a reduction in coppicing (Warren 1992).

The White-letter Hairstreak butterfly (*Satyrium*

w-album) has declined due to the loss of Elm, its food-plant, from Dutch Elm disease, a pathogen introduced into the region in 1973 (chapter ten, this volume). However, the loss of the Grizzled Skipper (*Pyrgus malvae*) is more puzzling. It was recorded in the early 1970s at Childer Thornton, Cheshire and although its foodplant, Wild Strawberry (*Fragaria vesca*), was still present in the late 1970s, there was no sign of the butterfly (Rutherford 1983).

Addition and expansion
Overlooked species
The discovery of species that have always been present in the region, illustrates how poorly understood are many groups. For example, the recent discovery of the cerylonid beetle, *Anommatus diecki,* in the River Weaver woodlands was also the first British record (Eccles & Bowestead 1987). Similarly, a grass midge new to science, *Sitodiplosis phalaridis*, was found infesting the inflorescence of Reed Canary-grass (*Phalaris arundi-nacea*), at Fletcher's Moss, Didsbury, Greater Manchester in 1982 (Abbas 1986). Others, such as the widespread Svensson's Copper Underwing moth (*Amphipyra berbera svenssoni*) are newly recognised.

Natural expansions
Seventeen macro-Lepidoptera species have been added to the Cheshire list since 1960 through natural expansion. They include Blair's Shoulder-knot moth (*Lithomoia leautieri*), which became resident in Britain 40 years ago and which first reached Cheshire in 1989 (Rutherford 1994). Other species, such as the generally distributed Red Underwing moth (*Catocala nupta*), are worthy of mention, because they were very rare 20 years ago.

Species such as the Broad-bodied Chaser (*Libellula depressa*), are more transitory, colonising newly created water bodies, then disappearing after a few years. Another dragonfly, the Ruddy Darter (*Sympetrum sanguineum*) which was first recorded in Cheshire in 1985, is now well established.

The changing distribution over time of the seed bug *Ischnodemus sabuleti* provides a classic example of range expansion (Figure 20.1). This species was confined to two locations in south-eastern England last century, but it is now found as far north as Cheshire and Yorkshire and is one of the more common seed bugs in Britain, occurring in 114 10 x 10km squares (Judd & Hodkinson 1998).

Four butterfly species, the Holly Blue (*Celastrina argiolus*), Speckled Wood (*Pararge aegeria*), Gatekeeper (*Pyronia tithonus*), and Small Skipper (*Thymelicus*

Pre-1900

Pre-1950

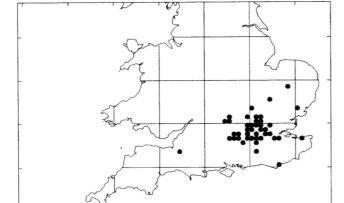

Pre-1970

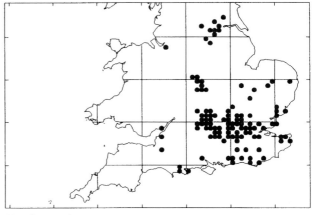

Total records

Figure 20.1. The changing distribution of *Ischnodemus sabuleti* in England over time. (From Judd & Hodkinson 1998)

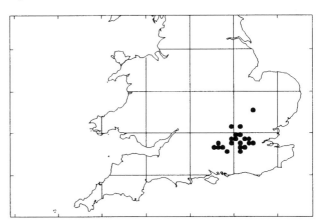

sylvestris), all inhabiting different biotopes, have crossed wide expanses of unsuitable terrain to become established in previously vacant habitats in northern Cheshire and Greater Manchester since 1989 (Hardy, Hind & Dennis 1993). Other species are spreading in a north or north-westerly direction to reach sites in the Mersey valley, thus expanding their range and density of distribution.

Accidental expansions and deliberate introductions

Some native species, such as the spider *Pholcus phalangioides* which was first recorded in the region in 1992, have been accidentally spread by man (Felton 1992a,b). The first north-western record of the Spitting Spider (*Scytodes thoracica*) was probably introduced to a Liverpool Museum store amongst packing cases.

Only two species have deliberately and successfully been translocated. A colony of Silver-studded Blue butterflies was reintroduced into Cheshire, VC58, at Thurstaston Common in 1994. Nearby on the Wirral Way at West Kirby, an introduced but forgotten colony of Scarlet Tiger moths (*Panaxia dominula*) was rediscovered in 1989. This had been founded in 1961 with a stock of 13,000 larvae and has since been used for studies on gene frequency (Clarke 1993).

Alien species

Most successful colonisers are synanthropic species or those introduced with their host plant. Other accidentally introduced alien species do not normally survive. A notable exception is the scarab beetle *Psammodius caelatus*, which originated from the western seaboard of North America, and, since its discovery in 1972, has spread along the Sefton coast (Johnson 1976; Eccles 1993).

Changes in the transport and packaging of fruit and vegetables have significantly reduced the number of 'stowaway' species that used to be imported through the Liverpool docks, such as the 25 orthopteroid species recorded by Ford (1972). Large theraphosid bird-eating spiders are also rarely recorded now, although the dangerous Black Widow spider (*Latrodectus mactans*) still turns up. A specimen of the dark and sinister spider *Badumna insignis*, a well known synanthropic species in Western Australia, was recently found at Widnes amongst imported *Eucalyptus* spp. timber from Perth. None of these is likely to become established here.

Garland & Appleton (1994) listed 10 introduced or vagrant species of ants found in Greater Manchester, the most successful being the Pharaoh ant (*Monomorium pharaonis*) which occurs in heated buildings in many parts of Britain. Recently established species in Merseyside include the gnaphosid spider *Urozelotes rusticus*, which was found in a house in Kirkby, and the house centipede (*Scutigera coleoptrata*), which was twice found close to the docks (Felton 1995, 1996). Other species, such as the 'cricket on the hearth' (*Acheta domestica*), which may have been present in Britain since the Crusades, have declined this century due to improving standards of hygiene. This last species can be found free-living in man-made habitats where there is constant warmth from fermenting organic matter (Marshall & Haes 1988), e.g., Bidston tip, Merseyside.

Most of the nine alien Mollusca species recorded from the region are found in canals (McMillan 1990). The Ramshorn snail *Menetus dilatatus*, which was discovered in 1869, was introduced with the discharging waste from cotton mills (Owen *et al.* 1962). Some, such as the Zebra mussel (*Dreissena polymorpha*), which was first recorded in 1844, and the *RDB* operculate water snail *Marstoniopsis scholtzi*, established since 1900, were once abundant but are now rare. A tiny freshwater limpet *Ferrissia wautieri*, is the most recent arrival and was first recorded in a Wirral pond in 1985.

Introduced plants are sometimes accompanied by host-specific insects. An extensively naturalised plant in the Mersey Basin is *Rhododendron ponticum*, which was brought to Britain as seed in 1763. Among the five alien species recorded from it in Britain, two, a leaf hopper *Graphocephala fennahi* and a lace bug *Stephanitis rhododendri*, occur in Cheshire and Merseyside, although the latter has not been recorded for many years (Judd & Rotherham 1992). A further 31 common polyphagous species (15 on Merseyside) are associated with it nationally.

Other notable colonisers include the Knopper Gall wasp (*Andricus quercuscalicis*) which has spread north and west across Europe, following the introduction of one of its principal hosts, Turkey Oak (*Quercus cerris*) (Lawton 1995).

The mirid bug *Alloeotomus gothicus*, which was first discovered in Britain in 1951, was found in 1985 at Nunsmere, Cheshire, probably originating from an adjacent Forestry Commission nursery (Judd 1987). The introduced pines at Ainsdale support an assemblage of beetles which were recorded by Eccles (1993). He also commented on the prettily marked Asparagus beetle (*Crioceris asparagi*), with its slug-like larvae, which may be found at this site, on naturalised Garden Asparagus (*Asparagus officinalis* ssp. *officinalis*).

This review of alien species is by no means complete and many other examples could be cited, e.g., the worm-eating flatworm *Australoplana sanguinea* and the money spider *Ostearius melanopygius*, both of which originate from New Zealand.

Fauna of natural habitats

Ainsdale Sand Dunes National Nature Reserve and Dunham Park with eleven and four *RDB* species respectively, are the two nationally important 'hotspots' for invertebrate conservation in the region, and are classified by Parsons (1987 a,b,c) as grade A sites. A further 14 Grade B sites are regional 'hotspots'. All but Stockton's Wood are natural or semi-natural habitats, and five of these top sites, supporting 23 (21%) of the region's *RDB* species, are on the Sefton coast.

The study of rarities is sometimes thought of as élitist,

but this has great value. These organisms may be very subtle indicators of environmental change, apart from being worthy of conservation in their own right (Mellanby 1974). Of the 110 *RDB* species recorded from the study region, 10 (9%) are now extinct nationally and a further 73 (66%) have not been recorded since 1970, many of which are probably regionally extinct.

The destruction of natural and semi-natural habitats, which support most of the region's *RDB* species, is the major threat to them. Another key threat to invertebrates in the changing British landscape is the fragmentation into small, isolated patches of habitats frequented by specialist species with poor dispersal powers (Luff & Woiwod 1995). This is a particular problem for isolated peat mosses in the region which support 18 (16%) of the region's *RDB* species.

Fortunately eight of the regional Grade A and B sites are statutory or private nature reserves or National Trust properties. The most important regional conservation achievement was the creation of an almost continuous strip of protected land along the Sefton coast. However, even on 'safe sites' the opportunity to manage change occurs all too rarely. Usually, management of the consequences of change is the only option, and nature conservation is forced to be reactive (Langslow 1992).

Man-made habitats

There are now more man-made habitats in Britain than ever before, providing greater scope for invasion. Likewise, the increase in disturbance to natural and semi-natural vegetation, by an increasingly mobile and affluent human population, together with the gradual loss of indigenous species through land use change, pollution, pesticides, etc., may collectively make the British countryside increasingly more accessible for alien species to become established (Eversham & Arnold 1992). In general anthropogenic features may increase variation in habitat and species richness locally, but often by the introduction or spread of more eurytopic species at the expense of native species requiring larger areas of natural habitat (Sheppard 1987).

Many species recorded in a study of the effects of current urban and past land use on beetle diversity in the Eccles area of Greater Manchester were those expected in the agricultural environment before town expansion (Terrell-Neild 1994). Species richness declines with increasing penetration into the town with a greater proportion of individuals coming from fewer species. This was most marked in areas with the longest history of human habitation.

Many studies have shown the importance of naturally colonised derelict land as a resource for wildlife (e.g., Bradshaw & Chadwick, 1980; Gemmell & Connell 1984), but there have been few on the insects of such sites. One exception is the work of Sanderson (1992a,b, 1993) who investigated the factors affecting the Hemiptera of 16, diverse, naturally colonised derelict sites, undergoing succession, in Merseyside and south Lancashire. He found that derelict land can often form relatively undisturbed ecological habitat-islands in an otherwise less habitable urban area. Hemipteran diversity indices were significantly correlated with site area, but not with soil, pH or site age, irrespective of the site's origin or history. The vegetation is of primary importance in predicting Hemiptera species composition, which is influenced by atypical plant communities on some of the nutrient poor soils, with extremes of pH. Although many of these sites had regionally rare plants growing on them, none of the 149 Hemiptera species recorded was of *RDB* status and only one species was new to Merseyside.

The artificial lime wastes around Northwich which are of high botanical interest, support a butterfly population, comprising common rough grassland species that have colonised from the surrounding countryside (Rutherford 1983). Old sand quarries, however, support an unusually rich aculeate fauna.

Urban parks provide important habitats for some invertebrates. A new British bark beetle, *Scolytus laevis* (Atkins, O'Callaghan & Kirby 1981) and three nationally scarce hoverflies are recorded from Sefton Park, Liverpool, including *Platycheirus tarsalis*, a species associated with lush wood edges. Nearby, an astonishing 18 nationally scarce species of beetle have been recorded from Clarke Gardens (Eccles 1987), including the rove beetle, *Hydrosmectina delicatissima*, new to Britain (Allen & Eccles 1988).

A few species have invaded Britain and adjusted themselves to the garden environment to the virtual exclusion of other habitats. There are several examples, two of the best known being noctuid moths: the Varied Coronet (*Hadena compta*) associated with cultivated *Dianthus*, which reached Cheshire in 1992, and the generally distributed but not common Golden Plusia (*Polychrysia moneta*) associated with *Delphinium*, has colonised gardens throughout much of the country over the last 100 years (Owen 1978; Rutherford 1994). Likewise, a few, previously rare native species, have spread rapidly with the planting of their food plants, or closely related species, in gardens. The Juniper Shield bug (*Cythostethus tristriatus*) and Juniper Carpet moth (*Thera juniperata*) have both increased with the planting of junipers and cypresses and have recently become established in Cheshire and Merseyside.

Most of the richest and most diverse butterfly habitats in Cheshire were made by humans but then abandoned (Rutherford 1983). High on this list are disused railway lines, which provide ready-made dispersal corridors; the first modern Cheshire location for the Small Skipper butterfly (*Thymelicus sylvestris*) was a disused railway line near Malpas, from which it has spread northwards.

The Heald Green railway cutting, mentioned earlier, supports 21 butterfly species which are notably absent in the heavily grazed adjacent meadows. This is because of the abundance of nectar-bearing plants in the cutting, the absence of insecticides and the shelter from prevailing westerly winds (Shaw 1993). New Ferry railway sidings support more butterfly species than any other site on Wirral and are a butterfly reserve. Former railway cuttings are also important for other invertebrates. The third British record of the nationally scarce leafhopper, *Cosmotettix caudatus,* was from Haskayne, now a small Lancashire Wildlife Trust nature reserve (Payne 1987) where limestone ballast has raised the pH of the soil, resulting in a flora similar to chalk grassland. The leafhopper, *Rhytistylus proceps,* which is normally associated with coastal or limestone habitats, also occurs here, about 10km inland (Sanderson 1992a).

A survey of 19 stretches of disused canals in Greater Manchester recorded 74 freshwater invertebrate species, including a number of nationally scarce and local species, which enhance the known importance of these sites for scarce vascular plants (Guest 1989). Recently, the freshwater winkle, *Viviparus contectus,* was reported from the Hollingwood Branch Canal (Parsons 1987b). This is primarily a southern species associated with calcareous slow flowing or standing water.

Flooded marl pits, which were dug from the 13th century well into the 19th century provide an important national aquatic habitat for invertebrates. The Cheshire Wildlife Trust estimated that 86,000, or over 25% of all English ponds, once occurred within the county although probably only 11,000 remain (chapter fourteen, this volume). Twelve species of dragonfly were recorded from the marl pits at Churton, including the nationally scarce Variable Damselfly (Gabb & Kitching 1992) and in 1995, the *RDB*1 water beetle, *Hydrochara caraboides,* was recorded from two ponds near Chester and Winsford (Guest 1996). Earlier, between 1940 and 1957, 27 species of freshwater molluscs were recorded in a study of 172 pits in the Bromborough area (McMillan 1959).

The extraction of boulder clay, sand and gravel in Cheshire has created new and important aquatic habitats for invertebrates, particularly dragonflies, as has the pumping of natural brine, which caused the formation of flashes or small lakes (Gabb & Kitching 1992). A large number of unpolluted, man-made pools, ranging from bomb craters and golf course reservoirs to scrapes excavated during the 1970s and 1980s for conservation purposes, make Ainsdale by far the most important single site for Odonata on the Sefton coast, with 14 species recorded (Hall & Smith 1991). Some species have only been recorded since their habitats were created, such as the Variable Damselfly and Emperor Dragonfly. Other species such as the Emerald Damselfly (*Lestes sponsa*), have shown marked population increases.

In addition to these man-made habitats specialised invertebrate faunas are associated with human habitation and the work place.

Conclusion

In the past man has had a positive effect on invertebrate biodiversity and abundance within the Mersey Basin. Sub-Boreal fragmentation of blanket woodland for

Neolithic agriculture created a habitat mosaic which benefited species associated with forest-edge, early successional and plagioclimax habitats. The heyday for British butterflies was probably the early medieval period with its warm, dry summers together with developing habitats maintained by traditional agricultural and forestry practices (Dennis 1992; Warren 1992).

Simplistic explanations of the pattern of invertebrate declines are misleading. However, habitat loss and fragmentation resulting from man's changing agricultural and forestry practices, industrialisation and urbanisation developments, have clearly had a major detrimental impact on invertebrate populations since the mid-19th century. Man-made areas, such as gardens, derelict land and the buildings in which humans live and work, provide new habitats, particularly for opportunist species. However, nearly all detailed investigations into the declines of British butterfly species have reached the same general conclusions: that they are ultimately caused by habitat changes or loss (Warren 1992).

Currently there are many more questions relating to the changing distribution and abundance of invertebrates in the Mersey Basin than there are answers. However, there is enormous potential for monitoring their response to environmental change and quality, in this rapidly changing and highly pressurised region.

Acknowledgements

I thank Brian Davis, Tom Eccles, Chris Felton, Eric Greenwood, Nora McMillan, Barry Shaw and Ian Wallace for their assistance.

References

Abbas, A.K. (1986). A new species of grass midge (Dipt. Cecidomyiidae) infesting the inflorescence of *Phalaris arundinacea* L. in Britain. *Entomologist's Monthly Magazine,* **122**, 65–71.

Allen, A.A. & Eccles, T.M. (1988). *Hydrosmectina delicatissima* Barnhauer (Col., Staphylinidae) new to Britain. *Entomologist's Monthly Magazine,* **124**, 215–20.

Anon. [1991]. Butterflies of Merseyside their history and status as recorded by members of the British Butterfly Conservation Society Merseyside Branch. Privately published.

Atkins, P.M., O'Callaghan, D.P. & Kirby, S.G. (1981). *Scolytus laevis* (Chapuis) (Coleoptera: Scolytidae) new to Britain. *Entomologist's Gazette,* **2**, 280.

Atkinson, D. & Houston, J. (eds) (1993). *The Sand Dunes of the Sefton coast.* National Museums & Galleries on Merseyside in conjunction with Sefton Metropolitan Borough Council, Liverpool.

Ball, S.G. (1992). *Recorder user manual.* Version 3.1, English Nature, Peterborough.

Bradshaw, A.D. & Chadwick, M.J. (1980). *The restoration of land.* Blackwell Scientific Publications, Oxford.

Brindle, A. (1952). The strange case of *Schiffemuelleria woodiella* Hub. (Lep: Oecophoridae). *Entomologist's Gazette,* **3**, 235–37.

Byerley, I. (1854). *Fauna of Liverpool.* H. Greenwood, Liverpool.

Chandler, P.J. (1991). Some corrections to the fungus gnats (Diptera, Mycetophiloidea) of Lancashire and Cheshire. *Annual Report and Proceedings of the Lancashire and Cheshire Entomological Society,* **114**, 38–53.

Clarke, C. (1993). *Panaxia dominula*, the Scarlet Tiger moth: queries arising from an artificial colony rediscovered after 28 years. *Antenna*, **17**, 177–83.

Creaser, A. (1992). The Wirral Peninsula, entomological past and present. *Annual Report and Proceedings of the Lancashire and Cheshire Entomological Society*, **115**, 72–75.

Cross, S. (1989). Provisional Lancashire and Cheshire checklists for Plecoptera, Ephemeroptera, Siphunculata and Siphonaptera. *Annual Report and Proceedings of the Lancashire and Cheshire Entomological Society*, **112**, 139–42.

Dennis, R.L.H. (1992). An evolutionary history of British butterflies. *The ecology of butterflies in Britain* (ed. R.L.H. Dennis), pp. 217–45. Oxford University Press, Oxford.

Eccles, T.M. (1987). Speke Hall Wood or Stockton Heath Wood. *Review of invertebrate sites in England, Merseyside and Greater Manchester* (ed. M. Parsons), (not paginated). Invertebrate site register 96. Nature Conservancy Council, Peterborough.

Eccles, T.M. (1993). Beetles (Coleoptera). *The Sand Dunes of the Sefton Coast* (eds D. Atkinson & J. Houston), pp. 99–103. National Museums & Galleries on Merseyside in conjunction with Sefton Metropolitan Borough Council, Liverpool.

Eccles, T.M. & Bowestead, S. (1987). *Anommatus diecki* Reitter (Coleoptera: Cerylonidae) new to Britain. *Entomologist's Gazette*, **38**, 225–27.

Ellis, J.W. (1889). *The coleopterous fauna of the Liverpool District*. Turner, Routledge, Liverpool.

Ellis, J.W. (1890). *The lepidopterous fauna of Lancashire and Cheshire*. McCorquodale, Leeds.

Emmet, A. & Heath, J. (1989). *Hesperidae – Nymphalidae, the butterflies. The moths and butterflies of Great Britain and Ireland*, 7:1. Harley Books, Colchester.

Eversham, B.C. & Arnold, H.R. (1992). Introductions and their place in British wildlife. *Biological recording of changes in British wildlife* (ed. P.T. Harding), pp. 44–64. Institute of Terrestrial Ecology Symposium, No. 26. HMSO, London.

Falk, S. (1991). *A review of the scarce and threatened bees, wasps and ants of Great Britain*. Research and survey in nature conservation, No. 35. Nature Conservancy Council, Peterborough.

Felton, C. (1991). Checklist of Lancashire and Cheshire spiders. *Annual Report and Proceedings of the Lancashire and Cheshire Entomological Society*, **114**, 57–70.

Felton, C. (1992a). Spider notes from Lancashire. *British Arachnological Society Spider Recording Scheme Newsletter*, **13**, 4.

Felton, C. (1992b). Foreigners in Cheshire. *British Arachnological Society Spider Recording Scheme Newsletter*, **13**, 4.

Felton, C. (1995). Urozelotes rusticus (L. Koch). (Gnaphosidae) new to Lancashire. *British Arachnological Society Spider Recording Scheme Newsletter*, **22**, 1–2.

Felton, C. (1996). The house centipede *Scutigera coleoptrata* (L.) in Lancashire. *British Myriapod Group Newsletter*, **24**, 1.

Felton, C. & Judd, S. (1997). *Carorita limnaea* (Araneae: Linyphiidae) and other Araneae at Wybunbury Moss, Cheshire – A unique refuge for two relict species of spider in Britain. *Bulletin of the British Arachnological Society*, **10**, 298–302.

Ford, W.K. (1953). Lancashire and Cheshire Odonata (a preliminary list). *The North Western Naturalist*, **6**, 227–33. New Series No. 2.

Ford, W.K. (1972). Orthopteroid stowaways. *Lancashire and Cheshire Fauna Society*, **61**, 17–21.

Foster, G.N. (1992). The effects of changes in land use on water beetles. *Biological recording of changes in British wildlife* (ed. P.T. Harding), pp. 27–30. Institute of Terrestrial Ecology Symposium, No. 26. HMSO, London.

Gabb, R. & Kitching, D. (1992). *The dragonflies and damselflies of Cheshire*. National Museums & Galleries on Merseyside, Liverpool.

Garland, S. & Appleton, T. (1994). Solitary wasps and ants (Sphecidae and Formicidae) of Lancashire and Cheshire. *Lancashire Wildlife Journal*, **4**, 1–25.

Gemmell, R.P. & Connell, R.K. (1984). Conservation and creation of wildlife habitats on industrial land in Greater Manchester. *Landscape Planning*, **11**, 175–86.

Guest, J. (1989). *Freshwater invertebrates in the canals of Greater Manchester*. Unpublished survey for the Nature Conservancy Council. Copy at Environmental Data Bank, Liverpool Museum, William Brown Street, Liverpool L3 8EN.

Guest, J. (1996). *Hydrochara caraboides* (Linnaeus) (Hydrophilidae) in Cheshire. *The Coleopterist*, **5**, 19.

Hall, R.A. & Smith, P.H. (1991). Dragonflies of the Sefton coast sand-dune system, Merseyside. *Lancashire Wildlife Journal*, **1**, 22–34.

Hammond, P.M. (1974). Changes in the British coleopterous fauna. *The changing flora and fauna of Britain* (ed. D.L. Hawksworth), pp. 323–69. The Systematics Association Special Volume No. 6. Academic Press, London.

Harding, P.T. (1979). *A survey of the trees at Dunham Massey Park, Greater Manchester*. Institute of Terrestrial Ecology Project No. 405, Huntingdon.

Harding, P.T. & Alexander, K.N.A. (1993). The saproxylic invertebrates of historic parklands: progress and problems. *Dead wood matters: the ecology and conservation of saproxylic invertebrates in Britain* (eds K.J. Kirby, & C.M. Drake), pp. 58–73. English Nature Science, No. 7. English Nature, Peterborough.

Hardy, P.B., Hind, S.H. & Dennis, R.L.H. (1993). Range extension and distribution-infilling among selected butterfly species in north-west England: evidence for inter-habitat movements. *Entomologist's Gazette*, **44**, 247–55.

Hull, M. (1987). Check-list of the Neuropteroidea of Lancashire and Cheshire. *Annual Report and Proceedings of the Lancashire and Cheshire Entomological Society*, **110**, 66.

Hull, M. (1990). Check-list of the sawflies of Lancashire and Cheshire. *Annual Report and Proceedings of the Lancashire and Cheshire Entomological Society*, **113**, 38-53.

Johnson, C. (1962). The scarabaeoid (Coleoptera) fauna of Lancashire and Cheshire and its apparent changes over the last 100 years. *The Entomologist*, **95**, 153–65.

Johnson, C. (1976). Nine species of Coleoptera new to Britain. *Entomologist's Monthly Magazine*, **111**, 177–83.

Johnson, C., Robinson, N.A. & Stubbs, A.E. (1977). *Dunham Park a conservation report on a parkland of high entomological interest*. Chief Scientist's Team Notes, No. 5, Nature Conservancy Council, London.

Johnson, C. & Eccles, T.M. (1983). *Plectophloeus erichsoni occidentalis* Besuchet (Coleoptera: Pselaphidae) new to Britain. *Entomologist's Gazette*, **34**, 267–69.

Judd, S. (1986). The past and present status of the damselfly *Coenagrion pulchellum* (Van Der Linden) (Odonata: Coenagriidae) – in Cheshire and parts of its adjacent counties, corresponding to the 100km square SJ3—3—. *Entomologists' Record and Journal of Variation*, **98**, 57–61.

Judd, S. (1987). A checklist of Lancashire and Cheshire Heteroptera. *Annual Report and Proceedings of the Lancashire and Cheshire Entomological Society*, **110**, 60–65.

Judd, S. & Rotherham, I.D. (1992). The phytophagous insect fauna of *Rhododendron ponticum* L. in Britain. *The Entomologist*, **111**, 134–50.

Judd, S. & Hodkinson, I.D. (1998). The biogeography and regional biodiversity of the British seed bugs (Hemiptera: Lygaeidae). *Journal of Biogeography*, **25**, 227–49.

Kendall, P. (1982). *Bromius obscurus* (L.) in Britain (Col., Chrysomelidae). *Entomologist's Monthly Magazine*, **117**, 233–34.

Kidd, L.N. & Brindle, A. (1959). The Diptera of Lancashire and Cheshire, Part 1. *Lancashire and Cheshire Fauna Committee*, **33**, 1–136.

Langslow, D.R. (1992). Legislation and policies – Managing the changes in British wildlife: the effects of nature conservation. *Biological recording of changes in British wildlife* (ed. P.T. Harding), pp. 65–70. Institute of Terrestrial Ecology Symposium, No. 26. HMSO, London.

Lawson, A.K. (1930). *A check list of the fauna of Lancashire and Cheshire. Part 1.* Lancashire and Cheshire Fauna Committee, Buncle, Arbroath.

Lawton. J.H. (1995). The response of insects to environmental change. *Insects in a changing environment* (eds R. Harrington & N.E. Stork), pp. 1–26. 17th Symposium of the Royal Entomological Society of London. Academic Press, London.

Luff, M.L. & Woiwod, I.P. (1995). Insects as indicators of land-use change: A European perspective, focusing on moths and ground beetles. *Insects in a changing environment* (eds R. Harrington & N.E. Stork), pp. 399–422. 17th Symposium of the Royal Entomological Society of London. Academic Press, London.

Mansbridge, W. (1940). *The lepidopterous fauna of Lancashire and Cheshire* (Revised Ellis list). Lancashire and Cheshire Entomological Society, Liverpool.

Marshall, J.A & Haes, E.C.M. (1988). *Grasshoppers and allied insects of Great Britain and Ireland.* Harley Books, Colchester.

Mellanby, K. (1974). Summing up. *The changing flora and fauna of Britain* (ed. D.L. Hawksworth), pp. 419–23. The Systematics Association Special Volume No. 6. Academic Press, London.

McMillan, N.F. (1959). The Mollusca of some Cheshire marl-pits: a study in colonization. *Journal of Conchology*, **24**, 299–315.

McMillan, N.F. (1990). The history of alien freshwater Mollusca in North-West England. *Naturalist*, **115**, 123–132.

Owen, D.E., Deyd, E.L., Smith, S.G., Brindle, A. *et al.* (1962). *Fauna of the Manchester area.* Manchester University Press, Manchester.

Owen, D.F. (1978). Insect diversity in an English suburban garden. *Perspectives in urban entomology* (eds G.W. Frankie, & C.S. Koehler), pp. 13–29. Academic Press, New York, USA.

Parsons, M. (1987a). *Review of invertebrate sites in England, Cheshire.* Invertebrate site register 95. Nature Conservancy Council, Peterborough.

Parsons, M. (1987b). *Review of invertebrate sites in England, Merseyside and Greater Manchester.* Invertebrate site register 96. Nature Conservancy Council, Peterborough.

Parsons, M. (1987c). *Review of invertebrate sites in England, Lancashire.* Invertebrate site register 98. Nature Conservancy Council, Peterborough.

Payne, K. (1987). Haskayne Cutting. *Review of invertebrate sites in England, Lancashire 98* (ed. M. Parsons), (not paginated). Nature Conservancy Council, Peterborough.

Rutherford, C.I. (1983). *Butterflies in Cheshire 1961–1982.* Supplement to the *1981–1982 Proceedings of the Lancashire and Cheshire Entomological Society.*

Rutherford, C.I. (1994). *Macro-moths in Cheshire 1961–1993.* Lancashire and Cheshire Entomological Society.

Sanderson, R.A. (1992a). Hemiptera of naturally vegetated derelict land in north-west England. *Entomologist's Gazette*, **43**, 221–26.

Sanderson, R.A. (1992b). Diversity and evenness of Hemiptera communities on naturally vegetated land in NW England. *Ecography*, **15**, 154–60.

Sanderson, R.A. (1993). Factors affecting the Hemiptera of naturally colonised derelict land in North West England. *The Entomologist*, **112**, 10–16.

Sharp, W.E. (1908). *The Coleoptera of Lancashire and Cheshire.* Lancashire and Cheshire Entomological Society. Gibbs and Bamforth Ltd, St. Albans.

Shaw, B.T. (1993). Results of a butterfly survey conducted along the Heald Green railway cutting (1984-1993 inclusive). Unpublished pamphlet – copy deposited in Liverpool Museum entomology library.

Shaw, B.T. (1994). *Cheshire butterfly recording scheme 1994 annual report.* Unpublished – copy deposited in Liverpool Museum entomology library.

Shaw, B.T. (1995). *1995 Cheshire butterfly report.* Unpublished – copy deposited in Liverpool Museum entomology library.

Smith, S.G. (1948). The butterflies and moths found in the counties of Cheshire, Flintshire, Denbighshire, Caernarvonshire, Anglesey and Merionethshire. *Proceedings of the Chester Society of Natural Science, Literature and Art*, **2**, 1–251.

Sumner, D.P. (1985). The geographical and seasonal distribution of the dragonflies of Lancashire and Cheshire. *Annual Report and Proceedings of the Lancashire and Cheshire Entomological Society*, **108**, 177–94.

Terrell-Neild, C. (1994). Beetle diversity and land use in the Eccles area of Greater Manchester. *Lancashire Wildlife Journal*, **4**, 35–55.

Thomas, J.A. (1991). Rare species conservation: case studies of European butterflies. *The scientific management of temperate communities for conservation* (eds I.F. Spellerburg, F.B. Goldsmith & M.G. Moriss), pp. 149–97. Blackwell Scientific Publications, Oxford.

Usher, M.B. (1995). A world of change: land-use patterns and arthropod communities. *Insects in a changing environment* (eds R. Harrington & N.E. Stork), pp. 371–422. 17th Symposium of the Royal Entomological Society of London. Academic Press, London.

Vincent, P. (1990). *The biogeography of the British Isles – an introduction.* Routledge, London.

Wallace, I.D. & Wallace, B. (1982). Land invertebrates, excluding Mollusca, spiders and harvestmen. *Hilbre the Cheshire Island – its history and natural history* (ed. J.D. Craggs), pp. 87–116. Liverpool University Press, Liverpool.

Warren, M.S. (1992). The conservation of British butterflies. *The ecology of butterflies in Britain* (ed. R.L.H. Dennis), pp. 246–74. Oxford University Press, Oxford.

Wyatt, B.K. (1992). Resources for documenting changes in species and habitats. *Biological recording of changes in British wildlife* (ed. P.T. Harding), pp. 20–26. Institute of Terrestrial Ecology Symposium, No. 26. HMSO, London.

CHAPTER TWENTY-ONE

'All the birds of the air' – indicators of the environment

D. NORMAN

Introduction

Birds are now probably the best known part of the fauna, having been greatly studied, with reliable identification, for almost two centuries, and avifaunas of all parts of the Mersey Basin were published in the 19th century. These were based on relatively limited information, however, depending mainly on the authors' network of correspondents. It is only in the last few decades that truly comprehensive information has become available, mainly through surveys organised by the British Trust for Ornithology (BTO), largely carried out by amateur participants who travel throughout the region. The most notable surveys are the national atlases, of the distribution of breeding birds in 1968–72 (Sharrock 1976), of the distribution and numbers of wintering birds in 1981–84 (Lack 1986), and of the distribution and numbers of breeding birds in 1988–91 (Gibbons, Reid & Chapman 1993). The local ornithological societies have organised atlases of the breeding distribution of birds on a 2 x 2km square (tetrad) basis in Greater Manchester (Holland, Spence & Sutton 1984) and Cheshire and Wirral (Guest et al. 1992) but, regrettably, not in Merseyside or Lancashire. Because most publications concentrate on descriptions of distribution rather than numbers, it is often difficult to tell if a species has increased or decreased if it has not also changed its range: nevertheless, birds are probably the only taxon for which some quantitative data exist.

This chapter considers various factors that have affected the birds of the Mersey Basin. Examples are given of species in each category, but these are illustrative rather than comprehensive, because of limited space, and I concentrate on the breeding season, with occasional discussion of wintering birds.

Key factors

Natural effects

Climatic change in Britain
Several species which used to breed in Cheshire and Lancashire no longer do so, including Woodlark (*Lullula arborea*), last recorded around the 1860s, Nightingale (*Luscinia megarhynchos*), Nightjar (*Caprimulgus*

europaeus), Red-backed Shrike (*Lanius collurio*), which nested at Bootle in the 19th century, and Wryneck (*Jynx torquilla*), the last two now being almost extinct in Britain. All are insect-eaters of southerly distribution, probably affected by climatic change (Burton 1995).

The Mersey Basin has long been on the edge of the distribution of the Turtle Dove (*Streptopelia turtur*), so its status in this area has fluctuated considerably. It underwent a northerly and westerly expansion in the 19th century, colonising Cheshire in the 1870s and first breeding in Lancashire in 1904, steadily increasing to 1930, possibly assisted by agricultural recession and the availability of more weed seeds. Southern Lancashire continued to be the most north-westerly regular breeding area until the late 1960s, when Turtle Doves again started to retreat south-eastwards. A comparison between the two BTO Atlases (Sharrock 1976 and Gibbons et al. 1993) shows a dramatic shift out of north-west England, and this species is now close to extinction in the region.

The Reed Warbler (*Acrocephalus scirpaceus*) is another species close to its north-western limit in the Mersey Basin. It expanded its range northward to reach Lancashire in about 1850, probably assisted by climatic amelioration, and by 1900, bred as far north as Morecambe and east to the Yorkshire border. By the 1930s the species had retreated towards the south – rather against the climatic trend – only being found near the coast in Lancashire and not in Wirral or the eastern hills. It has spread again in the last 20 or 30 years, with odd breeding sites now occupied along the coast almost as far as the Scottish border. The extensive drainage of the lowlands cannot have helped Reed Warblers, but many of the region's *Phragmites* reedbeds, their required breeding habitat, are now in the control of nature conservation organisations and are well managed and protected. Cuckoos (*Cuculus canorus*) in the area mainly use Dunnock (*Prunella modularis*) or Meadow Pipit (*Anthus pratensis*) hosts, but have extended to cuckold Reed Warblers in Cheshire recently: there were single records in 1934 and 1977, then annually from 1988 onwards at Rostherne and Woolston (Calvert 1989; Smith & Norman 1989).

Two species, Barn Owl (*Tyto alba*) and Song Thrush

(*Turdus philomelos*), have occasioned much concern for their decline over the last 30 or 40 years. Several factors are implicated, including agricultural habitat changes and pesticides, and climatic factors must be playing a part. They are both southern species which here reach close to their northern limit.

The Yellow Wagtail (*Motacilla flava*) used to be widespread in the lowlands here, but must have been severely hit by loss of habitat from drainage, intensification of agriculture and replacement of grasslands with cereals. However, when Stuart Smith studied Yellow Wagtails breeding alongside the River Mersey in suburban Manchester over the seven years 1939–45, he wrote in his New Naturalist Monograph (1950) 'there is little doubt that it is increasing'. Since then there has clearly been a contraction in range, south-eastwards, with some local declines or extinctions.

Climatic change outside Britain

The reducing rainfall in western Africa has drastically affected the populations of several of our summer visitors. The Sedge Warbler (*Acrocephalus schoenobaenus*) used to be regarded as common throughout the Mersey Basin, except for the eastern hills, and Oakes (1953) declared it to be '*the* warbler of the plains' of old Lancashire. Its population appeared stable from 1800 to 1968 although it had disappeared from areas where the habitat had been drained or developed. Then, along with other species – notably the Whitethroat (*Sylvia communis*) (Winstanley, Spencer & Williamson 1974) – the population crashed in 1969 and again in 1984, conclusively linked to west African drought (Peach, Baillie & Underhill 1991). Although their status in the Mersey Basin region has been poorly recorded until recently, my ringing studies of Sand Martins (*Riparia riparia*) breeding in mid-Cheshire quarries show that the survival of adults varies annually between about 8% and 50%, which correlates strongly with west African rainfall (Norman & Peach, unpublished). The local populations of Tree Pipit (*Anthus trivialis*), Whinchat (*Saxicola rubetra*), Grasshopper Warbler (*Locustella naevia*) and Redstart (*Phoenicurus phoenicurus*) have not been so well studied, but they are all probably mainly determined by African climate changes.

Severe winter weather

The breeding numbers of the Grey Heron (*Ardea cinerea*) are particularly well known, from the BTO censuses from 1928 onwards, the longest running census of any bird species. There are about 500 nests in the Mersey Basin, the great majority in Cheshire. Although pesticides can reduce the survival of adults, the most important factor affecting their numbers is severe winters, when their food becomes locked under ice.

Populations of insectivorous residents such as Goldcrests (*Regulus regulus*), Stonechats (*Saxicola torquata*) and Green Woodpeckers (*Picus viridis*) fluctuate with expansions and local extinctions, mainly correlated with hard winters.

Range expansion

The Little Ringed Plover (*Charadrius dubius*) first bred in the Mersey Basin (Cheshire) in 1954, and there are now regularly up to 40 or 50 pairs, mostly in sand quarries or lime beds. Collared Doves (*Streptopelia decaocto*) have spectacularly spread from the Balkans in the 1930s to reach the Mersey Basin in 1960, finding an available niche as a medium-sized grain-eater tolerant of man, and now it is one of our commoner species.

Black Redstarts (*Phoenicurus ochruros*) and Bearded Tits (*Panurus biarmicus*) bred here in the 1970s or early 1980s, but have failed to establish themselves. One of the most extraordinary events of recent years was the nesting of Marsh Warbler (*Acrocephalus palustris*) at Woolston in 1991, their most northerly breeding in Britain this century (Norman 1994). Regrettably this has not been sustained. Single pairs of Black-necked Grebe (*Podiceps nigricollis*) bred several times in Cheshire between 1938 and 1953 and then during the 1980s, and from the late 1980s onwards several pairs have bred each year.

Shelducks (*Tadorna tadorna*) and Oystercatchers (*Haematopus ostralegus*) built up during this century to a considerable breeding population on the coast and near the River Mersey, and are now moving inland more frequently to breed (Gibbons *et al.* 1993). Similarly the Redshank (*Tringa totanus*), previously a rare coastal breeder, completely changed its status during the late-19th and 20th century to become a common inland breeder (Oakes 1953), although usually close to the major rivers.

Unintentional human impacts

Agricultural changes

Species such as Skylark (*Alauda arvensis*) and Lapwing (*Vanellus vanellus*) must have been scarce up to about 5,000 BC, perhaps limited to the coastal marshes and the Pennine fringes, but clearance of trees for land cultivation would have allowed them to spread and become characteristic species of open farmland.

Skylarks largely shifted from natural pastures and grassland to arable fields, apparently with little change in distribution or numbers, until about 1980, since when their population has almost halved. Good habitat used to be provided by short-term leys of grass or clover, but the shift to autumn-sown cereals leaves fewer seeds for winter feeding, and by April the crops are too tall and dense for nesting. They have declined in my study area at Frodsham Marsh, however, where little change in habitat or farming practice has occurred, and I suspect that there may be other influences such as the recent prevalence of cold, wet springs.

Lapwings are still common in the region, but like Skylarks are declining fast with agricultural changes, mainly the transition from hay to silage, and autumn-sown cereals that grow too tall in spring for the species to nest in such fields.

Corncrakes (*Crex crex*) used to be quite common in north-west England, and their rapid decline from about

1880 onwards is a classic tale of inimical agricultural changes. Their habitat of tall grass and herbs, especially hay meadows, became much less common as farmers turned to making silage. What hay remained was grown more rapidly with inorganic fertilisers, leading to a season too short for Corncrakes to rear their young before the onslaught of mechanical harvesting. The species almost disappeared from the Mersey Basin during the Second World War, and has bred only sporadically since then.

The lowland mosses used to be grouse moors; Carrington Moss until 1886 and Chat Moss until the mid-1930s, but they were drained for agriculture, and Red Grouse (*Lagopus lagopus*) is now confined to the heather-dominated eastern hills. Their population has roughly halved in the last 50 years, as moorlands have been lost to pastoral farming and subsidies have encouraged heavy sheep grazing (chapter eleven, this volume). Twite (*Carduelis flavirostris*) and Short-eared Owls (*Asio flammeus*) also used to breed regularly on the mosses, but are now restricted to breeding in heather moorland.

The Corn Bunting's (*Miliaria calandra*) population declined in the agricultural depression of 1870–1930 with the much reduced area of cereals. It recovered from 1940–1970, but then dropped greatly again as winter survival suffered through the loss of stubble. A reduction in farmland invertebrates, taken as food for their young, is also thought to be a contributory factor. Despite this gloomy picture, the lowlands of west Lancashire are one of the most densely occupied areas of all Britain (Gibbons *et al.* 1993).

Tree Sparrows (*Passer montanus*) have shown puzzling, irregular cycles in numbers, being high from the 1880s to 1930s, dropping to a low about 1950 then peaking again in 1960–78. They are now in a major decline phase undoubtedly caused by the reduction of weeds through the use of herbicides. House Sparrows (*Passer domesticus*) increased substantially, along with the human population in the 19th century, and major attempts to destroy them had little general effect. Their population showed little change until the 1970s, but has decreased markedly since then, probably because of a decline in both invertebrates and weed seeds. Greenfinches (*Carduelis chloris*) and Linnets (*Carduelis cannabina*) survived the depredations of bird-catchers in the 19th century, but their population fluctuations in the 20th century, now sharply downwards, are apparently linked to the availability of seeds on agricultural land.

The Yellowhammer (*Emberiza citrinella*) used to be common through most of the region, but has undergone a serious contraction in range since 1930–50, especially noticeable in the east of the Mersey Basin (Holland *et al.* 1984). They are very dependent on hedgerows, mainly as breeding sites and song-posts. However, as much as 60% of Cheshire hedges have gone in this century, for agricultural production, urban and industrial growth, mineral extraction and road-building. Lesser Whitethroats (*Sylvia curruca*) became less common during the Second World War, which Boyd (1950) ascribed to the practice of trimming hedges lower to allow cultivation closer to the field edges.

The story of the disastrous effects of the organochlorine seed-dressings used in the 1950s and early 1960s is well known: the poisons were ingested by seed-eating birds, and populations of Stock Dove (*Columba oenas*) and many farmland finches were badly affected. The pesticide residues also accumulated up the food chain to devastate the populations of many bird-eating raptors. The effects were partly direct, with many birds killed outright, but also more insidious, with a reduction in breeding success caused by thinner egg-shells. Sparrowhawks (*Accipiter nisus*) were wiped out from much of England, but persisted in the region, probably because of the lower acreage of arable land. The Peregrine (*Falco peregrinus*) was also badly affected, but was not a common bird and certainly did not breed in the Mersey Basin at that time.

Poisoning by agricultural chemicals is not just a recent phenomenon: in the first half of the 19th century, Grey Partridges (*Perdix perdix*) were poisoned in large numbers through feeding on seedcorn that had been steeped in arsenic to kill wireworms.

In the last few years, pesticides have become still more efficient and now kill many of the farmland invertebrates, probably affecting species such as Rook (*Corvus frugilegus*) and Starling (*Sturnus vulgaris*). The Rook has always been common through most of the Mersey Basin, although it is missing from much of the lowlands north of the River Mersey because of the shortage of nesting trees. There used to be some sport shooting and collection of nestlings for food, but they were not persecuted as much as the other corvids because of the early (mid-19th century) recognition of its role in eating agricultural pests. Breeding Starlings, which also eat tremendous numbers of soil invertebrates, declined in the 18th century, but then increased greatly in the 19th century, perhaps due to climatic changes. They have decreased sharply in recent years, from 1980 on, although still attaining a very high density north of the River Mersey (Gibbons *et al.* 1993).

Finally, one species which has adapted its behaviour recently to take advantage of agricultural produce is the winter-visiting Fieldfare (*Turdus pilaris*). Their habit of feeding on orchard apples helps them to survive when the ground is frozen (Norman 1994).

Drainage of wetlands

The Bittern (*Botaurus stellaris*) became extinct in the Mersey Basin by 1850. Initially its decline was due to drainage of its reedbed habitat, but numbers were reduced further by shooting for the table and for its feathers to make flies for fishing; then, as they became rare, collectors of skins and eggs hastened the decline. Another reedbed specialist, the Marsh Harrier (*Circus aeruginosus*), probably bred until about 1820 in the Mersey valley and last nested in the region about 1860 around Martin Mere (Holloway 1995). Drainage and enclosure through the 18th and 19th centuries caused a widespread decline in Mallard (*Anas platyrhynchos*) and Teal (*Anas crecca*) breeding, and although the former is still common and widespread, Teal is still dwindling as a breeding species. Snipe (*Gallinago gallinago*) used to nest abundantly on the mosslands of Lancashire (Oakes 1953); it was common on the plains and very common on the moors, but has now gone from almost all the lowland areas.

Many water birds such as Little Grebe (*Tachybaptus ruficollis*) and Reed Bunting (*Emberiza schoeniclus*) have taken advantage of the patchwork of ponds created by marling since the 13th century and formerly such a feature of the Mersey Basin (chapter fourteen, this volume). However, the use of fertilisers and piping of water for stock to drink meant that the two reasons for marl pits to remain no longer applied, and many were filled in or left to become overgrown with scrub.

Urban and industrial development
Most rural species have suffered, often with local extinctions, when their habitats have been taken for development, and it would be tedious to list examples. There are, on the other hand, several examples where development has benefited birds. Some species now depend almost exclusively on man-made structures for their nest sites, including Swifts (*Apus apus*) and House Martins (*Delichon urbica*): when they had to find cliffs or tree-holes they must have been scarce in the Mersey Basin. Swallows (*Hirundo rustica*) must also have changed their breeding sites since historical time, almost all now nesting in buildings, but even during the Roman occupation commensal breeding was common. From about 1960 the vast majority of the Sand Martin population has nested in sand quarries. The Little Gulls (*Larus minutus*) that now congregate on spring passage at the mouth of the River Mersey benefit from the lagoons in the docks at Seaforth for feeding, bathing and resting (Smith 1995).

Conurbations also have a 'heat island' effect, whereby the mean temperature may be several degrees above that of surrounding areas, making a substantial difference to birds' overnight survival, especially in winter. The massive urban roosts of immigrant Starlings certainly take advantage of this effect.

The former coastal colony of up to 300 pairs of Common Terns (*Sterna hirundo*) at Ainsdale and some Arctic Terns (*Sterna paradisaea*) declined in the 1930s with adjacent house-building, and subsequent war-time activities – establishment of a naval station on the dunes – finished them off. The period between the wars saw a widespread decline in Ringed Plover (*Charadrius hiaticula*), as there was a dramatic increase in human use of the coasts, for recreation, holiday homes and sea defences, with consequent disturbance and loss of habitat. The species' salvation was a shift in habit, moving to breed inland, sporadically from 1946 and regularly for about the last 20 years. The Little Tern (*Sterna albifrons*), which used to nest on south Lancashire shores (Sefton coast), has been similarly affected, but has suffered much more since it has not moved inland to breed in this country as it commonly does in continental Europe.

Afforestation
The maturing conifer plantations are assisting Crossbills (*Loxia curvirostra*) and Siskins (*Carduelis spinus*) to breed in greater numbers. The Redpoll (*Carduelis flammea*) used to be scarce but has flourished, especially since the early 1960s, benefiting particularly from Birch (*Betula* spp.) on the mosslands and those planted around the new towns. Coal Tits (*Parus ater*) have increased substantially since the 19th century but are still scarce away from trees. Chiffchaffs (*Phylloscopus collybita*) expanded their range northwards in the 19th century, and are mainly associated with wooded areas. Although still present at low densities north of the River Mersey, they have increased and spread in recent years.

Several species that depend on woodland for breeding, notably Grey Heron, Sparrowhawk, Nuthatch (*Sitta europaea*), Wood Warbler (*Phylloscopus sibilatrix*) and Goldcrest showed an obvious gap in their distribution in the 1968–72 breeding Atlas north of the River Mersey in Merseyside and Greater Manchester, which had largely been filled in by the time of the 1988–91 Atlas. Other species are still missing from that area, including Woodcock (*Scolopax rusticola*), Green Woodpecker, Lesser Spotted Woodpecker (*Dendrocopos minor*), Rook, Jackdaw (*Corvus monedula*), Marsh Tit (*Parus palustris*), Redstart, Garden Warbler (*Sylvia borin*) and Tree Pipit. On the other hand the Willow Tit (*Parus montanus*) is more abundant in the Mersey valley and mosslands than anywhere else in the region (Gibbons *et al.* 1993). Also, the thousands of Bramblings (*Fringilla montifringilla*) that visited Liverpool in the winter of 1980–81 took advantage of the mature Beeches (*Fagus sylvatica*), planted in suburban avenues around 1810, by feeding avidly on the mast.

Water and air quality
The almost relentless decline of the Kingfisher (*Alcedo atthis*) in the 19th century was the product of persecution, hard winters and pollution of watercourses. There has been a general recovery in the 20th century following a reduction in persecution, and milder winters, but canalisation of streams and rivers has reduced the numbers of nesting sites and fishing perches. Dippers (*Cinclus cinclus*) and Grey Wagtails (*Motacilla cinerea*) are found in limited numbers in the hill-streams throughout the uplands, but the latter species also spreads into urban areas and is less sensitive to pollution or acidification of its watercourses because they take a wider range of insect prey.

The waterfowl wintering on the Mersey Estuary, especially Pintail (*Anas acuta*), Teal, Wigeon (*Anas penelope*), Shelduck, Dunlin (*Calidris alpina*) and Redshank, have undoubtedly benefited greatly from the improvement in water quality from an almost lifeless river before the 1970s (Thomason & Norman 1995).

The aerial pollution of the Industrial Revolution might

have suppressed flying insects and their predators such as House Martins. Both Long-tailed Tits (*Aegithalos caudatus*) and Chaffinches (*Fringilla coelebs*) were scarce in the Mersey valley and to the north of it, perhaps because of poor air quality limiting the lichens with which they camouflage their nests. Long-tailed Tits have recently spread into the Liverpool area, and Chaffinches might now be increasing (Marchant *et al.* 1990).

Recreational disturbance

Several scarce moorland breeders are endangered by the increasing numbers of walkers in the hills, with the very small populations of Golden Plover (*Pluvialis apricaria*) (Yalden & Yalden 1989), Common Sandpiper (*Actitis hypoleucos*) (Holland *et al.* 1982), Dunlin and Ring Ousel (*Turdus torquatus*) especially at risk.

Mute Swans (*Cygnus olor*) have been fairly common in the region for centuries, although often ignored as a domesticated species. They underwent a catastrophic decline between 1950 and 1985, attributed to poisoning through ingestion of lead weights discarded by anglers. The species reached its nadir around 1985 when it was one of the scarcest breeding birds in Cheshire (13 pairs), but since the phasing out of lead weights, the population has rapidly recovered to reach at least 70 pairs only ten years later.

Deliberate human impacts
Legislation

Laws such as the Sea Birds Preservation Act (1869), the Lapwing Protection Act (1926) and the Wildlife and Countryside Act (1981) have had major effects on conservation of some species, but affect the whole of the UK and are not specific to the Mersey Basin.

Provision of food and protection

Greenfinches and Siskins have benefited greatly from their recently-acquired habit of feeding on peanuts in gardens, which allows them to attain good condition at a time of year when natural seeds are scarce. Many tits likewise owe their over-winter survival to food put out by householders. Blackcaps (*Sylvia atricapilla*) appeared as a wintering species in the Mersey Basin from about 1964 onwards, as birds of southern German and Austrian breeding stock discovered the benefits of a shorter migration to an area with reasonably mild winters and ample food supplies: they favour well-stocked gardens, and perhaps 100 individuals are now recorded in the region each winter.

In the 19th century the Pied Flycatcher (*Ficedula hypoleuca*) was not present locally although it was common to the west (Wales) and north (Cumbria and northern Yorkshire). From 1939 onwards they nested sporadically in the Mersey Basin, with increasing numbers especially in the last decade or so as more nest-boxes were provided. The only Common Tern breeding records in our region since the Second World War have been in the last two decades on man-made nesting sites in Merseyside and Greater Manchester. Goldeneyes (*Bucephala clangula*) have bred recently in nest-boxes in Lancashire.

Reserves like Martin Mere have allowed hundreds of wild Bewick's Swan (*Cygnus columbianus*) and Whooper Swans (*Cygnus cygnus*) – previously very scarce birds – to winter here. The Ribble National Nature Reserve hosts tens of thousands of Pink-footed Geese (*Anser brachyrhynchus*) and Wigeon, manifold increases on the figures of 50 years ago.

It is probably protection, or at least the decline of shooting, that has allowed several duck species to breed from early this century, e.g., Shoveler (*Anas clypeata*) and Tufted Duck (*Aythya fuligula*), with other species, e.g., Gadwall (*Anas strepera*) and Pochard (*Aythya ferina*), colonising only in the last 20 years.

Persecution

During the 19th century, most wildlife was seen as competitors with humans for food, and widespread systematic persecution of almost any species of bird took place. The large estates employed many gamekeepers who killed anything they thought, rightly or wrongly, might threaten their sport. The effect was most noticeable when the numbers of keepers dropped markedly during both World Wars, and many birds took advantage. Sparrowhawks used to be heavily persecuted throughout the region, but their secretive breeding habits and high reproductive rate ensured they survived, even in heavily keepered woods. Some nests are still robbed in Merseyside, apparently by amateur would-be falconers. Red Kites (*Milvus milvus*) were persecuted into extinction around 1800, and Hen Harriers (*Circus cyaneus*) and Buzzards (*Buteo buteo*) a little later. Buzzards are now making a welcome resurgence, having bred in Cheshire from 1980 onwards. Peregrines, having survived the depredations of falconers for hundreds of years, mainly by nesting in inaccessible and dangerous nesting places, have also nested at several Cheshire sites in the last five years, as have Ravens (*Corvus corax*).

Jays (*Garrulus glandarius*) and Magpies (*Pica pica*) declined during the 19th century due to persecution, but increased during the First World War and afterwards, again increasing noticeably during the Second World War so that Boyd (1950) thought Magpies 'far too abundant'. The species has now changed its habits to tolerate man and to nest in hedgerows and in conurbations. Carrion Crows (*Corvus corone*), hated for so long, also increased during the Great War and afterwards, with another rise during the Second World War.

Kestrels (*Falco tinnunculus*) and Tawny Owls (*Strix aluco*) were uncommon in the 19th century, through direct persecution, but the former also through reduction of old corvid nests to take over. Both species have greatly increased during this century, particularly between 1928 and 1953, and have become common in towns, especially feeding on House Sparrows in Manchester.

The Bullfinch's (*Pyrrhula pyrrhula*) habit of eating

fruit-tree buds resulted in a bounty of a penny a head in the mid-17th century, about 50 pence at today's prices, but their population increased after the Wild Birds Protection Acts of the 1880s and 1890s.

There are modern-day calls to reduce numbers of some species. The Cormorant (*Phalacrocorax carbo*) is an abundant non-breeding visitor to the region and is spreading inland to gorge on artificially stocked fishing waters, much to the disgust of anglers who, dubbing it the 'black plague', are lobbying hard for licences to shoot it. Many of the region's migrant species are hunted in southern Europe, but there is little evidence on whether or not this actually affects their populations. Wildfowling is extensively practised in the Mersey Basin: properly exercised, with appropriate adherence to closed seasons and bag limits, it appears to have no effect on the populations of ducks or geese.

Collection for food
Large numbers of Lapwing eggs used to be collected for food, and the species decreased greatly in the 19th century, with loss of habitat as well. A rapid resurgence in fortunes occurred with the Lapwing Protection Act of 1926. Black-headed Gulls (*Larus ridibundus*) bred in the Delamere area of Cheshire from at least 1617, but a steady population decline throughout Britain during the 19th century, probably through large numbers of eggs being harvested from most colonies, brought them close to extinction. The Delamere colony survived, being recorded in 1860, and the Sea Birds Preservation Act (1869) helped the species to thrive, although they declined again after 1958, possibly due to changes in water-level caused by increased sand extraction in the area, and have not bred there since 1965.

Collection for fashion
The fashion for skins and feathers increased in the 19th century so that by 1860 the national population of the Great Crested Grebe (*Podiceps cristatus*) was reduced to about 42 breeding pairs, of which 20 were in Cheshire. Following legal protection and the formation of the Royal Society for the Protection of Birds (RSPB), the species increased so that a survey in 1931 found 78 pairs breeding in Cheshire. Green Woodpeckers and Jays were also shot for their feathers to make fishing flies and for women's fashions, and it is difficult now to comprehend that in the 1890s Robins (*Erithacus rubecula*) were popular in millinery, and that countless individuals of Britain's national bird were killed to adorn women's hats.

Collection as specimens
In the 19th century the Goldfinch (*Carduelis carduelis*) was a very popular cage-bird, and so easy to catch that it was rare in the area until its inclusion in the Wild Birds Protection Acts of 1880 and 1881 allowed slow increases in population and range. An increase in weeds, especially thistles, in the agricultural depression of the late 19th and early 20th centuries also helped them, but all publications up to 1950 indicate exceptional scarcity in

Greater Manchester. They are now widespread but not numerous across the Mersey Basin.

Many Victorian drawing rooms used to include a stuffed specimen, but no birds have been collected for this purpose for many years. The oologists of the 19th and the first half of the 20th centuries took many complete clutches, often from the rarer species, and must have affected their populations, before egg-collection was outlawed by various Acts of Parliament.

Introductions
Introductions have almost always benefited the species concerned, allowing an expansion of range beyond that naturally occupied, but many introductions have had deleterious effects on the indigenous species, either by competition or displacement. Pheasants (*Phasianus colchicus*) were introduced about 1,000 years ago but remained uncommon until the rise of modern game-keeping, and are now widespread and common, with extensive management and releasing. The Ruddy Duck (*Oxyura jamaicensis*) bred in Cheshire from 1968 and in Greater Manchester since 1981, but migrating individuals may now be endangering the closely related scarce White-headed Duck (*Oxyura leucocephala*) in Spain through hybridisation. At the end of the last century, the Canada Goose (*Branta canadensis*) was rare, but it has spread rapidly in recent decades, the Cheshire population trebling from 1953 to 1976 and still increasing, though they have bred in Greater Manchester only since 1974. The Little Owl (*Athene noctua*) was introduced to England in the 19th century, and first bred in several parts of the region around 1920. The population rocketed until about 1960, since when it has become less common, perhaps with reductions in prey from pesticides and tidier farm practices.

Introduced mammals can affect birds. Rabbits (*Oryctolagus cuniculus*), introduced probably around 1100, have shaped parts of the countryside so that some birds depend on the habitat they produce. Indirectly the decline of Wheatears (*Oenanthe oenanthe*) after the Second World War was accentuated by the catastrophic drop in rabbit populations from myxomatosis, since their burrows are the Wheatear's favourite nest site, and the rabbits graze the grass to the short sward the birds need. The Wigeon that winter on the Mersey Estuary themselves graze almost exclusively on the areas that have been cropped, first by summer cattle and then by rabbits. American Mink (*Mustela vison*), escaped or deliberately released from farms (chapter twenty-two, this volume), are now major predators on waterfowl in some areas, although their population appears to be cyclical and they have been checked by organised trapping.

Species showing little change
As well as those species discussed above that have changed their status, there are several whose range or numbers have kept stable, often because their catholic habits have enabled them to adapt to the changing environment. Pied Wagtails (*Motacilla alba*), Dunnocks,

Robins, Blue Tits (*Parus caeruleus*) and Great Tits (*Parus major*) have been common for at least two centuries, and have experienced no widespread changes, although local or temporary declines have occurred following severe winters. Similarly, the Wren (*Troglodytes troglodytes*) has long been abundant throughout the region, although less so north of the River Mersey (Gibbons *et al.* 1993); being mainly resident, and certainly not leaving the British Isles, and although insectivorous all year round, thus suffering huge losses in hard winters it can bounce back to become, in some years, Britain's most numerous bird.

Future prospects

Prophecy can be dangerous, but I feel there is room for cautious optimism. Most of the destructive actions of the past were taken in ignorance of their likely effect, whereas now there is a reasonable understanding of the way in which birds and habitats interact. Indeed, in recent years there is a greater awareness of the interdependence of all the components of our 'green and pleasant land'. Governments have enthusiastically embraced the concept of biodiversity, and action plans are devised for species and habitats. My main concern is that there is too much emphasis on special sites and species, and that the overview of the wider countryside could still be lost. Bitterns and Black-necked Grebes are important and must be encouraged and protected, but we must not concentrate on the rarities so much that we overlook agricultural policies that could drive Skylarks and Lapwings to the same state of rarity.

References

Included here are a number of publications used in compiling this chapter but not necessarily cited in the text.

Boyd, A.W. (1946). *The Country Diary of a Cheshire Man*. Collins, London.
Boyd, A.W. (1950). *A Country Parish*. The New Naturalist Series. Collins, London.
Burton, J.F. (1995). *Birds and Climate Change*. Christopher Helm, London.
Calvert, M. [1989]. Cheshire Reed Warblers as Cuckoo Hosts. *Cheshire & Wirral Bird Report*, **1988**, 87.
Cheshire County Council (1992). *Cheshire State of the Environment Project*. Cheshire County Council, Chester.
Coward, T.A. & Oldham, C. (1900). *The Birds of Cheshire*. Sherratt & Hughes, Manchester.
Coward, T.A. (1910). *A Vertebrate Fauna of Cheshire and Liverpool Bay*. Witherby, London.

Flegg, J.J.M. (1975). Bird Population and Distribution Changes and the Impact of Man. *Bird Study*, **22**, 191–202.
Gibbons, D.W., Reid, J.B. & Chapman, R.A. (1993). *The New Atlas of Breeding Birds in Britain and Ireland 1988–1991*. T. & A.D. Poyser, London.
Guest, J.P., Elphick, D., Hunter, J.S.A. & Norman, D. (1992). *The Breeding Bird Atlas of Cheshire and Wirral*. Cheshire & Wirral Ornithological Society.
Hardy, E. (1941). *Birds of the Liverpool Area*. Buncle, Arbroath.
Holland, P., Robson, J.E. & Yalden, D.W. (1982). The status and distribution of the Common Sandpiper (*Actitis hypoleucos*) in the Peak District. *Naturalist*, **107**, 77–86.
Holland, P., Spence, I. & Sutton, T. (1984). *Breeding Birds in Greater Manchester*. Manchester Ornithological Society.
Holloway, S. (1995). *The Historical Atlas of Breeding Birds in Britain and Ireland 1875–1900*. T. & A.D. Poyser, London.
Lack, P. (1986). *The Atlas of Wintering Birds in Britain and Ireland*. T. & A.D. Poyser, Calton.
Latham, F.A. (ed.) (1991). *Delamere: The History of a Cheshire Parish*. Local History Group, Tarporley.
Lever, C. (1977). *The Naturalized Animals of the British Isles*. Hutchinson, London.
Marchant, J.H., Hudson, R., Carter, S.P. & Whittington, P. (1990). *Population Trends in British Breeding Birds*. BTO, Tring.
Mitchell, F.S. (1892). *The Birds of Lancashire*. Gurney and Jackson, London.
Norman, D. [1994]. First Breeding of Marsh Warbler in Cheshire: Woolston 1991. *Cheshire & Wirral Bird Report*, **1993**, 94–96.
Norman, D. (1994). *The Fieldfare*. Hamlyn, London.
Oakes, C. (1953). *The Birds of Lancashire*. Oliver & Boyd, Edinburgh.
Peach, W.J., Baillie, S.R. & Underhill, L. (1991). Survival of British Sedge Warblers *Acrocephalus schoenobaenus* in relation to west African rainfall. *Ibis*, **133**, 300–05.
Sharrock, J.T.R. (1976). *The Atlas of Breeding Birds in Britain and Ireland*. T. & A.D. Poyser, Berkhamsted.
Smith, P.H. (1995). Gulls and Terns of the Mersey Estuary. *The Mersey Estuary – Naturally Ours* (eds M.S. Curtis, D. Norman, & I.D. Wallace), pp. 60–68. Mersey Estuary Conservation Group, Warrington.
Smith, M.G. & Norman, D. [1989]. Cuckoos at Woolston 1988. *Cheshire & Wirral Bird Report*, **1988**, 88.
Smith, S.E. (1950). *The Yellow Wagtail*. New Naturalist Monograph. Collins, London.
Thomason, G. & Norman, D. (1995). Wildfowl and Waders of the Mersey Estuary. *The Mersey Estuary – Naturally Ours* (eds M.S. Curtis, D. Norman, & I.D. Wallace), pp. 33–59. Mersey Estuary Conservation Group, Warrington.
Williamson, K. (1975). Birds and climatic Change. *Bird Study*, **22**, 143–64.
Winstanley, D., Spencer, R. & Williamson, K. (1974). Where have all the Whitethroats gone? *Bird Study*, **21**, 1–14.
Yalden, D.W. & Yalden, P.E. (1989). The sensitivity of breeding Golden Plovers (*Pluvialis apricaria*) to human intruders. *Bird Study*, **36**, 49–55.

A much extended version of this manuscript is available on request from the author.

CHAPTER TWENTY-TWO

The lost ark: changes in the tetrapod fauna of the Mersey Basin since 15,000 BP

C.T. FISHER AND D.W. YALDEN

Introduction

In discussing the history of amphibians, reptiles and mammals in the Mersey Basin, some historical licence is necessary. There are some instances where tetrapod species are known from local records, many more where tetrapods are only known certainly as records elsewhere on a national basis but which are assumed also to have occurred locally; yet others can only be surmised as existing here by analogy with what happened in other places and with other organisms. In trying to present a coherent story from fragmentary evidence, it is necessary to combine these elements.

15,000 BP

At the beginning of the record, the ice sheet of the last glaciation (Devensian) was just retreating, and the mammal fauna of Britain included Woolly Mammoth (*Mammuthus primigenius*), Woolly Rhinoceros (*Coelodonta antiquitatis*), Reindeer (*Rangifer tarandus*), Giant Deer (*Megaloceros giganteus*), lemmings (*Dicrostonyx torquatus* and *Lemmus lemmus*), Wolf (*Canis lupus*) and Brown Bear (*Ursus arctos*).

Direct evidence for the existence of these species locally comes from caves in the uplands surrounding the Mersey Basin (in the Peak District, Furness and in North Wales), and from more local peat and gravel deposits. The exact dating of such records is uncertain, and some remains (especially of Woolly Mammoth and Woolly Rhinoceros) may belong to earlier periods in the Devensian, but most are late-glacial (Figure 22.1; Table 22.1).

A Mammoth from Cae Gwynn is dated at 18,000 BP, so is certainly full-glacial in age, but the recently discovered mammoths from Condover, Shropshire, dated 12,400 BP (Lister 1991) are among the latest known from Britain, and confirm their presence here until the late glacial.

Reynolds (1933, after Dawkins 1875) comments that the abundant remains of Reindeer (and Bison (*Bos bonasus*), which is not discussed here) at Windy Knoll, just west of Castleton in Derbyshire, strongly indicate that this pass was a regular migration route from the

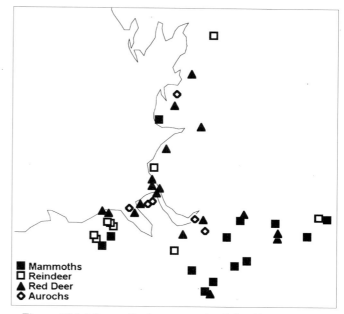

Figure 22.1. Mersey Basin mammals of the Glacial period and later Mesolithic – distribution of Mammoths, Reindeer, Red Deer and Aurochs.

Derwent Valley through to the plains of Lancashire and Cheshire.

Mersey Basin records of Giant Deer are few, but include those at Freshfield and Wallasey (Table 22.1). There is also Giant Deer material from Helsfell Point (near Kendal, Cumbria) in the collections at Liverpool Museum, National Museum & Galleries on Merseyside. Lemmings of both genera are recorded from the area (Table 22.1).

According to Rackham (1986) there can be little doubt that the larger mammals of this era died out as a result of human activity, including hunting; this may be an over-simplified view.

14,000 to 11,000 BP

During this period the climate became warmer and Birch scrub spread into the area. The most notable tetrapod record from these times is the specimen of an Elk (*Alces*

	North Wales	Merseyside	Lancashire	Cheshire	Derbyshire
Mammoth	Cefn Caves[1,7] Tremeirchion[1,7] Plas Heaton[GMC] Cae Gwynn[4]		Blackpool[3]	Adlington[2,6] Coppenhall[2,6] Marbury[2,6] Mere Hall[2,6] Sandbach[2,6] Wrenbury[2,6] Northwich[1] Bolesworth[7]	Buxton[1] Castleton[1]
Woolly Rhinoceros	Ffynnon Beuno[7] Cae Gwynn[7,GMC] Gop Cave[7] Gwaenysgor[7]				
Reindeer	Cefn Caves[7,10] Bont Newydd[7,10] Plas Heaton[7,10] Galltfaenan[7,10] Ffynnon Beuno[7,10] Cae Gwynn[7,10] Gop Cave[7,10] Gwaenysgor[7,10] Lynx Cave[JB]	Freshfield[10]	Whittington Hall[10]	Chester[10]	Castleton[3,10] Ravencliffe[3,10] Wirksworth[3,10]
Giant Deer	Cefn Caves[7,9] Ffynnon Beuno[7,9] Gwaenysgor[7,9]	Wallasey Pool[3,5,8]	Ravensbarrow Hole[12]		
Lemmings (D. torquatus, L. lemmus)	Gwaenysgor[7] (D.t) Lynx[JB] (D.t, L.l)		Wharton Crags[11] (D.t, L.l)		Dowel Cave[11] (D.t, L.l) Fox Hole[11] (D.t) Etches Cave[11] (L.l)

Key
1 = Adams (1877–79)
2 = Coward & Oldham (1910a)
3 = Fisher Card Index
4 = Lister (1991)
5 = Moore (1858)
6 = Morton (1898)
7 = Neaverson (1940–43)
8 = Rance (1875)
9 = Reynolds (1929)
10 = Reynolds (1933)
11 = Sutcliffe & Kowalski (1976)
12 = Whitehead (1964)
GMC = Collections of the Grosvenor Museum, Chester
JB = John Blore, pers. comm.

Table 22.1. Sites with fossil remains from the glacial period. Mammoth, Woolly Rhinoceros, Reindeer, Giant Deer and Lemmings.

alces) found at High Furlong near Blackpool, which was dated at 12,400 BP from analysis of bone from the skeleton (Hallam et al. 1973; Clutton-Brock 1991). This provides the earliest direct evidence locally of human hunting; from lesions on the long bones the Elk appears to have been attacked about the legs with barbed points about two weeks before death, and the subsequent multiple wounds – caused by both barbed points (found with the skeleton) and probably axes – show how the animal finally succumbed.

The large collections of Giant Deer from Ballybetagh Bog near Dublin date from this period (Barnosky 1985), and it is probable that they also still roamed the Mersey Basin at this time. Indeed many of the imprecisely dated late-Pleistocene tetrapod records cited above could belong to either the earlier or this later period.

11,000 to 10,000 BP

Between 11,000 and 10,000 BP the climate cooled again,

and this cold spell probably wiped out Giant Deer for good. However, during this time Horse (Equus caballus), Reindeer and lemmings returned to Britain. The nearest certain record of Reindeer dated to this period is that of 10,600 BP from Ossom's Cave, Manifold Valley, Staffordshire. Elsewhere, there are numerous records for this period (e.g., Chelm's Coombe and Gough's New Cave, Somerset; Currant 1991). Lemmings are referred to by Yalden (1982), and ^{14}C dates were compiled for Reindeer and Horse by Housley (1991).

10,200 BP to the present

The post-glacial or Flandrian period in which we live began rather abruptly at about 10,200 BP. From both records of beetle faunas and direct climatological evidence, the warming of about 8°C in summer temperature took only 50 years (Yalden 1982; Dansgaard, White & Johnsen 1989, and see also chapter one, this volume). The Reindeer may have lingered on in the uplands for the next 1,000 years, but the improved climate led to an equally rapid change in the fauna. Red Deer (*Cervus elaphas*), Roe Deer (*Capreolus capreolus*), Elk (Moose), Aurochs (*Bos primigenius*) and Wild Boar (*Sus scrofa*) became the predominant prey of Mesolithic hunters. There seem to be no local sites with bones of these species that are contemporary with the famous Star Carr, Yorkshire and Thatcham, Berkshire camps. However, there are numerous undated records of Red Deer and Wild Boar from the Mersey Basin flood plain which could belong to this period, and numerous records of Mesolithic flints (chapter four, this volume) which imply that hunters were active in the area.

One very interesting set of fossils from this period is the early amphibian fauna from the Whitemoor Channel, near Bosley in east Cheshire, dated to 10,000–8,800 BP, which includes Palmate Newt (*Triturus helveticus*), Common Newt (*T. vulgaris*), Common Toad (*Bufo bufo*), Natterjack (*B. calamita*) and Common Frog (*Rana temporaria*) (Holman & Stuart 1991). There has been some debate over the years about how the isolated Merseyside coastal populations of Natterjack and Sand Lizard (*Lacerta agilis*) reached this area, when their main British populations are on the heathlands of southern England (Beebee 1978, 1980; Yalden 1980a, 1980b). The Whitemoor fossil fauna strongly suggests that they did indeed migrate into the north-west of England, reaching the north Solway coast at an early post-glacial date before the spread of woodland made the English midlands too inhospitable for them (as argued by Yalden 1980a) – rather than after the Neolithic tree-clearance.

During the well-wooded Mesolithic and on into the Neolithic period, the Mersey Basin mammal fauna must have been dominated by the large ungulates (Figure 22.1; Table 22.2). An interesting picture of this fauna is provided by the footprints exposed at low tide from time to time, but especially in the 1990s, on the foreshore at

Formby and Hightown (see chapter two, this volume). These include Aurochs, Red Deer and Humans (*Homo sapiens*), the prints often appearing to hint at a state of pursuit – although which species is in flight is open to conjecture (C.T. Fisher, personal observation). Remains of large sub-fossil Red Deer have been recorded from several localities in the Mersey Basin (see Table 22.2).

Leigh (1700) included the location of most of the Lancashire Red Deer specimens in the following passage:

> … in which five Yards within the Marle I saw the Skeleton of a Buck standing upon his Feet, and his Horns on its Head, which are yet preserv'd at Ellel-Grange near Lancaster … eight Yards within Marle in Larbrick near Preston in Lancashire, was found the entire Head of a Stag, with the Vertebrae of the Neck whole… In a Place in Lancashire call'd the Meales, under the Moss four Yards within Marle was found an exotic Head … the Brow-Antlers were bigger than usually the Arm of a man is … the Beams were near 2 Yards in height …

Roe Deer sub-fossil bones seem less well recorded, but occur in several river deposits (see Table 22.2). There are many records of Aurochs from the Mersey Basin.

The Neolithic is marked faunally by the arrival of domestic Sheep (*Ovis aries*) and Goats (*Capra hircus*) with the new farmers from the Middle East, and the level of human interference in the ecology of the Basin increases steadily from this point to the present. Direct evidence is, however, poor compared with the south of England, until the Roman period. House Mice (*Mus musculus*) arrived in Iron Age times in southern England, and it was probably the Romans who brought Black Rats (*Rattus rattus*). Both House Mice and Yellow-necked Mice (*Apodemus flavicollis*) were recorded from Roman

	North Wales	Merseyside	Lancashire	Cheshire
Red Deer	Grognant Beach, Prestatyn[NMGM]	Blundellsands Shore[NMGM] Rimrose[7] Formby Bank[2] Dove Point, Leasowe[1] Meols[8] West Kirby[NMGM] New Brighton Shore[NMGM]	Ellel[3] Larbreck[3] Meols Hall[3] Preston[8]	Macclesfield[10] Norton[1] Tytherington[10] Combermere[8] Rostherne Mere[1] Thornton le Moors[NMGM]
Roe Deer	Ffynnon Beuno[8]	Meols[8]	Warton Crags[8]	Rushton[8]
Aurochs		Dove Point, Leasowe[NMGM,9] Moreton[NMGM] Hilbre Island[6] Wallasey Pool[4,5]	Preston[9] Pilling Moss[9]	River Weaver at Kingsley[NMGM] River Dee at Chester[NMGM] Northwich[9] Runcorn[1]

Key

1 = Coward & Oldham (1910a)
2 = Edwards & Trotter (1954)
3 = Leigh (1700)
4 = Moore (1858)
5 = Neaverson (1940–43)
6 = Newstead
7 = Reade (1872)
8 = Reynolds (1933)
9 = Reynolds (1939)
10 = Sainter (1878)

NMGM = Collections of National Museums & Galleries on Merseyside

Table 22.2. Sites with Mesolithic sub-fossil remains (from 10,200 BP). Red Deer, Roe Deer and Aurochs.

Manchester (Yalden 1984); the latter is now confined to southern Britain.

From Roman Chester come the remains of Red Deer, Roe Deer, Wild Boar and Wolf. Leigh's plate (1700) of 'The horn of the Rane-Deer found under the altar at Chester' actually depicts a Roebuck antler. Anglo-Saxon archaeological evidence is locally absent, but a clue to the fauna then comes from place-name evidence; the Beaver (*Castor fiber*) is recalled in two lost Cheshire names, Beuer'feld and Buernes, while the Wolf is remembered in at least twenty names in Cheshire and seven in Lancashire (Aybes & Yalden 1995). Wildboar Cloughs in Cheshire and Derbyshire, Wildboar Farm in Lancashire and Yeverleye (eofor – leah = boar clearing) in Cheshire record that species, and the Wildcat (*Felis silvestris*) is represented by Wildcathishevede, Cheshire (Aybes & Yalden 1995).

By Norman times, the English fauna had probably already lost Beaver, Brown Bear and Aurochs as a consequence of hunting, but species diversity was restored somewhat by the introduction of Fallow Deer (*Dama dama*) and Rabbit (*Oryctolagus cuniculus*) by the Normans (Corbet & Harris 1991). Rabbits were initially kept and protected in warrens as a source of meat and fur, while Fallow Deer, also originally from the Mediterranean, were kept in deer parks, being better adapted than the native woodland deer to grazing.

The herd-dwelling Red Deer were also imparked, as indeed were Wild Boar. Delamere Forest is obliquely mentioned in the Domesday Book of 1086, along with *haiae capreolorum* at Kingsley and Weaverham; there are in all 99 hays detailed in the Cheshire Domesday volume, and they were apparently enclosures for harvesting woodland game. Roe Deer would have been the most common of these, though other species were probably taken (Yalden 1987). One other intriguing entry appears in the Domesday Book for Cheshire: in the records for the county town, it is reported that the city paid in revenue £45 and 3 timbers of marten skins. A timber was a bulk quantity of 40–60 skins and presumably the martens were Pine Martens (*Martes martes*).

Deer played an increasingly important part in the economy and in the social standing of the ruling classes. Forests were originally designated by the king for deer hunting (Rackham 1986), and later by others of the nobility under licence from him. Many were in wooded areas, but others were largely treeless; the forest of High Peak, on the Pennine slopes of the Mersey Basin, was re-established in Elizabethan times, and contained a herd of Red Deer which increased under enhanced protection from under 30 in 1579, to over 120 in 1586, before finally being disestablished in 1650 (Shimwell 1977). Parks were created out of large estates, and the remnant Red Deer from the forest of High Peak were reputedly enclosed in Lyme Park. Other major parks were on the outskirts of Liverpool, at Croxteth, Knowsley and Toxteth (Harrison 1902), and one is still clearly marked in Sefton Park on the Ordnance Survey map of south Liverpool for 1908. Toxteth ('Stochestede', or 'woody place') was originally enclosed, with Smithdown, to form the park for Liverpool Castle in 1204. In 1337 Ranulf de Dacre, parson of Prescot, was brought before the assize for poaching deer in Toxteth Park; Robert de Barton, a priest from Aigburth, was also arrested for encouraging him. Toxteth's status as a forest was removed in 1596 (Griffiths 1907).

The Elizabethan period also marked the start of formal vermin control, with the infamous act of 1564 'for the preservation of Grayne'; this empowered churchwardens to pay bounties for various pest species, not only rats and mice but also many predators. Out of this antipathy seems to have developed the increasing persecution which led to the virtual extinction of many carnivores locally. The Pine Marten was last recorded in Cheshire in the 1880s (Coward & Oldham 1910; Forrest 1918) but survived in northern Lancashire until the 1950s (Ellison 1959). The Polecat (*Mustela putorius*) died out in Cheshire in 1900 and in Lancashire was gone by 1910. The Wildcat was extinct in Cheshire before 1800 and gone from Lancashire by 1825 (Langley & Yalden 1977).

The same story of persecution involves the Otter (*Lutra lutra*), which Lomax hunted in the north-west of England from 1829 to 1871; he caught 21 animals from the rivers Ribble and Hodder alone from 1830 to 1833 (Lomax 1892). Otters must once have been common in the undrained areas between Southport and Liverpool; the last record from the Blackpool area was at Marton Mere in 1955 (Ellison 1959, 1963). Otterspool, a creek off the Mersey in south Liverpool, clearly indicates their historical presence on the banks of this now most industrial of rivers. The last period when Otters appear to have been relatively common was the 1930s; for instance, two cubs were shot 'above Formby' in March 1933, according to the *Proceedings of the Liverpool Naturalists' Field Club* for 1934. Looking through those cards in the North West Biological Field Data Bank at the Liverpool Museum, which record historical occurrences of Otters in Lancashire and Cheshire (also see Ellison 1959), it is apparent how many were killed by trains, as the tracks were often laid across wetlands. Otters held on in north Lancashire, and by the mid-1990s appeared to be spreading south again. However, polluted waters still hinder their re-establishment in the Mersey Basin (Jefferies 1989).

During this period one other significant addition was made to the fauna; the Brown Rat (*Rattus norvegicus*) arrived, with human assistance, from Russia in the late 1720s and rapidly displaced the Black Rat. Brown Rats are now the major economic vertebrate pest in this country, while the Black Rat is almost extinct. Liverpool docks and the city centre were one of the last strongholds of this rather attractive species, but sadly it has not been recorded there for several years (Twigg 1992).

By Victorian times, when the predators were being enthusiastically exterminated, other species were being introduced for their 'attractive appearance'. The American Grey Squirrel (*Sciurus carolinensis*) was introduced to Cheshire at Henbury in 1876, the earliest introduction documented by Shorten (1954). From there it spread throughout the county and displaced the native Red Squirrel (*Sciurus vulgaris*), as it has done in many places in Britain. Red Squirrels survived in Wirral until the 1960s but they are now extinct there. The River Mersey and its associated industrial belt acted for a long time as a barrier to the Grey Squirrel but during the 1980s they spread north through Greater Manchester, and also spread westwards down the River Ribble from Yorkshire in a pincer movement. Red Squirrels still occur in some numbers along the Ainsdale – Formby pinewoods, but there are repeated claims that this population derives in part from German stock released in the early 1940s (Ellison 1959). Ecological research on this population is currently under way to determine the beneficial or other effect of all the supplementary food (peanuts) given to them by humans, and genetic research based at the Institute of Zoology in London is investigating the origins of this population. In view of the demise of the species elsewhere, this population should be regarded as of considerable conservation importance. Small populations of Red Squirrel occur in Lancashire and more widely further north, but they are endangered everywhere.

Other introductions include the Sika Deer (*Cervus nippon*) population in the Bowland Forest, released near Gisburn in 1907 (Ellison 1959). The Muntjac (*Muntiacus reevesi*) was accidentally released in Cheshire in 1989, although it has been present in southern England since the 1940s (Chapman, Harris & Stanford 1994). The American Mink (*Mustela vison*) has spread through the area since the 1950s after accidental escapes from fur farms in the north of Lancashire (Tapper 1992), although the oldest Mink record from north-west England is from Farnworth, Bolton in 1956 (Bolton Museum and Art Gallery collections).

The present

Currently, the pattern of change is as dynamic as ever. Deer are increasing in numbers and range in the Mersey Basin; Fallow Deer occur in a few parks (Dunham, Lyme and Knowsley) and small populations occur in small woodlands, but they are still scarce compared with their status elsewhere in England. Roe Deer are spreading back down the Pennines; *c*.100 Red Deer are established, but vulnerable to poaching, in the Cheshire Hills (albeit from mainly re-introduced stock), and the survivors of the Peak Forest herd remain in Lyme Park. Muntjac and Sika Deer are also increasing in range.

Among the carnivores, there is currently evidence of Otters and Polecats spreading back into Cheshire from Wales. On the other hand, Mink appear to be responsible for the final demise of many local Water Vole (*Arvicola terrestris*) populations, though this animal has been declining all this century in many parts of the country as a consequence of habitat change (Strachan & Jefferies 1993). Red Squirrels remain precariously poised in the face of the threat from Grey Squirrels, and the small Sand

Lizard population is being sustained in part by captive breeding. The Natterjack also seemed doomed to extinction during the drought years in the 1970s, but conservation efforts and improved rainfall have rescued them.

As for the bats, more than ten years of dedicated, organised recording by the county bat groups have started to show accurately the effect of human impact on members of this order. Daubenton's Bat (*Myotis daubentonii*), a species associated with water and thus vulnerable to the effects of pollution, is probably much less common than it was in the 19th century. Nevertheless, it holds on in some surprising places – such as in a river tunnel running underneath a factory which uses a vast variety of chemicals – and may now be increasing again. The woodland-loving Bechstein's Bat (*Myotis bechsteinii*) probably occurred historically in north-west England, though it has not been definitely recorded here – the species was once common in other parts of England, as is indicated by the large assemblages of bones in Grimes Graves in Norfolk (Corbet & Harris 1991). There are now only about 1,500 individuals in Britain (Morris 1993). Conversely, the Pipistrelle (at present alluded to as *Pipistrellus pipistrellus*, but actually two distinct species), although declining by an estimated 60% in Britain as a whole between 1978 and 1986, has found many new roost sites in houses, particularly those built since 1960, with easier access to roof spaces and wall cavities (Morris 1993).

Conclusion

Thus the mammal, particularly the large mammal, fauna of the Mersey Basin has been almost entirely shaped by humans. The original herds of large game were hunted and, together with partly man-induced habitat change, eventually led to actual or near-extinction. With the arrival of Neolithic farmers came domestic species, and a different attitude to harvesting animals. The large predators – like Wolf and Bear – were eliminated as a threat to man or livestock, and were hunted for their fur, along with Beavers and other species. The ungulates and other food animals (like the Rabbit and Hare) were carefully guarded as beasts of the chase, or even more strictly controlled in parks. The survival of deer in this region clearly depended on their inclusion in parks, and with the waning political correctness of hunting – and increased opportunities for the economy offered by forestry – they are establishing themselves again as part of the regional fauna.

Currently, however, the mammal fauna is dominated by some 250,000 dairy cattle, 330,000 pigs and over a million sheep on the surrounding uplands (Government Statistical Service: *Digest of Agricultural Census Statistics*, UK 1991). In addition, there are a large number of cats, dogs and other domestic animals. The human population of north-west England also occupies much of the land. Not much space or habitat is left for other species; recent discussions about re-introducing the Dormouse (*Muscardinus avellanarius*) to Cheshire almost foundered because there was scarcely anywhere suitable. Yet the willingness to consider such actions, along with the efforts to encourage species such as the Otter and Natterjack, offer the hope that a tetrapod fauna in the next millennium will be at least as rich as that of the 20th century. Changes in fashion in human food consumption away from meat and dairy products – whether temporary or permanent – may mean more land returns to habitats suitable for wild species. Attempts to re-establish the fauna of pre-Roman times are premature, if not impossible to achieve, but at least we can dream of the Lost Ark.

Acknowledgements

We are grateful for assistance from staff in the Local History Library and Municipal Research Departments of Liverpool City Libraries.

We would also like to thank Brian Davis and Peter Jones for their very pertinent remarks on, and improvements to, this manuscript. Dr A.J. Morton's DMAP programme produced Figure 22.1.

References

Adams, A.L. (1877–1879). *Monograph on the British fossil elephants*. Part 1. *Dentition and osteology of* Elephas antiquus *(Falconer)*. Part 2. *Dentition and osteology of* Elephas primigenius *(Blumenbach)*. The Palaeontographical Society, London.

Aybes, C. & Yalden, D.W. (1995). Place-name evidence for the former distribution and status of Wolves and Beavers in Britain. *Mammal Review*, **25**, 201–26.

Barnosky, A.D. (1985). Taphonomy and herd structure of the extinct Irish Elk *Megaloceros giganteus*. *Science*, **228**, 340–44.

Beebee, T.J.C. (1978). An attempt to explain the distributions of the rare herptiles *Bufo calamita*, *Lacerta agilis* and *Coronella austriaca* in Britain. *British Journal of Herpetology*, **5**, 763–70.

Beebee, T.J.C. (1980). Historical aspects of British herpetofauna distribution. *British Journal of Herpetology*, **6**, 105.

Cantor, L.M. (1982). *The English medieval landscape*. Croom Helm, London.

Cantor, L.M. (1983). *The medieval parks of England: a gazetteer*. Loughborough University of Technology, Loughborough.

Chapman, N., Harris, S. & Stanford, A. (1994). Reeves' Muntjac *Muntiacus reevesi* in Britain: their history, spread, habitat selection, and the role of human intervention in accelerating their dispersal. *Mammal Review*, **24**, 113–60.

Clutton-Brock, J. (1991). Extinct species. *The Handbook of British Mammals* (eds G.B. Corbett & S. Harris), pp. 571–75. The Mammal Society and Blackwell Scientific Publications, Oxford.

Corbet, G.B. & Harris, S. (1991), *The handbook of British mammals*, 3rd ed. The Mammal Society & Blackwell Scientific Publications, Oxford.

Coward, T.A. & Oldham, C. (1910). *The Vertebrate fauna of Cheshire and Liverpool Bay* Vol. 1. *The mammals and birds of Cheshire*. Part 2. *The reptiles and amphibians of Cheshire*, (ed. T.A. Coward). Witherby & Co., London.

Currant, A. (1991). A Late Glacial Interstadial mammal fauna from Gough's Cave, Somerset, England. *The Late Glacial in north-west Europe: human adaptation and environmental change at the end of the Pleistocene* (eds N. Barton, A.J. Roberts & D.A. Roe), pp. 48–50. Council for British Archaeology Research Report 77, London.

Dansgaard, W., White, J.W.C. & Johnsen, S.J. (1989). The abrupt

termination of the Younger Dryas climate event. *Nature*, **339**, 532–34.

Dawkins, W. Boyd. (1875). On the Mammalia found at Windy Knoll. *Quarterly Journal of the Geological Society*, **31**, 248.

de Rance, C.E. (1875). On the relative age of some valleys in the north and south of England, and of the various and post-glacial deposits occurring in them. *Proceedings of the Geological Association*, **4**, 221–53.

Edwards, W. & Trotter, F.M. (1954). *British Regional Geology (Geological Survey & Museum): the Pennines and adjacent areas, based on previous editions by D.A. Wray*. 3rd ed. British Geological Survey, HMSO, London.

Ellison, N.F. (1959). *A checklist of the fauna of Lancashire and Cheshire. Mammalia, reptilia, amphibia. Revised to the end of 1956*. In *Thirty-first report of the recorders*. Lancashire & Cheshire Fauna Committee, Buncle & Co., Arbroath.

Ellison, N.F. (1963). *Report on the mammals, reptiles and amphibians to the end of 1962*. In *Thirty-third report of the recorders*. Lancashire & Cheshire Fauna Committee, Buncle & Co., Arbroath.

Fisher, J.M.Mc. 'card index': refers to manuscript reference cards and bibliography relating to all vertebrate post-glacial records in Britain; index now amongst Fisher Collection Archive in the Archives Section of the Natural History Museum, London.

Forrest, H.E. (1918). Pine Marten in Shropshire. *The Naturalist*, **738**, 231.

Government Statistical Service, (1991). *The Digest of Agricultural Census Statistics, United Kingdom 1991*. HMSO, London.

Griffiths, R. (1907). *The history of the royal and ancient park of Toxteth, Liverpool*. Privately printed; copies in Liverpool City Library.

Hallam, J.S., Edwards, B.J.N., Barnes, B. & Stuart, A.J. (1973). The remains of a Late Glacial Elk associated with barbed points from High Furlong, near Blackpool, Lancashire. *Proceedings of the Prehistoric Society*, **39**, 115–21.

Harrison, W. (1902). Ancient forests, chases and deer parks in Lancashire. *Transactions of the Lancashire & Cheshire Antiquarian Society*, **19** (for 1901), 1–37.

Holman, J.A. & Stuart, A.J. (1991). Amphibians of the Whitemoor Channel early Flandrian site near Bosley, East Cheshire; with remarks on the fossil distribution of *Bufo calamita* in Britain. *Herpetological Journal*, **1**, 568–73.

Housley, R.A. (1991). AMS dates from the Late Glacial and early Postglacial in north-west Europe: a review. *The Late Glacial in north-west Europe: human adaptation and environmental change at the end of the Pleistocene* (eds N. Barton, A.J. Roberts & D.A. Roe), pp. 25–39. Council for British Archaeology Research Report 77, London.

Jefferies, D.J. (1989). The changing otter population of Britain 1700–1989. *Biological Journal of the Linnean Society*, **38**, 61–69.

Langley, P.J.W. & Yalden, D.W. (1977). The decline of the rarer carnivores in Great Britain during the nineteenth century. *Mammal Review*, **7**, 95–116.

Leigh, C. (1700). *The natural history of Lancashire, Cheshire and the Peak, in Derbyshire*. Oxford.

Lister, A. (1991). Late Glacial mammoths in Britain. *The Late Glacial in north-west Europe: human adaptation and environmental change at the end of the Pleistocene* (eds N. Barton, A.J. Roberts & D.A. Roe), pp. 51–59. Council for British Archaeology Research Report 77, London.

Lomax, J. (1892). *Diary of otter hunting from A.D. 1829 to 1871*. Henry Young & Sons, Liverpool.

Moore, T.J. (1858). Notice of mammalian remains discovered in the excavations at Wallasey for the Birkenhead New Docks. *Transactions of the Historical Society of Lancashire & Cheshire*, **1857–1858**, 265–68.

Morris, P.A. (1993). *A red data book for British mammals*. The Mammal Society, London.

Morton, G.H. (1898). The elephant in Cheshire. *Transactions of Liverpool Biological Society*, **12**, 155–58.

Neaverson, E. (1940–43). A summary of the records of Pleistocene and Postglacial Mammalia from North Wales and Merseyside. *Proceedings of Liverpool Geological Society*, **18**, 70–85.

Rackham. O. (1986). *The history of the countryside*. Dent, London.

Reade, T.M. (1872). The geology and physics of the post-glacial period as shewn in the deposits and organic remains in Lancashire and Cheshire. *Abstract and Proceedings Liverpool Geological Society*, **1871–1872**, 36–88.

Reynolds, S.H. (1929). *A monograph on the British Pleistocene Mammalia* Vol. III, part III. *The Giant Deer*. The Palaeontographical Society, London.

Reynolds, S.H. (1933). *A monograph on the British Pleistocene Mammalia* Vol. III, part IV. *The Red Deer, Reindeer and Roe*. The Palaeontographical Society, London.

Reynolds, S.H. (1939). *A monograph on the British Pleistocene Mammalia* Vol. III, part VI. *The Bovidae*. The Palaeontological Society, London.

Sainter, J.D. (1878). *Scientific rambles round Macclesfield*. Swinnerton & Brown, Macclesfield.

Shimwell, D.J. (1977). Studies in the history of the Peak District landscape: I Pollen analysis of some podzolic soils on the Limestone Plateau. *University of Manchester School of Geography Research Papers*, **3**, 1–54.

Shorten, M. (1954). *Squirrels*. New Naturalist Monograph. Collins, London.

Strachan, R. & Jefferies, D.J. (1993). *The Water Vole* Arvicola terrestris *in Britain 1989–1990: its distribution and changing status*. Vincent Wildlife Trust, London.

Sutcliffe, A.J. & Kowalski, K. (1976). Pleistocene rodents of the British Isles. *Bulletin of the British Museum (Natural History), Geology*, **27**, 31–147.

Tapper, S. (1992). *Game Heritage*. Game Conservancy, Fordingbridge.

Twigg, G. (1992). The Black Rat *Rattus rattus* in the United Kingdom in 1989. *Mammal Review*, 22: 33–42.

Whitehead, G.K. (1964). *The deer of Great Britain and Ireland*. Routledge & Kegan Paul, London.

Yalden, D.W. (1980a). An alternative explanation of the distribution of the rare herptiles in Britain. *British Journal of Herpetology*, **6**, 37–40.

Yalden, D.W. (1980b). Historical aspects of British herpetofauna distribution: a reply. *British Journal of Herpetology*, **6**, 105–06.

Yalden, D.W. (1982). When did the mammal fauna of the British Isles arrive? *Mammal Review*, **12**, 1–57.

Yalden, D.W. (1984). The Yellow-necked mouse *Apodemus flavicollis*, in Roman Manchester. *Journal of Zoology*, London, **203**, 285–88.

Yalden, D.W. (1987). The natural history of Domesday Cheshire. *Naturalist*, **112**, 125–31.

Conclusion

Figure 23.1. The south prospect of Prescot, engraving of 1743 by W. Winstanley. (Philpott 1988 p. 29).

CHAPTER TWENTY-THREE

The consequences of landscape change: principles and practice; problems and opportunities

J.F. HANDLEY AND R.W.S. WOOD

Introduction

The Industrial Revolution began in Britain with north-west England, and the Mersey Basin in particular, in the forefront. Consequently, it was one of the first regions in the world to experience the full force of industrialisation and urbanisation. The advent of a new millennium coincides with the end of that first industrial era. Indeed for the past two decades, the region has been undergoing a painful process of economic restructuring associated with the transition from a manufacturing to a knowledge-based economy. It is therefore timely to take stock, to assess the scale of change and to review the consequences for biodiversity.

Ecology and Landscape Development: A History of the Mersey Basin takes a long time frame from the last glaciation to the present day and beyond. Throughout this time there have been two major drivers of landscape change: climate and human influence. During the past two centuries these processes have become interlinked as the burning of fossil fuels has contributed to global warming and accelerated climate change. This chapter examines the causes and consequences of landscape change, draws out some underlying ecological principles and shows how these can be applied to overcoming problems and realising opportunities within the Mersey Basin. The study of the ecology of the Mersey Basin is interesting and worthwhile in its own right. However, it has a wider significance of providing lessons which can help guide environmental planners and managers, both here and elsewhere, along a new development path.

The Industrial Revolution replaced a rural economy which had lasted for a thousand years and which had itself profoundly changed the landscape, fauna and flora of the Mersey Basin. The publication of the Strategic Plan for the North West (SPNW) in 1973 (North West Joint Planning Team 1973) is an important bench-mark providing, for the first time, a systematic review of the state of the region's environment. This coincided with the end of two centuries of rapid population growth in the Mersey Basin and associated urbanisation. That development had taken place with little regard for environmental capacity and this was reflected in the poor quality of air, land and water throughout the Mersey Basin. There were clear signs by the 1970s that a once prosperous region was undergoing structural economic decline and SPNW broke new ground by recognising that improving the state of the environment was fundamental to addressing that decline. The subsequent period, from the mid-1970s to the present day, has been one of 'stabilisation and renewal'.

Progress in improving environmental quality has been uneven, with the reduction of smoke and sulphur dioxide in the urban centres perhaps the outstanding achievement. It might be expected, given the scale and intensity of industrialisation and urbanisation, and the limited progress in solving inherited problems from that era, that biodiversity in the Mersey Basin would have suffered grievously. The actual position is much more complex and the processes of change have had positive as well as negative consequences. There are important lessons to be learnt.

The tide of change

Woodland clearance and habitat modification

The tide of change has been flowing strongly since the end of the most recent glaciation around 10,000 years ago. Human influence was there to see even in the late-glacial (12,000 BP with the skeleton of an Elk (*Alces alces*) showing clear evidence of human predation (chapter twenty-two, this volume).

Fossil footprints of a later date on the shores of Liverpool Bay show Mesolithic hunters sharing the habitat with Aurochs (*Bos primigenius*) and Red Deer (*Cervus elaphus*) (Figure 2.3, chapter two, this volume). There is evidence even from these early times of significant habitat modification in the form of burning by Mesolithic hunters in the woodlands flanking the Pennine uplands (chapter eleven, this volume). The influence of human induced disturbance through fire, stock grazing and soil erosion in prehistoric times is well documented by Innes *et al.* (chapter four, this volume). Indeed it seems that many of the supposed 'natural environments', especially the heathlands and moorlands, of the Mersey Basin are in fact plagioclimax communities created by human intervention long before the Roman

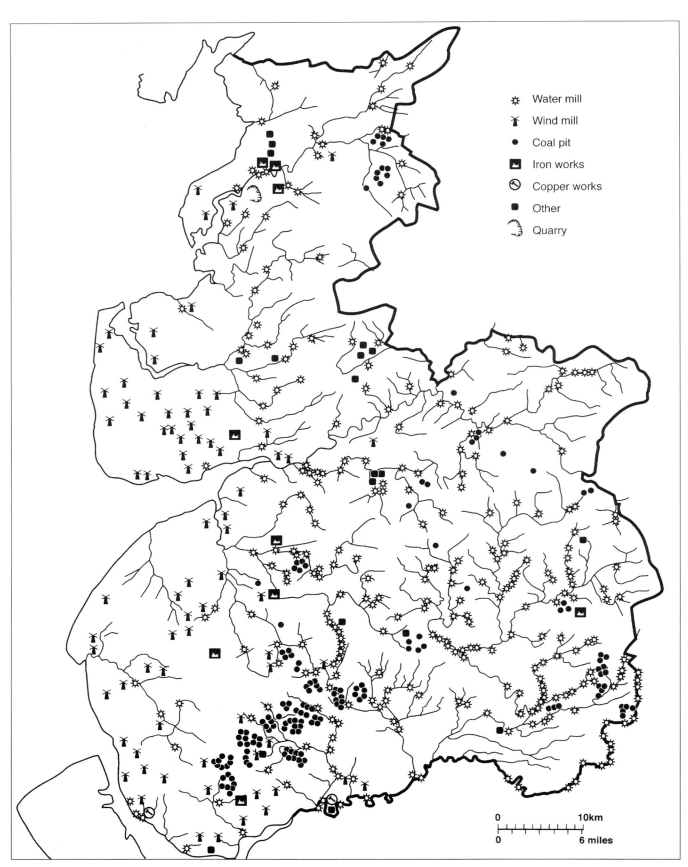

Figure 23.2. Industrial sites depicted on Yates' 1786 map of Lancashire. (Harley 1968).

conquest (chapters four and eleven, this volume).

Cowell (chapter four, this volume) concludes that

> the landscape pattern for approximately 9,000 years before the Domesday Survey was one rooted in woodland, fen, swamp, peat bog and long sweeps of coast. Early human intervention in this environment, due to low population pressure and the sustainable nature of human activity, meant that the effects were limited both in scale and distribution.

Nevertheless, by the time of the 1086 Domesday Survey the nature and extent of woodland cover had been profoundly altered (chapter three, this volume); the woodland matrix, which once stretched from the coast to the highest hills, had been permanently opened up and fragmented. For example, two estimates for Cheshire, based on a Domesday Survey, suggest only a 25–27% woodland cover (Rackham 1986; Yalden 1987). Forest clearance proceeded rapidly in subsequent centuries to fuel the demands of a burgeoning population. Climate change and disease in the 14th century caused social and economic dislocation and with it a switch to pastoral farming. As population growth resumed after the plagues which swept Europe, urban centres began to take shape within an increasingly enclosed pastoral landscape (chapter five, this volume; Philpott 1988). By the mid-17th century, Lancashire was described as a 'close county full of ditches and hedges' (Walker 1939) and we can see this tightly connected landscape in the 1745 tythe map for Newton-in-Makerfield (Figure 5.4, chapter five, this volume) and in the early 18th-century engraving of Prescot (Figure 23.1).

The Industrial Revolution

The second great shaping of the landscape begins with the Industrial Revolution. This profound change in the social and economic fortunes of the region had its roots in textiles and other putative industries of Elizabethan times, but gained pace rapidly in the 18th century (Walton 1987). We have seen the enclosure landscape of pre-industrial England in Figure 23.1, but the signs of change are already evident here. Coal mining is under way in the foreground and in the town itself we can see the first smoke stacks from large-scale industrial processes. But the real action was taking place in the south where in the 1750s and 1760s, as Walton (1987 p. 74) recounts

> a clear tendency was emerging for large-scale new industries to concentrate in Liverpool and close to the Mersey and its associated waterways. Brass, copper, salt and sugar boiling, brewing, pottery and glass-making all followed this pattern, and the initiatives of the mid-century were to provide the basis for a new heavy industrial economy in the classic 'Industrial Revolution' years, although ultimately this lucrative harvest was reaped in St Helens, Warrington and the surrounding areas rather than in Liverpool itself'. (see also chapter six, this volume).

The subsequent development of St Helens, the archetypal industrial town, and the nature of that 'lucrative harvest' has been graphically documented by Barker & Harris (1993).

Yates' map of Lancashire from shortly after this time (1786) shows an economy in transition from renewable energy to fossil fuel (Figure 23.2). Windmills are distributed along the coastal strip and water mills like strings of beads along the streams. However, the growing importance of coal is also evident with a cluster of coal pits on the exposed coalfield of south Lancashire and scattered pits along the higher Pennine valleys. As Jarvis & Reed observe (chapter six, this volume) there is 'only a finite number of foot-pounds of work in an entire river system'. The introduction of the steam engine 'changed the rules and it was now possible to employ almost any amount of power in any location where coal was obtainable at an acceptable price'.

Coal is such a bulky item that transportation costs rather than extraction costs had a great influence on its use in the Industrial Revolution period (von Tunzelmann 1986). The development of transport infrastructure was therefore critical and began with the creation of the canal system.

Which sources of coal grew most rapidly was determined by three principal factors: '...where the demand was greatest, where connections to supply more distant markets were best developed, and where the seams themselves were most easily accessible' (Freeman, Rodgers & Kinvig 1966 p. 90). All three conditions were met in three locations: in the Douglas Valley near Wigan, using the Leeds & Liverpool Canal (completed in 1816); St Helens using the Sankey Canal of 1757, providing a connection to the Mersey Estuary west of Warrington and via the Weaver navigation into the saltworks in Cheshire (which exhausted local wood supplies by the middle of the 17th century); and the area to the north and east of Manchester using the Ashton and Rochdale canals, supplementing local production at Ardwick and Pendleton. This was a profoundly symbiotic relationship where the growth of coal mining stimulated the growth of the textile industry and vice versa.

The pattern was further reinforced by the creation of the railway network (Figures 23.3 and 23.4). The rapid establishment of a net of lines covering the Mersey Basin was substantially completed by 1850, enabling strong inter- and intra-regional connections. 'The main effect of the railways was to open up much of Lancashire to a far wider market than had been known before and especially to stimulate the growth of Liverpool as a centre of both overseas and local trade' (Freeman et al. 1966 p. 89–90). Indeed Widnes and Crewe owed their existence to the railway and, more generally, the network of lines served further to strengthen local specialisation and contributed to industrial locational inertia. The pattern of industrial development which was substantiated and rapidly expanded in these early years of the railway largely persisted until the precipitous industrial decline of the middle and late 20th century.

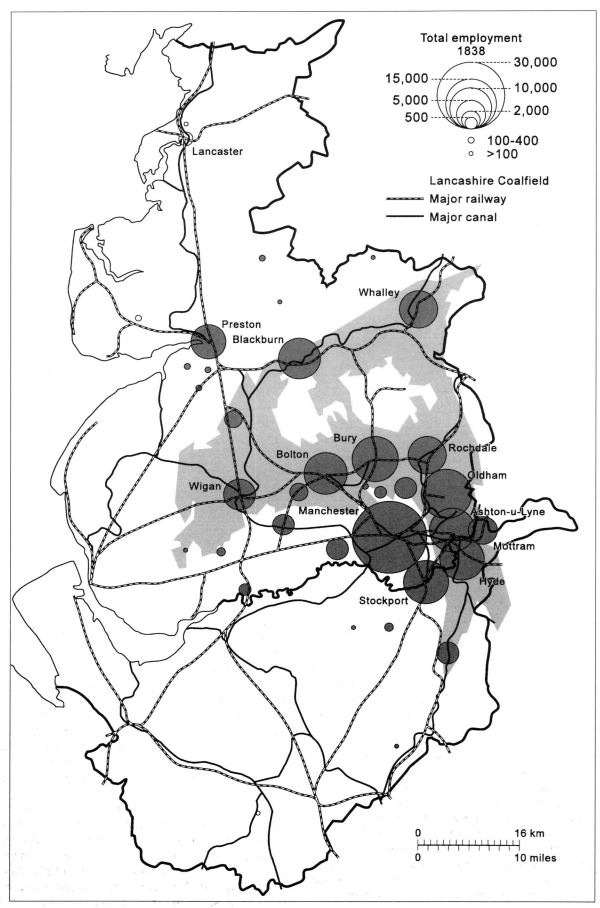

Figure 23.3. The location of the cotton industry in 1838. (Freeman *et al.* 1966 p. 91 and p. 96).

Figure 23.4. The Stockport railway viaduct 1986 with modern office block and 19th century mills by the River Mersey
(*Photo: John Davis*).

The Mersey Basin had by 1851 become the world's greatest manufacturing region. Its wealth was based primarily upon textile manufacture (Figure 23.5), accounting for some 63% of the British textile industry which itself yielded over 50% of the total value of the nation's exports. Industrial and commercial activity stretched throughout a network of industrial towns united by a complex web of waterways and latterly railways. The two great commercial centres of Liverpool and Manchester dominated the scene, the focus for the activities of a number of smaller towns which by now specialised in aspects of the textile, mining, chemical, and engineering industries. Together, these formed a unique industrial heartland and the model for the development of industrial regions throughout the world.

One of its more notable, and alarming, features was the rapidity with which this textile-based economy had expanded. Quite simply 'the growth of this single great staple industry had reshaped both the economy and the landscape of Lancashire at a speed unmatched in any other region of Great Britain' (Freeman *et al.* 1966 p. 103).

Despite the massive dominance of the cotton industry, regional industrial specialisation was nevertheless very important, and St Helens exemplifies the importance of local industrial tradition in setting a course for subsequent development induced by the supply of cheaper

fuel and the availability of growing markets both at home and in the colonies. The glass, chemical and copper refining industries have a long history in St Helens. Glass-making in the area was founded upon and largely tied to a silica-rich source of Shirdley Hill sand and soda ash, derived from the local salt refining industry (the origins of Shirdley Hill sand are discussed in chapter two, this volume). The glass-making process was revolutionised in 1773 by the construction of the first large factory, and a developing supply of cheap coal led to the rapid growth of this and the other power-hungry processes of chemical manufacture and copper refining (Barker & Harris 1993).

The urbanisation of the Mersey Basin

In the mid-19th century, some 68% of the population lived in urban areas at a time when the rest of Britain, let alone the world, had a primarily rural-based population. Though the exact definition of what constituted an urban area was by this time not yet substantiated, a dense settlement pattern had evolved on the Lancashire coalfield and along the line of the Mersey Valley, exploiting the natural resources of water and coal, and progressively forming a closely interconnected web which, even in 1851, would have appeared to form a great metropolis. Thus in 1801 Liverpool had some 83,000 inhabitants

Figure 23.5. Ashton-under-Lyne, 1985, with 19th-century cotton mills and houses as well as more recent housing. The Pennine hills are in the background. (*Photo: John Davis*).

which swelled to 375,000 by 1851; similarly, Manchester and Salford grew from some 93,000 to around 388,000 over this period; the influx of migrants from rural areas, other regions and countries was the key to the speed and scale of growth. Immigration from Ireland in the wake of the potato famine was a particularly important source, together with migrants from eastern Europe en route to the Americas who stayed to make a permanent home in north-west England.

As well as being fundamental to industrial growth and development, the railways also provided the first practical means of extensive suburban development and the consequent urbanisation of the hitherto largely agricultural hinterlands of the two dominant growth poles (Figure 23.6). The fine Victorian suburbs of Liverpool and Manchester such as Wirral and south Manchester were the result. The level of pollution in the city centres provided a further stimulus to the exodus from the increasingly commercial cores of both cities.

By the mid-19th century a complex settlement pattern was emerging, centred on the cities of Liverpool and Manchester. Long-established textile towns such as Burnley, Rochdale and Oldham were becoming increasingly linked to the commercial centre of Manchester, just as Liverpool was serving as the focus for satellite towns

such as Runcorn and St Helens. By 1851, the Mersey Basin was a predominantly urban area with the newly opened railways acting as a stimulus to growth and the increasing coalescence of urban areas.

The environmental legacy of industrialisation and urbanisation

The flowering of the economic fortunes of the Liverpool–Manchester urban-industrial area was coextensive with the greatest pressures upon biota, many of which continue into the present: industrial and urban development creating air and water pollution, and the extinguishing and fragmentation of natural habitats on an unprecedented scale. The contemporary accounts of those such as Frederic Engels (1844) of the conditions of the urban dwellers in Manchester give a startling picture of the unregulated environmental degradation which inevitably accompanied such growth; we can only begin to imagine the scale and intensity of the environmental pollution which accompanied so many to an early grave. Charles Dickens' evocative description of 'Coketown' in *Hard Times* – probably based on Preston, but nevertheless good for most of the region's industrial towns – gives us a flavour, albeit lyrical, of the fetid conditions which prevailed:

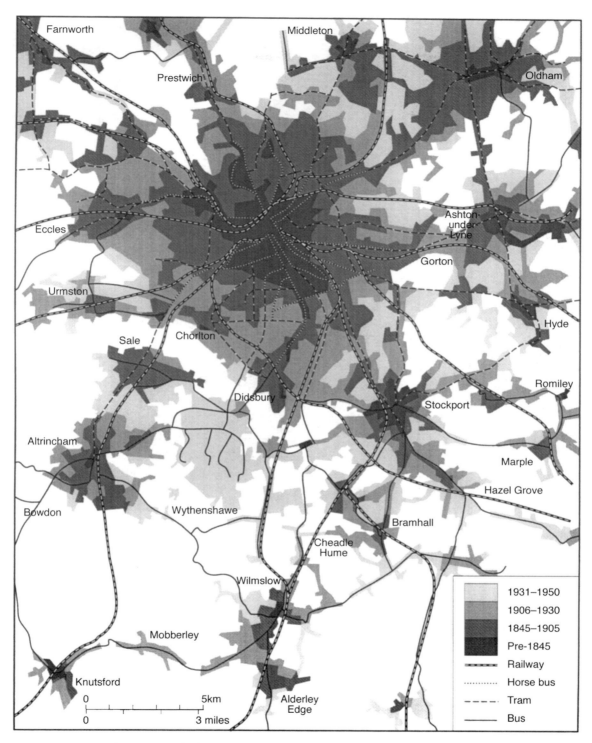

Figure 23.6. The pattern of urban growth in Manchester 1845–1950 (British Association 1962, p. 50).

It was a town of red brick, or of brick that would have been red if the smoke and ashes had allowed it; but as matters stood it was a town of unnatural red and black like the painted face of a savage. It was a town of machinery and tall chimneys, out of which interminable serpents of smoke trailed themselves for ever and ever, and never got uncoiled. It had a canal in it, and a river that ran purple with ill-smelling dye, and vast piles of buildings full of windows where there was a rattling and a trembling all day long, and where

the piston of the steam engine worked monotonously up and down like the head of an elephant in a state of melancholy madness. (Dickens 1854.)

Plant and animal communities thus faced the challenges of extinction, marginalisation and adaptation as the tide of industrial and concomitant urban development swept the Mersey Basin. Natural habitats such as the peat mosses were, by 1851, largely reclaimed for intensive agricultural production to supply the ever more demanding urban areas, and those same areas spewed forth choking atmospheric pollution from coal burning and poisonous discharges into the watercourses, the legacy of which is still being tackled today. In St Helens the alkali industry created 'one scene of desolation' in the surrounding countryside, with leafless trees and lifeless hedgerows whilst the nearby stream was 'an open sepulchre full of pestiferous odours' (Barker & Harris 1993, p. 350 and p. 416 respectively). A more extended account of the alkali industry, its environmental impact and the emergence of pollution control regulation is provided by Jarvis & Reed (chapter six, this volume).

Whilst the industrial heartland of the Mersey Basin formed the centrepiece of national economic boom in the period 1850 to 1875, the agricultural hinterland of Cheshire, though to an extent industrialised through the operations of the salt industry centred on Northwich, remained outside the immediate effects of the stimuli of town growth and improved communications. The broad pattern of dairy farming and market gardening observable today was established in this period.

There is much anecdotal evidence from these times for the impact of historic pollution on biodiversity in the Mersey Basin (see chapters six and eleven, this volume), but this topic deserves more systematic research. As this volume demonstrates, the consequences have in many respects been lasting, and include acute damage to biota from water pollution in rivers and canals (chapter thirteen, this volume) and the Mersey Estuary (chapter fifteen, this volume); air pollution damage to bryophytes in the uplands (chapter eighteen, this volume) and lichens in the lowlands (chapter eighteen, this volume). Nevertheless, it seems likely that urbanisation has had a more permanent impact through direct habitat loss, habitat fragmentation and indirectly through habitat modification (see chapter seven, this volume). Michael Dower (1965, p. 5) set the scene in graphic terms:

> Three great waves have broken across the face of Britain since 1800. First, the sudden growth of the dark industrial towns. Second, the thrusting movement along far flung railways. Third, the sprawl of car-based suburbs. Now we see under the guise of a modest word, the surge of a fourth wave which could be more powerful than all the others. The modest word is leisure.

We have had the tools to control the pattern of urban development since the Town & Country Planning Act of 1947. However, habitat loss to development continued unabated in the post-war years, and the impact of cumulative development has often gone unnoticed (Handley 1984). Taking but one example, the loss of precious sand dune habitat on the Sefton coast has been well documented (Figure 23.7), together with the consequences for vulnerable animal species such as the Sand Lizard (*Lacerta agilis*).

The first period of urbanisation in this case coincided with the construction of the Lancashire & Yorkshire Railway from Liverpool to Southport. The next wave of

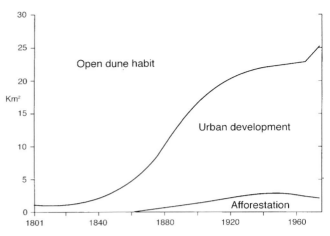

Figure 23.7. Loss of sand dune habitat to urbanisation and afforestation (Handley 1984, p. 229, after Jackson 1979).

development (post 1945) coincided with the expansion of car-based suburbs. The dune coastline itself bore the full brunt of Michael Dower's 'fourth wave' as the sand dunes were destabilised by intensive recreational use threatening habitat integrity and tidal inundation (Handley 1982). The Sefton Coast Management Scheme has been conspicuously successful in addressing these problems as we shall see later. However, it is only in the past two decades that the importance of protecting what remains of the Mersey Basin's critical natural capital has been properly recognised and, even today, primary habitats are still being lost to meet society's demand for transport infrastructure, waste disposal and minerals.

Stabilisation and renewal

Unsurprisingly, for an economy so heavily dependent upon one staple industry, adaptation to the changing demands of the world economy proved to be extremely difficult. Precipitous industrial decline began in the 1920s and gathered pace in the 1930s, reaching its peak during the 1950s and 1960s, where the high-wage textile industry of north-west England simply could not compete with the newly industrialising countries on the same terms. The industrial structure of the Mersey Basin did adapt, refocusing into high investment industries such as electrical engineering, car and aircraft manufacture, chemical production and oil refining, which grew in areas away from the traditional mining and textile centres. In turn, however, these 'new' industries have experienced decline in the face of fierce global competition.

Population growth in the North West Region (most of which is accounted for by the Mersey Basin) continued until 1971 but then declined and finally stabilised at around 6.4 million (Figure 23.8). Urban expansion continued during the post-war period (see for example Figure 23.10 for Merseyside). Between Liverpool and Manchester significant new development also took place in the New Towns of Runcorn and Warrington. Here service and distributive industries were able to take full

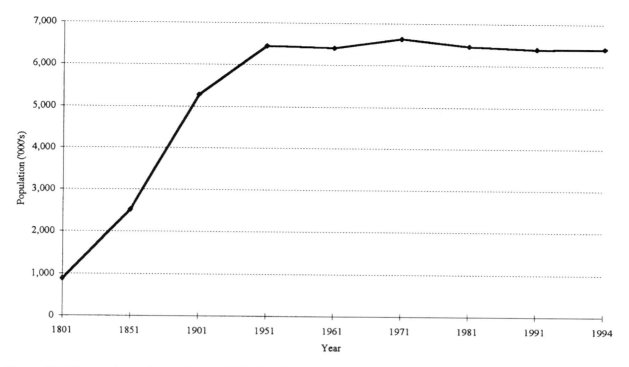

Figure 23.8. Regional population change 1801–1994 (Department of Environment *Longterm Population Distribution in Great Britain – a Study*. HMSO, London. 1971 Table 1.4, p. x; Office for National Statistics *Regional Trends*, 1996 HMSO, London. Table 3.1, p. 46).

advantage of their central location not only in the region but also in the UK. This reinforced the trend of population migration from the core of the older urban centres to new housing estates on the periphery.

The *Strategic Plan for the North West* [SPNW] (North West Joint Planning Team 1973) marked a very significant shift in policy with a new emphasis on urban renewal and a proposal to concentrate new development along 'growth corridors' between Liverpool and Manchester. In particular, 'the corridors should not be seen mainly as fringes of new development attached to the present urban areas. The concept implies action along corridors extending outwards from the conurbation centres. They should play their part in structuring renewal and rehabilitation of existing urbanisation as well as that of new development beyond existing urban boundaries.' (SPNW 1973, p. 241.)

One important policy tool was the creation of extensive tracts of Green Belt within the Mersey Basin to constrain and shape the future development pattern (Figure 23.9).

The Green Belt is an effective and well understood planning tool for containing development, but it has little or no influence on the quality of the countryside within it, which is all too often severely degraded in urban fringe locations (Elson 1986). Today, the physical integrity of the Green Belt is also under threat. Whilst the population has stabilised in the Mersey Basin, there is a continuing process of counter-urbanisation. This is being reinforced by an increased rate of household formation due to changes within society such as greater longevity, more one-person households, etc. (Office for National

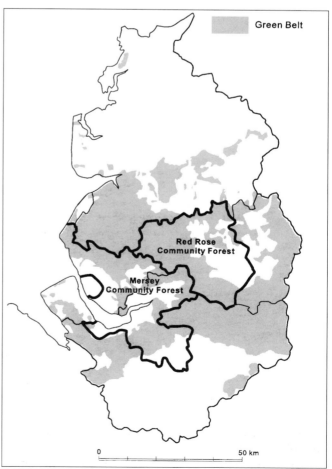

Figure 23.9. Green belt and the community forests in the Mersey Basin (Wood *et al.* 1996, p. 40).

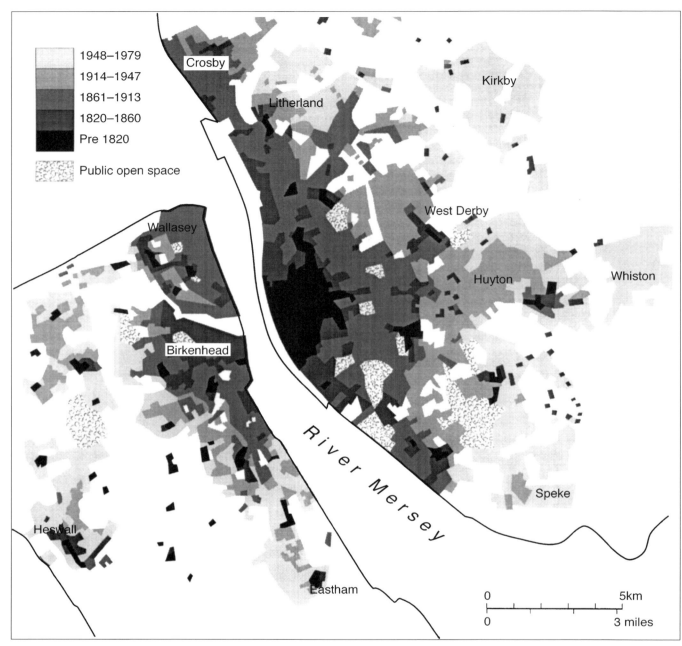

Figure 23.10. Urban expansion of Merseyside to 1979, (contrast this map of Merseyside with Yates' map of 1786 (Figure 5.5, p. 53, this volume) (Lawton 1982, p. 8).

Statistics 1996). The most recent policy statement – Regional Planning Guidance for the North West (RPG 13) (Government Office for the North West/ Government Office for Merseyside 1996) – anticipates that projected development can be accommodated without encroaching on the Green Belt, but given the continuing 'flight from the cities' this policy stance will be difficult to maintain.

SPNW also recognised that poor environmental quality was a contributing factor in regional decline, and that in this respect 'the North West is significantly worse than other regions'. The Report highlighted three priorities for action: river pollution, derelict land and air pollution. The subsequent progress on these fronts has

been mixed. For some time, despite an upturn in expenditure on infrastructure, water quality in the rivers continued to deteriorate. However, thanks to major investment during the past 15 years, there are now signs of significant progress both in river and canal systems (Figure 23.11) and in the Mersey Estuary (National Rivers Authority 1995; Mersey Basin Campaign, 1997 and chapter fifteen, this volume).

The reduction in urban concentrations of smoke and sulphur dioxide which resulted from smoke control programmes (combined with changing patterns of fuel consumption) is a remarkable achievement. These pollutants have now fallen below World Health Organisation guidelines in both towns and cities (Figure 23.13) (see

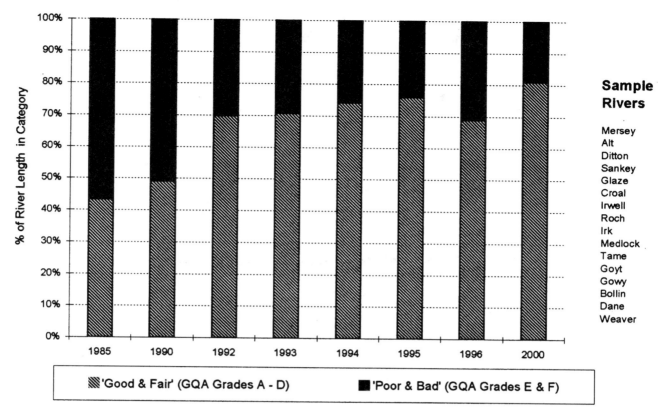

Figure 23.11. Water quality in the Mersey Basin 1985–2000 (Mersey Basin Campaign 1997).

chapter eighteen, Figure 18.2, this volume).

The position with regard to derelict land is less satisfactory. SPNW predicted that if current levels of investment in land reclamation were projected forward, the region's stock of derelict land, much of which had been inherited by the demise of the old wealth creating industries, would be finally cleared in 1994. In fact, despite huge investment, the stock of derelict land has actually increased (Figure 23.12). This is because the rate at which new dereliction has been created by industrial obsolescence has more than matched the rate of derelict land clearance. This situation presents one of the sternest

future challenges; not only must the 'engine of dereliction' be reversed, but the legacy of derelict land has to be used wisely as part of a wider strategy for the promotion of biodiversity and conservation.

Industrialisation, urbanisation and biodiversity

The Mersey Basin was at the forefront of the Industrial Revolution and is one of the first 'regions' in the world to cope with the socially painful process of adjustment

Figure 23.12. Derelict land in north-west England (ha) – Components of Change (Wood *et al.* 1996, p. 106, derived from DoE 1991b, 1995).

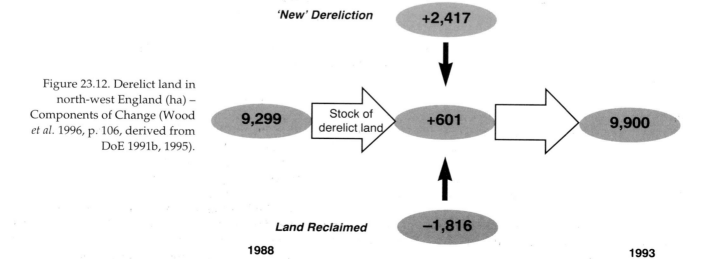

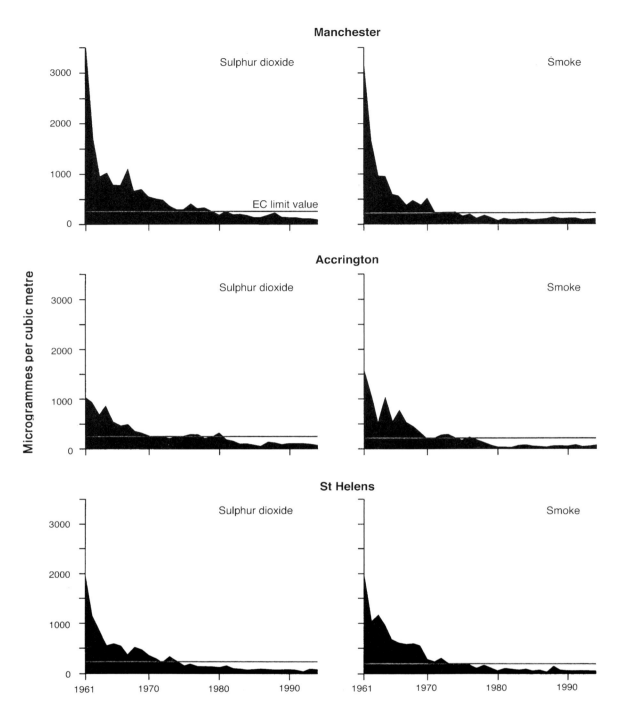

Figure 23.13. Sulphur dioxide and smoke trends in north-west England 1961–1994 (annual peak values).
(AEA Technology 1995).

to a post-industrial economy. As this volume demonstrates, it is also one of the best documented parts of Britain, and therefore the world, in terms of its natural history. Here we explore some of the key processes which drive landscape change, the consequences for flora and fauna, and any lessons learnt which may be transferable to other regions experiencing a similar transition.

We can identify two fundamental cultural drivers of landscape change in modern times: obsolescence and dysfunction.

Obsolescence/Loss of function

Obsolescence, or loss of function, is associated with changing patterns of land-use. This is a potent factor in the countryside of the Mersey Basin where cessation of traditional management practices has released successional processes in plagioclimax communities and initiated landscape change which threatens habitat integrity. Examples cited in this volume include scrub development following cessation or reduction of grazing on sand dunes (chapter sixteen, this volume) heathland (chapter eight, this volume), and the virtual disappearance of

	Number of Woods		
Use	*Wirral*	*North Merseyside*	*Total*
Major Uses			
Environmental protection	0	22	22
Nature conservation	10	5	15
Game management	19	67	86
Grazing	28	21	49
Timber production	0	17	17
Recreation	67	72	139
Visual amenity	26	70	96
No use	25	54	79
Ancillary uses			
Vandalism to trees	11	29	40
Refuse disposal	73	52	125

Table 23.1. The utilisation of woodlands in Merseyside 1974–1976. Note that many woods have two or three uses in either part or the whole of the wood
(Berry & Pullen 1982 p. 112).

traditional woodland management systems such as coppicing (chapter ten, this volume). A survey of woodland uses in Merseyside in the 1970s highlighted the poverty of woodland management (Table 23.1), and for all the commendable efforts of the Mersey and Red Rose Forests, the woodland management situation is little better today. The situation in the farmed countryside is a matter of particular concern where valuable (but often obsolete) features, such as hedgerows and marl pits, are especially at risk (see chapters seven and fourteen, this volume).

On a more positive note, obsolescence in the urban economy is a source of great biological opportunity (Handley 1996). The abandoned 'disturbance corridors' of the former transport system can quickly become 'regeneration corridors', providing new opportunities for people and wildlife (Foreman 1995 and chapters eight and twelve, this volume). Similarly, the abandoned spoil heaps and subsidence flashes of the post-industrial landscape provide a wide variety of starting points for natural recovery (see Figures 23.14 and 23.15 and chapter twelve, this volume). Derelict land is inherently variable, providing a wide range of starting points for natural succession with variation in pH, fertility, water relations, slope, aspect, stability and toxicity.

Those plant communities and their associated fauna which develop, represent the interaction between this inherent physical and chemical variability (often a product of industrial history) and the biological potential of the area (Ash 1991). It is no accident that in the more heavily urbanised parts of the region we find a strong match between designation of sites for nature conservation and industrial disturbance (Morrish 1996).

We can even see natural recovery at work in industrial water bodies notably the docks of Salford Quays ('fresh' water) and Liverpool (salt water) (see chapter fifteen, this volume). The recovery of the Liverpool Docks has been relatively self-sustaining since the initial dredging operation and installation of lock gates to re-

establish permanent water. However, by contrast, the establishment of an aquatic ecosystem at Salford Quays has faced a series of biological challenges which have been overcome by some imaginative ecological engineering (Hendry *et al.* 1993; Struthers 1997).

Dysfunction

Dysfunction refers to the disruption caused by a mismatch between the type and intensity of land-use and the character of the receiving landscape. Philip Grime recognised three fundamental challenges to existence for plants, and perhaps other components of the ecosystem (Grime 1979, 1986). These are:

Figure 23.14. Colonisation of a colliery spoil heap at Bold Moss, St Helens: heathland.

Figure 23.15. Colonisation of a colliery spoil heap at Bold Moss, St Helens: wetland.

1. competition – where conditions for growth are favourable;

2. stress – where some factor in the environment depresses growth potential; and

3. disturbance – the physical removal of biomass by processes such as grazing, burning and trampling.

In heavily urbanised areas, competition may be intensified by nutrient enrichment leading to a loss of biodiversity; examples in this volume are algal blooms in dockland ecosystems (chapter thirteen, this volume), and worries about enrichment of heathland by atmospheric pollution (chapter eight, this volume). Intensive agricultural production with heavy use of nitrogen fertilizers in the lowlands of Lancashire and Cheshire is leading to enrichment of lakes and streams (chapter thirteen, this volume) and ponds (chapter fourteen, this volume). There is also concern about groundwater pollution by nitrates. Part of Cheshire has been designated as a Nitrate Sensitive Area (Wood *et al.* 1996).

Stress is typically associated with environmental pollution of air, water and land. Figure 23.16 shows how the consequences of stress may be felt at different levels from the individual to the ecosystem. Examples are found at all levels in this account of the ecology of the Mersey Basin.

In some cases where organisms are simply not equipped to cope with new pressures, like sulphur dioxide pollution, whole taxa have been obliterated in the more polluted areas (*Sphagnum* spp. on blanket peat, chapter eleven and lichens in town centres, chapter eighteen, this volume) though for lichens at least we see an encouraging pattern of recovery as pollution levels have abated (see Figures 18.7 and 18.8, chapter eighteen, this volume).

Remarkable examples of both phenotypic and genotypic response of marine algae to stress are provided by Russell *et al.* (chapter seventeen, this volume). Classic examples of genotypic response to pollutants in the Mersey Basin include industrial melanism in lepidoptera (chapter twenty, this volume) and evolution of metal tolerant genotypes of both plants and animals in industrial centres such as Prescot (Bradshaw & McNeilly 1981, p. 43; Parry, Johnson & Bell 1984).

There are also good examples of the population response to opportunities created by stress such as the recent expansion of the halophyte, Danish Scurvygrass (*Cochlearia danica)* along the salt-laden road verges of the region (Figure 19.3, chapter nineteen, this volume). The influence of stress factors at the community level is illustrated by the post-industrial landscape where low fertility, extremes of pH, etc., hold back competitor species and create very distinct plant communities (Ash 1991; chapter eight, this volume). Stress conditions have even been introduced artificially by topsoil removal and mixing of industrial waste materials to produce sustainable wild flower meadows on otherwise fertile but species-poor urban grasslands (Ash, Bennet & Scott 1992).

The most significant impacts of stress are felt at the

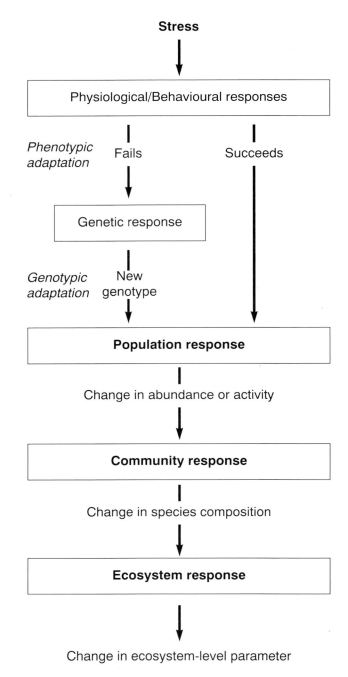

Figure 23.16. The effect of stress at different levels of biological organisation. Note: each box represents some level at which there is some buffering capacity, reducing the impact of the stress on the level above (Beeby 1993, p. 22).

level of the ecosystem. The complexity of ecosystem processes at this level of organisation is well exemplified by the recent work of Moss *et al.* on the Cheshire Meres (chapter thirteen, this volume). In the Pennine uplands, by contrast, the problem is one of soil impoverishment by acid rain. Acidification results from the long distance transport of sulphur and nitrogen from pollution sources in the lowlands which are then washed out by rainfall or captured by dry deposition in the uplands (Figure 23.17). Consequently, the Pennine uplands of the Mersey

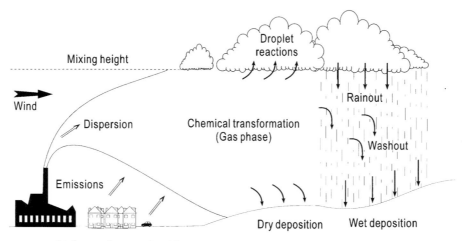

Figure 23.17. Processes which may be involved between the emission of an air pollutant and its ultimate deposition to the ground. (Harrison 1992).

Basin receive one of the highest acid pollution insults in rural Britain and this on an ecosystem of very low carrying capacity. Critical load exceedence maps point to severe problems for upland soils and water bodies (Critical Loads Advisory Group 1994; Handley & Perry 1995).

'Disturbance' is often associated with traditional vegetation management practices and we have already seen that the conservation of many relict habitats depends on the maintenance of the disturbance regime. By contrast, disturbance in the form of excessive (intensive recreation) and malignant (vandalism) use can be very damaging. Erosion problems from concentrated visitor use are a feature of heathland and sand dune habitats of the lowlands, and overused footpaths in the uplands. A systematic survey of vegetation damage on Merseyside in the late 1970s using colour infra-red aerial photography identified disturbance as a much more potent source of vegetation damage than environmental pollution (Handley 1980).

Managing over-load

In general, an effective response to dysfunction is to reduce the load from environmental stress or disturbance to within the carrying capacity of the receiving system. The Government's long-term pollution control strategy for large combustion plants will reduce levels of SO_2 and NO_x very significantly in the Pennine uplands (Critical Loads Advisory Group 1994). The same is true of water pollution to rivers, which is being addressed through the Mersey Basin Campaign. In the Mersey Basin area, over three quarters of all watercourses are now of 'good' or 'fair' water quality – that is, able to support coarse fish populations – with the ambitious target that by 2010 all watercourses will be of this standard. Just ten years ago, only some 40% of watercourses were of good or fair quality (Figure 23.11). Similar improvements are being achieved in the Mersey Estuary (chapter fifteen, this volume).

An alternative to load reduction is to increase the carrying capacity of the environment. This has been done successfully at pressure points created by concentrated visitor use in fragile dune systems of the coastal zone (Wheeler, Simpson & Houston 1991), and on eroding footpaths in the uplands (Ruff & Maddison 1994). However, effective countryside management requires more than technical solutions, and the Mersey Basin has been at the forefront of devising innovative management mechanisms which bring landowners, land users and government agencies together in a spirit of partnership (Wheeler *et al.* 1991; Countryside Commission 1976, 1993). One remarkable innovative exercise in capacity building is the creation of new community forests in the urban fringes of Manchester and Liverpool. Initiated in 1991, the two designated Community Forests cover around 170,000 hectares and are by far the largest of the twelve designated in England, and virtually encircle the conurbations (Mersey Community Forest 1995; Red Rose Community Forest 1994). Continuous woodland forming a bridge between town and country is not envisaged; rather a mosaic of planting which will give structure to the landscape in one of the least wooded areas of the country. The planting programme will extend over some 30 to 40 years and it is intended that tree cover will be increased by three to five times. The community forests cover five broad themes:

1. creating networks of wooded greenways;

2. greening transport routes;

3. returning farmland to forestry;

4. weaving woodland into new development; and

5. capitalising on woodland assets.

Rebuilding environmental capital through woodland creation and enhancement, and using that new structure intelligently, represents an overdue refocusing of environmental planning priorities towards a sensitive balance of ecology, development and amenity.

Ecology and sustainability

Towards sustainable development

If the publication of the Strategic Plan for the North West was a landmark in environmental consciousness within the region, the publication in 1990 of the Environment White Paper *This Common Inheritance* was equally significant in marking an official shift in Government policy towards a more sustainable development path. The White Paper presaged the emergence of an international consensus at the United Nations Conference on Environment and Development at Rio de Janeiro in 1992 (the Earth Summit). The UK Government responded to the Summit by approving the following commitments (Her Majesty's Government 1994a, b, c, d):

1. UK Strategy for Sustainable Development;

2. Climate Change Convention;

3. Biodiversity Convention; and

4. Sustainable Forestry.

This new national emphasis on sustainability is already being reflected in regional policy. The recently published Regional Planning Guidance for the North West (the successor to SPNW, Government Office for the North West/Government Office for Merseyside 1996) states (para. 2.9) that:

> the priority for the future is to maximise the competitiveness, prosperity and quality of life in the Region through *sustainable development*. It is envisaged that the North West can become:
>
> 1. a world class centre for the production of high quality goods and services;
>
> 2. a green and pleasant region; and
>
> 3. a region of first class links to the rest of Europe and the world.

Whatever the limitations of such rhetorical flourishes, and the underpinning motivations, land-use and economic planning are nevertheless beginning to explore how the demands of the environment, economy and society can be reconciled at the regional scale. Roberts (1994 p. 782) suggests that four principles might be used to guide sustainable regional planning:

1. the 'standard' elements of sustainable development related to the environment, futurity and equity;

2. elements related to the diversification of the regional economy, intended to make it better able to deal with adversity;

3. the question of self-sufficiency, intended to minimise environmentally and economically wasteful resource inputs or transfers; and

4. the question of territorial integration both within the individual region and between regions.

The exact interpretation of what constitutes a 'region' and hence the most appropriate scale for planning and

management is problematic. The establishment of the 'city region' as a basis for sustainable planning is one approach (see for example Breheny & Rookwood 1993; Ravetz 1994; Owens 1994; Roberts & Chan 1997) of particular relevance to the Mersey Basin.

Planning to conserve and enhance biodiversity

One of the key government publications following the Earth Summit was the *National Biodiversity Action Plan* (Her Majesty's Government 1994c). The Biodiversity Action Plan aims to 'conserve and enhance biological diversity within the UK and to contribute to the conservation of global diversity through all appropriate mechanisms'. The objectives of the Strategy are to conserve, and where practicable, to enhance:

1. overall population and natural ranges of species and quality and range of wildlife habitats and ecosystems;

2. internationally important and threatened species, habitats and ecosystems;

3. species, habitats and natural and managed ecosystems that are characteristic of local areas; and

4. the biodiversity of natural and semi-natural habitats where this has been diminished over recent decades.

The government established a Biodiversity Steering Group to lead implementation of the Plan and one of their early recommendations was for the establishment of regional biodiversity action plans. It is encouraging to note that the first steps have already been taken in establishing such a plan for the North West Region centred on the Mersey Basin (Bennett *et al.* 1996). The collected papers in this volume provide an invaluable bench-mark for biodiversity planning and many important pointers for effective action.

The biodiversity balance sheet

The long history of human settlement in the Mersey Basin, culminating in the Industrial Revolution and its aftermath, has had a profound effect on landscape ecology and hence on biodiversity. Woodland clearance gradually eroded the matrix of primary habitat, replacing it in time by a fragmented countryside with isolated habitat patches of woodland, moor and heath (chapter seven, this volume). The connectivity between habitats has been reduced by the progressive removal of landscape features such as hedgerows and the downgrading of stream corridors (chapters seven and nine, this volume). Urban development has resulted in the direct loss of habitat and indirect impacts through enrichment, stress and disturbance.

However, perhaps the most remarkable feature of the history of landscape development in the Mersey Basin is the resilience of nature in the face of this massive disruption. Among the more striking positive findings are:

1. contribution to species richness within the habitat (α

diversity) by environmental stress which reduces the dominance of competitor species;

2. contribution to habitat richness (β diversity) by industrial obsolescence initiating natural succession and creative conservation; and

3. contribution to the total species complement (δ diversity) by escapes, introductions and possibly climate change.

As the chapters in this volume show, not only are the latter findings cause for optimism about the future, they also suggest that there is much we can learn about the study of ecology in a heavily urbanised region; for example the importance of disturbance corridors (including motorways) for promoting species migration within the region. The tentative findings of Greenwood (chapter nineteen, this volume) about the increasing total species complement (at least of higher plants) are most unexpected, and, together with comparable data on avifauna, lepidoptera and certain other taxa, vindicates the efforts of local recorders in documenting the biological consequences of the tide of change in this remarkable region.

Conclusions and way forward

The urban and industrial challenge to the natural integrity of the Mersey Basin has abated somewhat, but its forces are by no means spent. There will be continuing demands for development, especially housing, waste disposal and transport infrastructure which will threaten what remains of the region's critical natural capital. Similarly, as historic problems of air and water pollution are overcome, new challenges are emerging such as the primary and secondary pollutants from motor vehicles (Royal Commission on Environmental Pollution 1995; Wood *et al.* 1996). In addition, we have hardly begun to tackle the deep-seated historic problems of contaminated land and its associated ground water pollution (Royal Commission on Environmental Pollution 1996).

One critical issue is that the two principal drivers of landscape change (climatic and cultural influence) are now inextricably linked through carbon forcing (chapter one, this volume; Department of the Environment 1991a, 1996). An examination of the likely consequences of climate change for landscape and biodiversity in the region must now be a high priority. More fundamentally, we need to recognise that, despite the closure of the region's coal mines, north-west England is still essentially a fossil fuel economy. A move back toward renewable energy (so important in 1786, Figure 23.2) would bring very significant environmental impacts, not least on the Pennine uplands (wind farms) and on the Mersey Estuary, Britain's second most favourable estuary for generating tidal power (Department of Energy 1992).

Despite these concerns for the future, we can take heart from the new emphasis on sustainability emerging in national and regional policy. This will involve not only conserving what remains of the long-established biota, but actively repairing past damage and rehabilitating the environmental capital of the Mersey Basin. The Mersey and Red Rose Community Forests are beginning the long haul of revitalising the region's woodland capital (at only 4% this is one of the most impoverished landscapes in Europe). Creative conservation is a powerful force which could be used to greater effect, especially in wetland creation, as the outstanding achievements at Martin Mere demonstrate (chapter twenty-one, this volume).

There has been an exponential growth in environmental initiatives addressing these and other issues (Kidd *et al.* 1996), but the targeting of these initiatives is uneven. The landscape infrastructure of the rural lowlands seems to be especially vulnerable and, with some notable exceptions (e.g., the Cheshire Special Landscapes Project) is not well served by current policy and practice. Similarly, whilst there is now a comprehensive coverage of management schemes in the coastal zone of the Mersey Basin, they are for the most part substantially under-resourced and therefore ineffective. The Sefton Coast Management Scheme is a notable and important exception.

What is evident is that the Mersey Basin is fortunate, despite being the test-bed for the world's first industrial economy, in possessing a rich ecological legacy, and action is needed to secure what remains for future generations. The way forward, as envisaged by Adams (1996) is likely to involve:

1. maintaining diversity of landscapes and ecosystems;

2. building room for nature into economic life;

3. building connections between people and nature; and

4. allowing nature to function and creating conditions for it to do so.

The development of environmental policy from international to local levels, but especially through the new regionalism, is putting these aspirations into practice. Environmental assessment is now enabling more informed judgements to be made about the likely impact of new developments on landscape and ecology and the potential for mitigation. We are only at the start of a process which is beginning to recognise the complexities of the interconnections between ecology and development. Industrialisation and urbanisation have taken a heavy ecological toll in the past, and in some respects continue to do so, but there now exists an unparalleled opportunity to develop new understandings of the relationship between conservation and development. The timely and authoritative contributions to this volume represent the establishment of an information base which will help to realise this aspiration.

References

Adams, W. (1996). *Future Nature*. Earthscan, London.

AEA Technology (1995). *Air Pollution in the UK: 1993/4*. AEA, Stevenage.

Ash, H. (1991). Soils and Vegetation in Urban Areas. *Soils in the Urban Environment* (eds P. Bullock & P. Gregory), pp. 153–70. Blackwell Scientific Publications, Oxford.

Ash, H., Bennett, R. & Scott, R. (1992). *Flowers in the Grass*. English Nature, Peterborough.

Barker, T. & Harris, J. (1993). *A Merseyside Town in the Industrial Revolution: St Helens 1750–1900*. Cass & Co., London.

Beeby, A. (1993). *Applying Ecology*. Chapman & Hall, London.

Bennett, C., Fox, P., Marhall, I., Bruce, N. & Jepson, P. (eds) (1996). *Biodiversity North West: Co-ordinating Action for Biodiversity in North West England*. Conference Proceedings Environment Agency, Warrington.

Berry, P. & Pullen, R. (1982). The Woodland Resource: Management and Use. *The Resources of Merseyside* (eds W. Gould & A. Hodgkiss), pp. 101–18. Liverpool University Press, Liverpool.

Bradshaw, A. & McNeilly, T. (1981). *Evolution and Pollution*. Studies in Biology No. 30. Edward Arnold, London.

Breheny, M. & Rookwood, R. (1993). Planning the Sustainable City Region. *Planning for a Sustainable Environment: a Report by the Town & Country Planning Association* (ed. A. Blowers), pp. 150–89. TCPA, London.

British Association (1962). *Manchester and Its Region*. Manchester University Press, Manchester.

Countryside Commission (1976). *The Bollin Valley: A Study of Land Management in the Urban Finge*. **CCP97**. Countryside Commission, Cheltenham.

Countryside Commission (1993*). Countryside Management Projects*. **CCP403**. Countryside Commission, Cheltenham.

Critical Loads Advisory Group (1994). *Critical Loads of Acidity in the United Kingdom: Summary Report*. HMSO, London.

Department of Energy (n.d.). *Survey of Tidal Energy in the U.K.* Report No. STP 102. Department of Energy, London.

Department of Energy (1992). *Tidal Power from the River Mersey: A Feasibility Study. Stage III Report*. Department of Energy, London.

Department of the Environment (1971). *Long Term Population Distribution in Great Britain: a Study*. HMSO, London.

Department of the Environment (1991a). *The Potential Effects of Climate Change in the UK*. UK Climate Change Impacts Review Group 1st Report. HMSO, London.

Department of the Environment (1991b). *Survey of Derelict Land in England, 1988*. HMSO, London.

Department of the Environment (1995). *Survey of Derelict Land in England, 1993*. HMSO, London.

Department of the Environment (1996). *Review of the Potential Effects of Climate Change in the UK*. UK Climate Change Impacts Review Group 2nd Report. HMSO, London.

Dickens, C. (1854). *Hard Times*.

Dower, M. (1965). *The Challenge of Leisure*. Civic Trust, London.

Elson, M. (1986). *Green Belts: Conflict Mediation on the Urban Fringe*. Heinemann, London.

Engels, F. (1844). *The Condition of the Working Class in England*.

Foreman, R. (1995). *Land Mosaics: the Ecology of Landscape and Regions*. Springer Verlag, New York, USA.

Freeman, T., Rodgers, H. & Kinvig, R. (1966). *Lancashire, Cheshire and the Isle of Man*. Nelson & Sons, London.

Government Office for the North West/Government Office for Merseyside (1996). *Regional Planning Guidance for the North West: RPG 13*. HMSO, London.

Grime, J. (1979). *Plant Strategies and Vegetation Processes*. John Wiley, Chichester.

Grime, J. (1986). Manipulation of Plant Species and Communities. *Ecology and Design in Landscape* (eds A. Bradshaw, D. Goode & E. Thorpe), pp. 175–94. Blackwell Scientific Publications, Oxford.

Handley, J. (1980). The Application of Remote Sensing to Environmental Management. *International Journal of Remote Sensing*, **1**, 181–95.

Handley, J. (1982). The Land of Merseyside. *The Resources of Merseyside* (eds W. Gould & A. Hodgkiss), pp. 83–100. Liverpool University Press, Liverpool.

Handley, J. (1984). Ecological Requirement for Decison-Making Regarding Medium Scale Developments in the Urban Environment. *Planning and Ecology* (eds R. Roberts & T. Roberts), pp. 222–38. Chapman & Hall, London.

Handley, J. (1996). *The Post Industrial Landscape: a Groundwork Status Report*. Groundwork Foundation, Birmingham.

Handley, J. & Perry, D. (1995). *The Regional Environment of the Transpennine Corridor*. Occasional Paper No. 41. Department of Planning & Landscape, University of Manchester.

Harley, J. (1968). *A Map of the County of Lancashire, 1786, by William Yates*. Historic Society of Lancashire & Cheshire.

Harrison, R. (1992). *Understanding Our Environment*. Royal Society of Chemistry, London.

Hendry, K., Webb, S., White, K. & Parsons, N. (1993). Water Quality and Urban Regeneration: a Case Study of the Central Mersey Basin. *Urban Waterside Regeneration: Problems and Prospects* (eds K. White, E. Bellinger, A. Saul, M. Symes & K. Hendry), pp. 271–82. Ellis Howard, Chichester.

Her Majesty's Government (1994a). *Sustainable Development: the UK Strategy*. HMSO, London.

Her Majesty's Government (1994b). *Climate Change: the UK Programme*. HMSO, London.

Her Majesty's Government (1994c). *Biodiversity: the UK Action Plan*. HMSO, London.

Her Majesty's Government (1994d). *Sustainable Forestry: the UK Programme*. HMSO, London.

Jackson, H. (1979). The Decline of the Sand Lizard, *Lacerta Agilis* L. Population on the Sand Dunes of the Merseyside Coast, England. *Biological Conservation*, **16 (3)**, 177–93.

Kidd S., Handley, J., Wood, R. & Douglas, I. (1996). *'Greening the North West': a Regional Landscape Strategy Working Paper 2 – Strategic Environmental Initiatives*. Occasional Paper No. 54. Department of Planning & Landscape, University of Manchester.

Lawton, R. (1982). From the Port of Liverpool to the Conurbation of Merseyside. *The Resources of Merseyside* (eds W. Gould & A. Hodgkiss), pp. 1–13. Liverpool University Press, Liverpool.

Mersey Basin Campaign (1997). *Mersey Basin Campaign: Mid Term Report*. Mersey Basin Campaign, Manchester.

Mersey Community Forest (1995). *The Mersey Forest: Forest Plan*. Mersey Community Forest, Warrington.

Morrish, B. (1997). *The Realisation of Ecological and Amenity Benefits through Land Reclamation Programmes in Greater Manchester*. MSc thesis, University of Manchester.

National Rivers Authority (1995). *The Mersey Estuary: a Report in Environmental Quality*. HMSO, London.

North West Joint Planning Team (1973). *Strategic Plan for the North West: SPNW Joint Planning Team Report*. HMSO, London.

Office for National Statistics (1996). *Regional Trends 1996*. HMSO, London.

Owens, S. (1994). Can Land Use Planning Produce the Ecological City? *Town & Country Planning* **63, (6) June**, 170–73.

Parry, G., Johnson, M. & Bell, R. (1984). Ecological Surveys for Metalliferous Mining Proposals. *Planning and Ecology* (eds R. Roberts & T. Roberts), pp. 40–55. Chapman & Hall, London.

Philpott, R. (1988). *Historic Towns of the Merseyside Area: a Survey of Urban Settlement to c.1800*. National Museums & Galleries on Merseyside Occasional Papers, Liverpool Museum No. 3. Liverpool Museum, Liverpool.

Rackham, O. (1986). *The History of the Countryside*. Dent, London.

Ravetz, J. (1994). Manchester 2020 – a Sustainable City Region Project. *Town & Country Planning*, **63 (6) June**, 181–85.

Red Rose Community Forest (1994). *Red Rose Forest Plan.* Red Rose Forest, Manchester.

Roberts, P. (1994). Sustainable Regional Planning. *Regional Studies,* **28 (8)**,781–87.

Roberts, P. & Chan, R. (1997). A Tale of Two Regions: Strategic Planning for Sustainable Development in East and West. *International Planning Studies*, **2 (1)**, 45–62.

Royal Commission on Environmental Pollution (1995). *Eighteenth Report: Transport and Environment.* HMSO, London.

Royal Commission on Environmental Pollution (1996). *Nineteenth Report: Sustainable Use of Soil.* HMSO, London.

Ruff, A. & Maddison, C. (1994). Footpath Management in the National Parks. *Landscape Research*, **19 (2)**, 80–87.

Struthers, W. (1997). From Manchester Docks to Salford Quays: Ten Years of Environmental Improvements in the Mersey Basin Campaign. *Journal of the Chartered Institute of Water & Environmental Management*, **11 (2)**, 1–7.

von Tunzelmann, N. (1986). Coal and Steam Power. *Atlas of Industrialising Britain 1760–1914* (eds J. Langton & R. Morris), pp. 72–79. Methuen, London.

Walker, F. (1939). Historical Geography of South West Lancashire Before the Industrial Revolution. *Chetham Society*, **103**, New Series.

Walton, J. (1987). *Lancashire: a Social History 1558–1939.* Manchester University Press, Manchester.

Wheeler, D., Simpson, D. & Houston, J. (1991). Dune Use and Management. *The Sand Dunes of the Sefton Coast.* (eds D. Atkinson & J. Houston), pp. 129–49. National Museums & Galleries on Merseyside in conjunction with Sefton Metropolitan Borough Council, Liverpool.

Wood, R., Handley, J., Douglas, I. & Kidd, S. (1996). *'Greening the North West': a Regional Landscape Strategy Working Paper 1 – Regional Landscape Assessment.* Occasional Paper No. 53. Department of Planning and Landscape, University of Manchester.

Yalden, D. (1987). The Natural History of Domesday Cheshire. *Naturalist,* **112,** 125–31.

Authors' Addresses

Allen, Dr J.R., Port Erin Marine Laboratory, School of Biological Sciences, University of Liverpool, Port Erin, Isle of Man, IM9 6JA.

Ash, Dr H.J., 5 Dearnford Avenue, Bromborough, Wirral, L62 6DX.

Atkinson, Dr D., Population Biology Research Group, School of Biological Sciences, Nicholson Building, University of Liverpool, Liverpool, L69 3BX.

Barr, C.J., Institute of Terrestrial Ecology, Merlewood Research Station, Grange-over-Sands, Cumbria, LA11 6JU.

Boothby, Dr J., Pond *Life* Project, Liverpool John Moores University, Trueman Building, 15–21 Webster Street, Liverpool, L3 2ET,

Bradshaw, Professor A.D., School of Biological Sciences, University of Liverpool, Liverpool, L69 3BX.

Butterill, G., Cheshire Wildlife Trust, Grebe House, Reaseheath, Nantwich, Cheshire, CW5 6DG.

Cowell, R.W., Liverpool Museum, National Museums & Galleries on Merseyside, William Brown Street, Liverpool, L3 8EN.

Davis, Dr B.N.K., Brook House, Easton, Huntingdon, Cambs., PE18 0TU.

Doody, Dr J.P., National Coastal Consultants, 5 Green Lane, Brampton, Huntingdon, Cambs., PE18 8RE.

Eaton, Dr J.W., School of Biological Sciences, University of Liverpool, Liverpool, L69 3BX.

Fairhurst, Dr J., Cheshire County Council, Environmental Planning, Commerce House, Hunter Street, Chester, CH1 2QP.

Fielding, Dr N.J., School of Biological Sciences, University of Liverpool, Liverpool, L69 3BX.

Fisher Dr C.T., Liverpool Museum, National Museums & Galleries on Merseyside, William Brown Street, Liverpool, L3 8EN.

Fox, Professor B.W., Tryfan, Longlands Road, New Mills, High Peak, Derbyshire, SK22 3BL.

Gonzalez, Dr S., School of Biological and Earth Sciences, Liverpool John Moores University, Byrom Street, Liverpool, L3 3AF.

Greenwood, E.F., Liverpool Museum, National Museums & Galleries on Merseyside, William Brown Street, Liverpool, L3 8EN.

Handley, Professor J.F., OBE, Department of Planning and Landscape, University of Manchester, Oxford Road, Manchester, M13 9PL.

Hawkins, Professor S.J., Biodiversity & Ecology Division, School of Biological Sciences and Centre for Environmental Sciences, University of Southampton, Shackleton Building, Highfield, Southampton, S017 1BJ.

Holland, D.G., The Environment Agency, Mirwell, Carrington Lane, Sale, Cheshire, M33 5NL.

Huddart, Dr D., School of Education and Community Studies, Liverpool John Moores University, I.M. Marsh Campus, Barkhill Road, Liverpool, L17 6BD.

Hull, Dr A., Pond *Life* Project, Liverpool John Moores University, Trueman Building, 15–21 Webster Street, Liverpool, L3 2ET.

Huntley, Professor B., Environmental Research Centre, Department of Biological Sciences, University of Durham, Durham, DH1 3LE.

Innes, Dr J.B., Environmental Research Centre, Department of Geography, University of Durham Science Laboratories, South Road, Durham, DH1 3LE.

Jarvis, A.E., Centre for Port & Maritime History, GWR Building, Merseyside Maritime Museum, National Museums & Galleries on Merseyside, Liverpool, L3 1DG.

Jemmett, Dr A.W.L., School of Biological Sciences, University of Liverpool, Liverpool, L69 3BX.

Judd, Dr S., Liverpool Museum, National Museums & Galleries on Merseyside, William Brown Street, Liverpool, L3 8EN

Lageard, Dr J.G.A., Division of Environmental Science, Crewe and Alsager Faculty, Manchester Metropolitan University, Crewe Green Road, Crewe, Cheshire, CW1 1DU.

Lewis, Dr J.M., University of Liverpool, P.O. Box 147, Liverpool, L69 3BX.

Long, Dr A.J., Environmental Research Centre, Department of Geography, University of Durham, Science Laboratories, South Road, Durham, DH1 3LE.

Mitcham, T., Lancashire Wildlife Trust, Cuerden Park Wildlife Centre, Shady Lane, Bamber Bridge, Preston, Lancashire, PR5 6AU.

Morries, G., Lancashire County Council, P.O. Box 160, East Cliff County Offices, Preston, Lancashire, PR1 7EX.

Moss, Professor B., School of Biological Sciences, University of Liverpool, Liverpool, L69 3BX.

Nolan, P., The Environment Agency, Mirwell, Carrington Lane, Sale, Cheshire, M33 5NL.

Norman, Professor D., Rowswood Cottage, Ridding Lane, Sutton Weaver, Runcorn, Cheshire, WA7 6PF.

Oldfield, P., Environmental Services Directorate, Halton Borough Council, Grosvenor House, Halton Lea, Runcorn Cheshire, WA7 2GW.

Oldfield, Professor F., Executive Director, Past Global Changes, International Geosphere-Biosphere Programme, Bärenplatz 2, CH - 3011 Bern, Switzerland.

Philpott, Dr R.A., Liverpool Museum, National Museums & Galleries on Merseyside, William Brown Street, Liverpool, L3 8EN.

Plater, Dr A.J., Department of Geography, University of Liverpool, Liverpool, L69 3BX.

Reed, P.N., Central Services Division, National Museums & Galleries on Merseyside, P.O. Box 33, 127 Dale Street, Liverpool, L69 3LA.

Russell, Dr G., School of Biological Sciences, University of Liverpool, Liverpool, L69 3BX.

Smart, R.A., 10 Elizabeth Crescent, Queens Park, Chester, CH4 7AZ.

Stark, G.J., Institute of Terrestrial Ecology, Merlewood Research Station, Grange-over-Sands, Cumbria, LA11 6JU.

Tallis, Dr J.H., School of Biological Sciences, University of Manchester, 3.614 Stopford Building, Oxford Road, Manchester, M13 9PT.

Tooley, Professor M.J., School of Geography and Geology, Purdie Building, North Haugh, University of St Andrews, Fife, KY16 9ST.

Walker, Professor S., Regional Water Manager, Environment Agency, North West Region, P.O. Box 12, Richard Fairclough House, Knutsford Road, Warrington, Cheshire, WA4 1HG.

Wallace, Dr I.D., Liverpool Museum, National Museums & Galleries on Merseyside, William Brown Street, Liverpool, L3 8EN.

Weekes, L., Cheshire Wildlife Trust, Grebe House, Reaseheath, Nantwich, Cheshire, CW5 6DG.

Wilkinson, Dr S.B., School of Biological Sciences, University of Liverpool, Liverpool, L69 3BX.

Wood, R.W.S., Department of Planning and Landscape, University of Manchester, Oxford Road, Manchester, M13 9PL.

Yalden, Dr D.W., School of Biological Sciences, University of Manchester, 3.614 Stopford Building, Oxford Road, Manchester, M13 9PT.